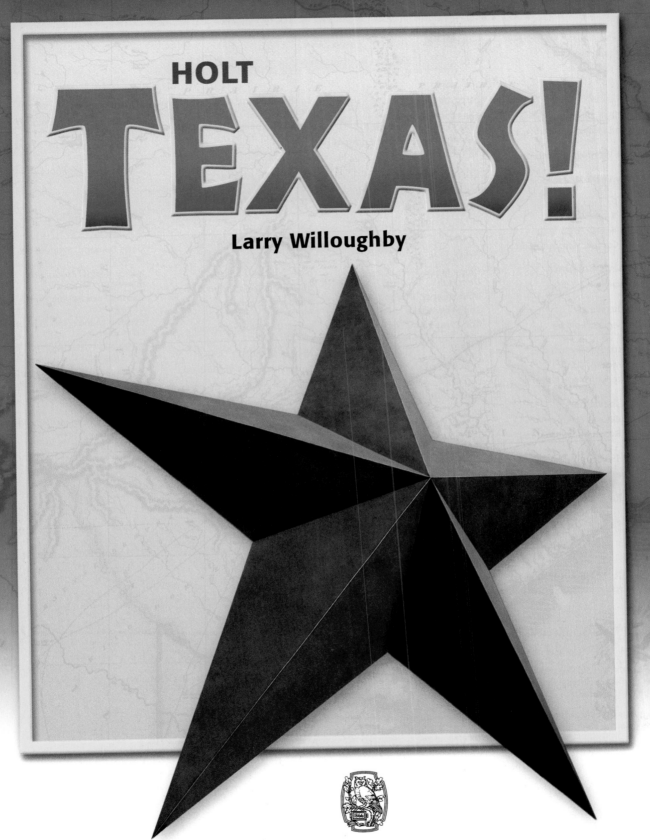

HOLT
TEXAS!

Larry Willoughby

HOLT, RINEHART AND WINSTON

A Harcourt Education Company

Austin • Orlando • Chicago • New York • Toronto • London • San Diego

STAFF CREDITS

Editorial

Sue Miller, *Director*

Steven L. Hayes, *Executive Editor*

Robert Wehnke, *Managing Editor*

Hadley Lewis Watson, *Senior Editor*

Pupil's Edition

Marc Segers, *Editor*

Lance Cooper, *Associate Editor*

Teacher's Edition

Joni Wackwitz, *Editor*

Ancillaries

Marc Segers, *Editor*

Technology Resources

Rob Hrechko, *Editor*

Annette Saunders, *Editor*

Fact Checking

Bob Fullilove, *Editor*

Jenny Rose, *Assistant Editor*

Copy Editing

Julie Beckman, *Senior Copy Editor*

Katelijne A. Lefevere, *Copy Editor*

Support

Gina Tasby-Rogers, *Administrative Assistant*

Sue Minkler, *Assistant Editorial Coordinator*

Editorial Permission

Lee Noble, *Permissions Editor*

Art, Design and Photo

Book Design

Diane Motz, *Senior Design Director*

Marc Cooper, *Design Manager*

Sonya Mendeke, *Designer*

Bob Prestwood, *Designer*

Liann Lech, *Traffic Coordinator*

Teacher's Edition

Lori Male, *Senior Designer*

Ed Diaz, *Design Associate*

Image Acquisition

Joe London, *Director*

Tim Taylor, *Photo Research Supervisor*

Bob McClellan, *Senior Photo Researcher*

Rick Benavides, *Photo Researcher*

Terry Janecek, *Photo Researcher*

Lyndol Descant, *Assistant Photo Researcher*

Sarah Hudgens, *Assistant Photo Researcher*

Nicole Mlakar, *Photo Coordinator*

Elaine Tate, *Art Buyer Supervisor*

Nicole McLeod, *Art Buyer*

Cover Design

Jason Wilson, *Designer*

New Media Design

Susan Michael, *Design Director*

Kimberly Cammerata, *Design Manager*

Grant Davidson, *Designer*

Media Design

Curtis Riker, *Design Director*

Graphic Services

Kristen Darby, *Manager*

Cathy Murphy, *Senior Image Designer*

Jeff Robinson, *Senior Designer*

Linda Wilbourn, *Image Designer*

Jane Dixon, *Image Designer*

Photo Studio

Sam Dudgeon, *Senior Staff Photographer*

Victoria Smith, *Staff Photographer*

Lauren Eischen, *Photo Specialist*

Prepress and Manufacturing

Gene Rumann, *Production Manager*

Nancy Hargis, *Production Supervisor*

Leanna Ford, *Production Coordinator*

Cynthia Munoz, *Production Coordinator*

Antonella Posterino, *Coordinator*

Jevara Jackson, *Manufacturing Coordinator, Book*

Rhonda Farris, *Inventory Planner*

Kim Harrison, *Manufacturing Coordinator, Media*

COVER: The Bob Bullock Texas State History Museum opened to the public in April of 2001. The state-of-the-art museum tells the "Story of Texas" through a variety of programs and exhibits.

Cover photo: HRW photo by Peter Van Steen

AUTHORS

About the author

Larry Willoughby is an Associate Professor of History at Austin Community College. His books include *Austin: A Historical Portrait* and *Texas Rhythm, Texas Rhyme: A History of Texas Music.*

Contributor

Dr. Janice C. May is Professor of Government at the University of Texas at Austin. Dr May is the author of *The Texas State Constitution, A Reference Guide* and has served on two Texas Constitutional Revision Commissions.

EDITORIAL REVIEW BOARD

Content

Dr. Randolph B. Campbell is a Regents Professor of History at the University of North Texas. Dr. Campbell is the author of several books, including *Sam Houston and the American Southwest* and *Grass-Roots Reconstruction in Texas, 1865–1880.*

Dr. Jesús F. de la Teja is Professor of History at Southwest Texas State University. Dr. de la Teja is the author of several books, including *San Antonio de Béxar: A Community on New Spain's Northern Frontier* and *A Revolution Remembered: The Memoirs and Selected Correspondence of Juan N. Seguín.*

Dr. Terry Jordan holds the Walter Prescott Webb Chair in History and Ideas at the University of Texas at Austin. Dr Jordan has published several books, including *German Seed in Texas Soil* and *Trails to Texas: Southern Roots of Western Cattle Ranching.*

Educational

Barbara Mayo
Program Facilitator
Austin ISD
Austin

Rick Rodriquez
San Juan Middle School
Pharr-San Juan-Alamo ISD
San Juan

Velma Stredic
Thomas Edison Middle School
Dallas ISD
Dallas

Elaine Parr
Truitt Middle School
Cypress-Fairbanks ISD
Houston

REVIEWERS

Content Reviewers

Dr. Armando C. Alonzo
Texas A&M University
Mexican American and Texas

Dr. Julia Kirk Blackwelder
Texas A&M University
20th century U.S. and women

Dr. Gregg Cantrell
University of North Texas
Texas and old South

Dr. Donald E. Chipman
University of North Texas
*Colonial Texas, Mexico, and
Spanish borderlands*

Dr. Nicole Etcheson
University of Texas at El Paso
Civil War and Reconstruction

Dr. Sam W. Haynes
University of Texas at
Arlington
19th-century U.S. and Texas

Dr. C. L. Higham
Texas A&M University
*American West and
Native American*

Yolanda Chavez Leyva
University of Texas
at San Antonio
*U.S. Southwest and
Mexican American*

Dr. John Miller Morris
University of Texas
at San Antonio
*Political science and
geography*

Dr. Roger M. Olien
University of Texas
at Permian Basin
*20th-century America,
business, and Texas*

Dr. Sherry Smith
Southern Methodist
University
*American West and
American Indian*

Dr. F. Todd Smith
University of North Texas
*Mexican borderlands,
colonial North America,
and Native American*

Educational Reviewers

Jeannie Adams
T. W. Browne Middle School
Dallas

David R. Blackmon
Oliveira Middle School
Brownsville

William Centeno
J. Wood Middle School
San Antonio

Shirley Collins
Covington Middle School
Austin

Don Cornman
Dueitt Middle School
Houston

M. L. Garcia
Miller Jordan Middle School
San Benito

Deborah Hardin
Crain Middle School
Victoria

Jerry Johnson
Franklin Middle School
Abilene

Deann Lee
Crockett Middle School
Paris

Lizette Lozano
L. J. Christen Middle School
Laredo

Saul Martinez
Lincoln Middle School
El Paso

John Pinkham
Austin Middle School
Amarillo

Hollye Reynolds
Fredericksburg Middle School
Fredericksburg

Sylvia Saldivar
Elliott Grant Middle School
Corpus Christi

Quintin G. Williams
W. E. Greiner Middle School
Dallas

Field Test Teachers

Gloria G. Aguirre
Bowie Junior High School
Odessa

Nanci Bush
Florence Middle School
Florence

Bill Cameron
Morris Middle School
McAllen

Patty Christian
Mann Middle School
Amarillo

Rebecca A. Corley
Evans Junior High School
Lubbock

Jesse DeLaRosa
Morris Middle School
McAllen

Steele Ewing
Zavala Middle School
Pecos

John Gambino
Walker Junior High School
Monahans

Victor Gonzales
Slider Middle School
El Paso

Lizettete Gutierrez
St. Augustine High School
Laredo

Lana Hamilton
Jackson Middle School
San Antonio

Shawn Hampton
Crowley Middle School
Fort Worth

Ronald L. Harden, Sr.
Mann Middle School
Abilene

Cindy Hathaway
Pflugerville Middle School
Pflugerville

Christine J. Hockensmith
Houston Middle School
Amarillo

Edna Martinez
Camino Real Middle School
El Paso

D. Q. Maynard
Balmorhea School
Balmorhea

Brent Olson
Coakley Junior High School
Harlingen

Lynne Smogur
Barbara Bush Middle School
San Antonio

M. Elaine Worthen
Flour Bluff Junior High School
Corpus Christi

HOLT
TEXAS!

Whooping crane

CONTENTS

How to Use Your Textbook . . . . . **xxvi**

Why History Matters Today . . . . . **xxx**

Themes in Texas History . . . . **xxxii**

Skills Handbook. . . . . **xxxvi**
Critical Thinking **S1**
Becoming a Strategic Reader **S4**
TAKS Test-Taking Strategies **S12**
Atlas **A1**

UNIT 1
The Geography of Texas

Texas Teens
Young Naturalists **1**

CHAPTER 1
The Geographer's Tools   **2**

1 The Six Essential Elements of Geography **4**
Connecting to Science and Technology
GIS **5**
Visualizing History *Texas Landforms* **6**
Biography *Roy Bedichek* **7**
That's Interesting! *Miles and Miles of Texas* **8**
2 Using Maps **9**
3 Using Graphs, Charts, and Tables **13**

CHAPTER 2
A Land Called Texas   **18**

1 The Physical Landscape of Texas **20**
Connecting to Literature *Goodbye to a River*
by John Graves **23**
2 The Texas Climate **24**
Global Connections *El Niño* **25**
That's Interesting! *Texas Tornadoes* **27**
Biography *Lady Bird Johnson* **28**
3 Texans and Geography **30**
Our Cultural Heritage *Religious Diversity*
in Texas **31**
Connecting to Geography *The Texas*
Population **34**
4 Natural Resources of Texas **35**
Daily Life *Future Farmers of America* **36**
Citizenship and You *Recycling* **37**

Texas wildflowers

Caddo woman

CHAPTER 3

The Regions of Texas............ **40**

1 A Regional Crossroads..................... **42**

2 The Gulf Coastal Plain **45**
  Texas Cities *Houston*..................... **47**
  Lone Star Legacy *Padre Island*............. **48**

3 The Central Plains **51**
  Biography *Walter Prescott Webb*........... **53**

4 The Great Plains **54**
  That's Interesting! *Llano Estacado*.......... **55**
  Connecting to Literature The Wind
  by Dorothy Scarborough.................... **56**

5 The Intermountain Basins and Plateaus..... **57**
  That's Interesting! *Vast Western Spaces*...... **58**

Social Studies Skills Workshop
  Posing and Answering Questions.......... **62**
History in Action Unit 1 Simulation **63**

UNIT 2

Exploration and Settlement

(Beginnings–1821)............ **64**

Texas Teens
  Young American Indians...................... **65**

CHAPTER 4

Texas Indians

(Beginnings–1700) **66**

1 The First Texans **68**
  Connecting to the Arts *Rock Art* **69**
  Lone Star Legacy *Alibates Flint Quarries*..... **71**

2 The Western Gulf Culture Area............ **72**

3 The Southeastern Culture Area............ **75**
  Linking Past to Present *Studying the Caddoan Mounds*................................. **76**
  Our Cultural Heritage *Our Caddo Name* **77**
  Connecting to Literature *Native American Stories* **78**

4 The Pueblo Culture Area.................. **79**
  Linking Past To Present *Pueblo Culture*...... **81**

5 The Plains Culture Area **82**
  That's Interesting! *Danger on the Plains* **83**

Big Bend National Park

Spanish conquistador

CHAPTER 5
The Search for Empire
(1492–1670). **88**

1 Europeans Reach the Americas **90**
    That's Interesting! *Pigs on the Loose* **91**
    Connecting to Economics and Math
    Gold and the Spanish Empire **93**

2 The Spanish Explore Texas **94**
    Linking Past to Present *Cartography* **95**
    Biography *Álvar Núñez Cabeza de Vaca* **97**

3 Searching for Cities of Gold **98**
    Biography *Estevanico* **99**
    Daily Life *What's for Dinner?* **102**

4 Consequences of Spanish Exploration **103**
    Global Connections *The Reformation* **104**
    Lone Star Legacy *Texas Mustangs* **105**
    Connecting to Geography *The Columbian*
    Exchange **107**

CHAPTER 6
The Spanish Missions
(1680–1760) **110**

1 Spanish Settlements on the Frontier **112**
    Visualizing History *Life in a Spanish*
    Mission **113**
    Our Cultural Heritage *Spanish*
    Place-Names **114**

2 The French Challenge **115**
    Connecting to Science and Technology
    La Belle **116**
    That's Interesting! *Mud Volcanoes* **119**

3 The Spanish Return to Texas **120**
    Texas Cities *San Antonio* **122**
    Biography *Martín de Alarcón* **124**

4 War and Expansion **125**
    Biography *Antonio Margil de Jesús* **126**

5 Life in Spanish Texas **128**
    Connecting to the Arts *Mission Architecture* . . **129**
    Connecting to Music *Romances Corridos* . . . **131**

CHAPTER 7
Conflicts of Empire
(1760–1821) **134**

1 Changes in Spanish Texas **136**
    Biography *Antonio Gil Ybarbo* **139**

2 Disputes with the United States **140**
    That's Interesting! *Bernardo de Gálvez* **141**

3 Unrest and Revolution **143**
    That's Interesting! *Goliad's*
    Spanish Name **144**
    Our Cultural Heritage *Diez y Seis*
    de Septiembre **145**
    Global Connections *Revolutions*
    in Latin America **146**

4 Spanish Rule Ends in Mexico **148**
    Biography *Martín de León* **151**

Social Studies Skills Workshop
    Decision-Making Skills **154**
History in Action Unit 2 Simulation **155**

Presidio near Goliad

vii

Stephen F. Austin

Oxen used on early Texas farms

CHAPTER 9
Life in Early Texas
(1820–1835) **180**

1 Texas Fever **182**
   That's Interesting! *Texas Panthers* **184**
   Lone Star Legacy *The Big Thicket* **185**

2 Daily Life on the Frontier **186**
   Connecting to the Arts *Texas Quilts* **187**
   Our Cultural Heritage *A Blending
   of Foods* **188**
   Daily Life *Leisure Time* **189**

3 Trade and Transportation **191**
   Biography *William Goyens* **193**
   Connecting to Literature *Texas: Observations,
   Historical, Geographical, and Descriptive by
   Mary Austin Holley* **194**

4 Government and Society **195**

UNIT 3
American Colonization
(1820–1835) **156**

Texas Teens
Young Settlers **157**

CHAPTER 8
Americans Settle in Texas
(1820–1835) **158**

1 Moses Austin and Texas **160**
   That's Interesting! *Baron de Bastrop* **161**
   Biography *Moses Austin* **162**

2 Stephen F. Austin in Texas **163**
   Biography *Stephen F. Austin* **164**

3 The Austin Colonies **168**
   Daily Life *Hospitality in Colonial Texas* **169**
   Biography *Jane Long* **170**

4 The *Empresarios* **172**
   Our Cultural Heritage *Tejano Culture* **175**
   Connecting to Geography and Math
   Land in Mexican Texas **177**

CHAPTER 10
The Road to Revolution
(1825–1835) **200**

1 Political Unrest in Texas **202**
   Texas Cities *Laredo* **204**
   Linking Past to Present *Trade Relations* **205**
   Global Connections *The Antislavery
   Movement Abroad* **206**

2 Tensions Grow **207**
   Historical Document *Turtle Bayou
   Resolutions* **209**
   Biography *Antonio López de
   Santa Anna* **210**

3 Conventions and Petitions **211**
   Citizenship and You *Political Protest* **212**
   That's Interesting! *Austin in Prison* **214**

4 The Move toward War **215**
   Visualizing History *Federalism and
   Centralism* **216**

Social Studies Skills Workshop
   Problem-Solving Skills **220**
History in Action Unit 3 Simulation **221**

UNIT 4 The Republic of Texas

(1835–1845) **222**

Texas Teens
Young War Supporters **223**

Plains Indians in Texas

CHAPTER 11
The Texas Revolution

(1835–1836) **224**

1 The War Begins **226**
   Biography *Juan Seguín* **229**
   Daily Life *The Home Front* **230**

2 The Consultation of 1835 . . . . **231**
   Historical Document *Declaration of the People of Texas* **232**

3 The Siege of the Alamo **234**
   Biography *William B. Travis* **235**
   Visualizing History *The Siege of the Alamo* . . **236**
   Historical Document *Travis's Letter* **237**
   That's Interesting! *Line in the Sand* **239**

4 The Convention of 1836 . . . . **240**
   Biography *Lorenzo de Zavala* **242**
   Historical Document *The Texas Declaration of Independence* **243**
   Biography *George C. Childress* **245**

5 Independence Is Won **246**
   Biography *Susanna Dickinson* **247**
   Biography *James Fannin* **248**

CHAPTER 12
A New Nation

(1836–1845) **254**

1 The Early Republic **256**
   Lone Star Legacy *The Lone Star Flag* **258**

2 Houston's First Term **259**
   Lone Star Legacy *Texas Rangers* **261**
   Biography *Sam Houston* **262**
   That's Interesting! *Houston: The Raven* **263**
   Biography *Chief Bowles* **264**

3 Lamar's Presidency **265**
   Biography *Mirabeau B. Lamar* **266**

4 Houston's Second Administration **271**
   Linking Past to Present *The Size of the Texas Government* **272**

CHAPTER 13
Life in the Republic

(1836–1845) **276**

1 The Texans **278**
   Biography *Greenbury Logan* **280**

2 European Immigration to Texas **282**
   That's Interesting! *Cow Horns* **283**
   Our Cultural Heritage *Little Alsace in Texas* **284**
   Connecting to Geography *Immigration to Texas* **285**

3 Texas Life **286**
   Texas Cities *Dallas* **287**
   Connecting to the Arts *Théodore Gentilz* **288**
   Daily Life *The Texas Schoolroom* **289**

The Convention of 1836

British platter
honoring the
Texas Revolution

CHAPTER 14
Texas Faces Foreign Challenges
(1836–1845) **292**

1 Foreign Recognition of Texas **294**
   Linking Past to Present *The French
Legation* **295**
   That's Interesting! *The Pig War* **296**
2 Conflict with Mexico.................... **297**
   Global Connections *The Pastry War*....... **298**
   Connecting to the Arts *Frederic Remington*.. **300**
   Connecting to Geography *Conflicts with
Mexico* **302**
3 The Last Years of the Republic **303**
   That's Interesting! *Counting the Votes* **304**
   Biography *Anson Jones*.................. **305**

Social Studies Skills Workshop
   Reading Skills.......................... **308**
History in Action Unit 4 Simulation **309**

UNIT 5 The Lone Star State
(1845–1861)................. **310**
Texas Teens
Young Texans on the Frontier **311**

CHAPTER 15
Texas Joins the United States
(1845–1860) **312**

1 The Annexation of Texas................. **314**
   Biography *Jane McManus Cazneau* **315**
   Daily Life *Statehood Celebrations* **317**
2 Forming a Government **318**
   Biography *José Antonio Navarro* **319**
   Visualizing History *The Separation of Powers* . **320**
   That's Interesting! *A Ban on Duels*........ **321**

3 Political and Economic Issues............. **322**
   Biography *Elisha M. Pease* **323**
   Linking Past to Present *The Governor's
Mansion* **324**
   Connecting to Economics and Math
The Republic's Debt **325**

CHAPTER 16
Western Expansion
and Conflict
(1845–1860) **328**

1 The Mexican War **330**
   That's Interesting! *Old Rough and Ready* ... **331**
   That's Interesting! *Behind Enemy Lines* **332**
   Biography *John Coffee Hays* **333**
2 Results of the Mexican War **334**
   Our Cultural Heritage *German Culture
in the Hill Country* **337**
3 The Texas Rangers and American Indians... **338**
   Texas Cities *Fort Worth* **340**
   Connecting to the Arts *Friedrich Petri* **341**
   Linking Past to Present *Military Bases* **342**
   Connecting to Geography *The Texas
Frontier* **343**

Ceremony celebrating the annexation of Texas

CHAPTER 17
Life in a Frontier State
(1845–1861) 346

1 Earning a Living 348
   That's Interesting! *The Mavericks* 350
   Connecting to Economics *Free Enterprise* . . . 352
2 Transportation 353
   Daily Life *Texas Roads* 354
3 Social and Cultural Institutions 357
   Biography *Gail Borden Jr.* 358
   Connecting to the Arts *Hermann Lungkwitz* . . 359
4 Slavery in Texas 360
   Our Cultural Heritage *African Traditions* 361
   Connecting to Literature *African American
   Folktales* 362

Social Studies Skills Workshop
   Interpreting Time Lines 366
History in Action Unit 5 Simulation 367

UNIT 6 Conflicts in Texas
(1861–1880) 368

Texas Teens
Young Soldiers 369

CHAPTER 18
Texas and the Civil War
(1861–1865) 370

1 Slavery and States' Rights 372
   Citizenship and You
   Serving during the War 375
2 The Civil War Begins 376
   Global Connections
   Global Trade and the Civil War 378
   That's Interesting! *Snowball Wars* 380
3 Campaigns in Texas and the Southwest 381
   Biography *Richard Dowling* 383
   Texas Cities *Brownsville* 384
   Daily Life *Camp Life* 385
4 The Texas Home Front 386
5 The End of the War 389

CHAPTER 19
Reconstruction
(1865–1877) 394

1 Presidential Reconstruction 396
   Lone Star Legacy *Juneteenth* 397
   Daily Life *African American Schools* 398
2 Congressional Reconstruction 400
   Biography *George T. Ruby* 402
   Citizenship and You *Your Vote Counts* 403
3 The Davis Administration 404
   That's Interesting! *Historically Black
   Colleges* 405
   Linking Past to Present *Party Politics* 406
   Connecting to Literature *Old Yeller
   by Fred Gipson* 407
4 Texas after Reconstruction 408
   Biography *Richard Coke* 409
   Visualizing History *The Sharecropping Cycle* . 410

CHAPTER 20
The Indian Wars
(1861–1880) 414

1 Changes in Indian Policy 416
   Biography *Satanta* 419
2 War on the Plains 420
   That's Interesting! *General Sherman's
   Near Miss* 421
   Biography *Cynthia Parker* 422
   Connecting to Math *The Buffalo Population* . . 424
3 The Red River War 425
   That's Interesting! *Bat Masterson* 426
4 The Indian Wars End in Texas 428
   Biography *Henry O. Flipper* 429
   Our Cultural Heritage *American Indian
   Celebrations* 430
   Connecting to Geography
   The Expanding Texas Frontier 431

Social Studies Skills Workshop
   Identifying Cause and Effect . . . 434
**History in Action Unit 6
Simulation** 435

Cowboy spur

Juneteenth parade rider

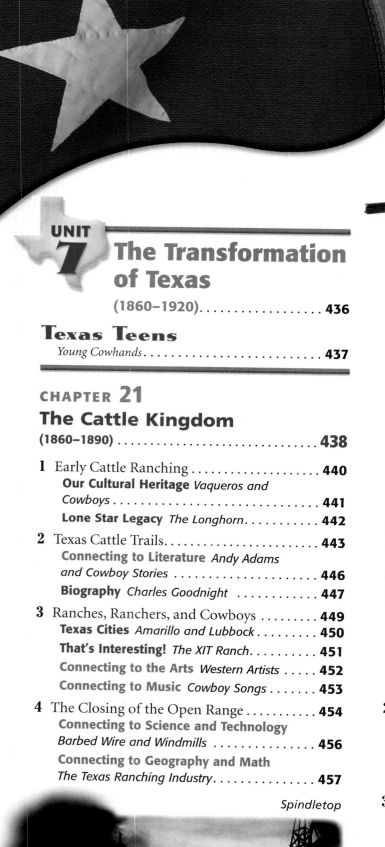

Rio Grande Railroad Engine 1

UNIT 7 The Transformation of Texas

(1860–1920) 436

Texas Teens
Young Cowhands 437

CHAPTER 21
The Cattle Kingdom

(1860–1890) 438

1 Early Cattle Ranching 440
 Our Cultural Heritage *Vaqueros and Cowboys* 441
 Lone Star Legacy *The Longhorn* 442

2 Texas Cattle Trails 443
 Connecting to Literature *Andy Adams and Cowboy Stories* 446
 Biography *Charles Goodnight* 447

3 Ranches, Ranchers, and Cowboys 449
 Texas Cities *Amarillo and Lubbock* 450
 That's Interesting! *The XIT Ranch* 451
 Connecting to the Arts *Western Artists* 452
 Connecting to Music *Cowboy Songs* 453

4 The Closing of the Open Range 454
 Connecting to Science and Technology
 Barbed Wire and Windmills 456
 Connecting to Geography and Math
 The Texas Ranching Industry 457

CHAPTER 22
Railroads and Farming

(1870–1900) 460

1 The Growth of Railroads 462
 Global Connections *Famine in China* 465
 Connecting to Economics and Math
 The Railroad Boom 466

2 Changes in Farming 467
 Connecting to Economics *King Cotton in Texas* 469
 Biography *Dora Nunn Roberts* 470

3 Agricultural Industries and Workers 471
 That's Interesting! *The Knights of Labor* 473

CHAPTER 23
The Oil Boom

(1890–1920) 476

1 The Birth of the Oil Industry 478
 Lone Star Legacy *Spindletop* 479
 Biography *Anthony F. Lucas* 480
 Daily Life *Life in the Oil Fields* 481
 Connecting to Geography *Oil and Natural Gas Fields* 482

2 The Growth of the Oil Industry 483
 Visualizing History *Vertical and Horizontal Integration* 484
 That's Interesting! *Oil Nicknames* 484
 Connecting to Economics *Wildcatters* 485

3 Effects of the Oil Boom 486
 Texas Cities *Midland and Odessa* 487
 Connecting to Science and Technology
 Oil Drilling 488

Social Studies Skills Workshop
 Study Skills 492
History in Action Unit 7 Simulation 493

Spindletop

UNIT 8 Prosperity and Crisis

(1870–1939) 494

Texas Teens
Young Relief Workers 495

CHAPTER 24
Texas in the Age of Reform
(1870–1920) 496

1 Farmers and Reform 498
   Citizenship and You *Getting Involved in Government* 499
2 Government in the Reform Age 503
   Biography *James Stephen Hogg* 504
   Connecting to Geography *The Greer County Dispute* 505
3 The Progressive Movement 507
   That's Interesting! *The Great Storm* 508
   Texas Cities *Galveston* 509
4 Women and the Progressive Movement 511
   That's Interesting! *Clara Driscoll and the Alamo* 512
   Biography *Jovita Idar* 513

CHAPTER 25
Texans at Home and Abroad
(1890–1920) 516

1 From Farm to City 518
   Connecting to Literature *O. Henry and the Modern Short Story* 519
   Biography *Carrie Marcus Neiman* 520
2 Urban Life in Texas 522
   Biography *Adina Emilia De Zavala* 523
   That's Interesting! *Moving the Bank* 524
   Connecting to Music *Scott Joplin* 525
   Connecting to the Arts *Elisabet Ney* 526
3 Texas and World Events 527
   Connecting to Literature *Jovita Gonzáles de Mireles* 529
   Global Connections *The Political Origins of World War I* 530

CHAPTER 26
Boom and Bust
(1920–1939) 534

1 The Transition to Peace. 536
   Biography *Miriam A. "Ma" Ferguson* 538
2 Economic and Cultural Change 540
   Biography *C. M. "Dad" Joiner* 541
   Texas Cities *Corpus Christi* 542
   Connecting to Music *Texas Blues* 543
3 The Great Depression 544
   That's Interesting! *Hoover Hogs*. 545
   Connecting to Economics and Math *Texans at Work* 546
   Visualizing History *The Causes of the Dust Bowl* 547
   Connecting to Geography *Drought and Farming in Texas*. 549
4 Texas and the New Deal 550
   Biography *Samuel Rayburn* 551
   Linking Past to Present *Social Security* 552
   Connecting to Music *Western Swing* 553
   Lone Star Legacy *The San Jacinto Monument* 554
   Connecting to Literature *"Mustang Gray" by J. Frank Dobie* 555

Social Studies Skills Workshop
   Using Primary and Secondary Sources. 558
History in Action Unit 8 Simulation 559

Women's suffrage poster

World War II poster

UNIT 9
The Modern Era
(1939–Present) 560

Texas Teens
Young Entrepreneurs 561

CHAPTER 27
World War II and the Cold War
(1939–1960) 562

1 World War II 564
   Daily Life *World War II Soldiers* 565
   That's Interesting! *Young Texans Help the War Effort* 566
2 Postwar Peace and Politics 568
   Global Connections *Roots of the Cold War* .. 569
   Biography *Dwight D. Eisenhower* 570
3 The Urbanization of Texas 572
   Connecting to Music *Buddy Holly and Rock 'n' Roll* 573
   Connecting to Literature *Katherine Anne Porter* 574
   Connecting to the Arts *Robert Rauschenberg* 575
   Connecting to Geography and Economics *Trade and Interstate Highways* 576
4 The Search for Equal Rights 577
   Biography *Hector P. García* 579
   Biography *Oveta Culp Hobby* 581

CHAPTER 28
Texas in Transition
(1960–1980) 584

1 A Texas President 586
   Biography *Lyndon B. Johnson* 588
2 The Civil Rights Movement 590
   Biography *James Farmer* 591
   Biography *Henry B. González* 593
   Biography *Barbara Jordan* 595
3 New Technology and the Space Race 596
   Biography *Walter Cunningham* 597
   Connecting to Economics *The Texas Aerospace Industry* 598
4 Texas in the 1970s 600
   Connecting to Science and Technology *Keeping Cool in Texas* 601
   Visualizing History *Urban Growth* 602
   That's Interesting! *The Astrodome* 602
   Our Cultural Heritage *The Chinese Lunar New Year* 603
   Connecting to Economics *Texas Boom-and-Bust Cycles* 605

CHAPTER 29
Challenges of a Modern State
(1980–Present) 608

1 Political Change in Texas 610
   That's Interesting! *Bob Bullock and the Story of Texas* 612

2 Texans in the White House **613**
   Biography *George W. Bush* **615**
   Historical Document *President Bush's
   Address to the Nation* **617**

3 The Texas Economy **619**
   Biography *Michael DeBakey* **621**
   Texas Cities *El Paso* **622**
   Connecting to Economics *Employment
   in Texas* **623**

4 Cultures of Texas **624**
   Connecting to Literature *Larry McMurtry* . . . **626**
   Connecting to the Arts *John Biggers* **627**
   Connecting to Music *Tejano Music* **628**

5 Texas Faces the Future **629**
   Connecting to Science and Technology
   Our Future **631**

Social Studies Skills Workshop
   **Distinguishing Fact from Opinion
   and Identifying Bias** **634**
History in Action Unit 9 Simulation **635**

UNIT 10 Handbook of Texas
(1845–Present) **636**

Texas Teens
   Young Politicians **637**

CHAPTER 30
Texas Government
(1845–Present) **638**

1 The Texas Constitution **640**
   Global Connections *English Common Law* . . **642**

2 The Texas Legislature **644**
   Biography *Thomas J. Lee* **645**
   Visualizing History *How a Bill Becomes a
   Law in Texas* **646**
   That's Interesting! *High-Tech Government* . . . **647**

3 The Texas Executive **648**
   Biography *Ann Richards* **649**
   Texas Cities *Austin* **650**
   Lone Star Legacy *The Texas Capitol* **651**

4 The Texas Judiciary **652**
5 The State Budget and Public Education **655**
   Linking Past to Present *Texas School Days* . . **657**

CHAPTER 31
Local Government
and Citizenship
(1845–Present) **660**

1 Local Government **662**
   That's Interesting! *Texans on the Road* **663**

2 The Bill of Rights **665**
3 Citizenship and Elections **668**
   Citizenship and You *Public Service* **669**
   Biography *Phil Gramm* **670**

4 Political Parties and Interest Groups **671**
   That's Interesting! *Every Vote Counts* **672**
   Daily Life *A Lobbyist's Day* **673**

Social Studies Skills Workshop
   Using the Internet **676**
History in Action Unit 10 Simulation . . . **677**

REFERENCE SECTION
Opener **678**
The Governors and Presidents of Texas **R1**
The Constitutions of Texas **R8**
Facts about Texas **R10**
Gazetteer **R12**
Glossary **R18**
Spanish Glossary **R28**
Index **R39**
Acknowledgments **R55**

The Texas Capitol

Primary Sources

Sam Houston

Texas Voices

Roy Bedichek, *Environmental Dangers* 7

Frederick Law Olmsted, *The Trinity River* 22

Francis Moore Jr., *Texas Northers* 25

William B. DeWees, *Plant life of the South Texas Plains* 48

Robert T. Hill, *The Beauty of Texas Canyons* 59

Simars de Bellisle, *The Nomadic Life of the Karankawa* 73

Don Juan de Oñate, *Wichita Houses* . . 77

Diego Pérez de Luxán, *Jumano Hairstyles* 80

Bernal Díaz del Castillo, *Tenochtitlán* . . 92

Álvar Núñez Cabeza de Vaca, *Surviving in Texas* 96

Álvar Núñez Cabeza de Vaca, *Pretending to be a Healer* 97

Pedro de Castañeda, *The High Plains of the Texas Panhandle* 101

Pedro de Castañeda, *Early Contact with the Apache* 106

Alonso de León, *Finding La Salle's Settlement* 118

Isidro Félix de Espinosa, *Meeting the Tejas in East Texas* 122

Miguel de Molina, *An Early Conflict between the Spanish and Apache* . . 126

Isidro Félix de Espinosa, *Life in the Missions* 128

Antonio Gil Ybarbo, *Life in Bucareli* . . 138

Juan Agustín Morfi, *The Lack of Settlement in East Texas* 141

Pedro de Nava, *Spanish Fears of Filibusters* 144

Antonio María Martínez, *Texas in Ruins* 149

Mary Brown Austin, *Moses Austin's Last Wish* 162

Stephen F. Austin, *Choosing Land for a Colony* 164

Noah Smithwick, *The Town of San Felipe* 170

Stephen F. Austin, *Success in Texas* . . 171

Noah Smithwick, *Life in DeWitt's Colony* 174

Michael Muldoon, *Our Great Founder* 176

Thomas White, *The G. T. T. Reputation* 183

Frances Trask, *An Early School in Cole's Settlement* 189

Charles Douglas, *Slavery in Colonial Texas* 197

Fredonian Declaration of Independence 203

Manuel de Mier Y Terán, *Report on the State of Affairs in Texas* 204

The *Ayuntamiento* of San Antonio, *The Advantages of U.S. immigration to Texas* 206

Stephen F. Austin, *Concerns Over the Convention of 1833* 213

Noah Smithwick, *The March to San Antonio* 228

James Bowie, *The Importance of the Alamo and San Antonio* 235

William B. Travis, *A Call for Reinforcements* 238

Anonymous, *The Ruins of the Alamo* 239

Colonel Pedro Delgado, *The Mexican Camp at San Jacinto* 250

Sam Houston, *Sparing the Life of Santa Anna* 251

Francis R. Lubbock, *Sam Houston* . . . 258

Sam Houston, *Peace Treaties and American Indian Policies* 264

Telegraph and Texas Register, *Opposition to Austin as the Capital* 266

Mirabeau B. Lamar, *The Republic of Texas Indian Policy* 268

W. B. DeWees, *People of the Redlands* 273

Prince Carl of Solms-Braunfels, *The Importance of the German Settlements in Texas* 283

William H. Wharton, *The U.S. View of Texas Annexation in 1836* 296

Samuel Maverick, *General Woll's Invasion* 299

James Morgan, *Anson Jones's Election* 304

John Tyler, *The Meaning of James K. Polk's Election* 316

W. B. DeWees, *The Annexation of Texas* 317

Thomas J. Rusk, *The Texas Constitution Ban on Banks* 320

Charles DeMorse, *Welcoming the Mexican War* 332

Matagorda Newspaper, *Banning Tejanos* 336

Muguara, *The Effects of Westward Expansion on American Indians* . . . 340

Tokaway, *Reservation Life* 341

James Buckner Barry, *Challenges Doctors Faced* 351

Jane McManus Cazneau, *Eagle Pass* . . 359

Anonymous, *Experiences of Slaves* . . 363

Sam Houston, *Texas Should Stay in the Union* 374

Jefferson Davis, *Texas Troops* 377

J. C. Bates, *Vicksburg* 380

Julius Eggeling, *The Battle of Glorieta Pass* 382

M. L. Clark, *Fighting at Galveston* . . . 383

Anonymous, *Juneteenth* 396

Flake's Bulletin, *Literacy during Reconstruction* 397

James J. Thornton, *Justice and Texas Courts during Reconstruction* 399

Maud Cuney Hare, *Jim Crow Laws* . . 410

Satanta, *Effects of Westward Expansion on American Indians* . . . 418

Ten Bears, *Opposition to Reservation Life* 418

Galveston News, *Support of Raids against American Indians* 422

Old Lady Horse, *The Effects of Buffalo Extermination* 424

Little Robe, *Importance of the Buffalo* 425

Grey Beard and Minimic, *Accept Reservation Life* **427**

H. P. Cook, *Life on the Cattle Trail* . . **447**

George Duffield, *Burdens Cowboys faced on Cattle Drives* **448**

Charles Siringo, *Cowboys' Financial Problems* **453**

Fort Worth Democrat, *Effects of the Railroad Boom on Fort Worth* **465**

Jerome Swinford, *The International Demand for Texas Lumber* **472**

Al Hamill, *The Spindletop Strike* . . . **480**

Allie V. Scott, *Life in a Texas Boomtown* **487**

Anonymous Farmer, *Problems Farmers Face* **498**

Southern Farmers' Alliance Song, *"The Alliance Goes Marching On"* . . **502**

Fort Worth Gazette, *The Texas Railroad Commission* **505**

Isaac Cline, *The Galveston Storm* . . . **508**

Anonymous Russian Immigrant, *Freedom in Texas* **521**

William Brumby, *The Mission of the Texas Department of Health* **524**

Theodore Roosevelt, *Texas Rough Riders* **528**

Bruce Turner, *Oil Field Work* **541**

William G. DeLoach, *The Bust in Cotton Farming* **542**

Stella Boone and Ethel Stringer, *Life during the Depression* **545**

Monroe Brannon, *Clothing during the Depression* **546**

Pauline Robertson, *Texas Dust Storms* **548**

Robert Hicks, *Pappy Lee O'Daniel's Campaign* **553**

Audie Murphy, *Supporting the War Effort* **566**

Holland McCombs, *Dallas in the 1950s* **573**

Lulu B. White, *Working for Civil Rights* **578**

Hector P. García, *Félix Longoria's Funeral* **579**

Abe Fortas, *Lyndon B. Johnson's Personality* **587**

James Farmer, *Freedom Rides* **591**

Lyndon B. Johnson, *It Is Time to Enact a Civil Rights Law* **592**

Severita Lara, *Crystal City Protests* **593**

William Clements, *My Political Style* . . **604**

Mark Furr, *A Texan's Experience in the Persian Gulf War* **614**

George W. Bush, *America's Resolve* . . **616**

Joe Sierra, *The Texas Culture and the Tigua Indians* **625**

Sandra Cisneros, *Texas Literature and the Spanish Language* **626**

Gordon Bennett, *A Long History of Global Connections in Texas* **631**

Thomas J. Rusk, *The Principles of a Constitution* **641**

George W. Bush, *The Meaning of a Vote for the Texas Governor* . . . **649**

Sam Rayburn, *Public Service* **669**

Karl Rove, *The Costs of Political Campaigns in Texas* **673**

James Farmer

Historical Document

Turtle Bayou Resolutions **209**

Declaration of the People of Texas **232**

Travis's Letter **237**

The Texas Declaration of Independence **243**

President Bush's Address to the Nation **617**

Stephen F. Austin

Interpreting Political Cartoons

Santa Anna's Surrender **275**

Texas Coming In **316**

Sam Recruiting **327**

The Mexican War **345**

Grant and Reconstruction **405**

Reconstruction in Texas **413**

The Development of Texas **475**

The Spindletop Oil Boom **480**

Problems Facing Cotton Farmers . . **557**

The Tidelands Dispute **571**

The Connally Caper **604**

The Growth of the Republican Party in Texas **633**

The Redistricting of Texas **659**

The Spindletop oil boom

Contents **xvii**

History and Your World

The Texas Landscape. 4
The Use of Maps. 9
The Use of Charts and Graphs 13
Water Resources 20
Severe Weather. 24
Population Changes 30
Texas Agriculture 35
Natural Landforms. 42
Rainfall. 45
Ranching in the Central Plains 51
Erosion. 54
National Parks 57
Native American Cultures 68
Commercial Fishing. 72
Archaeology. 75
Droughts 79
Buffalo and Endangered Animals . . . 82
Deep-sea and Space Exploration . . . 90
Regional Growth 94
Minerals and Natural Resources. . . . 98
Global Trade. 103
Farming Today 112
European Immigration Today 115
Trade Disputes. 120
Former Colonies Today 125
Spanish Influence in the
Southwest 128
Migration 136
Democracy. 140
Foreign Conflicts Today 143
Government Policy Changes 148
Why People Move 160
Reasons for Immigration. 163
Community Problems Today. 168
Population Booms. 172
Modern Migrations 182
Reliance on Agriculture 186
Trade in Texas 191
Troubles Facing New Governments. . 195
Protests 202
Constitutional Issues Today. 207
International Conferences 211

Taxes. 215
Military Funding. 226
Forming New Governments. 231
Battle Memorials 234
Independence Days. 240
Refugees 246
Elections 256
Economic Problems. 259
Political Leaders Today. 265
National Debt. 271
Influencing Government 278
Immigration Trends and Patterns. . . 282
Education. 286
Diplomatic Talks 294
International Conflicts 297
U.S. Political Issues Today 303
Political Debates Today 314
Public Participation in Government. . 318
Governors 322
Peace Efforts 330
Treaties Today 334
Conflicts Over Land 338
Large-scale Farming. 348
Advances in Transportation 353
Writers and Artists 357
Civil Rights Struggles Today. 360
Regional Issues 372
Peace Talks. 376
People in the Armed Forces 381
People Affected By War. 386
Rebuilding Nations 389
Government Aid Programs 396
Political Disagreements. 400
Funding of Government Programs. . 404
How Laws are Made 408
American Indian Policies 416
American Indian Life 420
U.S. Army Today. 425
Relocation of People. 428
Livestock Industry Today 440
Jobs that Require Travel 443

Modern-Day Cowboys. 449
Scientific Discoveries Today. 454
Transportation Today. 462
Boom-and-Bust Cycles 467
Recent Inventions 471
Energy Sources Today 478
Oil Industry Today 483
Causes of City Growth. 486
Reform Organizations 498
Business and Regulation. 503
Recent Labor Actions. 507
Women in Politics 511
Urban Growth Today 518
Challenges of City Life. 522
Mexican Immigration Today 527
Human Rights Groups. 536
Popular Consumer Items 540
The U.S. Economy Today. 544
Government Regulation 550
Protecting Freedoms 564
Military Bases. 568
Effects of Urban Growth Today 572
Civil Rights. 577
Social Programs. 586
Current Political Movements. 590
Weapons Technology. 596
Major Texas Industries. 600
Government Leaders 610
Terrorism. 613
Trade Between Texas and Mexico. . . 619
The Census 624
Leadership Qualities 629
Government and the Law. 640
How the Legislature Works 644
State Governor. 648
Trials and Court Rulings 652
Taxes and Government Spending. . 655
Public Services. 662
Recent Political Meetings 665
Recent Elections 668
Recent Political Campaigns. 671

Texas Teens

Young Naturalists 1
Young American Indians 65
Young Settlers 157
Young War Supporters 223
Young Texans on the Frontier 311

Young Soldiers 369
Young Cowhands 437
Young Relief Workers 495
Young Entrepreneurs 561
Young Politicians 637

Texas teen dancing

LINKING PAST to PRESENT

Studying the Caddoan Mounds . . . 76
Pueblo Culture 81
Cartography 95
Trade Relations 205

The Size of the Texas Government . . 272
The French Legation 295
The Governor's Mansion 324
Military Bases 342

Party Politics 406
Social Security 552
Texas School Days 657

Citizenship and You

Recycling 37
Political Protest 212
Serving during the War 375

Your Vote Counts 403
Getting Involved in Government . . . 499
Public Service 669

Texas Cities

Houston 47
San Antonio 122
Laredo 204
Dallas 287

Fort Worth 340
Brownsville 384
Amarillo and Lubbock 450
Midland and Odessa 487

Galveston 509
Corpus Christi 542
El Paso 622
Austin 650

Building the Capitol

LONE STAR LEGACY

Padre Island 48
Alibates Flint Quarries 71
Texas Mustangs 105
The Big Thicket 185

The Lone Star Flag 258
Texas Rangers 261
Juneteenth 397
The Longhorn 442
Spindletop 479

The San Jacinto Monument 554
The Texas Capitol 651

Our Cultural Heritage

Religious Diversity in Texas 31
Our Caddo Name 77
Spanish Place-Names 114

Diez y Seis de Septiembre 145
Tejano Culture 175
A Blending of Foods 188
Little Alsace in Texas 284
German Culture in the Hill Country . . 337

African Traditions 361
American Indian Celebrations 430
Vaqueros and Cowboys 441
The Chinese Lunar New Year 603

Interdisciplinary Activities

Connecting To Geography

The Texas Population 34
The Columbian Exchange 107
Land in Mexican Texas. 177
Immigration to Texas. 285

Conflicts with Mexico 302
The Texas Frontier 343
The Expanding Texas Frontier 431
The Texas Ranching Industry. 457
Oil and Natural Gas Fields 482

The Greer County Dispute. 505
Drought and Farming in Texas 549
Trade and Interstate Highways 576

CONNECTING TO THE ARTS

Rock Art. 69
Mission Architecture 129
Texas Quilts 187
Théodore Gentilz. 288
Frederic Remington. 300
Friedrich Petri. 341

Hermann Lungkwitz 359
Western Artists. 452
Elisabet Ney. 526
Robert Rauschenberg. 575
John Biggers 627

CONNECTING TO Music

Romances Corridos 131
Cowboy Songs. 453
Scott Joplin 525

Texas Blues 543
Western Swing. 553
Buddy Holly and Rock 'n' Roll. 573
Tejano Music 628

Jukebox

Connecting To Literature

Goodbye to a River by John Graves . . . 23
The Wind by Dorothy Scarborough . . 56
Native American Stories 78

Texas: Observations, Historical, Geographical, and Descriptive
by Mary Austin Holley 194
African American Folktales 362
Old Yeller by Fred Gipson 407
Andy Adams and Cowboy Stories. . . . 446

O. Henry and the Modern Short Story. . 519
Jovita González de Mireles. 529
"Mustang Gray" by J. Frank Dobie . . 555
Katherine Anne Porter. 574
Larry McMurtry. 626

CONNECTING TO SCIENCE AND TECHNOLOGY

GIS. 5
La Belle 116

Barbed Wire and Windmills. 456
Oil Drilling 488
Keeping Cool in Texas 601

Our Future 631
High-Tech Government 647

CONNECTING TO MATH

Gold and the Spanish Empire...... 93
Land in Mexican Texas.......... 177
The Republic's Debt 325
The Buffalo Population 424
The Texas Ranching Industry...... 457
The Railroad Boom 466
Texans at Work 546

CONNECTING TO ECONOMICS

Gold and the Spanish Empire...... 93
The Republic's Debt 325
Free Enterprise 352
The Railroad Boom 466
King Cotton in Texas 469
Wildcatters................... 485
Texans at Work 546
Trade and Interstate Highways 576
The Texas Aerospace Industry..... 598
Texas Boom–and–Bust Cycles 605
Employment in Texas 623

Historical Highlights

That's Interesting!

Miles and Miles of Texas.......... 8
Texas Tornadoes 27
Llano Estacado 55
Vast Western Spaces 58
Danger on the Plains 83
Pigs on the Loose 91
Mud Volcanoes................ 119
Bernardo de Gálvez 141
Goliad's Spanish Name 144
Baron de Bastrop.............. 161
Texas Panthers................ 184
Austin in Prison 214
Line in the Sand 239
Houston: The Raven 263
Cow Horns................... 283
The Pig War 296
Counting the Votes 304
A Ban on Duels 321

Old Rough and Ready.......... 331
Behind Enemy Lines 332
The Mavericks 350
Snowball Wars................ 380
Historically Black Colleges....... 405
General Sherman's Near Miss..... 421
Bat Masterson 426
The XIT Ranch 451
The Knights of Labor 473
Oil Nicknames 484
The Great Storm 508

Clara Driscoll and the Alamo...... 512
Moving the Bank.............. 524
Hoover Hogs 545
Young Texans Help the War Effort .. 566
The Astrodome 602
Bob Bullock and the Story of Texas................. 612
High-Tech Government 647
Texans on the Road........... 663
Every Vote Counts 672

Texas armadillo

Future Farmers of America jacket

Historical Highlights, *continued*

Daily Life

Future Farmers of America 36
What's for Dinner? 102
Hospitality in Colonial Texas 169
Leisure Time. 189
The Home Front. 230

The Texas Schoolroom 289
Statehood Celebrations 317
Texas Roads 354
Camp Life 385

African American Schools 398
Life in the Oil Fields. 481
World War II Soldiers. 565
A Lobbyist's Day 673

Biography

Lady Bird Johnson

Roy Bedichek 7
Lady Bird Johnson. 28
Walter Prescott Webb 53
Álvar Núñez Cabeza de Vaca. 97
Estevanico 99
Martín de Alarcón 124
Antonio Margil de Jesús 126
Antonio Gil Ybarbo 139
Martín de León. 151
Moses Austin 162
Stephen F. Austin. 164
Jane Long. 170
William Goyens 193
Antonio López de Santa Anna. 210
Juan Seguín. 229
William B. Travis. 235
Lorenzo de Zavala 242
George C. Childress. 245
Susanna Dickinson 247
James Fannin. 248
Sam Houston. 262

Chief Bowles 264
Mirabeau B. Lamar 266
Greenbury Logan. 280
Anson Jones. 305
Jane McManus Cazneau 315
José Antonio Navarro. 319
Elisha M. Pease 323
John Coffee Hays. 333
Gail Borden Jr. 358
Richard Dowling. 383
George T. Ruby 402
Richard Coke 409
Satanta 419
Cynthia Parker 422
Henry O. Flipper 429
Charles Goodnight. 447
Dora Nunn Roberts 470

Anthony F. Lucas 480
James Stephen Hogg. 504
Jovita Idar. 513
Carrie Marcus Neiman. 520
Adina Emilia De Zavala 523
Miriam A. "Ma" Ferguson 538
C. M. "Dad" Joiner 541
Samuel Rayburn. 551
Dwight D. Eisenhower. 570
Hector P. García 579
Oveta Culp Hobby 581
Lyndon B. Johnson 588
James Farmer. 591
Henry B. González. 593
Barbara Jordan 595
Walter Cunningham. 597
George W. Bush 615
Michael DeBakey. 621
Thomas J. Lee 645
Ann Richards 649
Phil Gramm 670

GLOBAL CONNECTIONS

El Niño. 25
The Reformation 104
Revolutions in Latin America. 146
The Antislavery Movement Abroad . . 206

The Pastry War. 298
Global Trade and the Civil War 378
Famine in China 465

The Political Origins of World War I . . 530
Roots of the Cold War. 569
English Common Law. 642

Technology Activities

Maps and Location 17
The Edwards Aquifer 39
Regions of Texas 61
Native Americans and their
Environment 87
Navigation Technology 109
Texas Culture 133
Texas Filibusters 153
Empresario Colonies 179
Life in Colonial Texas 199
Historical Documents that led
to the Texas Revolution 219
The Siege of the Alamo 253

Indian Conflicts of the
Republic of Texas 275
Immigrant Cultures in Texas 291
The Debate over Annexation 307
Early Texas Governors 327
Texas Rangers and the
Mexican War 345
Transportation Systems 365
Effects of the Civil War on Texas . . . 393
Effects of Reconstruction on Texas . . 413
American Indian Culture in Texas . . 433
The King Ranch 459
Railroads in Texas 475

Oil Industry 491
The Galveston Hurricane of 1900 . . . 515
The Effects of the Mexican
Revolution on Texas 533
The Great Depression 557
World War II and the Cold War 583
Effects of Urbanization 607
The Texas Economy and
Geographic Patterns 633
The Structure of the Texas
Government 659
Contributions of Elected
Leaders in Texas 675

Skill-Building Activities

Social Studies Skills WORKSHOPS

Interpreting Graphs Four Largest Texas Cities, 2000 17
Interpreting Maps Major Rivers of Texas 39
Interpreting Maps National Parks in Texas 61
Posing and Answering Questions 62
Interpreting Maps Migration Routes of Early Peoples 87
Interpreting Charts 2000 Values of Texas Livestock
Originally Native to Europe, Africa, or Asia 109
Interpreting Maps North America in 1754 133
Interpreting Maps The Neutral Ground 153
Decision-Making Skills 154
Interpreting Graphs Texas Population
Growth, 1783–1836 179
Interpreting Maps Texas Cultural Regions, 1836 199
Interpreting Charts Value of Texas Exports, 1833 219
Problem-Solving Skills 220
Interpreting Maps The Battle of San Jacinto, 1836 253
Interpreting Political Cartoons Santa Anna's Surrender 275
Interpreting Maps German Settlements in Texas,
1831–1860 291
Interpreting Graphs The Republic's
Indian-Policy Expenses 307
Reading Skills 308
Interpreting Political Cartoons Sam Recruiting 327
Interpreting Political Cartoons The Mexican War 345
Interpreting Maps Slaves in Texas, 1860 365
Interpreting Time Lines 366
Interpreting Maps Texas Vote on Secession, 1861 393

Interpreting Political Cartoons Reconstruction in Texas 413
Interpreting Graphs Texas Counties with the Largest
American Indian Population, 2000 433
Identifying Cause and Effect 434
Interpreting Maps Ethnic and Racial Background
of Cowboys, 1880 459
Interpreting Political Cartoons The Development of Texas . . 475
Interpreting Graphs Spindletop Oil Production,
1901–1921 491
Study Skills 492
Interpreting Maps Texas Counties That Regulate Alcohol,
c.2000 515
Interpreting Graphs Texas Urban and Rural Population,
1870–1920 533
Interpreting Political Cartoons Problems Facing Cotton
Farmers 557
Using Primary and Secondary Sources 558
Interpreting Graphs Texas Urban and Rural Population,
1920–1970 583
Interpreting Maps Growth of the Sunbelt, 1970–1980 . . . 607
Interpreting Political Cartoons The Growth of the
Republican Party in Texas 633
Distinguishing Fact from Opinion and Identifying Bias 634
Interpreting Political Cartoons The Redistricting of Texas . . . 659
Interpreting Graphs Voter Turnout in the Most
Populated Counties, 2000 675
Using the Internet 676

Skill-Building Activities, *continued*

History in Action UNIT SIMULATIONS

Problem Solving How Can You Help the State's Parks? **63**

Decision Making Should Spain Finance a New Expedition to Texas?. **155**

Problem Solving How Can Stephen F. Austin Convince Settlers to Move to Texas? **221**

Decision Making Should Texas Declare Independence?. . . **309**

Decision Making Should Texas Join the United States? . . . **367**

Decision Making Should Texas Support the Union or the Confederacy? **435**

Problem Solving How Will You Move Texas Cattle to Market? **493**

Problem Solving How Can Texas Farmers Raise Crop Prices? **559**

Decision Making Should Your Family Move to a City? **635**

Problem Solving How Can I Encourage Texans to Vote? **677**

MAPS

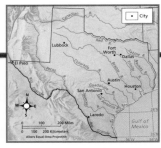

World: Political **A1**

United States of America: Political . . **A2**

United States of America: Physical . . **A4**

North America: Political **A6**

Texas: Physical. **A7**

Locating Texas **A8**

Texas Counties **A8**

Latitude and Longitude **10**

The Environment of Texas, 2000 . . . . **11**

Zones of Annual Average Precipitation **26**

Major Rivers of Texas **39**

Natural Regions of Texas **43**

Subregions of the Gulf Coastal Plain . . **46**

Subregions of the Central Plains . . . **52**

Subregions of the Great Plains **55**

The Intermountain Basins and Plateaus Region **58**

National Parks in Texas **61**

Native Americans in Texas, c.1500s and c.1800s **70**

Comanche Migration to Texas, 1700–1800 . . . . **84**

Migration Routes of Early Peoples . . . **87**

Spanish Explorers in Texas, 1519–1601 . . . . **96**

Non-Native Plants and Animals in Texas, 1990s **107**

La Salle and the French in Texas . . . **117**

Texas under Spanish Rule, c.1750 . . . **121**

North America in 1754 . . . . **133**

North America in 1763 . . . . **137**

The Louisiana Purchase and the Adams-Onís Treaty **141**

The Neutral Ground **153**

Austin's Colony **165**

Some *Empresarios'* Colonies and Land Grants, 1820s **173**

Mexican Land Grants, 1821–1836 . . **177**

U.S. Settlers Come to Texas, 1830s . **183**

Coahuila y Texas in 1825 . . . . **196**

Texas Cultural Regions, 1836 . . . . . **199**

Conflicts in Texas, 1825–1835 . . . . **208**

Early Conflicts of the Texas Revolution, 1835 . . . . **227**

Battles of the Texas Revolution, 1835–1836 . . . . **249**

The Battle of San Jacinto, 1836 . . . . **253**

The Republic of Texas, 1836 . . . . . . **257**

Indian Battles in Texas, 1836–1845 . . **268**

Immigration to Texas, 1836–1850 . . . **285**

Origin of European Immigrants . . . **285**

German Settlements in Texas, 1831–1860 . . . . **291**

Conflicts of the Republic, 1837–1842 . . . . **302**

The Mexican War, 1846–1848 . . . . . **331**

New Borders, 1853 . . . . **335**

Military Posts and Indian Reservations in Texas, 1846–1860 . . . . **343**

Transportation in Texas, 1860 . . . . . **355**

Slaves in Texas, 1860 . . . . **365**

The Union and the Confederacy, 1861 . . . . **374**

Major Battles of the Civil War **379**

The Civil War in Texas, 1862–1865 . . **382**

Civil War Trade, 1861–1865 . . . . **387**

Texas Vote on Secession, 1861 . . . . **393**

Reconstruction in the South **401**

Indian Wars in Texas, 1871–1874 . . **421**

Settlement of the Texas Frontier, 1880 . . . . **431**

The Cattle Kingdom of Texas, 1865–1890 . . . . **445**

Ranching in Texas, Today **457**

Ethnic and Racial Background of Cowboys, 1880 . . . . **459**

The Growth of Railroads, 1860–1902 . . . . **463**

Oil and Natural Gas Fields, 1930 . . **482**

Oil and Natural Gas Fields, 2000 . . **482**

Populism in Texas, 1890s **501**

The Greer County Dispute **505**

Texas Counties That Regulate Alcohol, c.2000 . . . . **515**

The Dust Bowl, 1930s **549**

Highways in Texas, 1950–2000 . . . . **576**

Growth of the Sunbelt, 1970–1980 . . **607**

GRAPHS AND CHARTS

Texas Counties. **A9**
Texas Population, 1900–2000. . . . . **14**
Texas Population Growth, 1990–2000 . . . . **14**
Origins of Immigrants to Texas, 1996 . . . . **15**
Four Largest Texas Cities, 2000 . . . . **17**
Cutaway View of Texas Elevation. **21**
Texas Population Pyramid, 1999. . . . . **34**
Racial and Ethnic Heritage of Texas, 2000 . . . . **34**
Texas Population, 2000–2010. . . . . **34**
Origins of Plants and Animals **107**
2000 Values of Texas Livestock Originally Native
to Europe, Africa, or Asia **109**
Causes and Effects of Mexican Independence **149**
Texas Population Growth, 1783–1836. . . . . **179**
Value of Texas Exports, 1833 . . . . **219**
Salaries of Texas Government Officials **304**
The Republic's Indian-Policy Expenses **307**
Texas Population **349**
Texas Occupations, 1850 and 1860 . . . . **352**
Total and Slave Populations, 1860 . . . . **362**
Texas Counties with the Largest American
Indian Population, 2000 . . . . **433**

The Cattle Boom In Texas **457**
Causes and Effects of the Railroad Boom. **464**
King Cotton in Texas **469**
Spindletop Oil Production, 1901–1921. . . . . **491**
Texas Urban and Rural Population, 1870–1920 . . . . **533**
Drought in Texas, 1920–1940. . . . . **549**
Transportation and Export Trade with Mexico,
1997 and 2000 . . . . **576**
Texas Urban and Rural Population, 1920–1970 . . . . **583**
Registered Voters in Texas, 1970–1980. . . . . **594**
Oil and Natural Gas Production in Texas, 1915–1995 . . . **605**
Oil Prices, 1970–1997 . . . . **605**
Governors' Elections, 1948–1998 . . . . **611**
Fastest-Growing Occupations in Texas, 1998–2008. . . . **623**
Growth of High-Tech Jobs in Texas, 1980–2000. . . . . . . **623**
Fastest-Growing Metropolitan Areas in Texas, 2000. . . . **630**
Texas Judicial System. **653**
Texas State Budget, 2002 . . . . **656**
Forms of Municipal Governments. **663**
Voter Turnout in the Most Populated Counties, 2000 . . . **675**

TIME LINES

Texas Indians: Beginnings–1700. . . . . **66**
The Search for Empire: 1492–1670. . . . . **88**
The Spanish Missions: 1680–1760. . . . . **110**
Conflicts of Empire: 1760–1821 . . . . **134**
Americans Settle in Texas: 1820–1835 . . . . **158**
Life in Early Texas: 1820–1835 . . . . **180**
The Road to Revolution: 1825–1835. . . . . **200**
The Texas Revolution: 1835–1836. . . . . **224**
A New Nation: 1836–1845 . . . . **254**
Life in the Republic: 1836–1845 . . . . **276**
Texas Faces Foreign Challenges: 1836–1845 . . . . **292**
Texas Joins the United States: 1845–1860 . . . . **312**
Western Expansion and Conflict: 1845–1860. . . . . **328**
Life in a Frontier State: 1845–1861 . . . . **346**

Texas and the Civil War: 1861–1865 . . . . **370**
Reconstruction: 1865–1877 . . . . **394**
The Indian Wars: 1861–1880 . . . . **414**
The Cattle Kingdom: 1860–1890 . . . . **438**
Railroads and Farming: 1870–1900 . . . . **460**
The Oil Boom: 1890–1920 . . . . **476**
Texas in the Age of Reform: 1870–1920 . . . . **496**
Texans at Home and Abroad: 1890–1920 . . . . **516**
Boom and Bust: 1920–1939 . . . . **534**
World War II and the Cold War: 1939–1960. . . . . **562**
Texas in Transition: 1960–1980. . . . . **584**
Challenges of a Modern State: 1980–Present **608**
Texas Government: 1845–Present. **638**
Local Government and Citizenship: 1845–Present. **660**

VISUALIZING HISTORY

Texas Landforms **6**
Life in a Spanish Mission **113**
Federalism and Centralism. **216**
The Siege of the Alamo. **236**
The Separation of Powers **320**

The Sharecropping Cycle **410**
Vertical and Horizontal Integration **484**
The Causes of the Dust Bowl **547**
Urban Growth **602**
How a Bill Becomes a Law in Texas **646**

How to Use Your Textbook

Use the chapter opener to get an overview of the time period.

The Chapter Time Line shows you a comparison of Texas and U.S. and global events.

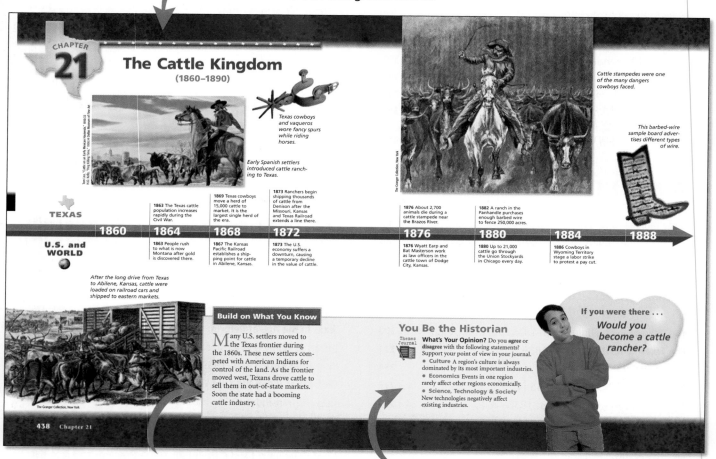

CHAPTER 21

The Cattle Kingdom
(1860–1890)

Texas cowboys and vaqueros wore fancy spurs while riding horses.

Early Spanish settlers introduced cattle ranching to Texas.

Cattle stampedes were one of the many dangers cowboys faced.

This barbed-wire sample board advertises different types of wire.

TEXAS

1863 The Texas cattle population increases rapidly during the Civil War.

1869 Texas cowboys move a herd of 15,000 cattle to market. It is the largest single herd of the era.

1873 Ranchers begin shipping thousands of cattle from Denison after the Missouri, Kansas and Texas Railroad extends a line there.

1876 About 2,700 animals die during a cattle stampede near the Brazos River.

1882 A ranch in the Panhandle purchases enough barbed wire to fence 250,000 acres.

| 1860 | 1864 | 1868 | 1872 | 1876 | 1880 | 1884 | 1888 |

U.S. and WORLD

1863 People rush to what is now Montana after gold is discovered there.

1867 The Kansas Pacific Railroad establishes a shipping point for cattle in Abilene, Kansas.

1873 The U.S. economy suffers a downturn, causing a temporary decline in the value of cattle.

1876 Wyatt Earp and Bat Masterson work as law officers in the cattle town of Dodge City, Kansas.

1880 Up to 21,000 cattle go through the Union Stockyards in Chicago every day.

1886 Cowboys in Wyoming Territory stage a labor strike to protest a pay cut.

After the long drive from Texas to Abilene, Kansas, cattle were loaded on railroad cars and shipped to eastern markets.

Build on What You Know

Many U.S. settlers moved to the Texas frontier during the 1860s. These new settlers competed with American Indians for control of the land. As the frontier moved west, Texans drove cattle to sell them in out-of-state markets. Soon the state had a booming cattle industry.

You Be the Historian

What's Your Opinion? Do you **agree** or **disagree** with the following statements? Support your point of view in your journal.
- **Culture** A region's culture is always dominated by its most important industries.
- **Economics** Events in one region rarely affect other regions economically.
- **Science, Technology & Society** New technologies negatively affect existing industries.

If you were there . . . *Would you become a cattle rancher?*

438 Chapter 21

Build on What You Know bridges the material you have studied in previous chapters with the material you are about to begin. As you read the Build on What You Know feature, take a few minutes to think about the topics that might apply to the chapter you are starting.

You Be the Historian puts you in the place of a historian looking at the past. In this feature, you will be asked to respond to three general statements about the chapter. Each statement is tied to one of the key themes of the program. You should respond based on your own knowledge and then record your responses in your journal. There are no right or wrong answers, just your informed opinion.

Use these built-in tools to read for understanding.

Read to Discover

questions begin each section of *Texas!* These questions serve as your guide as you read through the section. Keep them in mind as you explore the section content.

Why It Matters Today

is an exciting way for you to make connections between what you are reading in your history book and the world around you. In each section, you will be invited to explore a topic that is relevant to our lives today by using **CNNfyi.com** connections.

Interpreting the Visual Record

features accompany many of the book's rich images. Pictures are one of the most important primary sources historians can use to help analyze the past. These features invite you to examine the images and to interpret their content.

Define and Identify

terms are introduced at the beginning of each section. The terms will be defined in context.

The Story Continues

features an interesting episode from Texas history that shows you that history is not just a collection of facts but a blend of many individual stories and adventures.

Texas Voices

quotations appear frequently throughout the book. These exciting primary source quotations give you a glimpse into the lives of actual people who made history. Many of these quotations are accompanied by an Analyzing Primary Sources question to help you better interpret the sources and draw inferences about their importance.

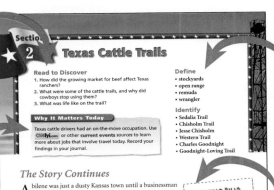

Reading Check

questions appear throughout the book to allow you to check your comprehension while you are reading. As you read each section, pause for a moment to consider each Reading Check. If you have trouble answering the question, go back and examine the material you just read.

Use these review tools to pull together all the information you have learned.

Graphic Organizers will help you pull together important information from the section. You can complete the graphic organizer as a study tool to prepare for a test or writing assignment.

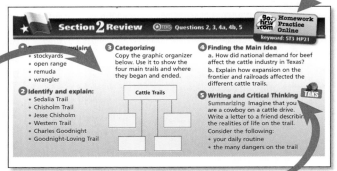

Homework Practice Online lets you log on to the go.hrw.com Web site to complete an interactive self-check of the material covered in the section.

Writing and Critical Thinking for TAKS activities allow you to explore a section topic in greater depth and to build your skills that will help you on the TAKS test.

The Chapter at a Glance is an interesting visual summary of the main ideas of the chapter.

Social Studies Skills Workshop is a way for you to build your skills at analyzing information and to practice answering standardized-test questions.

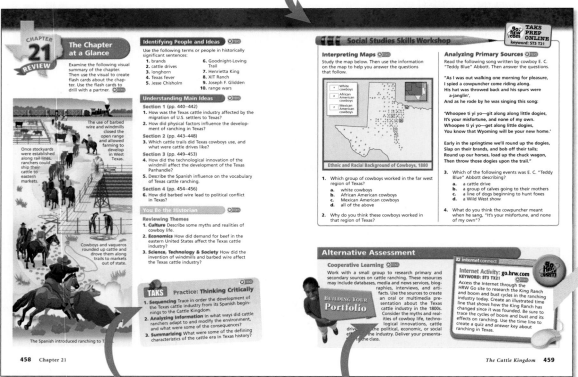

Thinking Critically for TAKS questions ask you to use the information you have learned in the chapter to extend your knowledge. You will be asked to analyze information by using your critical thinking skills.

Building Your Portfolio is an exciting and creative way to demonstrate your understanding of history.

Use these online tools to review and complete online activities.

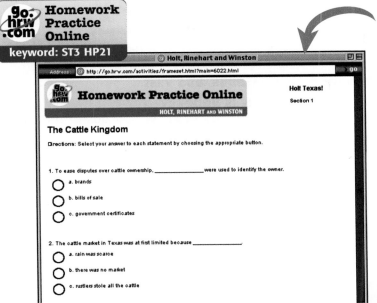

go.hrw.com Homework Practice Online
keyword: ST3 HP21

Holt, Rinehart and Winston

Address: http://go.hrw.com/activities/frameset.html?main=6022.html

go.hrw.com Homework Practice Online
HOLT, RINEHART AND WINSTON

Holt Texas!
Section 1

The Cattle Kingdom

Directions: Select your answer to each statement by choosing the appropriate button.

1. To ease disputes over cattle ownership, _____ were used to identify the owner.
   - a. brands
   - b. bills of sale
   - c. government certificates

2. The cattle market in Texas was at first limited because _____.
   - a. rain was scarce
   - b. there was no market
   - c. rustlers stole all the cattle

Homework Practice Online lets you log on for review anytime.

go.hrw.com TAKS PREP ONLINE
keyword: ST3 T

TAKS Prep Online helps you to prepare for the TAKS test.

---

internet connect

Internet Activity: go.hrw.com
KEYWORD: ST3 TX21 ★TEKS

Access the Internet through the HRW Go site to research the King Ranch and boom and bust cycles in the ranching industry today. Create an illustrated time line that shows how the King Ranch has changed since it was founded. Be sure to trace the cycles of boom and bust and its effects on ranching. Use the time line to create a quiz and answer key about ranching in Texas.

GO.HRW.COM

/gohrw_rls1/pKeywordResults?keyword=st3%20tx21&SPIDERSESSION=AAAAAgAAABoA

...STON   SOCIAL STUDIES

ST3 TX21

HOLT TEXAS!

The King Ranch: Then and Now

Activity: Use the links below to learn more about the King Ranch and boom and bust cycles in the ranching industry. Then create an illustrated time line that shows how the King Ranch has changed since it was founded. Be sure to trace the cycle of boom and bust and its effects on ranching. Use the time line to create a quiz and answer key about ranching in Texas.

Activity Links

The History of the King Ranch
An article on the formation of the King Ranch. The article features photographs.
Web site by: The King Ranch

A Virtual Tour of the King Ranch
A virtual tour of the King Ranch. The site features background information on the daily routine of the ranch.
Web site by: Corpus Christi Caller-Times

Return to Top | ST3 TX21

Copyright © by Holt, Rinehart and Winston. All rights reserved.
Terms of Use

Internet zone

Internet Connect activities are just one part of the world of online learning experiences that awaits you on the go.hrw.com Web site. By exploring these online activities, you will take a journey through some of the richest Texas history materials available on the World Wide Web. You can then use these resources to create real-world projects, such as newspapers, brochures, reports, and even your own Web site!

Why History Matters Today

" **T**exas history is as varied, tempestuous, and vast as the state itself. Texas yesterday is unbelievable, but no more incredible than Texas today."

—Edna Ferber

Right now, at this very second, somewhere in Texas, someone is making history. It is impossible to know who or in what way, but the actions of people today may become the history of tomorrow.

History and Your World

All you need to do is watch or read the news to see history unfolding. How many news stories do you see or hear about ordinary people doing extraordinary things? The Why It Matters Today feature beginning every section of *Texas!* invites you to use the vast resources of **CNNfyi.com** or other current events sources to examine the links between past and present. Through this feature you will be able to draw connections between the stories in Texas history and the events that are taking place in the nation and around the world.

Anyone Can Be a History Maker

When you think of the word *history,* what comes to mind? Do you picture politicians sitting around a table deciding the future of the nation? Or do you see a long list of dates and boring facts to be memorized? Of course, politicians, dates, and facts are part of history, but there is actually much more to understanding and exploring our past. Our state has developed through the efforts of many different people, from all backgrounds and walks of life. Many of them were teenagers like yourself. Did you know teenagers were involved in the early contacts between Europeans and Texas Indians? It's true. For example,

Student reporters contribute to CNNfyi.com.

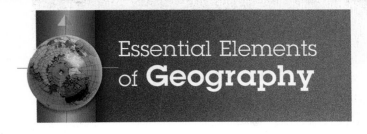

Essential Elements of Geography

History and geography share many elements. History describes important events that have taken place from ancient times until the present day. Geography describes how physical environments affect human events. It also examines how people's actions influence the environment around them. To describe a series of events without placing them in their physical settings is to tell only part of the story. Essential elements of geography include:

▶ **The World in Spatial Terms** This essential element refers to the way geographers view the world. They look at where things are and how they are arranged on Earth's surface. For example, geographers might be interested to learn why certain cities developed where they did.

▶ **Places and Regions** Geographers often focus on the physical and human characteristics that make particular parts of Earth special. A region is an area with common characteristics that make it different from surrounding areas. People create regions as a convenient way to study the world. Regions can be large, like North America, or small like a neighborhood.

▶ **Physical Systems** Geographers study the physical processes and interactions between four physical systems—Earth's atmosphere, land, water, and life. Physical processes shape and change Earth's physical features and environments.

▶ **Human Systems** As with physical systems, studying human systems can tell geographers much about the world around us. For example, studying population growth, distribution, and movement helps in understanding human events and their effect on the environment.

▶ **Environment and Society** One of the most important topics in geography is how people interact with the environment. People depend on the environment's natural resources for survival. However, human activities can have both positive and negative effects on Earth's environment.

▶ **The Uses of Geography** Historians use geography to understand the past. They look not only at when things happened but where and why they happened. But geography is important to the present as well as the past. People use geography every day to explore how to use Earth's limited resources, such as water and minerals, more effectively and in a way that ensures the success of future generations.

Texas teens can use the essential elements of geography to learn more about Texas geography.

Skills Handbook

Critical Thinking **S1**

Becoming a Strategic Reader **S4**

TAKS Test–Taking Strategies **S12**

Critical-thinking skills, reading skills, and test-taking strategies can help Texas teens become better students.

Critical Thinking

Throughout *Texas!*, you will be asked to think critically about the events and issues that have shaped Texas history. Critical thinking is the reasoned judgment of information and ideas. The development of critical thinking skills is essential to effective citizenship. Such skills empower you to exercise your civic rights and responsibilities. Helping you develop critical thinking skills is an important goal of *Texas!* The following critical thinking skills appear in the section reviews and chapter reviews of the book.

1 Analyzing Information is the process of breaking something down into its parts and examining the relationships between them. Analyzing enables you to better understand the whole. For example, to analyze the effects of the growth of the railroad in Texas, you might study the impact of the railroad on farming, settlement of the frontier, or urban growth.

2 Sequencing is the process of placing events in correct chronological order to better understand the historical relationships among the events. You can sequence events in two basic ways: according to absolute or relative chronology. Absolute chronology means that you pay close attention to the exact dates events took place. Placing events on a time line would be an example of absolute chronology. Relative chronology refers to the way events relate to one another. To put events in relative order, you need to know which one happened first, which came next, and so forth.

3 Categorizing is the process by which you group things together by the characteristics they have in common. By putting things or events into categories, it is easier to make comparisons and see differences among them.

4 Identifying Cause and Effect is a part of interpreting the relationships between historical events. A *cause* is an action that leads to an event. The outcome of the action is an *effect*. To explain historical events, historians often point out multiple causes and effects. For example, Mexican President Santa Anna's abandonment of the Constitution of 1824, Stephen F. Austin's arrest, and the arrival of Mexican troops in Texas were all factors that led to the Texas Revolution. The revolution had many effects, including the formation of the Republic of Texas.

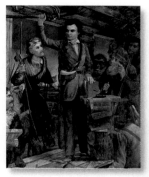

Stephen F. Austin

5 Comparing and Contrasting is examining events, situations, or points of view for their similarities and differences. *Comparing* focuses on both the similarities and the differences. *Contrasting* focuses only on the differences. For example, by comparing and contrasting the physical and human characteristics of a region, students can learn about the geographic diversity and patterns found in Texas.

Flint tool used by Native Americans

6 Finding the Main Idea is combining and sifting through information to determine what is most important. Historical writing often uses many examples and details to support the author's main ideas. Throughout *Texas!*, you will find numerous Reading Checks and questions in section reviews to help you focus on the main ideas in the text.

7 Summarizing is the process of taking a large amount of information and boiling it down into a short and clear statement. Summarizing is particularly useful when you need to give a brief account of a longer story or event. For example, the story of how cattle ranching developed in the Texas Panhandle is a detailed one. Many different events came together to make up the story. You could summarize the events by saying, "During the 1880s the Texas cattle industry was booming. With the removal of the Plains Indians from West Texas, the region was opened to ranching. The grassland in the region provided plenty of food for cattle. Although the region had little rainfall, ranchers used windmills to pump water from the Ogallala Aquifer to provide water for their livestock. With plenty of land, food, and water, ranching boomed in the Panhandle."

Early Texas farm

8 Making Generalizations and Predictions is the process of interpreting information to form more general statements and to guess about what will happen next. A *generalization* is a broad statement that holds true for a variety of historical events or situations. Making generalizations can help you see the "big picture" of historical events, rather than just focusing on details. It is very important, however, that when making generalizations you try not to include situations that do not fit the statement. When this occurs, you run the risk of creating a stereotype, or overgeneralization. A *prediction* is an educated guess about an outcome. When you read history, you should always be asking yourself questions like, "What will happen next? If this person does this, what will that mean for . . . ?", and so on. These types of questions help you draw on information you already know to see patterns throughout history.

9 Drawing Inferences and Conclusions is forming possible explanations for an event, a situation, or a problem. When you make an *inference,* you take the information you know to be true and come up with an educated guess about what else you think is true about that situation. A *conclusion* is a prediction about the outcome of a situation based on what you already know. Often, you must be prepared to test your inferences and conclusions against new evidence or arguments. For example, a historian might conclude that the contributions of African Americans and Mexican Americans who fought for their country during World War II helped spur the civil rights and equal rights movements in Texas.

World War II hero Doris Miller

10 Identifying Points of View is the process of identifying factors that influence the outlook of an individual or group. A person's point of view includes beliefs and attitudes that are shaped by factors such as age, gender, religion, race, and economic status. This critical thinking skill helps you examine why people see things as they do and reinforces the realization that people's views may change over time or with a change in circumstances.

11 Supporting a Point of View

involves choosing a viewpoint on a particular event or issue and arguing persuasively for that position. Your argument should be well organized and based on specific evidence that supports the point of view you have chosen. Supporting a point of view often involves working with controversial or emotional issues. For example, you

might consider the points of view involved in the Populists' effort to regulate Texas railroads during the late 1800s. Whether you choose a position in favor of the farmers or in favor of the railroads, you should state your opinion clearly and give reasons that defend it.

Railroad poster encouraging migration to Texas

12 Identifying Bias

is the process of evaluating the opinions of others about events or situations. Bias is an opinion based on prejudice or strong emotions, rather than on fact. It is important to identify bias when looking at historical sources, because biased sources often give you a false sense of what really happened. When looking at both primary and secondary sources, it is always important to keep the author's or speaker's point of view in mind and to adjust your interpretation of the source when you detect any bias.

13 Evaluating

is assessing the significance or overall importance of something, such as the success of a reform movement, the actions of a president, or the results of a major conflict. You should base your judgment on standards that others will understand and are likely to share. For example, you might consider the outcome of the Mexican War and the Treaty of Guadalupe Hidalgo, evaluating the importance of these events on Texas and its borders. You could also evaluate the effect of the war on the people already living in Texas.

14 Problem Solving

is the process by which you pose workable solutions to difficult situations. The first step in the process is to identify a problem. Next you will need to gather information about the problem, such as its history and the various factors that contribute to the problem. Once you have gathered information, you should list and consider the options for solving the problem. For each of the possible solutions, weigh their advantages and disadvantages and, based on your evaluation, choose and implement a solution. Once the solution is in place, go back and evaluate the effectiveness of the solution you selected.

15 Decision Making

is the process of reviewing a situation and then making decisions or recommendations for the best possible outcome. To complete the process, first identify a situation that requires a solution. Next, gather information that will help you reach a decision. You may need to do some background research to study the history of the situation, or carefully consider the points of view of the individuals involved. Once you have done your research, identify options that might resolve the situation. For each option, predict what the possible consequences might be if that option were followed. Once you have identified the best option, take action by making a recommendation and following through on any tasks that option requires.

Becoming a Strategic Reader

by Dr. Judith Irvin

Everywhere you look, print is all around us. In fact, you would have a hard time stopping yourself from reading. In a normal day, you might read cereal boxes, movie posters, notes from friends, t-shirts, instructions for video games, song lyrics, catalogs, billboards, information on the Internet, magazines, the newspaper, and much, much more. Each form of print is read differently depending on your purpose for reading. You read a menu differently from the way you read poetry, and a motorcycle magazine is read differently than a letter from a friend. Good readers switch easily from one type of text to another. In fact, they probably do not even think about it, they just do it.

When you read, it is helpful to use a strategy to remember the most important ideas. You can use a strategy before you read to help connect information you already know to the new information you will encounter. Before you read, you can also predict what a text will be about by using a previewing strategy. During the reading you can use a strategy to help you focus on main ideas, and after reading you can use a strategy to help you organize what you learned so that you can remember it later. *Texas!* was designed to help you more easily understand the ideas you read. Important reading strategies employed in *Texas!* include the following:

1 Methods to help you **anticipate** what is to come

2 Tools to help you **preview and predict** what the text will be about

3 Ways to help you **use and analyze visual information**

4 Ideas to help you **organize the information** you have learned

1. Anticipate Information

How Can I Use Information I Already Know to Help Me Understand What a New Chapter Will Be About?

Anticipating what a new chapter will be about helps you connect the upcoming information to what you already know. By drawing on your background knowledge, you can build a bridge to the new material.

1 Each chapter of *Texas!* asks you to explore the main themes of the chapter before you start reading by forming opinions based on your current knowledge.

You Be the Historian

Themes Journal

What's Your Opinion? Do you **agree** or **disagree** with the following statements? Support your point of view in your journal.

● **Culture** A region's culture is always dominated by its most important industries.

● **Economics** Events in one region rarely affect other regions economically.

● **Science, Technology & Society** New technologies negatively affect existing industries.

Create a chart like this one to help you analyze the statements.

A Before Reading Agree/Disagree		B After Reading Agree/Disagree
2	A region's culture is always dominated by its most important industries.	**4**
	Events in one region rarely affect other regions economically.	
	New technologies negatively affect existing industries.	

3 Read the text and discuss with classmates.

5 You can also refine your knowledge by answering the You Be the Historian—Reviewing Themes questions in the chapter review.

Anticipating Information

▶ **Step 1** Identify the major concepts of the chapter. In *Texas!*, these are presented in the **You Be the Historian** feature at the beginning of each chapter.

▼

Step 2 Agree or disagree with each of the statements and record your opinions in your journal.

▼

Step 3 Read the text and discuss your responses with your classmates.

▼

Step 4 After reading the chapter, revisit the statements and respond to them again based on what you have learned.

▼

Step 5 Go back and check your knowlege by answering the You Be the Historian—Reviewing Themes questions in the chapter review.

You Be the Historian— Reviewing Themes

1. **Culture** Describe some myths and realities of cowboy life.
2. **Economics** How did demand for beef in the eastern United States affect the Texas cattle industry?
3. **Science, Technology & Society** How did the invention of windmills and barbed wire affect the Texas cattle industry?

2. Previewing and Predicting

How Can I Figure out What the Text Is about before I Even Start Reading a Section?

Previewing and **predicting** are good methods to help you understand the text. If you take the time to preview and predict before you read, the text will make more sense to you during your reading.

1 Usually, your teacher will set the purpose for reading. After reading some new information, you may be asked to write a summary, take a test, or complete some other type of activity.

"After reading about ranching, you will work with a partner to create a historical museum exhibit describing . . ."

2 As you preview the text, use *graphic signals* such as headings, subheadings, and boldfaced type to help you determine what is important in the text. Each section of *Texas!* opens by giving you important clues to help you preview the material.

Previewing and Predicting

▶ **Step 1** Identify your purpose for reading. Ask yourself what will you do with this information once you have finished reading.

▼

Step 2 Ask yourself what the main idea of the text is and what key vocabulary words you need to know.

▼

Step 3 Use signal words to help identify the structure of the text.

▼

Step 4 Connect the information to what you already know.

Looking at the section's **main heading** and **subheadings** can give you an idea of what is to come.

Read to Discover questions give you clues as to the section's main ideas.

Define and Identify terms let you know the key vocabulary you will encounter in the section.

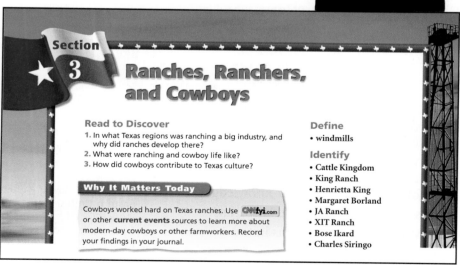

Section 3

Ranches, Ranchers, and Cowboys

Read to Discover
1. In what Texas regions was ranching a big industry, and why did ranches develop there?
2. What were ranching and cowboy life like?
3. How did cowboys contribute to Texas culture?

Why It Matters Today

Cowboys worked hard on Texas ranches. Use CNNfyi.com or other **current events** sources to learn more about modern-day cowboys or other farmworkers. Record your findings in your journal.

Define
• windmills

Identify
• Cattle Kingdom
• King Ranch
• Henrietta King
• Margaret Borland
• JA Ranch
• XIT Ranch
• Bose Ikard
• Charles Siringo

3 Other tools that can help you in previewing are **signal words**. These words prepare you to think in a certain way. For example, when you see words such as *similar to, same as,* or *different from,* you know that the text will probably compare and contrast two or more ideas. Signal words indicate how the ideas in the text relate to each other. Look at the list below of some of the most common signal words grouped by the type of text structures they indicate.

Signal Words

Cause and Effect	Compare and Contrast	Description	Problem and Solution	Sequence or Chronological Order
• because • since • consequently • this led to…so • if…then • nevertheless • accordingly • because of • as a result of • in order to • may be due to • for this reason • not only…but	• different from • same as • similar to • as opposed to • instead of • although • however • compared with • as well as • either…or • but • on the other hand • unless	• for instance • for example • such as • to illustrate • in addition • most importantly • another • furthermore • first, second…	• the question is • a solution • one answer is	• not long after • next • then • initially • before • after • finally • preceding • following • on (date) • over the years • today • when

4 Learning something new requires that you connect it in some way with something you already know. This means you have to think before you read and while you read. You may want to use a chart like this one to remind yourself of the information already familiar to you and to come up with questions you want answered in your reading. The chart will also help you organize your ideas after you have finished reading.

What I know	What I want to know	What I learned

3. Use and Analyze Visual Information

How Can All the Pictures, Maps, Graphs, and Time Lines With the Text Help Me Be a Stronger Reader?

Analyzing Information

▶ **Step 1** As you preview the text, ask yourself how the visual information relates to the text.

▼

Step 2 Generate questions based on the visual information.

▼

Step 3 After reading the text, go back and review the visual information again.

▼

Step 4 Make connections to what you already know.

Using visual information can help you understand and remember the information presented in *Texas!* Good readers form a picture in their minds when they read. The pictures, charts, graphs, cartoons, time lines, and diagrams that occur throughout *Texas!* are placed strategically to increase your understanding.

1 You might ask yourself questions like:

> Why did the author include this information with text? What details about this visual are mentioned in the text?

After you have read the text, see if you can answer your own questions.

2

What is loaded on these trains?

Where might these trains be going?

What does this picture reveal about the Texas economy?

3 After reading, take another look at the visual information.

4 Try to make connections to what you already know.

4. Organize Information

Once I Learn New Information, How Do I Keep It All Straight So That I Will Remember It?

To help you remember what you have read, you need to find a way of **organizing information**. Two good ways of doing this are by using graphic organizers and concept maps. **Graphic organizers** help you understand important relationships—such as cause-and-effect, compare/contrast, sequence of events, and problem/solution—within the text. **Concept maps** provide a useful tool to help you focus on the text's main ideas and organize supporting details.

Identifying Relationships

Using graphic organizers will help you recall important ideas from the section. They are also a study tool you can use to prepare for a quiz or test or to help with a writing assignment. Some of the most common types of graphic organizers are shown below.

> ### Cause and Effect
> Events in history cause people to react in certain ways. Cause-and-effect patterns show the relationship between results and the ideas or events that made the results occur. You may want to represent cause-and-effect relationships as one cause leading to multiple effects,

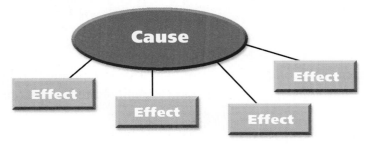

or as a chain of cause-and-effect relationships.

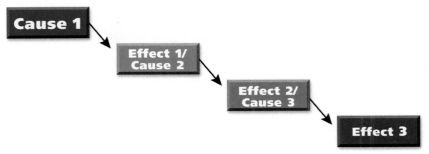

Constructing Graphic Organizers

▶ **Step 1** Preview the text, looking for signal words and the main idea.

▼

Step 2 Form a hypothesis as to which type of graphic organizer would work best to display the information presented.

▼

Step 3 Work individually or with your classmates to create a visual representation of what you read.

▶ Comparing and Contrasting

Graphic Organizers are often useful when you are comparing or contrasting information. Compare-and-contrast diagrams point out similarities and differences between two concepts or ideas.

▶ Sequencing

Keeping track of dates and the order in which events took place is essential to understanding history. Sequence or chronological-order diagrams show events or ideas in the order in which they happened.

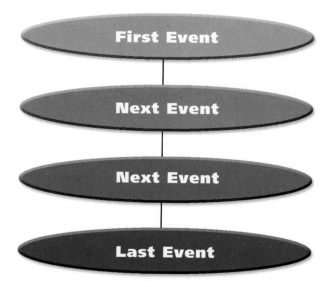

▶ Problem and Solution

Problem-solution patterns identify at least one problem, offer one or more solutions to the problem, and explain or predict outcomes of the solutions.

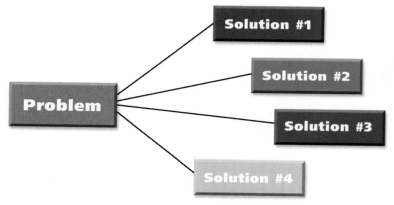

Identifying Main Ideas and Supporting Details

One special type of graphic organizer is the concept map. A concept map, sometimes called a semantic map, allows you to zero in on the most important points of the text. The map is made up of lines, boxes, circles, and/or arrows. It can be as simple or as complex as you need it to be to accurately represent the text.

Here are a few examples of concept maps you might use.

Constructing Concept Maps

▶ **Step 1** Preview the text, looking at what type of structure might be appropriate to display a concept map.

▼

Step 2 Taking note of the headings, boldfaced type, and text structure, sketch a concept map you think could best illustrate the text.

▼

Step 3 Using boxes, lines, arrows, circles, or any shapes you like, display the ideas of the text in the concept map.

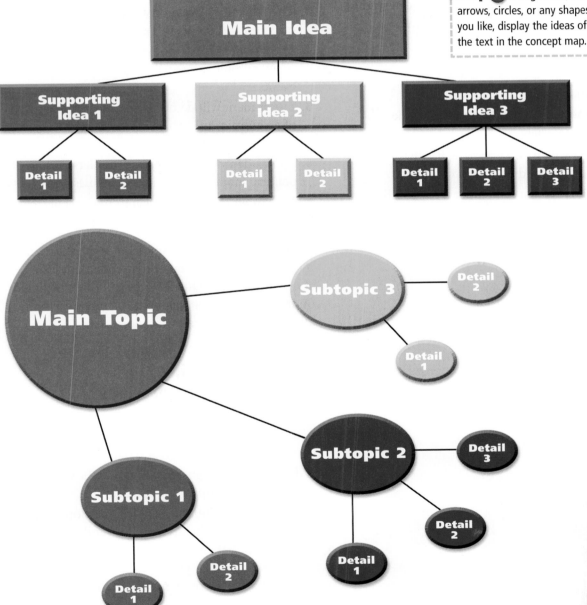

TAKS Test–Taking Strategies

Every year in school, from grade 2 through grade 11, you will be asked to take the TAKS (Texas Assessment of Knowledge and Skills) Test. The test is designed to demonstrate the content and skills you have learned. It is important to keep in mind that the best way to prepare for the test is to pay close attention in class and take every opportunity to improve your general social studies, reading, writing, and mathematical skills.

Tips for Taking the Test

1. Be sure that you are well rested.
2. Be on time and be sure that you have the necessary materials.
3. Listen to the instructions of the teacher.
4. Read directions and questions carefully.
5. **DON'T STRESS!** Just remember what you have learned in class, and you should do well.

▶ **Practice the strategies at go.hrw.com.**

go.hrw.com
TAKS PREP ONLINE
keyword: ST3 T

Tackling Social Studies

The social studies portions of the TAKS is designed to test your knowledge of the content and skills listed in the Texas Essential Knowledge and Skills (TEKS) that you have been studying in class. The objectives for TAKS are as follows:

1. The student will demonstrate an understanding of issues and events in Texas history.
2. The student will demonstrate an understanding of geographic influences on historical issues and events.
3. The student will demonstrate an understanding of economic and social influences on historical issues and events.
4. The student will demonstrate understanding of political influences on historical issues and events.
5. The student will use critical thinking skills to analyze social studies information.

The TAKS contains multiple-choice questions and may in the future contain open-ended questions also. The multiple-choice items will often be based on maps, tables, charts, graphs, pictures, cartoons, and/or reading passages and documents.

Tips for Answering Multiple-Choice Questions

1. If there is a written or visual piece accompanying the multiple-choice question, pay careful attention to the title, author, and date.
2. Then read through or glance over the content of the piece accompanying the question.
3. Next, read the multiple-choice question for its general intent. Then reread it carefully, looking for words that give clues. For example, words such as *most* or *best* tell you that there may be several correct answers, but you should look for the most appropriate answer.

4. Always read all of the possible answer choices, even if the first one seems like the correct answer. There may be a better choice farther down in the list.

5. Reread the accompanying information (if any is included) carefully to determine the answer to the question. Again, note the title, author, and date of primary-source selections. The answer will rarely be stated exactly as it appears in the primary source, so you will need to use your critical thinking skills to read between the lines.

6. Use your knowledge of the time in history or person involved to help limit the answer choices.

7. Finally, reread the question and selected answer to be sure that you made the best choice and that you marked it correctly on the answer sheet.

Strategies for Success

There are many strategies you can use to help you feel more confident about answering questions on social studies standardized tests. Here are a few suggestions:

1. Adopt an acronym—a word formed from the first letters of other words—that you will always use for analyzing a document or visual that might accompany a question.

Helpful Acronyms

For a document, use **SOAPS**, which stands for

S	Subject
O	Occasion
A	Audience
P	Purpose
S	Speaker/author

For a picture, cartoon, map, or other visual piece of information, use **OPTIC**, which stands for

O	Overview
P	Parts (labels or details of the visual)
T	Title
I	Interrelations (how the different parts of the visual work together)
C	Conclusion (what the visual means)

2. Form visual images of maps and try to draw them from memory. The standardized test will most likely include important maps from Spanish Texas, the colonial era, the Texas revolution, the Texas frontier, and many other subjects and eras. Be able to see in your mind's eye such things as the regions of Texas, the different borders of Texas over the years, and the areas of the state that have the largest population or amount of rainfall. Know major physical features, such as the Gulf of Mexico, the Rio Grande, the Hill Country, the Panhandle, the Piney Woods, and the mountains of West Texas, and be able to place them on a map.

3. When you have finished studying any Texas historical era, try to think of who or what might be important enough for the test. You may want to keep your ideas in a notebook to refer to when it is almost time for the test.

4. Pay particular attention to the Texas Constitution and its influences. Many standardized tests contain questions about this important document and the period during which it was written. Questions will address the influence of the U.S. Constitution and the Bill of Rights. Questions will also focus on the reasons Texas settlers might have had for supporting the structure of government created by the Texas Constitution.

5. For the skills area of the tests, practice putting major events and personalities in order in your mind. Sequencing people and events by dates can become a game you play with a friend who also has to take the test. Always ask yourself why this event is important.

6. Follow the tips under "Ready for Reading" on the next page when you encounter a reading passage in social studies, but remember that what you have learned about history can help you in answering reading-comprehension questions.

Ready for Reading

The main goal of the reading sections of most standardized tests is to determine your understanding of different aspects of a reading passage. Basically, if you can grasp the main idea and the author's purpose, then pay attention to the details and vocabulary so that you are able to draw inferences and conclusions, you will do well on the test.

Tips for Answering Multiple-Choice Questions

1. Read the passage as if you were not taking a test.

2. Look at the big picture. Ask yourself questions like, "What is the title?", "What do the illustrations or pictures tell me?", and "What is the author's purpose?"

3. Read the questions. This will help you know what information to look for.

4. Reread the passage, underlining information related to the questions.

Types of Multiple-Choice Questions

1. **Main Idea** This is the most important point of the passage. After reading the passage, locate and underline the main idea.

2. **Significant Details** You will often be asked to recall details from the passage. Read the question and underline the details as you read. But remember that the correct answers do not always match the wording of the passage precisely.

3. **Vocabulary** You will often need to define a word within the context of the passage. Read the answer choices and plug them into the sentence to see what fits best.

4. **Conclusion and Inference** There are often important ideas in the passage that the author does not state directly. Sometimes you must consider multiple parts of the passage to answer the question. If answers refer to only one or two sentences or details in the passage, they are probably incorrect.

5. Go back to the questions and try to answer each one in your mind before looking at the answers.

6. Read all the answer choices and eliminate the ones that are obviously incorrect.

Tips for Answering Short-Answer Questions

1. Read the passage in its entirety, paying close attention to the main events and characters. Jot down information you think is important.

2. If you cannot answer a question, skip it and come back later.

3. Words such as *compare, contrast, interpret, discuss,* and *summarize* appear often in short-answer questions. Be sure you have a complete understanding of each of these words.

4. To help support your answer, return to the passage and skim the parts you underlined.

5. Organize your thoughts on a separate sheet of paper. Write a general statement with which to begin. This will be your topic statement.

6. When writing your answer, be precise but brief. Be sure to refer to details in the passage in your answer.

Targeting Writing

On many standardized tests, you will occasionally be asked to write an essay. In order to write a concise essay, you must learn to organize your thoughts before you begin writing the actual composition. This keeps you from straying too far from the essay's topic.

Tips for Answering Composition Questions

1. Read the question carefully.

2. Decide what kind of essay you are being asked to write. Essays usually fall into one of the following types: persuasive, classificatory, compare/contrast, or "how to." To determine the type of essay, ask yourself questions like, "Am I trying to persuade my audience?", "Am I comparing or contrasting ideas?", or "Am I trying to show the reader how to do something?"

3. Pay attention to key words, such as *compare, contrast, describe, advantages, disadvantages, classify,* or *speculate.* They will give you clues as to the structure that your essay should follow.

4. Organize your thoughts on a separate sheet of paper. You will want to come up with a general topic sentence that expresses your main idea. Make sure this sentence addresses the question. You should then create an outline or some type of graphic organizer to help you organize the points that support your topic sentence.

5. Write your composition using complete sentences. Also, be sure to use correct grammar, spelling, punctuation, and sentence structure.

6. Be sure to proofread your essay once you have finished writing.

Gearing up for Math

On most standardized tests you will be asked to solve a variety of mathematical problems that draw on the skills and information you have learned in class. If math problems sometimes give you difficulty, use the tips below to help yourself work through the problems.

Tips for Solving Math Problems

1. Decide what the goal of the question is. Read or study the problem carefully and determine what information must be found.

2. Locate the factual information. Decide what information represents key facts—the ones you must use to solve the problem. You may also find facts you do not need to reach your solution. In some cases, you may determine that more information is needed to solve the problem. If so, ask yourself, "What assumptions can I make about this problem?" or "Do I need a formula to help solve this problem?"

3. Decide what strategies you might use to solve the problem, how you might use them, and what form your solution will be in. For example, will you need to create a graph or chart? Will you need to solve an equation? Will your answer be in words or numbers? By knowing what type of solution you should reach, you may be able to eliminate some of the choices.

4. Apply your strategy to solve the problem and compare your answer to the choices.

5. If the answer is still not clear, read the problem again. If you had to make calculations to reach your answer, use estimation to see if your answer makes sense.

ATLAS

World: Political

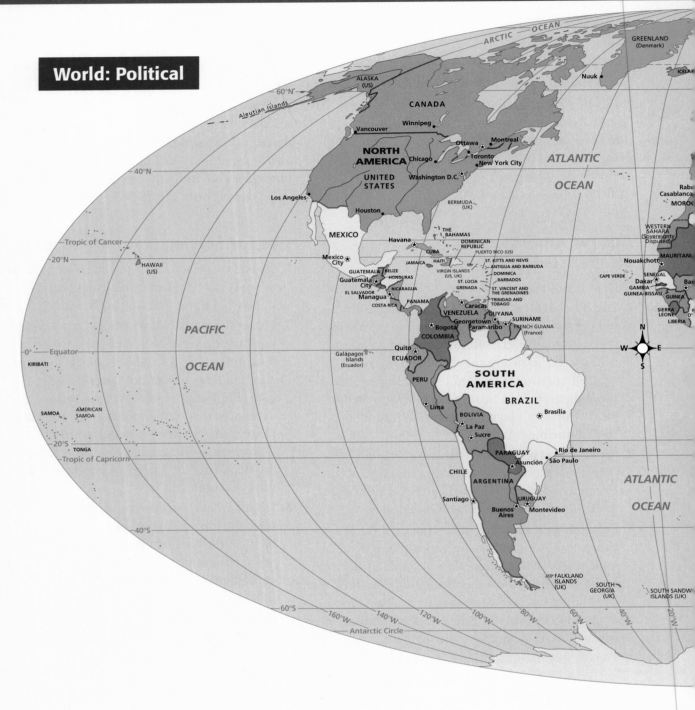

ARCTIC OCEAN

GREENLAND
(Denmark)

ICELA

Nuuk •

ALASKA
(US)

60°N

CANADA

Aleutian Islands

Vancouver
Winnipeg

NORTH
AMERICA

Ottawa
Montreal
Chicago
Toronto
New York City

ATLANTIC

40°N

UNITED
STATES

Washington D.C.

OCEAN

Rab
Casablanca
MOROC

Los Angeles

Houston

BERMUDA
(UK)

WESTERN
SAHARA
(Sovereignty
Disputed)

Tropic of Cancer

MEXICO

Havana

THE
BAHAMAS

DOMINICAN
REPUBLIC

20°N

HAWAII
(US)

Mexico
City

CUBA

PUERTO RICO (US)

Nouakchott

MAURITANI

ST. KITTS AND NEVIS
ANTIGUA AND BARBUDA

CAPE VERDE

SENEGAL

GUATEMALA
BELIZE

JAMAICA
HAITI

VIRGIN ISLANDS
(US, UK)

DOMINICA

Dakar
Ba

Guatemala
City

HONDURAS

ST. LUCIA
GRENADA

BARBADOS

GAMBIA
GUINEA-BISSAU

EL SALVADOR
NICARAGUA

ST. VINCENT AND
THE GRENADINES

GUINEA

Managua

COSTA RICA

PANAMA

Caracas

TRINIDAD AND
TOBAGO

SIERRA
LEONE

LIBERIA

VENEZUELA

GUYANA

N

Bogotá
Georgetown
Paramaribo

SURINAME

W E

COLOMBIA

FRENCH GUIANA
(France)

PACIFIC

Quito

S

0°
Equator

Galápagos
Islands
(Ecuador)

ECUADOR

KIRIBATI

OCEAN

PERU

Lima

SOUTH
AMERICA

BRAZIL

Brasília

SAMOA

AMERICAN
SAMOA

BOLIVIA

La Paz

Sucre

20°S

TONGA

Río de Janeiro

Tropic of Capricorn

PARAGUAY

São Paulo

Asunción

ATLANTIC

CHILE

ARGENTINA

OCEAN

40°S

Santiago

URUGUAY

Buenos
Aires

Montevideo

FALKLAND
ISLANDS
(UK)

SOUTH
GEORGIA
(UK)

SOUTH SANDW
ISLANDS (UK)

60°S

160°W
140°W
120°W
100°W
80°W
60°W
40°W
20°W

Antarctic Circle

Legend

⊛ National capitals

• Other cities

SCALE: at Equator

0   500   1,000   1,500   2,000 Miles

0   1,000   1,500 Kilometers

Mollweide Projection

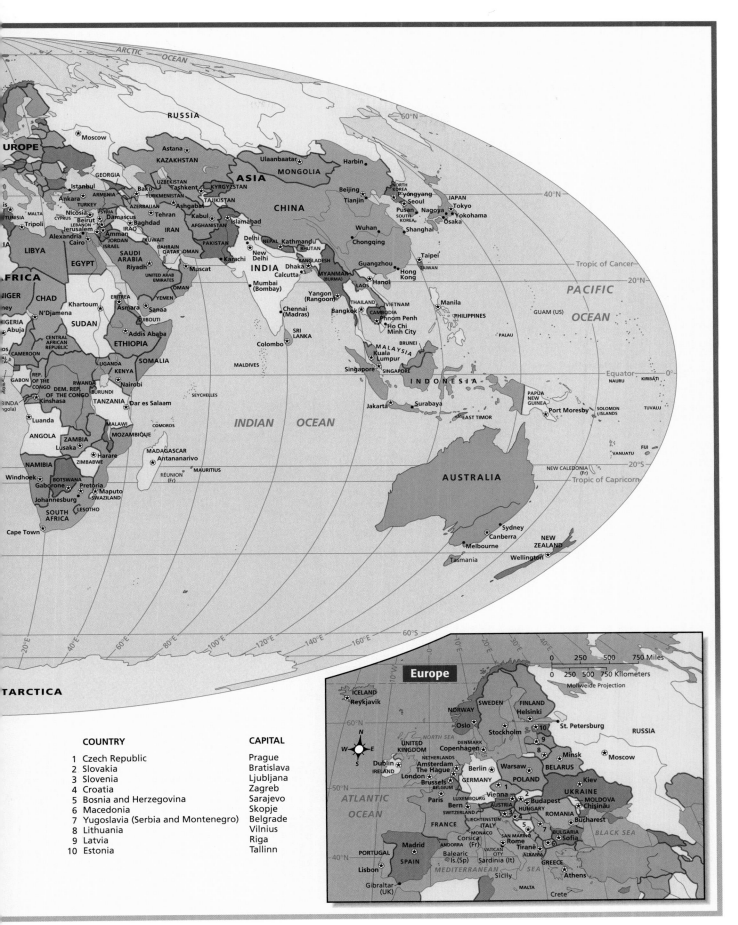

COUNTRY

1 Czech Republic
2 Slovakia
3 Slovenia
4 Croatia
5 Bosnia and Herzegovina
6 Macedonia
7 Yugoslavia (Serbia and Montenegro)
8 Lithuania
9 Latvia
10 Estonia

CAPITAL

Prague
Bratislava
Ljubljana
Zagreb
Sarajevo
Skopje
Belgrade
Vilnius
Riga
Tallinn

Europe

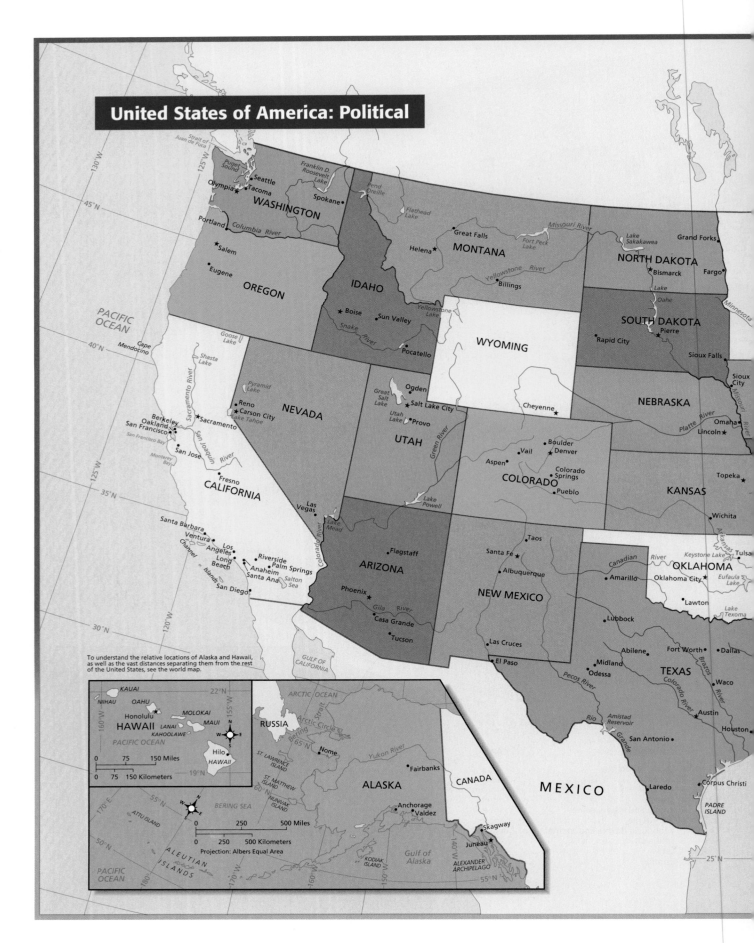

United States of America: Political

PACIFIC OCEAN

WASHINGTON
Seattle
Olympia★
Tacoma
Spokane
Portland
Columbia River
Salem★
Eugene
OREGON

Strait of Juan de Fuca
Puget Sound

Franklin D. Roosevelt Lake
Pend Oreille
Flathead Lake

MONTANA
Great Falls
Helena★
Billings
Yellowstone River
Fort Peck Lake
Missouri River

NORTH DAKOTA
Bismarck★
Grand Forks
Fargo
Lake Sakakawea

IDAHO
Boise★
Sun Valley
Pocatello
Snake River
Yellowstone Lake

SOUTH DAKOTA
Pierre★
Rapid City
Sioux Falls
Lake Oahe
Minnesota

WYOMING
Cheyenne★

NEBRASKA
Sioux City
Omaha
Lincoln★
Platte River
Missouri River

Cape Mendocino
Goose Lake
Shasta Lake
Pyramid Lake
Sacramento River

NEVADA
Reno
Carson City★
Sacramento★
Berkeley
Oakland
San Francisco
San Jose
San Francisco Bay
Monterey Bay
Fresno
CALIFORNIA
Lake Tahoe
San Joaquin River

Great Salt Lake
Salt Lake City★
Ogden
Utah Lake
Provo
UTAH
Green River
Lake Powell

COLORADO
Boulder
Vail
Denver★
Aspen
Colorado Springs
Pueblo

KANSAS
Topeka★
Wichita
Arkansas River

Santa Barbara
Ventura
Los Angeles
Long Beach
Anaheim
Santa Ana
San Diego
Riverside
Palm Springs
Salton Sea
Channel Islands

Las Vegas
Lake Mead
Colorado River

ARIZONA
Flagstaff
Phoenix★
Casa Grande
Tucson
Gila River

NEW MEXICO
Taos
Santa Fe★
Albuquerque
Las Cruces
El Paso

Amarillo
Lubbock
Midland
Odessa
Abilene
Pecos River

OKLAHOMA
Oklahoma City★
Lawton
Tulsa
Canadian River
Keystone Lake
Eufaula Lake
Lake Texoma

TEXAS
Fort Worth
Dallas
Waco
Austin★
Houston
San Antonio
Laredo
Corpus Christi
Padre Island
Brazos River
Colorado River
Amistad Reservoir
Rio Grande

GULF OF CALIFORNIA

MEXICO

CANADA

To understand the relative locations of Alaska and Hawaii, as well as the vast distances separating them from the rest of the United States, see the world map.

KAUAI
NIIHAU
OAHU
Honolulu★
MOLOKAI
LANAI
MAUI
KAHOOLAWE
HAWAII
Hilo
HAWAII
PACIFIC OCEAN

0   75   150 Miles
0   75   150 Kilometers

ARCTIC OCEAN
Arctic Circle
RUSSIA
Nome
Bering Strait
ST. LAWRENCE ISLAND
ST. MATTHEW ISLAND
NUNIVAK ISLAND
Yukon River
Fairbanks
ALASKA
Anchorage
Valdez
Skagway
Juneau★
KODIAK ISLAND
Gulf of Alaska
ALEXANDER ARCHIPELAGO

BERING SEA
ATTU ISLAND
ALEUTIAN ISLANDS
PACIFIC OCEAN

0   250   500 Miles
0   250   500 Kilometers
Projection: Albers Equal Area

CANADA

MINNESOTA
Duluth
Superior
Marquette
Sault Ste. Marie
Minneapolis
St. Paul
Green Bay
WISCONSIN
MICHIGAN
Saginaw
Madison
Milwaukee
Grand Rapids
Lansing
Ann Arbor
Detroit
Lake Michigan
Lake Huron
Lake Superior
Lake Erie
Lake Ontario

IOWA
Cedar Rapids
Rockford
Chicago
Davenport
Des Moines
Gary
South Bend
Fort Wayne
Peoria
Springfield
INDIANA
Indianapolis
ILLINOIS
Illinois River
East St. Louis
St. Louis

ansas City
MISSOURI
Jefferson City
Springfield
Fayetteville
Lake of the Ozarks

Buffalo
Rochester
Syracuse
Albany
NEW YORK
Cleveland
Youngstown
Akron
OHIO
Columbus
Dayton
Cincinnati
PENNSYLVANIA
Pittsburgh
Allentown
Harrisburg
Philadelphia
Newark
New York City
Jersey City
Trenton
Camden
NJ
Atlantic City
Susquehanna River
WEST VIRGINIA
Charleston
Louisville
Frankfort
Lexington
Evansville
KENTUCKY
Ohio River
Lake Barkley
Kentucky Lake

MAINE
Augusta
Burlington
Montpelier
VT
NH
Concord
Manchester
Portland
Lake Champlain
Boston
Worcester
MA
Springfield
Hartford
CT
RI
Providence
Cape Cod
Bridgeport
New Haven
LONG ISLAND
Long Island Sound
Yonkers
Hudson River
Connecticut River
St. Lawrence River

Baltimore
DE
MD
Dover
Annapolis
Washington, D.C.
DELAWARE BAY
VIRGINIA
Richmond
CHESAPEAKE
Norfolk
Newport News
Virginia Beach
Cape Hatteras

ATLANTIC OCEAN

ARKANSAS
Little Rock
Pine Bluff
Red River
Shreveport
LOUISIANA
Beaumont
New Orleans
Baton Rouge
MISSISSIPPI
Vicksburg
Jackson
Meridian
Montgomery
Mobile
Pensacola
Biloxi
CHANDELEUR ISLANDS

Memphis
Nashville
Knoxville
Asheville
TENNESSEE
Chattanooga
Huntsville
ALABAMA
Birmingham
Columbus
Macon
GEORGIA
Atlanta
Mississippi River

Winston-Salem
Greensboro
Durham
Raleigh
Charlotte
NORTH CAROLINA
Greenville
SOUTH CAROLINA
Columbia
Charleston
Savannah
Savannah River
SEA ISLANDS

Tallahassee
Jacksonville
Gainesville
FLORIDA
Orlando
Cape Canaveral
Tampa
St. Petersburg
Lake Okeechobee
Fort Myers
Fort Lauderdale
Miami
Cape Sable
FLORIDA KEYS
Straits of Florida
Chattahoochee River

GULF OF MEXICO

veston

THE BAHAMAS

CUBA

⊛	National capital
★	State capitals
•	Other cities

ARCTIC OCEAN
NORTH AMERICA
EUROPE
ASIA
ATLANTIC OCEAN
AFRICA
PACIFIC OCEAN
Equator
AUSTRALIA
SOUTH AMERICA
INDIAN OCEAN
ANTARCTICA
Robinson Projection

N
W E
S

0   250   500 Miles
0   250   500 Kilometers
Projection: Albers Equal Area

50° N
60° W
65° W
45° N
40° N
65° W
35° N
30° N
25° N
80° W
85° W
90° W
75° W
70° W

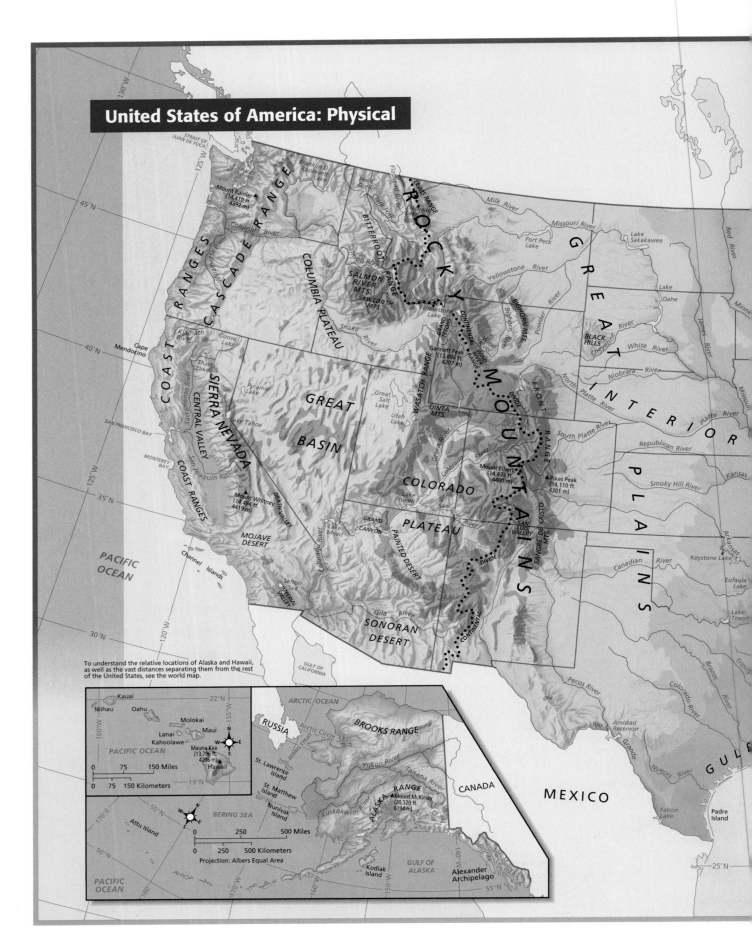

United States of America: Physical

To understand the relative locations of Alaska and Hawaii, as well as the vast distances separating them from the rest of the United States, see the world map.

Projection: Albers Equal Area

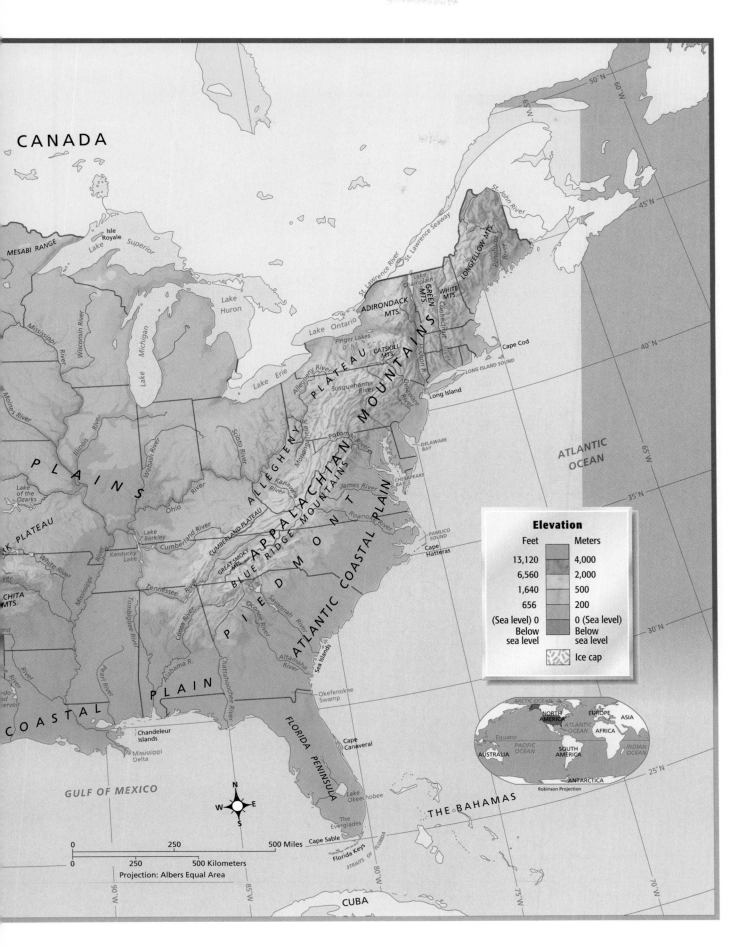

CANADA

MESABI RANGE
Isle Royale
Lake Superior
Lake Huron
Lake Michigan
Lake Ontario
Lake Erie
Wisconsin River
Mississippi River
Des Moines River
Illinois River
Wabash River
Scioto River
Ohio River
Allegheny River
Monongahela R.
Kanawha River
Potomac River

St. Lawrence River
St. Lawrence Seaway
Lake Champlain
ADIRONDACK MTS.
Finger Lakes
CATSKILL MTS.
ALLEGHENY PLATEAU
Susquehanna River
Delaware River

GREEN MTS.
WHITE MTS.
LONGFELLOW MTS.
St. John River
Penobscot River
Connecticut River
Hudson R.

Cape Cod
LONG ISLAND SOUND
Long Island

DELAWARE BAY
CHESAPEAKE BAY

ATLANTIC OCEAN

P L A I N S

Lake of the Ozarks
K PLATEAU
White River
Lake Barkley
Kentucky Lake
Cumberland River
CUMBERLAND PLATEAU
GREAT SMOKY MTS.
Tennessee River
CHITA MTS.
Mississippi River
Tombigbee River

A P P A L A C H I A N   M O U N T A I N S
BLUE RIDGE MOUNTAINS
P I E D M O N T
James River
Roanoke River
PAMLICO SOUND
Cape Hatteras

A T L A N T I C   C O A S T A L   P L A I N

red
...do...
...rvoir
...r River

C O A S T A L   P L A I N
Pearl River
Alabama R.
Coosa River
Oconee River
Ocmulgee River
Savannah River
Chattahoochee River
Altamaha River
Sea Islands
Okefenokee Swamp

Chandeleur Islands
Mississippi Delta

GULF OF MEXICO

FLORIDA PENINSULA
Cape Canaveral
Lake Okeechobee
The Everglades
Cape Sable
Florida Keys
STRAITS OF FLORIDA

THE BAHAMAS

CUBA

Elevation

Feet		Meters
13,120		4,000
6,560		2,000
1,640		500
656		200
(Sea level) 0		0 (Sea level)
Below sea level		Below sea level

Ice cap

ARCTIC OCEAN
NORTH AMERICA
EUROPE
ASIA
ATLANTIC OCEAN
AFRICA
Equator
PACIFIC OCEAN
SOUTH AMERICA
INDIAN OCEAN
AUSTRALIA
ANTARCTICA
Robinson Projection

0   250   500 Miles
0   250   500 Kilometers
Projection: Albers Equal Area

N
W   E
S

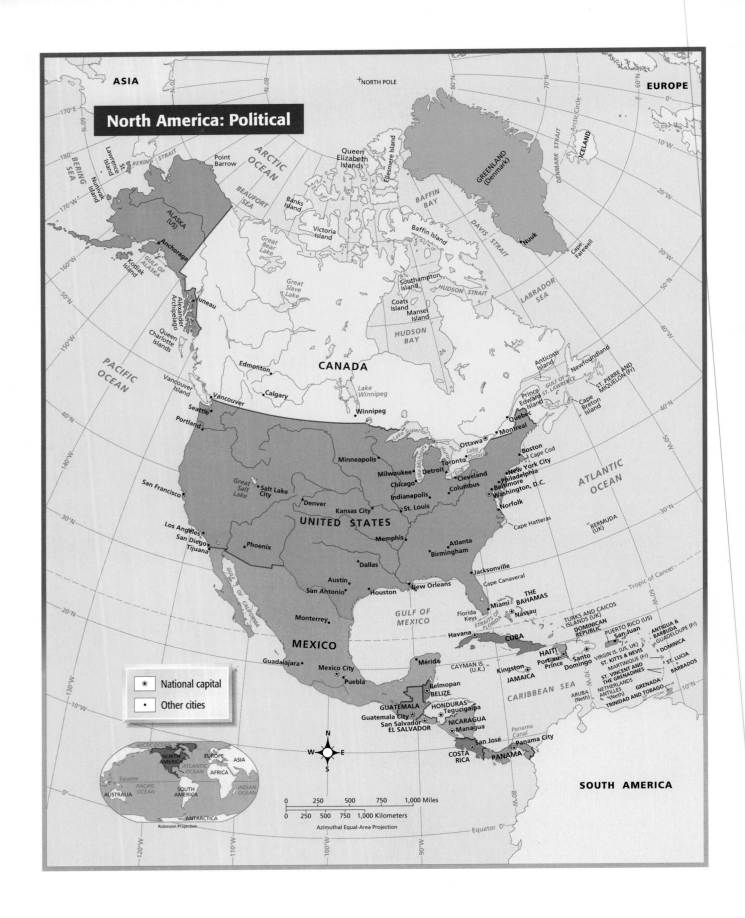

North America: Political

ASIA

EUROPE

ARCTIC OCEAN

NORTH POLE

Point Barrow

Queen Elizabeth Islands

Ellesmere Island

GREENLAND (Denmark)

ICELAND

ARCTIC OCEAN

BERING STRAIT

St. Lawrence Island

Nunivak Island

BEAUFORT SEA

Banks Island

BAFFIN BAY

DENMARK STRAIT

Arctic Circle

ALASKA (US)

Anchorage

Victoria Island

Baffin Island

Nuuk

DAVIS STRAIT

Cape Farewell

BERING SEA

Kodiak Island

GULF OF ALASKA

Great Bear Lake

Southampton Island

HUDSON STRAIT

LABRADOR SEA

Juneau

Alexander Archipelago

Great Slave Lake

Coats Island

Mansel Island

Queen Charlotte Islands

HUDSON BAY

PACIFIC OCEAN

Edmonton

CANADA

Anticosti Island

Newfoundland

ST. PIERRE AND MIQUELON (Fr)

Vancouver Island

Vancouver

Calgary

Lake Winnipeg

Prince Edward Island

GULF OF ST. LAWRENCE

Cape Breton Island

Seattle

Portland

Winnipeg

Quebec

Montreal

Ottawa

Lake Superior

Lake Michigan

Lake Huron

Lake Ontario

Lake Erie

Toronto

Boston

Cape Cod

Minneapolis

Milwaukee

Detroit

New York City

Philadelphia

Chicago

Cleveland

Baltimore

San Francisco

Great Salt Lake

Salt Lake City

Denver

Indianapolis

Columbus

Washington, D.C.

ATLANTIC OCEAN

Kansas City

St. Louis

Norfolk

UNITED STATES

Los Angeles

Memphis

Cape Hatteras

San Diego

Phoenix

Atlanta

BERMUDA (UK)

Tijuana

Birmingham

Dallas

Austin

Jacksonville

San Antonio

Houston

New Orleans

Cape Canaveral

Tropic of Cancer

Monterrey

Miami

GULF OF MEXICO

THE BAHAMAS

Florida Keys

STRAITS OF FLORIDA

Nassau

TURKS AND CAICOS ISLANDS (UK)

Guadalajara

Mexico City

Havana

CUBA

DOMINICAN REPUBLIC

PUERTO RICO (US)

San Juan

ANTIGUA & BARBUDA

GUADELOUPE (Fr)

Puebla

MEXICO

Mérida

CAYMAN IS. (U.K.)

HAITI

Port-au-Prince

Santo Domingo

VIRGIN IS. (US, UK)

ST. KITTS & NEVIS

DOMINICA

Kingston

MARTINIQUE (Fr)

JAMAICA

ST. VINCENT AND THE GRENADINES

ST. LUCIA

BARBADOS

Belmopan

BELIZE

NETHERLANDS ANTILLES (Neth)

GRENADA

GUATEMALA

HONDURAS

Tegucigalpa

CARIBBEAN SEA

ARUBA (Neth)

TRINIDAD AND TOBAGO

Guatemala City

San Salvador

EL SALVADOR

NICARAGUA

Managua

Panama Canal

San José

Panama City

COSTA RICA

PANAMA

SOUTH AMERICA

- ⊛ National capital
- • Other cities

NORTH AMERICA

EUROPE

ASIA

ARCTIC OCEAN

ATLANTIC OCEAN

AFRICA

Equator

PACIFIC OCEAN

SOUTH AMERICA

INDIAN OCEAN

AUSTRALIA

ANTARCTICA

Robinson Projection

Equator 0°

N
W E
S

0   250   500   750   1,000 Miles

0   250   500   750   1,000 Kilometers

Azimuthal Equal-Area Projection

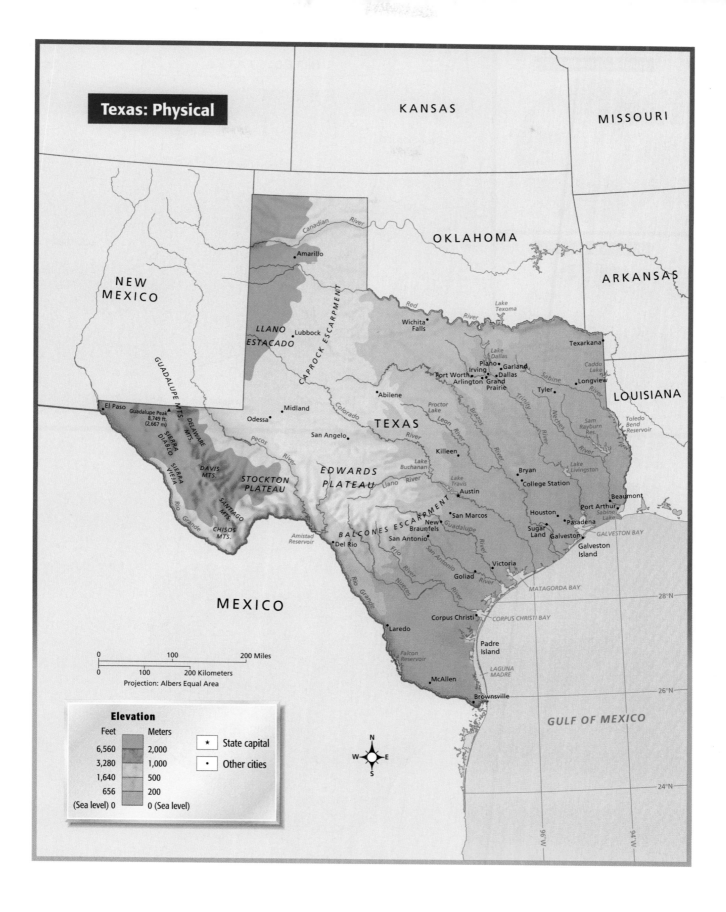

Texas: Physical

KANSAS

MISSOURI

OKLAHOMA

ARKANSAS

NEW MEXICO

Canadian River

•Amarillo

LLANO ESTACADO

•Lubbock

CAPROCK ESCARPMENT

Red River

Lake Texoma

Wichita Falls•

Texarkana•

Caddo Lake

Plano•
Irving• •Garland
Fort Worth• •Dallas
Arlington• Grand Prairie

Lake Dallas

Sabine River

•Tyler

•Longview

LOUISIANA

GUADALUPE MTS.

•Midland

Colorado River

•Abilene

Proctor Lake

Leon River

Brazos River

Trinity River

Neches River

Toledo Bend Reservoir

Sam Rayburn Res.

TEXAS

El Paso•
Guadalupe Peak 8,749 ft. (2,667 m)

SIERRA DIABLO
DELAWARE MTS.

•Odessa

Pecos River

San Angelo•

Killeen•

Lake Buchanan

Lake Travis

College Station•

Lake Livingston

Beaumont

DAVIS MTS.

SIERRA VIEJA

STOCKTON PLATEAU

SANTIAGO MTS.

CHISOS MTS.

Rio Grande

EDWARDS PLATEAU

Bryan•

Austin★

Houston•

Port Arthur•

Sabine Lake

Pasadena•

GALVESTON BAY

Llano River

BALCONES ESCARPMENT

San Marcos•
New Braunfels•

Guadalupe River

Sugar Land•

Galveston•

Galveston Island

Amistad Reservoir

Del Rio•

San Antonio•

Frio River

San Antonio River

Goliad•

Victoria•

MEXICO

Rio Grande

Nueces River

MATAGORDA BAY

28°N

Corpus Christi•

CORPUS CHRISTI BAY

Laredo•

Padre Island

Falcon Reservoir

LAGUNA MADRE

McAllen•

26°N

Brownsville•

GULF OF MEXICO

24°N

96°W

94°W

Scale

| 0 | 100 | 200 Miles |
| 0 | 100 | 200 Kilometers |

Projection: Albers Equal Area

Elevation

Feet	Meters
6,560	2,000
3,280	1,000
1,640	500
656	200
(Sea level) 0	0 (Sea level)

★ State capital

• Other cities

N W E S

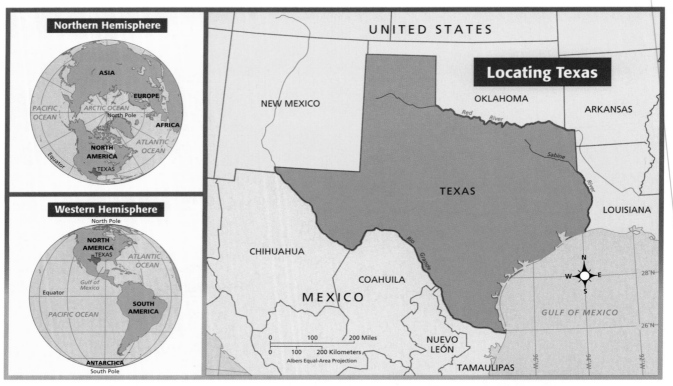

Locating Texas

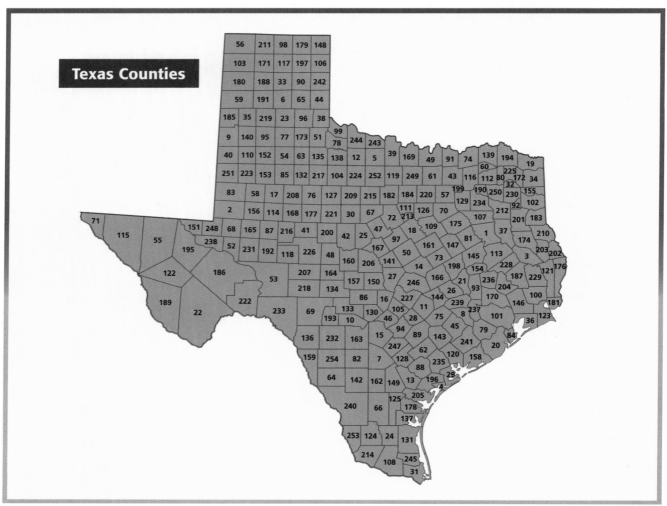

Texas Counties

Texas Counties

Counties of Texas	Number on Map	2000 Population	Area (sq. mi.)	County Seat	Date Created /Organized	Industries/Products
Anderson	1	55,109	1,078.0	Palestine	1846	timber, cattle, manufacturing
Andrews	2	13,004	1,501.0	Andrews	1910	oil, cattle, cotton
Angelina	3	80,130	864.4	Lufkin	1846	timber, cattle, manufacturing
Aransas	4	22,497	527.9	Rockport	1871	shipping, cattle, tourism
Archer	5	8,854	925.7	Archer City	1880	cattle, oil services, dairy, agriculture
Armstrong	6	2,148	913.7	Claude	1890	agribusiness, cattle, wheat
Atascosa	7	38,628	1,232.7	Jourdanton	1856	cattle, peanuts, strawberries
Austin	8	23,590	656.3	Bellville	1837	cattle, manufacturing, tourism
Bailey	9	6,594	827.3	Muleshoe	1917	manufacturing, dairy, agriculture, cattle
Bandera	10	17,654	797.5	Bandera	1856	tourism, hunting, cattle
Bastrop	11	57,733	895.9	Bastrop	1836	cattle, hay, tourism, high-tech
Baylor	12	4,093	901.0	Seymour	1879	cattle, agribusiness, crops
Bee	13	32,359	880.3	Beeville	1858	oil, cattle, agribusiness
Bell	14	237,974	1,087.1	Belton	1850	cattle, high-tech, corn, manufacturing
Bexar	15	1,392,931	1,256.7	San Antonio	1836	tourism, cattle, crops
Blanco	16	8,418	713.3	Johnson City	1858	tourism, agribusiness, cattle
Borden	17	729	906.0	Gail	1891	cattle, oil, agribusiness, cotton
Bosque	18	17,204	1,002.6	Meridian	1854	cattle, agribusiness, hunting
Bowie	19	89,306	922.7	Boston	1840	cattle, crops, paper manufacturing
Brazoria	20	241,767	1,597.4	Angleton	1836	cattle, petrochemicals, rice
Brazos	21	152,415	590.3	Bryan	1843	education, agribusiness, cattle
Brewster	22	8,866	6,193.1	Alpine	1887	cattle, tourism
Briscoe	23	1,790	901.6	Silverton	1892	agribusiness, cotton, wheat
Brooks	24	7,976	943.6	Falfurrias	1911	oil, gas, cattle, crops
Brown	25	37,674	956.9	Brownwood	1857	manufacturing, cattle, agribusiness
Burleson	26	16,470	677.8	Caldwell	1846	oil, gas, cattle, crops
Burnet	27	34,147	1,020.0	Burnet	1854	cattle, stone, agribusiness, hunting
Caldwell	28	32,194	547.3	Lockhart	1848	oil, agribusiness, cattle
Calhoun	29	20,647	1,032.1	Port Lavaca	1846	cotton, manufacturing, oil, grain
Callahan	30	12,905	901.2	Baird	1877	cattle, wheat, feed and fertilizer
Cameron	31	335,227	1,276.3	Brownsville	1848	agribusiness, trade, tourism, cotton, vegetables, citrus
Camp	32	11,549	203.1	Pittsburg	1874	agribusiness, poultry, timber
Carson	33	6,516	924.1	Panhandle	1888	wheat, cattle, agribusiness
Cass	34	30,438	960.3	Linden	1846	poultry, cattle, timber
Castro	35	8,285	899.3	Dimmitt	1891	agribusiness, cattle, corn
Chambers	36	26,031	868.5	Anahuac	1858	oil, chemicals, rice, cattle
Cherokee	37	46,659	1,062.0	Rusk	1846	nurseries, timber, dairy, cattle
Childress	38	7,688	713.5	Childress	1887	cotton, cattle, wheat
Clay	39	11,006	1,116.1	Henrietta	1873	oil, agribusiness, cattle, crops
Cochran	40	3,730	775.2	Morton	1924	agribusiness, oil, cotton, sunflowers
Coke	41	3,864	927.9	Robert Lee	1889	oil well supplies, agribusiness
Coleman	42	9,235	1,281.5	Coleman	1864	agribusiness, oil, cattle
Collin	43	491,675	885.8	McKinney	1846	manufacturing, cattle, grain
Collingsworth	44	3,206	919.4	Wellington	1890	peanuts, cotton, agribusiness
Colorado	45	20,390	973.6	Columbus	1837	agribusiness, oil services, rice
Comal	46	78,021	574.5	New Braunfels	1846	manufacturing, cattle, crops
Comanche	47	14,026	947.6	Comanche	1856	dairy, cattle, agribusiness
Concho	48	3,966	993.7	Paint Rock	1879	agribusiness, sheep, cattle, grain
Cooke	49	36,363	898.7	Gainesville	1848	agribusiness, oil, cattle, grain
Coryell	50	74,978	1,056.7	Gatesville	1854	agribusiness, cattle, grain, military
Cottle	51	1,904	901.6	Paducah	1892	agribusiness, cotton, peanuts

Texas Counties

Counties of Texas	Number on Map	2000 Population	Area (sq. mi.)	County Seat	Date Created /Organized	Industries/Products
Crane	52	3,996	785.6	Crane	1927	oil, oil services, cattle ranching
Crockett	53	4,099	2,807.6	Ozona	1891	sheep, cattle, oil, gas
Crosby	54	7,072	901.6	Crosbyton	1886	agribusiness, cattle, cotton
Culberson	55	2,975	3,812.8	Van Horn	1912	agribusiness, cattle, crops, tourism
Dallam	56	6,222	1,505.3	Dalhart	1891	agribusiness, cattle, hogs, grain
Dallas	57	2,218,899	908.7	Dallas	1846	telecommunications, electronics, textiles, banking
Dawson	58	14,985	902.1	Lamesa	1905	cotton, peanuts, cattle
Deaf Smith	59	18,561	1,498.3	Hereford	1890	meatpacking, farming, feedlots
Delta	60	5,327	277.8	Cooper	1870	agribusiness, tourism, cattle, crops
Denton	61	432,976	957.6	Denton	1846	horses, eggs, cattle, crops
DeWitt	62	20,013	910.4	Cuero	1846	wood, furniture, cattle
Dickens	63	2,762	905.2	Dickens	1891	agribusiness, cattle, cotton, horses
Dimmit	64	10,248	1,334.5	Carrizo Springs	1880	vegetables, cattle, agribusiness
Donley	65	3,828	933.0	Clarendon	1882	cattle, agribusiness, cotton
Duval	66	13,120	1,795.7	San Diego	1876	cattle, grain, oil, cotton
Eastland	67	18,297	931.8	Eastland	1873	agribusiness, cattle, peanuts
Ector	68	121,123	901.7	Odessa	1891	oil, cattle, horses, pecans
Edwards	69	2,162	2,120.0	Rocksprings	1883	goats, sheep, hunting, oil
Ellis	70	111,360	951.6	Waxahachie	1850	manufacturing, agribusiness, cattle
El Paso	71	679,622	1,014.6	El Paso	1850	trade, distribution, dairy, tourism
Erath	72	33,001	1,089.8	Stephenville	1856	dairy, cattle, horses
Falls	73	18,576	773.8	Marlin	1850	agribusiness, cattle, grain
Fannin	74	31,242	899.1	Bonham	1838	agribusiness, cattle, soybeans
Fayette	75	21,804	959.8	La Grange	1838	agribusiness, poultry, cattle, crops
Fisher	76	4,344	901.7	Roby	1886	agribusiness, oil, cattle, cotton
Floyd	77	7,771	992.5	Floydada	1890	cotton, livestock feedlots, cattle
Foard	78	1,622	707.7	Crowell	1891	agribusiness, wheat, cotton, clothes
Fort Bend	79	354,452	886.0	Richmond	1838	agribusiness, petrochemicals, crops
Franklin	80	9,458	294.7	Mount Vernon	1875	agribusiness, dairy, hay, fruits
Freestone	81	17,867	892.1	Fairfield	1851	mining, cattle, fruits, crops
Frio	82	16,252	1,134.3	Pearsall	1871	peanuts, agribusiness, oil, crops
Gaines	83	14,467	1,502.8	Seminole	1905	cotton, oil, gas, peanuts
Galveston	84	250,158	876.3	Galveston	1839	port activities, cattle, tourism
Garza	85	4,872	896.2	Post	1907	cotton, oil, cattle
Gillespie	86	20,814	1,061.5	Fredericksburg	1848	tourism, cattle, peaches, crops
Glasscock	87	1,406	900.9	Garden City	1893	cotton, cattle, hunting, oil, gas
Goliad	88	6,928	859.3	Goliad	1837	oil, agribusiness, cattle, corn
Gonzales	89	18,628	1,069.8	Gonzales	1837	agribusiness, poultry, cattle
Gray	90	22,744	929.2	Pampa	1902	oil, cattle, wheat
Grayson	91	110,595	979.1	Sherman	1846	manufacturing, cattle, horses
Gregg	92	111,379	276.3	Longview	1873	oil, manufacturing, cattle, horses
Grimes	93	23,552	801.2	Anderson	1846	manufacturing, cattle, timber, dairy
Guadalupe	94	89,023	714.2	Seguin	1846	manufacturing, cattle, poultry
Hale	95	36,602	1,004.8	Plainview	1888	agribusiness, cattle, cotton, hogs
Hall	96	3,782	904.0	Memphis	1890	grain, cotton, peanuts, cattle
Hamilton	97	8,229	836.3	Hamilton	1858	agribusiness, dairy, cattle, hunting
Hansford	98	5,369	920.4	Spearman	1889	agribusiness, cattle, corn
Hardeman	99	4,724	697.0	Quanah	1884	agribusiness, wheat, cattle, cotton
Hardin	100	48,073	897.3	Kountze	1858	paper manufacturing, wood, cattle
Harris	101	3,400,578	1,777.8	Houston	1837	petrochemicals, port activities, aerospace, rice
Harrison	102	62,110	915.1	Marshall	1842	oil, gas, lumber, cattle, hay
Hartley	103	5,537	1,463.3	Channing	1891	cattle, corn, wheat, gas

Texas Counties

Counties of Texas	Number on Map	2000 Population	Area (sq. mi.)	County Seat	Date Created /Organized	Industries/Products
Haskell	104	6,093	910.2	Haskell	1885	agribusiness, wheat, cotton, peanuts
Hays	105	97,589	679.8	San Marcos	1843	education, cattle, crops, tourism
Hemphill	106	3,351	912.0	Canadian	1887	oil, cattle, crops
Henderson	107	73,277	949.0	Athens	1846	agribusiness, cattle, manufacturing
Hidalgo	108	569,463	1,582.7	Edinburg	1852	food processing, sugarcane, citrus
Hill	109	32,321	985.6	Hillsboro	1853	agribusiness, cattle, manufacturing
Hockley	110	22,716	908.5	Levelland	1921	oil, gas, cotton, grain
Hood	111	41,100	436.7	Granbury	1866	tourism, cattle, hay, peanuts
Hopkins	112	31,960	792.7	Sulphur Springs	1846	dairy, cattle, horses, hay
Houston	113	23,185	1,236.8	Crockett	1837	livestock, poultry, timber
Howard	114	33,627	904.2	Big Spring	1882	agribusiness, oil, gas, cotton
Hudspeth	115	3,344	4,572.2	Sierra Blanca	1917	agribusiness, mining, cotton
Hunt	116	76,596	882.0	Greenville	1846	manufacturing, cattle, education
Hutchinson	117	23,857	894.9	Stinnett	1901	oil, gas, petrochemicals, cattle, corn
Irion	118	1,771	1,051.6	Mertzon	1889	cattle, sheep, goats, wheat, oil
Jack	119	8,763	920.1	Jacksboro	1857	oil, cattle, hay, wheat
Jackson	120	14,391	857.0	Edna	1836	oil, rice, cattle, cotton
Jasper	121	35,604	969.6	Jasper	1837	timber, oil, cattle, hogs, fishing
Jeff Davis	122	2,207	2,264.6	Fort Davis	1887	tourism, greenhouse nurseries, cattle
Jefferson	123	252,051	1,111.2	Beaumont	1837	petrochemicals, rice, soybeans, cattle
Jim Hogg	124	5,281	1,136.2	Hebbronville	1913	oil, cattle, hay, dairy
Jim Wells	125	39,326	868.2	Alice	1912	oil, gas, cattle, dairy, grain
Johnson	126	126,811	734.3	Cleburne	1854	agribusiness, dairy, cattle, horses
Jones	127	20,785	937.1	Anson	1881	agribusiness, cotton, wheat, peanuts
Karnes	128	15,446	753.5	Karnes City	1854	agribusiness, cattle, poultry
Kaufman	129	71,313	806.8	Kaufman	1848	manufacturing, nursery crops, cattle
Kendall	130	23,743	662.9	Boerne	1862	agribusiness, cattle, sheep, goats
Kenedy	131	414	1,945.5	Sarita	1921	oil, hunting, cattle, horses
Kent	132	859	902.8	Jayton	1892	agribusiness, oil, cattle, sheep, goats
Kerr	133	43,653	1,107.6	Kerrville	1856	tourism, cattle, sheep, goats, crops
Kimble	134	4,468	1,250.9	Junction	1876	livestock, goats, sheep, pecans
King	135	356	913.3	Guthrie	1891	minerals, cattle, horses, cotton
Kinney	136	3,379	1,365.3	Brackettville	1874	agribusiness, cattle, goats, hay
Kleberg	137	31,549	1,090.4	Kingsville	1913	chemicals, plastics, cattle, cotton
Knox	138	4,253	855.4	Benjamin	1886	agribusiness, cattle, horses, goats
Lamar	139	48,499	932.4	Paris	1841	manufacturing, cattle, hay, soybeans
Lamb	140	14,709	1,017.7	Littlefield	1908	agribusiness, cattle, corn, wheat
Lampasas	141	17,762	713.9	Lampasas	1856	cattle, goats, military
La Salle	142	5,866	1,494.2	Cotulla	1880	agribusiness, cattle, peanuts, hunting
Lavaca	143	19,210	970.3	Hallettsville	1846	manufacturing, poultry, cattle, leather
Lee	144	15,657	634.0	Giddings	1874	manufacturing, cattle, hogs, eggs
Leon	145	15,335	1,080.4	Centerville	1846	oil, gas, cattle, hogs, poultry
Liberty	146	70,154	1,176.3	Liberty	1837	chemicals, rice, soybeans
Limestone	147	22,051	933.1	Groesbeck	1846	manufacturing, cattle, dairy, horses
Lipscomb	148	3,057	932.2	Lipscomb	1887	agribusiness, cattle, wheat, oil
Live Oak	149	12,309	1,078.8	George West	1856	oil, cattle, hogs, corn, grain
Llano	150	17,044	966.1	Llano	1856	cattle, turkeys, hunting, hogs
Loving	151	67	676.8	Mentone	1931	oil, cattle
Lubbock	152	242,628	900.6	Lubbock	1891	cotton, cattle, feedlots, manufacturing
Lynn	153	6,550	893.4	Tahoka	1903	agribusiness, cotton, peanuts, grain
Madison	154	12,940	472.3	Madisonville	1854	manufacturing, nurseries, cattle
Marion	155	10,941	420.3	Jefferson	1860	timber, cattle hay, goats
Martin	156	4,746	915.6	Stanton	1884	oil, cotton, grain, cattle

Texas Counties

Counties of Texas	Number on Map	2000 Population	Area (sq. mi.)	County Seat	Date Created /Organized	Industries/Products
Mason	157	3,738	932.2	Mason	1858	cattle, peanuts, sheep, hunting
Matagorda	158	37,957	1,612.2	Bay City	1837	oil, rice, cotton, grain
Maverick	159	47,297	1,291.7	Eagle Pass	1871	oil, cattle pecans, vegetables
McCulloch	160	8,205	1,073.3	Brady	1876	agribusiness, manufacturing, cattle
McLennan	161	213,517	1,060.2	Waco	1850	distribution center, corn, wheat
McMullen	162	851	1,142.6	Tilden	1877	livestock, hunting, cattle, hay
Medina	163	39,304	1,334.5	Hondo	1848	agribusiness, cattle, crops, hunting
Menard	164	2,360	902.2	Menard	1871	agribusiness, oil, gas, sheep, goats
Midland	165	116,009	902.2	Midland	1885	oil, cattle, horses, sheep
Milam	166	24,238	1,021.6	Cameron	1837	aluminum, poultry, cattle, hay
Mills	167	5,151	749.8	Goldthwaite	1887	agribusiness, hunting, cattle, sheep
Mitchell	168	9,698	915.9	Colorado City	1881	agribusiness, oil, cotton, grain
Montague	169	19,117	938.4	Montague	1858	agribusiness, oil, cattle, dairy
Montgomery	170	293,768	1,076.8	Conroe	1837	lumber, oil, cattle, hay
Moore	171	20,121	909.6	Dumas	1892	oil, gas, cattle, manufacturing
Morris	172	13,048	258.6	Daingerfield	1875	steel, timber, cattle, hay
Motley	173	1,426	989.8	Matador	1891	cotton, cattle, peanuts, hunting
Nacogdoches	174	59,203	981.3	Nacogdoches	1837	agribusiness, timber, poultry, dairy
Navarro	175	45,124	1,086.2	Corsicana	1846	manufacturing, oil, cattle, cotton
Newton	176	15,072	939.5	Newton	1846	timber, cattle, crops, tourism
Nolan	177	15,802	913.9	Sweetwater	1881	manufacturing, oil, gas, cattle, sheep
Nueces	178	313,645	1,166.4	Corpus Christi	1846	oil, port activities, grain
Ochiltree	179	9,006	918.1	Perryton	1889	oil, cattle, hogs, wheat
Oldham	180	2,185	1,501.4	Vega	1880	cattle, ranching, crops
Orange	181	84,966	379.5	Orange	1852	petrochemicals, shipping, cattle, rice
Palo Pinto	182	27,026	985.4	Palo Pinto	1857	manufacturing, petroleum, cattle
Panola	183	22,756	801.0	Carthage	1846	gas, oil, cattle, forestry, dairy
Parker	184	88,495	910.0	Weatherford	1855	agribusiness, cattle, horses
Parmer	185	10,016	885.2	Farwell	1907	cattle, grain, crops, meat packing
Pecos	186	16,809	4,765.0	Fort Stockton	1872	agribusiness, oil, gas, vegetables
Polk	187	41,133	1,109.8	Livingston	1846	timber, lumber, hay, vegetables
Potter	188	113,546	922.0	Amarillo	1887	feedlots, cattle, petrochemicals, gas
Presidio	189	7,304	3,856.4	Marfa	1875	cattle, onions, hunting, bees, honey
Rains	190	9,139	258.8	Emory	1870	oil, tourism, cattle, vegetables
Randall	191	104,312	922.4	Canyon	1889	agribusiness, wheat, corn, education
Reagan	192	3,326	1,176.0	Big Lake	1903	oil, gas, cotton, cattle, sheep
Real	193	3,047	700.0	Leakey	1913	tourism, cattle, sheep, goats, hunting
Red River	194	14,314	1,057.6	Clarksville	1837	agribusiness, lumber, cattle, soybeans
Reeves	195	13,137	2,642.0	Pecos	1884	agribusiness, feedlots, cattle, cotton
Refugio	196	7,828	818.6	Refugio	1837	oil, cotton, cattle, grain
Roberts	197	887	924.1	Miami	1889	agribusiness, oil services, cattle
Robertson	198	16,000	865.7	Franklin	1838	agribusiness, cattle, cotton, hay
Rockwall	199	43,080	148.6	Rockwall	1873	grain, cattle, horses, cotton
Runnels	200	11,495	1,057.2	Ballinger	1880	agribusiness, oil, manufacturing
Rusk	201	47,372	938.6	Henderson	1843	oil, lumber, cattle, dairy, poultry
Sabine	202	10,469	576.5	Hemphill	1837	timber, tourism, poultry, cattle
San Augustine	203	8,946	592.2	San Augustine	1837	lumber, shipping, manufacturing
San Jacinto	204	22,246	627.9	Coldspring	1870	timber, oil, cattle, horses
San Patricio	205	67,138	707.0	Sinton	1847	oil, petrochemicals, cotton, grain
San Saba	206	6,186	1,138.2	San Saba	1856	agribusiness, stone, cattle, poultry
Schleicher	207	2,935	1,310.7	Eldorado	1901	oil, hunting, sheep, cattle, goats
Scurry	208	16,361	907.6	Snyder	1884	oil, textiles, cotton, grain, livestock
Shackelford	209	3,302	915.5	Albany	1874	oil, manufacturing, cattle, wheat

Texas Counties

Counties of Texas	Number on Map	2000 Population	Area (sq. mi.)	County Seat	Date Created /Organized	Industries/Products
Shelby	210	25,224	834.5	Center	1837	poultry, eggs, cattle, timber
Sherman	211	3,186	923.2	Stratford	1889	agribusiness, cattle, wheat, corn
Smith	212	174,706	949.4	Tyler	1846	agribusiness, oil, roses, cattle
Somervell	213	6,809	191.8	Glen Rose	1875	tourism, cattle, hay, grain, goats
Starr	214	53,597	1,229.3	Rio Grande City	1848	vegetable packing, shipping, cattle, trade
Stephens	215	9,674	921.5	Breckenridge	1876	oil, agribusiness, cattle, hogs, goats
Sterling	216	1,393	923.5	Sterling City	1891	cattle, sheep, hunting, oil, goats
Stonewall	217	1,693	920.2	Aspermont	1888	agribusiness, cattle, wheat, cotton
Sutton	218	4,077	1,454.4	Sonora	1890	oil, gas, agribusiness, hunting, cattle
Swisher	219	8,378	900.6	Tulia	1890	feedlots, grain, manufacturing, crops
Tarrant	220	1,446,219	897.5	Fort Worth	1850	aerospace, manufacturing, trade
Taylor	221	126,555	919.3	Abilene	1878	military, feedlots, wheat, cattle
Terrell	222	1,081	2,357.9	Sanderson	1905	ranching, oil, gas, tourism
Terry	223	12,761	890.8	Brownfield	1904	agribusiness, oil, cotton
Throckmorton	224	1,850	915.5	Throckmorton	1879	oil, agribusiness, hunting, cattle
Titus	225	28,118	425.6	Mount Pleasant	1846	agribusiness, manufacturing, poultry
Tom Green	226	104,010	1,540.5	San Angelo	1875	sheep, wool, mohair, cattle, cotton
Travis	227	812,280	1,022.1	Austin	1843	education, tourism, high-tech, government
Trinity	228	13,779	713.9	Groveton	1850	forestry, tourism, cattle, horses
Tyler	229	20,871	935.7	Woodville	1846	lumber, manufacturing, cattle, hay
Upshur	230	35,291	592.6	Gilmer	1846	manufacturing, agribusiness, poultry
Upton	231	3,404	1,241.8	Rankin	1910	oil, cotton, cattle, pecans, sheep
Uvalde	232	25,926	1,558.6	Uvalde	1856	agribusiness, cattle, vegetables
Val Verde	233	44,856	3,232.6	Del Rio	1885	agribusiness, sheep, goats, military
Van Zandt	234	48,140	859.5	Canton	1848	oil, tourism, cattle, dairy
Victoria	235	84,088	888.7	Victoria	1836	petrochemicals, oil, corn, cattle
Walker	236	61,758	801.4	Huntsville	1846	education, tourism, timber, cattle
Waller	237	32,663	518.4	Hempstead	1873	agribusiness, manufacturing, cattle
Ward	238	10,909	835.7	Monahans	1892	oil, gas, cattle, cotton, alfalfa
Washington	239	30,373	621.3	Brenham	1837	agribusiness, oil, cattle, poultry
Webb	240	193,117	3,375.6	Laredo	1848	international trade, manufacturing, tourism
Wharton	241	41,188	1,094.5	Wharton	1846	oil, rice, sulfur, cotton, hunting
Wheeler	242	5,284	915.3	Wheeler	1879	oil, agribusiness, cattle, horses
Wichita	243	131,664	632.9	Wichita Falls	1882	retail trade, cattle, wheat, oil
Wilbarger	244	14,676	978.1	Vernon	1881	agribusiness, wheat, alfalfa, cattle
Willacy	245	20,082	784.2	Raymondville	1921	oil, agribusiness, cotton, corn, vegetables, citrus
Williamson	246	249,967	1,136.4	Georgetown	1848	agribusiness, cattle, high-tech
Wilson	247	32,408	808.5	Floresville	1860	agribusiness, cattle, dairy, hogs
Winkler	248	7,173	841.2	Kermit	1910	oil, gas, cattle, goats, horses
Wise	249	48,793	922.7	Decatur	1856	agribusiness, oil, cattle, dairy
Wood	250	36,752	695.7	Quitman	1850	oil, gas, dairy, cattle, poultry
Yoakum	251	7,322	799.8	Plains	1907	oil, cotton, peanuts, watermelons
Young	252	17,943	930.8	Graham	1874	oil, agribusiness, cattle, wheat
Zapata	253	12,182	1,058.1	Zapata	1858	tourism, oil, cattle, onions, fruit
Zavala	254	11,600	1,301.7	Crystal City	1884	agribusiness, cattle, vegetables, corn

Sources: *Texas Almanac 2000–2001*
http://quickfacts.census.gov/qfd/states/48000.html
Handbook of Texas

internet connect

GO TO: go.hrw.com
KEYWORD: ST3 Almanac
FOR: More information on Texas counties

UNIT 1

The Geography of Texas

CHAPTER 1 **The Geographer's Tools**

CHAPTER 2 **A Land Called Texas**

CHAPTER 3 **The Regions of Texas**

Texas Teens
Young Naturalists

The beauty and diversity of the state's geography has inspired a tradition of naturalists, or nature lovers. These naturalists enjoy studying and exploring the landscape of Texas. Texas teenagers have participated in programs with the Boy Scouts, Girl Scouts, Explorers Clubs, and Texas Parks and Wildlife. These organizations have encouraged teens to explore and learn about the state's environment and wildlife.

Texas teens enjoy outdoor recreational activities such as canoeing on Texas lakes.

Texas Parks and Wildlife Department offers a summer camp program, where Texas teens can learn about outdoor recreation and facts about Texas geography. Texas Parks and Wildlife also sponsors an annual Wildlife Expo that explores activities available in the great outdoors of Texas. The Expo sponsors an art, poetry, and essay contest for Texas students. Joy Chou, the sixth-grade poetry winner for 2000, described the Gulf Coast.

> "The Ocean waves are crashing against the shore,
> As I breathe in the salty scent and wish to soar.
> Puffy clouds lace the blue sky,
> It seems like paradise, I can't deny."

The beauty of Texas also inspired eighth-grader Alejandra Villarreal.

> "Evenings like this
> In the state of the Lone Star
> Exist only in Texas;
> We are luckier by far."

In what ways do Texas teens enjoy the state's great outdoors?

In this unit you will learn more about the geography, climates, landforms, and regions of Texas. You will also learn about the people and culture of Texas.

LEFT PAGE: *The Texas landscape at Palo Duro State Park is characterized by rugged red cliffs and yucca plants.*

CHAPTER 1

The Geographer's Tools

This Texas snowman was made in Dallas.

The Rio Grande winds through the Big Bend region.

TEXAS

Coldest Spot The lowest recorded temperature in Texas was a chilly –23°F, occurring in 1899 at Tulia and in 1933 at Seminole.

Hottest Spot The highest recorded temperature in Texas was a blistering 120°F, occurring in 1936 at Seymour and in 1994 at Monahans.

Longest River The Rio Grande, which begins in Colorado and flows along the Texas-Mexico border, runs 1,896 miles.

U.S. and WORLD

Coldest Spot Vostok, Antarctica, had a record low of –129°F in 1983.

Hottest Spot El Azizia, Libya, had a record high of 136°F in 1922.

Longest River The Nile River flows some 4,160 miles through northeast Africa.

Penguins live in many areas including the cold climate of Antarctica.

Build on What You Know

Have you heard that everything is bigger in Texas? The state is second in the nation in size—behind Alaska. This large area offers a variety of terrain and natural scenery. To understand this large state, geographers use a variety of tools including maps and charts.

Horned lizards enjoy the dry climate of West Texas.

Guadalupe Peak is in West Texas.

Driest Place Wink received just 1.76 inches of rain in 1956.

Wettest Place In 1873 Clarksville received 109.4 inches of rain.

Highest Point Guadalupe Peak is the highest point in the state, at 8,749 feet above sea level.

Driest Place Arica, Chile, receives an average of just 0.03 inches of rain per year.

Wettest Place Lloro, Colombia, receives an average of 523.6 inches of rain per year.

Highest Point Mount Everest is the highest point in the world, at 29,035 feet above sea level.

If you were a geographer . . . *How would you describe Texas?*

You Be the Geographer

Themes Journal

What's Your Opinion? Do you **agree** or **disagree** with the following statements? Support your point of view in your journal.

● **Geography** Larger states have more geographic variety than smaller ones.

● **Culture** Geographers are not interested in human activity or cultures.

● **Economics** The economy of a region is directly dependent on its geography.

The Six Essential Elements of Geography

Read to Discover

1. What types of information do geographers study?
2. What do each of the six essential elements of geography address?

Why It Matters Today

People have lived in Texas and influenced its environment for thousands of years. Use CNNfyi.com and other **current events** sources to find information about the Texas landscape today. Record your findings in your journal.

Define

- geography
- environment
- culture
- geographic information systems
- ecosystem
- migration
- urbanization

Identify

- Roy Bedichek

The Geographer's World

Educator Roy Bedichek moved to a ranch near Austin in 1946. Writing to a friend, he described the natural beauty of the Hill Country. "A gentle rain started on the corrugated [grooved] iron roof a moment ago and I pulled the curtain of the southwest window to take a peep. . . . Suddenly as a flash on a motion-picture screen an *upright* rainbow in full and vivid [bright] colors appeared. . . . [I] stood there transfixed [motionless], a witness to a miracle."

Roy Bedichek saw a rainbow like this one in 1946.

★ The World in Spatial Terms

Geography is the study of the special physical and human characteristics of a place or region. An important part of geography is the relationship between humans and their **environment**, or physical surroundings. A geographer might also study **culture**, a learned system of shared beliefs, traits, and values. A geographer could describe Texas in many ways. Texas is big—it covers about 267,000 square miles and has a population of more than 20 million. It is the second largest state in both size and population. Most Texans live in cities rather than in rural, or agricultural, areas. Yet Texas has about 200,000 farms and some 130 million acres of farm and ranch land—more than any other state.

Geographers look at where things are on Earth's surface. For example, geographers studying Texas cities might find that they are typically located near sources of water, transportation centers, or other important cities. Changes in settlement patterns over time are also important.

Geographers use many tools in their studies, including maps, charts, and graphs. They also use field notes, interviews, photographs, reference books, and videos. High-tech tools such as satellites provide detailed images of Earth. Computer databases, like **geographic information systems** (GIS), store huge amounts of data, or information. Geography helps in future planning, including where new dams or roads should be built in Texas.

✔**Reading Check Finding the Main Idea** Why is geographic knowledge useful?

★ Places and Regions

People's culture and experiences affect their ideas of places and regions. A place has physical and human characteristics that make it special. Physical characteristics include animal and plant life, sources of water, climate and weather, landforms, and soils. Landforms are the natural shapes on Earth's surface, such as mountains, hills, and valleys. Human characteristics include ethnicity, language, political and economic systems, population distribution, religion, and standards of living.

A region is an area with common characteristics that make it different from surrounding areas. People define regions to organize the world. Regions can be as large as Texas, or as small as a neighborhood. A *formal* region has one or more shared characteristics. A formal region might be based on physical features such as plant life. Formal regions could also be cultural, economic, or political. Countries, states, and cities are examples of formal political regions. A *functional* region is made up of

Interpreting the Visual Record

Landscapes. The Texas landscape is diverse with deserts, forests, plains, mountains, and swamps. **What does this image of Guadalupe Mountains National Park tell you about some of the landscape?**

different places that function together as a unit. A newspaper's subscription area and a metropolitan area such as Dallas–Fort Worth are examples of functional regions. A *perceptual* region is defined by people's shared attitudes, culture, and feelings about an area. Perceptual regions, such as Central Texas or the Panhandle, often have vague borders. Geographers try to learn what defines a place or region and what makes it special.

✔**Reading Check** **Categorizing** Choose a place or region and list three of its physical features and three of its human features.

★ Physical Systems and Human Systems

Geographers study the physical processes and interactions among four physical systems—Earth's atmosphere, land, water, and life. Physical processes shape and change Earth's physical features and environments. For example, Padre Island's coastline changes as tides from the Gulf of Mexico move beach sand. Climate and weather affect humans. For example, people might choose to live in an area that has a mild climate. In some

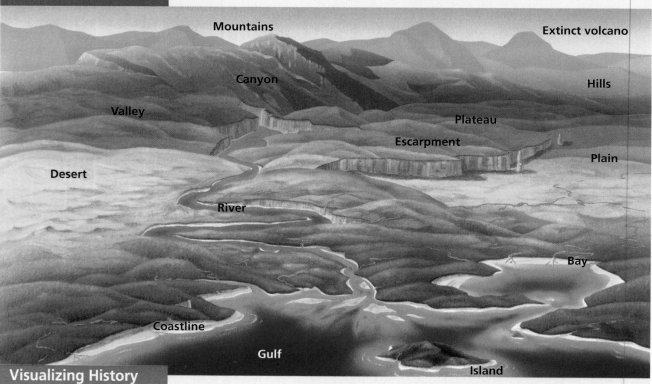

Texas Landforms

The Texas landscape is diverse. Traveling across the state, you could find plains, rivers, hills, deserts, and even mountains. Each of the landforms and waterways in this diagram can be found in Texas.

Mountains

Extinct volcano

Canyon

Hills

Valley

Plateau

Escarpment

Plain

Desert

River

Bay

Coastline

Gulf

Island

Visualizing History

1. **Geography** What can be learned about Texas geography from this diagram? ★TEKS

2. **Connecting to Today** What geographic features can you find near your school?

Central and North Texas areas the clay soil shrinks or swells depending on the weather. This knowledge affects building construction.

An **ecosystem** is all of an area's plants and animals together with the nonliving parts of their environment. A beach, an island, and a pond are ecosystems. Earth is the largest ecosystem. Natural events and human activity can change ecosystems. For example, in the 1930s drought and overgrazing led to the loss of topsoil and plant life in parts of North and West Texas. This hurt farming and ranching in the area. Studying physical processes and ecosystems is important because the environment is the setting for all life on Earth.

Studying human systems such as population distribution, growth, and movement helps in understanding human events and geography. Population growth is affected by a population's age, birthrate, death rate, and life expectancy. Changes in human activity such as advances in medical care and food production have led to population growth. Geographers also look at where people live and how crowded a region or place is when they study population density. They also study **migration**, or the movement of people. One specific type of migration is known as **urbanization**, which is an increase in people living or working in cities. Texas, like many places, is part of this trend.

Many geographers study the features of cultural groups. People often create groups that separate, organize, or unify areas. Geographers also consider human systems of communication, trade, and transportation in the global economy. Such human activities help explain how humans interact with one another and with the environment.

 Reading Check **Identifying Cause and Effect** How did the weather change in the 1930s? How did this change affect the Texas economy?

Biography

Roy Bedichek
(1878–1959)

Roy Bedichek was an educator, folklorist, and journalist who moved to Texas from Illinois when he was about six years old. He attended the University of Texas, earning a bachelor of science and a master's degree. After college he taught high school. Bedichek was a strong promoter of higher education. For many years he served as director of the University Interscholastic League (UIL). Bedichek was a gifted storyteller and wrote several books, including *Adventures with a Texas Naturalist*, *Karánkaway Country*, and a history of the UIL. **In what ways was Bedichek a leader in natural sciences and education?** TEKS

★ Environment and Society

One of the most important topics in geography is how people interact with the environment. Human activities can have positive effects on the environment. For example, people help restore the environment by planting trees in areas that have been deforested. However, human activities can also affect the environment negatively. As Houston's industry and population have grown, air pollution there has greatly increased. Some Texans have tried to limit the harm humans do to the environment. Texas naturalist **Roy Bedichek** warned of the dangers of pollution some 50 years ago.

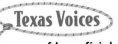 **Texas Voices** ❝The gentle gardener poisons his soil to kill pillbugs and in so doing annihilates [wipes out] great numbers of beneficial creatures, including the lowly and lovely earthworm.❞

—Roy Bedichek, quoted in *Three Men in Texas*, by Ronnie Dugger.

Analyzing Primary Sources
Identifying Cause and Effect According to Bedichek, why do some gardeners change the environment, and to what effect?

The environment affects humans as well. Physical features such as landforms and rivers can influence where people live, and people depend on the environment for survival. Human life requires three basic resources—air, water, and land. Other natural materials, such as wood and coal, are also important resources. As the world population grows, demands on resources increase. Geographers study the location, quality, and quantity of Earth's resources and the effect of human activity on these resources. Historians use geography to understand history. They not only look at when things happened but where and why they happened. For example, suppose you need to know when, where, and why the first settlement in San Antonio was built. You would need to know that water sources such as the San Antonio River influenced the settlement's location.

Geography helps people understand the present as well as the past. For example, the growing population of Texas has placed greater demands on the environment. In response, many communities in Texas have created water-conservation programs to help preserve this important natural resource. These programs are one way that Texans are using their knowledge of geography to plan for the future. Many geographers use the six essential elements to organize their studies and to help them understand the geography of Texas.

1. The World in Spatial Terms
2. Places and Regions
3. Physical Systems
4. Human Systems
5. Environment and Society
6. The Uses of Geography

 Reading Check **Analyzing Information** How might human actions cause water pollution?

 Section 1 Review  **TEKS** Questions 2, 4b

go.hrw.com Homework Practice Online
keyword: ST3 HP1

1 Define and explain:
- geography
- environment
- culture
- geographic information systems
- ecosystem
- migration
- urbanization

2 Identify and explain:
Roy Bedichek

3 Categorizing
Copy the table below. List the six essential elements of geography. Then describe each element.

Essential Element	Purpose

4 Finding the Main Idea
a. Describe the types of information geographers study.
b. How do humans adapt to and modify the physical environment?

5 Writing and Critical Thinking **TAKS**
Analyzing Information Imagine that you are a geographer scheduled to speak to a classroom. Write a speech describing geography and what you do. Consider the following:
- the definition of geography
- the importance of geography

Read to Discover

1. Why are maps useful?
2. What are the main parts of a map, and what information does each part provide?
3. How does a geographer decide what type of map to create?

Why It Matters Today

Maps are essential tools for geographers and many other professionals. Use CNNfyi.com and other **current events** sources to find a news article that uses a map to explain a subject. Record your findings in your journal.

Define

- **relative location**
- **absolute location**
- **latitude**
- **longitude**
- **equator**
- **prime meridian**
- **compass rose**
- **scale**
- **legend**
- **reference maps**
- **thematic maps**
- **map projections**

The Geographer's World

Harm de Blij, a world-famous geographer, was born in the Netherlands shortly before World War II. During the war, de Blij and his family had to stay inside much of the time for safety. He spent countless hours reading geography books that told of interesting, faraway lands. He later made geography his career. The work, he says, has brought him "a lifetime of discovery and fascination."

Harm de Blij is now a professor of geography and has written numerous geography books.

★ Map Grids

Maps are important tools for geographers and historians. A map is a graphic representation of a place or an area that illustrates the land, the seas, and even space. Maps may also show information about the physical and human features of a place. With maps, many types of information can be organized visually.

Most people use maps to locate places. Geographers describe location in two ways. **Relative location** is where a place is in relation to other places. The relative location of a place is described by its distance and direction from another place. For example, Dallas is 225 miles northwest of Houston. Dallas could also be described as being 33 miles east of Fort Worth. **Absolute location** is the exact position of a place on Earth. The absolute location of the Texas Governor's Mansion is the corner of Eleventh and Colorado Streets in Austin.

How do you find a place on a map? One common method is the grid system. If you look at a road map you might notice a grid made of lines that typically run east-west and north-south. Mapmakers—or cartographers—may place letters of the alphabet across the top or bottom of this grid. Numbers may run along one or both sides. These letters and numbers make it easier to find a specific place on a map.

✔**Reading Check** **Finding the Main Idea** Why do people use maps?

★ Latitude and Longitude

To locate an exact spot on Earth, people use a more complex grid system. This system uses **latitude** and **longitude**, which are imaginary lines circling the globe. While latitude lines run east-west, longitude lines run north-south. Lines of latitude and longitude measure distance in degrees—360 of which circle Earth. Each degree is divided into 60 minutes, and each minute is divided into 60 seconds. The symbol for degree is °. Minute is ′ and second is ″. Latitude lines measure distance north and south of the **equator**. The equator is an imaginary line circling the globe exactly halfway between the North and South Poles. Latitudes north of the equator are labeled *N* on maps. Those south of the equator are labeled *S*. Lines of latitude range from 0° at the equator to 90°N at the North Pole and 90°S at the South Pole.

Longitude lines measure distance east and west of the **prime meridian**. The prime meridian is an imaginary line that runs around the globe from the North Pole, through Greenwich, England, to the South Pole. Longitude lines range from 0° at the prime meridian to 180° at a line exactly halfway around the globe from the prime meridian. On maps, lines of longitude west of the prime meridian to 180° are labeled *W*. Those east of the prime meridian to 180° are labeled *E*.

The exact location of any place on Earth can be given as a combination of latitude and longitude. For example, the latitude of San Antonio, Texas, is 29°25′N. The city's longitude is 98°30′W. Because Texas is such a large state, it covers several degrees of latitude and longitude. From north to south, Texas stretches from latitude 36°30′N to 25°50′N. From east to west, the state extends from longitude 93°31′W to 106°36′W.

✔**Reading Check** **Contrasting** How do longitude and latitude differ?

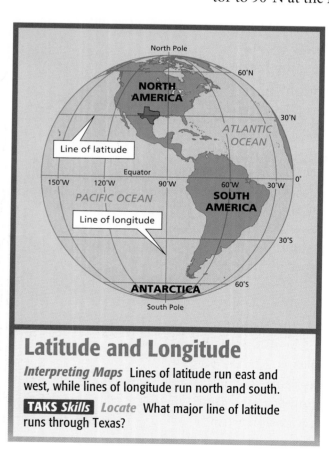

Latitude and Longitude

Interpreting Maps Lines of latitude run east and west, while lines of longitude run north and south.

TAKS Skills *Locate* What major line of latitude runs through Texas?

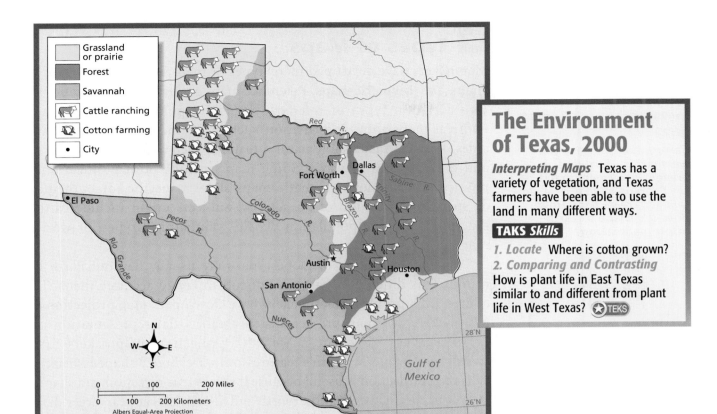

Grassland or prairie
Forest
Savannah
Cattle ranching
Cotton farming
• City

El Paso
Red R.
Fort Worth • • Dallas
Sabine R.
Colorado R.
Brazos
Trinity
Pecos R.
Rio Grande
Austin ★
San Antonio •
Houston •
Nueces R.
Gulf of Mexico
28°N
26°N
96°W   94°W

N
W   E
S

0   100   200 Miles
0   100   200 Kilometers
Albers Equal-Area Projection

The Environment of Texas, 2000

Interpreting Maps Texas has a variety of vegetation, and Texas farmers have been able to use the land in many different ways.

TAKS *Skills*

1. Locate Where is cotton grown?

2. Comparing and Contrasting How is plant life in East Texas similar to and different from plant life in West Texas? ⭐TEKS

★ The Parts of a Map

In some ways, maps are like coded messages. To decode them, map-makers provide elements that make maps easier to read, such as a map's title. The title for the map above tells you that the map shows the state's environmental regions. A map's directional indicator shows which directions are north, south, east, and west. North is usually at the top of a map. To show direction, some maps have a **compass rose** that points to all four cardinal points—north, south, east, and west.

A map's **scale** is the relationship between a measurement on the map and the actual distance on Earth's surface. Perhaps the most useful part of a map is the **legend**, or key. The legend explains the meaning of all the symbols on a map. This information typically appears in a box near the edge of the map. Map symbols may include colors, numbers, patterns, or small drawings.

Some maps include additional inset maps or locator maps, which are smaller maps set inside or next to the main map. Inset maps show more detail than the main map. For example, a map of Houston might have an inset map showing downtown Houston. Locator maps place the area in a map in its larger geographic surroundings.

✔**Reading Check** **Summarizing** List the parts of a map and what they do.

Texas students use maps to find locations and to learn about the characteristics of places and regions.

★ Types of Maps

Mapmakers have developed many types of maps, including **reference maps** and **thematic maps**. Reference maps are used to find locations. Two common types of reference maps are political and physical. Political maps show information such as boundaries, capitals, and cities. Physical maps show natural features such as landforms, rivers, and other bodies of water. Some maps include both political and physical information. Thematic maps show a specific topic, theme, or spatial distribution of an activity. Subjects might include cattle ranching, climates, population density, rainfall, soil types, or world religions.

With the exception of globes, maps are usually flat, but Earth is round. This difference makes it difficult to create accurate maps. To address this problem, mapmakers have developed **map projections**. Mapmakers use map projections to create a flat representation of Earth's surface. To create a Mercator projection, mapmakers first transfer an image of Earth's features onto a cylinder-shaped surface. This map projection is useful because it shows true direction and shape. However, landmasses near the North and South Poles appear larger than they really are. For example, the sizes of northern areas like Greenland, Canada, and Europe are enlarged while the sizes of tropical areas are diminished. Other types of projections show the sizes of landmasses more accurately but distort their shapes. The many types of map projections each have specific advantages and disadvantages.

✔ **Reading Check** **Contrasting** How do reference maps and thematic maps differ?

Section 2 Review

1 Define and explain:
- relative location
- absolute location
- latitude
- longitude
- equator
- prime meridian
- compass rose
- scale
- legend
- reference maps
- thematic maps
- map projections

2 Summarizing

Copy the graphic organizer below. Use it to describe how different map parts help decode a map.

Latitude and Longitude lines

Compass rose

Scale

Legend

3 Finding the Main Idea

a. Why do people make maps?

b. How do map grids differ from latitude and longitude, and when might a mapmaker use each?

4 Writing and Critical Thinking

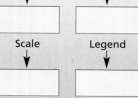

Evaluating Imagine that you are preparing a report on farming in Texas. Describe some maps you might use. Consider the following:
- physical, political, and thematic maps
- titles and dates of possible maps
- the information you want to show

Using Graphs, Charts, and Tables

Read to Discover

1. What types of information do bar graphs, line graphs, pie charts, and tables show, and why are they useful?
2. What are three types of charts, and when might you use each type?

Why It Matters Today

Lists of names, facts, and statistics are often clearest when presented visually. Use CNNfyi.com and other **current events** sources to find a news article that includes a chart or graph. What is the visual's purpose? Record your findings in your journal.

Define

- **statistics**
- **bar graph**
- **horizontal axis**
- **vertical axis**
- **line graph**
- **pie chart**
- **time line**
- **flowchart**
- **causation chart**

The Geographer's World

In the spring of 2000, the U.S. government began taking a census—a count of each person in a specific area. To ensure that everyone was counted, the government hired census takers. Josephine Jones of Dallas was one Texan who eagerly signed up. Jones and the other census takers collected a huge amount of data. The government then organized all this information for research and public use.

The census measures the growth of the Texas population.

★ Using Graphs

Sometimes the best way to convey an idea or information is graphically, or with pictures. Geographers and historians have many tools for presenting information visually. For example, graphs make it easier to compare facts and see the relationships between them. They are also useful for showing **statistics**—information in the form of numbers.

A **bar graph**, or bar chart, is useful in comparing information about different places or different time periods. Bar graphs use bars of different lengths to represent numbers and percentages. The bars may extend sideways or stand on end. Most bar graphs have a **horizontal axis** and a **vertical axis**. The horizontal axis is the line across the bottom of the

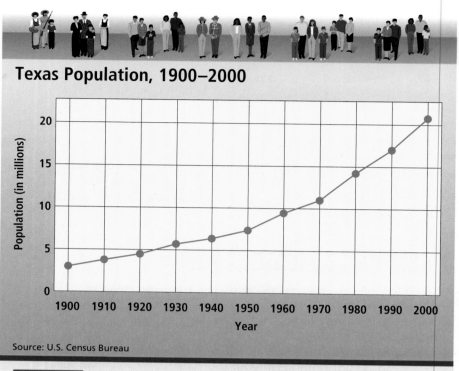

Texas Population, 1900–2000

Population (in millions)

20
15
10
5
0

1900 1910 1920 1930 1940 1950 1960 1970 1980 1990 2000

Year

Source: U.S. Census Bureau

TAKS Skills *Interpreting Graphs* The population of Texas has grown every 10 years since 1900. How have Texas population patterns changed since 1960? ★TEKS

Texas Population Growth, 1990–2000

Texas Counties	Population Growth
Harris	20.7%
Dallas	19.8%
Bexar	17.5%
Tarrant	23.6%
Travis	40.9%
Collin	86.2%

TAKS Skills *Interpreting Tables* During the 1990s many Texas counties experienced large population growth. What was the difference in population growth between Collin and Dallas Counties? ★TEKS

graph. The vertical axis is the line along the side. One axis usually has a number scale giving the measure or value shown by the bars. The other axis may represent another variable, such as a time period. Colors sometimes define the bars instead of labels. A legend then explains what each color means. The bar graph in the chapter review makes it easy to see which Texas city has the largest population.

A **line graph** indicates a trend, or pattern. It may show if something is increasing, decreasing, or staying about the same over time. Like bar graphs, line graphs have a horizontal and a vertical axis. The line graph above provides a simple visual record of population changes in Texas.

✔**Reading Check Finding the Main Idea** How are graphs useful to geographers and historians?

★ Using Charts and Tables

A **pie chart**—or circle graph—shows how the parts of a whole are divided. The pie—or circle—represents the whole item or total amount. The pie pieces—or segments of the pie—represent a percentage of the whole. To make pie charts easier to read, segments are often colored. A legend may be used to define each color. The pie chart on the next page shows the origins of immigrants to Texas in 1996. The circle represents the total number of immigrants. Each segment represents the percentage of immigrants from one part of the world. A pie chart clearly summarizes a large amount of information.

Tables help organize and categorize information. Tables are particularly useful when information is both descriptive and statistical. The table on the previous page lists names and statistical information. Tables use grids with columns and rows of boxes. Each box is called a cell. Labels often appear at the top of each column and at the left of each row.

Charts show the relationship between different subjects. A **time line** shows the sequence of events. Time lines are useful for studying how one event may have led to or caused later events. A **flowchart** uses boxes, arrows, and sometimes images to show a series of activities or steps. For example, a flowchart could describe the steps it takes to turn trees into paper. Although it is similar to a flowchart, a **causation chart** focuses on cause and effect. These charts can take several forms. They may use pictures or diagrams to show the causes and effects of events. Some causation charts have boxes and arrows pointing out the effects of an event or idea. Others show events as steps or as a ladder. When an event has many causes or effects, a web diagram is useful. In a web, an event appears in the center. Its causes or effects surround it. In general, most charts contain information that is difficult to show in graphs or tables or to describe in text.

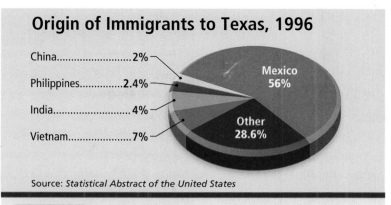

Origin of Immigrants to Texas, 1996

China.........................2%
Philippines...............2.4%
India.........................4%
Vietnam.....................7%
Mexico 56%
Other 28.6%

Source: *Statistical Abstract of the United States*

TAKS *Skills* *Interpreting Charts* New immigrants from Asian and Latin American countries have added to the diversity of Texas. What percentage of immigrants to Texas came from Asian countries? ⭐TEKS

✔**Reading Check** **Analyzing Information** When might a geographer or historian choose to use a pie chart or a table instead of a line or bar graph?

Section 3 Review   ⭐TEKS Question 4

go.hrw.com **Homework Practice Online** keyword: ST3 HP1

1 Define and explain:
- statistics
- bar graph
- horizontal axis
- vertical axis
- line graph
- pie chart
- time line
- flowchart
- causation chart

2 Categorizing
Copy the web diagram below. Use it to explain how different charts, graphs, and tables help geographers and historians.

Line Graphs
Bar Graphs
Pie Charts
Time Lines
Geographers and Historians
Tables
Causation Charts
Flow-charts

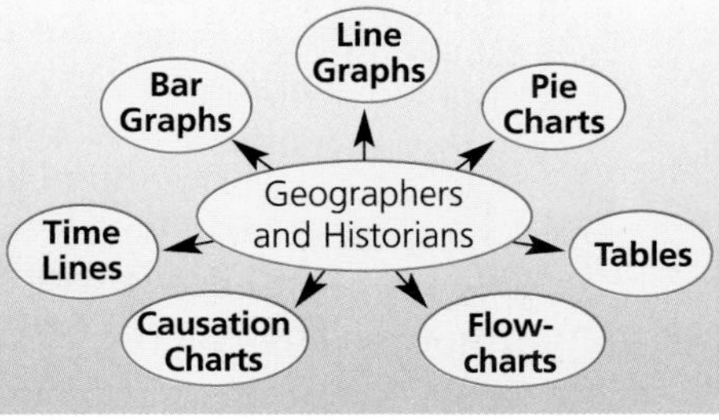

3 Finding the Main Idea
a. Why do people use graphs?
b. Describe three types of charts and explain their primary uses.

4 Writing and Critical Thinking TAKS
Drawing Inferences and Conclusions
Imagine that you are writing a newspaper article about a drought. Create a thematic chart or table for your article. Consider the following:
- the causes, events, and results
- the farmers, crops, and geography

The Chapter at a Glance

Examine the following visual summary of the chapter. Then use the visual to write a one-page chapter summary that a classmate can use as a study guide.

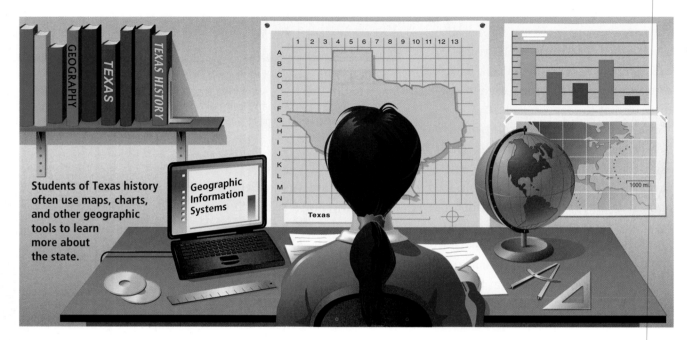

Students of Texas history often use maps, charts, and other geographic tools to learn more about the state.

Geographic Information Systems

Texas

1000 mi.

Identifying People and Ideas

Use the following terms or people in sentences.

1. geography
2. Roy Bedichek
3. longitude
4. equator
5. compass rose
6. legend
7. thematic maps
8. vertical axis
9. pie chart
10. causation chart

Understanding Main Ideas

Section 1 (pages 4–8)

1. What are the six essential elements of geography?
2. In what ways do humans modify the environment, and what are some results of those modifications?

Section 2 (pages 9–12)

3. Why do geographers find map grids and lines of longitude and latitude useful?
4. What are the parts of a map?

Section 3 (pages 13–15)

5. Why are graphs useful?
6. Why might a geographer choose to use a chart rather than a graph?

You Be the Geographer

Reviewing Themes

1. **Geography** How is the size of Texas related to its geographic diversity?
2. **Culture** How do geographers learn about human activities and cultures?
3. **Economics** How might geography affect the type of businesses and industries that develop in an area?

TAKS Practice: Thinking Critically

1. **Summarizing** Describe an idea for a Texas map showing regions based on one physical and one human characteristic.
2. **Drawing Inferences and Conclusions** Why are flowcharts and time lines often used by historians?
3. **Making Generalizations and Predictions** How will geography help in understanding Texas history?

Interpreting Graphs ✪TEKS

Study the graph below. Then use the information in the graph to help you answer the questions that follow.

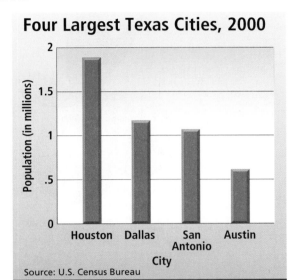

Four Largest Texas Cities, 2000

Population (in millions) — cities: Houston, Dallas, San Antonio, Austin

City

Source: U.S. Census Bureau

1. Approximately how much larger is Houston's population than that of the next largest city?

 a. 750,000 people
 b. .75 people
 c. 1,500,000 people
 d. 1.5 people

2. What advantages does a bar graph have in presenting the information on population distribution?

Analyzing Primary Sources ✪TEKS

Read the following quote from early Texas settler Noah Smithwick. Then answer the questions.

"[Growing corn] was no very difficult matter near the coast, where there were vast canebrakes all along the rivers. The soil was rich and loose from the . . . crops of [wild] cane that had decayed on it. In the fall, when the cane died down, it was burned off clean. The ground was then ready for planting, which was done in a very primitive manner, a sharpened stick being all the implement [tool] necessary. With this they made holes in the moist loam [soil] and dropped in grains of corn. . . . The only water obtainable was that of the sluggish river, which crept along between low banks thickly set with tall trees, from branches of which . . . [hung] long streamers of Spanish moss swarming with mosquitoes and malaria."

3. Which of the following statements would be least important to a geographer?

 a. The quote describes the arrangement of things in the landscape of an area.
 b. The quote describes a relationship between environment and society.
 c. The quote offers clues to the physical and human systems operating in Texas.
 d. The quote is of historical value.

4. Based on this quote, what conclusions could be drawn about where pioneers settled and why?

Alternative Assessment

Linking to Community ✪TEKS

Think about some of the physical and human characteristics that help define an area in your community. Physical characteristics might include the plant life, landforms, or climate of your community. The human characteristics might include the types of industry, location of roads, or where people live. Create a map of the area and label some of the characteristics you have included.

BUILDING YOUR Portfolio

☑ **internet** connect

Internet Activity: go.hrw.com
KEYWORD: ST3 TX1 ✪TEKS

Access the Internet through the HRW Go site to research how maps are made, what maps can illustrate, and how maps are formatted. Then apply what you have learned by creating a map that illustrates the relative and absolute location of your school. Make sure your map has a directional indicator, a legend, and a scale.

CHAPTER 2

A Land Called Texas

The Texas oil industry provides thousands of Texans with jobs.

South Texas produces large crops of oranges and other citrus fruits.

TEXAS	In 1997 Texas produced more than 465 million barrels of oil worth some $8.5 billion.	Texas has an estimated 23 billion tons of lignite, a type of coal.	More than 6 million acres of Texas land are irrigated.	The Ogallala Aquifer is the largest underground water source in Texas.
U.S. and WORLD	In 1997 the United States produced more than 2.3 billion barrels of oil worth some $40.6 billion.	The United States produced more than 85.8 million tons of lignite in 1998.	The United States used 81 billion gallons of water for irrigation in 1995.	The Ogallala Aquifer is also the largest aquifer in North America.

Large oil tankers ship millions of barrels of oil to markets around the world.

Build on What You Know

Texas is a large and diverse state. The tools of geography will help you learn about the climate, landforms, people, and resources of Texas. The state's diverse population and wide variety of physical features help make Texas unique.

Texas parks and natural areas provide a winter home for the endangered whooping crane.

Caddo Lake is a popular recreation area in East Texas.

		Toledo Bend Reservoir on the Sabine River holds more than 5.5 billion cubic meters of water.	
In 1999 there were more than 227,000 farms in Texas.	Agriculture added some $40 billion to the Texas economy in 1998.		Caddo Lake is the largest natural lake in Texas, covering more than 39 square miles.
In 1999 there were 2.2 million farms in the United States.	Agriculture added more than $220 billion to the U.S. economy in 1998.	The largest reservoir in the world is the Owen Falls Reservoir in Uganda, Africa.	The largest natural lake in the world is the Caspian Sea, which covers more than 143,000 square miles.

American farmers grow millions of bushels of corn each year.

You Be the Geographer

Themes Journal

What's Your Opinion Do you **agree** or **disagree** with the following statements? Support your point of view in your journal.

● **Geography** A region's physical features, such as land and water, are always modified by humans.

● **Culture** Immigrants moving into an area add to its cultural traditions.

● **Economics** A region's resources always influence its economy.

If you were a geographer . . .
What would you find most interesting about Texas geography?

The Physical Landscape of Texas

Read to Discover

1. What landforms are found in Texas?
2. What types of water resources exist in Texas?

Why It Matters Today

Texans have long relied upon the state's sources of water. Texas has many different water resources, including aquifers and reservoirs. Use **CNNfyi.com** or other **current events** sources to learn about water resources. Record your findings in your journal.

Define

- **plains**
- **plateaus**
- **ranges**
- **tributaries**
- **reservoirs**
- **irrigation**
- **aquifers**

Identify

- **Ogallala Aquifer**
- **Edwards Aquifer**

In 1966 the Caverns of Sonora were named a National Natural Landmark.

The Geographer's World

In the summer of 1956, Jack Burch and James Papadakis discovered a small opening in a West Texas limestone cliff. They decided to squeeze through the 18-inch hole. Once inside, the two adventurers found a large cave with beautiful rare stalactites—rock formations that hang like icicles. The men had discovered one of the hidden natural treasures of Texas. The cavern was opened for public tours four years later. The Caverns of Sonora are among the most beautiful caves in the world.

★ Landforms of Texas

The Caverns of Sonora are just one of many natural treasures in Texas. To locate Texas on a globe, find the Northern Hemisphere. This northern half of the planet lies between the North Pole and the equator. Texas is also in the Western Hemisphere—the half of the planet west of the prime meridian. Located in the southern half of the North American continent, Texas borders a large body of water called the Gulf of Mexico. The state is located in the central and southern region of the United States. Texas is just north of Mexico, west of Louisiana, south of Oklahoma, and east of New Mexico. Arkansas borders the northeastern corner of Texas.

The varied landscape of Texas includes canyons, islands, valleys, and even extinct volcanoes. The four major landforms in Texas are hills, mountains, plains, and plateaus. **Plains** are areas of flat or gently rolling land without a sharp rise or fall in elevation. **Plateaus** are areas of flat elevated land that drop sharply on one or more sides.

Plains cover much of the Gulf Coast, the Panhandle, North Texas, South Texas, and West Texas. These flatlands help to define the Texas landscape. One visitor noted that the Gulf Coast plains were "so perfectly flat that the eye embraced an extent [distance] of many miles." Many of the Texas plains are interrupted by hills. The easternmost part of Texas is covered by forests. To the west lie gently rolling prairies, or treeless grasslands. Central Texas has rugged hills, including those in the Hill Country. West of the Hill Country lies the Edwards Plateau, which rises in elevation from east to west.

West of the Edwards Plateau, the landscape becomes rocky. Several different **ranges**, or groups of mountains, rise west of the Pecos River. The highest point in Texas, Guadalupe Peak, is part of the Guadalupe Mountains. Although West Texas has some mountains, most of the state is covered by plains.

 Reading Check **Summarizing** How does the Texas landscape change from east to west?

★ The Texas River System

Texas has several water features, including lakes, rivers, and streams. The largest body of water is the Gulf of Mexico, which is an important resource for Texas. It provides a source for fishing and shrimping as well as an area for recreation. Water from all of the rivers and streams in Texas eventually flows into the Gulf of Mexico.

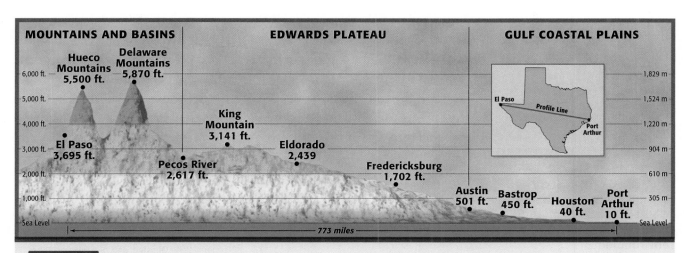

TAKS Skills *Interpreting Charts* Moving from east to west, the elevation of Texas rises and the landscape becomes more rugged. How much higher are the Delaware Mountains than Port Arthur? ★TEKS

Texas plant life. Many Texas rivers run through the prairies of Central Texas, providing water to plant and animal life. *What plant life can you identify in this photograph?*

Texas has more than a dozen major rivers and some 11,000 streams. The Texas river system can be divided into several groups. A number of rivers and smaller streams in the northern part of the state flow into the Mississippi River. These include the Red River and Canadian River. A second group of rivers begins in Texas and neighboring states. These rivers flow parallel with one another directly into the Gulf of Mexico. They include the Brazos, Colorado, Neches, Nueces, Sabine, and Trinity. The third group consists of the Rio Grande and its **tributaries**. A tributary is any smaller stream or river that flows into a larger stream or river. The Pecos River is an important tributary to the Rio Grande.

Every one of these Texas rivers has its own special character. The Rio Grande is by far the longest. It begins as a snow-fed mountain stream in Colorado. From there, it flows 1,896 miles through New Mexico down desert canyons and coastal lowlands to the Gulf of Mexico. For 1,254 miles the Rio Grande forms the international boundary between the United States and Mexico. The Comal—one of the shortest rivers in Texas—rises from a spring and flows for less than three miles. The Colorado River travels some 600 miles across Texas. Along the way it drains nearly 40,000 square miles of Texas landscape. It is the largest river contained entirely within the state. The Trinity River travels some 550 miles through the prairies of North Texas and the woods of East Texas. It then flows into the Gulf of Mexico. Park designer Frederick Law Olmsted traveled through Texas in the 1850s and commented on the river.

Analyzing Primary Sources
Summarizing What did Olmsted suggest about how Texans modify the environment?

Texas Voices ⟩ 66These bottom lands bordering the Trinity [River] are among the richest of Texas. . . . High up, in the region of the Forks of the Trinity [River], are lands equally suitable to cotton, wheat, and corn.99

—Frederick Law Olmsted, *Journey through Texas*

Reading Check Contrasting How do Texas rivers differ from each other?

★ Texas Lakes and Aquifers

Texas has few natural lakes. Caddo Lake, in Northeast Texas, is the largest. However, the state has hundreds of lakes built by people. Texans built dams along rivers to help control floods and to create **reservoirs**. These artificial lakes store water that is often used as drinking water for towns and cities. Reservoirs also serve as places for recreation. Some reservoirs are important sources for **irrigation**, or watering of crops.

Water is also found in the state's **aquifers**. Aquifers are formations of natural gravel, rock, and sand that trap and hold rainwater underground. Refilling, or recharging, them with water is typically a slow process. In Texas several major aquifers provide water for farms, homes, and industry. The **Ogallala Aquifer** is the largest underground water source in the state. The aquifer stretches from West Texas and New Mexico north to South Dakota. Almost 95 percent of the water pumped out of the aquifer is used for irrigation. Just to the south, the **Edwards Aquifer** provides water for San Antonio, Austin, and the rest of Central Texas. The largest springs in Texas come from the Edwards Aquifer. A spring is a natural outpouring of water from underground. These springs provide a place of recreation as well as a source of water.

Connecting To Literature

Goodbye to a River
John Graves

John Graves grew up near Fort Worth and visited the Brazos River as a child. As an adult, Graves traveled by boat down the Brazos. The following excerpt is from an account of his journey, published in 1961.

For scores of years no [population] boom has brought people to its banks; booms elsewhere have sucked them thence. Old respect for the river's occasional violence makes farmers and ranchers build on high ground away from the stream itself, which runs primitive and neglected. When you paddle and pole along it, the things you see are much the same things the Comanches and the Kiowas used to see, riding lean ponies down it a hundred years ago to raid the new settlements in its valley. **According to Graves, why do farmers and ranchers build on high ground away from the river?**

★ **Reading Check Analyzing Information** How have Texans used the state's natural resources?

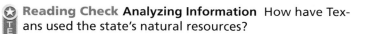

★ Section 1 Review

★TEKS Questions 3, 5

go.hrw.com **Homework Practice Online** keyword: ST3 HP2

1 Define and explain:
- plains
- plateaus
- ranges
- tributaries
- reservoirs
- irrigation
- aquifers

2 Identify and explain:
- Ogallala Aquifer
- Edwards Aquifer

3 Evaluating
Copy the graphic organizer below. Use it to explain how each feature of Texas geography affects life in the state.

Location   Landforms

Life in Texas

Water Resources

4 Finding the Main Idea
a. Describe the location of Texas.
b. What landforms and water resources exist in Texas?

5 Writing and Critical Thinking
Drawing Inferences and Conclusions
Write an interview with a geographer about the different geographical features of Texas. Be sure to include questions and potential anwers.
Consider the following:
- landforms and water resources
- how Texans use these resources

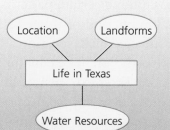

A Land Called Texas **23**

The Texas Climate

Read to Discover

1. How does the climate and weather of Texas affect the economy and life in the state?
2. How are Texas plants and animals affected by the state's landscape and climate?

Why It Matters Today

Texas experiences many types of severe weather. Use **CNN fyi.com** or other **current events** sources to learn about recent occurrences of severe weather. Record your findings in your journal.

Define

- **humidity**
- **drought**
- **erosion**
- **habitat**
- **extinct**

Identify

- **Lady Bird Johnson**

The Geographer's World

Severe weather such as tornadoes can cause deaths, injuries, and significant economic losses by destroying crops and homes.

In 1947, Texas Panhandle residents of Lipscomb County heard a loud trainlike noise. One rural resident stepped out of his front door and saw an approaching tornado. The tornado picked the man up hundreds of feet into the air. Another person went to the door after the man disappeared. The second man was also swept up by the tornado. After a few scary moments, both men were set down uninjured. When they searched for the house they found nothing but the foundation and a couch. Sitting on the couch was the first man's family, who were all unhurt—but understandably frightened.

★ Weather and Climate

Texas weather can change quickly and dramatically. But as in all places, weather in Texas follows certain patterns. Climate is an area's pattern of weather over a long period of time. The state's climate, particularly its temperature, is affected by its location. Texas is much closer to the equator than to the North Pole. The equator receives sunlight most directly. As a result, most of Texas experiences hot summers and long periods of sunshine. On some days temperatures rise above 110°F.

Wind patterns also affect the climate of Texas regions. The highest temperatures occur most often in the Rio Grande valley and areas of north-central Texas. These areas are hotter because of winds that blow in from the west. These western winds cross deserts and carry warmer drier air into the state.

The temperature of water rises and falls more slowly than that of land. Thus, the Gulf of Mexico acts as an air conditioner for the Texas coast. In the summer, sea breezes keep nearby land areas cooler than areas farther inland. In the winter the Gulf keeps coastal lands warmer. However, Texans who live along the Gulf Coast experience higher **humidity**—the amount of moisture in the air. The high humidity often makes the warm temperatures along the Gulf Coast feel even hotter.

The Panhandle is also affected by winds. Winds that blow in from the north usually bring cooler temperatures to the Panhandle during winter months. The area often experiences cold fronts, or air masses, called northers. Temperatures can drop in a matter of minutes when a norther hits. A norther's effects are sometimes felt as far south as Central Texas and along the coast of the Gulf of Mexico. In winter a northern air mass can blow in with freezing winds, ice, and snow. One Texan in the 1840s described a norther.

Texas Voices ❝These winds commonly burst forth so suddenly that the first notice of their advent [arrival] is a violent gust that almost checks respiration [takes your breath away]. . . . The temperature frequently falls fifteen to twenty degrees in as many minutes.❞

Francis Moore Jr., quoted in *Texas: A Geography*, by Terry G. Jordan, et al.

Elevation can also affect temperature. The temperature can be cooler in higher elevations because the air is not as dense. Air that is less dense does not absorb heat as well. Therefore, the mountains and higher elevations of West Texas generally have a cooler climate than the other parts of the state.

⭐ **Reading Check Summarizing** What weather patterns occur in different parts of Texas?

GLOBAL CONNECTIONS

El Niño

Sometimes global trends in weather affect Texas. Every few years, the ocean temperature rises along the west coast of South America. This trend, called El Niño, brings more winter rain than average to Texas. Most of this rain soaks the normally dry regions of West Texas and the Panhandle. **How does El Niño affect the Texas climate?**

Analyzing Primary Sources
Finding the Main Idea
According to Moore, how does one know a norther has arrived?

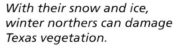

With their snow and ice, winter northers can damage Texas vegetation.

25

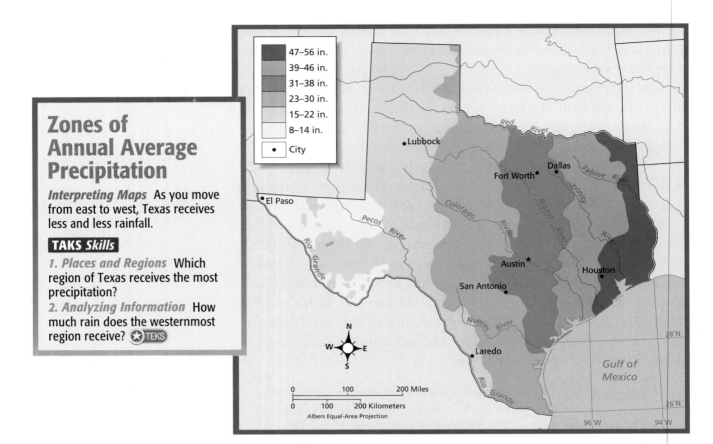

Zones of Annual Average Precipitation

Interpreting Maps As you move from east to west, Texas receives less and less rainfall.

TAKS *Skills*

1. Places and Regions Which region of Texas receives the most precipitation?

2. Analyzing Information How much rain does the westernmost region receive? ★ TEKS

Map legend:
- 47–56 in.
- 39–46 in.
- 31–38 in.
- 23–30 in.
- 15–22 in.
- 8–14 in.
- • City

★ Rainfall in Texas

An area's climate is also determined by precipitation, or moisture falling as rain, snow, sleet, hail, or mist. In Texas the amount of precipitation increases across the state from west to east. While the average rainfall total in West Texas is 8–14 inches per year, East Texas receives 39–56 inches of rain annually. One reason the eastern half of Texas receives more rain is that it is closer to the Gulf of Mexico. Warm moist air from the Gulf passes over East Texas. When this air passes over land, it meets cooler air masses. The warm air rises and often dumps rain on East Texas. The northern area of Texas receives part of its moisture from snow. The Panhandle usually gets several heavy snows each winter. The largest snowfall on record in Texas occurred in 1956, when the Amarillo area was blanketed by more than 30 inches of snow.

When rainfall is much less than the average, Texans experience a **drought**. These long periods without much rain can cause damage to crops. Texas had serious droughts in the 1890s, 1930s, 1950s, 1980s, and 1990s. Water shortages during droughts have become a greater problem as the state's population has grown. The growth of industry, irrigation, and population have placed greater demands on water resources such as aquifers. As a result, water supplies in some Texas towns have fallen to very low levels during dry summer months. Droughts are particularly damaging to the Texas farming and ranching industries.

Floods are another threat to Texans and their property. Within minutes, calm streams can become raging rivers. Rivers can overflow their banks and cover neighboring lands. Dams have helped control flooding in many areas of Texas. But other places, like the Hill Country, still have floods following heavy downpours.

Reading Check **Evaluating** How can changes in rainfall affect the economy of Texas?

★ Severe Weather

Texas gets its share of severe weather—including tornadoes, hurricanes, and blizzards. Tornadoes are violent funnel-shaped storms that develop inside severe thunderstorms. The swirling winds of tornadoes can reach speeds of more than 300 miles per hour. Texas is in the southern edge of "Tornado Alley," a region of the midwestern United States. In Texas, tornadoes usually appear in the Panhandle or the north-central part of the state. One account of a tornado in May 1868 described its effects. "[The tornado] blew cattle into the air, lodging them in trees, sucked all water from the Brazos River for a short distance and dumped a fifty-pound fish on dry land." In 1998 approximately 110 tornadoes struck Texas. Tornadoes have claimed hundreds of lives and caused millions of dollars in damage. The tornado season is usually from spring until the beginning of summer.

Toward midsummer, the season for hurricanes starts. The season lasts through early fall. These huge storms develop over the waters of the Atlantic Ocean and Gulf of Mexico. They come ashore with high

Interpreting the Visual Record

Hurricanes. Hurricanes can strike the Texas coast with winds of more than 100 miles per hour. **How do you think severe weather like this could affect the Texas economy?** ★TEKS

Lady Bird Johnson
(1912–present)

Claudia Alta "Lady Bird" Taylor grew up near the East Texas town of Marshall. Claudia was nicknamed Lady Bird as a child. After earning a master's degree at the University of Texas, Lady Bird married school-teacher Lyndon B. Johnson in 1934. Lady Bird helped her husband's political career as he rose to become a U.S. president during the 1960s.

Later in her life, Lady Bird Johnson became concerned about the decline of wild plant life. Lady Bird explained why she founded a center to study wildflowers in Austin. "The founding of the National Wildflower Research Center was my way of repaying some of the debt for the delight . . . Nature has given me all my life." **Why did Lady Bird Johnson establish the wildflower center?**

winds, heavy rains, and enormous tidal surges from the Gulf. In 1900 some 6,000 to 8,000 people were killed when a hurricane hit Galveston. An even larger storm, Hurricane Carla, came ashore in 1961 near Port Lavaca. Winds rose to 175 miles per hour, and storm tides reached 18.5 feet above normal. Despite early warnings, 34 people died. Hundreds more were injured.

Texas also gets hit by blizzards, or large snow storms. Those storms bring high winds, ice, and snow. They usually strike the Texas Panhandle or the north-central area of Texas. Blizzards are particularly dangerous to cattle and other livestock. The Great Blizzard of 1886–87 nearly destroyed the Texas cattle industry for almost a decade. With new research and technology, scientists are better able to predict when and where severe weather will strike. These developments have saved hundreds of lives.

Reading Check **Categorizing** When and where do Texans experience tornadoes, hurricanes, and blizzards?

★ Texas Vegetation

The diversity of the Texas climate has provided a hospitable place for native plants. All kinds of brush, bushes, native grasses, trees, and wildflowers are native to Texas. Climate, landforms, and soil all help to determine where a plant will grow. For example, only native plants that can survive long periods without water can grow in the dry lands of far West Texas. Short grasses grow in clumps there, as do cacti and plants such as yucca. Groups of coniferous, or cone-bearing, trees are found in the mountains. These trees include junipers, piñon pines, and ponderosa pines. In contrast, the prairies of the central and eastern regions of Texas have rich native grasslands.

The plains of South Texas are also hot and dry. However, they get a bit more rain than West Texas does. South Texas is often called "brush country" because it is covered by shrubs and small trees. Mesquite trees are scattered throughout this part of Texas. Oaks are also found in places with more rain. Palm trees grow along the warm Gulf Coast of South Texas. Cacti and various grasses add to the variety of the landscape. In the Panhandle, the plains stretch for miles without trees. However, the soil conditions and annual rainfall support many different kinds of grasses. Unlike in far West Texas, grasses cover most of the land in the Panhandle.

In contrast to dry western Texas, the eastern third of the state receives plenty of rain. The soil is also very fertile. As a result, bushes, forests, and tall grasses can easily grow there. Forests cover the Piney Woods in East Texas. Gideon Lincecum visited the region in the 1830s. He wrote that it was "the thickest woods I ever saw." The Piney Woods is full of loblolly, longleaf, and shortleaf pine trees. Elm, hickory, and oak trees are also common in East Texas.

Lady Bird Johnson, the wife of U.S. president Lyndon B. Johnson, worked to keep Texas highways beautiful by leading the effort to plant bluebonnets and other wildflowers along the state's roads. She also helped establish the National Wildflower Research Center in Austin. The center provides information on native plants. These plants help to prevent **erosion**, or soil loss, by holding soil in place with their roots. Many wild plants also contribute beauty to the Texas landscape.

★ **Reading Check** **Contrasting** How do the climate and geography of West Texas differ from those of East Texas? How do these factors affect plant life in Texas?

★ Texas Wildlife

The vegetation of Texas provides a **habitat**, or environmental home, to a wide variety of animals. The forests and prairies of Texas are home to many wild animals. These include armadillos, bears, deer, javelinas, prairie hens, raccoon, skunks, wildcats, wild turkeys, and wolves. Texas waters are also full of wildlife. These animals include alligators, catfish, oysters, redfish, shrimp, and hundreds of other types of sea life.

As the state's environment has changed, the habitats of some animals have been destroyed. The gray wolf and the whooping crane are just two animals that might become **extinct** in Texas. To be extinct means to die out completely or disappear. The populations of some animals that were once threatened with extinction have grown in recent years. For example, the buffalo population has grown dramatically.

Wildcats live in many areas of Texas.

★ **Reading Check** **Summarizing** What consequences have come from the modification of animal habitats in Texas?

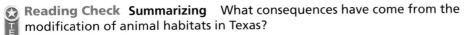

Section 2 Review ★(TEKS) Questions 3, 4a, 5

go.hrw.com **Homework Practice Online**
keyword: ST3 HP2

1 Define and explain:
- humidity
- drought
- erosion
- habitat
- extinct

2 Identify and explain:
- Lady Bird Johnson

3 Analyzing Information
Copy the graphic organizer below. Use it to explain how each type of weather affects Texas.

	Where they occur	Effects on life and economy
Droughts		
Floods		
Tornadoes		
Hurricanes		
Blizzards		

4 Finding the Main Idea
a. How does the climate of East Texas differ from that of West Texas?
b. What weather and geographic features affect plant and animal life?

5 Writing and Critical Thinking **TAKS**
Summarizing In a letter to a friend, describe how the weather differs between East and West Texas.
Consider the following:
- weather trends in different regions
- the time of year

3 Texans and Geography

Read to Discover

1. What groups came to Texas, and where did they settle?
2. What factors have led to the growth of the Texas population?

Define

- **immigration**
- **demography**
- **growth rate**
- **birthrate**
- **death rate**
- **age distribution**

Why It Matters Today

Texas has a growing population. Use CNNfyi.com or other **current events** sources to learn about population changes. Record your findings in your journal.

Texans of Czech descent often wear traditional clothing during festivals and cultural events.

The Geographer's World

Texas has become home for people from many different countries. These newcomers have brought cultural traditions with them. According to one Texan of Czech heritage, some Czech settlers practiced a special ritual. On Easter morning, a young Czech man would wash the face of the woman he liked. If the woman liked the young man as well, she would wash his face the day after Easter. This ritual marked the beginning of a relationship. While this old Czech tradition has faded from use, many other cultural traditions are preserved by Texans.

★ Who Texans Are

Texas is mostly populated by people who moved from other lands. As a result, Texans have many backgrounds, ethnicities, and races. New-comers have brought unique cultural traditions and beliefs from their homelands. These differences contribute to the state's cultural diversity.

The first people to live in Texas were Native Americans who moved to the area thousands of years ago. After Europeans arrived, the population of Native Americans began dropping rapidly. Many Texas Indians died from warfare and diseases that the Europeans carried. During the 1700s and 1800s some Native American groups migrated to Texas from other parts of North America. In 2000 about 118,000 American Indians lived in Texas. Many Texas Indians hold religious ceremonies and practice traditional ways of life. For example, the Alabama-Coushatta Indians hold traditional dances on their reservation near Lake Livingston.

Many Texans trace their ancestry to people who came from Europe. The movement of people from one country to another is called **immigration**. Some of the first European immigrants in Texas came from Spain. Most of these settlers came from Mexico, bringing with them the Spanish language and the Catholic faith. In recent times the largest number of immigrants to Texas have come from Mexico. In 2000 more than 6.6 million Hispanics lived in Texas. This number is more than 30 percent of the Texas population.

In 2000 the number of Texans who considered themselves white and not Hispanic was about 11 million. This number accounts for about 52 percent of the state's population. Some of these people's families first came to Texas in the early 1800s when settlers from the United States began coming to Texas. These settlers helped shape the economic system, education system, and laws of Texas. European immigrants also influenced Texas culture. Significant numbers of German, Czech, French, Irish, and other Europeans came to Texas during the 1800s and 1900s. Their presence is seen in place-names, foods, and other cultural traditions of Texas. For example, German polka music and food, such as sauerkraut, are common in some Texas Hill Country towns.

African Americans also have a long history in Texas. Many African Americans were brought to Texas as slaves during the early and mid-1800s. The African American population in Texas grew during the 1900s. In 2000 the state's African American population numbered more than 2.4 million, or about 12 percent of the Texas population that year. African Americans have influenced music, religious practices, and many other cultural traditions of Texas. For example, Scott Joplin, Huddie "Leadbelly" Ledbetter, and other African Americans in Texas helped develop ragtime, blues, and jazz.

In recent years more Asian Americans have made Texas their home. As of 2000 more than 560,000 Asian Americans lived in the state. An estimated 14 percent of immigrants to Texas in 2000 were Asian Americans. These immigrants have brought many foods and traditions. Asian Americans have brought religions such as Buddhism, Hinduism, and Islam to Texas, adding to the state's diversity.

Reading Check **Summarizing** What cultural activities have different racial and ethnic groups contributed to Texas?

Our Cultural Heritage

Religious Diversity in Texas

During its history, Texas has attracted many different groups of people. As new groups came, they brought their religious beliefs with them. Early Spanish settlers in Texas established Catholic churches. Later, American and European settlers built Methodist, Baptist, Lutheran, and other Protestant churches in their communities. Jewish settlers built synagogues. Today new groups continue to arrive in Texas. Buddhists from Vietnam and other Asian countries have built temples in several large Texas cities. Middle Eastern and Indian newcomers have established Islamic mosques and Hindu and Sikh temples. **How does the growing population of Texas affect the state's religious diversity?** TEKS

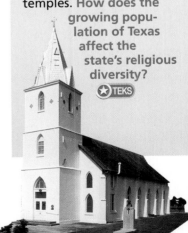

★ Where Texans Have Settled

Some regions of Texas have been settled by people with a similar ethnic background. These groups have influenced the areas they settled. For example, people from Mexico have been migrating to the Rio Grande

Cultural celebrations. These children are participating in a Hindu festival outside of Austin. Asian immigrants have brought new cultural traditions to Texas. **How do you think cultural celebrations like this one help Asian immigrants maintain their cultural heritage?**

⭐TEKS

valley for many years. As a result, Mexican influences are strong in South Texas. For example, many businesses and cultural institutions in this region have Spanish names.

Most early settlers from the southern United States made their home in East Texas. Many did so because the climate and soil are similar to those of the American South. Large groups of German and Czech immigrants have settled in Central Texas. These European immigrants have left their mark on the area. This can be seen in the place-names, foods, and cultural activities in the region. For example, German immigrants established the towns of Fredericksburg and New Braunfels. In these towns people still hold German music festivals called Sängerfests.

Historically, most Texans have lived in rural areas. As Texas industries grew, people began to move to cities. By 1950, more Texans lived in urban areas than on farms and ranches. As of 2000, about 85 percent of Texans lived in cities. Houston, Dallas, and San Antonio are three of the largest cities in the United States. Because most larger cities are in the central and eastern areas of Texas, the majority of Texans live in these regions. This growing population of city-dwellers marks a big change from the early days of rural settlement in Texas.

⭐ **Reading Check** **Finding the Main Idea** What settlement patterns have appeared in Texas?

⭐ The Growing Population of Texas

Texas is becoming more diverse as its population continues to increase. In 2000 Texas had a population of more than 20 million. To understand why the Texas population continues to grow, you must learn about **demography**. Demography is a branch of geography that studies human populations. When studying population **growth rate**—the speed of growth—demographers look at several factors. The **birthrate** is the number of births per 1,000 people. The **death rate** is the number of deaths per 1,000 people. In 1999 the birthrate in Texas was 17.5, and the death rate was 7.3. Better health care is allowing more Texans, like other Americans, to live longer. As a result, the death rate has dropped. More Texans are being born than are dying. These two factors are contributing to the growing population of Texas. Immigration and migration are also factors in the growth of the Texas population. In 1998 more than 44,000 people came to Texas from foreign countries. Many of these newcomers have arrived from such different countries as Mexico, India, and Vietnam.

The number of multi-generational families with grandparents and great-grandparents is growing as Texans continue to live longer.

The growing population has brought many changes to Texas, including the age of the Texas population as a whole. As Texans live longer and more are born, the **age distribution** of the state changes. The age distribution is the portion of the population at each age. Some populations are, on the average, younger than others. This means they have a greater percentage of young people than other regions. With a higher percentage of young people, Texas is a younger state than most.

Gender distribution also affects population. As is common throughout the United States, there are just a few more women in Texas than men. One reason for this is women tend to live longer than men. In 1998 there were 95.5 men for every 100 women. This has not always been the case, however. At the beginning of the 1900s, there were approximately 110 men for every 100 women. Because Texas has a growing population, the age distribution and diversity of the state will continue to change. In addition, the population growth rate of the state will most likely increase over time.

Reading Check **Summarizing** What factors have contributed to the growth rate of the Texas population?

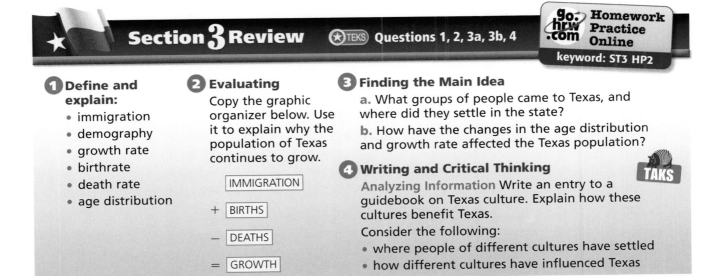

Section 3 Review
★TEKS Questions 1, 2, 3a, 3b, 4

go.hrw.com **Homework Practice Online**
keyword: ST3 HP2

1 Define and explain:
- immigration
- demography
- growth rate
- birthrate
- death rate
- age distribution

2 Evaluating
Copy the graphic organizer below. Use it to explain why the population of Texas continues to grow.

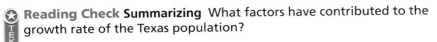

> IMMIGRATION
> + BIRTHS
> − DEATHS
> = GROWTH

3 Finding the Main Idea
a. What groups of people came to Texas, and where did they settle in the state?
b. How have the changes in the age distribution and growth rate affected the Texas population?

4 Writing and Critical Thinking
Analyzing Information Write an entry to a guidebook on Texas culture. Explain how these cultures benefit Texas.
Consider the following:
- where people of different cultures have settled
- how different cultures have influenced Texas

TAKS

Geography

The Texas Population

The population of Texas is expected to grow. Projections, or estimates, of future populations help the government and businesses plan to meet the future needs of populations. Geographers can use pie graphs and charts to show changes in the racial and ethnic make-up of Texas.

Geography Skills

Interpreting Data and Charts

1. What percentage of Texans have Hispanic and Asian American heritage?

2. In which age groups do women outnumber men in Texas?

3. How much is the total population of Texas expected to grow between 2000 and 2010?

4. Which group's population is expected to grow fastest between 2000 and 2010?

5. What effects do you think the changes in population will have on Texas? ⭐TEKS

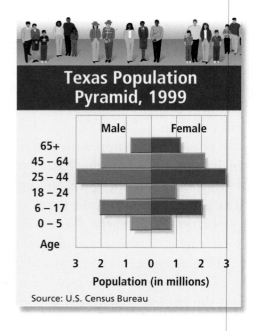

Texas Population Pyramid, 1999

Age	Male	Female
65+		
45 – 64		
25 – 44		
18 – 24		
6 – 17		
0 – 5		

3   2   1   0   1   2   3
Population (in millions)

Source: U.S. Census Bureau

Racial and Ethnic Heritage of Texas, 2000

Other.......................... **0.8%**

Asian American......... **2.7%**

American Indian........ **0.6%**

African American.....**11.5%**

White **52.4%**

Hispanic **32%**

Source: U.S. Census Bureau

Texas Population

	2000	2010*
Total Population	20,851,820	23,227,000
White	10,933,313	11,866,000
Hispanic	6,669,666	7,421,000
African American	2,404,566	3,058,000
American Indian	118,362	120,000
Asian American	562,319	762,000

Source: *Statistical Abstract of the United States* and U.S. Census Bureau
* Figures for 2010 are estimates.

Natural Resources of Texas

Read to Discover

1. What natural resources can be found in Texas?
2. How have Texans used natural resources?

Define

- **agriculture**
- **nonrenewable resources**
- **renewable resources**

Why It Matters Today

Texans raise a wide variety of crops and animals. Use **CNNfyi.com** or other **current events** sources to learn more about crops and animals in Texas today. Record your findings in your journal.

The Geographer's World

In June 1919 farmer Ruth Jones was planning to get married. Ruth and her sisters worked on their family's East Texas farm right up to the day before the wedding. Saturday afternoon, they leaned their hoes against a dead tree in the field and went home to prepare for the wedding on Sunday. On Monday morning they were back working in the fields. Farmers like Jones rarely take a break from their fields.

In the early 1900s Texas farmers used plows like this one in their field work.

★ Agricultural Resources

Texas has a wealth of natural resources that have contributed to the state's growth. The climate, soil, and water resources are all important to the Texas economy. Some Texans make their living from **agriculture**, or growing crops and raising animals. East Texas receives a lot of rainfall and has rich soil. Farmers in this region grow a wide range of crops, including fruits, nuts, and vegetables. Corn, tomatoes, and watermelon are some of the area's other important crops. The greater amount of rainfall in East Texas supports the growth of forests, which in turn supports a large timber industry. Along the southeastern Gulf Coast, farmers grow rice and vegetables. These crops do well in the region's warm wet climate.

Farmers in drier regions of Texas often use aquifers and rivers to irrigate their crops. The use of irrigation helps Texans overcome the climate limitations of many drier regions. In South Texas, farmers grow

crops such as alfalfa, citrus fruits, cotton, melons, and vegetables. The warm winters in the region allow farmers to grow crops year-round. Southern farmers can often grow two sets of crops per year. Farmers in the Panhandle can grow huge crops of wheat and cotton by drilling and pumping water from the Ogallala Aquifer to irrigate their fields.

The livestock industry is an important part of the Texas economy. The main livestock in Texas include cattle, chickens, horses, pigs, sheep, and turkeys. The native grasses and generally warm climate of Texas provide a natural place to raise livestock. Many livestock range the prairies of Central Texas, the Gulf Coast, and the Panhandle. In the dry Panhandle, ranchers pump water from aquifers and rivers for their livestock. Cattle ranching is a big business in Texas. In 1999, Texas ranchers had some 14 million head of cattle worth almost $7 billion. In the rockier regions of Texas, ranchers raise goats for their mohair, which is used in clothing. Texas produces more mohair than any other state in the nation.

 Reading Check **Evaluating** How do climate and other geographic features affect what crops and animals are raised in different regions of Texas?

★ Energy Resources

Some of the most valuable natural resources are energy resources such as coal, natural gas, and oil. Energy resources are important because they supply fuel to run automobiles, heat homes, and power industry. The production of oil and natural gas in Texas is worth almost $20 billion per year. Texans have drilled oil wells in almost every region of the state and built refineries to process these resources. Thousands of Texans depend on jobs in the oil industry.

Coal, natural gas, and oil are **nonrenewable resources**. They cannot be replaced by Earth's natural processes. As a result, there is a limited supply of nonrenewable resources. Some Texans have turned to **renewable resources**—ones that are easily replaced by Earth's natural processes. Examples of renewable energy resources include sunshine, trees, and wind.

Texas has a number of other resources that are important to its economy. For example, the construction industry uses sand and gravel to make concrete and other building products. Texans also mine minerals such as copper, salt, and sulfur. These natural resources provide important products for the daily lives of Texans. The production of these materials also provides many jobs to Texans.

 Reading Check **Analyzing Information** How have Texans developed technology to use the state's natural resources?

★ Using Resources Wisely

Texas has a wide variety of abundant natural resources. Many Texans have used these rich natural resources to build successful businesses. For example, the state's climate, soil, and water have enabled Texas farmers to raise crops, creating a multi-billion dollar agricultural industry in the state. Many other Texas industries, from oil production to construction, have grown by using fossil fuels and other natural resources of the state. A large part of the Texas economy relies upon these resources.

Texans work to balance the state's economic growth and the needs of the future. For example, an abundant supply of water in Texas aquifers is important to farmers and ranchers in drier regions of Texas. Every year billions of tons of water are pumped out of Texas aquifers for farming and human consumption. In some years enough water is pumped out of Texas aquifers to cover roughly 11 million acres of land to a depth of one foot. However, in many years only some 5 million acre-feet worth of water is refilled. The slow process of refilling aquifers has led some Texans to organize water conservation districts to manage water resources. These districts were created to help to ensure the long-term use of aquifers for irrigation and allow for a productive agricultural economy in the state.

Throughout the state's history, scientific and technological innovations have helped Texans use natural resources. Advances in drilling technology have made removing oil, natural gas, and water from underground more efficient and profitable. New advances in science and technology will bring further changes to the use of the state's natural resources.

★ **Reading Check** **Making Generalizations and Predictions** How do you think future scientific discoveries and technological innovations will affect the use of natural resources?

Citizenship and You

Recycling

Some Texas businesses have turned to recycling as a way to reduce costs and manage their use of resources. Recycling is the reuse of materials. Recycling can save energy, money, and natural resources. Texans have formed groups like the Recycling Coalition of Texas and the Texas Corporate Recycling Council. Organizations such as these have established conferences, education programs, and partnerships with Texas industries. **What have recycling organizations done to promote recycling?** ★TEKS

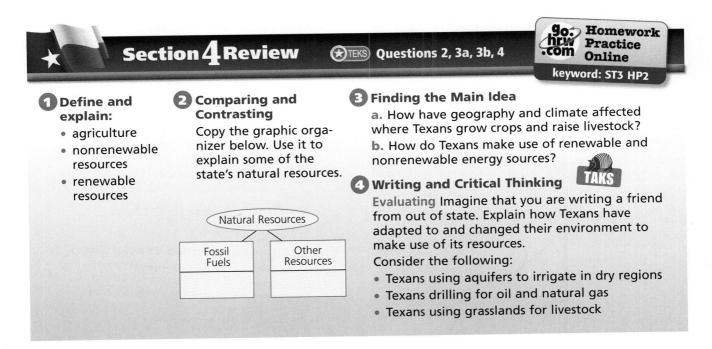

Section 4 Review   ★TEKS Questions 2, 3a, 3b, 4

go.hrw.com Homework Practice Online
keyword: ST3 HP2

1 Define and explain:
- agriculture
- nonrenewable resources
- renewable resources

2 Comparing and Contrasting
Copy the graphic organizer below. Use it to explain some of the state's natural resources.

Natural Resources

Fossil Fuels	Other Resources

3 Finding the Main Idea
a. How have geography and climate affected where Texans grow crops and raise livestock?
b. How do Texans make use of renewable and nonrenewable energy sources?

4 Writing and Critical Thinking   TAKS
Evaluating Imagine that you are writing a friend from out of state. Explain how Texans have adapted to and changed their environment to make use of its resources.
Consider the following:
- Texans using aquifers to irrigate in dry regions
- Texans drilling for oil and natural gas
- Texans using grasslands for livestock

The Chapter at a Glance

Examine the following visual summary of the chapter. Then use the visual to create a model of life in Texas. ★TEKS

Landforms, Water, and Weather

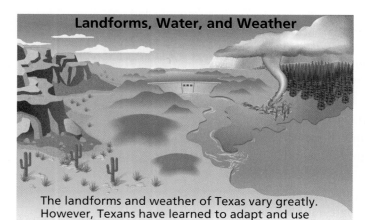

The landforms and weather of Texas vary greatly. However, Texans have learned to adapt and use these geographic features.

People of Texas

People have come to Texas from many different places. More Texans today live in cities than in rural areas.

Natural Resources

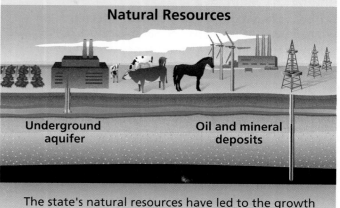

Underground aquifer   Oil and mineral deposits

The state's natural resources have led to the growth of farming, ranching, energy production, and many other industries.

Identifying People and Ideas ★TEKS

Use the following terms or people in sentences.

1. plains
2. irrigation
3. aquifers
4. humidity
5. drought
6. Lady Bird Johnson
7. growth rate
8. birthrate
9. death rate
10. age distribution

Understanding Main Ideas ★TEKS

Section 1 (pp. 20–23)
1. What types of landforms can be found in Texas?
2. How do some Texans use water resources?

Section 2 (pp. 24–29)
3. What types of severe weather threaten Texas?
4. How are Texas plants and animals affected by climate?

Section 3 (pp. 30–33)
5. What factors have contributed to a rising growth rate in Texas?
6. How has the age distribution of Texas changed?

Section 4 (pp. 35–37)
7. What types of crops and livestock are raised in Texas?
8. What natural resources can be found in Texas?

You Be the Geographer ★TEKS

Reviewing Themes
1. **Geography** How have Texas farmers and ranchers changed the landscape of Texas?
2. **Culture** How have people of different racial and ethnic backgrounds added to the diversity of Texas culture?
3. **Economics** In what ways have the natural resources and weather of Texas affected the economy of the state?

TAKS Practice: **Thinking Critically** ★TEKS

1. **Analyzing Information** How have Texans adapted to and modified the natural environment? What are some of the effects of these efforts?
2. **Evaluating** How does Texas benefit from the state's diversity of physical and human characteristics?
3. **Drawing Inferences and Conclusions** Make several predictions about how Texas and its natural resources will be affected by future scientific discoveries and technological innovations.

Interpreting Maps ⭐TEKS

Study the map below. Then use the information on the map to answer the questions that follow.

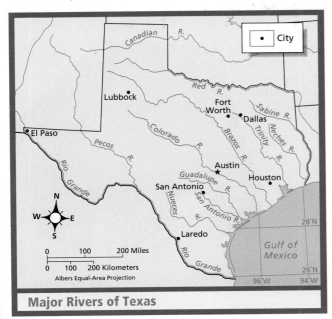

Major Rivers of Texas

1. Which region of Texas has the fewest rivers?
   a. East Texas
   b. the Gulf Coast
   c. South Texas
   d. West Texas

2. How do you think these sources of water have affected where Texans have settled?

Analyzing Primary Sources ⭐TEKS

Read the following quotes about the now extinct passenger pigeon. Then answer the questions.

"Wild pigeons . . . in large numbers visit us in the fall and winter. . . . The wild pigeons establish a roost to which they return at night, after having gone during the day a great distance in search of food. They . . . crowd upon one another on the limbs of trees and bushes, so as to bend and even break them down."—O. M. Roberts

"I saw pigeons pass in the millions. . . . These passenger pigeons ate the mast, or acorns, from trees—it was their favorite food—and settlers went to their roost in Anderson County and killed them in great numbers, leaving them on the ground. They killed them with sticks to keep the pigeons from eating the acorns they wanted the hogs to have."—Charles R. Yarborough

3. Why do pigeons leave their roosts during the day?
   a. They leave to find food.
   b. They leave to migrate.
   c. They like to fly.
   d. They leave to find a new roost.

4. How do Roberts's and Yarborough's accounts differ? How are they similar?

Alternative Assessment

Cooperative Learning ⭐TEKS

Work with a small group to complete the following activity. Each person in your group should select one of the following features of Texas geography: a) landforms b) water resources c) vegetation d) animal life e) weather. Each member should pose questions and provide answers for a quiz show based on some of the geographic features of Texas. Be sure to ask questions about the distribution and patterns of these features. Each group may wish to quiz its members, awarding points for correct answers.

BUILDING YOUR Portfolio

📶 **internet** connect

Internet Activity: go.hrw.com
KEYWORD: ST3 TX2 ⭐TEKS
Access the Internet through the HRW Go site to research the formation of the Edwards Aquifer and its importance to urban and rural residents, wildlife, and the local economies of South and Central Texas. Then write an informative essay to report what you have found. Make sure you use standard grammar, spelling, sentence structure, and punctuation.

CHAPTER 3

The Regions of Texas

Trucks loaded down with lumber travel East Texas roads, hauling timber to sawmills.

Texas cotton is made into textiles like these bolts of fabric.

TEXAS	The Texas timber industry earned more than $1 billion in 1997.	Texas contains more than 22 million acres of forests and woodlands.	In 1998 the value of Texas cotton production reached nearly $1.2 billion.
U.S. and WORLD	The American timber industry earned more than $46 billion in logging and sawmill production in 1997.	In 1996 the United States contained more than 746 million acres of forests and woodlands.	American farmers harvested more than $4.1 billion worth of cotton in 1998.

Forests in the United States provide timber for paper, furniture, and other products.

Build on What You Know

Texas has a wide variety of landforms, water resources, climates, and plant and animal life. In many cases, geographers use these physical features to describe the different regions of the state. From the Piney Woods of East Texas to the dry deserts in the west, Texas is a land of many contrasts.

Interpreting Maps ⭐TEKS

Study the map below. Then use the information on the map to help answer the questions that follow.

National Parks in Texas

Map legend:
- National Park
- National Forest
- National Preserve
- National Grassland
- National Seashore
- • City

RITA BLANCA NATIONAL GRASSLAND
Canadian R.
Lubbock
Red R.
Dallas
Sabine R.
SABINE NATL. FOREST
El Paso
GUADALUPE MOUNTAINS NATIONAL PARK
Colorado R.
Pecos R.
Brazos
Trinity R.
ANGELINA NATIONAL FOREST
DAVY CROCKETT NATIONAL FOREST
BIG BEND NATIONAL PARK
Rio Grande
Guadalupe R.
Austin
SAM HOUSTON NATIONAL FOREST
San Antonio
Houston
BIG THICKET NATL. PRESERVE
MEXICO
Corpus Christi
PADRE ISLAND NATIONAL SEASHORE
Gulf of Mexico
0 75 150 Miles
0 75 150 Kilometers
Albers Equal-Area Projection
28°N
26°N
96°W
94°W

1. Which region has the most national forests?
   a. West Texas
   b. South Texas
   c. East Texas
   d. the Panhandle

2. Locate the national park in Texas that borders another country.

Analyzing Primary Sources ⭐TEKS

Read the following quote by Walter Prescott Webb and answer the following questions.

"A plains environment is . . . sub-humid [dry]. . . . The Great Plains offered such a contrast to the [eastern] regions . . . as to bring about a marked change in the ways of pioneering and living. For two centuries American pioneers had been working out a technique for the utilization [use] of the humid regions east of the Mississippi River. . . . Then . . . they . . . came out on the Great Plains, an environment with which they had had no experience. . . . The ways of travel, the weapons, the method of tilling the soil, the plows and other agricultural implements, and even the laws themselves were modified."

3. In what ways did settlers have to adapt to deal with the physical features of the Great Plains?
   a. They had to develop new methods of farming in dry regions.
   b. They changed the farming practices they used in the East only slightly.
   c. The settlers were unable to farm.
   d. They had to develop new methods for farming in wet regions.

4. How do you think these early pioneers modified the environment of the Great Plains?

Alternative Assessment

Cooperative Learning ⭐TEKS

Work with a small group to complete the following activity. Each person in your group should select one of the following regions of Texas: a) Gulf Coastal Plain b) Central Plains c) Great Plains d) Intermountain Basins and Plateaus. Each member should complete a model that shows the region's features, including natural resources, economic activities, educational institutions, and recreational opportunities in the area. Then work together as a group to create a brochure that compares the regions for tourists.

BUILDING YOUR Portfolio

🖵 internet connect

Internet Activity: go.hrw.com
KEYWORD: ST3 TX3 ⭐TEKS

Access the Internet through the HRW Go site to research the location, wildlife, land features, and main cities of a region in Texas. Then create a radio script in which you tell an audience about your region. You might want to record your radio script on an audiotape. Make sure you cover each of the topics written above and use standard spelling, sentence structure, grammar, and punctuation.

Social Studies Skills
WORKSHOP

Posing and Answering Questions

Understanding the geography of Texas is essential to understanding its history. A good way to learn about geography is to know how to pose and answer questions about the topic.

Posing and Answering Questions These skills involve formulating questions and knowing how to respond to them. These skills will help you understand information that is presented to you in various forms such as texts or maps. Listed below are guidelines that will help you with posing and answering questions.

1. **Determine what information is presented in the source.** For example, if you are looking at a map, pose questions such as, "What does the map show?" and "Does it show any special geographic features?"

2. **Find out what can be learned from the information presented.** If the map displays towns and geographic features, ask why a town on the map is located in a certain area. For example, why might a town be located near a river? Studying the geographic features of a region can also shed light on historical events. If you are studying a map that displays battle locations, pose questions such as "Did geographic features influence who won the battles?"

3. **Identify the geographic distributions and patterns that are present.** Take an overall look at the map and think about how human and physical factors have affected what you see. Ask questions that help you understand how these factors have contributed to geographic distributions and patterns. Pose questions such as, "Why are many settlements located in regions where water is plentiful?", "What does this suggest about how the people in those settlements earn a living?", and "How have physical features affected the types of transportation available to people living the region?"

Example

Geographers pose and answer questions about geographic distributions and patterns to better understand the physical and human systems of Texas. The following questions and answers relate to the population of Texas.

1. **Determine what information is presented in the source.** If you are looking at a map of the San Antonio area, ask what physical and human features are shown.

2. **Find out what can be learned from the information presented.** What does the information tell you about the population of Texas?

3. **Identify the geographic distributions and patterns that are present.** Pose questions such as "What conclusions can be drawn about the geographic distributions and patterns of Texas?"

Practicing the Skill

Chapter 2, Section 3, Texans and Geography, describes where Texans have settled. Pose a question relating to where one group has settled, why they chose that location, and what the location suggests about how they earned a living. Then pose those same questions about another Texas group and answer the questions. ⭐TEKS

History in Action

UNIT 1 SIMULATION

You Solve the Problem . . .

How Can You Help the State's Parks?

Complete the following activity in small cooperative groups. You and other members of your community want to ensure that Texas state parks are well maintained. Your group would like to make a poster to encourage other Texans to help in the effort. Follow these steps to solve your problem.

1. Gather Information. Use your textbook and other resources to find information that might influence your plan of action for urging Texans to help preserve the state's parks. Remember that your poster must include information to persuade Texans to help. Be sure to use what you learned from this unit's Skills Workshop on Posing and Answering Questions to help you find an effective solution to this problem. You may want to divide up different parts of the research among group members.

2. List and Consider Options. After reviewing the information you have gathered, list, and consider the options you might recommend for successfully convincing Texans to take action to maintain their state parks. Your final solution to the problem may be easier to reach if you consider as many options as possible. Be sure to record your possible options for the preparation of your poster.

3. Consider Advantages and Disadvantages. Now consider the advantages and disadvantages of taking each option. Ask yourselves questions such as, "How will working together help the state's parks?" Once you have considered the advantages and disadvantages, record them as notes for use in preparing your poster.

4. Choose, Implement, and Evaluate a Solution. After considering the advantages and disadvantages, you should prepare your poster. Be sure to make your poster urging Texans to help maintain their state parks very clear. You will need to support your reasons by including information you gathered and by explaining why you rejected other options. Your poster needs to be visually appealing to attract the attention of other Texans. When you are ready, decide which group members will present the poster, and then take your solution to the community (the rest of the class).
Good luck!

UNIT 2

Exploration and Settlement

(Beginnings–1821)

CHAPTER 4 **Texas Indians** (Beginnings–1700)

CHAPTER 5 **The Search for Empire** (1492–1670)

CHAPTER 6 **The Spanish Missions** (1680–1760)

CHAPTER 7 **Conflicts of Empire** (1760–1821)

Texas Teens

Young American Indians

According to Spanish legend, a young Caddo Indian named Angelina was particularly helpful to the Spaniards at the San Francisco de los Tejas mission in 1690. According to the legend, Spanish explorer Alonso de León and Father Massanet were two of the first Europeans to meet Angelina. Her eagerness to help the explorers and learn Spanish impressed the newcomers. The young Indian was given the name "Little Angel" or Angelina.

Angelina was a member of a smaller group of American Indians called the Hainai. The Hainai were one of at least 13 groups that belonged to the Hasinai Confederacy, which was one of several groups that composed the Caddo Confederacy.

Like these Alabama-Coushatta teenagers, American Indians in Texas continue to practice traditional celebrations and performances.

Angelina was willing to become a Christian and learned both Spanish and French. She eventually served as a translator for both Spanish and French explorers in the region. As additional expeditions ventured into East Texas and new missions were established, other Spanish explorers recorded meeting an educated Caddo woman. At times Angelina may have lived and traveled with these explorers and missionaries.

Angelina made such an impression on the priests that they named a river after her, the Angelina. She is one of only a few American Indians honored by the Spanish in this way. The county of Angelina and the Angelina State Forest also bear her name today. A bronze statue honoring her can be found in Lufkin, across from the Museum of East Texas. **What role did Angelina play in Texas history?**

In this unit you will learn more about American Indians and Spanish settlement in Texas. You will also learn about the interactions between American Indians and the first European explorers and settlers.

LEFT PAGE: *Francisco Vásquez de Coronado and more than 300 Spanish soldiers set out across Texas in search of gold and American Indian settlements.*

CHAPTER 4

Texas Indians
(Beginnings–1700)

Early Texans used flint to make weapons and tools.

Large animals such as woolly mammoths roamed through Texas.

TEXAS

Native Americans hunt animals for food.	**c. 1500 B.C.** Coastal Native Americans make knives and scrapers from stone.	**c. A.D. 100** Native Americans living near Galveston Bay begin making pottery.	

10,000 B.C.	**1500 B.C.**	**500 B.C.**	**A.D. 500**

U.S. and WORLD

	c. 1000 B.C. A clay tablet made in Babylon is an early attempt to create a map of the world.	**c. A.D. 1** Native Americans now known as the Hohokam create farming communities in present-day Arizona.	**c. A.D. 900** The Anasazi start building large houses in Chaco Canyon in present-day New Mexico.

The ancient Anasazi built huge dwellings.

Build on What You Know

The environments of the different regions of Texas vary widely. Some regions are good for farming, while others are too dry. Native Americans adapted to these regions in various ways. The food they ate, the homes they lived in, and the tools they used reflected their environment.

Caddo Indians had a complex society based on farming.

Karankawa Indians used war clubs, fish spears, and fish traps.

c. A.D. 1000 The Caddo grow many kinds of crops in East Texas.

A.D. 1528 Europeans arrive in Texas and encounter the Karankawa.

A.D. 1000 **A.D. 1200** **A.D. 1400** **A.D. 1600**

The Anasazi wore woven shoes.

A.D. 1492 Explorer Christopher Columbus reaches islands off the south-eastern coast of present-day Florida.

You Be the Historian

Themes Journal

What's Your Opinion? Do you **agree** or **disagree** with the following statements? Support your point of view in your journal.

- **Geography** People doing the same work in different regions lead similar lives.
- **Culture** People who rely on the same resources for survival are always the same culturally.
- **Science, Technology & Society** Changes in technology affect a group's culture.

If you were there . . .
How would you survive in early Texas?

The First Texans

Read to Discover

1. What have scholars learned about the first Americans?
2. How did environmental changes affect early Americans, and what did they do to adapt?
3. What civilizations developed in the Americas?

Why It Matters Today

In 1929, scientists in East Texas discovered a large stone head. Native Americans had carved the head long ago. Use CNNfyi.com or other **current events** sources to learn more about the study of early peoples. Record your findings in your journal.

Define

• prehistory
• anthropologists
• archaeologists
• artifacts
• hunter-gatherers
• maize
• precontact

Identify

• Paleo-Indians
• Mesoamerica

The Story Begins

A work crew digging out an old streambed near Lubbock uncovered animal bones and a spearhead. They took the spearhead to a professor at a nearby university. He realized they had made an exciting discovery and took steps to protect the site. Since this discovery in the 1930s, many scientists have studied the remains of early Americans at Lubbock Lake.

Archaeologists use many tools to explore ancient Texas.

★ The First Americans

Early Texans lived and hunted at Lubbock Lake some 12,000 years ago, before recorded history. This period of time before written records is called **prehistory**. Scientists called **anthropologists** study and compare peoples to learn how they lived. Other scientists known as **archaeologists** use remains of materials that they find to study past peoples. Archaeologists sift through layers of earth and explore the oceans looking for **artifacts**—tools, weapons, and other objects made by people. Artifacts give clues about how people lived in the distant past.

Archaeologists also study human remains. For example, in 1953, archaeologists found the ancient bones of a woman near Midland. In 1983, archaeologists working near Leander found the remains of another woman. She lived more than 9000 years ago. These skeletons, nicknamed Midland Minnie and Leanderthal Lady, have helped scholars learn about prehistoric Texas.

Archaeologists use other evidence to learn about prehistoric times. People often drew or carved pictures on cave walls or on the sides of cliffs. This rock art provides clues about how early people lived and practiced their religions. Pictures usually show important activities, such as hunting, fighting enemies, or celebrating special days. Prehistoric people left pictures along the Rio Grande at Seminole Canyon and at Hueco Tanks State Historical Park. Archaeologists have also found rock art in Big Bend National Park.

Many scientists believe that the first people to live in North America came from Asia. This migration occurred sometime between 38,000 and 10,000 B.C. during the last Ice Age. The global climate was then much colder, and more of Earth's water was frozen into glaciers. When ocean levels dropped, a land bridge known as Beringia appeared between Asia and present-day Alaska. **Paleo-Indians**, or the first Americans, crossed this land bridge. They entered Texas at least 12,000 years ago. Paleo-Indians were **hunter-gatherers**, or people who hunt animals and gather wild plants for food. They used stone tools and flint-tipped spears to hunt animals, many of which were very large. The mammoth, an ancestor of the modern elephant, stood 14 feet tall with tusks up to 16 feet long.

When the last Ice Age ended about 8000 B.C., the climate became warmer. Short grasses replaced the tall grasses that had supported giant animals. Many large animals disappeared, so Native Americans developed weapons to hunt smaller animals. For example, they hunted with small spears propelled by a spear-thrower called an atlatl. Native Americans also made stone tools, including axes, knives, and scrapers. They made other tools from antlers, bones, and shells.

People began farming in the Americas around 7000 years ago. This first occurred in **Mesoamerica**, a region that includes present-day Mexico and northern Central America. **Maize**, a type of corn, was the most important crop for early farmers. Native Americans also grew beans, squash, and other vegetables. Farming provided a stable source of food and allowed people to remain in one place for long periods. Populations grew and more complex societies developed. Organized religious practices became more common, and people began to specialize in their work. Artists, priests, and soldiers appeared in some Native American groups. Although large farming societies developed to the south and east of Texas, most Texas Indians remained hunter-gatherers. Even so, their lives changed in other ways. Texas Indians made pottery and began to hunt with the bow and arrow.

CONNECTING TO

THE ARTS

Rock Art

Many colors and images appear in Texas rock art, like this example from Seminole Canyon State Historical Park. To make colored paints, Native Americans ground rocks into powder. They sometimes mixed animal fats into the powder. In Texas, Native Americans created images that were anywhere from 1 inch to 18 feet high. **Why did Native Americans use ground rocks and animal fat for rock art?**

⭐ **Reading Check** **Sequencing** List in order the events that shaped life in the Americas from the Ice Age to 7000 years ago.

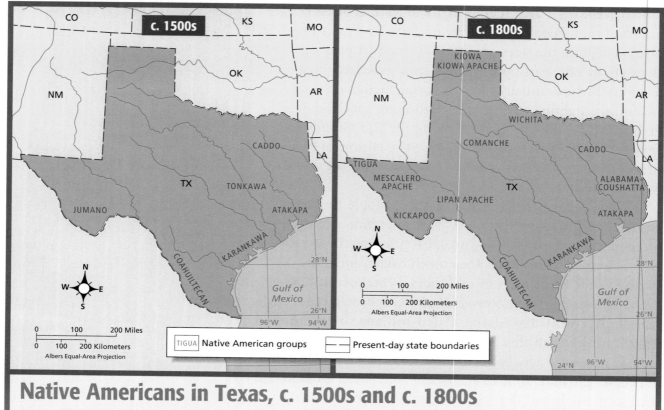

Native Americans in Texas, c. 1500s and c. 1800s

Interpreting Maps The westward migration of settlers in North America forced new American Indian groups to move to unsettled parts of Texas.

TAKS Skills *Human Systems* Why do you think these new American Indian groups settled in the northern and western regions of Texas? **TEKS**

★ Early Civilizations

Several early civilizations developed during the **precontact** period—the time before Europeans arrived in the Americas. These civilizations had large cities and complex religions and cultural practices. The Maya civilization in Mesoamerica thrived from about A.D. 300 to 900. The Maya had the only complete written language in the Americas. They also developed mathematical and astronomical systems. The Toltec and Aztec civilizations arose in Mesoamerica after the Maya civilization started to decline. Both of these civilizations had organized governments. The Toltec built great stone pyramids, some of which are still standing. In the Aztec city of Tenochtitlán (tay-nawch-teet-LAHN), people traded goods and traveled by canoe on the city's canals.

To the west of Texas, the Anasazi (ah-nuh-SAH-zee) traded jewelry and other goods with distant Native American communities. The Anasazi built huge dwellings that were several stories tall. By around A.D. 1150 they began to build these dwellings into cliffsides for defense. Some Anasazi dwellings had hundreds of rooms in which thousands

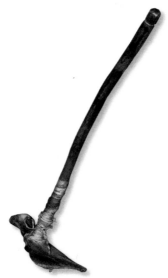

The Caddo used hoes to farm.

of people could live. At Chaco Canyon, in what is now northwestern New Mexico, there are nine of these huge structures.

The Mississippian culture developed to the east and north of Texas between A.D. 700 and 1600. There were hundreds of Mississippian villages along the Cumberland, Mississippi, and Tennessee Rivers. The Mississippians mostly farmed, but they also hunted with bows and arrows. The Mississippians built many huge flat-topped mounds of earth. Monks Mound, which can still be seen in present-day Illinois, stands more than 100 feet high. The Mississippians built a wooden structure on top of the mound. This structure served as a temple used for religious ceremonies or as a house for the ruler. Other important Mississippian mound sites are located in what are now Alabama, Georgia, and Oklahoma.

Although no large civilizations developed in Texas, it was home to many different groups of Native Americans. Native American cultures in Texas developed in response to their environments. Native Americans living near a river might fish or grow crops. Their celebrations and stories would reflect the importance of fishing or farming in their lives. In regions where the land was not good for farming, groups would hunt and gather. These groups valued hunting ability, and they became skilled at tracking the animals they hunted for food. They also developed tools and weapons suitable for hunting. Four general culture areas developed in Texas. These are the Western Gulf cultural region, the Southeastern cultural region, the Pueblo cultural region, and the Plains cultural region. Texas Indians adapted their lifestyles to respond to the unique challenges each region presented.

LONE STAR LEGACY

Alibates Flint Quarries

The Alibates flint quarries are located in the central Panhandle of Texas. The flint beds cover about 10 square miles. Native Americans used Alibates flint to make tools and weapons. Spearheads made from Alibates flint have been found as far away as Colorado. In 1965 the flint quarries were declared a national monument. Today visitors can see waste flint, broken tools, and stones that Native Americans used as hammers. **Why has Alibates flint been found far away from the quarries?**

Reading Check **Analyzing Information** Describe some of the defining characteristics of civilizations during the precontact era.

Section 1 Review

(TEKS) Questions 1, 3, 4b, 5

go.hrw.com **Homework Practice Online**
keyword: ST3 HP4

1 **Define and explain:**
- prehistory
- anthropologists
- archaeologists
- artifacts
- hunter-gatherers
- maize
- precontact

2 **Identify and explain:**
- Paleo-Indians
- Mesoamerica

3 **Identifying Cause and Effect**
Copy the graphic organizer below. Use it to show what innovation changed Native American life around 5000 B.C., and what the effects were.

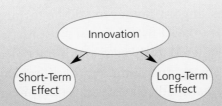

4 **Finding the Main Idea**
a. What have archaeologists discovered about Paleo-Indians in Texas?
b. When did Paleo-Indians come to the Americas, and what were the defining characteristics of the Paleo-Indian era in Texas?

5 **Writing and Critical Thinking**
Analyzing Information Write a paragraph analyzing the effects of physical factors such as climate and landforms on major prehistoric events in Texas.
Consider the following:
- climate changes during the Ice Age and the development of the land bridge
- later climate changes in the Americas

The Western Gulf Culture Area

Read to Discover

1. Where did the Karankawa live, and what was their life like?
2. How did the Coahuiltecan survive in a dry area?

Define

- **nomads**
- **wigwams**
- **mitotes**

Why It Matters Today

Native Americans near the Texas coast knew that the Gulf of Mexico could be an excellent food source. Use CNNfyi.com or other **current events** sources to learn more about commercial fishing today. Record your findings in your journal.

Some Texas Indians relied on available materials such as tall grasses to make their homes.

The Story Continues

A mystery had arisen. Archaeologists working north of Corpus Christi had unearthed human skeletons. The remains were ancient and unusually large. Who were these people? The archaeologists identified them as the remains of Karankawa Indians. But another puzzle remained. One skeleton came from a person who was six feet tall. The others were also unusually large for early Native Americans. Scientists struggled to explain why the Karankawa were larger.

★ The Karankawa

People of the Karankawa culture were hunter-gatherers who lived from the area near present-day Galveston south to Corpus Christi Bay. The Karankawa were **nomads**, or groups of people who moved from place to place. During the fall and winter months, they lived along the Gulf Coast. They used dugout canoes to paddle through the bays and inlets. For food, the Karankawa fished, hunted sea turtles, and collected shellfish. They also gathered birds' eggs and hunted deer and small animals.

During the spring and summer, the Karankawa moved away from the coast. They camped near rivers and springs on the flat coastal prairie. A French explorer described the life of the Karankawa.

"I passed the entire summer in this country with them in going everywhere in search of food because they possess no cabins or fields. That is why they travel in this manner the entire summer. The men kill a few deer and a few buffaloes and the women search for wild potatoes."

—Simars de Bellisle, quoted in *The Karankawa Indians of Texas*, by Robert A. Ricklis

Analyzing Primary Sources
Analyzing Information
What part of Bellisle's description shows that the Karankawa moved from place to place?

Karankawa men hunted with large wooden bows and arrows. To fish, they used bows and arrows or fish traps. Karankawa women collected plants, cooked the food, and took care of the camp. They built portable **wigwams**, or circular huts, from bent poles covered with animal skins and reed mats. Each wigwam could house seven or eight people.

Reading Check **Finding the Main Idea** Why did the Karankawa move to different regions at different times of the year?

★ Daily Life of the Karankawa

The Gulf Coast has hot summers and mild winters, so the Karankawa did not need much clothing. Some men did not wear anything. Others wore a deerskin breechcloth, a short cloth worn around the waist. Women wore skirts of deerskin or grass. In addition, both men and women painted themselves with bright colors. To keep insects away, the Karankawa rubbed alligator fat and dirt on their skin.

Europeans who arrived in Texas in the 1500s noted that the Karankawa treated their children with kindness. According to one explorer, the Karankawa "love their off-spring [children] . . . and treat them with the greatest mildness." The Karankawa gave their children two names, one of which was known only to close family members. The Karankawa believed that the secret name carried magic that protected children from danger.

Nothing could protect them from Euro-pean diseases, however. The Karankawa, like other Texas Indian groups, had never been exposed to European diseases. The Karankawa fell ill and died at an alarming rate. In addition, they fought with other Native Americans, the French, the Spanish, and later, Americans. By the mid-1800s there were no Karankawa left.

Reading Check **Evaluating** Analyze the impact of European contact on the Karankawa.

Interpreting the Visual Record

Fishing. The Karankawa used bows and arrows to obtain fish for food. **How did the Karankawa adapt to their environment?**

The Coahuiltecan and other Texas Indians hunted deer.

★ The Coahuiltecan

Groups belonging to the Coahuiltecan culture hunted and gathered food in southern Texas, where the climate was too dry to easily support farming. The Coahuiltecan were nomads who covered large distances in their search for buffalo, deer, and small mammals. The men dug pits to capture javelinas, mammals that look like wild pigs, and started fires to drive animals toward waiting hunters. The Coahuiltecan also fished and gathered wild plants. Their diet included ant eggs, lizards, snakes, spiders, and worms.

Many archaeologists believe that the Coahuiltecan made few tools. But they did have stone hammers and knives, and they used the bow and arrow to hunt. They used gourds, such as melons and squashes, and woven baskets to store food. The Coahuiltecan did not build permanent houses because they were always moving. Instead, they placed animal skins over bent branches for shelter. Inside these huts were fire for cooking and heating, and grass or deerskin beds. The men wore little clothing, and the women wore grass or deerskin skirts. Both men and women wore their hair long, hanging down to the waist.

The Coahuiltecan worked hard to survive, but they also made time for fun. At times groups would gather together for feasting and dancing at all-night celebrations called **mitotes**. These gatherings celebrated important events, such as special religious occasions, victory in battle, or a plentiful food supply.

The arrival of Europeans changed the lives of the Coahuiltecan. Many died from European diseases. They also faced attacks from Apache Indians. Many Coahuiltecan began to live among the Spanish and abandon their traditional ways of life. By 1800 few Coahuiltecan groups remained. The few surviving Coahuiltecan joined other Indian groups.

✔**Reading Check** **Analyzing Information** How did the Coahuiltecan use wildlife and plants to survive?

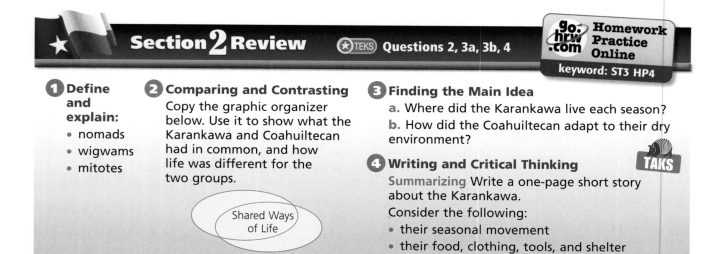

Section 2 Review

(★)TEKS Questions 2, 3a, 3b, 4

go.hrw.com **Homework Practice Online**
keyword: ST3 HP4

1 Define and explain:
- nomads
- wigwams
- mitotes

2 Comparing and Contrasting
Copy the graphic organizer below. Use it to show what the Karankawa and Coahuiltecan had in common, and how life was different for the two groups.

Shared Ways of Life

3 Finding the Main Idea
a. Where did the Karankawa live each season?
b. How did the Coahuiltecan adapt to their dry environment?

4 Writing and Critical Thinking
Summarizing Write a one-page short story about the Karankawa.
Consider the following:
- their seasonal movement
- their food, clothing, tools, and shelter

TAKS

The Southeastern Culture Area

Read to Discover

1. What was the Caddo culture like?
2. How were the Wichita similar to neighboring groups?
3. Where did the Atakapa live, and how did that affect their culture?

Define

- crop rotation
- confederacies
- allies
- matrilineal

Why It Matters Today

Important archaeological sites need to be preserved for future study. Use **CNN fyi.com** or other **current events** sources to learn more about working at an archaeological site. Record your findings in your journal.

The Story Continues

The Caddo Indians told many stories to their children. The following story taught the importance of farming. "As Snake-Woman gave each person the seeds, she told him that he must plant them, and must care for the plants that grew from them, but must allow no one, especially children, to touch them. . . . She said that until the seeds were ripe they belonged to her, and if any one gathered them too soon she would send a poisonous snake to bite him."

Squash was one of many crops grown by the Caddo.

★ The Caddo and Farming

The Caddo moved into eastern Texas from present-day Arkansas, Louisiana, and Oklahoma more than 1,000 years ago. The rich soil and abundant rain of eastern Texas made it possible to grow many crops. The Caddo built permanent villages and became expert farmers using farming methods commonly practiced today. For example, the Caddo practiced **crop rotation**—a system of growing different crops on the same land over a period of years—to prevent the soil from wearing out. The Caddo also set aside extra seeds for next year's crop. In addition, the Caddo burned forests to provide lands for growing crops. The Caddo grew beans, corn, squash, sunflower seeds, and tobacco.

In most other Texas Indian groups, women did all the farming. The Caddo valued farming so highly that the men shared the responsibility for growing crops. The men cleared the fields and made farm tools. To prepare the fields, the Caddo used hoes made from wood or the shoulder blades of buffalo. Women did the rest of the farm work. In addition, Caddo women gathered wild plants, cooked, and cleaned the houses.

Reading Check Summarizing What types of farming methods did the Caddo use that are still practiced today?

★ Caddo Society

With their plentiful supply of food, the Caddo had a large population. This allowed some people to take on special jobs not related to farming. Over time, the Caddo developed one of the more complex societies in Texas. The Caddo were organized into three **confederacies**. These groups shared a common language and were **allies**, or friends who supported one another. The three Caddo confederacies were the Hasinai, the Kadohadacho, and the Natchitoches. Although conflicts sometimes arose between the groups, they were usually on good terms with one another. Each confederacy built temples and mounds that were used for religious events. The mounds were also used as burial sites for important religious and political leaders. In addition to a religious and political structure, Caddo society included healers and craftspeople.

The Caddo were a **matrilineal** society. This means families were traced through the mother's side. Caddo family names came from the mother, not the father. In addition, when couples married, they lived with the wife's family. Women cared for the household and made the important decisions concerning the family. In each house, an older woman directed the activities of the 10 to 20 people who lived there.

The men built the houses, covering wooden poles with grass. Some Caddo may have plastered the outside of their houses with mud. In addition to building houses, men hunted and fished. When fishing, they would bait a series of hooks and tie them to a string that was stretched across a creek. The Caddo used bows and arrows to kill buffalo, deer, and small animals. Buffalo and deer served many purposes. During the cold winter months, men and women wore clothing made from animal skins. In the summer, men wore a deerskin breechcloth, while women wore clothes made from grass and straw. Both men and women tattooed and painted their bodies.

When European explorers came to Texas, the Caddo were one of the first groups they met. Despite the changes and difficulties the Europeans brought, the Caddo would continue to play a role in the state's history for years to come.

✔ Reading Check Analyzing Information What aspects of Caddo culture suggest that their society was successful?

LINKING PAST to PRESENT

Studying the Caddoan Mounds

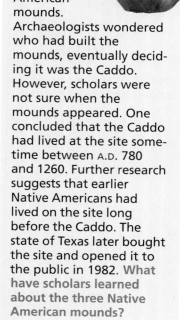

The Caddoan Mounds State Historic Site near Alto, Texas, is the location of three Native American mounds. Archaeologists wondered who had built the mounds, eventually deciding it was the Caddo. However, scholars were not sure when the mounds appeared. One concluded that the Caddo had lived at the site sometime between A.D. 780 and 1260. Further research suggests that earlier Native Americans had lived on the site long before the Caddo. The state of Texas later bought the site and opened it to the public in 1982. **What have scholars learned about the three Native American mounds?**

⭐ The Wichita

To the west of the Caddo along the Red River lived the Wichita Indians. The Wichita confederacy included four different groups—the Waco, the Taovaya, the Tawakoni, and the Wichita. Originally from present-day Kansas and Oklahoma, the Wichita moved into north-central Texas in the 1700s. Some Wichita lived as far south as present-day Waco.

The Wichita lived along creeks and rivers, where they grew beans, corn, melons, and squash. The Wichita used horses to hunt buffalo and deer. Although the Wichita hunted, they lived in permanent villages. One Spanish explorer in Kansas described a Wichita house.

> **Texas Voices** ❝[The houses are] all round, built of forked poles . . . and on the outside covered to the ground with dry grass. Within, on the sides, they had frameworks or platforms which served them as beds on which they slept. Most of them were large enough to hold eight or ten persons.❞
>
> —Don Juan de Oñate, quoted in *Spanish Exploration in the Southwest, 1542–1706,* by Herbert E. Bolton

Like the Caddo, the Wichita tattooed their bodies. However, the Wichita used more tattoos and made unusual designs. Women drew circles around their eyes and lines from their lips to their chins. Men tattooed their eyelids and drew a short line at the corner of each eye. Because these tattoos made them look like raccoons, the Wichita called themselves *Kitikiti'sh,* or "raccoon eyes."

⭐ **Reading Check Finding the Main Idea** What innovation allowed the Wichita to stay in one place?

Interpreting the Visual Record

Horses. Capturing wild horses was hard work. **How did horses help Texas Indians?**

Our Cultural Heritage

Our Caddo Name

In eastern Texas, the Spanish encountered a group of Caddo known as the Hasinai. The Spanish called the Hasinai by the group's word for friend—*Tejas* (TAY-hahs). The state of Texas takes its name from this word.

Native American Stories

Most cultures have stories and tales to explain the origin of people and animals. These tales are called origin or creation stories. The Wichita told how people got what they needed to survive. According to the story, people had many things but did not know how to use them. Then a man called Having-Power-to-carry-Light and a woman called Bright-Shining-Woman appeared. They traveled from village to village. Having-Power-to-carry-Light showed the men how to make a bow and arrow and how to hunt. Bright-Shining-Woman brought Mother-Corn and told the women to plant it. She explained that it would make the young strong and that the people could use it forever. Having-Power-to-carry-Light then became the first star seen in the morning, and Bright-Shining-Woman became the moon. **What does this story reveal about how the Wichita acquired new technology?** ⭐TEKS

⭐ The Atakapa

Between the Caddo and the Gulf of Mexico lived the Atakapa people. Their homeland ran from Galveston Island to the Sabine River and into parts of present-day Louisiana. The Atakapa who lived inland from the Gulf had good land for farming. They grew several vegetables, but corn was one of their most important crops. Some scholars think that the Atakapa learned about farming from the Caddo. In addition to farming, the Atakapa used bows and arrows to hunt wild game. Buffalo and alligators formed part of their diet.

Other Atakapa lived closer to the coast, where the land was marshy. Saltwater sometimes flooded the land, so farming was impossible in this area. The ocean, however, provided an abundant supply of food. The Atakapa used wooden traps to fish and canoes to gather shellfish, which they raked from the sea bottom. The Atakapa also gathered berries, birds' eggs, and nuts.

Although little is known about their houses, they probably lived in huts made from brush. The Atakapa also made pottery and wove baskets. Their clothing was simple, consisting of a breechcloth for men and a skirt for women. Some groups tattooed their faces and bodies. Little remains of the Atakapa culture. European diseases had a terrible effect on the Atakapa, and by the early 1900s there were very few left.

⭐TEKS **Reading Check Comparing and Contrasting** In what types of environments did Atakapa groups live, and how did these affect their way of life?

Section 3 Review   ⭐TEKS   Questions 2, 3a, 4

go.hrw.com **Homework Practice Online**
keyword: ST3 HP4

1 Define and explain:
- crop rotation
- confederacies
- allies
- matrilineal

2 Analyzing Information
Copy the graphic organizer below. Use it to describe four aspects of the Caddo culture.

Caddo

3 Finding the Main Idea
a. How did the Caddo culture adapt to and modify the environment?
b. Where did the Atakapa live, and how did they adapt to their environment?

4 Writing and Critical Thinking   TAKS
Comparing Write a short report noting the similarities of the Caddo, Wichita, and Atakapa.
Consider the following:
- how they obtained food
- houses and clothing

4 The Pueblo Culture Area

Read to Discover

1. Why did the Jumano come to the Rio Grande area, and how did they survive in their environment?
2. What problems did the Jumano face?

Define

- **adobe**
- **hides**

Why It Matters Today

Drought affected the lives of hunter-gatherers and farmers in early Texas. Use **CNN fyi.com** or other **current events** sources to learn more about drought problems today. Record your findings in your journal.

The Story Continues

The old buildings of sun-baked earth had withstood years of heat, rain, and wind. They had outlasted the people who built them. The empty village stood on the Texas plain, silent proof of a once-thriving society. The homes were built close to one another, as if huddled against the harsh elements. What happened to the people who lived there? Scholars had much to learn before they would know the secrets of the village.

Adobe is a building material still used today.

★ The Jumano

In northern New Mexico, a group of Native Americans called the Pueblo lived as farmers. They built permanent houses out of **adobe** bricks, which they made by drying clay mud in the sun. Sometime between A.D. 1000 and 1200, some Pueblo moved south along the Rio Grande into Texas. This group, known today as the Jumano, built villages along the Rio Grande. Although the region was dry and rugged, they grew corn and other crops by placing their fields near the river. When the Rio Grande overflowed, the fields filled with water.

The Jumano also gathered wild plants for food and hunted buffalo. Some Jumano became nomads and moved onto the plains of western and central Texas. They supplied the Jumano near the Rio Grande with meat and **hides**, or animal skins. The Jumano also traded goods with other Native American groups to the east and the west.

Farming. Many Native American groups farmed, growing and then drying corn in the Texas sun. **How did the environment affect Texas Indians?** ⭐TEKS

The Jumano near the Rio Grande lived in large villages. Some 10,000 people lived in the five Jumano villages near La Junta de los Ríos, north of Big Bend. In some villages, the Jumano built their houses around a central plaza. About 30 to 40 people lived in each house. The houses were made of adobe and wood, which helped the Jumano stay cool during the summer. The roofs were flat and probably made from tree branches. The Jumano often painted black, red, white, and yellow stripes on the inside walls. Jumano who did not live in the villages probably lived in separate adobe houses or in grass huts. Those Jumano who hunted buffalo on the plains lived in temporary shelters made from animal hides or grass.

The Jumano used bows and arrows to hunt buffalo. In battle, the Jumano fought with large, heavy clubs and carried shields made of buffalo hide. The Jumano were experts at making goods from animal hides, which they softened by beating with stones. Spanish explorers reported that the Jumano wore clothing and shoes made from hides. Jumano jewelry was made from copper, coral, and turquoise. They also tattooed or painted their faces with striped lines. One Spanish explorer described Jumano hairstyles.

Analyzing Primary Sources
Comparing and Contrasting
How did the hairstyles of Jumano women differ from those of the men?

Texas Voices

❝The women . . . wear their hair long and tied to the head. The men have their hair cut very short, up to the middle of their heads, and from there up they leave it two fingers long and curl it with . . . paint in such a way that it resembles a small cap. They leave on the crown [top] a large lock of hair to which they fasten [tie] feathers of white and black.❞

—Diego Pérez de Luxán, quoted in *The Indians of Texas,* by W. W. Newcomb Jr.

⭐ **Reading Check Analyzing Information** What innovation helped the Jumano acquire food?

★ Troubled Times for the Jumano

When the Spanish arrived in Texas, they traded goods with the Jumano. The Jumano were particularly interested in the horses the Spanish brought because horses made travel and buffalo hunting much easier. However, the Spanish arrival also marked the beginning of a difficult time for the Jumano. The Spaniards brought diseases that killed many Jumano.

The Jumano faced other problems as well. Drought had always made life in western and central Texas difficult. In the early 1500s some Jumano told a Spanish explorer that it had not rained for two years in a row. When periods of drought became longer during the 1600s and 1700s, many rivers in Texas dried up. Farming became very difficult, and many crops failed. Much of the grass on the plains also died, prompting the buffalo herds in western and central Texas to move away. The Jumano, who had depended on the buffalo for meat and hides, lost an important resource.

The Jumano also suffered from attacks by the Apache. The Apache wanted control of Jumano hunting territories and the trade between Plains Indian groups and the farming villages of New Mexico. In the early 1680s a group of Jumano, led by Juan Sabeata, asked the Spanish for protection against the Apache. Sabeata knew Spanish customs and the language, and he also knew the people of northern Mexico. Even so, the Spanish did little to help the Jumano. By the mid-1700s the Jumano had lost control of much of their land to the Apache. Historians think the Jumano probably survived in small groups that eventually joined other Native American groups.

★ **Reading Check** **Summarizing** What three major events caused problems for the Jumano?

LINKING PAST to PRESENT

Pueblo Culture

The Jumano were a part of the larger Pueblo culture. The Pueblo lived in buildings of sun-baked mud and straw. They farmed, growing several varieties of corn and other vegetables. Skilled pottery makers, they used decorated jars for food storage. The Pueblo also held elaborate dances and ceremonies, many of which reflected the importance of agriculture to their society. Although historians believe that the Jumano joined other Native American groups, the Pueblo culture survived and flourishes today in the American Southwest. **How did the Pueblo adapt to their environment in ways similar to Indian groups in Texas?**

★TEKS

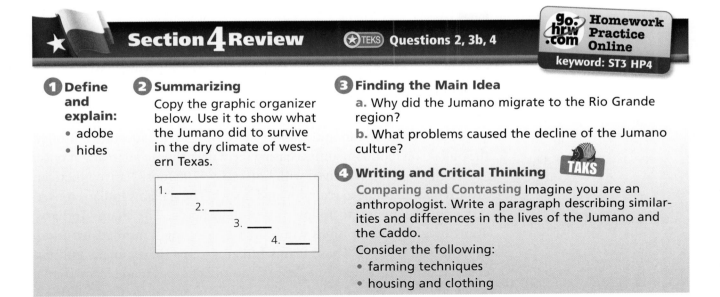

Section 4 Review ★TEKS Questions 2, 3b, 4

go.hrw.com **Homework Practice Online**
keyword: ST3 HP4

1 **Define and explain:**
• adobe
• hides

2 **Summarizing**
Copy the graphic organizer below. Use it to show what the Jumano did to survive in the dry climate of western Texas.

1. ____
2. ____
3. ____
4. ____

3 **Finding the Main Idea**
a. Why did the Jumano migrate to the Rio Grande region?
b. What problems caused the decline of the Jumano culture?

4 **Writing and Critical Thinking** **TAKS**
Comparing and Contrasting Imagine you are an anthropologist. Write a paragraph describing similarities and differences in the lives of the Jumano and the Caddo.
Consider the following:
• farming techniques
• housing and clothing

The Plains Culture Area

Read to Discover

1. How did the horse change Plains Indians' lives?
2. What were the common aspects of Plains Indian culture?

Why It Matters Today

The Plains Indian groups depended on the buffalo. Use **CNNfyi.com** or other **current events** sources to learn more about the buffalo or an animal that is in danger of disappearing. Record your findings in your journal.

Define

- **hunting grounds**
- **tepees**
- **bands**

Identify

- **Comanchería**

This Kiowa warrior's shield is made of painted buffalo hide, cloth, and eagle feathers.

Panhandle-Plains Historical Museum, Research Center, Canyon, Texas

The Story Continues

The hunters had finally killed their prey. The buffalo would provide food for everyone, but the hunters had to quickly prepare the buffalo and move on. If they lost track of the herds, the people might starve. A European explorer described how they removed the buffalo hide. "They cut the hide open at the back and pull it off . . . using a flint [stone tool] as large as a finger, tied in a little stick. . . . The quickness with which they do this is something worth seeing."

★ The Indians of the Plains

The Great Plains stretch from Canada into southern Texas. Before the arrival of Europeans, Native American groups lived on the edges of the plains where it was possible to farm. They entered the plains to hunt the buffalo. These animals were enormous—some weighed 1,600 pounds and were 6 feet tall at the shoulder and 10 feet long. Men and women hunted the buffalo on foot, sometimes chasing them over cliffs to kill many at once.

Then the Spanish arrived with horses. By 1700 most Native American groups on the southern plains owned horses. These Plains Indians moved out onto the plains to follow the buffalo herds. The Plains Indians' **hunting grounds**, or areas where they traditionally hunted for food, became much larger. These Plains Indian groups shared many cultural characteristics. Most lived in **tepees**, movable homes made from animal hides stretched over long poles. Plains Indians also made food, clothing, tools, and weapons from the buffalo. Women made a food called pemmican from dried buffalo meat pounded into a powder to which they added nuts and berries. Summer was an important time for Plains Indians groups. Food was plentiful, allowing **bands**, or small groups made up of a few families, to meet for celebrations.

★ The Tonkawa

The Tonkawa lived on the north-central plains of Texas and on the southeastern edge of the Edwards Plateau. The Tonkawa depended on the buffalo for their food, clothing, and shelter. Because they lived to the south of the largest buffalo herds, the Tonkawa were also hunter-gatherers. They hunted small animals, such as rabbits, rattlesnakes, and skunks, and gathered berries, fruits, and nuts. Like other Plains Indians, the Tonkawa wore clothing made from buffalo skins. During the warm summer months, Tonkawa children wore very little clothing. The men wore their hair long and parted in the middle, while women wore their hair either long or short. Both men and women painted their bodies.

In the 1700s the Tonkawa were driven from their hunting grounds by the Apache. The Tonkawa tried to adjust to the loss of their major source of food and hides—the buffalo—but had little success at farming. Surviving Tonkawa often joined other Native American groups, and by the 1900s the Tonkawa no longer existed as a separate Indian group.

✔**Reading Check** **Analyzing Information** Why did the Tonkawa lifestyle change after they were driven from their hunting grounds?

That's Interesting!

Danger on the Plains

Human hunters were not the only threat the buffalo faced on the Great Plains. Wolves followed the herds, killing the old, the sick, and the young. Buffalo trampled each other as they crossed rivers. Fires caused by lightning often killed everything in their path, including buffalo. In the winter, buffalo drowned if they fell through river ice.

Interpreting the Visual Record

Buffalo. *Texas Indians used a variety of techniques to hunt buffalo.* **What is one method Texas Indians used to hunt buffalo?**

Some Plains Indians hunted buffalo with bows and arrows.

★ The Apache

The Apache culture group originally lived in present-day Canada. Scholars believe that the Apache migrated to the American Southwest between A.D. 1000 and 1400. Two Apache groups, the Lipan and the Mescalero, settled in Texas. The Lipan lived from the western edge of the Texas Hill Country to the Rio Grande. The Mescalero, who lived in western Texas, eventually moved to present-day New Mexico.

The Apache were organized into bands that traveled, hunted, and fought together. The bands were made up of extended families, and the most prominent member led the band. Groups of bands often lived close together for defensive purposes or for ceremonies. The Apache were skilled at riding horses, and they often worked as a team when hunting buffalo. They surrounded buffalo herds and used bows and arrows to kill the animals. A Spanish explorer described what the Apache did with buffalo meat. "They dry their meat in the sun, cutting it into thin slices, and when it is dry they grind it, like flour, for storage." The Apache had many uses for buffalo hides. For example, if they needed to cross a river, they stretched hides over branches to make tub-shaped boats.

Some Lipan Apache farmed, which was unusual for Plains Indians. Crops included beans, corn, pumpkins, and watermelons. When the buffalo moved, however, the Lipan Apache followed. Some Apache who did not farm traveled to New Mexico to trade with Native American groups there for food. Most Lipan Apache men cut their hair very short on the left side but allowed the hair on the right side to grow long. The men tied feathers and other decorations to their hair. They also plucked out all their beard and eyebrow hair. Both men and women wore earrings. Women also wore copper bracelets.

The Apache often raided their neighbors for goods. Because horse-riding Apache could easily attack Pueblo villages and Spanish towns, they soon became feared throughout Texas. However, the arrival of the more powerful Comanche, along with pressure from the Spanish, led to the decline of the Apache. In addition, many Apache died from European diseases. By the early 1800s, many Apache had been driven from Texas into Mexico and New Mexico.

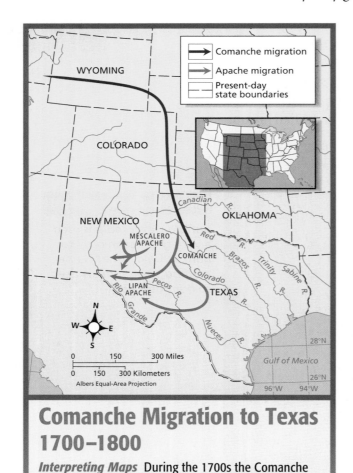

Comanche Migration to Texas 1700–1800

Interpreting Maps During the 1700s the Comanche migrated into the Great Plains region of Texas.

TAKS Skills *Human Systems* How did the migration of one Native American group affect the lives of other Native Americans? ⭐TEKS

⭐ **Reading Check** **Summarizing** How did the introduction of horses affect the Apache?

★ The Comanche and Kiowa

The Comanche originally lived in what is now the western United States. After they acquired horses the Comanche moved onto the Great Plains. To escape more powerful Plains groups and to have access to more buffalo and wild horses, the Comanche moved into Texas in the early 1700s.

The Comanche lived in bands headed by a peace chief, usually an older man. The best rider and fighter in the band served as its war chief. These leaders and other respected men helped make important decisions for the band.

Their skill as buffalo hunters quickly made the Comanche a wealthy group. They traded goods made from the buffalo with other Native Americans. The Comanche were also skilled fighters. They soon controlled much of the plains, including northern and western Texas, which the Spanish called the **Comanchería**.

The Kiowa were the last Plains group to arrive in Texas. They moved from the northern plains sometime in the early 1800s to escape from enemies. The Kiowa hunted buffalo and gathered berries, fruits, and nuts. Although the Kiowa did not farm, they did trade with neighboring groups. Kiowa men did the hunting and fighting. They wore their hair long, but over their right ear the hair was cut short. Kiowa women prepared the buffalo hides, sewed clothing, and made pemmican. Skilled fighters, the Kiowa became allies of the Comanche. Both groups fiercely resisted being forced from their Texas hunting grounds and abandoning their way of life.

The Comanche rode their horses bareback.

★ **Reading Check Comparing** How were the Comanche and Kiowa similar?

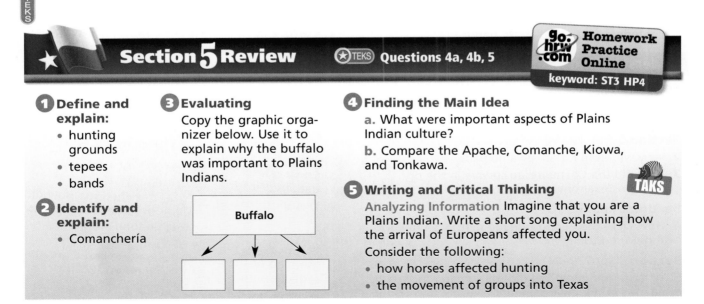

Section 5 Review ★TEKS **Questions 4a, 4b, 5**

go.hrw.com **Homework Practice Online**
keyword: ST3 HP4

1 Define and explain:
- hunting grounds
- tepees
- bands

2 Identify and explain:
- Comanchería

3 Evaluating
Copy the graphic organizer below. Use it to explain why the buffalo was important to Plains Indians.

Buffalo

4 Finding the Main Idea
a. What were important aspects of Plains Indian culture?
b. Compare the Apache, Comanche, Kiowa, and Tonkawa.

5 Writing and Critical Thinking
Analyzing Information Imagine that you are a Plains Indian. Write a short song explaining how the arrival of Europeans affected you.
Consider the following:
- how horses affected hunting
- the movement of groups into Texas

TAKS

The Chapter at a Glance

Examine the following visual summary of the chapter. Prepare a poster that illustrates the main ideas from each section. Present your poster to the class. ⭐TEKS

The Western Gulf Culture Area

The Southeastern Culture Area

The Pueblo Culture Area

The Plains Culture Area

These Native Americans were primarily hunter-gatherers who lived near the Gulf Coast. They were nomads who used dugout canoes to fish for food.

Many of these Native Americans were farmers who practiced crop rotation and used tools made of wood and animal bones. They also hunted wild game.

The Pueblo Indians were farmers who also hunted buffalo and other game. They lived in West Texas in houses built out of adobe bricks.

The Plains Indians were nomads who hunted buffalo and other game. They acquired horses by the 1700s and were skilled riders.

Identifying People and Ideas ⭐TEKS

Use each of the following terms or people in historically significant sentences.

1. artifacts
2. precontact
3. nomads
4. crop rotation
5. confederacies
6. matrilineal
7. adobe
8. hunting grounds
9. tepees
10. bands

Understanding Main Ideas ⭐TEKS

Section 1 (pp. 68–71)

1. What are the defining characteristics of the Paleo-Indian era in Texas?

Section 2 (pp. 72–74)

2. Why were the Karankawa nomads?
3. How did the Coahuiltecan survive in the dry western Texas environment?

Section 3 (pp. 75–78)

4. How were the Caddo farming methods similar to those used today?

Section 4 (pp. 79–81)

5. What farming method did the Jumano use to adapt to their environment?

Section 5 (pp. 82–85)

6. How did the horse aid the Plains Indians?

You Be the Historian ⭐TEKS

Reviewing Themes

1. **Geography** Why were the lives of the Caddo similar to and different from those of the Jumano?
2. **Culture** In what ways were Texas Plains Indian groups similar to one another?
3. **Science, Technology & Society** How did new tools and technologies affect Native Americans?

⭐TEKS

TAKS Practice: **Thinking Critically**

1. **Contrasting** How did the lives of hunter-gatherers in Texas differ from those of farmers?
2. **Drawing Inferences and Conclusions** How did the environment influence the way Texas Indians obtained food in the four cultural regions?
3. **Supporting a Point of View** Do you think farming or the arrival of the horse had a greater effect on the lives of Texas Indians? Provide reasons for your answer.

Social Studies Skills Workshop

Interpreting Maps ⭐TEKS

Study the map below. Then use the information on the map to answer the questions that follow.

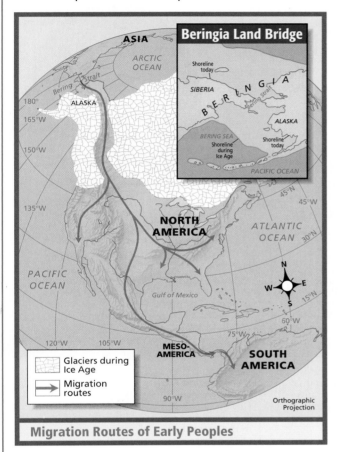

Migration Routes of Early Peoples

1. What geographic feature enabled people to travel to the Americas?
   a. Mesoamerica
   b. the Gulf of Mexico
   c. the Beringia Land Bridge
   d. the Arctic Ocean

2. How did this geographic feature affect the development of Texas?

Analyzing Primary Sources

Read the following quote by a Spanish explorer about the Karankawa. Then answer the questions.

"The Indians . . . left the island and passed over in canoes to the main [land], into some bays where [there] are many oysters. . . . There is [a] great want of wood; mosquitos are in great plenty. The houses are of mats, set up on masses of oyster shells, which they sleep upon."

3. Which of the following statements best describes the author's point of view?
   a. The Indians are not using all the resources available to them.
   b. The Indians were starving.
   c. The Indians did not trust the explorer.
   d. The Indians relied on food sources and materials that they could find.

4. What shows that the explorer observed the Indians adapting to their environment?

Alternative Assessment

Interdisciplinary Connection to Geography ⭐TEKS

Work with a small group to complete the following activity. Each person should select a Texas Indian group discussed in the chapter. Use the library to find information to create a section for a guide to Texas Indian life. Create illustrated maps showing how the groups obtained food in the four cultural regions. Be sure to use standard grammar, spelling, sentence structure, and punctuation.

BUILDING YOUR Portfolio

📄 **internet** connect

Internet Activity: go.hrw.com
KEYWORD: ST3 TX4 ⭐TEKS

Access the Internet through the HRW Go site to research the lifestyles of two Native American groups mentioned in the chapter and the environments in which they lived. Create an illustrated booklet that compares and contrasts how the groups adapted to their environment. Write at least one paragraph for both groups, describing their food sources and their environments.

CHAPTER 5

The Search for Empire
(1492–1670)

The first explorers in the Americas made maps of the lands they explored.

Viceroy Mendoza planned and supplied Coronado's expedition.

TEXAS

1519 Alonso Álvarez de Pineda maps the Texas coast.

1541 Explorer Francisco Vásquez de Coronado crosses the Texas Panhandle.

1554 A Spanish treasure fleet shipwrecks off of present-day Padre Island.

1581 Spaniard Hernán Gallegos writes about the lives of the Jumano Indians in Texas.

1490	1510	1530	1550	1570

U.S. and WORLD

1519 Hernán Cortés begins his conquest of the Aztec Empire.

1532 Francisco Pizarro begins his defeat of the Inca Empire in South America.

1565 Pedro Menéndez de Avilés founds St. Augustine, Florida, the first European settlement in the present-day United States.

1574 An estimated 152,500 Spanish settlers live in the Americas.

1492 Christopher Columbus first reaches the Bahamas.

Spanish conquistadores found gold treasures such as this Inca mask in the Americas.

Build on What You Know

Europeans arrived in Texas in the early 1500s. At the time, many different American Indian groups already lived in the area. Their lives would be permanently changed as Spanish explorers and others began to enter and settle on their land.

★ Cortés Conquers the Aztec

The Aztec had large amounts of gold, precious gems, and silver. Moctezuma gave Cortés peace offerings from this treasure, but the gifts were not enough. Cortés took Moctezuma captive and began planning how to conquer the Aztec. Before Cortés was prepared, fighting broke out between the Aztec and the Spaniards. On the night of June 30, 1520, the Spaniards fled the city. Cortés then began planning a new assault. He convinced more Mexican Indians to join him and had his men build boats armed with cannons. In May 1521 the Spaniards and their Indian allies attacked Tenochtitlán. After a long and brutal fight, they defeated the Aztec in August 1521. Many of the Aztec were killed or enslaved. Tenochtitlán lay in ruins.

Spain had captured the great wealth and land of the Aztec Empire. The Spanish sent much of the Aztec gold and silver, including treasures, to Spain. On top of the ruins of Tenochtitlán, Cortés built Mexico City. It became the capital of New Spain, which eventually extended from California to Florida to Mexico. Along with the Caribbean Islands, Mexico became a common starting point for Spanish exploration in the Americas. Such exploration increased the size of Spain's empire, which by 1600 included much of North and South America.

 Reading Check **Comparing** How were the Aztec Empire and Spanish America similar?

CONNECTING TO
ECONOMICS AND MATH

Gold and the Spanish Empire

Spanish explorers sent the gold and silver they found in the Americas back to Spain. As the amount of gold in Spain rose, prices of goods also rose. Spain produced few goods itself, so much of its wealth left the country to pay for goods made elsewhere.

The chart below lists the value of gold and silver sent to Spain from the Americas between 1516 and 1660. Use the information to create a bar graph.

YEAR	VALUE OF GOLD AND SILVER
1516–1520	993,000 pesos
1536–1540	3,938,000 pesos
1556–1560	7,999,000 pesos
1576–1580	17,252,000 pesos
1596–1600	34,429,000 pesos
1616–1620	30,112,000 pesos
1636–1640	16,315,000 pesos
1656–1660	3,361,000 pesos

Interpreting Data ★TEKS

1. During what years did the value of gold and silver sent to Spain peak?

2. By what percentage did the value of gold and silver increase between 1536 and 1560?

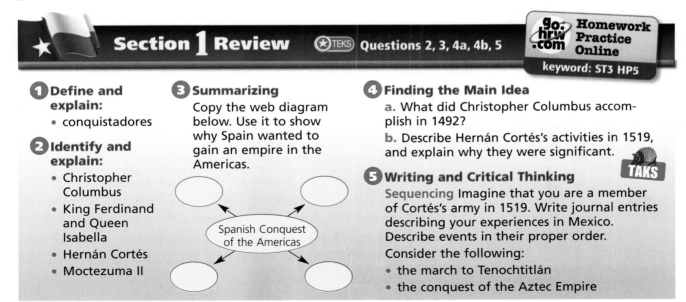

Section 1 Review ★TEKS Questions 2, 3, 4a, 4b, 5

go.hrw.com **Homework Practice Online** keyword: ST3 HP5

1 Define and explain:
- conquistadores

2 Identify and explain:
- Christopher Columbus
- King Ferdinand and Queen Isabella
- Hernán Cortés
- Moctezuma II

3 Summarizing
Copy the web diagram below. Use it to show why Spain wanted to gain an empire in the Americas.

Spanish Conquest of the Americas

4 Finding the Main Idea
a. What did Christopher Columbus accomplish in 1492?
b. Describe Hernán Cortés's activities in 1519, and explain why they were significant.

5 Writing and Critical Thinking
Sequencing Imagine that you are a member of Cortés's army in 1519. Write journal entries describing your experiences in Mexico. Describe events in their proper order.
Consider the following:
- the march to Tenochtitlán
- the conquest of the Aztec Empire

TAKS

2
The Spanish Explore Texas

Read to Discover

1. Why was Pineda's voyage in 1519 important to Texas?
2. How did the Narváez expedition end, and what events led to this outcome?
3. What experiences did Cabeza de Vaca and Estevanico have in Texas?

Identify

- **Alonso Álvarez de Pineda**
- **Pánfilo de Narváez**
- **Álvar Núñez Cabeza de Vaca**
- **Estevanico**

Why It Matters Today

Early Spanish explorers visited the Gulf Coast of Texas. Today the Gulf Coast contains several of our state's cities. Use CNNfyi.com or other **current events** sources to find information about regional growth. Record your findings in your journal.

The Story Continues

In 1519 Ferdinand Magellan (muh-JEL-uhn) began a famous voyage. With five ships and some 250 explorers, Magellan sailed west from Spain and then south around South America. During the voyage, storms and hunger threatened the crew. Ships were lost, and as supplies ran out the sailors ate rats to survive. Then Magellan was killed at a stop in the Philippines. His crew continued, however. The 18 sailors who returned to Spain were the first people to sail around the world.

The Granger Collection, New York

Ferdinand Magellan, like other sailors of his time, used a compass and the stars to help him navigate during his voyages.

★ Pineda Explores the Gulf Coast

Magellan had been looking for a southern waterway to the Pacific Ocean. The same year he set sail, Spanish explorer **Alonso Álvarez de Pineda** began searching for a northern waterway to the Pacific. In 1519 Pineda sailed with a fleet from Jamaica into the Gulf of Mexico. Heading west from Florida, he sailed along the Gulf Coast. After several months Pineda reached a large river along which were several American Indian villages and many palm trees. Pineda named the river Río de las Palmas, or "River of Palms." The explorers camped there for 40 days and then returned to Jamaica. Some historians claim this river was the Rio Grande. However, other historians claim that Pineda found the river Soto la Marina, 150 miles farther to the south.

Pineda and his crew were the first-known Europeans to see the Texas coast. In addition, Pineda was the first to map the northern Gulf of Mexico. Although no evidence exists that he and his crew entered Texas, their voyage increased Spanish interest in the region.

 Reading Check **Finding the Main Idea** What was the result of Pineda's voyage to the Gulf Coast in 1519?

1519

Alonso Álvarez de Pineda is the first European to map the Texas Gulf Coast.

★ Narváez and the "Island of Misfortune"

In 1527 <u>**Pánfilo de Narváez**</u> (PAHM-fee-loh day nahr-BAH-ays) led another voyage to the Gulf of Mexico. Like other Spanish explorers in the Americas, he dreamed of finding gold and riches. The Narváez expedition included five ships carrying some 600 soldiers as well as horses. The explorers reached Florida in April 1528 and went ashore near Tampa Bay. While exploring the coast, the Spaniards saw some American Indians with gold. They excitedly asked where they could find more of the metal. The American Indians described Apalachee, a northern region that they said was rich in gold. Eager to find treasure, Narváez divided his force. He sent the ships in search of a harbor, while he and 300 soldiers set off for Apalachee.

Struggling through the Florida swamps, the Spaniards soon became lost. They ran out of food and grew weak. Many were wounded or killed during American Indian attacks. When the explorers at last found Apalachee, there was not any gold. The discouraged Spaniards slowly began making their way back to the coast.

When the explorers neared shore, they searched for their ships without success. Unknown to the group, the ships had returned home after waiting for the soldiers for some time. The stranded and starving explorers had to eat their horses to survive. Explorer <u>**Álvar Núñez Cabeza de Vaca**</u> (kah-BAY-sah day BAH-kah) described their desperation. "It became clear that we could leave this terrible land only by dying."

As a last resort the Spaniards used what materials they could find to build several small boats. The flimsy crafts barely sat above water once the explorers crowded aboard. About a month after they set sail, a huge storm arose. Three of the boats, including Narváez's, washed up on the Texas coast, probably in or near Matagorda Bay. Narváez drowned when his poorly anchored boat washed out to sea. The other two boats shipwrecked on a Texas island—perhaps Galveston or San Luis. Cabeza de Vaca called this island Malhado, meaning "misfortune." Only about 80 explorers survived to reach this island.

Stranded once again, the explorers had lost most of their supplies. Many had even lost their clothes at sea and had nothing to wear. With winter approaching, the situation was grim. Just as they were losing all

LINKING PAST to PRESENT

Cartography

In 1519 Alonso Álvarez de Pineda created the first map of the northern Gulf of Mexico. To create the map, he used his observations and simple tools such as a compass. Today mapmakers create extremely accurate maps using computers and satellites. In 1999 NASA launched *Landsat 7*. This satellite provides detailed images of Earth that are used to make maps. **How have mapmaking techniques improved?** ⊘TEKS

The Granger Collection, New York

A map of the Texas coast made in the 1500s

A Landsat 7 image of the Texas coast

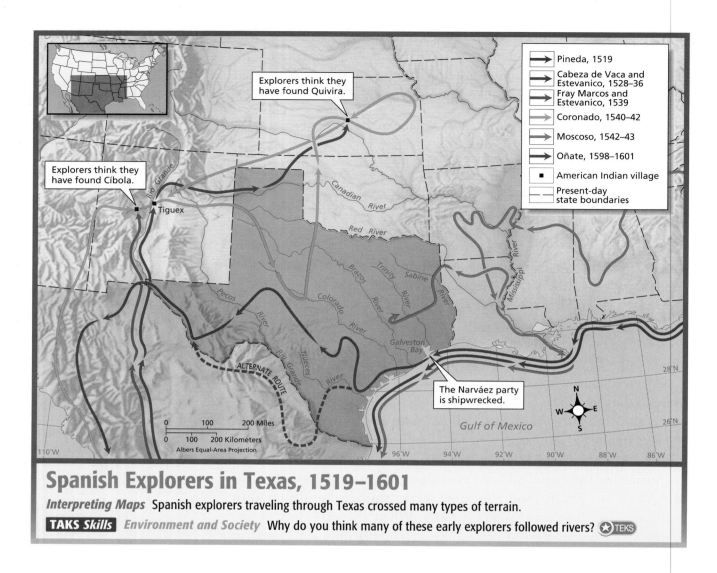

Spanish Explorers in Texas, 1519–1601

Interpreting Maps Spanish explorers traveling through Texas crossed many types of terrain.

TAKS Skills *Environment and Society* Why do you think many of these early explorers followed rivers? ⭐TEKS

Map labels:
- Explorers think they have found Quivira.
- Explorers think they have found Cíbola.
- The Narváez party is shipwrecked.
- Tiguex
- ALTERNATE ROUTE
- Gulf of Mexico

Legend:
- Pineda, 1519
- Cabeza de Vaca and Estevanico, 1528–36
- Fray Marcos and Estevanico, 1539
- Coronado, 1540–42
- Moscoso, 1542–43
- Oñate, 1598–1601
- ■ American Indian village
- Present-day state boundaries

hope, a group of Karankawa Indians appeared. Shocked by the strangers' condition, the Karankawa took the explorers in and shared their supplies with them. Food and clothing were scarce, however. Most of the Spaniards died during that winter. The few who lived were held captive and forced to work very hard.

For the next few years Cabeza de Vaca worked as a servant, a trader, and a healer. He traveled along the Texas coast gathering sea shells and mesquite beans to trade for animal skins. He later wrote about his experiences in Texas.

Analyzing Primary Sources
Summarizing How did the climate of Texas affect the Spaniards?

Texas Voices "Throughout all this country we went naked, and . . . twice a year we cast our skins like serpents. The sun and air produced great sores on our [chests] and shoulders. . . . The country is so broken and thickset, that often after getting our wood in the forests, the blood flowed from us in many places."

—Álvar Núñez Cabeza de Vaca, *The Narrative of Álvar Núñez Cabeza de Vaca*

⭐ **Reading Check** **Summarizing** What tragedy struck the Narváez expedition when the explorers tried to sail to Mexico?

★ The Spaniards' Adventures in Texas

Finally Cabeza de Vaca met three other explorers originally with the Narváez expedition who had become slaves of the Coahuiltecan Indians. Among these explorers was a North African named **Estevanico** (e-stay-bah-NEE-koh). The four men eventually escaped and set off along the coast in search of Mexico. They traveled from one American Indian village to another. At one village Cabeza de Vaca removed an arrowhead from a man's chest and then stitched up the wound. The operation amazed the American Indians who watched. Cabeza de Vaca later described how the explorers' growing fame as healers helped them survive.

Texas Voices **"This cure gave us control throughout the country. . . . We drew so many followers that we had no use for their services. . . . Frequently we were accompanied by three or four thousand persons, and . . . had to breathe upon and sanctify [bless] the food and drink for each."**

—Álvar Núñez Cabeza de Vaca, *The Narrative of Álvar Núñez Cabeza de Vaca*

Estevanico's skill at communicating with different American Indian groups also helped the explorers survive. Cabeza de Vaca wrote that Estevanico "talked with [the Indians] constantly, found out about the ways we wanted to go . . . and the things we wished to know."

In 1536, almost eight years after their shipwreck, the four lost explorers came across a group of Spanish soldiers. The explorers explained who they were, and the astonished soldiers took them to Mexico City. Cabeza de Vaca later returned to Spain. In 1542 he published the story of his travels as *The Narrative of Álvar Núñez Cabeza de Vaca.*

★ **Reading Check Identifying Points of View** Why did many American Indians in Texas follow the four Spanish explorers?

Álvar Núñez Cabeza de Vaca
(c. 1490–c. 1560)

From an early age, Álvar Núñez Cabeza de Vaca heard tales of exploration and conquest. His grandfather had conquered the Canary Islands. As a teenager, Cabeza de Vaca joined the Spanish army. He served in Spain and Italy. After the disastrous Narváez expedition, Cabeza de Vaca became governor of a colony in Paraguay. When the settlers rebelled, he returned to Spain in disgrace. **How did Cabeza de Vaca's early experiences help him on his travels through Texas?**

Section 2 Review ★TEKS **Questions 1, 2, 3a, 3b, 4**

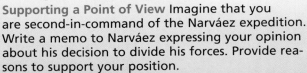
go.hrw.com **Homework Practice Online**
keyword: ST3 HP5

1 Identify and explain:
- Alonso Álvarez de Pineda
- Pánfilo de Narváez
- Álvar Núñez Cabeza de Vaca
- Estevanico

2 Summarizing
Copy the chart below. Use it to describe the actions and results of each expedition.

Pineda	Narváez
ACTIONS	ACTIONS
↓	↓
RESULTS	RESULTS

3 Finding the Main Idea
a. Explain the significance of Pineda's 1519 voyage to Texas history.
b. What adventures did Cabeza de Vaca and Estevanico have during their time in Texas?

4 Writing and Critical Thinking
TAKS
Supporting a Point of View Imagine that you are second-in-command of the Narváez expedition. Write a memo to Narváez expressing your opinion about his decision to divide his forces. Provide reasons to support your position.
Consider the following:
- the swamps the Spaniards would have to cross
- other actions Narváez might have taken

Searching for Cities of Gold

Read to Discover

1. What events occurred on Fray Marcos and Estevanico's journey to Cíbola?
2. Where did Coronado go on his expedition, and what did he learn?
3. What were the results of the Coronado and de Soto–Moscoso expeditions?

Why It Matters Today

Conquistadores explored the Americas in search of gold, silver, and other valuable metals. Use CNN**fyi**.com or other **current events** sources to learn more about the economic importance of minerals and other natural resources today. Record your findings in your journal.

Define
• viceroy

Identify
• Fray Marcos de Niza
• Francisco Vásquez de Coronado
• Hernando de Soto
• Luis de Moscoso Alvarado

The Story Continues

A Spanish legend described the Seven Cities of Gold. According to the story, seven bishops fled Portugal when it was invaded in the A.D. 700s. After crossing the Atlantic Ocean, they came to a land filled with gold and jewels. There, the bishops built seven fabulously wealthy cities. Although no one knew the cities' location, many Spaniards thought they might be in the Americas. Some wealthy empires had already been found. Surely others lay hidden away.

Spaniards often melted gold taken from the Americas into coins and bars such as these.

★ The Search for Lost Cities of Gold

Before returning to Spain, Cabeza de Vaca reported his adventures. He told of hearing of "mountains to the north, where there were towns of great population and great houses." He also said that he had seen signs of gold in the mountains. The report excited the **viceroy**, or royal governor, of New Spain. In 1539 the viceroy sent a Catholic friar named **Fray Marcos de Niza** north to find these cities. Fray Marcos was a skilled explorer. Because Estevanico knew the land, Fray Marcos chose him as his guide. Some 300 Mexican Indians went along to provide protection.

The explorers crossed what is now Arizona into New Mexico. Estevanico and several others went ahead of the main group to scout the way. Estevanico wore bright clothing and a cape and tied bells to his wrists and ankles so he would look like a healer.

Fray Marcos eventually received word that Estevanico and the advance group had seen a large city. As the friar continued on, he met some of the advance group fleeing his way. They reported that they had reached one of the seven cities and seen people wearing gold jewelry and drinking from golden cups. However, Estevanico had angered the villagers. They had attacked, killing him and many of the others.

To avoid a similar fate, Fray Marcos moved to high ground to view the city from afar. There, he saw it shining in the distance, with buildings that sparkled like gold in the desert sun. Satisfied that he had found great treasure, Fray Marcos returned home to Mexico City. He excitedly reported finding seven wealthy cities, which the Spanish called Cíbola. As wild rumors of Cíbola's wealth quickly spread, officials planned an expedition to claim its treasure.

 Reading Check **Analyzing Information** Why might officials in Mexico City have questioned Fray Marcos's description of the cities of Cíbola?

★ Coronado's Search for Cíbola

To conquer Cíbola, the Spanish organized the largest force they had ever sent into North America. Some 300 soldiers, several religious officials, and more than 1,000 Mexican Indians led herds of cattle, horses, and sheep. **Francisco Vásquez de Coronado**, a 30-year-old conquistador, commanded this force. Riding a stallion, Coronado made an impressive sight in gold-plated armor and a steel helmet with bright feathers. With Fray Marcos serving as guide, the force set off in April 1540.

The Granger Collection, New York

Biography

Estevanico
(c. 1501–1539)

Estevanico was born around 1501 in Morocco. During his late teens, he worked as a servant for a Spaniard named Andrés Dorantes. In 1527 the two men joined the Narváez expedition. Estevanico thus became the first African to explore Texas. Later, in 1539, he guided a small group searching for gold. He was the first in the party to reach a Zuni village. Although Estevanico had gotten along well with many other American Indians, some of his actions angered the Zuni. Outside the village, they killed him. **In what two expeditions did Estevanico participate?** TEKS

Interpreting the Visual Record

Searching for gold. This Spanish map from the 1500s shows the presumed location of the Seven Cities of Cíbola. How did geographic features such as rivers help the Spaniards determine the location of American Indian settlements? TEKS

Coronado. Coronado led his large expedition across the dry regions of what is now the southwestern United States. **How do you think they may have adapted to the environment of the region during their trip?**

When Coronado reached the city that Fray Marcos had seen, he found a force of Zuni Indians waiting. A short but hard-fought battle took place. The Spaniards, with their muskets and swords, soon defeated the Zuni. The conquerors' joy of victory did not last long, however. As they searched the cities, they did not find any gold or silver. The cities of Cíbola were not the legendary lost cities of gold but rather Zuni Pueblo villages. The Zuni had houses made of adobe brick, not gold. Coronado was furious and sent Fray Marcos back to Mexico City in disgrace.

 Reading Check **Drawing Inferences and Conclusions** How did physical and human features lead the Spanish to think Cíbola was made of gold?

★ Coronado Hears of Quivira

Although disappointed, Coronado sent groups out to explore the land and search for treasure. The members of one group, led by García López de Cárdenas, became the first known Europeans to see the Grand Canyon. Another group traveled east to Tiguex (tee-GWAYSH), an area containing several American Indian villages near the Rio Grande in what is now New Mexico. Coronado soon moved his main force to the area because the Tigua Indians who lived there were friendly.

While at Tiguex, the Spaniards met an American Indian from farther east whom they called the Turk. He told tales of Quivira, a nearby region where the cities were said to be full of gold. After the experience at Cíbola, many Spaniards doubted the Turk's story. Yet Coronado thought finding Quivira was worth the risk and planned an expedition for the coming spring. That winter, the Spaniards' supplies ran out and they began forcing the Tigua Indians to give them food and clothing.

The Tigua grew angry, and fighting soon broke out between them and the Spaniards. The Spaniards killed many Tigua before establishing control.

★ **Reading Check** **Finding the Main Idea** Who was the Turk, and why did the story he told interest Coronado?

★ Coronado Travels through Texas

Guided by the Turk, Coronado set out in search of Quivira in the spring of 1541. The explorers traveled onto the flatlands of the Texas Panhandle. One soldier described the area's high plains.

Texas Voices ❝The country . . . was so level and smooth that . . . if a man lay down on his back he lost sight of the ground. . . . Several lakes were found at intervals; they were round as plates. . . . The grass grows tall near these lakes; away from them it is very short. . . . In traveling over those plains, [we left] no more trace . . . than if nothing had been there.❞

—Pedro de Castañeda, quoted in *Spanish Explorers in the Southern United States, 1528–1543*

The expedition continued across the Llano Estacado. Deer, rabbits, and wolves lived on this plain. The explorers also saw strange hump-backed "cows," which were actually some American buffalo. As the explorers traveled, they met many American Indians. Coronado and his army noted how skilled these Plains Indians were at hunting the buffalo. Moving east, the expedition crossed onto the Caprock Escarpment. This area of cliffs and canyons divides the Texas High Plains from the lower interior plains. There the explorers came upon another unusual sight—a deep gorge cut into the land. This gorge was likely Palo Duro Canyon.

The explorers camped in this canyon, and then the expedition headed north. Near what is now Wichita, Kansas, they reached "Quivira" and once again met with disappointment. Instead of treasure, they found only grass huts and corn. Coronado became angry and asked the Turk why he had deceived them. The Turk explained that the Tigua had made him tell the story so that the explorers would leave their village. Coronado had the Turk killed for his actions.

Coronado returned to Mexico City in 1542. In his report of his journey he described the Llano Estacado as a fine land similar to parts of Spain. He noted that the huge buffalo herds might provide a source of wealth. Because he had not found any gold or other treasure, Spanish officials considered the expedition a failure, however.

★ **Reading Check** **Categorizing** What animals and geographic features did Coronado see while crossing the Texas Panhandle?

The Granger Collection, New York

Interpreting the Visual Record

Armor. Conquistadores wore armor to protect themselves in battle. *How might this armor have been a disadvantage during an expedition in Texas?*

Daily Life

What's for Dinner?

Before a voyage, explorers loaded their ships with barrels of flour, cattle, and other foods and livestock. These supplies often ran out before the ships landed. In such cases, some explorers ate wormy biscuits or rats to stay alive. When traveling overland in the Americas, hungry explorers copied the diets of local American Indians. Depending on where they were, explorers ate corn, fish, prickly pear fruit, and roots. In desperate times, explorers even ate bark or their horses to survive. **How did explorers in the Americas learn which local plants or animals were good to eat?**

★ Moscoso Explores East Texas

While Coronado marched to the cities of Cíbola from the south, a group led by Spanish explorer **Hernando de Soto** sought them from the east. De Soto and some 600 soldiers had landed on the Florida coast in 1539. For more than two years they had explored what is now the southeastern United States. Then in May 1542 de Soto died of fever. **Luis de Moscoso Alvarado**, another member of the group, took command.

Because the expedition had not found any treasure, Moscoso decided to head to Mexico City. He led the explorers west into East Texas, where they met many Caddo Indians. Soon, however, the explorers began having trouble finding food, and the Caddo had none to spare. Realizing they had little chance of making it to Mexico City on foot, Moscoso returned to the Mississippi River. Like Narváez, the explorers built small boats to sail to Mexico. Their attempt was successful, and in 1543 some 300 members of the original force of 600 reached Mexico.

In Mexico City, Moscoso made a report of his expedition much like Coronado's. Moscoso described Texas as a geographically varied land. He also mentioned seeing a thick, black goo seeping from the ground. Although he did not know it, Moscoso had seen petroleum, or oil. This would one day become the "black gold" of Texas. However, the Spanish were interested only in gold and silver, and neither Coronado nor Moscoso had found any. The expeditions to Texas had failed to produce the riches the Spanish desired.

⭐ **Reading Check** **Making Generalizations and Predictions** After Moscoso's report, do you think Spanish officials were eager to send other expeditions to Texas? Why or why not?

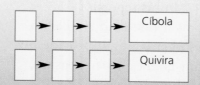

★ Section 3 Review ⭐TEKS Questions 2, 3, 4a, 4b, 5

go.hrw.com **Homework Practice Online**
keyword: ST3 HP5

1 **Define and explain:**
- viceroy

2 **Identify and explain:**
- Fray Marcos de Niza
- Francisco Vásquez de Coronado
- Hernando de Soto
- Luis de Moscoso Alvarado

3 **Sequencing**
Copy the graphic organizer below. Use it to identify in order the stories and events that led to Coronado's exploration of the American Southwest.

[ ] → [ ] → [ ] → Cíbola

[ ] → [ ] → [ ] → Quivira

4 **Finding the Main Idea**
a. What happened on the Fray Marcos expedition to Cíbola?

b. Compare and contrast the Coronado and de Soto–Moscoso expeditions.

5 **Writing and Critical Thinking** **TAKS**
Identifying Points of View Imagine that you are a Zuni Indian living in the American Southwest. Describe your opinion of the Spaniards who were looking for Cíbola.

Consider the following:
- Spanish actions toward the Zuni
- Zuni actions toward the Spanish

Consequences of Spanish Exploration

Read to Discover

1. What was the significance of Juan de Oñate's travels?
2. How did Spain profit from its exploration in Texas?
3. How did the Columbian Exchange affect American Indians in Texas?

Why It Matters Today

The transfer of plants and animals between the Americas and other parts of the world greatly changed people's lives. Use **CNNfyi.com** or other **current events** sources to find information about the worldwide exchange of goods or ideas today. Record your findings in your journal.

Define
- epidemics
- mustangs

Identify
- Juan de Oñate
- Columbian Exchange

The Story Continues

In January 1598 Juan Perex de Bustill, his wife, and nine children left their home in Mexico. With more than 500 other settlers, they headed north into the Chihuahuan Desert. The settlers brought more than 80 carts full of supplies for a colony and thousands of cattle, horses, oxen, and sheep. Water was often scarce. During one long dry stretch, the thirsty colonists prayed for a miracle. Suddenly, a rainstorm arose, forming pools of water. The grateful colonists named the spot Socorro de Cielo, or "Aid from Heaven."

Don Juan de Oñate was granted the right to settle and govern the new colony of New Mexico.

★ Oñate Founds New Mexico

After the Coronado and de Soto–Moscoso expeditions, Spanish officials lost interest in northern New Spain. The region had not produced any gold or other valuable metals. Yet rumors of marvelous golden cities to the north did not go away. In the late 1500s these tales again drew Spanish explorers to the Pueblo region in New Mexico. A few of these travelers also entered Texas. Some of the explorers who made the trips greatly exaggerated the region's potential wealth.

Juan de Oñate traveled across the rugged and dry terrain of the Texas Panhandle during his expedition.

CONNECTIONS

The Reformation

While the Spanish were spreading the Catholic faith in the Americas, Catholicism was under attack in Europe. In 1517 a Catholic priest named Martin Luther listed the problems he found with the Church. Luther posted his list on the door of Castle Church in Wittenberg, Germany. The event led to a religious reform movement called the Protestant Reformation. In time, this movement resulted in the development of Protestant churches. **What event sparked the Reformation?**

Between 1550 and the 1590s, settlement in New Spain had been slowly spreading northward. King Philip II of Spain, who wanted to control this expanding settlement, decided to colonize the land of the Pueblo Indians. By doing so, he also hoped to increase Spain's wealth and spread Christianity to the Pueblo. King Philip granted **Juan de Oñate** (ohn-YAH-tay) the right to settle and govern the colony, named New Mexico. Oñate was from a wealthy Spanish family that had profited from silver mining in Mexico.

In early 1598 Oñate led more than 500 colonists north across the Chihuahuan Desert. The settlers struggled through the hot, dry land. When they reached the Rio Grande, the river seemed like an oasis with its shady willow trees and cool water. One colonist wrote, "These were the . . . fields of happiness where we could forget our misfortunes [hardships] . . . and enjoy those comforts so long denied us." The thankful settlers held a feast to celebrate their survival. Near what is now San Elizario, Texas, Oñate claimed the Rio Grande region for Spain. The colonists then continued upriver until they reached several Pueblo villages, north of where Santa Fe, New Mexico, lies today. There the colonists built the first Spanish settlement in New Mexico.

Life in the colony was hard, and the settlers soon began to grumble. They had few comforts and were not finding any gold. Oñate decided to explore northeast toward Quivira, in hopes of finding treasure where Coronado had failed. In 1601 Oñate set out with a small group across the Texas Panhandle. Like Coronado, he too failed to find any gold, and unhappily returned to New Mexico. The lack of treasure in Texas and the surrounding areas caused the Spanish to lose interest in the region. Few explorers entered the area for the next 80 years.

⭐ **Reading Check** **Finding the Main Idea** What did Juan de Oñate accomplish in 1598?

★ The Effects of Spanish Exploration

Although the Spanish failed to find gold, their exploration of Texas was important. It gave Spain a strong claim to the area. The Spanish also gained valuable knowledge about the land and people of Texas. In addition, Texas served as a buffer between Spanish settlements to the south and American Indians and other, later European colonies.

At the same time, Spanish exploration greatly changed the lives of American Indians in Texas. During their travels, European explorers spread diseases such as measles and smallpox. Although most Europeans recovered from such illnesses, American Indians often died because they had never been exposed to these diseases. **Epidemics**, or widespread outbreaks of disease, killed thousands of American Indians. In time, many Indians in Texas died from European diseases and from conflicts with Europeans.

The spread of diseases from Europe to the Americas was part of the **Columbian Exchange**. This term refers to the transfer of plants, animals, and diseases between the Americas and other continents. The Columbian Exchange is so named because it began with Christopher Columbus's arrival in the Americas in 1492. The Spanish brought to the Americas new plants and animals, such as bananas, cattle, and horses. When they returned to Europe, explorers took back American plants and animals, such as corn, peanuts, and turkeys.

★ **Reading Check Summarizing** What is the Columbian Exchange, and how did it affect Texas Indians?

★ The Rise of a Plains Horse Culture

The wild offspring of the horses the Spanish brought to the Americas became known as *mesteños*, or **mustangs**. In the 1600s, American Indians in Texas began obtaining mustangs through trade and raids. Horses greatly changed Indian life, particularly on the plains. Using horses, Indians could move their belongings more easily. Some Indians became more nomadic, or mobile, as they used horses to follow the buffalo herds. On horseback, Indians became more effective hunters and fighters. They could ride deep into enemy territory, strike quickly, and then vanish into the plains.

Spaniards in New Mexico first recorded seeing Apache Indians riding horses in 1659. The sight horrified the Spanish—they had lost an important military advantage. They were no longer the only ones in the area with horses. The rise of a plains horse culture marked the start of a new phase in Spanish-Indian relations and warfare.

★ **Reading Check Identifying Cause and Effect** What led to the development of a Plains Indian horse culture, and how did this development affect the Spanish?

★ LONE STAR LEGACY

Texas Mustangs

The small horses brought by the Spanish to the Americas were tough and able to live off the land. In time, some escaped, and their wild offspring were called mustangs. By the mid-1800s more than 2 million mustangs roamed the North American grasslands. Hunting later decreased this number to as low as 20,000. A 1971 federal law protecting wild horses on public lands has helped restore the mustang herds. **How do mustangs represent the Spanish heritage of Texas?** ★TEKS

★ The Apache Dominate the Plains

The Apache in Texas and New Mexico had initially been friendly to the Spanish. While traveling through the Texas Panhandle, the explorers Coronado and Oñate both had met groups of Apache. A member of Coronado's force described them.

Apache used buffalo hides for shelter, clothing, and shields like this one.

Texas Voices ❝These folks live in tents made of the tanned skins of the cows [buffalo]. They travel around near the [buffalo], killing them for food. . . . They have better figures [than other Indians], are better warriors, and are more feared. They travel like the Arabs [nomads], with their tents and troops of dogs loaded with poles. . . . These people eat [the buffalo's] raw flesh and drink [its] blood. . . . They are a kind people and not cruel.❞

—Pedro de Castañeda, quoted in *Spanish Explorers in the Southern United States, 1528–1543*

After the Spanish began settling among the Pueblo, their relationship with the Apache changed. The Apache, who had raided the Pueblo for years, began to view the Spanish as enemies. Bands of Apache raided the New Mexico settlements, taking horses and supplies. They proved unstoppable on horseback despite the Spaniards' superior weapons. The Apache soon ruled the Texas Plains, which the Spanish called Apachería, meaning "Apache land."

The conflict between the Spanish and the Apache was one of many between Europeans and American Indians. The Spanish and other Europeans saw American lands as theirs to claim. American Indians—who had lived on this land for generations—saw it as their home. In Texas, clashes between these two points of view would continue for several hundred years.

Reading Check **Contrasting** How did relations between the Apache and the Spanish change?

 Section 4 Review ⊛TEKS Questions 2, 3, 4a, 4b, 5
go.hrw.com **Homework Practice Online**
keyword: ST3 HP5

1 **Define and explain:**
- epidemics
- mustangs

2 **Identify and explain:**
- Juan de Oñate
- Columbian Exchange

3 **Summarizing**
Copy the diagram below. Use it to list the effects of Spanish exploration in Texas.

Spanish Exploration in Texas

4 **Finding the Main Idea**
a. What did Juan de Oñate achieve, and how did his travels affect Texas?
b. How did the Spanish benefit from their exploration of Texas?

5 **Writing and Critical Thinking** **TAKS**
Analyzing Information Write one paragraph explaining positive and one paragraph explaining negative effects of the Columbian Exchange in Texas. Consider the following:
- the transfer of new animals and plants
- the spread of European diseases

Geography

The Columbian Exchange

The Columbian Exchange began when Columbus first arrived in the Americas. This process involved the transfer of plants, animals, and diseases between the Americas and Europe, Africa, and Asia. Explorers brought European plants and animals with them to the Americas. When explorers went home, they brought American plants and animals back with them. These plants and animals gradually spread from Europe to Africa and Asia.

Geography Skills

Interpreting Thematic Maps and Charts

1. What food crops native to Europe, Asia, or Africa now grow in the Texas Panhandle?

2. What animals native to Europe, Asia, or Africa are now raised in South Texas?

3. What animals native to Europe, Asia, or Africa are most commonly found in Texas today? ⭐TEKS

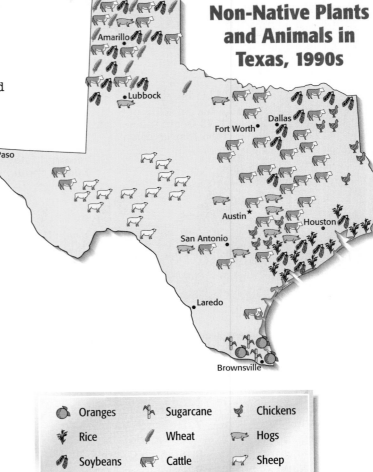

Non-Native Plants and Animals in Texas, 1990s

Legend:
- 🍊 Oranges
- 🌾 Rice
- Soybeans
- 🌿 Sugarcane
- Wheat
- 🐄 Cattle
- 🐔 Chickens
- Hogs
- 🐑 Sheep

Origins of Plants and Animals

	THE AMERICAS	EUROPE, ASIA, OR AFRICA
FOOD PLANTS	avocados, beans, cashews, cassava roots, cocoa beans, corn, papayas, peanuts, pecans, peppers, pineapples, potatoes, squash, tomatoes, vanilla beans, wild rice	barley, oats, rice, wheat, bananas, chickpeas, coffee, grapes, lemons, lettuce, okra, olives, onions, oranges, peaches, pears, radishes, soybeans, sugarcane, watermelons
OTHER PLANTS	cotton, marigolds, rubber, tobacco	bluegrass, couchgrass, crabgrass, daisies, dandelions, roses
ANIMALS AND INSECTS	gray squirrels, guinea pigs, hummingbirds, muskrats, potato beetles, rattlesnakes, turkeys	chickens, cows, domestic cats, goats, hogs, honey bees, horses, Japanese beetles, mice, rabbits, rats, sheep, sparrows, starlings

The Chapter at a Glance

Examine the following visual summary of the chapter. Then use the visual to write a one-page summary of this chapter that a classmate can use as a study guide. ★TEKS

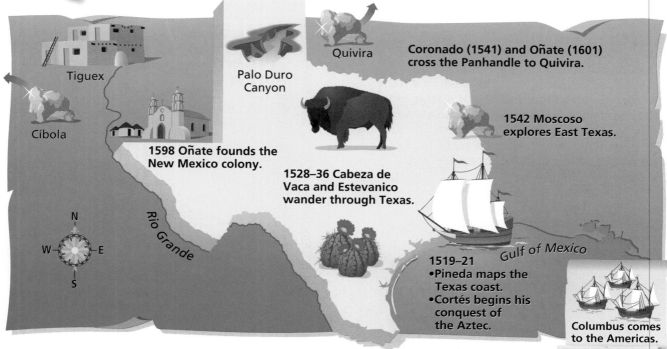

Tiguex

Cíbola

Palo Duro Canyon

Quivira

Coronado (1541) and Oñate (1601) cross the Panhandle to Quivira.

1542 Moscoso explores East Texas.

1598 Oñate founds the New Mexico colony.

1528–36 Cabeza de Vaca and Estevanico wander through Texas.

Rio Grande

N W E S

1519–21
• Pineda maps the Texas coast.
• Cortés begins his conquest of the Aztec.

Gulf of Mexico

Columbus comes to the Americas.

Identifying People and Ideas ★TEKS

Use the following terms or people in historically significant sentences.

1. Christopher Columbus
2. conquistadores
3. Hernán Cortés
4. Álvar Núñez Cabeza de Vaca
5. Estevanico
6. viceroy
7. Francisco Vásquez de Coronado
8. Juan de Oñate
9. Columbian Exchange
10. mustangs

Understanding Main Ideas ★TEKS

Section 1 (pp. 90–93)

1. What did Spain gain through its conquest of the Aztec Empire?

Section 2 (pp. 94–97)

2. Why was 1519 important to Texas history?

Section 3 (pp. 98–102)

3. Why did the Spanish want to find the Seven Cities of Cíbola? Who led these expeditions?

Section 4 (pp. 103–106)

4. How did exploration in Texas benefit Spain, and why did exploration end in the early 1600s?

You Be the Historian ★TEKS

Reviewing Themes

1. **Science, Technology & Society** How was the small army that Cortés started with able to defeat the Aztec?

2. **Economics** How did Spain's economy benefit from the exploration and conquest of the Americas?

3. **Culture** How did Spanish exploration affect Texas Indians?

TAKS ★TEKS **Practice: Thinking Critically**

1. **Analyzing Information** How do you think Texas Indians regarded healers?

2. **Contrasting** Explain how Coronado's dealings with American Indians differed from those of Cabeza de Vaca and Estevanico.

3. **Drawing Inferences and Conclusions** What effect do you think disease had on the Spaniards' ability to conquer American Indian groups?

Social Studies Skills Workshop

Interpreting Charts ⭐TEKS

Study the pie chart below. Then use the information on the chart to help you answer the following questions.

2000 values of Texas livestock originally native to Europe, Africa, or Asia

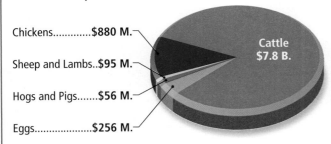

Chickens.............$880 M.

Sheep and Lambs..$95 M.

Hogs and Pigs.......$56 M.

Eggs..................$256 M.

Cattle $7.8 B.

Source: Texas Department of Agriculture

1. What animal or animal product native to Europe, Asia, or Africa accounted for the largest value in Texas in 2000?
   a. eggs
   b. hogs and pigs
   c. cattle
   d. chickens

2. What are some types of food that would not be available in Texas without the Columbian Exchange?

Analyzing Primary Sources ⭐TEKS

Read the following quote describing the Moscoso expedition in Texas. The quote is by the unknown "Gentleman of Elvas," from his account entitled *The Narrative of the Expedition of Hernando de Soto*. Then answer the questions.

"The residents [of the American Indian village of Guasco] stated, that ten days' journey from there, toward the sunset, was a river called Daycao [likely the Brazos], . . . whence [where] they had seen persons on the other bank, but without knowing what people they were. . . . Ten horsemen sent in advance . . . had crossed; and, following a road . . . , they came upon an encampment [camp] of Indians. . . . Taking two natives, they went back . . . , [but] no Indian was found in the camp who knew their language."

3. Based on the quote, why did the explorers travel to the Daycao River?
   a. They were curious about the people the Guasco Indians had seen there.
   b. They were looking for food.
   c. They were trying to find a river leading to Mexico City.
   d. They were looking for gold.

4. What does the quote show was one of the problems explorers faced when dealing with American Indians?

Alternative Assessment

Cooperative Learning ⭐TEKS

Work with a small group to complete the following activity. Each person in your group should select one of the following explorers: a) Hernán Cortés, b) Pánfilo de Narváez, c) Francisco Vásquez de Coronado, or d) Juan de Oñate. Work together as a group to create an illustrated book about the explorers' adventures. Research and write the section for the explorer you chose. Then work with other group members to create the book's cover. You may want to create and include maps to make your illustrated book clearer.

BUILDING YOUR Portfolio

📶 internet connect

Internet Activity: go.hrw.com
KEYWORD: ST3 TX5 ⭐TEKS

Access the Internet through the HRW Go site to research modern navigation technology and the technology European explorers in Texas may have used. Then write a report that compares the technology of the past and present. Include illustrations of the devices you have learned about. Use standard grammar, spelling, sentence structure, and punctuation in your report.

The Spanish Missions

(1680–1760)

The Granger Collection, New York

La Salle canoed down the Mississippi River claiming the region for France three years before coming to Texas.

Mission Concepción was one of the early Spanish missions established near what is now San Antonio.

TEXAS

1685 A group of colonists led by French explorer René-Robert Cavelier, Sieur de La Salle lands in Matagorda Bay in Texas.

1690 The Spanish build a mission named San Francisco de los Tejas.

1718 Martín de Alarcón establishes the San Antonio de Valero mission.

1680	1690	1700	1710

U.S. and WORLD

1688 The Glorious Revolution in England led to the removal of the Catholic ruler James II and the appointment of William and Mary to the English throne.

c. 1694 The French begin trading with American Indians along the Mississippi River for beaver pelts that are made into fur hats.

1700 More than 250,000 people live in the English colonies of North America.

1718 The French found New Orleans.

William and Mary ruled England from 1689 until 1702.

Build on What You Know

Many Spaniards came to the Americas seeking gold and glory. Their search for gold brought several explorers trekking through Texas, where they reported on the land and its people. In the 1680s the Spanish began building churches and forts in Texas to extend their influence into the area.

Horse races were a popular pastime in early Spanish Texas settlements.

Some Spanish missions had brightly decorated altars.

1731 Settlers from the Canary Islands arrive in San Antonio.

1755 Rancher Tomás Sánchez establishes the town of Laredo.

1720 **1730** **1740** **1750** **1760**

1732 Benjamin Franklin begins to publish *Poor Richard's Almanack.*

1759 Charles III takes the throne of Spain. He would later become known as one of the nation's best kings.

Charles III enacted a series of reforms during his reign.

You Be the Historian

Themes Journal

What's Your Opinion? Do you **agree** or **disagree** with the following statements? Support your point of view in your journal.

● **Culture** When people move to a new region, they adapt to the culture that is already there.

● **Geography** A settlement's chances of success are not affected by its location.

● **Global Relations** Conflicts between countries always affect their overseas territories.

If you were there . . .
Would you have settled in Texas?

Spanish Settlements on the Frontier

Read to Discover

1. How did Spanish officials try to control the borderlands of New Spain?
2. Why did the Spanish establish missions along the western Rio Grande during the 1680s?

Why It Matters Today

The crops that Spaniards and American Indians grew were important sources of food for the missions. Use **CNNfyi.com** or other **current events** sources to learn more on farming today. Record your findings in your journal.

Define

- missions
- presidios
- ranchos
- revolt

Identify

- **Pueblo Revolt**
- **Corpus Christi de la Isleta**

Francis di Bernardone of Assisi founded a Catholic religious group known as the Franciscans.

The Story Continues

Francis di Bernardone, a young Italian knight from Assisi, fought his first battle when he was 20. On his way to a second clash he became ill. As he lay sick in bed, he thought about the meaning of his life. When he recovered, he was a changed man. He gave up soldiering and devoted himself to a religious life. In 1209 he founded a religious group. Many of these Franciscans became missionaries. Some 400 years later, Franciscans came to Texas to convert American Indians to Catholicism.

★ The Mission System

At first, the Spanish were the only Europeans with settlements in North America. But by the early 1600s other nations had begun founding settlements. Royal officials wanted to protect New Spain's northern frontiers. Because few Spaniards lived in these borderlands, the Spanish sent missionaries there to establish **missions**, or religious communities. Spain used missions to convert American Indians to Catholicism and, eventually, to develop settlements in the borderlands. The mission system also represented the Spanish government in the borderlands.

The Spanish built missions near rivers to ensure a good water supply. Missions usually included churches, dormitories, workrooms, barns, fields, and gardens. The Spanish wanted local American Indians to live within the mission walls. Missionaries taught these Indians about Catholicism and an agricultural way of life. One priest noted, "This would also be the [best way] of achieving the civilization of many . . . peoples, who [might] accept . . . Christian instruction." Many American Indians helped build and maintain the missions. But many other Indians did not want missions on their lands and opposed Spanish attempts to change their ways of life. To protect the missions from attack, the Spanish usually built **presidios**, or military bases. Soldiers in these forts were generally responsible for protecting several missions.

When civilians came to the borderlands, they usually built their settlements near missions and presidios. Some of these civil settlements became small towns. Farmers and merchants in these towns provided products and services for the missions and presidios. Other Spaniards lived on **ranchos**, or ranches. Some ranchos belonged to missions, while others were privately owned. Over time, some of these ranches grew into small settlements, increasing the Spanish presence in the borderlands.

⭐ **Reading Check** **Analyzing Information** Describe some of the defining characteristics of Spanish Texas.

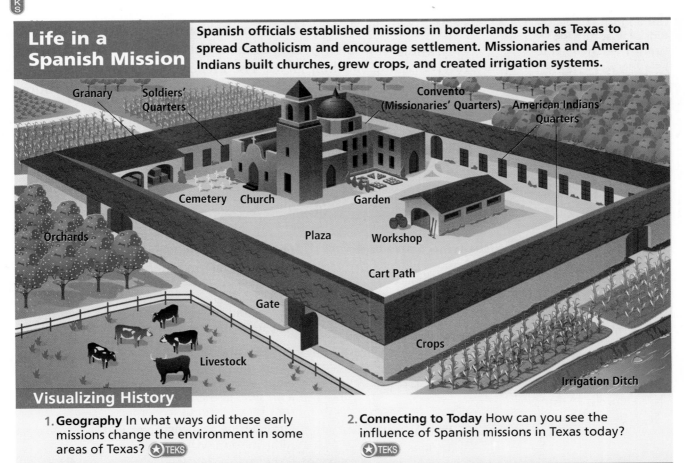

Life in a Spanish Mission

Spanish officials established missions in borderlands such as Texas to spread Catholicism and encourage settlement. Missionaries and American Indians built churches, grew crops, and created irrigation systems.

Granary
Soldiers' Quarters
Convento (Missionaries' Quarters)
American Indians' Quarters
Cemetery   Church
Garden
Orchards
Plaza
Workshop
Cart Path
Gate
Crops
Livestock
Irrigation Ditch

Visualizing History

1. **Geography** In what ways did these early missions change the environment in some areas of Texas? ⭐TEKS

2. **Connecting to Today** How can you see the influence of Spanish missions in Texas today? ⭐TEKS

★ New Missions along the Rio Grande

In the late 1600s the Spanish began building missions just south of the Rio Grande. They also built several missions among the Pueblo Indians in New Mexico. Life in the New Mexico missions was hard, and food was often scarce. The situation grew worse in the 1670s when a drought ruined many crops. At times, people even ate leather to survive. Tensions increased when missionaries tried to stop the Pueblo from following their traditional religious beliefs. In 1680 a Pueblo spiritual leader named Popé (poh-PAY) led a **revolt**, or revolution, against the Spanish. This __Pueblo Revolt__ forced the Spanish settlers out of New Mexico.

Spain wanted to give these settlers a place to live and build a base from which to retake New Mexico. To accomplish these goals, Spanish officials extended the mission system along the Rio Grande. In 1682 the Spanish founded the first mission in Texas. __Corpus Christi de la Isleta__ was along the western Rio Grande, just east of present-day El Paso. Over time, a town grew up on the site. The Tigua Indians called the settlement Ysleta (ees-LE-tah), which is probably the oldest European town in Texas. The settlement of El Paso was later founded near Ysleta.

Other missions were built in the area. Spaniards and Piro Indians fleeing the Pueblo Revolt founded a mission southeast of Ysleta, and another mission was built across the Rio Grande from Ysleta. Missionaries there hoped to convert the Apache, Jumano, Manso, Piro, Suma, and Tano Indians. In the midst of this activity, the Spanish received some shocking news. The French had entered the Gulf of Mexico—Spanish waters. The Spanish quickly focused their attentions on protecting their territory along the Gulf Coast.

 Reading Check **Finding the Main Idea** Why did the Spanish build missions along the Rio Grande in West Texas?

★ Section 1 Review ★TEKS Questions 2, 3, 4a, 4b, 5

go.hrw.com **Homework Practice Online**
keyword: ST3 HP6

1 Define and explain:
- missions
- presidios
- ranchos
- revolt

2 Identify and explain:
- Pueblo Revolt
- Corpus Christi de la Isleta

3 Identifying Cause and Effect
Copy the graphic organizer below. Use it to describe Spain's goals for the borderlands and how Spain tried to accomplish those goals.

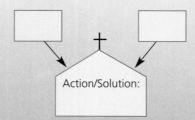

Action/Solution:

4 Finding the Main Idea
a. What types of Spanish settlements were in the borderlands? What was the purpose of each?
b. Why did the Spanish choose to build the first Texas missions along the Rio Grande?

5 Writing and Critical Thinking
Supporting a Point of View Write a letter to an official in Mexico City requesting a presidio in the borderlands. Include reasons for your request.
Consider the following:
- the mission system
- the Pueblo Revolt

The French Challenge

Read to Discover

1. Why did the French try to build a settlement near the Mississippi River, and what was the outcome?
2. What effect did the La Salle expedition have on Spanish policy in Texas?
3. What happened to the Spanish mission in East Texas?

Why It Matters Today

In the 1600s people from France, Spain, and other European nations settled in the Americas. Use CNN fyi.com or other **current events** sources to learn more about immigration today. Record your findings in your journal.

Identify

- René-Robert Cavelier, Sieur de La Salle
- La Salle expedition
- Matagorda Bay
- Fort St. Louis
- Alonso de León
- Damián Massanet
- Tejas
- San Francisco de los Tejas

The Story Continues

Diego de Peñalosa was bitter. The former Spanish governor of New Mexico had been found guilty of several crimes. He was exiled from all of New Spain in the 1660s. He went to England and then to France, seeking to undermine Spain's power in the Americas. To the French king Peñalosa proposed that France build a colony on the Rio Grande and slowly move into Texas. The king liked the idea. Peñalosa's hopes of leading the expedition soon died, however. The king picked another river and another explorer for the French colony.

The French king at the time was Louis XIV, also known as the Sun King.

★ La Salle's Expedition

Spain was no longer the only European power in North America in the 1600s. England was beginning to establish its thirteen colonies along the East Coast. France also posed a threat to Spain's control of the borderlands. To the north France had claimed Canada. French fur trappers were exploring the Great Lakes as well as the Ohio, Missouri, and Mississippi Rivers. In 1682 French explorer **René-Robert Cavelier, Sieur de La Salle** expanded France's empire. He canoed down the Mississippi River to its mouth at the Gulf of Mexico. There he planted the French flag and claimed all of the land drained by the Mississippi for France.

CONNECTING TO
SCIENCE AND TECHNOLOGY

La Belle

In 1686 La Salle's ship *La Belle* wrecked in Matagorda Bay. Divers discovered *La Belle* in 1995. Archaeologists wanted to examine the ship, so engineers designed an enormous steel structure to hold back the water. Scholars spent months examining *La Belle*. The ship and its artifacts were then taken to a laboratory at Texas A&M University for further study. The artifacts—such as bells, cannons, glass beads, and pottery—taught scholars much about the lives of the colonists. **How did scholars benefit from raising *La Belle*?**

This land extended from the Great Lakes to the Gulf of Mexico. La Salle named the region Louisiana for his king, Louis XIV.

After exploring the area, La Salle returned to France. He asked the king for permission to establish a settlement near the giant river's mouth. La Salle pointed out that the settlement would strengthen France's claim to Louisiana. The colony would serve as a military base and discourage other European colonists from moving into the area. The French would also gain a port for the valuable fur trade and perhaps even trade with the Spanish colonies. King Louis agreed to La Salle's proposal. Because a colony so close to Texas would anger the Spanish, the French kept their plan a closely guarded secret. They hoped to sneak up the Mississippi River and establish the colony before the Spanish found out.

The **La Salle expedition** left France in the summer of 1684. It had four ships and about 300 soldiers and settlers. The expedition ran into trouble when Spanish pirates captured one ship. Then some of the sailors deserted. They later told the Spanish of La Salle's plans. Despite these problems, La Salle sailed on. He became lost, however, and the ships missed the mouth of the Mississippi. The group finally came ashore in February 1685 at **Matagorda Bay** on the Texas coast. While entering the bay, one ship ran aground with valuable supplies aboard. Then another ship returned to France. The colonists were left with very little food and few other supplies. They were ill prepared for life in the wilderness.

 Reading Check Finding the Main Idea What was the purpose of the La Salle expedition?

★ Fort St. Louis

La Salle and the others quickly realized they could not live on the coast's marshy lowlands. They moved inland several miles and built a settlement called **Fort St. Louis** near Garcitas Creek. The settlement consisted of several simple houses and a five-room fort made out of timbers from the wrecked ship. One of the rooms in the fort served as a chapel. For protection, the settlers put eight cannons on the fort's walls.

As the settlement was being built, La Salle led a small group west toward the Rio Grande. They may have been searching for Spanish mines or food supplies. La Salle was away from the fort from October 1685 to March 1686. He probably reached the Rio Grande before he realized that Fort St. Louis was west of the Mississippi.

Meanwhile, life was not going well at the settlement. Hunger and disease killed many settlers. In addition, the colonists had to defend themselves against attack by the Karankawa Indians. By the end of July 1685, more than half the settlers were dead. The situation became worse as the colony's leaders quarreled. La Salle returned in March 1686 to a colony in crisis. The colonists' condition grew more desperate when the last remaining ship, *La Belle,* wrecked during a storm and stranded the settlers.

La Salle decided to go to Canada for help. However, the eastward journey through the wilderness to the Mississippi was difficult, and the expedition ended in failure. In early 1687 La Salle and 17 men went east again, looking for the Mississippi. While they marched through East Texas, tensions mounted. The men argued about how poorly things had turned out. Violence resulted, and La Salle was murdered by one of his own soldiers. Six members of La Salle's party eventually made their way back to Canada.

Back at the settlement, fewer than 30 people were left. Many were women and children. Karankawa Indians attacked and overran the fort in late 1688 or 1689. They killed all of the adult settlers and destroyed the fort. Five children were taken captive by the Karankawa. The children were kept by the Karankawa until they were rescued by later expeditions. The La Salle expedition had ended in disaster. Despite its failure, the expedition gave France a claim to Texas. It also challenged Spain's empire north of the Rio Grande.

 Reading Check **Analyzing Information** Why did Fort St. Louis fail?

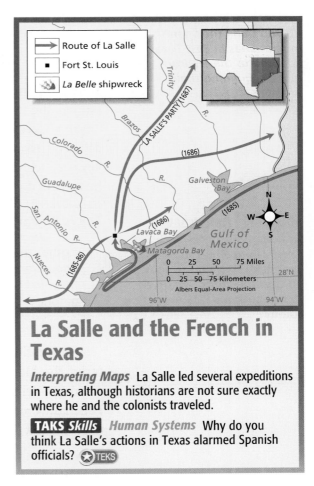

La Salle and the French in Texas

Interpreting Maps La Salle led several expeditions in Texas, although historians are not sure exactly where he and the colonists traveled.

TAKS Skills *Human Systems* Why do you think La Salle's actions in Texas alarmed Spanish officials? ★ TEKS

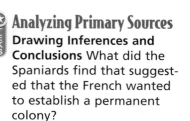

Interpreting the Visual Record

Missions. *The first mission in East Texas, San Francisco de los Tejas, was a simple building similar to this reconstructed mission.* **How do you think the Spanish missionaries in East Texas adapted to the environment in building their missions?** ★TEKS

Analyzing Primary Sources

Drawing Inferences and Conclusions What did the Spaniards find that suggested that the French wanted to establish a permanent colony?

★ The Spanish Search for La Salle

Soon after the founding of Fort St. Louis, the Spanish tried to remove the French from Texas. Officials sent six expeditions by land and five by sea. Attempts at locating the settlement in 1686 and 1687 failed, but the Spanish learned much about the geography of East Texas.

Alonso de León, a Spanish governor, led another expedition in 1689. A Spanish priest, Father **Damián Massanet** (mas-ah-NAY), accompanied the group. The expedition found two French survivors living among a group of American Indians. De León took the men back to Mexico City to be questioned. Spanish officials ordered de León back to Texas to search for the fort. When de León finally found the settlement, he recorded what the Spanish saw.

Texas Voices **❝We found three dead bodies strewn [scattered] in the field, one of which seemed to be a woman by the clothes that still clung to the bones. . . . We looked for more dead bodies, and could not find them, which caused us to conclude that they had been cast [thrown] into the arroyo [creek] and that the alligators, many in number, had eaten them.❞**

—Alonso de León, quoted in *Documents of Texas History*

In addition to finding the French settlement, the Spanish encountered the Hasinai. The Spaniards called the Hasinai by the Indians' word for "friend"—**Tejas** (TAY-hahs). Father Massanet believed that the Hasinai were interested in the establishment of a mission. After further exploration, the Spanish reported what they had learned to the viceroy.

Reading Check Summarizing What did the Spanish accomplish in the search for the French settlement?

★ Spanish Missions in East Texas

Alonso de León and Father Massanet had been impressed by the land and the Tejas. When they returned to Mexico City, they advised the viceroy to set up missions in the region. Spanish officials soon approved the plan. They feared that the French might gain control of Texas if there were no Spanish settlements there.

In early 1690 de León and Father Massanet returned to Texas with several missionaries and more than 100 soldiers. Arriving in the land of the Tejas, the Spanish claimed the region for their king. They then picked a site west of the Neches River. The Spanish set to work building the mission. After only a few days, they had finished building **San Francisco de los Tejas**. The Tejas promised to think about moving into the mission. De León and Father Massanet soon returned to Mexico, leaving three missionaries and three soldiers at the mission. The Tejas and the missionaries were hopeful about the mission's future.

In 1691 Father Massanet and Domingo Terán de los Ríos, the first governor of Texas, arrived in East Texas. Disputes between the two men created tension in the mission. In addition, droughts and floods ruined the mission's crops. Supplies were difficult to get, and the Spanish had to live on corn cakes. The Tejas at the mission ate cow skins to survive.

The Spanish became even more discouraged after discovering that the Tejas did not want religious instruction. An outbreak of disease worsened tensions between the Spaniards and the Tejas, who blamed the Spanish for the deadly disease. The Spaniards realized that they had to leave. On the night of October 25, 1693, the Spanish burned the mission to the ground. They buried the mission bells and fled to Mexico. The first Spanish attempt at settling East Texas ended in failure.

★ Reading Check **Finding the Main Idea** Why did the Spaniards leave East Texas?

 **Section 2 Review** **Questions 1, 2, 3a, 3b, 4**

go.hrw.com Homework Practice Online
keyword: ST3 HP6

① Identify and explain:
- René-Robert Cavelier, Sieur de La Salle
- La Salle expedition
- Matagorda Bay
- Fort St. Louis
- Alonso de León
- Damián Massanet
- Tejas
- San Francisco de los Tejas

② Analyzing Information
Copy the graphic organizer below. Use it to show why the Spanish decided to build a mission in East Texas.

Reasons for a mission
1.
2.

③ Finding the Main Idea
a. Why did La Salle establish Fort St. Louis, and what happened to it?
b. What steps did Spanish officials take to stop French settlement in Texas?

④ Writing and Critical Thinking **TAKS**
Identifying Cause and Effect Write a short article about the founding and failure of the East Texas mission.
Consider the following:
- why it was established
- the challenges it faced

The Spanish Return to Texas

Read to Discover

1. Why did the French send an agent to Texas, and what happened when he arrived?
2. What was the Spanish goal in East Texas?
3. Why did the Spanish settle in the San Antonio River area, and what was the result?

Why It Matters Today

The Spanish tried to protect their hold on Texas by barring foreign trade in the region. Use **CNNfyi.com** or other **current events** sources to learn more about free trade issues or a trade dispute between nations today. Record your findings in your journal.

Identify

- **Francisco Hidalgo**
- **Louis Juchereau de St. Denis**
- **Domingo Ramón**
- **Nuestro Padre San Francisco de los Tejas**
- **Martín de Alarcón**
- **Antonio de San Buenaventura y Olivares**
- **San Antonio de Valero**
- **San Antonio de Béxar**
- **Villa de Béxar**
- **San Fernando de Béxar**
- **El Camino Real**

Many Texas missions had simple altars.

The Story Continues

Father Francisco Hidalgo was a patient but persistent man. Since becoming a Franciscan at the age of 15, he had longed to become a missionary, travel, and spread the Catholic faith. After arriving in New Spain, the young priest heard many stories about Texas. He became determined to go there to teach Texas Indians about Catholicism. Delay after delay prevented Father Hidalgo from reaching them. But he knew that his chance would come.

★ A New French Threat

After the settlement failures in East Texas, the Spanish ignored most of Texas for more than 20 years. Father **Francisco Hidalgo** (ee-DAHL-goh) tried to change that policy. He had served at San Francisco de los Tejas. After that mission was abandoned, Father Hidalgo helped found the San Juan Bautista mission along the Rio Grande, but Father Hidalgo was not content there. He wanted to return to East Texas and work with local American Indians. He repeatedly asked Spanish officials to re-establish the East Texas mission, but they refused. Unwilling to give up, Father Hidalgo eventually looked elsewhere for help. He wrote a letter asking the French governor of Louisiana to help build missions in East Texas. Sending such a letter was a daring move because France and Spain were longtime enemies.

At their trading posts in the Mississippi River valley, the French traded with American Indians for furs. Spain prohibited the French from trading in New Spain. Nonetheless, Governor Cadillac of Louisiana saw Father Hidalgo's letter as a way to begin trading in Texas. In 1713 Cadillac sent **Louis Juchereau de St. Denis** (sand uh nee), an experienced explorer, to East Texas to find Father Hidalgo. In 1713 he built a trading post near the Red River that grew into the town of Natchitoches, Louisiana. St. Denis traveled west through East Texas, but he could not find Father Hidalgo in the region. After trading with some Tejas, he headed to the Spanish missions along the Rio Grande. He arrived at the San Juan Bautista presidio with a load of goods to trade. Faced with a French trader at his doorstep, the Spanish commander of the presidio arrested St. Denis. Commander Diego Ramón treated St. Denis well. The trader enjoyed his stay at the mission, even convincing Ramón's stepgranddaughter to marry him. Eventually, Ramón had to send St. Denis to Mexico City for questioning.

Reading Check **Finding the Main Idea** What action did the French take to begin trading in Texas?

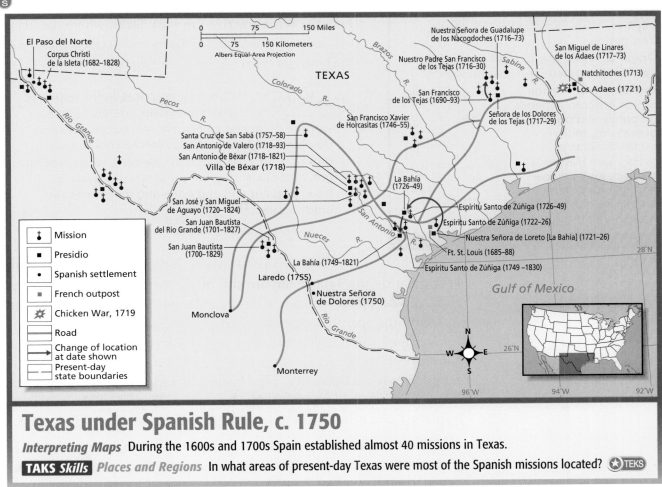

Texas under Spanish Rule, c. 1750

Interpreting Maps During the 1600s and 1700s Spain established almost 40 missions in Texas.

TAKS Skills *Places and Regions* In what areas of present-day Texas were most of the Spanish missions located? ⭐TEKS

Texas Cities

San Antonio

History: Martín de Alarcón, a Spanish official, founded a mission and presidio on the site of the city in 1718. The mission later became known as the Alamo. It became the site of an important battle in the Texas Revolution.

Population in 2000: 1,144,646

Relative Location: South-central Texas on the San Antonio River

Region: South Texas Plains

County: County seat of Bexar County

Special feature: San Antonio, with its historical Spanish architecture and winding River Walk, is a popular U.S. tourist destination.

Origin of name: Mission San Antonio de Valero was named for a Spanish viceroy.

Economy: The economy of San Antonio depends on public and private operations. Military establishments such as Fort Sam Houston, tourism, and medical research play important roles in the city's economy.

★ New East Texas Missions

St. Denis told Spanish officials that he had traveled to Texas to look for Father Hidalgo. The priest was not in East Texas, so St. Denis headed to the Rio Grande to continue his search. It is doubtful that the Spanish officials believed St. Denis. The presence of a French trader in Texas alarmed the officials, who feared that the French were once again a threat to Texas. In addition, the Spanish had heard that the Tejas wanted them to return to East Texas. The Spanish decided it was time to build new missions in East Texas. Father Hidalgo had achieved his goal.

In 1716 Diego Ramón's son, **Domingo Ramón**, led an expedition to East Texas. Even though St. Denis was not a Spaniard, he was hired as the guide. The expedition included Spanish priests, soldiers, civilians, and three French citizens. Some of the soldiers also brought their wives. These women were probably the first female Spanish settlers in Texas. The Spanish brought gifts for the Tejas, hand tools, and seed for crops. In late June the settlers arrived in East Texas, where the Tejas warmly welcomed them. A priest described the meeting between the settlers and the Tejas.

> **Texas Voices** ❝About eight o'clock in the morning thirty-four Indians arrived. . . . We went to greet and embrace them, our hearts overflowing with joy. . . . We . . . served chocolate to them. . . . This day was most pleasing to us, holding out, as it did, such great prospects of attaining [reaching] our end and achieving the purpose so much desired.❞
>
> — Isidro Félix de Espinosa, quoted in *Documents of Texas History*

The Spaniards soon built **Nuestro Padre San Francisco de los Tejas** near the site of the original mission. Father Hidalgo was placed in charge of the mission. With the assistance of St. Denis, the Spanish established five more missions in East Texas. The Tejas helped the Spanish choose sites for the missions. One mission, Nuestra Señora de Guadalupe de los Nacogdoches, was located on the future site of Nacogdoches. The mission San Miguel de Linares de los Adaes was located in present-day Louisiana. To protect the missions, Captain Ramón built the Nuestra Señora de los Dolores de los Tejas presidio.

 Reading Check **Analyzing Information** How did the Spanish re-establish their control over East Texas?

★ The San Antonio Settlements

The Spanish were determined to firmly establish the mission system in East Texas. Officials knew that the first mission failed partly because of its distant location. It was more than 500 miles from the nearest Spanish settlements. Getting supplies to the mission had been difficult. The journey was long and dangerous, with the threat of raids by Texas Indians. As a result, the Spanish in East Texas sometimes even turned to nearby French settlements for supplies. Because of these problems and the experiences of earlier East Texas missions, the Spanish decided to set up an outpost between the East Texas missions and the Rio Grande.

In 1716, officials approved a plan to build a mission-presidio outpost along the San Antonio River. In 1718 **Martín de Alarcón**, the governor of Texas, led a group of colonists to the area. A priest, **Antonio de San Buenaventura y Olivares**, traveled with a separate group. By the beginning of May, both parties had reached the San Antonio River. Near the river, they built **San Antonio de Valero**. This mission was a simple structure made of branches, mud, and straw. The group then moved about a mile away and built a presidio named **San Antonio de Béxar**. The Spanish also established a small civil settlement called **Villa de Béxar**.

The San Antonio River area was a good location for a settlement. Winters were usually mild. Summers were hot but not very humid—unlike those in East Texas. Cottonwood trees dotted the landscape. One Spaniard called it "the most beautiful part of New Spain." The Spaniards built several more missions along the San Antonio River. In 1720 Spanish missionary Antonio Margil de Jesús established San José y San Miguel de Aguayo. It was the finest mission in Texas. A two-story stone building served as the priests' residence. As the years passed, the mission built a sugar mill, where workers made delicious brown sugar cones. Many Indian groups, including the Coahuiltecan, lived and worked at

Missionaries used noise-makers to call mission residents to church services.

1718

Martín de Alarcón establishes a mission and a presidio at the site of present-day San Antonio.

Interpreting the Visual Record

San Antonio. *The town grew as new settlers came to San Antonio, attracted by its good farmland and pleasant climate.* ***Based on this piece of art, what geographic factors do you think affected the growth of San Antonio?*** ★TEKS

Martín de Alarcón
(dates unknown)

Martín de Alarcón arrived in the Americas sometime before 1691. He later became the governor of Spanish Texas. After founding San Antonio, Alarcón set out on a dangerous trip to supply the missions in East Texas. He distributed supplies and talked with the French. Shortly after his journey to East Texas, Alarcón returned to Mexico. **How did Alarcón contribute to Spanish settlement in Texas?** TEKS

the San Antonio missions. These missions soon became ranching centers, with many cattle roaming the area's pastures. They came to be the most successful missions in Texas.

Spanish officials developed a plan to bring immigrants to the San Antonio area. In 1731, 15 families of Canary Islanders arrived at the presidio. These 56 people eventually lived near the presidio in **San Fernando de Béxar**. This settlement had the first organized civil government in Texas. Together with the other missions and presidio, the area made up San Antonio de Béxar. It was commonly called Béxar or San Antonio.

San Antonio became the halfway point on the Texas part of **El Camino Real** (kah-MEE-noh ree-AHL), or "the Royal Road." This road led from the East Texas missions to the southern Rio Grande settlements. It then continued south to Mexico City. Some segments of the road began as trails linking American Indian settlements. Later, the Spanish traveled over El Camino Real to establish and then supply East Texas missions.

El Camino Real was a rough road. Governor Alarcón had traveled along the dangerous road to deliver supplies to the missions of East Texas in the early 1700s. Although the road was rough, the rivers he had to cross caused him even more problems. Alarcón almost drowned crossing one swollen stream. Despite its condition, the road was important because it linked the Texas settlements. It helped the growth of Spanish settlement in Texas, particularly in San Antonio.

Reading Check Summarizing What advantages did the San Antonio settlements have, and why was El Camino Real important to Spanish settlers?

 Section 3 Review TEKS Questions 1, 2, 3a, 3b, 4

go.hrw.com **Homework Practice Online**
keyword: ST3 HP6

1 Identify and explain:
- Francisco Hidalgo
- Louis Juchereau de St. Denis
- Domingo Ramón
- Nuestro Padre San Francisco de los Tejas
- Martín de Alarcón
- Antonio de San Buenaventura y Olivares
- San Antonio de Valero
- San Antonio de Béxar
- Villa de Béxar
- San Fernando de Béxar
- El Camino Real

2 Categorizing
Copy the graphic organizer below. Use it to identify the steps the Spanish took to settle San Antonio.

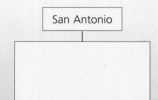
San Antonio

3 Finding the Main Idea
a. Why did St. Denis go to Texas, and how did the Spanish respond?
b. What did the Spanish hope to achieve in East Texas?

4 Writing and Critical Thinking TAKS
Identifying Cause and Effect Write a short story about why and how the Spanish founded the first mission and presidio in San Antonio in 1718.
Consider the following:
- the location of San Antonio and other Spanish settlements
- the events surrounding the founding of the first mission and presidio in San Antonio

War and Expansion

Read to Discover

1. How did the war between France and Spain affect Texas?
2. How did the Apache and the Comanche respond to the mission system?

Why It Matters Today

In the 1600s several European nations had many colonies in the Americas. Use **CNNfyi.com** or other **current events** sources to learn more about these nations and their territories today. Record your findings in your journal.

Identify

- Chicken War
- Marqués de San Miguel de Aguayo
- Aguayo expedition
- La Bahía

The Story Continues

In 1699 a French captain sailed into Pensacola Bay on the coast of western Florida. He was looking for the mouth of the Mississippi River, where he hoped to establish a French colony. But the Spanish had already reached the bay. When the Frenchman asked for permission to explore the area, the Spanish captain refused. The Frenchman protested, but the Spaniard remained firm. Finally, the French expedition left the bay and set up a settlement at what is now Biloxi, Mississippi.

French sailors explored the Gulf Coast in large sailing ships.

★ The Aguayo Expedition

Tensions between France and Spain had been high, and the two countries went to war in 1719. The war soon affected Texas. In June 1719 a French lieutenant and seven soldiers from Natchitoches attacked the nearest Spanish mission, San Miguel de Linares de los Adaes. The two Spaniards there quickly surrendered. The French soldiers gathered up supplies and raided the henhouse. Pleased with the capture of the chickens, the lieutenant tied several to his saddle. That was a mistake. The chickens squawked wildly, the horse reared, and the lieutenant was tossed to the ground. One Spaniard, seeing his chance to escape, ran into the woods. He made his way to a nearby mission. He claimed that French soldiers were marching on East Texas. The news of this **Chicken War** spread quickly. The frightened Spaniards left their missions and the

Antonio Margil de Jesús
(1657–1726)

Antonio Margil de Jesús dedicated his life to missionary work in New Spain. After serving in Mexico and Central America, he went to Texas. There he founded two missions in East Texas in 1717. The Spanish abandoned these missions during the Chicken War. Margil's work continued when he and the fleeing settlers arrived in San Antonio in late 1719. Margil kept the settlers busy. They had soon completed mission San José y San Miguel de Aguayo. In 1722 Margil returned to Mexico. He spent the rest of his life working for the Catholic Church. **Where in Texas did Margil establish missions?** ⭐TEKS

⭐ **Analyzing Primary Sources**
Identifying Points of View
How did the appearance of the American Indians affect the priest?

presidio and fled to San Antonio. The French did not attack any more missions, but the Spanish had already abandoned East Texas.

The Spanish did not abandon East Texas for long. The viceroy ordered the **Marqués de San Miguel de Aguayo**, the governor of Coahuila, to reoccupy the missions. The **Aguayo expedition** set out in 1720 with a large force of some 500 soldiers and 4,000 horses. It also included cattle, goats, and sheep. The expedition arrived in East Texas in 1721. The war between France and Spain had already ended, and the Spaniards quickly reoccupied the missions. Aguayo met with Louis Juchereau de St. Denis, the French commander in the area. The two agreed to separate control of French Louisiana and Spanish Texas. To keep the French out of East Texas, Aguayo built the presidio Nuestra Señora del Pilar de los Adaes. He staffed it with 100 soldiers. The Spanish settlements at the presidio and the mission San Miguel de Linares de los Adaes became known as Los Adaes. Eight years after the founding of the presidio, Los Adaes became the official capital of Spanish Texas.

From Los Adaes, Aguayo moved southwest. He established the mission Nuestra Señora del Espíritu Santo de Zúñiga near Matagorda Bay. A presidio was built nearby. Together these establishments came to be known as **La Bahía**. The mission was built to convert the Karankawa Indians of the area. It was moved farther inland several times in later years. Its final location is near present-day Goliad. After the Aguayo expedition, the Spanish once again had a presence in East Texas.

⭐ **Reading Check** **Identifying Cause and Effect** Why did the Spanish send Aguayo into East Texas, and what was the result?

⭐ Clashes on the Frontier

The Spanish soon faced another conflict when American Indians attacked Spanish settlements during the 1730s and 1740s. The Spanish particularly feared the Apache, an Indian group that had moved into South Texas during the early 1700s. Armed with guns and riding horses, the Apache were a deadly enemy. One missionary described an attack.

 Texas Voices ❝I saw nothing but Indians on every hand . . . arrayed [dressed] in the most horrible attire [clothing]. Besides the paint on their faces, red and black, they were adorned [decorated] with the pelts [skins] and tails of wild beasts, wrapped around them or hanging down from their heads, as well as deer horns.❞

—Miguel de Molina, quoted in *Spanish Texas, 1519–1821*, by Donald E. Chipman

Central Texas missions and San Antonio were hard hit by raids. The attacks increased as the Spanish moved into Apache territory and the Comanche pushed the Apache south toward San Antonio.

Missionaries hoped to convert the Apache and other Central Texas Indians to Catholicism. The Spanish thought this might create more peaceful relations. In 1746 the Franciscans began setting up three missions along the San Gabriel River. A presidio guarded these San Xavier missions. However, the missionaries and the presidio commander did not get along. The tension rapidly grew worse when a smallpox epidemic killed many of the mission Indians and a friar was murdered, probably by some presidio soldiers. With water in short supply and conflict brewing, the Spaniards moved the missions and presidio to another site in 1755.

Many supplies and soldiers from the failed San Xavier settlements ended up at Santa Cruz de San Sabá. This mission was established in 1757, and a presidio was built several miles away. The Spanish had little success converting the Apache, however. One March morning in 1758 a crisis occurred. About 2,000 American Indian enemies of the Apache, including some Comanche, appeared outside the mission gates. They attacked and burned the mission, killing two of the three missionaries. The presidio had fewer than 50 soldiers during the attack. They watched helplessly as survivors of the attack staggered into the presidio. The mission was never rebuilt.

The attack on San Sabá marked the beginning of warfare between the Comanche and the Spanish. The Comanche and the Apache fiercely resisted the Spanish threat to their land and culture. As a result, the Spanish were never able to maintain missions in the land of the Apache or Comanche. After a century of settlement activity in Texas, only a few locations were doing well. These included the San Antonio missions and settlements along the Rio Grande. Despite great effort and expense, Spain controlled only a few areas in Texas.

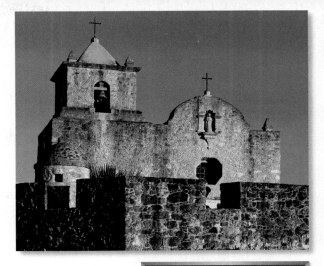

Presidios. *The presidio near Goliad once protected the mission Nuestra Señora del Espíritu Santo de Zúñiga. The presidio moved each time the mission was relocated.* **What features might have helped this presidio protect both its soldiers and the Spanish mission?** TEKS

★ **Reading Check** **Analyzing Information** What problems did the Central Texas missions face?

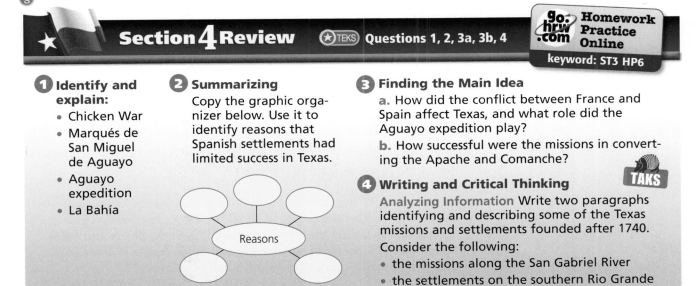

Section 4 Review   TEKS Questions 1, 2, 3a, 3b, 4

go.hrw.com **Homework Practice Online** keyword: ST3 HP6

1 Identify and explain:
- Chicken War
- Marqués de San Miguel de Aguayo
- Aguayo expedition
- La Bahía

2 Summarizing
Copy the graphic organizer below. Use it to identify reasons that Spanish settlements had limited success in Texas.

Reasons

3 Finding the Main Idea
a. How did the conflict between France and Spain affect Texas, and what role did the Aguayo expedition play?
b. How successful were the missions in converting the Apache and Comanche?

4 Writing and Critical Thinking

TAKS

Analyzing Information Write two paragraphs identifying and describing some of the Texas missions and settlements founded after 1740.
Consider the following:
- the missions along the San Gabriel River
- the settlements on the southern Rio Grande

Life in Spanish Texas

Read to Discover

1. What was life like in the Spanish missions and presidios?
2. What was life like for the residents of Spanish settlements?
3. How has Spanish culture influenced present-day Texas?

Define

- *ayuntamiento*
- **alcalde**
- **vaqueros**

Why It Matters Today

Many states in the American Southwest still show signs of a strong Spanish influence. Use **CNNfyi.com** or other **current events** sources to identify one way this influence is felt today. Record your findings in your journal.

Missionaries rang bells to call residents to morning chapel services.

The Story Continues

The mission bells rang as daylight began to brighten the dark Texas sky. Rising from buffalo-skin mattresses, American Indians walked to the chapel. The priests counted the churchgoers as they entered. Then the congregation chanted and prayed. Later, the Spaniards and the Indians rose to sing a song called *El Alabado*. It told the churchgoers to "Lift your heart and exalt [praise] Him [God]." It was the start of another day at a Spanish mission in Texas.

★ Life in the Missions

The Spanish wanted Texas Indians to live in the missions and learn the Spanish way of life. In the missions, life followed a daily pattern of worship and work. The day started at dawn with religious services. For at least an hour, priests taught mission Indians about the Catholic faith. Then the Indians' workday began under the direction of the priests and soldiers. One priest described the work.

Texas Voices ❝The labor of the Indians is to plant the fields, look after the cattle, to water the crops, to clear away weeds, and to gather their grain, to [build] their dwellings and other buildings. . . . Some work at weaving and in the forges [ironmaking areas], and others work as carpenters and bricklayers.❞

—Isidro Félix de Espinosa, quoted in *Spanish Expeditions into Texas, 1689–1768*, by Nancy Haston Foster

American Indian men tended crops of beans, corn, and cotton. The women made pottery, cared for the livestock, wove cloth, and ran the mission kitchen. The day ended with prayers and dinner—usually thin cereal. When they were not in church or working, mission Indians also learned Spanish songs and dances. The Spanish hoped these lessons would encourage Indians to abandon their traditional celebrations. This strategy rarely worked, as one missionary complained. "When the ministers are not watching them they [the Indians] go off to the woods, and there hold their dances." Some Indians also left the missions during hunting or fishing seasons. Most Texas Indians attempted to keep their own culture and traditions despite pressure from the missionaries.

Mission life was often harsh. Typically, the dwellings were uncomfortable, with dirt floors and open windows. People living at the mission sometimes went hungry. In the East Texas missions food was often scarce. One missionary wrote about the lack of food. "The meals consisted of nothing more than a little purslane [a wild herb] seasoned with salt and pepper." He noted that Indians sometimes helped in needy times. "Once in a while the Indians would give us a little corn, beans of a certain kind, and some wild fruits."

Conditions were better at other missions, particularly in San Antonio. By 1750, one mission had 2,000 cattle and 1,000 sheep. Mission Indians there harvested 2,400 bushels of corn that year. By 1780, Indians were irrigating the mission's crops. Missions near present-day El Paso and San Antonio thrived because Indians there adopted Spanish cultures. Other missions, such as those in East Texas and La Bahía, helped the Spanish gain a presence in the borderlands.

Reading Check **Evaluating** How did some Texas Indians adapt to Spanish culture while maintaining their Indian traditions?

★ Life in the Presidios

Missions were more likely to succeed if they had a presidio nearby. These military outposts were built of adobe, stone, and timber. Presidios had a chapel, barracks for soldiers, storage rooms, and a headquarters building. Sometimes a stockade, or wall, surrounded these buildings.

The soldiers in the presidios had several duties. They guarded the missions and helped supervise the American Indians who lived there. At times, the soldiers disagreed with the missionaries about how to treat the mission Indians. The missionaries and soldiers also argued about who had the higher authority in the borderlands. This tension added to the hardship of living in the small, isolated presidios.

CONNECTING TO
THE ARTS

Mission Architecture
Many of the early mission chapels in Texas were simple, rough structures made of wood. As the Spanish continued to settle in Texas, they began using stone to build mission villages. The buildings had baroque, or fancy, details. Carvings and sculptures decorated arched windows and doorways. Soaring bell towers stood high against the Texas sky. Mission San José in San Antonio is often called the Queen of Texas Missions. It includes a domed chapel and bright wall paintings. It also has a sculpted window known as Rosa's Window. **Why might Spanish missionaries have wanted to create beautiful and fancy chapels?** TEKS

Interpreting the Visual Record

Dances. *To take a break from the rough work of ranching and maintaining early settlements in Texas, Spaniards went to dances.* **Based on the clothing the men are wearing, what type of work do you think they did?**

Although their work was risky, the soldiers received low wages. Many soldiers fell into debt because their pay was late in coming. In addition, the soldiers had poor equipment. Their uniforms were often worn and ragged. Despite the harsh conditions, some soldiers brought their families with them. Eventually, a few of these families moved from the presidios and helped start Spanish settlements.

 Reading Check **Comparing** How was life in the presidios similar to life in the missions?

★ Life in the Settlements

Texas settlements had a diverse population of Spaniards, American Indians, and African Americans. Most of the Spanish had moved north from Mexico in search of good land for farming or ranching. Some settlers were former soldiers who had married Texas Indians. Although a few free African Americans lived in the settlements, most African Americans were brought to Texas as slaves.

A few permanent Texas towns grew from the mission system. These towns were scattered over a huge area. As they grew, these Spanish settlements shared some similarities with modern towns. Many had well-defined streets leading past houses and government buildings. There were many different stores, including bakeries and candle shops. In San Antonio, by far the largest settlement, dams were built to create an irrigation system of canals. San Antonio was the first town that allowed people to participate in their government. When the Canary Islanders first came, they were given lands and a charter for their settlement, San Fernando de Béxar. The *ayuntamiento* (ah-yoon-tah-MYEN-toh), or governing council, enforced royal and local laws. The **alcalde** (ahl-KAHL-day), served as mayor, sheriff, and judge of small cases. The viceroy in Mexico City had authority over all settlements in New Spain, including Texas. The governor represented the viceroy in Texas.

The economy of the settlements was mostly based on farming and ranching. Both men and women helped with the planting and harvesting of crops. The cattle business helped San Antonio and other towns grow. **Vaqueros** (vah-CARE-ohz), or cowboys, worked on ranches near the settlements. Vaqueros were well known for their skilled horse riding and cattle handling. The Spanish also used their skills at horse riding to provide entertainment. Horse racing was a popular event. Most social activities centered around the family and the church. Religious holidays offered opportunities for worship and socializing. On other special occasions, residents gathered at fandangos, or dances. As the Spanish settlements grew, they developed more cultural activities.

The Spanish strongly influenced the culture and history of Texas. Some Spanish missions are still active churches. The restored La Bahía presidio can be seen near present-day Goliad. The Spanish also laid out the first Texas roads, such as El Camino Real. Many of the place-names of cities and natural features such as rivers are Spanish.

Texas traditions reflect their Spanish influence. For example, the Spanish had introduced horses and cattle ranching to the Americas. They settled in Mexico and then moved north, bringing cattle with them. Cowboys later used the equipment developed by the vaqueros. Spanish law was also handed down. For example, early Spanish laws protected the property rights of women. Women continued to benefit from these laws when Texas became part of the United States. Spanish architecture, art, food, language, and music are alive in Texas today.

CONNECTING TO Music

Romances Corridos

Romances corridos, or folk songs, were very popular in Spanish settlements in the 1700s. These songs, sometimes accompanied by guitar, dealt with many different subjects—love, heartbreak, and bravery. *Romances corridos* continue to appeal to many Texans. The tunes have new words. Even so, they can be traced to the songs that Spanish settlers sang to entertain themselves on the frontier. **How are *romances corridos* from frontier times similar to many popular songs of today?**

The Metropolitan Museum of Art

⭐ **Reading Check Drawing Inferences and Conclusions** What influence did the Spanish have on Texas place-names and the cattle industry?

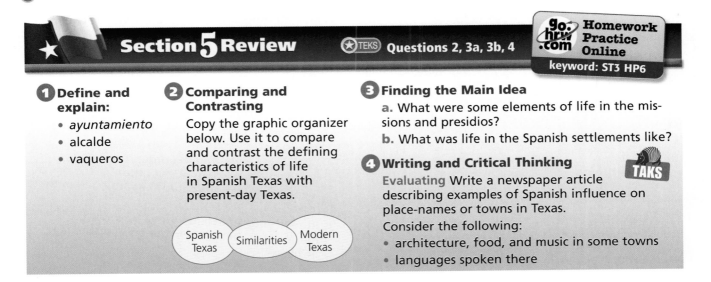

Section 5 Review

⭐TEKS Questions 2, 3a, 3b, 4

go.hrw.com **Homework Practice Online** keyword: ST3 HP6

1 Define and explain:
- *ayuntamiento*
- alcalde
- vaqueros

2 Comparing and Contrasting
Copy the graphic organizer below. Use it to compare and contrast the defining characteristics of life in Spanish Texas with present-day Texas.

Spanish Texas — Similarities — Modern Texas

3 Finding the Main Idea
a. What were some elements of life in the missions and presidios?
b. What was life in the Spanish settlements like?

4 Writing and Critical Thinking
Evaluating Write a newspaper article describing examples of Spanish influence on place-names or towns in Texas.
Consider the following:
- architecture, food, and music in some towns
- languages spoken there

TAKS

The Chapter at a Glance

Examine the following visual summary of the chapter. Then use it to create an oral presentation describing life in Spanish Texas.

Spanish Missions in Texas

Missions were built to spread the Catholic faith to American Indians and to gain control of the frontier.

Presidios in Texas

Presidios were built to protect the missions and guard against French forces and American Indians on the frontier.

Spanish Settlements in Texas

Spanish settlements grew near missions and presidios, providing valuable supplies. These settlements reinforced the Spanish presence in Texas.

Identifying People and Ideas

Use the following terms or people in historically significant sentences.

1. missions
2. Pueblo Revolt
3. La Salle expedition
4. San Francisco de los Tejas
5. Francisco Hidalgo
6. Domingo Ramón
7. San Antonio de Valero
8. El Camino Real
9. Marqués de San Miguel de Aguayo
10. *ayuntamiento*

Understanding Main Ideas

Section 1 (pages 112–114)

1. How did the Spanish try to control the borderlands?

Section 2 (pages 115–119)

2. How did René-Robert Cavelier, Sieur de La Salle change Spanish policy in Texas?

Section 3 (pages 120–124)

3. Why is 1718 an important year in Texas history?

Section 4 (pages 125–127)

4. How did the Chicken War lead to the Aguayo expedition, and what were the effects of this expedition?

Section 5 (pages 128–131)

5. What was life like for the Spanish and American Indians in the missions?

6. Identify some examples of Spanish influence on modern-day Texas.

You Be the Historian

Reviewing Themes

1. **Culture** How did the Spanish attempt to change American Indian culture?
2. **Geography** How did San Antonio's climate and location help the settlement become successful?
3. **Global Relations** How did the war between France and Spain affect Texas?

TAKS Practice: **Thinking Critically**

1. **Comparing** Compare how the French and Spanish interacted with Texas Indians.
2. **Sequencing** Identify the order in which the Spanish built missions in the different regions of Texas, and what prompted them to build in those regions.
3. **Identifying Points of View** How did the missionaries' beliefs affect Spanish settlement in Texas?

Interpreting Maps ⭐TEKS

Study the map below. Then use the information on the map to answer the questions that follow.

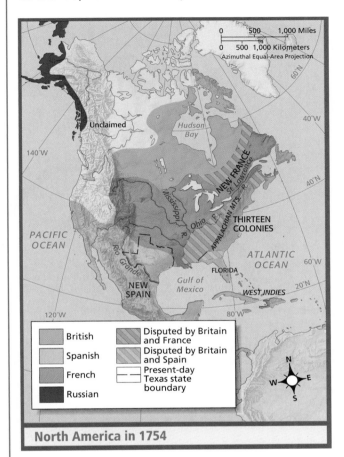

British

Spanish

French

Russian

Disputed by Britain and France

Disputed by Britain and Spain

Present-day Texas state boundary

North America in 1754

1. Which of the following statements is correct?
   a. France and Spain claimed the same area.
   b. England and Russia claimed the same area.
   c. Spain and France shared a border.
   d. Spain had no territory in present-day Texas.

2. Which countries claimed parts of present-day Texas?

Analyzing Primary Sources ⭐TEKS

Read the following quote about the presidio at San Sabá. Then answer the questions.

"The ease with which the enemy has been seen to maintain himself in its vicinity [area] . . . will some-day suggest to them the ease with which this pre-sidio can be surrounded. . . . Their numbers will not be small; the captain states that at times as many as three thousand [American Indians] have come to attack the presidio."

3. Which of the following statements best describes the author's point of view?
   a. The American Indians might soon realize how easy it would be to capture the presidio.
   b. The Spanish should not abandon the presidio because it is easy to defend.
   c. The Spanish outnumber the Indians.
   d. The Indians will never attack the presidio.

4. Based on the chapter, do you think the author's concerns were reasonable?

Alternative Assessment

Linking to Community ⭐TEKS

Create a list of all the things in your community that have Spanish place-names. Pick four of those names. Then do some research about the origins and meanings of these names. Finally, create a visual display about the place-names you have found. If the place-name is named for someone, be sure to include information about that person. Include any interesting facts related to the place-names. Present what you have learned to your class.

BUILDING YOUR Portfolio

📝 internet connect

Internet Activity: go.hrw.com
KEYWORD: ST3 TX6 ⭐TEKS

Access the Internet through the HRW Go site to research how people from different racial, ethnic, and religious groups maintain their cultural heritage while adapting to the larger Texas culture. Complete the interactive activity on cultural diversity. Write your answers in the text box provided. Be sure to use standard grammar, spelling, sentence structure, and punctuation.

CHAPTER 7

Conflicts of Empire

(1760–1821)

Spanish priest Juan Agustín Morfi
wrote an early history of Texas.

American Indians
battled Spanish
forces in Texas.

TEXAS

1766 The Marqués de Rubí expedition begins.

1779 Antonio Gil Ybarbo founds the town of Nacogdoches in East Texas.

1783 Spanish priest Juan Agustín Morfi, author of the *History of Texas, 1673–1779*, dies.

1791 Philip Nolan, a U.S. citizen, receives permission to capture wild horses in Texas.

1760	1770	1780	1790

U.S. and WORLD

1763 France, Great Britain, and Spain sign the Treaty of Paris, officially ending the Seven Years' War.

1775 The American Revolution begins.

1789 The French Revolution begins.

American Patriots fight
against British forces.

The Granger Collection, New York

Build on What You Know

The Spanish tried to control Texas by building missions, presidios, and small towns. When the French were no longer a threat, Spanish officials lost interest in Texas. However, Spain soon faced new threats to its control of Texas and the rest of Mexico.

The Granger Collection, New York

José Bernardo Gutiérrez de Lara led the Republican Army of the North against the Spanish forces.

Mexican rebels fought to win independence from Spain.

1819 U.S. citizen James Long and a small force invade Texas, only to be defeated by Spanish forces.

1821 Mexico, which includes Texas, wins its independence from Spain.

1800   1810   1820

1803 France sells Louisiana to the United States. The purchase doubles the nation's size.

1810 Father Miguel Hidalgo y Costilla's Grito de Dolores, or "Cry of Dolores," sparks Mexico's War of Independence.

1821 Venezuela joins other Latin American nations in winning independence from Spain.

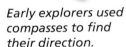

Early explorers used compasses to find their direction.

You Be the Historian

Themes
Journal

What's Your Opinion? Do you **agree** or **disagree** with the following statements? Support your point of view in your journal.

- **Economics** Economic ties promote goodwill between nations.
- **Geography** Changing borders do not affect national policy.
- **Global Relations** National leaders and other individuals can dramatically influence politics in other countries.

If you were there . . .
Would you join the movement for independence from Spain?

Changes in Spanish Texas

Read to Discover

1. What were the results of the Marqués de Rubí report?
2. How did relations between American Indians and Spaniards in Texas change during the late 1700s?

Why It Matters Today

Settlers in East Texas migrated to new homes in the 1770s. Use CNNfyi.com or other **current events** sources to find information about migration today. Record your findings in your journal.

Define

- cede

Identify

- **Treaty of Paris**
- **Marqués de Rubí**
- **Tejanos**
- **Antonio Gil Ybarbo**
- **Nacogdoches**
- **Athanase de Mézières**

Guns were used by groups fighting on the Texas frontier.

The Story Continues

At the San Sabá presidio, Colonel Diego Ortiz Parrilla was worried. War had broken out between British and French colonists northeast of Texas. Parrilla told Spanish officials that he had heard rumors about the fighting. The British and French were giving guns to the Wichita. American Indians with guns posed a serious threat to Spain's hold on Texas. Already, armed Indians had attacked his fort. Parrilla urged officials to strengthen the weak Texas defenses.

★ The Marqués de Rubí Report

In 1754 war had begun between France and Great Britain over control of the Ohio River valley. This conflict was called the French and Indian War. The fighting soon spread to Europe, resulting in the Seven Years' War. Fearing Britain's growing power, Spain sided with France in 1762. A year later the British defeated the French. The results of this war changed the map of North America.

The 1763 **Treaty of Paris** required France and Spain to **cede**, or officially give, territory to Britain. France gave up Canada and all its claims east of the Mississippi River. Spain ceded Florida. Under a separate treaty, Spain gained New Orleans and all French territory west of the Mississippi River. With the loss of this huge region, called Louisiana, the French threat to Texas was gone. France had no land left on the mainland of North America. Britain and Spain were now the main European powers on the continent.

With the changes to its empire, Spain decided to inspect its northern borderlands. In 1766 the **Marqués de Rubí** began an inspection tour of the region's presidios. As he traveled through Texas the next year, he grew increasingly concerned about conditions there. Most of the presidios needed repairs and were staffed by soldiers who lived in poverty, often without decent uniforms or equipment. One soldier reported, "This company lacks arms, horses, coats, and in a word everything necessary to carry out its obligations [duties]."

Rubí found better conditions at La Bahía and San Antonio de Béxar. Most other Texas missions and presidios were struggling, however. Rubí also noted that Spanish attempts to befriend and convert the Apache had failed. Enemies of the Apache, such as the Comanche, now saw the Spanish as enemies.

In all, Rubí spent some two years and traveled more than 7,000 miles touring northern New Spain. He understood—as did many Spanish officers stationed on the frontier—that Spain did not have the power, wealth, and people necessary to hold such a huge, remote region. In 1768 Rubí returned to Mexico City and issued a report. He urged Spain to pull back to the "real" frontier. To protect this frontier, he suggested running a string of 15 forts, each about 100 miles apart, from lower California to southern Texas. Only San Antonio and Sante Fe would remain north of this line of forts. Rubí did not think that a Spanish presence in East Texas was needed because the area no longer bordered French land. He recommended the following for Texas.

1. Spain should abandon all missions and presidios except those at La Bahía and San Antonio.

2. San Antonio should then replace Los Adaes as the capital of Texas.

3. The Spanish population in East Texas should be moved to San Antonio to strengthen the defenses of the settlement and missions there.

4. The Spanish should befriend the Comanche and use their help in fighting the Apache.

Reading Check **Summarizing** Why did Marqués de Rubí recommend withdrawing from much of Texas?

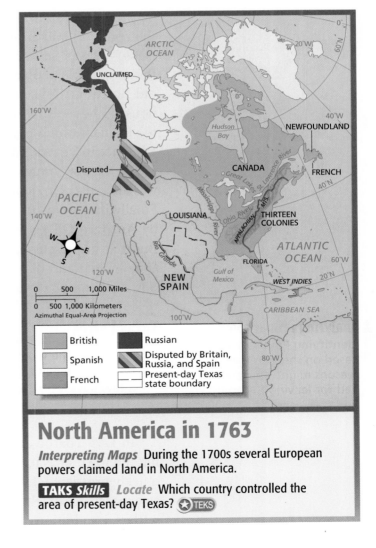

British
Spanish
French
Russian
Disputed by Britain, Russia, and Spain
Present-day Texas state boundary

North America in 1763

Interpreting Maps During the 1700s several European powers claimed land in North America.

TAKS Skills *Locate* Which country controlled the area of present-day Texas? **TEKS**

Antonio Gil Ybarbo and others founded Nacogdoches.

★ Changes in Texas Policies

The government approved Rubí's recommendations. In 1773, officials began the withdrawal from East Texas. Several hundred settlers lived in the region in and around Los Adaes. They included **Tejanos** (tay-HAH-nohs)—Texas settlers of Spanish descent—French, and American Indians. These people had established homes, farms, and ranches and did not want to leave. One man recalled how an official "went from house to house, driving the people from them." Some settlers died during the hard, three-month trek to San Antonio.

Once in San Antonio, which became the capital of Texas in the early 1770s, the newcomers were unhappy. They found that the best farmland was already taken. Many grew homesick and began asking to go home. Finally they were allowed to return east as far as the Trinity River. Led by **Antonio Gil Ybarbo** (ee-BAHR-boh), in 1774 the group founded Bucareli in present-day Madison County. At first, Bucareli prospered. Comanche raids, disease, and flooding soon became serious problems, however. Ybarbo described the situation in a letter.

Analyzing Primary Sources
Identifying Points of View
Based on the letter, what reasons might Ybarbo have had for leaving Bucareli?

Texas Voices ❝On the night of February 14, the river went out of its banks and inundated [flooded] everything on both sides. . . . [The women and children] were got out on boards and doors and taken to the highest point in the vicinity [area], where a few days later Comanches fell upon us.❞

—Antonio Gil Ybarbo, quoted in *Documents of Texas History*

In 1779 Ybarbo and the others decided to move farther east, founding the town of **Nacogdoches** on the site of an old mission. The town quickly prospered. It was set deep in the Piney Woods and thus was not as exposed to attack from American Indians that were hostile toward settlers. In addition, the Tejas who lived in the area were friendly to the

Spanish. Nacogdoches developed a brisk trade with Louisiana and nearby Texas Indians. Although Spain did not allow such trade, Nacogdoches was far from officials in San Antonio. The town soon became the main gateway for people and goods entering Texas from Louisiana.

Spanish policies in regard to American Indians changed during this time. The Spanish mission system had failed to secure peaceful relations with Plains Indians in Texas. Officials decided to copy the more successful French policy of befriending American Indians by trading with them and giving them gifts. **Athanase de Mézières** (mayz-yer), the son-in-law of Louis Juchereau de St. Denis, was chosen to direct the new Texas Indian policy. Mézières was a good choice. He had experience dealing with Indians and spoke several Indian languages. Mézières lost no time in contacting Texas Indians. During the 1770s he established peace with several northern Indian groups. Then in 1779 he was thrown from his horse and soon died.

Despite the death of Mézières, in 1785 Spanish and Comanche leaders signed a peace treaty. The Comanche agreed to stop raiding Spanish settlements in return for yearly gifts. These gifts included items such as beads, clothes, mirrors, and shoes. After a while, the Spanish even gave the Comanche guns. The treaty maintained a degree of peace with the Comanche for some 30 years.

Apache attacks in Texas continued, however. One Spanish official called the Apache "the enemies most to be feared [partly] because of their . . . knowledge of our strength [defenses]." In 1790 a large Spanish army joined with Comanche, Wichita, and other American Indian allies. At Soledad Creek, west of San Antonio, this force won a major victory over the Apache. This loss weakened Apache strength in Texas for many years.

Antonio Gil Ybarbo
(1729–1809)

Antonio Gil Ybarbo was born at Los Adaes. As an adult, he established a large and prosperous ranch, El Lobanillo, in present-day Sabine County. The ranch also served as a center for trade with American Indians and residents of Louisiana. Ybarbo became an important leader. In recognition, Spanish officials made him lieutenant governor, chief justice, and captain of the militia at Nacogdoches. **What role did Ybarbo play in Spain's colonization of Texas?** ⭐TEKS

⭐ **Reading Check** **Sequencing** List in order what happened to the East Texas settlers from 1773 to 1779.

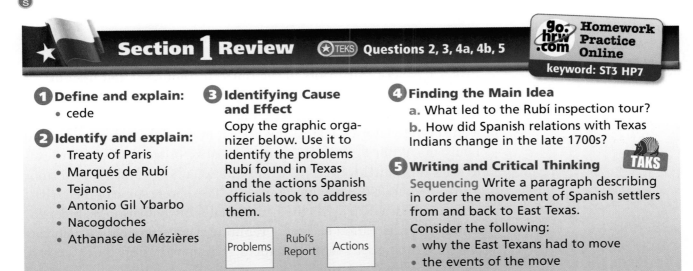

Section 1 Review ⭐TEKS Questions 2, 3, 4a, 4b, 5

Homework Practice Online

keyword: ST3 HP7

1 Define and explain:
• cede

2 Identify and explain:
• Treaty of Paris
• Marqués de Rubí
• Tejanos
• Antonio Gil Ybarbo
• Nacogdoches
• Athanase de Mézières

3 Identifying Cause and Effect
Copy the graphic organizer below. Use it to identify the problems Rubí found in Texas and the actions Spanish officials took to address them.

Problems	Rubí's Report	Actions

4 Finding the Main Idea
a. What led to the Rubí inspection tour?
b. How did Spanish relations with Texas Indians change in the late 1700s?

5 Writing and Critical Thinking TAKS
Sequencing Write a paragraph describing in order the movement of Spanish settlers from and back to East Texas.
Consider the following:
• why the East Texans had to move
• the events of the move

Disputes with the United States

Read to Discover

1. How did Spain contribute to the American Revolution, and why did the new nation threaten Texas?
2. How did the Louisiana Purchase affect Texas?

Why It Matters Today

In 1776 the United States declared its independence and established a republic. Use **CNNfyi.com** or other **current events** sources to learn about democracy in other countries. Record your findings in your journal.

Define
- republic
- diplomats

Identify
- Bernardo de Gálvez
- Louisiana Purchase
- Simón de Herrera
- James Wilkinson
- Neutral Ground
- Adams-Onís Treaty

The Story Continues

USA 15c

The Granger Collection, New York

Gen. Bernardo de Gálvez
Battle of Mobile 1780

Bernardo de Gálvez's victories gave the Patriots control of the Mississippi River.

Bernardo de Gálvez eyed the British fort in Pensacola, Florida, determined to take it at all costs. If he did, Spain would gain control of Florida. Gálvez directed the 7,000 soldiers and 35 ships at his command to begin the attack. Inside the fort the 1,600 British troops were not easily defeated. They held out for two months. Then on May 9, 1781, a huge explosion ripped through the fort—a Spanish shell had hit the main gunpowder site. Gálvez added another victory to his list.

★ The Growing U.S. Threat

In 1775, American Patriots in the thirteen colonies began fighting for independence from Great Britain. Later, Spain joined the fight against the British. **Bernardo de Gálvez**, the governor of Spanish Louisiana, won several victories against the British in the Bahamas, Florida, and Louisiana. While fighting in Louisiana, Gálvez ordered officials in Texas to send him cattle to feed his troops. Between 1779 and 1782, Tejanos drove some 10,000 cattle into Louisiana. These were some of the earliest Texas cattle drives. In 1783 the United States officially won its independence. The new nation became a **republic**, a government in which voters elect officials to represent them. The new nation quickly grew, leading some Spanish officials to see it as a threat.

U.S. settlers soon pushed to the Mississippi River. Without permission, some continued on into Spanish Louisiana as far as the Red River. Few Spanish settlers lived in upper Louisiana or East Texas. In 1783 one Spaniard criticized this sparse settlement in Texas.

Texas Voices

"All the souls, which on our part, populate such a rich and vast province [area], are to be found in one villa [town], two presidios, . . . six ranches, seven missions and . . . Bucareli. . . . If one thinks about the millions of souls who could maintain themselves there, . . . the fertility of the land . . . one would not see this abandon [lack of settlement] without indifference."

—Father Juan Agustín Morfi, quoted in *Spanish Texas, 1519–1810,* by David M. Vigness

Spanish officials in Louisiana decided to allow U.S. immigration to boost the population. But officials in Texas put troops at Nacogdoches to keep unwanted foreigners out. As the U.S. population grew, Spain watched anxiously. International events soon increased Spain's concerns. In 1800 France forced Spain to return Louisiana and then sold it to the United States for $15 million in 1803. The land deal, known as the **Louisiana Purchase**, doubled the size of the young nation.

★ **Reading Check** **Finding the Main Idea** Why did some Spanish officials see the United States as a threat to Spain's colonies?

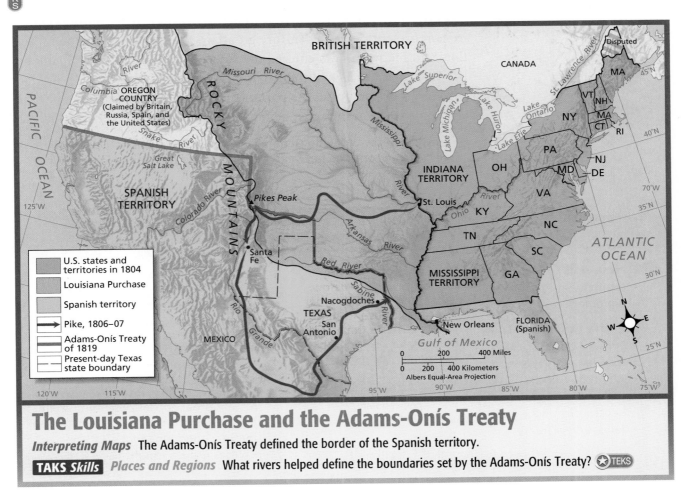

The Louisiana Purchase and the Adams-Onís Treaty

Interpreting Maps The Adams-Onís Treaty defined the border of the Spanish territory.

TAKS Skills *Places and Regions* What rivers helped define the boundaries set by the Adams-Onís Treaty? ★TEKS

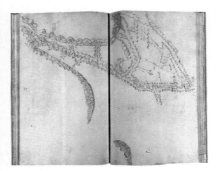

Zebulon Pike's journal includes a map prepared during his travels.

★ Border Disputes in Texas

The Spanish were alarmed by the Louisiana Purchase—the United States now bordered New Spain. A dispute quickly arose over the undefined boundaries of Louisiana. Some U.S. officials believed its western boundary was the Rio Grande and that Louisiana included Texas. Spanish officials strongly disagreed. They claimed the land at least to the Arroyo Hondo, a small stream between Natchitoches and the Sabine River. The Spanish began massing troops in East Texas.

Even more U.S. settlers began moving into Louisiana. One Spaniard commented, "Wherever these Americans go, they spread out like oil upon a cloth." Meanwhile, U.S. explorer Zebulon Pike set out for the upper Arkansas and Red Rivers in 1806. Spanish soldiers captured him near the upper Rio Grande and accused him of spying. After his release Pike wrote a report describing Texas as a land full of abundant game, herds of mustangs, and wild cattle. The report increased U.S. interest in the region.

In late 1806 Spanish lieutenant colonel **Simón de Herrera** met with General **James Wilkinson**, commander of U.S. forces in Louisiana. The two agreed to make the disputed territory neutral, or a region not belonging to either side. Both nations would stay out of this **Neutral Ground** until **diplomats** could meet to set an official border. Diplomats represent countries in foreign affairs. Despite the agreement, settlers and many outlaws entered the Neutral Ground. In 1819 Spain and the United States signed the **Adams-Onís Treaty**, setting the boundary between their territories. As part of the terms, the United States gave up all claims to Texas in exchange for the Neutral Ground and Florida.

★ **Reading Check** **Making Generalizations and Predictions** Do you think conflict will continue between New Spain and the United States? Why?

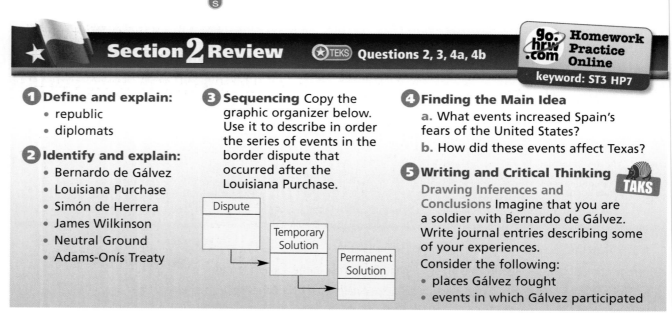

★ Section 2 Review ★TEKS Questions 2, 3, 4a, 4b

go.hrw.com Homework Practice Online
keyword: ST3 HP7

① **Define and explain:**
• republic
• diplomats

② **Identify and explain:**
• Bernardo de Gálvez
• Louisiana Purchase
• Simón de Herrera
• James Wilkinson
• Neutral Ground
• Adams-Onís Treaty

③ **Sequencing** Copy the graphic organizer below. Use it to describe in order the series of events in the border dispute that occurred after the Louisiana Purchase.

Dispute

Temporary Solution

Permanent Solution

④ **Finding the Main Idea**
a. What events increased Spain's fears of the United States?
b. How did these events affect Texas?

⑤ **Writing and Critical Thinking**
Drawing Inferences and Conclusions Imagine that you are a soldier with Bernardo de Gálvez. Write journal entries describing some of your experiences.
Consider the following:
• places Gálvez fought
• events in which Gálvez participated

Unrest and Revolution

Read to Discover

1. How did Philip Nolan affect events in Texas?
2. What did the Gutiérrez-Magee expedition achieve?
3. What filibuster activity occurred along the Gulf?

Why It Matters Today

In the late 1700s some U.S. citizens fought to free Texas and Mexico from Spain. Use **CNNfyi.com** or other **current events** sources to find information about U.S. involvement in foreign conflicts today. Record your findings in your journal.

Define

- filibusters
- siege

Identify

- **Philip Nolan**
- **Miguel Hidalgo y Costilla**
- **Republican Army of the North**
- **Jean Lafitte**
- **James Long**
- **Jane Long**

The Story Continues

To Philip Nolan, the mustangs roaming the Texas plains gleamed like gold. Horses were valuable items, and in Texas, they ran free. All you had to do was catch them. Nolan became a mustanger, capturing wild horses in Texas and driving them to Louisiana. There he sold them at a hefty profit. Then Spanish officials heard rumors of a U.S. plot to invade northern New Spain. Was Nolan a U.S. spy?

Horses were highly valued in early Texas.

★ The Philip Nolan Expeditions

At first, Spanish officials thought that **Philip Nolan** was searching for wealth. Nolan, a U.S. citizen who worked for James Wilkinson, had begun coming to Texas in 1791 as a mustang trader. Nolan entered Texas three times with permission, but in time, some Spanish officials grew suspicious of him. They heard rumors that Nolan was spying for Wilkinson.

In late 1800 Nolan and some 20 men returned to Texas, this time without permission. Spanish soldiers were sent to arrest them. About 40 miles northwest of Waco, they found the mustangers' camp. Nolan resisted arrest and was killed. Most of his men were captured, tried, and imprisoned. Only one, Ellis P. Bean, lived to return to the United States. Whatever Nolan's motives, his actions increased Spanish fears of U.S. expansion. A letter to the Texas governor expressed these concerns.

Philip Nolan's group clashed with Spanish soldiers in Texas.

Analyzing Primary Sources

Supporting a Point of View Do you think citizens have the right to declare independence from a government? Support your answer.

Texas Voices

❝The king [of Spain] has been informed . . . that the United States has ordered emissaries [agents] to move here and work to subvert [threaten] the population. . . . Avoid the entry of any foreigner or any suspected person.❞

—Pedro de Nava, quoted in *Spanish Texas, 1519–1821,* by Donald E. Chipman

In the early 1800s, Spanish suspicions increased because of what the Spanish called *filibusteros,* or military adventurers. Most **filibusters** wanted to free Texas or all of Mexico from Spain. Some wanted Texas to be a separate country or to join the United States. Other filibusters were looking for adventure or quick wealth.

Reading Check **Identifying Points of View** Why did Spanish officials grow suspicious of Philip Nolan?

★ The Gutiérrez-Magee Expedition

A growing movement for independence emerged in New Spain in the early 1800s. On September 16, 1810, Father **Miguel Hidalgo y Costilla** (ee-DAHL-goh ee kaws-TEE-yah), a priest in Dolores, Mexico, rang a church bell and called for an end to Spanish rule. "Will you not defend your religion and rights as true patriots? Long live our Lady of Guadalupe! Death to bad government! Death to the Spaniards!" This Grito de Dolores, or "Cry of Dolores," sparked a war for Mexican independence. Father Hidalgo soon led an army of more than 50,000. Support grew as this army marched across Mexico. Then in 1811, Spanish soldiers captured and executed Father Hidalgo.

Others continued the fight. José Bernardo Gutiérrez de Lara had gone to the United States to raise money and support for the rebellion. After Father Hidalgo's death, Gutiérrez decided to attack Texas. He hoped to use Texas as a base from which to continue fighting for

That's Interesting!

Goliad's Spanish Name

La Bahía's new name, Goliad, honored Father Hidalgo, the priest who first led the movement for Mexican independence. *Goliad* was a re-ordering of the letters in *Hidalgo,* without the letter *h.*

Mexican independence. With the secret support of the United States, Gutiérrez went to Louisiana to raise a private army. There, a U.S. agent introduced him to Augustus William Magee, a U.S. Army officer. Magee resigned from the army and joined Gutiérrez. The two soon raised about 130 volunteers, many of them U.S. citizens. Gutiérrez and Magee named this force the **Republican Army of the North**.

Flying a solid green flag, the Gutiérrez-Magee expedition invaded Texas in August 1812 and quickly took Nacogdoches. More volunteers, including many Tejanos, joined the army. In mid-September, the army headed to La Bahía, capturing the presidio there. Soon, some 800 Spanish soldiers laid **siege** to the fort. A siege is a military blockade of a city or fort. The filibuster force held the fort through the winter. Magee died during this time, and another U.S. volunteer, Samuel Kemper, took charge. The Spanish army failed to take the fort. The rebel army had grown to about 800 members. In March 1813 it attacked and defeated a Spanish force of 1,200 near San Antonio, capturing the town.

Reading Check **Drawing Inferences and Conclusions** Why do you think so many U.S. citizens joined Gutiérrez and Magee?

★ The Green Flag over Texas

On April 6, 1813, José Bernardo Gutiérrez de Lara issued a document declaring Texas independence. At a celebration, he spoke of freedom. "The bonds that kept us bound to the dominion [government] of Spain have been severed [broken] forever; we are free and independent."

The Republican Army's military success was soon overshadowed by problems. Several Spanish prisoners, including the Texas governor, were brutally executed. Many volunteers were upset by these executions. As a result, some soldiers began leaving, including Samuel Kemper. Gutiérrez then appointed himself the leader of the new government. This action angered those volunteers who wanted officials to be elected. Gutiérrez also wanted Texas to remain part of Mexico. Most of the U.S. volunteers hoped Texas would join the United States or become an independent nation. A group soon forced Gutiérrez from power and replaced him. These events left the Republican Army weak and confused.

Meanwhile, a Spanish army under General Joaquín de Arredondo moved into Texas from the south. In August 1813 the two armies clashed near Medina. After four hours of fighting, Arredondo won a decisive victory. More than 1,000 rebels lay dead. This loss crushed the rebellion. General Arredondo then led a campaign of revenge across Texas. Hundreds of Tejanos were executed or imprisoned. Many others fled. By the end, few people remained in Nacogdoches.

Reading Check **Identifying Cause and Effect** What problems arose within the Republican Army of the North, and how was the army affected by them?

Our Cultural Heritage

Diez y Seis de Septiembre

On September 16, 1810, Father Hidalgo delivered his historic Grito de Dolores. Today many Texans celebrate Diez y Seis de Septiembre, or the "Sixteenth of September." Festivities include speeches, parades, and traditional Mexican foods, music, and dancing. Some Texas towns also hold *charreadas,* Mexican-style rodeos exhibiting skilled horse riding. These celebrations honor an important day in Mexican and Texas history. **What event does Diez y Seis de Septiembre honor?** TEKS

Interpreting the Visual Record

Galveston. What geographic features might have made Galveston a good base for pirates and rebels? ⭐TEKS

GLOBAL CONNECTIONS

Revolutions in Latin America

The Mexican rebellion was part of a revolutionary wave that swept Latin America in the early 1800s. These revolts led to the creation of several nations including Argentina, Brazil, Peru, and Venezuela. Simon Bolívar, nicknamed the Liberator, led many of these struggles for independence. The nation Bolivia is named in his honor. By 1830 Spain had lost most of its American empire. Who was "the Liberator"?

⭐ Pirates and Rebels on the Coast

Despite General Arredondo's actions, filibuster and revolutionary activity continued along the Gulf Coast. Henry Perry, a U.S. volunteer in the Gutiérrez-Magee expedition, gathered a force of about 300. In 1815 he moved into Texas, eventually establishing a base on Galveston Island. This island was home to pirates, smugglers, and revolutionaries. Louis Michel Aury, a French pirate-adventurer, controlled Galveston Island. Aury was working with Mexican rebels and raiding Spanish ships in the Gulf of Mexico.

A second filibuster force, under Spaniard Francisco Xavier Mina, also came to the island. In April 1817 Aury led Mina's and Perry's forces to the coast of Mexico. Perry took about 50 men and entered Texas. In June 1817 they reached La Bahía, where Perry demanded the surrender of the Spanish garrison. When the Spanish refused and prepared to attack, Perry and his men fled. Spanish forces soon surrounded the group, killing or wounding most of them. Perry later died after being wounded in the fighting.

On returning to Galveston Island, Aury found French pirate **Jean Lafitte** in charge and soon left. Lafitte had been a pirate and smuggler in Louisiana. He had also fought for the United States at New Orleans in the War of 1812. To thank him, the U.S. president had given Lafitte a pardon, or official release from punishment, for his crimes. Like Aury, Lafitte began raiding Spanish ships in the Gulf. Although he too claimed to be fighting for Mexican independence, he most likely was interested only in Spanish treasure. When Lafitte began to attack American ships, the U.S. Navy forced him to leave Galveston Island in 1820. He continued to raid ships in the Gulf of Mexico until his death a few years later.

⭐ **Reading Check Finding the Main Idea** Where was filibuster activity based after the Gutiérrez-Magee expedition?

★ The Long Expeditions

One of the best-known filibusters was Dr. **James Long**, from Natchez, Mississippi. Like many U.S. citizens, Long was angry about the Adams-Onís Treaty. He thought that Texas should be either independent or part of the United States. From his home, he began organizing an army to invade Texas. In 1819 Long and a force of more than 120 invaded Texas and quickly captured Nacogdoches. Long declared Texas independent. He then traveled to Galveston Island, where he tried unsuccessfully to get Jean Lafitte's support. Meanwhile, more than 500 Spanish troops attacked and ran the invaders out of Texas.

Refusing to give up, Long planned a second invasion. In 1820 his new army sailed for Texas, landing at Point Bolivar. In late 1821 Long led the army inland to La Bahía. Spanish forces attacked, and Long was forced to surrender. While Long was awaiting trial, a soldier shot and killed him. Officials claimed the death was accidental, but Long's friends called it murder. His death ended the early filibuster period in Texas.

Jane Long had accompanied her husband to Texas and awaited his return at Point Bolivar. With Long were two young girls—her daughter, Ann, and a slave named Kian. When the army failed to return, Long, who was pregnant, chose to stay behind with the girls and wait. In December, Long gave birth to a second daughter, Mary James. They struggled through the winter. At one point, several Karankawa Indians appeared, but Long fired a cannon and scared them away. Long eventually learned of her husband's death. She traveled back to the United States, hoping one day to return to Texas.

After leaving Galveston, Jean Lafitte moved his base to an island off the coast of Mexico.

★ **Reading Check** **Identifying Points of View** Why did James Long oppose the Adams-Onís Treaty of 1819?

Section 3 Review TEKS Questions 2, 3, 4a, 4b, 5
go.hrw.com **Homework Practice Online**
keyword: ST3 HP7

1 **Define and explain:**
- filibusters
- siege

2 **Identify and explain:**
- Philip Nolan
- Miguel Hidalgo y Costilla
- Republican Army of the North
- Jean Lafitte
- James Long
- Jane Long

3 **Categorizing**
Copy the graphic organizer below. Use it to identify the filibusters and to describe their actions and goals.

Filibuster Expedition	Actions	Goals

4 **Finding the Main Idea**
a. What events took place when Philip Nolan entered Texas?
b. Why did the Texas Gulf Coast become the focus of filibuster activity?

5 **Writing and Critical Thinking** **TAKS**
Supporting a Point of View Imagine that you live in San Antonio de Béxar. Write an article either supporting or opposing the Republican Army of the North's activity in Texas.
Consider the following:
- the reasons the army was fighting
- the events that occurred during and after the army's expedition in Texas

Section 4

Spanish Rule Ends in Mexico

Read to Discover

1. How did the Mexican War of Independence affect Texas?
2. What was life like in Texas under Mexican rule?

Why It Matters Today

The missions closed as the government changed its policies in Texas. Use CNNfyi.com or other **current events** sources to find information about government policy changes today. Record your findings in your journal.

Define
- jacales
- secularize

Identify
- **José María Morelos y Pavón**
- **Agustín de Iturbide**
- **Vicente Guerrero**
- **Martín de León**

The Granger Collection, New York

Mexicans proudly flew their new flag after winning independence.

The Story Continues

Early on July 19, 1821, the people of San Antonio de Béxar gathered in the town's plaza. They had only recently learned the news—the war was over, and Mexico had won its independence from Spain. Texas governor Antonio María Martínez stood solemnly with the others. Slowly, the Spanish flag in the plaza was lowered, and another flag was raised in its place. Standing before a crucifix, the group began reciting an oath of loyalty to Mexico.

★ Mexico Wins Independence

While some people were trying to free Texas, others had continued to fight for Mexico's independence. After Father Hidalgo's death, a priest named Father **José María Morelos y Pavón** led the fight for Mexican independence. In 1815 the Spanish captured and executed him. The revolution seemed at an end. Then in 1820 events in Europe breathed new life into the rebellion. When political changes in Spain weakened the government, Mexican rebels saw their chance. Military officer **Agustín de Iturbide** (ee-toor-BEE-day) joined forces with rebels led by **Vicente Guerrero**. Together their army defeated the Spanish in 1821. Mexico had won its independence. In 1822 Iturbide declared himself emperor, but he proved to be an unpopular ruler. In the next year he was forced from power and Mexico was declared to be a republic.

The Mexican War of Independence took a heavy toll on Texas. Many Tejanos had fled or been killed. Relations with Texas Indians had worsened, resulting in increased American Indian attacks on settlements. The Texas economy was left in ruins, with livestock lost and crops destroyed. Governor Antonio María Martínez expressed his sorrow.

Texas Voices 66[The armies have] drained the resources of the country, and laid their hand on everything that could sustain [support] human life. [Texas] has advanced at an amazing rate toward ruin and destruction.99

—Antonio María Martínez, quoted in *The Mexican Frontier, 1821–1846,* by David J. Weber

Analyzing Primary Sources
Identifying Points of View
What effect did Martínez believe the war had had on the region's resources?

By 1821 only a few thousand Tejanos remained in Texas, about half of the population in 1810. They were not the only residents—about 30,000 American Indians also lived in the region. Most Tejanos were grouped in two settlements. About 1,500 people lived in San Antonio, the capital. Two of the town's important residents were Erasmo Seguín and José Antonio Navarro. Both men had left Texas during the Gutiérrez-Magee expedition, and Seguín had lost all his property. Later, both men returned. Seguín served as San Antonio's postmaster and alcalde, or mayor. To the southeast, about 1,000 Tejanos lived in La Bahía, renamed Goliad in 1829. In East Texas, the town of Nacogdoches was almost deserted.

Reading Check **Sequencing** Describe in order the final events leading to Mexican independence.

Causes and Effects of Mexican Independence

Causes
- Wide economic and social divisions between the rich and poor in New Spain
- Political corruption in Spain
- Examples of other revolutions, including the American Revolution and those occurring in Latin America
- Father Hidalgo's Grito de Dolores

Effects
- Creation of Mexico as an independent republic
- Economic ruin and loss of life in Mexico, including Texas
- Political instability in Mexico
- Attempts to increase the Texas population with immigrants from Europe and the United States

TAKS *Skills* *Interpreting Charts* Mexico was one of several colonies to revolt against Spain. What impact did Mexican independence have on Texas? **TEKS**

Interpreting the Visual Record

Ranchos. Ranching in early Texas was often hot, dusty work. **How did many Tejanos earn a living in frontier Texas?** ⭐TEKS

⭐ Tejano Ranchers

To the south and west, several thousand people lived along the Rio Grande. These settlers were grouped around El Paso del Norte and Laredo. Lush grasslands had helped the lower Rio Grande valley develop into a major ranching area. Livestock included cattle, horses, and sheep. **Martín de León**, Tomás Sánchez, and José Narciso Cavazos were several of the region's most successful ranchers. Sánchez also served as the alcalde of Laredo for many years. Cavazos raised a variety of stock on his huge 470,000-acre ranch. With the opening of a port at Matamoros in 1820, the lower Rio Grande region also developed into a trade center. This region continued to grow after Mexican independence.

Ranching also began growing in importance in the San Antonio River valley. A steady cattle trade existed between Texas and markets in Coahuila to the south and Louisiana to the east. Many wealthier Tejanos lived on ranches. Their stone ranch houses often resembled forts, with thick high walls. To guard against attacks by Texas Indians, ranchers put bars and shutters over their windows. For added protection, some houses included watchtowers and gun ports. Other Tejanos lived in **jacales** (huh-KAW-lays), small one-room huts made of sticks and mud. Settlers stacked short sticks or brush and rocks to form walls. Owners then plastered the walls with mud. Tejanos, whether living in stone houses or jacales, faced many difficulties and dangers on the frontier.

⭐ **Reading Check Analyzing Information** How did Tejanos adapt to their environment?

★ Mexican Policies in Texas

Mexico's new government had to decide which Spanish policies to continue in Texas. One of Spain's first policies in the region had been the creation of the mission system. Over the years, the Spanish founded many Texas missions, the last in 1793. Named Nuestra Señora del Refugio, this mission served the Karankawa along the south Texas coast. After being moved twice, the mission was located at what is now Refugio. In time, a settlement and several ranches grew up around the mission.

The same year the Refugio mission was founded, Spain began to **secularize** the Texas missions. Secularization is the process of moving from religious to civil control. Mission San Antonio de Valero was the first to be secularized. From 1801 to 1825 it housed the military unit, the Flying Company of San José y Santiago del Alamo de Parras. This unit gave the mission its famous nickname, the Alamo. After independence, Mexico continued the process. All Texas missions were secularized by 1831, and most mission Indians settled among the Spanish. The mission buildings and lands were placed under local control, given away, or sold. Tejanos acquired most of the mission lands and livestock.

In place of the mission system, Mexico had to develop a new policy for settling and governing Texas. Like Spain, Mexico worried that the Texas population was too small. The few Tejanos could hardly protect the vast land of Texas. In addition, few Mexicans wanted to live on the rough isolated frontier. Offers of free land lured few settlers northward. On the eve of Mexican independence, such concerns had led Spain to open Texas to U.S. immigration. Mexican officials would have to decide whether to continue this policy.

 Reading Check **Finding the Main Idea** What happened to the mission system after Mexican independence?

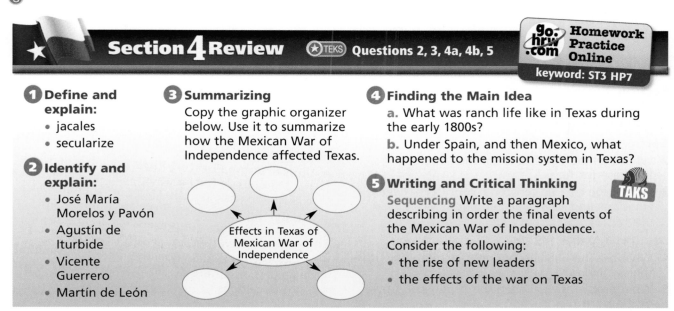

Section 4 Review ★TEKS Questions 2, 3, 4a, 4b, 5

go.hrw.com **Homework Practice Online** keyword: ST3 HP7

1 Define and explain:
- jacales
- secularize

2 Identify and explain:
- José María Morelos y Pavón
- Agustín de Iturbide
- Vicente Guerrero
- Martín de León

3 Summarizing
Copy the graphic organizer below. Use it to summarize how the Mexican War of Independence affected Texas.

Effects in Texas of Mexican War of Independence

4 Finding the Main Idea
a. What was ranch life like in Texas during the early 1800s?
b. Under Spain, and then Mexico, what happened to the mission system in Texas?

5 Writing and Critical Thinking
Sequencing Write a paragraph describing in order the final events of the Mexican War of Independence.
Consider the following:
- the rise of new leaders
- the effects of the war on Texas

TAKS

The Chapter at a Glance

Examine the following visual summary of the chapter. Then use the visual to organize the information into an outline that a classmate can use as a study guide for the chapter. ★TEKS

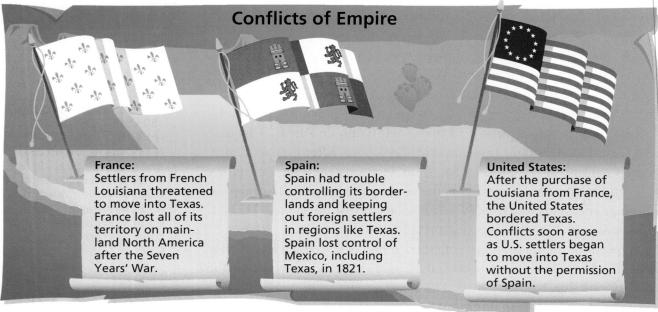

Conflicts of Empire

France: Settlers from French Louisiana threatened to move into Texas. France lost all of its territory on mainland North America after the Seven Years' War.

Spain: Spain had trouble controlling its borderlands and keeping out foreign settlers in regions like Texas. Spain lost control of Mexico, including Texas, in 1821.

United States: After the purchase of Louisiana from France, the United States bordered Texas. Conflicts soon arose as U.S. settlers began to move into Texas without the permission of Spain.

Identifying People and Ideas ★TEKS

Use each of the following terms or people in historically significant sentences.

1. Tejanos
2. Antonio Gil Ybarbo
3. Louisiana Purchase
4. Adams-Onís Treaty
5. Philip Nolan
6. filibusters
7. Miguel Hidalgo y Costilla
8. Jean Lafitte
9. James Long
10. Martín de León

Understanding Main Ideas ★TEKS

Section 1 (pages 136–139)

1. What actions did the Marqués de Rubí report lead to in Texas?

Section 2 (pages 140–142)

2. What was the significance of the Louisiana Purchase for Texas?

3. What issue created territorial conflicts between Louisiana and New Spain, and how was it resolved?

Section 3 (pages 143–147)

4. What did the filibusters hope to accomplish with their activities?

5. What problems weakened the Republican Army of the North?

Section 4 (pages 148–151)

6. How did Mexican independence affect Texas?

You Be the Historian ★TEKS

1. **Economics** What economic approach did the Spanish use to improve their relations with Texas Indians?

2. **Geography** How did the Louisiana Purchase affect Spanish policy in Texas?

3. **Global Relations** How did U.S. citizens try to influence events in Mexico and Texas?

TAKS Practice: Thinking Critically ★TEKS

1. **Supporting a Point of View** Do you agree with the Marqués de Rubí that defending East Texas was no longer important? Support your answer.

2. **Analyzing Information** Which country benefited more from the Adams-Onís Treaty, in your opinion, and why?

3. **Contrasting** Explain how the filibusters' views of their actions differed from Spanish officials' views of their actions.

Interpreting Maps ⭐TEKS

Study the map below. Then use the information on the map to help you answer the questions that follow.

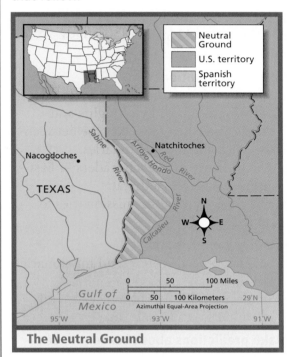

The Neutral Ground

1. Which streams and rivers helped define the boundaries of the Neutral Ground?

   a. the Sabine, the Arroyo Hondo, and the Red

   b. the Sabine and the Red

   c. the Calcasieu, the Sabine, and the Arroyo Hondo

   d. the Red and the Calcasieu

2. Why was the location of the Neutral Ground important?

Analyzing Primary Sources ⭐TEKS

Read the following quote by historian Anna Pennybacker, from her book *A History of Texas for Schools* (1895). Then answer the questions.

"In San Antonio lived many descendants of aristocratic [noble] Spanish families; the army officers were generally men of polished manners, as they often came from the Vice-Regal Court of Mexico; the priests were men of learning and refinement. The governor gave frequent receptions, while each night on the public square the people met to dance, converse [talk], to promenade [walk], and to visit."

3. According to the author, what were some of the qualities of the leaders in early San Antonio?

   a. social, talkative, liked to dance

   b. rugged, moderately wealthy, happy

   c. aristocratic, polished, educated, refined

   d. educated, ill-mannered, religious

4. Based on the above quote, what were some respected occupations in early San Antonio?

Alternative Assessment

Linking to Community ⭐TEKS

Work with your classmates to create a multimedia display illustrating Spanish heritage in Texas, and in particular, your community. You may need to do additional research about Spaniards and Tejanos who lived and worked in the area in the 1700s and 1800s. Prepare material showing what affect they had on the region where you live. Be sure to include brief biographical material on the people you are researching. Then hold a Spanish heritage day at your school for students, parents, and teachers.

BUILDING YOUR Portfolio

📝 **internet** connect

Internet Activity: go.hrw.com
KEYWORD: ST3 TX7 ⭐TEKS

Access the Internet through the HRW Go site to read primary and secondary sources on filibusters and revolutionaries in Spanish Texas. Then write a response to the questions in the interactive activity. As you read, think about the validity of the source based on language, corroboration with other sources, and information about the author.

Social Studies Skills

WORKSHOP

Decision-Making Skills

Like you, many figures in Texas history have faced difficult decisions. With the use of decision-making skills you will be better able to make a decision on important issues. The following activities will help you develop and practice these skills.

Decision Making involves choosing between two or more options. Listed below are guidelines that will help you with making decisions.

1. **Identify a situation that requires a decision.** Think about your current situation. What issue are you faced with that requires you to take some sort of action?

2. **Gather information.** Examine the causes of the issue or problem and consider how it affects you and others.

3. **Identify your options.** Consider the actions that you could take to address the issue. List these options so that you can compare them.

4. **Make predictions about consequences.** Predict the consequences of taking the actions listed for each of your options. Compare these possible consequences. Some options might be easier or seem more satisfying. But do they produce the results that you want?

5. **Take action to implement a decision.** Choose a course of action from your available options and put it into effect.

Example

During the early 1700s, Spanish officials decided to re-establish missions in East Texas after they fled the region in the 1690s. Here is an example of the decision-making process that the officials might have used.

1. **Identify a situation that requires a decision.** Should Spain re-establish missions in East Texas?

2. **Gather Information.**
   • Spanish missionaries left the area after crops were ruined by droughts and floods and when tensions rose between the Tejas and the missionaries.
   • The presence of French traders in East Texas was seen as a threat.
   • The Tejas wanted the missionaries to return.

3. **Identify your options.**
   • Spanish officials could send missionaries to East Texas.
   • Spanish officials could refuse to send missionaries to East Texas.

4. **Make predictions about consequences.**
   • If the missionaries return, the Tejas might welcome the missionaries and Spain's influence in the region could grow.
   • If Spanish officials refuse to send the missionaries to East Texas, the influence of Spain in the region might decrease.

5. **Take action to implement a decision.** Spanish officials decide to re-establish East Texas missions.

Practicing the Skill

Chapter 5, Section 3, Searching for Cities of Gold, describes Spanish explorers' search for the Seven Lost Cities of Gold. Imagine that you are a Spanish explorer aware of earlier failed attempts to find these cities. Use the decision-making guidelines above to help you decide whether to launch another expedition for the Lost Cities of Gold. Be prepared to defend your decision. ⭐TEKS

History in Action

UNIT 2 SIMULATION

You Make the Decision . . .

Should Spain Finance a New Expedition to Texas?

Complete the following activity in small cooperative groups. It is the era of exploration, 1492–1670. The Spanish king and queen are debating whether to finance an exploration expedition to Texas. Your group has been asked to provide the king and queen with information to help them decide whether to finance a new exploration expedition to Texas. Follow these steps to reach your decision.

1. Gather Information. Use your textbook and any other resources to find information that might influence whether Spain should finance an expedition to Texas. What advantages could be gained by exploring Texas? What challenges would explorers face? Be sure to use what you learned from this unit's Skills Workshop on Decision Making to help you make an informed choice. You may want to divide up different parts of the research among group members.

2. Identify Options. After reviewing the information you have gathered, consider the options you might recommend to the king and queen about whether Texas should be explored. Your final decision may be easier to reach if you consider as many options as possible. Be sure to record your possible options for your presentation.

3. Predict Consequences. Now take each option that your group came up with and consider what might be the outcome of each course of action. Ask yourselves questions like: "Are gold and treasure in Texas, as they are in South America?" and "Who would control the region if Spain does not explore it?" Once you have predicted the consequences, record them as notes for your presentation.

4. Take Action to Implement Your Decision. After you have considered your options, you should create your presentation. Be sure to make your decision about exploring Texas very clear to the king and queen. You will need to support your decision by including information you gathered and by explaining why you rejected other options. You may want to create cluster diagrams, maps, or charts to support your decision. When you are ready, decide who in your group will make which part of the presentation and take your decision to the king and queen (the rest of the class). Good luck!

UNIT 3
American Colonization
(1820–1835)

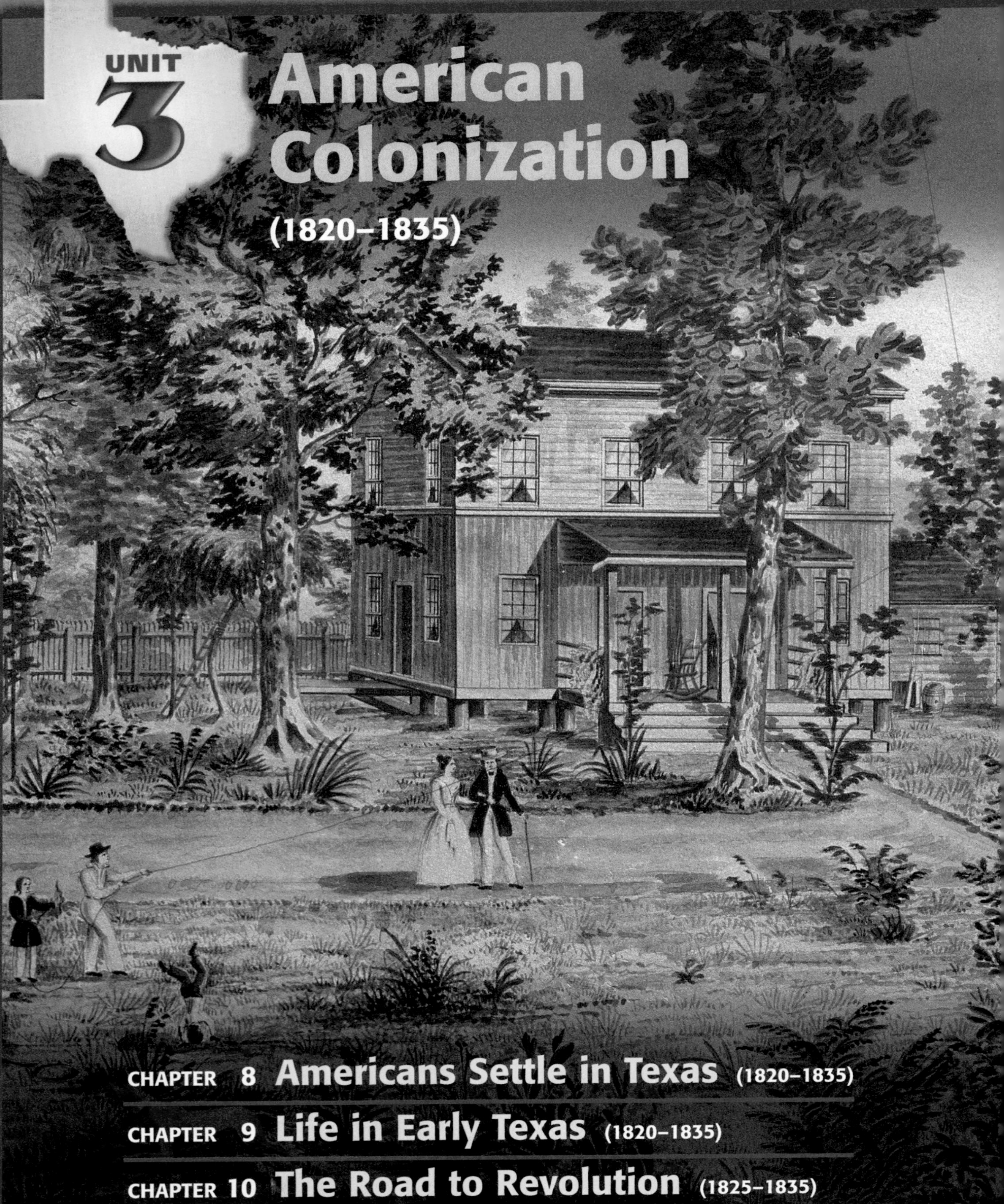

CHAPTER 8 **Americans Settle in Texas** (1820–1835)

CHAPTER 9 **Life in Early Texas** (1820–1835)

CHAPTER 10 **The Road to Revolution** (1825–1835)

Texas Teens
Young Settlers

When John Holland Jenkins was just a young boy his family moved to Texas from Alabama. While John was excited about moving to a new place, he was also frightened by the many stories of danger on the frontier his family heard as they traveled to Texas. Nevertheless, the family continued on to Texas and began looking for a place to settle.

Eventually, John and his family settled near Barton Creek, about 40 miles from Austin. Like most settlers, the first task the family faced was building a house. The entire family, including John, helped with the building. They constructed a cabin out of cedar logs. The family cut and shaped the logs by hand with axes. The cabin had a dirt floor, and the roof was made from split pine boards. Neighbors were few and far between—only two lived within six miles.

Texas teens across the state participate in frontier days, rodeos, and other activities that recall the early days of Texas.

Life on the Texas frontier was full of danger and excitement. John had an encounter with Buffalo Hump, a famous Comanche chief. A group of Comanche stopped at the family's cabin. The Jenkins family helped the hungry Comanche. With the family's permission, the Comanche killed a cow to eat. After eating their fill, the Comanche left in peace. As a teenager, John Jenkins had many more adventures in the Texas frontier. **What was life like for young settlers in Texas such as John Jenkins?**

In this unit you will learn more about the lives of early settlers of Texas. You will also learn about the events and issues in the Texas colonies that would soon lead to conflict between settlers and the Mexican government.

LEFT PAGE: *Many early settlers came to Texas hoping to establish farms or trade with other colonists.*

Americans Settle in Texas

(1820–1835)

U.S. immigrants settling in Texas brought candleholders like this one to light their new homes.

Stephen F. Austin fulfilled his father's plan to establish a colony in Texas.

TEXAS

1821 The Spanish government grants Moses Austin permission to found a colony in Texas.

1823 About 3,000 U.S. settlers live in Texas without the permission of the Mexican government.

1824 *Empresario* Martín de León settles families on the lower Guadalupe River.

1826 An American Indian attack on the Green DeWitt colony forces U.S. settlers to flee Gonzales.

1820	**1822**	**1824**	**1826**

U.S. and WORLD

1824 Charles Grandison Finney receives a license as a Presbyterian minister and begins preaching throughout the United States.

1826 Fur trapper and explorer Jedediah Smith blazes an overland route to California.

Traveling ministers held revivals throughout the American Midwest.

Build on What You Know

In the early 1800s many people in Mexico fought for independence from Spanish rule. In 1821 Mexico became an independent country. Many Tejanos were glad to be part of Mexico. However, the war had left Texas unprotected. Mexico needed a larger population if it was to maintain control of the region.

Publication of the Texas Gazette *begins soon after colonists settle in San Felipe de Austin.*

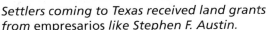

Settlers coming to Texas received land grants from empresarios *like Stephen F. Austin.*

1829 The *Texas Gazette* newspaper begins publication in Austin's colony.

1835 Texas settlers hold about 3,500 land grants.

1828	**1830**	**1832**	**1834**

1828 Andrew Jackson is elected president of the United States.

1830 A cholera epidemic spreads west from Asia across Europe.

1832 George Catlin paints portraits of American Indians as he travels across the American West.

1835 Samuel Colt obtains a British patent for his single-barreled revolver. He obtains a U.S. patent the next year.

This frog was a campaign item for Andrew Jackson.

You Be the Historian:

Themes Journal

What's Your Opinion? Do you **agree** or **disagree** with the following statements? Support your point of view in your journal.

● **Citizenship** Patience and persistence are important leadership qualities.

● **Economics** People usually immigrate to another country for financial reasons.

● **Geography** Many people choose where to live on the basis of climate and other geographic factors.

If you were there . . .
How would you encourage more families to settle in Texas?

Moses Austin and Texas

Read to Discover

1. Why did Moses Austin want to establish a colony in Texas?
2. Why did Moses Austin go to Texas, and was his trip a success?

Why It Matters Today

Moses Austin wanted to found a colony of U.S. settlers in Texas. Use CNNfyi.com or other **current events** sources to find information about why people move today. Record your findings in your journal.

Define
- **financial panic**
- **depression**

Identify
- **Moses Austin**
- **Panic of 1819**
- **Stephen F. Austin**
- **Baron de Bastrop**

Moses Austin had to purchase picks and other equipment for his mines.

The Story Continues

Moses Austin read the pamphlet carefully. Lead in upper Louisiana, it said, was so abundant that miners there just scooped it up. Austin's lead mines in Virginia were in serious financial trouble, so in 1796 he set out on the long journey to the Spanish territory. When Austin finally reached the mines six weeks later, he marveled at the lead just lying scattered on the ground. It is of "better quality than any I have ever seen," he wrote. He soon began making plans to start a new life in this new country.

★ Moses Austin's Texas Dream

In June 1798 **Moses Austin** moved to present-day Missouri, which was then part of Spanish Louisiana. Spanish officials allowed him to mine lead there. Austin became a Spanish citizen and formed strong ties with government officials. By the time the United States purchased Louisiana in 1803, he had become a wealthy part owner of the Bank of St. Louis. However, in 1819 the United States experienced a **financial panic**, or economic crisis. This **Panic of 1819** led to a **depression**, or period of low economic activity. Many banks failed, including the Bank of St. Louis. Austin was ruined. "I found nothing I could do would bring back my property again," he wrote.

Austin had profited once before by moving to a Spanish land. Perhaps such a move could work again. He came up with a bold plan to establish a colony of U.S. families in Texas. By charging them fees, he could regain his wealth. Hopeful again, Austin set out for Texas.

⭐ **Reading Check** **Finding the Main Idea** Why did Moses Austin decide to establish a colony in Texas?

⭐ Moses Austin Goes to Texas

On his way to Texas, Austin visited his son **Stephen F. Austin** in Arkansas Territory. The younger Austin had doubts about his father's plan. Despite these concerns, Austin's son gave him $50 and a horse. Moses Austin also took along a slave named Richmond as a traveling companion. In late November 1820 the two men crossed into East Texas. As they traveled to San Antonio, Austin admired the land. He passed through forests and prairies. Austin hoped the land's fertile soil and many streams would make the area good for farming. On December 23, 1820, Austin and Richmond rode into San Antonio. They made their way through the dusty streets to the residence of Texas governor Antonio María Martínez. Austin's timing was poor. Recent filibuster activity had made the governor suspicious of U.S. citizens. When he learned that Austin was from the United States, the governor ordered Austin out of the city. Disappointed, Austin gathered his papers and left.

Then a chance meeting occurred that changed history. Crossing the town plaza, Austin saw a man whom he had met years before in Louisiana. This man, **Baron de Bastrop**, was a Dutch businessman who had moved to San Antonio. Austin told Bastrop about his colonization plan and the governor's order to leave. Bastrop decided to help. Bastrop convinced Martínez to let Austin stay in town for a few days. During this

That's Interesting!

Baron de Bastrop

The Baron de Bastrop was not a true baron. His real name was Philip Hendrik Nering Bögel. In 1793 he fled the Netherlands after being accused of theft. He adopted his fake title and eventually settled in San Antonio. Although some people suspected his deception, no one ever proved it. Bastrop became a successful businessman and a respected statesman. Both the town of Bastrop and Bastrop County are named for him.

Interpreting the Visual Record

Texas rivers. Rivers flow through many regions of Texas. **What in this image would be appealing to people who might want to settle in Texas?** ⭐TEKS

Moses Austin
(1761–1821)

Moses Austin was born in Connecticut. In his twenties he entered the lead-mining business in Virginia. After a period of prosperity, several of Austin's business ventures failed. Austin then moved his family to present-day Missouri in 1798. There he used new techniques in his lead operations. His business expanded, amassing him a fortune of $190,000. When he journeyed to Texas in 1820, however, most of this fortune was gone. Austin was the first person to get permission to bring U.S. settlers into Texas. **How did Moses Austin shape Texas history?** TEKS

time, Bastrop rewrote Austin's colonization request in a formal Spanish style. The two men then went to see Martínez together. Austin described his plan to bring families from the United States to Texas. Bastrop pointed out that Austin had been a Spanish citizen and would be loyal to New Spain. Bastrop noted that the colony would improve the economy and help protect the region from American Indian attacks and U.S. invasions. Bastrop's arguments were persuasive. Martínez agreed to urge his superiors to approve Austin's plan. Austin was confident his trip was a success. "The Governor was pleased to say that if I returned I might depend on his friendship," Austin told Bastrop.

Their mission accomplished, Austin and Richmond headed home. Things then took a turn for the worse. A fellow traveler stole all their horses, mules, and supplies. The two men were forced to walk the rest of the way. Cold weather and flooded streams slowed their progress. By the time they reached shelter, both men were very ill. Austin's health remained poor after he returned to Missouri. Despite his illness, he began to make preparations for his colony. In the spring of 1821, Austin received good news. Spanish officials had approved his colonization request. Austin was granted the right to settle 300 Catholic families from Louisiana. However, Austin became extremely ill and asked his wife to write his son Stephen.

 Texas Voices "He called me to his bed side and with much distress and difficulty of speech, begged me to tell you to take his place . . . to go on with the business in the same way he would have done had not sickness, and oh dreadful to think of perhaps death, prevented him from accomplishing [it]."

—Mary Brown Austin, quoted in *Stephen F. Austin: Empresario of Texas,* by Gregg Cantrell

 Reading Check **Summarizing** What year did Austin receive permission to establish a colony, and what were the terms of that grant?

★ **Section 1 Review** TEKS Questions 2, 3, 4a, 4b, 5

go.hrw.com Homework Practice Online
keyword: ST3 HP8

1 **Define and explain:**
- financial panic
- depression

2 **Identify and explain:**
- Moses Austin
- Panic of 1819
- Stephen F. Austin
- Baron de Bastrop

3 **Analyzing Information**
Copy the graphic organizer below. Use it to show the reasons that Spanish officials had for and against giving Moses Austin his colony.

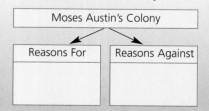

Moses Austin's Colony

Reasons For | Reasons Against

4 **Finding the Main Idea**
a. Why did Moses Austin try to form a colony?
b. What did Austin hope to accomplish in Texas? Was he successful?

5 **Writing and Critical Thinking** **TAKS**
Evaluating Write a short entry on Moses Austin for a Texas history book. Consider the following:
- Austin's contribution to the colonization of Texas
- the significance of the year 1821

Stephen F. Austin in Texas

Read to Discover

1. What steps did Stephen F. Austin take to carry out his father's colonization contract?
2. Why did U.S. settlers come to Austin's colony, and when did they first arrive?
3. Why did Austin go to Mexico City in 1822, and what were the results of his trip?

Why It Matters Today

During the 1820s many U.S. settlers came to Texas hoping to improve their lives. Use **CNNfyi**.com or other **current events** sources to find information about immigration today. Record your findings in your journal.

Define

- **cotton gins**
- **land titles**
- **militia**

Identify

- **Erasmo Seguín**
- **Joseph H. Hawkins**
- *Lively*
- **Imperial Colonization Law**

The Story Continues

Erasmo Seguín, the mayor of San Antonio de Béxar, was about to give up. He had traveled to Louisiana to meet Moses Austin, who was long overdue. Tired of waiting, Seguín decided to write Austin's son to see if he had any information. Suddenly, Stephen F. Austin arrived, having decided to help his father. Not waiting for Moses Austin, they set out for Texas. Near the Sabine River, a rider caught up to them with bad news—Moses Austin had died. The fate of the Texas colony now lay in the hands of his son.

Erasmo Seguín helped in Stephen F. Austin's efforts to establish a colony in Texas.

★ Stephen F. Austin Goes to Texas

Stephen F. Austin was 27 years old when he learned of his father's death. Austin became determined to carry out his father's plan to bring U.S. settlers to Texas. As he entered Texas in 1821, Austin made a promise to himself. "I determined [decided] to fulfill rigidly all the duties and obligations of a Mexican citizen," he wrote.

Austin arrived in San Antonio de Béxar in August 1821. **Erasmo Seguín**, a rancher and the alcalde, or mayor, of the town, led Austin to Governor Martínez. The Baron de Bastrop was on hand to translate. Martínez greeted Austin warmly and offered to support Austin's efforts

Stephen F. Austin
(1793–1836)

Born in Virginia on November 3, 1793, Stephen F. Austin grew up on the frontier in present-day Missouri. After attending school in Connecticut and Kentucky, Austin returned home to help manage his father's businesses. He was studying law in New Orleans when he decided to help with his father's Texas colony. The younger Austin was an energetic, intelligent, patient man. Soft-spoken, cultured, and soon fluent in Spanish, he was equally at ease with frontier settlers and Mexican officials. He was devoted to his colonists and served as their adviser, banker, diplomat, and judge. His efforts brought prosperity to many and earned him the title the Father of Texas. **What qualities and experiences helped Austin become an important Texas leader?** ⭐TEKS

to continue with his father's plans. Mexico had won independence from Spanish rule since the time Moses Austin's contract had been approved, so Austin needed a new contract from the Mexican government. Over the next few days, Austin worked out a proposal. Martínez then agreed to help him get approval from officials in Mexico City.

Austin spent the next few months exploring the land east of San Antonio. He picked the rich farmland in the area of the Brazos and Colorado River valleys as the location for his colony—some 11 million acres in the Gulf Coast Plain. A colony there would have a mild climate, fertile soil, water, and plenty of timber for building. Wild game was also plentiful. In addition, the site was near the coast, where settlers and supplies could arrive by ship. In his journal, Austin described the spot where he would later found his colony's capital.

Texas Voices ❝The Prairie comes [up] to the river . . . and affords [provides] a most beautiful situation for a Town or settlement. The bluff [low cliff] is about 60 feet high—The country back of this place and below for about 15 miles (as far as we went) is as good in every respect as man could wish for, Land all first rate, plenty of timber, fine water—beautifully rolling.❞

—Stephen F. Austin, quoted in *Stephen F. Austin: Empresario of Texas*, by Gregg Cantrell

⭐TEKS **Reading Check Summarizing** Where was Austin's colony located, and what geographic features led him to choose this site?

⭐ Austin Readies His Colony

Stephen F. Austin hurried back to the United States to make the final preparations. Once he returned to Natchitoches, Louisiana, Austin sent a report to Governor Martínez. It specified the colony's location, including extra land along the Gulf Coast for a port. Austin had already given the governor his proposed land terms. Heads of households would receive 640 acres of land. A married man could claim another 320 acres, plus 160 acres for each child. Slaveholders could claim 80 acres per slave. In addition, settlers who provided valuable services or who brought items such as **cotton gins**—devices that separate cotton fibers from seeds—might receive extra land. Where possible, these land grants would border on a river that would provide water for farming and transportation. Settlers would pay Austin a fee of 12.5 cents per acre for his services. This fee covered the costs of surveying the land and recording **land titles**—legal documents proving ownership.

Austin's terms were very attractive to people in the United States, where land cost at least $1.25 an acre. U.S. law also required settlers to buy a minimum of 80 acres and pay the full price in cash. After the Panic of 1819, few people had the $100 in cash needed to buy this much land. Austin, however, was willing to accept goods as payment for land fees or allow settlers to pay off the fees over time. As he advertised his colony's land terms, applications poured in from eager men and women. Austin developed strict guidelines for selecting settlers. He believed his colony's success depended upon having hardworking, law-abiding people. Settlers would also be required to become Mexican citizens and convert to Catholicism.

Austin went to New Orleans to make final arrangements for the colony's finances. While there, he formed a partnership with **Joseph H. Hawkins**, a friend and lawyer. Hawkins provided Austin with financial support. Austin used some of this money to buy and outfit a small ship called the *Lively*. In late 1821 the *Lively* sailed from New Orleans with colonists and a cargo of seeds, tools, and building materials. Austin planned to meet the ship at the mouth of the Colorado River and set out for his colony.

⭐ **Reading Check** **Identifying Cause and Effect** Why was buying land in the United States difficult, and how did this affect settlement in Texas?

Settlers relied on axes to build their homes.

⭐ Early Settlement of Austin's Colony

Austin reached the Colorado River in January 1822, but he could not find the *Lively*. The *Lively*'s crew had accidentally landed at the Brazos River. Failing to find Austin, the crew left the settlers and supplies, then returned to New Orleans. The settlers in turn also failed to find Austin, and most eventually made their way back to the United States. On a second attempt to reach Texas, the *Lively* wrecked near the tip of Galveston

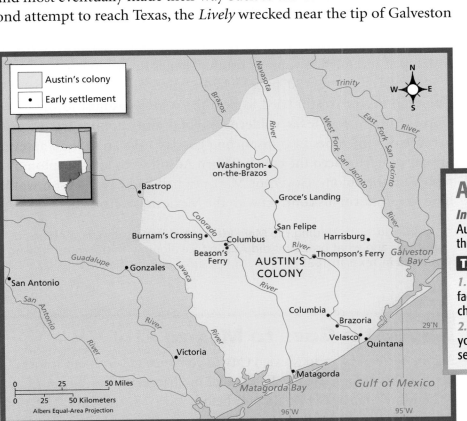

Austin's colony
• Early settlement

Navasota
Brazos
River
Trinity
West Fork San Jacinto
East Fork San Jacinto
River
N
W E
S

Bastrop
Washington-on-the-Brazos
Groce's Landing
Colorado
Burnam's Crossing • Columbus
San Felipe
Harrisburg
River
Beason's Ferry
AUSTIN'S COLONY
Thompson's Ferry Galveston Bay
Guadalupe • Gonzales
Lavaca
River
San Antonio
San
Antonio
River
Columbia
Brazoria
29°N
Velasco
Quintana
River
River
Victoria
Matagorda
0 25 50 Miles
0 25 50 Kilometers
Albers Equal-Area Projection
Matagorda Bay
Gulf of Mexico
96°W
95°W

Austin's Colony

Interpreting Maps Stephen F. Austin established his colony on the Gulf Coast Plain.

TAKS Skills ⭐TEKS

1. Physical Systems What physical factors might have influenced Austin's choice for the location of his colony?
2. Evaluating What advantages do you think rivers provided to early settlements?

Courtesy of the Witte Museum, San Antonio, Texas

Interpreting the Visual Record

Colonial life. Austin had supplies shipped to his new colony so that colonists could build cabins and plant crops. *Based on this painting, what types of building supplies did the early colonists use?* TEKS

1821

The first U.S. settlers arrive in Austin's colony.

Island. The loss of the ship's supplies was hard on Austin's colony. Several other settlers had already arrived in 1821. Andrew Robinson and his family were perhaps the first to reach the colony. They camped west of the Brazos River, where Robinson would later run a ferry. Soon afterward, brothers Abner, Joseph, and Robert Kuykendall and their families arrived in the colony. Joseph Kuykendall established the first settlement on the Colorado River. Other early settlers included Austin's old friend Josiah Bell and Austin's younger brother, James Brown Austin.

By March some 150 people had settled along the Brazos and Colorado Rivers. Austin tried to help the colonists adjust to the hardships of life in the Texas wilderness. Food and supplies were scarce because of difficulties in transporting goods to the area. Soon an even greater problem faced the colony. When Austin went to San Antonio to report on the colony, Governor Martínez had bad news. Austin would have to reconfirm his contract with the Mexican government.

⭐ **Reading Check** **Finding the Main Idea** What important event occurred in 1821, and what problems did Austin face along with the colonists who arrived in Texas in 1821?

⭐ Austin Goes to Mexico City

Austin decided to go to Mexico City to convince government leaders to approve his colony. He left Josiah Bell in charge and set out in March 1822. More than a year would pass before he saw Texas again. The journey was more than 1,000 miles through rugged and dangerous land.

At one point some 50 Comanche captured Austin's group, but the party was eventually released unharmed. At another point, Austin dressed as a beggar to fool robbers. Once he reached Mexico City, he found officials struggling to organize the new government. As a result, they had little time for Texas matters. Facing many delays, Austin passed the time by studying Spanish and meeting with officials.

Austin's patience eventually paid off. In January 1823 the Mexican government passed the **Imperial Colonization Law**. Under this law, Austin's land grant was secure and he could continue to bring in settlers from the United States. But then another political crisis occurred. Mexican leader Agustín de Iturbide fell out of power, and the new government canceled the colonization law.

Austin quietly pressed his case with officials. Once again, his determination led to success. The new government decided to uphold his contract under the terms of the canceled law. The Imperial Colonization Law had set land grants for couples at 4,428 acres for ranching and 177 acres for farming. In addition, settlers were exempt, or free, from paying taxes for six years. Austin would receive about 100,000 acres once he completed his contract by settling 300 families. The Mexican government also gave him permission to form a local government and serve as judge for the colony. In addition, he received the power to organize a **militia**, or an army made up of citizens who serve when necessary.

Austin's time had been well spent. He had formed strong ties with several Mexican officials. These leaders were impressed by his determination, honesty, intelligence, and loyalty. These ties would prove to be key to the future success of his colony. In April 1823 Austin headed back to Texas.

Stephen F. Austin created this map of his colony in 1833.

 Reading Check **Drawing Inferences and Conclusions** What personality traits helped Austin win approval for his colony?

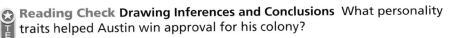

Section 2 Review ⭐TEKS Questions 2, 3, 4a, 4b, 5

go.hrw.com Homework Practice Online
keyword: ST3 HP8

1 **Define and explain:**
- cotton gins
- land titles
- militia

2 **Identify and explain:**
- Erasmo Seguín
- Joseph H. Hawkins
- *Lively*
- Imperial Colonization Law

3 **Summarizing**
Copy the graphic organizer below. Use it to describe Austin's colony.

Austin's Colony	
Location	
Size	
Final Land Terms	
Date of Start of Settlement	
Date of Final Approval	

4 **Finding the Main Idea**
a. Why did Austin's colony attract so many U.S. settlers, and what year did they first arrive?
b. Why did Stephen F. Austin travel to Mexico City, and what was the eventual outcome of his trip?

5 **Writing and Critical Thinking** **TAKS**
Sequencing Write a paragraph describing in order the steps Stephen F. Austin took to carry out his father's colonization contract.
Consider the following:
- Austin's travels in Texas
- Austin's trip to Mexico City

The Austin Colonies

Read to Discover

1. What problems did Austin's colony face, and how did Austin try to resolve them?
2. Who settled in Austin's colony, and what characteristics did they share?
3. How many colonies did Stephen F. Austin eventually form in Texas, and what was life there like?

Identify

- **Old Three Hundred**
- **Samuel May Williams**
- **John P. Coles**
- **Jane Long**
- **San Felipe de Austin**
- **Little Colony**
- **Bastrop**

Why It Matters Today

Austin's colony experienced many problems during its early years. Use **CNNfyi.com** or other **current events** sources to find out about community problems and solutions today. Record your findings in your journal.

Alligators can still be found along rivers near the Texas Gulf Coast.

The Story Continues

Life in the Texas colonies was hard. Early settlers lived in crude log cabins without any floors or windows. Frightened families huddled together in small villages in hopes of fending off American Indian attacks. Swarms of mosquitoes appeared along the hot and humid Gulf Coast, spreading deadly diseases. Alligators prowled at night, eating dogs and on rare occasions even people. Despite such harsh conditions, many settlers stayed, and even more kept coming.

★ Early Problems in Austin's Colony

Stephen F. Austin returned to his colony in August 1823. With him was the Baron de Bastrop, who had been appointed to issue the land titles. When they reached the colony, they found that many of the settlers were discouraged. Several were threatening to leave, while others had already gone. A number of problems had arisen during Austin's absence. A bad drought had ruined the colony's first crop. Low on food, the settlers had eaten wild game to survive. In addition, the Karankawa, Tonkawa, and other local American Indians did not like the colonists living on their land and had raided the colony.

Austin tried to reassure the settlers, telling them that Mexico had approved the contract for the colony. To help bring order to the colony, he established a headquarters near present-day La Grange. There he set up a system of government and created rules to guide the colony. These rules were a mixture of Mexican and U.S. law. Austin also formed a militia, which led several attacks against the Karankawa and Tonkawa. At the same time, Austin tried with limited success to form peaceful relations with some Texas Indians. As he dealt with these problems, Austin began to look upon the settlers "as one great family who are under my care."

Reading Check Summarizing What early problems affected settlers in Austin's colony, and how did Austin try to solve them?

★ The Old Three Hundred

As Austin tried to restore good spirits to the colonists, their number increased. By the fall of 1824, Austin had nearly fulfilled his contract. In all, 297 families and single men had received land in his colony. These settlers became known as the **Old Three Hundred**. Most of them came from the southern United States, particularly Louisiana. They were mostly farmers, and many were also slaveholders. Of the 1,790 colonists living in Austin's colony in 1825, about 440 were enslaved African Americans. Jared Groce, the wealthiest U.S. settler, brought some 90 slaves to the colony.

The settlers were fairly well educated. Only four of the white colonists could not read, a low figure for the time. Settlers tended to be law-abiding because of Austin's strict regulations.

Well-known members of the Old Three Hundred included **Samuel May Williams** and **John P. Coles**. Williams served as Austin's colonial secretary, and Coles built a sawmill that supplied lumber to the colony. The families of the Old Three Hundred included many women and

Jane Long
(1798–1880)

Jane Long was one of the Old Three Hundred. With her daughter Ann she obtained land in present-day Fort Bend and Waller Counties. Long also ran boardinghouses, started a farm, raised cattle, and even tried raising sheep. Like many colonists, Long used slave labor in these efforts. In 1850 Long's plantation was worth more than $10,000. She never remarried, but tradition holds that some of the leading men of Texas courted her. **How did Jane Long contribute to the colonization of Texas?** ★TEKS

Analyzing Primary Sources
Drawing Inferences and Conclusions Considering the colonists' building materials, how do you think they adapted to the environment of the region?

children. Some women held land grants on their own. **Jane Long**, the widow of filibuster James Long, received land in Austin's colony in 1824. She went on to become one of the most famous of the Old Three Hundred. Another widow, Rebekah Cumings, came to Austin's colony in 1822 with her five children. She claimed land in present-day Brazoria and Waller Counties.

★ **Reading Check Analyzing Information** Explain the significance of the term Old Three Hundred.

★ San Felipe de Austin

Austin's colony needed a capital. In 1824 Austin founded **San Felipe de Austin**, better known as San Felipe. The town was located in present-day Austin County along the Brazos River. This site had several advantages. It was in the center of the colony and halfway between the coast and El Camino Real. This road had become known as the Old San Antonio Road. The town sat on a high bluff, which aided in its defense. Below the bluff, the river provided a source of water. In addition, a ferry was located at the site.

San Felipe soon became the heart of Austin's colony. The town's population grew quickly as settlers moved to the capital. Austin placed his land office there and built a cabin on the edge of town. Gail Borden Jr. and Robert Williamson were two other well-known residents. Borden, with his brother Thomas and Joseph Baker, published the *Telegraph and Texas Register* newspaper. Borden also worked as a surveyor and inventor. Williamson was a judge who wore a wooden peg to support the knee of a weak leg. Known as Three-Legged Willie, Williamson would later help form the Texas court system. By 1827 San Felipe had between 100 and 200 residents. One settler described the town as it looked at the time.

Texas Voices ❝Twenty-five or perhaps thirty log cabins strung along the west bank of the Brazos River was all there was of it. . . . The buildings all being of unhewn [rough] logs with clapboard [planked] roofs, presented few distinguishing [different] features. . . . Every fellow built to suit himself . . . so that the town was strung along either side of the road something like half a mile . . . 'Pretty good as to length, but rather thin.'❞

—Noah Smithwick, *The Evolution of a State, or Recollections of Old Texas Days*

By the early 1830s San Felipe was the largest business center in Texas, after San Antonio. Homes and stores lined Atascosito Road, the town's main street. A lumber mill, newspaper office, and post office provided needed services. Soon, even a hotel was available for weary travelers. Austin's colony was a success.

★ **Reading Check Evaluating** What geographic factors helped San Felipe de Austin thrive?

Austin's Other Colonies

Several Tejano leaders helped Austin in his colonization efforts. José Miguel de Arciniega, Gaspar Flores de Abrego, José Antonio Saucedo, and Erasmo Seguín gave valuable assistance. With their help, Austin was able to acquire contracts for four more colonies between 1825 and 1831. They each partially overlapped his first, except for one. This colony became known as Austin's **Little Colony**.

Austin's contract for the Little Colony provided for settlement of 100 families north of the Old San Antonio Road and east of the Colorado River. This was an isolated location on the western edge of Texas settlement. The colony's main town of **Bastrop** was near Comanche hunting grounds and suffered attacks. Because of its isolation, the colony grew slowly. Austin tried to help the colony by organizing a militia and recruiting some Tonkawa as allies. Although these efforts helped, the colony remained small. In 1830 just one bachelor and two families lived in Bastrop.

Despite the slow growth of the Little Colony, Austin's other colonization efforts were a success. Austin described his feelings about his achievements in 1829.

Robert Williamson was one of the most famous residents of San Felipe.

Texas Voices

❝My ambition has been to succeed in redeeming [freeing] Texas from its wilderness state by means of the plough alone. . . . In doing this I hoped to make the fortune of thousands and my own amongst the rest. . . . I think that I derived [received] more satisfaction from the view of flourishing [thriving] farms springing up in this wilderness than military or political chieftains do from . . . their victorious campaigns.❞

—Stephen F. Austin, quoted in *Stephen F. Austin: Empresario of Texas,* by Gregg Cantrell

Analyzing Primary Sources
Analyzing Information
What pleased Austin the most about his work in Texas?

★ **Reading Check** **Contrasting** What geographic factors caused Bastrop to grow more slowly than San Felipe?

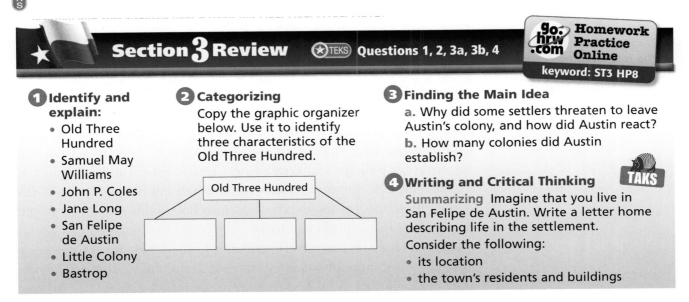

Section 3 Review

(TEKS) Questions 1, 2, 3a, 3b, 4

go.hrw.com **Homework Practice Online**
keyword: ST3 HP8

1 Identify and explain:
- Old Three Hundred
- Samuel May Williams
- John P. Coles
- Jane Long
- San Felipe de Austin
- Little Colony
- Bastrop

2 Categorizing
Copy the graphic organizer below. Use it to identify three characteristics of the Old Three Hundred.

Old Three Hundred

3 Finding the Main Idea
a. Why did some settlers threaten to leave Austin's colony, and how did Austin react?
b. How many colonies did Austin establish?

4 Writing and Critical Thinking
TAKS
Summarizing Imagine that you live in San Felipe de Austin. Write a letter home describing life in the settlement.
Consider the following:
- its location
- the town's residents and buildings

The Empresarios

Texas settlers cherished the few fancy pieces of clothing and jewelry that they managed to bring to Texas.

The Story Continues

Patricia de León struggled to improve her rough surroundings in the frontier town of Victoria. Although her simple log house had only a dirt floor, she arranged fine furniture in it. She ordered elegant clothing from abroad for herself and her 10 children and had the goods shipped to the small settlement of Victoria. De León also made certain that the town had a school and a Catholic church. Like many other settlers, she worked to build a new life in Texas.

★ Mexico's New Colonization Laws

Following the success of Austin's colony, the Mexican government passed a law intended to encourage more immigration. The **National Colonization Law of 1824** allowed each Mexican state to set its own colonization policies and created new restrictions. Unlike Stephen F. Austin, new U.S. immigrants were not free to establish colonies near the nation's borders or along the coast. Mexico hoped this restriction would help protect its northern territory.

In 1824 the Mexican government also formed the state of **Coahuila y Texas** by combining the separate states of Texas and Coahuila. The new state of Coahuila y Texas had its own immigration policy. Officials met in the state's capital, Saltillo, located 50 miles southwest of Monterrey. The first Texas citizen to serve in the Coahuila y Texas lawmaking body was the Baron de Bastrop. He and many well-to-do Tejanos wanted to see Texas grow. They hoped U.S. settlers and other immigrants would improve the Texas economy and provide extra defense against American Indians. They also believed that new settlement would raise land values in the region and provide new markets for Tejano merchants. As a result of the influence of Tejano leaders and others, Coahuila y Texas passed the **State Colonization Law of 1825**. This law further opened Texas to settlement and immigration.

Many people followed in the footsteps of Stephen F. Austin and became *empresarios*. These businesspeople promoted settlement in Texas. Under the State Colonization Law, *empresarios* received 67,000 acres of land for every 200 families they brought to Texas. The head of a household could receive 4,428 acres of land for $30. This was less than a penny an acre. New settlers also did not have to pay taxes for 10 years. The law's only requirements were that settlers become Catholics and Mexican citizens of good character. This law resulted in a huge wave of U.S. immigration to Texas.

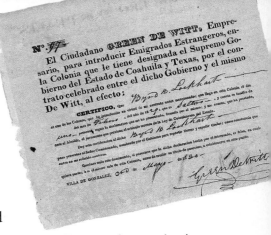

Empresarios *received contracts from the Mexican government to bring settlers to Texas.*

⭐ **Reading Check** **Finding the Main Idea** How did Mexico encourage settlement in Texas?

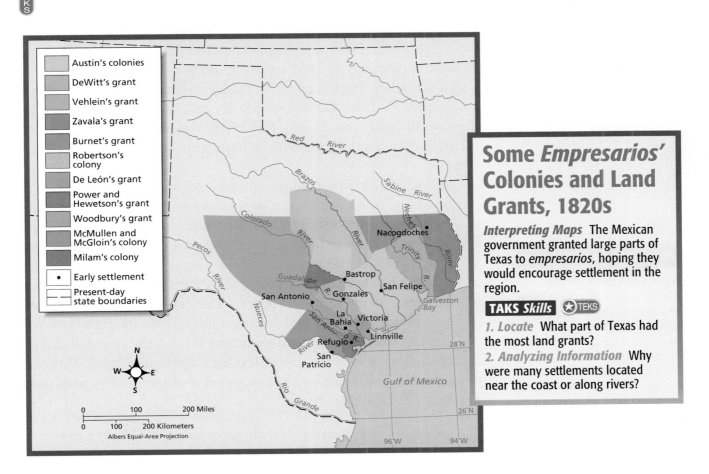

Some *Empresarios'* Colonies and Land Grants, 1820s

Interpreting Maps The Mexican government granted large parts of Texas to *empresarios*, hoping they would encourage settlement in the region.

TAKS Skills ⭐TEKS

1. Locate What part of Texas had the most land grants?

2. Analyzing Information Why were many settlements located near the coast or along rivers?

★ The DeWitt and de León Colonies

In 1825 **Green DeWitt**, who was from Missouri, and his partner, James Kerr, received a grant to settle 400 families in Texas. DeWitt's colony was located on the fertile soil of the Gulf Coast Plain and the Post Oak Belt. Gonzales, located along the Guadalupe River, was the colony's main town. The settlement's location exposed it to American Indian attacks. One Texas settler commented on life in the colony.

★ Analyzing Primary Sources
Identifying Points of View According to Smithwick, what was one of the most difficult factors of life in the colonial era of Texas?

Texas Voices
❝The rude log cabins, windowless and floorless, . . . were absolutely devoid [empty] of comfort. . . . There was no poultry, no dairy, no garden, no books, or papers as nowadays . . . no schools, no churches—nothing to break the dull monotony [boredom] of their lives, save an occasional wrangle [tussle] among the children and dogs.❞

—Noah Smithwick, *The Evolution of a State, or Recollections of Old Texas Days*

Despite these hardships, more than 525 people lived there by 1831. That year, **José Antonio Navarro**, a San Antonio businessman, was appointed the colony's land commissioner. Along with DeWitt and Kerr, Navarro became one of the colony's leading citizens.

In hopes of increasing Mexican migration to Texas, officials gave Tejano *empresarios* certain privileges, such as the first choice of available lands. **Martín de León** was the only *empresario* to found a Texas colony of primarily Mexican settlers. In 1824 he received permission to establish a colony along the lower Guadalupe River. The town of Victoria was its main settlement. By 1834 some 300 people—mainly Mexicans but also a few Irish, Tejano, and U.S. settlers—lived there. Unlike other *empresarios*, de León did not specify his colony's borders. As a result, they overlapped with those of DeWitt's colony. Numerous clashes occurred between the men, with officials usually deciding in de León's favor.

Although de León's colony was attacked by American Indians, it prospered and developed into an important ranching center. Thousands of cattle roamed the lush grass of the coastal plains. De León's own 22,000-acre ranch was located along Garcitas Creek, in present-day Victoria County. The de Leóns' house soon became a social and cultural center. After her husband's death in 1833, Patricia de León took over management of the family property. The colony also served as an important trade center. In 1831 Irishman John J. Linn founded the town of Linnville, which became an important Texas port. *Empresarios* like de León helped encourage some Mexican migration to Texas. Mexican migration to Texas remained low, however, and U.S. settlers soon outnumbered Tejanos three to one.

Interpreting the Visual Record

Tejano ranchers. In 1805 Martín and Patricia de León, along with their 10 children, settled on a large ranch near the Aransas River. He became an early trail driver, taking livestock to market in New Orleans. **What common cowboy clothing and tools is de León wearing and using in this image?**

★ **TEKS**

★ **Reading Check Evaluating** How did geographic and human factors affect the the DeWitt and de León colonies?

★ Other *Empresarios*

A few *empresarios* were Europeans. Scotsman Arthur G. Wavell tried to start a colony in northeast Texas along the Red River. Although Wavell was unable to attract British settlers, his partner, Benjamin Milam, did manage to attract a few U.S. settlers. Conflicts with the United States over the colony's eastern boundary caused problems, however, and the colony did not succeed.

Irishmen James Power and James Hewetson founded a colony north of the Nueces River, along the Gulf Coast. The main settlement, Refugio, was located on the site of an old mission. Both Irish and Mexican settlers came to the colony, which had 200 land grants by 1835. To the west of this colony, Irishmen John McMullen and James McGloin founded a colony along the Nueces. San Patricio de Hibernia, Spanish for "Saint Patrick of Ireland," served as its main town. Its growth slowed after a cholera epidemic swept through the settlement. Only 84 land titles had been issued by 1835.

Other Texas *empresarios* included David G. Burnet, Haden Edwards, and **Lorenzo de Zavala**. A native of Yucatán, Zavala was active in Mexican politics. In 1829 he received a contract to settle 500 families on a huge tract of land in East Texas. Zavala never established the colony, however, and later sold it to the Galveston Bay and Texas Land Company.

⬤ **Reading Check** **Analyzing Information** How successful was the *empresario* system?

Our Cultural Heritage

Tejano Culture

Tejanos have preserved their Spanish and Mexican culture. Early Tejano communities enjoyed many social activities, as shown in this Théodore Gentilz painting of San Antonio residents going to a ball. In Tejano communities today, people continue to maintain traditions while adapting to the larger culture. They eat Spanish-Indian foods such as corn tortillas and frijoles, or beans. Neighbors and relatives gather for dances, fiestas, and holidays. Tejanos also preserve their Spanish Catholic heritage. Tejano traditions remain a vibrant part of the state's diverse culture. **How have Tejanos maintained their culture?** ⬤TEKS

Alamo Collection, photograph courtesy the Daughters of the Republic of Texas Library

Texans have created works of art and memorials to honor Stephen F. Austin.

★ Austin's Contributions to Texas

In all, the Mexican government granted some 40 *empresario* contracts in Texas. The *empresario* system helped bring about a population boom in Texas. By 1834 an estimated 21,000 settlers lived in the region, up from only a few thousand in 1821. Settlement centered in the eastern Piney Woods, the Post Oak Belt, and the Gulf Coast Plain. The fertile soil, abundant rainfall, and mild climate in these areas provided good land for ranching and farming.

Although many *empresarios* helped settle Texas during the 1820s, Stephen F. Austin remained the most important. In just 10 years, he helped bring more than 1,500 families to Texas. To these people, Austin was more than just an *empresario*. He was also a friend and adviser. Quiet and soft-spoken, he had the ability to get along with many different people. Austin won the trust of Mexican officials, American Indian leaders, and strangers who came to his colonies. This skill, along with his drive and determination, helped him succeed in the face of enormous obstacles. Because of his many contributions, Austin is known today as the Father of Texas. A poem published after his death described his role in Texas history.

 **Texas Voices** ❝He peopled Texas, by a solemn clause
Of legal Treaty, and Religion's laws.
He bow'd obedience to the great Command
Till [plow] up the Desert—Cultivate the Land❞

—Michael Muldoon, quoted in *Stephen F. Austin: Empresario of Texas,* by Gregg Cantrell

 Reading Check **Analyzing Information** Why do people call Austin the Father of Texas?

 Section 4 Review TEKS **Questions 2, 3, 4a, 4b, 5**  **Homework Practice Online** keyword: ST3 HP8

① **Define and explain:**
• *empresarios*

② **Identify and explain:**
• National Colonization Law of 1824
• Coahuila y Texas
• State Colonization Law of 1825
• Green DeWitt
• José Antonio Navarro
• Martín de León
• Lorenzo de Zavala

③ **Comparing**
Copy the graphic organizer below. Use it to identify *empresarios* in Texas and to explain their effects on settlement in the region.

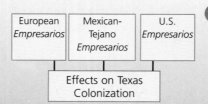

European *Empresarios* | Mexican-Tejano *Empresarios* | U.S. *Empresarios*

Effects on Texas Colonization

④ **Finding the Main Idea**
a. How did the Mexican colonization laws affect immigration to Texas?
b. What regions of Texas did *empresarios* help settle during the 1820s, and what geographic factors drew immigrants to those regions?

⑤ **Writing and Critical Thinking** **TAKS**
Supporting a Point of View Write a paragraph supporting or opposing Austin's title as the Father of Texas.
Consider the following:
• the success of Austin's colonies
• the contributions of other *empresarios* and Tejanos

Land in Mexican Texas

In the 1820s many U.S. and other settlers came to Texas in search of land. Cheap and plentiful land in Texas offered many economic opportunities.

Land Grants

The following table lists early settlers and the size of each of their land grants. A *sitio* of land equals about 4,428 acres, and a *labor* of land equals about 177 acres. Convert the *sitios* and *labores* to acres and create a bar graph of this information. ⭐TEKS

Name	Size of Grant
Elijah Alcorn	1.5 *sitios*; 1 *labor*
Stephen F. Austin	22.7 *sitios*; 3 *labores*
Josiah H. Bell	1.5 *sitios*
James Cummins	6 *sitios*; 1 *labor*
John Foster	2.5 *sitios*; 3 *labores*
Jared E. Groce	10 *sitios*
Jane Long	1 *sitio*; 1 *labor*

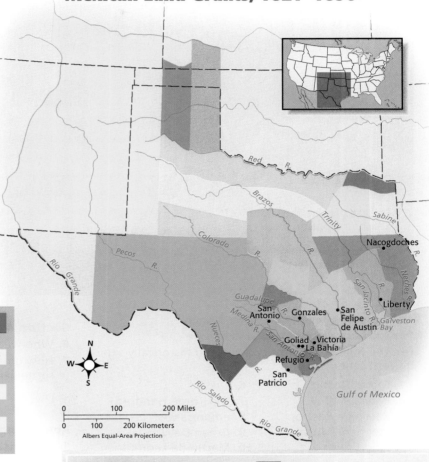

Mexican Land Grants, 1821–1836

Austin's colonies (1825–1828)
Austin and William's (1831) (Robertson's colony, 1825)
Burnet's grant (1826)
Cameron's grant (1827 and 1828)
De León's grant (1824)
DeWitt's grant (1825)
Filisola's grant (1831)
McMullen and McGloin's colony (1828)
Milam's colony (1826)
Powers and Hewetson's grant (1826)

Wavell's colony (1826)
Woodbury's grant (1826–1834)
Vehlein's grant (1828)
Zavala's grant (1828)
Grant and Beales (1832)
Padilla and Chambers (1830)
Col. Juan Domínguez (1829)
Exeter and Wilson (1826 and 1828)
• Early settlement
--- Present-day state boundaries

0 100 200 Miles
0 100 200 Kilometers
Albers Equal-Area Projection

Geography Skills

Interpreting Thematic Maps and Data ⭐TEKS

1. Which person in the table owned the largest amount of land, and how much did that person own?

2. In what part of Texas were the first land grants?

3. Who were the *empresarios* of these first grants?

The Chapter at a Glance

Examine the following visual summary of the chapter. Then use the visual to create a table that lists the benefits of the *empresario* system for the Mexican government, *empresarios,* and settlers. ⭐TEKS

The **Empresario System**

Stephen F. Austin

- Mexico used the *empresario* system to settle its northern territories.
- *Empresarios* such as Stephen F. Austin were given land grants by the Mexican government to bring in settlers to Texas.

- Following his father's plan, Austin established a colony and brought the first U.S. settlers, the Old Three Hundred.
- Many of the settlers who came for cheap land were from the southern United States.
- These new settlers were required to become citizens of Mexico and join the Catholic Church.

Identifying People and Ideas ⭐TEKS

Use the following terms or people in historically significant sentences.

1. Moses Austin
2. Panic of 1819
3. Baron de Bastrop
4. Stephen F. Austin
5. land titles
6. *Lively*
7. Old Three Hundred
8. *empresarios*
9. Green DeWitt
10. Martín de León

Understanding Main Ideas ⭐TEKS

Section 1 (pp. 160–162)

1. What were Moses Austin's plans for Texas, and when did Spain grant his request?

Section 2 (pp. 163–167)

2. What difficulties did Stephen F. Austin face in getting a contract for his colony?

3. Why did many U.S. settlers immigrate to Austin's colony?

Section 3 (pp. 168–171)

4. Where did most of the Old Three Hundred come from in the United States, and what did they have in common?

5. What was the capital of Austin's first colony, and how did Austin expand his colonization efforts in Texas?

Section 4 (pp. 172–176)

6. Who were some of the other *empresarios*?

7. How did Austin and the other *empresarios* affect settlement in Texas?

You Be the Historian ⭐TEKS

Reviewing Themes

1. **Citizenship** What qualities helped Stephen F. Austin succeed as the leader of his colonies in Texas?

2. **Economics** Why did so many U.S. settlers come to Texas during the 1820s?

3. **Geography** What factors did Texas settlers consider when deciding where they should live?

 ⭐TEKS

TAKS Practice: **Thinking Critically**

1. **Comparing and Contrasting** How were the mission system and *empresario* system similar? How were they different?

2. **Summarizing** Explain the significance of the year 1821 in Texas history.

3. **Drawing Inferences and Conclusions** How did the limits on where immigrants could settle reflect Mexico's concerns about U.S. settlers?

Interpreting Graphs ⭐TEKS

Study the bar graph below. Then use the information in the graph to help you answer the questions.

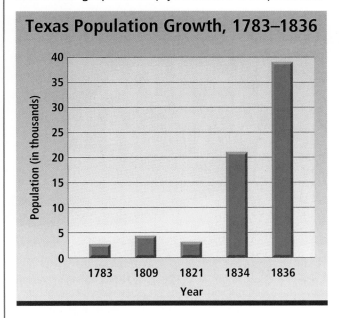

Texas Population Growth, 1783–1836

(Bar graph showing Population in thousands by Year. 1783: about 3; 1809: about 4; 1821: about 3; 1834: about 21; 1836: about 39.)

1. About how many times bigger was the Texas population in 1836 than in 1821?

   a. about 20 times
   b. about 3 times
   c. about 42 times
   d. about 10 times

2. What was the main reason for this growth?

Analyzing Primary Sources ⭐TEKS

Read the following quote by Texas colonist Noah Smithwick. Then answer the questions.

"**What the discovery of gold was to California the colonization act of 1825 was to Texas. In the following year Sterling C. Robertson, who had obtained a grant for a colony, . . . went up into Kentucky recruiting. The glowing terms in which he descanted on [described] the advantages to be gained by emigration [leaving], were well calculated [planned] to further his scheme [founding a colony]. To every head of a family . . . was promised 177 acres of farming land . . . and 4,428 acres of pasture land for stock. . . . Corn . . . was to be had for the planting. . . . Of the hardships . . . [and] danger from the . . . Indians . . . he was discreetly [carefully] silent.**"

3. What major arguments did Robertson use to persuade Kentuckians to move to Texas?

   a. the presence of prosperous towns and good schools and churches
   b. the good food supply and the easy availability of land
   c. the lack of American Indians that were hostile toward settlers
   d. a booming economy and easy access to transportation routes

4. What bias does Smithwick point out in Robertson's description of Texas?

Alternative Assessment

Interdisciplinary Connection to the Arts ⭐TEKS

Work with a small group to create a mural illustrating the events of Texas colonization in the 1820s and early 1830s. Be sure to identify important people involved in the colonization of Texas. You might want to organize your mural to show events in sequence, where possible. Provide a caption of one or two paragraphs explaining your design. When you have finished, review your work to check the grammar, spelling, and punctuation.

BUILDING YOUR Portfolio

📄 internet connect

Internet Activity: go.hrw.com
KEYWORD: ST3 TX8 ⭐TEKS

Access the Internet through the HRW Go site to research the location of an *empresario* colony in Texas. Then analyze physical factors that affected where colonies were established by creating a chart that displays the following information: the name, landforms, natural resources, and climate of the colony. You may want to illustrate your chart.

Life in Early Texas

(1820–1835)

Settlers in Texas lived in the newly created Mexican state of Coahuila y Texas.

Jared Groce's first house in Texas was located on the Brazos River in Waller County.

TEXAS

1822 U.S. settler Jared Groce plants a cotton crop, possibly the first in Stephen F. Austin's colony.

1824 Mexican officials adopt the Constitution of 1824. Coahuila and Texas are merged to form one state.

1827 Stephen F. Austin receives a contract to settle an additional 100 families in Texas.

1820	1822	1824	1826

U.S. and WORLD

1821 The first public high school opens in Boston, Massachusetts.

1823 Charles Macintosh invents waterproof fabric, which was used in raincoats.

1825 The Erie Canal is completed.

A Massachusetts law passed in 1827 required large towns to establish high schools like this one.

Build on What You Know

In the early 1820s *empresarios* such as Stephen F. Austin and Martín de León established colonies in Texas. Their actions and a generous colonization law for Texas led to a wave of immigration from the United States and other countries. These settlers worked hard to build a new life in Texas.

The Granger Collection, New York

The availability of cheap land drew thousands of U.S. settlers west to Texas and other regions during the early 1800s.

To prepare cotton for market, farmers often bound their harvests in large bales.

1829 Thomas J. Pilgrim organizes a Sunday school and private boys' school in San Felipe.

1833 Mary Austin Holley's letters, describing life in early Texas, are published.

1834 Texas farmers export some 7,000 bales of cotton, worth about $315,000, to New Orleans.
1835 An estimated 1,000 U.S. immigrants enter Texas each month.

1828   1830   1832   1834

1833 Great Britain abolishes slavery throughout its empire.

1834 Cyrus McCormick patents a reaping machine that allows farmers to harvest grains such as wheat three times faster.

The McCormick reaper helped increase farm productivity.

You Be the Historian:

Themes Journal

What's Your Opinion? Do you **agree** or **disagree** with the following statements? Support your point of view in your journal.

- **Constitutional Heritage** A constitution creating a strong central government is preferable to one giving more control to local governments.

- **Citizenship** Obeying the law is an important requirement of citizenship.

- **Geography** Transportation systems affect economic growth.

If you were there . . .
How would you improve frontier life?

Texas Fever

Read to Discover

1. Why did many early U.S. settlers go to Texas, and where did they and other groups settle?
2. How did settlers get to Texas and choose their land?

Define
- flatboats

Identify
- G.T.T.

Why It Matters Today

The early immigrants who came to Texas had to endure long, hard journeys. Use **CNN fyi.com** and other **current events** sources to find information about modern migrations. Record your findings in your journal.

Many early immigrants to Texas packed their belongings in wagons.

The Story Continues

The lone rider heard the wagon train before he saw it. Shouts and cries mixed with the thuds, clangs, and groans of the wagons and the oxen. Slowly bumping over ruts and stones, the wagon train rolled into view. The weary and muddy immigrants struggled past. Some rode, while others trudged forward on foot. Despite the hard journey, they kept going, eager to reach Texas.

★ Gone to Texas

The population of Texas grew quickly during the 1820s and 1830s. Some people moved to Texas from Europe and other parts of Mexico. However, most of the settlers flooding into Texas were farmers from the southern United States. Texas fever had swept the nation. The "pull" of cheap land and easy payment terms drew many immigrants. Several factors also "pushed" U.S. settlers to leave their country. Many immigrants were escaping debts resulting from the Panic of 1819 and the depression that followed it. Many settlers hoped to make a fresh start in Texas, where U.S. creditors had no authority to collect debts. For example, both Stephen F. Austin and Jared Groce had left behind large debts.

U.S. authorities could not follow criminals into Texas either. Gradually, a number of drifters and outlaws began entering the region. Word spread that Texas was filling with undesirable people. When someone left town owing money or accused of a crime, people said they had probably gone to Texas. Many overdue accounts were marked "<u>G.T.T.</u>" for "Gone to Texas." Such rumors made some people hesitant to move to Texas. One man wrote to Austin about his concerns.

Texas Voices ❝As I contemplate [think about] becoming a resident of Texas, I feel great solicitude [concern] about the nature of the population which will inhabit the country. . . . The planters here have a most desperate [low] opinion of the population there, originating . . . from such villains as . . . have taken shelter in that province [area].❞

—Thomas White, quoted in *Texas Siftings*, by Jerry Flemmons

⭐ **Reading Check** **Categorizing** What were the major push and pull factors of U.S. immigration to Texas?

Analyzing Primary Sources **Identifying Bias** What factors might have influenced White's opinion of Texas settlers? How might Stephen F. Austin respond to such criticism?

⭐ The People of Texas

In 1834 a Mexican official estimated that the Texas population had reached some 21,000, about 15,000 of whom were from the United States. Most of them were of English, Irish, or Scottish ancestry. They

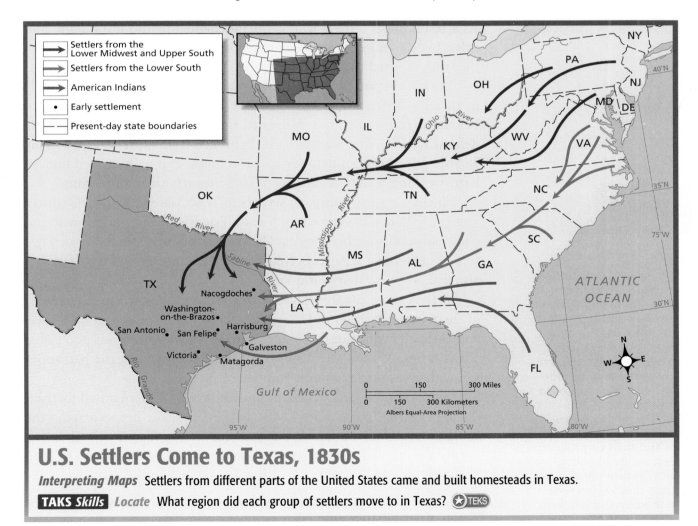

U.S. Settlers Come to Texas, 1830s

Interpreting Maps Settlers from different parts of the United States came and built homesteads in Texas.

TAKS Skills *Locate* What region did each group of settlers move to in Texas? ⭐TEKS

Interpreting the Visual Record

Getting to Texas. Many U.S. immigrants traveled on flatboats for part of their journey. *How do you think geographic factors such as rivers affected immigration to Texas?* ⭐TEKS

mainly settled in the fertile Brazos, Colorado, and Trinity River valleys along the Gulf Coast and in East Texas. While many U.S. settlers came to Texas with the help of *empresarios,* others came on their own. Mexican law allowed settlers to acquire land directly, but the process was difficult. As a result, most settlers who came independently did not obtain land titles. Instead, they became squatters, or people who do not legally own the land on which they live.

The Tejano population in 1834 was about 4,000. Tejanos lived mainly in the San Antonio and Nacogdoches areas. Many Tejanos welcomed U.S. immigration because it boosted the economy and helped provide defense against American Indians. Francisco Ruiz expressed how many Tejanos felt. "I cannot help seeing advantages . . . if we admitted honest, hard-working people, regardless of what country they come from."

The majority of European settlers in Texas were of British, German, French, or Italian backgrounds. Johann Friedrich Ernst and his wife and children were probably the first German family to come to Texas. They settled in Stephen F. Austin's colony in 1831. A number of Irish families also lived in San Patricio and Refugio.

In 1834 some 2,000 enslaved African Americans lived in Texas. Most of them came as slaves of U.S. settlers. Slaves lived mostly in East Texas and along the Gulf Coast. About 150 free African Americans also called Texas home. Under Mexican law, free African Americans had more rights than those living in the southern United States.

Members of several American Indian groups also migrated to Texas during the 1820s and early 1830s. Many Cherokee began leaving the southeastern United States as U.S. settlement expanded. Some Cherokee eventually settled in East Texas. Chickasaw, Creek, Delaware, and Shawnee Indians also settled in Texas during this period.

⭐ **Reading Check** **Summarizing** What immigrant groups came to Texas, and where did they settle?

That's Interesting!

Texas Panthers

Some early Texas settlers encountered wild panthers. These animals both horrified and fascinated the colonists. The panthers had several odd habits. They ate an incredibly wide range of food—anything from horses to grasshoppers. After killing large game, such as a deer, panthers ate their fill and then carefully covered the dead animal with branches and leaves. Later, they would return to feast on the leftovers.

★ Getting to Texas and Choosing Land

By 1835 an estimated 1,000 U.S. settlers were entering Texas each month. Many immigrants came to Texas in covered wagons pulled by horses, mules, or oxen. Colonist Jared Groce had one of the largest wagon trains, consisting of some 50 wagons filled with people and supplies. Other immigrants rode on horseback, with their belongings tied behind their saddles. Some even walked. For many, the fastest way to reach Texas was by boat. Water travel was typically more expensive than traveling overland, however. Some who went by water floated down the Mississippi River on long, low boats called **flatboats**. These travelers usually went to New Orleans, where they boarded ships headed to Texas.

On reaching Texas, settlers had to decide where to live. Although *empresarios* sometimes assigned specific grants of land, most settlers made their own choices. They usually settled along rivers and streams that provided water for drinking, farming, and transportation. The fertile soil and mild climate of the Gulf Coast Plain and the Piney Woods attracted many U.S. immigrants. Some settlers also chose land that resembled their old homes. For example, many people from hilly southern Tennessee settled in hilly areas in present-day Red River County.

The presence of American Indians also affected settlement patterns in Texas. Many settlers feared Plains Indians such as the Apache and Comanche. Colonists avoided their lands, settling east of the Guadalupe River and south of the Old San Antonio Road instead. Generally, however, most Texas Indians in this area accepted the newcomers.

★ **Reading Check** **Summarizing** Analyze the geographic factors that immigrants considered when choosing land and how that affected settlement in Texas.

★ LONE STAR LEGACY

The Big Thicket

Some people who moved to East Texas settled in an area called the Big Thicket. In the 1830s, yellow pines up to six feet in diameter covered the region. Bear, deer, panthers, and wolves roamed the area's hills and swamps. Today the Big Thicket offers one of the largest varieties of plant life in the world, including four meat-eating plants. The region is also home to some 350 bird species. How do you think the natural resources of the area affected settler life? ★ TEKS

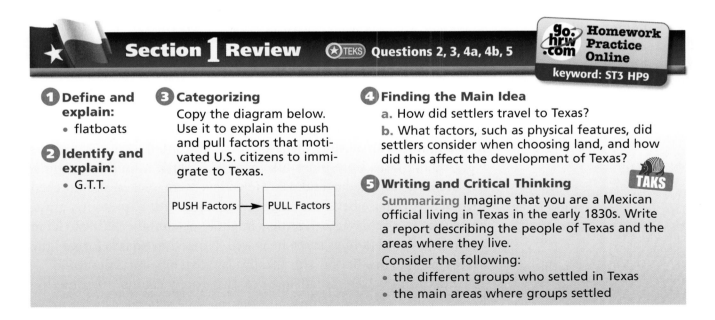

Section 1 Review   ★ TEKS Questions 2, 3, 4a, 4b, 5

go.hrw.com Homework Practice Online
keyword: ST3 HP9

1 Define and explain:
- flatboats

2 Identify and explain:
- G.T.T.

3 Categorizing
Copy the diagram below. Use it to explain the push and pull factors that motivated U.S. citizens to immigrate to Texas.

PUSH Factors → PULL Factors

4 Finding the Main Idea
a. How did settlers travel to Texas?
b. What factors, such as physical features, did settlers consider when choosing land, and how did this affect the development of Texas?

5 Writing and Critical Thinking TAKS
Summarizing Imagine that you are a Mexican official living in Texas in the early 1830s. Write a report describing the people of Texas and the areas where they live.
Consider the following:
- the different groups who settled in Texas
- the main areas where groups settled

Daily Life on the Frontier

Read to Discover

1. What types of houses did settlers build in Texas during the 1820s and early 1830s?
2. What were the clothing and diet of settlers in Texas like at that time?
3. What were religion and education like in early Texas?

Why It Matters Today

Many settlers in Texas relied on their crops for food. Use **CNNfyi.com** or other **current events** sources to find out how people rely on agriculture today. Record your findings in your journal.

Define

- **dogtrot cabins**
- **quilting bees**
- **buckskin**
- **venison**

Identify

- **Thomas J. Pilgrim**
- **Mary Wightman**
- **Frances Trask**

The Story Continues

After a long journey immigrant families often found a warm welcome in Texas. From miles around, settlers came to help them build a house. After greeting the new arrivals, they set to work. While the men cut down trees and hauled logs, the women barbecued meat and prepared cornbread. Children played games and learned to dance. Their work done, the settlers finally left as night fell.

Many of the homes built by early U.S. settlers were dogtrot cabins.

★ Frontier Homes

One of the first tasks for newcomers in Texas was to build a house. For this chore, settlers had to rely on the building materials at hand. To the south and west, many Tejanos lived in flat-roofed adobe or stone houses. Jacales, small huts made of sticks and mud, were common as well. Where trees were plentiful, many U.S. settlers built log cabins. Settlers used pine, cedar, and oak. Hewn logs were stacked and notched together. The space between the logs was filled with clay, stones, grass, and sticks. In warm weather, settlers might knock out this filling to let in a breeze. Of course, bugs came in as well. Long, thin boards formed the cabins' roofs, while floors were usually clay, dirt, or sometimes wood.

Most homes were small one- or two-room cabins. In some log homes, called **dogtrot cabins**, an open passage separated two rooms.

Breezes would flow through this passage, cooling the cabin. As time passed, some settlers enclosed the passage to form a third room. A settler described Stephen F. Austin's dogtrot cabin. "Austin's house was a double log cabin with a wide 'passage' through the center, a porch . . . on the front with windows opening upon it, and [a] chimney at each end."

Settlers usually furnished their homes with items they made themselves. This handmade furniture was often simple and sturdy. Some furnishings were both functional and beautiful, like the quilts that women made. **Quilting bees**, or quilting groups, were popular because women could socialize while they worked. As time passed, settlers often replaced their log cabins with larger, fancier homes and nicer furniture.

★ **Reading Check** **Analyzing Information** In what ways did Texans adapt to their environment when building their homes?

★ Clothing in Early Texas

Settlers also used local materials to make their clothes. Because Texas had plenty of wild cattle and game, leather clothing was common. Many men, women, and children wore **buckskin**, or tanned deer hide. Some settlers decorated their buckskin clothing with beads or fringe. Although extremely strong, buckskin was very uncomfortable and often smelly. As other fabrics became available, settlers gladly switched to them. By the early 1830s, homespun cotton began replacing buckskin. Women and girls began wearing cotton dresses and bonnets. Men wore cotton shirts in the fields and dark cotton suits for formal events. At dances and balls, some wealthier women wore elaborate dresses from the United States and Europe. Men who could afford it wore frock coats with vests, ruffled shirts, and stiff collars. During cold weather, men and women wore coats made of bearhide, blankets, or buffalo skin. Mexican ponchos, cotton blankets with a slit for the head, were also common.

Hats provided protection against the harsh sunlight and extra warmth on cold days. Women wore simple cotton bonnets or sun hats. Men usually wore wide-brimmed hats made of beaver, buckskin, or coonskin. Tejano men often wore sombreros. For more formal events, men sometimes wore stovepipe hats, while women wore fancy store-bought hats. As towns in early Texas grew, merchants began stocking ready-to-wear items, such as calico dresses, silk gowns, suits, and vests. These store-bought goods were expensive because merchants had to charge high prices to cover shipping costs. As a result, most Texans continued to make their own clothing.

★ **Reading Check** **Summarizing** How did settlers' clothing demonstrate how Texans adapted to their environment?

Our Cultural Heritage

A Blending of Foods

Immigrants brought their traditional recipes and cooking styles to Texas. For example, German immigrants introduced spicy sausages and sauerkraut. Settlers from the United States expanded their diets as they encountered new foods. Many U.S. settlers became fond of Mexican tortillas and tamales. Sometimes settlers combined traditional dishes to form a new tradition, such as Tex-Mex food. **How did immigrants adapt to Texas culture while maintaining their own heritage?** ⭐ TEKS

⭐ Frontier Foods

Most Texas settlers had to be self-reliant for food as well as clothing. For their meals, settlers depended on their crops and livestock, as well as wild game. Any extra crops or livestock were sold or traded. Most settlers planted corn, which grew well in Texas and was easy to harvest and prepare. It was also nutritious. A German settler described the crop's importance. "Raising corn was a matter of life and death, since upon it depended the existence of the colony." Tejano and U.S. settlers had learned many different ways to prepare corn from American Indians. Settlers roasted or boiled corn on the cob. They made cornmeal by drying the kernels and grinding them. Settlers used cornmeal to make tortillas. They would also add butter, milk, or molasses to the cornmeal to make cornbread. Cornmeal batter cooked over hot coals produced johnnycakes. Other corn dishes included fritters, hominy, and popcorn. Corn's uses did not stop there—settlers also fed it to their livestock and used it for fuel. They even found uses for corn cobs, making items such as back scratchers, bottle stoppers, and fishing floats.

Texas settlers grew vegetables such as cabbages, peas, pumpkins, sweet potatoes, and turnips. Wild berries, grapes, peaches, and other fruits were sometimes available. Pecan trees grew along many rivers. Butter, cheese, eggs, flour, and milk were rarely available, however. The typical settler's meal consisted of fried meat, cornbread, and black coffee. The most common meats were beef, pork, and **venison**, or deer meat. In coastal areas and along rivers, fish was standard fare. When these were not available, settlers hunted a variety of game. One popular recipe instructed cooks to "salt and pepper inside of 1 skinned and gutted possum."

⭐ **Reading Check Evaluating** How did the Texas settlers' use of corn demonstrate their ability to adapt to and modify their environment?

⭐ Religion in Early Texas

Mexico's official religion was Roman Catholicism. Most U.S. settlers in Texas, however, were Protestant and unwilling to change their beliefs. Publicly, they stated support for the Roman Catholic Church but privately worshiped as they pleased. Although some Tejano settlements had priests, most new Texas settlements had none. Stephen F. Austin pleaded with officials for a priest because his colonists needed someone to handle baptisms, burials, and other religious ceremonies. Finally, Father Michael Muldoon, an Irish priest, arrived in San Felipe in 1831. He was one of the few priests any of the early U.S. settlers ever saw.

While under Mexican rule, Texas did not have any organized Protestant churches because only the Catholic Church was legal. A fair amount of Protestant activity did exist, however. Traveling preachers

During the early 1830s Father Michael Muldoon performed mass weddings and baptisms for Texas settlers.

from the United States held camp meetings, while Protestant missionaries worked to spread their religion. Sumner Bacon, a Presbyterian, traveled through Texas giving sermons and handing out English and Spanish Bibles. Several Texans also organized Protestant Sunday schools. In 1829 **Thomas J. Pilgrim**, a Baptist, organized the first Sunday school in San Felipe. That same year, <u>Mary Wightman</u> began a Sunday school at Matagorda. Mexican officials usually just ignored such religious activity.

Reading Check Analyzing Information How did U.S. settlers maintain their cultural heritage?

★ Education on the Frontier

Protestant teachers also opened private schools. For example, Pilgrim ran a boys' school in San Felipe. In 1835 <u>Frances Trask</u> opened a girls' boarding school in Cole's Settlement. Trask described the school in a letter.

Texas Voices ❝My school is small, but profitable, as tuition is high, from $6.00 to $10.00 per quarter—I have but 7 boarders at $2.00 wk [a week]. . . . My buildings (for I have two) rank second to none in Texas. One is a frame building 15 by 20 ft. with two glazed windows on a side, and folding doors at each end. This answers for schoolroom, parlor, bed chamber, and hall. The other [building] is . . . a rugged black log house . . . that is my kitchen.❞

—Frances Trask, quoted in *The Texas Republic: A Social and Economic History*, by William Ranson Hogan

Daily Life

Leisure Time

Settlers in early Texas enjoyed many forms of entertainment. Riders and spectators alike loved horse racing, a favorite pastime of the first Spanish settlers. Frontier Texans also enjoyed music and dancing. One man remembered a dance that lasted almost 15 hours. Weddings and balls were also popular social occasions. At home, settlers often read aloud from the Bible and other books. Storytellers told tall tales as family members gathered around. **How did settlers entertain themselves in Texas?**

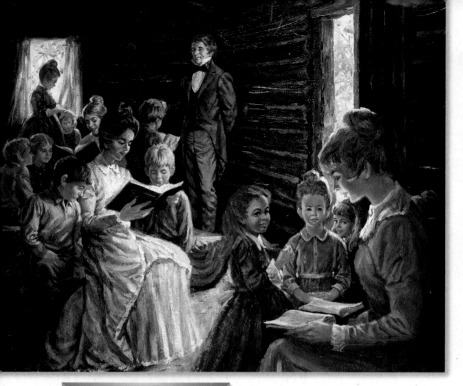

Colonial life. Students in frontier schools often shared their textbooks. How does this painting reflect the way children were taught in frontier Texas? ⭐TEKS

Education in early Texas was mainly limited to teaching in the home or small private schools. Wealthier settlers sent their children to schools in the United States, where the education system was better established. The Coahuila y Texas Constitution and an 1829 law provided for the creation of public schools in Texas. However, few settlements had the funds to establish such schools, and capable teachers were in short supply.

Some communities responded to these challenges by sharing the costs to set up schools. Juan Zambrano established a school in San Antonio in 1811. Other Tejanos started a public school in San Antonio in 1828 called the Public Free Primary School, supported partly by local funds. Teachers taught arithmetic, morals, reading, religion, and writing. Jonesborough, Nacogdoches, and San Augustine opened schools as well.

By 1836 Texas had more than 20 schools. However, many children did not have access to education. Even when schools were available, the demands of farm life kept many children in the fields. In addition, enslaved African Americans were not allowed to attend school.

⭐ **Reading Check** **Drawing Inferences and Conclusions** Why do you think the Mexican government tried to establish public schools in Texas?

⭐ **Section 2 Review** ⭐TEKS Questions 2, 3, 4a, 4b, 5

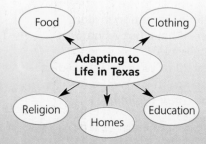
go.hrw.com **Homework Practice Online**
keyword: ST3 HP9

1 **Define and explain:**
- dogtrot cabins
- quilting bees
- buckskin
- venison

2 **Identify and explain:**
- Thomas J. Pilgrim
- Mary Wightman
- Frances Trask

3 **Summarizing**
Copy the graphic organizer below. Use it to describe life in Texas during the 1820s and early 1830s.

```
        Food              Clothing
              Adapting to
              Life in Texas
     Religion              Education
            Homes
```

4 **Finding the Main Idea**
a. How did U.S. settlers attempt to maintain their religious heritage while adapting to the local culture?
b. Why were public schools rare in Texas?

5 **Writing and Critical Thinking** TAKS
Analyzing Information Write a letter to a U.S. family planning to go to Texas in the early 1830s. Explain how they can adapt to life there.
Consider the following:
- available resources in Texas
- culture and policies of Texas

Read to Discover

1. What economic activities were important to the Texas economy in the early 1800s?
2. What was transportation like in Texas at that time?

Why It Matters Today

Settlers in early Texas traded a great deal with the United States. Use **CNN fyi.com** or other **current events** sources to find information about U.S. or Texas trade today. Record your findings in your journal.

Define

- **plantations**
- **free enterprise**
- **barter**
- **exports**
- **imports**
- **sawmills**

Identify

- **William Goyens**

The Story Continues

Once in Texas, Austrian immigrant George B. Erath realized that he lacked several important items. Looking through his few belongings, Erath selected some with which he was willing to part. Approaching other settlers, he traded his clothes for cattle and hogs. To obtain corn, he gave up his horse. Erath's partner, who was in a similar position, traded his ox for a pig and his feather bed for three cows. In Texas, livestock and corn were more important than luxuries.

Oxen and other farm animals were very important to settlers who used them to work the land and supply their families with food.

★ Farming and Ranching

Agriculture dominated the Texas economy during the 1820s and 1830s, when most settlers lived on small family farms. Farm families worked hard to prepare fields, harvest crops, and perform household tasks. With few nearby stores and little cash, families also produced many of the items they needed, such as tools and clothing. Settler Mary Rabb took care of her Texas farm alone for a period. "I would pick the cotton . . . and spin six hundred thread . . . every day and milk my cows and pound my [corn]meal . . . and cook . . . and churn and mind my children." A few Texas settlers established **plantations**—large farms that usually specialized in growing one kind of crop. Plantations often resembled small communities and sometimes covered thousands of acres. Enslaved African Americans provided the main labor force, often working from dawn to dusk in both the fields and in homes.

Interpreting the Visual Record

Farming and ranching. Early Texas farmers and ranchers often raised enough food to feed their families and to trade for other necessities. However, a few large ranchers also drove their cattle to markets in New Orleans and other areas. **How do you think farm life in this image compares to farming today?** TEKS

On both small and large farms, cotton became the main crop grown for profit. U.S. immigrants brought cotton farming to Texas, making the lower Brazos, Colorado, and Trinity River valleys the center of cotton production. Tejano farmers around Goliad and San Antonio also grew small amounts of cotton.

Some settlers also established ranches in Texas. The mild climate, prairies, and river valleys provided good pasture for cattle and other livestock. Spanish settlers had begun ranching in the Rio Grande valley. By the 1820s wealthy Tejanos such as Martín de León and Erasmo Seguín were ranching around San Antonio and Victoria. Family, friends, and hired hands typically all lived together on the ranch, which resembled a small community. A visitor in 1834 described the Seguín ranch. "It consists of a square, palisaded [walled] round, with the houses of the families residing there forming the sides." Life on Texas ranches was made up of branding, caring for, feeding, and herding the cattle.

Reading Check Contrasting How did the economic purposes of Spanish and U.S. settlers in Texas differ?

★ Business, Trade, and Transportation

Craftspeople and merchants also lived in Texas. Blacksmiths, carpenters, and shopkeepers offered their services in Nacogdoches, San Antonio, and San Felipe. These businesspeople made a profit by engaging in **free enterprise**, an economic system in which businesses operate with minimal government control. For example, **William Goyens** of Nacogdoches became wealthy by running a blacksmithing shop and various other businesses. In time, Brazoria and Matagorda joined Nacogdoches as important commercial trade centers.

Most business was conducted through **barter**, or the trade of one good or service for another, because the supply of money was limited. As the population grew, business and trade increased. In the 1830s Texas was producing **exports**. These are items that a country sells to other nations. Texas exports included cattle, corn, cotton, cowhides, furs, horses, pork, and salt. Texas exports, most of which went to Louisiana, were worth about $500,000 in the mid-1830s. There was also a demand for many U.S. **imports**, or items that a nation buys from other countries.

Despite this business growth, Texans manufactured few items. Blacksmiths and carpenters made essential items such as plows, tools, and wagons. A few Texans owned cotton gins. Jared Groce owned the largest cotton gin in Texas. Texans also operated **sawmills**, which cut wood into usable pieces. Most of these small industries helped support farming and ranching.

Poor transportation was the chief obstacle to economic growth in Texas in the early 1800s. The few roads that linked towns were little more than wide trails. These roads were bumpy and dusty in dry weather. In wet weather they became muddy impassable swamps. Traveling and transporting goods by river was not much better. Many Texas rivers were shallow and full of snags and sandbars. During heavy rains, rivers often overflowed or became blocked by driftwood. Although small boats and rafts could navigate some rivers, most large boats had difficulties.

Ships and steamboats arrived at Texas ports on the Gulf of Mexico. One of the busiest ports was located in Galveston Bay. In the early 1830s Brazoria and Matagorda became important port towns. Although these ports connected Texas to other regions, they did not solve its internal transportation problems.

Biography

William Goyens
(1794–1856)

Originally from North Carolina, William Goyens became a wealthy business owner in Nacogdoches. He worked as a blacksmith and a wagon maker, transported goods, and also ran an inn. Goyens also served Texas as a diplomat, assisting in important negotiations with the Cherokee. **What significant contributions did Goyens make to Texas?** ⭐TEKS

⭐TEKS **Reading Check Evaluating** How did Texas exports reflect its economy, and how did geographic factors limit transportation?

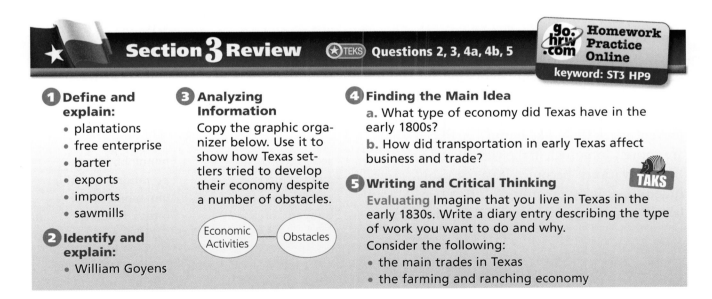

Section 3 Review ⭐TEKS Questions 2, 3, 4a, 4b, 5

go.hrw.com **Homework Practice Online**
keyword: ST3 HP9

1 Define and explain:
- plantations
- free enterprise
- barter
- exports
- imports
- sawmills

2 Identify and explain:
- William Goyens

3 Analyzing Information
Copy the graphic organizer below. Use it to show how Texas settlers tried to develop their economy despite a number of obstacles.

Economic Activities — Obstacles

4 Finding the Main Idea
a. What type of economy did Texas have in the early 1800s?
b. How did transportation in early Texas affect business and trade?

5 Writing and Critical Thinking
TAKS
Evaluating Imagine that you live in Texas in the early 1830s. Write a diary entry describing the type of work you want to do and why.
Consider the following:
- the main trades in Texas
- the farming and ranching economy

Life in Early Texas **193**

Connecting To *Literature*

Texas: Observations, Historical, Geographical, and Descriptive

Mary Austin Holley

The diaries, letters, and histories of Mary Austin Holley provide a detailed picture of life in early Texas. The cousin of Stephen F. Austin, Holley was a well-educated and sophisticated woman from Connecticut. Holley visited Texas in 1831. While there, she wrote many letters about the region to friends. In 1833 her letters were published in a book entitled Texas: Observations, Historical, Geographical, and Descriptive. *Holley visited Texas several more times and published her diary of one such trip. Holley followed this work with the book* Texas. *Published in 1836, it is the first known history of Texas written in English. The following excerpt is from an 1831 letter, in which Holley describes how settlers adapted to life in Texas.*

Mary Austin Holley

It is found to be easier to raise or manufacture such articles as are needed in the family, or to do without, than to obtain them from abroad, or to employ an individual to **scour**[1] the country, in search of such as may be desired. People live too far apart, to beg or borrow often. . . . If they want any article of first necessity, coffee, for instance, which is much used, they will send some of their chickens, butter, and eggs, to a neighboring family newly arrived, and propose an exchange, as most new comers bring with them some **stores**.[2] There is much of this kind of barter, **provisions**[3] being so much more plenty than money. . . .

The common concerns of life are sufficiently exciting to keep the spirits **buoyant**,[4] and prevent every thing like **ennui**.[5] Artificial wants are entirely forgotten, in the view of real ones. . . . Even **privations**[6] become pleasures: people grow **ingenious**[7] in overcoming difficulties. Many **latent**[8] faculties are developed. They discover in themselves, powers, they did not suspect themselves of possessing. Equally surprised and delighted at the discovery, they apply to their labours with all that energy and spirit, which new hope and conscious strength inspire.

Understanding What You Read ⭐TEKS

1. **Literature and History** How did human factors such as trade and communication contribute to the immigration of U.S. settlers?

2. **Literature and You** Based on information in this chapter, how accurately does this primary source describe Texas at this time?

[1] **scour:** search
[2] **stores:** goods
[3] **provisions:** goods
[4] **buoyant:** uplifted
[5] **ennui:** boredom
[6] **privations:** hardships
[7] **ingenious:** clever
[8] **latent:** hidden

Government and Society

Read to Discover
1. How did the Mexican Constitution of 1824 affect Texas?
2. Why did the issue of slavery begin to cause conflict?

Define
• federalism

Identify
• Constitution of 1824

Why It Matters Today

Mexico changed its form of government in the early 1820s. Use CNNfyi.com and other **current events** sources to find information about a nation where the form of government has recently changed. Record your findings in your journal.

The Story Continues

The news spread through Texas that the Mexican legislature had approved a new constitution. Stephen F. Austin had advised the officials who had written the document, and Erasmo Seguín had represented Texas at the constitutional assembly. Texas farmers had donated corn to cover Seguín's expenses. The people of Texas had done their part. They now waited to learn how the new constitution would affect them.

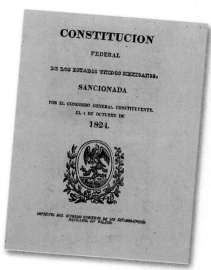

The Constitution of 1824 established a federal government for Mexico.

★ Texas under Mexican Rule

After Mexican leader Agustín de Iturbide lost power, Mexico became a republic. On October 4, 1824, officials adopted the Federal Constitution of the United States of Mexico, or the **Constitution of 1824**. Erasmo Seguín of San Antonio helped write this constitution. Most Texans—Tejanos and U.S. settlers alike—supported the Constitution of 1824. Like the U.S. Constitution, it gave limited power to the central government and broad local authority to the states. This division of power, called **federalism**, distributes power between a central and regional governments. The Constitution of 1824 also divided power among three branches of government. A president served as the head of state. At the same time, the two constitutions differed in many ways. Mexico's state lawmakers, not its citizens, elected the president. Unlike the United States, Mexico did not separate church and state or have freedom of religion. Roman Catholicism was the official religion of Mexico.

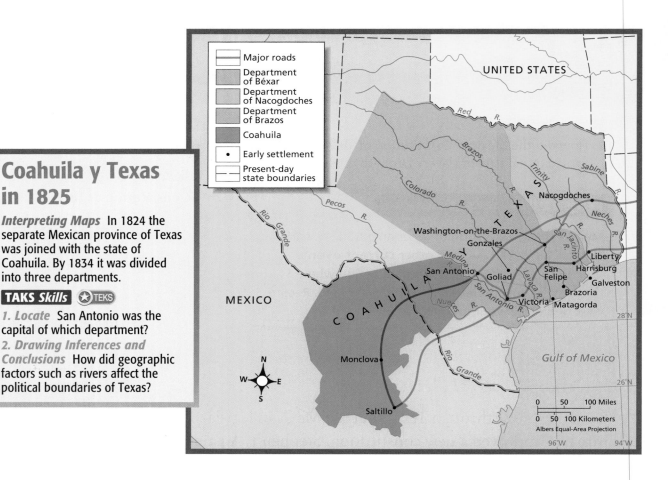

Coahuila y Texas in 1825

Interpreting Maps In 1824 the separate Mexican province of Texas was joined with the state of Coahuila. By 1834 it was divided into three departments.

TAKS Skills ⭐TEKS

1. Locate San Antonio was the capital of which department?

2. Drawing Inferences and Conclusions How did geographic factors such as rivers affect the political boundaries of Texas?

When conflicts erupted in the 1830s, Texans expressed their loyalty to the Constitution of 1824 by placing that date on flags.

The Constitution of 1824 also united Texas and the Mexican province of Coahuila into one state. Many settlers disliked this decision. They thought that separate statehood would provide more local control. In addition, the state's capital of Saltillo was far away. As a result, few Texans could participate in state government. In 1825 Texas became a department, or political subdivision, within Coahuila y Texas. Later, this department was further divided into three departments, with headquarters at Nacogdoches, San Antonio, and San Felipe. Tejanos held most government positions in San Antonio. However, U.S. settlers dominated politics wherever they were the majority of the population.

Many U.S. settlers wanted local control over rights and freedoms. This was because their political traditions differed from Mexican law. For example, U.S. settlers wanted the right to a trial by jury, as in the United States. The state constitution of Coahuila y Texas, adopted in 1827, allowed for trial by jury. However, authorities did not make any attempt to provide such trials. When U.S. settlers did not agree with Mexican laws, they often ignored or changed them. Mexican officials who wanted to encourage immigration frequently took no notice of such actions. As a result, local government in Texas became a mixture of Mexican and U.S. practices.

⭐ **Reading Check** **Comparing** How were the Mexican Constitution of 1824 and the U.S. Constitution similar?

★ The Issue of Slavery in Texas

Cultural and political differences between Texans—particularly U.S. settlers—and the Mexican government eventually led to conflicts. Through trade and other connections, most U.S. settlers remained more closely tied to the United States than to Mexico. In late 1825 an American newspaper described the situation. "The colonists in Texas will not be Mexicans more than in name."

One issue more than others divided U.S. settlers and the Mexican government. During the 1820s the Mexican and Coahuila y Texas state governments passed laws restricting slavery. Many U.S. settlers in Texas ignored such restrictions. However, many U.S. settlers and potential immigrants feared that Mexico might make slavery illegal. An Alabama farmer expressed this in a letter to Stephen F. Austin.

While Eli Whitney's cotton gin made it easier to process cotton, cotton farming still required a great deal of labor.

Texas Voices ❝Our most valuable inhabitants [residents] here own [slaves]. I am therefore anxious to know what the laws are upon that subject. . . . Our planters are not willing to remove [to Texas] without they can first be assured [promised] of their [slaves] being secured to them by the laws of your Govt.❞

—Charles Douglas, quoted in *Westward Expansion*, by Sanford Wexler

Analyzing Primary Sources ★
Identifying Points of View
Do you think the writer would go to Texas if he could not keep his slaves? Why or why not?

Some Tejanos and U.S. settlers opposed slavery. However, many Texans who opposed slavery—including Austin—believed that it was necessary for the economy because farming cotton required a great deal of labor. In 1827 the state constitution outlawed slavery. However, José Antonio Navarro helped pass a law allowing for contract labor. This law gave Texas slaveholders a way to work around the constitutional ban. As U.S. settlement in Texas increased, tensions with Mexican officials over the issue of slavery rose.

★ **Reading Check** **Making Generalizations and Predictions** How do you think U.S. settlers' unwillingness to adopt Mexican ways will affect Texas?

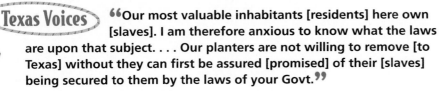

★ **Section 4 Review** ★TEKS Questions 2, 3, 4a, 4b, 5

go.hrw.com **Homework Practice Online**
keyword: ST3 HP9

1 **Define and explain:**
- federalism

2 **Identify and explain:**
- Constitution of 1824

3 **Comparing and Contrasting**
Copy the graphic organizer below. Use it to list the differences and similarities between the Mexican Constitution of 1824 and the U.S. Constitution.

Similarities	Differences

4 **Finding the Main Idea**
a. Identify how the Mexican Constitution of 1824 affected Texas.
b. Why did the issue of slavery cause increasing tensions in Texas?

5 **Writing and Critical Thinking**

TAKS

Identifying Cause and Effect Write a paragraph explaining why Mexican officials were concerned about the number of U.S. settlers in Texas.
Consider the following:
- tensions about the issue of slavery
- cultural and political differences

The Chapter at a Glance

Examine the following visual summary of the chapter. Then use the visual to write a one-page short story about life in Texas during the early 1800s. Use standard grammar, spelling, sentence structure, and punctuation to describe the economy, immigration, and Mexican government in Texas. ★TEKS

Some U.S. settlers brought slaves to Texas to help work the fields and do chores.

While most Texans supported the new Constitution of 1824, many settlers disliked several Mexican policies.

Many new settlers came to Texas for land to start their own farms. With them, they brought ideas about farming, religion, and government.

Identifying People and Ideas ★TEKS

Use the following terms or people in historically significant sentences.

1. G.T.T.
2. flatboats
3. dogtrot cabins
4. quilting bees
5. plantations
6. free enterprise
7. barter
8. exports
9. Constitution of 1824
10. federalism

Understanding Main Ideas ★TEKS

Section 1 (pp. 182–185)

1. Why did many U.S. immigrants come to Texas in the early 1800s?
2. What different groups settled in Texas during the 1820s and early 1830s?

Section 2 (pp. 186–190)

3. How did Texas settlers adapt to their environment?
4. How did U.S. settlers maintain their cultural heritage, particularly their religious beliefs, while adapting to Texas culture?

Section 3 (pp. 191–193)

5. Describe the Texas economy in the early to mid-1830s.

Section 4 (pp. 195–197)

6. How did the Constitution of 1824 affect Texas? How did Texas settlers feel about the document?

You Be the Historian ★TEKS

Reviewing Themes

1. **Constitutional Heritage** Why did many Texas settlers like how the Constitution of 1824 divided government power?
2. **Citizenship** Do you think that Texas settlers who broke Mexican laws were good citizens? Provide reasons for your answer.
3. **Geography** How did poor transportation networks in Texas affect the region's economy?

TAKS Practice: Thinking Critically ★TEKS

1. **Contrasting** How did the purposes and methods of Spanish and U.S. settlement in Texas differ?
2. **Summarizing** Describe the major characteristics of life in Texas during Mexican rule.
3. **Evaluating** How did physical and human factors, such as the Mexican government, affect the settlement of U.S. immigrants in Texas?

Interpreting Maps ⭐TEKS

Study the map below. Use the information on the map to help you answer the questions that follow.

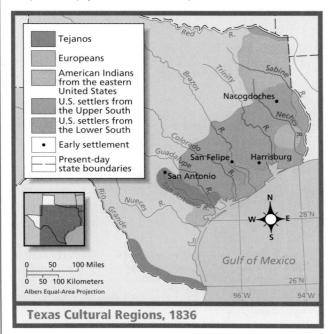

Texas Cultural Regions, 1836

Map legend:
- Tejanos
- Europeans
- American Indians from the eastern United States
- U.S. settlers from the Upper South
- U.S. settlers from the Lower South
- • Early settlement
- Present-day state boundaries

Labels on map: Red R., Sabine, Trinity, Brazos, Neches R., Nacogdoches, Colorado R., Guadalupe, San Felipe, Harrisburg, San Antonio, San Antonio R., Nueces R., Rio Grande, Gulf of Mexico, 28°N, 26°N, 96°W, 94°W

0 50 100 Miles
0 50 100 Kilometers
Albers Equal-Area Projection

1. In 1836 what group or groups occupied the largest part of Texas?
   a. settlers from the Upper South
   b. settlers from the Lower South
   c. Europeans and Tejanos
   d. American Indians and Tejanos

2. Summarize the settlement patterns in Texas.

Analyzing Primary Sources ⭐TEKS

Read the following story by Solomon Wright. Then answer the questions.

"A man moving to this promised land from Missouri drove two spans of powerful, spirited Thoroughbred horses [attached] to two brand new wagons. . . . Anybody would ask him where he was going, he'd boom out in the heartiest voice you can imagine, 'Goin' to Texas to get rich.'

After a couple of years in the alligator-swamp country, this man and his family had been shaken by so many chills and burned up by so much fever that they were as yellow as pumpkins, and just about as spirited. . . . Finally he started back to Missouri in an old shackly [rickety] wagon, each of its four wheels trying to go in a different direction, pulled by a pair of ewe-necked, rabbit-hipped prairie ponies. When anyone would ask him where he was going, he would squeak out in a weak, whiney voice, 'Goin'-back-to-Missouri.' "

3. This humorous story illustrates what serious fact about settling in Texas?
   a. Wagons often broke down in Texas.
   b. Failure struck many hopeful settlers.
   c. Hard work assured success on the Texas frontier.
   d. Prairie ponies sold well in Missouri.

4. Why do you think that East Texans enjoyed telling this sort of story?

Alternative Assessment

Cooperative Learning ⭐TEKS

Work with a small group to complete the following activity. You have been chosen to find ways to improve the economy of early Texas. As a group, use a problem-solving process to identify problems, gather information, and list and consider options. Then think about the advantages and disadvantages of each option. Next, pick and implement one or two of the best solutions. Finally, write an evaluation of how effective you think those solutions would have been. Your solutions must have been workable in early Texas.

BUILDING YOUR Portfolio

🖳 internet connect

Internet Activity: go.hrw.com
KEYWORD: ST3 TX9 ⭐TEKS
Access the Internet through the HRW Go site to research what life was like for the people who lived in Texas in the early 1800s. Then write an essay or build a collage or a model that demonstrates an aspect of the transportation, housing, education, diet, and entertainment of Texans during this time.

The Road to Revolution
(1825–1835)

Haden Edwards and his wife Susanna received a land grant near Nacogdoches.

After Mier y Terán issued his report, soldiers entered Texas to strengthen Mexico's control over the region.

Soldado Mexicano Presidial.

TEXAS

1826 The Fredonian Rebellion begins after Haden Edwards comes into conflict with settlers.

1828 General Manuel de Mier y Terán begins a tour of Texas for the Mexican government.

1829 President Guerrero issues a decree ending slavery in Mexico, but an exemption is made for Texas.

1830 On April 6 Mexico issues a law that changes rules on immigration and trade in Texas.

| 1825 | 1826 | 1827 | 1828 | 1829 | 1830 |

U.S. and WORLD

1827 The United States formally offers to purchase Texas from Mexico for $1 million.

1829 Spanish soldiers land at Tampico in a final attempt to reconquer Mexico. Forces led by Antonio López de Santa Anna defeat them, earning him the nickname Hero of Tampico.

1825 Bolivia wins its independence from Spain.

Simon Bolívar was known as the Liberator of South America and helped Bolivia win its independence.

Build on What You Know

During the 1800s thousands of U.S. immigrants came to Texas. As they did, conflict with the Mexican government soon developed. When President Antonio López de Santa Anna abandoned the Constitution of 1824, tensions increased in Texas.

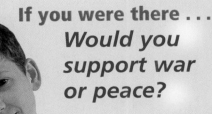

Cannons were important for defense of early settlements in Texas.

Stephen F. Austin was arrested while returning to Texas after an important visit with government officials in Mexico City.

1831 The town of Gonzales receives a cannon from the Mexican government to defend citizens against American Indian attacks.

1834 Stephen F. Austin is arrested in Saltillo.

1835 Texans become concerned when the Mexican government officially abolishes the Constitution of 1824.

1831 1832 1833 1834 1835

1831 A violent slave revolt, known as Nat Turner's Rebellion, takes place in Virginia.

1832 General Santa Anna leads a revolt against President Bustamante.

Tocqueville's book was based on observations he made during a tour of the United States.

1835 Alexis de Tocqueville begins publishing *Democracy in America*.

You Be the Historian

Themes Journal

What's Your Opinion? Do you **agree** or **disagree** with the following statements? Support your point of view in your journal.

● **Economics** Economic factors such as trade are usually the cause of conflicts between nations.

● **Constitutional Heritage** A president should be able to abolish the nation's constitution.

● **Government** New governments have more problems than old governments.

If you were there . . . *Would you support war or peace?*

Political Unrest in Texas

Read to Discover

1. What conflicts developed over land titles, and how did Mexico respond?
2. What conclusions did General Mier y Terán draw after his visit to Texas?
3. Why did Mexico pass the Law of April 6, 1830, and how did Texans react to it?

Define

• decree
• customs duties

Identify

• **Haden Edwards**
• **Fredonian Rebellion**
• **Manuel de Mier y Terán**
• **Vicente Guerrero**
• **Guerrero Decree**
• **Law of April 6, 1830**

Why It Matters Today

In the early 1830s many Texans were unhappy with the Mexican government and began to rebel. Use CNNfyi.com or other **current events** sources to find information on protests against governments today. Record your findings in your journal.

Decorated coaches such as this one were rare in Texas during the 1820s.

The Story Continues

On November 10, 1827, a large caravan left Mexico City for Texas. The main coach was decorated with silver and surrounded by a military escort for protection. Mexican general Manuel de Mier y Terán and a few others traveled inside the coach. The trip was rough. Muddy roads made traveling difficult. Along the way some of the travelers fell ill. But the group pressed on because they were on an important mission.

★ The Fredonian Rebellion

Part of the mission was to investigate conditions in East Texas, where a conflict had erupted the year before. Trouble began after **Haden Edwards**, a businessman from Kentucky, received an *empresario* contract in 1825. He had permission to settle some 800 families near Nacogdoches. When he arrived, Edwards found that a number of Mexican families, U.S. settlers, and Cherokee had been living on the land for years.

Edwards's contract required him to respect the property rights of all settlers who had titles to their land. So Edwards promptly ordered the settlers to prove their ownership. Many of the settlers could not find their land titles or had never received one. Edwards required these settlers to pay him for a title. If they did not pay, he threatened to sell their land. This enraged many of the settlers, who complained to the government. When an official named José Antonio Saucedo decided that Edwards could not charge for new land titles, he protested the decision.

In October 1826 the Mexican government canceled Edwards's contract. Benjamin Edwards, Haden's brother, took action. He gathered a small band of settlers, including some Cherokee. Then he claimed a part of East Texas as the independent Republic of Fredonia. On December 16, 1826, Benjamin Edwards and his supporters rode into Nacogdoches and took over a building known as the Old Stone Fort. On December 21 they adopted the Fredonian Declaration of Independence.

Analyzing Primary Sources
Identifying Points of View
According to this document, why did the Fredonians rebel?

Texas Voices ❝The Government of the Mexican United States have . . . reduced the . . . emigrants [newcomers] . . . in the Province of Texas . . . to the dreadful alternative [choice] of either submitting [giving] their freeborn necks to the yoke [harness] of . . . [a] despotic [unjust] government . . . or of taking up arms in defense of their . . . rights.❞

—Fredonian Declaration of Independence, quoted in *Documents of Texas History,* edited by Ernest Wallace

Most Texans—both Tejano and U.S. settlers alike—opposed the **Fredonian Rebellion**. Stephen F. Austin, who supported the Mexican government's decision, called out the militia. In January 1827 the Fredonians learned that Mexican troops and the militia were coming. The rebels, including Haden Edwards, fled. Some were captured but later released after Austin spoke with officials. Edwards later returned to Texas and settled in Nacogdoches, where he died in 1849.

⭐ **Reading Check** **Drawing Inferences and Conclusions** How do you think human factors such as land grants led to the Fredonian Rebellion?

Interpreting the Visual Record

Nacogdoches. The Fredonian rebels raised a red-and-white flag, with the words Independence, Liberty, Justice *written on it, over the Old Stone Fort in Nacogdoches.* **What does this image show about life in Nacogdoches?**

★ Mier y Terán's Report

The Fredonian Rebellion was a minor event, but it attracted a lot of attention. Newspapers in the United States carried stories about the revolt. This interest in the rebellion greatly worried the Mexican government. During the 1820s the U.S. government made several offers to purchase Texas from Mexico. These offers offended Mexican leaders. Many Mexicans suspected that the Fredonian Rebellion was part of a U.S. plot to acquire Texas. The Mexican government sent more troops into East Texas to protect the region. Mexican officials also sent General **Manuel de Mier y Terán** with a group to tour Texas and to investigate conditions there.

Mier y Terán began his inspection tour in Laredo in early 1828 and arrived in San Antonio on March 1. From there, he traveled on to San Felipe de Austin, where he met with Stephen F. Austin. They discussed many of the issues important to the U.S. settlers. Austin also expressed his loyalty to Mexico.

Mier y Terán continued his tour and soon arrived in Nacogdoches. While there, he wrote a letter to the president of Mexico. Mier y Terán noted that Mexican influence in Texas decreased as one moved northward and eastward. Settlers from the United States seemed to outnumber Tejanos by 10 to 1. He warned that the American influence, particularly in East Texas, was growing stronger every day.

> **Texas Voices** ❝I tell myself that it could not be otherwise than that from such a state of affairs [events] should arise an antagonism [unfriendly relationship] between Mexicans and foreigners. . . . Therefore, I am warning you to take timely [quick] measures [actions]. Texas could throw the whole nation into revolution.❞
>
> —Manuel de Mier y Terán, quoted in *Documents of Texas History,* edited by Ernest Wallace

Mier y Terán made several recommendations to the Mexican president. First, trade between Texas and Mexico should be increased in an effort to discourage trade with the United States. Second, more soldiers needed to be sent to Texas to increase Mexico's control over the region. Finally, Mexico should encourage more Europeans and Mexicans to settle in Texas. Mier y Terán hoped that these actions would reduce U.S. influence in the region and show Mexico's power and its determination to keep Texas.

Reading Check **Finding the Main Idea** What conclusion did Mier y Terán draw, and what did he advise?

Texas Cities

Laredo

History: Laredo was founded in 1755 when rancher Tomás Sánchez established a settlement there. Lying on a road from Mexico to Texas, Laredo served as an important location for trade and travel. The town prospered along with the growing population of Mexico's northern territories.

Population in 2000: 176,576

Relative location: On the Rio Grande southwest of San Antonio

Region: Gulf Coastal Plain

County: County seat of Webb County

Special feature: Located on the Texas-Mexico border, Laredo is a center of trade and tourism.

Economy: After the arrival of railroads in the late 1800s, Laredo's importance as a trade center grew even more. Laredo's economy was also boosted by the discovery of oil and natural gas in the 1920s. Since the passage of NAFTA, Laredo has grown as a center of import and export trade with Mexico.

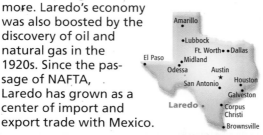

Amarillo
•Lubbock
Ft. Worth • • Dallas
El Paso • Midland
Odessa Austin
San Antonio ★ Houston
• Galveston
Laredo • • Corpus Christi
• Brownsville

The Mexican government sent troops to Texas to enforce the Law of April 6, 1830.

★ The Law of April 6, 1830

Before responding to Mier y Terán's proposals, the Mexican government took an action that greatly worried some settlers. In 1829 President **Vicente Guerrero** issued a decree, or official order, ending slavery in Mexico. Texas slaveholders, most of whom were from the United States, protested this **Guerrero Decree**. They argued that their businesses and farms depended on the labor of the some 1,000 slaves in Texas. Local officials listened to these arguments. They gained an exemption, or exception, from the decree for Texas.

In response to Manuel de Mier y Terán's report, the Mexican government passed the **Law of April 6, 1830**. It banned U.S. immigration to Texas and made it illegal for settlers to bring more slaves into Texas. The law also suspended unfilled *empresario* contracts. The government hoped to issue new contracts to bring more Mexicans and Catholic Europeans rather than U.S. families to Texas. The government also began to tax all U.S. imports coming into Texas. These **customs duties**, or import taxes, raised money for the government. They were also supposed to encourage internal trade within Mexico, as the duties would add to the cost of U.S. goods. Although the rest of Mexico had been paying these duties already, the new law now required Texans to pay customs duties on imports as well.

Mexican officials hoped that the Law of April 6, 1830, would strengthen Mexico's control over Texas. Instead, it angered many

LINKING PAST to PRESENT

Trade Relations

One source of conflict between Texans and the Mexican government was customs duties. Trade still plays an important role in Texas-Mexico relations. In 1994 the North American Free Trade Agreement (NAFTA) went into effect. NAFTA removed trade barriers—such as import and export taxes— between the United States, Canada, and Mexico. As a result of NAFTA, trade between Texas and Mexico has greatly increased. **What do you think the longterm effects of NAFTA will be?** ⊛TEKS

Tejanos and U.S. settlers. They feared that the new restrictions would hurt the growing Texas economy. Immigration had led to population growth and trade, which helped the economy.

Many U.S. settlers were also upset that their relatives and friends in the United States could not move to Texas. Stephen F. Austin disliked the new law, but he tried to work with Mexican officials and encouraged colonists to respect the law. However, Austin's own faith in the central government had been shaken by the change in its approach toward dealing with Texas. Austin realized that relations with the government in Mexico City had been badly damaged.

Tejanos who supported U.S. immigration, such as Erasmo Seguín, José Antonio Navarro, and young Juan Seguín, also opposed the Law of April 6, 1830. After it went into effect, the *ayuntamiento* of San Antonio held a special meeting. Its members, including Erasmo Seguín and Navarro, noted several of the advantages of having people from the United States move to Texas.

> **Texas Voices** ❝The advantages of liberal North American immigration are innumerable [not able to be counted]: (1) The colonists would afford a source of supply for the native inhabitants. (2) They would protect the interior from Indian invasions. (3) They would develop roads and commerce to New Orleans and New Mexico. (4) Moreover, the ideas of government held by North Americans are in general better adapted to those of the Mexicans than are the ideas of European immigrants.❞
>
> —The *ayuntamiento* of San Antonio, quoted in *Foreigners in their Native Land*, edited by David J. Weber

⭐ **Reading Check** **Evaluating** How did Mier y Terán's tour of Texas and report lead to the passage of the Law of April 6, 1830?

Section 1 Review   ⭐ TEKS Questions 2, 3, 4a, 4b, 5

go.hrw.com **Homework Practice Online** keyword: ST3 HP10

1 Define and explain:
• decree
• customs duties

2 Identify and explain:
• Haden Edwards
• Fredonian Rebellion
• Manuel de Mier y Terán
• Vicente Guerrero
• Guerrero Decree
• Law of April 6, 1830

3 Identifying Cause and Effect

Copy the graphic organizer below. As you move up the ladder, describe the events that led to the Law of April 6, 1830.

Law of April 6, 1830
Mier y Terán Report
Mier y Terán Investigation
Fredonian Rebellion

4 Finding the Main Idea

a. How did disputes over land titles lead to the Fredonian Rebellion, and what was the government's response to it?

b. What steps did Mier y Terán recommend in his report?

5 Writing and Critical Thinking

Supporting a Point of View Imagine that you are living in Texas in the 1830s. Would you have supported or opposed the Law of April 6, 1830? Explain why or why not. Consider the following:
• the importance of Texas to Mexico
• the growth of the Texas economy and population

Tensions Grow

Read to Discover
1. What events led to conflict at Anahuac?
2. Why were the Turtle Bayou Resolutions written?
3. What caused the violence at Velasco?

Why It Matters Today

In the early 1830s many Texans were upset by the Mexican government's violation of the Constitution of 1824. Use CNNfyi.com or other **current events** sources to find information on constitutional issues today. Record your findings in your journal.

Define
- resolutions

Identify
- **Juan Davis Bradburn**
- **George Fisher**
- **William B. Travis**
- **John Austin**
- **Turtle Bayou Resolutions**
- **Antonio López de Santa Anna**
- **José Antonio Mexía**
- **José de las Piedras**
- **Battle of Velasco**

The Story Continues

In the 1830s Asa Hill left his Georgia home for Texas. He wanted to start a new life for his family. He found some land in Stephen F. Austin's colony and then returned home to gather his loved ones. His family reached Matagorda Bay by boat, but they still had a long wagon ride ahead. After a week of camping in the Texas wilderness, the Hills arrived at their destination. They built a house and planted crops for food. They knew nothing of the growing tensions in Texas.

Asa Hill was one of many U.S. settlers who moved to Texas in the 1830s.

★ Conflicts at Anahuac

The Mexican government stationed hundreds of troops in Texas to enforce the Law of April 6, 1830. Before long, conflict developed between the military and some settlers. In the fall of 1830, troops built a fort at the mouth of the Trinity River on Galveston Bay near an important trade route and immigration point. The settlement became known as Anahuac. At this key location, troops could enforce the new trade and immigration laws. Colonel **Juan Davis Bradburn**, who was originally from the United States, commanded the troops stationed at the fort.

Francisco Madero, a surveyor from Coahuila, was approving land titles for settlers in the area. He had been appointed general land

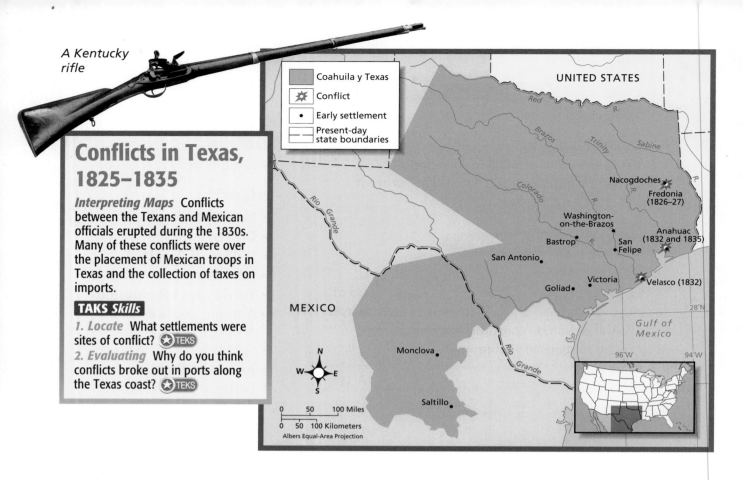

A Kentucky rifle

Conflicts in Texas, 1825–1835

Interpreting Maps Conflicts between the Texans and Mexican officials erupted during the 1830s. Many of these conflicts were over the placement of Mexican troops in Texas and the collection of taxes on imports.

TAKS Skills

1. Locate What settlements were sites of conflict? ⭐TEKS

2. Evaluating Why do you think conflicts broke out in ports along the Texas coast? ⭐TEKS

Map legend:
- Coahuila y Texas
- ✷ Conflict
- • Early settlement
- – – Present-day state boundaries

UNITED STATES

Nacogdoches
Fredonia (1826–27)
Washington-on-the-Brazos
Anahuac (1832 and 1835)
Bastrop
San Felipe
San Antonio
Victoria
Goliad
Velasco (1832)

MEXICO

Monclova

Saltillo

Gulf of Mexico

28°N
96°W   94°W

0   50   100 Miles
0   50   100 Kilometers
Albers Equal-Area Projection

---

commissioner for Texas in 1830. In February 1831 Bradburn arrested Madero, claiming that Madero's actions were illegal according to the Law of April 6, 1830. Many Texans became upset when Bradburn put Madero in jail. Bradburn then angered the settlers in Liberty, a nearby town. He disbanded the town government and used slaves for projects without paying the slaveholders for their labor.

In November 1831 tensions increased. **George Fisher**, a U.S. settler who had become a Mexican citizen, was a new customs official. He demanded that all ships landing in Texas pay their customs duties at Anahuac. This rule required some shippers to travel overland from Brazoria to Anahuac to get the necessary paperwork. Stephen F. Austin, responding to complaints, wrote to Bradburn. The rules were "utterly impracticable and their execution is impossible."

When several ship captains ignored Fisher's rules, he sent soldiers after them. During one chase, a soldier was wounded. An all-out battle was avoided because of Austin's quick reaction. He explained to Mexican officials that the event was not an act of disloyalty but a problem with Fisher. Fisher resigned soon after the incident. Yet conditions did not improve. In the spring of 1832, Bradburn arrested several citizens, including **William B. Travis** and Patrick Jack, and held them for a military trial. Texas settlers were enraged over the events in Anahuac.

⭐ **Reading Check** **Drawing Inferences and Conclusions** How did the enforcement of the Law of April 6, 1830 lead to problems at Anahuac?

★ The Turtle Bayou Resolutions

Patrick Jack's brother, William Jack, began to rally the townspeople. Soon groups of settlers at Liberty and Brazoria also demanded the prisoners' release. **John Austin**, a settler in Brazoria, helped organize a force of more than 150 people. They marched toward the fort at Anahuac. The angry Texans exchanged gunfire with Mexican troops and even captured some soldiers. Bradburn agreed to release the prisoners if the Texans would release the soldiers and leave. The settlers agreed to the terms and left. But Bradburn did not keep his promise.

After the conflict at Anahuac, the settlers withdrew a few miles to Turtle Bayou. John Austin and some other men left to get cannon from Brazoria. Those who stayed drew up several **resolutions**, or statements of a group's opinions. The **Turtle Bayou Resolutions** declared that the events at Anahuac were not a rebellion against Mexico. The settlers stated that they were defending their rights and the Constitution of 1824. They expressed support for General **Antonio López de Santa Anna**, who was trying to overthrow President Anastacio Bustamante.

Bustamante had taken complete control of the government, which violated the Constitution of 1824. Santa Anna had much support throughout Mexico, including important leaders like Colonel **José Antonio Mexía.** Mexía came to Brazoria with an army and was given a copy of the Turtle Bayou Resolutions.

Many Texans were upset with George Fisher for enforcing Mexican customs laws.

⭐ **Reading Check** **Finding the Main Idea** Why did the settlers create the Turtle Bayou Resolutions, and what did they declare?

Historical Document

Turtle Bayou Resolutions

On June 13, 1832, Texans at Turtle Bayou wrote a document explaining their actions at Anahuac. These statements are called the Turtle Bayou Resolutions.

" RESOLVED [It is determined] That we view with feelings of the deepest regret, the manner in which the Gover't [government] of the Republic of Mexico is **administered**[1] by the present **dynasty**[2]—The repeated violations of the constitution—the total disregard of the law—the entire **prostration**[3] of the civil authority; and the

substitution in the **stead**[4] of a military **despotism**[5] are **grievances**[6] of such a **character**[7], as to **arouse**[8] the feelings of every freeman, and **impel**[9] him to resistance. . . .

RESOLVED That the people of Texas be invited to cooperate with us, in support of the principles **incorporated**[10] in The **foregoing**[11] resolutions. — 13th June 1832. . . ."

Analyizing Primary Sources ⭐TEKS

1. **Finding the Main Idea** Why were these resolutions written?

2. **Evaluating** How does this document show the importance of freedom of speech?

---

[1]**administered:** managed
[2]**dynasty:** ruling government
[3]**prostration:** collapse
[4]**stead:** place

[5]**despotism:** unjust government
[6]**grievances:** sufferings
[7]**character:** nature
[8]**arouse:** excite

[9]**impel:** force
[10]**incorporated:** included
[11]**foregoing:** previous

Biography

Antonio López de Santa Anna
(1794–1876)

Antonio López de Santa Anna's long military career began in 1810. He fought for Spain against Mexican independence. In 1821 he switched sides and supported the rebel forces. In 1832 Santa Anna led a successful revolt, and in 1833 he was elected president of Mexico. He promised to restore the Constitution of 1824. He did not fulfill his promise and war soon erupted How did Santa Anna's policies affect Texas?

★ The Battle of Velasco

Soon after these events, a Mexican force led by Colonel **José de las Piedras** arrived from Nacogdoches. Piedras blamed Colonel Bradburn for much of the conflict with the U.S. settlers. To restore the peace, Piedras released Travis, Jack, and the other prisoners and recommended removing Bradburn from his post. Bradburn then resigned. With Bradburn gone, the settlers felt that the threat to their freedoms was removed. A serious battle had been avoided at Anahuac.

Unaware that the conflict at Anahuac was over, John Austin's group loaded their cannon on a ship at Brazoria. They soon reached the settlement of Velasco, near the mouth of the Brazos River. Colonel Domingo de Ugartechea, commander of the Mexican troops, refused to let the rebels pass. On June 26, 1832, fighting broke out. The Mexican soldiers soon ran out of ammunition and had to surrender on June 29. The colonists had won the **Battle of Velasco**. Men on both sides were killed and wounded during the battle.

After the battle, the Texans continued their journey to Anahuac. They triumphantly arrived with the cannon, only to find the conflict there settled. However, resistance to central Mexican authority grew stronger in Texas every day. Most of the Mexican troops soon left the region. The soldiers went to take sides in the war between the Federalists led by Santa Anna and the Centralists led by President Bustamante. Texans anxiously waited for news from Mexico City. They hoped Santa Anna would win the fighting and restore the Constitution of 1824.

Reading Check **Making Generalizations and Predictions** How do you think events at Velasco would have been different had John Austin and his group known about the Turtle Bayou Resolutions and Piedras's trip to Anahuac?

★ Section 2 Review ⊛TEKS Questions 2, 3, 4a, 4b, 5

go.hrw.com **Homework Practice Online**
keyword: ST3 HP10

1 Define and explain:
- resolutions

2 Identify and explain:
- Juan Davis Bradburn
- George Fisher
- William B. Travis
- John Austin
- Turtle Bayou Resolutions
- Antonio López de Santa Anna
- José Antonio Mexía
- José de las Piedras
- Battle of Velasco

3 Sequencing

Copy the graphic organizer below. Use it to show in order the steps that led to conflicts at Anahuac and Velasco.

Texans arrested

Law of April 6, 1830

4 Finding the Main Idea

a. How did physical factors, such as the location of Anahuac, contribute to the conflict there?

b. What led some Texans to write the Turtle Bayou Resolutions?

5 Writing and Critical Thinking TAKS

Analyzing Information Imagine that you are at Velasco during the battle. Write a letter informing a friend of the causes of the conflict.

Consider the following:
- the events at Anahuac
- events in other parts of Mexico

Conventions and Petitions

Read to Discover

1. Why did Texans hope the Constitution of 1824 would be restored?
2. What did the Conventions of 1832 and 1833 hope to achieve?
3. What events occurred when Stephen F. Austin went to Mexico City in April 1833?

Define

- reforms
- delegates

Identify

- Convention of 1832
- William H. Wharton
- Convention of 1833
- Valentín Gómez Farías

Why It Matters Today

Texans held two conventions to discuss government reforms. Use **CNN fyi.com** or other **current events** sources to find information on a recent national or international conference. Record your findings in your journal.

The Story Continues

As word of the conflict between Anastacio Bustamante and Antonio López de Santa Anna had traveled through Mexico, Texans realized that Santa Anna would probably take control of the government. Stephen F. Austin wanted to assure Santa Anna that Texas supported the general. Austin met with Colonel José Antonio Mexía in Matamoros to discuss the situation in Texas. Austin and other leaders convinced Mexía that Texas was loyal to Santa Anna and that the local disturbances were under control.

Some Mexican soldiers wore hats similar to this one during the 1820s and 1830s.

The Convention of 1832

Colonel Mexía traveled to Brazoria, where he was welcomed with a party. Despite having been given the Turtle Bayou Resolutions, Mexía gave a favorable report on Texas. Santa Anna defeated Bustamante's forces in 1832 and was popularly elected president of Mexico in 1833. He appointed his vice president to take care of the day-to-day affairs of Mexico's government. Santa Anna then spent much of his time at his hacienda near Veracruz. However, he still controlled the policies of the Mexican government.

William H. Wharton led a group that wanted the Mexican government to reform its policies and allow Texans to have more local control over their government.

Political Protest

The First Amendment to the U.S. Constitution protects the right of free speech. Participating in a convention, as Texans did in 1832 and 1833, can be one form of protest. There are many other ways to stage a protest. For example, some people hold marches or demonstrations. Many people draft petitions that express an opinion and are signed by citizens. Petitions are given to government officials or other leaders. Some people use the Internet to protest issues. There are Internet sites that keep track of the various protests occurring throughout the world. **Why do you think freedoms of speech and petition are important in a democratic society?**

Texans believed that Santa Anna would restore the Constitution of 1824. With a new government, some Texans thought that the time might be right for change. Since the Guerrero Decree in 1829 and the Law of April 6, 1830, many U.S. settlers and Tejanos had been unhappy with the central government. The settlers in San Felipe de Austin called a convention to discuss possible **reforms**, or changes in policy. Each district in Texas was asked to send **delegates**, or representatives, to San Felipe on October 1, 1832.

On October 1, delegates from 16 settlements attended the **Convention of 1832**. San Antonio, the largest Tejano settlement, was not represented. Its leaders had decided that the convention was unlawful. The delegates chose Stephen F. Austin as president of the convention. During the six-day convention, the delegates adopted several resolutions.

1. They asked the Mexican government to allow legal immigration from the United States.

2. The delegates requested that Texas become a separate Mexican state instead of being joined with Coahuila.

3. The Texans asked that customs duties be removed for three years.

4. The delegates asked for land for public schools.

The convention chose delegates **William H. Wharton** and Rafael Manchola to present the resolutions to the state and federal governments. Despite Manchola's experience as a legislator, the men could not get officials in San Antonio to accept the resolutions.

Reading Check **Finding the Main Idea** What did most Texans hope would happen with the Constitution of 1824, and what reforms did the Convention of 1832 propose?

★ The Convention of 1833

Stephen F. Austin realized that for reform to occur, Texans had to be in agreement and work together. The convention had lacked the backing of Tejanos in San Antonio, so Austin tried to gain their support. While he was meeting with leaders in San Antonio, a group of impatient Texans called for another convention.

The **Convention of 1833** met at San Felipe on April 1. Most of the 56 delegates had not attended the first convention. Delegate Sam Houston of Nacogdoches had only recently arrived in Texas. He had more political experience than most of the other delegates. He had been a member of the U.S. Congress and governor of Tennessee. Like many of the delegates, he wanted action. The delegates chose William H. Wharton as president. He led a group that wanted to push harder for changes in Mexican policy. Austin was upset that the convention had been called in his absence. In a letter, Austin explained his concerns.

Mexico City was a busy commercial center when Stephen F. Austin traveled there in 1833.

Texas Voices "That measure placed me in an awkward position. . . . I went there [San Antonio] to consult with the authorities of that place. I considered that very great respect . . . was justly due to them as native Mexicans, as the capital of Texas, and as the oldest and most populous town in the country, and I knew the importance of getting them to take the lead in all the politics of Texas."

—Stephen F. Austin, quoted in *The Life of Stephen F. Austin,* by Eugene C. Barker

Analyzing Primary Sources
Identifying Points of View
Why did Austin feel that he was in an awkward position?

In spite of his feelings, Austin supported the new convention. It adopted many of the same resolutions as the earlier convention. The members again asked that immigration from the United States be allowed. They requested that Texas be made a separate state from Coahuila so they could have more control over their own affairs. They even wrote a constitution for the proposed state. Stephen F. Austin, Erasmo Seguín, and Dr. James B. Miller were chosen to present the proposals to Santa Anna. Neither Seguín nor Miller could make the trip, so Austin set out for Mexico City alone on April 22, 1833.

Reading Check **Analyzing Information** Why was this second convention called?

★ Austin Is Arrested

The trip took Austin nearly three months. When he finally arrived, he faced one problem after another. Mexican officials were still trying to organize a new government. Santa Anna was out of the city, so Austin had to meet with Vice President **Valentín Gómez Farías** instead. Gómez Farías promised to present the Texans' requests to the Mexican

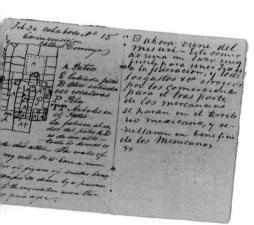

Stephen F. Austin kept a diary while he was in prison.

Congress. However, the government had many other problems to handle. A disease called cholera had swept through the city, and thousands of people were sick and dying.

In September, Austin was still waiting for the Congress to discuss the proposals. He asked Gómez Farías for a quick approval. Austin also noted that Texans might go ahead with organizing a state government without official approval. Gómez Farías thought Austin was threatening him, and the meeting ended in anger. In October a frustrated Austin wrote a letter to the local government in San Antonio. He had not yet received permission for Texas to become a separate state. Yet Austin advised Texans to meet "without a moment's delay for the purpose of organizing a local government for Texas."

When Santa Anna returned to Mexico City the following month, Austin was finally able to meet with him. Santa Anna agreed to nearly all of the resolutions of the Convention of 1833. He agreed to allow immigration from the United States and to lower taxes on U.S. imports. However, he refused to make Texas a separate state from Coahuila.

Austin left Mexico City on December 10, 1833. Although he had failed to gain permission to make Texas a state, he headed home full of hope because he had achieved his other goals. Austin's hopes were soon dashed, however. In January, when he reached Saltillo, the capital of Coahuila y Texas, Austin was arrested. Mexican officials had read his letter. The officials thought Austin had challenged Mexican authority.

Austin was taken back to Mexico City under armed guard and was put in prison without a trial. After nearly a year in prison, Austin was released on December 25, 1834. Even then, he was not permitted to return to Texas until July 1835. Back in Texas, many people worried and waited for him to return home.

Reading Check **Sequencing** List in order the events that led to Austin's arrest.

Section 3 Review

(TEKS) Questions 2, 3, 4a, 4b, 5

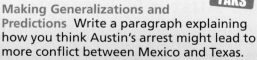

Homework Practice Online
keyword: ST3 HP10

1 Define and explain:
- reforms
- delegates

2 Identify and explain:
- Convention of 1832
- William H. Wharton
- Convention of 1833
- Valentín Gómez Farías

3 Categorizing
Copy the graphic organizer below. Use it to show what reforms Texans hoped to gain with the Convention of 1832 and 1833.

Convention of 1832

Convention of 1833

4 Finding the Main Idea
a. What impact did the Constitution of 1824 have on events in Texas?
b. Why was Stephen F. Austin arrested?

5 Writing and Critical Thinking
Making Generalizations and Predictions Write a paragraph explaining how you think Austin's arrest might lead to more conflict between Mexico and Texas. Consider the following:
- why Austin went to Mexico
- what happened in Mexico City

The Move toward War

Read to Discover

1. How did the Mexican government's policies increase tension between Texans and the Mexican government?
2. What led to a call for war?

Why It Matters Today

Part of the conflict between the Mexican government and the Texans was over taxes. Use **CNNfyi.com** or other **current events** sources to find information on a debate over taxes today. Record your findings in your journal.

Define
• faction

Identify
• Antonio Tenorio
• Martín Perfecto de Cos
• Lorenzo de Zavala
• Consultation

The Story Continues

Andrew Briscoe wanted to stir up trouble with the Mexican official at Anahuac. Briscoe loaded the front of his ship with bricks. He wanted his ship to look like it was weighed down with smuggled goods. He hoped to fool the commander at Anahuac into believing he was trying to avoid paying taxes on the goods. The commander was so irritated by the trick that he arrested Briscoe.

Texas merchants such as Andrew Briscoe usually shipped supplies in barrels or crates.

★ Mexico Tightens Control

Briscoe's actions reflected the concern many Texans had about the Mexican government's policies. In 1834 President Santa Anna declared that Mexico was not ready to be a republic and began to strengthen the power of the central government. In creating a centralist government, he violated the federal Constitution of 1824, which most Texans supported. Then in January 1835 he sent more troops and customs collectors to Texas. Santa Anna did honor some of Austin's requests, however. He legalized immigration from the United States and removed some customs duties.

In the spring of 1835 Captain **Antonio Tenorio** began collecting customs duties at Anahuac, where taxes had not been collected since 1832. This angered Texans at Anahuac, who believed that they were paying a greater share of taxes than at other Texas ports. Andrew Briscoe's arrest in June increased tensions.

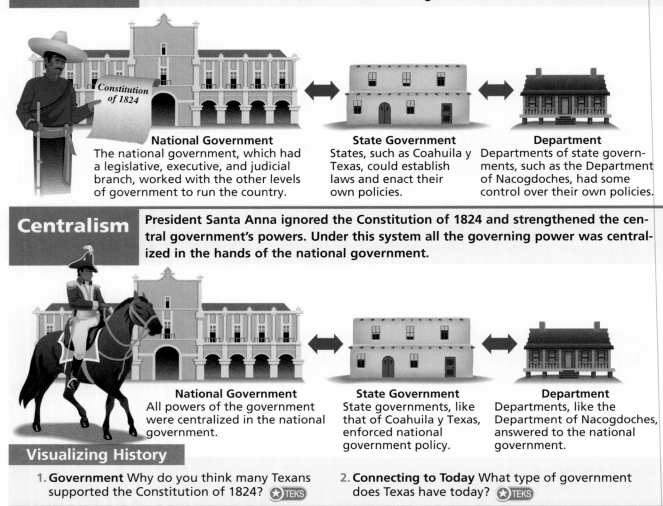

Federalism

The Constitution of 1824 created several levels of government that had the power to establish their own laws, hold elections, and create agencies. This system allowed for some local control of laws and regulations that affected Texas settlers.

Constitution of 1824

National Government
The national government, which had a legislative, executive, and judicial branch, worked with the other levels of government to run the country.

State Government
States, such as Coahuila y Texas, could establish laws and enact their own policies.

Department
Departments of state governments, such as the Department of Nacogdoches, had some control over their own policies.

Centralism

President Santa Anna ignored the Constitution of 1824 and strengthened the central government's powers. Under this system all the governing power was centralized in the hands of the national government.

National Government
All powers of the government were centralized in the national government.

State Government
State governments, like that of Coahuila y Texas, enforced national government policy.

Department
Departments, like the Department of Nacogdoches, answered to the national government.

Visualizing History

1. **Government** Why do you think many Texans supported the Constitution of 1824? TEKS

2. **Connecting to Today** What type of government does Texas have today? TEKS

In response, William Travis and about 25 U.S. settlers sailed the *Ohio* to Anahuac. There the group fired one shot and demanded Tenorio's surrender. When he refused, Travis ordered an attack. Tenorio quickly surrendered and agreed to leave Texas.

Travis's actions disturbed many Texans. Some feared that the conflict would cause more problems with the Mexican government, and they offered apologies to Mexican officials. General **Martín Perfecto de Cos**, the military commander of Texas, ordered the arrest of Travis, Robert Williamson, Samuel Williams, F. W. Johnson, and **Lorenzo de Zavala**. Zavala was a former Mexican cabinet member, state governor, and a firm supporter of federalism. He moved to Texas in 1835 after Santa Anna abandoned federalism. Cos also ordered more troops into Texas to better control the region.

 Reading Check **Analyzing Information** How did Santa Anna's policies and his refusal to follow the Constitution of 1824 increase tension in Texas?

★ Debating War and Peace

General Cos's orders greatly concerned Texans. Most U.S. settlers believed that citizens should have a right to a trial by jury. In 1834 the state legislature had granted Texas court reforms, such as trial by jury. But Cos planned to put any prisoners on trial in a military court, which, though legal, was unacceptable to many Texans. The arrival of more troops also upset Texans. A group led by William H. Wharton called a meeting to discuss these matters. The group decided to have delegates attend another convention, known as the **Consultation,** on October 15, 1835, in the settlement of Washington-on-the-Brazos.

In the meantime, Texans began debating how to respond to the growing problems with the Mexican government. One **faction**, or group, argued that Texans should remain calm. This faction wished to keep peaceful relations with the government. Another group, the war faction, argued for action. Some members of the war faction wanted Texas to declare its independence from Mexico.

While the debate continued, Stephen F. Austin returned from his imprisonment in Mexico. Austin's views on the conflict with the Mexican government had changed because of his arrest. Austin had gone to Mexico City to work for peace. Upon his return, Austin urged Texans to unite against Santa Anna and declared his support for the upcoming Consultation. Austin warned that Texans had no choice but to go to war. "There is no other remedy [solution] but to defend our rights, ourselves, and our country, but by force of arms."

Interpreting the Visual Record

The call for war. The time Austin spent in prison convinced him that Texas had no other choice but to go to war. *How does this painting show Austin's status as a leader in Texas?* ★TEKS

★ **Reading Check** **Evaluating** Why do you think the arrest of Austin and the conflicts in Texas led some Texans to call for war?

 Section 4 Review ★TEKS Questions 2, 3, 4a, 4b, 5

 **Homework Practice Online**
keyword: ST3 HP10

1 Define and explain:
- faction

2 Identify and explain:
- Antonio Tenorio
- Martín Perfecto de Cos
- Lorenzo de Zavala
- Consultation

3 Analyzing Information
Copy the graphic organizer below. Use it to explain how the Mexican government's actions led many Texans to call for war.

Actions ⟹ Call For War

4 Finding the Main Idea
a. How did the Constitution of 1824 factor into the events that led up to the call for war?
b. How did the events at Anahuac and Austin's advice lead to a push for war with Mexico?

5 Writing and Critical Thinking **TAKS**
Supporting a Point of View Write a statement supporting or opposing war with Mexico. Consider the following:
- the policies of the Mexican government and the Constitution of 1824
- the arrest of Stephen F. Austin and other Texans

CHAPTER 10

The Chapter at a Glance

Examine the following visual summary of the chapter. Then use the visual to create an expanded time line that you can use as a study guide. ★TEKS

The Road to Revolution

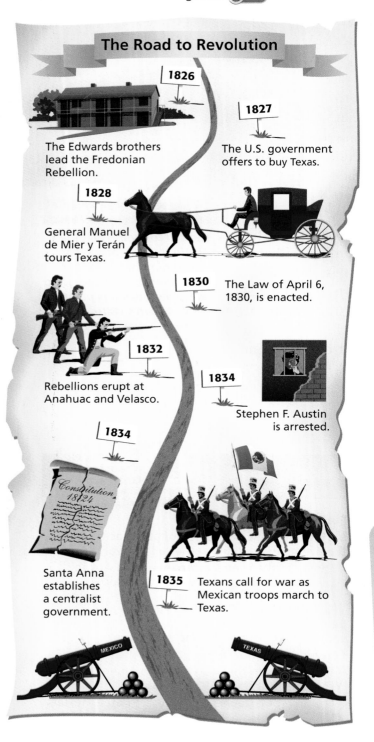

1826
The Edwards brothers lead the Fredonian Rebellion.

1827
The U.S. government offers to buy Texas.

1828
General Manuel de Mier y Terán tours Texas.

1830
The Law of April 6, 1830, is enacted.

1832
Rebellions erupt at Anahuac and Velasco.

1834
Stephen F. Austin is arrested.

1834
Santa Anna establishes a centralist government.

Constitution 1824

1835
Texans call for war as Mexican troops march to Texas.

MEXICO   TEXAS

Identifying People and Ideas ★TEKS

Use the following terms or people in historically significant sentences.

1. Fredonian Rebellion
2. Law of April 6, 1830
3. customs duties
4. Juan Davis Bradburn
5. Turtle Bayou Resolutions
6. Battle of Velasco
7. Convention of 1832
8. Convention of 1833
9. Martín Perfecto de Cos
10. Lorenzo de Zavala

Understanding Main Ideas ★TEKS

Section 1 (pp. 202–206)

1. What events led to the passage of the Law of April 6, 1830?

Section 2 (pp. 207–210)

2. In what ways did physical factors, such as the location of Anahuac, lead to conflict?
3. What events led to the Turtle Bayou Resolutions?

Section 3 (pp. 211–214)

4. Describe the reforms proposed by the Conventions of 1832 and 1833.

Section 4 (pp. 215–217)

5. How did Santa Anna's policies violate the Constitution of 1824, and what impact did this have?
6. Why were Texans split over the future of Texas as a part of Mexico?

You Be the Historian ★TEKS

Reviewing Themes

1. **Economics** What role did government regulation of trade play in the growing conflict between Texans and the Mexican government?
2. **Constitutional Heritage** How did Santa Anna's decision to set aside the Constitution of 1824 and create a centralist government affect Texas?
3. **Government** How do you think the problems facing a young nation like the Republic of Mexico affected its policies toward Texas?

★TEKS

TAKS Practice: Thinking Critically

1. **Making Generalizations and Predictions** What might have happened in Texas if Santa Anna had kept the Constitution of 1824 in place?
2. **Drawing Inferences and Conclusions** How might the creation of the Turtle Bayou Resolutions have contributed to the events that led to Texans' call for war?
3. **Supporting a Point of View** Do you think Texans should have taken up arms against the Mexican government? Explain your answer.

Interpreting Charts ⭐TEKS

Study the pie chart below. Then use the information in the chart to answer the following questions.

Value of Texas Exports, 1833

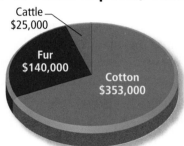

Cattle
$25,000

Fur
$140,000

Cotton
$353,000

Source: Rupert N. Richardson, et al., *Texas: The Lone Star State*

1. During the 1830s Texas had an agricultural economy. Which of the following sentences about the nature of the Texas economy is most accurate?
   a. The leading Texas export in 1833 was cattle.
   b. The leading Texas import was cotton.
   c. Cotton was the leading Texas export.
   d. People in Texas almost always wore more fur than cotton.

2. Cotton exports were about how many times more valuable than fur exports?

Analyzing Primary Sources ⭐TEKS

Read the following decree issued by the Mexican government in 1834. Then answer the questions.

"The Vice President of the Mexican United States . . . impressed by the necessity of aiding the multitude of persons whose fate has been, and still is, unfortunate . . . finds himself resolved to open its coffers [treasury] to remedy [solve the problem of] . . . such a pitiful condition. The territories situated next to the boundary line of our Republic . . . open to commerce . . . and extremely fertile, are offering, for robust [strong] Mexican arms, and industry, all kinds of things which are unavailable elsewhere. . . . The Republic finds itself plagued with families which, for one reason or another, have lost their fortune and their peace of mind. The Supreme Government invites all of them to better their fate in the peaceful pursuits of agriculture."

3. According to the Mexican government, why was the decree issued?
   a. to help the wealthy people of Mexico
   b. to help the poor farmers of Mexico
   c. to develop a plan that allows Texas to become an independent republic
   d. to make the government wealthy

4. How do you think the decree may have reflected the biases of the Mexican government at that time?

Alternative Assessment

Linking to Community

Today Texas and Mexico have a good relationship, and Americans travel to Mexico by the thousands each year. Interview someone in your school or community who has been to Mexico. Or, if possible, interview someone who has lived in Mexico. Ask the person to describe the place where he or she visited or lived and what he or she did there. Present an oral report of your interview to the class. You may want to include some visuals to accompany your report.

BUILDING YOUR Portfolio

📄 **internet** connect

Internet Activity: go.hrw.com
KEYWORD: ST3 TX10 ⭐TEKS

Access the Internet through the HRW Go site to research one of the following major documents in the chapter: the Law of April 6, 1830, Constitution of 1824, or the Turtle Bayou Resolutions. Create a chart or table with specific information from your research that shows the effects of one of the documents and how it led to the call for revolution.

Social Studies Skills

WORKSHOP

Problem-Solving Skills

Texans in the past and present have faced difficult problems. By using appropriate problem-solving skills you will be better able to choose a solution. The following activities will help you develop and practice this skill.

Problem solving is the process of finding an effective solution to a problem. Listed below are guidelines for the problem-solving process.

1. **Identify the problem.** Identify what the problem is that you are facing. Sometimes you face a difficult situation made up of several different problems.

2. **Gather information.** Conduct research on any important issues related to the problem. Try to find the answers to questions like the following: What caused this problem? Who or what does it affect?

3. **List and consider options.** Look at the problem and the answers to the questions you asked in Step 2. List and then think about your options—all the possible ways in which the problem could be solved.

4. **Examine advantages and disadvantages.** Consider the advantages and disadvantages of all the options that you have listed. Make sure that you consider the possible long-term effects of each solution. You should also determine what steps you will need to take to achieve each possible solution.

5. **Choose and implement a solution.** Select the best solution from your list and take the steps to achieve it.

6. **Evaluate the effectiveness of the solution.** After putting your plan into action, evaluate its effectiveness. Is the problem solved? Were the results worth the effort? Has the solution created any other problems?

Example

During the early 1800s conflicts erupted in Texas, which created a problem for Mexico. Here is an example of a problem-solving process that the Mexican government might have used.

1. **Identify the problem.**
   Conflicts are erupting between Texas settlers and Mexican soldiers.

2. **Gather information.**
   - Texans are upset over customs duties.
   - Texans are upset over the arrest of fellow settlers.

3. **List and consider options.**
   - Mexico can remove customs duties and free imprisoned Texas settlers.
   - Mexico can send more troops to Texas.

4. **Examine advantages and disadvantages**
   - If Mexico removes customs duties, the conflicts might end. But other Mexican states may not consider this fair.
   - If Mexico sends in more troops, it will show Mexico's authority over the region. But it might lead to more conflict.

5. **Choose and implement a solution.**
   Mexico sends more troops and releases some Texans.

6. **Evaluate the effectiveness of the solution.**
   The solution does not stop the conflicts.

Practicing the Skill

Chapter 8, Section 3, The Austin Colonies, discusses the challenges facing the first U.S. settlers in Texas. Imagine that you are a settler in Stephen F. Austin's colony. Use the problem-solving guidelines above to help you decide how best to solve the colony's problems. Be prepared to explain and defend your solutions. ⭐TEKS

History in Action

UNIT 3 SIMULATION

You Solve the Problem . . .

How can Stephen F. Austin convince settlers to move to Texas?

Complete the following activity in small cooperative groups. The year is 1821. Stephen F. Austin is developing a plan to convince people to move to Texas. Austin has requested your group to create a three-fold brochure. Follow these steps to solve your problem.

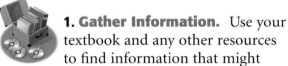

1. Gather Information. Use your textbook and any other resources to find information that might influence your plan of action for developing a brochure. Remember that your brochure must include information that will help Austin in convincing people to move to Texas. This information might include maps, charts, and graphs to show the land, plants, animals, climate, natural resources, and inhabitants of Texas. Be sure to use what you learned from this unit's Skills Workshop on Problem Solving to help you find an effective solution to this problem. You may want to divide up different parts of the research among group members.

2. List and Consider Options. After reviewing the information you gathered, list and consider the options you might use to help Austin in persuading people to settle in Texas. Your final solution to the problem may be easier to reach if you consider as many options as possible. Be sure to record your possible options for the preparation of your brochure.

3. Consider Advantages and Disadvantages. Now consider the advantages and disadvantages of taking each option. Ask yourselves questions such as, "How will this information persuade people to settle in Texas?" Once you have considered the advantages and disadvantages, record them as notes for use in preparing your brochure.

4. Choose, Implement, and Evaluate a Solution. After considering the advantages and disadvantages, you should plan and create your brochure. Be sure to make your proposal very clear. You will need to support your reasons for why people should settle in Texas by including information you gathered and by explaining why you rejected other options or reasons for moving to Texas. When you are ready, decide which group members will present the brochure, and then take your brochure to Austin (the rest of the class). Good luck!

UNIT 4

The Republic of Texas

(1835–1845)

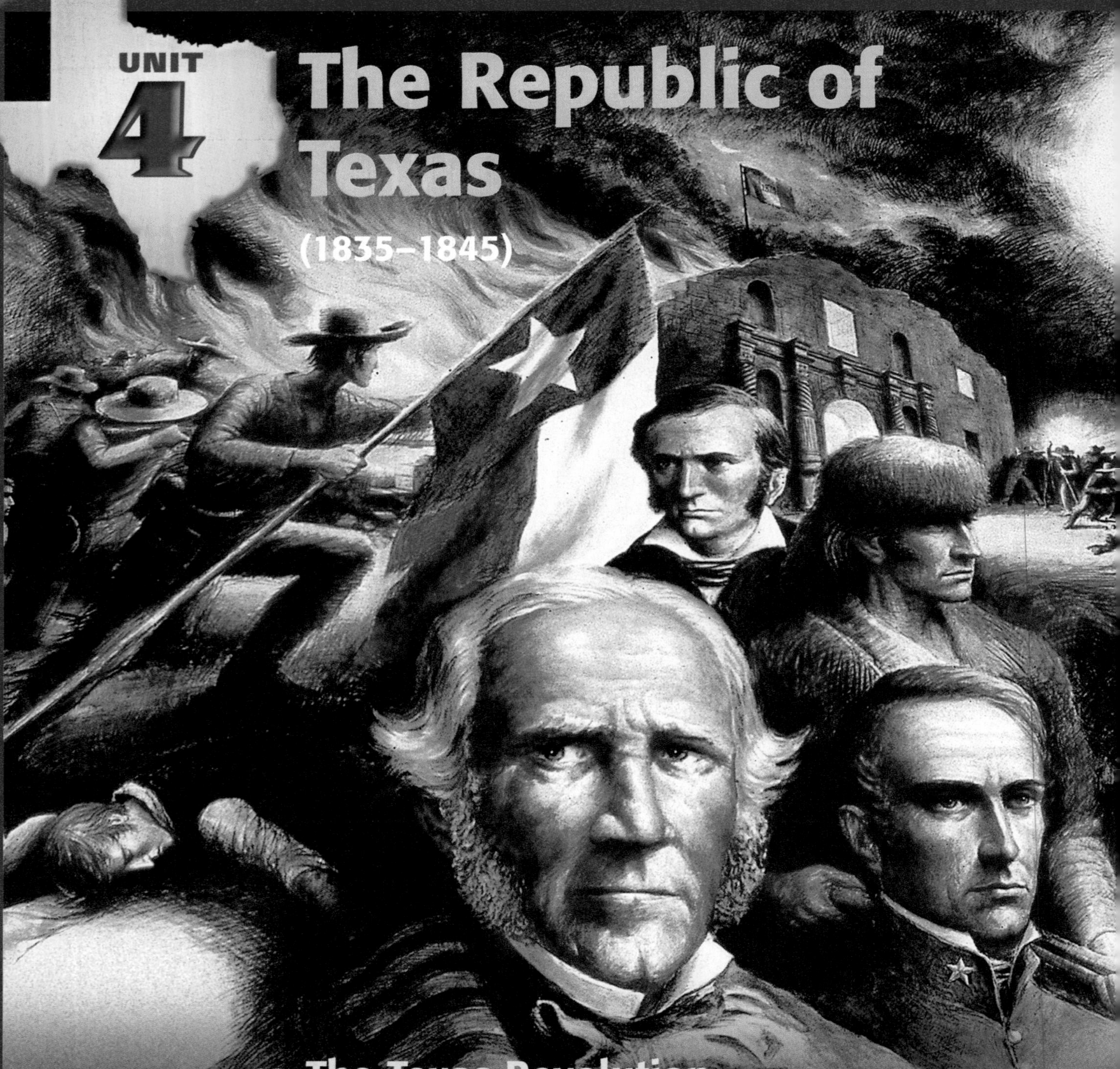

CHAPTER 11 **The Texas Revolution** (1835–1836)

CHAPTER 12 **A New Nation** (1836–1845)

CHAPTER 13 **Life in the Republic** (1836–1845)

CHAPTER 14 **Texas Faces Foreign Challenges** (1836–1845)

Texas Teens
Young War Supporters

Ten-year-old Dilue Harris, whose family had settled near present-day Houston, recalled that in 1835 settlers were "in a state of excitement during the winter." Tensions with Mexico were on the rise after a series of minor conflicts in Velasco, Anahuac, and other areas of Texas. Many settlers prepared for the worst. Even young Harris helped get ready for war. She melted lead in a pot to make bullets for settlers preparing to fight.

Students across Texas have learned about the state's history by visiting historic sites such as the Alamo.

Texans as young as 13 volunteered to fight to defend their homes. Thinking the war would be a great adventure, teenager John Holland Jenkins went off to fight against Mexican forces.

Other young Texans became caught up in the fighting that swirled around them. Eight-year-old Enrique Esparza, son of Alamo defender Gregorio Esparza, remembered when Mexican troops arrived in San Antonio. Enrique ran home to warn his family. Enrique's family then raced to the Alamo, hoping to get inside before Mexican forces sealed off the old mission. Enrique remembered that the mission church "was shut up, when we arrived. The window was opened to permit us to enter." The troops inside quickly closed the window. The Esparzas were among the last people to enter the Alamo before Mexican forces attacked. Enrique and other young Texans had entered into a very exciting but dangerous chapter in the history of Texas. **How was life during the Texas Revolution an exciting time for Texas teens?**

> **In this unit** you will learn about Texans' struggles for independence from Mexico. You will also learn about how Texans created a new nation.

LEFT PAGE: *This mural of the Texas Revolution honors key figures such as Sam Houston, William B. Travis, Davy Crockett, and James Bowie.*

The Texas Revolution
(1835–1836)

This mosaic honors the Texans' stand and victory at Gonzales.

During the Texas Revolution, some Mexican officers wore elaborate uniforms like this one.

 TEXAS

 U.S. and WORLD

August 1835	October 1835	December 1835	February 1836
	October 2 Texas settlers attack Mexican soldiers at Gonzales, forcing them to leave.	**December 9** Texas troops push Mexican troops out of San Antonio, capturing the city.	**February 23** The Siege of the Alamo begins. **March 2** The Texas Declaration of Independence is adopted.
September 9 In response to widespread demands for change, the British Parliament reforms local government in England.	**October 27** Santa Anna, the president of Mexico, decides to personally lead the campaign to put down the Texas rebellion.	**January 30** Richard Lawrence tries to assassinate U.S. president Andrew Jackson. Jackson is unharmed.	**March 30** Stephen F. Austin arrives in Washington to request aid for the Texas Revolution.

U.S. president Andrew Jackson was a friend of Sam Houston.

Build on What You Know

Different ideas about government, individual rights, and other matters had led to increasing conflict between settlers in Texas and the leaders of Mexico. During the early 1830s tensions grew, and fighting broke out. By late 1835, the first shots of the Texas Revolution had been fired.

After the Battle of San Jacinto, Santa Anna was captured and forced to surrender. Sam Houston injured his ankle during the battle.

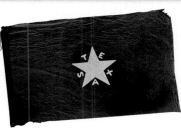

Texas adopted its first official flag in 1836.

April 21 Texans win the Battle of San Jacinto, ending the Texas Revolution.

December 10 The first official Texas flag is adopted by the Texas Congress.

April 1836	**June 1836**	**August 1836**	**October 1836**	**December 1836**

June 15 Arkansas is admitted as the 25th state of the United States.

August 10 Revolts erupt in several regions of Spain, forcing ruler María Cristina to restore the Constitution of 1812.

October 29 A revolt in Strasbourg led by French emperor Napoléon III fails, and he is banished from the country.

These medals belonged to Napoléon III of France.

You Be the Historian

Themes Journal

What's Your Opinion? Do you **agree** or **disagree** with the following statements? Support your point of view in your journal.

- **Constitutional Heritage** A constitution is necessary for good government.
- **Citizenship** Citizens should volunteer to serve their government during conflicts.
- **Geography** During a war, the geography of an area does not affect the outcome of a battle.

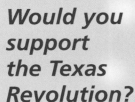

If you were there . . .

Would you support the Texas Revolution?

Read to Discover

1. How did the Battle of Gonzales significantly change relations between Texans and the Mexican government?
2. What events led to the siege of San Antonio?
3. What happened during the siege and capture of San Antonio?

Why It Matters Today

Providing the army with supplies, funds, and soldiers was a difficult task for Texas leaders in 1835. Use CNN**fyi**.com or other **current events** sources to learn about military funding in the United States today. Record your findings in your journal.

Define

- infantry
- cavalry

Identify

- **Antonio López de Santa Anna**
- **Battle of Gonzales**
- **Martín Perfecto de Cos**
- **Ben Milam**
- **Stephen F. Austin**
- **Juan Seguín**
- **Edward Burleson**
- **Erastus "Deaf" Smith**
- **Grass Fight**

The Story Continues

The conflict at Gonzales began when Texans refused to surrender their cannon to Mexican soldiers.

Nicolás Rodríguez, the Mexican commander at Fort Lipantitlán, sent word asking to borrow James McGloin's two-pound cannon. McGloin refused. The commander then sent another request for the cannon. McGloin still said no. Enraged, Rodríguez told his men to bring him the cannon—with McGloin tied to it. But McGloin still refused to give up the weapon.

★ The Capture of Gonzales and Goliad

One month earlier, a similar conflict had erupted at Gonzales. Many people in Texas were upset with the Mexican government because **Antonio López de Santa Anna** refused to follow the Constitution of 1824. When a Mexican officer in San Antonio ordered U.S. settlers at Gonzales to hand over a brass cannon, they refused. They then buried the cannon in an orchard and sent riders to ask for reinforcements. The U.S. settlers also removed the ferry that crossed the Guadalupe River to prevent Mexican soldiers from taking the cannon.

As reinforcements arrived, the settlers' force grew to at least 140 men. On October 1 they decided to attack the Mexican force of approximately 100 soldiers. The rebels dug up the cannon and mounted it on a wagon. They also made a flag with the challenge *COME AND TAKE IT*. Early on October 2, the settlers attacked. The fighting in the **Battle of Gonzales** was brief, leaving at least one Mexican soldier dead. No Texas settlers were killed, and the Mexican soldiers withdrew to San Antonio. After the Battle of Gonzales, many Texans realized that there was no turning back. A war had begun.

General **Martín Perfecto de Cos**, headquartered in San Antonio, ordered about 300 more Mexican soldiers to Texas to help put down the rebellion. In response, a group of settlers living near the coastal towns of Matagorda and Victoria formed a volunteer army. They decided to attack the Mexican garrison at Goliad, where Cos had left fewer than 30 soldiers. George Collinsworth commanded the Texan force of about 50 settlers. He was assisted by veteran **Ben Milam**. On October 10, 1835, the U.S. settlers attacked, and a brief fight occurred. The garrison, outnumbered and surrounded, surrendered.

After the victory at Goliad, more volunteers joined the rebel army. The rebels then set their sights on San Antonio, where Cos and a Mexican army were waiting. By capturing Goliad, the Texas rebels had cut off the Mexican army's supply route. Another force of some 300 Texas settlers had already gathered at Gonzales for an attack.

⭐ **Reading Check** **Sequencing** List in order the events that led to the Battle of Gonzales, the first battle of the Texas Revolution.

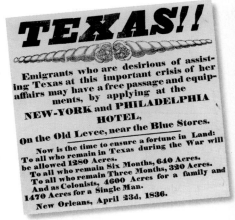

Pamphlets like this one were distributed to encourage U.S. settlers to come to Texas and support the Texas war effort.

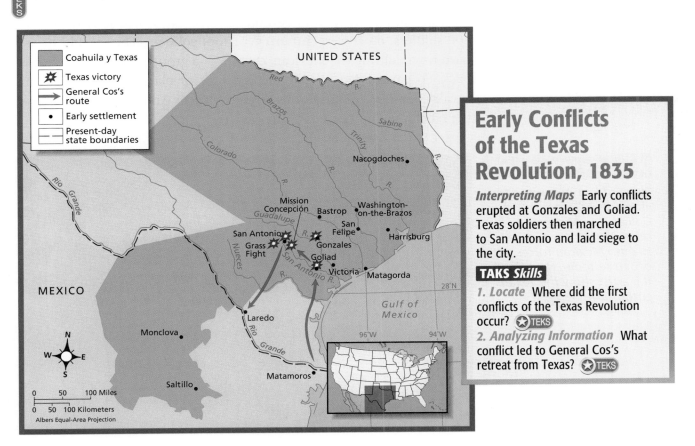

Early Conflicts of the Texas Revolution, 1835

Interpreting Maps Early conflicts erupted at Gonzales and Goliad. Texas soldiers then marched to San Antonio and laid siege to the city.

TAKS Skills

1. Locate Where did the first conflicts of the Texas Revolution occur? ⭐TEKS

2. Analyzing Information What conflict led to General Cos's retreat from Texas? ⭐TEKS

★ The March on San Antonio

In mid-October the volunteers in Gonzales began to organize their planned attack on San Antonio. They elected army officers, choosing **Stephen F. Austin** as their general. The difficult march to San Antonio began on October 12. Gunsmith Noah Smithwick described efforts to move a cannon.

 Analyzing Primary Sources
Identifying Points of View
Which phrase of Smithwick's reveals his opinion of the Texas army's condition?

> **Texas Voices** ❝We prodded [poked] up the oxen with our lances [spears] . . . until they broke into a trot. . . . But rapid locomotion [movement] was not congenial [friendly] to them. . . . Finally . . . the old cannon was abandoned in disgrace at Sandy Creek before we got halfway to San Antonio.❞
>
> —Noah Smithwick, *The Evolution of a State, or Recollections of Old Texas Days*

Austin set up camp on the outskirts of the city in late October. Austin's army was aided by Tejanos from San Antonio, many of whom had suffered after the arrival of General Cos. Leading Tejano citizens such as Erasmo Seguín had been forced to sweep the city streets. Tejano women had to bake tortillas for the Mexican troops. Mexican forces also took supplies and destroyed some citizens' homes.

Already opposed to Santa Anna's government, many Tejanos were further outraged by the actions of Cos and his troops. More than 100 Tejanos—including **Juan Seguín** and Plácido Benavides—joined the Texas army in San Antonio and other towns. The Texas army, however, was ill trained and ill equipped. Although it had grown to some 600 soldiers, most were **infantry**, or foot soldiers. They would have a hard time fighting the Mexican **cavalry**—a group of soldiers on horseback. So part of Austin's military strategy, or plan, was to increase his cavalry. Juan Seguín and other Tejanos in San Antonio who supported the rebellion volunteered for the cavalry.

Interpreting the Visual Record

Siege of San Antonio. *After victories at Gonzales and Goliad, Ben Milam and other Texans were eager to push Mexican forces out of San Antonio.* **How does the artist show the Texans' enthusiasm?** ★TEKS

Daughters of the Republic of Texas Library

Austin wanted to establish a good defensive position outside of San Antonio. To find a choice location, he sent out a search party of 90 men led by James "Jim" Bowie, James Fannin, and Andrew Briscoe. On October 28 the search party was attacked by 400 Mexican soldiers at the Mission Concepción. Bowie and the party had camped in a good defensive position and dug in behind a riverbank. The Mexican soldiers' shots missed the rebels. With more-accurate rifles, the Texas soldiers held back the Mexican forces. In the fight at Concepción, the Texas troops won a quick and clear victory. Like the capture of Goliad, this victory boosted the confidence of the Texas army. Some troops wanted to attack General Cos in San Antonio immediately. With advice from other officers, Austin decided to wait for reinforcements. The Texas army leaders were worried about the number of soldiers and artillery in San Antonio.

 Reading Check **Summarizing** How did geographic factors such as landforms affect Texans preparing to lay siege to San Antonio?

★ The Grass Fight

After the fight at Concepción, Stephen F. Austin moved his headquarters to the Old Mill just north of San Antonio. In this position, the Texas army could lay siege to San Antonio. A siege is a military action where an enemy is surrounded and routes for supplies and reinforcements are cut off. Because the Mexican troops had taken the supplies of local Tejanos, the siege seemed to have little effect. Many of the Texas troops became impatient, and some began to desert. Others fell ill as the weather grew colder. After a couple of weeks, Austin grew discouraged. On November 18 Austin received word of his appointment as a commissioner to the United States. The soldiers elected Colonel **Edward Burleson**, an experienced soldier, to take command of the Texas army. Burleson considered withdrawing from the area immediately and ending the siege.

Then on November 26 **Erastus "Deaf" Smith**, one of Burleson's scouts, rode into camp. He reported that more than 100 Mexican soldiers with pack animals were headed to San Antonio. A rumor quickly spread through the camp that they were carrying silver to pay the Mexican troops. About 40 Texas cavalry under Bowie and 100 infantry troops ambushed the Mexicans. The rebels captured the soldiers' horses and mules along with their cargo. The Texas troops eagerly opened the bags that supposedly held silver, only to find grass for feeding horses. This incident became known as the **Grass Fight**. Although the Texas troops were disappointed, some rebels realized that the siege was working because the Mexican forces needed feed for their starving animals.

 Reading Check **Identifying Cause and Effect** Why did the Grass Fight take place, and what was the result?

Daily Life

The revolution disrupted the daily lives of many Texans. This was true for Tejanos during the siege and capture of San Antonio. Both the Mexican and Texas armies took food, livestock, and other supplies from townspeople. During the battle, Texas troops broke down the doors of homes, tore holes in the walls and ceilings, and used the residents' furniture for cover. Many homes were left in ruins. **What types of hardships did some Texans suffer during the revolution?**

TEKS

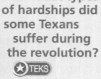

A settler's door lock

★ The Capture of San Antonio

After the Grass Fight, Colonel Burleson ordered a withdrawal from San Antonio to Goliad. On December 4, the day Burleson ordered the pullback, a captured Mexican officer was brought to camp. He reported that General Cos's troops were weak and disorganized. The siege and lack of supplies had worn down the Mexican soldiers. After hearing the report, Colonel Ben Milam shouted to the troops, "Who will go with old Ben Milam into San Antonio?" About 300 rebels answered Milam's call. They gathered that night at the Old Mill. Ben Milam and Francis W. Johnson each took command of a group for the attack on San Antonio.

The Texas troops attacked in the early morning hours on December 5, 1835. The fighting spread from house to house, and then on to the rooftops. One Texan described the frightened citizens' reaction. "Men, women and children began to run out, in their night clothes and unarmed." On the third day, Milam was killed. Although the Texas troops had lost Milam, the battle was turning in their favor. They were forcing the Mexican troops to retreat. By December 9 the Mexican forces had been pushed out of the center of San Antonio. On December 10 the two sides agreed to the terms of Cos's surrender. Cos was allowed to lead his troops out of Texas. The Texas army had forced nearly every Mexican soldier out of Texas.

The victory in San Antonio led many Texans to believe that the conflict was over. The rebels thought that they could form a separate state within Mexico and operate under the laws of the Constitution of 1824. Santa Anna had different plans for Texas, however.

★ **Reading Check** **Finding the Main Idea** What was the outcome of the siege of San Antonio?

TEKS

★ **Section 1 Review** ⬦TEKS Questions 2, 3, 4a, 4b, 5

go.hrw.com **Homework Practice Online**

keyword: ST3 HP11

1 Define and explain:
- infantry
- cavalry

2 Identify and explain:
- Antonio López de Santa Anna
- Battle of Gonzales
- Martín Perfecto de Cos
- Ben Milam
- Stephen F. Austin
- Juan Seguín
- Edward Burleson
- Erastus "Deaf" Smith
- Grass Fight

3 Summarizing
Copy the web diagram below. Use it to show how early victories gave confidence to the Texas troops during the Texas Revolution.

Battle of Gonzales

Capture of Goliad

Capture of San Antonio

Texans' Confidence

4 Finding the Main Idea
a. Describe the effects of the Battle of Gonzales on Texas-Mexico relations.
b. How did the victory at Goliad inspire Texas troops to head toward San Antonio?

5 Writing and Critical Thinking
Drawing Inferences and Conclusions
Imagine that you are a reporter covering the siege of San Antonio. Write a report that describes the events.
Consider the following:
- decisions that army officials made
- effects of geographic factors such as landforms on the battle

TAKS

The Consultation of 1835

Read to Discover

1. What issues were debated at the Consultation?
2. What kind of government did the Consultation establish, and why did problems with it arise?

Why It Matters Today

Texans held the Consultation to discuss the formation of a government. Use CNN**fyi**.com or other **current events** sources to learn about new governments being formed today. Record your findings in your journal.

Define
- provisional

Identify
- Branch T. Archer
- Declaration of November 7, 1835
- Henry Smith
- Sam Houston
- William Goyens

The Story Continues

Several Texas settlers had braved long distances and a hard journey to reach San Felipe de Austin. They had an important mission. As delegates to the Consultation, they would debate the future of Texas. Because only a few delegates had trickled into town by October 15, the meeting was delayed. The 30 or so delegates in San Felipe became restless waiting for others to arrive. Frustrated, some threatened to leave.

Delegates at the Consultation used quill pens.

★ Debating Independence

Finally, on November 4, 1835, enough delegates had arrived for the first session of the Consultation to begin. The delegates elected **Branch T. Archer** president of the convention and began debating the recent events. The pro-war delegates argued that Texas should declare its independence from Mexico. The pro-peace group feared that declaring independence would cost them the support of Tejanos. Many Tejanos wanted the Constitution of 1824 restored, but they worried about their future in an independent Texas. Peace party members stated that they were loyal Mexican citizens. Their goal was to restore the Constitution of 1824.

The pro-war and pro-peace groups reached a compromise in the **Declaration of November 7, 1835**. The delegates pledged their loyalty to Mexico, explaining that they had used force only to defend themselves. However, the document warned that if Mexico did not restore the Constitution of 1824, they would create an independent government.

Declaration of the People of Texas

The Consultation adopted the following statement on November 7, 1835.

"Whereas, *General Antonio Lopez de Santa Anna and other Military Chieftains have, by force of arms, overthrown the Federal Institutions of Mexico, and dissolved the Social Compact which existed between Texas and the other Members of the Mexican Confederacy—Now, the good People of Texas, availing themselves of their natural rights,*

SOLEMNLY DECLARE

1st. *That they have taken up arms in defense of their rights and Liberties, which were* threatened by the encroachments [advances beyond proper limits] of military despots, and in defense of the Republican Principles of the Federal Constitution of Mexico of 1824. . . .

These Declarations we solemnly avow to the world, and call GOD to witness their truth and sincerity. . . .

[P. B. Dexter], Secretary B. T. Archer, President"

Analyzing Primary Sources ⭐TEKS

1. **Finding the Main Idea** Why was the declaration issued?
2. **Drawing Inferences and Conclusions** According to the declaration, why did Texans take up arms?

The next order of business was to create a **provisional**, or temporary, government. The Consultation elected **Henry Smith** governor and James Robinson lieutenant governor. Governor Smith was a member of the pro-war group and had been active in public life since he came to Texas in 1827. He had served as a delegate to the Convention of 1833. To help run the provisional government, the Consultation created the General Council. In addition, the delegates chose three commissioners to travel to the United States. The commissioners were Stephen F. Austin, William H. Wharton, and Branch T. Archer. Their goals were to recruit volunteers for the army and to raise money.

The delegates also addressed military matters. They selected **Sam Houston** as commander in chief of a regular army, modeled after the U.S. Army. Houston was an experienced soldier and politician. He had served as a U.S. congressman and as governor of Tennessee. But Houston faced several problems. The delegates had left the volunteer forces under their existing organization and command. At that time, Texas forces were entirely made up of volunteers, so Houston had no regular army. There was little Houston could do to organize the volunteers. The Consultation did not give him the power or the money to pay soldiers.

The General Council did authorize the creation of a Texas navy to protect the Texas coast and supply ships traveling from New Orleans and other eastern ports. However, the first navy ships were not purchased until January. Once in action, the navy not only protected Texas settlements but also made many attacks on Mexican ships and towns during the revolution.

⭐ **Reading Check** **Finding the Main Idea** What role did the Constitution of 1824 play in the Declaration of November 7, 1835?

★ The Provisional Government

Disagreements over military strategy soon created conflict within the government. Some Texas rebels wanted to attack Matamoros, a city across the Rio Grande. This would bring the war closer to Santa Anna and might encourage other regions to revolt against him. In addition, some rebels were interested in claiming land in the region. Francis Johnson and James Grant organized the volunteer troops for this campaign. Sam Houston and Governor Smith did not support them, but the council voted to carry out the attack. Johnson and Grant left for Matamoros, hoping to gather volunteers along the way. This Matamoros expedition, however, only reached San Patricio and Agua Dulce Creek.

Meanwhile, Houston and **William Goyens** went to East Texas to negotiate a peace treaty with the Cherokee. Both men were well suited for the task. Houston had lived with the Cherokee as a teenager and adult. Goyens, an African American businessperson, had been appointed by the Mexican government to work with American Indians. Because of their efforts, the Cherokee agreed to remain neutral during the revolution.

Other efforts of the provisional government were less successful. Texas did not have clear goals or good leadership, and several conflicts emerged between members of the General Council. Disagreements also arose between Smith, who wanted immediate independence for Texas, and the council members of the pro-peace group. Despite protests from Smith, in December 1835 the General Council scheduled a new convention for March 1, 1836, to solve the government's problems.

Interpreting the Visual Record

American Indian relations. William Goyens and Sam Houston met with the Cherokee to form a peace treaty during the revolution. **How do you think their experiences with American Indians helped Goyens and Houston achieve their goal?** ★TEKS

★ **Reading Check** **Drawing Inferences and Conclusions** What caused the problems faced by the provisional government?

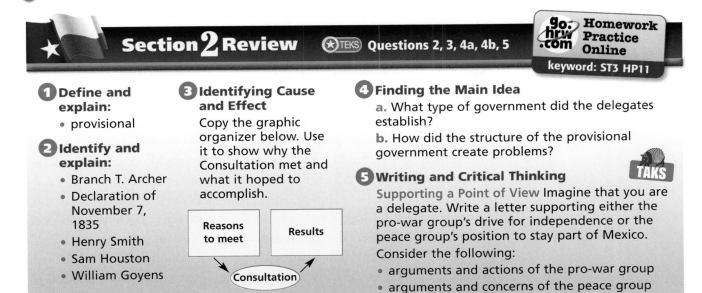

★ **Section 2 Review** ★TEKS Questions 2, 3, 4a, 4b, 5

go.hrw.com **Homework Practice Online** keyword: ST3 HP11

1 Define and explain:
- provisional

2 Identify and explain:
- Branch T. Archer
- Declaration of November 7, 1835
- Henry Smith
- Sam Houston
- William Goyens

3 Identifying Cause and Effect
Copy the graphic organizer below. Use it to show why the Consultation met and what it hoped to accomplish.

Reasons to meet → Results →

Consultation

4 Finding the Main Idea
a. What type of government did the delegates establish?
b. How did the structure of the provisional government create problems?

5 Writing and Critical Thinking TAKS
Supporting a Point of View Imagine that you are a delegate. Write a letter supporting either the pro-war group's drive for independence or the peace group's position to stay part of Mexico. Consider the following:
- arguments and actions of the pro-war group
- arguments and concerns of the peace group

The Siege of the Alamo

Read to Discover

1. What was the condition of the Texas forces when the Mexican troops arrived in Texas?
2. Why did Texans decide to defend the Alamo, and how did they prepare?
3. How did the Battle of the Alamo begin, and what occurred during its final hours?

Why It Matters Today

The battle at the Alamo became a rallying point for Texas troops. Use CNNfyi.com or other **current events** sources to learn how important battles are remembered today. Record your findings in your journal.

Define

- casualties
- noncombatants

Identify

- **Davy Crockett**
- **José de Urrea**
- **James Fannin**
- **James "Jim" Bowie**
- **William B. Travis**
- **James Bonham**
- **Siege of the Alamo**
- **Susanna Dickinson**

Even before he came to Texas, Davy Crockett was well known as a brave frontiersman.

The Story Continues

On January 9, 1836, Davy Crockett sat down to write a letter to his children. He had just arrived in Texas and described with enthusiasm his warm welcome. Settlers fired a cannon and held a dinner in honor of the famous frontiersman. He then looked for a place to settle and claim a piece of land. He also noted to his family that he had joined the Texas army as a volunteer and was happy with his choice. The letter would prove to be Crockett's last.

★ The Mexican Army Advances

More than a month after **Davy Crockett** wrote his letter to his children, Mexican forces began to approach San Antonio. Seeking revenge against rebellious Texans, Santa Anna decided that he would personally lead the attack. In February 1836 Santa Anna's army of approximately 6,000 soldiers reached the Rio Grande. Santa Anna led some of his forces to San Antonio. General **José de Urrea**, who entered Texas farther south near Matamoros, proceeded with an army toward Goliad.

The Texas army was unprepared for an advance by the Mexican troops, and Urrea quickly overtook the Texans that were headed to Matamoros. The rest of the Texas forces were scattered in small groups.

Colonel James Neill had just more than 100 troops in San Antonio. About 400 soldiers were in Goliad under the command of Colonel **James Fannin**.

Sam Houston was alarmed that the Texas army was so ill prepared and disorganized. On January 17 he notified Governor Smith that **James "Jim" Bowie** was on his way to San Antonio to evaluate the situation there. Houston recommended that the former San Antonio de Valero Mission, also called the Alamo, be destroyed and its artillery removed. Smith disagreed, believing it was important to defend the Alamo. Its defenses had been improved several years earlier to provide protection from American Indian attacks. The mission was also strategically located along the Old San Antonio Road—one of the two major routes through Texas. San Antonio would be one of the first Texas settlements the Mexican troops reached.

On January 19 Bowie arrived in San Antonio with 25 men. He examined Colonel Neill's improvements to the fort and its 21 cannons. He and Neill agreed that the Alamo and its artillery were too important to destroy. He wrote Governor Smith explaining why.

Texas Voices 66The salvation of Texas depends in great measure on keeping Bexar [San Antonio] out of the hands of the enemy. . . . Colonel Neill and myself have come to the solemn [serious] resolution that we will rather die in these ditches than give them up to the enemy.99

—James Bowie, quoted in *Lone Star*, by T. R. Fehrenbach

When Smith received Bowie's letter, he decided to send reinforcements. He ordered Colonel **William B. Travis** to raise a force and head to San Antonio. In spite of his efforts, Travis could gather only 30 soldiers. He and his troops rode in from San Felipe de Austin on February 3. As word spread of the rebellion, U.S. volunteers trickled into Texas. Davy Crockett led a dozen Tennessee volunteers into San Antonio a few days after Travis arrived. Although Crockett was a famous frontiersman and a former U.S. congressman, he did not want a position of authority. He told Travis, "Assign me some place and I and my Tennessee boys will defend it all right." **James Bonham** and a volunteer force from Alabama called the Mobile Grays also joined the Texas defenders. When Colonel Neill left the Alamo to care for an ill family member, he put Travis in command. Travis and Bowie argued over control, finally agreeing to share command.

⭐ **Reading Check** **Supporting a Point of View** Do you agree or disagree with Bowie's decision to defend the Alamo? Explain your answer.

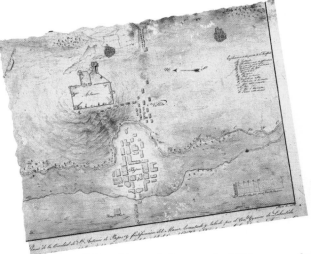

A Mexican soldier created this map of the Alamo and San Antonio for Santa Anna.

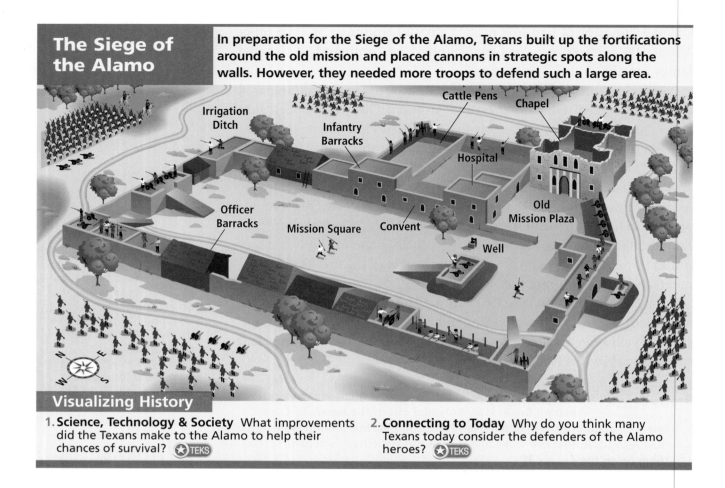

In preparation for the Siege of the Alamo, Texans built up the fortifications around the old mission and placed cannons in strategic spots along the walls. However, they needed more troops to defend such a large area.

Cattle Pens

Chapel

Irrigation Ditch

Infantry Barracks

Hospital

Officer Barracks

Old Mission Plaza

Mission Square

Convent

Well

Visualizing History

1. **Science, Technology & Society** What improvements did the Texans make to the Alamo to help their chances of survival? ★TEKS

2. **Connecting to Today** Why do you think many Texans today consider the defenders of the Alamo heroes? ★TEKS

★ The Siege Begins

As the Mexican forces approached San Antonio, the Texas troops at the Alamo built up their defenses. Green Jameson, a 29-year-old lawyer, was in charge of strengthening the plaza walls. He and the other defenders built up the walls to 12 feet high and 2 feet thick. Jameson directed the building of palisades—high fences made of stakes—behind which soldiers could fight. Jameson also worked with artillery officer Almaron Dickinson to place the 21 cannons around the Alamo. Even with such improvements, the Alamo would be difficult to defend without more troops. It was originally built as a mission, not a fort. The area enclosed by the two buildings and walls of the Alamo was about three acres, and likely required about 1,000 soldiers to defend it properly. The Texas soldiers in the Alamo at this time numbered little more than 150.

Travis and the rest of the Alamo defenders hoped for reinforcements. Juan Seguín organized scouts to look for Santa Anna's troops. Travis soon began hearing reports that Santa Anna's army was approaching. At first, the Texans doubted the reports. Travis and Bowie had thought that the rainy weather would delay the Mexicans until mid-March. However, Santa Anna had pushed hard. On February 23 a lookout spotted the Mexican troops marching down the road.

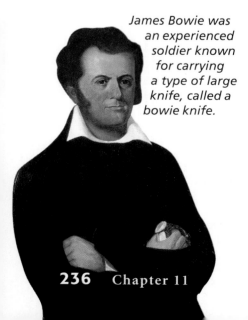

James Bowie was an experienced soldier known for carrying a type of large knife, called a bowie knife.

As Mexican troops marched into the city, the defenders, their families, and some local residents rushed to get inside the walls of the Alamo. Expecting a siege, the defenders gathered food, ammunition, and other supplies from local citizens. General Santa Anna arrived just after the defenders were safely inside and soon demanded their surrender. The Texas rebels responded by firing a cannon shot toward the Mexican army. Santa Anna reacted swiftly. He ordered that a large blood-red flag be raised so the defenders within the Alamo could see it. This "no quarter" flag meant that Santa Anna would leave no survivors. The **Siege of the Alamo** was under way.

On February 24, Mexican forces began firing on the Alamo. That day Travis wrote his famous plea "To the People of Texas and All Americans in the World." The letter was a request for aid in the face of certain death. Cannons bombarded the Alamo for hours at a time. Bowie, who had been ill, collapsed on the second day of the siege. Travis took charge. On the fourth day of the siege, Travis ordered the Texas troops to stop shooting and save their ammunition. He was worried that Santa Anna's army would soon launch a full-scale attack.

Reading Check Evaluating How did Texas troops prepare for the Siege of the Alamo, and was it adequate preparation in your point of view?

Historical Document

Travis's Letter

William B. Travis wrote this plea for help at the Alamo on February 24, 1836.

"Commandancy of the Alamo—

Bejar [San Antonio], Fby. 24th 1836—

To the people of Texas & all Americans in the world—

Fellow Citizens—& compatriots [fellow countrymen]—

I am **besieged,**[1] by a thousand or more of the Mexicans under Santa Anna—I have **sustained**[2] a continual Bombardment & **cannonade**[3] for 24 hours & have not lost a man—The enemy has demanded a surrender at **discretion,**[4] otherwise, the garrison are to be put to the sword, if the fort is taken—I have answered the demand with a cannon shot, & our flag still waves proudly from the walls—I shall never surrender or retreat. Then, I call on you in the name of Liberty, of patriotism & everything dear to the American character, to come to our aid, with all **dispatch**[5]—The enemy is receiving reinforcements daily & will no doubt increase to three or four thousand in four or five days. If this call is neglected, I am determined to **sustain**[6] myself as long as possible & die like a soldier who never forgets what is due to his own honor & that of this country—

VICTORY OR DEATH

William Barret Travis

Lt. Col. Comdt.

P.S. The Lord is on our side—when the enemy appeared in sight we had not three bushels of corn—we have since found in deserted houses 80 or 90 bushels and got into the walls 20 or 30 heads of **Beeves.**[7]

Travis"

Analyzing Primary Sources ⭐TEKS

1. **Finding the Main Idea** What request does Travis make?
2. **Making Generalizations and Predictions** What effect do you think this letter had?

[1]**besieged:** under attack	[3]**cannonade:** attack by cannons	[5]**dispatch:** speed	[7]**Beeves:** cattle
[2]**sustained:** suffered	[4]**discretion:** without demands	[6]**sustain:** protect	

"Fall of the Alamo" by Robert Onderdonk, courtesy of The Friends of the Governor's Mansion, Austin, Texas

Interpreting the Visual Record

The Alamo. *Fighting during the Mexican attack on the Alamo was fierce.* **How did the artist portray the bravery of Texas soldiers?**

TEKS

★ The Fall of the Alamo

Travis sent out several more requests for help. Bonham left to find aid for the Alamo, only to sneak back in on March 3. Juan Seguín also sneaked past Mexican troops to request help from Colonel James Fannin at Goliad. But no help arrived. Finally, on March 1, 32 volunteers from Gonzales rode into the Alamo. Led by Captain Albert Martin, they crept in under cover of early morning darkness. There would be no other help. The Texas force officially numbered 189, although some historians now believe there were more than 200 soldiers. Santa Anna sent at least 1,800 troops to take the Alamo. Travis made one last desperate appeal. On March 3 he sent a letter to Washington-on-the-Brazos.

Analyzing Primary Sources
Drawing Inferences and Conclusions What does Travis mean when he says he has to "fight the enemy on his own terms"?

Texas Voices 66 Colonel Fannin is said to be on the march to this place with reinforcements, but I fear it is not true, as I have repeatedly sent to him for aid without receiving any. . . . I look to the colonies alone for aid; unless it arrives soon, I shall have to fight the enemy on his own terms.99

—William B. Travis, quoted in *Documents of Texas History,* edited by Ernest Wallace

In the early morning hours of March 6 the Texas defenders were awakened suddenly. They heard shouts from Mexican soldiers and the sound of music. Santa Anna's army band was playing "El Degüello." The song meant that no mercy would be shown.

At about 5:00 A.M., four columns of Mexican soldiers attacked, but they were halted by the Texas artillery. The Mexican forces regrouped, however, and the four columns of troops overwhelmed the Texans. Mexican soldiers entered the Alamo by the hundreds. They captured a cannon, turned it inward, and opened fire. Hand-to-hand combat followed until almost every defender had been killed.

As the smoke cleared, at least 182 Texans were dead. The Tejano defenders who died included Juan Abamillo, Juan A. Badillo, Carlos Espalier, José María Esparza, Antonio Fuentes, Damacio Jiménez, José Toribio Losoya, and Andrés Nava. Accounts of Mexican losses vary. There were some 600 Mexican **casualties**—those killed, wounded, captured, or missing during war. There were some Alamo survivors, including **Susanna Dickinson**, wife of Almaron Dickinson, and her baby. Another survivor was Ana Salazar Esparza, wife of fighter José María Esparza. Santa Anna also spared a slave named Joe and several other **noncombatants**, or people who are not involved in fighting. One Tejano described the Alamo long after the attack.

Texas Voices ❝Ah Señor [Sir], had you but seen the Alamo on a feast day, as I have seen it, not like it is now, in ruins. . . . I never look into the ruins of the church without shedding a tear; not half the walls are now to be seen.❞

—Anonymous, quoted in *The Alamo Remembered,* by Timothy M. Matovina

General Santa Anna believed that the fall of the Alamo would convince Texans to surrender. In a letter, he wrote that he had achieved "a complete and glorious triumph." Instead, the Alamo became a symbol to many Texans that they must fight on at any cost.

Reading Check Analyzing Information Why do you think that the fall of the Alamo became a symbol that inspired many Texans to continue to fight?

1 Define and explain:
- casualties
- noncombatants

2 Identify and explain:
- Davy Crockett
- José de Urrea
- James Fannin
- James "Jim" Bowie
- William B. Travis
- James Bonham
- Siege of the Alamo
- Susanna Dickinson

3 Sequencing
Copy the diagram below. Use it show the path of events that led to the fall of the Alamo.

The Siege of the Alamo begins.
The Alamo falls.

4 Finding the Main Idea
a. What was the condition of the Mexican and Texas troops, and why was Sam Houston worried?
b. Why did James Bowie decide to defend the Alamo, and how did Texas troops prepare for battle?

5 Writing and Critical Thinking
Evaluating Imagine that you are at the Alamo during the siege. Describe in a journal the traits of leadership that Texans showed.
Consider the following:
- Bowie's decision to protect the Alamo
- Travis's actions

That's **Interesting!**

Line in the Sand
According to a famous Texas legend, on March 5 William B. Travis took his sword and drew a line on the ground. Those troops who wished to stay and defend the Alamo were asked to cross over the line. All but one person crossed the line. Some believe that one person may have been Louis Rose.

The Convention of 1836

Read to Discover

1. Who attended the Convention of 1836, and what did it achieve?
2. What kind of government did the Convention establish, and what problems did it face?

Why It Matters Today

On March 2, 1836, convention delegates adopted the Texas Declaration of Independence. Use **CNNfyi.com** or other **current events** sources to learn about how people around the world celebrate their nations' independence today. Record your findings in your journal.

Define

- **legislative branch**
- **executive branch**
- **judicial branch**
- **bill of rights**
- **petition**
- **ad interim**

Identify

- **Convention of 1836**
- **Lorenzo de Zavala**
- **George C. Childress**
- **David G. Burnet**

The Story Continues

Despite near-freezing weather, delegates met in an unfurnished building that looked much like this one.

Rain made travel rough. But on March 1, 1836, delegates slowly began to arrive in Washington-on-the-Brazos. At the newly built settlement, delegates found the streets full of ankle-deep mud. Organizers of the convention were using a small unfurnished building. Because only cloth covered its window openings, chilly winds blew through the building regularly. In spite of the uncomfortable conditions, the delegates were determined to accomplish their task.

★ Texas Declares Independence

The **Convention of 1836** was held at Washington-on-the-Brazos on March 1. Many of the 59 delegates had served in the U.S. government. They included Sam Houston, Richard Ellis, Robert Potter, Martin Parmer, and Samuel Carson. One of the delegates, **Lorenzo de Zavala**, had served in the Mexican Congress. The delegates named Richard Ellis of Pecan Point president of the convention.

The first order of business was to vote whether to declare independence. The vote passed quickly. **George C. Childress** chaired the committee in charge of drafting the document declaring independence. Childress wrote most of the declaration, using the U.S. Declaration of Independence as a guide. The Texas declaration listed the complaints the settlers had against Santa Anna's government. It stated that Mexico had denied them many rights guaranteed under the Constitution of 1824, and it declared Texas an independent country. The declaration was presented to the convention on March 2, 1836. The vote in favor of the declaration was unanimous—a decision in which everyone agrees. José Antonio Navarro and José Francisco Ruiz, the only Tejanos at the convention, signed the document. However, many Tejanos opposed the declaration, and some Tejanos left the Texas army after hearing the call for independence. Nevertheless, with the adoption of the declaration the Republic of Texas was born. Texans today celebrate March 2 as Texas Independence Day.

Reading Check **Summarizing** What was the first significant action of the Convention of 1836, and why did the delegates take that action?

★ The Constitution of 1836

A few days later, the delegates learned about the Siege of the Alamo. Many of them wanted to rush to San Antonio to aid the defenders. But Sam Houston urged the delegates to stay and create a constitution, or a plan for government, for the new republic. The delegates used the U.S. Constitution as a model and created a government with three branches. The **legislative branch** makes the laws, which are carried out by the **executive branch**. The Republic's legislative branch was called the Congress, and the executive branch was headed by a president. The **judicial branch** provides a court system. The powers of each branch were limited to only those listed in the document. The Texas Constitution also established a republican government in which representatives and executive officials are elected by the people. This idea, that the power to create or change the government comes from the people, is called popular sovereignty.

Interpreting the Visual Record

The Convention of 1836.
The Texas Declaration of Independence described Santa Anna's abuses against Texans, such as the arrest of Stephen F. Austin. The delegates approved the declaration's wording the second day they met. **How does the artist convey the serious nature of the convention's work?** ★TEKS

Lorenzo de Zavala
(1788–1836)

Lorenzo de Zavala was politically active during much of his life. He served as a Mexican congressman and governor. In 1829 Zavala received a land grant to settle 500 families in East Texas. In 1835 he became involved in the Texas independence movement. As a delegate to the Convention of 1836, Zavala played a key role in drafting the Texas Constitution. He was elected ad interim vice president. He also proposed a design for the first flag of Texas. **How was Zavala important to the Texas Revolution?**

Like the U.S. Constitution, the Constitution of 1836 contained a **bill of rights**. This is a statement of basic rights that the government cannot take away from individual citizens. The Texas bill of rights helps protect the rights of citizens and guarantees several freedoms. These include the freedom of speech, freedom of religion, freedom of the press, and the right to trial by jury. The Constitution of 1836 also called for a public school system and a policy of giving land to settlers.

The new constitution also resolved a controversial issue—slavery. The constitution ensured slavery as a legal institution, as well as the importation of slaves. The Texas Constitution also required free African Americans to **petition** Congress to stay in Texas. A petition is a formal request that is made to the government. Among those who had to do so was Samuel McCulloch Jr., the first Texan to shed blood during the revolution. He was wounded at Goliad in 1835.

The delegates then set up a new government. Because Texas was still at war, they created an **ad interim**, or temporary, government of leaders until elections could be held. **David G. Burnet** was selected as president, and Lorenzo de Zavala as vice president. Samuel P. Carson was named secretary of state. Bailey Hardeman was selected as secretary of the treasury. Thomas J. Rusk, Robert Potter, and David Thomas were named as secretary of war, secretary of the navy, and attorney general, respectively. The officers were sworn in on March 17, 1836, at Washington-on-the-Brazos. Later that day, they fled after hearing that the Mexican army was near. The government set up again at Harrisburg, but was forced to flee Santa Anna's advancing troops. Constantly on the move, the ad interim government had to leave the future of the Republic in the hands of Sam Houston and the army.

Reading Check **Comparing** How was the Texas Constitution similar to the U.S. Constitution?

Section 4 Review
(★)TEKS Questions 2, 3, 4a, 4b, 5

Homework Practice Online
keyword: ST3 HP11

1 **Define and explain:**
- legislative branch
- executive branch
- judicial branch
- bill of rights
- petition
- ad interim

2 **Identify and explain:**
- Convention of 1836
- Lorenzo de Zavala
- George C. Childress
- David G. Burnet

3 **Identifying Points of View**
Copy the graphic organizer below. Use it to explain why the convention delegates created the documents listed below.

Document	Delegates' Purpose
Declaration of Independence	
Constitution	

4 **Finding the Main Idea**
a. How did the political experiences of the delegates affect the convention?
b. What problems did the ad interim government have?

5 **Writing and Critical Thinking**
Comparing Imagine that you are reporting on the Convention of 1836. Write an article describing how the structure of the new government is a reflection of the ideas in the U.S. Constitution and Bill of Rights.
Consider the following:
- structure of the new government
- rights guaranteed in the Texas documents

THE
TEXAS
DECLARATION
of
INDEPENDENCE

On March 1, 1836, delegates met at Washington-on-the-Brazos to form a new government for Texas. One of the convention's first acts of business was to declare independence from Mexico. Below is the Texas Declaration of Independence, unanimously adopted on March 2.

THE DECLARATION OF INDEPENDENCE Made by the Delegates of The People of Texas in General Convention, at Washington, ON MARCH 2nd, 1836.

When a government has ceased to protect the lives, liberty and property of the people, from whom its legitimate powers are derived, and for the advancement of whose happiness it was instituted; and so far from being a guarantee for their inestimable and **inalienable** rights, becomes an instrument in the hands of evil rulers for their **suppression**. When the federal republican constitution of their country, which they have sworn to support, no longer has a substantial existence, and the whole nature of their government has been forcibly changed, without their consent, from a restricted federative republic, composed of sovereign states, to a consolidated central **military despotism**, in which every interest is disregarded but that of the army and the priesthood, both the eternal enemies of civil liberty, the ever ready **minions** of power, and the usual instruments of tyrants. When, long after the spirit of the constitution has departed, moderation is at length so far lost by those in power, that even the **semblance** of freedom is removed, and the forms themselves of the constitution discontinued, and so far from their petitions and **remonstrances** being regarded, the agents who bear them are thrown into dungeons, and mercenary armies sent forth to enforce a new government upon them at the point of the bayonet.

When, in consequence of such acts of **malfeasance** and **abdication** on the part of the government, **anarchy** prevails, and civil society is dissolved into its original elements, in such a crisis, the first law of nature, the right of self-preservation, the **inherent** and inalienable right of the people to appeal to first principles, and take their political affairs into their own hands in extreme cases, enjoins it as a right towards themselves, and a sacred obligation to their **posterity**, to abolish such government, and create another in its stead, calculated to rescue them from impending dangers, and to secure their welfare and happiness.

Exploring the Document

George C. Childress chaired the committee in charge of drafting the Texas Declaration of Independence. **How do you think Childress used the U.S. Declaration of Independence as a model for this document?** ★TEKS

---

inalienable: permanent

suppression: holding back

military despotism: military dictatorship

minions: faithful servants

semblance: likeness

remonstrances: protests

malfeasance: official's wrongdoing

abdication: giving up responsibility

anarchy: disorder

inherent: natural

posterity: future generations

Exploring the Document

Here the Declaration explains that Texans had a responsibility to call for independence. **Why do you think Texans felt that they had to demand their independence?** ★TEKS

Exploring the Document

Many Texas settlers were upset with Santa Anna for not enforcing the Constitution of 1824. What alternative did the Mexican government offer in the constitution's place? ⭐TEKS

Exploring the Document

The Declaration lists the charges that the settlers made against the Mexican government. What were some of their concerns? ⭐TEKS

amenable: answerable

habituated: accustomed to

acquiesced: accepted

privations: hardships

incarcerated: jailed

zealous endeavor: enthusiastic efforts

procure: gain

palladium: a protecting spirit

axiom: a rule

arbitrary: unreasonable

defiance: disregard

piratical attacks: robbery

desperadoes: outlaws

confiscation: taking of goods

dictates: principles

temporal: timely or earthly

functionaries: officials

formidable: causing fear

Nations, as well as individuals, are **amenable** for their acts to the public opinion of mankind. A statement of a part of our grievances is therefore submitted to an impartial world, in justification of the hazardous but unavoidable step now taken, of severing our political connection with the Mexican people, and assuming an independent attitude among the nations of the earth.

The Mexican government, by its colonization laws, invited and induced the Anglo American population of Texas to colonize its wilderness under the pledged faith of a written constitution, that they should continue to enjoy that constitutional liberty and republican government to which they had been **habituated** in the land of their birth, the United States of America.

In this expectation they have been cruelly disappointed, inasmuch as the Mexican nation has **acquiesced** to the late changes made in the government by General Antonio Lopez de Santa Anna, who, having overturned the constitution of his country, now offers us the cruel alternative, either to abandon our homes, acquired by so many **privations**, or submit to the most intolerable of all tyranny, the combined despotism of the sword and the priesthood.

It has sacrificed our welfare to the state of Coahuila, by which our interests have been continually depressed through a jealous and partial course of legislation, carried on at a far distant seat of government, by a hostile majority, in an unknown tongue, and this too, notwithstanding we have petitioned in the humblest terms for the establishment of a separate state government, and have, in accordance with the provisions of the national constitution, presented to the general congress a republican constitution, which was, without a just cause, contemptuously rejected.

It **incarcerated** in a dungeon, for a long time, one of our citizens, for no other cause but a **zealous endeavor** to **procure** the acceptance of our constitution, and the establishment of a state government.

It has failed and refused to secure, on a firm basis, the right of trial by jury, that **palladium** of civil liberty, and only safe guarantee for the life, liberty, and property of the citizen.

It has failed to establish any public system of education, although possessed of almost boundless resources, (the public domain,) and although it is an **axiom** in political science, that unless a people are educated and enlightened, it is idle to expect the continuance of civil liberty, or the capacity for self government.

It has suffered the military commandants, stationed among us, to exercise **arbitrary** acts of oppression and tyranny, thus trampling upon the most sacred rights of the citizens, and rendering the military superior to the civil power.

It has dissolved, by force of arms, the state congress of Coahuila and Texas, and obliged our representatives to fly for their lives from the seat of government, thus depriving us of the fundamental political right of representation.

It has demanded the surrender of a number of our citizens, and ordered military detachments to seize and carry them into the interior for trial, in contempt of the civil authorities, and in **defiance** of the laws and the constitution.

It has made **piratical attacks** upon our commerce, by commissioning foreign **desperadoes**, and authorizing them to seize our vessels, and convey the property of our citizens to far distant ports for **confiscation**.

It denies us the right of worshiping the Almighty according to the **dictates** of our own conscience, by the support of a national religion, calculated to promote the **temporal** interest of its human **functionaries**, rather than the glory of the true and living God.

It has demanded us to deliver up our arms, which are essential to our defense—the rightful property of freemen—and **formidable** only to tyrannical governments.

It has invaded our country both by sea and by land, with the intent to lay waste our territory, and drive us from our homes; and has now a large mercenary army advancing, to carry on against us a war of extermination.

It has, through its **emissaries**, incited the merciless savage, with the tomahawk and scalping knife, to massacre the inhabitants of our defenseless frontiers.

It has been, during the whole time of our connection with it, the **contemptible** sport and victim of successive military revolutions, and has continually exhibited every characteristic of a weak, corrupt, and tyrannical government.

These, and other grievances, were patiently borne by the people of Texas, until they reached that point at which **forbearance** ceases to be a virtue. We then took up arms in defense of the national constitution. We appealed to our Mexican **brethren** for assistance: our appeal has been made in vain; though months have elapsed, no sympathetic response has yet been heard from the interior. We are, therefore, forced to the melancholy conclusion, that the Mexican people have acquiesced in the destruction of their liberty, and the substitution therefore of a military government; that they are unfit to be free, and incapable of self government.

The necessity of self-preservation, therefore, now decrees our eternal political separation.

*We, therefore, the delegates, with **plenary** powers, of the people of Texas, in solemn convention assembled, appealing to a candid world for the necessities of our condition, do hereby resolve and declare, that our political connection with the Mexican nation has forever ended, and that the people of Texas do now constitute a* FREE, SOVEREIGN, *and* INDEPENDENT REPUBLIC, *and are fully invested with all the rights and attributes which properly belong to independent nations; and, conscious of the **rectitude** of our intentions, we fearlessly and confidently commit the issue to the supreme Arbiter of the destinies of nations.*

In witness whereof we have hereunto subscribed our names.

RICHARD ELLIS,
President and Delegate
  from Red River.
Albert H. S. Kimble,
  Secretary.
C. B. Stewart,
James Collinsworth,
Edwin Waller,
A. Brigham,
John S. D. Byrom,
Francisco Ruiz,
J. Antonio Navarro,
William D. Lacy,
William Menefee,
John Fisher,
Matthew Caldwell,
John S. Roberts,
Robert Hamilton,
Collin McKinney,
A. H. Latimer,
James Power,

Sam. Houston,
Edward Conrad,
Martin Parmer,
James Gaines,
William Clark, jun.,
Sydney O. Pennington,
William Motley,
Lorenzo de Zavala,
George W. Smyth,
Stephen H. Everett,
Elijah Stepp,
Claiborne West,
William B. Leates,
M. B. Menard,
A. B. Hardin,
John W. Bunton,
Thomas J. Gazley,
R. M. Coleman,
Sterling C. Robertson,
George C. Childress,
Bailey Hardeman,

Robert Potter,
Charles Taylor,
Samuel P. Carson,
Thomas J. Rusk,
William C. Crawford,
John Turner,
Benjamin Briggs
  Goodrich,
James G. Swisher,
George W. Barnet,
Jesse Grimes,
E. O. Legrand,
David Thomas,
S. Rhoads Fisher,
John W. Bower,
J. B. Woods,
Andrew Briscoe,
Thomas Barnett,
Jesse B. Badgett,
Stephen W. Blount.

emissaries: agents

contemptible: deserving scorn

forbearance: acceptance

brethren: brothers

plenary: full

rectitude: righteousness

Exploring the Document

Here the Declaration explains that Texans have carried the burden of the listed grievances. **What does the author hope Mexican citizens will do?** TEKS

Biography

George C. Childress
(1804–1841)

George C. Childress was born and raised in Tennessee. In 1835 he volunteered for the Texas army. Childress was elected to the Convention of 1836 and played a key role in it. He called the convention to order and served as the primary author of the document. **What role did Childress play in Texas history?** TEKS

Independence Is Won

Read to Discover

1. What events led to the Runaway Scrape?
2. What led to James Fannin's surrender at Goliad?
3. How did the Texas army defeat Mexican forces and win independence?

Why It Matters Today

Many U.S. and Tejano settlers fled from Santa Anna's army. Use CNN **fyi**.com or other **current events** sources to learn about refugees to the United States today. Record your findings in your journal.

Identify

- **Runaway Scrape**
- **Battle of Refugio**
- **Battle of Coleto**
- **Goliad Massacre**
- **Francita Alavez**
- **Battle of San Jacinto**

The Story Continues

In the spring of 1836, 10-year-old Dilue Rose Harris sadly packed up her belongings. Scouts had warned the Harris family that Santa Anna's soldiers were on their way. The Harrises believed that Santa Anna would destroy the Texas rebellion and Texans like them, so they ran for their lives. The Harris family packed their bed linens, clothes, and food on a sleigh pulled by a team of oxen. They left their farm as the sun was setting, wondering if they would ever see their home again.

During the Runaway Scrape, Texans abandoned their farms and homes, taking with them only the things they could easily carry.

★ The Runaway Scrape

General Sam Houston had the task of defeating Santa Anna so that Texans like the Harrises could return to their homes. During the Convention of 1836, the delegates had given Houston full command of both the regular army and the volunteers. This did not solve all of his problems, however. Houston was still short on troops, guns, ammunition, supplies, and money. He also had to quickly organize and train his army.

On March 6 Houston left Washington-on-the-Brazos and headed to Gonzales, still unsure of the outcome at the Alamo. When Houston reached Gonzales on March 11, he was greeted with rumors of the defeat. He sent out his best scouts to find out what had happened and where Santa Anna's forces were. Scouts Deaf Smith, R. E. Handy, and Henry Karnes left to investigate. The next day, the scouts escorted Susanna Dickinson and a few other survivors of the Alamo into Gonzales. Houston and the Texas army heard for the first time the details of the defenders' last stand at the Alamo.

He also learned that Santa Anna was heading to Gonzales, where Houston had fewer than 400 men. With more than 700 Mexican troops advancing on them, the Texans were in danger. Houston ordered a retreat. Many civilians packed their belongings and left as well. Houston then ordered the town of Gonzales burned so that the Mexican troops would not take any additional supplies.

Word began to spread through Texas about the Alamo. Fearing for their lives, Texans fled eastward. U.S. settlers—often accompanied by African American slaves—and many Tejanos left their farms, homes, and towns to avoid the advancing Mexican forces. This movement of settlers became known as the **Runaway Scrape**. Jeff Parson, a slave at the time, described the scene. "People and things were all mixed, and in confusion. The children were crying, the women praying. . . . I tell you it was a serious time." Conditions were made worse by heavy rains and flooding during the spring of 1836. Many died from disease and hardships during the Runaway Scrape.

Reading Check Identifying Cause and Effect What led to the Runaway Scrape, and how did it affect Texas?

★ Fannin's Surrender at Goliad

Many U.S. settlers in southern regions of Texas were fleeing before another Mexican army. General José de Urrea had crossed the Rio Grande with some 550 troops. He moved up the Texas coastline, attacking settlements along the way. On February 27, 1836, Mexican troops defeated 34 Texas soldiers holed up at San Patricio. At least eight Texas rebels were killed. On March 2, Urrea's troops ambushed and defeated some 26 Texas soldiers along Agua Dulce Creek.

While Santa Anna was stalled at the Alamo, Urrea continued toward Refugio. On March 14 he won the **Battle of Refugio**, defeating a number of Colonel James Fannin's troops who had been sent to evacuate the settlement. Some Texas soldiers escaped during the battle, only to be captured later by Urrea's forces. Urrea's next target was Fannin's army at Goliad.

On March 14 Fannin received an order from General Houston to withdraw to Victoria. Instead of acting immediately, Fannin waited for his troops to return from Refugio. Meanwhile, General Urrea was hurrying to catch up to Fannin. On March 18 Urrea's advance force met Fannin and his troops in a series of brief fights. Fannin then decided to leave the protection of the fort at Goliad and head northeast to Victoria.

James Fannin
(c. 1804–1836)

James Fannin is believed to have been born on January 1, 1804, in Georgia. He moved to Texas with his family in 1834. The next year Fannin joined the Texas army, fighting in the Battle of Gonzales. Later he commanded the Texas forces in the Battle of Concepción, in which 90 Texans defeated some 400 Mexican soldiers. In December Fannin took charge of at least 400 troops at Goliad. Fannin surrendered to General Urrea on March 20, 1836. He and many of his troops were executed on March 27 by order of General Santa Anna. In memory of Fannin and his troops, "Remember Goliad!" became a battle cry of the Texas Revolution. How did Fannin inspire Texans? TEKS

On March 19 the Texas troops marched into an open prairie outside of Goliad during a heavy fog. When they stopped to rest their animals, Urrea and his main army surrounded them. The Texas force numbered at least 300 soldiers, and the Mexicans had 300 to 500 troops. Fannin chose to stand and fight near Coleto Creek. In the **Battle of Coleto**, the Texas rebels were pinned down without cover and with a limited water supply. Fannin was wounded in the battle. The next morning, Mexican reinforcements arrived, giving Urrea several hundred more troops. Fannin decided to surrender. Following the surrender, he and most of the other Texas rebels were marched back to Goliad.

The prisoners were held in Goliad for a week. One U.S. settler described Urrea. "[Urrea] was not blood thirsty and when not overruled by orders of a superior . . . was disposed [likely] to treat prisoners with lenity [mercy]." Urrea wrote to Santa Anna, asking him for permission to hold the Texas troops as prisoners of war, rather than kill them. Santa Anna's response was swift and clear. Anyone who had taken up arms against the government of Mexico must be executed immediately.

On March 27, Mexican soldiers shot more than 400 Texans outside of Goliad. Those executed included Fannin's troops as well as Texas soldiers captured outside of Victoria. When the firing began, a few of the Texans ran and escaped. Some survived the **Goliad Massacre** during the smoky confusion. **Francita Alavez**, who was traveling with the Mexican troops, helped a few people escape. Texans later referred to her as the Angel of Goliad.

Reading Check Summarizing How did geographic factors and other events lead to Fannin's surrender?

★ Houston Prepares the Troops

With news of Goliad, some angry Texans began to demand an attack on Mexican forces. The Texas army had grown to more than 1,200 men after the fall of the Alamo. Houston, however, believed that his army was still too small and untrained to defeat the larger and better-supplied

During the conflict outside of Goliad, Fannin's troops were surrounded on the open prairie.

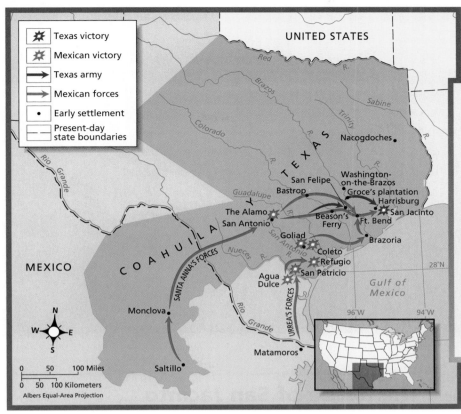

Battles of the Texas Revolution, 1835–1836

Interpreting Maps As Mexican forces marched across Texas, General Houston retreated eastward.

TAKS *Skills*

1. Locate Where did the major battles of the Texas Revolution occur? ⭐TEKS

2. Evaluating Why do you think Texas and Mexican forces traveled through towns and river crossings such as Beason's Ferry? ⭐TEKS

Mexican army. So he continued the retreat, moving eastward toward the Brazos River. Santa Anna's army was close behind. He was hoping to capture the ad interim government and Houston. Several Texas troops openly rebelled against Houston, criticizing him for retreating. Even President Burnet challenged Houston to fight. "The enemy are laughing you to scorn."

Houston ignored the criticism. He moved 500 men to Groce's Landing, 20 miles north of San Felipe de Austin. They camped at Jared Groce's plantation, where Houston trained and drilled his troops. The Texas troops also increased their stock of supplies and ammunition, some of which came from supporters in the United States. The citizens of Cincinnati, Ohio, had sent two cannons to the soldiers. The Texas rebels named the cannons the Twin Sisters.

Houston and the Texas army left Groce's Landing on April 12, marching southeast toward Harrisburg, where they arrived on April 18. That same day, Houston's scouts reported the location of Santa Anna and part of his army. They had crossed the Brazos River and were camped not far from Harrisburg. Houston made his decision. He wrote a friend, "We are in preparation to meet Santa Anna. It is the only chance of saving Texas." The stage was set for the final battle against Santa Anna.

Santa Anna carried a set of dishes like this one during his campaign in Texas.

⭐ **Reading Check** **Supporting a Point of View** Explain how, in your opinion, Houston's actions after the Alamo and Goliad were or were not an example of good leadership.

Interpreting the Visual Record

San Jacinto. During the Battle of San Jacinto, Texas forces crept onto the prairie that separated the Texan and Mexican camps. The Texans then launched a surprise attack crying, "Remember the Alamo! Remember Goliad!" **How does the artist show the confusion of battle?**

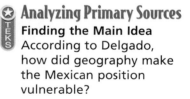

Analyzing Primary Sources

Finding the Main Idea According to Delgado, how did geography make the Mexican position vulnerable?

★ The Battle of San Jacinto

The Texas troops traveled down the Buffalo Bayou. On April 20 they camped in a grove of live oak trees, with a wide field in front of them. The only way the Mexicans could attack them would be to cross the field. Santa Anna and his forces arrived at the junction of the San Jacinto River and Buffalo Bayou that afternoon. They set up camp in a vulnerable spot. Santa Anna's forces were exposed to the Texas troops, who were partially hidden by the grove of trees. One of Santa Anna's officers, Colonel Pedro Delgado, was worried about the location.

Texas Voices ❝We had the enemy on our right, within a wood, at long musket range. Our front, although level, was exposed to the fire of the enemy, who could keep it up with impunity [without punishment] from his sheltered position.❞

—Colonel Pedro Delgado, quoted in *Texian Iliad*, by Stephen L. Hardin

On April 20 there were one or two clashes. In one of the fights, Private Mirabeau B. Lamar daringly saved the lives of two Texans. Lamar was promoted to colonel and placed in charge of the cavalry. In spite of the efforts of the Texas troops, the Mexican soldiers held their ground. The Texas rebels realized that defeating the more than 1,200 Mexican soldiers would not be easy. Shortly before noon on April 21, Houston called a meeting of the Texas army officers. They discussed a battle plan. After debating whether to attack immediately or wait for Santa Anna to attack, the group decided to attack that afternoon.

Houston assembled approximately 900 Texas troops—including Juan Seguín and a small group of Tejanos—at about 3:00 P.M. The

Texas soldiers moved from the woods onto the prairie, unseen by the Mexican forces. Many of the Mexican soldiers, exhausted from days of marching and the previous day's battle, were sleeping. Houston ordered the advance. Many Mexican troops were awakened by bullets and battle cries of "Remember the Alamo!" and "Remember Goliad!" The **Battle of San Jacinto** lasted only about 18 minutes. Surprised by the afternoon attack, many Mexican soldiers fled or tried to surrender. The Texas troops continued firing. When the shooting stopped, 630 Mexican soldiers had been killed. Only nine Texas troops had been killed or died of wounds from the fighting. Houston was among the wounded, with an ankle shattered by a rifle ball.

Santa Anna had disappeared during the battle. He was found the next day hiding in the marsh. Having captured Santa Anna, the Texas army won not only the Battle of San Jacinto but also the war. Houston refused to let the soldiers kill the Mexican general. He later explained his reasons.

Sam Houston was considered a hero after the Battle of San Jacinto.

Texas Voices ❝My motive in sparing the life of Santa Anna was to relieve the country of all hostile enemies without further bloodshed, and to secure his acknowledgment of our independence.❞

—Sam Houston, from an address to the citizens of Texas

⭐ **Reading Check** **Evaluating** What physical and human factors, such as landforms and military decisions, led to the Texas victory over the Mexican forces at San Jacinto?

April 21, 1836

Texans win the Battle of San Jacinto, and Texas gains its independence from Mexico.

 Section 5 Review ⭐TEKS Questions 1, 2, 3a, 3b, 4

 go.hrw.com **Homework Practice Online**
keyword: ST3 HP11

1 Identify and explain:
- Runaway Scrape
- Battle of Refugio
- Battle of Coleto
- Goliad Massacre
- Francita Alavez
- Battle of San Jacinto

2 Summarizing
Copy the graphic organizer below. Use it to explain the significant events in 1836 after the fall of the Alamo that led to Texas independence.

The Fall of the Alamo
Texas Independence

3 Finding the Main Idea
a. What led to the Runaway Scrape?
b. Why were Fannin's troops forced to surrender at Goliad?

4 Writing and Critical Thinking TAKS
Identifying Points of View Write a short news report explaining the Runaway Scrape and Sam Houston's leadership, and how these issues affected the Battle of San Jacinto.
Consider the following:
- Houston's retreat and training of troops
- Houston's decision to attack on the afternoon of April 21

CHAPTER 11 REVIEW

The Chapter at a Glance

Examine the following visual summary of the chapter. Then use the visual to create an oral presentation that describes the events of the Texas Revolution. TEKS

Texas wins independence!

April 21, 1836
Sam Houston's troops attack and defeat Santa Anna's forces at San Jacinto.

March 27, 1836
Texas troops captured outside of Goliad are executed.

March 6, 1836
Ending the siege, Santa Anna's troops capture the Alamo.

March 2, 1836
Texas declares independence.

December 5, 1835
Texas soldiers attack San Antonio and force Mexican troops out of Texas.

November 5, 1835
Texas delegates hold a consultation to debate independence.

October 2, 1835
Texas rebels win the Battle of Gonzales.

Identifying People and Ideas TEKS

Use the following terms or people in historically significant sentences.

1. Antonio López de Santa Anna
2. Sam Houston
3. James Fannin
4. William B. Travis
5. Siege of the Alamo
6. Convention of 1836
7. Lorenzo de Zavala
8. George C. Childress
9. Goliad Massacre
10. Battle of San Jacinto

Understanding Main Ideas (★)TEKS

Section 1 (pp. 226–230)
1. What early victories did Texans achieve in the revolution?

Section 2 (pp. 231–233)
2. How did the structure of the government created by the Consultation lead to problems?

Section 3 (pp. 234–239)
3. Describe the events that led to the fall of the Alamo in 1836.

Section 4 (pp. 240–242)
4. How did the ideas of the U.S. Constitution and Bill of Rights influence the Constitution of 1836?

Section 5 (pp. 246–251)
5. What led to the Runaway Scrape?
6. What was Sam Houston's strategy after the fall of the Alamo, and how successful was it?

You Be the Historian TEKS

Reviewing Themes

1. **Constitutional Heritage** What impact did the Mexican federal Constitution of 1824 have on the events of the Texas Revolution?
2. **Citizenship** How did Tejanos and other Texans participate in the revolution?
3. **Geography** How did the geography of Texas contribute to the outcome of several battles during the Texas Revolution?

TAKS Practice: Thinking Critically (★)TEKS

1. **Comparing** Examine both the Texans' victories and their defeats. What are some of the common elements of the victories? What are some of the common elements of the defeats?
2. **Summarizing** Why was the year 1836 significant to Texas?
3. **Supporting a Point of View** Do you think the Siege of the Alamo was a tragedy or an important rallying point for Texans? Explain your answer.

Interpreting Maps ⭐TEKS

Study the map below. Then answer the following questions.

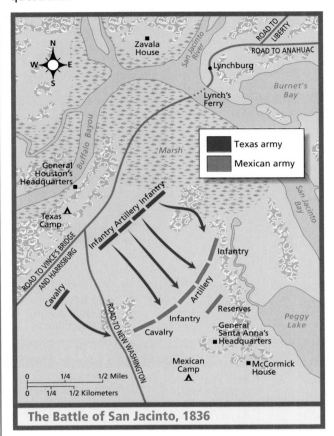

The Battle of San Jacinto, 1836

Texas army
Mexican army

1. Which of the following statements best describes the location of the Texas forces?
   a. near Peggy Lake
   b. on Lorenzo de Zavala's property
   c. in Lynchburg
   d. near the Buffalo Bayou

2. Based on this map, how do you think geography affected the Battle of San Jacinto?

Analyzing Primary Sources ⭐TEKS

Read the following quote by Sam Houston. Then answer the questions.

"War is raging on the frontiers. Bejar [San Antonio] is besieged by two thousand of the enemy. . . . By the last report, our force in Bejar was only one hundred and fifty men strong. The citizens of Texas must rally to the aid of our army, or it will perish. . . . *Independence is declared,* it must be maintained. Immediate action, united with valor [bravery], alone can achieve the great work."

3. Which of the following statements best summarizes how Houston inspired Texans to fight?
   a. Texans will be ashamed of themselves.
   b. The Alamo must be avenged.
   c. The enemy will destroy Texans if Texans do not defend themselves.
   d. The enemy has reinforcements.

4. What events in Texas influenced Houston's comments and point of view? Give specific examples.

Alternative Assessment

Cooperative Learning ⭐TEKS

Work with a small group to complete the following activity. Each person in your group should select one of the following participants in the Texas Revolution: (a) Sam Houston, (b) Antonio López de Santa Anna, (c) James Fannin, (d) William B. Travis, (e) Lorenzo de Zavala, (f) George C. Childress. Have each member create a biography for a news report on the important roles played by significant individuals in the Texas Revolution. Present your news report to the class.

BUILDING YOUR Portfolio

📶 **internet** connect

Internet Activity: go.hrw.com
KEYWORD: ST3 TX11 ⭐TEKS

Access the Internet through the HRW Go site to locate primary and secondary sources on the Battle of the Alamo. Write a short essay examining how geographic factors, transportation, communications, and other human factors affected the events. Also identify any biases and the points of view of the authors of the sources.

A New Nation
(1836–1845)

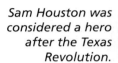

Sam Houston was considered a hero after the Texas Revolution.

Mirabeau B. Lamar disagreed with many of Sam Houston's policies.

1836 Sam Houston becomes the first popularly elected president of the Republic of Texas.

TEXAS

1837 The Texas government begins work in Houston, the new capital.

1838 Texans elect Mirabeau B. Lamar president.

1839 Texas passes a homestead law, protecting settlers' homes from being seized to pay debts.

1840 The new capital of Austin has 850 residents.

1836	**1837**	**1838**	**1839**	**1840**

U.S. and WORLD

1837 A financial panic leads to a depression in the United States.

1838 U.S. troops begin removing the Cherokee from Georgia to Indian Territory.

1839 The photographic process known as the daguerreotype is introduced at the Paris Academy of Sciences.

Many Cherokee died on the journey known as the Trail of Tears.

Build on What You Know

In the fall of 1835, increasing conflict between Texans and the Mexican government erupted in the Texas Revolution. With the crushing victory at the Battle of San Jacinto in April 1836, Texas won the war and became an independent nation. However, the new Republic of Texas faced many challenges.

Edwin Waller laid out the streets and oversaw the construction of the first government buildings in the new capital of Austin.

1841 Texans again elect Sam Houston president of the Republic.

1843 The Tehuacana Creek Councils lead to peace between Texans and several Texas Indian groups.

1844 President Sam Houston sends troops into East Texas to end the Regulator-Moderator War.

1841 1842 1843 1844 1845

1841 *Punch,* a periodical famous for its political humor, begins publication in London, England.

This first edition of Punch *featured a cartoon on its cover.*

1845 The U.S. Congress moves the presidential election day to the first week in November.

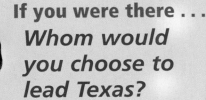

If you were there . . .
Whom would you choose to lead Texas?

You Be the Historian:

Themes Journal

What's Your Opinion? Do you **agree** or **disagree** with the following statements? Support your point of view in your journal.

• **Citizenship** Citizens express their points of view through voting.

• **Economics** A nation's economy is affected by events in bordering nations.

• **Government** Individuals can have a strong influence on the development of a nation.

The Early Republic

Read to Discover

1. What were the terms of the Treaties of Velasco, and how did both sides respond?
2. Why was the election of 1836 significant?

Why It Matters Today

Because Texas was a democratic republic, its citizens elected their leaders. Use **CNNfyi.com** or other **current events** sources to learn about elections in other countries today. Record your findings in your journal.

Define

• annexation

Identify

• **Treaties of Velasco**
• **Sam Houston**
• **Mirabeau B. Lamar**

Newspapers across the United States, such as this Baltimore publication, announced the Texas victory at San Jacinto.

The Story Continues

Several Texans were camped near Buffalo Bayou after fleeing their homes during the Runaway Scrape. Suddenly, a woman on the edge of the group began pointing and shouting, "Hallelujah! Hallelujah!" A man on horseback was racing toward them and yelling. "San Jacinto! The Mexicans are whipped and Santa Anna a prisoner!" Everyone laughed, hugged, and cried from happiness at the victory.

★ The Treaties of Velasco

The celebrations following the victory at San Jacinto were short-lived, partly because Mexican leaders had not yet recognized the war's end. As a result, some 2,000 Mexican troops under the command of General Vicente Filisola remained in Texas. Texans also needed to decide what to do with Mexican general and president Antonio López de Santa Anna, whom they had captured at San Jacinto. In exchange for his life, Santa Anna agreed to order the Mexican troops to leave Texas. Officials then took him to Velasco. On May 14, 1836, Santa Anna and Texas ad interim president David G. Burnet signed the two **Treaties of Velasco**. The first treaty, which was made public, included the following terms.

1. The war between Mexico and Texas was officially ended, and Texas was declared independent.
2. Santa Anna would not take up arms against Texas.
3. All Mexican forces would withdraw beyond the Rio Grande.

4. Prisoners would be exchanged.

5. The Mexicans would return all captured property.

6. Texas leaders would promptly return Santa Anna to Mexico.

The second treaty was kept secret. It provided for Santa Anna's immediate release. In exchange, he would try to persuade Mexican leaders to recognize Texas independence. Santa Anna also agreed to push for Mexican recognition of the Rio Grande as Mexico's border with Texas.

Many Texans wanted Santa Anna to be executed or imprisoned. Nonetheless, in June 1836 Santa Anna was put aboard the *Invincible* to sail to Mexico. Before the vessel could leave, a force led by Thomas J. Green blocked the port. This force was made up of volunteers who had only recently reached Texas and wanted the war to continue. Their actions convinced Burnet to imprison the Mexican leader.

Although Santa Anna was eventually released, Texas had violated a term of the treaties. Mexico also dealt a blow to the treaties—it refused to recognize the public treaty because Santa Anna had signed it while a prisoner. Mexico did not recognize the independence of Texas, and it still considered the region to be in rebellion. As a result, relations between Mexico and Texas remained unsettled.

★ **Reading Check** **Analyzing Information** What significant political event in Texas history occurred in 1836?

David G. Burnet was president through the troubled times of the Texas Revolution. The ad interim government had to move several times to avoid Mexican forces.

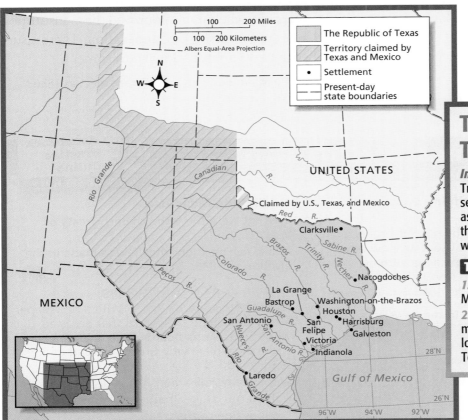

The Republic of Texas, 1836

Interpreting Maps In the second Treaty of Velasco, Santa Anna secretly pledged to recognize Texas as an independent nation. However, the boundaries of the new nation were not firmly established.

TAKS *Skills*

1. Locate What Texas regions did Mexico and Texas claim? ★TEKS

2. Evaluating Why do you think most of the Texas settlements were located in the eastern region of Texas? ★TEKS

The Lone Star Flag

The first official Texas flag was adopted by the Texas Congress on December 10, 1836. It had a blue background with a gold star in the center. It was replaced by the red, white, and blue Lone Star flag in 1839. The designer of the 1839 flag is unknown. Since then, changes have been made to the specifications for the flag, but the symbol of the state of Texas has remained essentially unchanged since 1839. **How did the appearance of the Lone Star flag change during the 1830s?**

★ The Election of 1836

A second major challenge facing the Republic of Texas was to form a new government. The Constitution of 1836 required that elections be held to select new leaders. Texans would also decide whether to approve the Constitution of 1836 and whether to pursue **annexation** of Texas to the United States. Annexation is the formal joining of one political region to another. Burnet wrote in a letter that the election would probably "be conducted with a good deal of spirit." Three well-known Texans ran for president—Stephen F. Austin, **Sam Houston**, and Henry Smith. Houston was the most popular candidate. "Old Sam Jacinto," as he became known, had led Texans to victory. Many Texans shared the view of this supporter.

Texas Voices

"No person ever met Sam Houston in the early days of the Republic without being impressed with his greatness. He was then about forty-two years of age, just the prime of life. Standing largely over six feet in height, with a massive, well formed hand, . . . a large head, a piercing gray eye, [and] a mouth and nose indicating character of fine proportions."

—Francis R. Lubbock, quoted in *A Political History of the Texas Republic, 1836–1845,* by Stanley Siegel

Houston won the presidency by a large majority. For vice president, voters elected **Mirabeau B. Lamar**, another hero of San Jacinto. Texans also elected 30 representatives and 14 senators to the Republic's new Congress. In addition, voters overwhelmingly approved the Constitution of 1836 and expressed a desire to pursue U.S. annexation. These issues decided, the Republic began to set up its national government.

★ **Reading Check** Finding the Main Idea Who did Texans elect in 1836?

Section 1 Review

(TEKS) Questions 2, 3, 4a, 4b, 5

go.hrw.com **Homework Practice Online**
keyword: ST3 HP12

1 Define and explain:
- annexation

2 Identify and explain:
- Treaties of Velasco
- Sam Houston
- Mirabeau B. Lamar

3 Identifying Cause and Effect

Copy the graphic organizer below. Use it to show how the Mexican government and Texans responded to the Treaties of Velasco, and why.

Treaties of Velasco

Cause of Texans' Response	Cause of Mexican Response
Response of Texans	Response of Mexico

4 Finding the Main Idea

a. What were the terms of each Treaty of Velasco?

b. List five decisions that Texans made in the election of 1836.

5 Writing and Critical Thinking

TAKS

Identifying Points of View Write a newspaper article describing the events that occurred when Santa Anna boarded the *Invincible*. In addition, explain why Green and Burnet acted as they did.

Consider the following:
- the terms of the Treaties of Velasco
- opposition to the treaties

Houston's First Term

Read to Discover

1. What were some actions of the first government of the Republic of Texas?
2. How did President Houston's administration try to solve problems with the military and the economy?
3. How did President Houston work to protect the rights of American Indians in Texas?

Why It Matters Today

Economic problems were one of the many challenges facing the Republic of Texas. Use **CNNfyi.com** and other **current events** sources to learn about current economic problems. Record your findings in your journal.

Define

- **administration**
- **cabinet**
- **expenditures**
- **revenue**
- **ratify**

Identify

- **Felix Huston**
- **Albert Sidney Johnston**
- **Texas Rangers**
- **Panic of 1837**
- **Chief Bowles**

The Story Continues

On October 22, 1836, Sam Houston stood before the leading citizens of Texas. His sword from the Battle of San Jacinto hung at his side. The audience grew quiet as he prepared to take the oath of office. Houston spoke briefly of his plans for Texas. Then he paused, removed his sword, and grasped it in both hands. In an emotional voice, he declared that the sword was a symbol of his past position. "I have worn it . . . in defense of my country," he said. Now Houston faced new challenges as president of the Republic.

Sam Houston carried this short sword during the Battle of San Jacinto.

★ Houston's Administration

Sam Houston became the first popularly elected president of the Republic of Texas on October 22, 1836. Addressing the first Texas Congress, Houston laid out his goals. He stressed the need for peace with American Indians and the need to stay alert and guard against an attack by Mexico. He also expressed his hope of seeing Texas annexed to the United States.

Houston faced many challenges during his **administration**, or term of office. He began addressing them by appointing a **cabinet** of executive department heads to assist him. He appointed Stephen F. Austin as secretary of state and Henry Smith as secretary of the treasury. Houston named Thomas J. Rusk as secretary of war and Samuel Rhoads Fisher as secretary of the navy. Austin served the Republic for only a few months. As a result of overwork and exposure to cold, he developed pneumonia. On December 27, 1836, Austin died at the age of 43. Texans mourned the loss of the leader who had dedicated his life to Texas. President Houston issued a statement expressing the nation's loss. "The father of Texas is no more. The first pioneer of the wilderness has departed." Houston ordered a 30-day period of mourning to honor Austin.

A second major task facing the Republic was the formation of a court system, as required by the constitution. The new Congress set up a supreme court, four district courts, 23 county courts, and justice courts. The Texas Supreme Court consisted of a chief justice and four associate justices, who also served as judges of the district courts. James Collinsworth was appointed the Republic's first chief justice.

Another order of business was to specify the Republic's boundaries. To the south and west, the Congress claimed the Rio Grande as the border. The Mexican government did not recognize this border, however. Many people who lived south and west of the Nueces River still considered themselves Mexicans.

Selecting a capital was also an early issue. President Burnet had moved the capital of the ad interim government from Velasco to Columbia. Officials found the town too small, so they began looking for a new site for the capital. Two brothers, John and Augustus Allen, had recently founded a town near Harrisburg on Buffalo Bayou. Named in honor of Sam Houston, the town was little more than a village. Nonetheless, the Allen brothers tried to persuade Congress to choose Houston as the new capital. They even offered to provide government buildings and lodging for officials. In late 1836 the Congress named Houston the new temporary capital. The Texas government moved there the following spring, and the town grew rapidly. In January 1837 it had 12 residents and one log cabin, but within four months, some 1,500 people lived there.

★ **Reading Check** **Summarizing** What were the early actions of Houston and the Texas Congress in the new Republic?

Interpreting the Visual Record

Houston. *During Sam Houston's term, the village of Houston was selected as the center of government. This engraving shows the capitol building there.* **How does this engraving reflect life in the new capital?**

★TEKS

★ Houston and Army Unrest

The new government soon faced a challenge from its own army. Many volunteers from the United States who had arrived too late to fight in the Texas Revolution were still eager for action. **Felix Huston**, the army's commander, and many others wanted to invade Mexico. President Houston considered such a move risky. To stop the growing unrest, he replaced Huston with **Albert Sidney Johnston**. This only led to more conflict. The decision angered Huston, and he challenged Johnston to a duel and severely wounded him.

With Johnston unable to take command, unrest in the army grew. One military commander urged soldiers to march on the capital. He wanted them to "chastise [scold] the President, kick Congress out of doors, and give laws to Texas." To regain control, Houston placed all but 600 troops on leave and never recalled them.

For defense and frontier protection, Houston relied instead on militia companies and the **Texas Rangers**. The Rangers were a defense force that tried to keep the peace along the frontier. Formed on November 24, 1835, the Texas Rangers had to be ready to ride at all times. In later years, the Rangers would become law officers. Although Houston's actions solved some problems, conflicts with the army continued to trouble the Republic.

★ **Reading Check Finding the Main Idea** What action did Houston take to solve growing unrest in the army? What role did the Texas Rangers play in his policies?

Sam Houston
(1793–1863)

When Sam Houston first rode into Texas in 1832, he was already a well-known hero in the United States. Although he was born in Virginia, his family had moved to Tennessee in 1807. Two years later he left home to live with the Cherokee. In 1813 he joined the U.S. Army, fighting under General Andrew Jackson. Houston then relied on his experience with the Cherokee as an Indian agent for the U.S. government. With the support of Jackson, Houston entered politics. He served Tennessee in the U.S. Congress and as governor. After again living with the Cherokee, Houston traveled to Texas in December 1832. Houston served his fellow Texans—first in the military and then in politics—for some 25 years. **What experiences helped Houston become a leader in Texas?**

★ Economic Policies

The new nation also had serious economic problems. The Republic's **expenditures**, or spending, far exceeded its **revenue**, or income. When Sam Houston took office, Texas had a national debt of $1.25 million. The new government collected taxes and placed customs duties on imported goods. Texas officials tried to get loans in the United States. The Republic also put public lands up for sale. Despite these efforts, the Republic's debt continued to rise as its expenses increased.

To make matters worse, the United States experienced a financial crisis in 1837. This **Panic of 1837** led to an economic depression. Texas, which traded heavily with the United States, soon felt the effects. Business slowed, and goods became scarce. The Republic's limited money supply posed another economic problem. Texans manufactured few goods and therefore had to import many items. As imports exceeded exports, money drained from the Republic. The government tried to increase the money supply by printing paper money. However, the Republic had no gold and silver to back this money. As the debt of the Republic grew and confidence in the government fell, the value of its money dropped.

Reading Check **Analyzing Information** How did economic problems in the United States affect Texas?

★ Land Policy under Houston

Although the Republic was in debt, it was rich in land. In 1836 Texas claimed more than 200 million acres of public land. The Constitution of 1836 provided for a land policy based on Spanish, Mexican, and southern U.S. practices. Heads of families living in Texas on March 2, 1836—excluding African Americans and American Indians—were guaranteed 4,606 acres. Single men aged 17 and over were guaranteed 1,476 acres of land. Veterans of the Texas Revolution received additional land. Later laws provided smaller land grants to more recent settlers. In all, the Republic distributed nearly 37 million acres under this land policy.

To encourage immigration, the Republic established a colonization policy in the early 1840s. Based on the Mexican *empresario* system, this policy gave agents contracts to settle immigrants in Texas. The Republic distributed another 4.5 million acres under this system.

Texas officials hoped the various land policies would help the economy by increasing settlement. Some of the early policies did not require settlers to live on the land they received, so some speculators acquired land in hopes of selling it for a quick profit. But land speculation was rarely profitable because land was so easy to obtain in the Republic.

Reading Check **Making Generalizations and Predictions** How do you think the Republic's land policy affected immigration to Texas?

Interpreting the Visual Record

Texas Indians. *Houston believed that American Indians and Texas settlers could live together in peace. Based on this engraving, how do you think Indians' lives differed from those of settlers in Texas?* ⭐TEKS

⭐ Houston's American Indian Policy

As settlements spread onto American Indian land, many conflicts arose. American Indians wanted to keep their land, but many Texans wanted to remove them from Texas—by force if necessary. President Houston opposed such action and supported a peaceful solution. He wanted to avoid a full-scale Indian war, which the Republic could not afford.

Houston sympathized with Indians' desire to control their land. During the Texas Revolution, he had negotiated a treaty guaranteeing the Cherokee title to and control of land in East Texas. The Texas Senate refused to **ratify**, or approve, the treaty, however. Some of the more than 400 Cherokee who lived to the north of Nacogdoches were angry that they had not received title to their land. In addition, Mexican agents had convinced some Cherokee to fight the Texans. President Houston urged the Cherokee to be patient. He told them that he would do everything in his power to help them hold on to their land. Houston wrote to **Chief Bowles**, a Cherokee leader and friend. "Do not be disturbed by the troubles which are around you, but be at peace." Houston set aside land for the Cherokee in an attempt to keep peace. This action angered Texas settlers who wanted the land and viewed the Cherokee as Mexican allies. Houston's efforts at peace seemed likely to fail.

Chief Bowles agreed to help Texas officials establish peace with Plains Indians to the west, where fighting had increased. New settlers were moving west by the hundreds. The Comanche, Kiowa, Wichita, and other Plains Indians viewed these newcomers as invaders. In May 1836, before Houston took office, Comanche and Kiowa forces had attacked Fort Parker. They killed most of the 34 residents and took five captives.

That's Interesting!

Houston: The Raven

When Sam Houston went to live with the Cherokee, Chief Oolooteka adopted him. Oolooteka gave Houston the name Colonneh, meaning "the Raven." Later, Houston married Diana Rogers Gentry and became a citizen of the Cherokee nation. Houston admired many American Indian customs. He also enjoyed wearing Cherokee clothing, even after he moved to Texas.

Houston's moccasins were highly decorated.

Chief Bowles
(c. 1756–1839)

Chief Bowles, whose Cherokee name was Duwali, was born in North Carolina. As U.S. settlement expanded in the South, he and his village were forced to move. In 1819 they settled in Texas. There, he served on a Cherokee decision-making council and later formed a strong friendship with Sam Houston. **Why do you think Chief Bowles chose to go to Texas?**

Houston and the Congress developed an American Indian policy to reduce conflict and protect Texas settlers. The policy established a line of forts along the frontier and encouraged trade with Indians. It was hoped the policy would promote peace and friendship with Texas Indians. While Texas Rangers patrolled the frontier, Houston tried to negotiate and sign treaties with Texas Indians. He described this approach.

 Texas Voices

66**Treaties of peace and amity [goodwill], and the maintenance of good faith with the Indians, present themselves to my mind as the most rational [reasonable] grounds on which to obtain their friendship. Let us abstain [cease] on our part from aggressions, establish commerce with the different tribes, supply their useful and necessary wants, maintain even-handed justice with them, and natural reason will teach them the utility [usefulness] of our friendship.**99

—Sam Houston, quoted in *Documents of Texas History*, edited by Ernest Wallace

Houston attempted to make peace with each American Indian group in Texas. He was one of the few Texas leaders who believed that Indians and settlers could live together in peace. Most Texans in the Republic disagreed with Houston, preferring to remove American Indians from Texas. Some Texans thought Houston's policy was slowing westward development. Ongoing conflict between American Indians and Texas settlers also made it difficult to maintain peaceful relations.

⭐ **Reading Check** **Identifying Points of View** Why did some Texans oppose President Houston's American Indian policy?

Section 2 Review ⭐TEKS Questions 2, 3, 4a, 4b, 5

go.hrw.com Homework Practice Online
keyword: ST3 HP12

1 Define and explain:
- administration
- cabinet
- expenditures
- revenue
- ratify

2 Identify and explain:
- Felix Huston
- Albert Sidney Johnston
- Texas Rangers
- Panic of 1837
- Chief Bowles

3 Analyzing Information
Copy the graphic organizer below. Use it to show how Sam Houston's administration tried to solve the Republic's problems.

Problem	Solution/Action
Unruly army	
Debt	
Lack of a clear land policy	
Conflict with American Indians	

4 Finding the Main Idea
a. What were two early actions of the Republic's Congress?
b. What economic policies did the Republic establish, and how successful were they?

5 Writing and Critical Thinking
Evaluating Imagine that you are a member of Sam Houston's cabinet. Write a short evaluation of Houston's American Indian policy explaining why you support it.
Consider the following:
- the cost of a full-scale war against American Indians
- recent conflicts with American Indians

TAKS

Lamar's Presidency

Read to Discover

1. What steps did Lamar's administration take to address the issue of public education?
2. What problems did Lamar's administration face?
3. How did changes in Texas policy lead to wars with Texas Indians?

Why It Matters Today

Mirabeau B. Lamar faced many challenges during his presidency. Use CNN**fyi**.com and other **current events** sources to learn about the problems facing a political leader today. Record your findings in your journal.

Define

- consecutive terms
- charter
- capitol
- homestead law
- red backs

Identify

- Rutersville College
- Edwin Waller
- Battle of the Neches
- Council House Fight
- Battle of Plum Creek

The Story Continues

Early one August morning, a few people in Linnville noticed a huge cloud of dust on the horizon. As the dust cloud neared, the residents realized that it was a Comanche raiding party. Some 1,000 Comanche swept down on the town. They captured and killed residents and stole horses. As they left, the Comanche burned the town. The raid was an angry response to a massacre that had occurred earlier at a peace conference.

The Comanche often carried shields like this one during raids and conflicts.

★ Lamar in Office

Sam Houston was no longer president when the Comanche raid on Linnville occurred. In September 1838, Texans had elected new leaders. Houston could not run for re-election because, under the Republic's constitution, a president could not serve **consecutive terms**, or two terms in a row. Even if Houston could have run, he might not have been re-elected. Many Texans disliked his policies, particularly his American Indian policy. Texans elected Mirabeau B. Lamar as their new president and David G. Burnet as vice president. Both men strongly disagreed with Houston's policies and personally disliked him.

On taking office in 1839, President Lamar stressed the need for a public education system. He stated that a "cultivated [educated] mind is

Mirabeau B. Lamar
(1798–1859)

A native of Georgia, Mirabeau B. Lamar came to Texas in 1835 to join the fight for Texas independence. After the war, Lamar served as vice president and then as president of the Republic. Lamar pursued an aggressive Indian policy and opposed annexation to the United States. He also faced many challenges, including a growing public debt and ongoing conflicts with Mexico. By the end of his presidency, Lamar had lost much popular support. He briefly retired from politics and focused on his love of writing poetry. In 1857 Lamar re-entered the political world, becoming U.S. minister to Nicaragua and Costa Rica. He died in 1859, two months after his assignment ended.

What political positions did Lamar hold in the Republic? TEKS

the guardian genius of Democracy." Following Lamar's lead, the Congress passed education acts in 1839 and 1840. These acts granted each county 17,712 acres of land to support public schools. The government also set aside 231,400 acres for the future establishment of two public universities.

The first college in the Republic to receive a **charter**—a document granting permission to operate—was <u>Rutersville College</u>. This private college opened in 1840 in Rutersville, near La Grange. However, the Republic never established a public school system or public universities. Because of low land prices, the land grants set aside to fund these schools were not yet worth much money. Nonetheless, because of his efforts, Lamar is known today as the Father of Texas Education.

Reading Check Finding the Main Idea How did Lamar's administration try to promote public education?

★ A New Capital

During Lamar's administration, the government also selected a permanent capital for Texas. President Lamar and many members of the Congress were unhappy with Houston as the capital. Lamar thought Houston was too far east. He wanted to move the political center of Texas west, closer to the edge of Texas settlement. Lamar believed this move would strengthen the Republic's control of the region.

In 1839 the Congress appointed a group to choose a site for a permanent capital. The group selected a village named Waterloo, located along the Colorado River. The government renamed this town Austin in honor of Stephen F. Austin. Judge <u>Edwin Waller</u> was sent to Austin to lay out the streets and begin building government offices. A temporary **capitol**, or a building in which government officials meet, was soon completed. Homes and other government offices were built, and businesses opened along the town's main street, Congress Avenue.

Not everyone was pleased with the new capital, however. Many Texans, including Sam Houston, claimed Austin was isolated and too far west. They feared it would be vulnerable to Mexican attack because of its location. Austin was also in Comanche territory and would therefore be exposed to Plains Indian raids. One such criticism appeared in a Houston newspaper on April 17,1839.

Analyzing Primary Sources
Identifying Bias Why else might the writer be critical of Austin becoming the Texas capital?

Texas Voices ❝The [capital's] location has been made at Waterloo [Austin], an inconsiderable [unimpressive] hamlet [village]. . . . The country around this point is represented to be exceedingly [very] fertile and beautiful, and the climate remarkably healthy. It is, however, almost entirely uninhabited [unsettled], and . . . more exposed than any other point on the frontier.❞

—*Telegraph and Texas Register.*

Life in frontier Austin was difficult and dangerous. However, as more people moved to Austin, the town began to prosper. By 1840 more than 850 people lived there, including diplomats from France, Great Britain, and the United States. Eventually, most Texans became satisfied with their new capital.

Reading Check *Identifying Points of View* What geographic factor made some Texans unhappy with Austin's location?

★ Land and Economic Policies

The Lamar administration continued the Republic's land policy. In January 1839 the Congress passed a **homestead law** that protected a family's home and up to 50 acres of land from seizure for debts. Thus, most creditors could not take a Texan's home and sell it to cover a debt.

This protection became important as the Republic's financial problems worsened. The public debt increased, while the value of Texas currency fell. The Republic responded by issuing new paper money certificates, which were commonly called **red backs**. The value of these red backs dropped quickly—they were worthless within three years of their printing. The Republic's debt was largely to blame. Because of rising military expenses, the government spent more than it collected in revenue. Military spending rose from $881,000 under Houston to more than $1.5 million under Lamar. Part of this money went to reoutfit the Texas navy with six new ships.

Reading Check *Summarizing* What were some of the Republic's financial problems during Lamar's administration?

Austin. The first capitol in Austin was a one-story building with a stockade to protect it from raids. *What types of transportation did early settlers use in Austin?* ★ TEKS

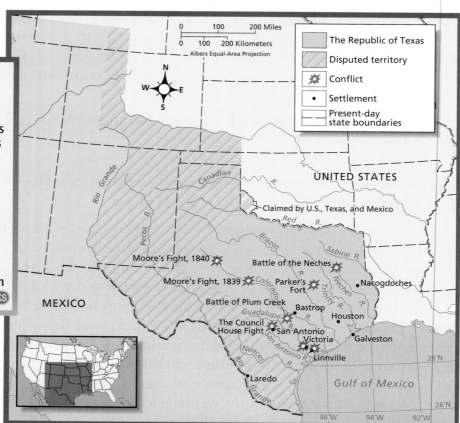

Indian Battles in Texas, 1836–1845

Interpreting Maps During Lamar's presidency, conflicts between Texas troops and American Indians erupted throughout the Republic.

TAKS Skills

1. Locate Where did the conflicts between Texas Indians and soldiers occur? ⭐TEKS

2. Drawing Inferences and Conclusions How do you think these conflicts affected settlement in the different regions of Texas? ⭐TEKS

Map labels:

- 0 100 200 Miles
- 0 100 200 Kilometers
- Albers Equal-Area Projection

Legend:
- The Republic of Texas
- Disputed territory
- ✶ Conflict
- • Settlement
- ☐ Present-day state boundaries

UNITED STATES
MEXICO
Rio Grande
Canadian R.
Pecos R.
Red R.
Claimed by U.S., Texas, and Mexico
Brazos R.
Sabine R.
Moore's Fight, 1840 ✶
Battle of the Neches ✶
Moore's Fight, 1839 ✶
Colorado R.
Parker's Fort ✶
Nacogdoches •
Neches R.
Battle of Plum Creek
Bastrop •
Trinity R.
Houston •
Guadalupe R.
The Council House Fight ✶
San Antonio •
Victoria •
Galveston •
San Antonio R.
Linnville •
Nueces R.
Laredo •
Gulf of Mexico
Rio Grande
28°N
26°N
96°W   94°W   92°W

⭐ Lamar's American Indian Policy

President Lamar's American Indian policy contributed to the rise in military spending. Lamar disliked Indians and wanted to remove them from Texas. Unlike Houston, he did not believe Indians had a right to their land. In his inaugural address, Lamar outlined his Indian policy.

Analyzing Primary Sources
Making Generalizations and Predictions What is Lamar's view of American Indians, and how do you think this will affect the Republic's Indian policy?

Texas Voices ❝The white man and the [American Indian] cannot dwell in harmony together. Nature forbids it. . . . I experience no difficulty in deciding on the proper policy to be pursued towards them. It is to push a rigorous [harsh] war against them; pursuing them to their hiding places without mitigation [relief] or compassion, until they shall be made to feel that flight from our borders without hope of return, is preferable to the scourges [horrors] of war.❞

—Mirabeau B. Lamar, quoted in *Lone Star,* by T. R. Fehrenbach

In 1839 Lamar ordered the Cherokee to leave Texas. When the Cherokee refused, Lamar sent some 500 soldiers led by Kelsey Douglass to forcibly remove them. In July fighting broke out near the Neches River. After several days of fighting in this **Battle of the Neches**, more than 100 Cherokee lay dead, including Chief Bowles. Texas forces then pursued most of the surviving Cherokee north into Indian Territory in the United States. Some other American Indians, including the Caddo and Shawnee, also left northeastern Texas during this time.

Conflict between Texas settlers and the Comanche had also worsened. In January 1839 Lamar sent Colonel John H. Moore to attack the Comanche living west of Texas settlements. Moore and his troops fought the Comanche in a series of conflicts. As a result of these raids, the Comanche eventually agreed to peace talks.

On March 19, 1840, about 65 Comanche men, women, and children arrived at the Council House in San Antonio for peace talks. Texas officials had ordered the Comanche to bring all their captives. However, the Comanche representatives brought only a few. One captive, a teenage girl named Matilda Lockhart, reported that the Comanche still held 15 Texans captive. When Texans demanded their release, the Comanche peace chief, Muk-wah-ruh, responded that he did not have authority over the Comanche holding those captives. Then the Texans tried to take the Comanche representatives hostage in exchange for the captives. The Comanche leaders called for help from their friends who were waiting outside. Fighting broke out in and around the Council House. By the battle's end, 35 Comanche lay dead, including 12 chiefs, 3 women, and 2 children. At least seven Texans also died. This **Council House Fight** probably destroyed any chance of peace.

When other Comanche heard about the massacre, they were outraged. First, they put their Texan captives to death. Then a large Comanche raiding party struck the settlements of Linnville and Victoria, killing more than 20 settlers, burning houses, and stealing supplies and livestock. Texas settlers called for revenge for the Comanche raids. A force of volunteers, regular soldiers, and Texas Rangers formed and began searching for the Comanche. Under the command of Edward Burleson, Mathew Caldwell, Felix Huston, and Ben McCulloch, the Texans found the Comanche on August 11, 1840. The Texas force attacked. During the **Battle of Plum Creek**, more than 130 Comanche were killed. One Texan was killed, and seven were wounded.

Reading Check **Identifying Cause and Effect** What was Lamar's policy toward American Indians, and what did he hope to achieve with it?

Interpreting the Visual Record

Battle of Plum Creek. *A volunteer force of settlers defeated the Comanche raiding party near present-day Lockhart, pushing the Comanche farther west.* ***What does this painting reveal about how the Commanche fought their enemies?*** ⭐TEKS

Texas settlers established small farms across the frontier.

★ The Results of Lamar's Policies

Despite this victory, many Texas settlers still feared the Comanche. Texas officials decided to strike farther into the frontier area known as Comanche country. In October, Colonel Moore led a force northwest in search of Comanche camps. Along the Colorado River, nearly 300 miles upriver from Austin, he found a Comanche village. The Texas force caught the Comanche by surprise and destroyed the village. Some 130 Comanche died in the conflict. Following these defeats, the Comanche moved farther north beyond the Red River, out of range of Texas forces.

By the end of his term, President Lamar had achieved his goal of removing the Cherokee from East Texas. The Comanche had also been pushed farther north and west, opening up vast lands for settlement. Speculators and settlers were pleased with the prospect of more land and a safer frontier.

However, Lamar's new policy proved a disaster for Texas Indians. American Indians in Texas had lost land and suffered severely. Some Texans were also concerned about the increased warfare and the expense that went with it. Lamar's American Indian policy had cost the Republic $2.5 million. It had also led to the loss of many lives.

In addition, Lamar's policies had contributed to a soaring national debt. During his term, the debt rose from $3.3 million to more than $8 million. One Texan wrote in 1840 that times had become "terribly severe." Once again, Texans were ready for a change.

Reading Check Finding the Main Idea In what ways was Lamar's Indian policy harmful to both American Indians and the Republic?

 **Section 3 Review** **Questions 2, 3, 4a, 4b, 5**

go.hrw.com Homework Practice Online
keyword: ST3 HP12

1 Define and explain:
- consecutive terms
- charter
- capitol
- homestead law
- red backs

2 Identify and explain:
- Rutersville College
- Edwin Waller
- Battle of the Neches
- Council House Fight
- Battle of Plum Creek

3 Summarizing
Copy the graphic organizer below. Use it to show how President Lamar dealt with the problems facing his administration.

Problem	Solution/Action

4 Finding the Main Idea
a. What did the Lamar administration do to promote education in Texas?
b. Why did the public debt continue to be a problem for the Republic?

5 Writing and Critical Thinking **TAKS**
Analyzing Information Imagine that you are a U.S. official sent to Texas. Write a short report on how changes in Texas policy led to wars with American Indians.
Consider the following:
- Lamar's American Indian policy
- conflicts between Texans and American Indians during Lamar's administration

Houston's Second Administration

Read to Discover

1. What policies did Sam Houston adopt during his second administration?
2. What were the causes of the Regulator-Moderator War?

Why It Matters Today

In 1841 the Republic's debt had become a major national problem. Use CNN **fyi**.com and other **current events** sources to learn about a current nation's debt. Record your findings in your journal.

Define
- **balanced budget**

Identify
- **Treaty of Tehuacana Creek**
- **Regulator-Moderator War**

The Story Continues

Texan James Morgan was worried about his future. Morgan hoped to make money in a new business deal but was concerned about land prices. A piece of land that had been worth $55,000 two years earlier had sold for only $800. Morgan was shocked by the price. "We're perfectly drained & times awfully hard indeed in the money way," he wrote a friend.

The Republic of Texas issued land grants to encourage settlement. Some Texans bought land, speculating that the value would rise.

★ Houston Returns to Office

In 1841, Texans returned to the polls to elect a new president. Sam Houston and David G. Burnet both ran for the office. Many people had grown unhappy with the last administration's American Indian policy, the worthless red backs, and the rising debt. Once again, Texans chose Sam Houston to lead them. They elected Edward Burleson as vice president.

In his second term as president, Houston struggled to reduce the growing national debt. He hoped to achieve a **balanced budget**, or a budget in which spending does not exceed revenue. To save money, Houston cut government jobs and salaries. He also cut the size of both the Texas army and the Texas Rangers. Houston even persuaded the Congress to sell the navy, but the sale was never carried out. As a result of these cutbacks, government spending dropped from $4.8 million

Treaty of Tehuacana Creek. During his second term, Sam Houston met with the Comanche to sign a peace treaty. **What do you think the white flags inside the circle symbolize?**

during Lamar's presidency to a little more than $500,000. Even with this drastic reduction, Houston could not balance the budget. The Republic's debt continued to rise, reaching $12 million by 1845.

In an attempt to solve the nation's money-supply problems, Houston had new paper money printed to replace the red backs. The government restricted how much of this money was issued to try to maintain its value. However, the value of the new money quickly fell because Texans had little faith in the money their government issued.

President Houston also returned Texas to the peaceful American Indian policy of his first term. He established more frontier trading posts to encourage trade with Texas Indians, and he signed peace treaties with various groups. Many Texas Indians began working for peace at the same time. In August 1842 the Caddo signed a peace treaty with the Texas government. They also agreed to help persuade 20 other Indian groups to attend a peace council. In March 1843 nine Indian groups—including the Caddo, Tawakoni, and Waco—met with Texas officials. This council was held at Tehuacana Creek, south of present-day Waco. The Indian and Texas leaders agreed to stop fighting. They planned a larger peace council to be held in September at Fort Bird on the Trinity River, near present-day Dallas. There Texas officials and nine Indian groups signed a treaty to put an end to fighting.

The Comanche, still angered by the massacre at the Council House, did not attend. However, in October 1844 Houston and Chief Buffalo Hump of the Penateka Comanche met at Tehuacana Creek and signed the **Treaty of Tehuacana Creek**. This peace and trade agreement did not establish boundaries for Comanche land. This issue later resurfaced and further strained relations between Texans and the Comanche. Nonetheless, under Houston's guidance, peace between American Indians and settlers returned to the Texas frontier.

 Reading Check **Making Generalizations and Predictions** Do you think Houston's peace policy will succeed? Explain your answer.

LINKING PAST to PRESENT

The Size of the Texas Government

The Texas government has grown tremendously since the days of the Republic. Today's government includes some 250 agencies, boards, and commissions. State employees number in the hundreds of thousands. Paying for this enormous government cost more than $49 billion in 2000. In contrast, the Republic of Texas government needed only about $130,000 to operate in 1845. This amount would equal about $2.1 million today. Why do you think state government costs so much more today?

★ The Regulator-Moderator War

While relations with Texas Indians were improving, violence broke out among settlers in Shelby County in East Texas. This region, known as the Redlands, bordered on the old Neutral Ground. Law enforcement was weak in the area, and as a result, many bandits and outlaws had moved there. One resident described the people who lived in the Redlands.

Texas Voices ❝It is nothing uncommon for us to inquire of a man why he ran away from the [United] States. Few persons feel insulted by such a question. They generally answer for some crime or other which they have committed.❞

—W. B. DeWees, *Letters from Texas*

In 1840 a feud began between Alfred George and Joseph G. Goodbread over fake land certificates. George persuaded Charles W. Jackson to kill Goodbread. Jackson then organized a group, called the Regulators, to "fight crime." In turn, Goodbread's supporters formed the Moderators. Both sides attacked each other and anyone else who got in their way. Local officials, many of whom had become involved, could not stop the feud. People were ambushed and shot. Judges were threatened, and prisoners hanged without trial. Houses were burned, and people were driven from their homes. Eventually, each side numbered in the hundreds. Finally, in August 1844 President Houston sent soldiers to stop the feud. These troops brought an end to the **Regulator-Moderator War**. Peace had again returned to East Texas.

Houston sent troops to end the Regulator-Moderator War. Few soldiers had fine uniforms like this one, which belonged to a Texas officer.

✪ **Reading Check** **Sequencing** Describe in order the events that led to the Regulator-Moderator War.

Section 4 Review ✪TEKS Questions 2, 3, 4a, 4b, 5

go. hrw .com **Homework Practice Online**
keyword: ST3 HP12

❶ Define and explain:
- balanced budget

❷ Identify and explain:
- Treaty of Tehuacana Creek
- Regulator-Moderator War

❸ Identifying Cause and Effect
Copy the graphic organizer below. Use it to list reasons that Sam Houston was elected to a second term. Then list the results of this election.

Causes	Event	Results
1. 2. 3.	Houston is elected to a second term as president.	1. 2. 3.

❹ Finding the Main Idea
a. How did Sam Houston attempt to solve the Republic's economic problems?
b. What were the results of Houston's peace policy toward American Indians?

❺ Writing and Critical Thinking TAKS
Supporting a Point of View Do you agree with Houston's decision to send in troops to put down the Regulator-Moderator War? Provide reasons to support your answer. Consider the following:
- violence resulting from the feud
- local officials' role in the feud

The Chapter at a Glance

Examine the following visual summary of the chapter. Then use the visual to create a short quiz about the major issues the Republic of Texas faced during the Houston and Lamar administrations. ★TEKS

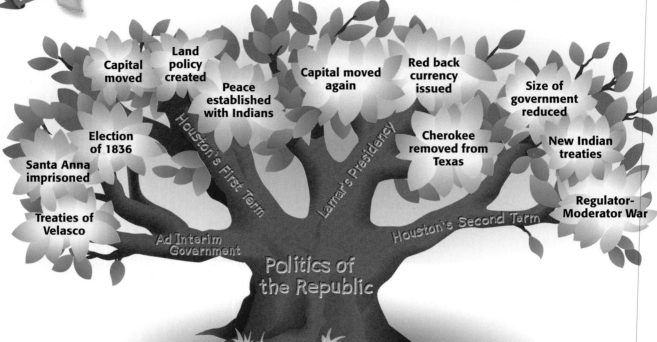

Capital moved

Land policy created

Peace established with Indians

Capital moved again

Red back currency issued

Size of government reduced

Election of 1836

Cherokee removed from Texas

New Indian treaties

Santa Anna imprisoned

Houston's First Term

Lamar's Presidency

Houston's Second Term

Regulator-Moderator War

Treaties of Velasco

Ad Interim Government

Politics of the Republic

Identifying People and Ideas ★TEKS

Use the following terms or people in historically significant sentences.

1. Treaties of Velasco
2. annexation
3. Sam Houston
4. Mirabeau B. Lamar
5. cabinet
6. Texas Rangers
7. red backs
8. Battle of the Neches
9. Battle of Plum Creek
10. balanced budget

Understanding Main Ideas ★TEKS

Section 1 (pp. 256–258)

1. What did Texas leaders and Santa Anna agree to in the Treaties of Velasco?

Section 2 (pp. 259–264)

2. What problems did Sam Houston face in his first term as president?

Section 3 (pp. 265–270)

3. How did President Lamar address the need for a public education system in the Republic?

4. Why did conflicts with American Indians increase during Lamar's administration?

Section 4 (pp. 271–273)

5. What policy changes did Sam Houston make during his second administration?

6. What was the Regulator-Moderator War, and how did Sam Houston end it?

You Be the Historian ★TEKS

Reviewing Themes

1. **Citizenship** Choose one of the early candidates for president of the Republic and explain why you would vote for that person.

2. **Economics** Analyze the impact of the U.S. economy and the Panic of 1837 on the Republic's economy.

3. **Government** How did Houston and Lamar shape the history of the Republic of Texas?

TAKS Practice: Thinking Critically ★TEKS

1. **Analyzing Information** Identify the major issues the Republic of Texas faced.

2. **Comparing and Contrasting** Compare and contrast the presidencies of Sam Houston and Mirabeau B. Lamar.

3. **Summarizing** Describe the defining characteristics of the Republic of Texas years.

Interpreting Political Cartoons (TEKS)

Study the political cartoon below. Then use the information in the cartoon to answer the questions.

1. Which statement best describes what is occurring in this political cartoon created after the Battle of San Jacinto?

   a. General Santa Anna and General Cos are surrendering to Sam Houston.
   b. Houston is ordering the execution of Santa Anna.
   c. Houston is surrendering to Santa Anna.
   d. Houston and Santa Anna are meeting to sign a treaty.

2. What is Santa Anna doing that helps you answer question 1?

Analyzing Primary Sources (TEKS)

Read the following quote from a letter that Sam Houston wrote to a council of Texas Indians. Then answer the questions.

"My brothers: The path between us . . . has become white . . . the sun gives light to our footsteps. . . . I send councillors with my talk. . . . Hear it, and remember . . . I have never opened my lips to tell [an American Indian] a lie. . . . Let the war-whoop be no more heard in our prairie—let songs of joy be heard upon our hills. In our valleys let there be laughter and in our wigwams let the voices of our women and children be heard . . . and when our warriors meet together, let them [have] peace and be happy."

3. What does President Houston hope to achieve by writing the letter?

   a. He would like to have all American Indians removed from Texas.
   b. He is explaining that the Texas government cannot afford to fight Indians.
   c. He would like to achieve peace with American Indians.
   d. He would like to convince Texas Indians that they do not have a right to their lands.

4. What does President Houston's letter reveal about his attitude toward American Indians in Texas?

Alternative Assessment

Linking to Community (TEKS)

Research events that happened in your area during the period of the Republic of Texas. Then create an illustrated time line showing some of these events, the dates, and the order in which they occurred. You might look for the development of new towns, elections of local officials, the start of new businesses or schools, raids or battles, or other events. Find at least one event to contribute to the class time line.

BUILDING YOUR Portfolio

internet connect

Internet Activity: go.hrw.com
KEYWORD: ST3 TX12 (TEKS)

Access the Internet through the HRW Go site to locate primary and secondary sources on the Council House Fight and the Battle of Plum Creek. Write a summary of one of the sources you find. Note any bias in the sources and how the bias influenced its conclusions. Make sure you use standard grammar, spelling, sentence structure, and punctuation in your summary.

Life in the Republic
(1836–1845)

Théodore Gentilz portrayed many aspects of Tejano life in works like this one, entitled Cart Returning from Town.

Horse racing was a popular activity for many Texans.

Courtesy of The Witte Museum, San Antonio, Texas

TEXAS

1838 Velasco citizens hold a horse race on the coast near the town.

1839 Repeated attacks and discrimination force more than 100 Tejano families to flee Nacogdoches.

1840 The first college chartered by the Republic, Rutersville College, is founded.

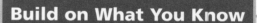

1836	**1837**	**1838**	**1839**	**1840**

U.S. and WORLD

1837 John Deere manufactures the steel plow.

1839 Tennessee produces some 45 million bushels of corn.

1840 The World's Anti-Slavery Convention is held in London.

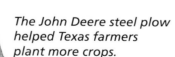

The John Deere steel plow helped Texas farmers plant more crops.

Build on What You Know

After the revolution, Texans faced new challenges. The Republic's land policy drew new immigrants from the United States and Europe to Texas, adding to the diversity of the young nation. Soon, Texans were building new towns, churches, and schools.

Steamboats like the Yellow Stone *helped immigrants move into Texas.*

Prince Carl of Solms-Braunfels helped bring immigrants to Texas before returning to Germany.

1841 William Kennedy publishes *Texas: The Rise, Progress, and Prospects of the Republic of Texas.*

1842 Snider de Pellegrini, director of a French colonization company, brings 14 settlers to Texas.

1844 Prince Carl of Solms-Braunfels comes to Texas followed by a group of German immigrants.

1845 At least 30,000 enslaved African Americans live in Texas.

1841   1842   1843   1844   1845

1843 Railroad lines from Paris to Rouen and Paris to Orléans are opened.

1845 A severe famine in Ireland begins, eventually killing hundreds of thousands of people.

Early railroads in France offered an efficient means of transportation.

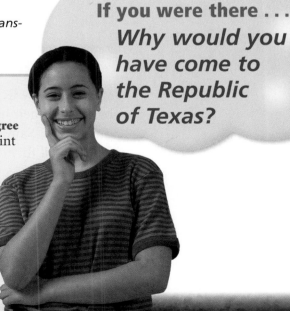

If you were there . . .
Why would you have come to the Republic of Texas?

You Be the Historian

Themes Journal

What's Your Opinion? Do you **agree** or **disagree** with the following statements? Support your point of view in your journal.

● **Citizenship** Citizens can change laws by creating petitions and exercising free speech.

● **Culture** Newcomers from different lands can both maintain their culture and adapt to a new culture.

● **Economics** Many immigrants move to find new economic opportunities.

1

The Texans

Read to Discover

1. What was life like in the Republic, and how did the government attract new settlers?
2. How did the Ashworth Act affect free African Americans?
3. How did the status of Tejanos change after the Texas Revolution?

Identify

- **Greenbury Logan**
- **Ashworth Act**
- **Juan Seguín**
- **José Antonio Navarro**

Why It Matters Today

Texans petitioned the Republic's government to change laws. Use **CNNfyi.com** or other **current events** sources to learn how Americans influence the government today. Record your findings in your journal.

The Story Continues

One hot summer day in Austin, seven-year-old W. C. Walsh and a group of boys disobeyed their mothers. Instead of playing in the backyard, they sneaked off to Shoal Creek to swim. The children were having a wonderful time when they heard someone cry out. Scared, they raced home. Walsh's mother scolded him for leaving the yard. Austin during the 1830s was no place for a child to be running around without supervision.

Fancy toys were rare in the Republic.

★ The Texas Population

Life in the new Republic presented many challenges. Many Texans had abandoned their homes during the Runaway Scrape. After the Battle of San Jacinto, Sam Houston made a call for Texans to return to their homes. "Tell them to come on, and let the people plant corn." Families returned home to find much of their property destroyed. Entire towns, including Harrisburg, Refugio, and San Felipe, had been burned or destroyed. Stephen F. Austin's home was among those burned. Texans had to rebuild their communities. To help them, the Constitution of 1836 granted land to many of the people who had lived in Texas before the revolution. In 1836 the population of Texas was approximately 52,700, including some 22,700 American Indians, African Americans, and Tejanos.

Hoping to encourage immigration, the Republic of Texas soon extended land grants to more individuals. The government also set up a land grant policy modeled after the *empresario* system. Agents received land grants in return for bringing immigrants and establishing settlements in the Republic. The government's land policy sparked an increase in immigration to Texas, and the population began to grow by leaps and bounds. From 1836 to 1847, the population of Texas increased by nearly 100,000.

⭐ **Reading Check** **Finding the Main Idea** What happened to the Republic's population, and why?

⭐ Immigration from the United States

By far the largest group of new immigrants to the Republic were from the United States. They came in search of land and economic opportunities, particularly after the economic depression caused by the Panic of 1837. Although they came from almost every state, most settlers were from the Mississippi Valley area south of the Ohio River. After arriving in Texas, many U.S. settlers began searching for land on which to farm or ranch. One Texan described the new settlers to a New Orleans newspaper. "All are land-hunting, seeking sugar, cotton and stock farm lands, but are as much at a loss in their selection as children in a toy shop." Many of the immigrants from the states of the Lower South settled in East Texas and along the Texas coast between Matagorda and Louisiana. People from the Upper South settled farther inland in East Texas and along the Red River in the northeast corner of the Republic.

Interpreting the Visual Record

Immigration to Texas. Many U.S. immigrants traveled to Texas in wagons like the ones shown below. **What transportation problems did people traveling in Texas face?** ⭐TEKS

The Granger Collection, New York

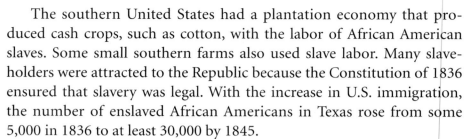

Greenbury Logan
(1799–date unknown)

Greenbury Logan was born into slavery in Kentucky in 1799 but was later freed. In 1831 he settled in one of Stephen F. Austin's colonies. He was wounded while fighting in the Texas Revolution. In 1837 Logan sent a petition to Congress, asking to remain in Texas. Some of the most respected men in the Republic signed his petition. **How does Logan's story demonstrate the challenges free African Americans faced in the Republic?** ⭐TEKS

Many African Americans in Texas worked on plantations and farms, planting and harvesting cotton and other crops.

The Granger Collection, New York

The southern United States had a plantation economy that produced cash crops, such as cotton, with the labor of African American slaves. Some small southern farms also used slave labor. Many slaveholders were attracted to the Republic because the Constitution of 1836 ensured that slavery was legal. With the increase in U.S. immigration, the number of enslaved African Americans in Texas rose from some 5,000 in 1836 to at least 30,000 by 1845.

Life for slaves was hard. Many worked long hours in cotton fields or did other farm chores. While most enslaved African Americans worked on small farms and plantations, a number lived in Texas towns. These slaves often worked as personal servants or day laborers. Slaveholders had broad control over the lives of slaves, who had no legal right to private property, to marriage, or to have a family. Almost every slave lived under threat of physical punishment.

⭐ **Reading Check** **Summarizing** Why did many immigrants from the U.S. South come to Texas, and where did they settle?

⭐ African Americans and the Ashworth Act

Life for free African Americans in Texas changed dramatically after Texas gained its independence. The Constitution of 1836 required free African Americans to get permission from the Texas Congress to continue living in Texas. In February 1840 Congress passed a new law that outlawed the immigration of free African Americans to Texas. The law stated that those already in the Republic would have to leave within two years or be sold into slavery. The law outraged many Texans who drew up petitions demanding that exceptions be made for their friends and neighbors. The petitions were often for veterans of the Texas Revolution like James Richardson and **Greenbury Logan**. Logan had fought in the battles at Concepción and San Antonio.

In November 1840, three petitions were presented to the Texas Congress on behalf of the Ashworth family. In response, Congress passed the **Ashworth Act**, which allowed the Ashworths and all free African Americans who were in Texas at the time of the Texas Declaration of Independence to stay. During his second term as president, Sam Houston extended the 1840 deadline that required some African Americans to leave Texas. Over the next several years, however, Texas passed new laws that strictly controlled the lives of free African Americans. Those who broke the laws faced whipping, branding, and other harsh punishments. By 1850 fewer than 400 free African Americans were reportedly living in Texas.

⭐ **Reading Check** **Drawing Inferences and Conclusions** Why do you think petitions were made for free African Americans who were veterans of the Texas Revolution?

★ Tejanos in the Republic

The Republic was also home to several thousand Tejanos. Some settled in large towns like San Antonio, where they lived in Tejano neighborhoods. Many Tejanos also lived in the Rio Grande valley, an area claimed by both the Republic of Texas and Mexico. Most Tejanos were laborers who owned no land and worked for hire. Of the Tejanos who owned ranches and farms, most worked small plots of land with only their families' help.

Tejanos often faced hostility, particularly from new U.S. immigrants. These settlers thought of Mexico as an enemy, and they often associated Tejanos with the Mexican government. Even Tejanos who had fought in the Texas Revolution faced discrimination. Tejanos often had their land and livestock stolen. In 1839, repeated attacks forced more than 100 Tejano families in Nacogdoches to leave their homes. Some Tejanos were forced to temporarily flee Texas. **Juan Seguín**, mayor of San Antonio from 1840 to 1842, witnessed several conflicts between Tejanos and U.S. settlers. "At every hour of the day and night, my countrymen ran to me for protection against the assaults . . . of these adventurers [new settlers]."

Despite these problems, many Tejanos remained in Texas. **José Antonio Navarro**, a signer of the Texas Declaration of Independence, served in the Republic's Congress. Tejanos maintained their culture, practiced their Catholic faith, ate traditional Mexican foods, and celebrated Mexican holidays. To these traditions they added some traditions of the other cultural groups, helping to create a unique Texas-Mexican cultural tradition.

Daughters of the Republic of Texas Library

José Antonio Navarro was an important figure in the Republic. He pushed for the protection of Tejano rights while serving in the Texas Congress.

★ **Reading Check** **Analyzing Information** Why might Tejanos have been disappointed by life in the Republic?

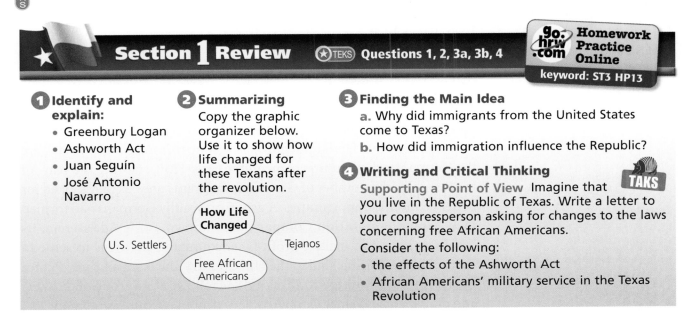

Section 1 Review ★ TEKS Questions 1, 2, 3a, 3b, 4

go.hrw.com **Homework Practice Online**
keyword: ST3 HP13

1 Identify and explain:
- Greenbury Logan
- Ashworth Act
- Juan Seguín
- José Antonio Navarro

2 Summarizing
Copy the graphic organizer below. Use it to show how life changed for these Texans after the revolution.

How Life Changed
- U.S. Settlers
- Free African Americans
- Tejanos

3 Finding the Main Idea
a. Why did immigrants from the United States come to Texas?
b. How did immigration influence the Republic?

4 Writing and Critical Thinking
Supporting a Point of View Imagine that you live in the Republic of Texas. Write a letter to your congressperson asking for changes to the laws concerning free African Americans.
Consider the following:
- the effects of the Ashworth Act
- African Americans' military service in the Texas Revolution

European Immigration to Texas

Read to Discover

1. Why did European immigrants come to Texas, and where did they settle?
2. How did these immigrants maintain their culture in Texas?

Why It Matters Today

Thousands of immigrants came to the Republic of Texas. Use CNNfyi.com or other **current events** sources to learn about immigration trends today. Record your findings in your journal.

Identify

- **German Emigration Company**
- **Prince Carl of Solms-Braunfels**
- **John O. Meusebach**
- **Henri Castro**

Daughters of the Republic of Texas Museum, Austin, Texas

Music and dances were sources of entertainment for Texas settlers.

The Story Continues

At about 10 P.M. in San Antonio, Théodore Gentilz and Auguste Frétellière set out with anticipation. They were going to a fandango—a dance being held by the local residents. As they neared Military Plaza, they heard the sounds of a violin. They followed the music to an adobe house. There they entered a candlelit room filled with people dancing and food. Newly arrived from France, Gentilz and Frétellière had never seen such a dance.

★ Germans Settle in Central Texas

Gentilz and Frétellière were just two of the many immigrants who soon called Texas home. The largest European group to immigrate to Texas were the Germans, who had first come in the early 1830s. During the years of the Republic, the number of German immigrants grew as they looked for better economic opportunities. A group of wealthy Germans had formed the **German Emigration Company**, also known as the Adelsverein. Its members hoped to make a profit by encouraging Germans to settle in Texas. After acquiring land in the Hill Country, the company sent **Prince Carl of Solms-Braunfels** to Texas in 1844 followed by a group of peasants and craftspeople. Prince Carl wrote letters home about his mission.

"The eyes of all Germany, no, the eyes of all Europe are fixed on us and our undertaking [task]: German princes, counts, and noblemen . . . are bringing new crowns to old glory while at the same time insuring [guaranteeing] immeasurable riches for their children and grandchildren."

—Prince Carl of Solms-Braunfels, quoted in
The Handbook of Texas

Once in Texas, Prince Carl established a port for the incoming settlers. The port, which was called Karlshafen by the Germans, was later renamed Indianola. In March 1845 the prince and a group of settlers established New Braunfels along the Guadalupe and Comal Rivers. When he returned home two months later, Baron Otfried Hans Freiherr von Meusebach replaced him. In Texas, the baron changed his name to **John O. Meusebach**. As Meusebach continued the work begun by Prince Carl, New Braunfels grew and prospered. By 1847 the German Emigration Company had sent more than 7,000 immigrants to Texas. Some stayed in established towns such as Houston and San Antonio, while other groups moved into the Hill Country. There they formed new settlements, including Fredericksburg, Boerne, and Comfort. These and other settlements extended the western frontier of Texas.

Before they left, Prince Carl instructed new immigrants headed to Texas to "stay together and remain faithful to German culture and habits." One German settler wrote to his relatives back home asking them to bring reminders of German culture. "Be sure to bring all the sheet music that you can collect. . . . And do not fail to bring the complete works of Goethe [a German poet]." Today many Texas Hill Country towns strongly reflect German traditions in their architecture, churches, food, and language.

Reading Check Analyzing Information Where did German immigrants settle, and how did they maintain their culture?

Analyzing Primary Sources
Identifying Points of View Why does Prince Carl think his task of bringing immigrants to the Republic is so important?

That's Interesting!

Cow Horns

To protect themselves from danger, German farmers on the Texas frontier would blow a horn made from cow horns. The sound would warn other settlers of approaching danger.

Interpreting the Visual Record

Religion. German immigrants brought many of their cultural traditions to Texas. These German immigrants in the Texas Hill Country are headed to church. *What does this picture suggest about the importance of church to these settlers?*

The Witte Museum, San Antonio, Texas

Little Alsace in Texas

The architecture of Castroville was distinctly European. Buildings had steep thatched roofs. The roads were often narrow lanes. The European-style construction has led Castroville to be called the Little Alsace of Texas. Many of these unique buildings can still be seen today. **What impact did the immigrants in Castroville have on that region of Texas?**

★ Other European Immigrants

In 1840 Texas and France signed a treaty that encouraged French immigration. **Henri Castro** brought one of the first groups of permanent French settlers to Texas. Many of them were from the province of Alsace, a mostly German-speaking area in France. Castro founded the Texas town of Castroville in 1844 near the Medina River. Many French immigrants became farmers and ranchers. By 1846 Castro had helped settle more than 2,000 colonists along the river. The cultural traditions of these French immigrants can still be found in the architecture, churches, and customs of Castroville and nearby towns such as D'Hanis, Quihi, and Vandenburg.

Irish settlers had been coming to Texas long before it was a republic. During the 1820s several Irishmen had received *empresario* contracts. One Irish *empresario*, James Hewetson, had accompanied Stephen F. Austin on his first trip to Texas in 1821. Many Irish immigrants fought with other Texas troops at the Alamo, Goliad, and San Jacinto. Irish settlers continued to come to Texas after the revolution, seeking economic opportunity. Irish-born William Kennedy encouraged this immigration in his 1841 book, *Texas: The Rise, Progress, and Prospects of the Republic of Texas.* By 1850 there were more than 1,400 Irish settlers throughout Texas.

Some Polish and Czech immigrants had also made their way to Texas, settling in South and Central Texas. During the revolution, Polish immigrants had fought at Goliad and San Jacinto. Polish and Czech immigration later increased as economic and political conditions pushed many from their homelands. Later immigrants from eastern Europe came to find good farmland.

Reading Check Summarizing Why did many Europeans come to the Republic?

★ Section 2 Review   ⊛TEKS Questions 1, 2, 3a, 3b, 4

go.hrw.com **Homework Practice Online** keyword: ST3 HP13

1 Identify and explain:
- German Emigration Company
- Prince Carl of Solms-Braunfels
- John O. Meusebach
- Henri Castro

2 Analyzing Information
Copy the table below. Use it to explain why immigrant groups came to the Republic and where they settled.

Immigrants	Why They Came	Where They Settled
German		
French		
Irish		
Polish		
Czech		

3 Finding the Main Idea
a. In what ways did new immigrants maintain their culture?
b. How did new immigrants from Europe influence life in the Republic?

4 Writing and Critical Thinking TAKS
Identifying Cause and Effect Explain how the settlement patterns of European immigrants affected the Republic.
Consider the following:
- locations of European settlements
- how this led to the development of the western frontier

Connecting To

Geography

Immigration to Texas

While most immigrants to Texas came from the United States, many others came from Europe. Many Europeans faced poverty and high taxes. Many found it difficult to own land and to make a comfortable living. Europeans came to Texas seeking better economic opportunities. Once in Texas, European immigrants formed their own communities, often located in frontier regions such as the Hill Country.

Geography **Skills**

Interpreting Thematic Maps

1. Based on this map, how would most European immigrants come to Texas? ⭐TEKS

2. How did the areas settled by people from the Upper South differ from those settled by people from the Lower South? ⭐TEKS

3. In what countries of Europe did most European immigrants originally live? ⭐TEKS

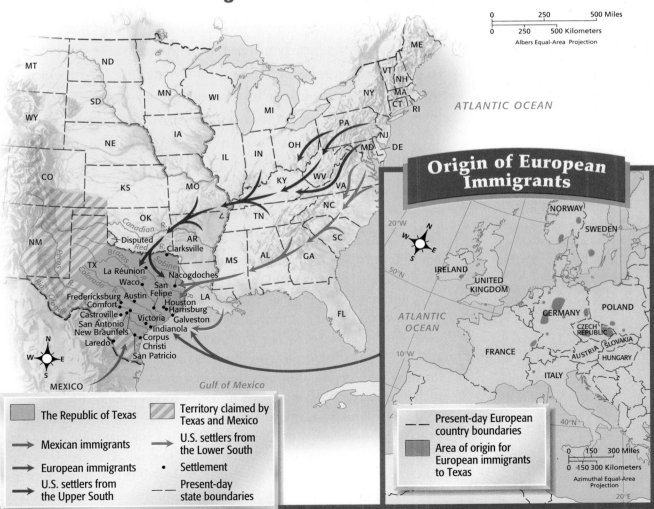

Immigration to Texas, 1836–1850

Origin of European Immigrants

Read to Discover

1. What was life like on farms and ranches and in towns in the Republic?
2. What roles did schools, churches, and leisure activities play in Texas?

Define
- denominations
- circuit riders
- academies

Identify
- Henry Austin

Why It Matters Today

Education was a major concern for people in the Republic. Use CNN.fyi.com or other current events sources to learn about education in other countries today. Record your findings in your journal.

The Story Continues

Before making their journey to Texas, many immigrants read a book by David Woodman Jr. called *Guide to Texas Emigrants*. This handy guide had many tips. He advised settlers to bring a reliable rifle and a strong dog. Woodman offered one other important recommendation. "It would be best to carry tents . . . for covering, until the house is built." Woodman also said it was important to bring farming tools, a wagon, and comfortable clothing.

Tools such as this mallet were important to early immigrants who needed them to build homes and farms.

★ Farming, Towns, and Transportation

Many Texans, whether old settlers or new immigrants, were farmers and ranchers. Their farms varied widely in size. Although some farms were large plantations, most were small family farms. Small-scale farmers generally had few or no slaves; instead, they did most farm tasks on their own. Farmers cleared acres of land to build homesteads, plant crops, and create pastures for grazing animals. Texas farmers mostly grew food for their own needs, although they often produced a small cash crop—such as corn, cotton, wheat, rye, or oats—to sell for a profit.

In the Republic, most cattle ranchers raised animals for their own use or to sell to other Texans. Ranchers supplied townspeople and farmers with food, hides, and other materials. A few ranchers, such as Taylor White, drove their cattle to New Orleans to sell them in markets there. Tejanos owned many ranches in the Rio Grande valley. Macedonio Vela,

Hipolito García, and Dionisio Guerra all owned large successful ranches. Some free African Americans such as Robert Thompson of Montgomery County also owned ranches. Ranchers worked hard to care for their livestock.

Texans also struggled to clear land and to build homes and businesses in the Republic's new settlements. Most of the jobs in the Republic's towns were related to agriculture. Doctors, shopkeepers, blacksmiths, silversmiths, tailors, cabinetmakers, and bankers operated in the largest towns. Towns like Houston and Galveston grew quickly as immigrants moved to them. Their founders had chosen locations that were beneficial for trade. New towns farther inland such as Dallas also began to grow.

Other new towns, such as Carolina, Geneva, Pompei, and Rome, were less fortunate. Many were founded by land speculators who gave away lots—small pieces of land—to persuade people to move there. These attempts often failed when they did not attract enough settlers. In some cases people were unable to pay for land they had agreed to buy. Cash was so rare in Texas that "not a man of them can pay me a dollar," one speculator wrote.

Travel between towns was difficult. The government tried to build new roads but had limited success. Texas roads remained poor, particularly in bad weather. Travel by horseback or stagecoach was often uncomfortable and dangerous. One traveler described the road conditions. "I was obliged [forced] in the worst places to relieve the mule by getting off and leading for a mile at a time, with water to my knees and sometimes to my britches pockets."

Some rivers were used for transporting goods and people. The first steamboat to enter a Texas river was the *Ariel*. **Henry Austin**, who was Stephen F. Austin's cousin, had begun operating this boat on the lower Rio Grande in 1829. He traded with Mexican merchants and later took the *Ariel* up the Brazos River. By the 1840s several steamboats traveled the Brazos, Colorado, and Trinity Rivers. These boats shipped cotton and other farm products from Texas farms and brought in needed goods to Texas settlers. Few Texas rivers were suited for steamboats, however. Floods, low water, and sandbars often prevented travel. The lack of a good transportation system slowed the growth of businesses and towns in the Republic.

⭐ **Reading Check** **Finding the Main Idea** How did geographic factors affect the economic development of Texas?

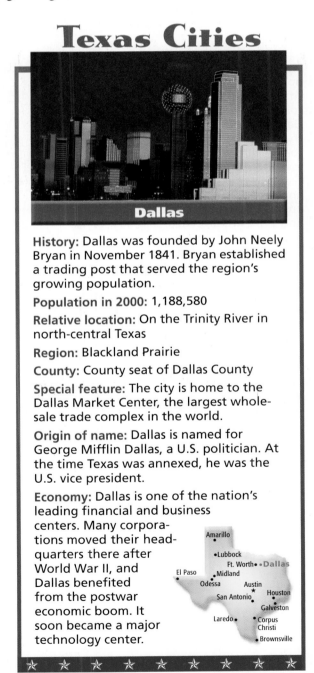

Texas Cities

Dallas

History: Dallas was founded by John Neely Bryan in November 1841. Bryan established a trading post that served the region's growing population.

Population in 2000: 1,188,580

Relative location: On the Trinity River in north-central Texas

Region: Blackland Prairie

County: County seat of Dallas County

Special feature: The city is home to the Dallas Market Center, the largest wholesale trade complex in the world.

Origin of name: Dallas is named for George Mifflin Dallas, a U.S. politician. At the time Texas was annexed, he was the U.S. vice president.

Economy: Dallas is one of the nation's leading financial and business centers. Many corporations moved their headquarters there after World War II, and Dallas benefited from the postwar economic boom. It soon became a major technology center.

Alamo Collection, Daughters of the Republic of Texas Library

⭐ Leisure, Literature, and Art

Texans enjoyed a number of leisure activities. Some were part fun and part work, such as building houses for newcomers, participating in log-splitting contests, and hunting and fishing. Other activities were all fun, such as songfests featuring popular tunes of the day, including "Yankee Doodle." Dances were one of the most popular pastimes, from the small rural affair to the large plantation ball. Many Texans also enjoyed concerts, horse races, and the theater.

Some citizens enjoyed literature and art, although both were scarce in frontier Texas. Most books published in the Republic dealt with its history or travel in Texas. Authors on these subjects included Mary Austin Holley and William Kennedy. Some Texans also wrote poetry. Two early Texas poets in the Republic were Mirabeau B. Lamar and Reuben M. Potter. The most common publications in the Republic were newspapers. In 1836 Texas had only one weekly newspaper, but by 1840 more than a dozen newspapers were being published in the Republic.

Artists, including portrait painters Charles Kneass and Jefferson Wright, practiced in Texas. Many of the Republic's artists were new immigrants. For example, French painter and surveyor Théodore Gentilz came to Texas with Henri Castro. Gentilz is known for his scenes of Texas life. Some sculptors also worked in the Republic.

⭐ **Reading Check** **Analyzing Information** How did Texans spend their leisure time?

★ Churches and Schools

In the towns and countryside, Texans established many churches. After Texas independence, Roman Catholicism was no longer the official state religion. Many Protestant **denominations**—organized religious groups with similar beliefs—soon built churches. The Methodist Church was the largest denomination in the Republic, followed by the Baptist Church. Presbyterians and Episcopalians were also active in Texas. Catholicism was the dominant religion in Galveston, San Antonio, and Tejano communities along the Rio Grande. Most Czech and Polish immigrants also belonged to the Catholic Church. Jews from central and eastern Europe lived in communities across Texas. Jewish immigrants established synagogues, or Jewish temples, in Galveston, Houston, and San Antonio.

Churches and temples served as the religious and social centers of most Texas communities. In addition to sermons and Sunday school, many churches sponsored revival meetings, picnics, and bazaars. **Circuit riders**, or traveling preachers, typically served a region on the frontier. They traveled to their areas on a regular basis to preach and to provide religious support to the settlers.

Churches also ran most schools. Rutersville College was founded by the Methodist Church in 1840. Later colleges included Galveston University and the University of San Augustine. Although President Mirabeau B. Lamar wanted Texas to establish a system of public education, funds for such an effort were scarce. Houston was the only town in the Republic to establish a public school. The school operated off and on throughout the 1840s. Several towns, however, established private **academies**—schools that offered classes at the high school level.

★ Reading Check Summarizing How did churches contribute to Texas communities during the years of the Republic?

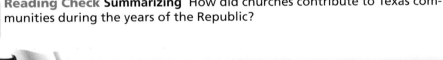

Section 3 Review ★TEKS Questions 2, 3, 4a, 4b, 5

1 Define and explain:
- denominations
- circuit riders
- academies

2 Identify and explain:
- Henry Austin

3 Summarizing
Copy the graphic organizer below. Use it to show how people made a living in Texas.

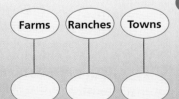

4 Finding the Main Idea
a. How did churches and schools contribute to life in the Republic?
b. What type of leisure activities and arts did Texans enjoy during the years of the Republic?

5 Writing and Critical Thinking

TAKS

Summarizing Write a summary explaining how geographic factors affected the economic development of Texas.

Consider the following:
- the state of the roads and rivers
- the importance of transportation

CHAPTER 13 REVIEW

The Chapter at a Glance

Examine the following visual summary of the chapter. Then use the visual to create a map that you can use to describe changes in life in the Republic. TEKS

---1840---

Texas Daily Life

September 9, 1840

New Immigrants Come to Texas

Immigrants came to the Republic from the United States and Europe, seeking cheap land and new opportunities.

The Farm Report

Many Texans worked on small farms and ranches. Even Texans living in towns worked in businesses that were related to agriculture.

STEAMBOAT ARRIVES

Traveling over Texas roads was often difficult. With new types of transportation, travel improved a little.

Big Dance

Texans worked hard to build homes, churches, and schools, but they still found time for entertainment.

Identifying People and Ideas TEKS

Use the following terms or people in historically significant sentences.

1. Ashworth Act
2. Juan Seguín
3. José Antonio Navarro
4. German Emigration Company
5. Prince Carl of Solms-Braunfels
6. John O. Meusebach
7. Henri Castro
8. denominations
9. circuit riders
10. Henry Austin

Understanding Main Ideas TEKS

Section 1 (pp. 278–281)

1. How did U.S. immigration change life in the Republic?
2. Did life in Texas become more diverse during the years of the Republic? Explain your answer.

Section 2 (pp. 282–284)

3. How did new immigrants from Europe influence Texas?
4. Where did European immigrants settle in the Republic?

Section 3 (pp. 286–289)

5. What was life like for the people who settled in the Republic?
6. How did churches serve the community in the Republic?

You Be the Historian TEKS

Reviewing Themes

1. **Citizenship** How do you think the actions of Texans filing petitions on behalf of the Ashworths reflected civic responsibility?
2. **Culture** How did immigrants to the Republic of Texas maintain their traditional cultures in their new home?
3. **Economics** Why did immigrants move to Texas?

TAKS   Practice: Thinking Critically   TEKS

1. **Drawing Inferences and Conclusions** How did the end of the Texas Revolution, the Republic's land grants, and immigration affect the population distribution in Texas?
2. **Supporting a Point of View** Do you think the Republic of Texas was a land of opportunity? Explain why or why not.
3. **Analyzing Information** Describe the defining characteristics of the Republic era.

Social Studies Skills Workshop

Interpreting Maps ⭐TEKS

Study the map below. Then use the information on the map to help you answer the questions that follow.

German Settlements in Texas, 1831–1860

1. In what region of Texas did German immigrants settle?
   a. Hill Country and Central Texas
   b. northeastern Texas
   c. West Texas
   d. Panhandle

2. What geographic factors influenced the German settlement patterns?

Analyzing Primary Sources ⭐TEKS

Read the following quote by Mary Austin Holley about the land owned by her brother Henry Austin. Henry Austin never earned the profit he and his sister had expected. Then answer the questions.

"**I am growing rich in Town Lots—all the town-makers, and they are not few, are ambitious to have me in their town & present me with a lot. . . . Brother [Henry Austin] will have a sale of town lots in Bolivar [on] 14 April . . . which can not fail to bring money. He expects at least $100,000. . . . He has a ware house already built, and contemplates a rail road towards Houston. . . . They say I should not know Houston it has grown so much since I was there.**"

3. Which of the following statements best describes the author's point of view?
   a. My brother's expectations for the growth of the town are too high.
   b. The sale of town lots will not bring in much money.
   c. I have already made a lot of money selling lots to new town residents.
   d. Texas towns are growing, and my brother and I will soon earn money selling lots in Bolivar.

4. Based on your knowledge of the chapter, why did Holley think the land in Bolivar would be profitable?

Alternative Assessment

Interdisciplinary Connection to Geography ⭐TEKS

BUILDING YOUR Portfolio

Work with a group of four or more classmates to complete the following activity. Create a map that shows the changes in geographic distributions of people during the years of the Republic of Texas. Write a caption that describes any geographic patterns in the population distribution. Use information from the chapter text and maps to complete the project. Based on the map, create questions for a quiz and provide an answer key.

🎵 **internet** connect

Internet Activity: go.hrw.com
KEYWORD: ST3 TX13 ⭐TEKS
Access the Internet through the HRW Go site to research why immigrant groups came to Texas and how their migration influenced Texas. Then write a newspaper article that explores how these groups maintained their cultural heritage while adapting to the larger Texas culture. Your article should accurately reflect life in the Republic and should include information from your research.

CHAPTER 14

Texas Faces Foreign Challenges
(1836–1845)

Before becoming a senator in 1838, William H. Wharton served as a diplomat for Texas in Washington.

Texas sought recognition from Great Britain, France, Belgium, and the Netherlands.

TEXAS

1837 The U.S. Congress authorizes a diplomat to go to Texas.

1838 William H. Wharton is elected to the Texas Senate.

1839 France becomes the first European nation to recognize Texas as an independent country.

1840 Galveston University opens its doors to five students.

1836	1837	1838	1839	1840

U.S. and WORLD

1837 Samuel Morse files for a patent for a telegraph.

1839 The Liberty Party, the first anti-slavery party in the United States, holds a national convention in New York.

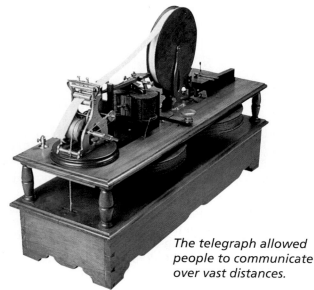

The telegraph allowed people to communicate over vast distances.

Build on What You Know

The Texas population increased dramatically after the revolution, as land policies and other factors encouraged immigration. The Republic soon sought recognition from other nations. Tensions with Mexico, however, led to several conflicts.

The Texas Navy had a number of large ships, including the schooner San Antonio.

Anson Jones served as the last president of the Republic of Texas.

1841 President Mirabeau B. Lamar orders the Texas Navy to the Yucatán coast.

1842 General Adrián Woll and about 1,400 Mexican soldiers capture San Antonio.

1844 Texans elect Anson Jones president of the Republic.

| 1841 | 1842 | 1843 | 1844 | 1845 |

1842 U.S. settlers from the Midwest flood the Oregon Trail on their way to Oregon Country.

Settlers traveling along the Oregon Trail packed many of their belongings in trunks.

1845 Florida becomes the 27th state to join the Union.

You Be the Historian

Themes Journal

What's Your Opinion? Do you **agree** or **disagree** with the following statements? Support your point of view in your journal.

● **Global Relations** Good relations with foreign nations can significantly benefit a country's economic and political affairs.

● **Government** The foreign policy of one administration has no effect on later presidencies.

● **Geography** The location of a nation affects its ability to remain independent.

If you were there . . .
Would you support efforts for foreign recognition?

Foreign Recognition of Texas

Read to Discover

1. Why was foreign recognition an important issue for Texas?
2. How successful was the Republic in gaining recognition from other nations?

Define
- foreign relations

Identify
- Alcée Louis La Branche
- James Pinckney Henderson

Why It Matters Today

The official recognition of Texas independence was important for a number of reasons, including improving the Republic's economy. Use CNNfyi.com or other **current events** sources to find information about ongoing diplomatic talks today. Record your findings in your journal.

The Story Continues

Sailors of the Texas Navy were proud. The navy's flagship, the *Independence,* had been repaired at great expense in New Orleans. The ship now sailed for home, carrying the Republic's representative to the United States, William H. Wharton. Then trouble struck. Off the Texas coast, the *Independence* encountered two Mexican warships. A fierce battle began. The *Independence* was soon captured, along with Wharton and all the Texas sailors. It seemed that no Texans would be safe until Mexico recognized the Republic.

Like the Independence, *this ship flew the Texas Navy flag.*

★ Establishing Diplomatic Ties

Relations with Mexico was one of the young Republic's greatest challenges in **foreign relations**—official dealings with other countries. Mexico did not accept Texas independence. Texas was therefore eager to have other nations recognize, or officially accept, its status as an independent nation. If other nations recognized the Republic's independence, Mexico too might change its position. This would lessen the possibility of a renewed war with Mexico. Any official recognition would demonstrate support for the Republic, which might encourage immigration to Texas. In addition to political motivations, officials of the Republic were driven by financial concerns. They hoped that recognition would lead to foreign trade and loans, both of which were desperately needed to improve the Republic's economy.

Recognition from the United States was particularly important. Some Texans hoped it might pave the way for the U.S. annexation of Texas. Many Texans, including Sam Houston, wanted Texas to be annexed as soon as possible. But U.S. officials were hesitant to recognize the Republic. Many Americans worried that recognition would anger Mexico, which still considered Texas part of its territory. In addition, the southern and northern states were at odds over the issue of slavery. Northerners who opposed slavery were against recognition because the Republic supported slavery and opposed any action to free slaves.

In 1836 U.S. president Andrew Jackson sent an agent—Henry Morfit—to find out if the struggling new nation could maintain its independence. Many Texas homes and farms had been abandoned or destroyed after the Runaway Scrape. Texas faced army unrest, debt, and the difficulties of establishing a new government. Because of these problems, Morfit submitted a negative report. He noted that the Republic's population was too small, that the young nation had too much debt, and that it had too powerful an enemy—Mexico. Jackson reported Morfit's findings to the U.S. Congress in December 1836. In Jackson's words, there was "an immense disparity [huge unevenness] of physical force on the side of Mexico." This would make it difficult for Texans to defend themselves if invaded. The decision to recognize Texas was left to the U.S. Congress.

Reading Check Finding the Main Idea Why was foreign recognition important to the Republic of Texas?

LINKING PAST to PRESENT

The French Legation

After France recognized the Republic, a luxurious home for French diplomat Alphonse Dubois de Saligny was built in Austin. De Saligny, however, sold the mansion before it was finished. Ownership of the house was passed down through a number of hands until it was finally purchased by the state in 1949. The Daughters of the Republic of Texas restored the mansion and now run it as a museum. Today the French Legation Museum is an Austin landmark. **Why do you think the French built this luxurious home?**

The Pig War

In 1841, pigs found a way into the French Legation, destroying papers and clothes belonging to Alphonse Dubois de Saligny. Even worse, they ate the corn set out for his prized horses. One of de Saligny's servants killed some of the pigs. The pigs' owner then attacked the servant. Word of the so-called Pig War spread quickly. Texas newspapers sided with the pigs, "Go it Texas! *Viva la pigs!*" Angry about the lack of response from Texas officials, de Saligny left Texas.

★ Foreign Recognition

William H. Wharton, who had been sent to Washington by President Houston, reported on the views of annexation in the United States.

Texas Voices "The recognition of our independence will certainly take place, but I have not . . . much hopes of our being annexed. . . . Already has the war [between slave and free states] violently commenced [begun] even on the prospect of our annexation."

—William H. Wharton, letter to Stephen F. Austin, December 11, 1836

While Wharton was in Washington, the U.S. representative to Mexico reported that the Mexican government was in chaos. The news convinced the U.S. government that it could recognize Texas without any serious threat from Mexico. In his last official act as president, Andrew Jackson appointed **Alcée Louis La Branche** as U.S. minister to Texas in 1837. The Republic sent Memucan Hunt as its first official representative to Washington. However, U.S. recognition did not lead to annexation. In October 1838, Texas leaders withdrew their request for annexation.

In 1837 Houston sent **James Pinckney Henderson** to Europe to try to gain recognition for Texas. Because of concerns about U.S. expansion, many European nations wanted Texas to stay independent. In September 1839 France recognized Texas, becoming the first European country to do so. France sent Alphonse Dubois de Saligny as its representative to the Republic. Recognition from Great Britain, Belgium, and the Netherlands followed. Texas leaders hoped that these nations would pressure Mexico to do the same. Mirabeau B. Lamar, the Republic's second elected president, used diplomacy and threats of attack to try to persuade Mexico to recognize Texas independence. But Mexico refused.

Reading Check Analyzing Information Why did the United States finally recognize Texas?

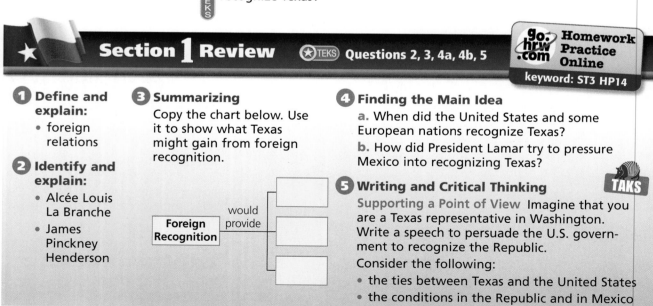

★ Section 1 Review ★TEKS Questions 2, 3, 4a, 4b, 5

go.hrw.com **Homework Practice Online**

keyword: ST3 HP14

1 Define and explain:
- foreign relations

2 Identify and explain:
- Alcée Louis La Branche
- James Pinckney Henderson

3 Summarizing
Copy the chart below. Use it to show what Texas might gain from foreign recognition.

Foreign Recognition — would provide → [ ] [ ] [ ]

4 Finding the Main Idea
a. When did the United States and some European nations recognize Texas?
b. How did President Lamar try to pressure Mexico into recognizing Texas?

5 Writing and Critical Thinking
Supporting a Point of View Imagine that you are a Texas representative in Washington. Write a speech to persuade the U.S. government to recognize the Republic.
Consider the following:
- the ties between Texas and the United States
- the conditions in the Republic and in Mexico

Conflict with Mexico

Read to Discover

1. What conflicts did the Republic have with Mexico?
2. What occurred during the Mier expedition?
3. How was peace with Mexico eventually achieved?

Why It Matters Today

Ongoing conflicts with Mexico made life in the Republic difficult. Use CNNfyi.com or other **current events** sources to find more information about international conflicts today. Record your findings in your journal.

Identify

- **Hugh McLeod**
- **Santa Fe expedition**
- **Ráfael Vásquez**
- **Angelina Eberly**
- **Archives War**
- **Adrián Woll**
- **Alexander Somervell**
- **William S. Fisher**
- **Mier expedition**

The Story Continues

It was early summer in 1841 as pioneers set out from Austin for Santa Fe. Their spirits were high, for they were on a mission. After a month, the travelers began to get discouraged. They still had not reached Santa Fe and were running out of food. Then their wagon got stuck at the Caprock. American Indian attacks claimed several lives. The rest of the pioneers had to eat stray dogs to survive.

President Lamar prepared this address to the citizens of Santa Fe.

★ The Santa Fe Expedition

In 1836 the Republic's Congress established the southern and western boundaries of Texas as the Rio Grande—from its mouth at the Gulf of Mexico to its source. This land included all of New Mexico east of the Rio Grande, which included Santa Fe. Mexican officials disputed such claims, as did most of the people living in New Mexico. Unlike President Houston, President Lamar attempted to enforce the Republic's claim. He wanted access to the valuable trade moving along the Santa Fe Trail and to expand the Republic's influence.

In June 1841 Lamar sent an expedition of about 320 people to Santa Fe to take control of the region. They took about $200,000 worth of trade goods. A number of well-known Texans, including José Antonio Navarro, accompanied the expedition. The expedition included five companies of soldiers under the leadership of **Hugh McLeod**. The **Santa Fe expedition** soon experienced great hardship. American

Interpreting the Visual Record

Santa Fe. Some Texans wanted to capture Santa Fe to gain control of valuable trade routes along the Santa Fe Trail. **What does this image suggest about life in Santa Fe at that time?**

GLOBAL CONNECTIONS

The Pastry War

The Mexican government experienced political difficulties after the Texas Revolution, including frequent leadership changes. It also experienced diplomatic troubles. In 1838 France declared war on Mexico after French citizens living in Mexico claimed that the Mexican government owed them money. One of them, a French pastry chef, said that Mexican army officers had damaged his restaurant. The conflict with France became known as the Pastry War. **What problems did Mexico face in the 1830s?**

⭐ TEKS

Indians attacked as the Texans passed through their lands. Food and water were in short supply as the expedition crossed the Texas plains. After the wagons got stuck near the Caprock and food supplies ran down, McLeod divided the soldiers. He sent one group to find Santa Fe, while he and another group stayed with the wagons.

When the exhausted Texans reached New Mexico, a Mexican force easily captured them in October 1841. McLeod's group later approached some towns in New Mexico, but they too were captured. The Mexicans marched the Texans about 1,200 miles to Mexico City and put them in prison. One of the prisoners described the hardships of the march. "We had not proceeded far when some of the guard . . . shot one of the men who was lame." The Texans were imprisoned until the following April. As the only Tejano captured, Navarro became a special target of Antonio López de Santa Anna's anger. He was sentenced to death and remained in prison even after the others had been released. Navarro eventually escaped and returned to Texas. Lamar's Santa Fe expedition was a failure. At least 60 Texans died, and the expedition cost a great sum of money.

⭐ **Reading Check Identifying Cause and Effect** What prompted Lamar to send the Santa Fe expedition, and why was it a failure?

⭐ The Texas Navy

In spite of the Santa Fe expedition's failure, President Lamar continued his campaign against the Mexican government. He placed Edwin W. Moore in command of the Texas Navy and in September 1841 sent it to the Yucatán coast. Rebels who were fighting the Mexican government agreed to pay $8,000 a month for the use of the navy. Lamar hoped this would pressure Mexican leaders to negotiate with Texas.

When Sam Houston began his second term as president in 1841, he ordered the navy to return home. Houston was determined to cut spending, and in 1843 he ordered that the navy ships be sold at auction in Galveston. Many people in Galveston opposed the sale and prevented bids from being submitted at the auction. The ships were not sold, but they were no longer in operation.

Reading Check **Analyzing Information** How did Lamar try to use the navy against Mexico?

★ The Archives War

Mexican leaders, upset by the actions of the Lamar administration, began launching raids into Texas. In the spring of 1842, a Mexican force under General **Ráfael Vásquez** entered Texas. Vásquez's 700 soldiers attacked San Antonio, Goliad, Refugio, and Victoria. However, Vásquez soon returned to Mexico.

Many Texans panicked when they heard that Mexican troops were invading. Fearing an attack on Austin, President Houston ordered that the government archives, or records, be withdrawn from the capital. Austin residents opposed this move, suspecting it meant the capital would be moved back to the city of Houston. Led by **Angelina Eberly**, they fired at officials who were loading documents onto wagons. This short conflict, called the **Archives War**, ended with the documents back in Austin.

Some Austinites saw the issue of where Texas archives would be located as important for the future of their town.

In September 1842 Mexico invaded Texas again. General **Adrián Woll** and 1,400 soldiers captured San Antonio. Texan Samuel Maverick described the morning invasion.

Texas Voices "We were aroused . . . by the firing of a . . . cannon . . . succeeded [followed] immediately by the . . . tramp of a body of men. A dense fog obscured [hid] them from actual observation until they had advanced into the public square . . . when the fog disappeared discovering [revealing] to us that we were surrounded on all sides by the bodies of regular [Mexican] troops."

—Samuel Maverick, quoted in *Memoirs of Mary A. Maverick*

Analyzing Primary Sources
Evaluating How did geographic factors such as weather affect events during Woll's invasion?

Hundreds of Texas militia and Texas Rangers made their way to San Antonio. They attacked Woll's force at Salado Creek, several miles from San Antonio. The Mexican troops retreated, taking captives with them.

Reading Check **Drawing Inferences and Conclusions** What did the Mexican raids on Texas demonstrate about the Republic's security?

Frederic Remington

Artist Frederic Remington painted many scenes of the American West. In this painting, he shows Texans captured during the Mier expedition picking beans to determine who would be executed. **How did Remington portray the drama of the event?** ⭐TEKS

★ The Mier Expedition

The Mexican attack on San Antonio angered Texans. "To arms! should be shouted throughout the Republic," one newspaper declared. Many people demanded war against Mexico. In November President Houston ordered General **Alexander Somervell** and some 750 soldiers to the Rio Grande. They were to recapture the prisoners taken by General Woll. When Somervell reached the Rio Grande, he realized that he did not have enough supplies or troops. He ordered his soldiers home, but about 300 of them disobeyed orders. They decided to invade Mexico. Under the command of Colonel **William S. Fisher**, the Texans headed toward the small Mexican town of Mier.

The Texans entered Mier on December 23 and demanded supplies, which the townspeople agreed to deliver the next day. When the supplies did not arrive, the Texans stormed the town. There, some 900 Mexican soldiers were waiting for them. After a daylong battle, about 100 Mexicans and 30 Texans were killed or wounded. Because they were running out of supplies, the Texans surrendered. The Mexican commander ignored an order to execute the prisoners.

The captured Texans began a long march toward Mexico City. Almost 200 of the prisoners escaped during the march south. Wandering in the mountains without food and water, most of them either died or were recaptured. Santa Anna, who once again ruled Mexico, ordered every 10th person to be shot. The 176 prisoners drew beans from a jar to see who would live and who would be executed. A prisoner described the scene. The beans were drawn from "a small earthen mug. The white ones signified *exemption* [no punishment], the black, *death*." The prisoners who drew the black beans were blindfolded and then shot. Of the remaining captives, 18 eventually managed to escape. At least 20 died in prison, and others were pardoned. In September 1844, Mexican officials released the last of the prisoners of the **Mier expedition**.

Through the efforts of Great Britain and France, peace was slowly restored between Texas and Mexico. Both European countries wanted the Republic to remain an independent nation to help slow the westward expansion of the United States, which they viewed as a rival. They put great diplomatic pressure on Mexico to recognize Texas. In the spring of 1845, a representative from Britain presented a document to the Mexican government. In it, the Texas government asked for peace and for Mexican recognition of Texas independence. In return, the Republic agreed not to be annexed by any nation.

However, the agreement was only to be a preliminary, or first, step toward a treaty. Annexation by the United States or continued independence would ultimately be decided by the people of Texas. Mexican leaders soon agreed to the terms of the proposal. Mexico wished to prevent U.S. annexation of Texas to block further U.S. expansion. Texas voters then had a choice. They could accept the Mexican offer, remain independent, and have a secure relationship with their southern neighbor. Or they could reject the agreement and try to join the United States.

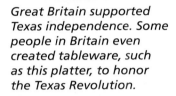

Great Britain supported Texas independence. Some people in Britain even created tableware, such as this platter, to honor the Texas Revolution.

⭐ **Reading Check** **Finding the Main Idea** Why was the Texas agreement not to be annexed by any nation critical to Mexico?

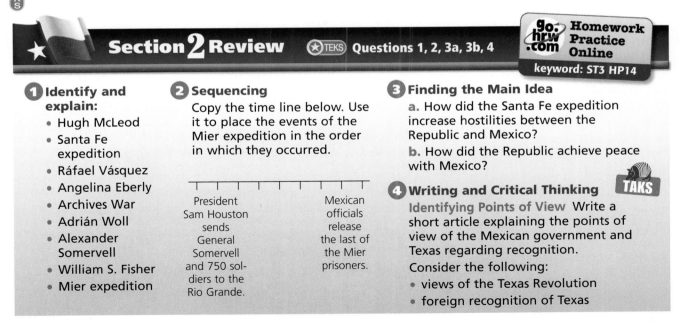

⭐ **Section 2 Review** ⭐TEKS Questions 1, 2, 3a, 3b, 4

go.hrw.com **Homework Practice Online**
keyword: ST3 HP14

1 Identify and explain:
- Hugh McLeod
- Santa Fe expedition
- Ráfael Vásquez
- Angelina Eberly
- Archives War
- Adrián Woll
- Alexander Somervell
- William S. Fisher
- Mier expedition

2 Sequencing
Copy the time line below. Use it to place the events of the Mier expedition in the order in which they occurred.

President Sam Houston sends General Somervell and 750 soldiers to the Rio Grande.

Mexican officials release the last of the Mier prisoners.

3 Finding the Main Idea
a. How did the Santa Fe expedition increase hostilities between the Republic and Mexico?
b. How did the Republic achieve peace with Mexico?

4 Writing and Critical Thinking TAKS
Identifying Points of View Write a short article explaining the points of view of the Mexican government and Texas regarding recognition.
Consider the following:
- views of the Texas Revolution
- foreign recognition of Texas

Texas Faces Foreign Challenges **301**

Geography

Conflicts with Mexico

Geography played a major role in the conflicts faced by the Republic. During the Santa Fe expedition, the Texans struggled across the rugged West Texas terrain. They had difficulty pulling their wagons up the 1,000-foot-high rise called the Caprock. During the Mier expedition, Texas soldiers traveled down the Rio Grande to Mier.

Conflicts of the Republic, 1837–1842

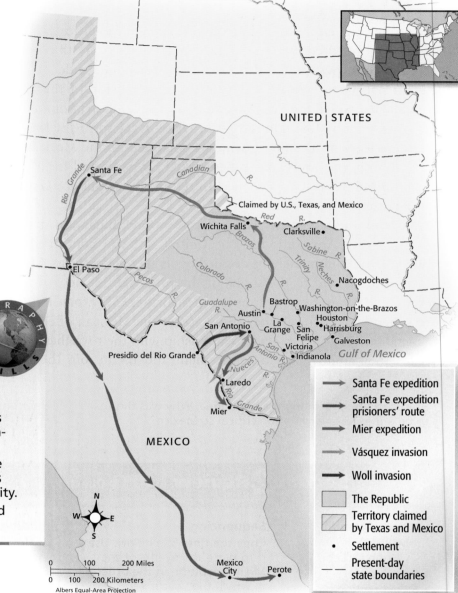

UNITED STATES

Claimed by U.S., Texas, and Mexico

Santa Fe
El Paso
Wichita Falls
Clarksville
Nacogdoches
Bastrop
Austin
Washington-on-the-Brazos
Houston
San Antonio
La Grange
San Felipe
Harrisburg
Galveston
Presidio del Rio Grande
Victoria
Indianola
Gulf of Mexico
Laredo
Mier
MEXICO
Mexico City
Perote

Rio Grande · Canadian · Red R. · Brazos · Sabine R. · Trinity · Neches R. · Pecos · Colorado R. · Guadalupe R. · San Antonio R. · Nueces R.

Legend
→ Santa Fe expedition
→ Santa Fe expedition prisoners' route
→ Mier expedition
→ Vásquez invasion
→ Woll invasion
▢ The Republic
▨ Territory claimed by Texas and Mexico
• Settlement
--- Present-day state boundaries

0   100   200 Miles
0   100   200 Kilometers
Albers Equal-Area Projection

Geography Skills

Interpreting Thematic Maps ⊛TEKS

1. Explain how geographic factors affected conflicts and foreign relations in the Republic.

2. Use the map scale to determine about how many miles the Texans marched from Austin to Mexico City.

3. What activity took place around San Antonio?

Texans on the Mier expedition traveled down the Rio Grande.

The Last Years of the Republic

Read to Discover

1. How did Mirabeau B. Lamar and Sam Houston influence the election of 1844?
2. What important issues did Texas face during Anson Jones's presidency?

Identify

- Anson Jones

Why It Matters Today

Annexation to the United States was a major issue for Texas. Use CNNfyi.com or other current events sources to find information about major political issues facing the United States today. Record your findings in your journal.

The Story Continues

In December 1844 Sam Houston stood before the Texas Congress to give his final speech as the Republic's president. He was pleased. Under his leadership, he reminded Congress, Texas had avoided war with Mexico. It had not invaded Texas since 1842, and all Texas prisoners but one had returned home. The economy was improving. Houston wanted the next president to continue his policies.

Sam Houston was known for his unusual clothes, such as this leopard-skin vest.

★ President Anson Jones

In the election of 1844, the Republic was divided. Newspapers printed harsh criticisms of the candidates, Vice President Edward Burleson and **Anson Jones**. Jones was a doctor from Brazoria and a veteran of the Battle of San Jacinto. He had served in the Texas Congress and as secretary of state under Houston. Because of their shared views, Jones received Houston's support in the election. Burleson had disagreed with the president over whether to attack Mexico. Because Burleson was at odds with Houston, Mirabeau B. Lamar and his followers supported him. As the election approached, the campaign reached a fever pitch. Voters either supported or opposed Sam Houston—there was no middle ground.

Jones easily defeated Burleson in the election. Many Texans associated the problems of the Republic with Lamar, so his support had hurt

Burleson. Kenneth Anderson, who was also supported by Houston, was chosen as vice president. Some citizens, however, claimed that Jones would not have won on his own merits. After the election, one Texan wrote a letter about the subject.

> **Texas Voices**   **❝Dr. *Anson Jones* is certainly elected to the Presidency—there is no doubt of it—though all the returns [ballots] are not in yet—He had no popularity of his own—rode in on Old Sam's Shadow! . . . But Old Sam can beat the Devil himself when he tries and make anyone president.❞**
>
> —James Morgan, letter to Samuel Swartwout, September 28, 1844

President Jones inherited the Republic's continuing economic problems. From its beginning, the Republic of Texas was in debt. The debt had grown during Lamar's presidency. When Sam Houston started his second term of office, the Republic's treasury was empty. In addition, the national debt had increased by millions of dollars. Houston had tried to limit government spending, but a partial failure of the Texas cotton crop in 1842 and 1843 prevented the nation's economy from recovering.

Jones continued Houston's policy of limited government spending. In addition, the new president continued to work for peace with Texas Indians, a policy that was also aimed at reducing spending. As annexation to the United States became more likely, the value of Texas currency slowly began to climb. By 1845 the value of Texas currency in many parts of the Republic had become equal to that of U.S. currency. Good crop years and increased trade were also helping to improve the Texas economy.

⭐ **Reading Check** **Drawing Inferences and Conclusions** What signs gave Texans hope that the Republic's economy was improving?

One of the most important issues in the annexation debate was finding a solution to the Republic's economic problems.

Salaries of Texas Government Officials

POSITION	1845 SALARY IN 1998 DOLLARS	1998
President/Governor	$82,500	$115,345
Secretary of State	$24,750	$76,966
Chief Justice	$28,875	$115,000
Attorney General	$16,500	$92,217
Land Commissioner	$24,750	$92,217

Source: *Texas Almanac* and *Laws of the Ninth Congress*

TAKS *Skills* *Interpreting Tables* Even after adjusting the salaries for inflation, officials today earn more money than officials of the Republic. Comparing the salary of the governor to the Texas president in 1998 dollars, how much more does the governor make?

★ Texans Debate Annexation

Although economic problems were a major concern, President Jones was more worried about the prospects of annexation. After winning independence, Texans had voted in favor of annexation. However, the U.S. government did not make an offer to annex the Republic. Houston's administration had supported annexation, while Lamar's administration had opposed it. As secretary of state, Jones had worked directly with Houston to map out foreign relations for Texas. This included plans for the Republic's possible annexation to the United States. In 1843 a newspaper had noted that "as great a proportion [percentage] of the people [are] in favor of annexation" as had been in 1836.

During his first months in office, Jones kept silent on the issue of annexation. Many Texans wanted decisive action, and became frustrated with Jones. They increasingly called for annexation. Jones wanted Texans to have the option of becoming part of their neighbor to the north or of maintaining independence. The latter depended on peaceful relations with Mexico, so he tried to obtain Mexico's recognition.

Few Texans were interested in negotiating with Mexico, as a newspaper expressed in 1845. "The object of the Mexican government is to lie and deceive us. . . . They may dupe [trick] some of our statesmen; but they will not dupe the people of Texas." As the demand for a convention to decide the matter grew stronger, word arrived that Mexico might soon recognize the Republic. Texans debated whether their country should stay independent or continue to seek annexation.

Anson Jones
(1798–1858)

Anson Jones was born in Massachusetts. He studied medicine as a young man and began practicing in 1820. He moved to Texas in 1833. After serving in the revolution, Jones returned to his medical practice. He also became interested in politics and served in a number of roles. Jones supported Houston's efforts to keep peace with Texas Indians. After serving as the last president of the Republic of Texas, Jones retired to his farm near Washington-on-the-Brazos. **What contributions did Jones make to Texas?** ★TEKS

 Reading Check Identifying Points of View Why did President Jones want to wait on the question of annexation?

 Section 3 Review ★TEKS Questions 1, 2, 3a, 3b, 4

 Homework Practice Online keyword: ST3 HP14

1 Identify and explain:
• Anson Jones

2 Analyzing Information
Copy the graphic organizer below. Use it to explain the choice President Jones wanted Texans to make regarding the future of the Republic.

The Future of the Republic

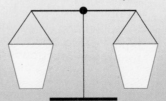

3 Finding the Main Idea
a. Who won the Texas presidential election of 1844, and how did Lamar and Houston influence this outcome?
b. In what ways had the Texas economy changed by 1844?

4 Writing and Critical Thinking
Making Generalizations and Predictions Write a paragraph explaining why you think Texans will or will not continue to support annexation. Consider the following:
• the reasons for annexation
• the improved economy and the possibility of recognition from Mexico

The Chapter at a Glance

Examine the following visual summary of the chapter. Then use the visual to create flash cards about the chapter. Use the flash cards as a study guide and drill with a partner. ⭐TEKS

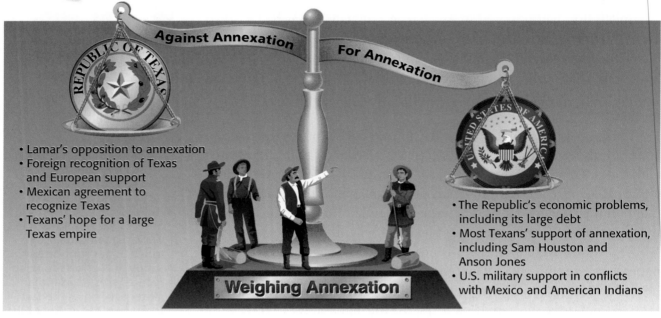

Against Annexation

REPUBLIC OF TEXAS

For Annexation

UNITED STATES OF AMERICA

- Lamar's opposition to annexation
- Foreign recognition of Texas and European support
- Mexican agreement to recognize Texas
- Texans' hope for a large Texas empire

- The Republic's economic problems, including its large debt
- Most Texans' support of annexation, including Sam Houston and Anson Jones
- U.S. military support in conflicts with Mexico and American Indians

Weighing Annexation

Identifying People and Ideas ⭐TEKS

Use the following terms or people in historically significant sentences:

1. foreign relations
2. Alcée Louis La Branche
3. Hugh McLeod
4. Santa Fe expedition
5. Ráfael Vásquez
6. Angelina Eberly
7. Archives War
8. Adrián Woll
9. Alexander Somervell
10. Anson Jones

Understanding Main Ideas ⭐TEKS

Section 1 (pp. 294–296)

1. Which nations were among the first to offer recognition of Texas?
2. How did President Lamar try to pressure Mexico into recognizing Texas?

Section 2 (pp. 297–301)

3. Describe what happened to the Santa Fe and Mier expeditions.
4. How did Texans hope to achieve peace with Mexico?

Section 3 (pp. 303–305)

5. What was the most critical issue during the presidency of Anson Jones, and how did Texans respond to it?

You Be the Historian ⭐TEKS

Reviewing Themes

1. **Global Relations** Describe the defining characteristics of the Republic's foreign relations.
2. **Government** How did Lamar's policy toward Mexico affect events during Houston's second administration?
3. **Geography** How did geographic features like nearness to Mexico affect the Republic's foreign relations?

⭐TEKS

TAKS Practice: Thinking Critically

1. **Comparing and Contrasting** How did Houston's and Lamar's foreign policies differ? How did this affect events in their presidencies?
2. **Analyzing Information** Identify in order the significant individuals and time periods of the Republic era of Texas history.
3. **Summarizing** What major issues did the Texas Republic face, and why did many Texans see annexation as a good solution?

Social Studies Skills Workshop

Interpreting Graphs ⭐TEKS

Study the bar graph below. Then use the information on the graph to help you answer the questions.

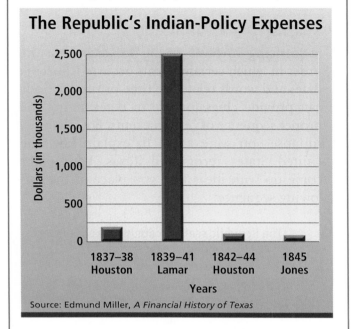

The Republic's Indian-Policy Expenses

Dollars (in thousands)

2,500
2,000
1,500
1,000
500
0

1837–38 Houston | 1839–41 Lamar | 1842–44 Houston | 1845 Jones

Years

Source: Edmund Miller, *A Financial History of Texas*

1. Approximately how many times more did Lamar spend than Houston and Jones combined?

   a. 2
   b. 8
   c. 15
   d. 25

2. In the 1840s, did the Republic's government spend less or more on fighting with American Indians in Texas?

Analyzing Primary Sources ⭐TEKS

Read the following quote by Sam Houston on events following the Santa Fe expedition. Then answer the questions.

"This moment I have learned that our Santa Fe prisoners have been released, and will soon return to Texas. At this I am much rejoiced for various reasons. First, because the sufferings of our countrymen are ended, and they are again free. We have one less cause of irritation, and so much the less food for . . . agitators. When the matter is understood of their release, it may give us a squint into the affairs of Mexico."

3. What does this quote reveal about Houston's point of view toward Mexico?

   a. Houston wants to better understand the positions of the Mexican government.
   b. He has no interest in Mexico.
   c. He favors an invasion of Mexico.
   d. Relations between Texas and Mexico are peaceful.

4. What does Houston mean when he refers to "agitators"?

Alternative Assessment

Cooperative Learning ⭐TEKS

BUILDING YOUR Portfolio

Work with a small group to complete the following activity. Imagine that you and the members of your group are diplomats of the Republic of Texas. Each of you should select one of the following countries and try to convince that country to recognize Texas: a) Mexico b) Great Britain c) France d) Belgium e) the Netherlands. Prepare a presentation to the officials of the nation you have selected. You may want to prepare visuals such as a map or poster to make your case more convincing.

🔲 **internet** connect

Internet Activity: go.hrw.com
KEYWORD: ST3 TX14 ⭐TEKS

Access the Internet through the HRW Go site to learn more about the debate over annexation. Locate, differentiate between, and use primary and secondary sources such as databases, biographies, and artifacts in your research. Choose which side of the debate you agree with and create a poster that supports your position. Present your poster to the class.

Social Studies Skills
WORKSHOP

Reading Skills

One of the biggest challenges you face in learning history is understanding what you read. By using appropriate Reading Skills, you will be able to understand more of what you read. Two important Reading Skills are Finding the Main Idea and Sequencing Information. The following activities will help you develop and practice these skills.

Finding the Main Idea

The main idea statement summarizes the most important point of a reading section. The main idea of a reading section is usually supported by sentences that provide details. Listed below are guidelines that will help you find the main idea of any reading assignment.

1. **Preview the material.** Read the title, introduction, and any other study clues that the assignment provides. These will often point to the main ideas being covered.

2. **Keep questions in mind.** Read the study questions that accompany the text. If the assignment does not provide study questions, create your own. Keeping these questions in mind will help you focus your reading.

3. **See how ideas are arranged.** Pay attention to the headings, subheadings, and opening paragraphs. Major ideas are often introduced in such material.

4. **Look for conclusions.** As you read, try to separate sentences that supply details from sentences that make general statements. Often a string of sentences providing detailed information leads to a conclusion that expresses a main idea.

Sequencing Information

Sequencing involves trying to determine the order in which certain events occurred. Specific dates and words related to time or time periods can provide clues for use in determining the proper sequence of certain events. For example, suppose you were asked to explain how the United States recognized Texas. You might come up with ideas that you place in the following sequence:

> The Republic seeks recognition from the United States.
>
> ▼
>
> Diplomats from Texas are sent to the United States.
>
> ▼
>
> Worried about Mexico's reaction, the United States rejects recognition.
>
> ▼
>
> Chaos in Mexico convinces the United States that it can recognize the Republic.
>
> ▼
>
> The United States recognizes Texas.

Practicing the Skill

TAKS

In Chapter 11, The Texas Revolution, find the section entitled Independence Is Won. Read the subsections Houston Prepares the Troops and The Battle of San Jacinto. Write four sentences that summarize the material in these subsections. Then condense your sentences into a single sentence that states the main idea. Brainstorm some important events and individuals of the Battle of San Jacinto. Then place these events and individuals in their proper sequence from first to last. ★TEKS

History in Action

You Make the Decision . . .

Should Texas Declare Independence?

Complete the following activity in small cooperative groups. It is 1835. You and your fellow delegates have been called to a convention. Your assignment is to decide whether Texas should declare independence from Mexico. The rest of the convention is about to begin debating the issue, so you need to make a decision quickly. Follow these steps to reach your decision.

1. Gather Information. Use your textbook and other resources to find information that might help you decide whether to declare independence. This might include your commitment to republican ideals, the actions of Santa Anna, and the views of people in your community, including Tejanos, African Americans, and recent arrivals from the United States. Be sure to use what you learned from this unit's Skills Workshop on Finding the Main Idea and Sequencing Information to help you make an informed decision. You may want to divide different parts of the research among group members.

2. Identify Options. After reviewing the information you have gathered, consider the options you might recommend to the convention. Your final decision may be easier to reach if you consider as many options as possible. Be sure to record your possible options for your presentation.

3. Predict Consequences. Now take each option you and the members of your group came up with and consider what might be the outcome of each course of action. Ask yourselves questions such as, "How might Texas benefit from doing this?", "How might Mexico respond if we do this?", and "What might be the long-term effects of following this course of action?" Once you have predicted the consequences, record them as notes for your presentation.

4. Take Action to Implement Your Decision. After you have considered your options, you should plan and create your presentation. Be sure to make your decision on whether to support independence very clear to the rest of the convention. You will need to support your decision by including information you gathered and by explaining why you rejected other options. Your presentation needs to be visually appealing to convince the other delegates. When you are ready, decide who in your group will make which part of the presentation and take your suggestion to the convention (the rest of the class). Good luck!

UNIT 5 The Lone Star State

(1845–1861)

CHAPTER 15 **Texas Joins the United States** (1845–1860)

CHAPTER 16 **Western Expansion and Conflict** (1845–1860)

CHAPTER 17 **Life in a Frontier State** (1845–1861)

Texas Teens

Young Texans on the Frontier

George Thomas Reynolds was a teenager when the Pony Express was being developed to send mail overland quickly by using skilled horseback riders. The youngest Pony Express riders were in their early teens. Riders had to be small, usually under 120 pounds, so that the extra weight of the mail—about 20 pounds—and another 25 pounds of equipment—did not overburden the horse. On longer runs, riders would change horses at stations in order to have a fresh horse. Riders generally rode a 75- to 100-mile route and received $25 a week along with free room and board.

The routes were often dangerous—heading through rugged American Indian territory. Rivers had to be crossed, and rain and flooding sometimes made this very hazardous. Riders, horses, and mail could be lost in river crossings. Extreme weather was also a danger. In one instance a Pony Express rider got lost making a December delivery and froze to death.

Richard Erastus Egan was in his late teens when he began riding for the Pony Express.

Although the work was often dangerous, Reynolds jumped at the chance for an exciting job as a Pony Express rider. Reynolds was only 15, but he was a good rider. In 1859 or 1860, Reynolds made a run for the Pony Express. He left his hometown of Palo Pinto loaded down with mail that needed to be delivered to Weatherford. Reynolds had to ride 35 miles through frontier territory where raids by American Indians were common. He reached Weatherford without a problem, however. Reynolds was lucky during his adventures as a Pony Express rider. **What challenges did Texans like Reynolds face on the frontier?**

In this unit you will learn more about the Texas frontier and the early history of the Lone Star State. You will also learn about the Mexican War, new American Indian policies, and many other changes.

LEFT PAGE: *The stagecoach was a common form of transportation across the Texas frontier in the days before the railroad.*

Texas Joins the United States

(1845–1860)

The annexation of Texas by the United States was celebrated with a flag-raising ceremony in Austin.

Before becoming a U.S. senator, Thomas J. Rusk served on the Texas Supreme Court.

TEXAS

1845 The United States annexes Texas.
1846 Thomas J. Rusk and Sam Houston become the first Texans to serve in the U.S. Senate.

1847 George T. Wood is elected governor of Texas.

1852 Work begins on the Port Isabel Lighthouse. When completed, its light could be seen from 16 miles away.

1845	**1847**	**1849**	**1851**

U.S. and WORLD

1845 Great Britain announces that it will seize all slave-carrying ships sailing to Brazil.

1848 The Seneca Falls Convention calls for equal rights for women, including the right to vote.

1850 California is admitted to the United States.

These British sailors are attempting to capture a slave ship.

Build on What You Know

The Republic of Texas had finally won recognition from the United States, Mexico, and several European countries. But annexation was still on many people's minds. In the United States, it was a matter of fierce debate. For Texas, annexation would bring many changes.

The Port Isabel Light-house was used as an observation tower and to signal sailors.

Some supporters of the Know-Nothing Party sang party songs from song sheets.

1854 The American, or Know-Nothing, Party becomes active in Texas.

1855 The Governor's Mansion is built in Austin.

1859 Sam Houston easily defeats incumbent Hardin Runnels in the election for Texas governor.

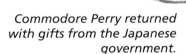

1853 **1855** **1857** **1859**

1853 Commodore Matthew C. Perry of the U.S. Navy sails into Edo (now Tokyo) Bay, Japan. Perry soon signs treaties of peace and commerce with the Japanese.

1855 The Kansas Territory's legislature passes harsh pro-slavery laws that spark criticism.

Commodore Perry returned with gifts from the Japanese government.

You Be the Historian

Themes Journal

What's Your Opinion? Do you **agree** or **disagree** with the following statements? Support your point of view in your journal.

● **Geography** Most people in a nation support adding new territory.

● **Citizenship** People should organize into groups to make government respond to their demands.

● **Economics** Nations should not be allowed to go into debt.

If you were there . . . *Would you support annexation?*

The Annexation of Texas

Read to Discover

1. How did slavery and westward expansion affect the debate over annexation?
2. What events led to the annexation of Texas?

Why It Matters Today

During the 1840s, politicians could not agree on the issue of whether or not to annex Texas. Use CNN**fyi**.com or other **current events** sources to find information about an issue that politicians are debating today. Record your findings in your journal.

Define

- **manifest destiny**
- **political parties**
- **nominated**
- **joint resolution**

Identify

- **John Tyler**
- **Jane McManus Cazneau**
- **James K. Polk**
- **Convention of 1845**
- **Texas Admission Act**

The Story Continues

The weather was cold and rainy, but William Henry Harrison was determined to give his first speech as president of the United States. He talked in the rain for an hour and 40 minutes. It proved to be his undoing—he caught pneumonia and died one month later. His vice president, John Tyler, became president. Tyler's position on Texas was clear: the Republic must be annexed.

This pitcher celebrates William Henry Harrison's campaign for president.

★ The Treaty to Annex Texas

The annexation debate was long-standing. In 1836, Texans had voted overwhelmingly to join the United States. However, in the United States, Americans were divided over annexation largely along regional lines. The North had developed an economy that relied heavily on commerce and manufacturing. The South relied on agriculture and slave labor. As a result, northerners and southerners generally disagreed on policies affecting business, slavery, and trade. Many northerners did not want Texas to be admitted to the Union as a slave state because it would tip the balance of power in Congress toward the South. Most southerners wanted Texas to join the Union. A New Orleans newspaper declared, "The South will almost to a man sustain [support] the policy of . . . annexation."

U.S. president **John Tyler**, a southerner, favored annexation. He and other Americans feared that Great Britain was gaining too much influence in Texas. In 1843, U.S. officials began to work toward annexation. The next year Tyler sent an annexation treaty to the U.S. Senate for approval. Under the treaty, Texas would become a U.S. territory—the first step toward becoming a state. The treaty called for the United States to pay the Republic's large public debt. In exchange, Texas would give all its public lands to the federal government.

When the treaty went to the Senate, former president John Quincy Adams wrote that "with it went the freedom of the human race." At a rally in New York City, some 3,000 people protested the treaty. The Senate debated the treaty in June 1844. Some senators warned that annexing Texas would spark a war with Mexico. But the most bitter debate on the Senate floor was over the issue of adding another slave state to the Union. After three weeks of debate, the Senate rejected the treaty.

The debate came at a time when many U.S. settlers were moving westward. The West was seen as a place of opportunity, where farming and trade would provide economic growth. Many Americans believed that the United States was meant to expand across North America. Newspaper editor John O'Sullivan used the term **manifest destiny** to describe this belief. "The American claim is by the right of our manifest destiny to overspread and to possess [own] the whole of the continent which Providence [divine guidance] has given us." Many Americans began to believe that it was the nation's manifest destiny to annex Texas. Columnist Jane McManus—**Jane McManus Cazneau** after her 1849 marriage—helped turn northern opinion in favor of annexation.

Reading Check **Supporting a Point of View** Would you have supported annexation? Explain your answer.

Interpreting the Visual Record

Manifest destiny. *John Gast's painting shows the westward movement of U.S. settlers across North America.* **How does this painting show Americans' belief that they had the right to expand across North America?**

The Granger Collection, New York

"Texas Coming In." This political cartoon forecasts the annexation of Texas and shows Stephen F. Austin and Sam Houston riding a boat into the United States. **According to this cartoon, is the United States pleased that Texas is joining the Union?** ★TEKS

Polk showed his support for annexation in his campaign material.

 Analyzing Primary Sources
Identifying Points of View
What conclusions did Tyler draw from Polk's election?

★ The Annexation Resolution

The annexation treaty and manifest destiny became important issues in the U.S. presidential election of 1844. The **political parties** held differing positions on these issues. Political parties are groups of people who help elect government officials and influence government policies. The Democratic Party **nominated**, or chose as its candidate, **James K. Polk** of Tennessee. Polk wanted the United States to annex Texas and expand west. Polk's chief opponent was Whig Party candidate Henry Clay of Kentucky. At first, Clay opposed annexation. He worried that it might result in war with Mexico. But in an effort to win votes in the South, he softened his opposition, while trying to reassure northern voters. But Clay's efforts to take both sides of the issue cost him the election. He offended voters in both the North and the South, giving Polk the victory.

Most Americans, including President Tyler, considered Polk's election a sign of the public's approval of annexation.

(Texas Voices) **"A controlling majority of the people and a larger majority of the states have declared in favor of immediate annexation. . . . It is the will of both the people and the states that Texas shall be annexed to the Union . . . immediately."**

—U.S. president John Tyler, annual message to Congress

Tyler therefore requested that both houses of Congress pass a **joint resolution**, or formal expression of intent, for annexation. A joint resolution required only a simple majority to pass. This was less than the two-thirds majority required for a treaty. In February 1845 the U.S. Congress passed the joint resolution to annex Texas.

★ **Reading Check** **Finding the Main Idea** How did Polk's election affect the annexation of Texas?

★ Texas Enters the United States

The joint resolution's terms were more favorable to Texas than the annexation treaty's terms had been. Texas would enter as a state rather than as a territory. Texans had to approve annexation and then write a new constitution. The new state could keep its public lands, but some would have to be sold to pay the public debt. Texas had to turn much of its public property, such as military supplies, over to the United States.

Texas president Anson Jones presented the offer of annexation from the United States to the Texas Congress along with the offer of recognition from Mexico. The final decision, he believed, should be made by the people of Texas. He also called for a convention to consider annexation. The delegates to the **Convention of 1845** assembled in Austin on July 4, 1845, and quickly approved annexation. Then they began work on a new constitution. Texans were proud of being independent, but there were good reasons for joining the United States. Most Texans were originally from the United States, and many still had families living there. Texas and the United States also shared strong business ties. The federal government would also provide Texas with military protection, a sound money system, and postal service. On October 13, Texas voters approved annexation by a vote of 4,254 to 267. Texans also approved the new state constitution. On December 29, 1845, President Polk signed the **Texas Admission Act**, making Texas the 28th state. One Texan explained,

Texas Voices ⟩ 66Truly we have every reason to be happy! To rejoice over the prosperity we enjoy! We are . . . united once more by the strong tie of national sympathy to all that we ever loved.99

—W. B. DeWees, *Letters from an Early Settler of Texas*

⊛ **Reading Check** **Evaluating** Why did most Texans favor annexation?

Newspapers and flyers asked readers whether they supported the annexation of Texas.

★ **Section 1 Review** ⊛TEKS Questions 2, 3, 4a, 4b, 5

go.hrw.com **Homework Practice Online**
keyword: ST3 HP15

1 Define and explain:
• manifest destiny
• political parties
• nominated
• joint resolution

2 Identify and explain:
• John Tyler
• Jane McManus Cazneau
• James K. Polk
• Convention of 1845
• Texas Admission Act

3 Categorizing
Copy the graphic organizer below. List the leaders and groups who favored or opposed annexation.

For Annexation	Against Annexation

4 Finding the Main Idea
a. What impact did slavery and westward expansion have on the annexation debate?
b. Beginning with the annexation treaty, identify in order the events that led to annexation.

5 Writing and Critical Thinking TAKS
Comparing and Contrasting Write a paragraph comparing a northerner's view of annexation with most Texans' views.
Consider the following:
• northerners' and southerners' views on slavery
• annexation's effect on the U.S. Congress

Forming a Government

Read to Discover

1. How did the Constitution of 1845 lay the foundation for new state government?
2. What steps were taken to organize the government of the new state?

Why It Matters Today

In 1845, Texans gathered to create a new constitution. Use CNNfyi.com or other **current events** sources to find information about public involvement in government today. Record your findings in your journal.

Define

- biennial
- corporations

Identify

- **James Pinckney Henderson**
- **Thomas J. Rusk**
- **José Antonio Navarro**

The Story Continues

During the ceremony for the annexation of Texas, the Republic of Texas flag was lowered, and the American flag raised.

Texans stood, some with tears in their eyes, as the Republic's flag was lowered from the capitol for the last time. Before the flag could touch the ground, Sam Houston caught it. President Anson Jones declared, "The final act in this great drama is now performed; the Republic of Texas is no more." Many Texans looked forward to their future as citizens of the United States, and when the American flag was raised, cheers erupted from the crowd.

★ The Convention of 1845

On February 19, 1846, President Anson Jones formally turned the Texas government over to **James Pinckney Henderson**, the state's first governor. Texans were thrilled. Noah Smithwick remembered the event. "When the stars and stripes, the flag of our fathers, was run up . . . cheer after cheer rent [tore] the air."

The Constitution of 1845 provided a framework for the new state government. The constitution was written at the Convention of 1845, which had assembled on July 4 in Austin. When the convention began, delegates chose **Thomas J. Rusk** as convention president. Rusk had helped write the constitution of the Republic of Texas in 1836. At the Convention of 1845 he received assistance from many able delegates who were experienced judges, lawyers, and legislators. As one newspaper reporter declared, "The delegates to the convention . . . would rank high in any country." Most delegates were originally from the southern United States. The only Tejano delegate, **José Antonio Navarro**, was also the only native Texan to serve at the convention. One delegate was missing. Sam Houston had traveled to Tennessee to pay his respects to former U.S. president Andrew Jackson, who had died in early June 1845. To honor Jackson, delegates wore black armbands as they formed committees to write the constitution.

The delegates used the constitutions of the United States, the Republic of Texas, and the state of Louisiana as models. They spent nearly two months working on the new state constitution. The resulting document was widely praised. Texans ratified the constitution in October 1845 by a vote of 4,174 to 312.

 Reading Check **Finding the Main Idea** What was the background of many of the delegates to the Convention of 1845?

★ The Constitution of 1845

Under the new constitution, the Texas government had three branches. The governor headed the executive branch and served a two-year term. The same person could not serve as governor more than four years in any six-year period. The legislative branch consisted of a senate and a house of representatives. House members served two-year terms, and senators served for four years. The state legislature met once every two years, or in **biennial** sessions. The judicial branch, or court system, consisted of the supreme court—the highest state court—and the district courts. The governor appointed judges, until 1850, when a constitutional

Biography

José Antonio Navarro
(1795–1871)

José Antonio Navarro had a long and distinguished career by the time he served as a delegate to the Convention of 1845. A business owner, rancher, and lawyer, he served in the Mexican Congress and in the Coahuila y Texas state legislature. Navarro supported Texas independence and signed the Republic's Declaration of Independence. He also helped write the Republic's constitution and served in its Congress. After statehood, he was twice elected to the Texas Senate. **How did Navarro contribute to Texas history?** ★TEKS

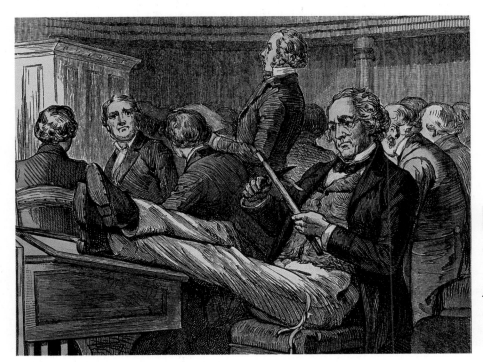

Interpreting the Visual Record

A new government. After the Constitution of 1845 was completed, Sam Houston joined the U.S. Senate. *What does this illustration reveal about how business was conducted in the U.S. Senate in the 1840s?*

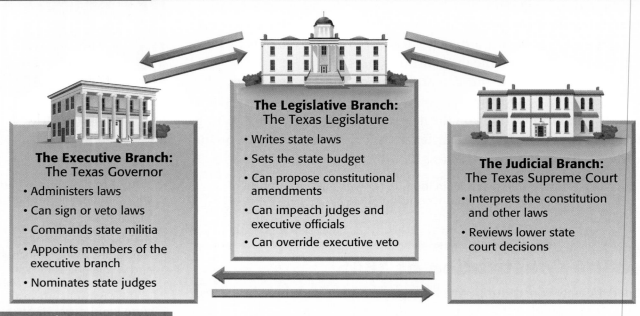

The Separation of Powers

The Texas Constitution of 1845 established a separation of governing powers, in which the powers of each branch are limited. The system is similar to the one established in the U.S. Constitution.

The Executive Branch:
The Texas Governor

- Administers laws
- Can sign or veto laws
- Commands state militia
- Appoints members of the executive branch
- Nominates state judges

The Legislative Branch:
The Texas Legislature

- Writes state laws
- Sets the state budget
- Can propose constitutional amendments
- Can impeach judges and executive officials
- Can override executive veto

The Judicial Branch:
The Texas Supreme Court

- Interprets the constitution and other laws
- Reviews lower state court decisions

Visualizing History

1. **Government** In what ways is each branch able to check or limit the powers of the other two branches? ★TEKS

2. **Connecting to Today** How does the separation of powers help provide limited government? ★TEKS

---

amendment allowed voters to elect judges. Voters also elected the governor and the members of the state legislature, but only white men 21 years of age or older could vote. African Americans, American Indians, and women could not vote or hold office. In this respect, Texas was like most other states in the Union. As with the Republic's constitution, the new state constitution continued to protect slavery.

The state constitution protected homesteads, or families' homes and lands up to 200 acres each, from creditors. It also provided legal protections for women. Proposals to protect the property rights of women had sparked considerable debate during the convention. The delegates decided that a husband could not sell the family homestead without his wife's permission. Married women could also own property separately from their husbands. Some of these legal protections for women stemmed from old Spanish laws.

The constitution also tried to protect Texans and the government from certain business practices. Thomas J. Rusk explained Texans' views.

★ **Analyzing Primary Sources**
Identifying Points of View
Why does Rusk dislike banks?

Texas Voices 66Thousands [of people] . . . have been ruined by banks. . . . I wish by no vote of mine . . . to authorize the institution [creation] of a bank which may benefit a few individuals but will carry here as elsewhere ruin, want, [and] misery.99

—Thomas J. Rusk, quoted in *Thomas J. Rusk: Soldier, Statesman, Jurist,* by Mary Whatley Clarke

The constitution banned banks because the vast majority of Texans were farmers who saw little need for banks and distrusted them. Many banks had failed during bad economic times in the Republic. The constitution also prevented the state legislature from taking on more than $100,000 in debt unless an emergency existed. **Corporations**, or companies that sell shares of ownership to investors to raise money, needed the legislature's permission to operate. A corporation's right to operate could be taken away if it used unfair business practices.

⭐ **Reading Check Summarizing** What were some of the main provisions of the Constitution of 1845?

⭐ The First State Election

The first state election was held on December 15, 1845. The major candidates had been delegates to the Convention of 1845. James Pinckney Henderson soundly won the governor's race, defeating Dr. James B. Miller. Albert C. Horton won the race for lieutenant governor. John Hemphill kept the post he had held in the Republic—chief justice of Texas. State officials took office on February 19, 1846.

The daily operations of government were transferred from the Republic to the state. Army posts, many public buildings, and other properties were turned over to the federal government. The state legislature met to decide who would represent Texas in the U.S. Senate. It came as no surprise that the legislators chose Sam Houston and Thomas J. Rusk. One Texan noted the appointments with approval. "These two great men placed the country before self." Within weeks, the two men left their homes for Washington.

⭐ **Reading Check Analyzing Information** Why did the Texas legislature select Sam Houston and Thomas J. Rusk as U.S. senators?

That's Interesting!

A Ban on Duels

The constitution banned anyone who took part in a duel from holding any state office. Some Texans had used dueling to settle arguments. For example, in 1837 President Houston appointed Albert Sidney Johnston commander of the Texas army. Felix Huston, the commander at that time, refused to give up control and challenged Johnston to a duel. Johnston accepted the challenge and was badly wounded.

Some Texans owned sets of dueling pistols.

Section 2 Review ⭐TEKS Questions 2, 3, 4a, 4b, 5

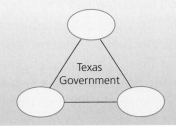

go.hrw.com Homework Practice Online
keyword: ST3 HP15

1 Define and explain:
- biennial
- corporations

2 Identify and explain:
- James Pinckney Henderson
- Thomas J. Rusk
- José Antonio Navarro

3 Summarizing
Copy the web diagram below. Use it to identify the three branches of the new state government established by the Constitution of 1845.

Texas Government

4 Finding the Main Idea
a. Who could vote and hold office under the Constitution of 1845?
b. After the Constitution of 1845 was approved, how was the state government formed?

5 Writing and Critical Thinking

TAKS

Supporting a Point of View Imagine that you are a delegate to the Convention of 1845. Write a letter to the voters of Texas, explaining why you voted for or against the sections that banned banks and restricted corporations.
Consider the following:
- Texans' experience with banks
- what the voters who elected you do for a living

Political and Economic Issues

Read to Discover

1. What were the positions of political parties, and how did they affect Texas politics?
2. Who were the early governors of Texas?
3. How was the state's public debt paid?

Why It Matters Today

Texas governors tried to improve conditions in the state. Use CNNfyi.com or other **current events** sources to find information about what issues governors face today. Record your findings in your journal.

Identify

- **Know-Nothing Party**
- **George T. Wood**
- **Peter Hansborough Bell**
- **Elisha M. Pease**
- **Hardin Runnels**

The Story Continues

In 1857, near the end of his career in the U.S. Senate, Sam Houston decided to run for governor of Texas as an independent candidate. Houston knew the race would be difficult, so he planned an aggressive campaign. "The people want excitement, and I had as well give it as anyone." Houston campaigned vigorously throughout the state. He traveled in a red buggy, sometimes sleeping on the ground.

Houston might have used this traveling dining set during his red buggy campaign.

★ Political Parties

Political parties did not exist in the Republic of Texas or in the state in the early years following annexation. Instead, groups of Texans supported particular persons, such as Sam Houston or Mirabeau B. Lamar. There were no parties to organize voters around political issues. In the late 1840s Texans started to join political parties that had been organized in the United States. The nation had a two-party system.

The Democratic Party generally represented the views of farmers and owners of small businesses. Andrew Jackson, a former U.S. president and a favorite of Texans, had been a Democrat. The party was very strong throughout the South, where most Texas leaders came from originally. In addition, many Democrats had supported the annexation of Texas.

Most Texas leaders joined the Democratic Party, and most Texans voted for Democratic candidate Lewis Cass in the 1848 presidential election. By 1856 some 90 percent of Texas counties sent delegates to the state Democratic convention. The Democratic Party was so strong in Texas that every governor elected between 1845 and 1857 was a Democrat. The popularity of the party led to some problems. Because they usually had little to fear from opposing political groups, the Democrats often fought among themselves. Splits within the party often involved Sam Houston, the most important figure in Texas politics.

Some Texans supported the Whig Party, the other major political party in the United States. Whigs supported banking and large business interests. They had opposed the annexation of Texas. These were not popular positions with most Texans. In the mid-1850s the Whig Party collapsed when its members became divided over the slavery issue. Many Whigs in the North joined with smaller groups to form the Republican Party. Republicans believed that slavery should not be allowed into any territories of the United States. For that reason, the Republican Party had almost no support in Texas and the South.

In the mid-1850s the American Party—commonly called the **Know-Nothing Party**—briefly appeared. This party acquired its name because when asked questions by outsiders, its secretive members answered, "I know nothing." This party supported slavery and wanted to keep immigrants and Catholics out of government. The Know-Nothings gained some support in Texas, but most Texans were not interested in their views. Many Texans were recent immigrants or Catholics or both. The Know-Nothing candidate for governor in 1855 lost the election but received some 18,000 votes. For a short time, Texans heard rumors that Sam Houston had joined the Know-Nothing Party. Houston denied this, saying, "Now, of the Know-Nothings I know nothing; and of them I care nothing." After the party faded in popularity, most Know-Nothing Texans became Democrats. By 1857 the Know-Nothing Party of Texas had disappeared.

⭐ **Reading Check** **Summarizing** What were the beliefs of each of the parties that challenged Democrats in Texas?

Elisha M. Pease
(1812–1883)

One of the popular early governors was Elisha M. Pease. Pease moved to Texas in 1835. He fought in the Battle of Gonzales and helped write the Republic's constitution. Pease was governor of Texas three times. Under his leadership, the legislature created the Permanent School Fund. In addition, he led the effort to pay off the state's debt. When Pease left office, the state was debt-free and in solid financial condition. **Why is Governor Pease considered an effective leader?** ⭐TEKS

⭐ Early Governors of Texas

James Pinckney Henderson, the state's first governor, served only one term in office. During part of that term, he was away leading Texas troops in a war between the United States and Mexico. Lieutenant Governor Albert C. Horton fulfilled the governor's duties during this time. Henderson chose not to run for re-election in 1847. Texas voters elected **George T. Wood** as their new governor. Wood was a plantation owner and friend of Sam Houston's. Frontier defense and disputes over the location of the state's northern and western boundaries were important issues during his administration. Wood ran for re-election in

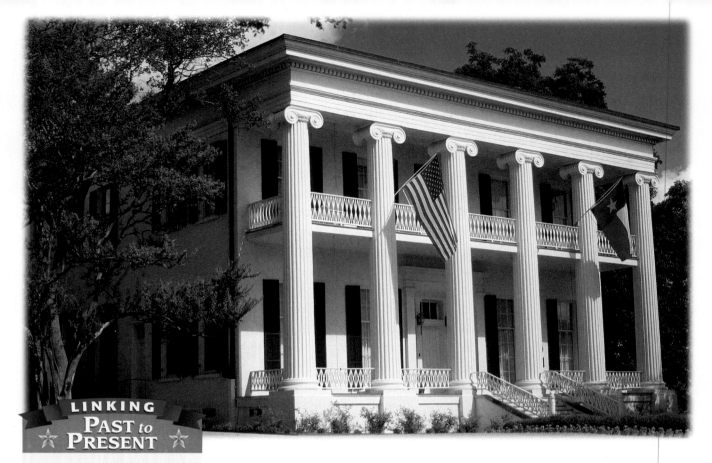

LINKING PAST to PRESENT

The Governor's Mansion

The Governor's Mansion in Austin is the fourth-oldest governor's mansion still in use in the United States. The early governors of Texas lived in Austin hotels or boarding-houses. In 1854 the legislature set aside $17,000 to build an executive mansion. The building was completed in 1856. Elisha M. Pease was the first governor to live in the mansion. In 1976 the mansion became a National Historic Landmark. Today visitors are welcome to tour the mansion. **Why is it important for the governor to have a residence in Austin?**

1849. One observer noted that Texans who disliked Houston "will move heaven and earth to defeat Wood."

Wood lost the election to **Peter Hansborough Bell**, a veteran of the Texas Revolution. Like Wood, the new governor tried to establish the extent of the state's territory. Bell claimed that part of New Mexico belonged to Texas. Texas voters re-elected him in 1851. Bell resigned from office a few months before his term ended to take a seat in the U.S. Congress. Lieutenant Governor J. W. Henderson became the governor for the remaining 28 days of Bell's term. In 1853, Texans elected **Elisha M. Pease** to the state's highest office. Pease was an active popular governor who supported education and other reforms. He defeated the Know-Nothing candidate to serve a second term in 1855.

In 1857 Sam Houston and **Hardin Runnels** ran for governor. Runnels, a wealthy cotton plantation owner from Bowie County, received the Democratic Party's nomination. Houston campaigned hard for the office. He gave 60 speeches in little more than two months during the hot Texas summer. Even so, Houston lost in a bitter campaign—the only election he ever lost. During Runnels's term in office, conflicts between settlers and American Indians increased. Runnels proved unable to deal with the problem effectively. When Houston ran against Runnels in 1859, he defeated Runnels easily. With that victory, Houston had served Texas as army commander, president of the Republic, senator, and governor.

⭐ **Reading Check** **Sequencing** Name in order the governors of Texas during the 1840s and 1850s.

★ Debts and Land Issues

The governors, like the presidents of the Republic, had to deal with the public debt and create a land policy. In 1845 the Republic of Texas owed some $10 million. The annexation resolution made the state responsible for paying this debt by selling some of its public lands. The state had plenty of land to sell. But buyers who did not homestead on the land had to purchase it. At the price of 50 cents per acre, there were few buyers. The debt continued to rise, reaching more than $12 million by 1850.

The federal government and Texas developed a plan to eliminate the debt. Texas gave up its claim to 67 million acres of land in present-day Colorado, Kansas, New Mexico, Oklahoma, and Wyoming. In return, the federal government gave Texas money to help pay the debt. The debt was paid off by 1855.

Texas still owned millions of acres of public land. The state gave much of it to settlers, each of whom could claim homesteads of 320 acres. The settlers had to live on the land and improve it in some way—typically by farming the land. The state set aside other lands for colleges, public schools, and universities. Additional lands were set aside for improvements such as roads, harbors, and railroads. By 1898 there were no unclaimed public lands left in Texas.

★ Reading Check Drawing Inferences and Conclusions
How did the state government use its public lands to improve the state?

CONNECTING TO ECONOMICS AND MATH

The Republic's Debt

Because the Texas government spent more than it received in revenue, the public debt grew by leaps and bounds. As the debt went unpaid and even increased, the interest mounted. By 1851, interest alone on the debt totaled $3.1 million.

The following chart shows how debt accumulated by the Republic grew from 1836 to 1851. Use the numbers in the chart to create a color-coded bar graph illustrating the increase of the debt.

YEAR	DEBT
1836	$1.25 million
1845	$9.9 million
1851	$12.4 million

Source: *Handbook of Texas*

Interpreting Data

1. By how many millions of dollars had the Republic's debt increased from 1836 to 1845? ★TEKS

2. How many times greater was the debt in 1851 than the debt in 1836? ★TEKS

Section 3 Review ★TEKS Questions 1, 2, 3a, 3b, 4

go.hrw.com **Homework Practice Online**
keyword: ST3 HP15

1 Identify and explain:
- Know-Nothing Party
- George T. Wood
- Peter Hansborough Bell
- Elisha M. Pease
- Hardin Runnels

2 Sequencing
Copy the time line below. Use it to show the winners in the race for governor between 1845 and 1859.

1845 _____
1847 _____
1849 _____
1851 _____
1853 _____
1855 _____
1857 _____
1859 _____

3 Finding the Main Idea
a. What were the positions of the political parties in Texas, and what effect did they have on Texas politics?
b. How did the state pay its debt?

4 Writing and Critical Thinking  TAKS
Identifying Points of View Write a paragraph describing the Democratic and Whig positions, and which was more popular.
Consider the following:
- which party opposed slavery
- the popularity of annexation in Texas

Texas Joins the United States **325**

CHAPTER 15 REVIEW

The Chapter at a Glance

Examine the following visual summary of the chapter. Then use the visual to create an outline of the major political and economic issues of Texas during the era of early statehood. Exchange your outline with a classmate to use as a study guide. ⭐TEKS

CONSTITUTION OF 1845

Texas governors adjust the state's land policy to encourage homesteading.

The U.S. government agrees to annex Texas. Texans overwhelmingly vote to join the United States in 1845. Texans adopt a new state constitution and create a new government.

After annexation, Texas governors face a large state debt and search for new solutions for the state's economic problems.

Identifying People and Ideas ⭐TEKS

Use the following terms or people in historically significant sentences.

1. nominated
2. joint resolution
3. James K. Polk
4. Texas Admission Act
5. biennial
6. corporations
7. James Pinckney Henderson
8. Thomas J. Rusk
9. Know-Nothing Party
10. Elisha M. Pease

Understanding Main Ideas ⭐TEKS

Section 1 (pp. 314–317)

1. Identify the different points of view of the Democratic and Whig Parties on annexation.
2. Why is 1845 a significant date in Texas history?

Section 2 (pp. 318–321)

3. Why did Texans create a new constitution in 1845?
4. How did the Constitution of 1845 affect women?

Section 3 (pp. 322–325)

5. Why did many Texans support the Democratic Party?

You Be the Historian ⭐TEKS

Reviewing Themes

1. **Geography** How did westward expansion affect the debate in the United States over the annexation of Texas?
2. **Citizenship** How did political parties change politics in Texas?
3. **Economics** Why was the public debt an important issue for Texas?

TAKS Practice: Thinking Critically ⭐TEKS

1. **Supporting a Point of View** Express your point of view on annexation. Offer reasons to defend your viewpoint.
2. **Analyzing Information** Analyze the causes and events that led to Texas statehood.
3. **Identifying Points of View** Identify the different points of view of the Democratic, Whig, Know-Nothing, and Republican Parties on the issue of slavery.

Interpreting Political Cartoons ★TEKS

Study the political cartoon below. Then use the information in the cartoon to help you answer the questions that follow.

1. During the 1850s the Know-Nothing Party was active in Texas. Which statement best explains why the cartoonist drew Sam Houston with a fishing net?

  a. to show Houston's efforts to capture support for the Know-Nothing Party

  b. to show Houston's luck winning support for the Know-Nothing Party

  c. because Houston liked politics

  d. because Houston liked to go fishing

2. Do you think the cartoonist agreed with Sam Houston? Why or why not?

Analyzing Primary Sources ★TEKS

Read the following quote by Charles Elliott, the British minister to the Republic of Texas. Then answer the questions.

"Since I have been here [in Great Britain], I have had some good opportunity of judging of the real state of feeling in this country respecting annexation, and I am persuaded it is entirely out of the question. . . . The single . . . practicable solution for all parties concerned is the acknowledgment of her independence by Mexico, and the steady adherence [loyalty] to it by Texas. I was concerned, indeed, to see that some movements had been made in your [Texas] Congress . . . for they are not calculated to work good effects in Mexico, or . . . elsewhere."

3. Which of the following statements best describes the author's point of view?

  a. Texas would benefit by being annexed by the United States.

  b. Texas would benefit by Mexican recognition and remaining independent.

  c. The United States would benefit by annexing Texas.

  d. Great Britain had no opinion on what Texas should do.

4. What might have influenced Elliott's point of view on the issue of annexation?

Alternative Assessment

Linking to Community ★TEKS

Texans elected state officials for the first time in 1845. There are many elected officials in your community. Choose one and find out what that person's responsibilities are. What are the qualifications for that person's office? What party does he or she belong to? What leadership qualities does the person bring to the office? Create a feature newspaper article that discusses your findings. Be sure to use standard grammar, spelling, sentence structure, and punctuation in your article.

BUILDING YOUR Portfolio

■ **internet** connect

Internet Activity: go.hrw.com
KEYWORD: ST3 TX15 ★TEKS

Access the Internet through the HRW Go site to research the lives and accomplishments of early Texas governors. Based on your research, create a database that includes when and where they were born, their years in office, their accomplishments, and any other information about these leaders that you find useful or interesting.

Western Expansion and Conflict
(1845–1860)

Many early illustrations of the Mexican War, such as this image of the Battle of Resaca de la Palma, were not very realistic.

Samuel H. Walker helped improve the design of the Colt revolver.

TEXAS

1846 Fighting breaks out between U.S. forces and Mexican troops at Palo Alto and Resaca de la Palma.

1847 Samuel H. Walker dies in combat during a conflict in Mexico.

1850 The Texas population reaches more than 200,000.

1845	1847	1849	1851

U.S. and WORLD

1846 The Bear Flag Revolt erupts as settlers in California declare independence from Mexico.

1848 Mexico cedes much of its territory to the United States in the Treaty of Guadalupe Hidalgo.

1850 Great Britain and the United States agree to build a canal in Central America to link the Pacific and Atlantic Oceans.

U.S. settlers in California raised this flag when they declared independence from Mexico.

Build on What You Know

In 1845 Texas joined the United States and formed a new state government. Relations between the United States and Mexico grew more tense after the annexation of Texas, and war broke out in 1846. The war's outcome greatly changed the political face of North America and the lives of Texans.

Comanche women often wore boots like these.

Fort Worth was established as a military post in 1849, but the army abandoned it only a few years later.

1853 U.S. Army troops abandon Fort Worth after settlers move farther west beyond the fort.

1859 A series of clashes occurs between Texas Rangers and Mexican Americans near Brownsville.

1853   1855   1857   1859

1853 Mexico sells the United States more than 29,000 square miles of territory along its border with present-day Arizona and New Mexico in the Gadsden Purchase.

1855 English clergyman Charles Kingsley publishes the novel *Westward Ho!*

1857 A financial panic begins in the United States.

Charles Kingsley's historical romance novel was set in Latin America.

If you were there . . .
How would you resolve a border conflict?

You Be the Historian

Themes Journal

What's Your Opinion? Do you **agree** or **disagree** with the following statements? Support your point of view in your journal.

- **Global Relations** Nations should always respect each other's borders.

- **Citizenship** Citizens' rights are affected during wartime.

- **Geography** The expansion of new settlements into a region affects both the land and the lives of people already there.

The Mexican War

Read to Discover

1. What led to war between Mexico and the United States?
2. What events took place during the Mexican War?
3. How did Texans participate in the war against Mexico?

Define
- **offensive**

Identify
- **Zachary Taylor**
- **Antonio López de Santa Anna**
- **John S. "Rip" Ford**
- **John Coffee Hays**
- **Winfield Scott**

Why It Matters Today

The United States and Mexico went to war in 1846. Use **CNNfyi.com** or other **current events** sources to learn about peace efforts around the world today. Record your findings in your journal.

U.S. troops stationed in Texas during the Mexican War looked forward to letters from home.

The Story Continues

U.S. lieutenant Napoleon Dana was stationed with his fellow soldiers along the Rio Grande. There he waited, anticipating a fight with Mexico. Many of the troops were becoming anxious, eager to prove themselves in battle. Dana, who dearly missed his wife, wrote a letter home. "Here we are at a dead standstill, doing nothing. . . . I wish I had all of my glory and was on my way home again."

★ Fighting Breaks Out

The border conflict arose from tensions between Mexico and the United States after the annexation of Texas and the signing of the Texas Admission Act on December 29, 1845. Many Mexicans feared that annexation was just the first step and that the United States wanted to take over all of Mexico. The Mexican minister to the United States left Washington in anger over annexation and several other issues.

First, Mexico claimed that the Nueces River marked the boundary between Texas and Mexico. The United States supported the Texas claim that the Rio Grande was the boundary. Second, many U.S. citizens wanted to be paid for damage done to their businesses and property in Mexico. Finally, U.S. leaders were angry because Mexico had ordered U.S. settlers to leave the Mexican territory of California.

President James K. Polk had sent diplomat John Slidell to Mexico in November 1845 to settle the disputes. Slidell was also to consider making an offer to purchase New Mexico and California. However, Mexican officials refused to meet with him.

Aware of the brewing conflict, Polk ordered General **Zachary Taylor** and thousands of U.S. soldiers into Texas. Their mission was to protect the new state from any attack. When Taylor's troops arrived along the Rio Grande in late March 1846, they discovered Mexican troops camped across the river. Taylor ordered his men to build a fort along the river— near what is now Brownsville.

In early April a Mexican general sent a message to Taylor, ordering him to "return to the east bank of the Nueces River." Taylor refused. On April 25 a force of 1,600 Mexican cavalry crossed the Rio Grande and attacked more than 60 U.S. soldiers. Most of the U.S. troops were captured, but 11 were killed and 5 were wounded. The next day, Taylor sent word to Washington that fighting had begun. When Polk heard this news, he asked the U.S. Congress to declare war. Congress acted swiftly, declaring war on Mexico on May 13, 1846. Before word of the declaration of war reached the border, more fighting had broken out. On May 8 and 9, U.S. troops fought General Mariano Arista's advancing forces at Palo Alto and Resaca de la Palma near Fort Brown. Taylor won both battles.

⭐ **Reading Check Analyzing Information** What role did the Rio Grande play in the events that led to the Mexican War?

The Mexican War, 1846–1848

Interpreting Maps After only a few months of fighting, U.S. forces had gained control of much of the territory north of Mexico City.

TAKS Skills

1. Places and Regions What region of Texas saw the most conflict during the Mexican War? ⭐TEKS

2. Drawing Inferences and Conclusions How do you think geographic factors such as mountains, rivers, and gulfs affected the war? ⭐TEKS

★ Texans in the Mexican War

Thousands of volunteers rushed to join the army when the call for war came. In Texas, many people welcomed a chance to fight against their old rival **Antonio López de Santa Anna**. One Texas newspaper editor expressed delight at the coming of war.

 **Texas Voices** ❝There is at last . . . an opportunity to pay off a little of the debt of vengeance [revenge] which has been accumulating [growing] since the massacre of the Alamo. . . . We trust that every man of our army . . . will think of his countrymen martyred [killed for their beliefs] at the Alamo, at Goliad, and at Mier.❞

—Charles DeMorse, quoted in *Documents of Texas History,* edited by Ernest Wallace

Some 6,000 Texans volunteered to fight in the Mexican War. Governor James Pinckney Henderson temporarily left office to serve in the army. Former president of Texas Mirabeau B. Lamar and Texas revolutionary Albert Sidney Johnston also volunteered. However, a few Texans, including Juan Seguín—a veteran of the Texas Revolution—fought for Mexico. Fearing for his safety in Texas, Seguín had fled San Antonio. When he arrived in Mexico, he was forced to fight or be arrested.

Several of the Texas Rangers who joined the U.S. forces during the war served as scouts. As one Ranger claimed, "[we] were . . . the eyes and ears of Taylor's army." Their fame as fighters spread quickly. Several Rangers, including **John S. "Rip" Ford**, **John Coffee Hays**, and Ben McCulloch, were recognized for their leadership and bravery during the war. Some Rangers' actions caused problems, however. At times they refused to follow the orders of U.S. Army officers. Rangers occasionally attacked Mexican villages with little reason, prompting General Taylor to threaten to throw all the Rangers in jail. Many Mexicans feared the Rangers, calling them *los diablos Tejanos*—"the Texas devils."

 Reading Check Evaluating How did Texas Rangers participate in the war?

★ A U.S. Victory

After winning battles in Texas, General Taylor began an **offensive**—a major troop advance—into northern Mexico. The U.S. forces first won an important victory at Monterrey. In 1847 Taylor's troops met a larger Mexican army at Buena Vista. General Santa Anna, in command of the Mexican forces, sent Taylor a note demanding that the U.S. forces surrender. Officer Thomas L. Crittenden replied, "General Taylor never surrenders." After two days of fighting, Santa Anna's forces retreated. The Texas Rangers played key roles at Buena Vista and Monterrey.

In the fall of 1846, U.S. Army general **Winfield Scott** had begun to carry out a new strategy. Under this plan, troops would land at Veracruz and march west to attack Mexico City, the nation's capital. President Polk liked the idea and transferred about 9,000 of Taylor's troops to Scott's command. In March 1847 Scott's force landed on the Mexican coast near Veracruz. From there they moved inland and captured Mexico City by mid-September. After fierce fighting, other U.S. forces took control of California and parts of New Mexico.

The major fighting ended September 14, 1847. On that day, U.S. troops raised the American flag over the National Palace in Mexico City. Of the approximately 116,000 U.S. soldiers who served in the war, nearly 13,000 lost their lives. Most of these soldiers died not in battle but from disease. More than 60 Texans died in battle, and more than 270 Texans died from disease or accidents. The war with Mexico had cost the United States nearly $98 million. In Mexico, countless lives were lost, and much property was destroyed.

Reading Check **Sequencing** List in order the events that led to the U.S. victory in the Mexican War.

★ Section 1 Review ★TEKS Questions 2, 3, 4a, 4b, 5

Homework Practice Online
keyword: ST3 HP16

1 Define and explain:
- offensive

2 Identify and explain:
- Zachary Taylor
- Antonio López de Santa Anna
- John S. "Rip" Ford
- John Coffee Hays
- Winfield Scott

3 Identifying Cause and Effect
Copy the graphic organizer below. Use it to show what problems arose between the United States and Mexico, and what the outcome was.

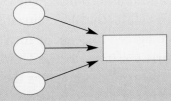

4 Finding the Main Idea
a. What events occurred during the Mexican War that led to the U.S. victory?
b. How did Texans and the Texas Rangers participate in the Mexican War?

5 Writing and Critical Thinking
Supporting a Point of View Write a story from either the Mexican or Texan perspective about the political and military events that led to the Mexican War.

Consider the following:
- the causes of tension
- the U.S. and Mexican troops stationed along the Rio Grande

TAKS

Results of the Mexican War

Read to Discover

1. What were the terms of the Treaty of Guadalupe Hidalgo, and what border issues remained for Texas?
2. How did the Mexican War and the treaty affect Texans and the state?
3. What happened to the population of Texas after the Mexican War?

Identify

- **Nicholas Trist**
- **Treaty of Guadalupe Hidalgo**
- **Mexican Cession**
- **Compromise of 1850**

Why It Matters Today

At the end of the Mexican War, the United States and Mexico signed a peace treaty. Use **CNNfyi.com** or other **current events** sources to learn about recent negotiations and treaties. Record your findings in your journal.

Nicholas Trist's negotiations with Mexican officials resulted in the Treaty of Guadalupe Hidalgo, ending the Mexican War.

The Story Continues

U.S. diplomat Nicholas Trist was in Mexico City trying to work out a peace treaty. But Mexican officials were reluctant to agree to U.S. terms, and the treaty talks dragged on for months. Frustrated with the negotiations, President Polk ordered Trist to return home. With peace in sight, Trist ignored the order. Furious, Polk called Trist a scoundrel!

★ The Treaty of Guadalupe Hidalgo

After the capture of Mexico City, Mexican officials had few options. Mexican officials met with U.S. diplomat **Nicholas Trist** near Mexico City, at the town of Guadalupe Hidalgo. On February 2, 1848, the diplomats signed the **Treaty of Guadalupe Hidalgo**, ending the Mexican War. Mexico's acting president, Manuel de la Peña y Peña, urged his fellow citizens to accept the treaty.

The treaty had several terms. Mexico recognized the annexation of Texas and the Rio Grande as its border. The United States agreed to cover the $3.25 million in claims that U.S. citizens had against the Mexican government. Mexico agreed to cede, or turn over, some 529,000 square miles of its northern territory to the United States for $15 million. Mexicans living in this region, known as the **Mexican Cession**, were to be granted all the rights of U.S. citizenship.

After the Mexican War, a heated debate erupted over slavery in the new U.S. territories. The U.S. Congress was divided. Pro-slavery legislators wanted to allow slavery in the new territories, while antislavery legislators wanted to ban it. Texans claimed that the Rio Grande formed not only their state's southern border but also its western one. Nearly half of present-day New Mexico, including the trading center of Santa Fe, lay east of the Rio Grande. The people in this region, particularly in Santa Fe, rejected the Texas claim. Some may have been angry with Texans for President Lamar's invasion during the early 1840s. In addition, most people in Santa Fe opposed slavery. They had no desire to become part of Texas because it allowed slavery. Pro-slavery members of the U.S. Congress supported the Texas claim. While the U.S. Congress debated, the Texas legislature acted. Early in 1848, it declared the huge disputed region to be Santa Fe County, Texas.

In 1850 Senator Henry Clay came up with a plan to resolve both the border conflict and the issue of slavery in the Texas–New Mexico territories of the Mexican Cession. His plan was called the **Compromise of 1850**. To settle the border conflict, the federal government offered to pay Texas $10 million to give up its claim. The state government needed the money to pay debts, so Texas voters approved the agreement. The U.S. government then established the present-day border between Texas and New Mexico.

U.S. senator Henry Clay urged Congress to reach a compromise on slavery.

Reading Check **Categorizing** List what the United States gained from the Treaty of Guadalupe Hidalgo and what Mexico gained.

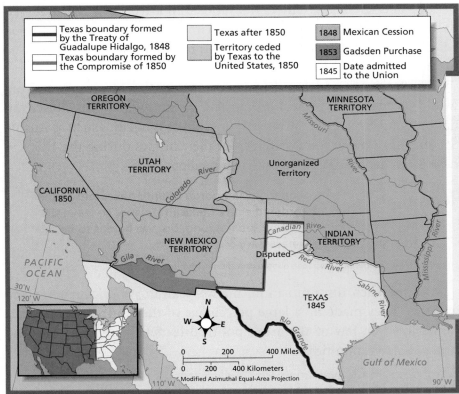

Texas boundary formed by the Treaty of Guadalupe Hidalgo, 1848

Texas boundary formed by the Compromise of 1850

Texas after 1850

Territory ceded by Texas to the United States, 1850

1848 Mexican Cession

1853 Gadsden Purchase

1845 Date admitted to the Union

OREGON TERRITORY

MINNESOTA TERRITORY

Missouri River

UTAH TERRITORY

River

Unorganized Territory

River

CALIFORNIA 1850

Colorado River

NEW MEXICO TERRITORY

Canadian River

INDIAN TERRITORY

Disputed

Red River

Mississippi River

Gila River

PACIFIC OCEAN

30°N

120°W

TEXAS 1845

Sabine River

Rio Grande

N
W E
S

0   200   400 Miles
0   200   400 Kilometers
Modified Azimuthal Equal-Area Projection

110°W

Gulf of Mexico

90°W

New Borders, 1853

Interpreting Maps The United States gained control of most of the Southwest by means of the Treaty of Guadalupe Hidalgo and the Gadsden Purchase.

TAKS Skills

1. Locate What river formed the western boundary of Texas before 1850? TEKS

2. Evaluating How did the Treaty of Guadalupe Hidalgo and the Compromise of 1850 help form the current borders of Texas? TEKS

Immigration. *Originally founded by German immigrants, Indianola was one of several ports of entry for immigrants to Texas. **What in this painting shows how transportation and geography affected immigration to Texas?*** ⭐TEKS

⭐ Tejanos and the War

The Mexican War and the Treaty of Guadalupe Hidalgo greatly affected Tejanos. Since the Texas Revolution, many U.S. settlers in Texas had been suspicious of Tejanos and had questioned their loyalty. As conflicts emerged with Mexico during the 1840s, discrimination against Tejanos increased. During the Mexican War, many Texans viewed Tejanos as enemies. Many Tejanos, fearing that they would lose ownership of their farms and ranches because of the war, sold their property—often at low prices—and left Texas. Others were forced to leave Texas under threats of violence and had their land taken without payment. Many of those who left Texas, particularly those living near the Rio Grande, went to Mexico.

The Treaty of Guadalupe Hidalgo guaranteed that Mexican Americans would receive equal protection under U.S. law. Nonetheless, discrimination against Tejanos continued. Some Tejanos in cities such as Austin, Seguin, and Uvalde were driven from their homes during the 1850s. A newspaper article described one such incident.

Analyzing Primary Sources
Identifying Bias What is the article's bias, and what words show the author's position?

Texas Voices 66The people of Matagorda County have held a meeting and ordered every Mexican [Tejano] to leave the county. To strangers this may seem wrong, but we hold it to be perfectly right, and highly necessary.99

—Matagorda newspaper, quoted in *A Journey through Texas,* by Frederick Law Olmsted

Despite such discrimination, many Mexican Americans remained in Texas. They made up a large percentage of the South Texas population. However, few of the area's political leaders were from Mexican American communities.

⭐ **Reading Check Evaluating** How did events during and after the Mexican War affect Tejanos?

New Migration to Texas

After the Mexican War, the state's population increased from 212,592 in 1850 to 604,215 by 1860. As in the past, most new Texans were farmers from the southern United States. Many of them brought slaves when they came. As a result, the African American population in Texas rose as well, from more than 58,000 in 1850 to 183,000 in 1860. However, fewer than 800 free African Americans lived in Texas during this time. The Texas population also included more than 12,000 Mexican Americans, who primarily lived in the southern region of the state.

Many Europeans came to Texas to escape hardships. Crop failures had left people starving in Ireland and parts of central and northern Europe. In addition, a series of revolutions in 1848 pushed many Europeans from their homelands. With a population of more than 20,000 in 1860, Germans were the largest European immigrant group in Texas.

Land agents such as Frenchman Victor Considerant brought groups of Europeans to Texas. Considerant established La Réunion, a colony of about 350 settlers in North Texas near the Trinity River. Other Europeans came to Central Texas. In 1854, Polish colonists founded Panna Maria in Karnes County. Czech immigrants settled at Cat Spring, Fayetteville, and Praha. Slavic settlers known as Wends also came to Central Texas. These settlements extended the line of the frontier westward. Hundreds of Jewish immigrants settled in cities such as Galveston, Houston, and San Antonio. The first Norwegian settlement in Texas was at Normandy, near Brownsboro. Immigrants from Italy, the Netherlands, and Belgium also arrived. Each group brought its traditional foods, celebrations, and architecture to Texas. The influence of these various cultural traditions spread across the state.

Reading Check **Analyzing Information** Why did immigrant groups come to Texas, and where did they settle?

Our Cultural Heritage

German Culture in the Hill Country

Several towns in the Hill Country show many traces of their German heritage. German architecture called *Fachwerk*—part timber and part stone—can be seen in many buildings. German food is popular throughout the state. In addition, the barbecue that many Texans enjoy originated in the smokehouses of early German settlers. Texans have adopted these and other German traditions as their own. **How has the culture of German immigrants influenced Texas?** TEKS

An old German stone house

go.hrw.com **Homework Practice Online** keyword: ST3 HP16

Section 2 Review

TEKS Questions 1, 2, 3a, 3b, 4

1 **Identify and explain:**
- Nicholas Trist
- Treaty of Guadalupe Hidalgo
- Mexican Cession
- Compromise of 1850

2 **Summarizing**
Copy the graphic organizer below. Use it to describe the Treaty of Guadalupe Hidalgo and its effects on the border of Texas.

Treaty

↓

New Borders → Effects on Texas

3 **Finding the Main Idea**
a. How did the Compromise of 1850 affect the borders of Texas?
b. How did immigration and migration to Texas after the Mexican War affect the state?

4 **Writing and Critical Thinking**
Identifying Cause and Effect Imagine that you are a Tejano in the 1850s. Write a diary entry describing how life in your community has changed since the war.
Consider the following:
- why a large number of Tejanos left Texas
- the changing population distribution

The Texas Rangers and American Indians

Read to Discover

1. How did Texas Rangers help shape events in Texas?
2. How did continued westward expansion affect the lives of American Indians and Texans?
3. How effective was the reservation system?

Define
• reservations

Identify
• Robert S. Neighbors
• Alabama-Coushatta

Why It Matters Today

Conflicts between American Indians and settlers erupted as more settlers moved west. Use CNNfyi.com or other **current events** sources to learn about ongoing conflicts over land today. Record your findings in your journal.

Without a set uniform, most Texas Rangers wore shirts and gloves similar to those of cowboys and western settlers.

The Story Continues

Texas Ranger Jack Hays wanted a road to be built from San Antonio to El Paso. To prove that the journey could be made safely, in 1848 Hays led an expedition with 71 people, including Rangers and American Indian scouts. The journey was tough. The Rangers had trouble finding water and food in this dry region of West Texas. The men even had to kill some of their horses for food. Finally, the expedition turned back for San Antonio.

★ Conflicts on the Frontier

During the 1850s, hundreds of new settlers moved westward into Texas. A newspaper reported, "For the last two weeks scarcely a day has passed that a dozen or more movers' wagons have not passed through our town." Many of these settlers moved onto the lands of American Indians, creating conflicts. As fighting erupted, frontier settlers asked the government for protection.

Once Texas had become a state, the federal government was responsible for solving conflicts with American Indians within the state. This task was difficult, partly because the state controlled all the public land that Indians claimed. Texas policies encouraged settlers to move west and did not recognize American Indians' land rights. At the time, the U.S. policy was to place troops along the frontier to guard settlements and keep settlers from moving farther west onto Indian lands. U.S. troops had difficulty fulfilling their task, however. Most troops sent to the frontier were infantry, or foot soldiers. They were no match for the Comanche and Kiowa, who were expert horse riders.

Texas governor George T. Wood called out the Texas Rangers to help. The Rangers had horses and could cover land as quickly as the Comanche and Kiowa did. In addition, the Rangers had the Colt six-shooter, a powerful new weapon that could fire six shots in a row. It gave the Rangers a great advantage in frontier warfare. The Rangers were so effective that the federal government agreed to pay them to guard the Texas frontier. Captain John S. "Rip" Ford and his Rangers established a camp east of Laredo, where they fought several battles with the Comanche. The Rangers patrolled the frontier throughout the 1850s.

Reading Check **Finding the Main Idea** What role did Texas Rangers play in shaping the Texas frontier?

★ Establishing Frontier Forts

While the Rangers fought on the open plains, the federal government tried to protect settlers by building forts. By 1849 a line of eight forts stretched from the Rio Grande to the Trinity River. Fort Duncan, near Eagle Pass, stood farthest to the south, while Fort Martin Scott protected the German settlers in Fredericksburg. To the north, Fort Worth guarded the banks of the Trinity River. In Medina County, Fort Lincoln was built on a high bank of Seco Creek. These forts protected not only settlers but also travel routes, which had become busier since the discovery of gold

Interpreting the Visual Record

Frontier settlement. *This painting by Charles M. Russell shows a farmer about to plow his new homestead as an American Indian approaches.* **Why do you think this farmer carried a gun while working on his farm?** TEKS

in California in 1848. The travelers and settlers altered American Indian life, as one Texas Indian explained.

Analyzing Primary Sources
Drawing Inferences and Conclusions How were Texas Indians affected by westward expansion?

Texas Voices

"The white man comes and cuts down the trees, building houses and fences and the buffaloes get frightened and leave and never come back, and the Indians are left to starve."

—Muguara, *The Evolution of a State, or Recollections of Old Texas Days,* by Noah Smithwick

Settlers soon established homesteads west of the original line of forts. The army abandoned those forts and built a new line of forts farther west. To the north, the army built Fort Belknap along the Brazos River. In the south, it built Fort Clark to protect people traveling from San Antonio to El Paso. The army built another line of forts across West Texas during the 1850s. These forts included Fort Lancaster and Fort Davis, which helped protect Texans from Mexican and American Indian attacks.

The line of forts did not stop conflicts between Texans and American Indians, however. The forts were too far apart to protect settlers or prevent them from moving west. The forts had too few troops and were often short on supplies.

Reading Check **Identifying Cause and Effect** How did settlement patterns change in the 1850s, and how did these changes lead to conflicts?

Texas Cities

Fort Worth

History: When the U.S. Army abandoned Fort Worth in 1853, settlers quickly moved to the area. During the 1870s, Fort Worth became a popular stopover for cowboys on cattle drives.

Population in 2000: 534,694

Relative location: In north-central Texas, 33 miles west of Dallas

Region: Grand Prairie subregion of the Central Plains

County: County seat of Tarrant County

Special feature: Known as Cowtown and Where the West Begins because of its ties to cattle trails

Origin of name: Originally an army post named for General William Jenkins Worth, who served in the Mexican War

Economy: Fort Worth's economy relies on meatpacking plants, petroleum production, and manufacturing, including aviation and electronics.

★ The Reservation Policy

As a result of continuing conflicts on the Texas frontier, the federal government worked with the state to create a new policy. The U.S. government planned to move the Texas Indians onto **reservations**—limited areas of land reserved for American Indians. The federal government would manage the reservations, while Texas would maintain ownership of the land.

In the 1850s Texas received federal aid and set aside thousands of acres of land for reservations. In 1854 the U.S. Army opened the Brazos Indian Reservation just south of Fort Belknap. About 2,000 American Indians, including Caddo, Tonkawa, and Waco, settled on the reservation. These Indians used part of their land for farming, receiving $80,000 worth of supplies and cattle a year from the federal government. Some 40 miles from the Brazos Indian Reservation, officials created another reservation. About 450 Penateka Comanche

CONNECTING TO
THE ARTS

Friedrich Petri

German immigrant Friedrich Richard Petri became friendly with American Indians who lived near Fredericksburg. Petri was one of the first artists to portray Texas Indians in paintings. **How does this painting portray the American Indians of the Texas plains?**

settled on this Comanche Indian Reservation. Government agents taught the Comanche, who were traditionally hunters, how to farm. But the Comanche did not have much luck. Drought in the mid-1850s made growing crops very difficult. The reservations did not attract many American Indians. A planned third reservation for the Lipan Apache failed when the Apache refused to move onto the land.

Many Plains Indians continued to live outside the reservation system. Most Indians wanted to maintain their traditional way of life, hunting and following the buffalo herds. Settlers, on the other hand, wanted to build farms and homes. They refused to recognize American Indians' right to their hunting grounds. As a result, violence continued on the Texas frontier.

Reading Check Analyzing Information What problems did the reservation system have?

★ The Removal of Texas Indians

The creation of reservations did not end conflicts in Texas. A Comanche leader recalled the Comanches' experiences.

 Texas Voices ❝Many years ago we lived in Texas where the government opened farms and supplied us with cattle and other domestic animals which prospered and made us happy for a while, but the citizens of that county soon said, the Comanches are bad, and drove us from these homes. . . . There we had a school like you, at which twenty-five of our children attended; we have none of these now and my heart is weak.❞

—Tokaway, quoted in *Indian Affairs and the Frontier of Texas, 1865–1880,*
by Bruce Logan Parker

Military Bases

During the mid-1800s the U.S. government built forts across West Texas. Today most of these forts are crumbling ruins. Fort Bliss, however, remains an active military post. First established in 1854, the fort has been relocated several times. During the 1990s more than 20,000 soldiers were stationed on the base, which houses an airfield and a hospital. **How do you think the purposes and uses of Texas forts have changed over the years?**

Today Fort Bliss is located near El Paso.

Settlers living near reservations often claimed that American Indians stole horses and cattle. Angry Texans formed armed groups to patrol the reservation boundaries. They sometimes killed Indians found off the reservations.

During the late 1850s some Texans began calling for an end to the reservation system. Settlers wanted American Indians totally removed from the state, and the federal government agreed. By 1859 the Indians living on the Brazos and Comanche Indian Reservations had been removed to Indian Territory in what is now Oklahoma. The removal of American Indians angered some Texans. Federal Indian agent **Robert S. Neighbors** had hoped that Indians on reservations would be treated fairly. Disappointed with the policy of removal, Neighbors helped the Indians in their difficult move. After returning to Texas, Neighbors was murdered by an angry Texan at Fort Belknap.

Texas recognized the right of one American Indian group to remain in the state—the **Alabama-Coushatta**. This small group was made up of the Alabama and Coushatta, who had moved from Louisiana into Texas in the late 1700s. During the Runaway Scrape, the Alabama-Coushatta aided settlers fleeing east. Because of this service during the Texas Revolution, many Texans were friendly to the Alabama-Coushatta. In 1854 Texas granted the Alabama-Coushatta 1,280 acres of land in Polk County. The federal government added more than 3,000 additional acres to the reservation in 1928. Today the Alabama-Coushatta Reservation, the Tigua Reservation near El Paso, and the Kickapoo Reservation near Eagle Pass are the only Indian reservations in Texas.

 Reading Check Evaluating How effective were U.S. policies in easing conflicts between Texans and American Indians? How did the policies affect Indian life?

★ **Section 3 Review** ★TEKS Questions 2, 3, 4a, 4b, 5

go.hrw.com **Homework Practice Online**
keyword: ST3 HP16

1 **Define and explain:**
- reservations

2 **Identify and explain:**
- Robert S. Neighbors
- Alabama-Coushatta

3 **Evaluating**
Copy the graphic organizer below. Use it to analyze the success or failure of the different frontier policies listed.

Policy/ Action	How Successful Was It?
Rangers	
Forts	
Reservations	

4 **Finding the Main Idea**
a. How did the Texas Rangers change life on the Texas frontier?
b. How did westward expansion affect American Indians in Texas?

5 **Writing and Critical Thinking**
Identifying Points of View Imagine that you are trying to resolve a conflict between U.S. settlers and American Indians in Texas. Write a letter that defines the issues and offers a solution to the conflict.
Consider the following:
- the westward expansion of U.S. settlers
- Texas Indians' views of U.S. settlers and opinions about reservation life

The Texas Frontier

As new settlers poured into Texas from elsewhere in the United States and Europe, the boundary of westward settlement moved farther west. New lines of forts were established to guard farms and settlements on the frontier.

Geography Skills

Interpreting Thematic Maps ⭐TEKS

1. What relationship exists between the line of the frontier and the location of forts?

2. Approximately how much farther from Houston was Fort Bliss than Fort Graham?

Military Posts and Indian Reservations in Texas, 1846–1860

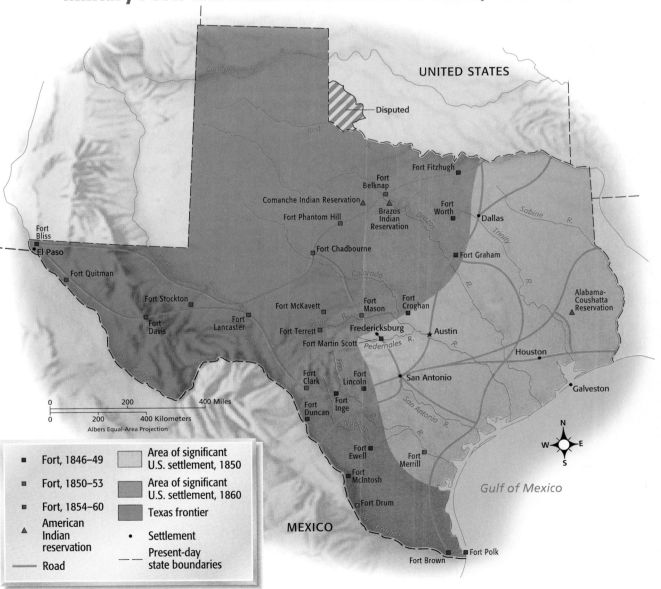

UNITED STATES

Disputed

Fort Fitzhugh
Fort Belknap
Comanche Indian Reservation
Fort Worth
Fort Phantom Hill
Brazos Indian Reservation
Dallas
Fort Chadbourne
Fort Graham
Colorado
Fort Bliss
El Paso
Fort Quitman
Fort Stockton
Fort McKavett
Fort Mason
Fort Croghan
Alabama-Coushatta Reservation
Fort Davis
Fort Lancaster
Fort Terrett
Fredericksburg
Austin
Fort Martin Scott
Pedernales R.
Houston
Fort Clark
Fort Lincoln
San Antonio
Fort Duncan
Fort Inge
Galveston
Fort Ewell
Fort Merrill
Gulf of Mexico
Fort McIntosh
Fort Drum
MEXICO
Fort Brown
Fort Polk

0   200   400 Miles
0   200   400 Kilometers
Albers Equal-Area Projection

Legend:
- Fort, 1846–49
- Fort, 1850–53
- Fort, 1854–60
- ▲ American Indian reservation
- — Road
- Area of significant U.S. settlement, 1850
- Area of significant U.S. settlement, 1860
- Texas frontier
- • Settlement
- – – Present-day state boundaries

The Chapter at a Glance

Examine the following visual summary of the chapter. Then use the visual to create a thematic cause-and-effect map of the expansion of the frontier.

The Mexican War

Growing conflict between the United States and Mexico led to war. Many Texans volunteered to fight, including the Texas Rangers.

The Results of the War

After the Mexican War and the signing of the Treaty of Guadalupe Hidalgo, new settlers from the United States and Europe came to Texas.

Texas Rangers and Indian Conflicts

As settlers moved to the Texas frontier, conflicts with American Indians increased. Officials used the Texas Rangers and a system of forts and reservations to try to stop the conflicts.

Identifying People and Ideas TEKS

Use the following terms or people in historically significant sentences.

1. John Coffee Hays
2. offensive
3. Winfield Scott
4. Nicholas Trist
5. Treaty of Guadalupe Hidalgo
6. Mexican Cession
7. Compromise of 1850
8. reservations
9. Robert S. Neighbors
10. Alabama-Coushatta

Understanding Main Ideas TEKS

Section 1 (pp. 330–333)

1. How did the annexation of Texas and fears of U.S. expansion lead to war with Mexico?
2. What contributions did Texans make during the Mexican War?

Section 2 (pp. 334–337)

3. What did Mexico cede to the United States in the Treaty of Guadalupe Hidalgo?
4. Who were some of the immigrant groups who came to Texas?

Section 3 (pp. 338–342)

5. What role did the Texas Rangers play on the Texas frontier?
6. What problems did the reservation system have, and how did this affect Texas?

You Be the Historian TEKS

Reviewing Themes

1. **Global Relations** How did a border dispute lead to war between the United States and Mexico?
2. **Citizenship** How were Tejanos' rights limited during and after the Mexican War?
3. **Geography** How did expansion of settlements on the frontier affect the region's landscape and the lives of American Indians?

 TEKS

TAKS Practice: **Thinking Critically**

1. **Analyzing Information** How did new immigration affect the population distribution of Texas in the 1850s?
2. **Drawing Inferences and Conclusions** Why do you think government officials agreed to remove American Indians from Texas?
3. **Summarizing** How did westward expansion lead Texans into conflicts with both Mexicans and American Indians?

Interpreting Political Cartoons ⭐TEKS

Study the political cartoon below. Then use the information to help you answer the questions that follow.

The Granger Collection, New York

PLUCKED

THE MEXICAN EAGLE BEFORE THE WAR!　THE MEXICAN EAGLE AFTER THE WAR!

1. Which of the following statements best describes the cartoonist's view of the effects of the Mexican War on Mexico?
   a. Mexico was humiliated.
   b. Mexico was the same as before the war.
   c. Mexico was in some ways stronger than it was before the war.
   d. Mexico was disorganized.

2. Which country do you think the cartoonist supported during the war? What, if any, biases do you see reflected in the cartoon?

Analyzing Primary Sources ⭐TEKS

Read the following quote by historian K. Jack Bauer about a battle that was fought during the Mexican War. Then answer the questions that follow.

"After two hours of fighting and the loss of 116 men killed, 665 wounded . . . [General] Worth held the mill. . . . The irony of the attack became clear when a search of the building produced only a few gun molds. . . . By one o'clock in the afternoon the American troops were back in their old positions. All that [General] Scott had to show for the casualties was 685 prisoners, fifty-three of them officers, and three additional trophy guns. . . . Perhaps 2,000 Mexican soldiers had been killed or wounded. Colonel Hitchcock spoke the truth when he called it a pyrrhic [worthless] victory."

3. Which of the following statements best describes the author's point of view about the battle?
   a. A victory at any cost is worthwhile.
   b. The loss of life in battle is almost never fruitless.
   c. War is exciting.
   d. War often results in many deaths for only the smallest gains.

4. How do you think the author's view of warfare might have influenced the way he reported the facts of the battle?

Alternative Assessment

Interdisciplinary Connection to Literature ⭐TEKS

Imagine that you are a Texas Indian who has moved to a reservation in 1854. Write a poem that expresses the changes that you and your family have experienced. Use information about the expansion of U.S. settlement, reservations, and the removal of Indians discussed in this chapter. Create an illustration to accompany the poem. You may want to refer to Chapter 4 for more information on Texas Indians.

BUILDING YOUR Portfolio

🖥 internet connect

Internet Activity: go.hrw.com
KEYWORD: ST3 TX16 ⭐TEKS

Access the Internet through the HRW Go site to research the history of the Texas Rangers or the history of the Mexican War. Take note of information about the authors of the sources you find and the language they use to evaluate the validity of the sources. Then create a political cartoon that refers to an event from your research. On a separate sheet of paper, write an explanation of your cartoon.

Life in a Frontier State
(1845–1861)

John O. Meusebach met with a group of Comanche chiefs in 1847. The meeting resulted in a treaty that allowed some German immigrants to settle in Comanche territory.

TEXAS

1846 Texas signs a peace treaty with the Penateka Comanche.

1847 A state census reports the state's population at more than 142,000.

1850 In her book *Texas in 1850,* Melinda Rankin describes the state and urges people to move to Texas.

1845	**1847**	**1849**	**1851**

U.S. and WORLD

1846 The Smithsonian Institution is established.

1848 Gold is discovered in California.

1852 *Uncle Tom's Cabin,* a novel that criticizes slavery, is published and sells 300,000 copies in the United States alone in its first year in print.

The California Gold Rush began after gold was discovered at Sutter's Mill.

Build on What You Know

Texas was a frontier state in the 1840s and 1850s. Settlers in Texas faced many challenges, but changes and improvements were occurring rapidly. Despite the difficulties, settlers continued to move to Texas. Many settlers brought slaves with them.

of 8,235. Other large towns included Houston, Jefferson, Marshall, Nacogdoches, and New Braunfels. Even though it was the state capital, Austin had fewer than 1,000 residents when Texas became a state.

Merchants in the towns provided farmers and ranchers with goods. Blacksmiths, masons, carpenters, and saddle and wagon makers also stayed busy. Other services included hotels and laundry businesses. Texas towns had numerous professionals, including doctors, lawyers, ministers, and teachers. Doctors faced many challenges, as one Texan recalled.

Texas Voices **"Injuries, deaths, and murders were to be expected by the frontiersman but, nevertheless, they always came as a shock. . . . Medicine and surgery were crude. It was my lot to help hold some patients for the doctor when he was amputating limbs without anesthetic [pain-killing drug]."**

—James Buckner Barry, quoted in *Scalpels and Sabers*, by Sylvia Van Voast Ferris and Eleanor Sellers Hoppe

Analyzing Primary Sources
Drawing Inferences and Conclusions Why does Barry say that "medicine and surgery were crude"?

Industry was only a small part of the Texas economy. As in the rest of the South, planters in Texas preferred to invest in land and slaves. Most local industries were family-owned and related to the agricultural economy. Flour milling was the largest industry in Texas. Most towns had **gristmills**—machines for grinding grain into meal or flour. Cotton gins were also common, while **tanneries** were built to prepare animal hides. In lumber-rich East Texas, there were a number of sawmills.

In an agricultural society like Texas, cash was scarce. Most people grew or made at home much of what they needed. Demand was low for **manufactured products**—items made either by hand or machine in large numbers for sale. Most manufactured items came from out of state.

Gristmills, like this one in Castroville, ground grains for local residents.

★ **Reading Check** **Identifying Cause and Effect** What was the basis of the Texas economy, and how did that affect Texas industry?

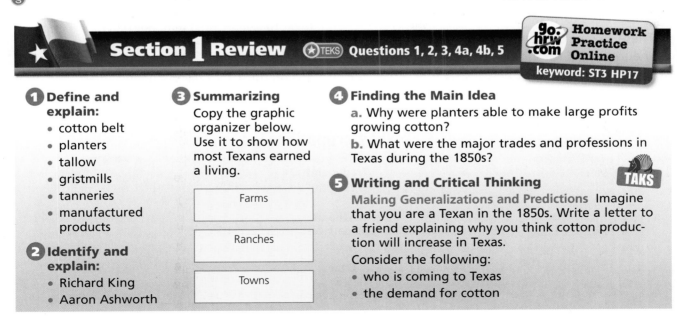

Section 1 Review ★TEKS Questions 1, 2, 3, 4a, 4b, 5

go.hrw.com **Homework Practice Online**
keyword: ST3 HP17

1 Define and explain:
- cotton belt
- planters
- tallow
- gristmills
- tanneries
- manufactured products

2 Identify and explain:
- Richard King
- Aaron Ashworth

3 Summarizing
Copy the graphic organizer below. Use it to show how most Texans earned a living.

| Farms |
| Ranches |
| Towns |

4 Finding the Main Idea
a. Why were planters able to make large profits growing cotton?
b. What were the major trades and professions in Texas during the 1850s?

5 Writing and Critical Thinking
Making Generalizations and Predictions Imagine that you are a Texan in the 1850s. Write a letter to a friend explaining why you think cotton production will increase in Texas.
Consider the following:
- who is coming to Texas
- the demand for cotton

Life in a Frontier State **351**

Economics

Free Enterprise

Many people moved to Texas in the 1850s hoping to earn a good living. Economic freedom in the United States meant that Texans had the right to exchange goods as they saw fit. They could decide what to produce, how to produce it, how much, and for whom. In the free enterprise system, government regulation is kept to a minimum and competition flourishes.

The right to private property was also important to many Texans. Owning land and growing a cash crop such as cotton was often the best way to make a profit. Demand for cotton had increased rapidly in the 1850s. Cotton prices rose when demand was greater than supply. Many farmers who supplied cotton profited from these high prices. The profit motive— or the desire to make a profit— is key to the free enterprise system. Other Texans saw opportunities in towns. Merchants profited by selling agricultural supplies. Tradespeople and professionals, including blacksmiths, lawyers, and doctors, provided services to Texans.

These Texans displayed the great entrepreneurial spirit for which the state is still known today. The chart below lists the occupations of Texans in 1850 and 1860.

Texans buy goods from a variety of sources— from small farmers' markets to large retail stores and over the Internet.

Understanding What You Read ⊛TEKS

1. Economics and History Analyze the impact of the free enterprise system, such as supply and demand, regulation, and profit motive, on the development of the Texas economy.

2. Economics and You How do businesses in your community participate in the free enterprise system?

Interpreting Charts

1. What occupational groups increased in Texas between 1850 and 1860? Which groups decreased?

2. How did Texans earn a living in 1850? How do you think that has changed today?

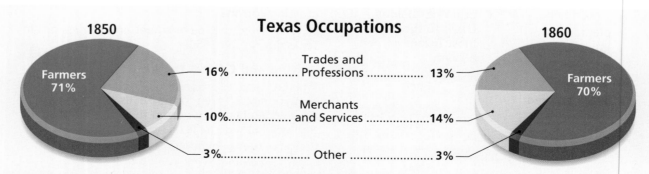

Texas Occupations

1850

Farmers 71%

1860

Farmers 70%

Trades and Professions .... 16% 13%

Merchants and Services .... 10% 14%

Other .... 3% 3%

Sources: Randolph Campbell, *An Empire for Slavery 1821–1865* and Richard Lowe and Randolph Campbell, *Planters and Plain Folk*

Transportation

Read to Discover

1. What geographic factors affected Texans' ability to sell what they produced?
2. What were some advantages and disadvantages of stagecoaches, steamboats, and railroads?

Why It Matters Today

Texans in the 1800s worked to improve transportation. Use **CNNfyi.com** or other **current events** sources to learn about modern advances in automobiles or other forms of transportation. Record your findings in your journal.

Define

- internal improvements

Identify

- Buffalo Bayou, Brazos, and Colorado Railway

The Story Continues

The U.S. Army wanted animals that could survive better than horses or mules in the dry climate of West Texas. In the 1850s the army experimented by bringing over 33 camels from Africa. A Texas boy remembered what happened the first time his horse saw a camel. "When my horse saw one of those things, he ran away with me. I just could not hold him." The camels were never used widely, and eventually the army sold some of them to freight companies.

Some army officials thought that camels would be well suited to the dry climate of the Texas frontier.

★ Stagecoach and Freight Lines

Transportation in early Texas was often slow. Most Texas roads turned to mud during wet weather and were little better than in the days of Spanish control. The lack of a good transportation system slowed the state's economic growth. Texans called for **internal improvements**, or advances in the state's transportation network.

Stagecoaches carried passengers and mail between Texas towns. Travel by stagecoach was often difficult and dangerous. Rugged or muddy roads were hard on both coaches and their travelers. Passengers could expect to help repair broken wheels, fight bandits, or push the coach through a stream. In the 1850s coaches improved, and stagecoach lines increased. A typical stagecoach could carry as many as nine

passengers inside and a few more outside. Four or six horses pulled the coaches. Stagecoach lines included routes between Houston and Austin, Houston and San Antonio, and San Antonio and Indianola.

In 1858 the Butterfield Overland Mail company began service in Texas. The line ran from St. Louis, through Texas, and on to San Francisco. Butterfield stagecoaches ran twice weekly, providing fast, reliable mail service to California. Butterfield's mail contract required them to make the 2,700-mile journey in 25 days. The trip cost $150 plus meals—about a year's wages for many Texans. The company built stations every 20 miles along the route, stocking them with fresh mules and water. U.S. troops at various forts provided protection, but travel could still be dangerous, as one customer noted. "The Comanches regard our soldiers much as they would a company of children armed with pop-guns and penny whistles."

The stagecoaches were not large enough to move heavy freight such as food products, dry goods, and the farm supplies Texans needed. To transport such goods, Texans used freight wagons—heavy wagons with iron axles and large wheels. Teams of 10 to 20 horses, mules, or oxen pulled these wagons. Most freight companies were located in Gulf Coast towns. Much of the state's goods were moved through Houston and Galveston. From Galveston, export goods could be shipped by water to ports outside the state. Mexican Americans played an important role in the freight business, particularly in San Antonio and South Texas.

⭐ **Reading Check** **Drawing Inferences and Conclusions** How did the vast distances and difficult terrain in Texas affect the state's economy?

Interpreting the Visual Record

*Steamboats. Although steamboats provided an alternative to wagon transportation, river travel in Texas was limited. **What benefits of steamboat transportation can you see in this image?*** ⭐TEKS

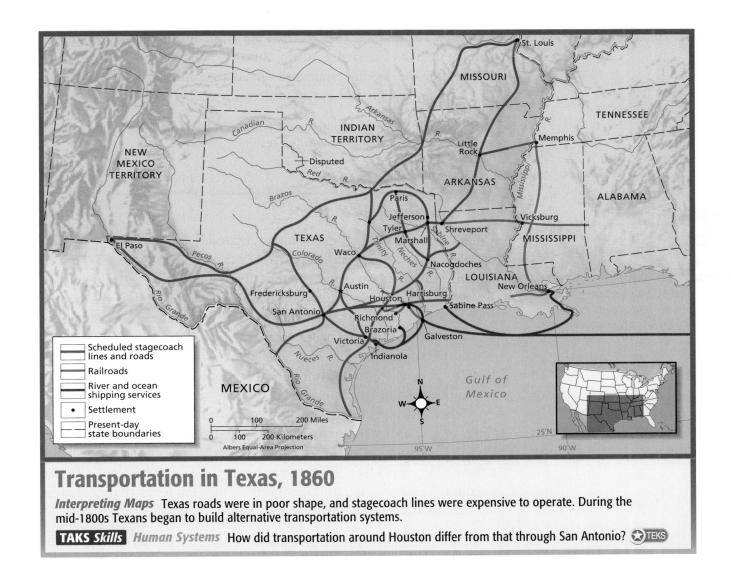

Transportation in Texas, 1860

Interpreting Maps Texas roads were in poor shape, and stagecoach lines were expensive to operate. During the mid-1800s Texans began to build alternative transportation systems.

TAKS Skills *Human Systems* How did transportation around Houston differ from that through San Antonio? ⭐TEKS

⭐ Steamboats

Freight wagons were unreliable and could not keep up with the state's transportation needs. Muddy roads often brought wagons to a stand-still. So Texans tried to use the state's rivers to transport goods. Steamboats could travel safely 250 miles up the Brazos River as far as Washington-on-the-Brazos. In northeastern Texas, steamboats were loaded with cotton at Jefferson. The boats traveled along Big Cypress Bayou to Caddo Lake. They then moved into the Red River and down the Mississippi River to New Orleans. When rainfall was plentiful, boats loaded with cotton could travel the Neches, Sabine, and Trinity Rivers.

Houston became a transportation center and the state's third-largest city. On Buffalo Bayou, steamboats carried goods, particularly cotton, from Houston to the busy port of Galveston. From there the goods were loaded onto larger ships for the trip to New Orleans, then the South's busiest port.

A few steamboats, such as the *Kate Ward* and the *Colorado Ranger*, had some luck in reaching Austin. But the shallowness of the Colorado River made the trip uncertain and even dangerous. Regular river service to Austin and much of the state's interior was never established.

⭐ **Reading Check** **Identifying Cause and Effect** Why did Texans use rivers for transportation, and what was the result?

Hand-powered carts were occasionally used as transportation on early rail lines.

⭐ Railroads

Unlike other forms of transportation, railroads could carry heavy loads even in bad weather. But they were very expensive to build, and Texans had difficulty financing them. Finally, in 1851 the **Buffalo Bayou, Brazos, and Colorado Railway** began construction on the first railroad line in Texas. Commonly called the Harrisburg Railroad, it charged five cents per mile for passengers. It charged one cent per mile for each 100 pounds of freight. By 1856 the line ran 32 miles from Harrisburg on Buffalo Bayou to Richmond on the Brazos River. The link soon expanded nearly 80 miles westward to the Colorado River.

Other railroads built lines in the Houston area during the 1850s. Lines also connected Victoria with Port Lavaca, and Marshall with Caddo Lake. Railroads boosted the economy by moving crops and other goods more quickly. The state gave grants of land to companies to encourage railroad construction. Even so, by 1860 fewer than 500 miles of railroad lines existed in Texas.

⭐ **Reading Check** **Analyzing Information** What benefits did railroad technology offer over other means of transportation?

⭐ **Section 2 Review** ⭐TEKS **Questions 3, 4a, 4b, 5**

go.hrw.com **Homework Practice Online**
keyword: ST3 HP17

1 **Define and explain:**
- internal improvements

2 **Identify and explain:**
- Buffalo Bayou, Brazos, and Colorado Railway

3 **Categorizing**
Copy the graphic organizer below. Use it to list the advantages and disadvantages of moving people and goods by stagecoach, steamboat, and railroad.

4 **Finding the Main Idea**
a. How did geographic factors affect the economic development of Texas?
b. How did the locations of Galveston and Houston affect their growth?

5 **Writing and Critical Thinking** TAKS
Supporting a Point of View Imagine that you are a Texas farmer in the 1850s. Write a newspaper editorial urging Texans to support or oppose railroad construction in the state.
Consider the following:
- a railroad's ability to carry heavy loads, even in bad weather
- the state's enormous potential for cotton production

Social and Cultural Institutions

Read to Discover
1. What were schools and churches like during early statehood?
2. What role did newspapers and the arts play in Texas?

Why It Matters Today

The arts were important to many Texans on the frontier. Use **CNN fyi.com** or other **current events** sources to learn about a writer or artist today. Record your findings in your journal.

Define
- telegraphs

Identify
- *Telegraph and Texas Register*
- Gail Borden Jr.
- Swante Palm

The Story Continues

The Cobb sisters of Galveston were determined to keep their school open. But starting and running a school in the young state was a challenge, even in an established town such as Galveston. The two teachers struggled throughout the 1850s to find enough money to keep the school's doors open. The local newspaper, the *Galveston News,* tried to help. The newspaper pleaded with the local community to support the school. "Will Galveston lose another school?" the newspaper asked.

School bells were used to call students to class in early Texas schools.

★ Frontier Schools and Churches

With Governor Elisha M. Pease's support, the state legislature set aside $2 million as a school fund in 1854. However, much of this money ended up being used for other purposes. For example, school funds were loaned out to support railroad construction in the state. As a result, there was little state money to build schoolhouses and pay teachers.

Towns like San Antonio and some German communities did build schools. One-room, log-cabin schools were common in rural areas where timber was available. Benches and desks, also cut from logs, rested on dirt floors. Some schools were built without windows and were lit by sunlight that came through the large gaps between logs. On

Some early Texas churches were simple buildings, such as this one in Castroville.

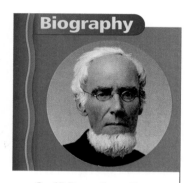
dark winter days, children did their lessons by the light of torches and lanterns. One student recalled the conditions of early schools in Texas. "Our seats . . . were long, two-foot-by-twelve-foot boards placed on top of two rocks. . . . We used our knees for desks to do our writing. In spite of all our handicaps . . . my school days were golden to me."

Schools combined strict discipline with a broad course of study. Even in the early grades, some schools taught students ancient world history and languages such as Latin and Greek. Eventually, more students took time off from farmwork to attend school. Students often found school a welcome relief from the never-ending work at home.

Churches also founded many schools and colleges in Texas. Baylor University was opened by the Baptist Church in 1845, and Austin College was organized in 1849 by the Presbyterian Church. In 1851 the Catholic Church in San Antonio founded the Ursuline Academy for girls. Churches also opened libraries, which made books—generally scarce on the frontier—available to Texans. Church membership grew as the state's population expanded in the 1850s. Churches provided spiritual and moral guidance and brought a social aspect to the often isolated lives of rural Texans. Several denominations stayed in touch with members by publishing newspapers. The *Texas Baptist,* the *Texas Presbyterian,* and the *Texas Catholic* kept members informed of church events.

Reading Check **Summarizing** How did schools and churches reflect aspects of life in Texas?

★ Newspapers

For a frontier region, Texas had a large number of newspapers—growing from 36 in 1852 to more than 80 in 1860. The **Telegraph and Texas Register**, first published in 1835, had the largest circulation of any Texas newspaper. Published in Houston, the newspaper was founded by **Gail Borden Jr.** and two other men. Other well-known papers were the *Galveston News,* the *Austin State Gazette,* and the *Dallas Herald.* Spanish-language newspapers were published in San Antonio and Brownsville. German newspapers, such as Galveston's *Zeitung,* also appeared. Most Texas newspapers were published only once or twice a week. They contained public notices, editorials, literary features, and information about local events.

Newspapers began carrying more national and world news in the 1850s after the first **telegraphs** were introduced. The telegraph allowed people to communicate across vast distances by sending coded signals over wires. In 1854 a telegraph line—strung from treetop to treetop—connected Galveston, Houston, Marshall, and several other towns. Texans could now receive news faster than ever.

Reading Check **Drawing Inferences and Conclusions** Why do you think that two major newspapers were based in Galveston and Houston?

★ Literature and Art

Texans also gathered information from libraries. Between 1850 and 1860 the number of libraries in the state rose from 12 to 132. **Swante Palm**, a Swedish settler in Austin, owned a large book collection. He later gave his books to the University of Texas.

Although books were scarce in Texas, most families had a Bible or a McGuffey's *Reader* to teach their children to read. Families also read local authors. Thomas Mayne Reid wrote about Texas legends in the *Headless Horseman.* Jane McManus Cazneau published the novel *Eagle Pass,* which described life on the Rio Grande. In this excerpt, the main character describes her first view of Texas.

Courtesy of Witte Museum, San Antonio, Texas

 Texas Voices ❝I landed in March, in Texas, and . . . was led captive by the fresh and verdant [green] beauty of the coast region. . . . Already green and laughing spring was holding her revels on a carpet of flowers in the bright sunshine. . . . All these sections [of Texas] offer independent homes on the easiest terms.❞

—Jane McManus Cazneau, *Eagle Pass*

Artists were also captivated by Texas. Painter Théodore Gentilz had already become known for his scenes of Texas life. Carl von Iwonski, Hermann Lungkwitz, and Friedrich Richard Petri were highly respected artists of the 1850s. Louise Heuser Wueste was San Antonio's most popular portrait painter. Eugenie Lavender was a famous painter in France before she moved to Texas. These artists skillfully illustrated the people and places of Texas.

Ⓣ Reading Check Categorizing Identify well-known writers and artists of early Texas.

CONNECTING TO THE ARTS

Hermann Lungkwitz

Hermann Lungkwitz was trained as a landscape painter in Germany before moving to Texas. He painted this image of Enchanted Rock in the 1860s. **How do you think immigrant artists influenced life in Texas during the 1800s?** Ⓣ TEKS

Section 3 Review
Ⓣ TEKS Questions 2, 3, 4a, 4b, 5

go.hrw.com Homework Practice Online
keyword: ST3 HP17

1 Define and explain:
- telegraphs

2 Identify and explain:
- *Telegraph and Texas Register*
- Gail Borden Jr.
- Swante Palm

3 Summarizing
Copy the graphic organizer below. Use it to describe education and religion in Texas during early statehood.

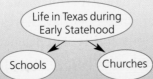

Life in Texas during Early Statehood

Schools　　Churches

4 Finding the Main Idea
a. What were some of the challenges faced by teachers and students in Texas?
b. What sort of information did newspapers carry during early statehood?

5 Writing and Critical Thinking
TAKS
Analyzing Information Imagine that you live in Texas in the 1850s. Write a letter to a friend describing how you spend your free time.
Consider the following:
- the availability of books in Texas
- Texas writers and artists

Slavery in Texas

Read to Discover

1. What was life like for enslaved Texans?
2. What were the major arguments against slavery?

Define

- abolition

Identify

- Elise Waerenskjold

Why It Matters Today

Slaves in Texas—as in most southern states—had no civil rights. Use **CNNfyi.com** or other **current events** sources to learn about a civil rights struggle in the world today. Record your findings in your journal.

The Story Continues

Slaveholder James Johnson of Travis County saw a chance to make some money. But as was common in the days of slavery, it involved breaking up a family. Nonetheless, he hired out a slave named Esther and her child to Ashbel Smith in Houston. Esther's husband, Jesse, desperate to be with his family, ran away to Houston. When Johnson caught up with him, he promised that Jesse could stay in Houston. But when Johnson instead started to take Jesse back to Travis County, Jesse ran away again.

Some slaves were forced to wear collars as a form of punishment.

★ Slave Labor

Slaves made up much of the East Texas population. Most of these slaves did farmwork. Slaves on small farms usually did a wide variety of tasks. On large plantations, slaves typically had specific jobs, with most of the men, women, and even children working in the fields. For them, work began at daybreak. They ate breakfast in the fields and then plowed, planted, or harvested. Men usually did the heaviest work, such as plowing fields. Lunch was eaten near the workplace. There was little time to stop, particularly during harvest time. Planters expected slaves to pick many pounds of cotton every day. An adult male slave could pick on average 150 to 200 pounds of cotton per day. Slaves also did other farm and household tasks. Men built and repaired fences, dug and cleaned out ditches, and hauled wood. Women often worked as cooks, laundresses, or seamstresses.

By 1850, slaves made up almost 20 percent of the population of Austin, Galveston, and Houston. Slaves who lived in towns did a variety of jobs. Men worked as carpenters or blacksmiths, while women were cooks, babysitters, or housekeepers. Slaves also helped build the state's transportation system, including its docks, railroads, roads, and warehouses. Some slaveholders hired out slaves to work for others, and a few were allowed to keep part of their wages and buy their freedom.

Reading Check **Categorizing** What jobs did enslaved men and women on plantations and in cities do?

★ Slave Culture

Slaves worked at least six days a week, but most had Sunday off. They spent any spare time doing personal chores or tending to their gardens. Some slaves worked extra jobs after completing their regular duties. They used the income to buy food, clothes, or special gifts for family members. Their food and shelter were often poor. Slaves ate a breakfast of corn bread, coffee, and sometimes bacon. Lunch might consist of bacon and corn bread or potatoes, or maybe a vegetable stew. Bacon, corn bread, and sweet potatoes made up the evening meal. Slaves working on plantations lived in small cabins with crude furniture.

Slaves spent evenings and time off in ways similar to most other Texans. They visited with their families and friends, and in the evening they told stories or played games. They held dances or family gatherings on Saturday nights. On Sunday, slaves had picnics or played music. Some slaveholders allowed slaves to attend a church. Slaves tried to worship even when it was forbidden, as one former slave recalled. "At night the slaves would gather round the fireplace on their knees and pray, and sing, and cry, but they dare not let the white folks know anything about it. . . . Thank the Lord we can now worship when we want to."

Interpreting the Visual Record

Slave life. Harvesting cotton was a common job for Texas slaves. **What other characteristics of slave life can you identify in this illustration?** TEKS

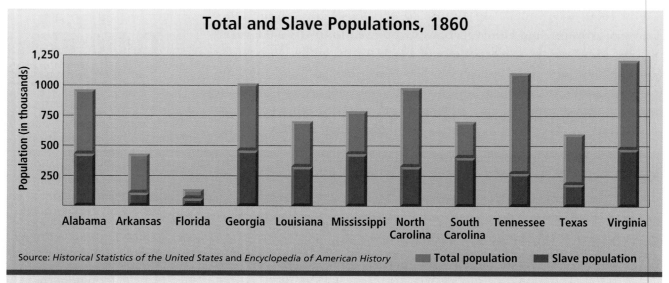

Total and Slave Populations, 1860

Source: *Historical Statistics of the United States* and *Encyclopedia of American History*   ■ Total population   ■ Slave population

TAKS Skills *Interpreting Charts* Many southerners considered slavery an important part of the South's agricultural economy. What states have a larger percentage of slaves than Texas? ★TEKS

Connecting To *Literature*

African American Folktales

Folktales are traditional stories, usually told by one person to another. Folktales were important to black communities in Texas. Some tales passed on moral lessons, while others were told simply because they were funny or entertaining. J. Mason Brewer collected stories from African Americans throughout Texas. In many of these stories, a dog spirit would appear to help people in need. In one story, a woman returns from the grave in the form of a ghost dog to give her daughter medicine. Why were folktales important to enslaved Texans? ★TEKS

Music and religion were important in slave communities. Slaves sang songs while working in the fields, and after work they played instruments such as fiddles or banjos. Urban slaves started the first African American churches in Texas. Music was a major part of the worship service. Spirituals rang through black churches, carrying messages of hope and faith. One song said, "When we all get to Heaven, They'll be no slaves no more!" Religion gave many African Americans strength to face the hardships of enslavement.

Reading Check Finding the Main Idea Why was religion an important part of of many slaves' lives?

★ Slave Escapes and Rebellions

Some Texas slaves were willing to risk their lives to escape slavery. Fleeing to Mexico was one option. Because of the likelihood of getting caught, however, the majority of slaves did not try to run away. Slaveholders severely punished those they caught, as a warning to others. Many slaves also feared that they would never again see family members left behind.

White Texans, particularly in areas with a large slave population, feared that slaves might rebel. One of the few planned uprisings took place in 1856 in Colorado County. Many slaves acquired guns, planning to rebel and escape to Mexico. Before the rebellion could take place, slaveholders learned of the plan. They hanged and whipped to death several slaves. In 1860, rumors spread that an outbreak of fire in North Texas was part of a slave plot. Although no uprising occurred, many African American and white Texans were executed for the supposed plot.

Reading Check Analyzing Information Why did many slaves not try to escape?

★ Debating Slavery

The Texas legislature, which was dominated by the state's planters, passed pro-slavery laws. Slaves could not own property or marry, and encouraging a slave to flee or hiding a runaway slave were serious crimes. Slaveholders and even many of those without slaves defended the system, noting that it supported the South's economy. Without slavery, they argued, cotton could not be grown, and money could not be earned from its export.

Some Texans supported **abolition**, or an end to slavery. Some opposed slavery for moral or religious reasons, believing that it was wrong for one person to own another. Many Texans bought, sold, and hired out slaves as property. One slave remembered families being broken apart.

Pottery made by Hiram Wilson, an enslaved African American, was sold around the state.

> **Texas Voices**   **"I gets to thinkin how Wash Hodges sold off Maw's chillen [children]. He'd . . . have the folks come for 'em when my maw was in the fields. When she'd come back, she'd raise a ruckus [complain loudly]. . . . But she allowed there weren't nothing could be done, cause it's the slavery law. She said, 'Oh Lord, let me see the end of it before I die!'"**
>
> —Anonymous, quoted in *Black Texas Women: A Sourcebook,* edited by Ruthe Winegarten

Analyzing Primary Sources
Identifying Points of View
What hardships did this slave witness in Texas?

Other abolitionists opposed slavery for political reasons, arguing that it went against the ideals of democracy and freedom. Many Mexican Americans and German Americans in Texas opposed slavery. **Elise Waerenskjold**, a Norwegian-born writer and journalist, spoke out against slavery. Another abolitionist, Melinda Rankin, was forced to leave Texas. Abolitionists were not welcome in Texas, and those who stayed generally kept their opinions to themselves.

★ **Reading Check** **Contrasting** What were the grounds for supporting or opposing slavery?

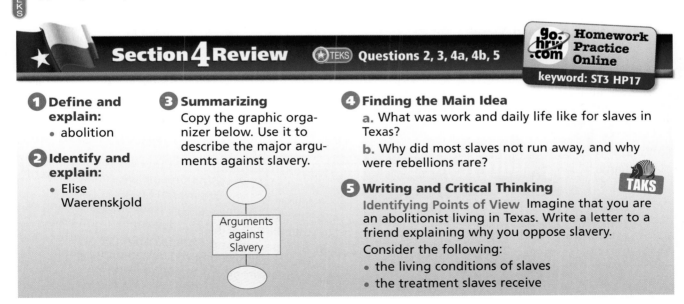

Section 4 Review ★TEKS Questions 2, 3, 4a, 4b, 5

go.hrw.com Homework Practice Online
keyword: ST3 HP17

① Define and explain:
- abolition

② Identify and explain:
- Elise Waerenskjold

③ Summarizing
Copy the graphic organizer below. Use it to describe the major arguments against slavery.

Arguments against Slavery

④ Finding the Main Idea
a. What was work and daily life like for slaves in Texas?
b. Why did most slaves not run away, and why were rebellions rare?

⑤ Writing and Critical Thinking
TAKS
Identifying Points of View Imagine that you are an abolitionist living in Texas. Write a letter to a friend explaining why you oppose slavery.
Consider the following:
- the living conditions of slaves
- the treatment slaves receive

CHAPTER 17 REVIEW

The Chapter at a Glance

Examine the following visual summary of the chapter. Then use the visual to write a one-page summary of this chapter that a classmate can use as a study guide. ★TEKS

Economy

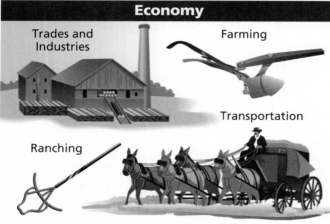

Trades and Industries

Farming

Transportation

Ranching

Society

Frontier Schools

Churches

Newspapers and the Arts

The Daily News

Slavery

Plantations

Slave Quarters

Fieldwork

Identifying People and Ideas ★TEKS

Use the following terms or people in historically significant sentences.

1. cotton belt
2. planters
3. Richard King
4. Aaron Ashworth
5. tanneries
6. manufactured products
7. *Telegraph and Texas Register*
8. Gail Borden Jr.
9. abolition
10. Elise Waerenskjold

Understanding Main Ideas ★TEKS

Section 1 (pp. 348–351)

1. What was the main source of income for Texans?
2. What were the major professions in Texas during the 1850s?

Section 2 (pp. 353–356)

3. Why did Texans need reliable transportation?
4. How did the locations of Galveston and Houston affect their growth?

Section 3 (pp. 357–359)

5. What role did churches and schools play in frontier Texas?

Section 4 (pp. 360–363)

6. Describe the daily life of enslaved African Americans in Texas.
7. Why did most Texas slaves not run away?

You Be the Historian ★TEKS

Reviewing Themes

1. **Government** What did the state government do to improve transportation within Texas?
2. **Geography** How did the weather and river systems affect transportation and the Texas economy in the mid-1800s?
3. **Economics** Analyze the effect of national and international markets on the production of goods and services in Texas.

TAKS Practice: Thinking Critically ★TEKS

1. **Identifying Points of View** Do you think that most planters would support the construction of railroads? Why or why not?
2. **Finding the Main Idea** How did the coming of the railroad affect the development of Texas?
3. **Comparing and Contrasting** How did Texans in the state's different regions adapt to and modify their environment to earn a living?

364 Chapter 17

Interpreting Maps ⭐TEKS

Study the map below. Then use the information on the map to answer the questions that follow.

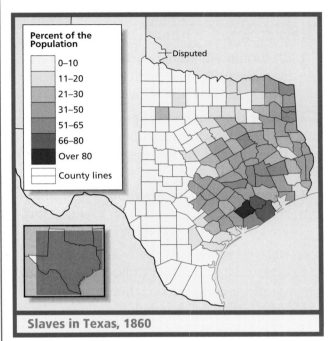

Slaves in Texas, 1860

Percent of the Population
- 0–10
- 11–20
- 21–30
- 31–50
- 51–65
- 66–80
- Over 80
- County lines
- Disputed

1. Which of the following correctly describes slavery in Texas in 1860?

   a. Slavery was limited to West Texas.
   b. Few slaves lived in East Texas.
   c. Many slaves lived in East Texas.
   d. Most slaves lived along the Rio Grande.

2. Using information from the map, support your choice of statements in question 1.

Analyzing Primary Sources ⭐TEKS

Read the following quote by Elise Waerenskjold. Then answer the questions.

"Let us now ask ourselves if we would be satisfied with being slaves, with being sold like animals, with being separated from our mates and our children whenever it might suit our master . . . without the slightest possibility of rising above the miserable state into which we were born, despite the fact that we might have the highest abilities and the greatest eagerness to learn. . . . I am convinced that in time slavery will be abolished either by gentle means or by force, because I believe that institutions founded on injustice cannot survive, but are doomed to fall."

3. Which of the following statements best describes the author's point of view?

   a. The state's booming economy was no reason to support slavery.
   b. She supports the institution of slavery.
   c. The African slave trade should be banned.
   d. Considering life from a slave's point of view reveals the injustice of slavery.

4. When interpreting a primary source, historians examine the historial context in which the source was written. What might have influenced the author's point of view?

Alternative Assessment

Cooperative Learning ⭐TEKS

Work with a small group to complete the following activity. Each person in your group should select a Texas historical figure, such as an artist, businessperson, farmer, or rancher, from the mid-1800s to research. Find out when and where the person was born, and how he or she contributed to Texas. Write a brief account about the person. You might want to include an illustration of the person or an aspect of his or her life. Then combine the results of your research with the other students in your group to create a "who's who" of frontier Texas.

BUILDING YOUR Portfolio

📶 **internet** connect

Internet Activity: go.hrw.com
KEYWORD: ST3 TX17 ⭐TEKS

Access the Internet through the HRW Go site to learn more about transportation systems and how the people of frontier Texas made a living in one of the following regions: a) lower East Texas, b) upper East Texas, c) the Gulf Coast, d) Central Texas. Create a thematic map of how Texans earned a living. Be sure to consider the various towns and transportation systems in the region.

Social Studies Skills

WORKSHOP

Interpreting Time Lines

Time lines display events in chronological order, or the sequence in which the events occurred. Knowing the chronological order of historical events is essential to understanding their significance. Time lines allow you to see relationships between events and help you to remember the dates of important events.

Sequence in a Time Line

Time lines are meant to be read from left to right, with the oldest dates on the left. The lines of the time line mark the time period between each event. For example, the lines might mark 10-, 5-, or 1-year periods. Each entry on the time line lists an important event and when it took place. These entries provide you with a sequence of events and may suggest a relationship to one another.

B.C. and A.D. Sometimes a time line will contain the abbreviations B.C. and A.D. The abbreviation B.C. stands for "before Christ." A.D. stands for "anno Domini," which means "in the year of the Lord." The year 1 B.C. was followed by A.D. 1. There was no year "0." When you read dates marked B.C. or A.D., remember that the abbreviation B.C. appears after the year—for example, 100 B.C. The abbreviation A.D. appears before the year—for example, A.D. 100.

How to Read a Time Line

1. **Determine its framework.** Note the years covered and the intervals of time into which the time line is divided.

2. **Study the sequence of events.** Study the order in which the events appear on the time line and the length of time between events.

3. **Supply missing information.** Think about the people, places, and other events associated with each item on the time line.

4. **Note relationships.** Ask yourself how an event relates to earlier or later events. Look for cause-and-effect relationships and long-term developments.

Practicing the Skill

Study the time line below, which lists important events in the history of Texas between 1845 and 1851. Then answer the following questions. ⭐TEKS

1. Into what periods is the time line divided?
2. How much time passed between the signing of the Texas peace treaty with the Penateka Comanche and the publication of Melinda Rankin's book?
3. Using the information you have just read about time lines, create your own time line about a subject in Texas history. List several significant events, individuals, and time periods in Texas history.

TEXAS

1846 Texas signs a peace treaty with the Penateka Comanche.

1847 A state census reports the state's population at more than 142,000.

1850 In her book, *Texas in 1850,* Melinda Rankin describes the state and urges people to move to Texas.

1845	1847	1849	1851

History in Action

You Make the Decision . . .

Should Texas join the United States?

Complete the following activity in small cooperative groups. It is 1845. Texans are debating whether their nation should join the United States. Your community has asked you to serve on a committee to develop a flyer that will identify reasons why Texas should or should not join the Union. Follow these steps to reach your decision.

1. Gather Information. Use your textbook and other resources to find information that might help you decide whether Texas should join the United States. Be sure to use what you learned from this unit's Skills Workshop on Interpreting Time Lines to help you focus on key points in your research. You may want to divide up different parts of the research among group members.

2. Identify Options. After reviewing the information you have gathered, consider the options you might recommend about whether Texas should join the United States or remain independent. Your final decision may be easier to reach if you consider as many options as possible. Be sure to record your possible options for the preparation of your flyer.

3. Predict Consequences. Now take each option you and the members of your committee came up with and consider what might be the outcome of each course of action. Ask yourselves questions such as, "How would Texas benefit from joining or not joining the United States?" Once you have predicted the consequences, record them as notes for the preparation of your flyer.

4. Take Action to Implement Your Decision. After you have considered your options, you should plan and create your flyer. Be sure to make your decision about joining the Union or remaining independent very clear. You will need to support your decision by including information you gathered and by explaining why you rejected other options. Your flyer needs to be visually appealing to convince the committee as well as the voters. When you are ready, decide which committee members will present each part of the flyer, and then take your flyer to the community board (the rest of the class). Good luck!

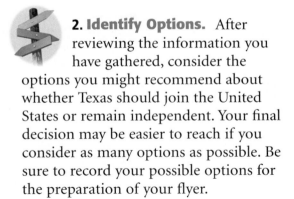

CHAPTER 18 **Texas and the Civil War** (1861–1865)

CHAPTER 19 **Reconstruction** (1865–1877)

CHAPTER 20 **The Indian Wars** (1861–1880)

Texas Teens
Young Soldiers

During the Civil War, 17-year-old Hugh Cooke of Waller County was angry that his commander thought Cooke was too young to fight. "Cap'n, come here. They've got me here holding horses; I didn't come here to hold horses. I came here to shoot Yankees." Cooke soon got his wish. At the beginning of the war, many young Texans shared Cooke's enthusiasm for fighting. Henry Elms was 17 when he signed up for the Confederate army at Victoria. Late one night as his unit attacked a large Union force in a heavily wooded area, they "raised a regular Texas Yell . . . and started forward through the brush." The fire of weapons flashed like lightning in the woods, revealing the position of the Union soldiers. Elms's unit won the battle.

As the war dragged on, soldiers began to miss their homes. One Texas teen, William Randolph Howell, wrote home as he lay sick in a field hospital. "Still remain at hospital. . . . My health improving slowly. Get a horse and prepare to go home. GLORIOUS THOUGHT!"

Teenagers who remained at home during the war faced challenges of their own. C. W. Ackerman and his 13-year-old brother were left to take care of the family farm while their father was away running a flour mill. One day, some Confederate soldiers came around gathering horses for use by the army. Ackerman begged the soldiers to let him keep his. "After frightening me real good they told me I could keep my horse." Ackerman was lucky—he was the only person in the area with a horse. Another young Texan who stayed behind when his father left for the war was not worried. "Mother was a fearless woman and the best marksman with a rifle I ever saw, so we felt able to take care of ourselves." **How did Texas teens play a role in the Civil War?**

Hugh Cooke was a teenager when he joined the Texas Volunteer Infantry and Cavalry, Company A, 3rd Batallion.

In this unit you will learn about the experiences of Texans during the Civil War and Reconstruction. You will also learn about the westward expansion of the frontier and its effects on American Indians in Texas.

LEFT PAGE: *During the Battle of Sabine Pass, Texas Confederate forces prevented a Union invasion of Texas.*

18

Texas and the Civil War
(1861–1865)

Thousands of Texans volunteered for the Confederate army.

Confederate troops regained control of Galveston in 1863.

TEXAS

	February 1861 Texans vote, by more than three to one, to secede from the United States.	**October 1861** Troops leave San Antonio for New Mexico, planning to capture the Southwest for the Confederacy.		**October 1862** Union forces capture Galveston.
	January 1861	**July 1861**	**January 1862**	**July 1862**

U.S. and WORLD

April 1861 The Civil War begins when Confederate forces open fire on Fort Sumter in South Carolina.	**July 1861** Union and Confederate armies clash in the First Battle of Bull Run, the first major battle of the war.	**April 1862** The Battle of Shiloh is fought.	

The first shot of the Civil War occurred at Fort Sumter.

Build on What You Know

In the 1850s slavery was firmly established in Texas and the South. Many northerners questioned whether slavery should be allowed anywhere in the United States. Soon, the whole nation was at war over issues that had divided the North and the South.

Some members of the Union cavalry wore uniforms such as this one.

During the Union advance on Brownsville, many Texans fled the community.

January 1863 President Lincoln issues the Emancipation Proclamation.

September 1863 A Union attempt to invade Texas is turned back at Sabine Pass.
November 1863 Union troops capture Brownsville.

April 1864 In a battle near Mansfield, Louisiana, Confederate forces stop a Union invasion of northeastern Texas.

May 1865 The last land battle of the war is fought at Palmito Ranch, Texas.

January 1863	**July 1863**	**January 1864**	**July 1864**	**January 1865**

July 1863 Union forces win major battles at Gettysburg, Pennsylvania, and Vicksburg, Mississippi.

September 1864 A Union army under General William Tecumseh Sherman captures Atlanta.

April 1865 General Robert E. Lee surrenders at Appomattox Courthouse.

The Museum of the Confederacy, Richmond, Virginia

Confederate general Robert E. Lee carried this sword in battle.

You Be the Historian

Themes Journal

What's Your Opinion? Do you **agree** or **disagree** with the following statements? Support your point of view in your journal.

• **Economics** War is always economically destructive for those who participate in it.

• **Citizenship** Citizens should be allowed to oppose a war even if their government has decided to fight in it.

• **Geography** A region's geography has little effect on how battles are fought there.

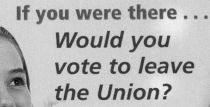

If you were there . . . *Would you vote to leave the Union?*

Slavery and States' Rights

Read to Discover

1. Why did the United States divide along sectional lines?
2. Why did many Texans want the state to leave the Union?

Why It Matters Today

Northerners and southerners disagreed about many issues. Use **CNNfyi**.com or other **current events** sources to learn about an issue that is important to a particular region today. Record your findings in your journal.

Define

- states' rights
- secede
- sovereignty

Identify

- Kansas-Nebraska Act
- *Dred Scott* decision
- Unionists
- Confederate States of America

The Dred Scott *decision outraged many abolitionists and led to increased tensions between the North and the South.*

The Granger Collection, New York

The Story Continues

After years of living as slaves, Dred and Harriet Scott faced a decision. They had lived in free territory for several years, and had recently been returned to the slave state of Missouri. White friends of the Scotts urged them to sue for their freedom. The Scotts decided to do so, believing that their residence in free territory had made them free. Dred Scott's case led to a landmark U.S. Supreme Court ruling.

★ Growing National Divisions

Slavery was one of the issues that divided the nation along sectional, or regional, lines. The North's population was growing as immigrants came to work in its factories. In contrast to the North's increasingly industrial economy, the South had an agricultural economy that used slave labor. These social and economic differences led to sectional disagreements. For example, the North wanted tariffs to protect its industries, while the South opposed tariffs because they increased the cost of imported items. During the tariff dispute, some southerners argued that states had a right to ignore tariffs and other federal laws. Under this **states' rights** argument, state power was greater than federal power.

As the United States expanded westward, Congress debated whether territories would enter the Union as free or slave states. This would affect the balance of power in Congress. After much debate, Texas entered the Union in 1845 as a slave state. Then under the Treaty of

Guadalupe Hidalgo of 1848 the United States gained vast stretches of land from Mexico. In the Compromise of 1850, Congress created a way for the new territories to become states. The compromise included a new Fugitive Slave Act, which made it a crime to assist runaway slaves. This act, along with Harriet Beecher Stowe's 1852 antislavery novel, *Uncle Tom's Cabin*, greatly increased support for the abolition movement.

In 1854 Congress passed the **Kansas-Nebraska Act**. This act allowed the Kansas and Nebraska Territories to decide whether to be free or slave states. Many northern members of the Whig Party were angry because this violated the 1820 Missouri Compromise, which prohibited slavery above the 36°30' line. They helped form the Republican Party in 1854 to stop the spread of slavery. Sam Houston, then serving in the U.S. Senate, was one of the few southerners who opposed the Kansas-Nebraska Act. Houston's stand was unpopular in Texas—even many of his old friends refused to speak to him.

In 1857 the U.S. Supreme Court dealt antislavery forces a blow with the ***Dred Scott* decision**. The Court ruled that African Americans were not citizens, and therefore could not sue in federal court. The Court also ruled that Congress could not ban slavery in any federal territory. The ruling shocked many northerners. Sectional tensions increased in 1859 when an abolitionist named John Brown led a raid on a federal armory in Harpers Ferry, Virginia, to start a slave revolt. He and his followers were hanged for treason.

★ **Reading Check** **Summarizing** Explain why divisions arose between the North and the South.

Slavery in the South. *Slaves spent many hours working in fields to produce cotton and other cash crops.* **What characteristics of slave life does this image show?**

A Confederate soldier's cap

The Museum of the Confederacy, Richmond, Virginia

The Union and the Confederacy, 1861

Interpreting Maps Texas joined the southern states that formed the Confederate States of America.

TAKS Skills

1. Human Systems List the states that made up the Confederacy.

2. Drawing Inferences and Conclusions What do you think Texas had in common with other Confederate states? ⭐TEKS

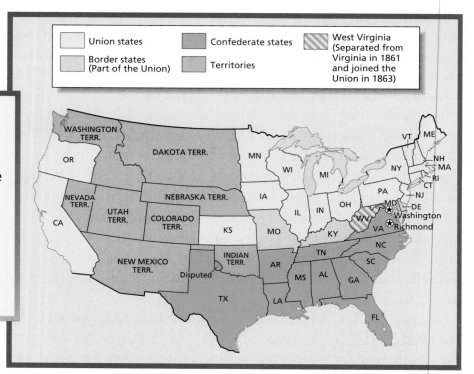

| Union states | Confederate states | West Virginia (Separated from Virginia in 1861 and joined the Union in 1863) |
| Border states (Part of the Union) | Territories | |

⭐ Texas Joins the Confederacy

In 1860 Republican Abraham Lincoln won the presidential election. He received no electoral votes from the South because many southerners feared that he would support abolition. After the election, South Carolina chose to **secede**, or formally withdraw, from the Union. Mississippi, Florida, Alabama, Georgia, and Louisiana also seceded.

Many Texas leaders called for a special meeting of the legislature to consider secession. This angered <u>Unionists</u>—people who wanted to stay in the Union and work out differences over slavery. About one out of four Texans were Unionists, including Sam Houston, Elisha M. Pease, David G. Burnet, Andrew J. Hamilton, and James W. Throckmorton. Houston, who had won the governor's election in 1859, urged Texans to stay in the Union.

Analyzing Primary Sources

Drawing Inferences and Conclusions Why does Houston describe the South's chance of independence as "a bare possibility"?

> **Texas Voices** ❝Let me tell you what is coming. Your fathers and husbands, your sons and brothers, will be herded at the point of the bayonet. You may, after the sacrifice of countless millions of treasure and hundreds of thousands of lives, as a bare possibility, win Southern independence . . . but I doubt it. The North is determined to preserve this Union.❞
>
> —Sam Houston, quoted in *The Raven,* by Marquis James

Houston tried to delay the legislative meeting, hoping the calls for secession would fade. Pro-secession leaders ignored him. They organized a secession convention to meet on January 28, 1861, adopting an ordinance, or order, of secession on February 1. The delegates voted 166 to 8 to leave the Union. They then scheduled a statewide vote on the issue. On February 23, 1861, Texans voted for secession by 46,153 to 14,747. A majority of people voted against it in only a few counties. On March 2, 1861, Texas became the seventh state to secede from the United States.

★ **Reading Check Analyzing Information** Describe the actions taken by the state's pro-secession leaders to have Texas join the Confederacy.

★ The Confederacy

In February 1861 Texas sent seven delegates to Montgomery, Alabama. There representatives from the seceding states formed a government called the **Confederate States of America**, or the Confederacy. The representatives wrote a constitution that was similar to the U.S. Constitution. It differed in several ways, however. The Confederate constitution emphasized the **sovereignty**, or supremacy, of the states and the right of people to hold slaves. The delegates elected a president, Jefferson Davis of Mississippi, and other officials to run the Confederacy. They chose Texan John H. Reagan as postmaster general.

On March 5, 1861, the Texas Secession Convention reassembled to write a new state constitution. The new document was basically the 1845 constitution with references to the Confederacy replacing references to the United States. When Governor Houston refused to take an oath of allegiance to the Confederacy, the delegates removed him from office. He was replaced with Lieutenant Governor Edward Clark. Sam and Margaret Houston left Austin and retired to Huntsville, where he died on July 26, 1863.

★ **Reading Check Finding the Main Idea** Why was Sam Houston removed from the governor's office in 1861?

Citizenship and You

Serving during the War

On the brink of the Civil War, Texans had to decide where their civic duty lay—with their state or with their country. Thousands of Texans served in the Confederate army. Others joined the Union army. Those who were neutral sometimes provided aid to the wounded of both sides. After the war, veterans of both armies assumed leadership positions in the state. Edmund J. Davis, who had organized a Union cavalry unit and eventually became a brigadier general, won election as governor in 1869. Today Texans fulfill their civic duties in many ways. **How do people in your community serve Texas and the nation?**

★ TEKS

Recruiting posters urged Union supporters to volunteer for combat.

TO ARMS!
RALLY FOR THE RIGHT!
Recruits Wanted
For THREE MONTHS SERVICE, IN
COMPANY A
GRAY RESERVES
CAPT. CHARLES S. SMITH
ARMORY,
810 MARKET STREET,
UP STAIRS.

Section 1 Review ★TEKS Questions 2, 3, 4a, 4b, 5

go.hrw.com Homework Practice Online
keyword: ST3 HP18

1 Define and explain:
- states' rights
- secede
- sovereignty

2 Identify and explain:
- Kansas-Nebraska Act
- *Dred Scott* decision
- Unionists
- Confederate States of America

3 Sequencing
Copy the time line below. List in order the events of 1861 that led to the secession of Texas.

Jan 28
Feb 1
Feb 23
Mar 2

4 Finding the Main Idea
a. Why was the United States divided along sectional lines?
b. Why did Texas secede?

5 Writing and Critical Thinking
Identifying Points of View Imagine that you live in Texas in the 1850s. Write a letter to a friend explaining how Texans are reacting to sectional tensions.
Consider the following:
- the Texas economy
- Texans' support of slavery

TAKS

The Civil War Begins

Read to Discover

1. How did Texans respond to the call to arms?
2. How did Texans prepare for war?
3. What were the main strategies and battles of the first half of the Civil War?

Why It Matters Today

The North and the South debated their differences for years before going to war. Use CNNfyi.com or other **current events** sources to learn about peace talks today. Record your findings in your journal.

Define
- **regiments**
- **cotton diplomacy**
- **ironclads**

Identify
- **Terry's Texas Rangers**
- **Hood's Texas Brigade**
- **Ross's Texas Brigade**
- **Albert Sidney Johnston**

The Story Continues

People gathered on balconies and rooftops overlooking Charleston Harbor. They watched Fort Sumter, wondering if the federal soldiers inside would surrender without a fight. The soldiers within the fort waited in the early morning darkness. They wondered if Confederate forces would actually fire upon them. They soon found out—at 4:30 A.M. cannons on the shore opened fire. Soon, as a Union soldier noted, "shot and shell went screaming over Sumter as if an army of devils were swooping around it."

When the federal soldiers surrendered at Fort Sumter, this flag was lowered and a Confederate flag was raised.

★ A Call to Arms

The Confederate attack on Fort Sumter in April 1861 marked the beginning of the Civil War. A civil war is a war between factions, or opposing groups, within the same country. The news of war "fell on the land like a thunderbolt," one person remembered. The day after Fort Sumter surrendered, President Lincoln called for 75,000 volunteers to help put down the rebellion. In response, Virginia, Arkansas, Tennessee, and North Carolina seceded from the Union.

Thousands of Texans responded to the Confederate call to arms. Even many Texas Unionists supported the Confederacy once the war began. "The North will never subdue [conquer] the South. Never, never!" vowed one Texas volunteer. By the end of 1861, some 25,000 Texans were in the Confederate army. Confederate president Jefferson Davis welcomed the first Texas troops in 1861.

Texas Voices ❝Texans! The troops from other States have their reputation to gain, but the sons of the defenders of the Alamo have theirs to maintain. I am sure you will be faithful to the trust.❞

—Jefferson Davis, address to Texas troops

Texas troops soon gained a reputation for spirit and daring in battle. Texans usually joined **regiments**—units of around 1,000 soldiers—from their hometowns or counties. The units took the names of the people who organized them. **Terry's Texas Rangers**, a cavalry unit organized by B. F. Terry, fought in battles throughout the Civil War. **Hood's Texas Brigade**, under the command of John Bell Hood, became a lead unit in the Army of Northern Virginia. It fought in some of the most important battles of the war. **Ross's Texas Brigade**, headed by Lawrence Ross, fought in Georgia, Mississippi, and Tennessee.

Texas also contributed many officers to the Confederacy. **Albert Sidney Johnston** was the second-highest-ranking officer in the army until his death in battle. Unionist James W. Throckmorton became a brigadier general. Texans Tom Green, Samuel Bell Maxey, Felix H. Robertson, and John Wharton were other key Confederate officers.

★ **Reading Check** **Making Generalizations and Predictions** How do you think the war will affect Texans?

Analyzing Primary Sources ★TEKS
Identifying Points of View
Why did Davis think that the Texan volunteers were different from soldiers of other southern states?

Interpreting the Visual Record

*Terry's Texas Rangers. Texas volunteers were known for their fighting skills and daring in battle. **What particular skills does this painting of Terry's Texas Rangers show?*** ★TEKS

Courtesy of the Witte Museum, San Antonio, Texas

Global Trade and the Civil War

Before the Civil War, the South had traded with European nations for many items it did not produce. The Union blockade greatly limited the South's ability to obtain supplies during the war. Texas, however, bordered Mexico, and the Union navy could not block Mexican ports. Texans took cotton across the Rio Grande to trade for supplies. Hundreds of ships from Europe brought military supplies to Mexico to trade for the cotton. **How did the location of Texas affect the South in the Civil War?** TEKS

The South traded cotton for guns and other supplies.

The Museum of the Confederacy, Richmond, Virginia

★ Texas Readies for War

Many of the Texas troops were ill-equipped, reporting with a variety of weapons, uniforms, and supplies. One Texas soldier remembered that "most of our blankets were pieces of carpets taken from floors." The Texans needed all the supplies they could get. Even before the state had officially seceded, the Texas government moved to seize federal property. In February 1861 a force led by Ben McCulloch surrounded the U.S. commander's headquarters in San Antonio. U.S. Army general David E. Twiggs quickly surrendered all federal property in Texas. Without firing a shot, the Texas militia captured more than $1 million in military supplies.

Texans also established new industries to get ready for the war. Thomas Anderson ran a gunpowder mill near Austin. A factory in Tyler made cannons and ammunition, while iron foundries opened in Jefferson and Rusk. Prisoners at Huntsville made 3 million yards of cloth during the war. Texas businesses made saddles, tents, uniforms, and wagons. The state's plentiful resources of cattle, cotton, and food crops such as corn were also a great help to the Confederacy.

Reading Check **Summarizing** How did preparation for war affect the Texas economy?

★ Resources and Strategies

The North had a number of advantages at the beginning of the conflict. With a larger population, it could recruit more soldiers. Because the North had more railroads, it could move troops and supplies more easily. The North had far more factories than the South did, so it could produce more weapons and supplies. The North also had an established government ready to conduct and raise money for the war.

The South did have some advantages. It had experienced military leaders, many of whom had served in the U.S. Army during the Mexican War. Many southerners, particularly Texans, were experienced in riding horses and using firearms. By the end of 1861, two thirds of Texans serving in the Confederate army were in the cavalry. A British observer noted Texans' preference for fighting on horseback. "No Texan walks a yard if he can help it."

At the beginning of the war, the Confederacy planned to stay on the defensive and wear down the Union's will to fight. The South hoped to maintain its ability to fight by getting war supplies from Europe. Southern leaders tried to gain foreign support, particularly from Great Britain, through the use of **cotton diplomacy**. The Confederacy withheld cotton shipments to British textile mills, hoping to force Britain to offer help. This strategy failed, partly because European storehouses had been fully stocked before the war.

The North faced the difficult task of having to conquer large amounts of enemy territory. The Union used a naval blockade to cut off southern seaports and prevent the Confederacy from importing war supplies. The blockade eventually extended from Virginia to Florida on the Atlantic coast and from Florida to the southern tip of Texas on the Gulf Coast. At the same time, Union forces planned to take control of the Mississippi River and cut the Confederacy in two. This would separate the important food-producing areas of Arkansas, Texas, and most of Louisiana from other southern states. Union forces also planned to capture Richmond, Virginia, the capital of the Confederacy.

These strategies resulted in three theaters, or regions, of war. The first theater was in the East, centered around Washington and Richmond. A second developed in Tennessee and Mississippi, and the third was west of the Mississippi River. Texans fought in all three theaters.

Reading Check Evaluating How do you think the northern strategy of taking control of the Mississippi River would affect Texas?

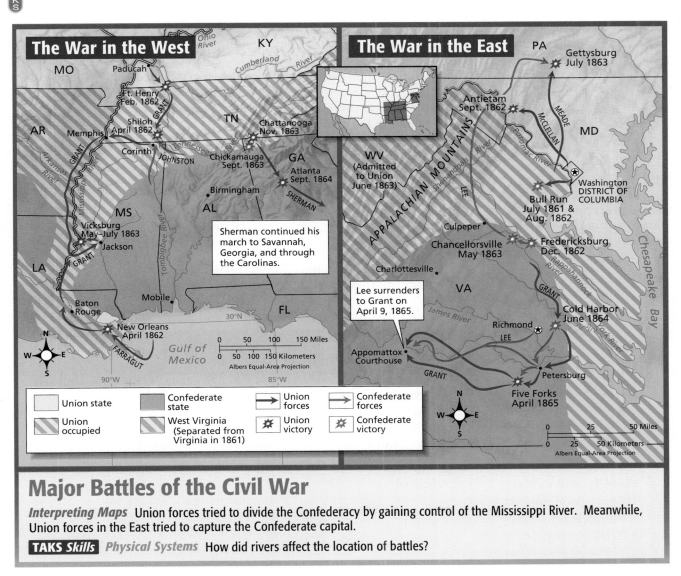

Major Battles of the Civil War

Interpreting Maps Union forces tried to divide the Confederacy by gaining control of the Mississippi River. Meanwhile, Union forces in the East tried to capture the Confederate capital.

TAKS Skills *Physical Systems* How did rivers affect the location of battles?

The Museum of the Confederacy, Richmond, Virginia

As the war continued, many soldiers lacked necessities such as these shoes. This caused great hardship, particularly during cold weather.

★ The Major Battles of the Civil War

The major battles of the war took place east of the Mississippi River. In July 1861 a Union army marched south to capture Richmond. Confederate forces stopped the advance at the First Battle of Bull Run. Confederate troops held off Union attacks the following year, eventually driving most Union troops from Virginia. In late September 1862 General Robert E. Lee's army clashed with a Union force in Maryland. The Battle of Antietam was an important Union victory. In late June 1863 Lee moved north again and battled Union forces at Gettysburg, Pennsylvania on July 1–3. They suffered heavy losses and retreated on July 4. The Battle of Gettysburg was a turning point—Lee was on the defensive for the rest of the war.

Meanwhile, Confederate and Union armies battled for control of the Mississippi River valley. Union general Ulysses S. Grant gained the upper hand in April 1862 in the Battle of Shiloh. It was a costly battle for both sides. General Albert Sidney Johnston of Texas was among those killed. Grant pressed on toward Vicksburg, Mississippi, which controlled traffic on the river. A Texas soldier noted the town's importance.

Texas Voices ❝Even if I could get leave of absence now I would not accept it when every man . . . will be so much needed in the coming contest before Vicksburg—which I regard as the hinging point in the destiny of our nation.❞

—J. C. Bates, quoted in *A Texas Cavalry Officer's Civil War*, edited by Richard Lowe

Grant began the six-week Siege of Vicksburg, supported by a fleet of **ironclads**—ships heavily armored in iron. When the town surrendered on July 4, 1863, the Confederacy was split in two. It became very difficult to get supplies from Arkansas, Louisiana, and Texas to the battlegrounds in the East.

★ **Reading Check** **Drawing Inferences and Conclusions** In addition to Gettysburg, what other battle could be considered a turning point, and why?

★ Section 2 Review ★TEKS Questions 2, 4a, 4b

go.hrw.com **Homework Practice Online**
keyword: ST3 HP18

1 Define and explain:
- regiments
- cotton diplomacy
- ironclads

2 Identify and explain:
- Terry's Texas Rangers
- Hood's Texas Brigade
- Ross's Texas Brigade
- Albert Sidney Johnston

3 Summarizing
Copy the chart below. Use it to describe the major battles of the Civil War and their significance.

Battle	Significance

4 Finding the Main Idea
a. How did Texans respond to news that war had begun?
b. What did Texans do to prepare for war?

5 Writing and Critical Thinking
Analyzing Information Write a paragraph describing each side's main strategies in the Civil War.
Consider the following:
- cotton diplomacy
- the blockade

Section 3

Campaigns in Texas and the Southwest

Read to Discover

1. What campaigns were fought in and near Texas?
2. What did the Confederacy hope to accomplish in the fighting in and around Texas?
3. How did geographic factors affect the battles?

Define

- cottonclads

Identify

- Henry H. Sibley
- Battle of Glorieta Pass
- Richard Dowling
- Davis Guards
- Battle of Sabine Pass
- Santos Benavides
- Red River Campaign

Why It Matters Today

Many Texans served in the military during the Civil War. Use CNNfyi.com or other **current events** sources to learn about men and women who serve in our nation's military today. Record your findings in your journal.

The Story Continues

Texan Val C. Giles shivered in the darkness. He was on guard duty, watching a Virginia swamp where many soldiers had died that day in battle. As he thought about his fallen comrades, something terrifying happened. He recalled, "The biggest ghost I had ever seen" slowly rose out of the swamp. He thought that it must be a dead soldier. Only later did he learn that the "ghost" was merely swamp gas.

Some Confederate soldiers wore gray jackets such as this one in battle.

The Museum of the Confederacy, Richmond, Virginia

★ The New Mexico Campaign

While many Texans served in the eastern theater of the Civil War, some served closer to home. Shortly after the war began, Texas forces led by Colonel John R. Baylor marched into New Mexico Territory and claimed the area. In the fall of 1861, General **Henry H. Sibley** took three Texas regiments to seize the Southwest—from New Mexico to California—for the Confederacy. The region had great wealth from its gold and silver mines as well as ports on the Pacific Ocean.

Sibley's 2,000 troops won a battle against 2,500 Union soldiers at Valverde, New Mexico. The Texas force then seized Albuquerque and Santa Fe. Gradually the army was weakened by disease and lack of food and water. One soldier remembered the march through the desert region. "We had suffered a lot, had gone hungry, and did not have

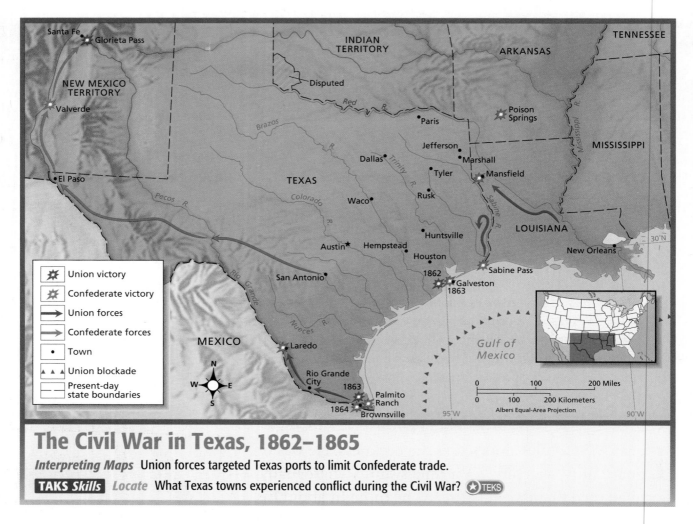

The Civil War in Texas, 1862–1865

Interpreting Maps Union forces targeted Texas ports to limit Confederate trade.

TAKS Skills *Locate* What Texas towns experienced conflict during the Civil War? ⭐TEKS

enough water. We sweated during the day and froze at night." Union troops met part of Sibley's force in the **Battle of Glorieta Pass** in New Mexico, on March 28, 1862. A Texas soldier recalled the battle.

Analyzing Primary Sources
Finding the Main Idea Why did the Texans retreat after the Battle of Glorieta Pass?

Texas Voices ❝We were under fire 6 hours, compelling [forcing] the enemy to retreat 3 miles and we won the battle. . . . On the day of the battle the enemy sent 200 men around to our camp and burned all our wagons together with all our clothing and provisions.❞

—Julius Eggeling, quoted in *Westward the Texans,* edited by Jerry D. Thompson

Stranded without supplies, Sibley and his small army had to retreat to Texas. Union forces kept control of the Southwest for the rest of the war.

⭐ **Reading Check** **Identifying Cause and Effect** What was the climate of New Mexico like, and how did that affect the Confederates' attempt to capture the region?

⭐ Fighting at Galveston Island

The Union navy had blockaded Texas ports by the summer of 1862. When a Union fleet sailed into Galveston Harbor in October, the small Confederate force there retreated. Galveston was vital to the Confederacy. If left in Union control, northern forces could easily sweep into Texas. General John B. Magruder, the commander of Confederate forces in Texas, made plans to recapture it.

Magruder's men converted two steamboats to gunboats, lining the sides with cotton bales for protection. Some soldiers doubted that these **cottonclads** would help much. Nonetheless, troops commanded by Colonel Tom Green boarded the *Neptune* and the *Bayou City* to attack Union ships in the harbor. At the same time, soldiers were preparing to attack the Union forces from the mainland. The attack began in the early morning hours of January 1, 1863. A Texan on the *Bayou City* remembered the events.

Texas Voices ❝The *Harriet Lane* [a Union ship] ran up beside us and I was ordered to cut the stays. When I cut them, the stage planks fell on the *Harriet Lane*. . . . Commodore Smith went aboard the hostile ship and after a moment's feeble resistance, she struck her colors and surrendered.❞

—M. L. Clark, quoted in *Reminiscences of the Boys in Gray, 1861–1865,* edited by Mamie Yeary

The remaining Union ships fled. Meanwhile, Confederate land forces overran the Union troops in Galveston, capturing several hundred soldiers. The Confederacy once again controlled the key Texas port.

⭐ **Reading Check** **Sequencing** List in order who controlled Galveston and the approximate dates of their control.

⭐ The Battle of Sabine Pass

The Union did not intend to leave Galveston in Confederate hands. In September 1863, Union troops set sail from New Orleans, which had been captured by the North in April 1862. General William B. Franklin and about 4,000 troops planned to invade Texas through Sabine Pass, march overland to Houston, and then capture Galveston. Confederate lieutenant **Richard Dowling** and about 45 soldiers in an all-Irish unit

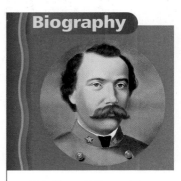

Biography

Richard Dowling
(1838–1867)

Richard Dowling of Houston joined the Confederate army and became a skilled artillery commander. In 1863 he was given command of Fort Griffin, which guarded Sabine Pass. Dowling knew that his men needed to be excellent shots to prevent Union vessels from simply steaming past the fort. When Union ships did attack, firing as they came, Dowling's men were ready. In his report of the fighting, Dowling praised his men. "All my men behaved like heroes; not a man flinched from his post. Our motto was 'victory or death.'" **Why was Dowling a good choice to command the fort?** ⭐TEKS

Interpreting the Visual Record

Sabine Pass. Sabine Pass is the outlet of the Sabine River into the Gulf of Mexico. **Based on this illustration of the Battle of Sabine Pass, how do you think geographic factors affected the battle?** ⭐TEKS

known as the **Davis Guards** were to protect the pass. They manned a small post called Fort Griffin, surrounded only by trenches and earthen mounds. The fort had six cannons, which the soldiers had used to practice hitting targets in the pass.

Union forces attacked on September 8, 1863. General Franklin planned to use gunboats to destroy Fort Griffin's cannons so that his troops could land. Union forces shelled the fort for more than an hour. The Davis Guards held their fire until the gunboats were close by. Dowling then ordered his men to fire. The Confederate gunners fired fast and accurately. They quickly crippled two gunboats and halted the Union attack. The rest of the Union ships turned back, but not before the Guards captured more than 300 Union soldiers. The victory excited people in Texas and the rest of the South. The Confederacy had lost two major battles that summer, and the **Battle of Sabine Pass** helped restore southern confidence. Lieutenant Dowling and the Davis Guards received special medals for their actions.

 Reading Check **Summarizing** Why was Sabine Pass a strategic location, and how did holding it affect events in Texas?

★ The Coast and South Texas

Despite the Confederate victories at Galveston and Sabine Pass, Union forces once again attacked Texas. Two months after the Battle of Sabine Pass, Union forces commanded by General Nathaniel Banks captured Brazos Island off the mouth of the Rio Grande. They wanted to take Brownsville and stop trade between Texas and Mexico. Texans like Sarah "Sally" Scull led wagon trains loaded with cotton across the border to Matamoros. From there, Texans shipped the cotton overseas and purchased supplies for the Confederacy. The Union wanted to cut off this supply route. This route was important as the blockade tightened. Ships known as blockade-runners sometimes slipped past the Union navy, but they could not carry on regular trade.

Union troops captured Brownsville in early November 1863. Banks then split his forces. One group of troops moved north up the coast, capturing Matagorda Island and occupying Indianola. Colonel Edmund J. Davis of Texas, leading the other column of Union troops, captured Rio Grande City. But his attack on Laredo failed. Texas troops led by Colonel

Texas Cities

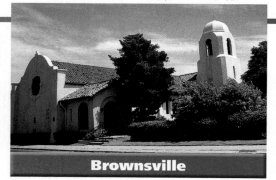

Brownsville

History: Spanish settlers arrived in the area of Brownsville in the late 1700s. In 1846 the U.S. Army established a post there. Over time Brownsville became an important trading post.

Population in 2000: 139,722

Relative location: Southern edge of the South Texas Plains

Region: South Texas Plains

County: County seat of Cameron County

Special feature: Brownsville has a twin city—Matamoros—across the Rio Grande in Mexico.

Origin of name: Originally a fort named Fort Brown, established at the beginning of the Mexican War

Economy: Brownsville's economy is based on agriculture, shipping, tourism, and the manufacture of a variety of goods, including garments, metal goods, and petrochemicals.

Santos Benavides, the highest-ranking Mexican American to serve in the Confederate army, turned back the attack. After Union forces were called away from Brownsville, Colonel John S. Ford quickly recaptured the town for the Confederacy. Although Union troops controlled Brazos Island, none remained on the mainland of the lower Texas coast.

⭐ **Reading Check** **Finding the Main Idea** What geographic feature made South Texas strategically important, and what was the goal of Union forces attacking the region?

⭐ The Red River Campaign

The Union troops had left Brownsville to take part in the **Red River Campaign**. Union leaders wanted to invade northeastern Texas from Louisiana along the Red River. They planned to attack in the spring, when the river was usually deep enough for boats. In March 1864 General Banks and 27,000 men began moving up the river, supported by a fleet of ironclads. Banks hoped to link with a smaller Union army of 15,000 men moving south from Arkansas.

On April 8, 1864, Confederate units commanded by General Richard Taylor intercepted Banks at Sabine Crossroads near Mansfield, Louisiana. The Confederate forces totaled fewer than 9,000 men, but in a stunning blow they forced Banks to turn back. Meanwhile, unusually low water levels on the Red River slowed the Union gunboats. They narrowly escaped destruction while retreating. The Union army moving south from Arkansas had no better luck. On April 18, Confederate forces defeated it at Poison Springs, Arkansas. Confederate troops had again turned back Union attacks in Texas.

⭐ **Reading Check** **Analyzing Information** How did the depth of the Red River affect General Banks's invasion of Texas?

Some soldiers took quinine to treat disease.

Section 3 Review

⭐TEKS Questions 4a, 4b, 5

Homework Practice Online
keyword: ST3 HP18

1 Define and explain:
- cottonclads

2 Identify and explain:
- Henry H. Sibley
- Battle of Glorieta Pass
- Richard Dowling
- Davis Guards
- Battle of Sabine Pass
- Santos Benavides
- Red River Campaign

3 Analyzing Information
Copy the graphic organizer below. Use it to list three of the Confederacy's goals for fighting in and around Texas.

Confederacy's Goals for Texas
1. _____
2. _____
3. _____

4 Finding the Main Idea
a. What battles were fought in and near Texas, and what was their significance?
b. What effects did geographic factors have on military campaigns in the region?

5 Writing and Critical Thinking
Supporting a Point of View Imagine that you are a Union or Confederate officer. Write a memorandum to your superior explaining why controlling Brownsville is important.
Consider the following:
- trade and transportation routes to Mexico
- the use of Brownsville as a launching point for an invasion of Texas

TAKS

The Texas Home Front

Read to Discover

1. What was life like for Texans during the Civil War?
2. How did the Civil War and the draft affect Unionists?

Define

- **draft**
- **martial law**

Why It Matters Today

The Civil War affected many people, even those who did not fight in it. Use **CNNfyi.com** or other **current events** sources to learn about a person who has been affected by war today. Record your findings in your journal.

Texans relied on harnesses and other equipment to keep their farms productive during the war.

The Story Continues

While her husband was in the army, Rebecca Adams ran the family's plantation and cared for nine children. Adams somehow found time to knit rabbit-fur gloves for her husband, Dr. Robert Adams. She summed up her situation in a letter to him. "I had to attend to your part of the work and mine too."

★ The Wartime Economy and the Draft

Although Texas suffered less than other Confederate States because few battles were fought in the state, Texans experienced many hardships. Goods became scarce and very expensive. Many newspapers stopped operation because of a lack of paper. Shortages were also created because supplies, particularly medicines, were sent to Confederate armies. Texans adapted to the wartime shortages, using thorns for pins and wallpaper as writing paper. When coffee became scarce, people used corn, okra, parched peanuts, or sweet potatoes to make drinks. Texans also made more homespun clothing.

To feed the army, farmers grew more corn and wheat and less cotton. Crop production also increased as slaveholders in other states sent slaves to Texas to prevent their being freed by Union occupation forces. Women and children ran farms and plantations, as did men who were unable to serve in the army. Women on the home front also worked in small factories, made items at home, and organized special groups to support the war effort. These groups made uniforms, bandages, and medical supplies. They also provided aid to the families of soldiers.

The state's political activity also focused on the war effort. All office-holders strongly supported the Confederacy. Francis R. Lubbock, who had been elected governor in 1861, joined the Confederate army in 1863. Pendleton Murrah was elected governor of Texas in 1863. Like Lubbock, Murrah struggled with state debts, defending the frontier against raids by American Indians, and raising troops for the Confederacy.

Although thousands of men had volunteered at the beginning of the war, they were not enough. In April 1862 the Confederate Congress passed a **draft**, or requirement of military service. All white males between the ages of 18 and 35 had to serve. The age limits were later broadened to 17 and 50. However, there were several loopholes in the law. People with certain key jobs were exempt. Men could also buy their way out of service or provide a substitute. Because of these loopholes, some southerners complained that the conflict was a "rich man's war, poor man's fight." Even with a draft, the Confederacy struggled throughout the war to put enough soldiers in the field.

Texas women made pillows and many other items for troops who were away fighting.

⭐ **Reading Check Analyzing Information** Why do you think the Confederacy had to pass a draft law?

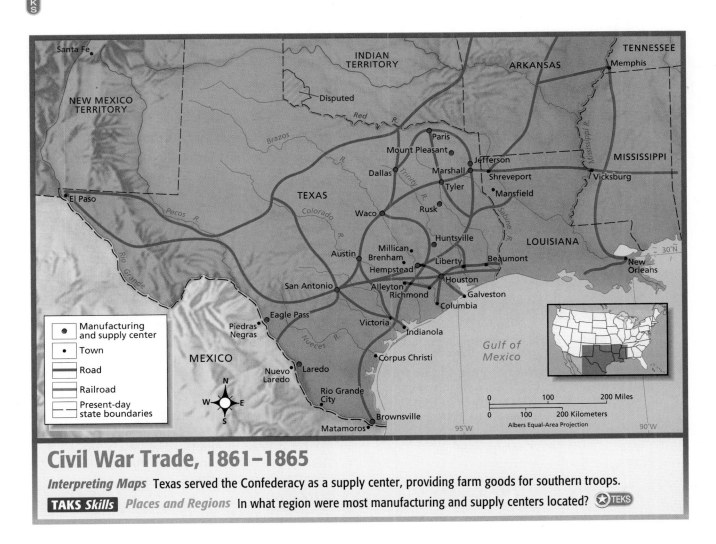

Civil War Trade, 1861–1865

Interpreting Maps Texas served the Confederacy as a supply center, providing farm goods for southern troops.

TAKS Skills *Places and Regions* In what region were most manufacturing and supply centers located? ⭐TEKS

Interpreting the Visual Record

Conflict at the Nueces. *Blood was shed when militia soldiers caught up with some fleeing Unionists at the Neuces River.* ***What effects of the Civil War do you think this illustration reveals?*** ★TEKS

★ Unionists in Texas

The Confederate draft sparked fierce opposition from some Unionists. Although many had joined the southern war effort, some refused to fight for either side. Many German Americans and Mexican Americans remained neutral. When the draft was passed, however, Texans had to choose sides. Some Unionists fled Texas to avoid the draft.

Confederate officials regarded many Texas Unionists as potentially dangerous traitors. Officials placed some areas with a large Unionist population under **martial law**, or rule by armed forces. Some Unionists were violently attacked. In August 1862 about 60 German Texans tried to flee to Mexico rather than be drafted into the Confederate army. The Texas militia caught and attacked them near the Nueces River, killing many. When German communities in Central Texas organized to protest, Confederates hanged 50 protesters.

Confederate leaders also worried about Unionists in North Texas. In October 1862 Confederate troops arrested more than 150 suspected Unionists and formed a court to try the accused people. A member of the jury remembered the events. "There were crowds in sight in every direction, armed, pressing forward prisoners under guard. . . . The mind of almost every man I saw seemed to be unhinged, and wild excitement reigned supreme." A mob soon took over. By the time the violence had ended, 40 suspected Unionists were hanged in Gainesville. Men were also killed in neighboring counties. This violence revealed how deep the feelings about the war ran.

★ **Reading Check Summarizing** What happened to some Unionists in Texas?

★ **Section 4 Review** ★TEKS Questions 2, 3a, 3b, 4

 go. hrw .com Homework Practice Online
keyword: ST3 HP18

1 Define and explain:
• draft
• martial law

2 Identifying Cause and Effect
What problems arose for Unionists during the Civil War, and how did these issues affect them?

| Problems | → | Effect on Unionists |

3 Finding the Main Idea
a. What was life like in Texas during the war?
b. Why did the Confederate government start drafting men into military service?

4 Writing and Critical Thinking
Analyzing Information Imagine that you are living in Texas during the Civil War. Write a journal entry describing what your life is like. Consider the following:
• what you eat
• what you wear

The End of the War

Read to Discover
1. What were the final events and battles of the Civil War?
2. How was Texas affected by the Civil War?

Identify
- **March to the Sea**
- **Emancipation Proclamation**

Why It Matters Today

The Civil War left much of the South in ruins. Use CNN**fyi**.com or other **current events** sources to learn more about a nation or group today that is rebuilding after a war. Record your findings in your journal.

The Story Continues

The Union advance had become unstoppable. General William T. Sherman's army pushed relentlessly through the South toward the Atlantic coast, destroying whatever lay in its path. After one battle, Texan Oscar Alexander rode out to look at the Georgia countryside. An elderly woman on crutches looked up at Alexander. "I do not know where those two little children and I are going to stay," she said. Alexander had no response. All he could see in every direction was the smoke of burning houses.

The Union army used drums to set the pace of their marching.

★ The War Draws to a Close

After the Battle of Gettysburg and fall of Vicksburg in July 1863, Union forces moved steadily into the South. In 1864 President Lincoln ordered General Ulysses S. Grant to take command in the eastern theater. Grant moved his army into eastern Virginia and engaged General Lee's troops in a series of battles. Lee's army was now on the defensive. Both sides suffered heavy losses, but Grant's army greatly outnumbered the Confederate forces. He continued to drive toward Richmond.

Meanwhile, Union general William Tecumseh Sherman led an army south from Tennessee toward Atlanta, an important railroad center. After capturing Atlanta in September 1864, Sherman set out across Georgia to Savannah. As he marched through the state, his army destroyed crops, livestock, railroads—any resources that could help the South. General John Bell Hood of Texas was unable to stop Sherman.

Surrender. General Lee surrenders to General Grant at Appomattox Courthouse, Virginia, marking the end of the Civil War. **How does the artist show the importance of this event?**

Sherman completed his **March to the Sea** when he reached Savannah in December. A Texas soldier remembered the ruin that Sherman's army left behind. "On Gen. Sherman's 'destruction' to the sea . . . the Yanks had burned and destroyed everything."

While Sherman marched on to the Carolinas, Grant was pursuing Lee. In April 1865, Union forces surrounded Lee's army near the town of Appomattox Courthouse, Virginia. With few options left, Lee met with Grant on April 9 and agreed to the Union's terms of surrender.

✔**Reading Check** **Analyzing Information** Why did Sherman destroy property on his March to the Sea?

★ Battle at Palmito Ranch

Word of Lee's surrender reached Confederate troops in the Brownsville area by May 1865. Hundreds of soldiers left their posts for home. But many stayed when General E. Kirby Smith, the commander of the western Confederate states, urged the soldiers to continue the war.

On May 12, Union troops moved inland to occupy Brownsville. The next day—more than a month after General Lee's surrender—Union and Confederate forces clashed at Palmito Ranch near Brownsville. Led by Colonel John S. Ford, the Confederate troops defeated the Union forces and captured more than 100 prisoners. A few days later, Union officers met with Ford to arrange a truce. The last land battle of the Civil War was a Confederate victory, but the South had already lost the war.

✔**Reading Check** **Supporting a Point of View** Do you agree or disagree with the soldiers' decision to continue fighting after Lee surrendered? Explain your answer.

★ Consequences of the War

About 620,000 Americans lost their lives in the Civil War, making it the deadliest conflict in U.S. history. Some 90,000 Texans served, and thousands were killed or wounded. Many soldiers suffered serious injuries such as the loss of an arm or leg. One Texas soldier remembered how he felt after the war. "I came home in May, 1865, not . . . scrappy as I started out, but . . . well versed [familiarized] in hardships, privations [loss], dangers and the art of war. . . . All I wanted in this life was some old clothes and something to eat."

Although Texas suffered few battles, the war left the state's economy in shambles. The cotton trade had nearly stopped. The deaths of many men placed hardships on Texas businesses, farms, and plantations. Fields needed to be plowed, and businesses needed to be reopened. Much work needed to be done to rebuild the state. When Governor Murrah and other officials fled to Mexico at the end of the war, the state's government had collapsed. No one seemed to know who was in charge. It took some time before Union forces could move in and restore order.

Enslaved Texans saw the war as a struggle for freedom. African American William Adams remembered, "we sure didn't want the South to win." After the war African Americans in Texas wondered about their future. In 1863 President Lincoln had issued the **Emancipation Proclamation**. This stated that slaves were free in those areas rebelling against the United States. As the Union army advanced into a Confederate state, slaves were freed. But the 250,000 freed slaves in Texas were uncertain what would happen next.

The Emancipation Proclamation freed all slaves in areas "in rebellion against the United States."

✪ **Reading Check** **Summarizing** How did the Civil War affect the Texas economy?

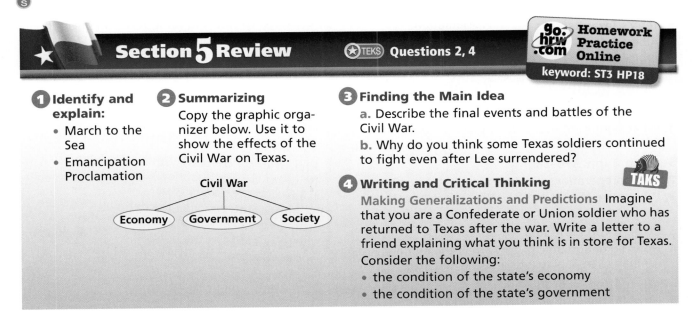

Section 5 Review ✪TEKS Questions 2, 4

go.hrw.com **Homework Practice Online**
keyword: ST3 HP18

1 Identify and explain:
- March to the Sea
- Emancipation Proclamation

2 Summarizing
Copy the graphic organizer below. Use it to show the effects of the Civil War on Texas.

Civil War
Economy — Government — Society

3 Finding the Main Idea
a. Describe the final events and battles of the Civil War.
b. Why do you think some Texas soldiers continued to fight even after Lee surrendered?

4 Writing and Critical Thinking

TAKS

Making Generalizations and Predictions Imagine that you are a Confederate or Union soldier who has returned to Texas after the war. Write a letter to a friend explaining what you think is in store for Texas.
Consider the following:
- the condition of the state's economy
- the condition of the state's government

The Chapter at a Glance

Examine the following visual summary of the chapter. Then use the visual to write a one-page story about the role of Texas in the Civil War. Use standard grammar, spelling, sentence structure, and punctuation to describe the battles in and near Texas and life on the Texas home front during the war. ⭐TEKS

Texas in the Civil War

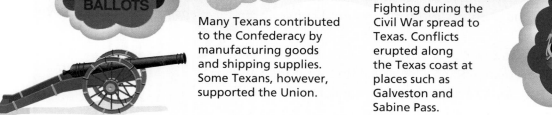

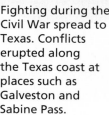
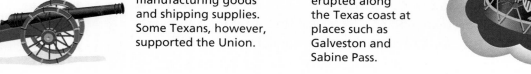

Texans voted to secede from the Union and join the Confederacy.

The war took a heavy toll on both sides. Many Texans were killed or wounded in the fighting.

Many Texans contributed to the Confederacy by manufacturing goods and shipping supplies. Some Texans, however, supported the Union.

Fighting during the Civil War spread to Texas. Conflicts erupted along the Texas coast at places such as Galveston and Sabine Pass.

Identifying People and Ideas ⭐TEKS

Use each of the following terms or people in historically significant sentences.

1. secede
2. states' rights
3. Unionists
4. regiments
5. Terry's Texas Rangers
6. Albert Sidney Johnston
7. Battle of Sabine Pass
8. Santos Benavides
9. Red River Campaign
10. Emancipation Proclamation

Understanding Main Ideas ⭐TEKS

Section 1 (pp. 372–375)
1. What significant events took place in Texas in 1861?

Section 2 (pp. 376–380)
2. What preparations did Texans make for war?
3. What were the North's and the South's strategies for fighting the war?

Section 3 (pp. 381–385)
4. How did geographic factors affect the military campaigns at Sabine Pass and the Red River?

Section 4 (pp. 386–388)
5. How did the Civil War affect life in Texas?

Section 5 (pp. 389–391)
6. How did the Civil War affect the Texas economy?

You Be the Historian ⭐TEKS

Reviewing Themes

1. **Economics** Why did Texas suffer less from the war than other areas of the South?
2. **Citizenship** How did some Texas Unionists lose their civil rights during the war?
3. **Geography** Why did most of the Union forces invade Texas by attacking coastal ports?

⭐TEKS

TAKS Practice: **Thinking Critically**

1. **Identifying Points of View** What were the points of view of abolitionists and southern leaders on the slavery issue?
2. **Summarizing** Describe the defining characteristics of the Civil War era in Texas history.
3. **Categorizing** List the political, economic, and social effects of the Civil War on Texas.

Interpreting Maps ⭐TEKS

Study the map below. Then use the information on the map to answer the questions that follow.

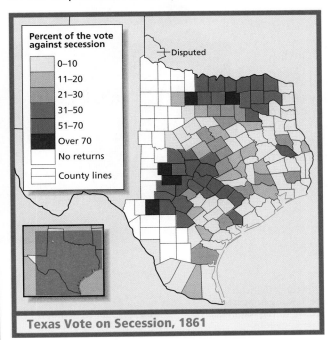

Percent of the vote against secession

- 0–10
- 11–20
- 21–30
- 31–50
- 51–70
- Over 70
- No returns
- County lines

Disputed

Texas Vote on Secession, 1861

1. Which of the following statements describes the pattern of voting on the secession issue?

   a. Few slaves lived in East Texas.
   b. Most plantations were in North Texas.
   c. Cotton grew well in the Hill Country.
   d. White Texans in good cotton-growing regions were likely to vote for secession.

2. Why do you think many counties in North Texas opposed secession?

Analyzing Primary Sources ⭐TEKS

Read the following quote by Texas soldier Ralph Smith. Then answer the questions.

"In great battles with thousands on each side . . . privates are like little screws in the wheel of a giant machine. All I remember for the first few minutes . . . was a terrible noise[,] great smoke, incessant [continual] rattling of small arms, infernal [terrible] confusion and then I realized that the whole line of the enemy was in disorderly retreat."

3. Which of the following statements best describes the author's point of view?

   a. His memory of the first few minutes of the battle is very clear.
   b. Individual soldiers often do not make a significant difference in large battles.
   c. He was always able to keep track of the battle's progress.
   d. He believes the enemy retreated in an orderly fashion.

4. What do you think Smith meant when he described privates as screws in a giant machine?

Alternative Assessment

Cooperative Learning ⭐TEKS

Work with a small group to complete the following activity. Each person in your group should select a significant individual such as the following: a) Sam Houston b) James W. Throckmorton c) John Bell Hood d) Albert Sidney Johnston e) Richard Dowling. You may want to select someone who lived in your county. Each member should research information about the person. Then work with your group to create a time line that shows the person's activities before, during, and after the war.

BUILDING YOUR Portfolio

internet connect

Internet Activity: go.hrw.com
KEYWORD: ST3 TX18 ⭐TEKS
Access the Internet through the HRW Go site to research the role of Texas in the Civil War. Then create a collage, diorama, or model that shows how the Civil War affected politics, the economy, and society in Texas. Write captions explaining your creation. Be sure to use standard grammar, spelling, sentence structure, and punctuation.

Reconstruction

(1865–1877)

The Emancipation Proclamation was issued in 1863 but did not go into effect in Texas until after the Civil War.

Senator George T. Ruby and other African Americans served in the Texas legislature during Reconstruction.

TEXAS

1865 The Emancipation Proclamation goes into effect in Texas, freeing the state's slaves.

1868 African American George T. Ruby is elected as a delegate to the Republican National Convention.

1869 Republican Edmund J. Davis is elected governor.

1865   1867   1869

U.S. and WORLD

1865 The Thirteenth Amendment, abolishing slavery, is put into effect.

1867 The U.S. Congress takes control of Reconstruction away from the president.

1868 Ulysses S. Grant is elected president.
1870 The Fifteenth Amendment gives African American men the right to vote.

African Americans celebrated the passage of constitutional amendments that ensured their rights, including the Fifteenth Amendment, which gave African American men the right to vote.

Build on What You Know

The Civil War had divided the country and badly damaged the South. The country needed to reunite and to help the millions of newly freed African Americans adjust to life after slavery. Leaders from the North and the South worked to rebuild the nation.

The 1873 election led to conflict between Republicans and Democrats, in which armed supporters took over parts of the state capitol.

1871 A public school system is created in Texas.

1874 The Democratic Party regains full control of state government.

1876 Texas adopts a new constitution.

1871　　1873　　1875　　1877

1872 The General Amnesty Act allows most former Confederates to once again hold public office.

1874 Republicans lose control of the U.S. House of Representatives.

1877 The Compromise of 1877 ends Reconstruction throughout the South.

Republican Rutherford B. Hayes won a close presidential election in 1876 after he promised Democrats that he would end Reconstruction.

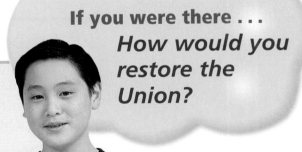

If you were there . . .
How would you restore the Union?

You Be the Historian

Themes Journal

What's Your Opinion? Do you **agree** or **disagree** with the following statements? Support your point of view in your journal.

- **Government** People who participate in a rebellion should be harshly punished.

- **Citizenship** People who have been on different sides in a war can work together to rebuild a country.

- **Economics** War always leads to dramatic changes in a nation's economy.

Presidential Reconstruction

Read to Discover

1. How did former slaves react to freedom, and how did the federal government help them?
2. What did Texas have to do to rejoin the Union?
3. How were the lives of freedpeople in Texas restricted after the Civil War?

Why It Matters Today

The federal government helped former slaves after the Civil War. Use **CNNfyi.com** or other **current events** sources to learn more about a government program that helps citizens today. Record your findings in your journal.

Define

- **freedpeople**
- **suffrage**
- **civil rights**

Identify

- **Juneteenth**
- **Reconstruction**
- **Thirteenth Amendment**
- **Freedmen's Bureau**
- **Andrew Johnson**
- **James W. Throckmorton**
- **Black Codes**

The Story Continues

One day after the Civil War ended, Tempie Cummins's mother was eavesdropping on their slaveholder. She heard him say that slaves in Texas had been freed. He also vowed to keep his slaves until "he had made another crop or two." Tempie's mother immediately told the other slaves that they were free and that they should quit working. The slaveholder chased her and shot at her, but she escaped with Tempie.

The Emancipation Proclamation was drafted on this table, which was located in the cabinet room of the White House.

★ Emancipation

U.S. troops took control of Texas at the end of the Civil War. When Union general Gordon Granger landed at Galveston in 1865, he issued a proclamation freeing Texas slaves. That day, June 19, is celebrated as **Juneteenth**. One former slave remembered hearing the news.

> **Texas Voices** **"We were working one day when somebody . . . came by and told us we were free, and we stopped working. . . . The boss man came up, and he said he was going to knock us off the fence if we didn't go back to work. . . . He called for his carriage, and said he was going to town to see what the government was going to do. Next day he came back and said, 'Well, you're just as free as I am.'"**
>
> —Anonymous, quoted in *Black Texas Women: A Sourcebook,* by Ruthe Winegarten

As the news of emancipation spread, many **freedpeople**, or former slaves, left the plantations. For many it was the first time they had the freedom to travel. During the summer and fall of 1865, Texas roads were crowded with former slaves loaded down with their possessions. Many freedpeople rushed to courthouses to legalize their informal slave marriages. Others searched for family members from whom they had been separated. Some gathered at military posts and towns, hoping to find paying jobs and military protection. Many who had been sent to Texas during the war returned to their prewar homes.

⭐ **Reading Check** **Summarizing** How did the end of the Civil War affect Texas slaves?

⭐ The Freedmen's Bureau

The U.S. government wanted to help freedpeople and bring the southern states back into the Union. **Reconstruction**—the process of reuniting the nation and rebuilding the southern states—lasted from 1865 to 1877. In February 1865 the U.S. Congress had proposed the **Thirteenth Amendment**, which abolished slavery. In March, Congress created the **Freedmen's Bureau** to provide help and legal aid to freedpeople. Because they had no land and few job opportunities, many freedpeople returned to their old plantations for work. Bureau agents tried to regulate freedpeople's employment contracts with landowners.

In addition, the bureau and churches helped African Americans open many schools in Texas. By 1870 more than 9,000 African Americans were enrolled in 150 schools. As a result, illiteracy—or the inability to read or write—among African Americans dropped from 95 percent in 1865 to 75 percent in 1880. A reporter toured one school.

Texas Voices ❝We saw fathers and mothers . . . with their grown up children, all anxiously engaged in the pursuit of knowledge. . . . We are informed that their progress is rapid, and from what we saw, the pupils are deeply interested in learning to read.❞

—*Flake's Bulletin*, quoted in *Republicanism in Reconstruction Texas*, by Carl H. Moneyhon

However, with only a few dozen agents assigned to Texas at any one time, bureau agents were limited in what they could achieve. There was also a limited number of federal troops assigned to support the agents' activities. Many Texans opposed the bureau's efforts to help freedpeople. One agent noted that former Confederates "seem to take every opportunity to vent [release] their rage and hatred upon the blacks. They are frequently beaten unmercifully." Bureau agents tried to protect freedpeople from such violence and to help them adjust to freedom.

⭐ **Reading Check** **Analyzing Information** Why might new educational opportunities for African Americans be considered an important social effect of Reconstruction in Texas?

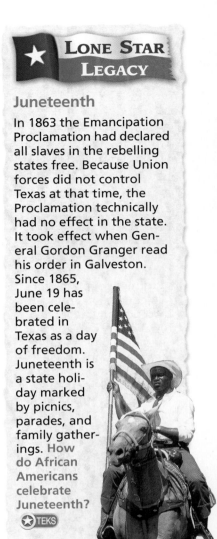

⭐ **LONE STAR LEGACY**

Juneteenth

In 1863 the Emancipation Proclamation had declared all slaves in the rebelling states free. Because Union forces did not control Texas at that time, the Proclamation technically had no effect in the state. It took effect when General Gordon Granger read his order in Galveston. Since 1865, June 19 has been celebrated in Texas as a day of freedom. Juneteenth is a state holiday marked by picnics, parades, and family gatherings. **How do African Americans celebrate Juneteenth?**

⭐TEKS

Analyzing Primary Sources
Drawing Inferences and Conclusions Why were adult African Americans in school alongside their children?

★ President Johnson's Plan

While the bureau was helping freedpeople, leaders in the federal government were debating how Reconstruction should proceed. Some people wanted to punish the South. Others, like President Abraham Lincoln, did not want to increase feelings of bitterness. Before the war ended he proposed a plan to reunite the country quickly. After Lincoln was assassinated in April 1865, **Andrew Johnson** became the new president.

Johnson also wanted Reconstruction to proceed quickly. Under his plan, voters in the former Confederate states had to take an oath of loyalty to the United States. High-ranking Confederate officials and wealthy property owners needed to apply for a presidential pardon. Afterward, they could take part in government once again. Before a state could rejoin the Union, it had to create a provisional, or temporary, government. The state had to write a new constitution that declared secession illegal and abolished slavery. Finally, the state had to agree not to pay any outstanding Confederate debts. After ratifying the new constitution, voters would elect a governor and legislature. The legislature then had to ratify the Thirteenth Amendment. Once a state's representatives had been seated in the U.S. Congress, the state would be fully restored to the Union. Johnson's Reconstruction plan was acceptable to many Texans.

Johnson appointed Unionist Andrew J. Hamilton as provisional governor of Texas in June 1865. Hamilton had previously represented Texas in the U.S. Congress from 1859 to 1861. When war broke out, he had gone north and become a general in the Union army. Nonetheless, many Texans welcomed him back to Austin in August 1865. Governor Hamilton soon appointed government officials, selecting Unionists as well as some former Confederates. In November he called an election to select delegates to a constitutional convention. Former Confederates, but not African Americans, could vote in the election.

The convention assembled in Austin on February 7, 1866. The delegates completed their work in two months. They declared secession illegal, recognized the end of slavery, and canceled the Confederate war debt. The remainder of the constitution was similar to the 1845 constitution. Debate was heated, however, over the status of freedpeople. The delegates failed to give African Americans equal rights. For example, black Texans could not testify in court cases involving white Texans or hold office. Nor were they granted **suffrage**, or voting rights. In June 1866, Texas voters approved the new constitution and elected government officials. **James W. Throckmorton** won the governor's race over Elisha M. Pease, a former governor. Former secessionists easily won control of the legislature. When it met on August 6, 1866, the legislature refused to ratify the Thirteenth Amendment.

★ **Reading Check** **Finding the Main Idea** Why did Governor Hamilton call a constitutional convention?

Daily Life

African American Schools

Reconstruction schools offered the first chance for freedpeople to get an education. But schools faced many challenges. The Freedmen's Bureau had difficulty recruiting teachers, and schools were often short of supplies. In September 1865 a Galveston teacher complained that he had 250 students but no books. Some schools were held in local churches. A teacher in Chambers County taught school in a grove of trees. **What challenges did black schools face during Reconstruction?** ★TEKS

★ The Black Codes

The Texas legislature, like others in the South, passed **Black Codes**. These laws denied African Americans' **civil rights**, or the individual rights guaranteed by the U.S. Constitution. Many Black Codes related to freedom of movement and work. For example, African Americans had to sign labor contracts that strongly favored their employers. African Americans could be jailed simply for not having jobs. Large landowners argued that such laws were needed to ensure that enough workers were available to harvest the state's crops.

African Americans also had to deal with threats and violence. Between 1865 and 1868, 468 freedpeople in Texas were murdered—90 percent of them by white men. Bringing the murderers to justice was difficult, as one Texas judge noted.

The Granger Collection, New York

Even after the Civil War, freedpeople who fell into debt could be auctioned as servants to pay off the debt.

Texas Voices

❝I regard it as almost an impossibility under existing arrangements to convict a white man of any crime . . . where the proof . . . depends upon the testimony of a black man, or where the violence has been against a black man. . . . I can suggest no means by which I think the civil courts can remedy the evil without a change in the public sentiment of the country.❞

—James J. Thornton, quoted in *Reconstruction in Texas,* by Charles William Ramsdell

Analyzing Primary Sources
Identifying Points of View
What did the judge think needed to happen before black Texans could receive justice in the courts?

★ **Reading Check** **Comparing and Contrasting** How was life similar and different for African Americans under the Black Codes and slavery?

Section 1 Review ★TEKS Questions 2, 3, 4a, 4b, 5

go.hrw.com **Homework Practice Online**
keyword: ST3 HP19

1 Define and explain:
- freedpeople
- suffrage
- civil rights

2 Identify and explain:
- Juneteenth
- Reconstruction
- Thirteenth Amendment
- Freedmen's Bureau
- Andrew Johnson
- James W. Throckmorton
- Black Codes

3 Sequencing
Copy the graphic organizer below. Use it to show, in order, the steps Texas had to take to be readmitted to the Union under President Johnson's plan.

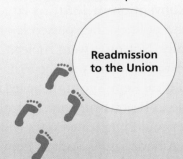

Readmission to the Union

4 Finding the Main Idea
a. How did the Freedmen's Bureau assist freedpeople in Texas?
b. In what ways were African Americans in Texas denied their civil rights after the Civil War?

5 Writing and Critical Thinking **TAKS**
Analyzing Information Imagine that you are living in Texas when General Granger announces the Emancipation Proclamation. Write a letter describing freedpeople's response.
Consider the following:
- activity at military posts and courthouses
- activity on the state's roads

Congressional Reconstruction

Read to Discover

1. Why did Congress take control of Reconstruction?
2. What did Congress require Texas to do to be readmitted to the Union?
3. How did Congressional Reconstruction affect Texans?

Why It Matters Today

Congress and the president disagreed about how Reconstruction should be handled. Use CNNfyi.com or other **current events** sources to learn about an issue that Congress and the president are debating today. Record your findings in your journal.

Define

• impeach

Identify

• **Radical Republicans**
• **Civil Rights Act of 1866**
• **Fourteenth Amendment**
• **Reconstruction Acts**
• **Philip Sheridan**
• **Edmund J. Davis**
• **George T. Ruby**
• **Union League**
• **Fifteenth Amendment**

Although James W. Thockmorton had voted against secession, he had served as a Confederate officer. He was elected governor in 1866.

The Story Continues

Allen Manning was frustrated. He and other African Americans had finally won their freedom. But many of the same people who controlled Texas before the war were regaining power. He wondered if life would truly become better for black Texans. To Manning, it seemed that many white Texans could not "get over us being free."

★ Radical Republicans React

The Black Codes raised new concerns in the U.S. Congress about President Johnson's Reconstruction plan. In addition, southern states had elected many of the people who had led the rebellion. For example, U.S. senator Oran M. Roberts had served as president of the Texas Secession Convention in 1861. As large-scale landowners took control of the South's politics, they passed laws that suited them economically and politically. Not only were African Americans denied equal rights but violence against them was occurring throughout the South.

Many **Radical Republicans** believed the U.S. Congress needed to take a greater role in Reconstruction. They thought that loyal southern state governments could be created only with the participation of Unionists and African Americans. As Radical Republicans gained power and influence, they passed the **Civil Rights Act of 1866**. This act gave citizenship to

African Americans and guaranteed them basic rights. President Johnson vetoed the act, arguing that it gave too much power to the federal government. He also rejected the principle of equal rights for African Americans. Congress overrode Johnson's veto. This marked a serious split between Congress and the president. Congress took an additional step to ensure that the act would not be overturned by a later Congress. In the summer of 1866, Republicans proposed the **Fourteenth Amendment** to guarantee citizenship and equal rights to African Americans. The Texas legislature and most other southern states refused to ratify it.

⭐ **Reading Check** **Identifying Cause and Effect** Who returned to power in the South, and how did this affect the actions of the U.S. Congress?

U.S. Army wagons appeared throughout Texas during Reconstruction.

⭐ The Reconstruction Acts

The 1866 elections gave the Republicans strong majorities in both houses of the U.S. Congress. Republicans now had enough votes to override any presidential veto. Congress passed a series of **Reconstruction Acts** beginning in March 1867. These acts marked the beginning of Congressional Reconstruction. The new southern state governments were once again declared provisional. Congress divided the South into

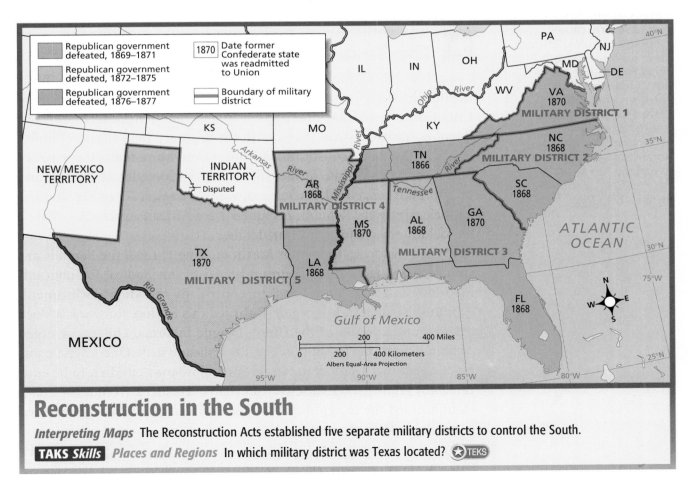

Republican government defeated, 1869–1871

Republican government defeated, 1872–1875

Republican government defeated, 1876–1877

1870 Date former Confederate state was readmitted to Union

Boundary of military district

PA
NJ
IL
IN
OH
MD
DE
WV
VA
1870
MILITARY DISTRICT 1
KS
MO
KY
NC
1868
MILITARY DISTRICT 2
NEW MEXICO TERRITORY
INDIAN TERRITORY
Disputed
AR
1868
MILITARY DISTRICT 4
TN
1866
SC
1868
MS
1870
AL
1868
GA
1870
ATLANTIC OCEAN
TX
1870
LA
1868
MILITARY DISTRICT 5
MILITARY DISTRICT 3
FL
1868
MEXICO
Gulf of Mexico
Rio Grande
Arkansas River
Mississippi River
Tennessee River
Ohio River

0 200 400 Miles
0 200 400 Kilometers
Albers Equal-Area Projection

Reconstruction in the South

Interpreting Maps The Reconstruction Acts established five separate military districts to control the South.

TAKS Skills *Places and Regions* In which military district was Texas located? ⭐TEKS

George T. Ruby
(1841–1882)

A native of New York, George T. Ruby moved to Texas in 1866 as an educator with the Freedmen's Bureau. He soon became involved in politics. In 1868 Ruby won election to the constitutional convention, where he pushed for equal rights for African Americans. In 1869, Texans elected Ruby to the state senate, where he served on several important committees. There he supported several causes, including bringing African American and white students together in the state's schools. After Reconstruction, Ruby moved to New Orleans, where he edited a newspaper for African Americans until he died of malaria. **How did George T. Ruby contribute to Texas?** **TEKS**

five military districts, with each placed under the command of an army officer. Southern states would have to do more than Johnson's plan had required to rejoin the Union. The states had to write new constitutions guaranteeing rights for African Americans, including suffrage for black men. The states also had to ratify the Fourteenth Amendment.

Texas and Louisiana made up the Fifth Military District, commanded by General **Philip Sheridan**. In July 1867 Congress gave military commanders wide authority to remove uncooperative southern leaders from office. That month Sheridan removed Governor Throckmorton, calling him "an impediment [obstacle] to Reconstruction." Sheridan appointed Elisha M. Pease to replace Throckmorton. Pease, a former two-term governor, was respected by most Texans. Over the next few months the military removed hundreds of other state and local officials.

President Johnson tried to block Congressional Reconstruction, prompting the House to **impeach** him. To impeach is to bring charges of wrongdoing against a public official. Johnson avoided being removed from office by one vote in the Senate, but his power had been broken. Ulysses S. Grant, who was more supportive of Congressional Reconstruction, won the 1868 presidential election.

★ **Reading Check** **Finding the Main Idea** What was the significance for Texas of the Republicans' success in the 1866 elections?

★ The Texas Republican Party

Congressional Reconstruction led to the development of the Texas Republican Party in 1867. In general, the party was made up mostly of Unionists and African Americans as well as many Mexican Americans. Republicans had a strong turnout in the February 1868 election for delegates to the state's constitutional convention. More than 80 percent of black men voted, while former high-ranking Confederate officials and most prewar officeholders could not vote. As a result, 78 of the 90 original delegates were Republicans and 9 were African Americans. Only a few delegates were former Confederates.

When the delegates met in Austin on June 1, 1868, the Republicans split into two factions. One group hoped to put Radical Republicans, including African Americans, in control of the state government. **Edmund J. Davis** and **George T. Ruby** led this faction. Ruby was a black delegate and a leader of the **Union League** in Texas. The league urged African Americans to support the Republican Party. One league pamphlet noted that Democrats would "not allow your children to be educated nor [allow] you to discuss your rights." Former governor Andrew J. Hamilton led the second faction. These moderate Republicans favored few changes from the past.

★ **Reading Check** **Identifying Points of View** Why did African American leaders in Texas try to rally support for the Republican Party?

The Constitution of 1869

The Constitutional Convention of 1868–69 was controlled largely by Radical Republicans. The delegates finished their work on the constitution in February 1869. The new Texas constitution gave equal rights to African Americans, including the right to vote. That same year the U.S. Congress proposed the **Fifteenth Amendment**, which gave suffrage to African American men.

In contrast to past constitutions, the new constitution gave the governor the power to appoint many state officials and judges. The governor's term of office was lengthened from two to four years, and the legislature was to meet every year. The constitution also made important changes in public education. The sale of public lands and a tax of one dollar per voter was to fund schools. In addition, one fourth of state revenue was to be set aside for schools. For the first time, attendance at school was required by law.

Texans voted in favor of the constitution by a wide margin. In the same election, Edmund J. Davis defeated Andrew J. Hamilton in a close race for governor. The Radical Republicans in the U.S. Congress now had a supporter in the Texas governor's office. Republicans also controlled the newly elected Texas legislature, which quickly ratified the Fourteenth and Fifteenth Amendments. This paved the way for Texas to be restored to the Union. In March 1870 President Grant signed an act of Congress admitting Texas senators and representatives. The next month, control of Texas was returned to the state government.

 Reading Check Contrasting How did the rights of African Americans differ under the Texas constitutions of 1866 and 1869?

 **Citizenship and You**

Your Vote Counts

Black Texans first registered to vote in 1867. About 98 percent of black men registered to vote that year. Later amendments to the U.S. Constitution gave the right to vote to women and younger people. More Texans have the power to vote today than at any time in the state's history. What was one way African Americans fulfilled their civic responsibilities? ⭐TEKS

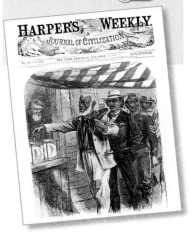

HARPER'S WEEKLY
JOURNAL OF CIVILIZATION

Section 2 Review ⭐TEKS Questions 2, 3, 4a, 4b, 5

go.hrw.com **Homework Practice Online** keyword: ST3 HP19

1 Define and explain:
- impeach

2 Identify and explain:
- Radical Republicans
- Civil Rights Act of 1866
- Fourteenth Amendment
- Reconstruction Acts
- Philip Sheridan
- Edmund J. Davis
- George T. Ruby
- Union League
- Fifteenth Amendment

3 Summarizing
Copy the graphic organizer below. Use it to list four major provisions of the Constitution of 1869.

4 Finding the Main Idea

a. Why did the Radical Republicans take control of Reconstruction away from President Johnson?

b. What did southern states have to do to be readmitted to the Union under Congressional Reconstruction?

5 Writing and Critical Thinking **TAKS**
Making Generalizations and Predictions Imagine that you are a newspaper editor in 1869. Write an editorial discussing how the new constitution and military control of the state will affect Texans.

Consider the following:
- who had the right to vote
- the military's role in Texas

The Davis Administration

Read to Discover

1. What were the major accomplishments and criticisms of the Davis administration?
2. What caused the end of Reconstruction in Texas?

Why It Matters Today

Texans during Reconstruction struggled to pay for Governor Edmund J. Davis's programs. Use CNNfyi.com or other **current events** sources to learn about how citizens pay for government programs today. Record your findings in your journal.

Define

• bonds
• scalawags
• carpetbaggers

Identify

• Matthew Gaines
• Ku Klux Klan
• Obnoxious Acts
• Richard Coke

The Story Continues

The First Texas Cavalry of the Union army was together again. This time they had gathered to celebrate, not to fight. The men, thrilled at their former leader Edmund J. Davis's victory in the governor's race, threw him a barbecue. Many Texans were there—"all the world hereabouts," according to the *Galveston News*. The time for celebration was short, however, as the Republicans turned to the business of rebuilding the state.

Before the Civil War, Edmund J. Davis had served as a state district judge in Brownsville.

★ The Davis Administration's Policies

Governor Edmund J. Davis had the support of the legislature that assembled in April 1870. It was dominated by Republicans, 11 of whom were African American. Senators **Matthew Gaines** and George T. Ruby led the legislative effort to stop the widespread crime in the state, particularly the actions of the **Ku Klux Klan**. This secret society had been threatening and murdering African Americans to keep them from expressing their political views. The legislature created a state militia and police force, which soon took action. As the police made arrests, crime dropped, and the influence of the Ku Klux Klan lessened.

The Republicans also tackled an important social issue—education. Davis wanted African Americans to be treated equally by the law. "I do not want to see white or black named in any law whatsoever." The legislature created free public schools for all the state's children. Money from public land sales and state and local taxes helped pay for school expenses. A state board of education and a superintendent of education oversaw the state's schools. Schools had a common course of study, teacher certification, and a central administration. Enrollment grew rapidly, with almost 130,000 students in the public schools during the 1872–73 school year.

The legislature also tried to help Texas recover economically after the war. To improve the state's transportation system, the legislature set aside money for roads and bridges. The state also issued **bonds** to help pay for railroad lines. Bonds are certificates that represent money the government has borrowed. The administration raised taxes to pay for schools, roads, and the larger central government.

⭐ **Reading Check** **Analyzing Information** How did Reconstruction affect the state socially and economically?

⭐ Opposition to Reconstruction

Many Texans opposed these policies. They referred to Texans who supported the Republicans as "**scalawags**," or "mean fellows." The few northerners who had come to Texas after the war were sometimes called "**carpetbaggers**" because some carried all they owned in bags made of carpet. An Illinois man explained why he moved to Texas. "I am going to introduce new ideas here in the farming line, and show the beauties of free over slave labor."

In the political arena, Democrats opposed Edmund J. Davis and the Radical Republicans at every opportunity. They clashed over the state police, the militia, and taxes. Democrats called many of the new laws **Obnoxious Acts**—obnoxious means very unpleasant. When Democrats complained of the rising state debt, Davis defended the spending. "If you have no government it will cost you nothing. If you have public schools and law and order, you must pay for it." Democrats also accused the Davis administration of taking money by fraud.

Democrats were also angered when Davis used the state police to guard voters in the 1872 elections. Davis's opponents claimed he was trying to frighten Democratic voters. In this election the Democrats regained control of the legislature.

⭐ **Reading Check** **Drawing Inferences and Conclusions** How did the policies of Davis's administration affect the state's economy?

Interpreting Political Cartoons

Reconstruction. *In this political cartoon, the South is shown carrying President Grant, who rides in a heavy carpetbag.* **How does this political cartoon reflect the southern point of view?** ⭐ TEKS

The Granger Collection, New York

LINKING PAST to PRESENT

Party Politics

Before the Civil War, the Democratic Party dominated Texas politics. This ended when Radical Republicans rose to power. Supported overwhelmingly by freedpeople, the Republicans in Texas brought a temporary halt to the Democrats' control. With the end of Reconstruction, the Democratic Party regained control of Texas politics. Not until the 1980s did the Republican Party play a major role in Texas politics. Both parties are now well represented in state government.

How did Reconstruction affect Texas politics?

⭐ TEKS

Bill Clements FOR GOVERNOR

A campaign pin for Bill Clements, the first Republican governor since Reconstruction.

★ The End of Reconstruction

In the 1873 election for governor Edmund J. Davis had the support of Radical Republicans. Most white Texans supported Democrat **Richard Coke**, a former Confederate officer. Coke won in a landslide—receiving 85,549 votes to 42,663 for Davis. Democrats also won the legislature. Some Republicans argued that the polls had closed too early. They brought the issue to the Texas Supreme Court, which ruled that the election was unconstitutional. Nonetheless, Democrats demanded control of the government. Davis was unsure what to do. He had been ready to turn the office over to Coke, but he did not want to ignore the court's ruling. Coke, meanwhile, "intended to become governor . . . no matter what it cost him or the state," according to one observer.

Davis allowed the legislature to meet, but he feared that the Democrats might take the governor's office by force. So he called in armed supporters to guard the first floor of the Capitol. Democratic leaders then brought in armed supporters to guard the legislative chambers on the second floor. When Davis learned that the federal government would not help, he stepped down. He turned the office over to Coke on January 19, 1874. This marked the end of Reconstruction in Texas.

Reconstruction was ending in other parts of the South as Radical Republican power faded. The party was hurt by scandals in President Grant's administration and a financial panic in 1873. In the 1876 presidential election, Republican Rutherford B. Hayes ran a close race against Democrat Samuel J. Tilden. Each candidate claimed to have won. In the Compromise of 1877, Democrats agreed to accept Hayes. In exchange for the Democrats' support, Hayes ended the involvement of federal troops in the South's political affairs. Reconstruction was over.

⭐ **Reading Check Identifying Cause and Effect** What happened in the election of 1876, and how did it affect Reconstruction in Texas?

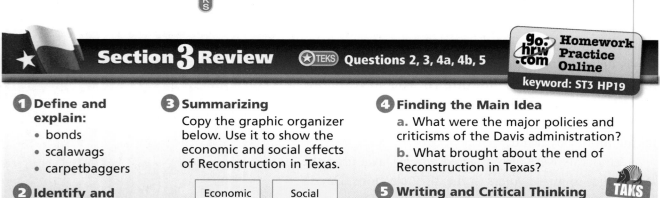

★ Section 3 Review   ⭐TEKS   Questions 2, 3, 4a, 4b, 5

go.hrw.com **Homework Practice Online**
keyword: ST3 HP19

1 Define and explain:
- bonds
- scalawags
- carpetbaggers

2 Identify and explain:
- Matthew Gaines
- Ku Klux Klan
- Obnoxious Acts
- Richard Coke

3 Summarizing
Copy the graphic organizer below. Use it to show the economic and social effects of Reconstruction in Texas.

Economic Effects

Social Effects

4 Finding the Main Idea
a. What were the major policies and criticisms of the Davis administration?
b. What brought about the end of Reconstruction in Texas?

5 Writing and Critical Thinking   TAKS
Supporting a Point of View Write a short speech for Governor Davis that strongly defends his policies.
Consider the following:
- crime in Texas
- internal improvements in Texas

Connecting To *Literature*

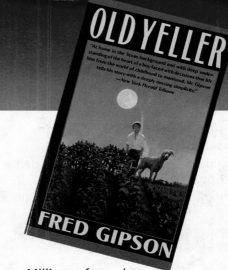

Old Yeller
Fred Gipson

Fred Gipson grew up in the Hill Country near Mason. His novel Old Yeller *tells the story of 14-year-old Travis, who protects the family while his father is away in the late 1860s. Settlers on the Texas frontier faced many day-to-day challenges as the state went through Reconstruction.* Old Yeller *is a stray dog taken in by Travis. In this excerpt, a bear is chasing Travis's younger brother Arliss, who somehow managed to grab onto the bear's cub.*

Millions of people have read about the adventures of Travis and Old Yeller.

Then, from way off to one side came a sound that I would have recognized anywhere. It was the coughing roar of a charging bear. . . . My heart went to pushing up into my throat, nearly choking off my wind. . . . I raced out into the open where I could see ahead. And what I saw sent a chill clear through to the marrow of my bones.

There was Little Arliss . . . holding onto the hind leg of a little black bear cub no bigger than a small coon. . . . Little Arliss was holding on for all he was worth, scared now and screaming his head off. Too scared to let go. . . .

Now the she bear was charging across the shallows in the creek. She was knocking sheets of water high in the bright sun, charging with her fur up and her long teeth bared, filling the canyon with that awful coughing roar. And no matter how fast Mama ran or how fast I ran, the she bear was going to get there first! . . .

Then, just as the bear went lunging up the creek bank toward Little Arliss and her cub, a flash of yellow came streaking out of the brush.

It was that big yeller dog. He was roaring like a mad bull. He wasn't one-third as big and heavy as the she bear, but when he piled into her from one side, he rolled her clear off her feet. They went down in a wild, roaring tangle of twisting bodies and scrambling feet and slashing fangs. . . . I didn't wait to see more. Without ever checking my stride, I ran in and jerked Little Arliss loose from the cub. I grabbed him by the wrist and yanked him up out of that water and slung him toward Mama like he was a half-empty sack of corn. I screamed at Mama. "Grab him, Mama! Grab him and run!" Then I swung my chopping axe high and wheeled, aiming to cave in the she bear's head with the first lick.

But I never did strike. I didn't need to. Old Yeller hadn't let the bear get close enough. . . . The minute Old Yeller saw we were all in the clear and out of danger, he . . . lit out for the house. The bear chased him for a little piece, but at the rate Old Yeller was leaving her behind, Mama said it looked like the bear was backing up.

Understanding What You Read ⊛TEKS

1. **Literature and History** What does the fact that Old Yeller saved Arliss's life tell you about life in Texas at that time?

2. **Literature and You** Do you think Gipson included this passage to suggest that the Texas frontier was too dangerous for families like the one portrayed in *Old Yeller*? Explain your answer.

Texas after Reconstruction

Read to Discover

1. How did Texas politics change with the Constitution of 1876 and one-party rule?
2. How were African Americans denied equal rights after Reconstruction?
3. How did Reconstruction affect Texas farmers?

Why It Matters Today

Texans wrote a new constitution in 1876. Use CNNfyi.com or other **current events** sources to learn about how laws are made in Texas today. Record your findings in your journal.

Define

- **segregation**
- **tenant farmers**
- **sharecroppers**

Identify

- **Norris Wright Cuney**
- **Redeemers**
- **Jim Crow laws**

The Story Continues

The Constitutional Convention of 1876 was celebrated with this poster honoring the delegates.

The Democratic delegates to the constitutional convention were determined to cut costs. They refused even to keep a journal of the convention proceedings, convinced that doing so would be a waste of money. Many delegates argued that state officials earned too much. But they could not agree on what the governor's salary should be. Was $5,000 a year, as provided in the Constitution of 1869, too high? Delegate J. L. German, a teacher, thought so. "The position should not be one that men would aspire to [desire] for the sake of money," he argued. "But rather for the honor attached to it."

★ The Texas Constitution of 1876

Democrats soon called for another constitutional convention, and in 1875 delegates met to write a new constitution. Of the 90 delegates, 15 were Republicans. Six of the Republicans were African American. Under the new constitution, the governor's term again became two years rather than four. The governor's power to appoint officials was reduced, and the legislature was again scheduled to meet once every two years instead of every year.

To limit government spending, the constitution did not let the legislature go into debt for more than $200,000. Many spending proposals had to be approved by Texas voters. The issue of education prompted considerable debate. Delegate Richard Sansom called for reduced support for public schools because Texans had complained about taxes. Most delegates agreed, and the new constitution dramatically cut back public school funding. Texas voters approved the constitution in February 1876. The Constitution of 1876 is still the state's basic law.

In addition to writing a new constitution, the Democrats immediately began to reverse the policies of the Davis administration. They removed Republican officials and cut government spending. Richard Coke's victory marked the beginning of 100 years of Democratic control in Texas. During this period of one-party rule, Democrats in Texas won nearly all state and local offices. Democrats continued to limit taxes and government spending, including education spending. School attendance was no longer required, and local authorities were allowed to take control of schools.

 Reading Check **Finding the Main Idea** What was the Democrats' goal in writing the Constitution of 1876?

★ Segregation and Jim Crow

African Americans' political power, which had peaked during the years of Radical control, fell along with the influence of the Republican Party in Texas. Nonetheless, African Americans remained active in the Republican Party throughout the late 1800s. In counties with large numbers of African Americans, local offices were sometimes won by black Republicans. At least one African American served in every Texas legislature except one before 1897. During these years, African American **Norris Wright Cuney** led the Republican Party in Texas. He was a delegate to every Republican national convention between 1872 and 1892.

As African Americans' political power declined, they once again lost many of their civil rights. After Reconstruction ended, many Texas and other southern leaders—mostly Democrats—tried to "redeem," or restore, the South to its prewar days. These "**Redeemers**" limited the size of state government and cut back on political participation by African Americans.

They also supported social separation of the races. At first this separation was customary and informal. But then **segregation**—the forced separation of people of different races in public—was written into the law. The Democrats passed what were called **Jim Crow laws** to enforce segregation. It became illegal for African Americans—and in some cases Mexican Americans—to eat in the same restaurants as white Texans. Nor could

Richard Coke
(1829–1897)

A native of Virginia, Richard Coke moved to Waco in 1850. Coke attended the Secession Convention and fought for the Confederacy. After the war he served on the Texas Supreme Court. He was removed from office by federal military authorities in 1867. As governor he reversed many policies put in place by the Radical Republicans. Coke was re-elected governor in 1876 but resigned that year to take a seat in the U.S. Senate. **What positions did Richard Coke hold in Texas government?** ★TEKS

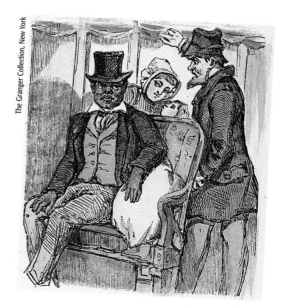
The Granger Collection, New York

Jim Crow laws spread across the South as African Americans' political power declined.

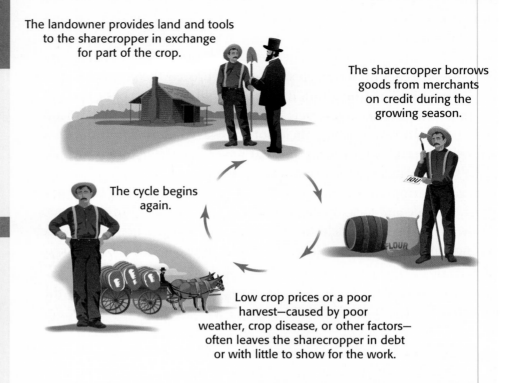

The Sharecropping Cycle

Many Texans who could not afford land became sharecroppers or tenant farmers. Because of debt, it was hard to get out of the sharecropping cycle.

Visualizing History

1. **Geography and Economics** How do you think geographic factors influenced the sharecropping system? ⭐TEKS

2. **Connecting to Today** How do you think debt and geographic factors affect farmers today? ⭐TEKS

The landowner provides land and tools to the sharecropper in exchange for part of the crop.

The sharecropper borrows goods from merchants on credit during the growing season.

The cycle begins again.

Low crop prices or a poor harvest—caused by poor weather, crop disease, or other factors—often leaves the sharecropper in debt or with little to show for the work.

they stay in the same hotels, attend the same schools, or ride in first-class railcars. One white southerner described segregated areas as "in every instance . . . the most uncomfortable, uncleanest, and unsafest place[s]." Norris Wright Cuney's daughter Maud remembered when her mother tried to take a seat in a first-class railcar.

⭐ **Analyzing Primary Sources**

Drawing Inferences and Conclusions Why did the conductor believe it necessary to lock the door?

Texas Voices 66My uncle Joseph had gone to the depot with mother to see her off to Houston. . . . The conductor of the first-class coach saw them coming, and, . . . he quickly locked the door of the coach, as he knew from experience that no argument or force could compel [force] mother to enter a second-class car. . . . Mother looked around and then innocently turning to Uncle Joseph, said: 'Well Joe . . . I see but one means of entrance and that is the window, so give me your hand. . . .' She got in the window and took her seat.99

—Maud Cuney Hare, *Norris Wright Cuney: A Tribune of the Black People*

The Jim Crow laws did far more than keep the races separate. They denied African Americans equal rights, equal opportunity, and equal protection under the law. African Americans challenged these laws in court. In 1883, however, the U.S. Supreme Court ruled that the Fourteenth Amendment applied only to the actions of state governments. This allowed private businesses and individuals to continue practicing discrimination and segregation.

⭐ **Reading Check** **Summarizing** How did the end of Reconstruction affect African Americans in Texas?

★ The Growth of Tenant Farming

With Reconstruction over, large landowners once again returned to political power. Agriculture continued to be the most important part of the economy. But many Texans—particularly freedpeople—could not afford land. Many of them became **tenant farmers**, or people who rent land to grow crops. A landowner would usually receive a part of a tenant farmer's crop as payment for using the land.

Farmers who lacked land and necessary supplies, such as mules, plows, and seed, promised a larger part of the crop in return for these items. These farmers were called **sharecroppers**. To make a profit, landowners usually made tenant farmers grow the most valuable cash crop—cotton. A tenant farmer who was unable to grow enough cotton to cover the land rental would have to take out more loans. Another bad crop would force the farmer to borrow even more money. As long as they owed money, tenant farmers and their children could not leave the land. This system gave landowners a great deal of control over tenant farmers and sharecroppers.

Many Texans worked as tenant farmers during Reconstruction. The highest numbers of tenant farmers were in counties where slavery had flourished before the Civil War. For example, about three fourths of farmers worked as tenant farmers in Fort Bend County. Both white and black Texans were tenant farmers, but a far greater percentage of African Americans survived by tenant farming. By 1880 about 40 percent of all Texas farmers worked as tenant farmers.

Sharecroppers worked long hours with plows and other equipment to grow crops.

★ **Reading Check** **Finding the Main Idea** What were the economic effects of Reconstruction on farming?

★TEKS | Questions 2, 3, 4a, 4b, 5

go.hrw.com **Homework Practice Online**
keyword: ST3 HP19

★ **Section 4 Review**

1 Define and explain:
- segregation
- tenant farmers
- sharecroppers

2 Identify and explain:
- Norris Wright Cuney
- Redeemers
- Jim Crow laws

3 Comparing and Contrasting
Copy the graphic organizer below. Use it to show the differences between the 1869 and 1876 constitutions.

	1869	1876
1. Public schools		
2. Governor's term		
3. Legislature's term		
4. Debt		

4 Finding the Main Idea
a. Explain how the Constitution of 1876 and one-party rule changed Texas politics.
b. How did Jim Crow laws affect the rights of black Texans?

5 Writing and Critical Thinking **TAKS**
Analyzing Information Imagine that you are a tenant farmer in Texas in the 1870s. Write a letter to a friend describing some of the challenges you face.
Consider the following:
- why you grow cotton
- how you obtained the tools and supplies you need

The Chapter at a Glance

Examine the following visual summary of the chapter. Then use the visual to prepare an oral presentation on Reconstruction in Texas. ⭐TEKS

Reuniting the Nation

With the end of the Civil War, slaves were emancipated in Texas. African Americans received new rights including suffrage and citizenship. However, many of these rights were not enforced.

The Reconstruction Acts placed Texas in a military district. Texans elected pro-Union Republicans such as Edmund J. Davis. Eventually, Democrats returned to power, and Texas became a one-party state.

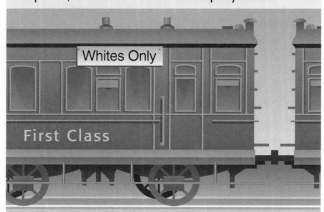

Whites Only

First Class

The Compromise of 1877 ended Reconstruction. Segregation was enforced in Texas and the South through Jim Crow laws.

Identifying People and Ideas ⭐TEKS

Use the following terms or people in historically significant sentences.

1. Juneteenth
2. freedpeople
3. Freedmen's Bureau
4. Black Codes
5. Radical Republicans
6. Reconstruction Acts
7. Richard Coke
8. Norris Wright Cuney
9. Jim Crow laws
10. segregation

Understanding Main Ideas ⭐TEKS

Section 1 (pp. 396–399)

1. In what ways did the Freedmen's Bureau help African Americans in Texas?
2. How did the Black Codes restrict the rights of freedpeople?

Section 2 (pp. 400–403)

3. What were the major provisions of the Texas Constitution of 1869?
4. What did Texas have to do under Congressional Reconstruction to be readmitted to the Union?

Section 3 (pp. 404–406)

5. What were the Republicans' major actions during Edmund J. Davis's administration?
6. What brought Reconstruction in Texas to a close?

Section 4 (pp. 408–411)

7. How did Jim Crow laws affect African Americans in Texas?

You Be the Historian ⭐TEKS

Reviewing Themes

1. **Government** In what ways was Congressional Reconstruction more demanding of southern states than Presidential Reconstruction?
2. **Citizenship** What role did Texas leaders who had supported or opposed secession play during Reconstruction?
3. **Economics** How did Reconstruction affect Texas economically?

⭐TEKS

TAKS Practice: **Thinking Critically**

1. **Identifying Points of View** What were the positions of the Texas Republican and Democratic Parties on suffrage for African Americans?
2. **Summarizing** What were the major political and social effects of Reconstruction in Texas?
3. **Drawing Inferences and Conclusions** What were the defining characteristics of the Reconstruction era in Texas?

Social Studies Skills Workshop

Interpreting Political Cartoons ⭐TEKS

Study the political cartoon below. Then use the information in the cartoon to help you answer the questions.

Young Texas.

1. Which sentence best explains why the knife has the words "For Reconstruction" on it?

  a. Texans wanted to undo Reconstruction policies.
  b. Texans supported Reconstruction policies.
  c. Texans sold many weapons.
  d. Texans liked to hunt.

2. What bias did the artist have that may have influenced this cartoon?

Analyzing Primary Sources ⭐TEKS

Read the following quote by former slave Felix Haywood about when he was freed. Then answer the questions.

"**Everybody went wild. We all felt like heroes, and nobody had made us that way but ourselves. . . . We thought we were going to get rich like the white folks, because we were stronger and knew how to work . . . and we didn't have to work for them any more. But it didn't turn out that way. We soon found out that freedom could make folks proud but it didn't make them rich.**"

3. Which of the following statements best describes the author's point of view?

  a. He was pleased that many freedpeople were able to earn a good living.
  b. He was proud that African Americans won their freedom but disappointed in their economic opportunities.
  c. He expected white Texans to help freedpeople.
  d. He believed freedpeople would succeed because of their work experience.

4. What do you think Haywood meant when he said freedpeople "felt like heroes"?

Alternative Assessment

Cooperative Learning ⭐TEKS

Working with a partner, create a large poster-size time line of the Reconstruction era in Texas. Include as many major events, issues, and people of the era as possible. Illustrate your time line with colorful drawings of people and symbols to better explain the era. Write captions to help describe the events and people that you have included on your time line. Be sure to use standard grammar, spelling, sentence structure, and punctuation.

BUILDING YOUR Portfolio

📄 **internet** connect

Internet Activity: go.hrw.com
KEYWORD: ST3 TX19 ⭐TEKS

Access the Internet through the HRW Go site to analyze some of the political, economic, and social effects of Reconstruction in Texas. Then write an editorial in which you support the election of either Edmund J. Davis or Richard Coke. Be sure to support your answer. Identify any bias you discover in the sources used for your editorial.

CHAPTER 20

The Indian Wars
(1861–1880)

Settlers and U.S. Army troops hauled supplies to the frontier in wagons.

Artist George Catlin painted images of the Comanche like this portrait of Little Spaniard.

1861 The Texas Frontier Regiment is established.

TEXAS

1864 Colonel Christopher "Kit" Carson leads an attack against Plains Indians in the Panhandle.

1868 Fort Richardson is established near Jacksboro.

1861	**1863**	**1865**	**1867**	**1869**

U.S. and WORLD

1865 U.S. negotiators sign the Treaty of the Little Arkansas with Comanche and Kiowa leaders.

1867 Railroads cut through the Great Plains, dividing the buffalo into northern and southern herds.

1870 The Illinois Central Railroad extends its line west, reaching Sioux City, Iowa.

Rail lines such as the Illinois Central Railroad brought new settlers to the U.S. frontier, changing life in the region.

Build on What You Know

Many of the soldiers stationed in Texas during Reconstruction guarded the frontier. Tensions between Texans and American Indians had increased as more and more settlers moved westward. Soon wars erupted on the frontier between the U.S. Army and American Indians in Texas.

Buffalo hunting was an important part of the lives of Plains Indians in Texas.

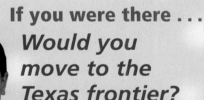

The Granger Collection, New York

Quanah Parker led the Comanche in battles against U.S. forces.

1874 Plains Indians attack a group of buffalo hunters in the Battle of Adobe Walls.

1875 Comanche leader Quanah Parker surrenders, ending the Red River War.

1879 Apache leader Victorio launches raids along the Texas-Mexico border.

1871   **1873**   **1875**   **1877**   **1879**

1871 Manufacturers begin to use buffalo hides to produce leather for industrial purposes.

The Sioux lived in the central Great Plains. This Sioux doll is dressed in horseback-riding clothes.

1875 A gold rush in the Black Hills of Dakota Territory leads to war between the Sioux and the United States.

1879 War breaks out between the British and the Zulu in South Africa.

If you were there . . .
Would you move to the Texas frontier?

You Be the Historian

Themes Journal

What's Your Opinion? Do you **agree** or **disagree** with the following statements? Support your point of view in your journal.

● **Geography** Groups moving into a region usually have little effect on people already living there.

● **Science, Technology & Society** As humans rely more on machines, they have less need for animals.

● **Culture** Groups rarely try to maintain their traditional values as their ways of life change.

Changes in Indian Policy

Read to Discover

1. How did the Civil War and Reconstruction affect relations between American Indians and settlers in Texas?
2. What steps did the federal government take to end American Indian raids in Texas?

Why It Matters Today

During the 1800s Texas and federal officials debated American Indian policy. Use CNNfyi.com or other **current events** sources to learn about American Indian policies today. Record your findings in your journal.

Define

- commissioners

Identify

- **Treaty of the Little Arkansas**
- **Satanta**
- **Treaty of Medicine Lodge**
- **Quakers**
- **Lawrie Tatum**

The Kiowa carried food and other supplies in beaded pouches.

The Story Continues

Mary and Britton Johnson wanted to build a new life in Young County. Their hopes were dashed in October 1864, when some Kiowa and Comanche attacked the settlement along Elm Creek. Johnson's son was killed and his wife and two daughters were taken captive. He rode into Indian Territory, determined to get them back. After some negotiation, Johnson managed to pay for their return.

★ American Indian Relations

The raid along Elm Creek was not an unusual event in the early 1860s. Many settlements were open to attack because soldiers and civilian men had left the Texas frontier to fight in the Civil War. As a result, many Plains Indians in Texas saw an opportunity to stop westward expansion. The Comanche took action, raiding along a line from Gainesville in North Texas to Fredericksburg in Central Texas. When the Civil War ended, federal troops arrived to guard the frontier. However, there were not enough troops to protect the scattered frontier settlements.

Federal **commissioners**—government representatives—met with leaders of the Comanche, Kiowa, and other southern Plains Indians in October 1865 to negotiate a peace treaty. In the **Treaty of the Little Arkansas**, Comanche and Kiowa leaders agreed to settle on a reservation in the Texas Panhandle. The peace was short-lived, partly because the reservation was never created. As settlers continued to move westward, some Comanche and Kiowa renewed their attacks. In 1866 a group of citizens from Lampasas County asked for help. "The frontier at this time is falling back, a standpoint must be made somewhere."

Texas governor James W. Throckmorton estimated that American Indians had killed 162 Texans and captured 43 more between 1865 and 1867. Between 1860 and 1870, more than half the population of Denton, Wise, and Young Counties moved away to safer areas. As many settlers left their homes, the frontier line was pushed back to the east.

⭐ **Reading Check** **Identifying Cause and Effect** What happened on the Texas frontier during the Civil War and Reconstruction, and how did this affect settlement?

⭐ The Treaty of Medicine Lodge

In 1867 the federal government sent commissioners to negotiate a new peace treaty with Comanche, Kiowa, and other Plains Indians at Medicine Lodge Creek in Kansas. The commissioners brought gifts of blankets, clothing, and even pistols and ammunition. They offered some 3 million acres of land for a reservation in Indian Territory. The

Courtesy of the Witte Museum, San Antonio, Texas

The Granger Collection, New York

The meeting at Medicine Lodge. During the meeting, U.S. officials encouraged the Plains Indians to move to reservations. **Based on this illustration, who participated in this meeting?** TEKS

Analyzing Primary Sources
Identifying Points of View What is Satanta's view of westward expansion?

government also promised to provide buildings, farming tools, and a total of $25,000 a year for 30 years. In return, the Plains Indians had to stop raiding, stay on the reservation, and take up farming.

Kiowa chief **Satanta** bitterly opposed the reservation policy. He argued that the Panhandle belonged to the Kiowa and the Comanche. At the meeting, Satanta made a famous speech.

Texas Voices "I have heard that you intend to settle us on a reservation near the mountains. I don't want to settle. I love to roam over the prairies. There I feel free and happy, but when we settle down we grow pale and die. . . . A long time ago this land belonged to our fathers; but when I go up to the river I see camps of soldiers on its banks. These soldiers cut down my timber; they kill my buffalo; and when I see that, my heart feels like bursting."

—Satanta, quoted in *Bury My Heart at Wounded Knee,* by Dee Brown

Others disagreed with Satanta. Kiowa leader Kicking Bird and Comanche chief Horseback argued that their survival depended on moving to the reservations. Many Plains Indians agreed to the terms of the **Treaty of Medicine Lodge** and several thousand moved to Indian Territory. Others remained on the plains, determined to maintain their hunting grounds. Ten Bears, a famous Texas Comanche chief, expressed a view of reservation life held by many Comanche.

Texas Voices "You said that you wanted to put us upon a reservation, to build us houses and make us medicine lodges. I do not want them. I was born upon the prairie, where the wind blew free. . . . I know every stream and every wood between the Rio Grande and the Arkansas. I have hunted and lived over that country. I live like my fathers before me and like them I lived happily."

—Chief Ten Bears, quoted in *Documents of Texas History,* edited by Ernest Wallace

Reading Check **Summarizing** What were the terms of the Treaty of Medicine Lodge?

★ The Peace Policy

In 1869 President Ulysses S. Grant established a Board of Indian Commissioners to carry out the terms of the peace treaty. Grant appointed many **Quakers**, members of a Protestant sect called the Society of Friends, to act as American Indian agents. The Quakers believed in religious tolerance for all peoples and in nonviolence. Many Quakers and Christian missionaries became active in Indian affairs in hopes of preventing war on the frontier by helping American Indians adjust to reservation life. The government hoped to teach the Plains Indians to make a living by farming, and agents arranged for the construction of schools and churches on the reservations. **Lawrie Tatum**, a Quaker, was the Indian agent for the Comanche and Kiowa at the reservation in Indian Territory.

There were serious problems with the reservation system. Although the government hoped that the Plains Indians would become farmers rather than buffalo hunters, the land the government set aside for them had poor soil. The few Indians who tried farming thus had trouble growing enough food to survive. Government food supplies failed to make up the difference. In addition, goods sent by the government to the reservation were sometimes sold illegally by contractors and never reached their proper destination. Some buffalo hunters entered the reservation, further threatening the Indians' food supply. As a result, American Indians living on reservations often went hungry and lacked basic supplies.

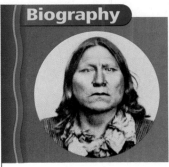

Biography

Satanta
(c. 1820–1874)

When Kiowa leader Satanta was born, Plains Indians were at the height of their power. Over the course of his life, he watched the Kiowa suffer military defeat and confinement to reservations. Satanta used both diplomacy and warfare to protect the Kiowa. He never adjusted to reservation life. Satanta was arrested several times and died in a prison at Huntsville. **What changes did Satanta see on the Texas frontier during his life?** ★TEKS

★ **Reading Check** **Summarizing** Explain how the Treaty of Medicine Lodge affected Plains Indians in Texas.

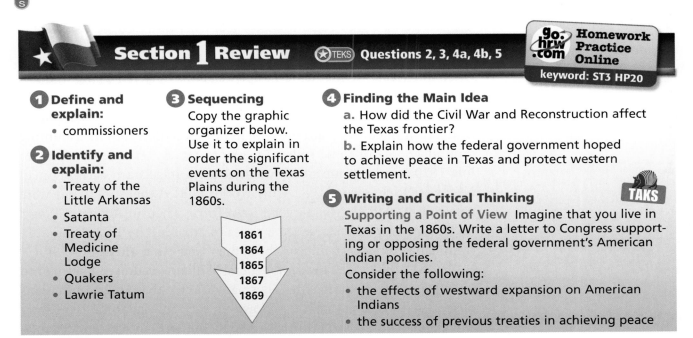

Section 1 Review ★TEKS Questions 2, 3, 4a, 4b, 5

go.hrw.com **Homework Practice Online** keyword: ST3 HP20

1 **Define and explain:**
- commissioners

2 **Identify and explain:**
- Treaty of the Little Arkansas
- Satanta
- Treaty of Medicine Lodge
- Quakers
- Lawrie Tatum

3 **Sequencing**
Copy the graphic organizer below. Use it to explain in order the significant events on the Texas Plains during the 1860s.

1861
1864
1865
1867
1869

4 **Finding the Main Idea**
a. How did the Civil War and Reconstruction affect the Texas frontier?
b. Explain how the federal government hoped to achieve peace in Texas and protect western settlement.

5 **Writing and Critical Thinking**
Supporting a Point of View Imagine that you live in Texas in the 1860s. Write a letter to Congress supporting or opposing the federal government's American Indian policies.
Consider the following:
- the effects of westward expansion on American Indians
- the success of previous treaties in achieving peace

TAKS

War on the Plains

Read to Discover

1. What was the result of the Salt Creek Raid?
2. What happened to the buffalo, and how did that affect Plains Indians?

Why It Matters Today

The Plains Indians relied heavily on the buffalo for clothing, food, and shelter. Use CNNfyi.com or other **current events** sources to learn about how American Indian life today. Record your findings in your journal.

Define

- **buffalo guns**

Identify

- **Salt Creek Raid**
- **Ranald S. Mackenzie**
- **Mackenzie's Raiders**
- **Quanah Parker**
- **Cynthia Parker**

The Story Continues

Fannie Beck's parents were away at the funeral of her cousin, Jesse, who had been killed by Texas Indians while hunting. Fannie and her brother Milton had been left overnight to watch the younger children. They huddled together by the fire. "We suffered an agony of fear every time Sue, the baby, stirred. . . . We didn't want her to cry and let the Indians know there was a houseful of unprotected children."

Fannie Beck had no time for toys. She was responsible for keeping her siblings safe while her parents were away.

★ The Salt Creek Raid

After the Treaty of Medicine Lodge, tensions between Plains Indians and settlers remained high. Indians living on the reservation were frustrated with the quality of life there. Other American Indians were upset by the continued westward movement of U.S. settlers into their hunting grounds. Some of these Indians began to attack Texas settlements. In July 1870 a large group of Kiowa attacked a stagecoach carrying mail near Fort Richardson. U.S. Army troops chased the raiders but were defeated in battle by the larger Kiowa force. Then in August a Kiowa leader named White Horse led a series of attacks. The Texas legislature complained to federal officials about these and other attacks.

In 1871 the U.S. Army sent General William Tecumseh Sherman to investigate Texans' complaints. Sherman doubted that American Indians posed a serious threat in Texas. However, early in May some 100 Kiowa and Comanche crossed into Texas. Led by Big Tree, Satank, and Satanta, they attacked a wagon train near Salt Creek on May 18, killing seven men. A wounded survivor of this **Salt Creek Raid** made his way to Fort Richardson and reported the raid to Sherman. The general sent troops after the raiders and then traveled to Fort Sill near Indian Territory.

When the raiders came to the Indian Territory reservation for food supplies, Lawrie Tatum asked them about the attack. Satanta responded, "If any other Indian comes here and claims the honor of leading the party he will be lying to you, for I did it myself." Satanta defended the raid by charging that the government had not treated the Indians fairly. He also accused Tatum of stealing supplies. The hardships of reservation life would result in more attacks, warned Satanta.

When Sherman learned of Satanta's statements, he had Big Tree, Satank, and Satanta arrested in a tense confrontation at Fort Sill. Satank was later killed while trying to escape. Big Tree and Satanta were tried for murder and sentenced to death. Tatum and other supporters of the peace policy worried that hanging the men would only make matters worse on the frontier. Texas governor Edmund J. Davis shared this concern, and he changed the death sentence to life in prison. Big Tree and Satanta were released from prison on parole, or let go under condition of good behavior, in 1873.

Reading Check **Summarizing** What significant events occurred on the Texas frontier in the early 1870s?

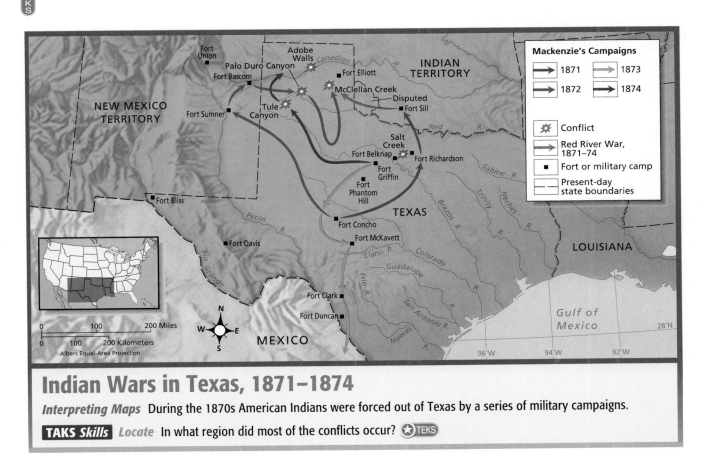

Indian Wars in Texas, 1871–1874

Interpreting Maps During the 1870s American Indians were forced out of Texas by a series of military campaigns.

TAKS Skills *Locate* In what region did most of the conflicts occur?

Biography

Cynthia Parker
(c. 1825–c. 1871)

On May 19, 1836, Comanche raiders attacked Parker's Fort in what is now Limestone County. The Comanche captured five settlers, including Cynthia Ann Parker, who was then 10 or 11 years old. Parker remained with the Comanche for almost 25 years. During that time she married Peta Nocona and had two sons and one daughter. One of her sons, Quanah Parker, became one of the most important Comanche leaders of his time. In 1860, Texas Rangers attacked a Comanche camp and captured Cynthia Parker. Relatives forced Parker to settle with them. Parker, however, regarded herself as Comanche. She tried several times, without success, to escape from her relatives. **Why did Parker consider herself to be a Comanche?** ⭐TEKS

⭐ Mackenzie's Raids

In response to the Salt Creek Raid, the U.S. War Department planned a series of attacks against Plains Indians who refused to live on the reservations. Colonel **Ranald S. Mackenzie**, whom Ulysses S. Grant had once called the most talented young officer in the U.S. Army, led the campaign. He commanded the 4th Cavalry regiment, which was stationed at several posts along the Texas frontier in the 1860s and 1870s. Mackenzie and his troops, called **Mackenzie's Raiders**, achieved great fame fighting on the Texas frontier. The *Galveston News* expressed the views of many Texans.

> **Texas Voices** ❝Go into the heart of their country. . . until the Indians are caught. . . . Lay waste [destroy] their villages, burn everything within reach, kill every warrior found in fighting trim [equipped to fight], and so utterly desolate [ruin] their regions that by sheer weakness they will never be able to send another war party to our border.❞
>
> —*Galveston News,* March 14, 1873

Mackenzie began his raids in the fall of 1871, traveling northwest from Camp Cooper on the Clear Fork of the Brazos River. Mackenzie's troops were guided by Tonkawa Indian scouts. At Blanco Canyon, Mackenzie's troops fought a minor battle against a Comanche group led by **Quanah Parker**. Parker was the son of **Cynthia Parker**, a captured settler, and Peta Nocona—a Comanche. Mackenzie pursued the Comanche into uncharted regions of the Panhandle. However, the Comanche escaped during a heavy snowstorm. Following several Indian raids in the spring of 1872, Mackenzie renewed his attacks on the Comanche in northwest Texas. He also crossed the Panhandle into New Mexico, chasing cattle thieves.

On September 29, 1872, Mackenzie's troops defeated a Comanche force at McClellan Creek, near present-day Pampa. They killed many Comanche, destroyed their village, and took some 120 women and children prisoner. Parker led an attack on Mackenzie's camp the following night and stampeded the animals that the Texans had captured. But Parker could not free the Comanche prisoners. Mackenzie kept the prisoners at Fort Concho to pressure the others to surrender. As a result, many Comanche abandoned life on the plains and moved to the reservation. It was a major victory for Mackenzie.

With the raids temporarily halted in northwest Texas, Mackenzie and the 4th Cavalry headed for the Mexican border. Stationed at Fort Duncan near Eagle Pass, Mackenzie led the effort to stop Kickapoo and Lipan Apache raids along the Rio Grande. By the end of 1873, Mackenzie had brought a stop to most of the border raids.

⭐ **Reading Check** **Sequencing** Describe in order the actions Colonel Mackenzie took against the Comanche.

★ The Slaughter of the Buffalo

Other events also threatened Plains Indians. For generations, they had depended on the buffalo. By the 1870s the survival of the buffalo—and the Plains Indians' way of life—was at serious risk. As railroad companies built lines across the Great Plains, hunters killed hundreds of buffalo to feed the rail crews. Once railroads reached towns in Kansas, buffalo hides could be moved quickly and cheaply to eastern cities. The buffalo hide industry began in 1871 when J. Wright Mooar shipped 56 hides to his brother John in New York City. John sold the hides to a tanning firm, which soon ordered 2,000 more. A new method for tanning buffalo hides into high quality leather led to a sharp rise in demand and price. With an average hide worth more than three dollars on the market, buffalo hunters swarmed onto the plains to make their fortune.

These hunters used a method called still hunting. In the early morning, hunters would sneak downwind of a herd and set up powerful rifles known as **buffalo guns**. These guns had telescopes, allowing hunters to slowly pick off members of the herd from a distance. One Texan later recalled, "A remarkably good hunter would kill seventy-five to one hundred [buffalo] a day."

Under the terms of the Medicine Lodge Treaty, buffalo hunters were not allowed onto Indian hunting grounds south of Kansas. The U.S. Army was supposed to patrol the Kansas–Indian Territory border but failed to do so. As a result, by 1873 hunters were pouring into Texas. Many U.S. military officials encouraged the extermination, or complete

Amon Carter Museum

Buffalo. *During the late 1800s the buffalo were hunted to nearly extinction.* **How did buffalo hunters' means of hunting differ from those of American Indians?** ★TEKS

The Buffalo Population

Scholars have had great difficulty determining the size of the buffalo population over time. Historians agree that during the late 1800s the herds were nearly wiped out. The following are estimates of the population.

YEAR	BUFFALO POPULATION
1800	30 million
1850	20 million
1889	835
2000	200,000

Interpreting Data ⭐TEKS

1. Use the information above to create a graph showing the buffalo population from 1800 to 2000.

2. By what percentage did the buffalo population decrease from 1800 to 1850?

3. By how much did the buffalo population grow between 1889 and 2000?

destruction, of the buffalo herds. General Philip Sheridan, who commanded the region including Texas, believed that killing off the buffalo would force Plains Indians onto reservations. In 1875 he urged the Texas legislature to allow the hunters to continue the slaughter. "Let them [hunters] kill, skin, and sell until the buffaloes are exterminated. Then your prairies can be covered with speckled cattle." One Kiowa, Old Lady Horse, described the effect this had on the buffalo.

Texas Voices ❝The buffalo were the life of the Kiowa. . . . Then the white men hired hunters to do nothing but kill the buffalo. Up and down the plains those men ranged, shooting sometimes as many as a hundred buffalo a day. Behind them came the skinners with their wagons. They piled the hides and bones into the wagons . . . and then took their loads to the new railroad stations that were being built. . . . Sometimes there would be a pile of bones as high as a man, stretching a mile along the railroad track.❞

—Old Lady Horse, quoted in *Native American Testimony*, edited by Peter Nabokov

Between 1872 and 1874, hunters killed an estimated 4.3 million buffalo. The buffalo hunters' activities—particularly their practice of taking the hides and leaving the meat to rot—outraged Plains Indians. As a Comanche named He Bear explained, "Just as it makes the white man feel to have his money carried away, so it makes us feel to see others killing and stealing our buffaloes."

⭐TEKS **Reading Check** **Finding the Main Idea** What technological factors led to the slaughter of buffalo herds in the late 1800s?

 Section 2 Review ⭐TEKS Questions 2, 3, 4a, 4b, 5

go.hrw.com **Homework Practice Online**
keyword: ST3 HP20

1 **Define and explain:**
- buffalo guns

2 **Identify and explain:**
- Salt Creek Raid
- Ranald S. Mackenzie
- Mackenzie's Raiders
- Quanah Parker
- Cynthia Parker

3 **Analyzing Information**
Copy the graphic organizer below. Use it to explain how the destruction of the buffalo affected American Indians.

Why Buffalo were Killed
↓
Effect on American Indians

4 **Finding the Main Idea**
a. How did the Salt Creek Raid affect the military's policy toward American Indians on the frontier?
b. What role did Colonel Mackenzie play in Texas?

5 **Writing and Critical Thinking** **TAKS**
Identifying Points of View Imagine that you are a Plains Indian. Write a poem that describes the importance of the buffalo.
Consider the following:
- how Indians used the buffalo
- the effect that hunters had on buffalo herds

The Red River War

Read to Discover

1. Why was the attack on Adobe Walls significant?
2. What occurred at the Battle of Palo Duro Canyon?

Identify

• Battle of Adobe Walls
• Battle of Palo Duro Canyon

Why It Matters Today

American Indians and U.S. Army soldiers fought in many regions of Texas. Use CNNfyi.com or other **current events** sources to learn about the U.S. Army today. Record your findings in your journal.

The Story Continues

The hot summer sun had not yet risen. Arapaho, Cheyenne, Comanche, and Kiowa waited in the dark. In the distance stood Adobe Walls, a trading post that served buffalo hunters on the Texas plains. Isatai, a powerful medicine man, promised that "those white men can't shoot you. . . . I will stop all their guns." With that, the Indians rode at full speed toward the settlement.

★ The Battle of Adobe Walls

By the spring of 1874, the situation had become desperate for Plains Indians. They were starving on the reservations, and the buffalo were being slaughtered by white hunters. Little Robe, a Cheyenne, reminded reservation agents of the importance of the buffalo.

Texas Voices "Your people make big talk and sometimes make war, if an Indian kills a white man's ox to keep his wife and children from starving; what do you think my people ought to say when they see their [buffalo] killed by your race?"

—Little Robe, quoted in *The Buffalo War,* by James L. Haley

Isatai called for a war to drive out the buffalo hunters. In response, several Plains Indians leaders met in June 1874. Quanah Parker led the Comanche, and Lone Wolf led the Kiowa. Encouraged by Isatai, they targeted the trading post at Adobe Walls in the Texas Panhandle.

On June 27 about 700 Indians attacked Adobe Walls. Only 28 men and one woman were at the trading post, but they had an important

Southern members of the Cheyenne wore fringed shirts during battle.

Palo Duro Canyon. During the Red River War many American Indians sought protection in the Palo Duro Canyon. **What geographic features of the canyon influenced the Indians' decision to stay there?** ⭐TEKS

advantage—buffalo guns. These powerful weapons could shoot long distances. Despite repeated attacks, the hunters held their ground at the **Battle of Adobe Walls**. Four defenders died in the battle, while Indian casualties are estimated at 12 to 30. Although the attack failed, Plains Indians remained determined to protect their hunting grounds. They began a widespread war against buffalo hunters and settlers, launching attacks in Colorado, Kansas, New Mexico, Oklahoma, and Texas.

⭐ **Reading Check** **Sequencing** Explain in order the events leading to American Indian attacks on the Texas frontier.

Bat Masterson

One of the defenders at Adobe Walls was a young man named Bartholomew "Bat" Masterson. He later became a respected lawman and one of the most famous figures of the American West.

⭐ The Battle of Palo Duro Canyon

After the attack at Adobe Walls and other American Indian raids, U.S. officials ordered General William Tecumseh Sherman to attack raiding Indians "wherever found. . . . The Reservation lines should be no barrier." Generals Sherman and Philip Sheridan organized a military campaign to kill or remove remaining American Indians in the Panhandle.

In August 1874 the army began a major offensive known as the Red River War. Some 3,000 troops in five different groups headed toward the Indian villages along the upper parts of the Red River. They were joined by the Frontier Battalion of the Texas Rangers, commanded by Major John D. Jones. Colonel Nelson Miles led a force of 750 soldiers into Texas from Fort Dodge in Kansas. These soldiers fought continuously against some 600 Cheyenne, who finally escaped in late August.

Major William Price led troops eastward from Fort Union in New Mexico Territory. Price defeated a band of Indians near Sweetwater Creek in the eastern Panhandle. Meanwhile, Colonel John Davidson and Lieutenant Colonel George Buell commanded two other military forces patrolling the region. Both forces destroyed many American Indian villages. The soldiers forced hundreds of Indians, mainly women and children, onto reservations, where supplies were already short.

Colonel Ranald S. Mackenzie struck the final blow to the Texas Plains Indians. In August, Mackenzie's forces marched north from Fort Concho. Mackenzie learned that many Comanche, Kiowa, and a few Cheyenne were camping in Palo Duro Canyon, which had provided safe shelter to Indian families for centuries.

Just before dawn on September 28, 1874, Mackenzie and about 500 troops quietly worked their way down into the canyon. The soldiers surprised the Indian villages and killed three Comanche. Panic-stricken, women and children fled out onto the plains. The **Battle of Palo Duro Canyon** took a terrible toll on the Comanche. In their haste to escape, the Comanche left behind most of their supplies—including more than 1,400 horses. Mackenzie had most of the horses shot to prevent the Comanche from recapturing them. He also ordered his men to burn the villages in the canyon. Lacking clothing and horses, few Indians could hope to survive the winter in the Panhandle. They had no choice but to move to the reservations in Indian Territory.

The battle marked a turning point in the Red River War. The era of American Indian control of the Texas Plains was quickly coming to an end. Indian leaders advised the Cheyenne to accept reservation life.

Panhandle-Plains Historical Museum, Research Center, Canyon, Texas

Comanche leader Quanah Parker, who wore this headdress, eventually surrendered.

 Texas Voices 66**We want them to travel in the white man's road. The white men are as many as the leaves on the trees and we are only a few people, and we should do as the white man wants us to, and live at peace with him.**99

—Grey Beard and Minimic, quoted in *The Military Conquest of the Southern Plains,* by William H. Leckie

Analyzing Primary Sources
Drawing Inferences and Conclusions Why did Grey Beard and Minimic advise the Cheyenne to adopt the ways of white Americans?

 **Reading Check Identifying Cause and Effect** What was the outcome of the Battle of Palo Duro Canyon, and how did it affect Texas Plains Indians?

Section 3 Review ⭐TEKS Questions 1, 2, 3a, 3b, 4

go.hrw.com **Homework Practice Online** keyword: ST3 HP20

1 Identify and explain:
- Battle of Adobe Walls
- Battle of Palo Duro Canyon

2 Identifying Cause and Effect
Copy the graphic organizer below. Use it to explain the main events of the early 1870s and how they led to the Red River War.

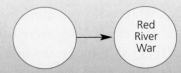

Red River War

3 Finding the Main Idea
a. How did the Battle of Adobe Walls affect Plains Indians on the frontier?
b. How did Mackenzie and his troops win the Battle of Palo Duro Canyon?

4 Writing and Critical Thinking TAKS
Drawing Inferences and Conclusions Write a short report explaining why some Plains Indians groups in Texas believed it was necessary to attack the buffalo hunters and settlers.
Consider the following:
- life on the reservations
- the effect of hunters on the buffalo

4 The Indian Wars End in Texas

Read to Discover

1. Why did Indian raids along the Rio Grande end?
2. What was the major consequence of the Indian wars?

Identify

- Victorio
- buffalo soldiers
- Henry O. Flipper
- Dawes General Allotment Act

Why It Matters Today

Texas Indians were forced onto reservations during the Red River War. Use **CNNfyi.com** or other **current events** sources to learn about people who are forced to relocate because of war or natural disaster today. Record your findings in your journal.

The Arizona desert, where the Apache were sent, was poor land for hunting and farming.

The Story Continues

Victorio never forgot what the U.S. Army had done to his mentor, Mangas Coloradas. Under a flag of truce, soldiers had killed the Apache chief. Now an Apache chief himself, Victorio would never trust the U.S. Army. When troops ordered Apache families to move to a hot barren reservation in Arizona, Victorio led many of them to Mexico.

★ Fighting on the Rio Grande

The departure of the group led by **Victorio** marked the beginning of one of the last Indian wars in the United States. Victorio and other American Indians began raids into Texas from Mexico. The Apache could easily attack travelers on the miles and miles of lonely roads of the Trans-Pecos region. In response to the raids, the U.S. Army ordered more troops to the Rio Grande area. Stopping the raids was not an easy task—the army chased Victorio for two years. Troops following the Apache had to carry their own food and water to survive in the dry rugged area.

Most of the some 2,500 troops stationed along the border served in the 9th and 10th Cavalries as well as in the 24th and 25th Infantry Regiments. Although white officers commanded these regiments, all the troops were African American. They were called "**buffalo soldiers**" by American Indians. **Henry O. Flipper**, the first black graduate of the U.S. Military Academy at West Point, took part in a campaign against the Apache while stationed at Fort Davis. Troops from this fort and Fort

Bliss sometimes trailed the Apache for weeks, only to find they had crossed the Rio Grande back into Mexico. The raids were not stopped until the Mexican army became active in the chase. Victorio died in 1880 while being pursued by Mexican troops.

⭐ **Reading Check** **Analyzing Information** What problems did the climate create for the U.S. Army in the Trans-Pecos region?

⭐ Reservation Life

As Apache resistance was overcome, most Texas Indians were facing the challenge of living on reservations in what is now Oklahoma. When they moved onto the reservation, Plains Indians had to give up their traditional way of life—hunting buffalo—and take up farming. Their efforts to farm and ranch often failed. They usually received poor land, and they had little experience raising crops using the techniques taught by the reservation agents. When government officials did not supply food, Indians often faced starvation. General Nelson Miles described conditions on the reservations. "[Indians] were sometimes for weeks without their rations." Few American Indians prospered on the reservations.

Indians on the reservations faced other challenges to their traditional ways of life. In 1883 the federal government banned many American Indian religious practices, including the Sun Dance. When some Kiowa planned the dance in 1889, soldiers stopped the event. Indians often had to hold traditional celebrations and ceremonies in secret. Many Indians continued to use their own languages as well as English. Indians also preserved many of their customs, myths, and styles of dress, despite government officials' efforts to eliminate these traditional aspects of the Indians' lives.

Henry O. Flipper
(1856–1940)

Henry O. Flipper was born into slavery in 1856. In 1878 he became the first African American to graduate from the U.S. Military Academy. After graduating, Flipper served as a second lieutenant in the 10th Cavalry. He worked as an army engineer, supervising the construction of roads and telegraph lines in Texas. Today West Point offers an award named after Flipper to students who succeed in the face of severe obstacles. **What role did Flipper play in the development of Texas?** ⭐TEKS

Soldiers from Fort Davis patrolled far western Texas.

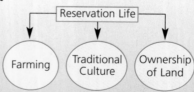

Quanah Parker, who had surrendered and moved to the reservation in 1875, worked to better relations between the federal government and American Indians. On occasion Parker went to Washington, D.C., to negotiate on behalf of American Indians. Parker managed to live successfully in the cultures of American Indians and white Americans alike. He once remarked about his mother, "If she could learn the ways of the Indian, I can learn the ways of the white man." Parker continued to try to improve the lives of the Comanche until his death in 1911.

Quanah Parker and other Indians on reservations shared the land they farmed. Some government officials believed that the Indians would be better off if they owned the land they worked. The **Dawes General Allotment Act** of 1887 divided up reservation lands and promised Indians U.S. citizenship. Some of the reservation lands were allotted, or divided, among individual families. But many Indians did not receive enough land to support themselves, as DeWitt Duncan noted. "What a condition! I have 60 acres of land. . . . What am I going to do with it?" After dividing the reservations, the government sold the remaining lands. As a result, Indians lost an enormous amount of land. The act also failed to grant Indians full citizenship as promised. All American Indians were not granted citizenship until 1924.

The difficulties of reservation life, the Dawes Act, military attacks, and the slaughter of the buffalo took a terrible toll on Texas Indians. By the 1880s their population had been greatly reduced. Most had either been killed or moved out of the state. This opened vast stretches of land on the Texas plains to farming and ranching. Settlers quickly moved onto lands that Texas Indians had called home for hundreds of years.

 Reading Check **Analyzing Information** How did the Indian wars affect migration patterns in Texas?

Section 4 Review

★ TEKS Questions 1, 2, 3a, 3b, 4

go.hrw.com **Homework Practice Online**
keyword: ST3 HP20

1 Identify and explain:
- Victorio
- buffalo soldiers
- Henry O. Flipper
- Dawes General Allotment Act

2 Summarizing
Copy the graphic organizer below. Use it to show how living on reservations changed the lives of American Indians.

```
              Reservation Life
       ┌───────────┼───────────┐
       ▼           ▼           ▼
   ( Farming ) (Traditional) (Ownership
                  Culture    of Land )
```

3 Finding the Main Idea
 a. Why did the Apache raids along the Rio Grande stop?
 b. What effect did the Indian wars have on migration patterns?

4 Writing and Critical Thinking TAKS

Supporting a Point of View Imagine that you live in the 1870s. Write an editorial explaining how you think the reservation system will affect American Indians in the future.

Consider the following:
- farming on the reservations
- government policy toward American Indian cultures

Geography

The Expanding Texas Frontier

Most American Indians had been removed from East Texas during the years of the Republic. In the 1860s settlement along the Texas frontier slowed. American Indian raids prevented white settlers from claiming new lands. During the 1870s, however, settlement along the frontier boomed as American Indians were removed from the land.

Geography Skills

Interpreting Thematic Maps ★TEKS

1. About what percent of Texas was frontier land in 1860?

2. How did the location of forts relate to the lines of frontier settlement?

3. Why did frontier settlement increase in the 1870s?

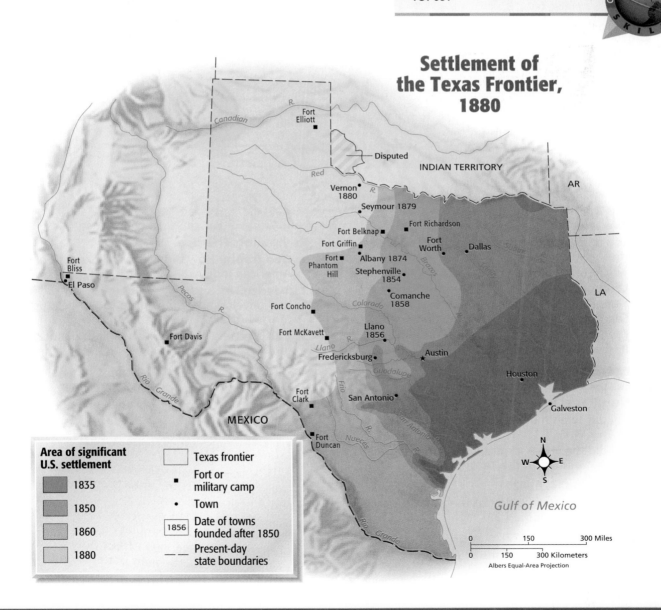

Settlement of the Texas Frontier, 1880

Area of significant U.S. settlement

- 1835
- 1850
- 1860
- 1880

☐ Texas frontier

■ Fort or military camp

• Town

1856 Date of towns founded after 1850

– – – Present-day state boundaries

0   150   300 Miles
0   150   300 Kilometers
Albers Equal-Area Projection

The Chapter at a Glance

Examine the following visual summary of the chapter. Then use the visual to create a chart that shows the causes of conflicts on the Texas frontier and their effects. ⭐TEKS

During the Civil War, American Indian raids increased on the Texas frontier until some Plains Indians signed a treaty and agreed to move onto reservations.

The U.S. Army began a campaign to remove all Plains Indians to reservations. The killing of the buffalo herds also threatened Plains Indians.

With most Indians driven out of Texas, settlers began moving farther west.

Identifying People and Ideas ⭐TEKS

Use the following terms or people in historically significant sentences.

1. Treaty of Medicine Lodge
2. Satanta
3. Salt Creek Raid
4. Lawrie Tatum
5. Ranald S. Mackenzie
6. Quanah Parker
7. Cynthia Parker
8. Battle of Palo Duro Canyon
9. buffalo soldiers
10. Victorio

Understanding Main Ideas ⭐TEKS

Section 1 (pp. 416–419)

1. Why did Texas Indians increase their raids during the Civil War?
2. Why did the Treaty of the Little Arkansas fail to resolve conflicts on the Texas plains?

Section 2 (pp. 420–424)

3. Why was the destruction of the buffalo a serious threat to Plains Indians?

Section 3 (pp. 425–427)

4. Why did American Indians attack Adobe Walls?

Section 4 (sec. 428–430)

5. What were conditions like on the reservations?

You Be the Historian ⭐TEKS

Reviewing Themes

1. **Geography** How did westward expansion affect American Indians?
2. **Science, Technology & Society** How did industrial development contribute to the destruction of the buffalo?
3. **Culture** How did American Indians maintain some of their traditional values even while living on the reservation?

TAKS Practice: Thinking Critically ⭐TEKS

1. **Evaluating** How effective was the reservation policy at dealing with conflicts between settlers and American Indians?
2. **Summarizing** What events led to the decline of the American Indian population in Texas?
3. **Identifying Cause and Effect** How did the Civil War affect settlement patterns on the Texas frontier?

Interpreting Graphs (TEKS)

Study the graph below. Then use the information on the graph to help you answer the questions that follow.

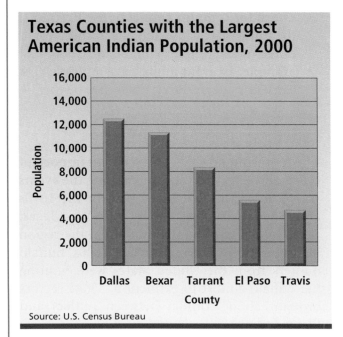

Texas Counties with the Largest American Indian Population, 2000

Source: U.S. Census Bureau

1. What is the difference in the American Indian populations between Dallas and Travis counties?
   a. 12,000
   b. 5,000
   c. 17,000
   d. 7,000

2. Based on this graph, what conclusions can you draw about the population distribution of American Indians in Texas?

Analyzing Primary Sources (TEKS)

Read the following quote from a 1867 government committee report on the status of American Indians. Then answer the questions that follow.

"The Indians everywhere, with the exception of the tribes within the Indian Territory, are rapidly decreasing in numbers from various causes . . . by disease; . . . by wars . . . by the steady and restless emigration of white men into the territories of the west, which, confining the Indians to still narrower limits, destroys that game [wildlife], which in their normal state, constitutes [provides] their principal means of subsistence [food]."

3. According to the report, which of the following is a cause of American Indians' decline?
   a. Indians selling their lands
   b. the government policy of signing treaties with Indians
   c. the growing number of white settlers in Indian homelands
   d. drought that ruins crops on the Plains

4. When interpreting a primary source, historians examine the historical context in which the source was written. What recommendations do you think the committee made regarding the future of American Indians?

Alternative Assessment

Cooperative Learning (TEKS)

BUILDING YOUR Portfolio

Work with a small group to complete the following activity. Create a colorful illustrated map showing where American Indians lived in Texas before 1880 and today. Each person in your group should create questions about geographic distributions and patterns for the map's legend. Be sure to ask questions about how migration and settlement have affected American Indians in Texas.

internet connect

Internet Activity: go.hrw.com
KEYWORD: ST3 TX20 (TEKS)

Access the Internet through the HRW Go site to research traditional cultural practices of an American Indian group living in Texas. Take note of the group's traditional celebrations, styles of dress, myths, and customs. Create a painting or thematic model that you can use to show the class what you have learned about the American Indian group.

Social Studies Skills
WORKSHOP

Identifying Cause and Effect

Identifying and understanding cause-and-effect relationships is crucial to the study of history. To investigate why events happen and what else may have happened because of these events, historians often ask several questions. These questions include the following: What immediate activities may have triggered the event? What past activities may have led up to the event? Who was involved?

How to Identify Cause and Effect

1. **Look for clues.** Certain words and phrases are immediate clues. They reveal the existence of a cause-and-effect relationship in history. The following chart lists some examples of clue words and phrases.

Clue Words and Phrases

Cause	Effect
because	aftermath
brought about	as a consequence
gave rise to	as a result of
inspired	depended on
led to	originating from
produced	outcome
provoked	proceeded from
spurred	resulting in
the reason	this led to

2. **Identify the relationship.** Read closely to identify how historical events may be related. Writers do not always state the link between cause and effect. Therefore, you must read very carefully. You may sometimes have to infer, or draw your own conclusions about, the cause or the effect of an event.

3. **Check for complex connections.** Beyond the immediate cause and effect, check for other, more complex connections. For example, an event might have multiple causes or effects. Effects may also be the cause of further events.

Example

The following flowchart presents an important cause-and-effect relationship among the events surrounding the Red River War. In the 1870s and 1880s settlers began to move to West Texas. Texas Indians had hunted buffalo in the region for generations. During the late 1800s, buffalo hunters from the United States were hunting the buffalo almost to extinction. These factors brought about conflict between settlers and Plains Indians.

Cause
westward movement of settlers

Cause
widespread killing of the buffalo

Effect
war between Texas Indians and settlers

Practicing the Skill

Reread Chapter 19, Section 2, of your textbook, which discusses the causes of Congressional Reconstruction. Draw a diagram like the one above, showing the relationships between the important events leading up to Congressional Reconstruction. ★TEKS

History in Action

UNIT 6 SIMULATION

You Make the Decision . . .

Should Texas Support the Union or the Confederacy?

Complete the following activity in small cooperative groups. The day is April 12, 1861. The Confederates have opened fire on Fort Sumter in Charleston Harbor. The people in Texas have strong feelings on both sides of the conflict. The Texas legislature has asked you to make a recommendation about which side of the Civil War Texas should support—the Union or the Confederacy. Follow these steps to reach your decision.

1. Gather Information. Use your textbook and other resources to find information that might help you decide whether to support the Union or the Confederacy in this conflict. Be sure to use what you learned from this unit's Skills Workshop on Identifying Cause and Effect to help you make an informed decision. You may want to divide up different parts of the research among group members.

2. Identify Options. After reviewing the information you have gathered, consider the options you might recommend to the legislature. Your final decision may be easier to reach if you consider as many options as possible. Be sure to record your possible options for your presentation.

3. Predict Consequences. Now take each option you and your group came up with and consider what might be the outcome of each course of action. Ask yourselves questions such as, "What would be the consequences of supporting the Union or the Confederacy?" Once you have predicted the consequences, record them as notes for your presentation.

4. Take Action to Implement Your Decision. After you have considered your options, you should plan and create your presentation. Be sure to make your decision on whether to support the North or the South very clear. You will need to support your decision by including information you gathered and by explaining why you rejected other options. Your presentation needs to be visually appealing to gain the support of the legislature. When you are ready, decide which group members will make each part of the presentation, and then take your decision to the legislature (the rest of the class). Good luck!

UNIT 7 The Transformation of Texas

(1860–1920)

CHAPTER 21 **The Cattle Kingdom** (1860–1890)

CHAPTER 22 **Railroads and Farming** (1870–1900)

CHAPTER 23 **The Oil Boom** (1890–1920)

Texas Teens

Young Cowhands

Teenagers played a crucial role in the growth of the state's cattle industry. With so many men in the military, the numbers of Texas cattle that roamed free on the frontier grew rapidly during the Civil War. When the war ended, ranchers needed help gathering, herding, and caring for these cattle. Teenagers like L. B. Anderson of Seguin participated in roundups, spent many years working on ranches, and went on cattle drives.

As parts of western Texas were opened up for ranching, many young Texans found work on cattle ranches. Occasionally, young women also participated in the ranch work. These teens did many jobs, including roping and herding cattle, mending fences, breaking horses, and maintaining the ranch's equipment.

Ranchers also needed people who could tolerate the hardships of driving cattle over hundreds of miles to northern stockyards. Many young Texans jumped at the chance for adventure. Cowhands faced a variety of dangers, including cattle thieves, bad weather, and stampedes. S. H. Woods, a 16-year-old from Alice, remembered a stampede.

Some women on the Texas frontier became accomplished riders and ranch workers.

"About 10 o'clock at night we were greeted with a terribly loud clap of thunder. . . . That started the ball rolling. Between the rumbling, roaring and rattling of hoofs, horns, thunder and lightning, it made an old cow-puncher long for . . . some dug-out on the banks of some little stream."

For many young Texans, the excitement of life on the trail more than made up for the dangers. J. M. Custer recalled, "We endured many hardships . . . but, just the same . . . the world is better for it." **Why did some Texas teens want to be cowhands?**

In this unit you will learn about the Texas cattle industry. You will also learn about the expansion of farming and railroads into the Texas frontier and how the Texas oil boom began.

LEFT PAGE: *Frederic Remington's painting* Turn Him Loose *shows the adventure and work of cowboy life.*

The Cattle Kingdom
(1860–1890)

Tom Lea, "Cattle on an Early Mexican Hacienda." 1950.32

Texas cowboys and vaqueros wore fancy spurs while riding horses.

Early Spanish settlers introduced cattle ranching to Texas.

TEXAS

1863 The Texas cattle population increases rapidly during the Civil War.

1869 Texas cowboys move a herd of 15,000 cattle to market. It is the largest single herd of the era.

1873 Ranchers begin shipping thousands of cattle from Denison after the Missouri, Kansas and Texas Railroad extends a line there.

1860	1864	1868	1872

U.S. and WORLD

1863 People rush to what is now Montana after gold is discovered there.

1867 The Kansas Pacific Railroad establishes a shipping point for cattle in Abilene, Kansas.

1873 The U.S. economy suffers a downturn, causing a temporary decline in the value of cattle.

After the long drive from Texas to Abilene, Kansas, cattle were loaded on railroad cars and shipped to eastern markets.

The Granger Collection, New York

Build on What You Know

M any U.S. settlers moved to the Texas frontier during the 1860s. These new settlers competed with American Indians for control of the land. As the frontier moved west, Texans drove cattle to sell them in out-of-state markets. Soon the state had a booming cattle industry.

The Granger Collection, New York

Cattle stampedes were one of the many dangers cowboys faced.

This barbed-wire sample board advertises different types of wire.

1876 About 2,700 animals die during a cattle stampede near the Brazos River.

1882 A ranch in the Panhandle purchases enough barbed wire to fence 250,000 acres.

1876   1880   1884   1888

1876 Wyatt Earp and Bat Masterson work as law officers in the cattle town of Dodge City, Kansas.

1880 Up to 21,000 cattle go through the Union Stockyards in Chicago every day.

1886 Cowboys in Wyoming Territory stage a labor strike to protest a pay cut.

You Be the Historian

Themes Journal

What's Your Opinion? Do you **agree** or **disagree** with the following statements? Support your point of view in your journal.

● **Culture** A region's culture is always dominated by its most important industries.

● **Economics** Events in one region rarely affect other regions economically.

● **Science, Technology & Society** New technologies negatively affect existing industries.

If you were there . . .

Would you become a cattle rancher?

Read to Discover

1. How did the Texas cattle industry develop from its Spanish beginnings?
2. What made the longhorn well suited for life in Texas?
3. How did the Civil War affect the Texas cattle industry?

Define

- **brands**
- **cattle drives**
- **rustlers**
- **longhorn**
- **Texas fever**

Why It Matters Today

People have been ranching in Texas for about 300 years. Use **CNN fyi.com** or other **current events** sources to learn more about the modern-day livestock industry. Record your findings in your journal.

The Story Continues

For years, traders regularly herded goats, hogs, and horses through the busy streets of New York City. Residents paid little attention to such livestock until longhorn cattle from Texas arrived. One local newspaper reported that the longhorns had "something of a wild look." The newspaper also noted that their meat was "a little tough." Beef-hungry New Yorkers did not mind. They paid about $80 apiece for the scrawny longhorns.

Longhorns resulted from the breeding of Spanish cattle with English cattle.

★ Spanish Beginnings

The Spanish had firmly established cattle ranchos, or ranches, in Mexico in the 1500s. By the early 1700s the Spanish were moving herds north into Texas to support the missions they had established in the Rio Grande and San Antonio River valleys. These regions had a good climate and water supply, as well as plentiful grasses. Eventually, ranching in Texas shifted from missions to private owners. Tomás Sánchez de la Berrera y Garza owned one of the largest ranches, which was located near Laredo. Martín de León owned another huge cattle ranch in present-day Victoria County.

As the number of cattle ranches grew, disputes sometimes arose when ranchers lost track of which cattle they owned. The Spanish government began ordering cattle owners to put **brands**, or identification marks made with hot metal, on their cattle. For example, de León's brand was EJ, which stood for Espíritu de Jesús, or "Spirit of Jesus." Tejano ranchers staged the first **cattle drives** in Texas, herding groups of cattle south of the Rio Grande to supply beef to Spanish military outposts. Ranchers also drove cattle from southeast Texas to Louisiana. Cattle ranching soon became an important part of the region's economy.

As U.S. settlers arrived in the early 1800s, ranching spread to other areas. Each region had its advantages. East Texas was relatively close to the cattle markets in New Orleans, while Central and South Texas had rich prairie grasses and moderate climates. After seeing the lush prairies, some U.S. settlers decided to become ranchers rather than farmers.

The Texas cattle industry slowly expanded in the 1840s. For example, Aaron Ashworth of Jefferson County had ranch holdings worth more than $30,000. Some Texans began driving cattle to out-of-state markets. James Taylor White began to drive cattle from Liberty County to market in New Orleans, and in 1846 Edward Piper took a herd of Texas cattle to Ohio. After gold was discovered in California, some Texans drove a number of cattle west to help feed the growing population of miners.

Despite the growth of the cattle industry, ranchers faced several challenges. Cattle **rustlers**, or thieves, threatened the herds. A bigger hurdle was access to markets. The demand for cattle within Texas was limited because of the region's fairly small population. Ranchers could herd their stock to sell outside of Texas, but it was a difficult and often dangerous process.

Reading Check **Sequencing** Describe in order the development of the cattle industry in Texas from its Spanish beginnings.

Our Cultural Heritage

Vaqueros and Cowboys

Vaqueros were the first cowboys in Texas. Most vaqueros were skilled ropers and riders. Over time, Spanish practices combined with the practices of U.S. settlers to create a Texas cowboy tradition. Many Texans still wear cowboy fashions, particularly boots and hats. Museums and events around the state celebrate vaqueros and cowboys. For example, the Texas Cowboy Reunion in Stamford features wild-horse races. **How have cowboys influenced the culture of Texas?** TEKS

Courtesy of the Witte Museum, San Antonio, Texas

Many Texas artists, such as Théodore Gentilz, focused their works on the life of vaqueros and cowboys.

★ The Texas Longhorns

During the mid-1800s the **longhorn** appeared in Texas. This new breed of cattle developed as Spanish breeds mixed with English cattle brought by U.S. settlers. The longhorns were well suited to life in Texas, thriving on its native grasses. These lean strong animals could endure hot weather as well as cold. They even ate prickly pear cacti during droughts and could survive on little water. In addition, longhorns were resistant to the cattle disease commonly called **Texas fever**.

While older longhorns weighed up to 1,600 pounds, some people said the longhorn had too little meat. They called it "8 pounds of hamburger on 800 pounds of bone and horn." However, long legs allowed longhorns to travel great distances, and their horns protected them from mountain lions, wolves, and other predators. Mature animals had enormous pointed horns—some were five or more feet across. Early Texas settlers displayed these horns on their walls. They made buttons, cups, decorations, furniture, and household utensils from the horns. They even stored gunpowder in hollowed-out horns. Few animals were as useful to people on the Texas frontier.

The longhorns became more valuable as cattle ranching grew in the late 1850s. When the Civil War broke out, the demand for Texas beef increased rapidly. The Confederate army needed to feed the troops. However, as the war dragged on, Texans found it difficult to move their cattle to the front. By 1863 the Union army had blocked trade from Confederate states, including Texas. As a result, the number of cattle in Texas grew rapidly. By the end of the Civil War, about 5 million cattle roamed the state. Many of these animals were mavericks, or unclaimed cattle. After the war, Texans looked for new markets to sell their cattle.

★ **Reading Check Finding the Main Idea** How did the migration of U.S. settlers to Texas affect the cattle industry?

★ Section 1 Review   ★TEKS Questions 1, 2, 3a, 3b, 4

go.hrw.com Homework Practice Online
keyword: ST3 HP21

1 Define and explain:
- brands
- cattle drives
- rustlers
- longhorn
- Texas fever

2 Analyzing Information
Copy the graphic organizer below. Use it to explain how the Texas cattle industry developed from its Spanish beginnings and throughout the Civil War.

Cattle Ranching in Spanish Texas
↓
Early Ranching in Texas
↓
Ranching during the Civil War

3 Finding the Main Idea
a. How did physical factors influence the development of cattle ranching in Texas?
b. Why were longhorn cattle important to the Texas cattle industry?

4 Writing and Critical Thinking
Drawing Inferences and Conclusions Imagine that you are an economist. Explain how free enterprise affected the Texas cattle industry. Consider the following:
- demand for cattle
- supply of cattle

TAKS

Texas Cattle Trails

Read to Discover

1. How did the growing market for beef affect Texas ranchers?
2. What were some of the cattle trails, and why did cowboys stop using them?
3. What was life like on the trail?

Why It Matters Today

Texas cattle drivers had an on-the-move occupation. Use CNNfyi.com or other **current events** sources to learn more about jobs that involve travel today. Record your findings in your journal.

Define

- stockyards
- open range
- remuda
- wrangler

Identify

- Sedalia Trail
- Chisholm Trail
- Jesse Chisholm
- Western Trail
- Charles Goodnight
- Goodnight-Loving Trail

The Story Continues

Abilene was just a dusty Kansas town until a businessman named Joseph McCoy decided to build a cattle market there. He formed a giant Wild West show that traveled by train to advertise his operations. The show featured trick riders and ropers as well as a 2,300-pound buffalo. Every time the train stopped, the performers and animals went into action. The show thrilled spectators. As word spread, many cattle buyers from the northeastern United States came to Abilene.

Wild West shows were popular attractions during the late 1800s and early 1900s.

★ The Cattle Drives

Demand for beef outpaced supply in the Northeast. The region had a large population, and its cattle supply had been greatly reduced by the Civil War. But in Texas the supply of cattle was greater than the demand for beef. As a result, cattle that sold for $3 or $6 a head in Texas sold for $38 in Kansas or $80 in New York.

Such high prices convinced Texas ranchers that they could make large profits by raising more cattle. However, ranchers could not drive longhorns to eastern markets because of the distance and the many populated farm areas the herds would have to cross. By 1865, **stockyards**, or huge holding pens, and packing houses were opening in Chicago. Soon,

Cattle drives. Texas ranchers and cowboys drove their herds of cattle hundreds of miles to sell them in out-of-state markets. **How do you think geographic factors, such as landforms and climate, affected cattle drives?** ⭐TEKS

more beef-processing plants were built farther west, in St. Louis and Kansas City. These plants were built to prepare the beef for shipment to cities in the North and East. Railroads connected cities in midwestern states such as Missouri with the larger cities in the Northeast. To reach these additional markets, Texas ranchers needed a way to get their cattle to the nearest railroad lines.

Cattle drives provided the answer. During the fall and winter, cattle grazed on the **open range**, or unfenced lands, of Texas. One rancher wrote, "Cattle are permitted to range . . . over a large surface of the country, thirty, forty, and even fifty miles in extent [size]." As spring approached, cowboys gathered cattle together in a roundup. Cowboys caught as many mavericks as possible and branded them to establish ownership of the animals. When the grass turned green in the spring, cowboys drove the cattle north. Along the way, the cattle grazed on the open range.

During one large cattle drive in 1866, cowboys moved about 260,000 cattle north over the **Sedalia Trail**, which became known as the Shawnee Trail. This trail led from South Texas through Indian Territory to Sedalia, Missouri. Toward the end of the trail, problems arose. In Missouri and eastern Kansas, there was little open range left—much of the land was farmed. As the huge herds passed through, farmers' crops were sometimes trampled. The longhorns also infected many other cattle by giving them ticks that carried Texas fever. Farmers became angry as their cattle died. Kansas and Missouri had already passed laws in an attempt to stop the cattle drives, and farmers began to turn back the Texas herds. The future of Texas cattle drives seemed uncertain.

⭐ **Reading Check** **Identifying Cause and Effect** Why was there a national market for beef, and how did demand affect the Texas cattle industry?

★ The Chisholm and Western Trails

Entrepreneur Joseph McCoy stepped in with a solution. McCoy knew that rail lines were moving farther west—by early 1867 tracks were being built in Kansas. State legislators there passed a law allowing cattle drives west of farm areas. McCoy arranged for the building of a cattle market complete with holding pens and loading chutes in Abilene, Kansas. McCoy made many improvements to the small town. Before he began, Abilene was, in McCoy's words, "a very small dead place, consisting of about one dozen log huts." McCoy even bargained with the Kansas Pacific Railroad to get special rates for shipping cattle to Chicago. To drum up business, McCoy sent scouts southward to urge Texas ranchers to bring their cattle to Abilene.

In 1867, Texas cowboys herded about 35,000 longhorns over the **Chisholm Trail**. The route to Abilene was named after **Jesse Chisholm**, a fur trader. The child of a Cherokee woman, Chisholm blazed the original trail in the mid-1860s to trade with American Indians. His trail went through Indian Territory to Kansas. The Chisholm Trail was an ideal route for the Texas cattle drives because it was not near farms. Over

After years of work, some ranchers became wealthy and could afford luxuries like this gold bull clock.

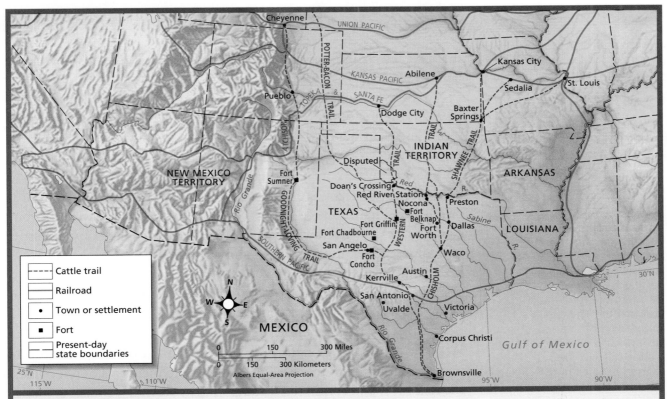

The Cattle Kingdom of Texas, 1865–1890

Interpreting Maps The use of cattle trails and railroads allowed Texas ranchers to sell their livestock in national markets.

TAKS Skills *Human Systems* How did railroad technology and cattle drives encourage an interdependence between Texas ranching and out-of-state cattle markets? ★TEKS

The Cattle Kingdom **445**

Andy Adams and Cowboy Stories
Some cowboys wrote about their adventures on cattle drives. Andy Adams wrote *The Log of a Cowboy,* in which he recalled a common but dangerous event—a stampede. "The cattle jumped from the bed ground and were off like a shot." The cowboys managed to calm the cattle, but their horses were a different matter. "The horses . . . gave us a long, hard run." What does *The Log of a Cowboy* reveal about the cowboys' way of life? ⭐TEKS

the next few years, even more cowboys used this trail to move their herds to Abilene.

In 1871 some 600,000 to 700,000 longhorns arrived in the cow town. At the end of the drive, most ranchers sold the animals for a good profit and paid the cowboys in cash. Weary cowboys spent their hard-earned money on hot baths, clean clothes, and good food. The large number of rowdy cowboys sometimes made cattle towns violent—at least until regular governments could be set up. Law-enforcement officials worked hard to keep the peace in the rough cattle towns. Cowboy Andy Adams warned that the Kansas cow town of Dodge City had strict law enforcement. "You can wear your six-shooters into town, but you'd better leave them at the first place you stop."

Farms and towns eventually sprang up along the Chisholm Trail as Texas Indians were pushed farther west. Texas ranchers soon needed a new trail across the open range to the west of settled territory. The **Western Trail** was forged in 1874. The route ran north from Kerrville to Fort Griffin—well to the west of the new settlements. The trail crossed the Red River and continued through Indian Territory, ending at Dodge City in southwestern Kansas. By 1879 the Western Trail was the primary route for Texas cattle being moved north. This trail was very successful and was used until the closing of the open range.

⭐ **Reading Check** **Analyzing Information** Why did Texas ranchers stop using the Chisholm Trail and begin using the Western Trail?

The Goodnight-Loving Trail

Not all of the cattle drives ended at railroad stockyards in Kansas. Ranchers also saw opportunities to profit by supplying cattle to military posts, mining camps, and American Indian reservations. **Charles Goodnight** and Oliver Loving were two cattlemen who looked beyond the eastern markets. In 1866 Goodnight and Loving combined their herds and set out for Fort Sumner, New Mexico. Their route became known as the **Goodnight-Loving Trail**. The trail ran from Young County west of Fort Worth, through San Angelo, across West Texas, north through New Mexico, and into Colorado. Over time, this trail became one of the most-traveled routes in the Southwest. Ranchers stopped using the trail when railroads came to Texas and eliminated the need for long cattle drives to rail lines.

Cowboy H. P. Cook participated in many drives to American Indian reservations in the West. He described his experiences on one trip:

Texas Voices 66The trip must have taken about six weeks going and returning. It was really tough, sleeping on the ground this trip, it was so wet and cold. I had just a couple of cotton quilts, and by morning there wasn't a dry thread in them, it was so wet. I used my saddle for a pillow. We would move the fire over and flop down on the ground where the fire had been, which would stay warm for a while.99

—H. P. Cook, quoted in *Texas Cowboys,* edited by Jim Lanning

Reading Check Finding the Main Idea Why did Goodnight and Loving blaze a cattle trail?

Life on the Trail

Cowboys represented many ranchers and supervised many herds on the cattle drives. Some ranchers drove their own cattle, but most hired a drover, or a cattle drive operator. John Henry Stephens, a well-known drover, made large sums of money herding other people's cattle to market. Cattle-herding outfits also included a trail boss, or a drive leader.

A typical cattle drive had 8 to 12 cowboys to care for 2,000 to 3,000 cattle. Mary Bunton, one of the few women to go on a trail drive, remembered the sight of so many cattle on the move. "I would turn in my saddle and look back, and it would look as if the entire face of the earth was just a moving mass of heads and horns." Each cowboy used several horses in relays of two or three, so that a fresh mount was always available. The herd of these animals was known as the **remuda**, the Spanish word for "remount." A **wrangler** cared for the crew's horses.

The camp cook was another important member of the drive crew. Good food meant happy cowboys. The cook traveled ahead of the herd

Loaded down with supplies and food for the cowboys, chuck wagons traveled ahead of the herd.

and had meals prepared when the rest of the outfit arrived. The cook's supplies were carried in the chuck wagon, or the covered supply wagon. A day on the trail began before sunrise. After a hot breakfast of bacon, beans, and biscuits, the cowboys would choose their horses from the remuda and start to move the cattle.

Two highly experienced cowboys called point men guided the herd, while other cowboys rode on the sides of the herd. Drag men traveled behind the herd. This was the drive's worst position because drag men "ate" dust the whole trip. On a good day, the herd would move 15 to 18 miles. About 5:00 P.M. or later, the crew stopped for the night. The dinner menu was usually beef or pork, but sometimes included "son-of-a-gun" stew. This thick soup was made from cow brain, heart, kidneys, liver, and tongue.

Trail drives were difficult and often dangerous. The sunshine was hot, and water was sometimes in short supply. Prairie fires swept across the plains, sometimes moving fast enough to overtake a cowboy on a galloping horse. Cowboys encountered bad weather, and rustlers tried to steal the livestock. In his diary, one cowboy described an unpleasant cattle drive.

Analyzing Primary Sources
Making Generalizations and Predictions Why might cowboys like George Duffield have continued to go on cattle drives despite the hardships?

Texas Voices "Awful night . . . not having a bit to eat for 60 hours . . . Tired. . . . Oh! what a night—Thunder Lightning & rain—we followed our Beeves [cattle] all night as they wandered about. . . . We Hauled cattle out of the Mud with oxen half the day. . . . My back is Blistered bad. . . . Found a Human skeleton on the Prairie to day."

—George Duffield, quoted in *The Cowboys,* by William H. Forbis

⭐ **Reading Check** **Categorizing** Who made up a typical cattle-driving crew, and what were their responsibilities?

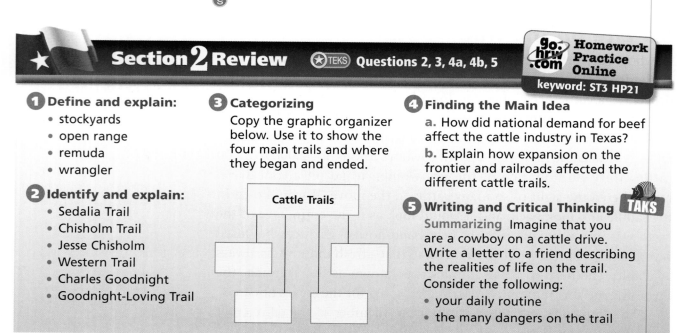

Section 2 Review ⭐TEKS Questions 2, 3, 4a, 4b, 5

go.hrw.com **Homework Practice Online**
keyword: ST3 HP21

1 Define and explain:
- stockyards
- open range
- remuda
- wrangler

2 Identify and explain:
- Sedalia Trail
- Chisholm Trail
- Jesse Chisholm
- Western Trail
- Charles Goodnight
- Goodnight-Loving Trail

3 Categorizing
Copy the graphic organizer below. Use it to show the four main trails and where they began and ended.

> Cattle Trails

4 Finding the Main Idea
a. How did national demand for beef affect the cattle industry in Texas?
b. Explain how expansion on the frontier and railroads affected the different cattle trails.

5 Writing and Critical Thinking **TAKS**
Summarizing Imagine that you are a cowboy on a cattle drive. Write a letter to a friend describing the realities of life on the trail. Consider the following:
- your daily routine
- the many dangers on the trail

Ranches, Ranchers, and Cowboys

Read to Discover

1. In what Texas regions was ranching a big industry, and why did ranches develop there?
2. What were ranching and cowboy life like?
3. How did cowboys contribute to Texas culture?

Why It Matters Today

Cowboys worked hard on Texas ranches. Use **CNNfyi.com** or other **current events** sources to learn more about modern-day cowboys or other farmworkers. Record your findings in your journal.

Define
- windmills

Identify
- Cattle Kingdom
- King Ranch
- Henrietta King
- Margaret Borland
- JA Ranch
- XIT Ranch
- Bose Ikard
- Charles Siringo

The Story Continues

Molly Goodnight, the wife of Texas rancher Charles Goodnight, loved to entertain. But visitors were rare on the isolated JA Ranch in the Panhandle. One evening a visiting cowboy brought three live chickens as a gift. He wanted Mrs. Goodnight to cook them, but she decided to keep them as pets. In a letter to her sister, she wrote, "You've no idea how much company a chicken can be."

Molly Goodnight owned a herd of cattle that was marked with her brand.

Panhandle-Plains Historical Museum, Research Center, Canyon, Texas

★ Ranching in South Texas

During the 1800s the cattle ranches that arose on the open range from Texas to Canada formed the **Cattle Kingdom**. The **King Ranch** in South Texas was one of the most important cattle operations in the state. Richard King and Gideon Lewis established the ranch in Nueces County in the early 1850s. King died in 1885, leaving his wife to run the ranch. **Henrietta King** and her son-in-law, Robert Kleberg, built the King Ranch into a thriving operation. By 1925 it included more than 1 million acres of land. King used her wealth to develop South Texas. She gave land for the towns of Kingsville and Raymondville, and she donated land and money for churches and schools. King also helped establish Texas A&M University–Kingsville.

Texas Cities

Amarillo and Lubbock

History: Businesspeople established Amarillo in 1887. It boomed as a large cattle-shipping location. Ranchers and farmers settled the general area of present-day Lubbock in the 1870s. The town was formed in 1890.

Amarillo population in 2000: 173,627

Lubbock population in 2000: 199,564

Relative location: Northwest Texas

Region: Panhandle

County: Amarillo is the county seat of Potter County, and Lubbock is the county seat of Lubbock County.

Origin of Name: Spanish herders called the area of present-day Amarillo *amarillo,* or "yellow," to describe the local soil and flowers. The county of Lubbock was named for Thomas S. Lubbock, a Texas Civil War veteran.

Economy: Amarillo relies on ranching, oil, and manufacturing. Lubbock has important industrial, technological, and agricultural businesses. Lubbock is the home of Texas Tech University. Lubbock is also a leading cotton producer.

Other large ranches developed in South Texas, where the climate was well suited to cattle ranching. Manuel Guerra owned a large ranch in Starr County. Like King and other big ranchers, Guerra was an important leader in South Texas. Another successful South Texas rancher, **Margaret Borland,** owned more than 10,000 cattle by 1873. That same year she led a trail drive to Kansas. Borland is believed to be the only woman to head up a trail drive. She took three of her children—all under age 15—and her granddaughter on the drive.

Reading Check Analyzing Information How did cattle ranchers like Henrietta King affect the social development of Texas towns?

★ Ranches in the Panhandle

By the early 1880s cattle ranching was a thriving and profitable industry in many parts of Texas. As Plains Indians were removed from West Texas, the Panhandle was opened up for ranching. The grass that covered the plains provided plenty of food for the cattle. In addition, the region's flat open land was well suited for cattle ranching because it allowed ranchers to keep close watch on the livestock. Although there were not enough rivers to water the cattle, the Ogallala Aquifer lay underneath the region. Ranchers adapted to the environment by using **windmills** to reach this huge supply of water. Windmills operate on a simple principle. The wind blows against a vane that turns the blades into the breeze. The wind then hits the blades, creating power to operate a pump. This power brings underground water to the surface.

In the mid-1870s Charles Goodnight and John Adair established one of the first ranches in the Panhandle—the **JA Ranch** in Palo Duro Canyon. The canyon had a good supply of grass and offered shelter from the harsh winds that swept across the region. The JA Ranch became large and successful. By the mid-1880s it covered more than 700,000 acres and supported about 40,000 cattle. Other pioneers also established ranches in the Panhandle. Thomas Sherman Bugbee built the Quarter Circle T Ranch in Hutchinson County. Another large ranch, the Matador, was founded in 1878. These ranches helped bring prosperity to the Panhandle.

Corporations, often funded by investors from the northern United States and from Great Britain, moved into the Panhandle along with the ranchers. The **XIT Ranch** was established in 1885 when the state gave the land to the Capitol Freehold Land and Investment Company. This company was funded by investors from Chicago and Britain. In return, the investors agreed to construct a new state capitol building to replace the one that had burned in 1881. The new capitol was completed in 1888 and is still the seat of Texas government.

Over time, the XIT Ranch became one of the largest and most famous ranches in Texas. The XIT covered about 3 million acres, extending nearly 200 miles along the Texas–New Mexico border—an area almost the size of Connecticut. At its peak, the XIT employed about 150 cowboys to care for roughly 150,000 cattle.

 Reading Check Summarizing Why did ranching develop in the Panhandle, and what are some of ranching's political legacies?

★ Ranchers and Cowboys

★ Ranchers and Cowboys

Most Texas ranches were located far from towns. Ranchers had to rely on their own resources to solve the many challenges they faced. Mary Jaques outlined the skills needed by ranchers. "The ideal ranchman must be butcher, baker, carpenter, . . . blacksmith, plain cook, milker." Female ranchers handled many tasks. In addition to herding and branding livestock, they raised children and operated households. Mrs. C. C. West helped manage a sheep ranch in West Texas. She remembered

That's Interesting!

The XIT Ranch

The ranch took its name from the XIT brand that a drover created. The block letters made it difficult for cattle rustlers to change. Some people disagree with this story about the ranch's name, however. They claim— because the roman numeral X stands for 10— that XIT stood for "ten In Texas," or the 10 counties that contained the ranch-land. Other people argue that it stood for "biggest in Texas."

Interpreting the Visual Record

Ranch life. Cowboys who worked on Texas ranches had many jobs, including training horses and branding cattle. **What traditional cowboy clothing are these ranch workers wearing?**

Western Artists

In this painting, *Roping a Steer*, artist and former cowboy Edward Borein shows a cowboy at work. Roping cattle was an essential skill for cowboys. How does this painting capture the difficulty of roping a running steer? ⭐TEKS

"living under a tree, herding sheep with my babe in my arms and using one big skillet for a whole kitchen outfit."

Ranchers could never have succeeded without cowboys, who did countless daily tasks on the ranches. Most cowboys were young men, and many were Mexican American or African American. One cowboy remembered his ranch crew. "There were about 50 cowboys at the headquarter ranch; a few Mexicans, and a few [African Americans] among them." Although they sometimes faced discrimination, some African American cowboys went on to own their own ranches and farms. For example, **Bose Ikard** supervised trail drives and directed some of the operations at Charles Goodnight's ranch. He eventually bought land in Parker County. African American Daniel W. Wallace went on many trail drives as a teenager. Even as a young cowboy, Wallace carefully saved and managed his earnings. He eventually bought a ranch that covered at least 1,200 acres and included some 500 head of cattle.

Texas cowboys wore clothes and used tools that were suited to the state's environment. Some cowboys wore the familiar cowboy hat, while others wore the vaqueros' broad felt hat. Many cowboys wore sombreros to protect themselves from the harsh sunlight and rain. Cowboys relied on leather chaps worn over their pants to protect them from thorny brushes. All cowboys used a long light rope called a lariat, from the Spanish *la reata*. Cowboys sometimes called their ropes "lassos" instead of lariats. The word *lasso* came from the Spanish word *lazo*. These and other terms reflect the Spanish heritage of ranching in Texas.

⭐ **Reading Check** **Finding the Main Idea** Identify examples of Spanish influence on vocabulary that originated in Texas cattle ranching.

★ Cowboy Culture

Over time, cowboys became an important part of American popular culture. Inexpensive novels featured countless cowboy heroes such as Arizona Joe, Denver Dan, and Fancy Frank. The novels glorified cowboy life. Wild West shows were also popular, using colorful posters to attract large crowds. Some people believed that western novels and shows accurately portrayed cowboy life. According to the myths, cowboys were fearless, happy, and worry free. They spent their days roaming through rugged but gorgeous landscapes.

The realities of cowboy life were far different from the myths. Cowboys faced many dangers, including blizzards, floods, and stampedes. These hazards injured and killed many cowboys. Cowboys also worked hard for hours on end. During trail drives, some cowboys rode 24 hours at a stretch and slept in their saddles. For their work most cowboys earned low salaries of about $300 per year. Cowboy **Charles Siringo** worked for the Rancho Grande Company for two years without receiving a regular paycheck. After subtracting his purchases at the ranch store, he earned just 75 cents for two years. Some, like Siringo, found it very difficult to make ends meet after buying what they needed for work.

> **Texas Voices** ❝We had unlimited credit at the company store. My credit was stretched almost to the breaking point in purchasing a cowboy outfit, such as saddle, bridle, spurs, pistol, bowie-knife, bedding, sombrero, silk handkerchiefs, slicker [rain coat], high-heel boots, etc.❞
>
> —Charles Siringo, *A Lone Star Cowboy*

★ **Reading Check** **Contrasting** How did the myths differ from the realities of the cowboy way of life?

CONNECTING TO Music

Cowboy Songs

Cattle were nervous creatures, particularly at night, so cowboys sang to help keep them calm and peaceful. Some trail bosses even auditioned cowboys before hiring them. Cowboy songs were often slow and sad. Cattle seemed to like these soothing tunes. "The Old Chisholm Trail" was one popular song.

"I'm up in the mornin'
    afore daylight
And afore I sleep the
    moon shines bright.

Oh, it's bacon and beans
    most every day–
I'd as soon be a-eatin'
    prairie hay."

Why might the "The Old Chisholm Trail" have been soothing to cowboys as well as their cattle? ★ TEKS

Section 3 Review ★ TEKS Questions 2, 3, 4a, 4b, 5

go.hrw.com Homework Practice Online
keyword: ST3 HP21

1 Define and explain:
- windmills

2 Identify and explain:
- Cattle Kingdom
- King Ranch
- Henrietta King
- Margaret Borland
- JA Ranch
- XIT Ranch
- Bose Ikard
- Charles Siringo

3 Categorizing
Copy the graphic organizer below. Use it to identify some of the myths and realities of cowboy life that became part of Texas culture.

Myths

Realities

4 Finding the Main Idea
a. In what parts of the state was ranching a big industry, and why did ranches develop there?
b. List examples of the Spanish influence on vocabulary related to cattle ranching in Texas.

5 Writing and Critical Thinking
Analyzing Information Write an advertisement that encourages ranchers to establish operations in the Panhandle.
Consider the following:
- the availability of land and water
- innovations such as the windmill

TAKS

The Closing of the Open Range

Read to Discover

1. How did barbed wire affect the development of Texas?
2. What contributed to the decline of the Cattle Kingdom?

Why It Matters Today

Technological innovations changed the Texas frontier. Use **CNN fyi.com** or other **current events** sources to learn more about new technology and scientific discoveries that affect the world today. Record your findings in your journal.

Define
- **barbed wire**
- **range wars**

Identify
- **Joseph F. Glidden**

The Granger Collection, New York

Joseph F. Glidden invented barbed wire in the 1870s. This advertisement shows the benefits of the new technology.

The Story Continues

John Warne Gates, an eager salesman, saw a golden opportunity to increase sales of barbed wire in Texas. In 1878 he held a demonstration in downtown San Antonio to advertise his product. Gates fenced a holding pen with barbed wire and stocked it with a herd of wild longhorns. Although the longhorns were strong and mean, the barbed wire held them back. The crowds were very impressed, and sales of barbed wire in Texas skyrocketed.

★ Fencing the Open Range

Farmers moving into West Texas wanted to fence their land to protect their crops from stray cattle. Some ranchers also tried to fence in their land. But building long fences was difficult because wood was scarce on the open plains. <u>**Joseph F. Glidden**</u>, a farmer in De Kalb, Illinois, answered this challenge. After his wife asked him to create a fence to keep dogs out of her garden, he developed **barbed wire** in 1873. These barbs kept cattle off the fences without hurting the animals. Glidden quickly opened a factory to make his product. Soon, inexpensive barbed wire was readily available. The sharp wire fences even survived the strong Texas winds. One advertisement described barbed wire as "light as air . . . and cheap as dirt."

Many people, particularly small-scale ranchers, disliked the idea of fencing the range. Over time, however, the idea became more popular.

The new invention made large-scale fencing both easy and inexpensive. By the end of the 1880s, there were barbed-wire fences in nearly every Texas county. This marked the end of the open range in Texas.

 Reading Check **Identifying Cause and Effect** What innovation was widely used in the 1880s, and how did it affect the use of land?

★ The Range Wars

Widespread fencing led to conflict in Texas in the early 1880s. Owners of small properties complained that they were being surrounded by the fences of giant cattle companies. Fencing became so extensive that public roads were blocked and mail delivery was interrupted. Many large ranchers fenced off water sources even though they did not own the land. Ranchers who let their cattle roam free complained that fencing cut their cattle off from water sources. This issue became critical when Texas was hit by a drought in 1883 and cattle began to die of thirst. Before long, **range wars** broke out. Under the cover of darkness, ranchers snipped the barbed-wire fences. A Gainesville farmer found a note that read, "If you don't make gates, we will make them for you." In Coleman County, cutters destroyed 500 miles of barbed-wire fences. Other ranchers, usually wealthy cattle operators, struck back. They hired guards to protect their fences, and gunfights sometimes broke out.

Fence cutting soon became an important political issue. In 1884 Governor John Ireland called an emergency session of the legislature. After heated debate, it passed a law making fence cutting illegal. The law also required a gate in every three miles of fence to allow passage for roads and railroads. In addition, the law banned people from fencing land they did not own or lease. The governor sent out the Texas Rangers to enforce the law.

Cattle ranchers also came into conflict with sheep ranchers. The Spanish had introduced sheep ranching to Texas in the early 1700s. By the time of the range wars, most sheep ranching in Texas took place in the state's southern and western regions. Cattle ranchers were angry because sheep ate the grass all the way to the root, making it useless for cattle.

 Reading Check **Analyzing Information** How did the ranchers' use of fencing spark a political controversy?

Interpreting the Visual Record

Sheep ranching. As sheep ranching expanded in the late 1800s, many Mexican Americans worked as pastores, *or herders, on Texas ranches.* **In what ways do you think sheep ranching is similar to and different from cattle ranching?**

Barbed Wire and Windmills

Barbed wire consists of two wires. The first wire is long. The second is cut into short sharp pieces that are twisted around the long portion. The wire is very effective at keeping livestock in or out of fields. Inventors tinkered with windmills by adding a vane to allow the windmill's wheel to turn into the wind. This ensured that the wheel would turn whenever a breeze was present, continuously pumping water. **How did these technical innovations affect Texas?** TEKS

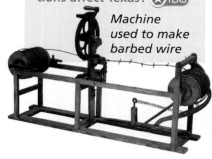

Machine used to make barbed wire

★ Legacy of the Open Range

Toward the end of the 1880s, the open range began to disappear. After the introduction of windmills, farmers and their crops were expanding onto the plains. Sheep ranching was also expanding in the late 1800s. Greater demand for woolen textiles in New England led to a rise in wool prices. Texas ranchers, particularly in regions with dry climates and more-rugged land, began to turn to sheep herding. Many cattle ranchers resented these changes.

The cattle industry changed in other ways as well. Severe winters in the 1880s caused the death of thousands of open-range cattle and thus cut down on the number of cattle drives. Many ranches went out of business. Many ranchers had expanded too quickly and allowed overgrazing of their land to occur. Years of heavy use had stripped the grass and damaged the soil itself. Some cattle operators sold their land to farmers. The new trends limited job opportunities for cowboys. In addition, the extension of railroad lines to Texas eventually ended the need for long cattle drives. Newly invented refrigerator cars could move processed beef to eastern cities. Large ranches remained, but the era of the open range was over.

Despite the decline of the cattle era, the industry created an important legacy in Texas. Throughout the world, people associate Texas with cowboys and cattle ranchers. Many Texans still raise and sell cattle. In addition, tourists visit Texas to watch rodeos and tour cattle operations such as the King Ranch. Cattle ranching continues to contribute to the state's economy.

 Reading Check **Summarizing** What two technological innovations came to the open range, and how did they affect the cattle industry?

★ Section 4 Review TEKS Questions 2, 3, 4a, 4b, 5

 **Homework Practice Online**
keyword: ST3 HP21

1 **Define and explain:**
- barbed wire
- range wars

2 **Identify and explain:**
- Joseph F. Glidden

3 **Identifying Cause and Effect**

Copy the graphic organizer below. Use it to explain what innovations came into use in the 1870s and 1880s and how they influenced the development of Texas.

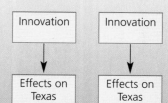

4 **Finding the Main Idea**
a. How did the development of the railroad affect the Texas cattle industry?
b. How did the cattle and sheep ranchers use of land contribute to the decline of the Cattle Kingdom?

5 **Writing and Critical Thinking**

Supporting a Point of View Imagine that you are a Texas rancher who either supports or opposes fencing the open range. Write a letter to your neighbor expressing your viewpoint. Consider the following:
- the economic consequences of fencing
- the political consequences of fencing

TAKS

The Texas Ranching Industry

Cattle and sheep ranching were important to the state's economy in the 1800s. These industries are still important in Texas. Today there are more than 280,000 cattle ranches and 7,000 sheep and lamb ranches.

Ranching in Texas, Today

Cattle
Sheep
Goat

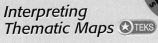

Interpreting Thematic Maps ⭐TEKS

1. In what region of Texas are most cattle raised?

2. In what region of Texas are most goats and sheep raised?

3. Use the information in the table below to create a bar graph showing the growth in the cattle population in Texas.

4. What was the increase in the number of cattle in Texas between 1840 and 1850?

5. How many more cattle were raised in Texas c. 2000 than in 1860?

The Cattle Boom in Texas

YEAR	NUMBER OF CATTLE
1840	124,397
1850	917,524
1860	3.8 million
c. 2000	14.5 million

CHAPTER 21 REVIEW

The Chapter at a Glance

Examine the following visual summary of the chapter. Then use the visual to create flash cards about the chapter. Use the flash cards to drill with a partner. ⭐TEKS

The use of barbed wire and windmills closed the open range and allowed farming to develop in West Texas.

Once stockyards were established along rail lines, ranchers could ship their cattle to eastern markets.

Cowboys and vaqueros rounded up cattle and drove them along trails to markets out of state.

The Spanish introduced ranching to Texas.

Identifying People and Ideas ⭐TEKS

Use the following terms or people in historically significant sentences:

1. brands
2. cattle drives
3. longhorn
4. Texas fever
5. Jesse Chisholm
6. Goodnight-Loving Trail
7. Henrietta King
8. XIT Ranch
9. Joseph F. Glidden
10. range wars

Understanding Main Ideas ⭐TEKS

Section 1 (pp. 440–442)

1. How was the Texas cattle industry affected by the migration of U.S. settlers to Texas?
2. How did physical factors influence the development of ranching in Texas?

Section 2 (pp. 443–448)

3. Which cattle trails did Texas cowboys use, and what were cattle drives like?

Section 3 (pp. 449–453)

4. How did the technological innovation of the windmill affect the development of the Texas Panhandle?
5. Describe the Spanish influence on the vocabulary of Texas cattle ranching.

Section 4 (pp. 454–456)

6. How did barbed wire lead to political conflict in Texas?

You Be the Historian ⭐TEKS

Reviewing Themes

1. **Culture** Describe some myths and realities of cowboy life.
2. **Economics** How did demand for beef in the eastern United States affect the Texas cattle industry?
3. **Science, Technology & Society** How did the invention of windmills and barbed wire affect the Texas cattle industry?

TAKS Practice: Thinking Critically ⭐TEKS

1. **Sequencing** Trace in order the development of the Texas cattle industry from its Spanish beginnings to the Cattle Kingdom.
2. **Analyzing Information** In what ways did cattle ranchers adapt to and modify the environment, and what were some of the consequences?
3. **Summarizing** What were some of the defining characteristics of the cattle era in Texas history?

Interpreting Maps ⊛TEKS

Study the map below. Then use the information on the map to help you answer the questions that follow.

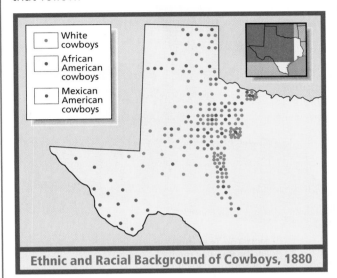

White cowboys
African American cowboys
Mexican American cowboys

Ethnic and Racial Background of Cowboys, 1880

1. Which group of cowboys worked mostly in the far west region of Texas?
   a. white cowboys
   b. African American cowboys
   c. Mexican American cowboys
   d. all of the above

2. Why do you think these cowboys worked in that region of Texas?

Analyzing Primary Sources ⊛TEKS

Read the following song written by cowboy E. C. "Teddy Blue" Abbott. Then answer the questions.

"As I was out walking one morning for pleasure,
I spied a cowpuncher come riding along.
His hat was throwed back and his spurs were
    a-janglin',
And as he rode by he was singing this song:

'Whoopee ti yi yo—git along, little dogies,
It's your misfortune, and none of my own.
Whoopee ti yi yo—git along, little dogies,
You know that Wyoming will be your new home.'

Early in the springtime we'll round up the dogies,
Slap on their brands, and bob off their tails;
Round up our horses, load up the chuck wagon,
Then throw those dogies upon the trail."

3. Which of the following events was E. C. "Teddy Blue" Abbott describing?
   a. a cattle drive
   b. a group of calves going to their mothers
   c. a line of dogs beginning to hunt foxes
   d. a Wild West show

4. What do you think the cowpuncher meant when he sang, "It's your misfortune, and none of my own"?

Alternative Assessment

Cooperative Learning ⊛TEKS

Work with a small group to research primary and secondary sources on cattle ranching. These resources may include databases, media and news services, biographies, interviews, and artifacts. Use the sources to create an oral or multimedia presentation about the Texas cattle industry in the 1800s. Consider the myths and realities of cowboy life, technological innovations, cattle drives, and the political, economic, or social effects of the industry. Deliver your presentation to the class.

BUILDING YOUR Portfolio

📶 **internet** connect

Internet Activity: go.hrw.com
KEYWORD: ST3 TX21 ⊛TEKS
Access the Internet through the HRW Go site to research the King Ranch and boom and bust cycles in the ranching industry today. Create an illustrated time line that shows how the King Ranch has changed since it was founded. Be sure to trace the cycles of boom and bust and its effects on ranching. Use the time line to create a quiz and answer key about ranching in Texas.

CHAPTER 22

Railroads and Farming

(1870–1900)

The Houston and Texas Central Railway was one of the first railroad companies in Texas.

Early Texas locomotives provided a reliable and inexpensive form of transportation.

TEXAS

1870 Texas has 583 miles of rail lines.

1876 The Texas legislature passes a law that allows the state to fund railroads with land grants.

1881 The Texas and Pacific Railway meets the Southern Pacific line near El Paso, forming the first transcontinental railroad route through Texas.

1870	**1874**	**1878**	**1882**

U.S. and WORLD

1875 The Huber Manufacturing Company, which builds threshers and other farm machinery, is incorporated.

1880 American farmers grow almost $325 million worth of cotton.

1882 Thomas Edison installs electrical power plants in New York City and London.

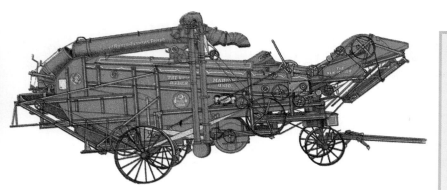

Early threshing machines were powered by horses or other livestock.

Build on What You Know

Soon after cattle ranchers settled on the Texas frontier, railroads and farmers began to press westward. The growth of farming and railroads helped spur economic progress in Texas. New businesses and technologies boomed in Texas and changed life in the state.

Railroad conductors relied on watches to keep trains on time.

With new technology such as the windmill, Texas farms became more productive.

1886 The Knights of Labor begin a major strike against Jay Gould's railroad company.
1889 There are more than 8,000 miles of railroad track in Texas.

1891 The Texas Railroad Commission is established to regulate railroads in Texas.

1900 Texas has more than 350,000 farms, and almost half of all farmers are tenant farmers.

1886   1890   1894   1898

1886 A labor rally in Chicago's Haymarket Square erupts in violence.

1892 The first gasoline-powered tractor is developed in Waterloo, Iowa.

1900 There are more than 5.7 million farms in the United States.

You Be The Historian

Themes Journal

What's Your Opinion? Do you **agree** or **disagree** with the following statements? Support your point of view in your journal.

● **Geography** The settlement of frontier land is only possible with new technologies.

● **Science, Technology & Society** The growth of industries is dependent on new transportation technologies.

● **Economics** Only in recent times has national and international demand for agricultural goods driven local economies.

If you were there . . . *How would the growth of railroads change your life?*

The Growth of Railroads

Read to Discover

1. How did railroads compare to other means of transportation in Texas?
2. How did railroads affect life in rural and urban Texas?
3. How did railroads lead to the development of the Texas frontier?

Define

- **transcontinental railroad**
- **junctions**

Why It Matters Today

Railroads brought an economic boom to many towns. Use **CNNfyi.com** or other **current events** sources to learn about transportation today. Record your findings in your journal.

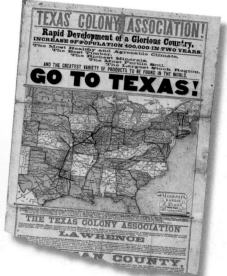

Railroad company advertisements promised a good climate, rich resources, and a thriving population in Texas.

The Story Continues

On Christmas morning in 1871, hundreds of people gathered outside of Austin. They hoped to get a glimpse of the first locomotive to enter the capital city. By mid-afternoon the crowd had moved to the downtown terminal. Officials hammered in the last spike of the railroad line as Austinites cheered. The crowd celebrated the completion of the rail line connecting Austin with Houston and Galveston.

★ New Railroad Lines

Many Texans eagerly awaited the arrival of rail lines, hoping they would spur economic growth. The state's economic development had been slowed by its transportation problems. Most Texas rivers were either too shallow or too unreliable for shipping goods, and dirt roads turned to mud during wet weather. As a result, moving people and goods was time-consuming and expensive. Railroads promised cheap, fast, and reliable transportation. A 35-mile trip that took a day and a half to travel by horse took less than two hours by rail. It was also cheaper to ship goods by railroad than by wagon. In the 1870s wagon freight rates averaged $1 for every 100 pounds shipped 100 miles, while railroad rates were less than 50 cents for the same amount over the same distance.

In 1861 there were about 470 miles of rail lines in Texas. However, the Civil War interrupted plans for new railroad construction. At the end of the decade, Texas continued to lag behind the rest of the country, which had almost 53,000 miles of track in 1870. The United States even had a **transcontinental railroad**—one that runs across a continent.

Community leaders in Texas offered to fund, or help pay for, railroad construction. Many cities issued bonds to help pay for rail construction. A bond is a certificate that represents money owed by the government to private citizens. San Antonio had issued the first Texas railroad bonds in 1850. Between 1850 and 1876, Texas cities and counties issued about $2.4 million in railroad bonds.

The Constitution of 1876 banned these local bonds but allowed the legislature to pass a general land grant law. For every continuous mile of track completed, a company could receive 16 square miles of land. The railroads were required to sell the land to finance surveying and construction of their lines. Texas eventually gave more than 32 million acres of land to more than 40 railroad companies.

Reading Check **Comparing and Contrasting** List the advantages of railroads over other forms of transportation in Texas.

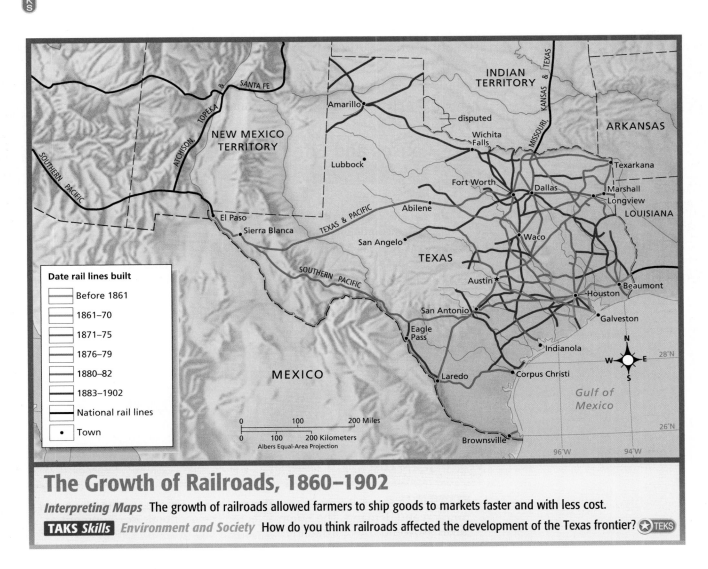

The Growth of Railroads, 1860–1902

Interpreting Maps The growth of railroads allowed farmers to ship goods to markets faster and with less cost.

TAKS Skills *Environment and Society* How do you think railroads affected the development of the Texas frontier? ★TEKS

The GH&SA Railway Company offered guide-books to immigrants thinking about moving to West Texas.

★ The Railroad Boom

Land grants and other forms of government aid helped create a Texas railroad boom. In the early 1870s the Houston and Texas Central Railway (H&TC) built a line from Galveston to Dallas and Denison. At Denison, it met the Missouri, Kansas, and Texas line, which provided service north to St. Louis, Missouri. Between 1876 and 1879, railroad companies laid more than 750 miles of track in Texas.

During the boom, railroad companies began a race west. The Southern Pacific was building a rail line from California to Texas. Other railroad companies competed to meet the Southern Pacific first. The company with the most miles of track would profit by receiving the largest government land grants and the biggest share of business. The Galveston, Harrisburg, and San Antonio Railway Company (GH&SA) had already built a line from Galveston to San Antonio. The line eventually earned the nickname the Sunset Route. In 1881 GH&SA work crews started building a line west from San Antonio toward El Paso. However, the Texas and Pacific Railway (T&P) had a jump on the GH&SA. Jay Gould, a national-railroad owner, had bought the T&P and begun construction on a westward route. In December 1881 the T&P met the Southern Pacific line in Sierra Blanca, some 90 miles east of El Paso. Gould was disappointed that his line did not reach El Paso, but he had helped complete the first transcontinental route through Texas.

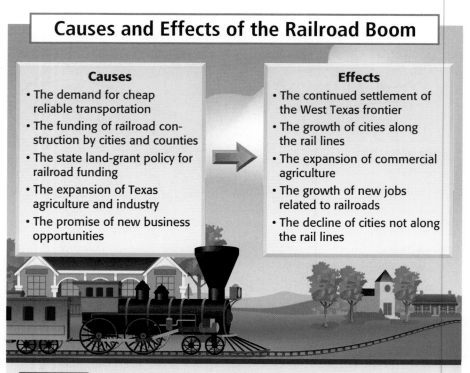

Causes and Effects of the Railroad Boom

Causes
- The demand for cheap reliable transportation
- The funding of railroad construction by cities and counties
- The state land-grant policy for railroad funding
- The expansion of Texas agriculture and industry
- The promise of new business opportunities

Effects
- The continued settlement of the West Texas frontier
- The growth of cities along the rail lines
- The expansion of commercial agriculture
- The growth of new jobs related to railroads
- The decline of cities not along the rail lines

TAKS Skills *Interpreting Charts* The railroad boom was spurred by public funding and demand. The boom affected the economic development of Texas. How did the railroad industry affect city growth? ★TEKS

Texas railroad companies also encouraged trade between Texas and Mexico by running lines to the Mexican border. In the early 1880s the International and Great Northern Railway extended its line from San Antonio to Laredo. The Panhandle was one of the last regions to receive rail service. The Fort Worth and Denver City Railway (FW&DC) began construction north of Fort Worth in 1881. New towns such as Amarillo emerged along the railroad stops in the Panhandle. Many of these towns boomed with the business that the railroads brought. Between 1879 and 1889, railroad crews laid 6,000 miles of track in Texas.

Reading Check Drawing Inferences and Conclusions Why did railroads compete to build lines in Texas, and how did they help expand settlement on the Texas frontier?

★ The Effects of the Rail Boom

The arrival of railroads greatly affected Texas. New cities were born, new areas were settled, and Texas became more connected to the rest of the country. Farm goods raised in Texas could be shipped out of state more easily, and goods produced elsewhere could be purchased in Texas. Towns such as Abilene, Big Spring, Eastland, and Sweetwater were established or grew with the arrival of the Texas and Pacific Railway (T&P). Cities grew rapidly at **junctions**, or the meeting places of two or more lines. These cities included Dallas, Houston, San Antonio, Galveston, Waco, El Paso, and Austin. Railroad-car repair shops and many other railway-related businesses appeared in these towns. Farmers and ranchers brought their crops and cattle to ship from cities along the railroad.

The economic boom in railroad towns attracted new residents. For example, Fort Worth grew up around a busy railroad junction. One local newspaper reported on the city's population boom.

Texas Voices

❝Work on the T&P . . . has already produced a good effect on the businesses of our town. It has infused [brought in] a new life and vigor [energy] into our people which reacts on those coming here with good results. Vacant houses are filling up; hotels are crowded.❞

—*Fort Worth Democrat,* quoted in *How Fort Worth Became the Texasmost City,* by Leonard Sanders

Towns that were bypassed by new rail lines often experienced drops in population and economic activity. For example, Jefferson was the sixth-largest Texas city in 1870. Tons of cotton and other farm products were shipped from Jefferson to New Orleans by water. But in 1873 the T&P built a rail line from Texarkana to Marshall, bypassing Jefferson. Jefferson declined in importance as goods were increasingly sent by rail.

Reading Check Identifying Cause and Effect How did railroads encourage business in some Texas cities, and what effects did this have on city populations?

GLOBAL CONNECTIONS

Famine in China

Many Chinese immigrated to the United States and found work building railroads. The first group of Chinese to arrive in Texas, some 250 people, came in 1870. More Chinese immigrated after a three-year drought struck China in 1876, destroying crops and causing a famine that killed nearly 10 million people. In 1881 approximately 2,600 Chinese workers arrived to build the Southern Pacific line east from El Paso. After the railroad was built, some of these workers stayed. **Why did Chinese immigrants come to Texas in the late 1800s?** TEKS

Analyzing Primary Sources
Drawing Inferences and Conclusions According to this newspaper, what effects were railroads having on Fort Worth?

The Railroad Boom

The growth of railroads allowed farmers to get goods to markets faster and at lower cost. The agricultural economy of Texas grew as more railroads were constructed.

YEAR	MILES	YEAR	MILES
1850 –	0	1930 –	17,569
1860 –	470	1940 –	17,057
1870 –	583	1950 –	16,296
1880 –	2,440	1960 –	15,445
1890 –	8,710	1970 –	14,683
1900 –	9,971	1980 –	13,075
1910 –	14,339	1990 –	11,541
1920 –	16,383	1998 –	11,383

Interpreting Data ⭐TEKS

1. Use the information in the table to create a line graph of the miles of tracks in Texas from 1850 to 1998.

2. How many more miles of rail lines were operating in 1900 than in 1870?

★ Farmers Move West

Railroads played a major role in opening up the Texas frontier to farming. As railroad companies built tracks through West Texas, settlers followed these lines and purchased land near railroad stops. Railroad companies encouraged this settlement, hoping to make money by selling parcels of land grants to farmers. These farmers would then raise crops or livestock and ship their goods over the companies' rail lines.

The railroad companies advertised the region's rich farmland, sending brochures out to all parts of the country. To ease farmers' concerns about the West Texas climate, some companies created demonstration farms with a wide variety of crops. The companies then brought potential land buyers to see what crops could be grown in the region. Partly as a result of such efforts, people began flocking to the frontier to find inexpensive land. The population of West Texas boomed. For example, the population of Jack County, which is northwest of Fort Worth, jumped from 694 in 1870 to more than 6,600 in 1880. Even a New Orleans newspaper commented on this trend. "Farmers are pouring into western Texas so fast that ranchmen have just time enough to move their cattle out and prevent their tails being chopped off by the advancing hoe." The number of farms in Texas rose from some 61,000 in 1870 to 350,000 in 1900.

 Reading Check Evaluating How did railroad transportation contribute to the settlement and development of the West Texas frontier?

 Section 1 Review ⭐TEKS Questions 2, 3a, 3b, 4

go.hrw.com **Homework Practice Online**
keyword: ST3 HP22

1 Define and explain:
- transcontinental railroad
- junctions

2 Identifying Cause and Effect

Copy the graphic organizer below. Use it to trace the development of the railroad boom and its effects on Texas.

```
Causes  →  Effects
```

3 Finding the Main Idea
a. Compare the types and uses of new transportation technology in Texas in the late 1800s.
b. How did the railroad have both positive and negative effects on urban growth in Texas?

4 Writing and Critical Thinking

Drawing Inferences and Conclusions Write a short memo describing how railroads affected the development of the Texas frontier.

Consider the following:
- the rail lines into the frontier
- the rail lines that connected Texas with U.S. and Mexican railroads

2 Changes in Farming

Read to Discover

1. How did new farming technology help Texans adapt to life on the frontier?
2. What were the effects of the commercial cotton-farming boom?

Why It Matters Today

In the late 1800s, Texans experienced a major farming boom that was followed by a bust in crop prices. Use CNN**fyi**.com or other **current events** sources to learn about boom-and-bust business cycles today. Record your findings in your journal.

Define

• **dry farming**
• **threshers**
• **commercial farming**
• **supply and demand**
• **boll weevil**

Identify

• **Dora Nunn Roberts**

The Story Continues

In 1891 General Robert St. George Dyrenforth began a series of government-sponsored experiments in West Texas. He believed that a big explosion in the sky might lead to rain in the dry region. Dyrenforth hauled more than 60 balloons, 100 kites, and thousands of pounds of explosives to a rural area outside of Midland. He then sent large balloons filled with hydrogen and loaded with dynamite into the air. The explosions produced gray clouds of smoke but little rain. After further experiments also failed, Dyrenforth returned $5,000 to the U.S. government and earned the nickname Major Dry-henceforth.

General Dyrenforth used a balloon to conduct his rainfall experiments.

★ New Farming Technology

Although West Texas was dry, many farmers had moved into the region during the late 1800s because the land there was inexpensive. Farmers soon learned that certain crops grew well in West Texas. Instead of growing corn like some East Texas farmers, West Texas farmers turned to wheat and other grains such as sorghum.

Even so, farmers needed new techniques to help them grow crops in the dry climate. Many farmers practiced **dry farming** techniques such as terracing to keep moisture in the soil. Farmers built terraces, or small

Steam-powered tractors were rare in Texas during the early 1900s.

*Railroads and farming. Railroads junctions, like this Houston depot, were busy with farmers bringing their cotton and other goods to be shipped to out-of-state markets. **How do you think the national demand for cotton affected the local market in Houston?*** ★TEKS

ridges, to catch runoff from rainfall and to help stop soil erosion. The soil in the Panhandle and some areas of West Texas was quite rich but was often very hard on the surface. John Deere's deep steel plow—widely used by 1845—helped West Texas farmers break through the hard soil. This type of plow left a layer of loose soil on top to allow crops to better absorb moisture from the air. During the 1880s a few farmers, following the lead of ranchers, began to use windmills to pump water from aquifers for crop irrigation.

Texans also began to use new mechanical farm tools. Farmers quickly gave up their old walking plows for horse-drawn ones that plowed several rows at once. Two-row planters also made planting faster and less difficult. **Threshers**—machines that separate grain or seeds from plants—made harvesting crops faster and easier. In the late 1800s a few Texas farmers even began to use steam-powered threshers and tractors. Steam-powered machines were rare and often attracted public interest. One Abilene newspaper reported the arrival of a steam-powered thresher. "The steam thresher received by T. & B. Gardner last week was a considerable source of amusement and curiosity while it remained in town." Although often amazed by these new machines, farmers used them to increase production.

★ **Reading Check** **Analyzing Information** How did new technology compare to past technologies and help farmers adapt to farming in West Texas?

★ Commercial Farming

New machinery, the increase in the number of farms, and the availability of railroads to ship products all encouraged agricultural growth in Texas. The increase in the state's agricultural production resulted in a boom in **commercial farming** during the late 1800s. Commercial farming is the large-scale growing of crops to sell for profit. Because cotton brought larger profits per acre than other crops, some Texas farmers began to grow only cotton. It grew well in the state's drier western regions as well as in East Texas. In 1880, Texas farmers produced about $57 million worth of cotton. Texas had just a few textile mills in the late 1800s, so much of this cotton was shipped out of state. Railroads provided a cheap way to ship cotton to national markets. This contributed to the boom in commercial cotton farming. The development of cottonseed oil further spurred cotton production. Cottonseed oil was used in cooking products, cosmetics, and roofing material.

Railroads also opened up new areas to commercial farming. Spur lines were extended off main lines into regions where cotton could be grown. Railroad companies offered lower rates for shipping cotton and built large cotton loading platforms at each railroad stop. From 1874 to 1878, the number of cotton bales shipped on the Texas and Pacific Railway more than tripled. Railroad companies also transported other crops, including fruits, rice, and vegetables.

As commercial farming boomed, the value of Texas agricultural goods shot up. In East Texas their value rose from more than $10 million to almost $40 million during the late 1800s. West Texas experienced an even more dramatic shift, increasing from $574,000 to more than $8 million during that same period. This rise in value was the result of increased crop production rather than a rise in farm prices.

 Reading Check **Finding the Main Idea** What geographic and other factors led to the boom in commercial farming of cotton in Texas?

King Cotton in Texas

Cotton production expanded rapidly during the late 1800s. Overproduction of cotton eventually led to a drop in prices.

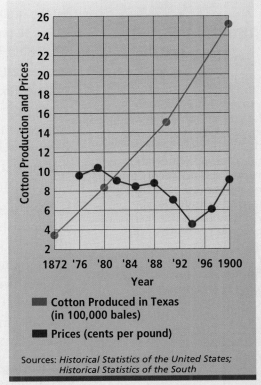

Cotton Production and Prices

Year

■ Cotton Produced in Texas (in 100,000 bales)

■ Prices (cents per pound)

Sources: *Historical Statistics of the United States; Historical Statistics of the South*

Interpreting Graphs

1. How many more bales were produced in 1900 than in 1880?

2. In general, what happened to the price of cotton as production increased? Why did this happen?

3. Based on this chapter, what historical and geographic factors might have led to the rise in cotton production?

★ Farming Troubles

The boom in commercial farm production eventually led to a bust in prices. As farmers grew more crops, supply began to exceed demand, and thus prices fell. This is the economic law of **supply and demand**. If

Dora Nunn Roberts
(1863–1953)

Born in Alabama, Dora Nunn moved to Texas and married Andrew Griffin. The couple settled in Howard County in 1884. The family used a windmill to pump water and irrigate vegetables. After her husband died, Nunn married John Roberts. When he died, she managed the farm. After oil was discovered on her property, she made large donations to several Texas colleges and hospitals. **How did Dora Nunn Roberts adapt to life on the frontier?**

supply is more than demand, prices fall. But if demand is greater than supply, prices rise. For example, between 1874 and 1897 national production of wheat rose by 250 million bushels, and the price fell from 94 to 63 cents per bushel. Around this same period, national cotton production increased from more than 3.8 million to about 10.9 million bales. Cotton prices also fell from 11 to 6 cents per pound. Railroads had integrated Texas with the national and international markets for cotton. Therefore, the price of a bale of cotton in Texas was determined by the quantity of cotton produced in all parts of the world. Texas farmers were now vulnerable to supply and price changes in world markets.

The drop in prices hit farmers hard because the cost of farming was on the rise. Prices for farmland rose once most of the inexpensive land on the Texas frontier had been purchased. Some of the best farmland rose in cost from $10 an acre in 1870 to more than $500 in 1900. Many migrants from the United States and immigrants from Mexico and Europe who could not buy land worked as farm laborers, tenant farmers, or sharecroppers. Between 1880 and 1900 the number of tenant farms in Texas tripled. Texas farmers such as **Dora Nunn Roberts** also struggled to survive a lengthy drought in the 1880s. In addition, cotton farmers suffered from crop-destroying pests and weeds during the 1890s. For example, the **boll weevil**, a type of beetle, first infested cotton fields in the Rio Grande valley and then quickly spread throughout Texas. Despite the pest problems, many farmers refused to grow anything but cotton. Farm organizations and scientists tried to encourage farmers to diversify and grow a variety of crops. However, even with the falling prices, farmers still made more money on cotton than on other crops.

Reading Check **Drawing Inferences and Conclusions** How do you think the interdependence of Texas and national and international markets and the economic law of supply and demand affected Texas farmers?

Section 2 Review

 Questions 1, 3, 4a, 4b, 5

go.hrw.com Homework Practice Online
keyword: ST3 HP22

1 Define and explain:
- dry farming
- threshers
- commercial farming
- supply and demand
- boll weevil

2 Identify and explain:
- Dora Nunn Roberts

3 Summarizing
Copy the graphic organizer below. Use it to explain how railroads and farming led to the integration of the Texas economy with national and international markets.

| Farming and Railroads | — | International Markets |

4 Finding the Main Idea
a. Compare the new types of farming technology. How did they help Texans adapt to and modify their environment?
b. Why did a boom in cotton farming occur, and what were its effects?

5 Writing and Critical Thinking
Categorizing Imagine that you had visited Texas twice, once in 1870 and again in 1900. Write a letter explaining how the commercial boom in cotton farming had both positive and negative effects on life in Texas.
Consider the following:
- the value of farm goods and changes in farming costs
- the effects of the law of supply and demand on farmers

Agricultural Industries and Workers

Read to Discover

1. What were the major Texas industries in the late 1800s?
2. What problems did labor unions face in Texas?

Why It Matters Today

New inventions helped Texas industries grow and become even more productive. Use CNNfyi.com or other **current events** sources to learn more about recent inventions. Record your findings in your journal.

Define

- labor unions
- strike

Identify

- Great Southwest Strike of 1886

The Story Continues

In 1876 a newspaper owner named Colonel A. H. Belo left his Galveston home for an exhibition in Philadelphia. He was eager to see all the new inventions that would be on display there. At the exhibition Belo and many others saw Alexander Graham Bell's new invention—the telephone. Thoroughly impressed, Belo decided that he had to have one. The telephones that he had installed at his home and at his office at the *Galveston News* were among the first in the United States.

Alexander Graham Bell exhibited this telephone in Philadelphia in 1876.

★ Leading Industries

New inventions like the telephone helped newspapers report on the state's expanding industries. The most important Texas industries continued to be ones that helped turn farm goods into products. Flour milling was the state's leading industry after agriculture. By 1870 there were more than 530 flour mills in Texas, and mills in Dallas County alone produced nearly $3 million worth of flour.

By the 1890s lumber had overtaken flour milling in value. Between 1870 and 1900 the production of lumber in Texas increased more than eightfold to more than $16 million. Much of the cutting and processing of timber in sawmills was done in the Piney Woods region. The growth of railroads created greater demand for lumber. Railroads used timber

Courtesy of the Witte Museum, San Antonio, Texas

Texas industries. Carl Hilmar Guenther built this mill in 1859 on the San Antonio River. **Why do you think Guenther located his mill near a river?** ⭐TEKS

⭐ **Analyzing Primary Sources**
Identifying Points of View
How does Swinford think international trade will affect the lumber industry in Texas?

for rail ties and bridges and for fuel. Railroads also provided cheap transportation for timber products, which were used for building in the treeless frontier of western Texas and in other parts of the United States. Timber was also transported to port cities such as Galveston, where it could be shipped by boat to national and international markets. International demand for Texas lumber boosted the state's economy. One Texas businessman recognized this trend.

Texas Voices 66Three large [lumber] mills at Beaumont . . . [have] built up an enormous trade. . . . They will go after the foreign trade harder than ever, when they have a surplus of stock and they expect to bring to Texas for the enrichment [benefit] of this section [region] and especially of the toilers [laborers] who seek their fortunes in this business, the trade and the cash of other countries.99

—Jerome Swinford, quoted in *The Road to Spindletop*, by John Stricklin Spratt

Other industries also developed. By 1900 Texas was the number one producer of cottonseed oil for the U.S. market. Meatpacking was another leading Texas industry. Stockyards and meatpacking plants were built near railroad junctions to take advantage of refrigerated railroad cars that could transport beef across great distances.

The Texas mining industry did not develop until the 1880s, when railroad locomotives began to use coal instead of wood as fuel. Coal burned more efficiently, and trains could run faster with this fuel. Railroads in Texas continued to grow as the 1800s drew to a close.

⭐ **Reading Check** **Analyzing Information** How did the growth of railroads affect Texas industries and the use of natural resources?

472 **Chapter 22**

★ Industrial Workers

Although these growing industries created new job opportunities, most Texans still worked in agriculture. In 1900 less than 2 percent of the population worked in manufacturing. Wages and hours for industrial workers varied from job to job. Some workers joined **labor unions**—organizations that formed to support the interests of workers. Unions pushed for improvements in the hours, wages, and working conditions of laborers. However, most unions did not allow African Americans to become members. One of the first unions in Texas was the Screwmen's Benevolent Association of Galveston. The union formed in 1866 and organized workers on the shipping docks of Galveston who used screw jacks to load cotton onto ships.

In 1882 the first national labor union arrived in Texas. The Knights of Labor organized to support skilled and unskilled workers of almost every trade, including farmers. Unlike most national unions, membership in the Knights was open to women and African Americans. In Texas the Knights organized railroad workers. The union led a successful **strike** against Jay Gould's Wabash Railroad in 1885. A strike occurs when workers refuse to do their job until a company meets their demands. Another railroad strike, known as the **Great Southwest Strike of 1886**, led to violence in Fort Worth. Labor unrest continued until the state militia and Texas Rangers restored order. Many Texans were upset by the violence, while others believed that strikes and other labor actions threatened the production and transportation of goods. As a result, support for unions decreased in Texas.

That's Interesting!

The Knights of Labor

When union members working for Gould's Wabash Railroad were fired in 1885, the rest of the union workers went on strike. The strike shut down the entire Wabash line in the Southwest and forced Gould to agree to the union's demands. The victory led to a dramatic rise in membership.

★ **Reading Check** **Identifying Cause and Effect** Why did labor unions grow in Texas, and what led to their decline?

Section 3 Review ⊛TEKS Questions 2, 3, 4a, 4b, 5

go.hrw.com **Homework Practice Online**
keyword: ST3 HP22

1 **Define and explain:**
- labor unions
- strike

2 **Identify and explain:**
- Great Southwest Strike of 1886

3 **Categorizing**
Copy the graphic organizer below. Use it to describe how agricultural industries contributed to the growth of the Texas economy.

Industry	Effect on Agriculture	Effect on Texas Economy
Flour milling		
Lumber		
Cottonseed oil		

4 **Finding the Main Idea**
a. What were the leading manufacturing industries in Texas for 1870 and 1890?
b. List two reasons why labor unions did not succeed in Texas.

5 **Writing and Critical Thinking**

TAKS

Analyzing Information Imagine that you are traveling through Texas in 1870 looking for industries in which to invest money. Write a memo to other investors on the effect of national and international markets on Texas.

Consider the following:
- the growth of railroads
- the demand for natural resources

The Chapter at a Glance

Examine the following visual summary of the chapter. Then use the visual to pose and answer questions about how Texas industries were affected by geographic factors and natural resources. ⭐TEKS

Farming and Railroads

Farmers began to use new farm machinery such as threshers and two-row planters, increasing productivity.

The construction of railroads opened up the western frontier and led to a boom in Texas farming and industry.

The largest Texas industries such as lumber mills were involved in processing the state's natural resources.

Identifying People and Ideas ⭐TEKS

Use the following terms or people in historically significant sentences.

1. transcontinental railroad
2. junctions
3. dry farming
4. thresher
5. commercial farming
6. supply and demand
7. Dora Nunn Roberts
8. boll weevil
9. labor unions
10. Great Southwest Strike of 1886

Understanding Main Ideas ⭐TEKS

Section 1 (pp. 462–466)

1. How did the railroad boom affect the growth of Texas towns and local economies?
2. How did railroads become a factor in settling the West Texas frontier?

Section 2 (pp. 467–470)

3. Identify ways that Texans used new farming technologies to adapt to and modify their environment.
4. Analyze the impact of supply and demand and international markets on Texas farmers.

Section 3 (pp. 471–473)

5. What goods did Texas industries supply for national and international markets?

You Be the Historian ⭐TEKS

Reviewing Themes

1. **Geography** How did technology help Texans adapt to and settle the Texas frontier?
2. **Science, Technology & Society** How did the development of the railroad help the growth of Texas industries and cities?
3. **Economics** How was the Texas economy affected by the national and international demand for farm and industrial goods?

⭐TEKS

TAKS Practice: Thinking Critically

1. **Drawing Inferences and Conclusions** How do you think new technology in Texas made the state more connected with the United States and the rest of the world? What were the effects?
2. **Identifying Cause and Effect** What factors led to the development of the West Texas frontier, and how did this affect the social, political, and economic life of the area?
3. **Evaluating** How did physical factors of Texas geography and human factors lead to the growth of agriculture and industry in Texas?

Interpreting Political Cartoons (TEKS)

Study the political cartoon below. Then use the information in the cartoon to answer the following questions.

Let Texas be Developed.

1. Which sentence best explains why Texas has both southern resources and northern capital yoked to her plow?
   a. Texas is producing goods with the aid of these two forces.
   b. These two forces are getting in the way of Texas industry.
   c. These two forces limit Texas agriculture.
   d. Texans dislike these two forces.

2. Based on this cartoon, how do geographic and human factors affect farming?

Analyzing Primary Sources (TEKS)

Read the following quote by a Texas newspaper editor who urged farmers to diversify their crops and thus avoid relying too heavily on cotton. Then answer the questions.

"Diversity in farming has so many advantages that it should find favor in the practice of every sensible agriculturalist [farmer]. It puts on the home table a great variety and prevents the necessity of many purchases; distributes both the labor and cash receipts pretty evenly throughout the year; prevents the overstocking in any single department, and so tends to keep up prices; is favorable to the rotation of crops, the advantage of which all appreciate; and finally is an insurance against heavy loss by distributing among many products the risks of failure of one."

3. Which of the following is not a reason the editor gives in support of crop diversification?
   a. Crop rotation provides a number of advantages.
   b. It helps protect the farmer against losses from droughts.
   c. Diversification provides the farmer with a variety of foods.
   d. It helps protect farmers by distributing the risk of failure among many crops.

4. Why do you think some Texas farmers would not want to diversify their crops?

Alternative Assessment

Linking to Community (TEKS)

Many Texans today work on farms or in industries. Interview someone in your community who works on a farm or in an industry. Ask that person what role new machinery or technology plays in his or her work. How has that person adapted to the region's environment? How have geographic and human factors influenced his or her work? Create a model or collage of a machine or other type of technology the person uses in his or her work.

BUILDING YOUR Portfolio

internet connect

Internet Activity: go.hrw.com
KEYWORD: ST3 TX22 (TEKS)

Access the Internet through the HRW Go site to research the coming of the railroads to Texas. Then create an advertisement promoting a new railroad line. Be sure your advertisement points out the social impact and economic benefits that the new line will bring to the area's residents. You may want to include a poster with maps and colorful illustrations with your presentation.

The Oil Boom
(1890–1920)

Texas Normal College was opened as a school to train teachers and other professionals.

When the Spindletop well struck oil, a huge plume of oil erupted from the ground.

TEXAS

1890 Texas Normal College and Teachers' Training Institute, now called the University of North Texas, opens in Denton.

1894 Drillers strike oil in Corsicana.

1901 The Spindletop well strikes oil, producing more than 17 million barrels of oil the next year.

1905 A large oil strike is made in the Humble oil field in Harris County.

1890	1894	1898	1902

U.S. and WORLD

1890 American inventor John Lambert builds the first automobile that uses an internal combustion engine.

1896 B. F. Goodrich Company manufactures the first automobile tires.

B. F. Goodrich Company advertised its tires in the early 1900s.

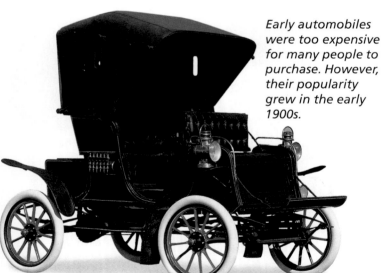

Early automobiles were too expensive for many people to purchase. However, their popularity grew in the early 1900s.

Build on What You Know

Texans witnessed many economic changes in the late 1800s. The growth of industry, commercial farming, and railroads affected the way Texans lived and worked. As the new century approached, Texans would witness another major economic change—the growth of the oil industry.

Oil from the Santa Rita No. 1 helped fund Texas universities during the 1920s and 1930s.

Humble Oil Company was founded in 1911

1908 Oil is discovered at Goose Creek along Galveston Bay.

1914 The Houston Ship Channel opens, and Houston soon becomes an important oil-refining center.

1919 An application is filed to drill for oil on state-owned land in West Texas. Several years later the Santa Rita No. 1 strikes oil.

1906   1910   1914   1918

1908 The Ford Motor Company introduces the Model T, one of the most popular cars in American history.

1911 The U.S. Supreme Court orders the Standard Oil Company to break up into several smaller companies.

1917 A French inventor builds a gyroplane—a flying craft much like a helicopter.

You Be the Historian

Themes Journal

What's Your Opinion? Do you **agree** or **disagree** with the following statements? Support your point of view in your journal.

● **Science, Technology & Society** The uses for natural resources do not change over time.

● **Culture** The rapid growth of industry affects all aspects of social life, including urban growth, education, and the arts.

● **Economics** National markets always influence local businesses and industries.

If you were there ...
Would you work in the oil industry?

The Birth of the Oil Industry

Read to Discover

1. How did the Texas oil industry begin?
2. What happened at Spindletop, and how did that event affect the Texas economy?

Define
• **petroleum**
• **fossil fuel**
• **derricks**
• **refinery**

Identify
• **Lyne T. Barret**
• **Pattillo Higgins**
• **Anthony F. Lucas**
• **Spindletop strike**

The Story Continues

Spindletop was a small hill just outside Beaumont. Although it was only 12 feet high, people often called it Big Hill. One day Pattillo Higgins took a girls' Sunday school class on an outing to Big Hill. He noticed gas bubbles in the spring on the hill. When Higgins poked his cane into the ground, gas escaped. This visit convinced Higgins that there was oil under Big Hill.

Pattillo Higgins thought that the gas bubbles at Spindletop meant that there was oil beneath the ground.

★ The Search for Oil

The demand for oil had risen dramatically after scientists developed kerosene in the mid-1800s. Kerosene was a new form of fuel for lighting that could be made from coal or **petroleum**. Commonly called oil, petroleum is a dark, thick, liquid **fossil fuel**. A fossil fuel is a fuel formed underground from plant or animal remains. Compared to other fuels, such as whale oil, kerosene was less expensive and less dangerous to use. The first major U.S. oil strike occurred in the late 1850s. An oil company sent Edwin Drake to northwestern Pennsylvania to search for oil. He drilled holes to try to reach petroleum deep underground but had little luck. One day when the drill reached 69 feet, a black liquid oozed out of the well. Local farmers ran through a nearby town shouting, "The Yankee has struck oil!"

Drake's success led others to search for oil. In Texas a Civil War veteran named **Lyne T. Barret** drilled for oil outside Nacogdoches in 1866.

He struck oil at 106 feet. His oil well was soon producing 10 barrels of oil a day. However, Barret could not raise the money necessary to continue drilling and had to shut the well down. Other Texans accidentally discovered oil. George Dullnig, a rancher in Bexar County, struck oil while drilling for water in 1886. Dullnig drilled two more wells but did not find enough oil to continue drilling. Other efforts at finding oil in Texas met with little success. Texas produced only 48 barrels of oil in 1889, compared to the 35 million barrels of oil produced in the rest of the United States.

It was not until 1894, when drillers searching for water in Corsicana struck oil, that the Texas oil industry truly began to grow. The Corsicana landscape was soon dotted with **derricks**, or towers that support oil-drilling equipment. During 1896 the Corsicana oil field produced 1,450 barrels of oil. Just four years later, Texans took more than 839,000 barrels of oil out of the oil field. To process the oil, business leaders constructed a **refinery**. A refinery is a factory where crude oil is refined, or made pure, and then made into various products. The oil refined at Corsicana was used to lubricate machinery and provide kerosene for lamps. It was also sprinkled on dirt roads to keep down dust.

⭐ **Reading Check** **Identifying Cause and Effect** What scientific innovation occurred in the mid-1800s, and how did that affect Texas?

LONE STAR LEGACY

Spindletop

After the discovery of oil at Spindletop, hundreds of derricks dotted the Spindletop skyline. By 1985 some 153 million barrels of oil had been taken out of the ground at Spindletop. To celebrate the oil field, Texans erected a granite monument in 1941. Today visitors can tour the Spindletop/Gladys City Boomtown Museum. **How does the monument symbolize the importance of Spindletop to Texas?** ⭐TEKS

⭐ The Spindletop Strike

The success at Corsicana was quickly overshadowed by a discovery at an oil field near Beaumont. **Pattillo Higgins**, a brick-factory owner, believed that oil would be found under a salt dome at a place called Spindletop Hill, or Big Hill. Salt domes are underground formations

Interpreting the Visual Record

Spindletop. The Spindletop strike led to an oil boom in the Gulf Coast region. **How does this image of the Spindletop oil field six years after the first strike reflect the oil boom?** ⭐TEKS

that often trap oil and natural gases. In 1892 Higgins and some friends worked together to form the Gladys City Oil, Gas, and Manufacturing Company. Although the company drilled three wells at Spindletop, it did not strike oil. But Higgins refused to give up.

Higgins ran an advertisement calling for a drilling engineer. In 1899 an engineer named **Anthony F. Lucas** responded to Higgins's ad. Lucas was an expert on salt domes, and he agreed that oil was probably beneath the Spindletop dome. He started drilling there in June 1900. At 575 feet, Lucas found traces of oil, but his equipment was not strong enough to continue. After finding business leaders willing to invest in new equipment, Lucas continued drilling. A man who worked at Spindletop described the big oil strike that occurred on January 10, 1901.

Texas Voices

❝All of a sudden, a chunk of mud came out of the six-inch hole . . . with an explosion just like a cannon popping off. . . . I walked over and looked down in the hole there . . . this frothy [foamy] oil was coming up . . . each flow a little higher and a little higher and a little higher. Finally it came up with such momentum [speed] that it just shot up clear through the top of the derrick.

—Al Hamill, quoted in *Tales from the Derrick Floor*,
by Mody C. Boatwright and William A. Owens

The giant plume of oil shooting into the air at Spindletop could be seen from more than 10 miles away. People came from miles around to see it. Over the next nine days some 800,000 barrels of oil shot out of the Spindletop well before workers could cap the gusher. Word of the strike quickly spread around the world, with newspapers calling it the great gusher in Texas. The **Spindletop strike** marked the beginning of the Texas oil boom.

⭐ **Reading Check** **Finding the Main Idea** What was the significance of the strike at Spindletop?

THE ONLY PLACE ON THE MAP.

BEAUMONT

⭐ Boom and Bust after Spindletop

The discovery of oil at Spindletop led to a boom in the Texas economy and created many jobs. Hundreds of oil companies formed to drill new wells, and the population of Beaumont swelled by nearly 40,000 people. By 1902 more than 500 oil companies were operating there. The *Galveston Daily News* reported on the growth and excitement in Beaumont. "The town continues to fill up. The street resembles a great holiday event. . . . Physicians are becoming real estate men. The lumber industry is forgotten in the wild rush for oil land. . . . Throngs of people frequent the streets until late at night and everything is oil."

Spindletop oil production peaked in 1902 at more than 17 million barrels of oil. That year, nearly 20 percent of the oil produced in the United States came from Spindletop. The discovery of this huge oil field soon affected oil prices. With large quantities of oil being produced, the supply of oil outpaced the national demand. As a result, the price of oil dropped. By 1902 oil prices had hit an all-time low of three cents a barrel. The rush of companies drilling oil at Spindletop also drained its oil reserves. By 1904 Spindletop was producing only 10,000 barrels of oil a day.

Most of the new companies that had formed went out of business when their wells dried up. Of those Texas companies that survived, several grew into major businesses. J. S. Cullinan, who owned the Corsicana refinery, founded the Texas Fuel Company in Beaumont in March 1901. The company soon changed its name to the Texas Company—later Texaco—and grew rapidly. By 1905 it owned oil wells and a refinery as well as railroad cars and pipelines for transporting oil. Another Spindletop oil company, the J. M. Guffey Petroleum Company, was formed in May 1901. Its owners—J. M. Guffey, A. W. Mellon, R. B. Mellon, and other associates—also founded the Gulf Refining Company. The two companies struggled for several years until merging in 1907 to become the Gulf Oil Corporation.

The Magnolia Petroleum Company and the Humble Oil Company, both founded in 1911, also became major businesses. By 1917 Humble—which was later bought by the Standard Oil Company of New Jersey—owned 217 wells that together produced 9,000 barrels of oil a day. Oil companies that survived the early boom were important to the Texas economy. They employed thousands of Texans, which in turn helped boost many of the state's other businesses.

⭐ **Reading Check** **Evaluating** How did the Spindletop oil boom affect the local economy and national oil prices?

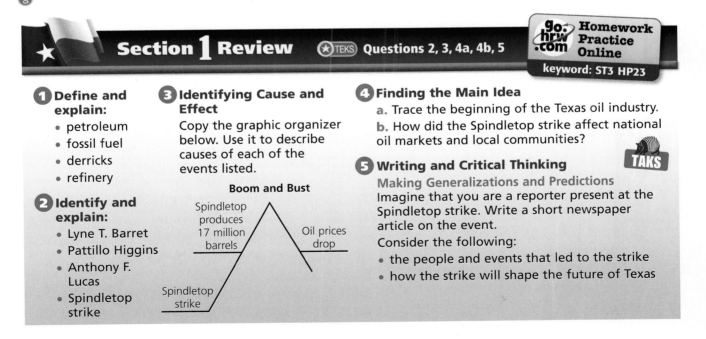

Section 1 Review ⭐TEKS Questions 2, 3, 4a, 4b, 5

1 Define and explain:
- petroleum
- fossil fuel
- derricks
- refinery

2 Identify and explain:
- Lyne T. Barret
- Pattillo Higgins
- Anthony F. Lucas
- Spindletop strike

3 Identifying Cause and Effect

Copy the graphic organizer below. Use it to describe causes of each of the events listed.

Boom and Bust

Spindletop produces 17 million barrels

Oil prices drop

Spindletop strike

4 Finding the Main Idea
a. Trace the beginning of the Texas oil industry.
b. How did the Spindletop strike affect national oil markets and local communities?

5 Writing and Critical Thinking

Making Generalizations and Predictions
Imagine that you are a reporter present at the Spindletop strike. Write a short newspaper article on the event.
Consider the following:
- the people and events that led to the strike
- how the strike will shape the future of Texas

Oil and Natural Gas Fields

While the Spindletop oil strike brought a surge of drilling to the Gulf Coast, oil fields were later discovered in many regions of Texas. Oil was soon discovered in North Texas, the Panhandle, and the Permian Basin. Natural gas was also found in these regions. These natural resources spurred Texas industries and economic growth.

Oil and Natural Gas Fields

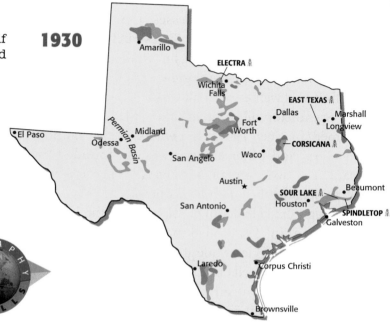

1930

Geography Skills

Interpreting Thematic Maps ⭐TEKS

1. Which region of Texas had the fewest oil fields in 1930?

2. Which region had the most natural gas fields in 2000?

3. Based on these maps, what conclusions can you draw about changes in the oil and natural gas industry, and how those changes affected regional economies in Texas?

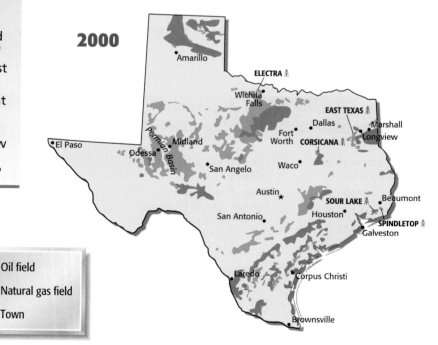

2000

Oil field

Natural gas field

• Town

The Growth of the Oil Industry

Read to Discover

1. How did Texans contribute to the oil boom, and what Texas regions produced oil?
2. How did new business ideas change the oil industry?

Define

- **wildcatters**
- **natural gas**
- **vertical integration**
- **horizontal integration**

Why It Matters Today

The oil industry was important to the Texas economy in the early 1900s. Use **CNN fyi**.com or other **current events** sources to learn about the oil industry today. Record your findings in your journal.

The Story Continues

The Spindletop strike lured thousands of people to Beaumont. They came with the hope of making huge profits. Soon it seemed as if everyone owned an oil company. In Beaumont a newspaper reporter saw two men looking at a map. The next day he learned that the newcomers had formed the What-Not Oil Company. This new company was just one of the hundreds that appeared in Beaumont in 1901.

New oil companies such as the Texas Consolidated Oil Company placed advertisements like this one.

★ Wildcatters and New Oil Fields

Some of these companies were owned by wildcatters—independent oil operators who searched for new fields. These entrepreneurs saved and borrowed money to invest in the oil business. In particular, wildcatters competed with one another to find salt domes in the Gulf Coast Plain just like the 1901 Spindletop strike. They found salt domes some 20 miles outside Beaumont at Sour Lake. Drilling began there in 1893, but the first big strike did not occur until 1902. That year a gusher produced as many as 50,000 barrels a day. By 1903 there were some 150 wells at Sour Lake. Overdrilling soon led to a drop in underground pressure, making oil drilling difficult. By the end of 1903, more than half of the wells at Sour Lake were abandoned. Other Gulf Coast oil fields faced a similar drop in oil production when they were overpumped.

Oil production extended beyond the Gulf Coast to North Texas. In 1903 North Texas rancher W. T. Waggoner struck oil. He later

Vertical and Horizontal Integration

Many corporations used horizontal and vertical integration to increase their business. Some large oil companies owned smaller companies that made products for each step of the oil-production process. Oil companies also bought many refineries or oil fields.

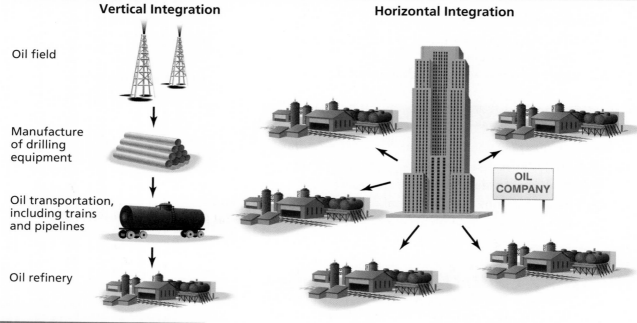

Vertical Integration

- Oil field
- Manufacture of drilling equipment
- Oil transportation, including trains and pipelines
- Oil refinery

Horizontal Integration

OIL COMPANY

Visualizing History ★TEKS

1. **Economics** How do you think these business practices would affect a company's profits?

2. **Connecting to Today** How do you think these practices affect local markets and businesses in Texas today?

---

complained that he was only drilling for water. "I wanted water, and they got me oil. I was mad, mad clean through." This Electra oil field made Waggoner a wealthy man, however. Other major North Texas oil fields included Wichita Falls and Burkburnett. In 1919 the Burkburnett field produced some 31.6 million barrels of oil.

After their success in North Texas, oil companies began drilling in the Panhandle. The first successful strike there took place in 1921. Six years later, Panhandle oil fields produced some 39 million barrels of oil in a single year. Oil was also discovered in the Permian Basin region of West Texas in 1921. During the 1920s several large oil fields were discovered in the area, including the Yates, Hobbs, and Big Lake oil fields. South and Central Texas were also the sites of oil production. However, these regions never produced the amount of oil that made other parts of the state famous. An oil strike deep in the heart of East Texas gave the oil industry its greatest surprise. Geologists had claimed that there was very little oil in East Texas north of the Gulf Coast. But a wildcatter's 1930 strike proved them wrong—the East Texas oil field turned out to be one of the largest in the world.

★ **Reading Check** **Sequencing** Identify in order where and when oil was discovered in the major regions of Texas.

That's Interesting!

Oil Nicknames

People in the oil business had special names for just about everything. A "boll weevil" was a worker who knew nothing about the oil business. A "roustabout" looked after the well and made necessary repairs. A "roughneck" worked on the derrick and took care of the pipe lowered into the well.

★ Oil Business Is Big Business

Texas oil fields produced more than just oil. **Natural gas**—a gas that can be used as a fuel—was also abundant. However, there was no way to get it to market safely in the early years of the oil industry. As a result, gas coming out of oil wells was allowed to burn. In the 1890s scientists invented a leakproof pipeline that could safely move natural gas about 100 miles. The first Texas gas pipeline stretched 19 miles between the Petrolia oil field and Wichita Falls. Further advances in pipeline technology during the 1920s and 1930s expanded the distance gas could be shipped. This new pipeline technology opened the market for Texas natural gas.

As more oil and gas fields were discovered, the Texas oil industry grew into a big business. In 1915, Texans sold more than 13 million dollars' worth of oil. Some Texas oil companies began to use a business strategy called **vertical integration**—owning the businesses involved in each step of a manufacturing process. For example, the Texas Company began by purchasing and transporting oil from Spindletop. As its profits grew, the company expanded into oil drilling, production, and refining. The company also bought items it needed for its business, such as barges and railroad tanker cars. By streamlining the processes of drilling, transporting, and refining oil, the Texas Company was able to develop into a huge corporation.

Most large oil companies also practiced **horizontal integration**—owning many businesses in a particular field. The larger oil corporations would run many refineries, sharing supplies and resources to make their businesses more efficient.

Reading Check **Drawing Inferences and Conclusions** How did oil companies expand to control a large part of the oil industry?

Section 2 Review ✪TEKS Questions 2, 3a, 3b, 4

Homework Practice Online
keyword: ST3 HP23

1 **Define and explain:**
- wildcatters
- natural gas
- vertical integration
- horizontal integration

2 **Sequencing**
Copy the graphic organizer below. Use it to trace the discovery of oil in the various regions of Texas.

Region	When oil was discovered
Gulf Coast	
North Texas	
Panhandle	
Permian Basin	
East Texas	

3 **Finding the Main Idea**
a. What role did wildcatters play in the oil boom?
b. Explain how new business strategies affected the oil industry.

4 **Writing and Critical Thinking**
Evaluating Imagine that you are a wildcatter traveling from region to region in 1919. Create a journal entry describing what businesses in the oil-production process you would want to own.
Consider the following:
- the steps of oil production
- getting oil to market

Read to Discover

1. How did the oil boom affect Texas towns?
2. How did new technology change the oil industry?
3. What effects did the oil industry have on the politics, economy, and social life of Texas?

Why It Matters Today

During the early 1900s oil production created boomtowns. Use CNNfyi.com or other **current events** sources to learn about how industry affects city growth today. Record your findings in your journal.

Define

- **boomtowns**
- **internal combustion engines**
- **gasoline**
- **philanthropy**

Identify

- **Texas Railroad Commission**
- **Permanent University Fund**
- **Santa Rita No. 1**

The Story Continues

Excited by stories of the Texas oil boom, Howard Hughes quit his job at a mining company in Missouri and moved to Beaumont. However, he quickly encountered a problem faced by all oil producers—drill bits could not cut through hard rock. Hughes decided to take a vacation to visit his parents and think about the problem. After two weeks, he had a solution. Hughes outlined the basic design of the Hughes Rock Bit, which could cut through rock 10 times faster than other bits.

Howard Hughes's rock bit had rotating drills that were able to cut through hard rock.

★ Boomtowns

The spectacular fortunes made in the oil business drew thousands of people to the Texas oil fields and nearby towns. Before Spindletop, Beaumont had 9,000 residents. Within two years of the big strike, some 50,000 people called Beaumont home. Nearby Sour Lake went from a small village to a city of 10,000 people within a matter of months.

Called **boomtowns** because they grew along with economic booms, these towns were crowded, dirty, and rough places. Thousands of Texans arrived at these towns seeking work in the oil industry. Oil-field workers often lived in tents or wooden shacks. The dirt streets of these towns became rivers of mud when it rained. Above all, boomtowns were busy places, where everyone was trying to make money. Businesses that served the oil industry benefited economically from the oil boom. A Texas schoolteacher described life in her boomtown.

❝In McCamey, they worked twenty-four hours a day. Everything stayed open twenty-four hours, the eating places and all, because the men worked night shifts and day shifts. I've seen my brother-in-law stay up twenty-four hours at the lumberyard. Businessmen had their living quarters at their place of business. They worked Sunday. It was no different from any other day.❞

—Allie V. Scott, quoted in *Life in the Oil Fields,* by Roger M. Olien and Diana Davids Olien

Analyzing Primary Sources
Identifying a Point of View
According to Scott, how did the oil boom affect other industries in Texas?

Reading Check **Drawing Inferences and Conclusions**
How did the development of the oil industry lead to urban growth in Texas?

★ The Automobile and Petrochemical Industries

Oil companies grew at a time when electricity was rapidly replacing kerosene for lighting homes and industries. Fortunately for oil producers, new uses for petroleum were being discovered. Because oil was cheaper than coal, it quickly replaced coal as the fuel for steam engines that ran ships and railroad locomotives. The use of automobiles with **internal combustion engines** was also increasing. These engines used **gasoline**, an oil by-product, for power instead of steam. These new uses for oil allowed the oil industry to remain profitable.

Before the development of the internal combustion engine, oil producers had little use for gasoline because demand for it was low. This changed as more Americans began to buy cars. Between 1895 and 1906 the number of registered cars in the United States rose from 5 to some 619,000. By 1916, Texans were driving about 195,000 of the 3.4 million cars in the United States. As Americans continued to purchase cars and drove longer distances, the demand for gasoline grew. Between 1916 and 1920, gasoline production in the United States rose from 49 million barrels to more than 116 million barrels. The Texas oil industry's production of gasoline helped keep Americans traveling the nation's roads and highways.

The growing popularity of the automobile guaranteed the Texas oil industry millions of customers.

Texas Cities

Midland and Odessa

History: Odessa was established in 1881 as a stop on the Texas and Pacific Railway. Farming families established Midland in 1884. Both cities grew slowly until the oil boom of the 1920s.

Midland population in 2000: 94,996

Odessa population in 2000: 90,943

Relative location: In the Permian Basin of West Texas

Region: Southern edge of the High Plains where the Edwards Plateau meets the Mountains and Basins region

County: Midland is the county seat of Midland County, and Odessa is the county seat of Ector County.

Origin of name: Midland was named for its location midway between Dallas and El Paso. Odessa was named after a city in Russia.

Economy: The major source of income and jobs for both cities is the petroleum industry. Banking, farming, and ranching are also important to their economies.

Interpreting the Visual Record

Boomtowns. People flocked to boomtowns seeking jobs in the oil business. **What type of work do you think these wagon drivers found in Texas boomtowns?** ★TEKS

CONNECTING TO
SCIENCE AND TECHNOLOGY

Oil Drilling

The first oil wells were drilled with a heavy drill bit attached to a long cable. This cable was lowered into the hole. The drill bit was lifted up and down, pounding deeper and deeper into the rock. Drillers also used the cable to pull dirt and rock out of the hole. Rotary drilling quickly became the preferred method. In rotary drilling the drill bit turns or spins as it pushes downward. As the bit turns, workers shoot drilling mud into the well. This mud prevents gushers and explosions. It also carries loose rock to the top of the well, so that workers do not have to stop as often. How was new oil-drilling technology similar to and different from past technology? ★TEKS

Offshore oil platform

In addition, scientists continued to develop new uses for petroleum. Petrochemicals, products made from oil and gas, became an important part of the Texas economy. Petrochemical products include synthetic rubber, plastics, and carbon black, which is used to make ink, tires, and other products.

 Reading Check **Analyzing Information** How did the development of new technologies affect the use of fossil fuels such as oil in Texas?

★ The Effects of the Oil Boom

While the oil boom boosted the state's economic growth, it also affected Texas in many other ways. The oil boom attracted many young farmworkers to jobs in the oil fields. Most drilling and production jobs were reserved for white workers. Despite facing discrimination in the oil fields, some African American and Mexican American workers found jobs as teamsters, hauling goods to and from the oil fields. Many oil workers lived a very mobile life, moving from town to town as they followed new oil strikes.

The oil boom also affected Texas politics and the environment. State officials began to pass restrictions designed to control parts of the oil industry. In 1899 the legislature passed laws concerning abandoned wells and the protection of groundwater from oil pollution. Some 20 years later, the legislature made it illegal to waste oil and natural gas. In 1917 the legislature gave the **Texas Railroad Commission**, an agency originally created to regulate railroads, authority to enforce laws concerning the petroleum industry. The commission set standards for spacing between wells and for pipeline transportation of oil and gas. These rules helped to prevent overdrilling.

The state government also began collecting taxes on oil production in 1905, taking in more than $101,000 in taxes that year. By 1919 the amount of money collected from taxes on oil production rose to more than $1 million. This money helped fund the state government and education programs for Texas children. Higher education in Texas also benefited from the state's oil production. In 1876 the Texas legislature had set aside 1 million acres of land in West Texas for the **Permanent University Fund**. Texas universities received money from the sale or use of this land. However, many people considered the land worthless until the **Santa Rita No. 1** oil well struck oil in 1923. Income from oil production went into the Permanent University Fund, which grew by more than $2,000 a day in 1925. The University of Texas system and the Texas A&M system continue to share the money in this fund. Their campuses have become two of the most important education centers in the state.

Texas also benefited from oil producers' philanthropy—the giving of money or gifts. Many of the wildcatters who became wealthy gave generous gifts to public institutions that influenced life in Texas. Wildcatters such as Hugh Roy Cullen gave large gifts to the University of Houston, Texas Medical Center, and many charitable organizations. Oil producers Sid Richardson and Walter William Fondren both gave money and gifts to Texas schools, hospitals, and other social institutions. Other oil producers have given generously to the arts in Texas. For example, John and Dominique de Menil established a collection of more than 10,000 works of art for public display. Oil producers have provided many jobs and spurred related industries in Texas. They have also had a major effect on the state's social life through philanthropy and education funding.

The University of Houston benefited from the philanthropy of oil wildcatters. The new funds created construction and education opportunities.

 Reading Check **Summarizing** How did the oil boom affect the politics, economy, and society of Texas?

Section 3 Review

(★)TEKS Questions 2, 3, 4a, 4b, 5

go.hrw.com Homework Practice Online
keyword: ST3 HP23

1 Define and explain:
- boomtowns
- internal combustion engines
- gasoline
- philanthropy

2 Identify and explain:
- Texas Railroad Commission
- Permanent University Fund
- Santa Rita No. 1

3 Categorizing
Copy the graphic organizer below. Use it to show how the oil industry affected the economy, politics, and social life of Texas.

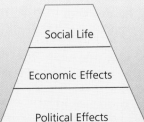

Social Life

Economic Effects

Political Effects

4 Finding the Main Idea
a. In what ways did the oil industry contribute to urban growth in Texas?
b. How did new technological developments such as the internal combustion engine, automobile, and petrochemicals affect the demand for and use of oil?

5 Writing and Critical Thinking
TAKS
Supporting a Point of View Write a letter to a member of Congress supporting a position for or against taxation and government regulation of the oil industry.
Consider the following:
- wildcatters and the spirit of free enterprise
- the Permanent University Fund and taxes collected on oil production

CHAPTER 23 REVIEW

The Chapter at a Glance

Examine the following visual summary of the chapter. Sketch a map that illustrates where these events of the oil boom occurred. Be sure to record the date of each event on the map. ⭐TEKS

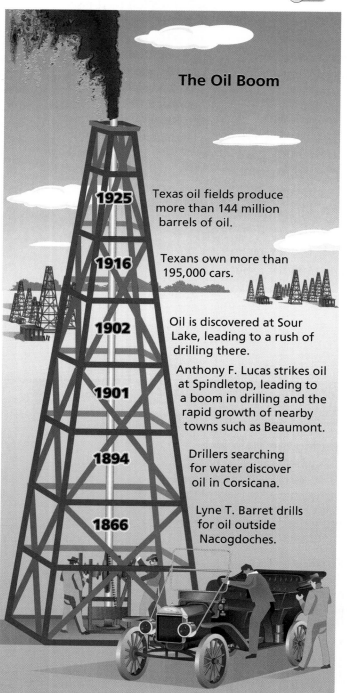

The Oil Boom

1925 Texas oil fields produce more than 144 million barrels of oil.

1916 Texans own more than 195,000 cars.

1902 Oil is discovered at Sour Lake, leading to a rush of drilling there.

1901 Anthony F. Lucas strikes oil at Spindletop, leading to a boom in drilling and the rapid growth of nearby towns such as Beaumont.

1894 Drillers searching for water discover oil in Corsicana.

1866 Lyne T. Barret drills for oil outside Nacogdoches.

Identifying People and Ideas ⭐TEKS

Use the following terms or people in historically significant sentences.

1. petroleum
2. Pattillo Higgins
3. Anthony F. Lucas
4. Spindletop strike
5. wildcatters
6. natural gas
7. vertical integration
8. boomtowns
9. internal combustion engines
10. Permanent University Fund

Understanding Main Ideas ⭐TEKS

Section 1 (pp. 478–481)

1. List in chronological order the events that led up to the discovery of oil at Spindletop.
2. How did the Spindletop strike affect national oil markets?

Section 2 (pp. 483–485)

3. Compare the levels of oil production in various regions of Texas.

Section 3 (pp. 486–489)

4. How did new technology such as the automobile affect the use of natural resources in Texas?
5. How did the oil boom affect education in Texas?
6. How did the growth of the oil industry affect sources of revenue for the state?

You Be the Historian ⭐TEKS

Reviewing Themes

1. **Science, Technology & Society** How did technological advances lead to the oil boom and contribute to the growing use of the state's natural resources?
2. **Culture** In what ways did the oil boom affect Texas society and urban growth?
3. **Economics** How did the national demand for oil affect local businesses in Texas, and how did Texas oil discoveries affect the national oil market?

TAKS Practice: Thinking Critically ⭐TEKS

1. **Evaluating** In what ways did the Spindletop strike lead to a boom-and-bust cycle in the oil industry?
2. **Summarizing** How did geographic factors such as natural resources affect the economy and politics of Texas?
3. **Drawing Inferences and Conclusions** What role did the desire for profit play in the growth of the oil industry in Texas?

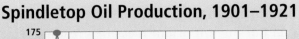
Interpreting Graphs ⊗TEKS

Study the graph below. Then use the information on the graph to answer the questions that follow.

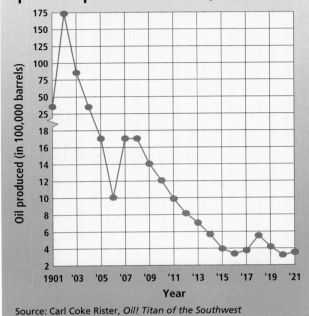

Spindletop Oil Production, 1901–1921

Oil produced (in 100,000 barrels)

Year

Source: Carl Coke Rister, *Oil! Titan of the Southwest*

1. Approximately how much did Spindletop oil production change between 1902 and 1910?
   a. dropped 16 million barrels
   b. rose 16 million barrels
   c. dropped 18 million barrels
   d. rose 18 million barrels

2. Based on your reading of the chapter what do you think may have caused the change?

Analyzing Primary Sources ⊗TEKS

Read the following excerpt from an oral history of oil drilling as remembered by Electra resident E. M. Friend. Then answer the questions.

"Doc got hold of a little old spudding [digging] machine and got to drilling those shallow wells. . . . His old machine didn't amount to much. He kept it fixed up with bailing wire and anything he could get hold of. . . . And so his brother had a little money and his father had a little money. They kind of throwed in together and bought them a rotary drill. And they got some contracts and I imagine they were just about the luckiest drillers in the country. And they had the one rig, then they built it up to three or four. And when things got quiet in Electra, the East Texas field opened up and they went down there. And their luck still held good, by George."

3. What led to Doc's success as an oil producer?
   a. using bailing wire on his old drilling machine
   b. luck and buying new technology
   c. drilling in many different regions at once
   d. only drilling in Electra

4. Is this a primary source of the events in Electra or a secondary source? Explain your answer.

Alternative Assessment

Interdisciplinary Connection to the Arts ⊗TEKS

Imagine that you are an artist hired by the city of Beaumont to design a mural to celebrate the Spindletop strike. Be sure that your mural has captions that explain the chronology of the events, individuals, and issues that led up to the historic Spindletop strike. You might include images in your mural that reflect the political, economic, and social effects of Spindletop and the Texas oil boom that soon followed.

BUILDING YOUR
Portfolio

▱ internet connect

Internet Activity: go.hrw.com
KEYWORD: ST3 TX23 ⊗TEKS

Access the Internet through the HRW Go site to research the impact of the oil industry on local Texas communities. Then create a poster or model that illustrates products made from petrochemicals, analyzes technological innovations in the oil industry, or evaluates the effects of those innovations on the use of resources such as fossil fuels, water, and land.

go.hrw.com

Social Studies Skills

WORKSHOP

Study Skills

Taking Notes and Summarizing are key study skills. The following activities will help you develop and practice these skills.

Taking Notes

Taking notes helps you identify the main points of whatever you are studying. Write your notes in your own words. Your notes should include the main idea, interesting and supporting details, examples, and key vocabulary words. You should be able to use your notes to write a detailed summary. Try to use the following steps when taking notes:

- Identify your subject or main topic.
- Identify the main ideas.
- Note interesting and important details.
- Identify key vocabulary terms.
- Review your notes shortly after you write them.

Example

In the following example, all important words have been underlined. Looking just at the underlined words, you can learn a lot. To grasp the basic information contained in this section, you need only those words that are underlined.

> **Texas Agriculture**
>
> Many _Texans eagerly awaited_ the arrival of new _rail lines_, hoping they would _spur economic growth_. The economic _development_ of Texas had been _slowed by its transportation problems_. Most Texas _rivers_ were either _too shallow_ or _too unreliable_ for shipping goods, while _roads_ turned to _mudholes_ during wet weather. Moving people and goods was time-consuming and expensive. _Railroads_ promised _cheap, fast, and reliable_ transportation.

Summarizing   A summary is a brief statement of the important ideas in a reading selection. Summaries are a good tool to use when you are doing research for a report. The following strategies will help you write a summary.

1. Briefly state the main ideas.
2. Look for key words or facts to use in your summary.
3. Write the summary in paragraph form.
4. Review your summary.

Example

The key words in the following passage are underlined. Notice how they are used in the summary that follows the passage.

> **Ranching in the Panhandle**
>
> _As Plains Indians were removed_ from West Texas, the _Panhandle was opened up for ranching_. The region's _flat, open land_ was _well suited for cattle ranching_ because it allowed ranchers and cowboys to keep close watch on the livestock. In addition, the _grass_ that covered the Plains _provided plenty of food_ for the cattle.

Summary   The Texas Panhandle was opened up for ranching as the Plains Indians were removed from the region. The Panhandle's grasslands were well suited for cattle ranching.

Practicing the Skill

1. Look at Chapter 23, Section 2. Read the subsection titled Wildcatters and New Oil Fields. On your own paper, take notes by writing down the key words from each paragraph.
2. Now look at Chapter 22, Section 2. Read the subsection titled Commercial Farming. Use the strategies outlined above to write a short summary of each paragraph.

History in Action

UNIT 7 SIMULATION

You Solve the Problem . . .

How Will You Move Texas Cattle to Market?

Complete the following activity in small cooperative groups. It is 1866. You and your family own a cattle ranch. You would like to prepare a brochure to encourage other ranchers in the area to sell their cattle in out-of-state markets. Follow these steps to solve your problem.

 1. Gather Information. Use your textbook and other resources to find information that might influence your plan of action for moving Texas cattle to market. Remember to include in your brochure information that will show ranchers how they can get their cattle to market. Be sure to use what you learned from this unit's Skills Workshop on Summarizing and Taking Notes to help you find an effective solution to this problem. You may want to divide up different parts of the research among group members.

2. List and Consider Options. After reviewing the information you have gathered, list and consider the options you might recommend for successfully moving Texas cattle to market. Your final solution to the problem may be easier to reach if you consider as many options as possible. Be sure to record your possible options for the preparation of your brochure.

 3. Consider Advantages and Disadvantages. Now consider the advantages and disadvantages of taking each option. Ask yourselves questions like: "Will this information persuade other ranchers to move cattle to markets?" and "Will this information convince the ranchers that a profit can be made by using this method?" Once you have considered the advantages and disadvantages, record them as notes for use in preparing your brochure.

4. Choose, Implement, and Evaluate a Solution. After considering the advantages and disadvantages, you should create your brochure. You will need to support your proposed solution on how to move Texas cattle to market by including information you gathered and by explaining why you rejected other options. When you are ready, decide which group members will present the brochure, and then take your brochure to the ranchers (the rest of the class). Good luck!

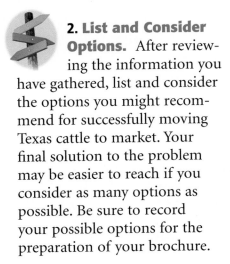

UNIT 8 Prosperity and Crisis
(1870–1939)

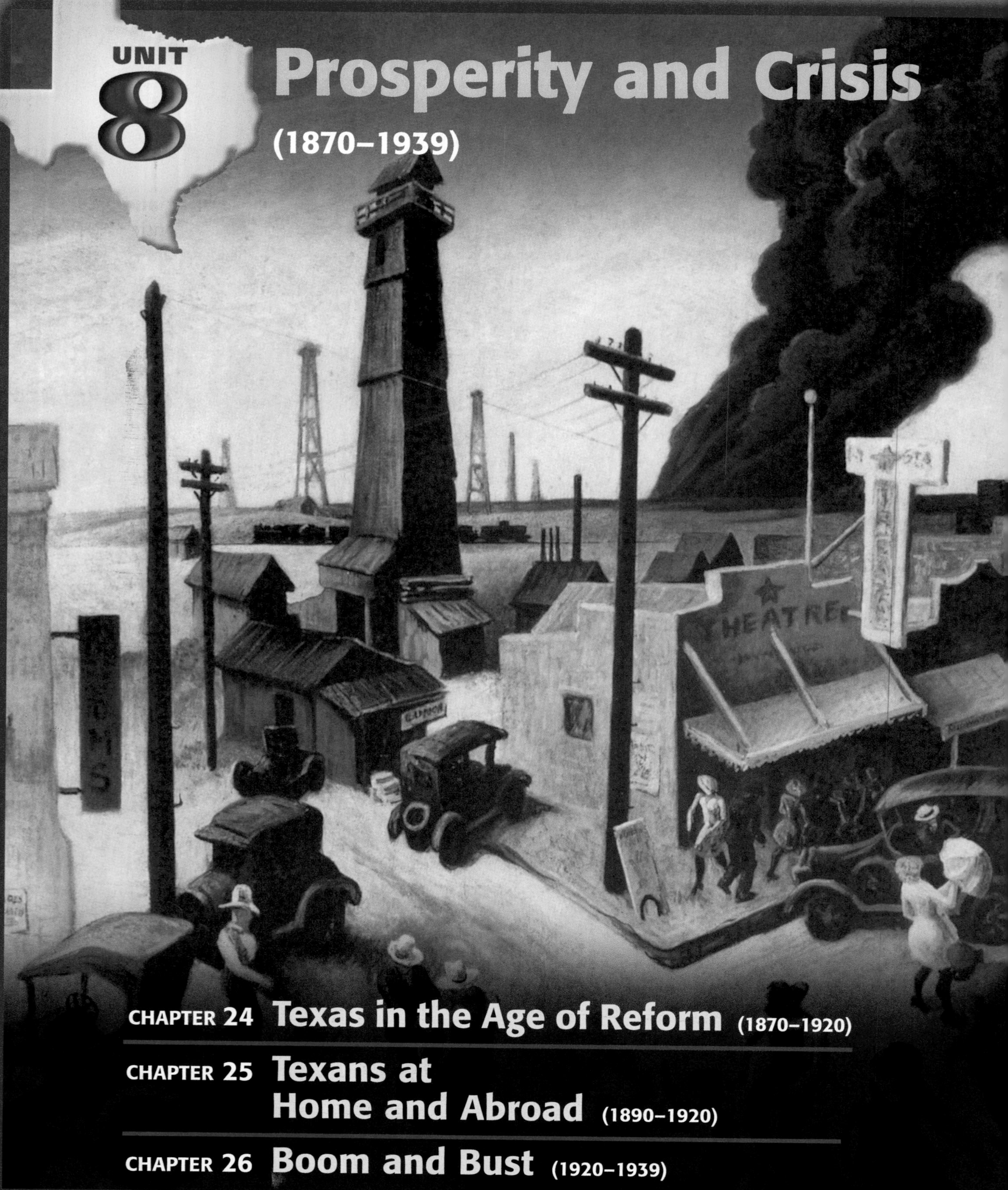

CHAPTER 24 **Texas in the Age of Reform** (1870–1920)

CHAPTER 25 **Texans at Home and Abroad** (1890–1920)

CHAPTER 26 **Boom and Bust** (1920–1939)

Texas Teens

Young Relief Workers

Benito Rodriguez was not even a teenager when the Great Depression struck Texas. Many people were out of work, and Texas youth had to do whatever they could to help their families. Rodriguez found one way to help— he joined the Civilian Conservation Corps (CCC). The CCC was designed to put unemployed young people to work in the nation's forests and parks, employing more than 3 million young people at the height of the depression. Although the CCC was

Young CCC workers in the Company 879 Survey Crew conducted surveys of Garner State Park near Uvalde in 1936.

only supposed to take young men between 18 and 25, Rodriguez enrolled early, at the age of 16. He worked for $30 a month and, as was required, sent $25 of that home. This much needed money allowed his family to purchase necessities. The government provided room, board, clothing, and tools for CCC workers.

The CCC performed many tasks, but one of the most long-lasting was the work they performed in the national and state parks systems. The CCC helped develop 800 state parks and plant 2 to 3 billion trees across the country. At Indian Lodge in Davis Mountains State Park, the CCC built the lodge and its furnishings. The CCC also built stone structures at Caddo Lake State Park and constructed buildings and trails, as well as planted trees, at Lake Brownwood State Park.

The CCC left a legacy of education by training teenage workers in Texas. One CCC worker explained that "getting up at 4 in the morning" gave him discipline. **How did some Texas teens help their families during the depression?**

> **In this unit** you will learn more about the Great Depression in Texas. You will also learn about reform movements in Texas, changes in rural and urban life, and Texans' involvement in world affairs.

LEFT PAGE: *Thomas Hart Benton's painting of a Texas boomtown portrays the leading industries and the trend of urbanization during the early 1900s.*

Texas in the Age of Reform
(1870–1920)

Students at the University of Texas participated in many activities and sports, including rowing.

Texas A&M University students were required to join the Corps of Cadets.

TEXAS

1876 Texas A&M University opens as an all-male military institution.

1883 The University of Texas formally opens.

1889 The Texas legislature passes the Antitrust Act of 1889.
1892 A leading association of farmers endorses the Populist Party.

1870	**1876**	**1882**	**1888**	**1894**

U.S. and WORLD

1881 The Knights of Labor, the first union to allow female members, establishes a local women's chapter in Philadelphia.

1886 A riot erupts in Chicago's Haymarket Square during a nationwide strike by unions.

1891 More than 1,400 delegates from 33 states and territories gather in Cincinnati to form the Populist Party.

Female members of the Knights of Labor attended the organization's 1886 convention as delegates.

Build on What You Know

The Texas oil boom led to rapid growth of oil-related industries, and soon big business prospered. Texans on farms and in the cities demanded that their government ensure fair treatment from big business. Across Texas, reformers took up the call for change.

The 1900 Galveston hurricane flooded the city and destroyed many of the downtown buildings.

The prohibition of alcohol was an increasingly popular idea in Texas.

1900 A hurricane hits Galveston, killing some 6,000 to 8,000 people.

1911 Jovita Idar becomes the first president of the League of Mexican Women.

1918 Texas ratifies the Eighteenth Amendment to the U.S. Constitution, which bans the sale or manufacture of alcohol.

1900   1906   1912   1918

1901 New Zealand passes a third Factory Act designed to protect the rights of workers.

1909 The National Association for the Advancement of Colored People (NAACP) is founded.

1920 The Nineteenth Amendment is adopted, granting women the right to vote.

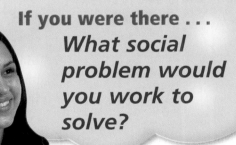

The NAACP led efforts to stop the lynching of African Americans.

You Be the Historian

Themes Journal

What's Your Opinion? Do you **agree** or **disagree** with the following statements? Support your point of view in your journal.

● **Economics** Free enterprise is harmed by government regulations.

● **Government** People are rarely able to bring about changes in government to correct social or economic problems.

● **Citizenship** People must work in groups to bring about social change.

If you were there . . .
What social problem would you work to solve?

Farmers and Reform

Read to Discover

1. How were Texas farmers caught in a boom-and-bust cycle?
2. What were the goals of the Grange and the Southern Farmers' Alliance?
3. Why was the People's Party formed?

Why It Matters Today

During the late 1800s Texas farmers joined organizations to push for reforms. Use CNNfyi.com or other **current events** sources to find information about an organization seeking reforms today. Record your findings in your journal.

Define

- cooperative stores
- pooling
- platform

Identify

- **Grange**
- **Southern Farmers' Alliance**
- **Populist Party**
- **Populists**
- **John Rayner**

Texas farmers often fell into debt when crop failures left them unable to pay off loans for supplies.

The Story Continues

Farmers in Lampasas County were angry and worried. Crop prices remained low. Year in, year out the only thing that seemed to grow was their debt. They gathered in 1877 at J. R. Allen's farm to come up with a plan of action. The farmers wanted to discuss how to fight the wealthy few they thought controlled their economic well-being.

★ Farmers Demand Reform

Many farmers in Texas and other parts of the United States faced serious hardships. The movement of farmers and railroads into the Plains sparked a boom in farm production in the late 1800s. But the supply of crops outpaced the demand. This, combined with problems in the national economy, caused prices to fall. Cotton farmers were particularly vulnerable to the changing national market. In the 1880s, cotton was selling for less than 10 cents a pound. On most farms, it cost 8 cents a pound just to produce the cotton. One rural man noted the difficulties farmers faced.

Texas Voices ❝We were told . . . to go to work and raise a big crop, that was all we needed. We went to work and plowed and planted; the rains fell, the sun shone, nature smiled, and we

The Progressive Movement

Read to Discover

1. What changes did progressives bring to politics and local government?
2. How did progressives try to reform society?

Why It Matters Today

To force changes in working conditions, union laborers have occasionally gone on strike. Use **CNNfyi.com** or other **current events** sources to find information about a recent labor action. Record your findings in your journal.

Define

• **progressives**
• **commission plan**

Identify

• **Terrell Election Law**
• **Seventeenth Amendment**

The Story Continues

Elizabeth Gaertner moved from New York City to Galveston as a young girl. After marrying a successful merchant, Alphonse Levy, she took care of her children and joined some clubs. Although she raised her own children in a comfortable home, she was aware of the less fortunate around her. She soon became active in her community. She was one of the many women working to solve social problems in Texas cities.

Elizabeth Gaertner took baskets of food to poor Texans.

★ Government Reform

In the early 1900s reformers known as **progressives** worked to improve society. *Progressive* means "forward-looking" or "relating to progress." Progressives tackled a variety of issues, including election reform. In 1905 the Texas legislature passed the **Terrell Election Law**, named after its sponsor Alexander W. Terrell. The law established primary elections to choose candidates for all state, district, and county races. Candidates who won would represent their party in the later general elections. The law also attacked election fraud—for example, by requiring the use of official ballots. The passage of the **Seventeenth Amendment** to the U.S. Constitution in 1913 allowed American voters—rather than the state legislatures—to vote directly for U.S. senators.

Another of the progressives' goals was to make local government more efficient. A major natural disaster in Galveston in September 1900

The Great Storm

After the disastrous 1900 hurricane, Galveston residents struggled to rebuild. One of their efforts involved raising the city to a greater height above sea level. To do this, they pumped sand into the city from the ocean floor. Any buildings that had survived the hurricane were then jacked up and placed on new foundations. In addition, a 17-foot-high seawall was built along the beach for protection.

The great storm. *The hurricane of 1900 left much of Galveston a pile of rubble.* **Based on this photo, how would you have felt if you had experienced the Galveston storm?**

spurred this reform effort. On September 8 a huge hurricane was moving toward the city. Residents went on about their business—they had been through hurricanes before. While observing the ocean early that Saturday morning, Galveston weather reporter Isaac Cline began to worry.

Texas Voices **"Unusually heavy swells [waves] from the southeast . . . overflowing low places [in the] south portion of the city three to four blocks from beach. . . . Such high water with opposing winds never observed previously."**

—Isaac Cline, quoted in *Texas: An Album of History,* by James L. Haley

The hurricane hit later that day. Waves battered Galveston, drowning people and destroying buildings. Some 6,000 to 8,000 people lost their lives, and half the city lay in ruins.

Many people in Galveston felt that the city government could not cope with the disaster. To rebuild the city, a new form of local government called the **commission plan** was established. Under this plan, an elected city commission shares both executive and legislative powers. Each commissioner supervises different city services. The new government of Galveston oversaw the rebuilding of the city, including the construction of a six-mile seawall to protect the island. Progressives liked the commission plan because of its efficiency. In choosing commissioners, emphasis was placed more on knowledge of city services and less on politics. The commission plan was a major reform of the progressive movement, and it was soon adopted by other U.S. cities.

Reading Check **Analyzing Information** How did geographic factors such as weather lead to a reform in the structure of local government in Texas?

★ Workplace and Health Reform

Progressives also tried to help Texas workers, many of whom labored long hours but earned little. Along with unions, progressives fought for higher wages, better working conditions, and a shorter workweek for factory workers. Progressives also opposed child labor. Children who worked in factories faced serious illness from long hours and poor conditions. Many received little education or exercise. Texas passed its first child labor law in 1903. Laws that regulated child labor more strictly soon followed.

Progressives also worried about unregulated food and drugs. Eating poorly processed food or taking unsafe medications made many people sick each year. Progressives such as the members of Texas Federation of Women's Clubs backed candidates who favored food and drug regulation. The clubs helped elect progressive candidate Thomas M. Campbell in 1906. During Campbell's administration, the legislature passed laws to regulate the food and drug industries and created the Dairy and Food Commission to set health standards. These laws led to increased costs for businesses that had to meet the higher standards. However, most Texans agreed that the benefits outweighed the costs because the laws helped improve the lives and health of many in the state.

Reading Check **Finding the Main Idea** What social reforms and government regulations did progressives pursue?

★ Education Reform

Many progressives, particularly women, also tried to improve Texas schools. Texas ranked near the bottom in the nation for its education system. About 15 percent of Texas children older than 10 could not read or write. Teachers were often untrained, and schools lacked the proper resources and facilities.

In the late 1800s and early 1900s the state established several schools to train teachers. These included Sam Houston Normal Institute in Huntsville and Southwest Texas State Normal School in San Marcos. The state also established medical schools such as the University of Texas Medical School near Galveston. During the early 1900s the legislature passed a number of laws to improve the public school system.

Texas Cities

Galveston

History: The city of Galveston was founded in 1836. With its good natural harbor and growing trade, the city had a booming local economy. The city was also a popular arrival spot for immigrants to Texas.

Population in 2000: 57,247

Relative location: Located on the eastern end of Galveston Island, some 50 miles southeast of Houston.

Region: Gulf Coastal Plain

County: County seat of Galveston County

Special feature: Located on an island, the city is a popular destination for tourists and beachgoers.

Origin of name: The city was named after Galveston Bay, which was named by explorer José de Evia in 1785. Evia named the bay in honor of Bernardo de Gálvez, then the viceroy of New Spain.

Economy: Galveston's economy today is largely based on tourism and shipping. The city's port is still active, and large numbers of people come to Galveston for recreation.

★ ★ ★ ★ ★ ★ ★ ★ ★

Education reformers pushed for more money to fund schools and to help pay for books, teachers' salaries, and other supplies such as desks.

Under the new laws, rural schools could borrow money and raise tax rates. More local funds could also be used to provide free textbooks. In addition, the legislature raised teachers' salaries and lengthened school terms. The reforms helped some 1 million Texas children attend school by 1910. The number of children in school increased after the legislature passed a law in 1915 requiring school attendance.

The reforms in the school system changed the lives of many Texans. More women gained access to education in the late 1800s than ever before. By 1890 more girls than boys attended Texas schools. Some women went on to get a higher education. Several colleges, including the University of Texas, began allowing women to attend. The Girls' Industrial College—now Texas Woman's University—opened in 1903. As educational opportunities for women increased, so too did their job prospects, particularly in the field of education. So many women became teachers that by 1900 they outnumbered men in teaching positions in Texas.

Education reform did not reach all Texans, however. African American and Mexican American students generally did not benefit from Progressive Era changes in education. The Constitution of 1876 had established separate funding for schools based on race. As a result, many Mexican Americans and African Americans did not have equal educational opportunities. The schools they attended often lacked adequate funding for facilities and supplies. Prairie View Normal Institute—now known as Prairie View A&M University—had been founded for African Americans, but it struggled for decades to obtain sufficient funding. African Americans seeking to earn law or medical degrees had to attend out-of-state schools. The fight to make public schools serve all Texans was only just beginning.

★ **Reading Check** **Categorizing** List some of the successes and some of the failures of education reform in the Progressive Era.

Section 3 Review ★TEKS Questions 2, 3, 4a, 4b, 5

go.hrw.com Homework Practice Online
keyword: ST3 HP24

❶ **Define and explain:**
- progressives
- commission plan

❷ **Identify and explain:**
- Terrell Election Law
- Seventeenth Amendment

❸ **Summarizing**
Copy the chart below and use it to show the progressives' reforms in the workplace, society, and education.

Progressive Reforms in Texas	
Workplace	
Society	
Education	

❹ **Finding the Main Idea**
a. How did reformers change the state's political system?
b. How did the structure of local government change in Texas during the Progressive Era?

❺ **Writing and Critical Thinking** **TAKS**
Evaluating Choose an issue that progressives were attempting to reform. Then write a paragraph in which you analyze progressives' success in reform regarding the issue.
Consider the following:
- reforms proposed
- how these reforms affected life in Texas

Women and the Progressive Movement

The Story Continues

Carry Nation and her new husband, a physician, looked forward to their life together. The young couple soon had a baby girl, but her husband's alcohol abuse had already destroyed the marriage. Nation remarried in 1877 and moved to Texas in 1879. She became a strong opponent of alcohol sales and even used hatchets to destroy saloons.

Prohibition backers wore hatchet pins such as this one in support of Carry Nation and her efforts.

★ The Temperance Movement

Like Carry Nation, many Texans worried about the effects alcohol abuse had on families. This led to the growth of the **temperance movement**, a social reform effort that encouraged people to drink less alcohol. Support for **prohibition**—the banning of the manufacture, distribution, and sale of alcohol—increased during the late 1800s and early 1900s. Many men and women supported prohibition as part of their religious beliefs. Organizations such as the Woman's Christian Temperance Union and the Anti-Saloon League pushed for prohibition. In 1895 more than half of the state's counties had placed limits on the production and sale of alcohol.

Prohibition became an even more important political issue in the early 1900s. The *Dallas Morning News* described prohibition as the

Clara Driscoll and the Alamo

Texas women took up many causes. Between 1903 and 1905 Clara Driscoll worked with the Daughters of the Republic of Texas to save the Alamo. The old mission had been purchased by a wholesale grocery company and fallen into poor condition. Driscoll used her personal fortune to buy the Alamo property, helping to save it for future generations.

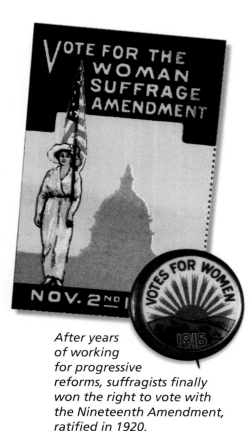

After years of working for progressive reforms, suffragists finally won the right to vote with the Nineteenth Amendment, ratified in 1920.

"paramount [dominant] . . . issue in our politics." The Democratic Party was split between those against and those for prohibition. Candidates often ran for election chiefly on the prohibition issue. In 1917 U.S. senator Morris Sheppard of Texas sponsored a constitutional amendment for national prohibition. The **Eighteenth Amendment** won the support of enough state legislatures—including the Texas legislature—to be ratified in 1919. As a result, the manufacture and sale of alcohol became illegal throughout the nation in 1920.

 Reading Check **Analyzing Information** How did prohibition affect the Texas Democratic Party?

★ The Suffrage Movement

Women played a vital role not only in prohibition but also in most progressive reforms. They fought to protect working mothers' rights and for new laws limiting child labor, ensuring food safety, and requiring school attendance. Some women even held political office. In 1918 **Annie Webb Blanton** became the first woman to win election to a Texas state office. She served as the state's superintendent of public instruction. As state superintendent, she helped establish a system of free textbooks, revise the teacher certification process, and improve rural education.

An overriding issue for women of the time was the effort to gain the right to vote. In 1913 **Eleanor Brackenridge** was chosen president of the Texas Woman Suffrage Association, later known as the Texas Equal Suffrage Association. Minnie Fisher Cunningham, Annie Webb Blanton, and **Jane McCallum** were other important suffrage leaders in Texas. Association leaders believed that "no state can be a true democracy in which one half of the people are denied the right to vote." They campaigned across the state in favor of voting rights for women. However, the suffragists faced strong opposition in Texas. Cunningham and the other suffrage leaders struggled to convince Texans that women should be allowed to participate in the state's politics.

Women in other states were also working for suffrage. Finally, in 1919 the U.S. Congress proposed the **Nineteenth Amendment** to the U.S. Constitution, granting women suffrage. The Texas legislature ratified the amendment in June 1919. In 1920 the amendment won ratification nationally, giving American women the right to vote.

Jane McCallum and other leaders went on to work with the Women's Joint Legislative Council. This group focused on education, prison reform, and child-labor issues. Nicknamed the Petticoat Lobby, this group was an influential force in Texas politics for years to come.

Reading Check **Summarizing** How did Texas women exercise their civic responsibilities in the early 1900s?

★ Limits of Reform

African American and Mexican American women in Texas also fought for reforms. In many cases, however, they were not welcomed by white reformers. For example, many women's suffrage groups were white only. Nonetheless, Christia Adair, a black Texan, worked for women's suffrage and equal rights for all black Texans. In South Texas, <u>Jovita Idar</u> organized people to support women's rights as well as rights for Mexican Americans in Texas. She also campaigned for education for poor children. Like many Texas women, Idar played an active role in reform efforts during the Progressive Era. Despite the efforts of Adair, Idar, and others, measures were passed in Texas denying suffrage to members of minority groups. Voting in local Democratic primary elections was restricted to white Texans only. In 1902 Texas began to require a **poll tax**, a tax on voting. As a result, poor Texans, many of whom were African American and Mexican American, could not afford to vote.

African Americans in Texas were denied the benefits of reform in other areas as well. The state legislature and city governments passed more Jim Crow laws during the early 1900s. Between 1910 and 1925, several Texas towns imposed segregated housing laws. Public facilities, restaurants, and hotels—even drinking fountains—were segregated. African Americans also faced racial violence. Increased racial hostility sometimes led to the lynching—or killing by a mob—of black citizens. Many years would go by before laws were passed to help protect the rights of African Americans in Texas.

 Reading Check **Finding the Main Idea** What were some of the limits of reform?

Biography

Jovita Idar
(1885–1946)

As a young woman, Jovita Idar of Laredo worked for her father's newspaper, *La Crónica*. The newspaper became a vocal political tool for Mexican Americans. Idar helped establish the League of Mexican Women. Idar was its first president. After her marriage in 1917, Idar moved to San Antonio. There she was active in community service, including serving as an interpreter for Spanish-speaking patients in a hospital. **How did Jovita Idar exercise her civic responsibilities in her lifetime?** ★TEKS

Section 4 Review ★TEKS Questions 2, 3, 4a, 4b, 5

go.hrw.com Homework Practice Online
keyword: ST3 HP24

1 Define and explain:
- temperance movement
- prohibition
- poll tax

2 Identify and explain:
- Eighteenth Amendment
- Annie Webb Blanton
- Eleanor Brackenridge
- Jane McCallum
- Nineteenth Amendment
- Jovita Idar

3 Analyzing Information
Copy the graphic organizer below. Use it to show how activists in Texas affected national progressive reforms.

> Eighteenth Amendment

> Nineteenth Amendment

4 Finding the Main Idea
a. Explain the different points of view held by members of the Democratic Party on prohibition. How did differing points of view affect the party?
b. Who did not benefit from the progressives' reforms?

5 Writing and Critical Thinking **TAKS**
Summarizing Write an editorial on the achievements and the limitations of the effort to expand democracy in the Progressive Era.
Consider the following:
- the Nineteenth Amendment
- the poll tax and Jim Crow laws

The Chapter at a Glance

Examine the following visual summary of the chapter. Then used the visual to create an outline of the chapter you can use to study with a classmate. ★TEKS

Farmers and Populism
- Regulate railroad companies
- Form cooperative stores
- Government ownership of railroads and telegraphs
- Reduce influence of big business on government

Business Reform
- Break up trusts and monopolies
- Reform insurance companies

City Government
- Establish a commission plan for local government
- Support efficient government

Education and Health
- Reform school funding
- More colleges to train teachers
- Regulate food and drugs

Women's Rights and Temperance
- Ban the production and sale of alcohol
- The right to vote for women

Identifying People and Ideas ★TEKS

Use the following terms or people in historically significant sentences.

1. Grange
2. Populists
3. monopoly
4. James Stephen Hogg
5. James E. Ferguson
6. progressives
7. commission plan
8. prohibition
9. Eleanor Brackenridge
10. Nineteenth Amendment

Understanding Main Ideas ★TEKS

Section 1 (pp. 498–502)

1. Explain the effect of the national agricultural market on Texas farmers' lives in the late 1800s.
2. What effect did railroad companies' practices have on farmers' lives?
3. What were the reform policies of the Populist Party?

Section 2 (pp. 503–506)

4. What were the effects of trusts and monopolies on the Texas economy?
5. What reforms did James Stephen Hogg fight for as attorney general and governor?

Section 3 (pp. 507–510)

6. What social, educational, and governmental reforms did the progressives support?

Section 4 (pp. 511–513)

7. What role did women play in the progressive movement, and what important right did they gain?

You Be the Historian ★TEKS

Reviewing Themes

1. **Economics** How did government regulations in the late 1800s and early 1900s try to protect business competition?
2. **Government** How did reformers change national, state, and local government?
3. **Citizenship** How did farmers, laborers, and women work to solve problems during the late 1800s and early 1900s?

TAKS Practice: **Thinking Critically** ★TEKS

1. **Analyzing Information** What effect did weather have on the reform of local government in Texas?
2. **Summarizing** Describe some of the defining characteristics of the Progressive Era.
3. **Sequencing** List in order and by date significant reforms achieved by women.

Interpreting Maps (TEKS)

Study the map below. Then use the information on the map to answer the questions that follow.

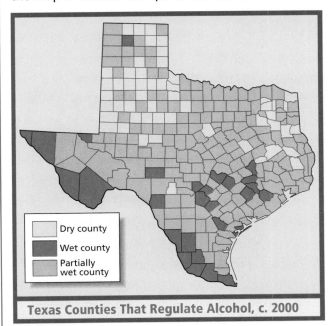

Texas Counties That Regulate Alcohol, c. 2000

Legend:
- Dry county
- Wet county
- Partially wet county

1. Many Texas counties have laws banning the sale of alcohol. These counties are called dry counties. What region had the most dry counties?
   a. the Rio Grande valley
   b. the Panhandle
   c. the Gulf Coast
   d. West Texas

2. How do you think this map reflects the legacy of the temperance movement in Texas?

Analyzing Primary Sources (TEKS)

Read the following quote from the platform of the Populist Party of Texas. Then answer the questions.

"We demand the most rigid, honest, and just national control and supervision of the means of public communication and transportation, and if this control and supervision does not remove the abuses now existing, we demand the government ownership of such means of communication and transportation."

3. Which of the following statements best describes the party's point of view?
   a. Private ownership of railroads is the best policy for Texas.
   b. Government should not interfere with how railroad companies decide to conduct their business.
   c. The government should take control of railroads if railroads are unsupervised.
   d. Free enterprise supports government ownership of railroads.

4. Why do you think the platform of the Populist Party singles out transportation for reform?

Alternative Assessment

Interdisciplinary Connection to Literature (TEKS)

Imagine that you are a farmer in Texas during the late 1800s and early 1900s. Write a poem or song in which you express your fears about your livelihood and your hopes for the future. Be sure to include the sources of your problems such as the effects of international and national markets, overproduction of crops, falling crop prices, debt, and droughts. Create an illustration to accompany your poem or song. The illustration should include images from your everyday life as a farmer in Texas.

BUILDING YOUR Portfolio

📄 **internet connect**

Internet Activity: go.hrw.com
KEYWORD: ST3 TX24 (TEKS)

Access the Internet through the HRW Go site to research how the Galveston hurricane of 1900 affected the political, economic, and social development of Texas. Then locate, differentiate, and use primary and secondary sources to create a pamphlet that shows the various ways in which the hurricane changed Galveston's people, infrastructure, and government.

Texas in the Age of Reform **515**

Texans at Home and Abroad
(1890–1920)

The Austin Baseball Club was one of the founding teams of the State Base Ball League.

Lieutenant Colonel Theodore Roosevelt sits at an officer's table during the training of the Rough Riders in San Antonio.

TEXAS

1894 The first football game is played between the University of Texas and Texas A&M.

1898 Teddy Roosevelt organizes and trains the Rough Riders in San Antonio.

1902 The Corsicana Oilers set a baseball record by defeating the Texarkana team 51 to 3.

| **1890** | **1894** | **1898** | **1902** |

U.S. and WORLD

1895 Cuban rebels revolt against Spanish rule.

1898 The United States declares war on Spain.

1904 The United States begins construction on the Panama Canal to provide a shorter route from the Atlantic Ocean to the Pacific Ocean. It takes 10 years to build.

U.S. ships fire on Spanish forces in the Battle of Santiago in 1898.

Build on What You Know

In the late 1800s the economy of Texas and the daily lives of Texans were changing. By 1900 industrialization, the oil boom, and the progressive movement had reshaped the state. In addition, many people from all over the world were moving to Texas.

This Neiman Marcus advertisement appealed to the fashion tastes of Texas women in the early 1900s.

The Houston Ship Channel and the city's bayous increased trade and spurred the growth of Houston.

1907 The first Neiman Marcus department store opens in Dallas.

1914 The Houston Ship Channel is completed, leading to the growth of industry in the Houston area.

1918 Texas troops are sent to France to fight in World War I.

1906   1910   1914   1918

1911 Mexican dictator Porfirio Díaz is overthrown.

1917 The United States declares war on Germany and enters World War I.

This advertisement celebrates the completion of the Panama Canal.

If you were there . . .
Would you move from a farm to a city for a job?

You Be the Historian

Themes Journal

What's Your Opinion? Do you **agree** or **disagree** with the following statements? Support your point of view in your journal.

• **Geography** Conflicts within a country rarely affect neighboring nations.

• **Economics** Immigrants are only attracted to a country or state because of jobs.

• **Global Relations** It is important for citizens to support their country's actions in other parts of the world.

From Farm to City

Read to Discover

1. How did rural life change in the early 1900s?
2. What spurred population growth in Texas cities?
3. Why did immigrants come to Texas, and where did they settle?

Define
- urbanization

Identify
- **Houston Ship Channel**
- **Federal Reserve System**

Why It Matters Today

Four out of five Texans lived in rural areas in 1900. Use **CNNfyi.com** or other **current events** sources to find information about city growth today. Record your findings in your journal.

The Story Continues

Panhandle-Plains Historical Museum, Canyon, Texas

Because of their many chores, girls who grew up on Texas farms during the early 1900s had little time to play with dolls.

aggie Washington was just six years old when she began doing all her family's housework. On top of these chores, she also took care of her baby sister. Maggie lived in rural Navarro County in the early 1900s. Like many farm children, Maggie was doing adult work when she was still a child herself. Maggie later explained, "When I was six years old I was keeping house like a woman. I had the babies to care for, the food to cook, clothes to wash and iron."

★ Life in Rural Texas

Like Maggie Washington, most family members in rural Texas helped with farmwork during the early 1900s. Texas farm families worked year-round. Crops had to be planted before spring and harvested before winter. Fields required constant attention to keep them clear of weeds. At the same time, family members raised livestock, fixed fences, and took care of one another.

Life on Texas farms required a lot of hard work and offered few luxuries. Before the 1930s few rural families had electricity in their homes. The majority of farmers continued to use kerosene lamps for light and outdoor pumps for water. Because less than 10 percent of Texas farmers had indoor plumbing in the 1920s, most farms had outhouses. However, mechanical farm machinery like threshers, binders, and reapers had become more common in Texas. More farmers used gasoline-powered tractors to do field work. Some farmers also used gasoline-powered or electric pumps instead of windmills to pump water for irrigation.

Farm production increased as new tractors and other machines made farming more efficient. The resulting surplus of agricultural products led to a drop in the prices of farm goods. With prices falling, it became hard for many farmers to pay their debts. The numbers of sharecroppers and tenant farmers rose. Texas newspapers published reports on these issues. "There is something rotten in Texas when more than half of our farm families are landless tenants." The struggles of farm life led many rural families to move to cities for new opportunities.

⭐ **Reading Check** **Summarizing** How did new technology change farm life and lead to both a boom in production and a bust in farm prices?

Some Texas farmers began using gasoline-powered tractors during the early 1900s.

⭐ Industry and the Growth of Cities

Although half of the nation lived in cities in 1920, only about one third of Texans lived in cities. Between 1910 and 1920, the populations of San Antonio, Dallas, and Houston each nearly doubled. This **urbanization**, or the growth of cities, was directly tied to the development of industry.

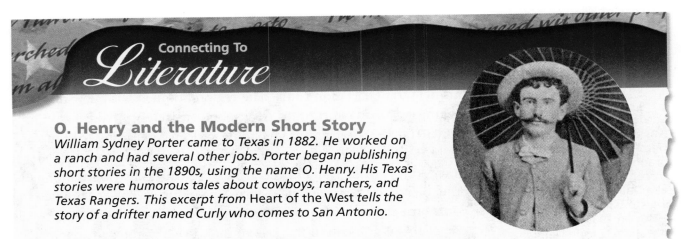

Connecting To *Literature*

O. Henry and the Modern Short Story
William Sydney Porter came to Texas in 1882. He worked on a ranch and had several other jobs. Porter began publishing short stories in the 1890s, using the name O. Henry. His Texas stories were humorous tales about cowboys, ranchers, and Texas Rangers. This excerpt from Heart of the West *tells the story of a drifter named Curly who comes to San Antonio.*

Curly stood a few moments in the narrow, mesquite-paved street. San Antonio puzzled and disturbed him. Three days he had been a non-paying guest of the town, having dropped off there from a box car of an I. & G. N. freight, because Greaser Johnny had told him in Des Moines that the Alamo city has **manna**[1] fallen, gathered, cooked and served free with cream and sugar. Curly had found the tip partly a good one. There was hospitality in plenty . . . [but] the town itself was a weight upon his

spirits after his experiences with the rushing, business-like, systematized cities of the North and East. . . . The winding, doubling streets, leading nowhere, **bewildered**[2] him.

Understanding What You Read

1. **Literature and History** Why does O. Henry describe San Antonio as a weight upon Curly's spirits?
2. **Literature and You** What do you think it would have been like to live in San Antonio in the early 1900s?

[1] **manna:** food from heaven   [2] **bewildered:** confused

Coming to Texas. *Many European immigrants sailed to Texas in ships.* **What does this photograph reveal about traveling conditions for immigrants in the early 1900s?**

Biography

Carrie Marcus Neiman
(1883–1953)

Carrie Marcus Neiman was the daughter of German Jewish immigrants. She began her career as a salesperson at a Dallas women's clothing store in the early 1900s. In 1905 she married Abraham Lincoln Neiman. Together with her brother and husband, Neiman cofounded the Neiman Marcus department store. As head buyer, her eye for fashion was central to the store's success. She oversaw the growth of Neiman Marcus from a local store to a national chain. How did Carrie Marcus Neiman contribute to the growth of Texas business in the early 1900s?

Cattle markets, oil, railroads, textiles, and other industries created jobs that attracted people to Texas cities. During the 1910s the number of Texans who worked in industry rose from almost 12 to nearly 16 percent. At the same time, the number of Texans involved in agriculture declined by about 24 percent.

City growth was concentrated in the more populated eastern half of the state, which had ports and markets for farm goods. Houston's location near the Gulf of Mexico had helped spur its growth. In 1914 the Buffalo Bayou, a waterway between Houston and the Gulf, was deepened and widened to allow larger ships to travel on it. The new **Houston Ship Channel** gave the city a direct link to the Gulf. Texans built oil refineries and factories near the channel to take advantage of this new transportation route. The region boomed with new residents seeking jobs in factories, on docks, and in freight yards. These jobs attracted many rural Texans, including African Americans, to Houston.

In 1914 the federal government built a district bank of the **Federal Reserve System** in Dallas. Federal Reserve banks distribute money to other banks and help regulate the banking industry. The Federal Reserve Bank brought new finance-related businesses to Dallas. The city was one of the largest cotton markets in the world. Manufacturing and the cotton trade contributed to the city's growth.

San Antonio was rapidly becoming an important military center. Businesses sprang up to provide services for the military base and the many troops stationed there. Between 1900 and 1920 San Antonio was the largest city in Texas. Dense settlement in West Texas and the Panhandle was more difficult because of a lack of water and timber. El Paso was the only West Texas city whose population had reached 50,000 by 1920. El Paso grew in part because of railroad connections with Mexico and the American Southwest.

Reading Check **Identifying Cause and Effect** How did different industries contribute to the growth of Texas cities?

★ Migration and City Growth

The booming oil industry, the expansion of commercial farming, and industrial jobs attracted many people to Texas. Continuing the trend of the 1800s, the largest group of new Texans came from other southern states. The majority of immigrants came from Mexico—almost 180,000 Mexicans arrived between 1900 and 1920. By 1930 nearly 700,000 Mexican Americans lived in the state, many of them settling in San Antonio and cities along the Rio Grande. Many of these immigrants lived in Mexican American communities and traveled to farms when labor was needed.

The German American population in Texas also grew—reaching more than 170,000 by 1910. Many German immigrants hoped to start their own farms in the rolling farmland of the Hill Country. Other European newcomers included Czechs, Irish, Italians, and Poles. Many of these groups settled in Central Texas and took up farming. Because of limits on Asian immigration, few Asians immigrated to Texas during the early 1900s. Although some Chinese Americans from California came to work on Texas railroads, in 1900 only about 800 lived in Texas.

Galveston was the main port of entry for immigrants from Europe. When one group of Jewish immigrants from Russia arrived in Galveston, their spokesperson thanked the mayor for greeting them.

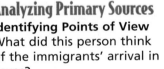

Some immigrants to Texas cities opened small businesses to sell goods to other immigrants.

Texas Voices ❝We are overwhelmed that the ruler of the city should greet us. We have never been spoken to by the officials of our country except in terms of harshness, and although we have heard of the great land of freedom, it is very hard to realize that we are permitted to grasp the hand of the great man. We will do all we can to make good citizens.❞

—Anonymous Russian immigrant, quoted in *Galveston Daily News,* July 2, 1907

Analyzing Primary Sources ★
Identifying Points of View
What did this person think of the immigrants' arrival in Texas?

★ **Reading Check** **Finding the Main Idea** Why did migrants and immigrants come to Texas, and where did they settle?

 Section 1 Review ⊛TEKS Questions 3, 4a, 4b, 5

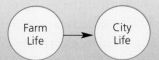 **Homework Practice Online**
keyword: ST3 HP25

1 **Define and explain:**
- urbanization

2 **Identify and explain:**
- Houston Ship Channel
- Federal Reserve System

3 **Summarizing**
Copy the graphic organizer below. Use it to list the factors that pulled people to Texas cities. Also list the difficulties of farm life that pushed Texans off of farms.

Farm Life → City Life

4 **Finding the Main Idea**
a. How did new technology change life on Texas farms in the early 1900s?
b. How did the population trends of Texas change in the early 1900s? Why was this?

5 **Writing and Critical Thinking**
Evaluating Write a letter to a friend explaining how you think Texas changed between 1900 and 1920. Consider the following:
- what opportunities attracted immigrants
- where immigrants settled

TAKS

Urban Life in Texas

Read to Discover

1. How did new technologies affect the lives of people in Texas cities during the early 1900s?
2. Why were Texas cities growing, and how did that create problems?
3. What new forms of leisure, entertainment, and art did Texans enjoy in the early 1900s?

Why It Matters Today

During the early 1900s city life presented many challenges. Use CNN**fyi**.com or other **current events** sources to find information about the challenges of urban life today. Record your findings in your journal.

Define

- suburbs
- ragtime

Identify

- **Adina Emilia De Zavala**
- **Texas Highway Department**
- **Texas Department of Health**
- **Texas Water Commission**
- **Scott Joplin**
- **William Sydney Porter**
- **Elisabet Ney**

The Story Continues

In 1902 young Jesse Illingsworth of Dallas made one of the first long-distance car trips in Texas. Illingsworth stood out with his gloves, goggles, and racing cap. It took him three days to make the 40-mile trip from Terrell to Dallas. He was unable to drive at night because the car had no headlights. Illingsworth sent scouts ahead on horseback to warn other travelers that a car was coming. He did so to avoid spooking travelers' horses with the racket of his engine.

Early automobile drivers wore goggles to protect their eyes because cars did not have windshields.

★ Urban Technology

The availability of new technologies made city life different from country life. In 1878 Colonel A. H. Belo installed the first telephone line in Texas. It ran between his house and his office at the *Galveston News*. Telephone switchboards soon opened in several Texas cities. By 1906 more than 100,000 Texans had telephones. Electricity came into use more slowly in Texas than the telephone. The first electrical power plant in Texas was built in Galveston during the early 1880s. In the next decade, several steam and hydroelectric, or water-powered, plants were built. These power plants provided electricity for industries, lighting, and transportation. Electric streetlights were introduced to Texas cities in the early 1900s. Elm Street in central Dallas was lined with such lights in 1911. Stores along the street also lit up their windows. Elm Street was called the "great white way" because it was so brightly lit.

Electricity also played a role in the development of new forms of mass transit, or public transportation. By 1920 Texas had more cities with electric streetcars than any state west of the Mississippi River. Streetcars led to the development of the first Texas **suburbs**, or residential neighborhoods built outside of a central city. Streetcars provided efficient transportation, so people could live in suburbs and work in cities. Texans began to move to suburbs for fresh air and a lifestyle that was more like that in the country.

Texas cities grew not only outward but also upward. Texans began to construct taller buildings to make room for new industries and the growing population. Skyscrapers, or multistory buildings, became common after the development of steel frames and elevators. The tallest building in Texas in the early 1900s was the 20-story Amicable Building in Waco. Skyscrapers like the Rice Hotel in Houston were built to catch breezes coming off the Gulf of Mexico. As new buildings were rising, some Texans like **Adina Emilia De Zavala** worked hard to keep the state's historic buildings from being torn down.

The new technology that eventually had the greatest effect on Texas cities was the automobile. In 1900, however, cars were rare and not very practical. Except for a few streets paved with bricks or wood, most cities had bumpy dirt roads and few bridges. In 1900 a 10-block stretch of Main Street was the only paved road in Dallas. Even the largest urban areas in Texas were still "walking cities"—small enough so people could walk wherever they needed to go.

Reading Check **Analyzing Information** How did new transportation technologies affect the development of Texas?

Biography

Adina Emilia De Zavala
(1861–1955)

Adina Emilia De Zavala helped to preserve Texas history while cities were changing life in the state. During the early 1900s she tried to prevent the destruction of parts of the Alamo. She even barricaded herself inside the Alamo for three days in protest. De Zavala helped organize the Texas Historical and Landmarks Association, and she fought for the preservation of other historic sites. **How did De Zavala try to preserve the state's cultural heritage?** TEKS

Electric streetcars, such as this one in Houston, ran along rails laid in the middle of downtown streets.

Moving the Bank

Because of heavy traffic on Commerce Street in San Antonio, the city government decided to pave and widen the street in 1913. The Alamo National Bank, which occupied a five-story stone structure, was located on the street. The busy bankers there had little time for road construction. When the construction crew came, the bank was simply jacked up, put on wheels, and moved back. The employees inside continued business as usual while the building was moved.

★ Urban Problems and Reform

The new urban technologies and the growth of cities caused some problems for city residents. Cars were considered dangerous. For example, drivers in Fort Worth were required by law to warn pedestrians by sounding their horn each time they came to an intersection. Texans had to pave roads, build bridges, and pass safety laws to manage increasing traffic. The first speed limit, 18 miles per hour, was passed in 1907. In 1917 the state government formed the **Texas Highway Department** to help build and maintain highways. As roads improved and cars became less expensive, automobile use expanded rapidly. This contributed to the changing life in Texas cities as streets became even busier with automobile traffic.

The booming Texas cities also faced housing shortages. Dallas had grown so fast—almost doubling in size between 1900 and 1910—that new residents had trouble finding housing. Some people even had to live in tents. Poorer city dwellers often lived in older homes, which they sometimes shared with several families. A survey of Austin in 1917 found people "crowded together in small huts, one and two families in a one-room shanty [cabin]."

Rapid urban growth made it difficult for cities to provide services such as electricity, garbage collection, sewers, police, health care, and fire protection. As a result, public health was a major concern. Lack of sewage as well as garbage disposal services led to high death rates from disease. Progressive reformers pushed for changes in these conditions. In 1903 the agency that became the **Texas Department of Health** was formed to help prevent disease. Dr. William Brumby, the head of the department in 1908, explained its mission.

★ Analyzing Primary Sources
Identifying Points of View
Why do you think Dr. Brumby wanted to act upon these reforms?

Texas Voices

❝[Our mission] is to preserve water supply by preventing pollution; to guard the neighbors by draining all premises; to protect the community by exterminating rodents; to promote the general welfare by proper sanitary law.❞

—Dr. William Brumby, quoted in *The Handbook of Texas*

The growing use of automobiles in the early 1900s led to some traffic and safety problems in busy Texas cities.

Some cities grew so fast that their water supplies could not meet the demand. For example, in 1910 a water shortage in Dallas forced residents to buy water from people who had wells. To solve these problems, cities began building more dams on creeks and rivers to create reservoirs. The **Texas Water Commission** was formed in 1913 to help cities and counties manage water resources.

Because many city buildings were built of wood, fire was also a serious threat. Without fire trucks and fire hydrants, volunteer firefighters could not keep fires under control. In 1912 a fire burned down much of the northern part of Houston. No one died, but the fire reduced 46 blocks to ashes. To prevent such fires, city governments began replacing volunteers with full-time firefighters. The first fire truck in Texas was purchased by Big Spring in 1909. This West Texas town bought the truck—which had a hose, pump, and water tank—after experiencing several fires. Like Big Spring, many Texas towns had to find solutions to problems created by growth and new technology.

Reading Check **Summarizing** How did changes in population distribution, such as urban growth, affect Texas cities?

This baseball glove was used in Texas during the early 1900s.

★ Sports, Leisure, and the Arts

During the early 1900s Texans looked for new ways to relax to escape the fast pace of city life and the hard work of rural life. Texans loved sports. Horse racing had long been a favorite Texas pastime. Professional baseball came to Texas in 1888 when the Texas League of Professional Baseball Clubs was formed. The best team in the league's early years was the Corsicana Oilers. Their 51 to 3 defeat of the Texarkana team in 1902 set a professional baseball record. Football, one of the most popular sports in the state today, was new to Texas in the 1890s. The state's oldest college football rivalry began in 1894 when the University of Texas beat Texas A&M 38 to 0. Many Texans also enjoyed boxing. Jack Johnson of Galveston won a heavyweight title by defeating Tommy Burns in 1908. Johnson went on to become the first African American world heavyweight boxing champion.

While sports were becoming more popular, Texans also enjoyed a good show. Children and adults alike loved the circus. Mollie Bailey, who was called the Circus Queen of the Southwest, ran one of the most popular circuses in the state. Her show was billed as "A Texas Show for Texas People." Bailey's circus traveled from town to town, entertaining crowds with dozens of acrobats and animal acts.

Nearly every town had a concert hall or theater where traveling shows performed. Local concert halls often featured **ragtime**, a new form of popular music. One of the earliest and best-known ragtime musicians was **Scott Joplin** of Texarkana. Ragtime musicians toured the state and played in vaudeville shows, which featured music, comedy, dance, and acrobatics acts together in one place. The first movies in Texas were shown in cities during the early 1900s. In Fort Worth the first movie house used bedsheets for a screen, and admission was five cents. San Antonio was home to one of the state's first film studios—Star Film Ranch. Silent movies filmed at Star included *Cyclone Pete's Matrimony* (1910) and *The Immortal Alamo* (1911).

Many Texans also read books for leisure and entertainment. Books about frontier times in Texas were particularly popular. Among the most celebrated Texas authors was Charles A. Siringo. One of his most popular books, *A Texas Cowboy,* told the story of his experiences on the Chisholm Trail. Siringo also wrote a biography of the outlaw Billy the Kid. His books helped establish the romantic myth of the Old West. **William Sydney Porter**, known as O. Henry, became famous for short stories about Texas cowboys. Texas artists also portrayed the state's past. For example, sculptor **Elisabet Ney** specialized in statues of early Texas heroes. Today her statues of Sam Houston and Stephen F. Austin can be seen in the Capitol in Austin.

To encourage interest in the arts and culture, Texas citizens paid for the construction of libraries and museums in cities across the state. During the late 1800s only the largest Texas towns, such as Houston, El Paso, and San Antonio, had libraries. However, with funding from wealthy businessman Andrew Carnegie, a national public library–building boom began. Between 1898 and 1917 Carnegie gave some $645,000 for the construction of 32 libraries in Texas. One of the first museums in Texas was established in 1879 by the Sam Houston Normal Institute to preserve its collection of Sam Houston's documents and materials.

✔**Reading Check Drawing Inferences and Conclusions** How did Texas artists, musicians, and writers contribute to life in the state in the early 1900s?

★ Section 2 Review   ⓉTEKS Questions 2, 3, 4a, 5

go.hrw.com Homework Practice Online
keyword: ST3 HP25

1 Define and explain:
- suburbs
- ragtime

2 Identify and explain:
- Adina Emilia De Zavala
- Texas Highway Department
- Texas Department of Health
- Texas Water Commission
- Scott Joplin
- William Sydney Porter
- Elisabet Ney

3 Analyzing Information
Copy the graphic organizer below. Use it to show the problems of city life and reforms.

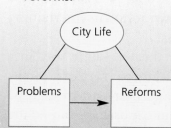

City Life

Problems → Reforms

4 Finding the Main Idea
a. How did new technology change city life and encourage the development of Texas?

b. What did Texans do for leisure and entertainment during the early 1900s?

5 Writing and Critical Thinking
TAKS
Summarizing Imagine that you are living in Dallas in the early 1900s. Write a journal entry describing how the changing population distribution has altered city life.
Consider the following:
- the growing populations of cities
- transportation and health issues

Texas and World Events

Read to Discover

1. How did the Spanish-American War affect Texas?
2. How did the Mexican Revolution of 1910 and raids along the Texas-Mexico border affect the state?
3. What were the effects of World War I on Texas?

Why It Matters Today

During the early 1900s many Mexicans immigrated to Texas. Use CNNfyi.com or other **current events** sources to find information about Mexican immigration today. Record your findings in your journal.

Define

- **refugees**
- **neutral**

Identify

- **Theodore Roosevelt**
- **Rough Riders**
- **Battle of San Juan Hill**
- **Francisco "Pancho" Villa**
- **John J. "Black Jack" Pershing**
- **Plan de San Diego**

The Story Continues

Texas soldiers of the 1st U.S. Volunteer Cavalry were on a mission. Their orders were to capture the port of Santiago de Cuba. First, however, they had to take San Juan Hill and Kettle Hill. The soldiers were scared but well trained. The cavalry unit joined forces with the African American 9th and 10th Cavalries and other regulars to capture Kettle Hill. The soldiers charged up the hill in the tropical heat against fierce gunfire. They captured the hill from the Spanish forces, but at the cost of hundreds of U.S. casualties.

COL. ROOSEVELT
Tells the story of THE ROUGH RIDERS in Scribner's Magazine. It begins in January and will run for six months, with many illustrations from photographs taken in the field.
JANUARY SCRIBNER'S
NOW READY PRICE 25 CENTS

Magazine and newspaper articles spread stories of the 1st U.S. Volunteer Cavalry, also known as the Rough Riders.

★ The Spanish-American War

In 1895, Cubans revolted against Spain. Many Americans supported their fight for independence. When the U.S. battleship *Maine* exploded in Havana Harbor in 1898, some Americans blamed Spain. Newspapers called for war, crying "Remember the *Maine*!" In April 1898 the U.S. government declared war on Spain. Some 10,000 Texans, many still of school age, showed up at recruiting stations volunteering to fight. Soldiers from all over the country learned about weapons and conducted drills on Texas army bases. Texas was an ideal training ground for the war because its hot weather and terrain were similar to those of Cuba.

When Lieutenant Colonel **Theodore Roosevelt** came to Texas to recruit troops, both cowboys and college students joined his 1st U.S.

The Spanish-American War. During the conflict Texas soldiers fought alongside "buffalo soldiers" from the 9th and 10th Cavalries. **How do you think geographic factors affected the fighting in Cuba?**

 Analyzing Primary Sources
Identifying Points of View What was Theodore Roosevelt's general opinion of his Texas troops?

Volunteer Cavalry. This outfit, known as the **Rough Riders**, trained in San Antonio. Roosevelt was proud of his recruits, particularly the Texans.

Texas Voices ❝We drew a great many recruits from Texas. . . . They were splendid shots, horsemen, and trailers [scouts]. They were accustomed [used] to living in the open, to enduring great fatigue [tiredness] and hardship.❞

—Theodore Roosevelt, *The Rough Riders*

The Rough Riders were the first U.S. troops to land in Cuba. They became famous for helping to defeat Spanish troops in the **Battle of San Juan Hill**. Other U.S. forces fought in Cuba, the Philippines, and Puerto Rico. U.S. forces defeated Spain and gained control of these islands. With its victory in the Spanish-American War, the United States expanded its role in world affairs. As a result, Texas continued to be a major training ground for U.S. troops.

⭐ **Reading Check Analyzing Information** What geographic features of Texas made the state a good place to train troops for battle in Cuba?

Pancho Villa (left) met with General John J. Pershing in 1914 near El Paso. During the Mexican Revolution the citizens of El Paso watched rebels capture Ciudad Juárez.

⭐ The Mexican Revolution

Closer to home for Texans was the conflict that erupted in Mexico as rebels overthrew President Porfirio Díaz. Although he was initially an elected leader, Díaz had since ruled as a dictator for many years. Democratic reformers like Francisco Madero were commonly arrested. After getting out of jail in 1910, Madero headed to San Antonio to organize an overthrow of Díaz. Madero joined with other rebels, including **Francisco "Pancho" Villa**, and attacked Mexican forces. At times the fighting was close to the Texas border. The Mexican Revolution forced Díaz to leave office in May 1911. Madero then became president. However, the fighting continued. The violence increased after General Victoriano Huerta had Madero assassinated. For the next several years, various forces fought for control. While Emiliano Zapata led forces in southern Mexico, Villa led forces in the north. The former governor of Coahuila, Venustiano Carranza, also led a force against Huerta. During the revolution, more than 1.5 million Mexicans were killed, and many more lost their homes and land. Many became **refugees**—people forced to leave their homeland because of war or persecution. Thousands of these refugees came to Texas, settling in the Valley and San Antonio.

Fearing that the violence would spill over the border, U.S. leaders closely watched the events in Mexico. Some worried that the war would hurt the American businesses that had invested some $1 billion in Mexico. In April 1914 President Woodrow Wilson sent U.S. Marines to seize Veracruz, Mexico's main port. Wilson hoped to prevent the arrival of a German ship loaded with guns and ammunition for Huerta. After negotiations, Huerta left office and Carranza became president. But civil war broke out again, and violence continued in Mexico until the 1920s.

⭐ **Reading Check** **Evaluating** What was a major social effect of the Mexican Revolution on Texas?

⭐ Border Troubles

Pancho Villa was angered by U.S. recognition of his rival, Carranza, as president. In 1916 Villa's forces stopped a train headed south from El Paso and shot 18 American passengers. In March, Villa's forces raided Columbus, New Mexico, leaving 17 of its citizens dead. In response to these raids, Wilson sent General **John J. "Black Jack" Pershing** and some 15,000 U.S. troops from Fort Bliss into northern Mexico to find Villa. The U.S. troops searched the rough landscape but failed to capture Villa. Pershing returned home in January 1917.

The Mexican Revolution also led to conflicts in South Texas. Many people from the midwestern United States had recently moved to the region to start their own farms and ranches. Clashes broke out with many Mexican American families who had lived on the land for generations.

Inspired by the Mexican Revolution, some Mexican Americans began to talk about rebelling against Texas. The radicals drafted a document called the **Plan de San Diego**. The plan called for Mexican Americans to take control of South Texas and declare it independent. From 1915 to 1917, supporters of the rebellion raided the property of many new residents in the Rio Grande valley. They killed 21 people and caused millions of dollars in property damage. Some angry citizens and Texas Rangers killed about 300 Mexicans and Mexican Americans in revenge. The conflicts on the border led to greater distrust between Mexican Americans and other Texans.

⭐ **Reading Check** **Summarizing** How did the Mexican Revolution and the migration of people from the Midwest to South Texas lead to conflict there?

Connecting To *Literature*

Jovita González de Mireles
Jovita González de Mireles was born in 1903 on a ranch in South Texas. González de Mireles was a public school teacher who became known for her novels, folk songs, and folktales about Tejano culture. Her novel *Dew on the Thorn* explores the relations between Mexican Americans and other Texans. One character declares that her family will stay on their land. "This land is ours. . . . It was blessed by the blood of our ancestors who fought and suffered for it and conquered it, that we, their children, might have a home!" **How has González de Mireles's work helped Tejanos maintain their cultural heritage?** ⭐TEKS

Interpreting the Visual Record

World War I. This Fort Worth parade honored returning Texas troops in 1918. **What does this photograph reveal about life in Fort Worth in the early 1900s?**

GLOBAL CONNECTIONS

The Political Origins of World War I

In 1914 Europe was divided between two major alliances: the Central Powers and the Allied Powers. A conflict erupted when Gavrilo Princip, a Serb, assassinated Austrian archduke Franz Ferdinand in Sarajevo in June 1914. In response, Austria-Hungary declared war on Serbia. Russia then declared war on Austria-Hungary. Germany, an ally of Austria-Hungary, declared war on Russia and its allies France and Britain. Soon, much of Europe was drawn into the war. **What were some of the causes of World War I?**

★ Texans and World War I

While the Mexican Revolution was being fought, World War I erupted in Europe in 1914. The Allied Powers—Great Britain, France, and Russia—battled the Central Powers. These were Germany and its allies—Austria-Hungary and Turkey. Most Americans wanted to remain **neutral**—not aligned with either side in a conflict—but this was difficult. In 1915, German submarines sank the British passenger ship *Lusitania*, killing 1,198 passengers, including 128 Americans. The German government also tried to ally itself with Mexico, promising to help it regain territory lost to the United States—including Texas. These actions greatly angered most Americans.

The United States declared war on Germany on April 6, 1917. More than 2 million Americans, including nearly 200,000 Texans, went to fight. Before going to Europe, many U.S. soldiers trained in Texas. The army sent them to Camp MacArthur in Waco, Camp Logan in Houston, and Camp Travis in San Antonio. Military pilots trained at Hicks Field in Fort Worth and at Kelly Field in San Antonio. Katherine and Marjorie Stinson owned the Stinson School of Flying in San Antonio, where some pilots were trained.

Once they arrived in Europe, soldiers spent weeks living in trenches, often ankle-deep in mud. These long shoulder-deep holes were dug in the ground to protect soldiers from bullets and artillery shells. Soldiers also faced German machine guns, artillery, and poison gas. In October 1918 one U.S. company was stopped by heavy machine-gun fire. Using hand grenades captured from the enemy, Texan Samuel M. Sampler attacked the German trenches. The young Texan single-handedly captured 28 German soldiers. Sampler was one of four Texans to win the Congressional Medal of Honor in World War I.

Other Texans played important roles in President Wilson's government. Edward M. House of Austin was a close adviser to the president. Albert Sidney Burleson and Thomas Watt Gregory served as the postmaster general of the United States and the U.S. attorney general, respectively. President Wilson also asked Jesse Jones of Houston to serve as the director of general military relief for the American Red Cross.

Back home, Texans showed their support for the war effort. They bought Liberty bonds, which the U.S. government issued to pay for the war. Texans also observed meatless Mondays and wheatless Wednesdays, so that more food would be available for soldiers. Texans stepped up agricultural production. Farmers borrowed money for more land and equipment, which led to a farming boom. Texas oil and lumber production also boomed to meet military needs. Businesses near military bases provided goods and services to troops stationed there. As the Texas economy expanded during the war, the state reached almost full employment. Women took on more responsibilities, working in the fields as well as in businesses.

Because the war was with Germany, some Texans accused German Americans of being unpatriotic and of not supporting the United States. These feelings ran high. Even the name of the popular German food sauerkraut was changed to "liberty cabbage." The war ended when Germany surrendered in November 1918. Texas soldiers came home, and the nation returned to a peacetime economy.

This World War I poster encourages U.S. citizens to plant gardens and raise crops to support the war effort.

★ **Reading Check Finding the Main Idea** How did World War I affect the Texas economy?

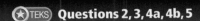

Section 3 Review ⊕TEKS Questions 2, 3, 4a, 4b, 5

go.hrw.com Homework Practice Online
keyword: ST3 HP25

1 Define and explain:
- refugees
- neutral

2 Identify and explain:
- Theodore Roosevelt
- Rough Riders
- Battle of San Juan Hill
- Francisco "Pancho" Villa
- John J. "Black Jack" Pershing
- Plan de San Diego

3 Evaluating
Copy the graphic organizer below. Use it to show how events in Mexico and along the border affected Texas.

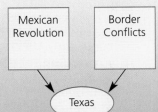

Mexican Revolution → Texas
Border Conflicts → Texas

4 Finding the Main Idea
a. What effect did the Spanish-American War have on Texas?
b. How was the Texas agricultural industry affected by World War I?

5 Writing and Critical Thinking TAKS
Evaluating Imagine that you lived in Texas during World War I. Write a letter to a friend explaining how the war affected your hometown.
Consider the following:
- the social, economic, and political effects
- Texans who fought in the war

The Chapter at a Glance

Examine the following visual summary of the chapter. Then use the visual to create a one-page summary of the chapter that you and a classmate can use as a study guide. ⭐TEKS

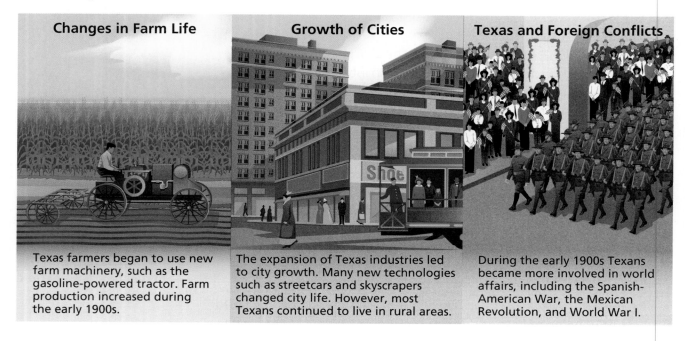

Changes in Farm Life

Texas farmers began to use new farm machinery, such as the gasoline-powered tractor. Farm production increased during the early 1900s.

Growth of Cities

The expansion of Texas industries led to city growth. Many new technologies such as streetcars and skyscrapers changed city life. However, most Texans continued to live in rural areas.

Texas and Foreign Conflicts

During the early 1900s Texans became more involved in world affairs, including the Spanish-American War, the Mexican Revolution, and World War I.

Identifying People and Ideas ⭐TEKS

Use the following terms or people in historically significant sentences.

1. urbanization
2. Houston Ship Channel
3. suburbs
4. Scott Joplin
5. William Sydney Porter
6. Elisabet Ney
7. refugees
8. Rough Riders
9. Francisco "Pancho" Villa
10. Plan de San Diego

Understanding Main Ideas ⭐TEKS

Section 1 (pp. 518–521)
1. How did new technologies affect agricultural development in Texas?
2. What economic factors led to increased urbanization in Texas?

Section 2 (pp. 522–526)
3. How did new technologies contribute to the urban development of Texas?
4. How did the changing population distribution in Texas affect cities during the early 1900s?

Section 3 (pp. 527–531)
5. How did the Mexican Revolution affect Texas?

6. How did World War I affect the economy and society of Texas?

You Be the Historian ⭐TEKS

Reviewing Themes

1. **Geography** How did its shared border with Mexico affect events in Texas during the early 1900s?
2. **Economics** How did the state's economy affect immigration and migration to Texas?
3. **Global Relations** What role did Texans play in the Spanish-American War and World War I?

TAKS Practice: **Thinking Critically** ⭐TEKS

1. **Comparing and Contrasting** Compare and contrast the uses of technology on farms and in cities before and after the new developments of the early 1900s.
2. **Drawing Inferences and Conclusions** How do you think the use of machines in farming contributed to city growth?
3. **Evaluating** How did immigration and migration to Texas lead to political conflict?

Interpreting Graphs ⭐TEKS

Study the bar graph below. Then use the information in the graph to help you answer the questions that follow.

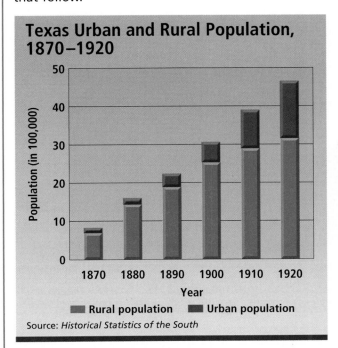

Texas Urban and Rural Population, 1870–1920

Rural population ▪ Urban population

Source: *Historical Statistics of the South*

1. Approximately how many more people lived in urban areas of Texas in 1920 than in 1870?
   a. 1.4 million
   b. 25 million
   c. 1 million
   d. 4 million

2. What factors do you think may have contributed to this change in population distribution?

Analyzing Primary Sources ⭐TEKS

Read the following lyrics to a popular song from the late 1800s. Then answer the questions.

"Come, boys, I have something to tell you,
Come near, I would whisper it low;
You are thinking of leaving the homestead.
Don't be in a hurry to go.
The city has many attractions,
But think of the vices [bad habits] and sins,
When once in the vortex [whirl] of fashion,
How soon the course downward begins.
(Chorus:)
Stay on the farm, stay on the farm,
Though profits come in rather slow,
Stay on the farm, stay on the farm;
Don't be in a hurry to go."

3. What problems does the author of this song see with city life?
   a. Its profits come in slowly.
   b. Everyone is in a hurry.
   c. It is full of dangers.
   d. Everyone talks too loudly.

4. What change in the population distribution does this song characterize as a negative trend?

Alternative Assessment

Cooperative Learning ⭐TEKS

Work with a small group to complete the following activity. Each person should select one of the following themes: a) immigration and geographic patterns, b) the Spanish-American War and World War I, c) new technology, d) the growth of Texas cities. Each member should pose questions and create answers based on the theme chosen. Combine the questions and answers and hold a quiz show about the chapter.

BUILDING YOUR Portfolio

 internet connect

Internet Activity: go.hrw.com
KEYWORD: ST3 TX25 ⭐TEKS

Access the Internet through the HRW Go site to research events of the Mexican Revolution and its impact in Texas. Some refugees wrote *corridos*—or ballads—about their experiences. Create your own *corrido* with the information you have found. Include a short explanation of how Mexican Americans have maintained their cultural heritage while adapting to the larger Texas culture.

CHAPTER 26

Boom and Bust

(1920–1939)

Ma Ferguson was a popular governor despite charges of corruption in her administration.

Republican Herbert Hoover won the majority of Texas votes for president in 1928.

1920 Governor William Hobby breaks a dockworkers' strike in Galveston.

TEXAS

1924 Texans elect Miriam A. "Ma" Ferguson as the state's first female governor.

1926 Automobile registrations reach 1 million.

1928 For the first time in the state's history, the majority of Texans vote for a Republican presidential candidate—Herbert Hoover.

| **1920** | **1922** | **1924** | **1926** | **1928** |

U.S. and WORLD

1922 Americans spend some $60 million on radios.

1924 Jazz music reaches a wider audience with the first public performance of George Gershwin's *Rhapsody in Blue.*

1926 The United States imports some $4.4 billion worth of goods.

1929 The U.S. stock market crashes, leading to business failures and massive unemployment.

1920 The Nineteenth Amendment is ratified, giving women the right to vote.

Women held parades and rallies to build public support for suffrage.

The Granger Collection, New York

Build on What You Know

Texas had become increasingly urbanized during the early 1900s. The Texas economy had expanded to meet the military's needs during World War I. But the postwar period brought social unrest and economic troubles. Although some enjoyed boom times in the 1920s, hard times lay ahead.

A MULE AND A PLOW

RESETTLEMENT ADMINISTRATION
Small Loans Give Farmers a New Start

During the Great Depression the U.S. government established programs to help farmers.

TEXAS

CENTENNIAL·CELEBRATIONS

The Texas Centennial was celebrated with a world's fair in Dallas.

1932 Some 300,000 Texans are unemployed.

1934 James V Allred is elected governor of Texas.

1936 Texas celebrates the 100th anniversary of the Texas Revolution.

1938 Texans elect W. Lee "Pappy" O'Daniel as governor.

1930   **1932**   **1934**   **1936**   **1938**

1932 U.S. voters choose Democrat Franklin D. Roosevelt to be their next president.

1934 The Federal Farm Bankruptcy Act extends credit to farmers in danger of losing their farms.

1936 The U.S. government creates a program to promote soil conservation.

1938 The Fair Labor Standards Act sets a minimum wage for some American workers.

Franklin D. Roosevelt won wide support from Americans who were unhappy with President Hoover's policies.

If you were there . . .
How would you help others during an economic depression?

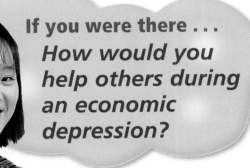

You Be the Historian

Themes Journal

What's Your Opinion? Do you **agree** or **disagree** with the following statements? Support your point of view in your journal.

● **Economics** War affects industries but not the agricultural economy.

● **Geography** Farmers change the environment, without any environmental consequences.

● **Citizenship** To fight for equal rights is an act of civic responsibility.

The Transition to Peace

Read to Discover

1. In what ways did World War I affect Texas?
2. What steps were taken to protect the civil rights of Texans following World War I?
3. Why was Miriam A. "Ma" Ferguson a controversial governor?

Why It Matters Today

Civil rights organizations became active in Texas during the 1920s. Use CNNfyi.com or other **current events** sources to learn about civil and human rights organizations today. Record your findings in your journal.

Define

- demobilization
- primary election
- white primary

Identify

- **Pat Neff**
- **Miriam A. "Ma" Ferguson**
- **Dan Moody**
- **National Association for the Advancement of Colored People**
- **Lawrence A. Nixon**
- **League of United Latin American Citizens**

The Story Continues

A crisis hit Galveston on March 19, 1920. A national dockworkers' strike that had swept down the East Coast had reached the Texas port. In the days that followed, Texans anxiously waited as they heard reports of beatings and even shootings. Governor William Hobby took action and declared martial law. National Guard troops shut down the city and watched as workers loaded 8,700 tons of freight that had been sitting on the docks.

Galveston dockworkers used pulleys to lift heavy bales of cotton and other cargo.

★ Demobilization and Labor Unrest

The dockworkers were struggling to make ends meet in the slowing U.S. economy that followed World War I. During the war, farms and factories had increased production to keep up with the U.S. military's needs. Many Texans had moved from farms to cities to take jobs in industries that were offering high wages to attract workers. When the war ended, the United States began the process of **demobilization**, or moving from a wartime to a peacetime economy. Soldiers returning home needed jobs, often displacing female and African American workers who had taken jobs in industry during the war. As military spending was cut, the economy slowed and competition for jobs increased. Some businesses laid off workers or reduced wages, creating hardships for many workers.

In 1919 some 4 million American workers went on strike for higher wages and better working conditions. Texas had its share of labor troubles. Two years after the Galveston dockworkers' strike, a railroad strike erupted in Denison and other Texas towns. **Pat Neff**, whom Texans had elected governor in 1920, declared martial law. Order was soon restored, and the railroad workers returned to their jobs.

Labor issues were not the only challenges Texans encountered. During World War I various groups had faced discrimination. Because the United States was fighting Germany, some Americans turned against everything German. For example, in 1919 Governor Hobby vetoed a bill to provide money for the German department at the University of Texas. Racial tension had also increased. African Americans made up some 31,000 of the nearly 200,000 Texans who served in the war. When black soldiers who were serving their country began demanding equal rights, many white Texans responded angrily. A riot in Houston involving African American soldiers and local residents resulted in 20 deaths. On questionable evidence, 19 soldiers were hanged for their part in the conflict.

African American veterans. Some African Americans who served in World War I returned to Texas to find discrimination and a slowing economy. **Why might African American veterans join veterans organizations?**

Violence increased with the formation of a new Ku Klux Klan in the early 1920s. Wearing hoods to hide their identities, Klan members threatened, attacked, and sometimes murdered people whom they disliked. They targeted African Americans, Jews, Roman Catholics, and recent immigrants. The Klan became a powerful political force in Texas. It helped elect mayors, members of the legislature, and U.S. senator Earle Mayfield. Many law enforcement officials had Klan connections. As one black Texan recalled, "A person couldn't trust nobody. Even the law was hooked up with them a lot of the time." In the mid-1920s internal disagreements and growing opposition to the Klan led to a decline in its power and influence in Texas.

Reading Check Analyzing Information What challenges did Texans face after World War I?

Biography

Miriam A. "Ma" Ferguson
(1875–1961)

Miriam Amanda Wallace was born in Bell County, Texas. In 1899 she married James Ferguson, who became governor of Texas in 1915. At first, Miriam Ferguson showed little interest in politics. She ran for governor in 1924 only because her husband could not. After a controversial first term, Ferguson was defeated in her 1926 re-election campaign. However, Texans elected her as governor again in 1932. Ferguson limited state spending while increasing state aid to Texans during the 1930s. Ferguson ran for a third term in 1940. **What actions did Ferguson take in her second term?**

Ma Ferguson's supporters celebrated her election by wearing inauguration pins and other festive items.

★ The Ferguson Administration

The influence of the Ku Klux Klan was a major issue in the 1924 governor's election. Candidate **Miriam A. "Ma" Ferguson** took a strong stand against the Klan. During the campaign she also promised Texans "two governors for the price of one." James E. Ferguson, her husband and campaign manager, had been governor from 1915 to 1917. Because he had been impeached and removed from office, he could not run for governor again. Nonetheless, the Fergusons were popular among many Texans. Reporters referred to Miriam Ferguson as Ma, and James Ferguson as Pa. Miriam Ferguson won the election, becoming the first female governor of Texas and the second female governor in U.S. history.

Miriam Ferguson was a controversial governor. Critics accused her husband of using his wife's influence to sell pardons to raise money. She pardoned more than 1,000 prisoners, many more than other Texas governors had pardoned. Unlike other governors of the 1920s, Ferguson did little to help education. For example, William Hobby's administration had led the effort to have the state provide students with free textbooks. Governor Neff had signed a bill creating Texas Technological College, now Texas Tech University, which opened in Lubbock in 1925.

Critics also accused the Fergusons of giving Highway Department contracts to friends instead of to the lowest bidder. In one lawsuit, Texas attorney general **Dan Moody** charged that the state was paying $7 million for work worth only $2 million. As a result of Moody's actions, several highway contracts were changed or canceled. In 1926 Ferguson lost her bid for re-election to Moody. At age 33, Moody became the youngest governor ever elected in Texas. He reorganized the highway department and reformed the prison system. He also appointed Jane McCallum, a reformer active in child care, education, and women's rights, as secretary of state. Moody easily won re-election in 1928.

Reading Check **Finding the Main Idea** How was the election of Miriam Ferguson a first in Texas history?

★ Early Civil Rights Efforts

Many Texans were becoming politically active by joining civil rights organizations such as the **National Association for the Advancement of Colored People** (NAACP). Founded in New York City in 1909, the NAACP opened its first Texas chapter in El Paso in 1915. The state soon had 31 NAACP chapters claiming some 7,000 members. However, many Texans violently opposed the NAACP's efforts. By 1923 only five Texas chapters remained in operation. Only in the late 1930s did the NAACP again become an important force in Texas.

In the 1920s many politically active African Americans centered their efforts on gaining voting rights. Texas had used a variety of methods—including a poll tax—to stop African Americans from voting. In 1923 a new law barred black Texans from voting in the Democratic **primary election**, which selected candidates to run in the later general election. Because the Republican Party was weak in Texas, this **white primary** effectively prevented African Americans from voting. When <u>Lawrence A. Nixon</u>, a black doctor from El Paso, was not allowed to vote in a Democratic primary in 1924, he filed suit against the state. The U.S. Supreme Court struck down the Texas law in 1927. The Texas legislature then gave the Democratic State Committee the power to exclude African Americans from primary elections. This move barred black Texans from voting for years to come.

African Americans faced discrimination in other areas. Teacher Lula Byars described her school. "I remember . . . nailing a piece of cardboard over the window to keep the cold wind out." African American newspapers such as the *Dallas Express* and the *San Antonio Register* called for an end to discrimination. Clifford Richardson of the *Houston Informer and Texas Freeman* and other black editors wrote editorials attacking racial violence.

Mexican Americans also struggled for equal rights. They were discriminated against in hotels, restaurants, and schools. In some counties, Mexican Americans could not vote in the Democratic primary. As one woman later recalled, "We Mexicanos had to fight for everything we ever had, even the right to go to school." To fight for their rights, Mexican Americans organized the <u>League of United Latin American Citizens</u> (LULAC) in Corpus Christi in 1929. It soon became the best-known Mexican American civil rights organization in the nation.

The Crisis, a monthly magazine published by the NAACP, documented cases of racial inequality and discrimination.

★ **Reading Check** **Summarizing** Describe the civil rights efforts of various groups in Texas during the 1920s.

Section 1 Review

★TEKS Questions 3, 4a, 5

Homework Practice Online
keyword: ST3 HP26

1 Define and explain:
- demobilization
- primary election
- white primary

2 Identify and explain:
- Pat Neff
- Miriam A. "Ma" Ferguson
- Dan Moody
- National Association for the Advancement of Colored People
- Lawrence A. Nixon
- League of United Latin American Citizens

3 Sequencing
Copy the chart below. Use it to discuss some of the significant actions Texas governors took during the 1920s, and the order in which they occurred.

Neff
↓
| Ferguson |
↓
| Moody |

4 Finding the Main Idea
a. Describe civil rights efforts in Texas after World War I.
b. What problems arose during Miriam Ferguson's administration?

5 Writing and Critical Thinking **TAKS**
Summarizing Write a paragraph explaining how World War I affected Texans economically, socially, and politically.
Consider the following:
- the wartime boom and demobilization
- civil rights efforts

Economic and Cultural Change

Read to Discover

1. What Texas industries boomed during the 1920s?
2. How did the boom-and-bust cycle affect Texas farmers?
3. How did life change in Texas during the Jazz Age?

Why It Matters Today

Consumer goods became an important part of the Texas and U.S. economies during the 1920s. Use CNNfyi.com or other **current events** sources to learn about how a consumer item affects people today. Record your findings in your journal.

Define

- **blues**
- **consumer goods**

Identify

- C. M. "Dad" Joiner

The Story Continues

The oil workers could not decide where to place the old, worn-out rig to begin drilling. Mrs. Daisy Bradford, who owned the land, had suggested they move the rig downhill. When the rig reached the bottom of the hill, Mrs. Bradford shouted, "Stop boys. Drill right there." Although she did not know it at the time, Mrs. Bradford had chosen a spot that would yield one of the greatest oil strikes in Texas history.

Oil workers used rotary drill bits to drill hundreds of feet to reach oil deposits.

★ Economic Growth

The oil boom that had boosted the Texas economy since the Spindletop strike in 1901 continued into the 1920s. New fields were discovered during and just after World War I at Ranger and Burkburnett. Other fields opened at Big Spring, Borger, and Mexia, and a discovery in Nueces County led Corpus Christi to become a major port for oil products. One of the biggest oil discoveries in Texas history was made by a wildcatter named <u>**C. M. "Dad" Joiner**</u>. He had leased land in East Texas from Daisy Bradford. In October 1930 his third well—the Daisy Bradford No. 3—"blew in," opening one of the largest oil fields in the world. The East Texas oil field extended from Henderson and Kilgore to Longview and Gladewater. By midsummer 1931 this oil field produced some 900,000 barrels of oil per day. In 1933 it produced more than 216 million barrels, accounting for more than 20 percent of U.S. oil production.

Oil discoveries made fortunes for a number of other Texans, including Howard Hughes, H. L. Hunt, Clint Murchison, and Sid Richardson. Hughes had developed a drill bit that could drill through very hard rock, allowing producers to reach previously unavailable oil reserves. Oil production in Texas increased as a result of this technological innovation. His son, Howard Hughes Jr., used the family wealth to become a leader in the aviation and filmmaking industries. Some Texans grew wealthy in the oil fields, but the work was hard, as one oilman recalled.

Texas Voices "When I went to work for the Magnolia Petroleum Company in '27, we worked eighty-four hours a week. We worked seven twelve-hour days with an occasional day off once or twice a month. . . . Most of the work was done with shovels, teams [of mules], and wagons, and a few trucks. And it took lots of men and lots of man-hours to do the work that we can do in a few hours today."

—Bruce Turner, quoted in *Tales from the Derrick Floor*, by Mody C. Boatright and William A. Owens

Cotton mills and clothing manufacturers also employed many Texans. Meatpacking and other industries that processed farm and ranch products continued to be important to the Texas economy.

Reading Check **Analyzing Information** What influence do you think Texas oil production had on local and national markets?

⭐ Hard Times for Farmers

Despite this industrial growth, most Texans still worked in agriculture. Farmers had expanded production to meet the military's demands during World War I. New irrigation methods, such as advanced windmills, made it possible to grow cotton and wheat in areas that were once too dry for farming, such as the Panhandle. As one farmer noted, "This land we're standing on is just a crust over a great big underground lake [Ogallala Aquifer]." With its flat, treeless land, the Panhandle was well suited for large farm machines. Irrigation and mechanization increased West Texas cotton production from 51,000 bales in 1918 to 1.1 million in 1926. As farming boomed, Panhandle ranches were divided into small farms. By 1924, more than 2.3 million acres were being farmed in the Panhandle, up from just 45,000 acres in 1909.

As farming increased in the Panhandle, many ranchers moved their herds to the south and east. Central Texas, the Gulf Coast, and the Pecos River region became important ranching centers. In much of these areas topsoil was thin and rainfall was spotty, making farming difficult. Conditions were better for farming in some parts of South Texas. Farmers there planted vast citrus-fruit orchards that produced oranges, grapefruits, lemons, and limes.

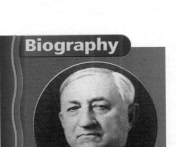

Biography

C. M. "Dad" Joiner
(1860–1947)

Born in Alabama, Columbus Marion Joiner served in the Tennessee legislature before moving to Oklahoma Territory in 1897. Although trained as a lawyer, he became involved in the oil business. In 1926 he moved to Texas to search for oil. In Rusk County, Joiner struck oil on his third try in 1930. He earned the nickname "Dad" for being the "father" of the East Texas oil field he had discovered. By 1938 Joiner was worth some $3 million. Joiner faced many legal problems, however, and lost much of his wealth. **How did C. M. "Dad" Joiner contribute to the economic development of Texas?** ⭐TEKS

Texas Cities

Corpus Christi

History: In 1839 Henry L. Kinney established a trading house and ranch on the site of present-day Corpus Christi. Tourism and industry increased, and Corpus Christi grew rapidly.

Population in 2000: 277,454

Relative location: On the Gulf Coast at the mouth of the Nueces River

Region: Southern edge of the Gulf Coast Plain

County: County seat of Nueces County

Special feature: Largest city on the coastal bend

Origin of name: Legend has it that Álvarez de Pineda named the nearby bay Corpus Christi because he arrived there on the festival day of Corpus Christi, which is Latin for "body of Christ."

Economy: Corpus Christi is a major port city. Ocean freighters and oil supertankers serve the entire South Texas area through Corpus Christi Bay. Industries include fishing, oil refining, and tourism.

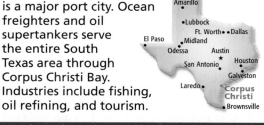

The prosperity that most farmers enjoyed during World War I did not last. Growth in the use of synthetic, or artificial, fabrics hurt demand for cotton. Farmers soon grew more cotton than Americans wanted to buy. Overproduction meant lower prices and profits. In April 1920, cotton sold for 42 cents a pound. A year later, it sold for less than 10 cents a pound. Even as farmers received less money for their crops, the cost of operating farms was rising. Farmers had to invest in farm machinery, and land prices in the Panhandle increased. One West Texas farmer recorded his thoughts about the crisis in his diary.

 Texas Voices ❝Cotton down to 4 cents per pound. How can a man pay his debts and live at such prices. Things one has to have is as high as if cotton was 25 to 35 cents per lb. One can not pay his debts. I have nothing to show for my year's work. Only some new debts.❞

—William G. DeLoach, *Plains Farmer*, edited by Janet M. Neugebauer

 Reading Check Identifying Cause and Effect Describe the boom-and-bust cycle of farming during and following World War I, and explain why it occurred.

★ The Jazz Age in Texas

While cotton farmers were experiencing hard times, many Texans were enjoying the social changes brought by the 1920s. The decade has several nicknames including the "Jazz Age" and the "Roaring Twenties." Jazz arose from the **blues**, a musical form with lyrics that often reflected the difficulties people faced in life. African American artists created jazz, which soon became associated with the decade's energy and excitement. Dances such as the bunny hug, the Charleston, and the fox-trot also became popular in the 1920s. In addition, families and friends liked attending baseball and football games. The development of a new technology—the radio—changed entertainment in Texas. Texans listened to music, news reports, and sports broadcasts. By the end of 1922 Texas had 25 commercial radio stations operating.

Texans also loved going to the movies, particularly westerns. Early films were in black and white and had no sound. A piano player or a phonograph typically provided music to accompany the scenes on the movie screen. It was not until 1927 that a movie with sound, *The Jazz*

Singer, was released. *Wings,* one of the five major movies filmed in Texas during the 1920s, won the first Academy Award for best motion picture.

Texans had more leisure time partly because of **consumer goods**—items intended for personal use—that made household tasks much easier. Electric sewing machines and household appliances such as refrigerators, toasters, and vacuum cleaners became more common in the 1920s. The demand for these and other consumer goods also led to the growing popularity of large department stores in cities such as Dallas and Houston.

One of the most popular consumer goods was the car. In 1916, Texans registered some 195,000 cars, a number that grew to 1 million just 10 years later. The automobile industry's growth boosted both demand for oil products and the Texas economy. Automobiles, trucks, and buses brought other economic changes to Texans. By using trucks to haul products to markets, farmers became less reliant on railroads. Bus lines competed with railroads for passengers. The popularity of cars soon created a need for more roads. In 1922 Governor Pat Neff called for "a big road building program for this State, not a little, sickly, puny one." The following year the Texas Highway Department received money from a tax on gasoline to build roads. Road construction moved slowly, however—in 1930 only 7,300 miles of paved roads crossed Texas.

Despite these advances, not all Texans were pleased with the changes the Jazz Age was bringing. Some worried that the automobile was destroying traditional values. Young people were more likely to drive around in the family car than to spend time with other family members. Texans also worried that people were drinking too much alcohol. As a result, many Texans supported prohibition, which was in effect throughout the 1920s until its repeal in 1933.

✔**Reading Check** **Summarizing** How did life in Texas change during the Jazz Age?

CONNECTING TO Music

Texas Blues

The blues is a form of music that African Americans living in the South created in the late 1800s. Blues singers and performers drew upon both African and American musical traditions to create music that told of the suffering African Americans endured. Several Texans contributed to the development and popularity of the blues. Blind Lemon Jefferson performed in the Dallas area, and his records were popular in northern states. One of the most famous Texas bluesmen, Robert Johnson, came from Mississippi, but recorded his music in Dallas and San Antonio. **How does the blues reflect the cultural diversity of Texas?** ⭐TEKS

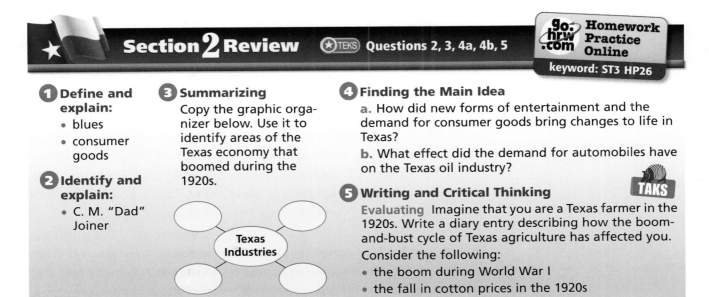

Section 2 Review ⭐TEKS Questions 2, 3, 4a, 4b, 5

go.hrw.com **Homework Practice Online**
keyword: ST3 HP26

1 Define and explain:
- blues
- consumer goods

2 Identify and explain:
- C. M. "Dad" Joiner

3 Summarizing
Copy the graphic organizer below. Use it to identify areas of the Texas economy that boomed during the 1920s.

Texas Industries

4 Finding the Main Idea
a. How did new forms of entertainment and the demand for consumer goods bring changes to life in Texas?
b. What effect did the demand for automobiles have on the Texas oil industry?

5 Writing and Critical Thinking TAKS
Evaluating Imagine that you are a Texas farmer in the 1920s. Write a diary entry describing how the boom-and-bust cycle of Texas agriculture has affected you. Consider the following:
- the boom during World War I
- the fall in cotton prices in the 1920s

Read to Discover

1. How did the Great Depression affect life in Texas?
2. How did Texans respond to the crisis?
3. What caused the Dust Bowl, and how did it affect Texans?

Why It Matters Today

The U.S. economy greatly affected the lives of Texans during the 1920s and 1930s. Use **CNNfyi.com** or other **current events** sources to learn about the U.S. economy today. Record your findings in your journal.

Define

- stocks
- soup kitchens
- breadlines
- scrip
- proration

Identify

- **Great Depression**
- **Ross Sterling**
- **Dust Bowl**

The Story Continues

At stockbrokers' offices throughout the United States, boys posted cards displaying the latest stock prices from the New York Stock Exchange. On one day in October 1929, they could not keep up with the changing prices. At the end of the day, the reporting of stock prices had fallen more than an hour behind. Investors had no idea what the values of their stocks were. They did know one thing for certain—prices were falling faster than anyone had ever seen before.

Stock tickers recorded the dropping stock prices during the crash of 1929.

★ An Economic Crisis

Companies sell **stocks**—shares of ownership—to raise money. Many people buy stocks hoping to sell them later and make a profit. During the 1920s the price of many stocks rose steeply. Many Americans began to speculate, buying stocks in an attempt to make a quick profit. Then in late October 1929, a panic spread at the New York Stock Exchange as people rushed to sell their stocks. This panic led to a stock market crash. Thousands of shares rapidly lost their value. Many people who had invested their savings in stocks were left with nothing.

The effects of the stock market crash were soon felt throughout the United States. Many banks that had been successful in Texas and other states were forced to close because they had made too many loans to people who now could not repay them. People who had savings in these banks sometimes lost all of their money. As people lost their savings, they bought less. Businesses began laying off workers to reduce expenses. Workers who were unemployed, or without work, could not buy as much food, clothing, or other goods as they once had. When demand for these goods fell, business was hurt even more. As this cycle continued, the economic slowdown became a depression.

During the first year of the depression, many people believed the economy would improve quickly. A Houston newspaper editor dismissed the stock market crash. "The changes in stock prices are purely an affair of and for the stock speculators." This optimistic spirit did not last long, however. The global economic slowdown in the 1930s was so severe that it became known as the **Great Depression**. Millions of people throughout the world became unemployed. By 1933 some 15 million American workers were unemployed and millions of families were on relief, or public assistance. Thousands of families lost their homes, and many people had to beg for money on the streets.

Governor **Ross Sterling** announced in 1932 that some 300,000 Texans were unemployed. African Americans and Mexican Americans were hit particularly hard. They were often the first to be laid off from work so that white employees could keep their jobs. As a result, many Mexican Americans returned to Mexico. Two San Antonio women later described life during the depression.

Texas Voices ❝Some of us had lost our homes which were nearly paid for, had sold our furniture, piece by piece, our jewelry, and even most of our clothes, hoping against hope that something in the way of a job would materialize [appear].❞

—Stella Boone and Ethel Stringer, quoted in *Women of the Depression,* by Julia Kirk Blackwelder

⭐ **Reading Check** **Finding the Main Idea** How were the banking industry and the production of goods and services in Texas affected by the boom-and-bust cycle after the stock market crashed?

Dallas Museum of Art, Otis Dozier, *The Annual Move*, 1985.125

Interpreting the Visual Record

Effects of the depression. This painting, entitled The Annual Move, *shows a depression-era family being forced to move.* **Based on the landscape, how do you think the family's harvest might have affected their situation?**

The Great Depression left many Texans out of work and seeking relief.

★ The Depression in Texas

The depression was somewhat less severe in Texas than it was in many other states. Most Texas farmers could at least feed their own families, and the oil industry continued to provide many jobs. Texans' need for assistance grew as the depression continued. Churches and private organizations tried to help as many people as possible, setting up **soup kitchens** and **breadlines** to give out food. Charitable organizations also donated clothing and provided shelters. Basic necessities were scarce, as one Texan recalled.

> **Texas Voices** ❝People around here just didn't have much money for anything, including clothes. During that time, people used cloth feed sacks to make garments to wear. People that had those sacks . . . made clothes for their children. All of our children's underwear was made out of the sacks.❞
>
> —Monroe Brannon, quoted in *The Loblolly Book II*, edited by Thad Sitton and Lincoln King

The Red Cross helped some 3,000 people in Dickens County—a county of fewer than 9,000 residents. However, charitable organizations could not assist everyone who needed aid. As the depression deepened, many Texans and other Americans grew frightened and angry.

Local governments also struggled to deal with the Great Depression. To reduce spending, many cities and counties cut jobs. One Texan complained, "This thing of cutting salaries and laying off employees, is one of the main things that has brought on this depression era." Local governments also issued **scrip**, or paper notes, to save money. These paper notes were a promise to pay at a later date. For example, teachers in San Antonio received scrip for their salary. Such measures did little to help the Texas economy or to boost confidence.

President Herbert Hoover and Governor Ross Sterling—like many Texans—opposed government programs such as unemployment relief because they worried about destroying individuals' self-reliance. They supported limited government aid to businesses. They believed that once businesses had recovered, new jobs would be created and the economy would revive. However, Texans and other Americans grew increasingly unhappy with these policies as the depression continued.

⭐ Reading Check Summarizing How did the Great Depression affect Texans?

★ A Crisis in the Oil Industry

As the depression deepened, the Texas oil industry faced a crisis. The East Texas oil discovery led to overproduction. The price of oil dropped from more than $1 per barrel to a dangerously low 8 cents per barrel. These low prices threatened to ruin profits and the Texas oil industry.

CONNECTING TO
ECONOMICS AND MATH

Texans at Work

Texans worked in a variety of industries during the Great Depression. Create a pie chart of the jobs Texans had in 1930.

INDUSTRY	NUMBER EMPLOYED
Agriculture	838,571
Manufacturing and mechanical	386,184
Trade	260,399

Interpreting Data ⭐ TEKS

1. How many more people worked in agriculture than in the second leading Texas industry?

2. How do you think life in Texas was affected by the types of work Texans did during the Great Depression?

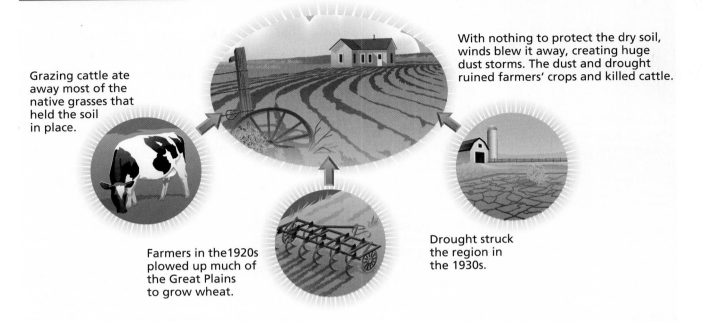

The Causes of the Dust Bowl

The Dust Bowl was caused by both physical and human factors. The drought and dust storms resulted in millions of dollars in damage.

Grazing cattle ate away most of the native grasses that held the soil in place.

With nothing to protect the dry soil, winds blew it away, creating huge dust storms. The dust and drought ruined farmers' crops and killed cattle.

Farmers in the 1920s plowed up much of the Great Plains to grow wheat.

Drought struck the region in the 1930s.

Visualizing History

1. **Geography** How did physical factors combine with human factors—like farming and ranching practices—to cause the Dust Bowl? ⭐TEKS

2. **Connecting to Today** What measures would you recommend to help people who change the environment avoid another Dust Bowl? ⭐TEKS

Governor Ross Sterling tried to get producers to limit production, but had little success. In August 1931 he declared martial law in four East Texas counties. He sent in the National Guard to enforce **proration**, or the proportionate division of oil production. Under proration, each well could produce only a certain amount of oil each day. Oil producers complained that the state government had no right to tell them how to use their property. In response, the state legislature passed laws granting the Railroad Commission more authority to regulate the oil industry. These laws helped prevent overproduction, thereby increasing stability within the oil industry.

⭐ **Reading Check** **Analyzing Information** How did the boom-and-bust economic cycle affect the Texas oil industry?

⭐ The Dust Bowl and Farmers

Although Texas farmers could grow much of their own food, the depression hit them hard economically. Farmers had experienced difficult times during the 1920s, but life grew even harder during the 1930s. Crop prices continued to drop. In 1932, cotton sold for less than six cents a pound. Prices fell so low that some farmers burned their crops.

YEARS OF DUST

RESETTLEMENT ADMINISTRATION
Rescues Victims
Restores Land to Proper Use

Many farmers were forced to move from the Panhandle because of dust storms.

As one newspaper noted, "There is no waste in burning something that . . . is hardly worth hauling to town."

An environmental disaster made matters worse. Ranching and farming were changing the environment. Cattle grazing had already damaged the native grasses that held the soil in place. In the 1920s farmers in Texas and other states plowed up much of the Great Plains to grow wheat. Wheat did not hold the soil as well as the native grasses. Then drought struck in the 1930s, leaving the soil dry and loose. When the spring winds came, they lifted the soil into the air, creating huge clouds of dust. The worst of these storms were called black blizzards, with walls of dirt reaching more than a mile high. In 1935 Amarillo suffered a black blizzard that blocked out the sun for more than 11 hours. One Amarillo resident remembered seeing a huge dark cloud approaching.

Texas Voices

"We were running . . . toward home when the wind hit, pelting our bare legs with gravel. We choked and gasped . . . as the air thickened with brown dust. . . . Just as we reached my front porch everything went completely black. The porchlight was consumed by the blackness. We couldn't see each other's faces. We couldn't see our own hands. I remember gasping, 'I can't breathe.'"

—Pauline Robertson, *Panhandle Pilgrimage*

Analyzing Primary Sources
Evaluating Based on this eyewitness account, how did changes to the environment affect the Panhandle?

Parts of the southern Great Plains soon came to be called the **Dust Bowl**. Drought and dust ruined crops, and thousands of cattle died. Many cattle ranchers struggled financially during this time. One third of Panhandle farm families received charity or relief. About 90 percent of the local farmers had to take out crop loans to be able to buy necessities.

Reading Check **Finding the Main Idea** How did weather affect the Panhandle and Texas farmers and ranchers during the Great Depression?

Section 3 Review (TEKS) Questions 3, 4a, 4b, 5

go.hrw.com **Homework Practice Online**
keyword: ST3 HP26

1 Define and explain:
- stocks
- soup kitchens
- breadlines
- scrip
- proration

2 Identify and explain:
- Great Depression
- Ross Sterling
- Dust Bowl

3 Analyzing Information
Copy the graphic organizer below. Use it to show the effects of the Great Depression on the Texas economy.

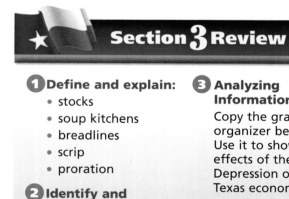

Depression — farming and ranching — oil — banking — manufacturing

4 Finding the Main Idea
a. How did government regulation affect the Texas oil industry?
b. How did Texas farmers and ranchers modify the environment during the 1920s, and what were the consequences of these modifications?

5 Writing and Critical Thinking
Analyzing Information Imagine that you live in Texas during the 1930s. Write a letter to a friend in New York describing how Texans have responded to the Great Depression.
Consider the following:
- the social effects of the Great Depression
- the environmental crisis that created the Dust Bowl

TAKS

Drought and Farming in Texas

Drought has long been a problem for Texas farmers and ranchers. Spanish explorer Álvar Núñez Cabeza de Vaca provided the first recorded information about a drought in West Texas. The map shows the regions of Texas affected by drought in the 1930s. The chart shows years of drought in different regions of Texas. Between 1920 and 1940 the only region that had no years of drought was the Low Rolling Plains. Crops failed during this time, and the state's cattle industry suffered. Texans endured droughts again in the 1950s, 1980s, and 1990s. In addition to having trouble with water, ranchers had trouble obtaining enough feed for their cattle because of the effects of erosion.

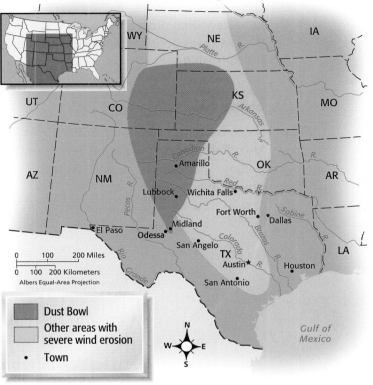

The Dust Bowl, 1930s

Geography Skills

Interpreting Thematic Maps and Graphs ⭐TEKS

1. What region of Texas was most affected by the drought and erosion that led to the Dust Bowl?

2. Which regions suffered the greatest number of drought years?

3. How do you think years of drought affected the cattle industry?

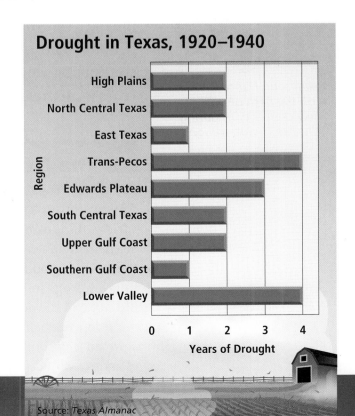

Drought in Texas, 1920–1940

Source: *Texas Almanac*

Section 4 Texas and the New Deal

Read to Discover

1. How did Texans help President Roosevelt during the depression?
2. How did New Deal programs improve life in Texas?
3. What were Texas politics and culture like during the Great Depression?

Define

- **centennial**

Identify

- **New Deal**
- **Social Security**
- **John Nance Garner**
- **Jesse Jones**
- **Lyndon Baines Johnson**
- **Sam Rayburn**
- **Civilian Conservation Corps**
- **James V Allred**
- **W. Lee O'Daniel**
- **J. Frank Dobie**

Why It Matters Today

The U.S. government tried to boost the economy in the 1930s. Use CNNfyi.com or other **current events** sources to learn about government regulation today. Record your findings in your journal.

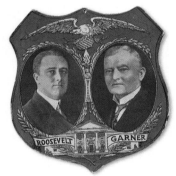

Texan John Nance Garner took the oath of office as the vice president during the 1933 inauguration.

The Story Continues

A young Texan named Lyndon Baines Johnson stood in the crowd on March 4, 1933. The sky over Washington, D.C., was cloudy, but the rain of the past few days had stopped. The audience watched Franklin D. Roosevelt take the oath of office. The new president told the American people, "The only thing we have to fear is fear itself." His comforting words provided hope to a nation battered by years of depression.

★ The New Deal

President Franklin D. Roosevelt had promised "a new deal for the American people." Roosevelt and his advisers asked Congress to pass a variety of measures—called the **New Deal**—to fight the depression. One act helped banks remain open, while another program gave money to the states for food and other aid to people. Another act paid farmers not to grow crops in order to cut down on overproduction. The New Deal did not end the depression, but it gave hope to millions of Americans.

Roosevelt believed that if workers had money to spend it would help spur an economic recovery. Business would benefit and the whole economy would improve. New Deal programs created jobs by funding public works—government-sponsored building projects for public use. People worked for New Deal agencies such as the Public Works Administration (PWA) and the Works Progress Administration (WPA). Workers constructed schools, dams, parks, and roads. These programs became so well known that many people wrote directly to Roosevelt looking for work. Lulu Gordon of San Antonio wrote, "I am willing to do any kind of work because I have to support myself and my children. . . . Please give me some work."

Roosevelt also wanted to provide Americans with economic security for the future. In 1935 Congress created the **Social Security** system. This program provided payments to retired citizens and benefits for unemployed workers. The Social Security system collected the money it needed for its payments from employers and from workers.

Several Texans served under Roosevelt and helped with his New Deal efforts. **John Nance Garner** of Uvalde served as vice president from 1933 to 1941. He had previously been Speaker of the U.S. House of Representatives. Under President Hoover, **Jesse Jones** of Houston had headed a government agency that loaned money to businesses. President Roosevelt then appointed Jones to head all government lending programs and to the position of secretary of commerce. **Lyndon Baines Johnson** of Johnson City served as state director of the National Youth Administration (NYA), which employed young people between the ages of 16 and 25. Johnson was only 27 years old when he became the NYA director. An NYA official complimented Johnson's service. "You have the best Youth Director in the nation in Lyndon Johnson."

Among the well-known Texans in the U.S. Congress was **Sam Rayburn** of Bonham. Rayburn held a seat in Congress for almost 50 years and served for many years as Speaker of the House. Rayburn was generally a loyal supporter of Roosevelt. Like Rayburn, other members of Congress from Texas usually supported New Deal programs.

Reading Check **Summarizing** Which Texans played a role in the New Deal, and what were their contributions?

Hard times. *Many teenagers tried to find jobs to support their families during the depression.* **How have these Texas boys managed to earn some money during the Great Depression?**

Social Security

When Congress passed the Social Security Act in 1935 as part of the New Deal, it was intended to help Americans deal with the depression. Since that time Social Security benefits have continued to help Texans and other Americans. Social Security provides financial assistance to retired persons, people with disabilities, and families of deceased workers. **How does Social Security help Texans?**

★ New Deal Programs in Texas

Several New Deal agencies offered assistance to Texans during the Great Depression. In 1934 some 13 percent of Texans received aid. The Federal Emergency Relief Administration provided millions of dollars to assist Texans. The **Civilian Conservation Corps** (CCC) created jobs for some 100,000 Texans. CCC workers built and repaired bridges, dams, and roads. Workers received $30 a month but were required to send $25 of their pay back home to their families. The families could then spend the money in their local economies. By January 1938, Texans had received some $23 million from family members in the CCC. Other Texans found jobs with the WPA. The WPA aided in the construction of dams along the Colorado River. NYA workers in Texas built many highway rest stops—an idea that soon spread throughout the nation. As a result of these jobs, Texans had money to spend on goods and services, thereby helping the state's small businesses.

The Rural Electrification Administration (REA) helped Texas farms gain access to electricity. This program was important to Texans because fewer than 10 percent of Texas farms had electricity in 1935. By 1965, 98 percent of Texas farms had electricity. The federal government also helped Texas farmers by purchasing farmland to keep it out of production and allow it to recover. Agents of the Soil Conservation Service taught farmers how to plant trees and grass to prevent soil from blowing away. They also advised farmers to plow in the direction of the natural shape of the land. That way the ridges and furrows would prevent further erosion by water and wind.

Many Texans welcomed the federal assistance, but as the depression continued some people began to criticize the New Deal. They feared that the rapid expansion of government would threaten individual liberty.

⭐ **Reading Check Drawing Inferences and Conclusions** How did New Deal programs affect the production of goods and services in Texas?

Interpreting the Visual Record

New Deal programs. *During the Great Depression the Works Progress Administration funded public works including murals.* **How did the artists of this mural show aspects of depression-era life in Texas?**

★ Texas Politics during the New Deal

Miriam Ferguson, who had been elected governor again in 1932, supported New Deal policies. In 1933 she convinced Texans to approve $20 million in bonds for relief aid. She also issued an order creating the Texas Relief Commission to assist Texans.

Ferguson chose not to run for office in 1934, opening the way for Texas attorney general **James V Allred** of Wichita Falls to win election as governor. Allred worked hard to bring New Deal programs and federal money to Texas, and he was re-elected in 1936. He once declared, "I'm gonna grab all I can for the State of Texas." Allred also helped create a state old-age pension program and a retirement plan for public school teachers. In addition, during Allred's administration the Texas Unemployment Compensation Commission—now known as the Texas Workforce Commission—was established. This commission gives Texans information about available jobs and distributes payments to unemployed workers.

In 1938 a candidate with a style unlike anyone else's ran for governor. **W. Lee O'Daniel** was the sales manager of a flour-milling company in Fort Worth. During the late 1920s O'Daniel had begun airing a radio show that featured a country music group called the Light Crust Doughboys. The show opened with the words, "Please pass the biscuits, Pappy!" Soon the show's host was known as Pappy Lee O'Daniel. In May 1938 O'Daniel announced that he had received some 54,000 letters in one week urging him to run for governor. Much to the surprise of political experts, O'Daniel ran a successful campaign. Texas journalist Robert Hicks described an O'Daniel campaign rally.

Texas Voices ❝The rally opens with hillbilly songs, then the candidate tells the crowd that the singing is over, and anyone who came for the show can leave. But no one does. He admits that when he first started talking about running [for governor] he was simply looking for a new way to help sell his flour. But when the people became serious about it he did so too. O'Daniel is as mystified [bewildered] as his opponents in regard to his large crowds.❞

—Robert Hicks, quoted in *Texas after Spindletop*, by Seth S. McKay and Odie B. Faulk

Texans elected O'Daniel by a wide margin in 1938. Some 100,000 people jammed Memorial Stadium in Austin to watch O'Daniel take the oath of office. Pappy O'Daniel's lack of political experience began to show after he took office, however. He had a poor relationship with the legislature, and few of his proposed programs became law. Nevertheless, Texans re-elected him in 1940. O'Daniel gave up the governor's office in 1941 to take a seat in the U.S. Senate. By that time, the depression was nearing its end.

✔**Reading Check Analyzing Information** Identify the accomplishments of the Texas governors elected during the 1930s.

CONNECTING TO Music

Western Swing

During the 1930s a new style of music appeared in Texas. Western swing featured traditional country music instruments such as the fiddle and the guitar. James Robert "Bob" Wills, a fiddle player, was the most influential western swing musician of the 1930s. Wills borrowed from the various musical traditions that he heard growing up in Texas. Mexican ballads, the blues of black Texans, and the sounds of rural southern music all inspired his music. In 1934 Wills formed a new band, the Texas Playboys. It became the most popular western swing band in the United States. How does western swing reflect how the diversity of Texas has blended to form a unique Texas culture? ★TEKS

Analyzing Primary Sources
Identifying Points of View
Why did Hicks claim that O'Daniel was "mystified" by his popularity?

LONE STAR LEGACY

The San Jacinto Monument

During the Texas centennial, construction began on a monument at the San Jacinto battleground. When it was completed in 1939, the monument stood some 570 feet high—five inches taller than the Washington Monument. The monument is topped by a 34-foot star, and a museum is located in the tower's base.

For what event does the San Jacinto Monument serve as a memorial?

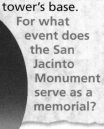

Life and Culture during the Depression

Life during the depression was difficult for many Texans. In 1934 journalist Lorena Hickok toured Texas. She noted, "I've been out on this trip now for a little more than two weeks. In all that time I've hardly met a person who seemed confident and cheerful." Music provided a welcome distraction to Texans. African American musicians such as Huddie Ledbetter and Aaron "T-Bone" Walker played the blues. Bob Wills and his band the Texas Playboys offered a new kind of dance music called western swing. Other musicians such as Woody Guthrie, who lived in the Panhandle from 1929 to 1937, wrote songs about the experiences of Texans in the depression. Guthrie's song "So Long, It's Been Good to Know You" was written in response to a huge dust storm that convinced some Texans that the world was about to end.

Texans also enjoyed other forms of music during the depression. Some Texans attended symphonies in Dallas, Houston, and San Antonio. Many Texans went to the movies. Texans also read the works of **J. Frank Dobie**, whose stories and collections of folktales captured many aspects of life in Texas. Another bright spot came in 1936, when Texas celebrated its **centennial**, or 100th birthday since independence. With federal assistance, the state spent $25 million to stage a world's fair in Dallas to mark the occasion. President Roosevelt visited the fairgrounds. The centennial provided an opportunity for Texans to enjoy the efforts of the Daughters of the Republic of Texas and other groups who worked to preserve the state's historic buildings and sites.

 Reading Check Summarizing What kind of celebrations, cultural activities, and performances did Texans enjoy during the depression?

Section 4 Review

(TEKS) Questions 3, 4a, 4b

Homework Practice Online
keyword: ST3 HP26

1 Define and explain:
- centennial

2 Identify and explain:
- New Deal
- Social Security
- John Nance Garner
- Jesse Jones
- Lyndon Baines Johnson
- Sam Rayburn
- Civilian Conservation Corps
- James V Allred
- W. Lee O'Daniel
- J. Frank Dobie

3 Categorizing
Copy the graphic organizer below. Use it to identify the significant achievements of Texas leaders during the depression.

Texan	Achievements
Rayburn	
Johnson	
Jones	

4 Finding the Main Idea
a. Explain how New Deal programs affected the production of goods and services in Texas.
b. How did New Deal programs affect rural Texans?

5 Writing and Critical Thinking TAKS
Summarizing Write a paragraph describing Texas politics and culture during the Great Depression.
Consider the following:
- governors of Texas during the depression
- music, movies, and celebrations in Texas

"Mustang Gray"
J. Frank Dobie

J. Frank Dobie was born on a ranch in Live Oak County. He joined the faculty of the University of Texas in 1914, but left the university for a year to manage his uncle's ranch. The western tales he heard from the ranch hands sparked his interest in the folklore of Texas and the American Southwest. By the 1930s, Dobie's writings and folktales were recognized in Texas and across the United States. His short story "Mustang Gray" tells the story of Mayberry B. Gray's efforts to capture a mustang.

Not long after coming to Texas, [Gray] was a-ranging after buffalo, far away from the settlements, when his horse fell, throwing him to the ground. He held to the reins, but the charge of a buffalo **mortally**[1] shot so frightened the horse that he jerked away and ran out of sight. After trailing him for a long time and finding his tracks mingled with those of wild horses, Gray came back to the slain buffalo for a meal. He took some of the meat to a pond nearby, built a fire, and cooked it.

Tracks . . . told him that mustangs were watering here. If he but had a rope, he might catch one. He climbed a tree over the main horse trail for a look. Before long he saw a band of mustangs galloping to water. Some of them, including a heavy-set stallion, passed beneath him. . . .

After the mustangs had water and left, Gray came down from the tree with a plan. If he attempted to walk back to the settlements, he would certainly suffer from thirst. Walking was against his principles anyhow. . . .

Animals have regular hours for watering, and when the time approached on the fourth day for the mustangs to come to the pond, Gray was ready for them. Having tied one end of the **reata**[2] to a low, stout branch, he took the other up the tree to an open space immediately over the trail and made it into a loop. He knew that he would have but one throw at one mustang. He wanted the heavy-set stallion. He did not miss.

The stallion jerked himself flat, but got up. For hours he plunged, ran, jerked, snorted but gradually as the man talked to him in low tones and moved gently, he calmed down. It was the next day before he tremblingly allowed a hand on his neck. . . . The taming process went on until Gray . . . got the stallion to stand until he was firmly seated. Then, headed towards the settlements, he pulled the bandanna free. For many miles the prairie was open. The mustang ran until he was completely exhausted. That evening Gray watered him and hobbled him short. The next morning he had comparatively little trouble keeping him under control. Riding bareback, he came to the camp of men who knew him. They dubbed him Mustang Gray, a name still attached to a place as well as to legend and song.

---

[1]**mortally:** fatally   [2]**reata:** rope

Understanding What You Read

1. **Literature and History** Why did Gray need to capture the mustang?
2. **Literature and History** What does this story reveal about the dangers of hunting on the Texas frontier?
3. **Literature and You** What folktales and stories are told in your community?

Texans have enjoyed reading collections of Dobie's works for decades.

The Chapter at a Glance

Examine the following visual summary of the chapter. Create an outline of the major events of the boom era of the 1920s and the depression era in Texas. Then compare your outline with a classmate's. ★TEKS

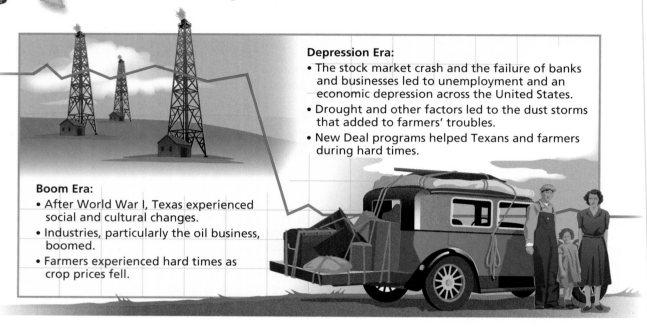

Depression Era:
- The stock market crash and the failure of banks and businesses led to unemployment and an economic depression across the United States.
- Drought and other factors led to the dust storms that added to farmers' troubles.
- New Deal programs helped Texans and farmers during hard times.

Boom Era:
- After World War I, Texas experienced social and cultural changes.
- Industries, particularly the oil business, boomed.
- Farmers experienced hard times as crop prices fell.

Identifying People and Ideas ★TEKS

Use the following terms or people in historically significant sentences.

1. Pat Neff
2. Miriam A. "Ma" Ferguson
3. Dan Moody
4. Lawrence A. Nixon
5. consumer goods
6. Great Depression
7. Ross Sterling
8. Dust Bowl
9. Sam Rayburn
10. J. Frank Dobie

Understanding Main Ideas ★TEKS

Section 1 (pp. 536–539)

1. What problems arose while Miriam Ferguson was governor?
2. What was the white primary, and how did it influence civil rights efforts in Texas?

Section 2 (pp. 540–543)

3. How did the geographic distribution of farming and ranching change during the 1920s?
4. What was life like in Texas during the Jazz Age?

Section 3 (pp. 544–548)

5. How did government regulation affect East Texas oil producers during the Great Depression?
6. How did falling crop prices affect farmers' profits?

Section 4 (pp. 550–554)

7. How did Texans contribute to the New Deal?

8. How did New Deal programs help the Texas economy?

You Be The Historian ★TEKS

Reviewing Themes

1. **Economics** How did World War I contribute to the boom-and-bust cycle of Texas agriculture?
2. **Geography** How did farmers in the Panhandle adapt to and modify the environment, and what were the consequences of the modifications?
3. **Citizenship** What steps did Texans take to fight for equal rights in the 1920s?

TAKS Practice: Thinking Critically ★TEKS

1. **Drawing Inferences and Conclusions** Many Texas businesses experienced boom-and-bust cycles during the depression. What part of this economic cycle did banking and ranching experience during this time?
2. **Analyzing Information** Describe the defining characteristics of the Jazz Age and the Great Depression era of Texas history.
3. **Summarizing** What effect did the New Deal have on farming and ranching in Texas?

Interpreting Political Cartoons

Study the political cartoon below. Then use the information in the cartoon to help you answer the questions that follow.

1. Texas farmers faced many environmental challenges in the 1930s. Why would the Texas farmer call Uncle Sam for help?

 a. He wanted federal assistance.
 b. Bollworms were good for cotton.
 c. Bollworms spread from the United States.
 d. The cotton belt spread across the entire southern United States.

2. Based on this cartoon, what crops did the pink bollworm eat?

Analyzing Primary Sources

Read the following quote by Annie Mae Hunt, an African American who lived in Texas during the depression. Then answer the questions.

"When I was raising [my] first three kids during the Depression . . . I had jobs. . . . Like on Monday morning, I'd get up, I'd go out to Mrs. X's house, wash for her, hang her clothes up. Then I'd go on down to wash for another woman. I've done four washes in one day. I'd come on back, and these things hung out for Mrs. X, they'd be ready. . . . And I cooked. I was a very good cook. Everybody liked my cooking. I didn't have to worry about no jobs, because I always had a job as long as I was cleanin' house and cookin'. And I did that for a long time."

3. Hunt earned money during hard times by doing laundry for

 a. her three daughters.
 b. her relatives.
 c. one other family.
 d. several other families.

4. How might the fact that Annie Mae Hunt was African American have affected her life during the Great Depression?

Alternative Assessment

Linking to Community

The Great Depression remains a vivid memory for many Americans who lived during the 1930s. Interview a member of your community who lived through the depression. Ask the person what kind of work his or her family did to make enough money to survive. Prepare a scrapbook of that individual's life and your community during the depression. You may want to include images of the era in your scrapbook.

BUILDING YOUR Portfolio

☑ internet connect

Internet Activity: go.hrw.com
KEYWORD: ST3 TX26 ⭐ TEKS
Access the Internet through the HRW Go site to research the Great Depression and to analyze the impact of national and international markets on the production of goods and services in Texas. Then create a chart that has the following information: the cause of the depression, whether the cause was national or international, and ways people attempted to solve challenges presented by the depression.

Social Studies Skills

WORKSHOP

Using Primary and Secondary Sources

There are many sources of firsthand historical information. These sources often include diaries, artifacts, newspaper editorials, interviews, letters, and legal documents. All of these are *primary sources.* Newspaper reports are also considered primary sources. However, they are typically written after an event has taken place. The same is true for personal memoirs and autobiographies. These works are usually written late in a person's life. The editorial cartoons, paintings, and photographs that make up history's visual record are also primary sources. These primary sources are valuable historical tools that allow a close-up look at the past.

Secondary sources are descriptions or interpretations of historical events written after the events have occurred. These sources are written by persons who did not take part in or witness the events. Biographies, encyclopedias, history books, and other reference works are examples of secondary sources. Writers of secondary sources have the advantage of knowing the long-range consequences of events. This knowledge helps shape their viewpoints.

How to Study Primary and Secondary Sources

1. **Study the material carefully.** Consider the nature of the material. Is it verbal or visual? Is it based on firsthand information or on the accounts of others? Note the major ideas and supporting details.

2. **Consider the audience.** Ask yourself: For whom was this message originally meant? Whether a message was intended, for example, for the general public or for a specific private audience may have influenced its style or content.

3. **Check for bias.** Watch for certain words or phrases that signal a one-sided view of a person or event.

4. **When possible, compare sources.** Study more than one source on a topic if you can. Comparing sources gives you a more complete and balanced account.

The Evolution of a State or Recollections of Old Texas Days by Noah Smithwick with new illustrations by Charles Shaw

Practicing the Skill

Select a topic from Unit 8. Write a brief report on this topic, using one primary source and one secondary source. Explain why each source is considered a primary or a secondary source. Your sources may include databases, media and news services, biographies, interviews, or artifacts. Be sure to check for bias and evaluate the validity of the sources by comparing the sources to each other, analyzing the language used in the sources, or researching the authors.

History in Action

UNIT 8 SIMULATION

You Solve the Problem . . .

How Can Texas Farmers Raise Crop Prices?

Complete the following activity in small cooperative groups. It is the late 1800s. You and your fellow Texas farmers want to work with other farmers to find a way to earn more money. You and the other farmers in your group would like to make a presentation to encourage other farmers to join the Southern Farmers' Alliance. Follow these steps to solve your problem.

1. Gather Information. Use your textbook and other resources to find information that might influence your plan of action for convincing farmers to join the Southern Farmers' Alliance. Remember that your presentation must include information that farmers will need to persuade them to join the Alliance. Be sure to use what you learned from this unit's Skills Workshop on Using Primary and Secondary Sources to help you find an effective solution to this problem. You may want to divide up different parts of the research among group members.

2. List and Consider Options. After reviewing the information you have gathered, list and consider the options you might recommend for successfully convincing Texas farmers to join the Alliance. Your final solution to the problem may be easier to reach if you consider as many options as possible. Be sure to record your possible options for the preparation of your presentation.

3. Consider Advantages and Disadvantages. Now consider the advantages and disadvantages of taking each option. Ask yourselves questions such as, "How will joining the Alliance help bring about political changes that will help us?" Once you have considered the advantages and disadvantages, record them as notes for use in preparing your presentation.

4. Choose, Implement, and Evaluate a Solution. After considering the advantages and disadvantages, you should prepare a presentation. Be sure to make your proposal to convince farmers to join the Southern Farmers' Alliance very clear. You will need to support your reasons by including information you gathered and by explaining why you rejected other options. When you are ready, decide which group members will make each part of the presentation, and then take your solution to the farmers (the rest of the class). Good luck!

UNIT 9 The Modern Era
(1939–Present)

CHAPTER 27 **World War II and the Cold War** (1939–1960)

CHAPTER 28 **Texas in Transition** (1960–1980)

CHAPTER 29 **Challenges of a Modern State** (1980–Present)

Texas Teens
Young Entrepreneurs

Millions of students across the nation eagerly watched as NASA launched its *Apollo 11* spacecraft to the Moon in 1969. They listened excitedly as astronauts spoke to flight controllers at the NASA Mission Control in Houston. The phrase "This is Houston" became famous. The interest created by the space race inspired many Texas students to study science and math. Some of these students have taken their interest in science and technology and created their own businesses.

Many Texas students study math and science helping Texas to continue to prosper with new technological advances.

One young Texan took his hobby of building customized computers and turned it into a profitable corporation. Michael Dell developed his first business at age 13—a mail order stamp-trading business. At 16, Dell took a job selling subscriptions for the *Houston Post* over the telephone. Even while working, he found time to tinker with computers. Dell realized that he could lower costs and be more competitive by building computers from different manufacturers' parts. In 1984 at the age of 18, while attending the University of Texas at Austin, Dell founded a computer company called PC's Limited. Dell quickly made a profit. At the end of the first year, the company's sales cleared more than $6 million. By 2000, it was one of the world's leading computer makers. Many other young entrepreneurs have found Texas to be a welcoming place for establishing new companies. **How have Texas teens embraced technology and free enterprise?**

In this unit you will learn more about Texas entrepreneurs. You will also learn about the many changes in Texas since World War II, including urban growth, civil rights movements, a changing economy, and the emergence of a two-party political system.

LEFT PAGE: *The first space shuttle launch began a new era of space exploration during the 1980s.*

World War II and the Cold War
(1939–1960)

Some Texas soldiers wore patches with the saying "Remember the Alamo" during World War II.

Texan Audie Murphy earned many medals and honors for his service in World War II.

TEXAS

1941 Large numbers of Texans volunteer for military service in World War II.

1944 The U.S. Supreme Court declares the Texas white primary unconstitutional.

1945 Texan Audie Murphy receives the Medal of Honor for stopping a German tank attack in France.

1939	1942	1945	1948

U.S. and WORLD

1939 Germany invades Poland, leading to World War II.
1941 Japanese forces attack U.S. Navy ships at Pearl Harbor.

1944 Allied troops launch D-Day, an invasion on the European continent.

1947 President Harry S Truman announces that the United States will help other nations that are fighting communism.

Many Americans saw the expansion of communism as a threat to democracy.

In early 1945, U.S. troops won a significant battle against Japanese forces on the Pacific island of Iwo Jima.

Build on What You Know

The New Deal helped Texans during the Great Depression. Nations around the world also struggled during this time. Another world war broke out after nations in Europe and Asia threatened their neighbors. War brought many changes to Texas.

As Texas cities grew in population and size, more people commuted to work and other places.

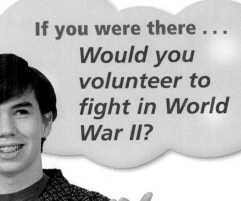

Lubbock native Buddy Holly was an early rock 'n' roll star.

1951 More than 3 million automobiles are registered in Texas.

1954 Allan Shivers successfully runs for a third term as governor.

1957 Texas women call for an equal rights amendment to the state constitution.
1959 Texas musician Buddy Holly is killed in a plane crash.

1960 The U.S. Supreme Court rules that Texas owns Gulf coastal tidelands up to a 10.35-mile limit.

1951   1954   1957   1960

1957 The Soviet Union launches *Sputnik*, the first artificial satellite.

1960 The Soviets shoot down a U.S. spy plane.

The launch of the Sputnik *satellite* stunned Americans and began a space race.

If you were there . . . *Would you volunteer to fight in World War II?*

You Be the Historian

Themes Journal

What's Your Opinion? Do you **agree** or **disagree** with the following statements? Support your point of view in your journal.

● **Economics** A war can transform and improve a nation's economy.

● **Constitutional Heritage** Individuals must sometimes struggle to protect their constitutional rights.

● **Science, Technology & Society** Industrial development always affects population distribution.

World War II

Read to Discover

1. What events led to World War II?
2. In what ways did Texans contribute to the war effort?
3. How did World War II affect Texans and the state?

Why It Matters Today

Democratic nations went to war to preserve their freedoms in World War II. Use CNNfyi.com or other **current events** sources to learn about a nation's efforts to guard the freedoms of its citizens. Record your findings in your journal.

Define

- **victory gardens**

Identify

- **Doris Miller**
- **Audie Murphy**
- **Dwight D. Eisenhower**
- **Chester W. Nimitz**
- **Oveta Culp Hobby**
- **Women's Auxiliary Army Corps**
- **Holocaust**

The Story Continues

December 7, 1941, dawned just like any other day for Texan Doris Miller. A sailor in the U.S. Navy, Miller was hard at work on board the USS *West Virginia* in Pearl Harbor, Hawaii, when a loud explosion rocked the ship. Miller raced to the main deck and could not believe what he saw. The skies were filled with Japanese warplanes. With bombs exploding around him, he helped his wounded captain to safety. Running back to the deck, Miller did his best to defend his ship by firing a machine gun at the attacking planes.

"above and beyond the call of duty"

Doris Miller became a hero during the Japanese attack on Pearl Harbor.

★ World War II Begins

Just over 20 years after World War I, thousands of Texans like **Doris Miller** served in yet another world war. After World War I, Germany and Italy had turned to a political theory known as fascism, which features a strong government headed by one individual. Under fascism the nation is seen as being more important than the individual. In the 1930s fascist leaders Adolf Hitler of Germany and Benito Mussolini of Italy expanded their nations' military forces. When German forces invaded Poland on September 1, 1939, Great Britain and France declared war on Germany. World War II had begun.

In Asia, Japan had built up its military strength and invaded China in 1937. Japan's leaders feared that the United States would try to stop

Japan's aggressive expansion. On December 7, 1941, Japan launched a surprise attack on Pearl Harbor, Hawaii. The Japanese sank or caused major damage to 19 U.S. naval ships. Doris Miller of Waco was awarded the Navy Cross for his efforts in defending his ship during the attack. The following day, the United States declared war on Japan. Three days later, Germany and Italy declared war on the United States. The United States was now fighting with the Allies—Britain, France, and the Soviet Union—against the Axis Powers of Germany, Italy, and Japan.

After the attack on Pearl Harbor, thousands of Texans rushed to enlist. Sara Castro Vara of San Antonio had six sons serve in the war. She said, "If I had a seventh son, I would have been proud to send him too to fight for his country." Of the 750,000 Texans who served in the armed forces during World War II, about 75 percent joined the army. The rest served in the navy, marines, or coast guard. These Texans served with distinction—33 Texans received the Congressional Medal of Honor. Five of them were Mexican Americans. **Audie Murphy** of Hunt County was the nation's most decorated soldier of the war, with 33 awards and medals. Many Texans served as officers. Some 150 generals and a dozen admirals in World War II were from Texas. General **Dwight D. Eisenhower**, who was born in Denison, served as commander of all Allied forces in Europe. Admiral **Chester W. Nimitz** of Fredericksburg commanded the U.S. fleet in the Pacific. These two men led the Allies to many important victories.

Thousands of Texas women served in noncombat positions in the military. **Oveta Culp Hobby** of Houston organized and commanded the **Women's Auxiliary Army Corps** (WAAC). In three years she managed nearly 100,000 women in posts around the globe. About 8,000 female Texans joined the WAAC, and another 4,000 served in Women Accepted for Volunteer Emergency Service (WAVES), a branch of the navy. At Avenger Field in Sweetwater, about 1,000 women trained for the Women's Airforce Service Pilots (WASPs). WASPs flew new planes from the manufacturers to military bases, gave instrument instruction to pilots, and tested damaged planes.

⭐ **Reading Check Summarizing** How did Texans serve in World War II?

Daily Life

World War II Soldiers

In 1944 the average U.S. soldier was 26 years old. He was five feet eight inches tall. In all likelihood, he had not finished high school. While in training in the United States, he woke up at 6:05 A.M., trained throughout the day, and went to bed at 9:45 P.M. A private earned $50 a month.

Once in Europe, the fighting was rough, Texan Audie Murphy recalled. "When you are moving into combat . . . fear is right there beside you. It strikes first in the stomach. . . . I got so scared the first day in combat I just decided to go along with it." **What experiences did Texas soldiers like Audie Murphy have during World War II?**

Interpreting the Visual Record

Texas military bases. During World War II, soldiers from all over the United States came to Texas military bases, such as Camp Swift near Bastrop. **What does this photo show about life on a military base?**

Factory work. *Women found jobs in Texas factories operating punch presses, working on assembly lines, and riveting metal parts.* **How do you think this woman's work on an airplane helped the U.S. war effort?**

That's Interesting!

Young Texans Help the War Effort

Young people in Texas took on extra responsibilities during the war. Some schools adjusted their schedules so that students could have more time to plant and harvest. Other young Texans searched their towns for scrap metal that could be used by the military.

★ The Texas Home Front

About 1.2 million army soldiers and 200,000 pilots trained at military bases in Texas. The U.S. Army operated 15 camps and 40 airfields in the state. With Brooks, Kelly, Lackland, and Randolph air bases, San Antonio became the world's largest aviation training center. The navy had bases at Beeville, Corpus Christi, Grand Prairie, and Kingsville. Many local economies within the state were boosted as Texas businesses provided services to military bases. Industry and agriculture also geared up to meet new demands. Hardworking Texans built aircraft at plants in Fort Worth, Garland, and Grand Prairie. Ships were built in the ports of Beaumont, Corpus Christi, Galveston, Houston, and Port Arthur. The chemical, oil, and steel industries also expanded production to meet war needs. As thousands of new jobs were created, the state's economy boomed and the depression came to an end.

The growing economy provided new opportunities for people. Some 500,000 Texans, including many African Americans, moved from rural areas to cities to work in booming industries. In addition, many Mexicans moved to Texas to take advantage of the strong job market. As Texas men enlisted, women took their factory jobs. "Rosie the Riveter"—a song about one of these hardworking women—became very popular. Governor Coke R. Stevenson described women's contributions to the war effort. "I talked with one [woman] whose husband is with General MacArthur in the Philippines. She was building a plane which she hoped would reach him before it is too late. 'I must hurry,' she said, 'and this ship must be good.' I said, 'yes, and it will be good. No Texas wife or mother will neglect a single detail in any plane or tank or truck or ship which might preserve the life of husband or son.'"

Like other Americans, Texans made sacrifices for the war effort. Many goods valued by the military, such as gasoline, meat, rubber, and sugar, were in short supply. The government rationed, or set aside for each family, a specific amount of these goods. In addition to reducing their own use of scarce items, Texans found ways to help the military. To help feed troops, Texas farmers devoted more land than usual to food crops rather than to cotton. Some Texans planted **victory gardens**, or small vegetable gardens, to grow extra food. Texans also purchased war bonds to finance the war. In a speech, Audie Murphy applauded such efforts.

> **Texas Voices** **❝I would like to . . . pay a tribute to the Mothers and Fathers who are here. For, it is they who perhaps suffer most in time of war. Too, I would like to express my gratitude for the swell job you have done on the home front. You have given us everything we asked for in the way of tools for modern warfare.❞**
>
> —Audie Murphy, quoted in *No Name on the Bullet,* by Don Graham

 Reading Check **Identifying Cause and Effect** How did World War II affect Texas economically and socially?

★ Victory for the Allies

While Texans worked hard on the home front, Texas soldiers fought alongside Allied troops that attacked in North Africa and the Pacific during 1942 and 1943. The first U.S. division to invade Europe was the 36th Infantry Division, based in Brown County. The 90th Infantry, based at Abilene, suffered heavy casualties as it fought its way across Europe. On D-Day—June 6, 1944—Allied troops invaded France to drive out the Germans. After months of hard fighting, they succeeded. Germany finally surrendered on May 8, 1945. As Allied forces entered Germany, they discovered death camps in which millions of people had been killed. Some 6 million Jews died in this **Holocaust**—Germany's attempt to kill the Jews of Europe.

The war in Europe had ended, but the war in the Pacific continued. Many Texas units, including the 103rd Infantry Division and 144th Infantry Regiment, saw extensive action in the Pacific. Allied forces moved steadily toward Japan, capturing important islands along the way. With this island-hopping strategy, the Allies moved into position to bomb and invade Japan. On August 6, 1945, the United States dropped an atomic bomb, a powerful new weapon, on the Japanese city of Hiroshima. Three days later, another atomic bomb was dropped on the city of Nagasaki. These devastating attacks convinced Japanese leaders that they could not win the war. Japan formally surrendered on September 2, 1945. World War II was over.

Some 50 million people died worldwide as a result of the war. Of the more than 400,000 Americans who died, 23,000 were from Texas. Texans and people around the world turned to the task of rebuilding.

BUY WAR BONDS

The U.S. government required citizens to ration goods, encouraged them to grow vegetable gardens, and urged them to buy bonds to help the war effort.

★ **Reading Check Analyzing Information** How did troops based in Texas contribute to the war effort?

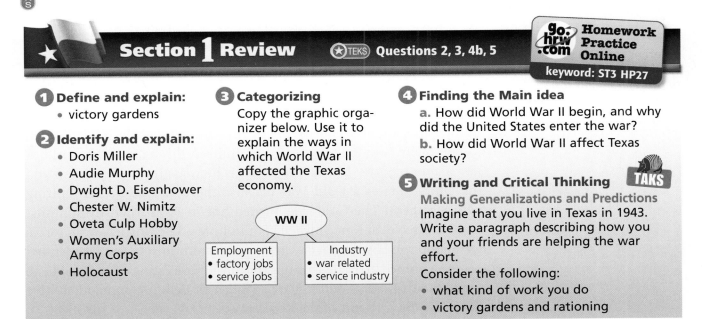

Section 1 Review

★TEKS Questions 2, 3, 4b, 5

go.hrw.com **Homework Practice Online**
keyword: ST3 HP27

1 **Define and explain:**
- victory gardens

2 **Identify and explain:**
- Doris Miller
- Audie Murphy
- Dwight D. Eisenhower
- Chester W. Nimitz
- Oveta Culp Hobby
- Women's Auxiliary Army Corps
- Holocaust

3 **Categorizing**
Copy the graphic organizer below. Use it to explain the ways in which World War II affected the Texas economy.

WW II

Employment
- factory jobs
- service jobs

Industry
- war related
- service industry

4 **Finding the Main idea**
a. How did World War II begin, and why did the United States enter the war?
b. How did World War II affect Texas society?

5 **Writing and Critical Thinking** TAKS
Making Generalizations and Predictions
Imagine that you live in Texas in 1943. Write a paragraph describing how you and your friends are helping the war effort.
Consider the following:
- what kind of work you do
- victory gardens and rationing

2 Postwar Peace and Politics

Read to Discover

1. How did government programs for veterans benefit Texans?
2. How did postwar events affect the Texas economy?
3. What major political events occurred in Texas during the 1950s?

Why It Matters Today

Many military bases opened in Texas during and after World War II. Use **CNNfyi.com** or other **current events** sources to learn about military bases today. Record your findings in your journal.

Define

- aerospace
- tidelands

Identify

- **Cold War**
- **GI Bill of Rights**
- **Gilmer-Aikin Laws**
- **Allan Shivers**

The Story Continues

Veterans returning after World War II had to adapt to postwar life, as this magazine cover illustrates.

Salvador Guerrero of San Angelo saw combat during World War II. When he returned home after the war he had trouble finding a good job. A friend told Guerrero about a job in Monahans. Guerrero later recalled that Monahans "seemed to hold a good future for me." The job paid well. It was not long, however, before Guerrero heard about a better job in Odessa. He moved his family there to start work at a weekly salary of $75.

★ The Cold War

The booming postwar Texas economy was partly the result of international tensions. The Soviet Union's forces had remained in Eastern Europe after the war ended. Americans believed that the Soviet leader, Joseph Stalin, wanted to spread communism throughout the world. A newspaper reporter labeled the tensions between the Soviet Union and the United States a **Cold War** because there was no actual fighting between them. The Cold War turned hot in 1950 when Communist forces from North Korea invaded South Korea. The North Korean forces were supported by the Soviet Union and Communist China. The United Nations immediately sent troops, primarily consisting of U.S. soldiers, to aid South Korea. Walton Harris Walker of Belton commanded these forces for the first part of the Korean War.

Many bases and military installations in Texas that had closed after World War II were quickly reopened, including Avenger Field, Dyess Air Force Base, and Harlingen Air Force Base. Texas industries once again produced much-needed war supplies. After several years of fighting, many Americans called for an end to the conflict. Dwight D. Eisenhower, who had been elected president in 1952, helped bring about peace. The next year, after intense negotiations, the two sides signed a cease-fire that effectively ended the war. Some 1.8 million U.S. soldiers, many of them Texans, had fought in the war, and some 54,000 lost their lives. Benito Martinez of Fort Hancock was one of the Texans who died in combat. Martinez single-handedly defended his position for hours despite attacks by a large enemy force. A fellow soldier recalled, "Even though he knew he would probably die, he was determined to stay on his position and fight off the enemy." Martinez was awarded the Congressional Medal of Honor for his sacrifice.

The Cold War did not end with the Korean War. As a result, national military spending increased, and Texas industries boomed. By 1955 Texas led the United States in the production of helium, oil, petrochemicals, and sulfur. The aircraft industry continued to thrive because of increased civilian travel and military demands. The military's need for rockets contributed to the state's **aerospace** industry. This industry manufactured airplanes and missiles. Missile research was carried out at Texas plants owned by Boeing and General Dynamics Corporation. The electronics industry also gained a strong presence in the state as firms such as Texas Instruments assisted in the development of missiles. Many military bases in Texas remained major training installations during the 1950s. Because much of the state's industry produced goods and services for the military, the Texas economy grew during the Cold War.

★ Reading Check **Analyzing Information** How did the Korean War and Cold War affect the Texas economy?

GLOBAL CONNECTIONS

Roots of the Cold War

At the end of World War II, the United States was the most powerful nation on Earth. Its economy was strong, and the nation had developed nuclear weapons. Although the Soviet Union had suffered greatly during the war, it quickly became a leading force in global politics. It too developed nuclear weapons. Americans worried that the Soviet Union planned to expand its control beyond Eastern Europe. At the same time, the Soviets resented America's efforts to stop the spread of communism. Suspicion on both sides led to the Cold War, which lasted more than 40 years. **Why did Americans not trust the Soviet Union?**

During World War II and the Cold War, Texas was home to a growing aircraft manufacturing industry.

Dwight D. Eisenhower
(1890–1969)

Born in Denison, Dwight D. Eisenhower served as Supreme Allied Commander during World War II. He was president of the United States from 1953 to 1961. As president, Eisenhower was dedicated to preventing the expansion of communism. Nonetheless, he did his best to keep the nation out of armed conflicts. During the 1952 presidential campaign, Eisenhower promised to go to Korea. It was early in his first term in office that the Korean War ended. **What kind of leadership did Eisenhower offer the United States during his presidency?** ⭐TEKS

The GI Bill offered many new educational opportunities to Texas veterans.

⭐ Postwar Politics

The state government benefited from the good economy. Under the guidance of Coke R. Stevenson, who served as governor from 1941 to 1947, the state paid off its debt. During the economic good times the Democratic Party, which still dominated Texas politics, passed several education programs. However, some Democrats claimed these programs would be too expensive for the state. This split the party into liberal and conservative groups—furthering a division that had begun in the 1930s. Some Democrats supported labor unions, civil rights for minorities, and the continuation of President Roosevelt's New Deal policies. Conservative Democrats generally opposed these positions.

Most political leaders did agree in supporting education. Education in Texas got a boost from federal and state laws. Before World War II ended, government leaders made plans to help returning veterans. In 1944 the U.S. Congress passed the Servicemen's Readjustment Act, commonly called the **GI Bill of Rights**. Under this new law, veterans received unemployment payments for up to one year and low-interest loans to buy homes or farms or to establish businesses. The GI Bill also provided money for veterans to attend college. Other legislation helped veterans with tuition at state universities. As a result of these policies, college enrollment in Texas and throughout the nation rose dramatically. Veterans welcomed the opportunity to get a fresh start at an education and a career.

Beauford Jester, who was elected governor in 1946 and again in 1948, also made education a priority for his administration. During Jester's terms, one of the most important education programs in the state's history was adopted. The **Gilmer-Aikin Laws** provided an educational framework that is still used today. An elected board of education sets the state's educational policy. The state Department of Education—later known as the Texas Education Agency—was to set and review standards for schools and teachers. It was also given the task of providing uniform textbooks for students throughout the state. These laws provided funds ensuring that children could attend school at least nine months a year. Additional funding was provided for teachers' salaries.

Governor Jester died in 1949 while still in office. Lieutenant Governor **Allan Shivers** became governor and later was elected to three terms of his own. Shivers backed several important laws passed by the legislature during his tenure. He helped expand government services by pushing tax increases through the legislature. This gave the state government enough money to fund schools and pay for teachers' salaries and retirement benefits for state employees. During this time the legislature also expanded juries and grand juries to include women in 1955.

✔**Reading Check** **Summarizing** Describe the important laws passed during Governor Jester's and Governor Shivers's terms.

★ The Tidelands Dispute

Governor Shivers is perhaps best known for his efforts to defend the state's ownership of tidelands—underwater lands bordering the coast. Texas and other states had long claimed ownership of their tidelands. When oil began to be discovered in these tidelands, however, the federal government claimed that the states had given up their control upon joining the Union. Many states, including Texas, objected. U.S. senator Lyndon B. Johnson declared his "determination to do all that I can to keep the tidelands of Texas away from federal control." The issue was particularly important to Texans because revenue from the tidelands went to the Permanent School Fund.

The tidelands issue soon became one of the most important struggles between the state and federal governments in the nation's history. Texas claimed the tidelands out to three leagues—or 10.35 miles—from the shoreline. Texas argued that it had established the boundary when it won its independence from Mexico. Texas claimed that the federal government had agreed to the boundary when Texas joined the Union. The Justice Department disagreed. In 1960 the U.S. Supreme Court ruled in favor of Texas. This ruling gave Texas clear title to some 2.4 million acres of tidelands. The Permanent School Fund has since received hundreds of millions of dollars in oil-related revenue from these tidelands.

A key figure in the state's victory was Price Daniel, who served Texas as attorney general and as U.S. senator. Daniel became governor in 1957 and served three terms. During his time in office the state passed its first sales tax, or tax paid by consumers when they buy certain goods.

By BOB TAYLOR, Times Herald Staff Cartoonist

—AND BUOYS WILL BE BUOYS

Interpreting Political Cartoons

The tidelands dispute. This cartoonist wanted to show the positions of the state of Texas and the U.S. government over the boundary of Texas coastal lands. **Why do you think the Texas buoy is located farther away from land than the Justice Department buoy?** ⊙TEKS

⊙ **Reading Check** **Finding the Main Idea** How did ownership of the tidelands lead to a dispute between Texas and the federal government?

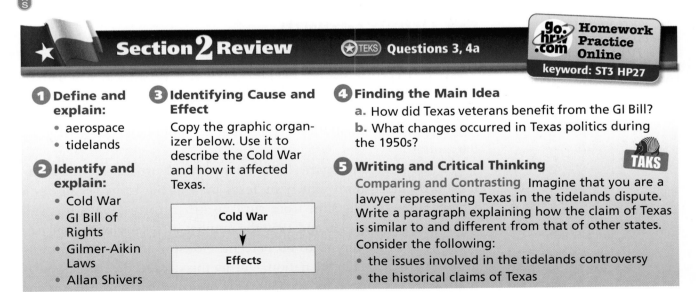

★ Section 2 Review   ⊙TEKS Questions 3, 4a

go.hrw.com Homework Practice Online
keyword: ST3 HP27

① Define and explain:
- aerospace
- tidelands

② Identify and explain:
- Cold War
- GI Bill of Rights
- Gilmer-Aikin Laws
- Allan Shivers

③ Identifying Cause and Effect
Copy the graphic organizer below. Use it to describe the Cold War and how it affected Texas.

Cold War
↓
| Effects |

④ Finding the Main Idea
a. How did Texas veterans benefit from the GI Bill?
b. What changes occurred in Texas politics during the 1950s?

⑤ Writing and Critical Thinking
Comparing and Contrasting Imagine that you are a lawyer representing Texas in the tidelands dispute. Write a paragraph explaining how the claim of Texas is similar to and different from that of other states.
Consider the following:
- the issues involved in the tidelands controversy
- the historical claims of Texas

World War II and the Cold War **571**

Read to Discover

1. What industries contributed to the urbanization of Texas, and what kind of jobs did those industries provide?
2. How did American culture change in the 1950s?

Why It Matters Today

Texas cities grew rapidly in the 1950s. Use CNNfyi.com or other **current events** sources to learn about the effects of growth of Texas cities today. Record your findings in your journal.

Define
• **commute**

Identify
• **Robert Rauschenberg**
• **Katherine Anne Porter**
• **Buddy Holly**
• **Roy Orbison**

The Story Continues

Lubbock High School student Buddy Holly wanted to be a rock 'n' roll star. His parents had encouraged his musical talents, and he had performed publicly since he was five. He was already a regular on Lubbock radio station KDAV's *Sunday Party.* Not long after graduating from high school he signed a recording contract. His song "That'll Be the Day" became a huge hit. Soon he and his band were playing concerts at packed houses across the country.

Buddy Holly's popularity increased after he appeared on national TV variety shows.

★ Urban Growth

Buddy Holly's career began in a time of major change in Texas. During World War II some 450,000 people moved to Texas to take advantage of the state's economic growth. Most of these people settled in urban areas. By 1950 some 7.7 million people lived in Texas, a 20 percent increase over the 1940 population. In 1960 the state's population reached some 9.6 million.

As the population grew, Texans experienced urbanization. Urbanization occurred more slowly in Texas than in the United States as a whole. However, the shift from rural to urban in the 1940s was still dramatic. Between 1940 and 1950 the number of Texans living in urban areas increased from 45 to 60 percent. Houston became the fastest-growing urban area in the nation. During this decade, the rural population of Texas dropped by 600,000. This occurred partly because many

African Americans left the state's rural communities to seek better jobs in the cities of Texas or the North.

Industries that had grown rapidly during World War II continued to draw people to cities. Texans worked for aircraft manufacturers, electronics firms, oil refineries, and ship manufacturers, among other businesses. These and other industries dramatically changed the look of Texas cities. In 1955 a national news magazine noted that "quiet [Texas] towns are being transformed, almost violently, into large cities with towering skylines." A journalist offered his description of Dallas.

Texas Voices ❝It is . . . the undisputed leader of finance, insurance, distribution, culture and fashion for this land. . . . Everything in Dallas is bigger and better; the parties are plushier, the buildings are more air-conditioned. . . . And in all of these things, it is finally a monument to sheer determination.❞

—Holland McCombs, quoted in *Dallas Public and Private,* by Warren Leslie

Analyzing Primary Sources
Identifying Bias What statements in this primary source reflect the biases of the author?

⭐ **Reading Check** **Finding the Main Idea** What major industries contributed to the urbanization of Texas?

⭐ Transportation

The continued popularity of the automobile helped the process of urbanization. Between 1945 and 1950, the number of cars in Texas rose from 1.7 million to some 3 million. To handle these cars, Texans built thousands of miles of new roads. Between 1940 and 1950, the number of paved roads in Texas increased from some 19,000 to 34,000 miles. These roads linked Texas cities to one another. Cities such as Dallas and Houston also built four-lane expressways to speed the movement of traffic within these cities. These expressways became part of the interstate highway system that the U.S. Congress authorized in 1956.

Rural Texans also benefited from the spending on roads. In 1945 the state began paving rural roads to help farmers get their goods to market. The program proved popular, and in 1949 the state government agreed to spend $15 million a year to upgrade rural farm-to-market roads.

Texas air transportation also expanded. As early as 1927, airlines had begun offering passenger service to Texans. Dallas became a stopover for many coast-to-coast flights because of its central location. Love Field in Dallas soon became one of the nation's busiest airports. Texas also served as a gateway for people traveling to and from Latin America. Brownsville served as a hub for many of these flights. In addition, an increasing number of Texas businesses bought and operated private airplanes. Although not as common as today, air transportation during the 1950s was increasingly important.

⭐ **Reading Check** **Analyzing Information** How did improvements in transportation affect the development of Texas?

CONNECTING TO
Music

Buddy Holly and Rock 'n' Roll

One of the most popular early rock 'n' roll musicians was Lubbock native Buddy Holly. He taught himself how to play guitar and in 1957 formed a band, the Crickets, with two friends. Their second record, "Oh Boy!" sold nearly 1 million copies. Holly and the Crickets toured widely and appeared on popular TV shows. In 1959 Holly died in a plane crash. Artists including the Beatles and Bruce Springsteen have pointed to Holly as an important influence.
What influence did Holly have on music in the United States?

Katherine Anne Porter

Texas author Katherine Anne Porter is a nationally known fiction writer. Born in Indian Creek, Porter grew up in San Antonio, Kyle, and Victoria. On the various occasions when her family came together, family stories were told and retold. Many of Porter's stories focus on family life and are set in Central Texas. She won the 1966 Pulitzer Prize for The Collected Stories of Katherine Anne Porter. *In this excerpt from a collection of essays, Porter describes her subject matter and writings.*

I write about Mexico because that is my familiar country. I was born near San Antonio, Texas. My father lived part of his youth in Mexico, and told me enchanting stories of his life there; therefore the land did not seem strange to me even at my first sight of it. . . . I have been accused by Americans of a taste for the exotic. . . . Maybe so, for New York is the most foreign place I know, and I like it very much. But in my childhood I knew . . . the German colonists in Texas and the Mexicans of San Antonio country, until it seemed to me that all my life I had lived among people who spoke broken, laboring tongues, [and] who put on with terrible difficulty. . . . I have never thought of these people as any other than American. . . . All the things I write of I have first known, and they are real to me.

Understanding What You Read ⭐TEKS

1. Literature and History How does Porter's writing reflect the history of cultural groups in Texas?

2. Literature and You How do different culture groups in your community maintain their culture while adapting to a larger Texas culture?

⭐ 1950s Culture

The rise of urban areas and the popularity of cars led to the boom in suburbs. The postwar economic prosperity allowed many Texas families to buy their own homes. By 1960 tens of thousands of Texans lived in suburban neighborhoods. Parks, schools, and public services were provided in the suburbs. Suburban life depended heavily on the car. Texans living in the suburbs chose to **commute** to their jobs, meaning they lived in one area but drove elsewhere to work. Rather than going to town to shop, people in the suburbs drove to small roadside shopping centers, often called strip malls. Fewer than 10 such malls existed in the United States in 1946, but by the late 1950s, there were some 4,000.

During the 1950s wages for many Texans in the suburbs and elsewhere increased even as their work hours declined. With more leisure time, many Texans went to art galleries, concerts, theater productions, and the movies. Texans such as **Robert Rauschenberg** became well-known artists. Movies about Texas and the American West were very popular. The hit movie *Giant*, starring James Dean, Rock Hudson, and Elizabeth Taylor, showed wildcatters and life on an enormous Texas ranch. Texas literature also grew in popularity as writers such as **Katherine Anne Porter** published works about Texas.

The movie Giant *was filmed near the West Texas community of Marfa.*

Texans also enjoyed a new form of communication and entertainment that arrived in the late 1940s—television. The first Texas television station was WBAP-TV in Fort Worth. In 1950 the Dallas–Fort Worth area had three stations, San Antonio had two, and Houston had one. The nation's first educational station, KUHT, began broadcasting in Houston in 1953. Although few Texans owned TV sets in 1950, television soon became a common feature in every Texas home. People began receiving much of their news and entertainment from television.

Television allowed Texans to see performances of a new kind of music that was popular with American teenagers. Rock 'n' roll had roots in African American blues music. In the 1950s white performers such as Elvis Presley brought this music to teenagers. The young people of America loved it. Texans such as **Buddy Holly**, **Roy Orbison**, and J. P. Richardson, known as the "Big Bopper," became popular rock 'n' roll artists. After Holly performed on *The Ed Sullivan Show*, the host asked him about his rapid success. Holly responded, "Well, we've had a few rough times, I guess you'd say, but we've been real lucky getting it this quick."

Texans also entertained themselves by playing or watching sports. Towns and cities formed teams for children and adults in baseball, football, and softball. Fans turned out to support high school and college teams across Texas. Millions of Texans swam or played golf or tennis. In addition, the first professional sports teams were organized in Texas in the postwar years. Texas women formed the first two organizations of female athletes in the United States, the Women's Professional Rodeo Association in 1948 and the Ladies Professional Golf Association in 1949. Texans across the state enjoyed their leisure time as never before.

✔ **Reading Check Summarizing** How did many Texans spend their leisure time in the 1950s?

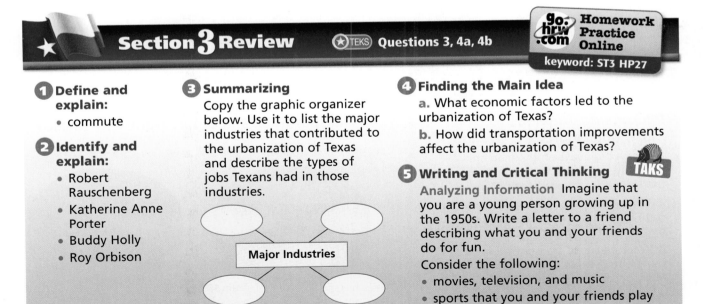

Section 3 Review

TEKS Questions 3, 4a, 4b

go.hrw.com **Homework Practice Online** keyword: ST3 HP27

1 Define and explain:
- commute

2 Identify and explain:
- Robert Rauschenberg
- Katherine Anne Porter
- Buddy Holly
- Roy Orbison

3 Summarizing
Copy the graphic organizer below. Use it to list the major industries that contributed to the urbanization of Texas and describe the types of jobs Texans had in those industries.

Major Industries

4 Finding the Main Idea
a. What economic factors led to the urbanization of Texas?
b. How did transportation improvements affect the urbanization of Texas?

5 Writing and Critical Thinking TAKS
Analyzing Information Imagine that you are a young person growing up in the 1950s. Write a letter to a friend describing what you and your friends do for fun.
Consider the following:
- movies, television, and music
- sports that you and your friends play

Geography and Economics

Trade and Interstate Highways

The United States and Mexico have been trading partners for decades. The pie graphs below show the value of exports from the United States to Mexico in the years 1997 and 2000. Much of this trade is carried out over the highways of Texas.

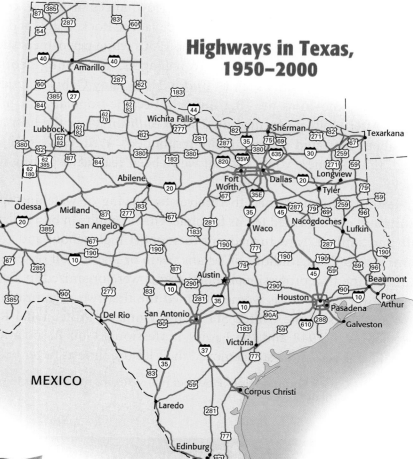

Highways in Texas, 1950–2000

Interstate highway
U.S. highway
• City

MEXICO

Geography **Skills**

Interpreting Thematic Maps and Charts

1. Which highways on the map are probably important trade routes between the United States and Mexico?

2. What Texas cities are located on interstate highways and the border between the United States and Mexico?

3. What means of transportation carries the greatest value of exported goods into Mexico from the United States?

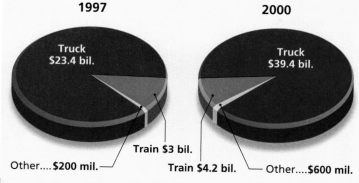

Transportation and Export Trade with Mexico

1997

Truck $23.4 bil.

Train $3 bil.

Other....$200 mil.

2000

Truck $39.4 bil.

Train $4.2 bil.

Other....$600 mil.

Source: U.S. Department of Transportation

The Search for Equal Rights

Read to Discover

1. What changes took place in the area of civil rights for Texas, and how were they accomplished?
2. How did Hispanic Texans fight for their civil rights?
3. What steps did women take to protect their rights?

Why It Matters Today

Many Texans struggled for decades to be treated equally under the law. Use **CNNfyi.com** or other **current events** sources to learn about civil rights efforts in the United States. Record your findings in your journal.

Define

- desegregate
- nonviolent resistance

Identify

- Christia Adair
- Martin Luther King Jr.
- James Farmer
- Hector P. García
- American GI Forum
- Heman Sweatt

The Story Continues

Dorothy Robinson was angry. When she rode the train from California to Texas in 1944, she had not been allowed in the dining car because she was African American. She later recalled, "White prisoners-of-war (Germans, I suppose) were marched under guard through my coach to enjoy a meal in the dining car to which I had been denied admittance."

In many places across Texas restrooms, restaurants, transportation facilities, and drinking fountains were segregated.

★ Discrimination in Texas

Although African Americans were fighting abroad for their country during World War II, at home they faced discrimination. Laws and customs denied minorities voting rights and equal opportunities, such as education or well-paying jobs. Tensions between African American and white Texans sometimes flared into large-scale violence. In 1943, thousands of white shipyard workers in Beaumont rioted. They were worried that they might lose their jobs to black Texans. Two people lost their lives, and several black-owned businesses were burned. It took the Texas Rangers to restore order to the town.

Organizations like the National Association for the Advancement of Colored People (NAACP) tried to stop discrimination. With the support of the NAACP, Lonnie Smith, a black dentist from Houston, filed a lawsuit to gain the right to vote in the Texas Democratic primary. In the 1944 case *Smith* v. *Allwright*, the U.S. Supreme Court struck down the white primary. NAACP leader William Hastie learned of the victory while reading a newspaper on a plane. He recalled, "I am sure the people on the plane thought I was crazy because I just let out one whoop and had it not been for the seat belt I would have gone straight up in the air." Black Texans responded enthusiastically. The number of African Americans registered to vote in Texas rose from some 30,000 in 1940 to about 100,000 in 1947.

Reading Check Analyzing Information How did African Americans protect their right to participate in the political system?

★ Working for Social Change

African Americans also struggled against other forms of discrimination. In the 1896 case *Plessy* v. *Ferguson,* the U.S. Supreme Court had ruled that as long as public facilities were "separate but equal," segregation was constitutional. African Americans had to use different bathrooms and public parks—in some areas they even had to use separate water fountains. These public facilities were rarely equal. NAACP leader **Christia Adair** noted that African Americans could not use many facilities in the Houston airport. They "could not sit in the waiting room . . . get a cold drink, couldn't buy a cold soda water or anything." During World War II African Americans—who made up more than 10 percent of Texas troops—even served in segregated units. It was not until 1948 that the U.S. government required the military to **desegregate**, or stop the practice of separating people by race.

Members of the NAACP demanded that the civil rights of African Americans be recognized. The NAACP scored many significant victories. Under the leadership of Lulu B. White from 1943 to 1949, the Houston chapter became the largest in the South. White urged other members to continue the struggle for civil rights.

> **Texas Voices** "If we can work together just a little harder—all our aims and objectives will be reached. . . . The enemies of democracy are concentrating their efforts to destroy our most effective Civil Rights—the right to vote and to be candidates for office— the right to jobs at equal pay—and the equal right to education. Only a united effort can meet this attack."
>
> —Lulu B. White, quoted in *Black Texas Women: A Sourcebook,* edited by Ruthe Winegarten

In addition to using the court system, African Americans held demonstrations and marches demanding recognition of their civil rights. A young pastor in Alabama named **Martin Luther King Jr.** called for **nonviolent resistance**. This involved peaceful public demonstrations to call attention to the problem of racial discrimination. He soon gained the support of millions of Americans from all backgrounds. With this support, King put pressure on leaders in the federal

Interpreting the Visual Record

Nonviolent resistance. During the 1950s Texans began to take action to end segregation by protesting and boycotting businesses that banned African Americans. **How are the people in the photo trying to end segregation?** ★TEKS

government to pass laws supporting equal rights. Texans also helped lead the struggle to end discrimination. <u>James Farmer</u> of Marshall was a co-founder of the Congress of Racial Equality (CORE) in Chicago in 1942. Like King, Farmer and other members of CORE called for non-violent resistance to Jim Crow laws. CORE initially did most of its work in northern states. During the next decade, however, CORE members worked in the South to train civil rights protesters.

⭐ **Reading Check** **Summarizing** How did civil rights leaders try to end discrimination?

⭐ The American GI Forum

Like African Americans, Hispanics in Texas also experienced discrimination despite their service in the war effort. "We have proven ourselves true and loyal Americans by every test that has confronted us," declared one Hispanic newspaper. In 1948 <u>Hector P. García</u>, a highly decorated U.S. Army surgeon, founded the <u>American GI Forum</u> to protect the rights of Hispanics. The GI Forum focused on helping veterans with education and health care. The American GI Forum received national attention in 1949. That year the Longoria family had tried to hold a memorial service for their son, Félix Longoria, who had been killed in the Philippines during the war. When the funeral director refused to let the family use the whites-only chapel of a Three Rivers funeral home, they contacted García. He used the GI Forum to inform political leaders about the developing controversy. García sent telegrams to members of congress encouraging them to take action.

Texas Voices ❝The denial was a direct contradiction of those same principles for which this American soldier made the supreme sacrifice in giving his life for his country, and for the same people who deny him the last funeral rites deserving of any American hero regardless of his origin.❞

—Hector P. García, quoted in American Forces Information Services Web site

Senator Lyndon B. Johnson of Texas arranged for Longoria's remains to be buried with honors in Arlington National Cemetery.

The Longoria affair motivated many Hispanics to take action. The GI Forum, along with LULAC, filed many desegregation lawsuits. In *Delgado* v. *Bastrop ISD* (1948), the U.S. Supreme Court declared that the segregation of Mexican Americans in public schools violated the U.S. Constitution. In 1957 the GI Forum won a lengthy lawsuit to end segregation of Hispanic children in Texas schools. The Forum also began voter registration drives and awarded scholarships to Hispanic students. In 1958 the GI Forum became a national organization, and it continued to assist Hispanics nationwide for decades to come.

⭐ **Reading Check** **Finding the Main Idea** How did Hector P. García and the American GI Forum assist Hispanics in Texas?

Biography

Hector P. García
(1914–1996)

Born in Mexico, Hector P. García and his family moved to Texas in 1918. García attended the University of Texas Medical School, receiving his degree in 1940. Because Hispanics had few opportunities to practice medicine in Texas, he moved to Nebraska. After the Pearl Harbor attack, he joined the U.S. Army. In addition to his civil rights work, García served as an adviser to several U.S. presidents. He received many awards for public service. In 1984 President Ronald Reagan awarded him the Medal of Freedom. García died in Corpus Christi in 1996. **How did García serve his country?** ⭐TEKS

The American GI Forum was founded to extend civil rights to Hispanic veterans who had fought to preserve democracy in World War II.

The effort to desegregate Texas public schools was controversial in some Texas communities.

★ Desegregating Public Schools

Although Mexican Americans had won their desegregation case, African Americans were still forced to attend schools separate from white students. Segregation supporters used the "separate-but-equal" principle to justify school segregation. Although the schools were separate, they were not equal. Schools for minority students were typically of much poorer quality.

In 1946 **Heman Sweatt** applied for admission to the University of Texas School of Law. The school denied his application but created a separate law school for African Americans. With the NAACP's backing, Sweatt filed a lawsuit against the university. Sweatt argued that he would receive a much better education at the regular law school. In *Sweatt* v. *Painter,* the U.S. Supreme Court ruled that segregated facilities in professional schools violated the U.S. Constitution. That year Sweatt enrolled at the University of Texas School of Law.

The *Sweatt* decision led the way for *Brown* v. *Board of Education,* a lawsuit that challenged the segregation of public schools. In 1954 the U.S. Supreme Court ruled in *Brown* that "separate educational facilities are inherently [by definition] unequal." This was a major victory for minority groups. The decision shocked and angered many white Texans, however. In 1956 a court ordered the Mansfield school district south of Fort Worth to desegregate. In response, a mob formed around the school. Governor Allan Shivers sent Texas Rangers to stop the court order from going into effect, and the federal government took no action to enforce it. Encouraged by their success, the Texas legislature passed laws that kept most Texas schools segregated until the 1960s.

⊙ **Reading Check** **Sequencing** Describe in order the events leading to the desegregation of Texas public schools.

★ New Opportunities for Women

Texas women also fought for recognition of their civil rights in the 1950s. Many women had gone to work during World War II, and some women wanted to continue working when the war ended. They began to express their dissatisfaction at the limited opportunities available to them. Leaders such as Oveta Culp Hobby believed that women deserved to be treated equally. Hobby was the first woman to win the U.S. Army's Distinguished Service Medal. She also served in President Dwight D. Eisenhower's cabinet as secretary of health, education, and welfare.

In the 1950s women began attending colleges and universities in greater numbers. More women were pursuing careers. In 1956 Hattie Briscoe became the first black woman to graduate from St. Mary's School of Law in San Antonio. She remembered being told during her first semester there that women had no business being in law school. She responded, "I am a woman, I am in law school and I am going to become a lawyer." She later graduated at the top of her class.

Working women demanded pay equal to the wages that men working similar jobs received. Gladys Humphrey recalled working in a meatpacking plant. "We felt like we should make a fair wage. Sometimes our jobs were just as hard and complicated as the men but women never made quite the same wage." Women did not gain equal pay, but they did lay the foundation for later achievements. For example, in 1957, Texas women proposed that the state constitution be amended to guarantee the equal rights of all Texans regardless of sex. After a 15-year struggle by its supporters, Texas voters approved the Texas Equal Rights Amendment.

★ Reading Check **Finding the Main Idea** How did women in Texas seek to gain equal rights during the 1950s?

Biography

Oveta Culp Hobby
(1905–1995)

Oveta Culp was born in Killeen. She became interested in politics at an early age. After earning a law degree from the University of Texas School of Law, she served as an advisor to the Texas legislature. In 1931 Culp married former Texas governor William Hobby. During the 1930s she served as president of the League of Women Voters of Texas. She later became publisher of the *Houston Post. Texas Business* once listed her as the only woman among "the 20 most powerful Texans." **How did Hobby work to improve the lives of Texas women?** ★ TEKS

Section 4 Review

★ TEKS Questions: 2, 3, 4a, 4b, 5

go.hrw.com
Homework Practice Online
keyword: ST3 HP27

1 Define and explain:
- desegregate
- nonviolent resistance

2 Identify and explain:
- Christia Adair
- Martin Luther King Jr.
- James Farmer
- Hector P. García
- American GI Forum
- Heman Sweatt

3 Analyzing Information
Copy the table below. Use it to trace the key developments of the civil rights movement in the 1940s and 1950s.

Event	Significance

4 Finding the Main Idea
a. What organizations struggled for civil rights, and what were their achievements?
b. How did Texas women pursue equal rights during the 1950s?

5 Writing and Critical Thinking TAKS
Analyzing Information Write a newspaper story that explains the effect of the *Brown* v. *Board of Education* decision in Texas.
Consider the following:
- the Supreme Court's ruling
- the crisis in Mansfield

The Chapter at a Glance

Examine the following visual summary of the chapter. Then use the visual to create a time line that shows some of the changes occurring in Texas in the 1940s and 1950s. ★TEKS

The Road to Prosperity

By the 1950s Texans living in cities began to outnumber rural Texans.

The ruling on the tidelands dispute allowed Texas to control the land and resources beyond the state's coast.

Fighting for civil rights, Hispanics and African Americans continued to press for an end to discrimination.

The GI Bill of Rights helped many Texas veterans go to school.

Texas musicians and artists influenced American popular culture during the 1950s.

Texas industries that emerged during World War II continued to grow during the Cold War.

Identifying People and Ideas ★TEKS

Use the following terms or people in historically significant sentences.

1. Doris Miller
2. Audie Murphy
3. Chester W. Nimitz
4. Oveta Culp Hobby
5. Cold War
6. tidelands
7. commute
8. Christia Adair
9. James Farmer
10. Hector P. García

Understanding Main Ideas ★TEKS

Section 1 (pp. 564–567)
1. How did World War II affect the daily lives of Texans?

Section 2 (pp. 568–571)
2. What effect did the Korean War have in Texas?
3. How might the Texas economy have been affected had the federal government won control of the tidelands?

Section 3 (pp. 572–575)
4. How did the distribution of the Texas population change in the 1940s and 1950s, and how did that change affect life in Texas?
5. What major industries attracted Texans to urban areas in the 1940s and 1950s?

Section 4 (pp. 577–581)
6. How did World War II affect relations between different racial groups in Texas?
7. What were some of the goals of Texas women in the 1950s?

You Be the Historian ★TEKS

Reviewing Themes

1. **Economics** How did World War II affect the local and state economies in Texas?
2. **Constitutional Heritage** How did civil rights leaders in Texas end the white primary?
3. **Science, Technology & Society** How did the state's industries contribute to urbanization in the 1940s and 1950s?

TAKS ★TEKS Practice: **Thinking Critically**

1. **Analyzing Information** Why did Texas experience urban growth? What do you think are the effects of urbanization?
2. **Summarizing** What kind of leisure activities did Texans enjoy in the 1950s?
3. **Identifying Cause and Effect** How did World War II contribute to the demand for civil rights?

Social Studies Skills Workshop

Interpreting Graphs ⭐TEKS

Study the graph below. The graph shows changes in the Texas rural and urban population from 1920 to 1970. Use the graph to answer the questions below.

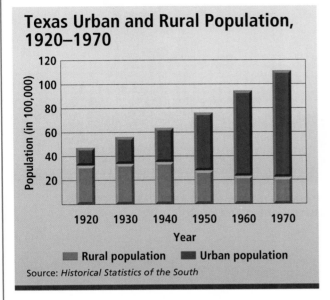

Texas Urban and Rural Population, 1920–1970

Population (in 100,000)

Rural population   Urban population

Source: *Historical Statistics of the South*

1. Between what years did the rural portion of the total Texas population decrease?

    a. 1940–70
    b. 1930–40
    c. 1920–40
    d. It never decreased.

2. Using information from the graph, create a list of questions and answers about the changing population distribution of Texas that occurred during the years presented in the graph.

Analyzing Primary Sources ⭐TEKS

Elmer Kelton was the son of a foreman who worked on a ranch near Crane, Texas. Kelton remembered that when ranchhands learned of the attack on Pearl Harbor, many of them joined the military. Read his description of the effect of the war on ranching in Texas. Then answer the questions.

"The ranching industry changed drastically during and after the war. The severe manpower shortage led to technological innovations that forever reduced the labor needs on ranches as well as farms. Another was the ranches' much heavier dependence upon family men than on the bachelor cowboys of an earlier era. Family men as a group were less likely to drift over the hill to see what was on the other side."

3. The main effect of the war on ranching was

    a. the loss of land to military training centers.
    b. the decline of family-owned ranches.
    c. a manpower shortage that led to technological developments.
    d. a reduced demand for beef.

4. Oral histories can reveal information about the ways that social change affects the lives of individuals. How did World War II change the lives of ranching families?

Alternative Assessment

Interdisciplinary Connection to the Arts

Robert Rauschenberg and other Texas artists used everyday objects to create works of art. Using materials that you find in your classroom, community, or home, create your own work of "found art." Try to incorporate the events of the 1940s and 1950s such as World War II, the Cold War, urbanization, or the civil rights movement into your work. Show it to your classmates and explain what the art means to you.

BUILDING YOUR Portfolio

internet connect

Internet Activity: go.hrw.com
KEYWORD: ST3 TX27 ⭐TEKS

Access the Internet through the HRW Go site to access online databases to analyze the political, economic, and social impact of World War II and the Cold War in Texas. Then use the Holt Grapher or other computer software to create databases and graphs that show the impact of World War II and the Cold War over the decades covered in the chapter.

Texas in Transition
(1960–1980)

The Job Corps was one of Lyndon B. Johnson's Great Society programs.

Astronauts on the Moon kept in contact with Mission Control in Houston.

TEXAS

1961 Henry B. González is elected to the U.S. House of Representatives, and John Tower is elected to the U.S. Senate.

1963 Lyndon B. Johnson becomes president of the United States after President John F. Kennedy is assassinated.

1967 Texas singer Janis Joplin's career takes off after a successful performance at the Monterey International Pop Festival.

| 1960 | 1963 | 1966 |

U.S. and WORLD

1962 A crisis erupts between the United States and the Soviet Union over Soviet missiles in Cuba.

1965 Civil rights leader Martin Luther King Jr. and about 800 other protesters are arrested in Selma, Alabama.

1966 Leaders of the women's movement in the United States found the National Organization for Women.

Martin Luther King Jr. organized non-violent marches to demand civil rights for African Americans.

Build on What You Know

Life changed for many Texans during the post–World War II years. Cities in Texas grew rapidly, and new business opportunities developed. However, some members of the population, particularly those belonging to minority groups, benefited less from these changes.

La Raza Unida Party helped Hispanic activists run for political office in Texas.

Willie Nelson performed at the 25th anniversary of Austin City Limits, *a TV program featuring uniquely American styles of music.*

1969 The National Aeronautics and Space Administration sends the *Apollo 11* mission to the Moon.

1970 Members of the Chicano movement and the Mexican American Youth Organization form La Raza Unida Party.

1972 Barbara Jordan is elected to the U.S. House of Representatives.

1974 *Austin City Limits* goes on the air with Willie Nelson as its first guest musician.

1980 The Texas population reaches 14 million.

1969   1972   1975   1978

1970 Four Kent State University students are killed by the Ohio National Guard during a Vietnam War protest.

1973 The Organization of Petroleum Exporting Countries (OPEC) cuts off oil supplies to the United States, leading to a jump in oil prices.

1975 The Vietnam War comes to an end.

1980 Eleven European countries form the first commercial firm to market the launching of satellites.

The OPEC oil crisis led to a serious energy shortage during the 1970s.

If you were there . . .
How would you promote equal rights?

You Be the Historian

Themes Journal

What's Your Opinion? Do you **agree** or **disagree** with the following statements? Support your point of view in your journal.

● **Citizenship** Citizens have a responsibility to defend everyone's rights.

● **Science, Technology & Society** New technological developments can be beneficial to a state's economy.

● **Geography** Geographic factors have substantial effects on the development of a society.

A Texas President

Read to Discover

1. What leadership qualities and experience did Lyndon B. Johnson have before he became the U.S. president?
2. What new legislation was passed as a result of the Great Society program?
3. How did the Vietnam War affect Texas?

Identify

- **Lyndon B. Johnson**
- **Great Society**
- **Economic Opportunity Act**
- **Tonkin Gulf Resolution**

Why It Matters Today

During the 1960s U.S. leaders expanded the use of government resources to try to help Americans. Use **CNNfyi.com** or other **current events** sources to find information about U.S. government social programs today. Record your findings in your journal.

The Story Continues

On Friday, November 22, 1963, Lyndon B. Johnson was on board *Air Force One* preparing to fly from Dallas to Washington, D.C. Johnson stood next to First Lady Jacqueline Kennedy as he took the presidential oath of office. Her husband, President John F. Kennedy, had been assassinated earlier that day. As the new president, Johnson faced the difficult challenge of pulling the nation together after the tragic event.

Lyndon B. Johnson's first job as president was to help the nation overcome the tragedy of President Kennedy's assassination.

★ A Texan in the White House

President John F. Kennedy, who had been elected in 1960, believed that the United States stood "on the edge of a New Frontier." His administration planned to cut taxes, reduce unemployment, protect African Americans' civil rights, and increase international trade. In 1963 Kennedy came to Texas to attend several political gatherings. As he was riding in a motorcade through downtown Dallas on November 22 with Texas governor John Connally and Vice President **Lyndon B. Johnson**, shots rang out. The president and Governor Connally were hit. Kennedy died a short time later at a Dallas hospital. At 2:38 P.M. on the day of the assassination, Johnson was sworn in as the new president.

Johnson was born near Stonewall, Texas, in 1908 and grew up in nearby Johnson City. He attended Southwest Texas State Teachers College in San Marcos. After earning a teacher's certificate, Johnson taught school and served as principal. Ambitious and hardworking, Johnson became involved in politics during his college and teaching years. In 1935 he became director of the Texas division of the National Youth Administration. Johnson was a strong supporter of the New Deal and President Franklin Roosevelt.

Johnson was elected to the U.S. House of Representatives in 1937 and to the U.S. Senate in 1948. He became one of the most skilled politicians in the national government. As senator, he was expert at getting bills passed that he supported. Abe Fortas, a close friend and former U.S. Supreme Court justice, once described Johnson's personality.

Texas Voices 66He was a very emotional man and a very sensitive man, a man of enormous power, power that was communicated to others. There was a physical element [trait] in his communication of power. There was also an element of his own dedication and his own intense commitment to achieve a chosen objective [goal]. Johnson was fervently [very] result-oriented [driven].99

—Justice Abe Fortas, quoted in *The Johnson Presidency,* by Kenneth W. Thompson

As a Democrat, Johnson became majority leader in the Senate in 1955. This is a leadership position held by a member of the party that has the majority of seats. In this powerful position, Johnson influenced policy in a number of areas, including civil rights and space exploration. These issues would become even more important during his presidential administration.

⭐ **Reading Check** **Finding the Main Idea** What characteristics did Lyndon B. Johnson have that led to his becoming a political success?

Analyzing Primary Sources
Drawing Inferences and Conclusions Which words in the quotation describe President Johnson's leadership qualities?

Interpreting the Visual Record

Johnson and education. *President Johnson returned to his childhood school and met with his first-grade teacher when he signed an education bill into law.* **How might Johnson's experiences have helped his political career?**

The Great Society was intended to help disabled Americans, among others.

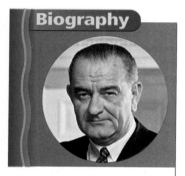

Lyndon B. Johnson
(1908–1973)

Lyndon B. Johnson was born on a farm in the Texas Hill Country. Johnson's interest in politics began at an early age—his father had served in the Texas legislature. Johnson's experiences teaching and working with poor students helped spur his belief in government programs to help the needy. As president of the United States, he worked to improve the lives of poor Americans. After retiring from public office in 1969, Johnson returned home to his ranch near Johnson City. He died in 1973 and was buried in his beloved Hill Country. **What early experience contributed to Johnson's belief in government programs to help Americans?** ⭐TEKS

⭐ The Great Society

When Lyndon B. Johnson became president, he took up and expanded many of John F. Kennedy's plans. President Johnson believed that the United States should provide equal rights, education, jobs, and decent housing for all its citizens. Johnson won the 1964 presidential election by a landslide. Using this support, he launched a program that he called the **Great Society**. Under this program, Congress passed laws establishing health care for older and disabled Americans. The Elementary and Secondary Education Act provided funding for public schools, while another act set up scholarships for poor students. Congress also passed acts to protect natural resources and to regulate water and air quality.

The **Economic Opportunity Act** launched another Great Society program. Part of this act provided funds for job training and created community action programs. The act also provided funds for the Job Corps, which trained young people for employment. In addition, Congress passed a new immigration act that allowed more people from Latin America and Asia to come to the United States. Partly as a result of this act, Hispanic and Asian immigration contributed significantly to the growth of Texas during the 1960s and 1970s.

Although many Americans supported Johnson's Great Society programs, some people argued that the federal government was spending too much on social programs. Others thought that these acts gave the federal government too much power over the states.

⭐ **Reading Check** **Supporting a Point of View** Do you believe that government programs like the Great Society benefit Texas and the United States? Explain your answer.

⭐ The Vietnam War

At the same time that President Johnson was working for change in the United States, conflict was brewing in Southeast Asia. The government of South Vietnam was fighting against communist forces backed by North Vietnam. Presidents Eisenhower and Kennedy had supported sending American military advisers to South Vietnam to help train its military forces. Then in 1964, upon Johnson's request, Congress passed the **Tonkin Gulf Resolution**. This measure gave the president the authority to order troops into combat. U.S. soldiers, bombers, and weapons were sent to Vietnam by the thousands. More than 500,000 Texans served in the military during the Vietnam War. In addition, industrial production increased a great deal to meet the military's growing needs. The booming defense industry boosted the Texas economy.

As casualties mounted, so did opposition to the war. Some Americans criticized President Johnson's handling of the war. Others demanded that he bring U.S. troops home. On college campuses across the country, students demonstrated against the war. Protesters followed Johnson everywhere he went, including in his home state. Johnson worried about the deep division in the country over the war, and about his own health. On March 31, 1968, he announced that he would not run for re-election. Johnson had little success in finding a way to end the war, which continued into the 1970s. Of the some 58,000 Americans who lost their lives in the war, more than 2,100 were Texans. In Vietnam and other Southeast Asian countries, millions were killed. Thousands of others became refugees, many of whom came to Texas. Large Vietnamese American communities grew in Texas cities such as Houston.

Thousands of U.S. troops fought in the Vietnam War, while many people protested the war.

Reading Check **Identifying Cause and Effect** How did war in Vietnam affect the economy and society in Texas?

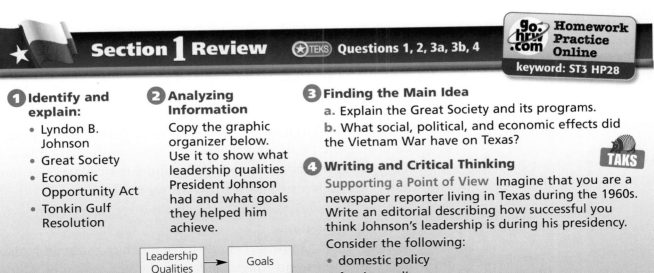

★ **Section 1 Review** ⊛(TEKS) **Questions 1, 2, 3a, 3b, 4**

go. hrw .com **Homework Practice Online** keyword: ST3 HP28

1 **Identify and explain:**
- Lyndon B. Johnson
- Great Society
- Economic Opportunity Act
- Tonkin Gulf Resolution

2 **Analyzing Information**
Copy the graphic organizer below. Use it to show what leadership qualities President Johnson had and what goals they helped him achieve.

Leadership Qualities → Goals

3 **Finding the Main Idea**
a. Explain the Great Society and its programs.
b. What social, political, and economic effects did the Vietnam War have on Texas?

4 **Writing and Critical Thinking**
TAKS
Supporting a Point of View Imagine that you are a newspaper reporter living in Texas during the 1960s. Write an editorial describing how successful you think Johnson's leadership is during his presidency.
Consider the following:
- domestic policy
- foreign policy

The Civil Rights Movement

Read to Discover

1. How did the civil rights movement develop during the 1960s?
2. What led to the expansion of equal rights for Hispanics?
3. How did the women's rights movement develop in Texas?

Why It Matters Today

During the 1960s, African Americans, Mexican Americans, and women became increasingly involved in politics. Use CNNfyi.com or other **current events** sources to find information about current political movements. Record your findings in your journal.

Define
- sit-ins

Identify
- James Farmer
- Civil Rights Act of 1964
- Voting Rights Act
- Barbara Jordan
- Henry B. González
- Chicano movement
- La Raza Unida Party
- Texas Women's Political Caucus

The Story Continues

Christia Adair was a leader of the civil rights movement in Texas.

Christia Adair of Houston was tired of segregation. One day while shopping in a department store she asked a clerk if she could try on an item in the fitting room. The clerk tried to steer her toward an alteration room because African Americans were not allowed in the store's fitting rooms. Adair insisted that she only wanted to try the item on and that it did not need alterations. The clerk called the manager who said, "Show the customer to the fitting room."

★ Nonviolent Protest

The movement for civil rights that had begun after World War II picked up speed during the 1960s. African Americans across the nation began to practice nonviolent resistance to end discrimination and segregation. Protesters staged boycotts and **sit-ins**—protests that involve sitting down in a location such as a public facility and refusing to leave—to bring an end to segregation.

A number of Texas students held sit-ins at lunch counters and other dining facilities. A group in Kingsville forced the integration of a local drive-in restaurant. One of the protesters recalled, "We started just parking our cars up in there . . . and wouldn't move. . . . [Finally] they started serving us." Texans also worked to integrate other facilities. In 1962 a group of Austin mothers protested an ice rink that would not allow African Americans to skate. Members of the Mothers Action Committee and their children marched every day for a year until the skating rink owners changed their policy. Press coverage of civil rights protests often helped the movement.

Texan **James Farmer** was a national leader of the civil rights movement. Through his organization, the Congress of Racial Equality (CORE), Farmer led civil rights protests. He also organized activists on bus rides—called Freedom Rides—through the South. He recalled why these Freedom Rides were held.

Texas Voices ❝Federal law said that there should be no segregation in interstate travel. The Supreme Court had decided that. But still state laws in the southern states and local ordinances ordered segregation of the races on those buses. Why didn't the federal government enforce its law? . . . We decided . . . to have an interracial group ride through the South. . . . We would be doing merely what the Supreme Court said we had a right to do. . . . The blacks would sit in the front of the bus, and would refuse to move when ordered.❞

—James Farmer, quoted in *Voices of Freedom,* by Henry Hampton and Steve Fayer

When Martin Luther King Jr. led peaceful demonstrations throughout the South, he drew national attention to the civil rights movement. In 1963 King and thousands of Americans participated in a March on Washington in support of civil rights. Some 900 Texans of all races participated in a march on the state Capitol. Like those in the national march, these protesters pushed for an end to discrimination and segregation.

⭐ **Reading Check Drawing Inferences and Conclusions** How did the right to free speech, press, and assembly affect the civil rights movement?

Biography

James Farmer
(1916-2000)

James Farmer of Marshall attended Wiley College and Howard University. After helping to found CORE in 1942, Farmer dedicated his life to the civil rights movement. He served as national director of CORE from 1961 to 1966. After leaving CORE, Farmer directed an adult literacy project and worked in the Department of Health, Education, and Welfare. Farmer also published the books *Lay Bare the Heart* and *Freedom—When?* **How did Farmer fulfill his civic responsibilities?** ⭐TEKS

Interpreting the Visual Record

A sit-in. Some young civil rights workers organized sit-ins—such as this one in Austin—to protest public facilities that were segregated. What in this image shows how sit-ins might be effective?

President Lyndon B. Johnson signed the Civil Rights Act of 1964 into law in front of legislators and other officials.

★ President Johnson and Civil Rights

In his first address to Congress, President Johnson urged passage of a civil rights law. He believed that the federal government needed to take action to ensure the rights of all Americans.

 Analyzing Primary Sources
Identifying Points of View
Why do you think Johnson thought it was time to pass civil rights laws?

Texas Voices 66We have talked long enough in this country about equal rights. We have talked for 100 years or more. It is time now to write the next chapter—and to write it in the books of law. I urge you . . . to enact a civil rights law so that we can move forward to eliminate from this Nation every trace of discrimination and oppression [injustice] that is based upon race or color.99

—President Lyndon B. Johnson, Address to Joint Session of the House and Senate, November 27, 1963

Congress soon passed the **Civil Rights Act of 1964**, which banned segregation in public places. The act also barred employers, unions, or universities with federal government contracts from discriminating on the basis of race, sex, religion, or national origin. In 1965 Congress passed the **Voting Rights Act**, which gave the federal government the power to check state voting procedures and to protect citizens' right to vote.

With the successes of the civil rights movement, African Americans gained more positions in the government. In Texas, African Americans began to win state offices for the first time since Reconstruction. In 1966 **Barbara Jordan** of Houston was elected as a state senator. Jordan was elected to the U.S. House of Representatives in 1972, becoming the first African American to represent Texas in the U.S. Congress.

 Reading Check **Finding the Main Idea** How did President Lyndon B. Johnson contribute to the civil rights movement?

★ Hispanic Rights

Hispanics also pushed for civil rights through protests, marches, and political organizations. The Political Association of Spanish-Speaking Organizations, the American GI Forum, and the League of United Latin American Citizens (LULAC) led the movement for equal rights in the 1960s. With leadership from Hector P. García and Albert Peña Jr., these groups hoped to spur Hispanic voters to become more active.

In 1956 Democrat **Henry B. González** had become the first Mexican American elected to the Texas Senate in the 1900s. In 1961 he was elected to the U.S. House of Representatives, where he served for 37 years. He became chairman of the Banking Committee in 1988. In 1964 Eligio "Kika" de la Garza of Hidalgo County was also elected to the House.

Because of new laws and the work of civil rights organizations during the 1960s, large numbers of Hispanics were registering to vote. Mexican Americans in Texas were elected to city, county, and state offices. Despite such gains, many Hispanics still faced discrimination by local officials. Schools that served the Mexican American population were often poor and continued to be segregated in reality, if not by law. The Mexican American Legal Defense and Education Fund (MALDEF) was founded in San Antonio in 1968 to fight discrimination, particularly in public education.

 Reading Check **Analyzing Information** Who were the early leaders of the Hispanic rights movement, and what successes did they have?

★ The Chicano Movement

Many Hispanics were concerned about their economic situation. Poverty was a persistent problem, particularly among farm laborers known as *campesinos*. In June 1966, farm laborers in Texas went on strike to demand a minimum wage. They marched 290 miles, from the Rio Grande valley to Austin. The growing demand for political change became known as the **Chicano movement**, or *el movimiento*. The movement took inspiration from César Chávez, a Mexican American who had organized migrant farmworkers in California. The success of the Chicano movement increased cultural pride within Mexican American communities and established Mexican Americans as a political force.

Students also became active in the Chicano movement. In Crystal City, Texas, Mexican American students walked out of school in 1969 to protest discrimination. Severita Lara described how the protests began at the school, which had an 85 percent Hispanic student body.

Texas Voices ❝In all of our activities, like for example, cheerleaders . . . there's always three Anglos and one mexicana. . . . We started questioning. Why should it be like that? . . . [We] started looking at other things.❞

—Severita Lara, quoted in *Chicano!* by F. Arturo Rosales

Biography

Henry B. González
(1916–2000)

Henry B. González was a political role model for many Mexican Americans. González was born in San Antonio to Mexican immigrants. He attended St. Mary's University Law School, where he earned a law degree. His first political office was as a member of the San Antonio City Council. His 1958 run for the Democratic Party's nomination for governor of Texas encouraged Mexican Americans to become more involved in Texas politics. In 1994 González received the Profile in Courage award from the John F. Kennedy Library. **How did Henry B. González contribute to Texas history?** ⭐TEKS

Analyzing Primary Sources
Identifying Points of View Considering that 85 percent of the school was Hispanic, why might Lara find the number of Hispanic cheerleaders important?

Crystal City. *During the school walkout in Crystal City, the Chicano activists established an alternative school.* **How do you think the words on the blackboard relate to the experiences of these students?**

In January 1970 the students returned to school after they won broad changes and the school board promised reforms. The students were supported by the Mexican American Youth Organization (MAYO), which was founded by José Angel Gutiérrez and Mario Compeán in 1967. In 1970 Gutiérrez formed a new political party, called **La Raza Unida Party** (RUP). The RUP hoped to highlight issues affecting Hispanics and to elect more Hispanics to political office.

The RUP achieved some success in Texas. In Crystal City, for example, Gutiérrez and other RUP members were elected to the school board and the city council. Hispanic women were important to the RUP. Party leader Marta Cotera explained that women "were very much in evidence as . . . candidates, [and] as organizers in leadership position[s]." RUP members helped create government policies to improve the lives of local Mexican Americans. The movement began to decline during the mid-1970s because party members disagreed over policy and as fundraising became more difficult. RUP disappeared after 1978.

New federal laws, however, helped expand Hispanic participation in the political process. A 1975 extension to the Voting Rights Act required that, in areas with large immigrant populations, ballots be provided in the voters' preferred language. This, in part, helped more Hispanic candidates win elections in many regions.

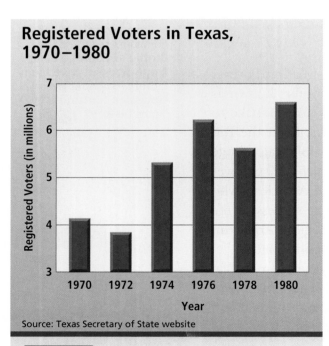

Registered Voters in Texas, 1970–1980

Source: Texas Secretary of State website

TAKS *Skills* *Interpreting Graphs* During the 1970s the number of registered voters rose with the growth of population and changes in voting rights laws. By how much did the number of voters increase between 1970 and 1980?

⭐ **Reading Check** **Summarizing** Describe the development of the Chicano movement.

The Women's Movement

During the 1960s and 1970s women's groups also made political gains. In 1966 author Betty Friedan and other feminists founded the National Organization for Women (NOW). NOW's statement of purpose declared that "the time has come for a new movement toward true equality." NOW chapters sprang up across Texas. Members pushed for new legislation and filed lawsuits on behalf of women who claimed workplace discrimination. They also staged marches, protests, and other demonstrations.

The **Texas Women's Political Caucus**, founded in 1971, worked to get more women elected to political office. The organizers of this group included Liz Carpenter and Jane Wells. When the caucus was founded there were only two women in the state legislature: Barbara Jordan and Frances Farenthold. Women made significant political gains the following year. Five women were elected to the state legislature, and Jordan was elected to Congress. In addition, Farenthold made a serious bid for governor. On the national level, the Republican Party chose Texan Anne Armstrong as speaker and co-chair of the National Republican Committee. She was the first woman co-chair and the first female to give a keynote address at a national party convention.

In the mid- to late 1970s, women were increasingly successful in their bids for local office. For example, Carole Keeton McClellan (now Strayhorn) became the first female president of the Austin school board and, later, mayor of Austin. She later served on the Railroad Commission and as state comptroller. By 1980 many more women had been elected to political office.

 Reading Check **Sequencing** Trace in order the development of the women's rights movement in Texas.

Section 2 Review

★TEKS Questions 2, 3, 4a, 4b, 5

go.hrw.com **Homework Practice Online**
keyword: ST3 HP28

1 Define and explain:
- sit-ins

2 Identify and explain:
- James Farmer
- Civil Rights Act of 1964
- Voting Rights Act
- Barbara Jordan
- Henry B. González
- Chicano movement
- La Raza Unida Party
- Texas Women's Political Caucus

3 Sequencing
Copy the graphic organizer below. Use it to trace in order the development of the civil rights movement for African Americans and to identify its key leaders.

Civil Rights
5.
4.
3.
2.
1.

4 Finding the Main Idea
a. What were some of the key events in the Hispanic civil rights movement?
b. Describe the development of the women's rights movement in Texas.

5 Writing and Critical Thinking TAKS
Summarizing Imagine that you are a participant in an equal rights movement. Write a pamphlet about nonviolent resistance and the freedoms of speech and press.
Consider the following:
- how freedom of speech and of the press helped your cause
- the importance of nonviolent protest

New Technology and the Space Race

Read to Discover

1. Why did the aerospace and defense industries in Texas grow, and what impact did they have on the state?
2. In what ways did developments in the high-tech industries affect Texas?

Identify

- *Sputnik*
- **National Aeronautics and Space Administration**
- **Manned Spacecraft Center**
- **Walter Cunningham**
- **Michael DeBakey**

Why It Matters Today

The defense industry developed new technology during the 1960s. Use **CNNfyi.com** or other **current events** sources to find information about today's weapons technology. Record your findings in your journal.

The Story Continues

NASA astronauts wore patches such as this on their space suits.

Part of the U.S. space program was moving to a new location. Gene Kranz had 30 days to find housing for himself and his family in Houston. But Kranz was in the middle of research and did not want to go to Houston. He called in his newest employee, Dutch, and told him to "scout around and find the best place to live." Dutch went and picked out houses for 10 families in southwest Houston, an area that later became known as Flight Controller Alley.

★ Texas in the Space Age

As a leader in aircraft and weapons production, Texas was a logical choice to become a center for the nation's developing space program. The launching of the Soviet **Sputnik** satellite in 1957 had prompted the creation of the **National Aeronautics and Space Administration** (NASA) in 1958. NASA took charge of the U.S. space program and worked to make U.S. goals in space a reality.

In 1961 NASA chose Houston as the headquarters for its astronauts. The **Manned Spacecraft Center** occupied 1,000 acres of ranchland formerly owned by James Marion West. The center officially opened that same year and became the Mission Control Center for all manned space flights. From the moment a rocket lifts off, the Mission Control Center monitors the flight and helps solve any problems.

The astronauts at Houston attracted worldwide attention as the space race intensified. After the Soviet Union sent the first human into space in 1961, President John F. Kennedy addressed a joint session of Congress. "I believe this nation should commit itself to achieving the goal . . . of landing a man on the moon and returning him safely." On May 5, 1961, Alan Shepard Jr. became the first American to enter space. In 1968 NASA launched the *Apollo 7* mission, the first manned flight of the Apollo program. Astronaut **Walter Cunningham** was a participant in the flight. On July 16, 1969, NASA sent *Apollo 11* into space, and astronaut Neil Armstrong achieved what many had thought impossible. He took his first step on the Moon's surface on July 20, 1969.

The Manned Spacecraft Center—renamed the Lyndon B. Johnson Space Center in 1973—researched, developed, and built the first space shuttle in the 1970s. In 1981 *Columbia* became the first shuttle launched into space. With much of the U.S. space program located in Texas, the center brought many jobs to the Houston area. The center had thousands of employees and was a primary site for U.S. research and development of manned spacecraft. The space center was also home to space station research, astronaut training, and aerospace medicine. Federal funding and the aerospace industry attracted many high-tech specialists to Texas.

Reading Check **Analyzing Information** How did the aerospace industry affect the economic development of Texas?

★ The Defense Industry

The defense industry grew along with the space industry. Texas had been a center of military aircraft and weapons production since World War II. As the Cold War continued, the push for new weapons technology grew, and the defense industry in Texas expanded. Several Texas firms, including General Dynamics Corporation and Texas Instruments, had U.S. government defense contracts to build weapons systems.

By 1965 General Dynamics was the number one weapons exporter in the nation. Texas also ranked second in aircraft production during the

Walter Cunningham
(1932–)

A native of Iowa, Walter Cunningham received a master's degree in physics from the University of California at Los Angeles. He then joined NASA in 1964, participating in the Apollo program. Although he left NASA in 1971, Cunningham remained a Houston resident. He has served on the board of directors of technology companies and has received several awards. These include the NASA Exceptional Service Medal and the Medal of Valor from the American Legion. Cunningham is a member of the International Space Hall of Fame and the Houston Hall of Fame. **How has Walter Cunningham been a leader in science and technology?** ⭐TEKS

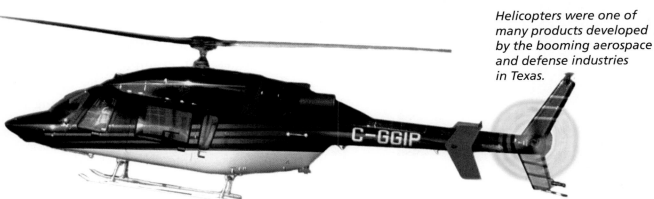

Helicopters were one of many products developed by the booming aerospace and defense industries in Texas.

The Texas Aerospace Industry

Aircraft manufacturing had been occurring in Texas since the early 1940s. By the 1960s it was one of the state's leading industries. In 1967 some 58,000 Texans worked in aircraft manufacturing. With the development of new weapons technology, Texas also became the site for companies in the defense industry. Aerospace technology firms began to do business in Texas in the 1950s, specializing in the manufacture and testing of rockets for the military. Texas was well known for aeronautics and aerospace technology even before it was chosen as home for the Manned Spacecraft Center. Texas companies created products to support NASA projects, while educational facilities such as Rice University assisted NASA in its space research. The Texas aerospace industry continues to lead the industry with its work with the International Space Station.

1. Economics and History How did the aeronautics and aerospace industries affect the development of Texas? ⭐TEKS

2. Economics and You How do you think the Texas aerospace industry has affected local, national, and international markets? ⭐TEKS

1960s. In addition, the state continued to be home to many military bases and personnel during the 1980s. By adding millions of dollars to the Texas economy, the defense industry—both military bases and weapons production—had become critical to the state's economy.

⭐ **Reading Check Finding the Main Idea** How did the development of new weapons technology during the Cold War affect the economy of Texas?

⭐ High-Tech Industries

In addition to becoming a center for defense and space research, Texas rapidly became a leader in other high-tech industries. Texas companies manufactured a variety of electronic devices, including transistors, television sets, and computers. Firms were drawn to Texas because of affordable labor and a good climate. By the late 1950s, Dallas, Fort Worth, and Houston had become centers for the electronics industry.

New technological developments in communications, radar, and other systems led to even greater growth in the industry. By 1963 nearly 300 businesses in Texas produced electronic devices. Firms such as Texas Instruments and Tracor grew as their sales reached millions of dollars a year. Several Texas companies became world leaders in the electronics industry, which added billions of dollars to the Texas economy. These companies also provided national and international markets with technology developed and manufactured in Texas.

As computer technology became more advanced, computers became important to the daily operations of businesses all over the world. The Texas high-tech industry began to design and manufacture semiconductors and microchips to meet the national and international demand for computers. The demand for these goods boosted and expanded the high-tech economy in Texas. For example, Austin became another Texas high-tech research center as companies such as IBM built facilities there during the 1960s and 1970s.

⭐ **Reading Check Drawing Inferences and Conclusions** How do you think scientific discoveries and high-tech industries in Texas made the state more interdependent with the world?

★ Medical Technology

Scientific research in medicine also spurred the Texas economy. With the development of medical centers such as the Texas Medical Center in Houston, the state has been at the forefront of medical research and treatment. Texas doctors and scientists studied treatments for cancer, evaluated new drugs, and developed other medical innovations. Texas doctors such as **Michael DeBakey** and Denton Cooley helped revolutionize the treatment of heart disease. In 1964 DeBakey performed the first arterial bypass operation to repair a damaged heart. In 1968 Cooley performed the first heart transplant.

As a center for medical research, Texas has attracted patients seeking quality health care from all over the world. Medical technologies that were developed in the state, such as the artificial heart, have been used throughout the world to treat patients. As a result of these scientific and medical advances, many medical technology companies have located their operations in Texas.

The booming Texas high-tech and medical technology industries affected not only the markets in which they operated but also the cities in which they were based. The population of these cities grew rapidly. As the population and economy expanded in Texas cities, world-class buildings and new sports arenas were built. Museums and other attractions were established or improved. People moved to Texas in increasing numbers to take advantage of not only the jobs in these industries but also the quality of life that a growing economy helped provide.

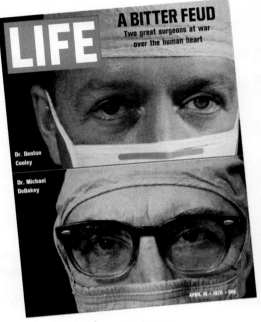

Texas heart surgeons Michael DeBakey and Denton Cooley became internationally known in the 1960s.

 ★ **Reading Check** **Analyzing Information** How has the medical technology industry affected markets in Texas, the United States, and the world?

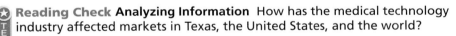

Section 3 Review
★TEKS Questions 2, 3a, 3b, 4

go.hrw.com **Homework Practice Online**
keyword: ST3 HP28

1 Identify and explain:
- *Sputnik*
- National Aeronautics and Space Administration
- Manned Spacecraft Center
- Walter Cunningham
- Michael DeBakey

2 Summarizing
Copy the graphic organizer below. Use it to show how new technology has affected the development of Texas.

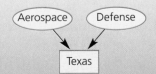

3 Finding the Main Idea
a. Explain how world events led to the growing defense industry in Texas in the 1960s.

b. How was the development of Texas affected by the growth of the high-tech and medical industries?

4 Writing and Critical Thinking

TAKS

Analyzing Information Imagine that you are an economist living in the 1960s. Write a short speech on how technology has led to an increasing dependence among Texas, the United States, and the world.

Consider the following:
- the military weapons produced in Texas
- the booming high-tech industries

Read to Discover

1. What were the effects of changes in the population distribution of Texas?
2. How did international events lead to a boom in the Texas economy in the 1970s?
3. How did a two-party system and other developments affect Texas politics in the 1970s?

Why It Matters Today

During the 1970s the Texas economy thrived as a result of high oil prices and booming industry. Use **CNNfyi.com** or other **current events** sources to find information about major Texas industries today. Record your findings in your journal.

Define

• two-party system

Identify

• Sunbelt
• John Tower
• Sharpstown stock-fraud scandal
• William Clements

Texans use cranes and other large construction equipment to build the state's skyscrapers.

The Story Continues

In the 1950s a writer described Austin's famous landmarks. "From a point of higher ground, one can see the college tower and the Capitol building." By the early 1970s, the beautiful old downtown buildings were being overshadowed by a new arrival—a skyscraper. The new building was a sign of the times. During the mid-1970s and early 1980s, Austin would become known for the thousands of newcomers flocking there to take part in a high-tech revolution.

★ The Sunbelt and Urban Growth

Austin was part of a new trend of growth in the <u>Sunbelt</u>—the South and Southwest—that had begun in the mid-1900s. The Sunbelt offered employment opportunities, a mild winter climate, and an appealing standard of living. Quality of life was an important factor in the Sunbelt migration. As one person wrote, "The Sun Belt offers both more 'sun' and more 'fun.' Outdoor living, informal entertaining, and golf year round—all afford [offer] the new lifestyles which Americans have adopted." Between 1940 and 1980, the population of the Sunbelt grew by more than 110 percent. In 1980 about one third of the U.S. population lived in this region.

A good deal of this growth took place in Texas. During the 1970s oil and gas companies and other successful industries drew people by the hundreds of thousands. Between 1970 and 1980 the Texas population grew from more than 11 million to more than 14 million. Most of these new Texans moved to cities. Houston and Dallas in particular grew rapidly, as industry boomed there. Immigration also contributed to urban growth. Most immigrants were from Mexico and came hoping to find better economic opportunities in Texas. Between 1970 and 1980 the Hispanic population grew from nearly 2.1 million to approximately 3 million—more than 20 percent of the Texas population.

⭐ **Reading Check** **Finding the Main Idea** Why did so many people move to Texas in the 1970s, and where did they settle?

⭐ New Jobs and City Life

As the population of Texas cities continued to grow, the economy entered a cycle of expansion. Most newcomers moved to cities because jobs and housing were plentiful. These newcomers added to the growing labor force in Texas. The prospect of a large labor pool of highly educated workers attracted new business to Texas cities. During the 1970s and 1980s several major national companies moved their headquarters to Texas. These businesses in turn attracted more job-seekers to the state.

The increase in city populations also created new demands for a variety of services, from restaurants to utilities. The new industries in Texas attracted national and international business to Texas cities. This increased the demand for hotels, airports, and other service industries. The number and size of service industries grew to meet the rising

CONNECTING TO SCIENCE AND TECHNOLOGY

Keeping Cool in Texas

Home air-cooling technology dates back to the early Spanish settlers who built houses of adobe—sun-dried brick. The adobe cooled down at night and stayed cool inside until afternoon. Texans began making simple devices to cool their homes as early as the late 1800s. These usually involved air blown over ice in various ways. Gradually, the machines became more complex, and by the 1940s Texas had become a national center for the manufacture of air-conditioning equipment. **How might new air-conditioning technology contribute to Sunbelt migration?** ⭐TEKS

Sunny climate and growing industries attracted people to Texas cities such as Dallas.

Texas cities began to grow more rapidly during the mid- and late 1900s. This growth was encouraged by several factors, including the sunny climate, improved transportation, economic opportunities, and air-conditioning.

Booming industries such as oil, electronic technology, and aerospace attracted many workers to Texas cities.

City Growth

The sunny climate attracted many companies and people to Texas.

The development of efficient air-conditioning made life during hot Texas summers more enjoyable. This led to even more migration to Texas.

The expansion of the highway system and the affordability of cars led to the growth in city size in Texas.

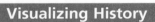

Visualizing History

1. **Geography** What geographic factors contributed to the growth and development of Texas? 🌟TEKS

2. **Connecting to Today** How do you think these geographic factors affect the economy of Texas today? 🌟TEKS

That's Interesting!

The Astrodome

Completed in 1965, the Houston Astrodome was the first fully air-conditioned domed stadium in the world. The Astrodome is huge. Inside, it reaches a height of 208 feet from the ground to the roof. The roof spans a distance of 642 feet.

demand, thus creating jobs for Texans. Manufacturing jobs, particularly in high-tech fields, increased. The number of manufacturing jobs grew by more than 100 percent in Dallas, Fort Worth, and Houston.

The growth of industries and jobs led to a growing demand for new houses, offices, and other buildings. The real estate market boomed in Texas to meet this demand. Construction cranes dominated the landscape in the major cities. Many people put all of their money into real estate investments. New tax laws made it easier for Texas banks and financial institutions to loan money to finance new construction. As a result, the banking industry expanded rapidly. During this economic boom, Texas cities grew at an unheard-of rate, both in numbers of buildings and in population.

As Texas cities grew, many people chose to live in new housing developments outside the central city. However, many of these people still worked downtown. State and city leaders responded by building new freeway systems that allowed Texans to commute more easily from suburbs into cities. Leaders also began to develop more public transportation systems such as buses to help people travel throughout the growing urban areas.

🌟 **Reading Check** **Evaluating** How did the types of jobs in cities change, and what led to the real estate boom?

★ The Oil Boom and Bust

Booming industries sparked rapid population growth in Texas. One of the most important industries that experienced a major boom in the 1970s was the oil business. In 1973 the Organization of Petroleum Exporting Countries (OPEC) banned oil shipments to the United States for political reasons. Although the situation lasted only a few months, it drove up world oil prices substantially. While much of the U.S. economy was hurt by the higher gas prices, Texas businesses that produced and sold oil and natural gas benefited greatly.

The spike in the price of oil produced a boom in the Texas oil industry. With the rising prices, profits for oil companies grew. Oil companies expanded production to meet the high demand. This created many new jobs in the industry, and salaries of oil workers grew—to almost three times their earlier level. Offshore oil drilling also increased. With the boom in production, Texas was supplying more oil to national and international markets.

This boom came to a halt in 1982 when oil prices dropped. More than 200,000 jobs were lost in Houston alone. The oil bust of the 1980s hurt other businesses in Texas, such as service industries that catered to the oil industry. The bust also led to a slowdown in the Texas real estate market.

 Reading Check Analyzing Information How did the international market for oil and boom-and-bust cycles affect Texas?

★ Politics in the 1970s

Texas government changed along with the state's population and economy. With the successes of the civil rights movements of the 1960s, Texans of all backgrounds became involved in deciding the direction of state government. Another major change during the 1970s was the growth of the Republican Party in the state. Texas had been primarily a one-party state since Reconstruction.

Texas eventually developed a **two-party system**—a political system in which two parties of comparable strength compete for political office. Republicans had gained some support in Texas in the 1950s. A majority of Texans had supported Republican Dwight D. Eisenhower in the 1952 and 1956 presidential elections. In 1961 **John Tower** became the first Republican to be elected to the U.S. Senate from Texas since Reconstruction. Republican Richard Nixon carried Texas in the 1972 presidential election.

The Democrats still held the state's executive office, however. They had won every election for governor in Texas for nearly 100 years. Beginning in 1950, Democrats Allan Shivers, Price Daniel, and John Connally had each been elected to three consecutive terms. Preston Smith was elected governor in 1968 and again in 1970. When Dolph

The Chinese Lunar New Year

The Chinese immigrants who came to Texas brought many of their cultural traditions with them, including holidays and festivals. For example, many Chinese Americans hold banquets and parades and shoot off firecrackers for the Chinese Lunar New Year. Family celebrations usually involve a dinner, staying up until the New Year arrives, and sealing the doors with red paper for good luck. The following day, the paper is broken, bringing in the New Year. **How have Chinese immigrants contributed to Texas culture?** ⊘ TEKS

Chinese New Year celebration in Austin.

THE CONNALLY CAPER —

The Connally caper.
Governor John Connally was such a strong conservative Democrat while in office that some people believed he slowed the development of the Republican Party in Texas. In 1973 he switched to the Republican Party. **How does this cartoonist show this event?**

Briscoe defeated Smith in the 1972 Democratic primary, this three-term pattern was broken.

Briscoe took office amid demands for reform in state government. In 1971 several officials had been accused and convicted of accepting bribes from Frank Sharp, a Houston businessman. In exchange for the bribes, these officials passed legislation that was favorable to Sharp. As a result of this **Sharpstown stock-fraud scandal**, the next legislature passed several reforms. Elected officials had to report how they acquired and spent donations to their campaigns. The laws also required records to be opened to the public.

Other changes to Texas government were also proposed. The length of the governor's term of office was changed from two to four years in 1972. In 1974 an unsuccessful attempt was made to rewrite the Texas Constitution.

Dolph Briscoe ran for re-election in 1978 but lost the Democratic nomination to Attorney General John Hill. Texas had not had a Republican governor since 1874, and many people thought that Hill could not lose. They were wrong. Republican **William Clements** won by nearly 17,000 votes. Clements described his style.

 Texas Voices ❝**They talk about how I'm direct, I'm abrupt, so forth and so on. Nonsense. I'm certainly straightforward, there's no question about that. You know, I don't have time to willy-nilly around the issues and blow a lot of smoke about this and that and so forth.**❞

—Governor William Clements, quoted in *The Texas Governor's Mansion*, by Jean Daniel, Price Daniel, and Dorothy Blodgett

★ **Reading Check** **Summarizing** How and when did a two-party political system develop in Texas?

Section 4 Review ★TEKS Questions 1, 3, 4a, 4b, 5

 go. hrw .com **Homework Practice Online**
keyword: ST3 HP28

1 **Define and explain:**
- two-party system

2 **Identify and explain:**
- Sunbelt
- John Tower
- Sharpstown stock-fraud scandal
- William Clements

3 **Analyzing Information**
Copy the graphic organizer below. Use it to show why people moved to Texas during the 1970s, where they settled, and how the changing population distribution affected Texas.

Why they moved

↓

Where they settled

↓

Effect on Texas

4 **Finding the Main Idea**
a. Describe the effect of high oil prices on international markets and booming industry on Texas.

b. Trace the development of a two-party system and other changes in Texas politics in the 1970s.

5 **Writing and Critical Thinking**
Summarizing Write a paragraph describing the effects of the Sunbelt migration on Texas in the 1970s.
Consider the following:
- economic growth
- effects on society

Texas Boom-and-Bust Cycles

Texas experienced a dramatic boom-and-bust cycle in its economy during the 1970s and 1980s. The years from 1973 to 1982 were the boom period, fueled by high prices for oil and natural gas. The initial cause of the increased prices was an OPEC ban on the sale of oil to the United States. The ban created an energy shortage in the United States and drove up prices. But oil prices dropped in 1982, leading to a bust in the oil industry. By September 1982, 17 Dallas-area oil companies had gone out of business.

Many Texans work on offshore oil platforms in the Gulf of Mexico.

Interpreting Charts ⓉTEKS

1. By how much did the production of oil increase between 1925 and 1975?

2. How much did production drop after 1975?

3. How did international markets affect production of oil and natural gas in Texas?

4. How do you think a state or nation can avoid serious effects of a boom-and-bust cycle in its economy?

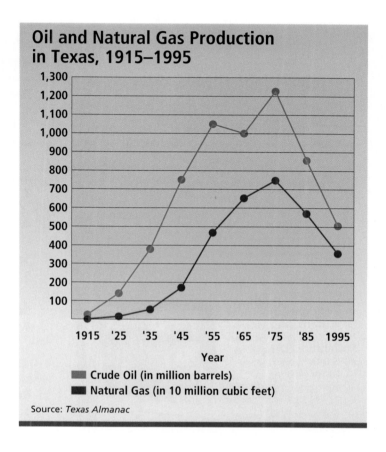

Oil and Natural Gas Production in Texas, 1915–1995

- ■ Crude Oil (in million barrels)
- ■ Natural Gas (in 10 million cubic feet)

Source: *Texas Almanac*

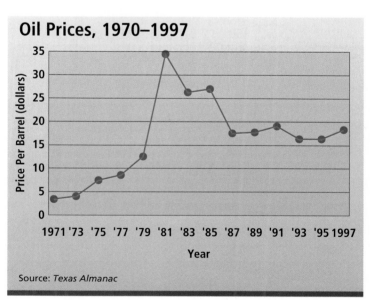

Oil Prices, 1970–1997

Source: *Texas Almanac*

CHAPTER 28 REVIEW

The Chapter at a Glance

Examine the following visual summary of the chapter. Then use it to create a time line that includes the significant individuals and time periods discussed in the chapter. ⭐TEKS

Texas in the 1960s–1970s

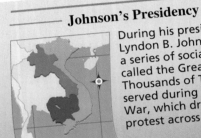

Johnson's Presidency

During his presidency Lyndon B. Johnson launched a series of social programs called the Great Society. Thousands of Texans served during the Vietnam War, which drew much protest across the nation.

Texans Fight for Civil Rights

Texans made progress in civil rights, as African Americans, Mexican Americans, and women pushed for changes to laws and won election to public office.

Booming Technology Industries

The growth of defense, aerospace, and electronics industries led to a booming Texas economy during the 1960s and 1970s.

Sunbelt Migration

Attracted to the warm climate, many businesses and people moved to Texas. This migration spurred urban growth. During the 1970s the oil industry and real estate business also grew.

Identifying People and Ideas ⭐TEKS

Use the following terms or people in historically significant sentences.

1. Lyndon B. Johnson
2. Great Society
3. sit-ins
4. Voting Rights Act
5. Barbara Jordan
6. Henry B. González
7. Chicano movement
8. Manned Spacecraft Center
9. Walter Cunningham
10. two-party system

Understanding Main Ideas ⭐TEKS

Section 1 (pp. 586–589)

1. Describe the leadership qualities of President Lyndon B. Johnson.
2. How did the Vietnam War affect the politics, society, and economy of Texas?

Section 2 (pp. 590–595)

3. Trace the development of the women's rights movement in Texas.
4. What steps did African Americans take in the 1960s to secure civil rights?

Section 3 (pp. 596–599)

5. What effect did aerospace technology have on the development of Texas?

Section 4 (pp. 600–604)

6. How did the Sunbelt migration lead to new types of jobs in Texas cities?

You Be the Historian ⭐TEKS

Reviewing Themes

1. **Citizenship** How do you think Texans who participated in the civil rights and equal rights movements exercised civic responsibilities?
2. **Science, Technology & Society** How did the development of new technologies affect the growth of Texas, particularly its cities, from the 1960s to the 1980s?
3. **Geography** How did geographic factors affect the political, economic, and social development of Texas during the 1970s?

TAKS Practice: Thinking Critically ⭐TEKS

1. **Analyzing Information** How did the boom in the aerospace, high-tech, and oil and gas industries affect the development of Texas and Texas cities?
2. **Summarizing** Trace the development of the Hispanic rights movement.
3. **Identifying Cause and Effect** What international event increased oil and natural gas prices, and how did that affect Texas?

Interpreting Maps ⭐TEKS

Study the map below. Use the information on the map to help you answer the questions that follow.

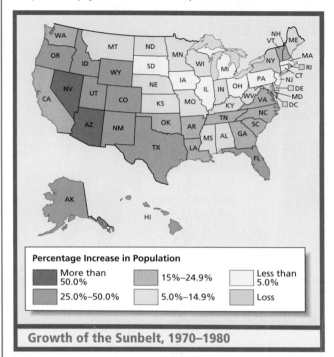

Percentage Increase in Population

- More than 50.0%
- 25.0%–50.0%
- 15%–24.9%
- 5.0%–14.9%
- Less than 5.0%
- Loss

Growth of the Sunbelt, 1970–1980

1. What geographic pattern is shown on this map?
   a. New England grew fastest in the 1970s.
   b. Texas was the fastest-growing state.
   c. The Southwest was one of the fastest-growing regions.
   d. Texas was the slowest-growing state.

2. What geographic factors, such as climate and weather, contributed to the Sunbelt's growth?

Analyzing Primary Sources ⭐TEKS

When Barbara Jordan began her campaign for a seat in the U.S. House of Representatives, Lyndon B. Johnson urged people to vote for her. Read the quote by Johnson. Then answer the questions.

"Barbara Jordan proved to us that black is beautiful before we knew what that meant. She is a woman of keen intellect and unusual legislative ability, a symbol proving that We Can Overcome. Wherever she goes she is going to be at the top. Wherever she goes all of us are going to be behind her. Those with hurting consciences because they have discriminated against blacks and women can vote for Barbara Jordan and feel good."

3. What leadership traits did Johnson say Jordan had?
   a. She could convince people to vote for her.
   b. She was a native Texan.
   c. She was a friend of Johnson's.
   d. She was a symbol of people's ability to overcome.

4. What role do you think bias may have played in Johnson's praise of a fellow Democrat?

Alternative Assessment

Cooperative Learning ⭐TEKS

Work with a small group to complete the following activity. Imagine that you and your group are members of the Texas Chamber of Commerce, and that you want to encourage companies to relocate to Texas. Each person in your group should select one of the following industries: a) aerospace, b) high-tech, c) medical, d) defense. Work together to prepare a colorful brochure that should convince companies to move to Texas. You might want to include visuals such as charts, diagrams, graphs, or maps to make your case more convincing.

BUILDING YOUR Portfolio

📶 **internet** connect

Internet Activity: go.hrw.com
KEYWORD: ST3 TX28 ⭐TEKS

Access the Internet through the HRW Go site to research the changes in the types of jobs that have resulted from urbanization, such as the growth of service industries. Then use the Holt Grapher to create a database and generate a graph that illustrates the data you have found. On a separate sheet of paper, write a paragraph telling how the growth of Texas cities affects the state's economy.

go.hrw.com

Challenges of a Modern State

(1980–Present)

Larry McMurtry's novel Lonesome Dove *is made into a movie for television starring Texan Tommy Lee Jones.*

LONESOME DOVE
The Pulitzer Prize-Winning Novel
LARRY McMURTRY

Texas blues musician Stevie Ray Vaughan was honored in Austin with this statue.

TEXAS

1986 Texas writer Larry McMurtry receives the Pulitzer Prize for his novel *Lonesome Dove.*

1990 Texas musician Stevie Ray Vaughan is killed in a helicopter crash.

1994 Tejano singer Selena Quintanilla's album *Amor Prohibido* sells some 600,000 copies in the United States.

1980	**1983**	**1986**	**1989**	**1992**

U.S. and WORLD

1984 American banks continue to experience financial trouble and fail at an increasing rate.

1988 Vice President George Bush is elected president of the United States.

1992 Canada, Mexico, and the United States sign the North American Free Trade Agreement (NAFTA), which goes into effect in 1994.

1980 Republican Ronald Reagan is elected president of the United States.

Ronald and Nancy Reagan received support from many Texans during their years in the White House.

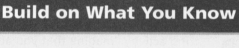

Build on What You Know

Texas had recently seen many changes, including the civil rights movement and the rise of a two-party political system. The development of new technologies that brought the state into the space age also brought opportunities and challenges as Texas entered the new century.

Republican George W. Bush defeated Democrat Ann Richards in the 1994 governor's race. Bush later became president of the United States.

The Dallas Area Rapid Transit system includes light-rail, buses, and other forms of public transportation.

1995 George W. Bush takes office as governor.

2000 Rick Perry becomes the 47th governor of Texas.

2001 Dallas Area Rapid Transit marks its fifth year of providing light-rail service to Dallas residents.

1995　　1998　　2001　　Present

1996 Democrat Bill Clinton is elected to a second term as U.S. president.

2000 Vicente Fox Quesada is elected president of Mexico.

2001 George W. Bush is inaugurated as the 43rd president of the United States.

On September 11, terrorists attack the World Trade Center and the Pentagon.

As a Texan . . .
What do you think your state will be like in the future?

You Be the Historian

Themes Journal

What's Your Opinion? Do you **agree** or **disagree** with the following statements? Support your point of view in your journal.

● **Science, Technology & Society** Advances in technology always improve people's lives.

● **Global Relations** One nation's economy can grow only by weakening another nation's economy.

● **Culture** Ethnic groups are rarely able to maintain traditional celebrations and activities while living within a larger culture.

Political Change in Texas

Read to Discover

1. How did Texas become a two-party state?
2. What were the goals of Texas leaders during the 1990s?

Why It Matters Today

Both Democrats and Republicans served as the Texas governor during the 1970s, 1980s, and 1990s. Use CNN**fyi**.com or other **current events** sources to learn more about appointed and elected leaders. Record your findings in your journal.

Identify

- **Mark White**
- **Phil Gramm**
- **Lloyd Bentsen**
- **Kay Bailey Hutchison**
- **Ann Richards**
- **George W. Bush**
- **Bob Bullock**
- **Rick Perry**

The Story Continues

Bill Clements faced a difficult challenge. Not only was he a latecomer to the race for governor of Texas, but no Republican had held the office in more than 100 years. He campaigned hard, crisscrossing the state to urge Texans to vote Republican. Clements won the election, shocking many political observers. At his inauguration, he spoke enthusiastically about his state. "Texas . . . is a place where people can realize their dreams."

Pins and other campaign items encouraged Texans to vote for Clements.

★ A Two-Party State

The election of Bill Clements in 1978 marked a turning point in state politics. Many Texans had turned to the Republican Party, which promised to control government spending and keep taxes low. As a result, Texas was rapidly becoming a two-party state. In the four elections for governor from 1978 to 1990, Republicans won two, and Democrats won two.

Clements promised to boost the state's economy by lowering taxes and reducing government regulation of business. In 1982 he ran for governor again, but lost to Democrat **Mark White**. White put improvements to the state's educational system as one of his top priorities. In a rematch of the 1982 race, Clements won a second term as governor in 1986.

The makeup of the Texas legislature also reflected the development of a two-party political system. In 1961 only two Republicans held seats in the 181-seat Texas legislature. These numbers gradually rose during the 1960s and 1970s.

Texans also increasingly supported the Republican Party on the national level. In 1970 only 4 members of the state's 25-member congressional delegation belonged to the Republican Party. As with the number of Republican state legislators, this number increased during the 1970s. Republican leaders such as John Tower, who served in the U.S. Senate for more than 20 years beginning in 1961, worked to increase their party's visibility in the state.

In 1984 Republican congressman **Phil Gramm**, a former Democrat, won Tower's seat when Tower retired. A former economics professor at Texas A&M University, Gramm won re-election in 1990 and 1996. As chairman of the Senate Banking Committee, Gramm supported legislation that reformed the nation's banking laws. Gramm served in the Senate with Democrat **Lloyd Bentsen** until Bentsen resigned to become U.S. secretary of the treasury in 1993. Bentsen's seat was won by Republican **Kay Bailey Hutchison**, who thus became the state's first female U.S. senator.

Reading Check **Summarizing** Trace the emergence of the two-party system in Texas.

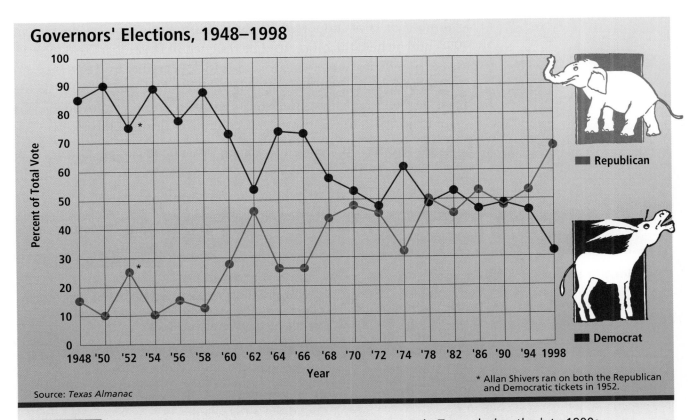

Governors' Elections, 1948–1998

Source: *Texas Almanac*

* Allan Shivers ran on both the Republican and Democratic tickets in 1952.

TAKS Skills *Interpreting Charts* The rise of the two-party system in Texas during the late 1900s led to greater competition between Republican and Democratic Party candidates. What years did Republican candidates defeat Democratic candidates?

★ Politics in the 1990s

The growing power of the Republican Party in Texas was put to the test in the 1990 governor's election. The Democratic Party nominated **Ann Richards**, the state's treasurer since 1983. Republicans chose Clayton Williams, a businessman from Midland. Richards won the election, which featured the highest voter turnout for a governor's race since 1970. Richards promised to support the state's businesses while ensuring strong protection for the environment. She also called for more women and members of minority groups to participate in leadership positions in state government.

Richards ran for governor again in 1994. The Republican Party nominated **George W. Bush** as their candidate. Bush had worked in the Texas oil industry and was a part owner of the Texas Rangers baseball team. Bush won after a vigorous campaign. Bush called for improvements to the economy and schools, lower property taxes, and stronger criminal laws. Bush recognized that he needed the cooperation of the legislature—which was controlled by Democrats—to achieve his goals. Bush urged both parties to engage in bipartisanship, or cooperation between parties. The governor developed a strong working relationship with Democratic leaders such as **Bob Bullock**, who served as lieutenant governor during much of Bush's time as governor. The legislature soon passed a number of laws supported by Bush. Bush easily won re-election in 1998, and he held the office until he resigned in December 2000 to serve as U.S. president. Lieutenant Governor **Rick Perry** became governor.

Meanwhile, in 1996 the Republican Party had won control of the Texas Senate for the first time since Reconstruction. Democrats held a small majority in the House of Representatives through the 1990s.

 Reading Check **Analyzing Information** What goals did Ann Richards and George W. Bush set for Texas?

 Section 1 Review ⊛TEKS Questions 2, 3a, 3b, 4

go.hrw.com **Homework Practice Online**
keyword: ST3 HP29

1 Identify and explain:
- Mark White
- Phil Gramm
- Lloyd Bentsen
- Kay Bailey Hutchison
- Ann Richards
- George W. Bush
- Bob Bullock
- Rick Perry

2 Categorizing
Copy the table below. Use it to list what national and state offices Republicans held.

National Offices	State Offices

3 Finding the Main idea
a. How did the two-party system develop in Texas?
b. What did the governors who were elected during the 1990s want to achieve?

4 Writing and Critical Thinking
Analyzing Information Write a paragraph describing how having a two-party system affects the legislative process in Texas.
Consider the following:
- bipartisanship
- the changing numbers of Democrats and Republicans in office

Read to Discover

1. What did George Bush accomplish as president, and what major events occurred during his presidency?
2. How was the United States attacked on September 11, 2001, and how did George W. Bush's administration respond?
3. How did the events of September 11 affect the nation?

Define
- terrorism

Identify
- George Bush
- War on Drugs
- Operation Desert Storm
- George W. Bush

Why it Matters Today

The terrorist attacks of September 11, 2001, continue to affect American life and U.S. foreign policy. Use **CNNfyi.com** or other **current events** sources to learn about the latest issues and events stemming from the fight against terrorism. Record your findings in your journal.

The Story Continues

For the Texans who had gathered in Houston on the evening of September 16, 1980, it was no ordinary night out. The 2,500 well-dressed guests had gathered to see some of the most important figures in the Republican Party. Guests saw presidential candidate Ronald Reagan and his running mate, Texan George Bush. The dinner raised some $2.8 million for the Republican Party, leading one Republican to declare it "the biggest political fundraiser ever held."

Texan George Bush ran for vice president on the Republican ticket with Ronald Reagan in 1980 and 1984.

★ President George Bush

George Bush, who had run on the Republican ticket in 1980 and in Ronald Reagan's successful re-election bid in 1984, served as Reagan's vice president for eight years. Americans chose Bush as president in 1988. Originally from Massachusetts, Bush became at age 18 the youngest pilot in the U.S. Navy. Bush was awarded several medals during World War II. After he graduated from Yale University, George and his wife, Barbara, moved to Texas. He worked in the oil industry and in 1966 won the first of two elections to the U.S. House of Representatives. During the 1970s Bush served in several important government leadership positions, including the director of the Central Intelligence Agency.

President George Bush met with U.S. troops during Operation Desert Shield before the Persian Gulf War.

Upon becoming president, Bush brought several Texans into his administration, including Secretary of State James Baker. Bush promised to provide "steady, experienced leadership." His administration addressed a number of issues. Bush increased support for the **War on Drugs**—an organized effort that had begun in the 1970s to end the trade and use of illegal drugs. In 1990 Bush signed the Americans with Disabilities Act (ADA). The ADA guaranteed people with disabilities equal access to public places, transportation, and jobs.

Overseas, dramatic changes were occurring in the Soviet Union as that nation gradually moved toward democracy. By 1991 the Soviet Union had broken apart, and many of the former Soviet republics had formed an alliance, the Commonwealth of Independent States. The Cold War had ended, but President Bush soon faced another challenge from overseas.

 Reading Check **Analyzing Information** What major policy actions did President Bush take during his presidency?

★ The Persian Gulf War

A crisis in the Middle East tested the Bush administration. On August 2, 1990, Iraq invaded its neighbor, Kuwait. Iraq's action threatened much of the world's oil supplies. Bush and leaders from many other nations quickly demanded that Iraqi forces withdraw from Kuwait. When Iraq refused, the United States and eventually some 30 other nations formed a military coalition, or alliance, to drive Iraqi forces out of Kuwait.

In mid-January 1991 the international coalition launched **Operation Desert Storm**. Aircraft and missiles from navy ships bombarded Iraq for six weeks. Texan Mark Furr recalled the beginning of the attack.

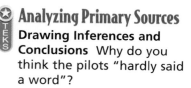 **Analyzing Primary Sources**
Drawing Inferences and Conclusions Why do you think the pilots "hardly said a word"?

Texas Voices ❝I remember the night the air war began as being very dark and still. I was on guard duty and all the airport lights were turned off. The pilots came out to the KC-135 tanker aircraft . . . and hardly said a word. . . . The seriousness of our mission set in hard.❞

—Mark Furr quoted in "Reservist called up," virtual texan.com Web site

Ground forces from the United States and other coalition nations then attacked. They swept through Kuwait, quickly freeing the nation from Iraqi control.

Many Americans approved of the way Bush handled the war, but a downturn in the economy became a major issue in the 1992 presidential race. Bush was defeated in that election by Democrat Bill Clinton, who went on to serve two terms as president.

Reading Check **Evaluating** What leadership qualities did President George Bush exhibit during his presidency?

★ George W. Bush Becomes President

In 2000 George Bush's son, Governor <u>George W. Bush</u> of Texas, ran for president against Vice President Al Gore. The race was extremely close. Television and other news outlets predicted victories for Gore then Bush based on estimates of election returns in Florida, the last major state to be decided. Whoever won Florida would receive enough electoral votes to win the presidency. When Bush was declared the winner, Democrats requested hand recounts in several counties. Republicans argued that this was unfair, and both parties took their cases to court.

After more than a month of court cases and counting, the U.S. Supreme Court ruled on December 12 that it was unconstitutional to perform hand recounts in only some counties. With little time to complete a recount of every vote, Gore conceded the next day. Bush had received 537 more votes than Gore in Florida, thus gaining the state's 25 electoral votes. The victory in Florida gave Bush more electoral votes than Gore, while nationally Gore had received more popular votes than Bush. George W. Bush was sworn into office on January 20, 2001. He soon appointed a number of Texans to key posts, including Rod Paige of Houston as secretary of education.

✔ **Reading Check** **Summarizing** Explain the events leading up to George W. Bush's inauguration as president.

★ America Attacked

President Bush soon had to deal with a national crisis. On Tuesday morning, September 11, 2001, it was business as usual in the financial district of New York City. The daily routine was shattered at 8:48 A.M. when a hijacked American Airlines jet, Flight 11, crashed into the north tower of the World Trade Center. The impact was devastating. Then at 9:03 A.M. a second plane—United Airlines Flight 175—slammed into

A New York City police officer leads a woman and child away from the World Trade Center.

President Bush greets firefighters at the site of the collapsed World Trade Center towers.

the south tower. Shocked observers began to realize that these were not accidents but deliberate acts of **terrorism**—violent acts by a person or small group to advance a political goal.

Hundreds of rescue workers struggled to aid victims. The south tower suddenly collapsed at 9:59 A.M., followed half an hour later by the fall of the north tower. Nearly 2,800 people still inside or near the towers were killed, including hundreds of firefighters, police officers, and other rescuers. Teams of rescue workers, including specialists from Texas, rushed to New York to participate in the rescue effort. They found few survivors.

New York was not the terrorists' only target. At approximately 9:40 A.M. a third plane, American Airlines Flight 77, hit the west side of the **Pentagon** near Washington, D.C., killing 184 military and civilian personnel. A fourth plane—United Airlines Flight 93—was also hijacked. It crashed southeast of Pittsburgh shortly after the collapse of the World Trade Center's north tower. In total, 265 passengers and crew aboard the four hijacked flights had been killed.

✔**Reading Check** **Sequencing** In what order did the events on the morning of September 11, 2001, take place?

★ The Nation Responds

The terrorist attacks shocked and horrified Americans, many of whom saw the tragic events live on television. Political leaders tried to rally the public's spirits on the day of the attack. That evening President George W. Bush addressed the nation.

 "Terrorist attacks can shake the foundations of our biggest buildings, but they cannot touch the foundations of America. These acts shatter steel, but they cannot dent the steel of American resolve."

—George W. Bush, September 11, 2001

Congress soon approved a $40 billion relief package to help the country recover from the attacks. The government also passed legislation to provide compensation to the families of victims.

Perhaps the greatest show of unity came from the American people. Many proudly displayed American flags. A group from the Dallas area trucked in 1,000 pounds of barbecue to feed the rescue workers. People donated blood and sent millions of dollars in aid.

The terrorist strikes on the World Trade Center also resulted in billions of dollars in financial losses. One area of particular concern was the airline industry, which had been forced to shut down for several days. Airlines, including Fort Worth–based American Airlines and Continental Airlines of Houston, laid off workers. Congress and the president rushed to authorize $15 billion in economic aid to help keep the nation's airlines operating.

After the attacks the Federal Bureau of Investigation (FBI) immediately began an investigation. The FBI soon released the names of 19 suspected hijackers from several Middle Eastern countries. Even more crucial was the identity of those who had planned these attacks. A prime suspect was identified almost immediately—Osama bin Laden, a wealthy Saudi Arabian exile who supported an extreme form of Islamic fundamentalism. He had publicly called for attacks on the United States. Officials believed that bin Laden's global terrorism network—known as al Qaeda (KY-duh), or "the Base"—was one of the few terrorist groups that had the resources and organizational structure necessary to carry out the attacks.

Immediately after September 11, U.S. leaders began to call for increased security measures. On September 20, 2001, President Bush announced the appointment of Tom Ridge as head of the Office of Homeland Security. Created to coordinate the domestic national-security efforts of various government agencies, the office later became a cabinet-level department. Federal agencies, along with commercial airlines, took significant steps to prevent future hijackings and other terrorist acts.

Burnet Middle School students sent thousands of stuffed animals to survivors of the attacks.

✔ **Reading Check Analyzing Information** What measures has the federal government taken to protect the nation's domestic security?

Historical Document

President Bush's Address to the Nation

On September 20, 2001, President George W. Bush addressed Congress and the American people. The following is an excerpt from his speech.

"Tonight we are a country awakened to danger and called to defend freedom. Our grief has turned to anger, and anger to resolution [determination]. Whether we bring our enemies to justice, or bring justice to our enemies, justice will be done. . . .

Every nation, in every region, now has a decision to make. Either you are with us, or you are with the terrorists. From this day forward, any nation that continues to harbor or support terrorism will be regarded by the United States as a hostile regime. . . .

This is the world's fight. This is civilization's fight. This is the fight of all who believe in progress and pluralism, tolerance and freedom. We ask every nation to join us. . . .

The advance of human freedom—the great achievement of our time, and the great hope of every time—now depends on us. Our nation—this generation—will lift a dark threat of violence from our people and our future. We will rally the world to this cause by our efforts, by our courage. We will not tire, we will not falter, and we will not fail."

Analyzing Primary Sources

1. **Analyzing Information** What did President Bush call on other nations to do?

2. **Evaluating** How did the president say the United States would react to terrorist acts?

★ War on Terrorism

The U.S. government also took action to limit terrorist threats abroad. On September 20, 2001, President Bush called the September 11 attacks "an act of war." The Bush administration built an international coalition and used economic, diplomatic, and military means to fight terrorism.

One of the first steps the U.S. government took was to stop the flow of money to terrorist organizations. By April 2002, some 192 individuals and organizations suspected of having ties to terrorist organizations had their financial assets frozen.

U.S. officials focused on the Taliban—a group that governed Afghanistan and allowed al Qaeda leaders to operate terrorist training camps in that country. The United States issued several warnings for the Taliban to turn over bin Laden, but the Taliban government refused. By late September, U.S. special forces had reportedly begun missions in Afghanistan. U.S. and allied forces conducted bombing raids on al Qaeda training camps and Taliban military targets beginning on October 7.

The Taliban was forced from power by mid-November, and a new democratic government was established. However, small groups of al Qaeda and Taliban fighters remained hidden in Afghanistan and in neighboring Pakistan.

The military action in Afghanistan was the first phase of the War on Terrorism. The United States and its allies around the world continued the effort to break up terrorist cells and disrupt terrorist plans. President Bush and his administration made the prevention of terrorist attacks a top priority. During this War on Terrorism, the American people have shown a great deal of strength and cooperation.

✔**Reading Check** **Drawing Inferences and Conclusions** Why do you think the initial stages of the War on Terrorism included both economic actions and military operations in foreign countries?

Soldiers from Fort Bliss are trained to use Patriot missiles.

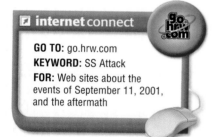

internet connect

GO TO: go.hrw.com
KEYWORD: SS Attack
FOR: Web sites about the events of September 11, 2001, and the aftermath

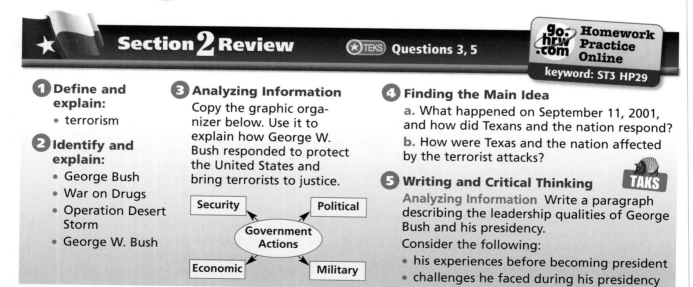

★ Section 2 Review

⭐TEKS Questions 3, 5

go.hrw.com **Homework Practice Online**
keyword: ST3 HP29

1 Define and explain:
- terrorism

2 Identify and explain:
- George Bush
- War on Drugs
- Operation Desert Storm
- George W. Bush

3 Analyzing Information
Copy the graphic organizer below. Use it to explain how George W. Bush responded to protect the United States and bring terrorists to justice.

```
Security          Political
        ↘      ↗
      Government
       Actions
        ↗      ↘
Economic          Military
```

4 Finding the Main Idea
a. What happened on September 11, 2001, and how did Texans and the nation respond?
b. How were Texas and the nation affected by the terrorist attacks?

5 Writing and Critical Thinking TAKS
Analyzing Information Write a paragraph describing the leadership qualities of George Bush and his presidency.
Consider the following:
- his experiences before becoming president
- challenges he faced during his presidency

The Texas Economy

Read to Discover

1. In what ways did the Texas economy continue its boom-and-bust cycle in the late 1900s?
2. How have growing industries and the North American Free Trade Agreement affected the Texas economy?

Why It Matters Today

Trade worth billions of dollars is carried out between Texas and Mexico every year. Use **CNN fyi.com** or other **current events** sources to learn more about this trade. Record your findings in your journal.

Define

- **Internet**
- **agribusiness**
- **infrastructure**
- **maquiladoras**

Identify

- **North American Free Trade Agreement**

The Story Continues

Ed Jones and his wife Jackie moved from Indiana to Texas in 1976. Ed soon found work as a roughneck in the Texas oil fields. In less than a year, he had worked his way up the company ladder to a position as personnel manager. However, during the oil bust of the early 1980s, Ed lost his job. He was lucky to find work as a roughneck again. Despite his troubles, Ed was optimistic about the future. He declared, "If you do your job right, you will get ahead."

★ Boom and Bust in the 1980s

The Joneses were living through an economic downturn, or decline in business activity. The boom-and-bust cycle that marked the Texas economy had again led to a bust. During the mid-1970s the price of oil skyrocketed in international markets, and the state's oil industry boomed. The entire Texas economy continued to grow until oil prices dropped in the early 1980s because of international overproduction. Companies reduced oil production in the state, and one third of workers in the Texas oil industry lost their jobs between 1982 and 1994.

The economic downturn soon affected other businesses in the state. Real estate sales had boomed along with the oil industry during the 1970s and early 1980s. Texas banks—which had greatly profited from the strong real estate market—were hit particularly hard when real

The Texas oil boom of the 1970s turned into a bust during the 1980s, hurting many Texas industries.

*Economic downturn. During the economic downturn of the late 1980s, Texas businesses were forced to close. This further hurt the Texas real estate market. **What does the image suggest about how economic busts affect Texas towns and cities?*** ⭐TEKS

estate prices collapsed in the 1980s. Defaulted, or bad, loans to oil companies and other industries that were in trouble made matters worse. Between 1985 and 1992, some 470 Texas banks went out of business. Texas savings and loan (S&L) institutions also failed at alarming rates. Many S&Ls had placed funds in risky investments, which resulted in the S&L crisis. Despite attempts to help banks and S&Ls, the Texas and national economies soon fell into a recession.

⭐ **Reading Check Analyzing Information** Trace the steps that led to a bust in the oil, real estate, and banking industries and the impact on the state's economy.

⭐ The Diversifying Economy

The changing demand for goods in national and international markets prompted Texans to diversify the state's industrial base. Sources of state revenue began to reflect this change. In 1983 the state government received more than 25 percent of its income from oil activities. By 1993, money from the oil industry made up only 7 percent of the state's income. Texans worked in high-tech industries as well as more traditional industries such as manufacturing and retail trade. Many Texans also found work in service industries such as health care and tourism. In addition, the Texas banking industry revived in the 1990s.

High-tech industries such as computers, electronics, and telecommunications experienced dramatic growth in the 1980s and 1990s. The Dallas–Fort Worth area became a national telecommunications and transportation center. Some 500 telecommunications companies in the region employed more than 70,000 people. One business executive explained why his high-tech company was located in Dallas. "It was strictly a matter of geography. You can reach anyplace [in the United States] with a nonstop flight."

The growth of communications technologies such as the **Internet** further spurred the Texas economy. The Internet is a worldwide system

The growing use of computers has helped Texans become more productive and has created many service and manufacturing jobs for Texans.

of computer networks. International corporations such as Motorola have established networking and Internet technology offices in Texas. In the late 1990s two Texas companies, Compaq Computer Corporation of Houston and Dell Computer Corporation of Round Rock, led the world in computer production. Some 25 percent of Texans who worked in manufacturing jobs produced computers or other electronic devices, and the value of Texas high-tech exports totaled more than $40 billion in 2000. Texas communications and computer industries have influenced national and international markets and brought new services and technologies to people around the world.

Although industry dominated the Texas economy, **agribusiness**— or the farming and the processing of crops—remained important. At the end of the 1990s agribusiness contributed about $40 billion to the state economy. Texas was the nation's leading producer of cotton and hay. The state also exported grapefruit, oranges, peanuts, and pecans.

The state's diversified economy allows many Texans to enjoy a high standard of living. It also enables Texas to compete with other regions of the United States and the world. In 1998 state officials announced that if Texas were a nation, it would be the world's 11th-largest economy.

Reading Check Evaluating How have high-tech and communication industries and national and international demand for goods affected the Texas economy?

★ The Medical Industry

Medical researchers in Texas have worked hard to meet the health needs of the state and the world. As a result, Texas has earned a reputation as a leader in medicine. Medical research centers around Texas have drawn millions of dollars in funding for medical research. In 1991 Texas medical centers spent $560 million on biomedical research. Research and technological developments have led to the growth of the medical industry in Texas. By 1995 Texas had more than 550 hospitals, 8 medical schools, and 75 nurse-training programs. The state provides services and medical devices to people and hospitals around the world.

Researchers such as Houston surgeon Michael DeBakey have contributed to the state's leading position in the medical field. Dr. DeBakey helped design a telemedicine system that relies upon satellite communications to treat patients in remote areas. In the late 1990s DeBakey and NASA worked together to produce a sophisticated device designed to help patients recover from heart surgery. Other Texans have also received international attention. In 1998 Dr. Ferid Murad of the University of Texas received the Nobel Prize in medicine for his research on the relationship between chemicals and the heart.

Reading Check Analyzing Information How has the medical technology industry affected Texas, the United States, and the world?

Biography

Michael DeBakey
(1908–)

While still in medical school, Michael Ellis DeBakey invented a device that later became an important part of the heart-lung machine. During World War II DeBakey developed the idea for the Mobile Army Surgical Hospital (MASH). In 1960 DeBakey began developing the first artificial heart. During the 1960s he created a plan in which doctors work together to treat diseases. DeBakey evaluated the medical condition of Russian president Boris Yeltsin in 1996, a testament to his importance in the field of medicine. How have the innovations pioneered by Michael DeBakey affected Texans and people around the world? ★TEKS

Texas Cities

El Paso

History: In 1659, the Spanish established a mission at the site of present-day Ciudad Juárez, Mexico. In 1682 they built the Corpus Christi de la Isleta mission across the Rio Grande—now a part of El Paso.

Population in 2000: 563,662

Relative location: On the Rio Grande in the far western tip of Texas

Region: Mountains and Basins

County: County seat of El Paso County

Origin of name: Spanish explorer Juan de Oñate named a nearby site El Paso del Norte, "The Pass of the River of the North."

Economy: El Paso's economy can be summarized by the "four C"s: cattle, clothing, copper, and cotton. The city is a center for cement manufacturing, cotton ginning, meatpacking, milling, mining operations, and oil refining. El Paso also has a thriving tourism industry.

★ Global Trade

The economy of Texas reflects the state's growing interdependence with the world. The Texas economy received a big boost in 1994 when the **North American Free Trade Agreement** (NAFTA) went into effect. This agreement eliminated many trade barriers. Many of the trade goods flowing between the United States and Mexico pass through Texas. On an average day during the late 1990s, more than 200,000 vehicles crossed the border between Texas and Mexico. In 1999 some $41 billion worth of goods—almost half of the state's exports—went to Mexico. Texas towns such as El Paso and Laredo boomed as trade increased. Laredo was one of the fastest growing cities in the country during the 1990s.

Increased border trade also created challenges as Texas cities along the border experienced rapid population growth. Many of these cities could not build an **infrastructure**—public works such as roads and water systems—fast enough to keep pace with the growth. Hundreds of **maquiladoras**—factories near the border—have also appeared in Mexico. Many of these factories are owned by American companies. These factories have provided many jobs, but pollution has increased in the border region. The resulting environmental and health issues continue to challenge Texas leaders.

 Reading Check **Summarizing** How has NAFTA affected the Texas economy?

★ Section 3 Review ⊛TEKS Questions: 2, 3, 4a, 4b, 5

go.hrw.com
Homework Practice Online
keyword: ST3 HP29

1 **Define and explain:**
- Internet
- agribusiness
- infrastructure
- maquiladoras

2 **Identify and explain:**
- North American Free Trade Agreement

3 **Summarizing**
Use the graphic organizer below to explain the decline and recovery of the Texas economy between 1980 and 2000.

1980	2000

4 **Finding the Main Idea**
a. What effect did NAFTA have on the Texas economy?
b. How has medical technology developed in Texas affected local, national, and international markets?

5 **Writing and Critical Thinking**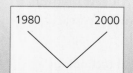
Drawing Inferences and Conclusions Write a paragraph discussing how the state's boom-and-bust economy and the demands of national and international markets encouraged Texas to diversify its industrial base. Consider the following:
- the oil, banking, and high-tech industries
- world competition and globalization

Economics

Employment in Texas

The growth of Texas cities and industries has created new demands for services. The number of teachers, retail salespersons, and other service providers needed in Texas cities has risen rapidly. Service jobs are among the fastest-growing occupations in Texas. Employment in the high-tech market has also increased. Texas high-tech workers have found employment in manufacturing, programming, and other fields. Texas high-tech workers design video games, software programs, hardware, and provide many other services. These jobs reflect the changing Texas economy in the early 2000s.

Fastest-Growing Occupations in Texas, 1998–2008

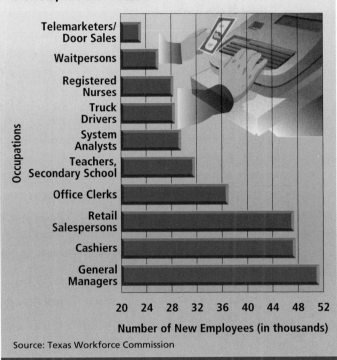

Source: Texas Workforce Commission

Growth of High-Tech Jobs in Texas, 1980–2000

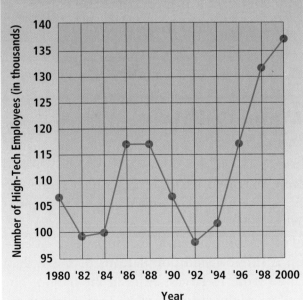

Source: Texas Workforce Commission

Interpreting Graphs and Charts ⊛TEKS

1. What are the three fastest-growing occupations in Texas?

2. How many more high-tech jobs were there in 2000 than 1992?

3. How has the growth of Texas cities affected the types of jobs available to Texans?

4. What general trend in employment can you recognize? How might this affect you?

Cultures of Texas

Read to Discover

1. How did the Texas population change during the 1990s?
2. How have ethnic groups in Texas celebrated their heritage?
3. In what ways do Texas musicians, writers, and artists reflect the state's diversity?

Why It Matters Today

The 2000 census offered information about who Texans were, where they lived, and how they worked. Use **CNNfyi.com** or other **current events** sources to learn more about the census and other population statistics. Record your findings in your journal.

Identify

- **Cinco de Mayo**
- **Larry McMurtry**
- **Sandra Cisneros**
- **John Biggers**
- **Van Cliburn**
- **Willie Nelson**
- **Stevie Ray Vaughan**
- **Selena Quintanilla**

The Story Continues

Tom and Debbie Lowell lived near Detroit, Michigan. Tom was laid off from his job as a plumber, and neither he nor Debbie could find work. They packed all their belongings into their car and headed south for Houston to look for work. When Tom went to his first job interview, the interviewer asked him, "So you've decided to come down to the land of opportunity?"

I WASN'T BORN IN TEXAS, BUT I GOT HERE AS FAST AS I COULD

Many new residents of Texas have expressed pride in their adopted state.

★ A Land of Many Cultures

As many Americans moved to Texas, its population grew from some 14 million in 1980 to close to 17 million in 1990. Between 1990 and 2000, the Texas population increased by more than 20 percent—to almost 21 million people. As a result, Texas ranked second in population only to California. By the 1990s Texas cities had also grown in size, with more than 80 percent of Texans living in cities. Three Texas cities—Houston, Dallas, and San Antonio—had populations of more than 1 million, placing them among the 10 largest cities in the nation. The 2000 census results also confirmed the diversity of the Texas population. Non-Hispanic white Texans made up slightly more than 52 percent of the state's population, with 10.9 million people. More than 6.6 million Texans—more than 30 percent of the state's population—claimed

Hispanic heritage. The more than 2.4 million African Americans made up about 12 percent of the Texas population. The more than 560,000 Texans of Asian heritage made up 2.7 percent of the state's population. Some 118,000 people, or less than 1 percent of the Texas population, claimed Native American background.

The diversity of Texas is also reflected in the ethnic heritage and celebrations of different groups in the state. Joe Sierra, a former governor of the Tigua, offered this insight into the state's culture.

Texas Voices ❝We have three cultures that we are trying to fit into: our own, the Spanish, and the American. . . . Some people today even claim that since we speak Spanish, we were never Indian. But, remember that we were Indians before the Spanish came and we conversed first in Tiwa, second in Spanish, and third in English. But our Spanish is even older than the Mexican or border Spanish that is today's Spanish: we speak a Castillian Spanish.❞

—Joe Sierra, quoted in *Exiled: The Tigua Indians of Ysleta del Sur,* by Randy Lee Eickhoff

Analyzing Primary Sources ✪ TEKS
Drawing Inferences and Conclusions How does Sierra's comment reflect the concept of diversity within unity?

Today the Tigua continue to preserve their traditional culture. The Tigua, who live outside El Paso, operate tourist attractions such as a museum that showcases the group's history. They also celebrate St. Anthony's Day on June 13 every year. On this day, they carry a statue of St. Anthony from their pueblo to their mission. During the ceremony the Tigua also carry a sacred 300-year-old drum. This blending of Catholic and traditional Tigua ceremonies and performances reflects how the Tigua have combined their Spanish and American Indian heritage.

Other groups in Texas also observe special days that remind them of their ethnic heritage. Each year on May 5, Mexican Americans celebrate **Cinco de Mayo**. It was on May 5, 1862, that a Mexican army defeated an invading French force at the Battle of Puebla. Mexican Americans also celebrate Diez y Séis de Septiembre, Mexico's Independence Day.

Other festivals held throughout Texas also celebrate the state's many cultures. The Texas Folklife Festival is held every August on the grounds of the University of Texas Institute of Texan Cultures in San Antonio. The Wurstfest, which is held every year in New Braunfels, celebrates the state's German heritage. African Americans throughout Texas celebrate Juneteenth on June 19 to mark the day in 1865 when the Emancipation Proclamation was announced in the state, freeing enslaved Texans. These and other celebrations reflect the diversity of the people of Texas.

✪ **Reading Check** **Summarizing** What cultural activities, celebrations, and performances reflect the ethnic heritage of Texas?

Interpreting the Visual Record

Hispanic culture. Texas Hispanics celebrate holidays with traditional performances and costumes. **How are these Hispanic students maintaining their cultural heritage?** ✪ TEKS

Challenges of a Modern State **625**

★ Texans in Art and Literature

Texas writers and artists have also provided the world with glimpses of the state in their work. Pulitzer Prize–winning author **Larry McMurtry** is one of the most well-known Texas writers. He has written several novels about life in Houston and on the Texas frontier. McMurtry once commented on why he writes about the frontier. "It's . . . fun to reinvent a western myth. . . . I'm renovating the cowboy." A. C. Greene and John Graves are two other well-known writers who have observed the relationship between the land of Texas and its effect on people's lives. Greene once called Graves's book *Goodbye to a River* "the best book ever written about Texas."

Other Texas writers focus on the people of Texas. For example, Américo Paredes wrote about the folklore of Mexican Americans. Lionel Garcia and **Sandra Cisneros** have also received national attention for their work. Cisneros often focuses on the experiences of Hispanic families in America. She occasionally uses Spanish phrases in her works. In an interview, Cisneros explained why she does this.

★ Analyzing Primary Sources

Evaluating How do you think Cisneros has maintained her Hispanic culture while adding to the larger Texas culture?

Texas Voices 66 What it does is change the rhythm of my writing. I think that incorporating the Spanish, for me, allows me to create new expressions in English—to say things in English that have never been said before. . . . All of a sudden something happens to the English, something really new is happening, a new spice is added to the English language. 99

—Sandra Cisneros, from an interview with Reed Dasenbrock

Connecting To *Literature*

Larry McMurtry

Larry McMurtry is perhaps the most noted Texas writer today. Many of his works have focused on life on the Texas frontier. In this excerpt from a collection of essays on Texas, In a Narrow Grave, *McMurtry described the importance of the history of the Texas frontier in his works.*

"Myself, I dislike frontiers, and yet the sense that my own has vanished produces in me the strongest emotion I have felt in connection with Texas, or with any place. It has **embedded**[1] itself in the titles of each of my books, and just as I think I have worn the emotion out it seizes me again, usually at some unlikely moment. I see my son, age five, riding a mechanical horse in front of the laundromat on Sunday morning, and the sight calls up my Uncle Johnny, when he was age

five, sitting on top of the McMurtry barn watching the last trail herd go by. It is indeed a complex distance from those traildrivers who made my father and my uncles determined to be cowboys to the mechanical horse that helps convince my son that he is a cowboy, as he takes a vertical ride in front of a laundromat."

Understanding What You Read ★ TEKS

1. **Literature and History** How do you think the closing of the frontier and the myths and realities of cowboy life have affected McMurtry's stories?

2. **Literature and You** What aspects of Texas life have you seen change, and what stories could be written about those changes?

---

[1] **embedded:** rooted

CONNECTING TO
THE ARTS

John Biggers

A native of North Carolina, John Biggers established the art department at Texas Southern University in 1949. Biggers became well known for his murals that showed aspects of African American history. Biggers taught his students to look to their African heritage and their local communities for inspiration. **How does this painting focus on Texas culture and daily life?**

The internationally known novelist James Michener wrote the novel *Texas* and spent his later years living in Austin.

Texans have also excelled in the visual arts. **John Biggers** of Texas Southern University has produced works of art that portray African American views and experiences. Texans can view the work of sculptor Charles Umlauf at the Umlauf Sculpture Garden in Austin. Donald C. Judd spent the last year of his life in Marfa, where he designed large sculptures made from industrial metals. These artists and others changed the way Texans have perceived their state.

Reading Check Categorizing How is the diversity of Texas reflected in the works of Texas authors and artists?

★ Music and Popular Culture

The Texas music scene also reflects the state's diversity. As author Rick Koster has noted, "Texas is a big state. But regardless of one's background or interests, it's probably possible to find the sort of music you want to hear—and find someone who's . . . good at playing it." Texans have written and performed blues, country, folk, jazz, rap, rock, Tejano, and classical music.

Classical pianist **Van Cliburn** of Fort Worth became world-famous in 1958. That year the 23-year-old Cliburn won an important piano competition in Moscow. Newspapers around the world carried the story, and Cliburn received a ticker-tape parade in New York City. Cliburn went on to enjoy a successful career as a classical musician. To encourage young piano players, he created the Van Cliburn International Piano Competition, which is held every four years in Fort Worth.

Texans such as George Jones and George Strait perform traditional country music. In the 1970s a group of Texas musicians developed what would become known as progressive country. These performers, who worked in and around Austin, included **Willie Nelson**, Waylon Jennings, and Jerry Jeff Walker. They had a number of hit songs. Nelson's popular "Blue Eyes Crying in the Rain" made him a national star. Lyle Lovett of Klein has also become an internationally known country singer.

Several of Texas's most popular music stars died tragically during the 1990s. **Stevie Ray Vaughan**, a gifted guitarist, studied the work of blues greats such as Freddie King of Gilmer and Albert Collins of Houston. During the 1980s Vaughan released a series of popular albums that combined blues and rock. However, he died in a helicopter crash after a concert in 1990. **Selena Quintanilla** was born in Lake Jackson in 1971. Her father recognized her musical talent and taught her how to perform. At age 15 Selena won the Tejano Music Award for best female vocalist. She continued to win awards, including a Grammy. Tragically, a member of Selena's business enterprises killed the young star in 1995.

People around the world learned about Texas and Texans from sources other than music. During the 1980s the popular TV show *Dallas* brought worldwide attention to the state. Starring Larry Hagman, who was born in Weatherford, the show told the story of a fictional wealthy Texas oil and ranching family. Many other TV shows and movies have been filmed in Texas, particularly in Austin and Dallas. People throughout the world continue to enjoy movies that are about Texas or that are made in the state.

⭐ **Reading Check** **Drawing Inferences and Conclusions** What does the music and popular culture reveal about the state?

Section 4 Review   ⭐TEKS Questions: 1, 2, 3a, 3b, 4

go.hrw.com **Homework Practice Online** keyword: ST3 HP29

1 **Identify and explain:**
- Cinco de Mayo
- Larry McMurtry
- Sandra Cisneros
- John Biggers
- Van Cliburn
- Willie Nelson
- Stevie Ray Vaughan
- Selena Quintanilla

2 **Analyzing Information**
Copy the graphic organizer below. Use it to show how Texas musicians, writers, and artists reflect the diversity of Texas.

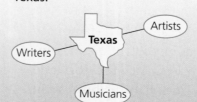

Artists

Texas

Writers

Musicians

3 **Finding the Main Idea**
a. In what ways did the state's population change in the 1990s?
b. How do Texans celebrate their ethnic heritage?

4 **Writing and Critical Thinking**
Summarizing Write a short story about how life in Texas has changed over time. Consider the following:
- the state's history
- the people of Texas

Texas Faces the Future

Read to Discover
1. What challenges do Texans face in the 2000s?
2. What have Texans done to protect their environment?

Define
- globalization

Identify
- Environmental Protection Agency
- Texas Natural Resources Conservation Commission
- Foreign-Trade Zones

Why It Matters Today

Texas leaders, both appointed and elected, face many different issues. Use CNNfyi.com or other current events sources to learn how Texas and other government leaders tackle these issues, and what leadership qualities they display while doing so. Record your findings in your journal.

The Story Continues

Texas governor Rick Perry grew up on a farm near the small West Texas community of Paint Creek. Perry's family valued education, and his father served on the local school board. As governor, Perry recognized the need for good schools as Texas entered a new century. In a State of the State address, Perry called upon Texans to continue to provide educational opportunities for everyone.

Rick Perry described his goals for Texas after being sworn into office.

★ Challenges of the Future

In his speech Governor Perry pointed to the various challenges facing the state. As technology became more important to the state's economy, Texas needed a better-educated labor force. To make certain that public school students were learning necessary skills, the state continued to use the Texas Assessment of Knowledge and Skills (TAKS) test.

As jobs in the high-tech, medical research, and other fields have contributed to the state's economic growth and population, the need for expanded transportation infrastructure has increased. State and local governments have tried to ease traffic congestion by building more roads and freeways. In 2000 the state spent more than $2.4 billion on road construction. Some Texas cities have also explored alternative means of public transportation. Dallas, for example, created the Dallas Area Rapid Transit (DART). This system consists of buses, light-rail, and vans that carry some 200,000 people per day.

Fastest-Growing Metropolitan Areas in Texas, 2000

Metropolitan Area (vertical axis)

- McAllen–Edinburg–Mission
- Austin–San Marcos
- Laredo
- Dallas–Fort Worth
- Brownsville–Harlingen–San Benito

Percentage of Growth in the 1990s: 10 20 30 40 50

Source: U.S. Census Bureau

TAKS Skills *Interpreting Charts* Migration and immigration contributed to urban growth in Texas. What was the fastest-growing metropolitan area? ★TEKS

Health care is another issue facing Texas. Health care in Texas improved overall during the 1980s and 1990s, but providing medical care for all Texans continues to present state leaders with a challenge. Although many Texas children do not have medical insurance, the state has worked to change this situation. Most Texans now enjoy access to better medical care than they have in the past.

★ **Reading Check** **Making Generalizations and Predictions** What challenges lie ahead for the state?

★ The Environment

Economic growth has led to greater industrialization, which, along with the growing population, has increased demand on the state's water supplies and other natural resources. Texas leaders have worked hard to successfully manage the state's resources. They do so to ensure that the people and businesses of Texas will have enough water to meet their needs.

In some parts of the state, air and water pollution have become an issue. Stopping pollution has become a goal for many Texans and other Americans. In 1970 the federal government created the **Environmental Protection Agency** (EPA) to direct efforts to control pollution. At the state level, the **Texas Natural Resource Conservation Commission** (TNRCC) was created in 1993. This commission tries to balance the increased costs businesses must bear to protect the environment with efforts to safeguard the state's air and water. It tracks air and water quality and enforces state and federal regulations regarding the environment. Through the combined efforts of citizens, businesses, and government, Texans are working to have a cleaner environment as well as a strong economy.

★ **Reading Check** **Analyzing Information** How has economic and population growth affected the state's natural resources?

Interpreting the Visual Record

These "Light Spikes" were placed outside a Houston office building. **How do they reflect the city's role as a global trade center?**

★ Globalization

During the late 1900s the nations of the world had become increasingly interdependent as goods, ideas, and people moved all across the globe. This process of **globalization** has boosted the state's economy as Texas businesses have gained greater access to global markets. This also means that Texas industries are sometimes affected by international events. For example, when Mexico experienced a financial crisis in 1995, computer exports from Texas to that country fell. Even so, the Texas economy has generally benefited from global interdependence. Many nations have offices in Texas to improve trade with the state. Texas also maintains several **Foreign-Trade Zones**. These are areas in which export regulations are reduced to promote trade. The increased trade in these areas has boosted the state's economy. In 2000 Texas had 26 such zones.

The state government has also played a role in advancing globalization. This has helped Texas become a major exporter of goods. Houston ranked seventh among exporting cities in the United States in 1997. Interaction between people from different parts of the world is not new, of course. Author Gordon Bennett noted that Texas had long been involved in international events.

Texas Voices ❝Pioneer settlers represented many European nationalities: German, Norwegian, Scot, Swedish, and more. . . . Our premier oil and gas industry ebbs and flows with Middle Eastern production and international demand. Houston and Dallas are world trade centers.❞

—Gordon Bennett, *Global Connections*

★ **Reading Check** **Finding the Main Idea** How has globalization transformed the Texas economy?

CONNECTING TO SCIENCE AND TECHNOLOGY

Our Future
The development of the computer has changed how many Texans study, work, and spend their leisure time. One important computer-related development is the Internet. The Internet has become an important research tool for Texas businesses, scholars, and students. During the early 2000s Texas remained a leader in producing computer and communications technologies. How might future computer and other technological innovations affect the Texas economy and society? ★TEKS

Section 5 Review ★TEKS Questions: 3, 4a, 4b, 5

go.hrw.com **Homework Practice Online** keyword: ST3 HP29

1 **Define and explain:**
- globalization

Identify and
2 **explain:**
- Environmental Protection Agency
- Texas Natural Resources Conservation Commission
- Foreign-Trade Zones

3 **Summarizing**
Copy the graphic organizer below. Use it to explain some of the challenges Texans face in the 2000s.

Education	Environment

Challenges for the future

4 **Finding the Main Idea**
a. How did Foreign-Trade Zones affect the Texas economy?
b. What are some of the environmental consequences of the state's growth?

5 **Writing and Critical Thinking**
Analyzing Information Imagine you are a reporter for a Texas newspaper. Write an article describing the challenges of the future.
Consider the following:
- the benefits and consequences of economic and population growth
- the economic, social, and environmental consequences that may result from future discoveries and technological innovations

TAKS

The Chapter at a Glance

Examine the following visual summary of the chapter. Prepare a pamphlet entitled Texas Looks to the Future based on the visual summary. Be sure to illustrate your pamphlet. ⭐TEKS

The boom in the computer and medical technology industries led to new jobs and a growing economy in the 1990s. NAFTA also affected the Texas economy as international trade expanded.

During the 1980s Republicans gained increasing power in Texas politics. Texas Republicans, George Bush and his son George W. Bush were elected president in 1988 and 2000, respectively.

A growing population has contributed to cultural diversity in Texas and to the state's growing economy.

Education, transportation, globalization, and population growth will all be important issues to the next generation of Texans.

Identifying People and Ideas ⭐TEKS

Use the following terms or people in historically significant sentences.

1. George W. Bush
2. Phil Gramm
3. Kay Bailey Hutchison
4. Internet
5. Cinco de Mayo
6. Van Cliburn
7. Selena Quintanilla
8. Larry McMurtry
9. John Biggers
10. globalization

Understanding Main Ideas ⭐TEKS

Section 1 (pp. 610–612)

1. Trace the development of the two-party system.

Section 2 (pp. 613–618)

2. Describe the leadership qualities of George Bush.
3. How did George W. Bush respond to terrorism in America?

Section 3 (pp. 619–622)

4. Why did the Texas banking industry experience both a boom and a bust during the 1980s?
5. How has medical technology affected the Texas economy?

Section 4 (pp. 624–628)

6. What did the 2000 census reveal about the geographic distribution of the Texas population?

Section 5 (pp. 629–631)

7. How has globalization affected Texas?

You Be the Historian ⭐TEKS

Reviewing Themes

1. **Science, Technology & Society** How has technology changed the lives of Texans?
2. **Global Relations** Why did Canada, Mexico, and the United States sign NAFTA, and how has NAFTA affected Texas?
3. **Culture** How is the diversity of Texas reflected in a variety of cultural activities, celebrations, and performances?

TAKS Practice: Thinking Critically ⭐TEKS

1. **Drawing Inferences and Conclusions** How might government protection of the environment affect the Texas economy?
2. **Analyzing Information** Explain how the state's boom-and-bust economy and the demands of national and international markets led Texas to diversify its industrial base.
3. **Making Generalizations and Predictions** How do you think Texas will change in the future?

Interpreting Political Cartoons ⭐TEKS

Study the political cartoon below. Use the political cartoon to answer the questions below.

WELL, LOOK AT US TEXANS!

SENATE VICTORY

G.O.P.

GAYLOR HOUSTON POST

1. How does the elephant's clothing reflect the state's Republican Party?

    a. The elephant's coat helps him stay warm.
    b. The cowboy hat and boots are often associated with Texas.
    c. The elephant's boots are stylish.
    d. The elephant is holding a mirror.

2. Based on this cartoon, why were members of the Republican Party of Texas happy?

Analyzing Primary Sources ⭐TEKS

Read the following quote from George Bush. Then answer the questions.

"Great nations of the world are moving toward democracy through the door to freedom. Men and women of the world move toward free markets through the door to prosperity. The people of the world agitate [push] for free expression and free thought through the door to the . . . satisfaction that only liberty allows. We know what works: Freedom works."

3. Which of the following statements best describes George Bush's point of view?

    a. Free markets do not help the people of the world.
    b. The people of the world are not calling for more freedom.
    c. Freedom and free markets will help people.
    d. Few of the world's great nations are moving toward democracy.

4. How does George Bush believe free markets will affect people throughout the world?

Alternative Assessment

Linking to Community ⭐TEKS

BUILDING YOUR Portfolio

Many communities hold celebrations or performances to recognize their ethnic and cultural heritage. Contact your local chamber of commerce, tourist bureau, or a person familiar with the activities of your community. Ask them to describe a local performance or celebration related to the community's past and heritage. Find out whether the person you are speaking with has first-hand information about what you need to know. Create a poster that advertises the event, focusing on the community's cultural heritage.

📶 **internet** connect

Internet Activity: go.hrw.com
KEYWORD: ST3 TX29 ⭐TEKS

Access the Internet through the HRW Go site to locate databases and media sources on the Texas economy and on the changing geographic distributions and patterns in the state. Then create a new database with the Holt Grapher that contrasts economic trends and geographic patterns of the 1980s with those of the 1990s. Students should then create a graph to represent this information.

Social Studies Skills

WORKSHOP

Distinguishing Fact from Opinion and Identifying Bias

Historical sources may contain both facts and opinions. Sources such as diaries, letters, and speeches usually express personal views. The ability to distinguish facts from opinions is very important. It allows you to judge the accuracy of an argument or the reliability of a historical account.

When reading historical sources, try to identify a writer's bias—prejudices or strong feelings. Many famous historical people had strong opinions that appear in their writings and speeches. Remember that just because a person is famous does not mean that you must agree with his or her opinions.

How to Distinguish Fact from Opinion

1. **Identify the facts.** Ask yourself: Can the statement be proven? Determine whether the idea can be checked for accuracy in a source such as an almanac or encyclopedia. If so, the statement concerns a factual matter. If not, it probably contains an opinion.

2. **Identify the opinions.** Look for clues that indicate a statement of opinion. These clues include phrases such as *I think* and *I believe*, comparative words like *greatest* and *more important*, and value-filled words like *extremely* and *ridiculous*. All of these words imply a judgment and, thus, an opinion.

How to Identify Bias

1. **Evaluate the information presented.** What are the sources of information? How reliable are they? Why might a historical figure have supported one view over another? Be sure to distinguish between provable facts and someone's opinions.

2. **Make your own judgment.** Remember that many of the historical documents you read are created by people who have their own opinions and points of view. It is up to you to read each document critically and to draw your own conclusions.

Practicing the Skill

Read the excerpt below, in which Holland McCombs discusses Dallas, and then answer the questions that follow.

"It is . . . the undisputed leader of finance, insurance, distribution, culture and fashion for this land. . . . And now it is becoming a great manufacturing center as well. . . . Everything in Dallas is bigger and better; the parties are plushier, the buildings are more air-conditioned. . . . And in all of these things, it is finally a monument to sheer determination."

1. Is this excerpt an example of a fact or an opinion? Which words let you know?

2. Compare this excerpt to other sources on Dallas and information about Holland McCombs. Describe how these help you evaluate the validity of the excerpt.

History in Action

UNIT 9 SIMULATION

You Make the Decision . . .

Should Your Family Move to a City?

Complete the following activity in small cooperative groups. It is 1943. Because of the U.S. military's need for weapons and supplies, industry in Texas has boomed. Many Texans have moved from rural areas to the state's cities to take advantage of the strong job markets there. Other Texans have chosen to stay on farms and ranches. You have to decide whether your family will move to a city. You have to prepare a presentation that will convince the rest of your family that your decision is best for them. Follow these steps to reach your decision.

1. Gather Information. Use your textbook and other resources to find information that might help you decide whether to move to a Texas city. Be sure to use what you've learned from this unit's Skills Workshop on Distinguishing Fact from Opinion and Identifying Bias to help you make an informed decision. You may want to divide up different parts of the research among group members.

2. Identify Options. Based on the information you have gathered, consider the options you might recommend for moving or not moving to a city. Your final decision may be easier to reach if you consider as many options as possible. Be sure to record your possible options for your presentation.

3. Predict Consequences. Now take each option you and your group came up with and consider what might be the outcome if you followed each course of action. Ask yourselves questions such as, "What job opportunities are available in a city that are not available where we now live?" Once you have predicted the consequences, record them as notes for your presentation.

4. Take Action to Implement Your Decision. After you have considered your options, you should plan and create your presentation. Be sure to make your decision on whether to move to a city very clear. You will need to support your decision by including information you gathered and by explaining why you rejected other options. Your presentation needs to be visually appealing to gain the support of your family. When you are ready, decide who in your group will make each part of the presentation, and then take your decision to your family (the rest of the class). Good luck!

UNIT 10

Handbook of Texas

(1845–Present)

CHAPTER 30 **Texas Government** (1845–Present)

CHAPTER 31 **Local Government and Citizenship** (1845–Present)

Texas Teens

Young Politicians

Chelsea Richards was 14 when she first became interested in Texas politics. When she started high school she joined the speech and debate team. She also decided to join the Young Democrats club because she seemed to share the same views as the Democratic Party. Organizations such as the Young Democrats and Young Republicans provide ways for Texas teens to participate in politics. Some members of these organizations later found success in political careers. For example, U.S. representative Pete Sessions of Dallas was a Young Republican before being elected to the U.S. Congress in 1996.

Texas teens have gotten involved in politics by working on petitions and participating in voter registration campaigns.

Richards participated as a delegate to the 2001 Texas Young Democrats Convention in Austin. She attended lectures and workshops that introduced her to the workings of the political system. Richards was the youngest representative there, and was a little nervous about speaking to the large group. Nonetheless, she successfully argued for the removal of an issue from the platform until the group had more information on the topic. While she was at the convention, she met some Texas politicians. The politicians offered her advice and assistance in her future political career.

Sometimes teenagers get the impression that their opinion does not matter. Richards has found that your voice does count. Involvement in politics not only gives back to the community but also makes sure the interests of the community are protected. Richards says, "Whether you join the Democrats, Republicans, or even a third party you are helping to guarantee our future." **How can Texas teens influence the government and future of the state?**

In this unit you will learn about the structure of Texas government. You will also learn about the rights and responsibilities of citizenship and other aspects of Texas politics.

LEFT PAGE: *The Texas Capitol is home to the Texas legislature and the site of many state government meetings.*

CHAPTER 30

Texas Government
(1845–Present)

Construction began on the Texas Governor's Mansion in 1854.

The Texas Education Agency reviews standards for learning materials, schools, and teacher certification.

TEXAS

1845 On December 29 the U.S. Congress officially admits Texas to the Union and approves its first state constitution.

1876 Texans adopt the constitution that governs the state today.

1890 James Stephen Hogg—the first native-born Texan to become governor— is elected.

1915 The Texas legislature passes the first state law requiring children to attend school.

1845	**1865**	**1885**	**1905**

U.S. and WORLD

1861 The Civil War breaks out in the United States between the North and the South.

1886 The Statue of Liberty, a gift from France to the United States, is installed on what is now Liberty Island.

1924 U.S. citizen- ship is granted to all American Indians born in the United States.

The Statue of Liberty is a symbol of the freedoms Americans possess under the U.S. Constitution.

Build on What You Know

Since their state's founding, Texans have taken an active role in determining the structure of government and have participated in its day-to-day processes. Many aspects of government have changed over the years. But the state's fundamental law, the Texas Constitution, has guided the state for more than 125 years.

In 1995 Governor George W. Bush celebrated the 150th anniversary of the annexation of Texas.

2000 The Texas state government employs more than 230,000 people in more than 200 agencies, with a two-year budget totaling more than $98 billion.

1930 Texas legislators receive their first pay raise since 1876.

1955 Women are allowed to serve on Texas juries for the first time.

1974 A major attempt to adopt a new Texas constitution fails.

1925   1945   1965   1985   Present

1933 President Franklin D. Roosevelt begins nationwide radio broadcasts, or "fireside chats," to explain his administration's policies.

1945 The United Nations is established.
1954 The U.S. Supreme Court's ruling in *Brown* v. *Board of Education* leads to the racial integration of American public schools.

1981 Sandra Day O'Connor becomes the first woman appointed to the U.S. Supreme Court.

1991 The Soviet Union dissolves, and many of the republics become independent nations.

You Be the Historian

Themes Journal

What's Your Opinion? Do you **agree** or **disagree** with the following statements? Support your point of view in your journal.

● **Constitutional Heritage** State constitutions rarely reflect the influence of other constitutions.

● **Government** A weak leader results in an ineffective government.

● **Economics** All government agencies should receive equal amounts of money.

As a Texan . . . *How are you affected by government?*

1 The Texas Constitution

Read to Discover

1. How have ideas from the U.S. Constitution influenced the Texas Constitution?
2. What basic principles are reflected in the Texas Constitution, and why is each one important?
3. Why does the Texas Constitution include a bill of rights?

Why It Matters Today

The Texas Constitution shapes the state government. Use **CNNfyi.com** or other **current events** sources to examine the relationship between government and the law. Record your findings in your journal.

Define

- **popular sovereignty**
- **republic**
- **limited government**
- **separation of powers**
- **legislative branch**
- **executive branch**
- **judicial branch**
- **checks and balances**
- **veto**
- **override**
- **federalism**
- **bill of rights**
- **amendments**

The Story Continues

On March 2, 1836, war raged in Texas. While Mexican troops laid siege to the Alamo, a group of Texas leaders in Washington-on-the-Brazos took a vote. Their decision was unanimous. Texas declared its independence from Mexico. Now began the task of forming a government. Most of these delegates were originally from the United States and were determined to form a government like that of the country they had left behind. The delegates debated for two weeks. At midnight on March 16, they concluded. The Republic of Texas had its constitution.

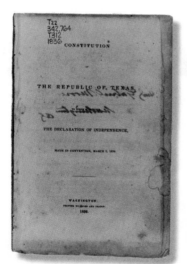

The Texas Declaration of Independence spelled out the problems Texans had experienced under Mexican control.

★ Basic Principles of Democracy

The Texas Constitution is the basis of the state's government and provides the fundamental, or basic, law of the state. The current Texas Constitution was approved in 1876 and is the fifth constitution Texas has had as a state. It is modeled after the Texas Constitution of 1845, which some national politicians considered to be the best of all state constitutions. Thomas J. Rusk headed the group that wrote the 1845 document. Rusk defined the principles he thought a constitution should express.

Texas Voices "Our Duties here, although important, are plain and easy of performance [easy to do]. The formation of a State Constitution upon republican principles, is the only act to be performed. . . . We insert those great principles which have been sanctioned [approved] by time and experience."

—Thomas J. Rusk, *Journals of the Convention*

Analyzing Primary Sources
Finding the Main Idea On what type of principles did Thomas J. Rusk think the Texas Constitution should be based?

The "great principles" Rusk referred to are those found in the U.S. Constitution. Today's Texas Constitution reflects six principles found in the U.S. Constitution—popular sovereignty, limited government, separation of powers, checks and balances, federalism, and protection of individual rights.

Popular sovereignty (SAH-vruhn-tee) forms the basis of both the U.S. and Texas governments. This principle asserts that all political power comes from the people. The Texas Constitution clearly states this principle. "All political power is inherent in [natural to] the people, and all free governments are founded on their authority, and instituted [created] for their benefit." Because Texans give the state government its authority, the constitution is sometimes called the people's document. Its purpose is to serve Texans, protect individual rights, and promote the common good.

Popular sovereignty is a characteristic of democratic government and of a **republic**, a government in which voters elect officials to represent them and to serve in the government. These officials are then responsible to the voters. Both Texas and the United States have the republican form of government. The Texas Constitution restricts, or limits, government power. This principle is known as **limited government**. Most limits protect Texans' individual rights. For example, the state cannot take away Texans' right to free speech.

Reading Check **Finding the Main Idea** What documents influenced the ideas in the current Texas Constitution?

Interpreting the Visual Record

Principles of democracy. *Rick Perry took an oath of office in January 1999 after being elected lieutenant governor.* **What in this photo reflects the importance of the office Perry is assuming?**

641

★ Balancing Governmental Power

The other principles reflected in the Texas Constitution help balance power in government. The **separation of powers** divides power among different government branches. This principle helps prevent any one branch from becoming too powerful. Article II of the Texas Constitution divides state government into three branches—legislative, executive, and judicial. This structure matches that of the U.S. government. Each branch has different powers and duties. The **legislative branch** makes the laws. The **executive branch** carries out the laws. The **judicial branch**, or court system, decides legal cases and interprets laws.

To further balance power, the Texas Constitution includes a system of **checks and balances**. Under this system, each branch has ways to check, or restrain, the other two. These checks help prevent one branch from controlling the government. For example, the governor can check the legislature by rejecting a proposed law. This rejection is called a **veto**. In turn, the legislature can check the governor with an **override**, or reversal, of a veto. These checks and balances are patterned on those found in the U.S. Constitution.

Federalism also balances power by distributing functions between a central government and regional governments. The U.S. Constitution divides authority between the federal government and state governments. For example, only the federal government can coin money. Only state governments can establish public school systems. Some powers are shared—both the federal and state governments can collect taxes.

★ Reading Check Analyzing Information How does the principle of federalism affect the federal and state governments?

★ The Texas Bill of Rights

The protection of individual rights is another basic principle of a republic. To protect Texans' rights, Article I of the state constitution provides a **bill of rights**. A bill of rights outlines the civil liberties, or individual rights, that a government promises to protect. The U.S. Constitution's Bill of Rights served as the model for the first Texas Bill of Rights.

The state's bill of rights includes several rights and freedoms. The freedoms of speech and of the press protect Texans' right to express their ideas and opinions. The freedom of worship protects Texans' right to practice whatever religion they choose. Several rights relate to crime. Some protect the rights of the victims of crime, while others protect the rights of people accused of crimes. For example, the Texas Bill of Rights ensures Texans' right to a trial by jury. The bill of rights concludes by declaring that the state can never take away these basic rights.

★ Reading Check Supporting a Point of View Explain why you think the Texas Bill of Rights is important.

★ Changing the Constitution

Like the U.S. Constitution, the Texas Constitution is a flexible document. It can be changed to address citizens' needs and views. Additions, changes, and corrections to a constitution are called **amendments**. For example, in 1995 a constitutional amendment was passed to increase the amount of state funds set aside for educational loans.

The political climate of the 1870s strongly affected the current Texas Constitution. Its writers wanted to set limits on the power of the state government. So they created a constitution that restricts the state government's powers. In many cases the state must ask the permission of the voters to take on new activities.

Some changes require voters to approve amendments to the constitution. Article XVII of the Texas Constitution provides the method for changing the document. A member of the Texas legislature can propose an amendment. Next, two thirds of the members of each chamber must approve the amendment. Last, a majority of Texans must vote to pass the amendment. Since 1876 the Texas Constitution has been amended about 400 times. In comparison, the U.S. Constitution has only 27 amendments.

The Texas Constitution has been the basic law of the state for more than 125 years. On three occasions, organized efforts have been made to replace the constitution entirely. These efforts—put forth in 1917, 1919, and 1972—were all defeated.

Texas House of Representatives Speaker James E. "Pete" Laney signs a bill.

Reading Check Drawing Inferences and Conclusions Why might people consider the Texas Constitution to be a living document?

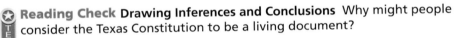

Section 1 Review

★TEKS Questions 1, 2, 3a, 3b, 4

go.hrw.com Homework Practice Online
keyword: ST3 HP30

1 Define and explain:
- popular sovereignty
- republic
- limited government
- separation of powers
- legislative branch
- executive branch
- judicial branch
- checks and balances
- veto
- override
- federalism
- bill of rights
- amendments

2 Summarizing

Copy the chart below. Use it to explain the importance of the basic principles in the Texas Constitution.

Texas Constitution
1.
2.
3.
4.
5.
6.

3 Finding the Main Idea

a. In what ways have ideas from the U.S. Constitution influenced the Texas Constitution?

b. What is the purpose of the Texas Bill of Rights?

4 Writing and Critical Thinking

Supporting a Point of View Imagine that you are attending a constitutional convention. Write a short speech explaining which two individual rights you think are most important and why.

Consider the following:
- who holds the power in a republic
- why a bill of rights is important

The Texas Legislature

Read to Discover

1. What are the Texas legislature's powers and duties?
2. How does a bill become a law?

Define

- **bicameral**
- **sessions**
- **bill**
- **conference committee**

Why It Matters Today

Texans can influence the laws that the state legislature passes. Use **CNNfyi.com** or other **current events** sources to learn how the Texas legislature or U.S. Congress works today. Record your findings in your journal.

The Story Continues

After the Civil War the U.S. Army took control of Texas. In 1870 military control ended. General Joseph J. Reynolds, the commanding officer, expressed his relief. He addressed the Texas legislature. "Here, take your state and run it. . . . I feel like a great weight has been lifted from me; . . . I am through with the heaviest contract [task] I ever undertook."

During Reconstruction, U.S. Army soldiers stayed in this Austin house.

★ The Two Houses

Article III of the Texas Constitution describes the legislative branch, which makes the laws that govern the state. Like the U.S. Congress, the Texas legislature is **bicameral**—made up of two houses: the House of Representatives and the Senate. The House has 150 members, called representatives, who serve two-year terms. The Senate has 31 members, called senators, who serve four-year terms.

Each representative and senator represents Texans in a particular district. Each type of district is sized to contain roughly the same number of people. Thus, all Texans have equal representation in the legislature. Every 10 years, the legislature uses the new census, or population count, to adjust the size of the districts. As of the 2000 census, each House member represented approximately 135,000 Texans. Each senator represented on average 655,000 Texans.

To serve as legislators, Texans must meet several requirements. All legislators must be residents of their election districts for at least one year before running for office. In addition, representatives must be at least 21 years old and have been Texas citizens for two years. Senators must be at least 26 years old and have been Texas citizens for five years. Legislators receive a salary of $7,200 per year. The Texas Constitution sets this sum. As a result, an amendment is necessary to change it. Legislators also receive money to cover work-related expenses.

Reading Check **Categorizing** What are the requirements and duties of Texas representatives and Texas senators?

★ Legislative Duties and Powers

Legislators serve the people in their districts, primarily by making laws. Some of the most important laws involve raising and spending public funds. Legislators can pass laws to spend and borrow money and to raise funds through taxes. Both houses have this "power of the purse." However, laws that raise money must originate in the House.

The legislature has several other duties and powers. Legislators can propose constitutional amendments. The Senate must approve all executive appointments. The legislature also has the power to impeach, or bring charges against, judges and executive officials. Impeachment is a two-step process. First, the House of Representatives brings impeachment charges against an official. If the House votes to impeach, the Senate then puts the official on trial. If the trial ends in a conviction, the legislature removes the official from office. The best-known case is the impeachment and conviction of Governor James Ferguson in 1917.

The Texas legislature does most of its work during periods called **sessions**. These sessions are held starting on the second Tuesday of January in odd-numbered years. Regular sessions last for up to 140 days. The governor can call special sessions of the legislature when necessary. A special session may last up to 30 days. The governor specifies the topics, such as the state budget, for the session.

Reading Check **Summarizing** What are the legislature's main powers and duties?

Biography

Thomas J. Lee
(1923–)

In 1964 Thomas J. "T. J." Lee became the first Chinese American to serve in the Texas legislature. After emigrating from China, his family eventually settled in San Antonio. Lee earned a law degree and became a successful attorney. In 1964 he ran for the Texas House of Representatives. The district in which Lee campaigned had a diverse population. During the campaign Lee spoke to voters in three languages: Chinese, English, and Spanish. How might speaking in three languages have helped Lee get elected?

The Texas legislature meets in the Capitol, where each house has its own chamber.

How a Bill Becomes a Law in Texas

Before a bill can become a law, it must pass through several committees, votes, and potential changes.

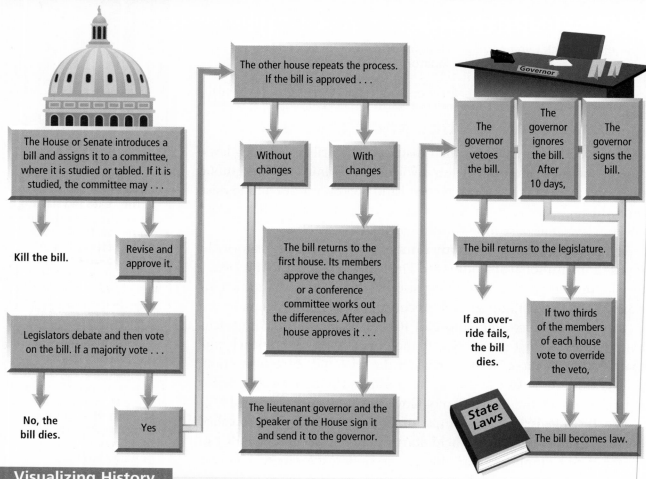

The House or Senate introduces a bill and assigns it to a committee, where it is studied or tabled. If it is studied, the committee may . . .

Kill the bill.

Revise and approve it.

Legislators debate and then vote on the bill. If a majority vote . . .

No, the bill dies.

Yes

The other house repeats the process. If the bill is approved . . .

Without changes

With changes

The bill returns to the first house. Its members approve the changes, or a conference committee works out the differences. After each house approves it . . .

The lieutenant governor and the Speaker of the House sign it and send it to the governor.

Governor

The governor vetoes the bill.

The governor ignores the bill. After 10 days,

The governor signs the bill.

The bill returns to the legislature.

If an override fails, the bill dies.

If two thirds of the members of each house vote to override the veto,

State Laws

The bill becomes law.

Visualizing History

1. **Government** What options does the governor have after the legislature approves a bill? ★TEKS

2. **Connecting to Today** How do you think this process affects your life today? ★TEKS

★ How a Bill Becomes a Law

The lawmaking process is complex. The leaders in each of the houses have a great deal of power. They have the ability to set the agenda and can influence which **bill**, or proposed law, gets considered. The leader of the House of Representatives is the Speaker of the House. Representatives elect the Speaker. The leader, or president, of the Senate is the lieutenant governor. This person, although involved with the legislature, is officially part of the executive branch.

Most of the duties of both the Speaker and lieutenant governor involve committees, or working groups. The leaders appoint all committee members and chairpersons. The Speaker and lieutenant governor also assign all bills to these committees. The committees consider, or study, the bills and decide which ones to recommend to the entire house. Each committee focuses on a specific area, such as education or finance. As a result, some committees are more powerful than others. Committees that meet during sessions are called standing committees. Those that meet between sessions are called interim committees.

In most cases, legislators in either house can create a bill. A clerk then reads the title of the bill aloud to the members of that house. Next, the house leader assigns the bill to a committee. The committee chairperson can table, or refuse to examine, the bill. Otherwise, the committee then studies the bill and sometimes changes it. Committee members may also hear citizens' opinions about the bill. After discussion, the committee approves or rejects the bill. A rejected bill "dies."

If the committee approves the bill, the entire house debates it and votes on the bill. If it is approved, the entire process repeats in the other house. The other house can reject the bill—in which case it dies—or approve the bill and send it to the governor. Or, the other house can approve a revised version of the bill. In this case, the two houses usually hold a **conference committee**. This committee works to revise the bill to satisfy both houses. After the committee is finished, both houses vote again on the bill. An approved bill then goes to the governor.

The governor can deal with a bill in three ways. He or she can sign the bill, in which case it becomes law. If the governor ignores the bill, it automatically becomes law after 10 days. The governor can also veto the bill. A vetoed bill returns to the legislature, which can then override the veto. If two thirds of the members of each house vote to override a veto, the bill becomes law. However, the legislature must be in session to do so. Of the thousands of bills proposed each session, fewer than half become law.

★ **Reading Check** **Sequencing** What are the steps that occur for a bill to become a law?

5-28-01   3:

THE HOUSE STANDS ADJOURNED
SINE DIE
PENDING RECEIPT OF MESSAGES

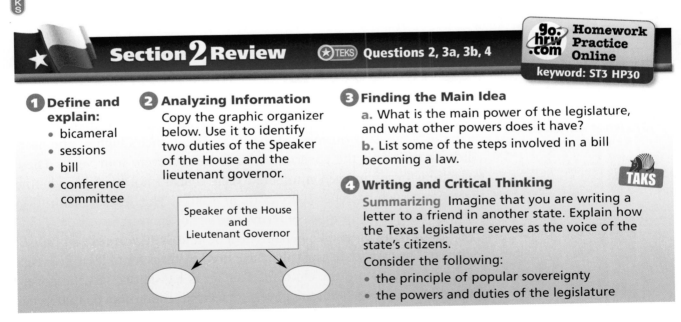

Section 2 Review   ★TEKS Questions 2, 3a, 3b, 4

go.hrw.com **Homework Practice Online**
keyword: ST3 HP30

1 Define and explain:
- bicameral
- sessions
- bill
- conference committee

2 Analyzing Information
Copy the graphic organizer below. Use it to identify two duties of the Speaker of the House and the lieutenant governor.

Speaker of the House and Lieutenant Governor

3 Finding the Main Idea
a. What is the main power of the legislature, and what other powers does it have?
b. List some of the steps involved in a bill becoming a law.

4 Writing and Critical Thinking
Summarizing Imagine that you are writing a letter to a friend in another state. Explain how the Texas legislature serves as the voice of the state's citizens.
Consider the following:
- the principle of popular sovereignty
- the powers and duties of the legislature

Section 3

The Texas Executive

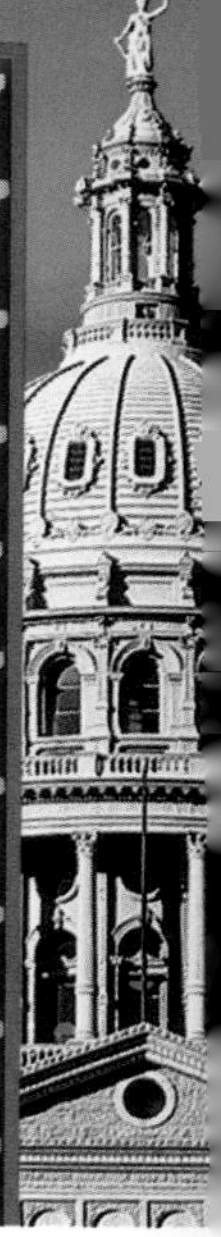

Read to Discover

1. What are the governor's primary powers and duties?
2. What officials and agencies make up the executive branch?

Define

- **line-item veto**
- **pardon**

Why It Matters Today

The decisions the governor makes affect Texans in many ways. Use CNNfyi.com or other **current events** sources to find information about a state governor or national leader today. Record your findings in your journal.

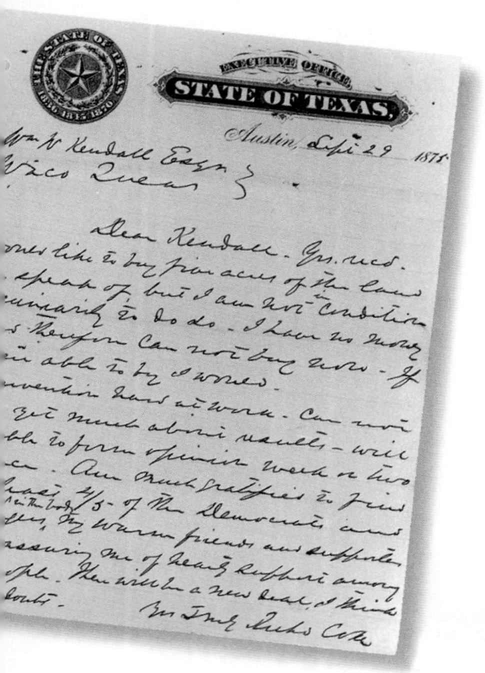
EXECUTIVE OFFICE
STATE OF TEXAS.
Austin, Sept 29 1875
Dear Kendall -

The state seal is in the upper left corner of this 1875 letter written by Richard Coke.

The Story Continues

During Reconstruction Texas governors had greater power than they do today. A controversy arose in the 1870s when Republican governor Edmund J. Davis lost his bid for re-election in 1873 and claimed that the election was corrupt. Richard Coke, the Democrat who had won the election, disagreed. Despite a court ruling in Davis's favor, a standoff took place in the Texas Capitol. After the state militia sided with Coke, Davis gave up. In 1875, delegates met to write a new state constitution. They decided they would prevent a governor from ever being as powerful as Davis had been.

The Governor

Article IV of the Texas Constitution describes the executive branch. This branch enforces the laws passed by the legislature. It also manages and conducts the daily business of the state. The branch's highest and best-known official is the governor, who is elected every four years. These elections occur in even-numbered years that do not have presidential elections, such as 2002, 2006, 2010, and 2014. The Texas Constitution does not limit the number of terms a governor can serve.

To run for governor, a person must be at least 30 years old and a U.S. citizen. The candidate must also have lived in Texas for at least five years immediately before the election. The Texas legislature sets the governor's salary. As of 2000, the governor receives more than $115,000 per year. The state also provides the governor with a house, a staff, and money for job-related expenses.

⭐ **Reading Check Finding the Main Idea** What state government official heads the executive branch in Texas?

⭐ The Powers and Duties of the Governor

The governor's powers involve the management of the state. He or she oversees many of the state's agencies, boards, and commissions and appoints officials to these agencies. During one term, a governor appoints some 3,000 officials. These appointments include the secretary of state, who oversees elections. The Senate must approve most appointments. The governor has the power to remove appointed officials from office with the Senate's approval. Because the 1876 constitution limits many of the governor's powers, Texas is said to have a weak governor.

An informal but important executive power is the governor's role as "first citizen" of Texas. In this role, the governor represents Texas at state functions and presents awards to outstanding Texans. The governor also issues proclamations, such as declaring a site a disaster area after a flood or a tornado. The governor also serves as the state's leader. His or her main job is to guide the state into the future. George W. Bush was twice elected governor of Texas.

Texas Voices ❝Every vote cast [in an election] is a hope. A hope that a child will get a good education. A hope that a neighborhood will be free from . . . crime. A hope that the years ahead will bring a better life.❞

—Texas governor George W. Bush, 1999 Inaugural Address

⭐ **Reading Check Summarizing** What are the governor's executive powers?

George W. Bush left his position as governor of Texas to become president of the United States.

Texas Cities

Austin

History: When settlers first arrived in the Austin area about 1835, Tonkawa Indians lived in the region. In 1839 the city was chosen as the new capital of the Republic of Texas. Edwin Waller, the first mayor, designed the original plan for the city. The grid pattern of Waller's plan is still visible in the layout of downtown.

Population in 2000: 656,562

Relative location: On the Colorado River, 75 miles northeast of San Antonio

Region: Edge of the Edwards Plateau: subregion of the Great Plains

County: County seat of Travis County

Special feature: The capital of Texas

Origin of name: Named for Stephen F. Austin

Economy: The state government employs a large part of Austin's workforce. The University of Texas also employs many people in the Austin area. In recent years, the city has become a center for high-tech industries and for research. Of the area's largest employers, 7 of 10 produce computer-related equipment.

★ Other Responsibilities

Every two years, the governor submits a budget proposal to the state legislature. This budget has little effect on the final version, however, because the legislature writes the budget bill. This limited financial control represents one of the weaknesses of the governor's office.

The Texas legislature has more power than the governor. However, the governor can influence the legislature in several ways. The governor can speak to the legislature and urge it to take certain actions. The governor does this in a "State of the State" address at the beginning of each legislative session. The governor gives the speech again when leaving office. The legislature may ignore the governor's suggestions, but a governor with a powerful personality can have a strong impact. For example, in 1891 Governor James Stephen Hogg urged the legislature to establish a railroad commission. Despite strong opposition, the legislature created the agency, now one of the state's most powerful.

The governor can also strongly influence the legislature by calling a special session. The legislature may deal only with topics specified by the governor. The Texas Constitution does not limit the number of special sessions a governor may call.

The governor's strongest legislative check is the veto. Because overrides rarely occur, the governor can often influence a bill's content by threatening a veto. The governor also has a **line-item veto**. This is the power to delete specific lines, or parts, of budget bills. This power increases the governor's influence on how state money is spent.

The governor also has responsibilities that involve the judicial branch. The governor appoints judges when vacancies occur. On the recommendation of the Board of Pardons and Paroles, the governor can also **pardon**, or free, people convicted of crimes. In addition, the governor can grant a 30-day reprieve, or delay, to a person facing the death penalty.

The governor also has duties involving the military. As commander in chief of the state's military, the governor can mobilize the Texas National Guard in times of crisis. The governor can also declare martial law, putting an area under military control.

★ **Reading Check** **Analyzing Information** List the governor's responsibilities.

★ Executive Officials and Agencies

The executive branch includes other elected officials besides the governor. Because they are not appointed, these officials are not under the governor's control. The lieutenant governor is one of the most important executive officials. This official serves a four-year term. His or her main duty is to act as the leader of the Texas Senate. The lieutenant governor also chairs the powerful Legislative Budget Board. These duties can give the lieutenant governor more power than the governor. The lieutenant governor also serves as acting governor when the governor is out of Texas.

The other senior executive officials provide important state services. The attorney general gives legal advice and represents Texas in certain court cases. The comptroller of public accounts oversees the collection of taxes. The commissioner of agriculture enforces agricultural laws and aids farmers. The commissioner of the General Land Office manages the state's land and mineral rights.

The executive branch also includes some 200 agencies, boards, and commissions. These departments enforce state laws and provide Texans with various services. The Texas Railroad Commission is one of the most important. The agency originally regulated the state's railroads when it was formed in 1891. Today it regulates the oil, natural gas, and mining industries in Texas. One of the largest agencies is the Department of Mental Health and Mental Retardation. This agency provides services to Texans who are mentally ill or disabled. These numerous agencies and officials help keep the state government running smoothly.

★ **Reading Check** **Comparing** In what ways are the offices of governor and lieutenant governor similar?

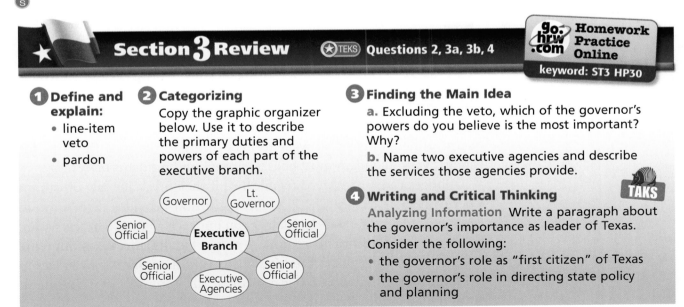

Section 3 Review

go.hrw.com **Homework Practice Online** keyword: ST3 HP30

★TEKS Questions 2, 3a, 3b, 4

1 **Define and explain:**
- line-item veto
- pardon

2 **Categorizing**
Copy the graphic organizer below. Use it to describe the primary duties and powers of each part of the executive branch.

Governor · Lt. Governor · Senior Official · Senior Official · **Executive Branch** · Senior Official · Senior Official · Executive Agencies

3 **Finding the Main Idea**
a. Excluding the veto, which of the governor's powers do you believe is the most important? Why?
b. Name two executive agencies and describe the services those agencies provide.

4 **Writing and Critical Thinking**
Analyzing Information Write a paragraph about the governor's importance as leader of Texas. Consider the following:
- the governor's role as "first citizen" of Texas
- the governor's role in directing state policy and planning

The Texas Judiciary

Read to Discover

1. How is the Texas court system structured?
2. What role do juries play within the judicial system?

Why It Matters Today

Many Texans will appear in one of the courts of the state at least once in their lives. Use **CNNfyi.com** or other **current events** sources to find information about a recent trial or court ruling. Record your findings in your journal.

Define

- civil law
- criminal law
- misdemeanors
- felonies
- trial courts
- appellate courts
- judicial review
- grand jury
- petit jury

The Story Continues

Governor Pat Neff had a problem. An important case had come before the Texas Supreme Court. However, every one of the justices had a personal interest in the case. Neff decided to appoint three women to serve as a temporary court. In January 1925, the only all-woman Supreme Court in Texas history met. The court heard the case, ruled on it, and then disbanded. More than 50 years passed before a woman served full-time on the high court.

These women served as Texas Supreme Court justices for one case after the regular judges disqualified themselves.

★ Judges and Courts

Article V of the Texas Constitution describes the judiciary. This branch makes up the state's court system. The Texas courts decide legal cases by interpreting and applying the law. More than 2,500 judges hear cases in some 3,000 Texas courts. Most of these officials are elected. Texas judges serve either four- or six-year terms. Although the qualifications for judges vary, all judges must be U.S. citizens and residents of Texas.

Judges can be removed from office if they break the law or cannot perform their duties. The Texas Constitution provides three ways to remove judges. The state legislature can impeach a judge. The legislature can ask the governor to remove a judge. Finally, the Texas Supreme Court can remove district judges. The governor appoints new judges to fill vacancies that occur because of death, removal, or retirement. Appointed judges serve until the next general election.

The Texas courts hear millions of cases each year involving either **civil law** or **criminal law**. Civil cases are legal disputes between individuals. Criminal cases are brought by the government against persons accused of crimes. **Misdemeanors** are minor crimes, such as littering or speeding, and **felonies** are major crimes, such as robbery or murder. Many defendants—people accused of crimes—plea bargain, or agree to admit guilt in exchange for a lighter punishment.

⊗ **Reading Check** **Finding the Main Idea** What is the main role of the judicial branch?

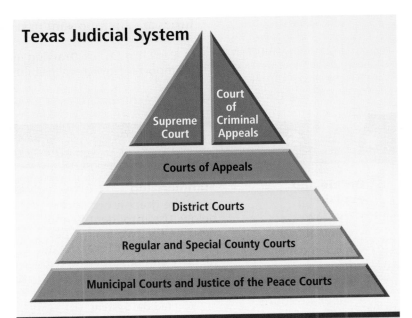

Seal of the Texas Supreme Court

★ The Structure of the Texas Courts

Cases that do go to trial are heard in one of the state's many **trial courts**, which hear new cases and give a verdict, or ruling. Texas has three levels of trial courts. Each level has a specific jurisdiction, or authority to hear certain types of cases. Municipal courts and justice of the peace courts hear misdemeanor cases punishable by fines. Justice of the peace courts hear civil cases that involve sums less than $5,000. Each county has at least one county court, called a constitutional county court. These courts hear more serious misdemeanor cases and civil cases involving amounts between $200 and $5,000. Many counties also have county courts at law. The jurisdiction of these courts varies greatly by county. District courts are the third level of trial courts. They hear all civil cases involving sums greater than $5,000, divorce cases, and some misdemeanor cases. District courts also hear all felony cases. Several Texas cities have separate district courts for criminal, family-law, and civil cases.

Appellate courts review trials to determine whether correct procedures were followed. Based on its review of a case, an appellate court may order a new trial or overturn a trial's verdict. Texas has two levels of appellate courts. The first level consists of 14 courts of appeals that review cases from district and county courts. The Supreme Court and the Court of Criminal Appeals are the state's highest courts. They mainly review the rulings of the appellate courts. The Supreme Court reviews civil cases. The Court of Criminal Appeals reviews criminal cases and all cases involving the death penalty.

Texas Judicial System

Supreme Court | Court of Criminal Appeals

Courts of Appeals

District Courts

Regular and Special County Courts

Municipal Courts and Justice of the Peace Courts

TAKS *Skills* *Interpreting Charts* The Texas judicial system is complex, with several thousand courts. What are the highest courts in the Texas judicial system? ⊗TEKS

Both high courts also have the power to judge the constitutionality of a law. This power is called **judicial review** and provides a check on the other two branches of government. In addition, the two high courts have the power to interpret the Texas Constitution when disagreements arise as to the constitution's meaning. Their interpretations affect how the constitution is applied. These two powers give the judicial branch an important role in state government.

⭐ **Reading Check** **Analyzing Information** How does judicial review reflect the principle of checks and balances in the Texas Constitution?

⭐ The Jury System

Texas courts use two types of juries. A **grand jury** decides whether a person accused of a felony should be indicted. An indictment is a formal charge of a crime. Grand juries consist of 12 people. Nine must vote to indict for a felony case to go to trial. A **petit jury** (PE-tee) decides the verdict in a trial.

The Texas Bill of Rights guarantees all Texans the right to a trial by jury. Juries give the accused the chance to have citizens decide their case. Defendants can decline their right to a jury trial. As a result, judges rule on many trials. Juries also give Texans a way to participate in the legal system. Texans must meet several requirements to serve on a jury. For example, jurors must be qualified to vote. Jurors must be able to read and write English. They cannot have been convicted of a theft or felony. Juries are an important part of the state's judicial system.

⭐ **Reading Check** **Drawing Inferences and Conclusions** Why is jury duty an important civic responsibility?

Section 4 Review ⭐TEKS Questions 2, 3a, 3b, 4

Homework Practice Online
keyword: ST3 HP30

1 **Define and explain:**
- civil law
- criminal law
- misdemeanors
- felonies
- trial courts
- appellate courts
- judicial review
- grand jury
- petit jury

2 **Summarizing**
Copy the graphic organizer below. Use it to identify and describe the two main types of cases heard in Texas. Next, identify and describe the two main types of courts in Texas.

Judicial System

Cases
1. _____
2. _____

Courts
1. _____
2. _____

3 **Finding the Main Idea**
a. What are the two highest courts in Texas, and what cases do they hear?
b. What is the role of each type of jury?

4 **Writing and Critical Thinking** **TAKS**
Evaluating Write a paragraph explaining why serving on juries is an important civil duty.
Consider the following:
- the right to a trial by jury
- the importance of the jury system

The State Budget and Public Education

Read to Discover

1. How is the Texas budget prepared, and what are the state's major sources of revenue?
2. How is Texas public education structured and governed?

Why It Matters Today

Many Texans are affected when the government raises taxes or cuts services. Use **CNNfyi.com** or other **current events** sources to find information related to taxes or government spending today. Record your findings in your journal.

Define

- appropriation bill
- revenue

Identify

- Office of Budget and Planning
- Legislative Budget Board

The Story Continues

In 1927 a young Texan named Lyndon B. Johnson began attending Southwest Texas State Teachers College. He had little money. To pay for his schooling, he worked as a janitor and a secretary. Johnson graduated in 1930. He would go on to become the 36th U.S. president. For Texans like Johnson, state colleges make obtaining a higher education possible.

LYNDON B. JOHNSON
Johnson City
B. S.; History.
B. A. Club, Press Club, Student
Council, Harris Blair, College
Star, Pi Gamma Mu.

SENIORS

Lyndon B. Johnson's experiences as a student and teacher influenced his work as a member of Congress and as president.

★ The State Budget

State funding helps keep tuitions low at public colleges. As a result, more Texans can afford college. For the years 2000 and 2001, the Texas budget gave more than $12 billion to higher education. The Texas state government requires billions of dollars to function. The cost of government for 2000 and 2001 totaled $98.1 billion. The state budget specifies how much of this money will go to different parts of the government.

Texas uses a biennial, or two-year, budget. Every two years all state agencies and offices prepare funding requests. These requests go to two state agencies. One is the **Office of Budget and Planning**, which is part of the executive branch. The other and more powerful agency is the **Legislative Budget Board**. It includes nine senior legislators and the lieutenant governor, who chairs the board. The two agencies analyze

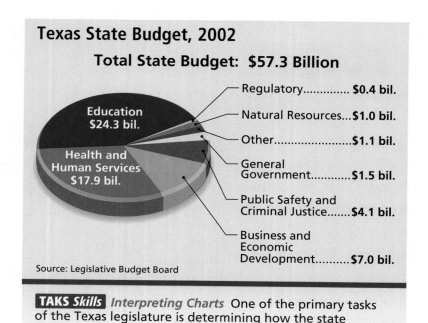

Texas State Budget, 2002

Total State Budget: $57.3 Billion

Education $24.3 bil.

Health and Human Services $17.9 bil.

Regulatory.............. $0.4 bil.

Natural Resources...$1.0 bil.

Other..................... $1.1 bil.

General Government........... $1.5 bil.

Public Safety and Criminal Justice....... $4.1 bil.

Business and Economic Development......... $7.0 bil.

Source: Legislative Budget Board

TAKS Skills *Interpreting Charts* One of the primary tasks of the Texas legislature is determining how the state government will spend its money. What area received the most funding in 2002? **TEKS**

funding requests and send a budget proposal to the Senate Finance Committee and to the House Appropriations Committee. The two committees study the proposals independently, and each recommends a budget to its house. Each house then prepares and approves an **appropriation bill**. This spending bill is the state budget. Both houses must then pass a final version of the bill.

The budget bill then goes to the Texas comptroller of public accounts. This official determines whether the state will receive enough **revenue**, or income, to cover the budget. The Texas Constitution requires a balanced budget—that is, one in which spending does not exceed income. Once the comptroller approves the budget bill, it goes to the governor to be signed.

Reading Check **Summarizing** What steps does the Texas budget go through to get approved?

★ Revenue and Spending

The Texas state government obtains the billions of dollars it needs from several sources. In 2000 the sales tax made up about 55 percent of the state's tax revenue. The sales tax gives the state a small percentage of the price of many goods and services. This tax is taken at the time of sale. Three other important taxes contributed about 15 percent of the state's income. The motor fuels tax and the vehicle sales and rental tax each raised more than $2.6 billion in 2000. The franchise tax, which applies to corporations based in Texas, raised some $2 billion. Much of the rest of the state's income comes from federal grants. In 2000 Texas received almost $15 billion from the federal government. Other sources of revenue include investments, license fees, and lottery fees.

State funds are used to build highways, pay state employees, and provide many other public services. The two areas that receive the most state money are health and human services and education. In 2000 Texas spent about $16 billion on health and human services. These services include medical treatment and other services for Texans in need. That same year the government spent some $19 billion on education.

Reading Check **Finding the Main Idea** What are the major sources of revenue for state government?

Restaurants and other businesses are required by the state of Texas to display their sales tax permits.

★ Texas Public Education

Article VII of the Texas Constitution requires the legislature to maintain "an efficient system of public free schools." Some 4 million students attend Texas public schools. State and local government contribute the most financial support to schools. The state provides money through the Permanent School Fund. This fund receives money from state taxes and investments. Local property taxes contribute heavily to school funding. The federal government also provides some funds. Much of this money funds specialized programs such as job training.

The administration of Texas public schools is divided between state and local governments. Although its role in education is limited, the federal government can occasionally get involved. For example, in the mid-1950s the federal courts ordered all public schools to integrate.

At the state level, the Texas legislature passes the laws governing public schools, including the subjects they teach. Two state agencies assist the legislature with these matters. The Texas Board of Education sets education policy and reviews textbooks for use in schools. This board has 15 elected members. The Texas Education Agency puts education policy into effect. This agency reviews standards for learning materials, schools, and teacher certification. The governor appoints a commissioner of education to direct this agency.

More than 1,000 independent school districts run schools at the local level. Boards of trustees or school boards govern these districts. School boards arrange for school construction, select textbooks, and set property tax rates. They also hire superintendents to run the day-to-day business of the school district. By providing a strong system of public education, Texans hope to ensure a successful future for their state.

★ **Reading Check Summarizing** How are Texas public schools funded?

LINKING PAST to PRESENT

Texas School Days

In the days when most children lived on farms, the school year was much shorter than it is today. Schools had long summer breaks because that was when farmers were busiest. In 1915 a Texas law required children aged 8 to 14 to attend school 100 days a year. Today school-age children in Texas are required to attend school at least 180 days a year. Some Texas schools have gone to year-round schedules. In such schools, the traditional summer break is divided into several two- to three-week vacations. **How did the state's farm-based economy affect the development of the Texas school year?** ⊙TEKS

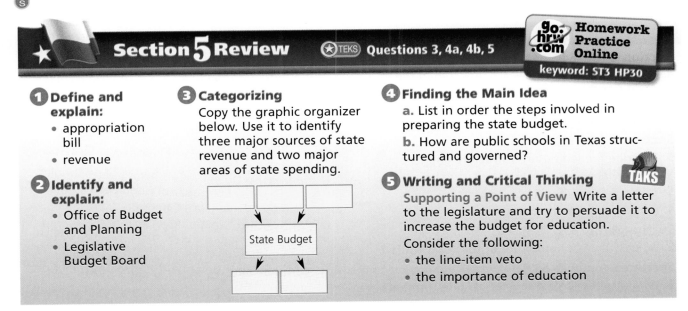

★ Section 5 Review ⊙TEKS Questions 3, 4a, 4b, 5

go.hrw.com **Homework Practice Online** keyword: ST3 HP30

1 Define and explain:
- appropriation bill
- revenue

2 Identify and explain:
- Office of Budget and Planning
- Legislative Budget Board

3 Categorizing
Copy the graphic organizer below. Use it to identify three major sources of state revenue and two major areas of state spending.

[graphic organizer: three boxes → State Budget → two boxes]

4 Finding the Main Idea
a. List in order the steps involved in preparing the state budget.
b. How are public schools in Texas structured and governed?

5 Writing and Critical Thinking TAKS
Supporting a Point of View Write a letter to the legislature and try to persuade it to increase the budget for education.
Consider the following:
- the line-item veto
- the importance of education

The Chapter at a Glance

Examine the following visual summary of the chapter. Then use the visual to pose and answer questions about the structure and function of the government of Texas. ★TEKS

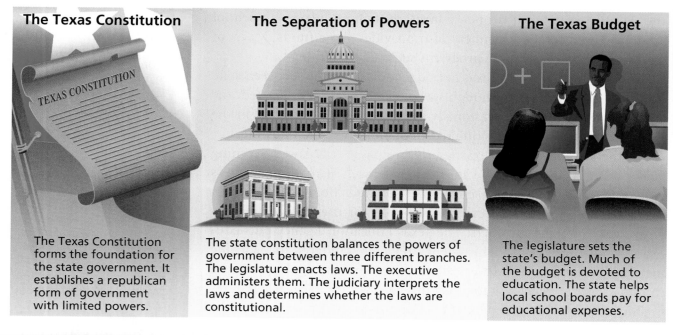

The Texas Constitution

The Texas Constitution forms the foundation for the state government. It establishes a republican form of government with limited powers.

The Separation of Powers

The state constitution balances the powers of government between three different branches. The legislature enacts laws. The executive administers them. The judiciary interprets the laws and determines whether the laws are constitutional.

The Texas Budget

The legislature sets the state's budget. Much of the budget is devoted to education. The state helps local school boards pay for educational expenses.

Identifying People and Ideas ★TEKS

Use each of the following terms or people in historically significant sentences.

1. popular sovereignty
2. limited government
3. separation of powers
4. checks and balances
5. federalism
6. bill of rights
7. bicameral
8. line-item veto
9. appellate courts
10. appropriation bill

Understanding Main Ideas ★TEKS

Section 1 (pp. 640–643)

1. What six basic principles are reflected in the Texas Constitution?
2. How does the Texas Constitution protect the individual rights of Texans?

Section 2 (pp. 644–647)

3. Describe the legislature's structure and its powers and duties.

Section 3 (pp. 648–651)

4. List some of the governor's powers.

Section 4 (pp. 652–654)

5. What is the basic structure of the Texas courts?

Section 5 (pp. 655–657)

6. What are the largest sources of state revenue?

7. Describe the structure of the state's public education system.

You Be the Historian ★TEKS

Reviewing Themes

1. **Constitutional Heritage** How was the Texas Constitution influenced by ideas found in the U.S. Constitution? Why do you think the two documents have similarities?
2. **Government** What are some of the advantages and disadvantages of having a weak governor?
3. **Economics** Name the public service that you think should receive most state funds. Give three reasons to support your choice.

TAKS **Practice: Thinking Critically** ★TEKS

1. **Evaluating** Do you think Texas judges should be elected by the public or appointed by the governor? Explain your answer.
2. **Contrasting** Explain how the powers of the judiciary differ from those of the executive branch and legislature.
3. **Summarizing** Describe the structure of the state government.

Social Studies Skills Workshop

Interpreting Political Cartoons

Study the political cartoon below. Then use the information in the cartoon to help you answer the questions that follow.

BILL McCLANAHAN.
TOUGH BIRD TO CARVE. 1964

1. What is the main point of the cartoon?

   a. Redistricting will be easy.
   b. Creating new districts will be difficult.
   c. Few people are aware of what is involved in the redistricting process.
   d. Political parties rarely disagree during the redistricting process.

2. What issues might arise during the redistricting process?

Analyzing Primary Sources ⊛TEKS

Read the following quote from Ann Richards, taken from her inaugural address, January 15, 1991. Then answer the questions.

"Today, we have a vision of a Texas where the government treats every citizen with respect and dignity and honesty, where consumers are protected, where business is . . . valued, where good jobs are plentiful, where those in need find compassion and help, where every decision is measured against a high standard of ethics and true commitment to the public trust. . . . Nothing is more fundamentally important to me than the understanding that this administration exists to serve the taxpayers. . . . Service to the people is government's bottom line."

3. Which of the following statements best describes Ann Richards's point of view?

   a. Government is too large.
   b. Government should serve the people.
   c. Government exists to strictly regulate business behavior.
   d. Government should not help the poor.

4. What do you think Richards means when she says that the "government's bottom line" is to serve the people?

Alternative Assessment

Linking to Community ⊛TEKS

Many people work in leadership positions in the state government. Research information about an elected or appointed leader of Texas, such as the governor, the secretary of state, a legislator, or a judge. Find out if the person was elected or appointed to office. Determine what the official's duties are and identify the leadership qualities that the person brings to the job. Then create a collage that illustrates the person's duties and leadership qualities for the class.

BUILDING YOUR Portfolio

🖅 **internet** connect

Internet Activity: go.hrw.com
KEYWORD: ST3 TX30 ⊛TEKS

Access the Internet through the HRW Go site to research the state's government. Then create a visual display or model on the structure and function of Texas government. Include information on the Texas Constitution, the branches of government, the major state agencies, and the specific powers and duties of each branch or agency. Include drawings, photographs, or 3-D models.

Local Government and Citizenship

(1845–Present)

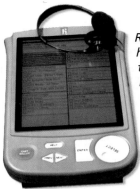

Recent technology has been used to make vote recorders that are very accurate.

WILLIAM PERRY CLEMENTS, JR. ★ GOVERNOR OF TEXAS

INAUGURATION
JANUARY 16, 1979

With his election in 1978, Bill Clements became the first Republican governor in more than 100 years.

TEXAS

1848 Texans cast their first votes as U.S. citizens in a presidential election.

1869 Edmund J. Davis is elected governor, the last Republican to hold the office until Bill Clements was elected in 1978.

1918 After decades of fighting for the right to vote, women are allowed to vote in Texas primary elections.

1845	**1865**	**1885**	**1905**

U.S. and WORLD

1848 The Seneca Falls Convention calls for equal rights for women, including the right to vote.

1868 The Fourteenth Amendment, which expands and protects citizenship, is adopted.

1892 A third party, the Populist Party, holds its first national convention.

1920 The Nineteenth Amendment is adopted, giving women the right to vote.

ELLIS ISLAND - IMMIGRATION DEPOT, NEW YORK.

Ellis Island was the nation's busiest immigration entry point during the early 1900s. Many immigrants have become naturalized citizens.

Build on What You Know

The Texas Constitution divided state government into three branches. Below the state government are many local governments. Texans make important contributions to their state by participating in elections and by fulfilling their many other civic responsibilities.

Texas teenagers participated in the 1992 Republican National Convention in Houston.

The state government encourages citizens to vote.

1925 The legislature begins to allow Texans to vote early if they are unable to go to the polls on election day.

1972 Texan Barbara Jordan is elected to the U.S. House of Representatives. She is the first black woman from the South to serve in Congress.

1986 Raul Gonzalez is elected to the Texas Supreme Court. He is the first Hispanic elected to statewide office in Texas.

1925 | 1945 | 1965 | 1985 | Present

1965 Congress passes the Voting Rights Act to protect citizens' right to vote.

2000 Texan George W. Bush is elected president of the United States.

Poll taxes prevented many poor and minority Americans from voting.

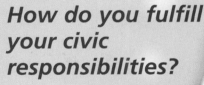

As a Texan . . .
How do you fulfill your civic responsibilities?

You Be the Historian

Themes Journal

What's Your Opinion? Do you **agree** or **disagree** with the following statements? Support your point of view in your journal.

● **Constitutional Heritage** Free speech and press contribute little to democratic society.

● **Citizenship** Civic participation is important in a republic.

● **Government** In a democracy, citizens rarely express different political views.

Local Government

Read to Discover

1. What are the structures and functions of local Texas governments?
2. How are local governments funded?

Why It Matters Today

Fire protection is just one example of a service provided by local governments. Use **CNNfyi.com** or other **current events** sources to find information on local public services today. Record your findings in your journal.

Define

- precincts
- commissioners' court
- mayor-council government
- council-manager government
- commission plan
- home-rule charters
- general-law cities
- special districts

The Story Continues

Trucks rumbled up and down the neighborhood streets. More and more businesses had moved into the area. Their arrival meant that many of the neighborhood's residents would soon have new jobs. The job opportunities were made possible because citizens had urged the town's city council to allow the businesses to move to the neighborhood.

Texas citizens regularly attend local government meetings to present issues that are important to them.

★ County Governments

Thousands of local governments throughout Texas provide police protection, roads, water, and other services to Texans. The state has 254 counties, each with its own government. Counties are divided into four **precincts**, or county subdivisions, and voters in each precinct elect a county commissioner. Voters countywide elect a county judge. These elected officials serve four-year terms and make up the **commissioners' court** that governs the county.

The judge directs the commissioners' meetings, in which they prepare the county budget and address local issues. The court also sets the county property tax rate. This is an important responsibility because property taxes are the major source of revenue for counties. If the voters approve, counties can also raise money by issuing bonds for the construction of buildings, roads, and other projects. Bonds are certificates that represent money the government has borrowed from citizens. Despite its name, the commissioners' court does not handle legal cases. However, in less populated counties the judge may hear certain cases.

Other officials also serve at the county level. The sheriff provides police protection and runs the county jail. The county attorney advises officials and prosecutes misdemeanor criminal cases. Each county has justices of the peace that hear minor criminal and civil cases. The county clerk keeps records of the commissioners' court and keeps deed records of all land in the county. The receiving and paying out of county funds is handled by the county treasurer. The county tax assessor-collector makes sure taxes are collected and issues vehicle titles. These and other officials work hard to keep counties running smoothly.

Reading Check Contrasting How do the duties of the commissioners' court and a regular court differ?

Municipal Governments and Special Districts

More than 85 percent of Texans live in urban areas run by municipal governments. There are several types of municipal governments. In a **mayor-council government**, voters elect a mayor and a city council to directly run the government. The mayor serves as the city's chief executive officer and directs the council meetings. Many cities have a **council-manager government** in which voters elect a mayor and members of a city council. These elected officials decide the city's policies. The council then chooses a city manager to carry out those policies and handle the city's day-to-day business. With a council-manager government, the city's administration rests in the hands of a hired professional.

The **commission plan**, also known as the Galveston Plan, was developed in 1901. Voters elect five to seven commissioners to serve as a city council. Each commissioner also supervises a city department. This

That's Interesting!

Texans on the Road

Maintaining the state's roads is an important function of local governments. The number of licensed drivers in Texas—more than 13 million—continues to grow each year. More than 14 million cars and trucks travel Texas highways, a number second in the nation only to California.

Forms of Municipal Government

Council-Manager

People — elect → Mayor*
People — elect → Council
Council — selects → Manager
Mayor* ← designates
Manager → Municipal Departments

*Mayors are either elected by the people or designated by councils.

Mayor-Council

People — elect → Mayor
People — elect → Council
Mayor → Municipal Departments

Commission

People — elect → Council
Council — designates → Mayor
Council → Each member heads a municipal department.

TAKS Skills *Interpreting Charts* Municipal departments often include police, fire, roads, utilities, and parks. In which form of government does the mayor have the most power?

Municipal services. One of the most important city services is fire protection. *How do you think these firefighters, who are receiving training, are important to Texas cities?*

form of government worked well for a time, but commissioners had difficulty working together toward citywide goals. As problems arose, cities switched to mayor-council or council-manager governments. There are no true commission governments in Texas today.

There are two types of municipalities in Texas. Municipalities with populations of more than 5,000 qualify for **home-rule charters**. These charters allow citizens to choose among the three forms of municipal government. Cities draft and adopt these charters within guidelines set by the state legislature. The cities then pass ordinances, or local laws. Unless an ordinance conflicts with state law, the state will not interfere with the local law. Most small towns and villages are known as **general-law cities**. They operate under the general laws of the state. Some of these towns have a charter from the legislature outlining the form of government they can use.

City governments raise revenue, or money, from bonds and from property and sales taxes. The government uses this money to provide services such as police and fire protection, garbage collection, and utilities. Many cities have parks, swimming pools, and sports leagues for recreation.

Special districts—particularly school districts—are the most numerous form of local government in the state. These districts are formed for a particular purpose, often handling services that other local governments do not provide. Special districts might serve Texans living in several communities. For example, some special districts provide flood control across several cities in the same region, such as the Lower Colorado River Authority. Texas also has hospital districts and transportation districts. The people in charge of special districts may be either appointed or elected.

Reading Check **Summarizing** How are city governments run, and why do special districts exist?

Section 1 Review

 Questions 1, 2, 3a, 3b, 4

 **Homework Practice Online**
keyword: ST3 HP31

1 Define and explain:
- precincts
- commissioners' court
- mayor-council government
- council-manager government
- commission plan
- home-rule charters
- general-law cities
- special districts

2 Categorizing
Copy the graphic organizer below. Use it to list the types of local governments. Describe how they are run and what services these governments provide.

County	Municipal	Special District

3 Finding the Main Idea
a. Describe the structure and function of county government.
b. What are the major sources of revenue for local governments?

4 Writing and Critical Thinking
Evaluating Imagine that you are a county commissioner. A citizens group has asked the county to repair a road. Write a letter explaining why you will or will not agree to this.
Consider the following:
- the road's need for repair
- the county's budget

Read to Discover

1. What are the freedoms of speech, the press, and assembly, and why are they important?
2. What legal protections does the Bill of Rights give Texans?
3. What are the other major rights protected by the Bill of Rights?

Define

- slander
- libel
- due process
- bail
- eminent domain

Why It Matters Today

The Texas Bill of Rights guarantees the right to assemble. Use **CNNfyi.com** or other **current events** sources to find information about a recent political meeting. Record your findings in your journal.

The Story Continues

For days a drama had unfolded on the sidewalk in front of the governor's mansion. Angry citizens were protesting some of the governor's environmental policies. The police had ordered the protesters to leave so that others could use the sidewalk. After several protesters were arrested, they went to court to defend their right to gather and protest. Their lawyer pointed to the Texas Bill of Rights and its protection of free speech and the right to assemble.

Some environmental activists exercise free speech by wearing pins that support their positions.

★ Basic Rights and Freedoms

The Texas Bill of Rights protects the individual liberties of Texans. Its placement at the front of the Texas Constitution emphasizes its importance. The Texas Bill of Rights begins by stating that Texas is an independent state, and it recognizes the U.S. Constitution as the only higher legal authority. Section 2 of the Texas Bill of Rights states that all political power stems from the people.

Sections 3 and 3a declare that Texans have equal rights under the law. This protects against laws that discriminate on the basis of gender, race, or national origin. Sections 4 through 7 protect Texans' freedom of worship. The government cannot support a religion or interfere with

Free speech and assembly. Occasionally, Texans have found it necessary to conduct public protests to make their opinions heard. *Why are these students protesting?*

anyone's decision to practice a religion or not. These sections bar the government from having an official religion or favoring any particular one.

Section 8 protects the freedoms of speech and of the press. These freedoms are crucial to democracy. For democracy to work, the people must be able to stay informed and to freely discuss issues. Texas media such as newspapers and magazines are published without the control of the government. These rights are not unlimited, however. **Slander**— a false statement made on purpose that damages another's reputation—is not protected. **Libel**, an intentionally false written statement, is not protected either. Nor does freedom of speech protect statements that seriously threaten the public's safety. For example, falsely shouting "Fire!" in a crowded theater is unprotected speech.

Section 27 of the Texas Bill of Rights ensures that Texans can freely assemble, or gather together. Generally, government officials cannot break up a meeting unless the people are disruptive or breaking the law. Texans can also petition, or make a request, for particular government action.

 Reading Check **Finding the Main Idea** What rights are protected in Sections 3 through 8 of the Texas Bill of Rights?

★ Protection of the Accused

The Texas Constitution includes safeguards that require the government to take certain legal actions before it can seize a person's property or punish a person. This is known as **due process**. Sections 9 through 16 of the Texas Bill of Rights deal with the rights of persons accused of a crime. Section 9 prohibits "unreasonable seizures or searches" of Texans' property. This means that, in most cases, a judge must approve a search before the police can carry it out.

Defendants in criminal cases have a number of protections. All defendants are presumed innocent until proven guilty. A person cannot be charged with a serious crime unless a grand jury decides that there is enough evidence. The defendant has the right to know the charge and to review the evidence. The accused must be allowed to question witnesses who testify for the government. The defendant is also entitled to a trial by jury. Convicted persons are guaranteed not to receive "cruel or unusual" punishment. If the person is found not guilty, he or she cannot be tried again for the same offense. In addition, the government cannot pass a law punishing someone for conduct that was lawful when committed.

Most people accused of a crime can get out of jail until their trial has ended by paying **bail**. This is money that defendants promise to pay to the court as a guarantee that they will show up for trial. Persons facing very serious criminal charges can be denied bail.

⭐ **Reading Check** **Analyzing Information** What are some of the rights protected by Sections 9 through 16 of the Texas Bill of Rights?

⭐ Other Rights

Texans benefit from other protections as well. The government can use **eminent domain**—taking land for public use. However, the property owner must be paid for the property. In addition, Texans cannot be jailed for unpaid debts.

Section 22 defines treason and the rights of persons accused of that charge. Under Section 23, Texans have the right to keep and bear arms. Section 24 places the state's military forces under the control of the state's civilian authorities. The government cannot force citizens to provide housing for soldiers in peacetime.

The Texas Bill of Rights protects a variety of other liberties. A citizen cannot be outlawed, or banished from the state. Section 28 limits the power to suspend state law to the legislature. Section 29 provides that the government cannot change the Texas Bill of Rights. In addition, laws that contradict the Bill of Rights will have no effect. Crime victims are given rights in Sections 30 and 31, including the right to be notified of court proceedings. These protections help ensure the freedom of all Texans.

⭐ **Reading Check** **Summarizing** What are some of the other rights guaranteed to Texans?

Many trials have been held in Texas courthouses such as the Ellis County courthouse in Waxahachie.

⭐ **Section 2 Review** ⭐TEKS Questions 1, 2, 3a, 3b, 4

go.hrw.com Homework Practice Online
keyword: ST3 HP31

1 Define and explain:
- slander
- libel
- due process
- bail
- eminent domain

2 Analyzing Information
Copy the table below. Use it to describe the freedoms of speech, press, and assembly.

Freedom of Speech	
Freedom of the Press	
Freedom of Assembly	

3 Finding the Main Idea
a. Describe the rights that a person accused of a crime has under the Texas Bill of Rights.
b. What other rights do Texans have under the Bill of Rights?

4 Writing and Critical Thinking
TAKS
Analyzing Information Write a paragraph explaining why freedoms of speech, the press, and assembly are important rights in a democracy.
Consider the following:
- where people get information about political issues
- how people can express their political views

Citizenship and Elections

Read to Discover

1. What are the responsibilities of citizenship?
2. What are the different types of Texas elections?

Why It Matters Today

Texans go to the polls regularly. Use CNNfyi.com or other **current events** sources to find information on a recent election. Record your findings in your journal.

Define

• primary elections
• runoff election
• general elections
• special election
• direct democracy
• referendum

The Story Continues

The Rio Grande needed help. Over time, littering and neglect had taken their toll. Citizens of El Paso saw this and started Dia del Rio—"Day of the River"—to clean up and beautify the river. Keith Floyd, a Dia del Rio volunteer, explained why he helped out. "Sometimes I think we take the Rio Grande for granted. I think people forget how beautiful it is." Local teenagers also volunteered. They planted trees, built trails, and cleaned up along the river.

Texas teenagers have volunteered for many community service projects such as this Texas beach cleanup.

★ Rights and Responsibilities

Texans who participate in volunteer activities like Dia del Rio are fulfilling their civic responsibilities. Citizens have both rights and responsibilities. U.S. citizens have the right to vote in elections and to run for government office. People born in the United States or a U.S. territory are U.S. citizens. In most cases, persons who are born outside the United States to a U.S. citizen are citizens. Those who are born in foreign countries to people who are not U.S. citizens can become naturalized citizens. Adult legal immigrants can apply for citizenship after meeting certain requirements, including tests of the applicants' understanding of the English language, U.S. history, and government. After passing the tests, immigrants take an oath of allegiance to the U.S. Constitution and become naturalized citizens.

Texans also have civic responsibilities such as obeying the law. Citizens must know what the laws are in order to obey them. The government can punish a lawbreaker even if the person is unaware of the law. If Texans disagree with a law, they can try to change it by speaking to their local representative or by challenging the law in court. They can also petition the government or vote for officials who oppose the law.

An important part of citizenship is public service. Serving in the military is one form of public service. Citizens can also participate in projects that help the community. Leading citizens have set an example of public service. Sam Rayburn recalled his years of public service.

Texas Voices ❝When I was a boy . . . I made up my mind that I was going to make politics and public affairs my life's work. I have never regretted that decision for a moment. . . . It has been interesting and satisfying all the way.❞

—Sam Rayburn

Paying taxes is another important civic responsibility. The government needs taxes to pay for important public services. Without taxes, the government could not provide schools, roads, and police and fire protection. Texans pay several state taxes, including sales and property taxes, as well as federal income taxes. Citizenship also requires people to serve on juries when called to do so. For the right to trial by jury in the Texas Bill of Rights to have any meaning, citizens must serve when called.

Voting is the basic way for citizens to participate in government. Texans cast their votes for or against particular candidates and issues. Because these votes affect government policy, citizens have a duty to stay informed about political issues and leaders. By staying informed, citizens can better judge the quality of the leadership. Citizens can then voice their approval or disapproval of the leaders' positions.

⭐ **Reading Check** **Drawing Inferences and Conclusions** Why is political participation important in a republic?

⭐ Elections

A voter must be a U.S. citizen and 18 years old. Texas voters must also have lived in the state for at least 30 days before the election. Citizens must register before they can vote. Registration ensures that a person's qualifications to vote have been checked before election day. To register, a potential voter fills out a simple form and sends it to the voter registrar—a county official. Within 30 days, the voter receives a registration certificate to present when it is time to vote. Citizens vote in the area where they live, either in person or by mail. The secretary of state supervises Texas elections. Most of the hands-on work of carrying out elections is handled by county officials. Local officials print ballots and provide voting equipment. Volunteers also help the process run smoothly.

There are many elections in Texas. Political parties hold **primary elections** at all levels of government to decide who will represent the party in later elections. The candidate who receives more than 50 percent

Analyzing Primary Sources ⭐
Drawing Inferences and Conclusions How did Sam Rayburn fulfill a civic responsibility?

Citizenship and You

Public Service

There are many ways people of all ages can contribute to their communities and be good citizens. Many Texas teenagers have donated their time to library reading programs for young children. Others volunteer with church groups, community centers, and hospitals. In what ways can Texans fulfill their civic responsibilities? ⭐TEKS

One way Texans meet their civic responsibilities is by registering to vote and taking part in elections.

Phil Gramm
(1942–)

William Philip Gramm was born in Georgia. After earning a Ph.D. in economics, he started teaching at Texas A&M University in 1967. In 1978 Gramm was elected to the U.S. House of Representatives, where he won two more terms as a Democrat. He then resigned to run as a Republican in a special election. In 1984 Gramm won John Tower's U.S. Senate seat when Tower declined to run for re-election. Gramm was re-elected in 1990 and 1996. He has served as chairman of the National Republican Senatorial Committee. **How has Gramm served the people of Texas?** TEKS

of the votes wins. If no one receives more than 50 percent, the top vote getters compete in a **runoff election**. Voters can only participate in one party primary. For example, someone who voted in the Democratic primary cannot vote in the Republican primary that same year. Primary elections are held in March of even-numbered years. Runoff elections, if needed, are held in April.

When the primary elections are over, the parties are ready to compete directly. **General elections** decide who wins a particular state or local office. The voters may also be asked to decide certain issues, such as constitutional amendments. All registered voters may participate in general elections. General elections for statewide office are held in November of even-numbered years when there is no presidential race. General elections at the local level are usually held in odd-numbered years. A vacancy may occur in an office before the next general election is held. When this happens, voters return to the polls for a **special election** held to fill the vacancy. For example, when Phil Gramm decided to switch parties he resigned from the U.S. House of Representatives. He ran as a Republican during a special election to fill this vacancy. Special elections can also be held for constitutional amendments and local bond issues.

In a representative democracy like Texas, elected officials represent the people. Texas also has **direct democracy**—voters decide issues directly rather than going through their representatives. Direct democracy takes several forms in Texas. A **referendum** allows citizens to vote on public issues such as constitutional amendments. A referendum can also be used to repeal, or do away with, a law. Initiatives allow voters to propose local laws and then require a vote on the measure. Citizens can propose initiatives if a given percentage of the voters sign petitions for the measure. The final example of direct democracy in Texas is the recall. This election gives voters the chance to remove a local official from office.

★ **Reading Check** **Analyzing Information** In what types of elections can Texas citizens vote?

 Section 3 Review ★TEKS Questions 3a, 4

go.hrw.com **Homework Practice Online**
keyword: ST3 HP31

1 **Define and explain:**
- primary elections
- runoff election
- general elections
- special election
- direct democracy
- referendum

2 **Sequencing**
Copy the graphic organizer below. Use it to show in order the steps that a citizen must take before voting.

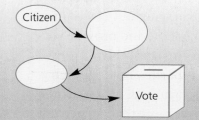

3 **Finding the Main Idea**
a. Why should citizens participate in elections?
b. What types of elections are held in Texas?

4 **Writing and Critical Thinking** TAKS
Evaluating Write a paragraph about the two civic responsibilities that you believe are most important.
Consider the following:
- benefits of civic responsibilities
- civic responsibility and democracy

Political Parties and Interest Groups

Read to Discover

1. What are political parties, and why are they formed?
2. How do interest groups and political action committees participate in the political process?

Define

- platform
- interest groups
- lobby
- political action committees

Why It Matters Today

Political races—whether for national or local office—are exciting events. Use CNNfyi.com or other **current events** sources to find information on a recent political campaign. Record your findings in your journal.

The Story Continues

Molly Beth Malcolm's parents taught her about the importance of voting. Voting, she learned, was a key way to participate in the political process. She carried this belief into adulthood, becoming chairperson of the Texas Democratic Party. She enjoys competing with the Republican Party. "I'm glad Texas is a two-party state. That's how democracy should be."

Joining political parties is one way of taking part in the political process.

★ Political Parties

Political participation is an important duty of citizens in a democracy. Political parties are one way for citizens to participate. Political parties organize to nominate and elect government officials and to shape government policy. Delegates are elected or appointed to attend their party's convention, where they decide the party's **platform**, or stated goals. Delegates also nominate candidates for office and elect party officers.

The two major political parties in Texas—and the United States—are the Democratic Party and the Republican Party. The Democratic Party dominated Texas politics for about 100 years after Reconstruction. Texas was virtually a one-party state during this time. Since the late 1970s the Republicans have held many statewide political offices, and Texas has become a two-party state. Although third parties sometimes

Learning about government. *Many Texas teens have participated in mock government sessions such as this one held in the Capitol.* **How do you think these students will benefit from their experience?** TEKS

have influenced Texas politics in different eras, they have not greatly affected state politics in recent years.

Parties tend to disagree with one another on political issues. For example, although Democrats and Republicans agree that education is important, the parties disagree on the best way to pay for good schools. Republicans argue that all school taxes collected within a district should pay for schools within that district. Democrats have argued that taxes from wealthier school districts should be used to help poorer districts. Environmental issues highlight another difference. Republicans generally believe that individuals, not the government, can best protect the environment. Democrats argue that the government should take the lead in protecting the environment. Democrats and Republicans want Texas to have a strong economy, but they differ on the role government should play in reaching that goal. Both parties work hard to win the support of Texans on these and other issues.

★ **Reading Check** **Identifying Points of View** How are Democrats' and Republicans' views on some issues similar and different?

Every Vote Counts

Whether you are a voter or an elected government official, voting is crucial. In 1845 Texas became the 28th state by a very slender margin. The final vote in the U.S. Senate was 27 to 25. In 1912 Woodrow Wilson was elected president by less than one vote per precinct in one state. In the 2000 presidential election Texan George W. Bush won the electoral college vote by receiving 537 more popular votes than Vice President Al Gore in Florida.

★ Interest Groups and Political Action Committees

Many Texans take part in the political process by forming or joining **interest groups**. These groups try to affect decisions made by those in government. They **lobby**, or try to persuade, public officials to support the group's goals. Interest groups hire lobbyists to meet with public officials. Lobbyists are often former government officials such as legislators.

Many interest groups direct their lobbying efforts on the state's legislators. Business groups such as the Texas Mortgage Bankers Association focus on economic issues. The League of United Latin American Citizens (LULAC) works to protect the civil rights of the state's Hispanics. Mothers Against Drunk Driving (MADD) supports the passage of laws designed to prevent drunk driving.

Interest groups have different points of view on important Texas issues. For example, a group called Texans for Lawsuit Reform organized to try to change how civil lawsuits are handled. They believe that the large amounts of money that Texas juries sometimes award are harming the state's businesses. The Texas Trial Lawyers Association believes that the Texas justice system should not be changed significantly. Each of these interest groups has lobbied the Texas legislature to support its point of view.

Fund-raising is also an important part of the political process. Contributions to political candidates can be made directly or through **political action committees** (PACs). PACs are groups that raise and spend money for a candidate. Contributions are important to political campaigns, particularly in races for statewide office. One political consultant noted the expense of these campaigns.

 **Texas Voices** "[Texas has] grown to be a very big state, and, when you have state senatorial districts that rival the size of congressional districts, you are trying to reach an awful lot of people and it costs a lot of money to run. . . . Television costs continue to escalate [rise] year after year."

—Karl Rove, quoted in *The World of Texas Politics*, edited by George Christian

The money pays for advertisements on radio, television, and in the newspapers. Texas sets no limit on how much money a PAC can accept or spend. But PACs must report information about their contributors and how the money is spent. PACs provide another way for Texans to participate in the political process.

Reading Check **Identifying Points of View** Describe the different points of view two interest groups have on how civil lawsuits should be handled.

MADD employs a lobbyist to support strengthening drunk-driving laws.

Section 4 Review (TEKS) Questions 3a, 4

go.hrw.com **Homework Practice Online**
keyword: ST3 HP31

1 Define and explain:
- platform
- interest groups
- lobby
- political action committees

2 Evaluating
Copy the graphic organizer below. Use it to show why interest groups form and the activities in which they engage.

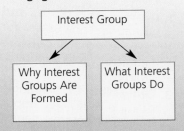

Interest Group

Why Interest Groups Are Formed

What Interest Groups Do

3 Finding the Main Idea
a. What are political parties, and how do they give Texans a way to participate in the political process?
b. What role do political action committees play in Texas politics?

4 Writing and Critical Thinking
Supporting a Point of View Imagine that you are running for governor. Write an e-mail to an interest group explaining why it should support you.
Consider the following:
- the interest group's positions
- why you support these positions

CHAPTER 31 REVIEW

The Chapter at a Glance

Examine the following visual summary of the chapter. Then use the visual to create an outline about local government and citizenship that you could use as a study guide. ⭐TEKS

Local Government

Local Government

| County Government | Municipal Government | Special District (such as school districts) |

Rights and Responsibilities

Rights

Responsibilities

The Texas Bill of Rights ensures that each citizen has the rights to freedom of press, speech, and religion as well as a trial by jury.

Texas citizens have responsibilities such as obeying the law, paying taxes, and public service. A responsible citizen is also an educated voter.

Politics

Political Parties

Interest Groups

Texas politics is dominated by two political parties, the Democratic and Republican Parties. These parties create platforms and raise funds for their candidates.

Interest groups and political action committees lobby the legislature to pass laws.

Identifying People and Ideas ⭐TEKS

Use the following terms or individuals in sentences.
1. commissioners' court
2. special districts
3. due process
4. eminent domain
5. primary election
6. general elections
7. special election
8. referendum
9. interest group
10. lobby

Understanding Main Ideas ⭐TEKS

Section 1 (pp. 662–664)
1. Describe the structure and function of local governments.
2. Describe the major sources of revenue for local governments.

Section 2 (pp. 665–667)
3. What rights are guaranteed in the Texas Bill of Rights?
4. How did the Texas Bill of Rights help protect Texans' freedom of speech and their right to assemble?

Section 3 (pp. 668–670)
5. What are the civic responsibilities of Texas citizens?
6. Describe the different elections in Texas, and explain why they are held.

Section 4 (pp. 671–673)
7. How do political parties and interest groups try to influence government policy?

You Be the Historian ⭐TEKS

Reviewing Themes
1. **Constitutional Heritage** Describe the importance of freedoms of speech and the press in a democratic society.
2. **Citizenship** What are the rights and responsibilities of Texas citizens, and why are they important?
3. **Government** How does the Texas Bill of Rights allow Texans and political parties to debate important issues?

TAKS Practice: Thinking Critically ⭐TEKS

1. **Drawing Inferences and Conclusions** Why do you think many Texans form interest groups?
2. **Comparing and Contrasting** How are the Democratic and Republican Parties similar and different?
3. **Evaluating** Explain how being informed on political issues is an important civic responsibility in a representative democracy.

674 Chapter 31

Interpreting Graphs ⭐TEKS

Study the graph below. Use it to answer the following questions.

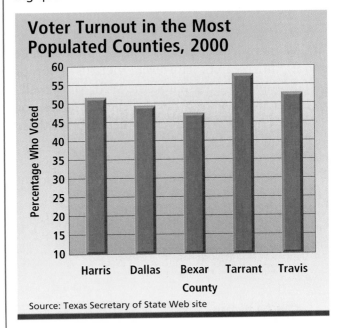

Voter Turnout in the Most Populated Counties, 2000

Source: Texas Secretary of State Web site

1. Which Texas county had the highest voter turnout, and what was the difference between the next highest county?

- **a.** Tarrant; 57.5 percent
- **b.** Travis; 5 percent
- **c.** Tarrant; 5 percent
- **d.** Bexar; 10 percent

2. What was the average voter turnout in these counties? Why might some people argue that more people should vote?

Analyzing Primary Sources ⭐TEKS

Read the following quote by former governor Bill Clements. Then answer the questions.

"You too have a responsibility to help achieve good government, and that responsibility goes beyond voting on election day. When we as individuals, and as a state are silent—when we let others make decisions for us without stating our beliefs—we forfeit [give up] our freedom. When we stand up and speak out, when we express our desires and concerns, then and only then, will we have effective government."

3. Which of the following statements best describes the author's point of view?

- **a.** Voting is the only way for people to express their points of view.
- **b.** Speaking out rarely results in better government.
- **c.** Only governmental leaders can bring about good government.
- **d.** People can best protect their freedom by speaking out.

4. What does Clements believe the people of Texas should do to create more effective government?

Alternative Assessment

Interdisciplinary Connection to the Arts

Imagine that you and several of your classmates belong to a political party and are delegates to your party's convention. Create a platform for your party, describing the issues that are most important to you and considering the rights and civic responsibilities of Texans. You might want to research the platforms of the Democratic and Republican Parties for ideas and to learn their points of view on issues that are important to Texans. Work as a group to write a catchy song that expresses your party's stance on an issue.

BUILDING YOUR Portfolio

🖥 internet connect

Internet Activity: go.hrw.com
KEYWORD: ST3 TX31 ⭐TEKS

Access the Internet through the HRW Go site to research and analyze the contributions of one of the following Texas leaders: Henry B. Gonzáles, Phil Gramm, Barbara Jordan, Sam Rayburn, President George Bush, President George W. Bush, or President Lyndon B. Johnson. Then write a biography in which you focus on the person's accomplishments and his or her leadership skills.

Social Studies Skills

WORKSHOP

Using the Internet

There is a wealth of information on the Internet. However, it takes a careful approach to find information that is both accurate and useful for your needs.

Finding the Information You Need

There are many types of search tools available. Directories, search engines, and subject guides are three of the major types of search tools. Each search tool is constantly changing. Get to know the strengths and weaknesses of your search tool choice. Many search engines use keywords to improve search speed and accuracy. Be sure to examine the "Help" files of any search tool to get the full details on search information.

Some large Web sites—such as America Online, MSN, Netscape, and Yahoo!—offer links to a broad range of information. In addition, there are many government sites that provide information on public policy and government organizations. Sites such as CNNfyi.com allow you to access current news and information.

Check the Reliability of the Web Page

Users must be able to determine whether a Web page contains reliable information. Ask yourself these questions:

- Is the information clear and easy to read?
- Is a well-respected organization sponsoring the site?
- Does the text contain any obvious mistakes?
- Is the Web site easy to navigate, and are most of the page links active?
- Does the Web site indicate updates, and are they recent?
- Is the information biased?

Warnings to Students The Internet contains many resources, making it an excellent tool for research. However, there is a lot of inappropriate material on the Web. Many well-respected sites have developed safe areas for youth, known as child-safe zones. Even at these sites you must be careful.

- Never chat with or meet with strangers.
- Never give out any personal information.
- If you get into an unsecured area, get out immediately and tell your parent or teacher.
- Stay within well-respected search engines.

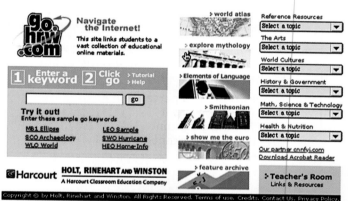

Practicing the Skill

Search the Internet to find information on Texas government. This could include information on the Texas Constitution, state or local government, or citizens' rights and responsibilities. Use this information to create an illustrated poster using charts or graphs to display the facts and figures about what you have found.

History in Action

You Solve the Problem . . .

How Can I Encourage Texans to Vote?

Complete the following activity in small cooperative groups. U.S. citizens over the age of 18 living in Texas can register to vote. Yet many qualified Texans have not registered to vote. You have to prepare a flyer to convince all eligible Texans to vote. Follow these steps to solve your problem.

1. Gather Information. Use your textbook and other resources to find information that might influence your plan of action for encouraging Texans to vote. Remember that your flyer must include information that Texans will need to persuade them to vote. Be sure to use what you learned from this unit's Skills Workshop on Using the Internet to help you find an effective solution to this problem. You may want to divide up different parts of the research among group members.

2. List and Consider Options. After reviewing the information you have gathered, list and consider the options you might recommend for successfully convincing Texans to vote. Your final solution to the problem may be easier to reach if you consider as many options as possible. Be sure to record your possible options for the preparation of your flyer.

3. Consider Advantages and Disadvantages. Now consider the advantages and disadvantages of taking each option. Ask yourselves questions such as, "What motivates a person to vote?" Once you have considered the advantages and disadvantages, record them as notes for use in preparing your flyer.

4. Choose, Implement, and Evaluate a Solution. After considering the advantages and disadvantages, you should plan and prepare your flyer. Be sure to make your proposal for convincing Texans to vote very clear. You will need to support your reasons by including information you gathered and by explaining why you rejected other options. Your flyer needs to be visually appealing to attract potential voters' attention. When you are ready, decide which group members will present each part of the flyer, and then take your flyer to the community (the rest of the class). Good luck!

Vaquero spur

Palo Duro
Canyon

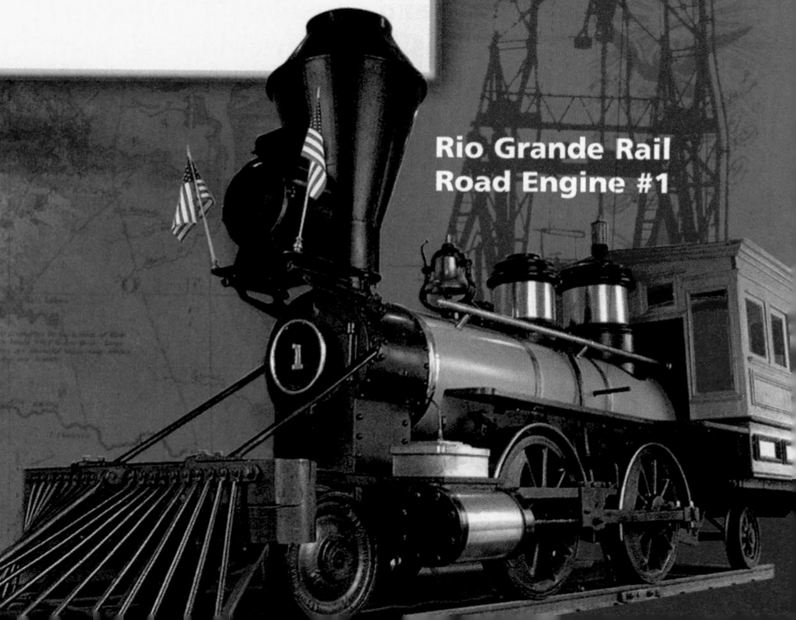

HOLT
TEXAS!
Reference

**Governors and
Presidents of Texas**...... **R1**

Constitutions of Texas .. **R8**

Facts about Texas **R10**

Gazetteer **R12**

Glossary **R18**

Spanish Glossary....... **R28**

Index................. **R39**

Acknowledgments **R55**

Rio Grande Rail
Road Engine #1

Governors and Presidents of Texas

Spanish Royal Governors of Texas

Domingo Terán de los Ríos
1691–1692

Gregorio de Salinas Varona
1692–1697

Francisco Cuerbo y Valdéz
1698–1702

Mathías de Aguirre
1703–1705

Martín de Alarcón
1705–1708

Simon Padilla y Córdova
1708–1712

Pedro Fermin de Echevers y Subisa
1712–1714

Juan Valdéz
1714–1716

Martín de Alarcón
1716–1719

José de Azlor, Marqués de San Miguel de Aguayo
1719–1722

Fernando Pérez de Almazán
1722–1727

Melchor de Media Villa y Azcona
1727–1730

Juan Antonio Bustillos y Ceballos
1730–1734

Manuel de Sandoval
1734–1736

Carlos Benites Franquis de Lugo
1736–1737

Prudencio de Orobio y Basterra
1737–1741

Tomás Felipe Wintuisen
1741–1743

Justo Boneo y Morales
1743–1744

Francisco García Larios
1744–1748

Pedro del Barrio Junco y Espriella
1748–1751

Jacinto de Barrios y Jáuregui
1751–1759

Ángel de Martos y Navarrete
1759–1766

Hugo Oconór
1767–1770

Barón de Ripperdá
1770–1778

Domingo Cabello
1778–1786

Bernardo Bonavía
1786 *(appointed but never served)*

Rafael Martínez Pacheco
1786–1790

The office of governor was ordered suppressed, and the province put under a provincial captain.
1788–1789

Manuel Muñoz
1790–1798

José Irigoyen
1798 *(appointed but never served)*

Juan Bautista Elguézabal
1800–1805

Antonio Cordero y Bustamante
1805–1808

Manuel María de Salcedo
1808–1813

Juan Bautista de la Casas
1811 *(revolutionary governor)*

Cristóbal Domínguez
1813–1814

Mariano Varela
1815–1816

Ignacio Pérez
1816–1817

Manuel Pardo
1817

Antonio Martínez
1817–1821

Mexican Governors of Texas

José Felix Trespalacios
1822–1823

Luciano García
1823–1824

Rafael Gonzales
1824–1826

Victor Blanco
1826–1827

José María Viesca
1827–1831

José María Letona
1831–1832

Juan Martín de Veramendi
1832–1833

Juan José de Vidaurri y Villasenor
1833–1834

Juan José Elguézabal
1834–1835

Agustín M. Viesca
1835

Provisional Colonial Governors before Independence

Henry Smith
1835–1836

James W. Robinson
1836 *(served as acting governor after Smith was impeached)*

Presidents of the Republic of Texas

David G. Burnet
March 16, 1836–October 22, 1836
(ad interim president)

Sam Houston
October 22, 1836–December 10, 1838

Mirabeau B. Lamar
December 10, 1838–December 13, 1841

Sam Houston
December 13, 1841–December 9, 1844

Anson Jones
December 9, 1844–February 19, 1846

Governors since Annexation

J. Pinckney Henderson
February 19, 1846–December 21, 1847
(Albert C. Horton served as acting governor while Henderson was away in the Mexican War.)

George T. Wood
December 21, 1847–December 21, 1849

Peter Hansbrough Bell
December 21, 1849–November 23, 1853

J. W. Henderson
November 23, 1853–December 21, 1853

Elisha M. Pease
December 21, 1853–December 21, 1857

Hardin R. Runnels
December 21, 1857–December 21, 1859

Sam Houston
December 21, 1859–March 16, 1861

Edward Clark
March 16, 1861–November 7, 1861

Francis R. Lubbock
November 7, 1861–November 5, 1863

Pendleton Murrah
November 5, 1863–June 17, 1865

Andrew J. Hamilton
June 17, 1865–August 9, 1866
(provisional governor)

James W. Throckmorton
August 9, 1866–August 8, 1867

Elisha M. Pease
August 8, 1867–September 30, 1869
(Between September 30, 1869, and
January 8, 1870, Texas was without an
acting head of government.)

Edmund J. Davis
January 8, 1870–January 15, 1874

Richard Coke
January 15, 1874–December 1, 1876

Richard B. Hubbard
December 1, 1876–January 21, 1879

Oran M. Roberts
January 21, 1879–January 16, 1883

John Ireland
January 16, 1883–January 18, 1887

Lawrence Sullivan Ross
January 18, 1887–January 20, 1891

James Stephen Hogg
January 20, 1891–January 15, 1895

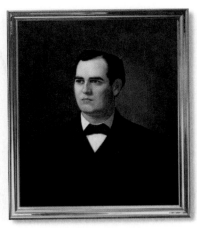

Charles A. Culberson
January 15, 1895–January 17, 1899

Joseph D. Sayers
January 17, 1899–January 20, 1903

S. W. T. Lanham
January 20, 1903–January 15, 1907

Thomas Mitchell Campbell
January 15, 1907–January 17, 1911

Oscar Branch Colquitt
January 17, 1911–January 19, 1915

James E. Ferguson
January 19, 1915–August 25, 1917

William P. Hobby
August 25, 1917–January 18, 1921

Pat M. Neff
January 18, 1921–January 20, 1925

Miriam A. Ferguson
January 20, 1925–January 17, 1927

Dan Moody
January 17, 1927–January 20, 1931

Ross S. Sterling
January 20, 1931–January 17, 1933

Miriam A. Ferguson
January 17, 1933–January 15, 1935

James V Allred
January 15, 1935–January 17, 1939

W. Lee O'Daniel
January 17, 1939–August 4, 1941

Coke R. Stevenson
August 4, 1941–January 21, 1947

Beauford H. Jester
January 21, 1947–July 11, 1949

Allan Shivers
July 11, 1949–January 15, 1957

Price Daniel
January 15, 1957–January 15, 1963

John Connally
January 15, 1963–January 21, 1969

Preston Smith
January 21, 1969–January 16, 1973

Dolph Briscoe
January 16, 1973–January 16, 1979

William P. Clements
January 16, 1979–January 18, 1983

Mark White
January 18, 1983–January 20, 1987

William P. Clements
January 20, 1987–January 15, 1991

Ann Richards
January 15, 1991–January 17, 1995

George W. Bush
January 17, 1995–December 21, 2000

Rick Perry
December 21, 2000—Present

The Constitutions of Texas

The Constitution of 1824

The first constitution that governed the people of Texas was the Mexican federal Constitution of 1824. Erasmo Seguín served as the representative for Texas in the assembly that created the document. Stephen F. Austin also consulted with the Mexican leaders who framed the document. The constitution used the U.S. Constitution and the Spanish Constitution of 1812 as models. Under this constitution a president and vice president were chosen for four-year terms by the legislative bodies of the states of Mexico. The constitution also created a national congress with a lower house of deputies and an upper house of senators. Judicial power was given to a Supreme Court and superior courts of departments and districts. The Catholic faith was given a special place in the government as the state religion and was supported by the treasury.

The Constitution of 1827

The Constitution of 1827 provided a government for the newly created state of Coahuila y Texas. The Constitution of Coahuila y Texas was published in 1827 after more than two years of debate. Baron de Bastrop represented Texas in the assembly at Saltillo. The constitution divided the state into three departments and created a unicameral legislature. Executive power was delegated to a governor and vice governor who were elected to four-year terms by popular vote. The right to trial by jury was addressed by the constitution but not clearly established. The document banned slavery. As in the Constitution of 1824, the Catholic religion was made the state religion.

The Constitution of 1836

After Texas declared its independence from Mexico, a new constitution was created for the Republic of Texas. On March 1, 1836, 59 delegates assembled at Washington-on-the-Brazos to create the document, which was ratified by a popular vote in September 1836. The U.S. Constitution and other state constitutions were used as models for the new government. The Constitution of 1836 divided the government into three branches. The Congress was bicameral with a House of Representatives and a Senate. The executive branch was led by a popularly elected president. The judiciary was composed of a justice, county, and district courts, headed by a supreme court. The constitution barred ministers and priests from holding public office. The document included a bill of rights and laws to protect homesteaders.

The Constitution of 1845

The Constitution of 1845 provides the framework of government for Texas as a state in the United States. The framers of the state constitution used the Constitution of 1836, the Constitution of Louisiana, and the constitution created at the Convention of 1833 as models. The legislature included a Senate and a House of Representatives. Representatives served for two years, and senators served for four years. The executive branch was headed by a governor who served a two-year term but could only serve four years of any six-year period. The judiciary was composed of a supreme court, district courts, and inferior courts established by the legislature. Ministers were ineligible to be legislators. Banks were outlawed.

The Constitution of 1861

The Constitution of 1861 was created after Texans voted to secede from the Union. The new document was an amended version of the Constitution of 1845. Some wording was replaced such as the replacement of the "United States of America" by "Confederate States of America." Slavery and states' rights were more directly addressed. All current state officials were required to take a loyalty oath to the Confederacy.

The Constitution of 1866

The Constitution of 1866 was created in accordance with the orders of Presidential Reconstruction. The term of the governor was increased from two to four years. The governor was given more powers including the ability to veto items of appropriations. The terms of office for legislators remained the same, but their salaries were increased. The number of judges on the Supreme Court was increased from three to five. The constitution also outlined improvements for public education and school funding.

The Constitution of 1869

The Constitution of 1869 was created in compliance with the Reconstruction Acts of 1867. The U.S. Constitution was declared the supreme law, and equal rights of all persons before the law were recognized. The term of office for the governor and representatives remained the same, but the term of senators was increased from four to six years. Legislative sessions were held annually. The number of judges on the Supreme Court was reduced from five to three. All judicial officers were appointed. African Americans were given the right to vote. A poll tax was also instituted to help fund public schools.

The Constitution of 1876

The Constitution of 1876 is the current constitution governing Texas. The document was created by a constitutional convention in 1875 and adopted after a popular vote in 1876. The convention was held after Democrats regained control of the legislature following Reconstruction. The Constitution of 1876 was influenced by provisions in the previous constitutions of Texas including some laws that can be traced to Mexican and Spanish laws. The document contains special sections dealing with land titles and debtor relief. The constitution also prohibited banks and required a strict separation of church and state. The powers of the governor were decreased and the term was reduced to two years. The governor's term in office was later extended to four years by a 1972 amendment. The term of representatives was set at two years and senators at four years. The legislature was to meet every two years. County courts were reinstated. All judges were to be elected by popular vote with the Supreme Court and Court of Criminal Appeals judges serving six-year terms. District court judges serve four-year terms, and all other judges serve two-year terms. Changes to the constitution are made through amendments. Since 1876 about 400 amendments to the constitution have been adopted. Several calls have been made over the years for a new constitution. With more than 90,000 words it is one of the longest state constitutions.

Facts about Texas

State Seal

A white star of five points on an azure blue field encircled by olive and live oak branches is pictured on the front side of the present seal. The seal bears the inscription "The State of Texas." The reverse side of the seal, adopted in 1961, shows a shield with symbols of the Texas war for independence from Mexico, surrounded by the six flags that have flown over Texas.

Six Flags over Texas

Through the years, six different national flags have flown over Texas. Early Spanish explorers claimed the region for Spain. The French flag also briefly flew over Texas. After Mexico won its independence from Spain, the Mexican flag flew over Texas. With the Texas Revolution, Texans established a new republic and created the lone star flag. The American flag replaced the Texas flag after annexation. During the Civil War, the Confederate flag was flown. When the Civil War ended in 1865, the American flag once again flew over Texas.

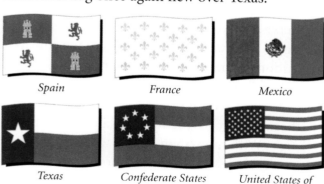

Spain

France

Mexico

Texas

Confederate States of America

United States of America

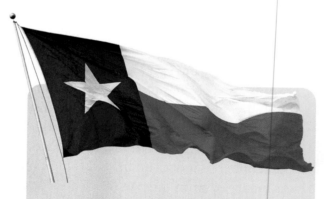

The Pledge to the Texas Flag

On April 3, 1965, Governor John Connally signed an act of the 59th legislature, officially designating the following as the pledge to the Texas flag:

Honor the Texas Flag.
I pledge allegiance to thee,
Texas, one and indivisible.

State Bird

The mockingbird was designated the Texas state bird by the legislature on January 31, 1927. The mockingbird has the ability to imitate many things it hears. It has been characterized as fearless and aggressive in protecting itself and its offspring against enemies.

State Song

The Texas state song is "Texas, Our Texas." The music was written by William J. Marsh, and the words by Gladys Yoakum Wright and William J. Marsh. It was adopted by the legislature in 1929.

State Flower

The bluebonnet was adopted on March 7, 1901, as the state flower of Texas by the 27th legislature. The flower is said to have received its name from its resemblance to a woman's sunbonnet. It also has been called wolfflower, buffalo clover, and *el conejo* (the rabbit).

Gazetteer

Abilene City in northwest-central Texas (32°N 100°W) **A7**; city in east-central Kansas. (39°N 97°W) **443**

Adobe Walls Location of a fort and trading post in the late 1800s in North Texas. **425**

Africa Second-largest continent on Earth; located in both the Northern and Southern Hemispheres. **A1**

Agua Dulce Creek Creek in South Texas. **233**

Alabama Southern state of the United States. Capital: Montgomery. (33°N 87°W) **A3**

Alaska State of the United States located in northwest North America. Capital: Juneau. (64°N 150°W) **A2**

Albany City in north-central Texas. (33°N 99°W) **431**

Albuquerque City in central New Mexico. (35°N 107°W) **A2**

Alpine Town in West Texas. (30°N 104°W) **58**

Alsace Region in northeast France. (48°N 7°E) **284**

Alto Community in East Texas. (32°N 95°W) **76**

Amarillo City in northwest Texas. (35°N 102°W) **A7**

Anahuac City on Galveston Bay in Texas. (30°N 95°W) **207**

Angelina National Forest Preserve of more than 153,000 acres in East Texas. **46**

Appomattox Town in central Virginia. (37°N 97°W) **390**

Aransas Pass City on a peninsula in Aransas Bay. (28°N 97°W) **350**

Aransas River River in South Texas. **174**

Arizona Southwestern state of the United States. Capital: Phoenix. (34°N 113°W) **A2**

Arkansas State of the south-central United States. Capital: Little Rock. (35°N 93°W) **A3**

Arkansas River River that flows through central Colorado, southern Kansas, northeast Oklahoma, and Arkansas. **A3**

Arkansas Territory Territory organized in 1819 that included present-day Arkansas and most of present-day Oklahoma. **161**

Arroyo Hondo Small stream between Natchitoches and the Sabine River. **142**

Asia Largest continent on Earth. **A1**

Atlanta Capital of Georgia. (34°N 84°W) **A3**

Atlantic Ocean Body of water separating North and South America from Europe and Africa. **A1**

Austin Central Texas city that serves as the state's capital. (30°N 98°W) **A7**

Austin County County in southeast-central Texas. **A8**

Balcones Escarpment Long fault or cliff running through south-central Texas. **A7**

Bastrop City in south-central Texas. (30°N 97°W) **161**

Bastrop County County in south-central Texas. **A8**

Beaumont City in southeast Texas. (30°N 94°W) **A7**

Beeville City in South Texas. (28°N 98°W) **566**

Bell County County in east-central Texas. **A8**

Belton City in Central Texas. (31°N 97°W) **568**

Bexar County County in south-central Texas. **A8**

Big Bend National Park National park in West Texas of about 1,250 square miles in the Big Bend of the Rio Grande. **58**

Big Cypress Bayou Bayou in northeast Texas. **355**

Big Spring City in northwest Texas. (32°N 101°W) **465**

Big Thicket National Preserve Wilderness area in East Texas. **46**

Blackland Prairie Subregion of the Gulf Coastal Plain in Texas that has a wet, mild climate and rolling prairies. **43**

Blanco Canyon Canyon in northwest Texas. **422**

Boerne City in south-central Texas. (30°N 99°W) **283**

Bonham City in northeast Texas. (34°N 96°W) **551**

Borger City in northwest Texas. (36°N 101°W) **540**

Brazil Federal republic in east-central South America. Capital: Brasília. (9°S 53°W) **A1**

Brazoria City in southeast Texas. (29°N 96°W) **209**

Brazoria County County in southeast Texas. **A8**

Brazos Island Barrier island south of Padre Island off the Texas coast. **385**

Brazos River River in Central Texas. **A7**

Brenham City in southeast-central Texas. (30°N 96°W) **349**

Brown County County in Central Texas. **A8**

Brownsboro Town in northeast Texas. (32°N 96°W) **337**

Brownsville City in South Texas. (26°N 97°W) **46**

Brownwood City in Central Texas. (32°N 99°W) **52**

Bryan City in east-central Texas. (31°N 96°W) **A7**

Buena Vista Battlefield site in northeast Mexico of a U.S. victory in the Mexican War. **333**

Buffalo Bayou Stream that flows through Houston, Texas. **250**

Burkburnett City in North Texas. (34°N 99°W) **540**

Caddo Lake Lake on the border of Texas and Louisiana. **A7**

California Western state of the United States. Capital: Sacramento. (38°N 121°W) **A2**

Canada Country in northern North America. Capital: Ottawa. (50°N 100°W) **A1**

Canadian River River in the southwestern United States that flows through southern Colorado, northeastern New Mexico, northwestern Texas, and into Oklahoma. **A7**

Canary Islands Islands in the Atlantic Ocean off the northwest coast of Africa. (28°N 16°W) **97**

Caprock Hard bed of rock below the soil of the High Plains subregion. **A7**

Caribbean Sea Arm of the Atlantic Ocean that connects with the Gulf of Mexico. **A6**

Castroville Town in south-central Texas. (29°N 99°W) **284**

Cat Spring Town in southeast-central Texas. (30°N 96°W) **337**

Caverns of Sonora Caverns in southwest-central Texas. **20**

Central Plains Region of Texas characterized by gently rolling prairies with abundant resources for ranching and farming. **43**

Chaco Canyon Canyon in present-day northern New Mexico. **71**

Chambers County County in southeast Texas. **A8**

death rate Number of deaths per 1,000 people. **33**

Declaration of November 7, 1835 Agreement signed at the Consultation in which delegates pledged their loyalty to Mexico but warned that they would create an independent government if the Constitution of 1824 was not restored. **231**

decree Official order. **205**

delegates Representatives, as to a convention. **212**

demobilization Moving from a wartime to a peacetime economy. **536**

demography Branch of geography that studies human populations. **32**

denominations Religious groups with similar beliefs. **289**

depression Period of low economic activity. **160**

derricks Towers that support oil-drilling equipment. **479**

desegregate To free a place or institution from laws or practices separating the races. **578**

diplomats Individuals who represent countries in foreign affairs. **142**

direct democracy System of government in which voters decide issues directly rather than through elected representatives. **670**

dogtrot cabins Log homes with two rooms separated by an open passage. **186**

draft Requirement of military service. **387**

***Dred Scott* decision** Ruling by the U.S. Supreme Court in 1857 in which the Court determined that African Americans were not citizens and thus could not sue in federal court. **373**

drought Long period without rain. **26**

dry farming Farming techniques, such as terracing, used in a dry climate to keep moisture in the soil. **467**

due process The legal process that governments must follow before taking away a person's property or punishing a person. **666**

Dust Bowl Parts of the southern Great Plains in which dust and drought ruined crops and killed thousands of cattle during the 1930s. **548**

Economic Opportunity Act Legislation passed as part of the Great Society that provided funds for job training and created community action programs. **588**

ecosystem All of an area's plants and animals together with the nonliving parts of their environment. **7**

Edwards Aquifer Underground water source that provides water for Central Texas. **23**

Eighteenth Amendment Amendment to the U.S. Constitution that established national prohibition. **512**

El Camino Real (kah-MEE-noh ree-AHL) "Royal Road" that led from the East Texas missions to the southern Rio Grande settlements and southward to Mexico City. **124**

Emancipation Proclamation President Abraham Lincoln's declaration of freedom for slaves in areas rebelling against the United States. **391**

eminent domain A government's power to claim privately owned land for public use. **667**

empresarios Businesspeople who promoted migration to the Texas colonies. **173**

environment Physical surroundings. **4**

Environmental Protection Agency Federal government agency that directs efforts to control air and water pollution. **630**

epidemics Widespread outbreaks of disease. **105**

equator An imaginary line circling the globe exactly halfway between the North and South Poles. **10**

erosion Process by which something such as soil is worn away. **29**

escarpments Cliffs. **54**

executive branch Branch of government that enforces, or carries out, the laws. **241, 642**

expenditures Government expenses. **262**

exports Items made in a country and sold to other countries. **193**

extinct Died out completely. **29**

faction A group acting together within a larger group, usually in opposition. **217**

fault Break in Earth's crust. **55**

federalism System of government that balances powers by distributing them between one central and many regional governments. **195, 642**

Federal Reserve System Central banking system that distributes money to other banks and helps regulate them. **520**

felonies Major crimes. **653**

Fifteenth Amendment Change to the U.S. Constitution that gave suffrage to African American men. **403**

filibusters Military adventurers who came to Texas from the United States in the early 1800s. **144**

financial panic Economic crisis. **160**

flatboats Long, low boats used for river travel. **185**

flowchart Chart using boxes, arrows, or images to show a series of activities or steps. **15**

foreign relations Dealings between a country and other countries. **294**

Foreign Trade Zones Areas in which export regulations are reduced to promote trade. **631**

Fort St. Louis Settlement built by members of the La Salle expedition possibly near Garcitas Creek in Texas. **117**

fossil fuel Fuel such as coal, oil, or natural gas formed underground from plant or animal remains. **478**

Fourteenth Amendment Change to the U.S. Constitution designed to guarantee citizenship and equal rights to African Americans. **401**

Fredonian Rebellion Revolt led by Texas colonist Benjamin Edwards that began in 1826 after conflict with the Mexican government ended in the cancellation of his colony's contract. **203**

Freedmen's Bureau Organization created by the U.S. Congress in 1865 to give legal aid to freedpeople. **397**

freedpeople Former slaves. **397**

free enterprise Economic system in which businesses operate with little interference from government. **192**

gasoline A by-product of oil used as a fuel. **487**

general elections Elections in which voters cast their ballots for candidates for a particular state or local office or for deciding certain issues. **670**

general-law cities Small towns or cities that operate under the general laws of the state of Texas; some have a charter from the legislature outlining their form of government. **664**

geographic information systems (GIS) Computer systems that gather, store, and organize geographic information. **5**

geography The study of the special physical and human characteristics of places or regions. **4**

German Emigration Company Company formed by a group of wealthy Germans that bought land in Texas and planned to profit by encouraging Germans to settle there. **282**

GI Bill of Rights Name for the Servicemen's Readjustment Act, which gave war veterans unemployment payments, loans, and money for college. **570**

Gilmer–Aikin Laws Acts that provided for the existing educational framework for Texas. **570**

globalization The interdependence of the nations of the world that has been created as goods, ideas, and people move across the globe. **631**

Goliad Massacre Execution of Colonel James Fannin and his troops by the Mexican army after its victory in the Battle of Coleto. **248**

Goodnight-Loving Trail Cattle trail that ran from Young County in Texas through New Mexico to Colorado. **447**

grand jury Jury that decides if a person accused of a felony should be indicted, or formally charged. **654**

Grange Organization of farmers created in the late 1860s, formally called the Patrons of Husbandry. **499**

Grass Fight Incident in November 1835 in which a group of Texans ambushed Mexican troops who were supposedly carrying silver; however, the Mexicans' sacks were only filled with grass for feeding their horses. **229**

Great Depression Severe global economic slowdown in the 1930s. **545**

Great Society Program launched by President Lyndon B. Johnson that included laws improving health care, education, environmental protection, job training, and immigration. **588**

Great Southwest Strike of 1886 Railroad strike in which a dispute between the Knights of Labor and Jay Gould's railroad company led to violence. **473**

gristmills Machines for grinding grain into meal or flour. **351**

growth rate Speed of growth. **32**

G.T.T. "Gone to Texas"—phrase popular during early colonization of Texas. **183**

Guadalupe Peak Part of the Guadalupe Mountains; peak is highest in Texas. **57**

Guerrero Decree Law issued by Mexican president Vicente Guerrero in 1829 that abolished slavery in Mexico. **205**

habitat Environmental home of an animal. **29**

hides Animal skins. **79**

Hogg Laws Laws passed during Texas governor James Hogg's administration to regulate business. **505**

Holocaust Nazi Germany's attempt to kill the Jews of Europe during World War II. **567**

home-rule charters Charters that allow citizens in Texas municipalities of more than 5,000 people to choose their form of government. **664**

homestead law Law passed by the Republic Congress in 1839 that protected a family's home and up to 50 acres of land from seizure for debts. **267**

Hood's Texas Brigade A leading unit of the Army of Northern Virginia that fought in some of the most important battles of the Civil War. **377**

horizontal axis Line across the bottom of a graph or chart that shows the value, measure, or other information presented in the graph or chart. **13**

horizontal integration Owning many businesses in a particular field. **485**

Houston Ship Channel Channel that connects Houston with the Gulf of Mexico. **520**

humidity The amount of moisture in the air. **25**

hunter-gatherers People who hunt animals and gather wild plants for food. **69**

hunting grounds Areas where a group traditionally hunts for food. **82**

immigration Movement of people from one country to another. **31**

impeach To bring charges against a public official. **402**

Imperial Colonization Law Mexican law passed in 1823 that increased land grants in Texas for ranching and farming and freed settlers from paying taxes for six years. **167**

imports Items that a nation buys from other countries. **193**

infantry Foot soldiers. **228**

infrastructure Public works such as roads and water systems. **622**

interest groups Groups united by a common interest that try to affect government policy. **672**

internal combustion engine Engine in which the combustion, or burning, that generates power takes place inside the engine. **487**

internal improvements Advances in a state's transportation network. **353**

Internet Worldwide system of computer networks. **620**

Interstate Commerce Commission Former government agency created in 1887 to regulate railroads. **504**

ironclads Ships used during the Civil War that were heavily armored with iron plates. **380**

irrigation Supplying water to crops by artificial methods. **23**

jacales (huh-KAW-lays) Small, one-room huts made of sticks and mud. **150**

JA Ranch Ranch in the Panhandle established by Charles Goodnight and John Adair. **450**

Jim Crow laws Laws passed in the southern states to enforce segregation. **409**

joint resolution Measure passed by both houses of Congress that is a formal expression of intent. **316**

judicial branch Branch of government in which courts decide legal cases and interpret laws. **241, 642**

judicial review Courts' power to determine if a law is constitutional. **654**

Texas Water Commission State government department established in 1913 to help cities and counties manage water resources. **525**

Texas Women's Political Caucus Group founded in 1971 that worked to get more women elected to political office. **595**

thematic maps Maps that show a specific topic, theme, or spatial distribution of an activity. **12**

Thirteenth Amendment Amendment to the U.S. Constitution that abolished slavery. **397**

threshers Machines that separate grain or seeds from plants. **468**

tidelands Underwater lands bordering the coast. **571**

time line Chart showing a sequence of events. **15**

Tonkin Gulf Resolution Resolution passed by the U.S. Congress that gave President Lyndon B. Johnson the authority to order troops into combat in the Vietnam War. **589**

tourism Business of attracting visitors to a region or place. **58**

transcontinental railroad Railroad that runs across the continent. **463**

transportation center Place where goods arrive to be reshipped to many destinations. **51**

Treaties of Velasco Two treaties signed by General Antonio López de Santa Anna and Texas ad interim president David G. Burnet ending the Texas Revolution. **256**

Treaty of Guadalupe Hidalgo Treaty signed by U.S. and Mexican officials on February 2, 1848, ending the Mexican War. **334**

Treaty of the Little Arkansas Treaty signed in October 1865 by federal commissioners and southern Plains Indian leaders in which Comanche and Kiowa leaders agreed to settle on a reservation in the Panhandle. **416**

Treaty of Medicine Lodge Treaty signed in 1867 in Kansas between federal commissioners and Plains Indians in which some American Indians agreed to move to reservations in Indian Territory. **418**

Treaty of Paris Treaty signed in 1763 ending the Seven Years' War; France and Spain agreed to give territory in North America to Great Britain. **136**

Treaty of Tehuacana Creek Peace and trade agreement signed by Republic of Texas president Sam Houston and Comanche chief Buffalo Hump in October 1844. **272**

trial courts Courts that hear new cases and give a verdict, or ruling. **653**

tributaries Small streams or rivers that flow into a larger stream or river. **22**

trusts Legal arrangements in which a number of companies are grouped under a single board of trustees. **503**

Turtle Bayou Resolutions Document drawn up after the conflict at Anahuac in 1832 in which Texans declared their support for the Constitution of 1824 and General Antonio López de Santa Anna. **209**

two-party system Political system in which two major parties compete to gain political office. **603**

Unionists Southerners who wanted to stay in the Union and work out differences over slavery in the mid-1800s. **374**

Union League Political group in Texas in the mid-1800s that urged African Americans to support the Republican Party. **402**

urbanization An increase in people living or working in cities. **7, 519**

vaqueros (vah-CARE-ohz) Cowboys. **131**

venison Deer meat. **188**

vertical axis Line across the side of a graph or chart that shows the value, measure, or other information presented in the graph or chart. **13**

vertical integration Owning the businesses involved in each step of a manufacturing process. **485**

veto Power exercised by the executive branch of government to reject a law. **642**

viceroy Royal governor. **98**

victory gardens Small vegetable gardens planted on the home front during World War II for extra food. **566**

Villa de Béxar Civil settlement established by the Spanish near the San Antonio de Béxar presidio. **123**

Voting Rights Act Legislation passed by the U.S. Congress in 1965 that gave the federal government the power to check voting procedures in the states to protect citizens' right to vote. **592**

War on Drugs U.S. government effort to end the trade and use of illegal drugs both in the United States and abroad. **614**

Western Trail Cattle trail that ran north from San Antonio to Dodge City, Kansas. **446**

white primary Primary elections established in the 1920s in Texas in which Africans Americans were excluded from voting. **539**

wigwams Circular huts. **73**

wildcatters Oil operators who worked on their own in search of new fields. **483**

windmills Devices using wind power to pump water from underground to the surface. **450**

Women's Auxiliary Army Corps Group of women who served in noncombat positions during World War II. **565**

wrangler One who herds or cares for livestock on the range. **447**

XIT Ranch Ranch established by the Capitol Freehold Land and Investment Company, which was funded by investors from Chicago and Great Britain. **451**

Glossary/Glosario

abolition/abolición Fin de la esclavitud. **363**

absolute location/posición absoluta Posición exacta de un lugar en la Tierra, con frecuencia definido en términos de latitud y longitud. **9**

academies/academias Escuelas que imparten clases de enseñanza secundaria. **289**

Adams-Onís Treaty/Tratado Adams-Onís Tratado firmado por Estados Unidos y España en 1819 para definir la frontera entre sus territorios. **142**

ad interim/interino Temporal. **242**

administration/administración Término durante el que ocupa su cargo un funcionario. **259**

adobe/adobe Material de construcción hecho de arcilla humedecida. **79**

aerospace/espacio aéreo Atmósfera de la Tierra y el espacio más allá de ésta. **569**

age distribution/distribución por edad Porción de la población que representa un grupo de determinada edad. **33**

agribusiness/agroindustria Agricultura a gran escala y procesamiento de los cultivos. **621**

agriculture/agricultura Siembra de cultivos y cría de animales. **35**

Aguayo expedition/expedición Aguayo Misión encabezada por el gobernador de Coahuila para recuperar las misiones del este de Texas después de la Guerra del pollo. **126**

Alabama-Coushatta/Alabama-coushatta Grupo indígena de Texas al que se le permitió permanecer en ese estado a mediados del siglo XIX a pesar de que otras tribus fueron obligadas a emigrar a otras tierras. **342**

alcalde/alcalde Funcionario español que se desempeñó como alcalde, comisario y juez de una población española de Texas. **131**

allies/aliados Amigos que se apoyan unos a otros. **76**

amendments/enmienda Agregados, cambios o correcciones hechas a una constitución. **643**

American G.I. Forum/Foro Estadounidense G.I. Organización formada por Héctor P. García para proteger los derechos de los hispanos. **579**

annexation/anexión Unión formal de una región política a otra. **258**

anthropologists/antropólogos Científicos que estudian y comparan diferentes culturas para aprender cómo viven o vivían. **68**

Antitrust Act of 1889/Ley Antimonopolio de 1889 Ley aplicada en Texas para evitar la creación de monopolios, especialmente en las compañías de ferrocarril. **504**

appellate courts/cortes de apelación Cortes que revisaban los casos para determinar si se habían seguido los procedimientos correctos. **653**

appropriation bill/carta de apropiación Carta que asigna una cantidad de dinero al gobierno para sus gastos. **656**

aquifers/acuíferos Formaciones naturales de grava, roca o arena debajo de la tierra en las que se almacena el agua de lluvia. **23**

archaeologists/arqueólogos Científicos que buscan restos de materiales y los usan para analizar las condiciones de vida en el pasado. **68**

Archives War/Archivos de Guerra Revuelta iniciada por ciudadanos de Austin cuando el presidente Sam Houston ordenó la eliminación de todos los registros y archivos del gobierno en Austin. **299**

artifacts/artefactos Herramientas, armas y otros objetos hechos por el hombre. **68**

Ashworth Act/Ley de Ashworth Ley del Congreso de la República de Texas que excluyó a la familia Ashworth de las leyes que prohibían a los afroestadounidenses liberados permanecer en Texas. **280**

ayuntamiento/ayuntamiento Consejo de gobierno de las poblaciones españolas en Texas. **130**

bail/fianza Suma de dinero que un acusado deposita en una corte como garantía de que se presentará cuando ésta se lo pida. **667**

balanced budget/presupuesto equilibrado Presupuesto en el que los gastos de un gobierno no son superiores a sus ingresos. **271**

bands/bandas Grupos de personas, como las tribus indígenas. **83**

barbed wire/alambre de púas Material con puntas filosas usado para construir cercas. **454**

bar graph/gráfica de barras Diagrama que usa barras de diferente longitud para representar números o porcentajes y comparar información sobre distintos lugares o épocas. **13**

barter/trueque Intercambio de bienes o servicios sin usar dinero. **193**

basins/cuencas Tierras bajas rodeadas por terrenos de mayor altitud. **57**

Bastrop/Bastrop Población principal de la pequeña colonia fundada por Stephen F. Austin; territorio que actualmente ocupa una ciudad de la parte centro sur de Texas. **171**

Battle of Adobe Walls/Batalla de Adobe Walls Batalla librada en junio de 1874 en la que unos 700 indígenas estadounidenses atacaron un campamento de cazadores de búfalos cerca de Adobe Walls. **426**

Battle of Coleto/Batalla de Coleto Batalla de la Revolución de Texas en la que el general mexicano José de Urrea derrotó a las tropas estadounidenses y capturó al coronel James Fannin. **248**

Battle of Glorieta Pass/Batalla del Paso de Glorieta Batalla de la Guerra Civil en la que las fuerzas de la Unión recuperaron el control del suroeste, excepto Texas, y lo mantuvieron hasta terminar la guerra. **382**

Battle of Gonzales/Batalla de González Breve batalla entre texanos y el ejército mexicano realizada en 1835 en la población de González, que dio inicio a la Revolución de Texas. **227**

Battle of the Neches/Batalla de los Neches Batalla que tuvo lugar en 1839 entre texanos y la tribu cheroqui luego de que el presidente Mirabeau B. Lamar ordenara a esta tribu que abandonara Texas. **268**

Battle of Palo Duro Canyon/Batalla del Cañón de Palo Duro Batalla llevada a cabo en septiembre de 1874 en la

que los Invasores de Mackenzie atacaron las aldeas indígenas del Cañón de Palo Duro y obligaron la retirada de la tribu comanche, con lo cual aumentaron su dominio en la Guerra del Río Rojo. **427**

Battle of Plum Creek/Batalla de Plum Creek Batalla entre texanos y la tribu comanche luego de que ésta iniciara ataques violentos a partir de la lucha de la Cámara del Consejo. **269**

Battle of Refugio/Batalla de Refugio Batalla de la Revolución de Texas en la que el general mexicano José de Urrea derrotó a las tropas del coronel James Fannin. **247**

Battle of Sabine Pass/Batalla del Paso de Sabine Batalla de la Guerra Civil en la que los Guardias Davis derrotaron al ejército de la Unión, con lo cual se recuperó la confianza en la victoria del sur. **384**

Battle of San Jacinto/Batalla de San Jacinto Última batalla de la Revolución de Texas en la que Sam Houston y el ejército de Texas atacaron por sorpresa y derrotaron a las tropas mexicanas de Santa Anna en apenas 18 minutos. **251**

Battle of San Juan Hill/Batalla de la Colina de San Juan Batalla de la Guerra entre España y Estados Unidos en la que los *Rough Riders* (jinetes rudos) ayudaron a derrotar a las fuerzas españolas. **528**

Battle of Velasco/Batalla de Velasco Batalla iniciada el 26 de junio de 1832 a causa de varios desacuerdos con funcionarios mexicanos en Anáhuac en la que el ejército texano obtuvo la victoria. **210**

bayous/brazo de río Tributarios provenientes de grandes cuerpos de agua en los que la corriente avanza lentamente. **47**

bicameral/cámara dual Que tiene dos cámaras de legisladores. **644**

biennial/bianual Que sucede cada dos años. **319**

Big Bend National Park/Parque Nacional de Big Bend Parque de 800,000 acres de extensión localizado al oeste de Texas. **59**

Big Thicket National Preserve/Reserva Nacional de Big Thicket Entorno natural de 85,000 acres poblados de árboles y diversos tipos de vida salvaje que se localiza en la región de Piney Woods. **46**

bill/iniciativa Ley presentada para su aprobación. **646**

bill of rights/declaración de derechos Documento en el que el gobierno otorga derechos civiles o individuales y se compromete a respetarlos. **242, 642**

birthrate/tasa de natalidad Número de nacimientos por cada 1,000 habitantes. **32**

Black Codes/códigos negros Leyes aprobadas por el Congreso estadounidense después de la Reconstrucción que niegan los derechos civiles a las personas de raza negra. **399**

blues/blues Tipo de música cuya letra refleja con frecuencia las dificultades de la vida cotidiana. **542**

boll weevil/gorgojo de algodón Tipo de escarabajo que infesta las plantas de algodón. **470**

bonds/bonos Certificados que representan el dinero que un gobierno debe a ciudadanos particulares. **405**

boomtowns/pueblos en auge Poblados que crecieron rápidamente debido al desarrollo económico de una región. **486**

brands/marcas Señales de identificación hechas en la piel del ganado con hierros calientes. **440**

breadlines/filas del pan Hileras de personas en espera de una ración gratuita de alimentos. **546**

buckskin/cuero Piel curtida de algún animal. **187**

Buffalo Bayou, Brazos, and Colorado Railway/Buffalo Bayou, Brazos y Colorado Railway Compañía que construyó la primera línea de ferrocarril en Texas. **356**

buffalo guns/rifles de búfalo Rifles poderosos con miras telescópicas usados para cazar búfalos. **423**

buffalo soldiers/soldados búfalo Nombre dado por los indígenas a las tropas estadounidense. **428**

C

cabinet/gabinete Grupo de consejeros de un jefe de estado como el presidente. **259**

capitol/capitolio Edificio en el que se reúnen los funcionarios del gobierno de Estados Unidos. **266**

Caprock/rocas de cubierta Capa de suelo duro bajo la superficie en la región de las Grandes Planicies. **54**

carpetbaggers/carpetbaggers "Aventureros"; habitantes del norte que emigraron al sur después de la Guerra Civil, llamados así porque llevaban sus pertenencias en sacos. **405**

casualties/bajas Personas fallecidas, heridas o capturadas durante una guerra. **239**

cattle drives/travesías de ganado Arreo de grandes manadas de ganado de campo abierto a los puntos de venta. **441**

Cattle Kingdom/reino del ganado Industria basada en la cría de ganado que se popularizó en la zona ganadera de Texas a Canadá durante el siglo XIX. **449**

causation chart/diagrama de causa y efecto Diagrama que usa dibujos, recuadros y flechas para mostrar las causas y efectos de un suceso. **15**

cavalry/caballería Grupo de soldados a caballo. **228**

cede/ceder Entrega oficial de territorio de un país a otro. **136**

centennial/centenario Aniversario número cien. **554**

charter/carta Documento que otorga permiso de operación. **266**

checks and balances/revisión y balance Acuerdo entre los poderes de un gobierno para revisar o restringir la autoridad de los demás poderes. **642**

Chicano movement/Movimiento Chicano Creciente demanda de cambios políticos y el final de la discriminación iniciada por los hispanos en la década de 1960. **593**

Chicken War/Guerra del Pollo Expansión de un conflicto entre Francia y España a territorio de Texas en el que soldados franceses atacaron la misión española de San Miguel de Linares de los Adaes. **125**

Chisholm Trail/sendero de Chisholm Ruta ganadera entre el Valle del Río Grande en Texas y Kansas. **445**

Cinco de Mayo/Cinco de Mayo Celebración mexicana del 5 de mayo de 1862, fecha en que el ejército mexicano derrotó a las fuerzas invasoras francesas en la Batalla de Puebla. **625**

circuit riders/jinetes de circuito Predicadores viajeros. **289**

Civilian Conservation Corps/Corporación de Conservación Civil Agencia creada con el *New Deal* para ofrecer empleos a los jóvenes durante la Gran Depresión. **552**

civil law/ley civil Ley que supervisa la aplicación de los derechos y obligaciones privados. **653**

civil rights/derechos civiles Derechos individuales garantizados por la Constitución. **399**

Civil Rights Act of 1866/Ley de derechos civiles de 1866 Ley que otorgó la ciudadanía a los afroestadounidenses y les garantizó los derechos civiles básicos. **400**

Civil Rights Act of 1964/Ley de derechos civiles de 1964 Ley aprobada durante el mandato del presidente Lyndon B. Johnson que prohibía la segregación en lugares públicos y sancionaba a empleadores, sindicatos y universidades relacionados con el gobierno que discriminaran a cualquier persona por su raza, género, religión o nacionalidad. **592**

Coahuila y Texas/Coahuila y Texas Estado creado por el gobierno mexicano en 1824 mediante la unión de los estados de Texas y Coahuila. **172**

Cold War/guerra fría Término que describe las tensiones entre Estados Unidos y la Unión Soviética después de la Segunda Guerra Mundial. **568**

Columbian Exchange/intercambio colombino Término que describe el intercambio de plantas, animales e incluso enfermedades entre continentes desde la llegada de Cristóbal Colón a América. **105**

Comanchería/comanchería Nombre español del territorio del norte y el oeste de Texas controlado por la tribu comanche. **85**

commercial farming/agricultura comercial Cultivo a gran escala de productos con fines de lucro. **469**

commissioners/comisionados Representantes de un gobierno. **416**

commissioners court/corte de comisionados Panel de comisionados electos para gobernar los condados de Texas. **662**

commission plan/plan de la comisión Plan del gobierno en el que un panel de comisionados electos se encarga de la prestación de servicios públicos. **598, 663**

commute/conmutar Viajar de ida y vuelta al lugar de trabajo cuando se vive en otro. **574**

compass rose/rosa de los vientos Figura de los mapas que indica la posición del norte, sur, este y oeste. **11**

Compromise of 1850/Compromiso de 1850 Acuerdo presentado por el senador Henry Clay para resolver la disputa fronteriza entre Texas y Nuevo México en la que Texas recibió 10 millones de dólares a cambio de que cediera la parte reclamada a Nuevo México. **335**

confederacies/confederaciones Alianzas entre grupos. **76**

Confederate States of America/Estados Confederados de América Nombre dado al gobierno formado por los 11 estados del sur que se separaron de Estados Unidos entre 1860 y 1861. **375**

conference committee/comité de conferencia Comité de legislatura que revisa las propuestas de ley para satisfacer las demandas de ambas cámaras. **647**

conquistadores/conquistadores Soldados españoles y aventureros en busca de gloria, oro y tierras. **91**

consecutive terms/términos consecutivos Dos periodos presidenciales seguidos. **265**

Constitution of 1824/Constitución de 1824 Constitución mexicana que limitó el poder del gobierno central y dio mayor autoridad a los estados. **195**

Consultation/Consulta Reunión realizada en noviembre de 1835 en la que Texas analizó el tema de la guerra contra México y redactó la Declaración del 7 de noviembre de 1835. **217**

consumer goods/bienes de consumo Productos fabricados para uso personal. **543**

Convention of 1832/Convención de 1832 Reunión de texanos en la que un grupo de delegados presentó varias reformas al gobierno mexicano, incluida la legalización de la migración de Estados Unidos a México y la separación de Texas de Coahuila. **212**

Convention of 1833/Convención 1833 Reunión de texanos impacientes con la falta de reformas en las políticas mexicanas hacia Texas, luego de la cual Stephen F. Austin fue enviado a la ciudad de México para presentar diversas propuestas. **212**

Convention of 1836/Convención de 1836 Reunión de delegados en Washington-on-the-Brazos en la que los texanos declararon su independencia de México. **240**

Convention of 1845/Convención de 1845 Reunión llamada por el presidente Anson Jones en la que un grupo de delegados aprobaron la anexión de Texas a Estados Unidos. **317**

cooperative stores/tiendas cooperativas Negocios de una organización operados para el beneficio de sus integrantes. **499**

corporations/corporaciones Compañías que se venden parcialmente en forma de acciones para recaudar fondos. **321**

Corpus Christi de la Isleta/Corpus Christi de la Isleta Primera misión española de Texas, localizada en la parte oeste del río Grande. **114**

cotton belt/región algodonera Región del sur de Estados Unidos en la que se cosechaba la mayor parte del algodón cultivado en el país. **349**

cottonclads/algodoneros Botes de vapor aislados con fardos de algodón que se usaron como botes de combate durante la Guerra Civil. **383**

cotton diplomacy/diplomacia del algodón Bloqueo de los envíos de algodón al extranjero por parte de los líderes del sur hasta obtener el apoyo de esas naciones durante la Guerra Civil. **378**

cotton gins/desmotadora de algodón Dispositivos usados para separar las fibras de algodón de las semillas. **164**

Council House Fight/Batalla de la Cámara del Consejo Batalla librada en San Antonio en 1840 entre texanos y comanches en la que los líderes de esta tribu no aceptaron liberar a todos sus prisioneros. **269**

council-manager government/gobierno de concejo Gobierno municipal en el que los votantes eligen a un alcalde y el concejo de la ciudad determina las políticas locales, elige a la persona que aplica dichas políticas y se encarga de los asuntos cotidianos. **663**

criminal law/ley criminal Ley que determina cuáles son las acciones ilegales en una sociedad. **653**

crop rotation/rotación de cultivos Sistema en el que se siembra diferentes productos en periodos alternados para evitar el desgaste de la tierra. **75**

culture/cultura Conjunto de creencias, valores y conductas aprendidas y compartidas por un grupo de personas. **4**

customs duties/derechos de aduana Impuestos de importación. **205**

Davis Guards/Guardias Davis Unión de soldados confederados de origen irlandés formada durante la Guerra Civil para proteger el Paso de Sabine. **384**

Dawes General Allotment Act/Ley Dawes de lotificación Ley aprobada en 1887 con la finalidad de dividir el territorio indígena en reservaciones con la promesa de otorgarles la ciudadanía estadounidense. **430**

death rate/tasa de mortalidad Número de personas fallecidas por cada 1,000 habitantes de una región. **33**

Declaration of November 7, 1835/Declaración del 7 de noviembre de 1835 Acuerdo firmado en la Consulta en el que los delegados juraron lealtad a México pero advirtieron que crearían un gobierno independiente si no se reformaba la Constitución de 1824. **231**

decree/decreto Orden oficial. **205**

delegates/delegados Representantes; por ejemplo, en una convención. **212**

demobilization/desmovilización Transición de la economía de tiempos de guerra a tiempos de paz. **536**

demography/demografía Rama de la geografía que estudia a las poblaciones humanas. **32**

denominations/sectas Grupos religiosos con creencias similares. **289**

depression/depresión Periodo de baja actividad económica. **160**

derricks/torre de perforación Bases donde se instala el equipo usado para la extracción del petróleo. **479**

desegregate/desegregar Anulación de leyes o prácticas que separan a las razas humanas en determinado lugar o institución. **578**

diplomats/diplomáticos Individuos que representan a sus países en los asuntos internacionales. **142**

direct democracy/democracia directa Sistema de gobierno en el que los asuntos de un país son resueltos por los votantes y no por un grupo de representantes electos. **670**

dogtrot cabins/cabañas de dos alas Cabañas de troncos que tienen dos habitaciones separadas por un pasillo. **186**

draft/reclutamiento militar Registro obligatorio para el servicio militar. **387**

Dred Scott decision/decisión *Dred Scott* Decisión adoptada por la Suprema Corte en 1857 que determinó que los afroestadounidenses no tenían derecho a la ciudadanía y por lo tanto no podían presentar demandas legales. **373**

drought/sequía Largo periodo sin lluvias. **26**

dry farming/cultivo de sequía Técnicas agrícolas usadas en climas secos para conservar la humedad del suelo. **467**

due process/proceso debido Proceso legal que las autoridades deben seguir antes de sancionar a una persona por una falta cometida. **666**

Dust Bowl/Cuenca del Polvo Parte de las Planicies del sur donde la sequía y el polvo arruinaron las cosechas y causaron la muerte del ganado en la década de 1930. **548**

Economic Opportunity Act/Ley de oportunidades económicas Ley incluida en la Gran Sociedad que otorgó fondos para ofrecer capacitación laboral y crear programas de acción para la comunidad. **588**

ecosystem/ecosistema Plantas, animales y formas no vivas que comparten el entorno de una región. **7**

Edwards Aquifer/acuífero Edwards Fuente de agua subterránea que abastece de agua a la parte central de Texas. **23**

Eighteenth Amendment/Decimoctava enmienda Enmienda constitucional que decretó la Prohibición en Estados Unidos. **512**

El Camino Real/El Camino Real Camino que comunicaba las misiones del este de Texas con las poblaciones al sureste de río Grande y llegaba hasta la ciudad de México. **124**

Emancipation Proclamation/Proclama de Emancipación Declaración del presidente Abraham Lincoln en la que otorgaba la libertad a los esclavos de cualquier territorio que se rebelara contra Estados Unidos. **391**

eminent domain/dominio eminente Autoridad del gobierno para declarar una propiedad privada como de uso público. **667**

***empresarios*/empresarios** Comerciantes que promovieron la migración a las colonias de Texas. **173**

environment/medio ambiente Entorno natural que nos rodea. **4**

Environmental Protection Agency/Agencia de Protección al Ambiente Departamento del gobierno federal creado para evitar y controlar la contaminación del aire y del agua. **630**

epidemics/epidemia Brote de una enfermedad que afecta a un área grande. **105**

equator/ecuador Línea imaginaria que rodea a la Tierra justo a la mitad de la distancia entre ambos polos. **10**

erosion/erosión Proceso de desgaste de un material, como el suelo. **29**

escarpments/acantilados Riscos. **54**

executive branch/Poder Ejecutivo Poder del gobierno que aplica las leyes. **241, 642**

expenditures/egresos Gastos del gobierno. **262**

exports/exportaciones Productos que un país compra a otros países. **193**

extinct/extinguida Especie que se ha agotado por completo. **29**

faction/facción Grupo que por lo general actúa en oposición de un grupo mayor. **217**

fault/falla Abertura importante en la corteza de la Tierra. **55**

federalism/federalismo Sistema de gobierno que reparte su poder entre un organismo federal y varios regionales para equilibrar fuerzas. **195, 642**

Federal Reserve System/Sistema de la Reserva Federal Sistema central que distribuye dinero a otros bancos y los ayuda a controlar sus operaciones. **520**

felonies/delitos Crímenes importantes. **653**

Fifteenth Amendment/Decimoquinta enmienda Enmienda constitucional que otorgó el derecho al voto a la mujer. **403**

filibusters/filibusteros Aventureros militares que llegaron de Estados Unidos a Texas a principios del siglo XIX. **144**

financial panic/pánico financiero Crisis económica. **160**

flatboats/pangas Largos botes planos usados como transporte en los ríos. **185**

flowchart/diagrama de flujo Diagrama que usa recuadros, flechas e imágenes para mostrar los pasos a seguir en un proceso. **15**

foreign relations/relaciones exteriores Asuntos que trata un país con los demás. **294**

Foreign Trade Zones/zonas de intercambio comercial Áreas donde se regulan las exportaciones con la finalidad de promover el intercambio comercial. **631**

Fort St. Louis/Fuerte St. Louis Base de la expedición de La Salle, posiblemente ubicada cerca de Garcitas Creek en Texas. **117**

fossil fuel/combustible fósil Combustible natural, como carbón o gas, que se forma en el subsuelo con restos de plantas y animales. **478**

Fourteenth Amendment/Decimocuarta enmienda Enmienda constitucional que otorgó a los afroestadounidenses la ciudadanía y los mismos derechos que a los demás. **401**

Fredonian Rebellion/Rebelión Fredoniana Revuelta iniciada en 1826 por el colono de Texas Benjamin Edwards después de un conflicto con el gobierno mexicano que canceló el contrato de su colonia. **203**

Freedmen's Bureau/Oficina de liberados Organización creada por el Congreso estadounidense en 1865 para brindar ayuda legal a las personas liberadas. **397**

freedpeople/liberados Esclavos puestos en libertad. **397**

free enterprise/libre empresa Sistema económico en que el gobierno no interfiere demasiado en la operación de los negocios. **192**

gasoline/gasolina Producto derivado del petróleo que se usa como combustible. **487**

general elections/elecciones generales Elecciones en las que los votantes usan boletas para elegir a los candidatos para un cargo particular o toman decisiones sobre ciertos asuntos. **670**

general-law cities/ciudades de ley general Pequeños pueblos y ciudades sujetos a las leyes del estado de Texas; algunos de ellos recibieron una carta de la legislatura que definía su propia forma de gobierno. **664**

geographic information systems/sistemas de información geográfica (GIS) Sistemas computarizados que recopilan, almacenan y organizan información geográfica. **5**

geography/geografía Estudio de las características físicas y humanas de cada lugar o región. **4**

German Emigration Company/German Emigration Company "Compañía Alemana de Inmigración"; compañía formada por un grupo de alemanes adinerados que compró tierras en Texas con la finalidad de promover la migración alemana a este lugar y obtener buenas ganancias. **282**

G.I. Bill of Rights/Carta de Derechos G.I. Ley de reajuste de prestaciones militares que ofreció a los veteranos de guerra seguros de desempleo y préstamos para comprar casas o pagar la educación de sus hijos. **570**

Gilmer–Aikin Laws/Leyes Gilmer-Aikin Leyes que crearon la base de la actual estructura educativa de Texas. **570**

globalization/globalización Interdependencia de las naciones del mundo mediante el intercambio de bienes, ideas y personas. **631**

Goliad Massacre/Matanza de Goliad Ejecución del coronel James Fannin y sus tropas después de su derrota en la Batalla de Loreto ante el ejército mexicano. **248**

Goodnight-Loving Trail/sendero Goodnight Loving Ruta ganadera que partía de Young County, Texas, y llegaba a Colorado, pasando por Nuevo México. **447**

grand jury/gran jurado Jurado que decide si una persona acusada de un delito debe someterse a cargos formales. **654**

Grange/*Grange* "Granja"; organización de agricultores creada a finales de la década de 1860, llamada popularmente los Protectores de la Agricultura. **499**

Grass Fight/Batalla de la Pastura Incidente ocurrido en noviembre de 1835 en el que un grupo de texanos emboscaron a tropas mexicanas creyendo que llevaban un cargamento de plata, aunque en realidad sólo llevaban sacos llenos de pasto para alimentar a sus caballos. **229**

Great Depression/Gran Depresión Severa reducción en las actividades económicas mundiales ocurrida en la década de 1930. **545**

Great Society/Gran Sociedad Programa del presidente Lyndon B. Johnson que incluía mejoras de salud, educación, protección ambiental, capacitación laboral y reformas de inmigración. **588**

Great Southwest Strike of 1886/Gran Huelga del Suroeste de 1886 Huelga de ferrocarrileros que ocasionó brotes de violencia a causa de una disputa entre los Caballeros del Trabajo y la compañía de Jay Gould. **473**

gristmills/molinos Máquinas usadas para triturar granos y elaborar harina. **351**

growth rate/tasa de crecimiento Velocidad con la que crece la población. **32**

G.T.T./G.T.T. (por sus siglas en inglés: "Gone to Texas"; "Se fue a Texas", en español) Frase popular en los primeros años de la colonización de Texas. **183**

Guadalupe Peak/Pico de Guadalupe Pico más alto de la región montañosa de Texas. **57**

Guerrero Decree/Decreto de Guerrero Ley aprobada por el presidente mexicano Vicente Guerrero en 1829 que abolió la esclavitud en México. **205**

habitat/hábitat Ambiente en que vive un animal. **29**

hides/cuero Piel de animal. **79**

Hogg Laws/Leyes de Hogg Leyes aprobadas por el gobernador de Texas James Hogg para reglamentar los negocios. **505**

Holocaust/holocausto Intento del movimiento nazi por acabar con los judíos de Europa durante la Segunda Guerra Mundial. **567**

home-rule charters/cartas de leyes ciudadanas Cartas que permiten a los ciudadanos de las localidades de Texas con más de 5,000 habitantes elegir su propia forma de gobierno. **664**

homestead law/Ley de posesión de tierras Ley aprobada por el Congreso de la República en 1839 para proteger 50 acres de terreno que no puede ser embargado como propiedad de cada familia. **267**

Hood's Texas Brigade/Brigada Hood de Texas Unidad líder del ejército de Virginia del Norte que participó en las batallas más importantes de la Guerra Civil. **377**

horizontal axis/eje horizontal Línea trazada a lo ancho en una gráfica para mostrar el valor o medida de los datos presentados. **13**

horizontal integration/integración vertical Posesión de todos los negocios de una rama particular. **485**

Houston Ship Channel/canal de Houston Canal que conecta Houston con el Golfo de México. **520**

humidity/humedad Cantidad de agua que flota en el aire. **25**

hunter-gatherers/cazadores-recolectores Personas que cazan animales y recolectan plantas para subsistir. **69**

hunting grounds/tierras de cacería Áreas en las que un grupo caza tradicionalmente en busca de alimento. **82**

immigration/inmigración Movimiento de personas que abandonan un país para irse a vivir a otro. **31**

impeach/encausar Levantar cargos contra un funcionario público. **402**

Imperial Colonization Law/Ley de colonización imperial Ley mexicana aprobada en 1823 que dio mayores garantías a los ganaderos y agricultores de Texas, además de exentar de impuestos por seis años a todos los colonos. **167**

imports/importaciones Productos que una nación compra a otras naciones. **193**

infantry/infantería Soldados a pie. **228**

infrastructure/infraestructura Obras públicas como carreteras y sistemas de suministro de agua. **622**

interest groups/grupos de interés Grupos unidos por un interés común que tratan de afectar las políticas de un gobierno. **672**

internal combustion engine/máquina de combustión interna Máquinas que utilizan la combustión, es decir, la quema de un combustible para generar energía en su interior. **487**

internal improvements/mejoras internas Avances en la red de transporte de un estado. **353**

Internet/Internet Sistema mundial de redes de computadoras. **620**

Interstate Commerce Commission/Comisión Interestatal de Comercio Departamento del gobierno creado en 1887 para regular la operación de las compañías ferrocarrileras. **504**

ironclads/acorazados Barcos equipados con placas protectoras de acero usados durante la Guerra Civil. **380**

irrigation/riego Suministro de agua por medios artificiales para regar los cultivos. **23**

jacales/jacales Pequeñas viviendas de una sola habitación hechas con lodo y varas. **150**

JA Ranch/rancho JA Rancho de Charles Goodnight y John Adair localizado en la saliente de Texas. **450**

Jim Crow laws/Leyes de Jim Crow Leyes aprobadas en los estados del sur para apoyar la segregación. **409**

joint resolution/resolución conjunta Medida aprobada por las dos cámaras del Congreso para formalizar una propuesta. **316**

judicial branch/Poder Judicial Rama del gobierno en la que una corte toma decisiones sobre asuntos legales e interpreta leyes. **241, 642**

judicial review/revisión judicial Autoridad de la Corte para determinar si una ley es aniticonstitucional. **654**

junctions/empalme Puntos de encuentro de dos o más conductos, como las líneas ferroviarias. **465**

Juneteenth/19 de junio Fecha en que el general de la Unión Gordon Granger emitió en Galveston la Proclama de emancipación que liberó a los esclavos de Texas. **396**

Kansas-Nebraska Act/Ley Kansas-Nebraska Ley aprobada en 1854 que daba a los residentes de Kansas y Nebraska autoridad para decidir si la esclavitud debía ser abolida o permitida. **373**

King Ranch/rancho King Rancho localizado al sur de Texas en el que se realizaban las operaciones de manejo de ganado más importantes. **449**

Know-Nothing Party/Partido de No sé nada Partido político oficialmente conocido como Partido Estadounidense, creado a mediados de la década de 1850; apoyaba la esclavitud y rechazaba la participación de inmigrantes y católicos en el gobierno. **323**

Ku Klux Klan/Ku Klux Klan Sociedad secreta formada después de la Guerra Civil; amenazaba y hasta asesinaba a personas de raza negra para restringir sus opiniones políticas; en 1915 se creó la versión moderna de este grupo. **404**

La Bahía/La Bahía Prisión y misión construida por el Marqués de San Miguel de Aguayo cerca de la bahía de Matagorda. **126**

labor unions/sindicatos Organizaciones formadas para defender los intereses de los trabajadores. **473**

land titles/títulos de propiedad Documentos legales que otorgan la posesión de la tierra. **164**

La Raza Unida Party/Partido de La Raza Unida Partido político fundado en 1970 por líderes hispanos con la finalidad de analizar los asuntos que afectaban a los latinoamericanos y obtener mayor representación política. **594**

La Salle expedition/expedición La Salle Exploración encabezada por René-Robert Cavelier, Sir de La Salle para fundar una colonia cerca de la desembocadura del río Mississippi; aunque el grupo se extravió, llegó a territorio de Texas y estableció el Fuerte St. Louis. **116**

latitude/latitud Líneas imaginarias que corren de este a oeste en el globo terrestre y miden la distancia al norte y al sur del ecuador. **10**

Law of April 6, 1830/Ley del 6 de abril de 1830 Ley emitida por el gobierno mexicano para prohibir la inmigración a Texas, la importación de esclavos y la creación de derechos de aduana para las importaciones estadounidenses; esta medida provocó el enojo de muchos colonos de Texas e inició el conflicto de ese estado con el gobierno de México. **205**

League of United Latin American Citizens/Liga de Ciudadanos Unidos de América Latina (LULAC, por sus siglas en inglés) Organización creada en 1929 por mexicanos estadounidenses residentes de Texas para luchar por sus derechos. **539**

legend/leyenda Clave que explica los símbolos, colores y características de un mapa. **11**

legislative branch/Poder Legislativo Rama del gobierno que crea las leyes. **241, 642**

Legislative Budget Board/Consejo Legislativo de Presupuesto Departamento del gobierno de Texas, creado como parte del Poder Legislativo, que incluye un cuerpo de nueve legisladores principales y un teniente gobernador para atender las solicitudes de fondos de otros departamentos del gobierno. **655**

libel/libelo Escrito con declaraciones falsas intencionales. **666**

lignite/lignito Tipo de carbón mineral. **49**

limited government/gobierno limitado Principio de un gobierno en el que el uso de los poderes es limitado por leyes establecidas, como la Constitución. **641**

line graph/gráfica lineal Gráfica que muestra una tendencia en un periodo, es decir, algo que aumenta o disminuye con el paso del tiempo. **14**

line-item veto/veto de artículos en línea Autoridad del Poder Ejecutivo para anular ciertas leyes total o parcialmente. **650**

Little Colony/Colonia Pequeña Colonia fundada por Stephen F. Austin como parte separada de otra colonia; en ella residían 100 familias de manera aislada, al oeste de la colonia principal. **171**

Lively/Lively Barco pequeño adquirido por Stephen F. Austin para transportar a los colonos y los bienes que formarían su colonia. **165**

lobby/cabildear Tratar de convencer a los legisladores en un tema específico. **672**

longhorn/cuernos largos Raza de ganado desarrollada mediante la cruza de razas españolas e inglesas traídas por los colonizadores. **442**

longitude/longitud Líneas imaginarias que corren de norte a sur en el globo terrestre y miden la distancia al este y al oeste del primer meridiano. **10**

Louisiana Purchase/Compra de Louisiana Acuerdo firmado en 1803 en el que Estados Unidos compró a Francia el territorio de Louisiana por 15 millones de dólares. **141**

Mackenzie's Raiders/Jinetes de Mackenzie Tropas dirigidas por el coronel Ronald S. Mackenzie que realizaron varios ataques sorpresa a las tribus indígenas de las Planicies. **422**

maize/maíz Tipo de granos originarios del continente americano. **69**

manifest destiny/destino manifiesto Creencia de que por destino Estados Unidos debía extenderse y ocupar América del Norte. **315**

Manned Spacecraft Center/Centro de Vuelos Espaciales Tripulados (por sus siglas en inglés) Cuartel general de entrenamiento de la NASA de astronautas y control de vuelo, localizado en Houston. En 1973 cambió su nombre a Centro Espacial Lyndon B. Johnson. **596**

manufactured products/productos manufacturados Productos fabricados manualmente o con máquinas para su venta en grandes cantidades. **351**

map projections/proyecciones en mapa Medios usados por los cartógrafos para crear representaciones planas de la superficie de la Tierra. **12**

maquiladoras/maquiladoras Fábricas mexicanas establecidas cerca de la frontera entre México y Texas. **622**

March to the Sea/Marcha hacia el Mar Campaña de la Guerra Civil dirigida por el general William Tecumseh Sherman en la que las fuerzas de la Unión destruyeron recursos sureños a su paso por Georgiato, Carolina del Sur. **390**

martial law/ley marcial Ley creada por autoridades militares. **388**

Matagorda Bay/bahía Matagorda Caleta localizada en el Golfo de México. **116**

matrilineal/matrilineal Descendencia originada en la parte materna de la familia. **76**

mayor-council government/gobierno de alcalde y concejo Gobierno municipal en el que los votantes eligen a su alcalde, pero un concejo administra el gobierno. **663**

Mesoamerica/Mesoamérica Región cultural que abarca el territorio ocupado actualmente por México y América Central. **69**

Metroplex/Metroplex Área de Dallas a Forth Worth. **50**

Mexican Cession/cesión mexicana Resultado del Tratado de Guadalupe Hidalgo en el que México cede a Estados Unidos parte de su territorio del norte a cambio de 18.25 millones de dólares. **334**

Mier expedition/expedición de Mier Ataque texano al poblado mexicano de Mier, luego de los ataques mexicanos a Texas en la década de 1840; en este ataque fueron capturados una gran cantidad de texanos por las tropas mexicanas. **301**

migration/migración Desplazamiento de un grupo de personas que abandona su lugar de origen. **7**

militia/milicia Ejército de civiles. **167**

misdemeanors/fechoría Crimen menor. **653**

missions/misiones Comunidades religiosas establecidas por católicos españoles. **112**

mitotes/mitotes Celebraciones de los coahuiltecos que duraban toda la noche. **74**

monopoly/monopolio Control absoluto de una rama comercial. **503**

mustangs/mustangs Tipo de caballos salvajes traídos a América por los colonizadores españoles. **105**

Nacogdoches/Nacogdoches Pueblo fundado por Antonio Gil Ybarbo en la región de Pinney Woods en Texas. **138**

National Aeronautics and Space Administration/Administración Nacional de Aeronáutica y el Espacio (NASA, por sus siglas en inglés) Agencia creada en 1958 para desarrollar el programa espacial estadounidense y lograr las metas propuestas. **596**

National Association for the Advancement of Colored People/Asociación Nacional para el Desarrollo de Personas de Color (NAACP, por sus siglas en inglés) Organización de defensa de derechos civiles fundada en 1909 cuya primera representación en Texas se estableció en El Paso en 1915. **538**

National Colonization Law of 1824/Ley nacional de colonización de 1824 Leyes aprobadas por el gobierno de México que permitían a sus estados definir sus propias políticas de colonización y fomentaba la inmigración a Texas. **172**

natural gas/gas natural Gas que puede usarse como combustible. **485**

natural regions/regiones naturales Zonas distintas con un ambiente físico común. **44**

neutral/neutral No aliado con ninguna de las partes que intervienen en un conflicto. **530**

Neutral Ground/territorio neutral Área sujeta a disputa entre Estados Unidos y España después de la compra de Louisiana. **142**

New Deal/New Deal Programa iniciado por el presidente Franklin D. Roosevelt para acabar con la Gran Depresión. **550**

Nineteenth Amendment/Decimonovena enmienda Enmienda constitucional que garantizó a la mujer el derecho al voto. **512**

nomads/nómadas Grupos de personas que viajan de un lugar a otro sin establecerse. **72**

nominated/nominado Persona elegida como candidato para un puesto en el gobierno. **316**

noncombatants/no combatientes Personas que no participan en los combates de una guerra. **239**

nonrenewable resources/recursos no renovables Recursos como el carbón, el gas natural y el petróleo que los procesos naturales de la Tierra no pueden regenerar. **36**

nonviolent resistance/resistencia sin violencia Demostraciones públicas pacíficas. **578**

North American Free Trade Agreement/Tratado de Libre Comercio (NAFTA, por sus siglas en inglés; TLC, en español) Acuerdo entre Estados Unidos, Canadá y México que eliminó muchas barreras comerciales. **622**

Nuestro Padre San Francisco de los Tejas/Nuestro Padre San Francisco de los Tejas Misión construida por los españoles cerca del sitio donde se estableció sin éxito la misión de San Francisco de los Tejas. **122**

Obnoxious Acts/Leyes Ofensivas Nombre dado por los demócratas a las leyes aprobadas durante la Reconstrucción. **405**

offensive/ofensiva Avance de tropas militares. **333**

Office of Budget and Planning/Oficina de Planeación y Presupuesto Dependencia del Poder Ejecutivo del gobierno de Texas creada para atender las solicitudes de otras dependencias, junto con el Consejo Legislador del Presupuesto. **655**

Ogallala Aquifer/acuífero Ogallala Fuente subterránea natural de gran extensión que se extiende desde el oeste de Texas y Nuevo México hasta Dakota del Sur. **23**

Old Three Hundred/Los Viejos Trescientos Nombre dado a las 300 familias y hombres solteros que recibieron tierras en la pequeña colonia de Stephen F. Austin. **169**

open range/campo abierto Tierras no protegidas con cercas. **444**

Operation Desert Storm/Operación Tormenta del desierto Invasión de las Naciones Unidas encabezada por Estados Unidos para obligar a Irak a retirar sus tropas de Kuwait. **614**

override/predominio Autoridad que tiene el Poder Legislativo para cancelar un veto. **642**

Paleo-Indians/paleoindígenas Los primeros estadounidenses. **69**

Panic of 1819/Pánico de 1819 Crisis económica estadounidense iniciada en 1819 que produjo el cierre de muchos bancos y una depresión generalizada. **160**

Panic of 1837/Pánico de 1837 Crisis financiera estadounidense que produjo una depresión general. **262**

pardon/indulto Autoridad que tiene el Poder Ejecutivo para liberar a personas acusadas de algún crimen. **650**

Permanent University Fund/Fondo de Universidad Permanente Fondo creado en 1876 por la legislatura de Texas para reservar 1 millón de acres al oeste de Texas y construir universidades; los ingresos generados por el petróleo obtenido en la zona se usaron en beneficio de las universidades. **489**

petition/petición Solicitud formal hecha por ciudadanos al gobierno. **242**

petit jury/pequeño jurado Jurado que decide el veredicto de un juicio. **654**

petrochemicals/petroquímica Productos químicos derivados del petróleo y el gas natural. **47**

petroleum/petróleo Líquido fósil espeso y oscuro usado como combustible. **478**

philanthropy/filantropía Ofrecimiento de dinero para causas de beneficencia. **489**

pie chart/gráfica de pastel Diagrama que muestra cómo se dividen las partes de un entero. **14**

plains/planicies Áreas planas o de pendiente ligera en las que no hay grandes elevaciones ni hundimientos. **21**

Plan de San Diego/Plan de San Diego Documento redactado por mexicanos estadounidenses a principios del siglo XX para hacer un llamado a la toma del sur de Texas. **529**

plantations/plantaciones Grandes granjas que por lo general se especializan en la siembra de un solo cultivo. **191**

planters/hacendados Agricultores importantes que tenían al menos 20 esclavos. **349**

plateaus/mesetas Áreas de elevación plana con bordes de pendiente pronunciada en uno o más lados. **21**

platform/plataforma Declaración de objetivos por parte de un partido político. **502, 671**

political action committees/comités de acción política (PAC, por sus siglas en inglés) Grupos que recaudan fondos para apoyar la campaña de un candidato. **673**

political parties/partidos políticos Grupos de personas que eligen a funcionarios del gobierno e influyen en las políticas del gobierno. **316**

poll tax/impuesto de voto Impuesto pagado para tener derecho a votar. **513**

pooling/consorcio Combinación de esfuerzos de varias compañías para evitar la competencia en cierta industria. **500**

popular sovereignty/soberanía popular Principio de gobierno en el que el poder político proviene de los habitantes. **641**

Populist Party/Partido Populista Partido político oficialmente llamado Partido del Pueblo, formado por integrantes de la Alianza Agrícola para reducir la influencia de las grandes empresas en el gobierno. **501**

Populists/populistas Miembros del Partido Populista o Partido del Pueblo. **501**

precincts/distritos Subdivisiones de un país. **662**

precontact/precolombino Periodo anterior a la llegada de los europeos al continente americano. **70**

prehistory/prehistoria Periodo anterior a los registros históricos escritos. **68**

presidios/presidios Bases militares de las colonias españolas en América. **113**

primary elections/elecciones primarias Elecciones en que los votantes eligen a los candidatos que participarán en las elecciones generales. **539, 669**

prime meridian/primer meridiano Línea imaginaria de la Tierra que va del Polo Norte al Polo Sur, y pasa por Greenwich, Inglaterra. **10**

progressives/progresistas Reformistas de finales del siglo XIX y principios del siglo XX que lucharon por mejorar la sociedad. **507**

prohibition/prohibición Cancelación del permiso legal para la fabricación, distribución y venta de bebidas alcohólicas. **511**

proration/prorrateo División o distribución proporcional. **547**

provisional/provisional Temporal. **232**

Pueblo Revolt/Revuelta de los indígenas pueblo Revolución dirigida por Popé, el líder de los indígenas pueblo contra los españoles de Nuevo México. **114**

Quakers/cuáqueros Miembros de una secta protestante conocida como la Sociedad de Amigos. **419**

quilting bees/*quilting bees* "Abejas tejedoras"; grupos de mujeres tejedoras. **187**

Radical Republicans/republicanos radicales Bando del Partido Republicano que a mediados del siglo XIX creía que el gobierno federal necesitaba tener un papel más activo en la Reconstrucción. **400**

ragtime/ragtime Tipo de música popular que surgió a principios del siglo XX. **525**

ranchos/ranchos Fincas de ganado. **113**

ranges/cordilleras Grupos de montañas. **21**

range wars/batallas a campo abierto Violentas disputas ocasionales por el control de las tierras a campo abierto. **455**

ratify/ratificar Aprobación y aceptación formal. **263**

Reconstruction/Reconstrucción Proceso de reunificación de Estados Unidos después de la Guerra Civil y la recuperación de los estados del sur. **397**

Reconstruction Acts/Leyes de reconstrucción Leyes federales aprobadas por el Congreso a partir de 1867 que marcaron el inicio de la Reconstrucción. **401**

red backs/espaldas rojas Papel moneda emitido por la República de Texas durante la administración de Mirabeau B. Lamar para detener la crisis económica. **267**

Redeemers/redentores Nombre dado a los líderes sureños que trataron de restaurar su territorio a las condiciones en que se encontraba antes de la Guerra Civil por medio de restricciones a los gobiernos estatales y a la participación política de los afroestadounidenses. **409**

Red River Campaign/Campaña del Río Rojo Intento fallido de la Unión de invadir Texas durante la Guerra Civil en parte para apoderarse de sus campos de algodón. **385**

reference maps/mapas de referencia Mapas para encontrar lugares específicos. **12**

referendum/referéndum Práctica que permite a los votantes tomar decisiones sobre temas legislativos. **670**

refinery/refinería Lugar donde se refina el petróleo crudo para fabricar productos útiles como la gasolina. **479**

reforms/reformas Cambios en las políticas de un país para mejorar ciertas condiciones. **212**

refugees/refugiados Personas obligadas a abandonar su lugar natal por causas de guerra o persecución. **529**

regiment/regimiento Unidad militar de varios batallones o tropas. **377**

Regulator-Moderator War/Guerra entre Reguladores y Moderados Enfrentamiento entre dos grupos del este de Texas que repartieron certificados falsos de propiedad, lo cual generó brotes de violencia. **273**

relative location/posición relativa Ubicación de un lugar en relación con la de otros. **9**

remuda/remuda Palabra española que significa "montura de reemplazo", se usaba para referirse a los caballos de repuesto que los vaqueros reservaban en las travesías de ganado. **447**

renewable resources/recursos renovables Recursos como los árboles y el viento, que son generados de nuevo por los procesos naturales de la Tierra. **36**

republic/república Gobierno en el que el poder proviene de la población y es ejercido por funcionarios electos de acuerdo con ciertas normas legales. **140, 641**

Republican Army of the North/Ejército de la República del Norte Ejército privado organizado por José Bernardo Gutiérrez de Lara y Augustus William Magee para luchar por la independencia mexicana de España. **145**

reservations/reservaciones Áreas exclusivas para los indígenas estadounidenses. **340**

reservoirs/embalses Lagos artificiales en los que se almacena agua que por lo general se suministra como agua potable a las ciudades. **23**

resolutions/resoluciones Declaraciones que expresan opiniones. **209**

revenue/ingresos Dinero que recibe el gobierno. **262, 656**

revolt/revuelta Revolución. **114**

Rio Grande valley/Valle del Río Grande Parte de las planicies de Texas, considerada como una de las zonas agrícolas más ricas de la nación. **48**

Ross's Texas Brigade/Brigada de Ross en Texas Tropas texanas que combatieron en Georgia, Mississippi, y Tennessee durante la Guerra Civil. **377**

Rough Riders/jinetes rudos Primer cuerpo voluntario de caballería estadounidense, al mando del teniente coronel Theodore Roosevelt, que se hizo famoso por haber derrotado a las tropas españolas en la Batalla de la colina de San Juan. **528**

Runaway Scrape/Gran Escape Huida de los colonos de Texas, quienes dejaron atrás granjas, hogares y poblaciones para evitar ser alcanzados por el ejército mexicano, luego de enterarse de la caída de El Álamo. **247**

runoff election/elecciones de desempate Elecciones que designan al ganador en una competencia en la que ninguna de las partes recibe la mayoría del voto. **670**

rustlers/abigeos Ladrones de ganado. **441**

Rutersville College/Universidad de Rutersville Primera universidad de Texas, inaugurada en 1884 cerca de La Grange. **266**

Salt Creek Raid/Ataque de Salt Creek Ataque de unos 100 indígenas de las tribus kiowa y comanche a una caravana cerca de Salt Creek en 1871. **421**

San Antonio de Béxar/San Antonio de Béxar Presidio construido por los españoles a aproximadamente una milla de la misión de San Antonio de Valero. **123**

San Antonio de Valero/San Antonio de Valero Misión construida por los españoles cerca del río San Antonio en la que tuvo lugar el sitio de El Álamo. **123**

San Felipe de Austin/San Felipe de Austin Capital de la pequeña colonia de Stephen F. Austin. **170**

San Fernando de Béxar/San Fernando de Béxar Población cercana al presidio de San Antonio de Béxar que se convirtió en la ciudad de San Antonio; lugar donde se estableció el primer gobierno civil de Texas. **124**

San Francisco de los Tejas/San Francisco de los Tejas Misión construida por los españoles al este de Texas que terminó en un fracaso. **119**

Santa Fe expedition/Expedición Santa Fe Expedición de más de 300 personas enviadas por el presidente Mirabeau B.

Lamar a Santa Fe para reclamar esa región de Nuevo México en nombre de Texas. **297**

sawmills/aserraderos Lugares en los que los troncos de los árboles son cortados en piezas de tamaño útil. **193**

scalawags/scalawags "Bribones"; nombre dado a los habitantes del sur que apoyaban la Reconstrucción con fines de lucro. **405**

scale/escala Medida que muestra la relación entre las distancias usadas en un mapa y las distancias reales. **11**

scrip/certificado Papel moneda. **546**

secede/secesión Retiro formal de un cuerpo organizado. **374**

secularize/secularizar Pasar de términos religiosos a términos civiles. **151**

Sedalia Trail/sendero de Sedalia Ruta ganadera que cruzaba territorio indígena para comunicar el sur de Texas con Sedalia, Missouri. **444**

segregation/segregación Separación obligada de blancos y afroestadounidenses en público. **409**

separation of powers/separación de poderes Principio de gobierno que divide los poderes en varias ramas. **642**

session/sesión Periodo de reuniones legislativas. **645**

Seventeenth Amendment/Decimoséptima enmienda Enmienda constitucional que otorgó a los estadounidenses el derecho de votar para elegir directamente a sus senadores. **507**

sharecroppers/cultivo compartido Sistema en el que los campesinos carecen de tierras y herramientas, por lo que siembran en tierras ajenas a cambio de recibir una parte de la cosecha. **411**

Sharpstown stock-fraud scandal/escándalo del fraude de Sharpstown Escándalo generado en el gobierno de Texas en 1971 cuando varios funcionarios fueron acusados de aceptar sobornos de un industrial de Houston. **604**

siege/sitio Bloqueo militar de una ciudad o un fuerte. **145**

Siege of the Alamo/sitio de El Álamo Ataque del ejército mexicano al fuerte de El Álamo en 1836 que concluyó con la derrota de las tropas texanas. **237**

sit-ins/plantones Protestas de personas que se sientan en un lugar y se niegan a abandonarlo. **590**

slander/calumnia Declaración falsa que daña la reputación de alguien. **666**

Social Security/seguridad social Programa creado con el *New Deal* para ofrecer pensiones de retiro y seguros de desempleo a los trabajadores. **551**

soup kitchens/comedores de beneficencia Lugares administrados por organizaciones de beneficencia en los que se ofrecen alimentos gratuitos a personas sin hogar. **546**

Southern Farmers' Alliance/Alianza de Agricultores del Sur Organización creada en 1877 por un grupo de agricultores de Texas; este grupo tuvo mayor influencia política que el Grange. **500**

sovereignty/soberanía Supremacía de poder. **375**

special districts/distritos especiales Organismo del gobierno local creado con un propósito específico, que por lo general ofrece servicios no ofrecidos por otros organismos locales. **664**

special elections/elecciones especiales Elecciones en las que los votantes pueden elegir a un funcionario para ocupar un puesto vacante o solicitar enmiendas constitucionales en temas locales. **670**

Spindletop strike/Huelga de Spindletop Huelga petrolera importante iniciada en Spindletop el 10 de enero de 1901 con la que inició el auge de las compañías petroleras en Texas. **480**

Sputnik/Sputnik Satélite artificial soviético cuyo lanzamiento en 1957 promovió la creación de la Agencia Nacional de Aeronáutica y el Espacio (NASA) en Estados Unidos. **596**

State Colonization Law of 1825/Ley estatal de colonización de 1825 Ley aprobada por el gobierno estatal de Coahuila y Texas que abrió Texas a la inmigración. **173**

states' rights/derechos estatales Derechos que limitan la autoridad del gobierno federal sobre los gobiernos de los estados. **372**

statistics/estadísticas Información presentada en forma de cantidades. **13**

stocks/acciones Títulos parciales de propiedad de una empresa. **544**

stockyards/corrales Lugares de concentración de cabezas de ganado. **443**

strike/huelga Negativa de los trabajadores a realizar sus labores hasta que su compañía cumpla con sus demandas. **473**

subregions/subregiones Partes en que se divide una región. **45**

suburbs/suburbios Zonas residenciales construidas en las afueras de una ciudad. **523**

suffrage/sufragio Derecho al voto. **398**

Sunbelt/franja del sol Región del sur de Estados Unidos caracterizada por tener un clima soleado. **42, 600**

supply and demand/oferta y demanda Sistema económico en el que si la oferta es mayor que la demanda, se reducen los precios, pero si la demanda es mayor, los precios suben. **469**

tallow/sebo Grasa animal usada para fabricar jabón y velas. **350**

tanneries/curtiduría Lugar donde se preparan pieles de animales para su uso. **351**

Tejanos/tejanos Colonos de ascendencia española o mexicana establecidos en Texas. **138**

Tejas/tejas Palabra tomada por los españoles del dialecto de los hasinai para nombrarlos; en español esta palabra significa *amigo*. **118**

Telegraph and Texas Register/Telegraph and Texas Register Periódico publicado por primera vez en 1835 que se convirtió en el de mayor circulación en Texas a mediados del siglo XIX. **358**

telegraphs/telégrafo Dispositivo eléctrico de comunicación a distancia con el que se envían mensajes codificados por medio de alambres. **358**

temperance movement/movimiento de abstinencia Reforma social que fomentaba la disminución en el consumo de bebidas alcohólicas. **511**

tenant farmers/agricultores arrendatarios Personas que rentaban tierras de cultivo. **411**

tepees/tipis Tiendas portátiles hechas con pieles de animales estiradas sobre postes, usados por los indígenas de las Grandes Planicies. **82**

Terrell Election Law/Ley Terrell de elecciones Ley con que la legislatura de Texas aprobó en 1905 la realización de elecciones primarias para elegir a los candidatos de las elecciones estatales, distritales y federales. **507**

terrorism/terrorismo Uso de ataques violentos por individuos o pequeños grupos con el propósito de conseguir ciertas metas políticas. **616**

Terry's Texas Rangers/*Terry's Texas Rangers* Unidad de caballería organizada por B. F. Terry, que libró varias batallas durante la Guerra Civil. **377**

Texas Admission Act/Ley de admisión de texas Ley firmada por el presidente James K. Polk que incluyó a Texas como el estado número 28 de la Unión. **317**

Texas Department of Health/Departamento de Salud de Texas Departamento del gobierno estatal fundado en 1903 para ayudar a prevenir enfermedades. **524**

Texas fever/fiebre de Texas Epidemia que atacó al ganado, con excepción de los cuernos largos, que fueron resistentes a la enfermedad. **442**

Texas Highway Department/Departamento de Carreteras de Texas Departamento estatal creado en 1917 para construir y dar mantenimiento a las carreteras de Texas. **524**

Texas Natural Resource Conservation Commission/Comisión para la Conservación de los Recursos Naturales de Texas Agencia estatal creada con el propósito de equilibrar el desarrollo económico y la protección del medio ambiente. **630**

Texas Railroad Commission/Comisión de Ferrocarriles de Texas Agencia creada en 1891 para regular la operación de las compañías de ferrocarril y otros transportes; a principios del siglo XX, esta agencia amplió sus acciones de supervisión a la industria petrolera. **488**

Texas Rangers/*Rangers* de Texas Cuerpo de defensa creado con la finalidad de mantener la paz en las fronteras de Texas. **261**

Texas Water Commission/Comisión de Aguas de Texas Departamento del gobierno estatal establecido en 1913 para ayudar a las ciudades y condados a administrar sus reservas acuíferas. **525**

Texas Women's Political Caucus/Junta Político de Mujeres de Texas Grupo fundado en 1971 para luchar por la obtención de más cargos políticos para las mujeres. **595**

thematic maps/mapas temáticos Mapas que muestran un tema específico o la distribución de espacios en una actividad. **12**

Thirteenth Amendment/Decimotercera enmienda Enmienda constitucional que abolió la esclavitud. **397**

threshers/trilladoras Máquinas usadas para separar los granos de las semillas de las plantas. **468**

tidelands/marismas Tierras ubicadas debajo del nivel del mar en zonas costeras. **571**

time line/línea del tiempo Diagrama que muestra una secuencia de sucesos en el tiempo. **15**

Tonkin Gulf Resolution/Resolución del Golfo de Tonkin Ley del Congreso que permitía al presidente Lyndon B. Johnson tomar decisiones sobre el envío de tropas estadounidenses a la guerra de Vietnam. **589**

tourism/turismo Negocio que consiste en atraer visitantes a un lugar o región. **58**

transcontinental railroad/ferrocarril transcontinental Ferrocarril que cruza la parte continental de Estados Unidos. **463**

transportation center/centro de transporte Lugar de recepción de productos que son distribuidos a otros lugares. **51**

Treaties of Velasco/Tratados de Velasco Serie de dos tratados firmados por el general Antonio López de Santa Anna y el presidente interino de Texas David G. Burnet para dar por terminada la Revolución de Texas. **256**

Treaty of Guadalupe Hidalgo/Tratado de Guadalupe Hidalgo Tratado firmado por funcionarios estadounidenses y mexicanos el 2 de febrero de 1848 para dar por terminada la guerra con México. **334**

Treaty of the Little Arkansas/Tratado de Little Arkansas Tratado firmado en octubre de 1865 por varios comisionados federales y líderes indígenas del sur de las Planicies en el que éstos, los líderes de los comanches y los kiowas, aceptaron establecerse en una zona de reserva de Panhandle. **416**

Treaty of Medicine Lodge/Tratado de Medicine Lodge Tratado firmado en 1867 entre comisionados federales y líderes indígenas de las Planicies en el que algunos grupos de indígenas estadounidenses aceptaron vivir en una zona de reserva del territorio indígena. **418**

Treaty of Paris/Tratado de París Tratado firmado en 1763 que dio por terminada la Guerra de los Siete Años; en este acuerdo, Francia y España decidieron ceder a la Gran Bretaña el norte del continente americano. **136**

Treaty of Tehuacana Creek/Tratado de Tehuacana Creek Acuerdo de paz firmado por el presidente de la República Sam Houston y el jefe comanche Búfalo Hump en octubre de 1844. **272**

trial courts/juicios civiles Cortes que analizan casos relacionados con la sociedad y dan un veredicto o decisión. **653**

tributaries/tributarios Pequeñas corrientes o ríos que desembocan en corrientes mayores. **22**

trusts/consorcio Acuerdo legal en el que varias compañías se agrupan en un solo consejo. **503**

Turtle Bayou Resolutions/Resoluciones de Bahía Tortugas Documento redactado después del conflicto de Anáhuac en 1832 en el que los texanos declararon su apoyo a la Constitución de 1824 y al general Antonio López de Santa Anna. **209**

two-party system/sistema bipartidista Sistema político en el que los dos partidos más importantes compiten para ganar el control de un país. **603**

Unionists/unionistas Sureños que deseaban permanecer en la Unión y resolver diferencias relacionadas con el tema de la esclavitud a mediados del siglo XIX. **374**

Union League/Liga de la Unión Grupo político creado en Texas a mediados del siglo XIX que invitaba a los afroestadounidenses a dar su apoyo al partido republicano. **402**

urbanization/urbanización Aumento del número de personas que viven o trabajan en las ciudades. **7, 519**

vaqueros/vaqueros Arrieros. **131**

venison/*venison* Carne de venado. **188**

vertical axis/eje vertical Línea trazada a lo largo en una gráfica para mostrar el valor o medida de la información presentada. **13**

vertical integration/integración vertical Apropiación de los medios usados en un proceso de fabricación. **485**

veto/veto Autoridad del poder ejecutivo para rechazar una ley del congreso. **642**

viceroy/virrey Gobernador real. **98**

victory gardens/huertos del triunfo Pequeños huertos que se sembraban en los hogares como fuente adicional de alimentos durante la Segunda Guerra Mundial. **566**

Villa de Béxar/villa de Béxar Población civil fundada por los españoles cerca del presidio de San Antonio de Béxar. **123**

Voting Rights Act/Ley de derecho al voto Ley aprobada por el Congreso estadounidense en 1965 que dio al gobierno federal autoridad para revisar las votaciones en los estados y garantizar el derecho al voto. **592**

War on Drugs/guerra contra las drogas Esfuerzo del gobierno para terminar con la venta y consumo ilegal de drogas tanto en Estados Unidos como en el extranjero. **614**

Western Trail/sendero del oeste Ruta ganadera de San Antonio, Texas, a Dodge City, Kansas. **446**

white primary/Elecciones Primarias de Blancos Ronda de elecciones primarias establecida en Texas en la década de 1920 en las que no se permitía el voto a los afroestadounidenses. **539**

wigwams/*wigwams* Chozas indias circulares. **73**

wildcatters/buscadores de petróleo Trabajadores que buscan petróleo por su cuenta. **483**

windmills/molinos de viento Dispositivos que usan la fuerza del viento para impulsar agua de mantos subterráneos a la superficie. **450**

Women's Auxiliary Army Corps/Corporación Auxiliar de Mujeres en el Ejército Grupo de mujeres que ocuparon puestos no incluidos en el combate directo durante la Segunda Guerra Mundial. **565**

wrangler/arriero Persona que conduce manadas de ganado en campo abierto. **447**

XIT Ranch/rancho XIT Rancho fundado por la Capitol Freehold Land and Investment Company, con la participación de inversionistas de Chicago y la Gran Bretaña. **451**

Key to Index
c=chart
f=feature
m=map
p=photo

A

Abbott, E. C., 459
Abilene, 53, 468
Abolition of slavery, 206, *f206,* 363, 374
abolitionists, 292, 373
Abrego, Gaspar Flores de, 171
absolute location, 9
academies, 289
Ackerman, C. W., 369
Adair, Christia, 513, 578, 590, *p590*
Adair, John, 450
Adams, Andy, *f446*
Adams, John, 612
Adams, John Quincy, 315, 612
Adams–Onís Treaty, *m141,* 142, 147
Adelsverein, 282
ad interim government, 242, 260
adobe, 79, *p79,* 80
aerospace industry, 569, 596–98, *f598;*
  effects of scientific and technological
  innovations on, 596–598; and impact on
  international markets, 598; and impact
  on local markets, 569, 596–98; and
  impact on national markets, 598
Affleck, Thomas, 349
Africa, 90, 107
African Americans: and African traditions, 360–361, *f361;* cattle ranching
  and, 287, 452, *m459;* and civil rights,
  399, 400, 538–39, 577–80, *p578,* 590–92,
  p590; and Civil War, 375; and citizens
  rights, 373, 403; in Congress, 655; and
  cowboys, 452, *m459;* cultural contributions of, 31, *f362,* 525–26, *f526,* 619; discrimination against, 539; and education,
  397, *f398, p398, f405,* 510; farming and
  411; free African Americans, 184, 192,
  280; in Houston, 520; industry and 473,
  488, 536, 566; and Juneteenth, 396–97,
  f397, 619; and labor unions, 473;
  National Association for the
  Advancement Colored People (NAACP),
  538, 577, 580; population in Texas, *c34,*
  338, 619; and segregation, 409–10,
  577–80; in settlements, 130; sharecropping and, 410–11, *c410;* and slavery,
  184, 191, 197, 360–63, *p361;* as soldiers,
  428–29, 527–28, *p528,* 537; Texas
  Republic and, 280; Texas Revolution and,
  233, *p233;* and veterans 536–37, *p537;*
  and World War I, 536–37, *p537;* and
  World War II, 564, *p564,* 566
age distribution, 33, *c34*
agribusiness, 469, 615

agriculture: and American Indians, 69,
  75–76, 78–81, 341, 429; in Central Plains,
  51–53; climate and, 467, 547–48, *c547;*
  commercial farming, 469; and drought,
  26, 81, 470, *c547,* 548; in East Texas,
  45–46; and economy, 19, 35, 41, 372,
  469, 519, 520; in Grand Prairie, 51; and
  Great Depression, 547–48, *c547;* and
  Gulf Coastal Plains, 45–50; and High
  Plains, 54–56; and irrigation, 18, 26, 468;
  and natural resources, 35; and plantations, 191–92; and production, 519; production for war, 531; in Rio Grande
  valley, 48; in South Texas, 18; in South
  Texas Plains, 519; technology of, 467–68;
  and teenagers, *f36;* on Texas Frontier,
  188, 191–92, 466–67; and windmills,
  450, 456, 468. *See also* farming, individ-
  ual crops
Agua Dulce Creek, 233, 247
Aguayo, Marqués de San Miguel de, 123,
  126
Aguayo Expedition, 125–26
air conditioning, *f601*
Air Force bases, 566
Alabama, 71, 157, 374–75
Alabama-Coushatta, 31, 342
Alabama Mobile Grays, 235
Alamo, 151, 223, 236–241, *p236, p238,*
  246–47, 523, 634
Alamo National Bank, *f524*
Alarcón, Martín de, 123–24, *f124, p124*
Alaska, 2, 41, 69
Alavez, Francita, 248
alcalde, 131
Alibates Flint Quarries, *f71*
Allen, Augustus, 260
Allen, John, 260
Allied Powers, 530
Allies, 565
allies, 76
alligators, 168, *p168*
Allred, James V., 553, R6
Alpine, 59
Alto, 76
Amarillo, 26, 55, 450, *f450,* 465
amendments, 402–03, 643
American GI Forum, 579
American Indians, 30–31, *m70;*
  Alabama–Coushatta, 31, 38, 342;
  Anasazi, 66–67, 70; Apaches, 74, 81, 83,
  84, 89, 105–06, 126–27, 137, 341; archeo-
  logical finds of, 68–69, *p68;* artifacts
  of, 68; Atakapa, 77; and buffalo, 76–85,
  423–24; Caddoes, 65, 67, 75–76, 102,
  340, *p67;* Cherokees, 203, 233;
  Coahuiltecan, 74, 97, 123; Comanches,
  23, 84–85, 126–27, 134, 139, 157, 167,
  171, 269, 338–41, 346, 416–17, *m84, p85;*
  confederacies of, 65, 76–77; conflicts
  with settlers, 268–70, *m268,* 338–42,
  416–17, 420–22, *m421,* 425–29; crops of,
  69; cultural regions of, 71; culture of, 71,
  74, 78, 81, 85–87; cultures compared, 74,
  78, 81, 85–87; customs of, 30–31, 69,

  p80; demise of, 30, 73–74, 78, 81, 84; disease effects on, 73–74, 78, 81, 84, 105,
  119; and environment, 66, 80; and
  Europeans, 65; festivals, *f430;* Hasinai,
  118; Hohokam, 66; homes of, 73, 82–83;
  and horses, 105; Jumano, 79–81, 114;
  Karankawa, 67, 72–73, *p73,* 87, 96, 117,
  147, 168–69; Kiowa, 23, *p82,* 85, 338–39,
  417; Lipan, 84; Mayas, 70; Mescalero, 84;
  migration of, 30–31, *m70, m84;*
  Mississippians, 71; as original Texans, 30;
  paintings of, 159; Piro, 114; Plains
  Indians, 82–85, 414–31; population of,
  30, *c34,* 76; Pueblo Culture, 79–81, *f81;*
  Pueblos, 79–81, 104, 106, *p86;* religious
  conversion of, 112–13, 120, 128–29; religious practices of, 69, 76; removal of
  from Texas, 341–42; and reservations,
  340–42, *m343,* 427, 429–30; rock art, *f69;*
  and Spanish relations, 105, 136, 139;
  Suma, 114; Tano, 114; Taovaya, 77;
  Tawakoni, 77; teenagers, *f65;* Tiguas,
  100–01, 114, 619; Toltec, 70; Tonkawa,
  83, 168–69, 171, 340; tools of, 66, *p66,*
  69, 71, 74, 76, 83, *p66;* and trade with
  French, 110; Wichita, 77; Zunis, 100. *See
  also* individual tribes
American Party. *See* Know-Nothing Party
American Red Cross, 531
American Revolutionary War, 134,
  p134, 141
Amicable Building, 523
Amor Prohibido (Selena), 609
Anahuac, 207–10, 215
Anasazi, *p66,* 66–67, 70
Anderson, Kenneth, 304
Anderson, L. B., 437
Anderson, Thomas, 378
"Angel of Goliad." *See* Francita Alavez
Angelina National Forest, 46
animal hides, 79–80, 82, 84–85, 96, 106,
  p106
annexation, 258, 295–96, 301, 304–05,
  312, 314–17, 323, 325, 330, 334
Antarctica, 2
anthropologists, 68
antislavery. *See* abolitionists
Antislavery Law of 1829, 205, 212. *See*
  Guerrero Decree
Antitrust Act of 1889, 504
Apachería, 106
Apaches, 74, 81, 83–84, 89, 105–06, 114,
  126–27, 137, 341
Apalachee, 95
appellate courts, 653–54
Appomattox Courthouse, 371
appropriation bill, 656
aquifers: Edwards, 18, 23; Ogallala, 18, 23,
  36, 450; use of, 35, 37, *p38*
Aransas River, 174
archaeologists, 68–69, 74, 76, 116
Archer, Branch T., 231
architecture: early settlers, 186–87, *p186;*
  French, 284, *f284, p284;* German, 337,

f337, p337; mission, *f129, p129;* Spanish, *f129*

Archives War, 299

Arciniega, Miguel de, 171

Argentina, 146

Ariel (boat), 287

Arista, Mariano, 331

Arizona, 66, 98

Arkansas, 20, 75, 161, 376, 385

Arkansas River, 142

armor, 91, *p101*

Armstrong, Neil, 597

Arnold, Ripley, 51

Arredondo, Joaquín de, 145–46

Arroyo Hondo, 142

art: during the Republic, 288, *f288, p288;* in a frontier state, 359, *f359, p359;* modern art, *f575, p575;* mission architecture, *f129, p129;* quilting, 187, *f187, p187;* rock art, *f69, p69;* sculpture, *f526, p526;* and Texas, 626–27, *p627. See also* specific artists and works

artifacts, 68–69

artillery, 530

Ashworth, Aaron, 350, 441

Ashworth Act, 280

Asia, 90, 564

Asian Americans: culture, 31, *p32;* as first Americans, 69; immigration of, 31, 69, 521; plants from, 107; population of in Texas, *c34;* spices, 90, *p90*

Assisi, Italy, 112

Atakapa, 78

Atascosito Road, 170

Atlantic Ocean, 27, 45, 90, 98, 328

atmosphere, 6

atomic bomb, 567

attorney general, Texas, 651

Aury, Louis Michel, 146

Austin, *f650;* artwork on, 176; and Barton Creek, 157; as capitol, 266–67, 600; colony of, 164–67, *m167,* 169–71; and Edwards Plateau, 56; and fault line, 55; history of, 650; and National Wildflower Research Center, 28–29; population of, *c17,* 524, 650; settlement of, 165, 167; water sources for, 23

Austin, Henry, 287

Austin, James Brown, 166

Austin, John, 209–10

Austin, Mary Brown, 162

Austin, Moses, 158, 160–64, *f162, p162*

Austin, Stephen F., 158–59, *p158,* 161–62, 164, *f164, p164,* 213; arrest of, 213–14, *f214;* and a call for war, 217; colonies of, 164–73, *m165;* and contributions to Texas, 158, 163–64, 166–67, 171, 176, *p176,* 208, 211, 214, 217, 259; and convention of 1832, 212; and the convention of 1833, 212–13; debts of, 182; and early conflicts between settlers and Mexico, 203, 208; and Edwards, 203; during the Republic, 259–60; and Law of April 6, 1830, 206; and Mier Y Terán, 204; and role in Consultation, 232; statue of, 526; and the Texas Revolution, 228–29; and Wharton, 296

Austin Baseball Club, *p516*

"Austin City Limits," 585, *p585*

Austin College, 358

Austin County, 170

Austria-Hungary, 530

automobiles, 487–88, 522–24, *p524,* 663

Aviation training. *See* Air Force bases

Avenger Field, 569

ayuntamiento, 130

Aztecs, 70, 88, 92–93

Babylon, 66

Bahamas, 91, 140

bail, 667

Bailey, Mollie, 525

Baker, James, 617

Baker, Joseph, 170

Baker, Thomas, 170

balance of power, 642

balanced budget, 271, 656

Balcones Escarpment, 55

banking industry, 50, 321, 323, 520, 619; boom–and–bust cycles in, 619–20

Banks, Nathaniel P., 384–85

Baptist, 31, 289, 358

bar chart. *See* bar graph

bar graph, 13

barbed wire, 454–56, *f456;* impact on farming and ranching, 454–56

Barret, Lyne T., 478–79

barter, 193

Barton Creek, 157

baseball, 525

basins, 44, 57–58

Bastrop, 161, 171

Bastrop, Baron de, 161–62, *f161,* 163, 168, 173

Bastrop County, 161

Battle of Adobe Walls, 425–26

Battle of Coleto, 248

Battle of Glorieta Pass, 382, *m382*

Battle of Gonzales, 227

Battle of the Neches, 268

Battle at Palmito Ranch, *m382,* 390

Battle of Palo Duro Canyon, 426–27, *p426*

Battle of Plum Creek, 269, *p269*

Battle of Puebla, 625

Battle of Refugio, 247

Battle of Resaca de la Palma, 328

Battle of Sabine Pass, *m382,* 383–84

Battle of San Jacinto, *p225, m253,* 254, 303

Battle of San Juan Hill, 528

Battle of Santiago (1898), 516

Battle of Shiloh, 370

Battle of Velasco, 210

Bauer, Jack K., 345

Baylor University, 358

bayous, 47

Bean, Ellis P., 143

Bear flag, *p328*

Beaumont, 47, 478, 480, 486, 566

Bedichek, Roy, 4, 7, *f7, p7*

Beeville naval base, 566

Belgium, 292, 296, 337

Bell, Alexander Graham, 471

Bell, Josiah, 166

Bell, Peter Hansborough, 324, R3

Belo, Colonel A. H., 471, 522

Belton, 568

Benavides, Plácido, 228

Benavides, Santos, 385

Bentsen, Lloyd, 611

Beringia, 69, *m87*

Bernardone, Francis di, 112

Bexar County, *c14*

Béxar, San Antonio de, 123, 163

bicameral, 644

biennial, 319

Big Bend National Park, 41, *p41,* 46, 57, 59, *p59,* 69, 80

Big Cyprus Bayou, 355

Big Spring, 525

Big Thicket National Preserve, 46, *f185*

Biggers, John, 627, *p627*

bill becoming law, 646–47

bill of rights, 242, 642. *See also* Texas Bill of Rights

Billy the Kid, 526

Biloxi (Mississippi), 125

birthrate, 32–33

Black Codes, 399–401

black Texans. *See* African Americans

Blackland Prairie, 50, 52

Blanton, Annie Webb, 512

blizzards, 27–28

bluebonnets, 29

blues, 31, *f543,* 554

Bob Bullock Texas State History Museum, 612

Bögel, Philip Hendrik Nering, 161

Bolivia, 146, 200

boll weevil, 470

bonds, 463, 662, 664

Bonham, James, 235

boomtowns, 486–87

boom–and–bust cycles, *f605,* 613–14; in banking, 619–20; in cattle ranching, 449–51, *c457, f457, m457,* 459, 548, *f549;* in cotton production, 467–70, *f469,* 472, 541–42; in farming, 466, 467–70, 547–48, *f549;* in oil and natural gas industry, 546–47, 603, *c605, f605,* 619–20; in real estate, 603, 619–20. *See also* free enterprise

Borden Jr., Gail, 170, 358, *f358, p358*

borderlands, 112–13, 115

Borland, Margaret, 450

boundaries of Texas: and the Compromise of 1850, 335, *m335;* and dispute with Mexico, 257, *m257;* and Greer county dispute, 505, *f505, m505;* after the Texas Revolution, 256–57, *m257;* and Treaty of Guadalupe Hidalgo, 335, *m335*

Bowie, James "Jim," 235–36

Bowie County, 324

Bowles, Chief, 264, *f264, p264*

Brackenridge, Eleanor, 512

Bradburn, Juan Davis, 207–08, 210

Bradford, Daisy, 540

branding, 440. *See also* cattle industry

Brazil, 146, 312

Brazoria, 170, 208–09, 303

Brazos Indian Reservation, 340
Brazos River, 22–23, 27, 164–66, 170, 210, 340, 355
breadlines, 546
Briscoe, Andrew, 215
Briscoe, Dolph, 603–04, R7
Brooks Air Force Base, 566
Brown, John, 373
Brown v. *Board of Education,* 580, 639
Brownsboro, 337
Brownsville, 49, 331, 371, *p371, f384,* 390
Brownwood, 53
Brumby, Dr. William, 524
Bryan, William Jennings, 501–02
Bryan–College Station, 49
buckskin, 187
Buddhism, 31
budget, state, 655–57, *c656*
Buena Vista, *m331, 333*
buffalo, 29, 76, 77–85, 101, 105–06, *f424*
Buffalo Bayou, Brazos, and Colorado Railway, 356
buffalo guns, 423
buffalo soldiers, 428–29, 527–28, *p528*
Bugbee, Thomas Sherman, 450
Bullock, Bob, 612
Bunton, Mary, 447
Burch, Jack, 20
Burleson, Albert Sidney, 531
Burleson, Edward, 229–30, 303–04
Burnet, David G., 175, 242, *f257, p257,* 265, 374, R2
Burns, Tommy, 525
Bush, Barbara, 613
Bush, George H. W., 608, 613–15, *p613,* 633
Bush, George W., 609, 615–618, *f615, p615, p616,* 632, R7
business. *See* economy
Bustamante, Anastacio, 209–10
Butterfield Overland Mail Company, 354
Byars, Lula, 539

Cabeza de Vaca, Álvar Núñez, 95–98, *f97, p97*
cactus, 28, 58
Caddo, 65, 67, *p67,* 75–78, *f77,* 102, 340
Caddoan mounds, *f76*
Caddo Lake, 19, *p19,* 77–78, 355
Caldwell, Mathew, 269
California, 93, 111, 137, 158, 179, 312, 330, 333, 339–40, 441, 521
Camino Real. *See* El Camino Real
Camp Logan, 530
Camp MacArthur, 530
Camp Travis, 530
Campbell, Thomas M., 505, 509, R5
Canada, 12, 50, 82, 84, 115, 117, 136, 205, 449
Canadian River, 22
Canary Islands, 97, 111, 124, 130
canyons, 21, 44, 55–57, 59, 69–70, 101
capitals of Texas, 260, 266–67

Capitol building, 600
Capitol Freehold Land and Investment Company, 451
Caprock Escarpment, 54, 55, 101, 297, 298
Cárdenas, García López de, 100
Caribbean Islands, 91, 93
Carl of Solms–Braunfels, Prince, 282–83
Carnegie, Andrew, 526
carpetbaggers, 405
Carranza, Venustiano, 529
Carson, Samuel P., 242
cartographers, cartography, 10, *f95*
Cass, Lewis, 322
Castañeda, Pedro de, 101, 106
Castro, Henri, 284, 288
Castroville, 284
Catholicism, 31, 98, 104, 112–13, 120, 126–28, 162, 165, 172–73, 281, 289, 323, 358. *See also* missions
Catlin, George, 159
cattle industry, *m11,* 36, 41, 43, 45, 49, 51, 53–55, 58, 105, *m107,* 126, 140, 437, *m445, f457, m457,* 520; and African Americans, 287, 350, 452, *m459;* art of, *f452;* and barbed wire, 454–56, *f456;* boom-and-bust cycles in, 449–51, *c457, f457, m457,* 459, 548, *f549;* in Central Plains, 51, 53; and the close of the open range, 454–56; and cowboys, *f441, m459;* drought and, 547–48, *f549;* in Great Plains, 55–56; in Gulf Coastal Plains, 47–49; longhorn, *p440,* 442, *f442;* and range wars, 455; Spanish beginnings and, 113, 131, 174, 440–41; and Spanish vocabulary, 447, 452; and Tejanos, 286–87, 452, *m459;* and teenagers, *f437;* and vaqueros, 131, 150, *f441. See also* ranching
cattle drives, 441, 443–48
Cattle Kingdom, *m445,* 449
cattle rustlers, 442
cattle trails, 443–48, *m445*
causation chart, 15
cavalry, 228
Cavazon, José Narciso, 150
caverns, 20
Caverns of Sonora, 20
Cazneau, Jane McManus, 315, *f315, p315,* 332, 359
Cazneau, William, 332
CCC. *See* Civilian Conservation Corps
census, 13, 644
centennial celebration, 554, *f554*
Central America, 69
Central Intelligence Agency (CIA), 611
Central Plains, *m43,* 44, 51–53, *m52, m60*
Central Texas, 6–7, 21, *p22,* 23, 25, 36, 521
Chaco Canyon, 66, 70
Charles III, King of Spain, 111
Charleston Harbor, 376
charreadas (rodeo), 145
charts, 13–15
checks and balances, 641–42
Cherokees, 203, 233
Chicago (Illinois), 439, 496
Chicano movement, 593–94, *p594*
Chicken War, 125–26
Chihuahuan Desert, 103–04
Childress, George C., 240, 245, *f245, p245*

Chile, 3, 206
China, 90, 465, 568
Chinese Americans, *f465,* 521, *f603*
Chinese Lunar New Year, *f603*
Chisholm, Jesse, 445
Chisholm Trail, 445–46, 526
Chisos Mountains, 58
cholera, 159
Christianity, 91
churches, 31, *f31, p31,* 110. *See also* missions, religion
CIA. *See* Central Intelligence Agency
Cíbola. *See* Seven Cities of Gold
Cinco de Mayo, 625
circuit riders, 289
circus, 525
Cisneros, Sandra, 626
cities. *See* individual listings by name
citizenship, 135, 660, 665, 668–70, *f669,* 671, 674; and elections, *f403,* 669–70; and government, *f499,* 668–70; and interest groups, 672–73; and jury duty, 654, 669; and political parties, 671–72
city council, 663–64
city manager, 663
city services, 524, 664
civic responsibility: and involvement in government, *f499,* 668–70; and voting, *f403,* 668–70
civil law, 653
civil rights, 399
Civil Rights Act of 1866, 400
Civil Rights Act of 1964, 592
civil rights movement, 608
Civil War: battles in Texas, 381–85, *m382;* battles outside of Texas, 376, 379–80, *m379,* 389–90; and the confederate states, *m374;* and cotton diplomacy, 378–79; definition of, 376; effects on Texas, 391; and emancipation, 396–97; end of, 389–90, 437, 638; events leading to, 372–75; and Fort Sumter, 370; and secession, 374–75, *m393;* soldiers in, 369–70, *f380;* start of, 376, 442; and trade, 378, *f378, m387;* teenagers, *f369;* Texans in the, 376–78, 381–85; and the Union states, 374, *m374;* and Union supporters, *f375,* 388, *p388*
Civilian Conservation Corps (CCC), *f495*
Clark, Edward, 375, R3
Clarke, Mary Whatley, 320
Clarksville, 3
Clay, Henry, 316, 335, *p335*
Clements, William "Bill," 406, 604, 610, *p654,* R7
Cliburn, Van, 627
climate: and elevation, 25; and humidity, 25; and landforms, 6; patterns of, 24–25; and precipitation, 26, *m26;* and regions, 44–50, 58; and vegetation, 28. *See also* weather
Clinton, Bill, 614
Coahuila (Mexico), 207, 529
Coahuila y Texas, 150, 172–73, *m196*
Coahuiltecan, 74, 97, 123
coal, 18, 36, 49
Coastal Bend, 42, 47
Coastal Plain, 44
Coke, Richard, 406, 409, *f409, p409,* 648, R4
Cold War, 568–69, 614; origin of, *f569*

Coles, John P., 169

colleges, f405. See also universities and specific schools

Collin County, c14

Collins, Albert, 628

Collinsworth, George, 227

Colombia, 3

colonization, 104–05, 110, 115–16, 158, 161–66, 169–73, 175, 179

Colorado, 71, 325

Colorado River, 22, 56, 164–66, 171

Colquitt, Oscar, R5

Colt, Samuel, 159

colt revolver, 159, 328, 339

Columbian Exchange, 105, f107

Columbus, Christopher, 67, 88, 90–91, 105, 108

Columbus (New Mexico), 529

Comahchería, 85

Comal River, 22

Comanche Indian Reservation, 340–42

Comanches, 23, 84, m84, 85, p85, 126–27, 134, 139, 157, 167, 171, 269, 338–40, 346, 416–17

commercial farming, 469. See also agribusiness, agriculture, farming

commission plan, 663

commissioners, 662–64

commissioners court, 662–64

communication, 292, 358, 471, 522, 575, 620–21

communism, 562, 568

Compaq Computer Corporation, 621

compass rose, 11

Compromise of 1850, 335, 373

comptroller of public accounts, 651, 656

computer industry, 41, 50, 598, 614–15. See also technology

Confederate army, 369–70, 376–78, 385, 397

Confederate States of America, 76–77, m374, 375–77, 398

conference committee, 641

Congressional Medal of Honor, 530, 565

Congressional Reconstruction, 402; See also Reconstruction

Congress of Racial Equality (CORE), 579, 591

coniferous trees, 28

Connally, John B., 603, R7

Connecticut, 162, 164

conquistadores, 88, p89, 91–104, m96, f102

Considérant, Victor, 338

constitutional amendments, 664

Constitution of 1824, 195, 216, 231–32, 234

Constitution of 1836, 241–42

Constitution of 1845, 319–32

Constitution of 1876, 463

construction industry, 36

Consultation, The, 217, 231

Convention of 1832, 211–12

Convention of 1833, 212

Convention of 1836, 240–41

Convention of 1845, 317–19

Convention of 1866, 398

Convention of 1868, 403

Convention of 1875, 408

Cooke, Hugh, 369

cooperative stores, 499

corn, 35, 69, 75, 105, 188

Coronado, Francisco Vásquez de, 88, 99–102, p100, 103–04, 106

corporations, 321; See also economy, individual industries

Corpus Christi, 42, 47, 72, 539–40, 542, f542, 566

Corpus Christi Bay, 72

Corpus Christi de la Isleta, 114

Corsicana Oilers, 516, 525

Cortés, Hernán, 88, 92–93

Cós, Martín Perfecto de, 216–17, 230

cotton, m11, 36, 40, 47–50, 53, 55, 180–81, 304, 349, 469–70, 520, 621; boom–and–bust cycles in, 467–70, f469, 472, 541–42; as a cash crop, 348–49, 469–70; and mechanization, 164, 197, p197, 468–70; prices, 469–70, f469, 542; and slavery, 164, 191–92, 197, 348–49, 360. See also agriculture, farming

cotton belt, 349

cotton diplomacy, 378

cotton gin, 164

cottonclads, 383

Council House Fight, 269

council–manager government, 663

county clerks, 663

county courts, 464, 653

county treasurer, 663

court of criminal appeals, 653

courts, 652–54

court system, 319–20, 653–54

cowboys, 441, f441, 444–48, 451–53, m459; and music, f453; myth and realities of, f446, 451–53; stories, f446

creation stories, 78

criminal law, 653

Crittenden, Thomas L., 333

Crockett, Davy, 234–35, p234

crop rotation, 76

crops, 18, 35–36, 47–51, 53, 69, 75–79, 84, 131, 337, 518. See also agriculture, farming

crossroad of natural regions, 44

Cross Timbers, 51–53

Cuba, 92, 527–28

Culberson, Charles, 505, R5

Cullen, Roy, 489

culture: African American, 31, 337, 360–62, f362, 525–26, f526, 542, f543, 554, 625; of American Indians, 70–85, f78; 105, 184, 625; Asian Americans, 31, p32; Chinese, f465, f603; Czech, 30, p30, 31–32, 284, 337, f628; definition of, 4, 5, 618; and diversity, 30–31, 38, p38; and European, m199, 337; features of, 7, 603; French, 31, 284, f284; German, 31–32, 184, f188, 282–83, 358, 337, f337; 625, f622; Irish, 31, 284, 337; Mexican American, 31–32, f145, f188, f529, 625–26, 628; Polish, 284; popular of, 572, 574–75; Pueblo, f81; regions of Texas, m199; and Swedish, 359; Tejano, 31–32, f175, 184, 187–88, m199, 281, 625–26, 628, f628; Texas Culture, m199, 288, 359, 542–43, 554, 625–28; and Wends, 337

Cumberland River, 71

Cumings, Rebekah, 170

Cummins, Tempie, 396

Cuney, Norris Wright, 409–10

Cunningham, Minnie Fisher, 512

Cunningham, Walter, 597, f597, p597

currency. 304; See also red backs

customs duties, 205

Cyclone Pete's Matrimony (film), 526

Czech, p30, 30–32, 337, 521

Dairy and Food Commission, 509

Dallas, f287; in Blackland Prairie, 50; census in, 13; economy of, 50, 287; Elm Street in, 523; Federal Reserve banks in, 50, 520; history of, 287; Neiman Marcus in, 517; population of, c17, 32, 524; and railroads, m463, 464–65; relative location of, 9; streetlights in, 523; transit system in, 609, 629

Dallas, 628

Dallas Area Rapid Transit (DART), 609, p609, 629

Dallas Express, 539

Dallas-Fort Worth: as functional region, 6, 614–15; Metroplex of, 50, 53

Dallas-Fort Worth International Airport, 50

Dallas Morning News, 511

dams, 27, 525

Dana, Napolean, 330

Daniel, Price, 571, 603, R6

DART. See Dallas Area Rapid Transit

Daughters of the Republic of Texas, 295, 523

Davis, Edmund J., 375, 394, 402–05, 648, 654, R4

Davis, Jefferson, 375, 377

Davis Guards, 384

Davis Mountains, 58

Davis Mountain State Park, 495

Davy Crockett National Forest, 46

Dawes General Allotment Act, 430

Dead Horse Canyon, 42

death penalty, 653

death rate, 33, 514

de Avilés, Pedro Menédez, 88

DeBakey, Michael, 599, 621, f621, p621

de Blij, Harm, 9, p9

debt, 325, c325

de Bustill, Juan Perex, 103

Declaration of Independence, Texas. See Texas Declaration of Independence

Declaration of Independence, United States. See United States Declaration of Independence

Declaration of November 7, 1835, 231

Declaration of the People of Texas, 232, f232

decree, 205

deer, 74, p74, 76–77, 101

Deere, John, 468

defense industry, 597–98

del Castillo, Bernal Díaz, 92

de León, Alonso, 118–19

de León, Martín, 150–51, 158, 174

de León, Patricia, 172, 174

Dell Computer Corporation, 621

Del Rio, 56

demobilization, 536–37

democracy, 562, 640–641, 666, 670

Democratic National Convention, 649

Democratic Party, 316, 322–24, 395, 402, 506, 603, 609–10, 612, 670–672, 674

Democratic State Committee, 539

demography, 32–33; *See also* population

DeMorse, Charles, 332

de Narváez, Pánfilo, 195

Denison, 464

Denton, 53, 417

Department of Mental Health and Retardation, 651

depression (economic), 160, 535; *See also* Great Depression

desegregation, 577–80, 590–94

deserts, 40, 58

de Soto, Hernando, 102–03, 109

de Soto–Moscoso expedition, 102–03

Detroit (Michigan), 624

Dew on the Thorn (de Mireles), 529

DeWees, William B., 48, 317

DeWitt, Green, 158, 174

Dia del Rio, 668

Díaz, Porfirio, 528

Dickinson, Almaron, 236

Dickinson, Susanna, 239, 247, *f247, p247*

dictator, 528

Diez y Seis de Septiembre, f145

diplomacy, 142

direct democracy, 664

Director of Homeland Security, 618

diseases, 73–74, 78, 81, 84, 105, 107, 119, 127, 159, 524. *See also* Columbian Exchange

district courts, 653

districts, 644

diversity. *See* culture

Dobie, J. Frank, 554, *f555, p555*

Dodge City (Kansas), 446

dogtrot cabins, 186–87, *p186*

Dolores (Mexico), 144

Dowling, Richard, 383, *f383, p383*

Dred Scott **decision,** 373

Driscoll, Clara, 512

drought, 7, 26, 79, 81, 168, 341, 547–48, *f549*

dry farming, 467–68

duels, 321, *f321*

due process, 666

Dullnig, George, 479

Dust Bowl, 547–48, *f549, m549*

Dutch, 161

Dyess Air Force Base, 569

Dyrenforth, General Robert St. G., 467

Eagle Pass, 339

Eagle Pass (Cazneau), 359

Earp, Wyatt, 439

East Texas, 22, 26, 28, 35, 40, 42, 68, 119, 122–24, 126, 129, 137–38

Eastern Cross Timbers, 52

Eastern Europe, 568

Eberly, Angelina, 299

Economic Opportunity Act, 588

economy: and agriculture, 19, 35, 41, 372, 469, 519–20; and banks, 320, 619–20; of the Central Plains, 51–53; and Civil War, 378, 386–87, 391; of Dallas, 50; and debt, 325; and depression, 160, 535, 544–45; diversifying, 620–21; downturn in, 438, 619–20; and employment, 617; and expenses, *c307;* and exports, *c219;* of Fort Worth, 51; free enterprise, 192, 286–87, 350–51, *f352,* 354, 443–44, 457, 479–81; and geography, 3; and globalization, 631; of the Great Plains, 55–56; of the Gulf Coastal Plain, 45, 47–50; and high–tech industry, 56, 598–99, 602, 620; of Houston, 47, 601; and immigration, 31, 517; impacts on, 38, 516, 544–54; and industry, 520, 598–99; of the Intermountain Basins and Plateaus, 58; and oil and gas industry, 46–47, 49, 53, 485–86, 603, 605; and railroad, *c466;* of San Antonio, 122; and service industry, 58, 602, 623; and Spain, 93; and timber industry, 40, 45; and tourism, 58; and weather, 7, 27; and World War I, 531, 536–37; and World War II, 566, 572–73. *See also* cattle industry, farming, free enterprise, ranching

ecosystem, 7

Edison, Thomas, 460

education: in Age of Reform, 496, 499, 509–10; and civil rights efforts, 579–80; in colonial Texas, 172, 180, 189–90; in early statehood, 357–58; and Freedmen's Bureau, 397–98, *f398;* and GI Bill of Rights, 570; during late 1900s, 629–30, 657; during Reconstruction, 395, 397–98, 404–05, 409; in the Republic of Texas, 276, 289, *f289,* 292

Edwards, Benjamin, 203

Edwards, Haden, 175, 200, 202–03

Edwards Aquifer, 23

Edwards Plateau, 21, *c21, m43,* 54, *m55,* 55–56, 83

Eighteenth Amendment, 512

Eisenhower, Dwight D., 565, 569, *f570, p570,* 603

El Alabado, 128

El Camino Real, 124, 131, 170. *See also* Old San Antonio Road

El Degüello, 239

elections, 321, 539, 669–70

Electra, 491

electricity, 518, 522–23

elevation, 25, 57, *c21*

Elliott, Charles, 327

Ellis, Richard, 240

Ellis County courthouse, *p667*

Ellis Island, 660

Elms, Henry, 369

El Niño, 25

El Paso, 8, 58–59, 129, 150, 338, 340, 464, 520, 526, 529, 625, 668

Emancipation Proclamation, 371, 394, 625

eminent domain, 667

employment, 623. *See also* occupations

empresarios, 173–76, 178

Enchanted Rock, 333

endangered species, 19, 29, 59

energy resources, 36–37

England. *See* Great Britain

English Common Law, 642

English language, 668

"The Entertainer" (Joplin), 525

entrepreneur, 348, 445, 483

environment: and ecosystems, 7; and industrialization, 630; influences on, 4, 6, 29; mapping, *m11;* and population, 630; and society, 7–8

Environmental Protection Agency (EPA), 630

EPA. *See* Environmental Protection Agency

epidemics, 105

equal rights, 665

equator, 10, 20, 24

erosion, 29, 54, 56

escarpments, 54

Esparza, Enrique, 223–24

Esparza, Gregorio, 223–24

Estevanico, 97–99, *f99, p99*

Europe, 12, 107, 136, 159, 337, 530–31, 562, 567

Europeans, 31–32, 65, 67, 70, 73–78, 82–84, 90–91, 100, 105–06, 116, 175, 183, *p520. See also* individual countrymen such as French, Germans, Spanish, et al.

executive branch. *See* government

expeditions, 143–45, 147

expenditure, 262

explorers, 88, 93–97, 101–03, 105–06, 110, *m96*

exports, 193

extinct, 29, 39. *See also* endangered species

faction, 217

Fair Labor Standards Act, 535

famine, 465

Fannin, James, 235, 238, 247–48, *f248, p248*

Farmer, James, 579, *f591, p591*

farming: and American Indians, 76–81, 84; and Catholic missions, 113, 119, 122–23; in the Central Plains, 51–53; commercial farming, 469, 518–19, 521; and cotton farming, 40, 47–50, 286, 347–49, 351, 360, 373, 498–99, 541–42; and drought, 26; in East Texas, 35, 45–46; and the Great Depression, 547–48; in the Gulf Coastal Plain, 45, 47–48, 50; in the Panhandle, 36; and sharecropping, 410–11; in South Texas, 35; and tenant farming, 410–11. *See also* agriculture, cotton, ranching

farm life, 518–19

fault, 55

Federal Farm Bankruptcy Act, 535

federal grants, 656

federalism, 195, *f216,* 642

Federal Reserve Bank, 50, 520

Federal Reserve System, 520

felonies, 647

fence cutting, 455

Fender, Freddie, 628

Ferdinand, Archduke Franz, 530

Ferdinand, King of Spain, 90

Ferguson, James E., 506, *p506*, 645, R5

Ferguson, Miriam A. "Ma," 534, *f534*, 538, *f538, p538*, R5, R6

Fifteenth Amendment, 403

filibusters, 144–46

financial panic, 160

Finney, Charles Grandison, 158

fire fighters, 525, 669

fire protection, 664

First Texas Cavalry, 404

1st United States Volunteer Cavalry, 527–28

Fisher, George, 208, *p209*

Fisher, Samuel Rhoads, 260

Fisher, William S., 300

fishing, 21, 47, 71

flags, 148, 258, 318, 328

flint, 71

Flipper, Henry O., 428, *f429, p429*

flood control, 664

floods, 26

Florida, 93–95, 125, 136, 140, 142, 292, 374, 615

flowchart, 15

Floyd, Keith, 668

Flying Company of San José y Santiago del Alamo Parras, 151

folktales, *f362*

football, 516, 525

Ford, John S. "Rip," 332, 339

foreign relations, 294

foreign trade, 295

Foreign-Trade Zones, 631

forests, 21, 28–29, 35, 37, 40, 46, 52

formal region, 5

Fort Belknap, 340

Fort Bend County, 170

Fort Bliss, 342, 529

Fort Brown, 331

Fort Clark, 340

Fort Davis, 57, 340

Fort Duncan, 339

Fort Griffin, 383, 446

Fort Hancock, 569

Fort Lancaster, 340

Fort Lincoln, 339

Fort Martin Scott, 339

Fort St. Louis, 117–18

Fort Sumter, 370, 376

Fort Worth, 9, 43, 50–53, p 329, 339–40, 465, 524, 526, 530, *p530*, 566

Fort Worth and Denver City Railway (FW&DC), 465

fossil fuel, 478

Fourteenth Amendment, 401, 660

France: and colonies in Texas, 110, 115–16; and Great Britain, 134, 136; and Louisiana, 136–37, 141; and Mexico, 619; and New Orleans, 136–37; and Spain, 125–26, 136; and Statue of Liberty, 632; and Texas independence, 292, 295–96, 301, 530; and World War II, 564

franchise tax, 650

Franciscans, 112, 126

Franklin, Benjamin, 111

Fredericksburg, 32, 339, 416

Fredonian Rebellion, 200, 203

freedpeople, 397

free enterprise, 160–61, 170, 352, 572–73, 576, 597–98, 621–22, *f623*; and agriculture, 19, 35, 40–41, 45, 53, 55–56, 181, 192, 219, 286–287, 348–50, 438, 443–59; and high-tech industry, 598, 602, 620–21; and meatpacking industry, 472; and oil and gas industry, 46–47, 55, 58, 476–91, 521, 540–41, 603, *f605*, 619; and railroads, 462–66, 503–05; during the Republic, 262, 286–87; during early statehood, 348–51, *f352*; and timber industry, 471–72

free speech, 660

Freedmen's Bureau, 397, 402

freedom of assembly, 666

freedom of the press, 666

freedom of worship, 665–66

French, 31, 72, 73, 110, 115, 138, 284, 337

French and Indian War, 136

French Legation, 295, 296

Friend, E. M., 491

frontier: after Civil War, 414–31, 438–56; during early statehood, 317–43, 346–359; during Mexican control, 163–77, 180–97; during Republic, 276–89

Fugitive Slave Act, 373

functional region, 5–6

fur trade, 116

Future Farmers of America, 36

FW&DC. *See* Fort Worth and Denver City Railway

G. T. T. *See* "Gone to Texas"

Gaertner, Elizabeth, 507

Gaines, Matthew, 404

Gainesville, 416, 455

Gallegos, Hernán, 88

Galveston, 28, 47, 72, 95, 141, *p146*, 299, 370, 507–08, 521–22, 525, 566

Galveston, Harrisburg and San Antonio Railway Company (GH&SA), 464

Galveston Bay, 66, 175, 207

Galveston Island, 146–47

Galveston News, 404, 471, 522

Galveston University, 292

Gálvez, Bernardo de, 140, 141

García, Hector P., 579, *f579, p579*

Garcia, Lionel, 620

Garcitas Creek, 117, 174

Garland, 50, 566

Garner, John Nance, 551

gas (natural), 36, 48–49, 53, 55, *m482*, 485 651. *See also* oil

gasoline, 487

Gates, John Warne, 454

gem stones, 93, 98

gender, 665

gender distribution, 33

General Dynamics Corporation, 569, 598

general elections, 670

General Land Office, 651

General-law cities, 664

Gentilz, Théodore, 282, 288, *f288*, 359, 441

geographic tools, 5

geographical information systems (GIS), 5

geography, geographers: and conflict, 302; definition of, 4–5, 8; and economy, 3; elements of, 4–8, 38; and exploration, 30; and graphs, 13; and immigration, 30–34; six essential elements of, 8

geologists, 484

Georgia, 71, 374, 377

German, J. L., 408

German Emigration Company, 282

Germans, 31–32, 283, 336, 339, 520–21, 531, 625

Germany, 89, 104, 517, 529–31, 562, 564–65

Gettysburg (Pennsylvania), 371

GH&SA. *See* Galveston, Harrisburg, and San Antonio Railway Company

GI Bill of Rights, 570

Giles, Val C., 381

Gilmer, 628

Gilmer–Aikin Laws, 570

Gipson, Fred, *f407*

GIS. *See* geographical information systems

Glidden, Joseph F., 454

globalization, 631

global markets, 47, 631

global trade, 378, 621–22, 631

goats, 36, 56, 58, 126

gold, 92–93, 95, 98–100, 102, 104, 110

Goliad, 126–27, 144, 149, 234, 238, 248, 284, 299

Goliad Massacre, 248

Gómez Farías, Valentín, 213–14

Gone to Texas (G.T.T.), 183

Gonzales, 158, 174, 247

González, Henry B., 593, *f593, p593*

Gonzalez, Raul, 661

Goodbye to a River (Graves), *f23*, 620

Goodnight, Charles, 447, *f447, p447*

Goodnight, Molly, *p449*, 449

Goodnight–Loving Trail, 447

Gore, Al, 615, 672

Gould, Jay, 461, 464

government: and balance of power, 641; branches of, 319–20; county, 662–64; county commissioners, 662–64; executive branch, 241, 642, 651; forms of, 319, *c663*; judicial branch, 241, 642; legislative branch, 241, 642, 644; local level, 662–63; municipal, 663; role in education, 190, 357, 403–05, 409, 505–06, 509–10, 570, 664; and separation of powers, 319–20, *c320*, 641; special districts, 664

governor, 319, 648–51

Governor's Mansion, *f324, p324, p638*

Goyens, William, *f193, p193*, 233

grains, 47, 49–51

Gramm, Phil, 611, 670, *f670, p670*

Grand Canyon, 100

grand jury, 654, 666

Grand Prairie, 50–52, 566

Grange, The, 499–500

Granger, Gordon, 396

Grant, Ulysses S., 394, *p390*, 402–03

Grass Fight, 229

grasslands, 28, 36, 44, 47–48, 51, 53–55

Graves, John, 23, 626

gray wolf, 29

lieutenant governor, 646, 651
lignite. *See* coal
limestone, 20, 55–56
limited government, 641
Lincecum, Gideon, 28
Lincoln, Abraham, 371, 374, 376, 398
line graph, 14
line-item veto, 644
Linn, John J., 174
Lipan Apache, 84
Lipscomb County, 24
Little Colony, 171
Lively (ship), 165–66
livestock, 36, 41, 49, 51–53, 58, 91, 105, *c107, c109, m107,* 150, 456, 518
Llano Basin, 56
Llano Estacado, 54–55, 101
lobby groups, 672–73
locator map. *See* inset map
Logan, Greenbury, 280, *f280, p280*
London (England), 460
Lonesome Dove (McMurtry), 608
Long, Ann, 147, 170
Long, James, 135, 147
Long, Jane, 147, *f170, p170*
Long, Mary James, 147
longhorn cattle, 440, *p440,* 442, *p442*
longitude, 10
Longview, 46
Los Adaes, 138
Louis XIV of France, 16
Louisiana, 20, 75, 116, 121, 126, 136–41, 143, 160–64, 169, 319, 374
Louisiana Purchase, 135, 141–42, *m141*
Lovett, Lyle, 628
Loving, Oliver, 447
Lowell, Tom and Debbie, 624
Lower Colorado River Authority, 664
Lubbock, 55, 68, 450, 538
Lubbock, Francis R. 387, R3
Lubbock Lake, 68
Lucas, Anthony F., 480, *f480, p480*
Lufkin, 66
LULAC. *See* League of United Latin American Citizens
lumber. *See* timber
Lungkwitz, Hermann, 359
Lusitania, 530
Luther, Martin, 104
Luxán, Diego Pérez de, 80
Lyndon B. Johnson Space Center, 585

MacArthur, Douglas, 566
Macintosh, Charles, 180
Mackenzie, Ranald S., 422, 428
Mackenzie's Raiders, 422
Macune, Charles W., 500–01
MADD. *See* Mothers Against Drunk Driving
Madero, Francisco, 207–08, 528
Madison County, 138
Magee, Augustus William, 145–46, 149
Magellan, Ferdinand, 94, *p94*
Maine (ship), 527

maize (corn), 69
Malcolm, Mary Beth, 671
Malinche, 92
Malintzin, 92
mammoths, 66, *p66,* 69
manifest destiny, 315
Manned Spacecraft Center, 596. *See also* Lyndon B. Johnson Space Center
Manning, Allen, 400
Mansfield (Louisiana), 371
Manso, 114
manufactured products, 351
manufacturing, 49, 52, 520, 602, 614
"Maple Leaf Rag, The" (Joplin), 525
mapmakers. *See* cartographers
maps: of colonies, *m173;* of explorers, *m88, m96;* and grids, 9–10; immigration, 284; insets in, 11; interpreting, *m10, m11;* and land grants, *m177;* and latitude, 10; and longitude, 10; making of, 12; parts of, 10; physical, 12; political, 12; projections, 12; reference, 12; of regions, *m43;* symbols on, 11; thematic, 12, 284; types of, 12; uses of, 9
maquiladoras, 622
March to the Sea, 390
Marcos de Niza, Fray, 98–100
Marfa, 59
Margil de Jesús, Antonio, *f126, p126*
Marshall, 28, 465
martial law, 388
Martin, Albert, 238
Martínez, Antonio María, 148–49, 161–64, 166
Martínez, Benito, 569
MASH. *See* Mobile Army Surgical Hospital
Massachusetts, 180, 611
Massanet, Damián, 118–19
Masterson, Bartholomew "Bat," 426, *p426*
Matagorda Bay, 116, 126, 207
Matamoros (Mexico), 150, 211, 233, 234
matrilineal societies, 76
Maverick, Mary Ann, 299, 350
Maverick, Samuel, 299, 350
Maxey, Samuel Bell, 377
Maya, 70
mayor–council governments, 657
mayors, 657
McAllen, 49
McCallum, Jane, 512
McCormick, Cyrus, 181
McCoy, Joseph, 443, 445
McCulloch, Ben, 269, 332, 378
McCulloch, Samuel Jr., 242
McGloin, James, 175, 226
McGuffey's *Reader,* 359
McLeod, Hugh, 297–98, 301
McManus, Jane. *See* Cazneau, Jane McManus
McMullen, John, 175
McMurtry, Larry, 608, 626
measles, 105
medical industry, 598–99, 621–22. *See also* health care
Medicine Lodge Creek, 418
Medina, 145, 339
Mercator projection, 12
merchants, 90

Mescalero Apache, 84
Mesoamerica, 69–70
Mesquite, 50
mesquite trees, 28, 49, 56, 58
mesteños. *See* mustangs
Methodist, 31
Metroplex, 50, 53
Meusebach, John O., 283
Mexía, José Antonio, 211
Mexican Americans: and cattle industry, 450, 452, 459; and civil rights, 409, 510, 513, 539, 579, 593; and Civil War, 384–85, 388; contributions to Texas culture, 609, 619–20, 622; folklore, 620; and free enterprise, 354; and immigration, 521; and the Mexican Revolution, 529; population, 31, 624–25, and World War II, 565, 568. *See also* Hispanics, Tejanos
Mexican Cession, 334–35
Mexican long–nose bat, 59
Mexican Revolution, 528–30
Mexicans: cultural influences of, 31–32; immigration to Texas, 31–33, 174, 521; Indians, 92, 93; and Texans conflict, 298–301, 529; in World War II, 565. *See also* Hispanics, Tejanos
Mexican War: and California, 330; and cavalry, 331; results of, 334–35, *m335;* and Tejanos, 336; Texans in, 331; troop movement of, *m331;* United States victory of, 333
Mexico: citizens of, 173; colonies of, 104–05, 158, 161–62, 164, 167–69; exploration of, 94–97, 102; and France, 619, 619–20, and Germany, 530; government of, 296; independence of, 135, 146, 148–50, 210, 529, 619; invasion of, 300; and Mesoamerica, 69; military of, 298; national palace of, 333; and New Spain, 93, 124; siege by, 236–48; Spanish control of, 158; Texas as part of, 144, 153, 158, 166–67; and Texas border, 20, 172, 297; Texas independence from, 144–45, 294, 296, 305, 640; trade route to, 50, 56, 58, 205, 520, 615; and United States border, 22, 330–31; United States investment in, 529; and United States relations, 295, 328; and war with United States, 323; and war with Texas, 294–95, 299–300, 315–16, 324, *m302;* and World War I, 530
Mexico City, 93, 97, 99–102, 118–19, 131, 137, 164–67, 213, 298, 300, 333
Mézières, Athanase de, 139
Michener, James, 627
Michigan, 624
Midland, 55, 68, 467, 487
Midland Minnie, 68
Mier expedition, 300–301, *m302, p302*
Mier y Terán, Manuel de, 200, 204
migration, 7, 30, 33, 69, *p70, m84, m87,* 174, 337, 521
Milam, Benjamin, 175, 227, 230
military bases, 49, 58, 334, 342, *m343,* 520, 530, 569, 598
military blockade, 145
military protection, 317
militia, 167, 171, 299
Miller, Doris, 564–65, *p564*
Miller, James B., 213, 321
Mina, Francisco Xavier, 146
Mineral Wells, 53
minimum wage, 535

INDEX

mining, 160

Mireles, Jovita González de, 529

misdemeanors, 647

missile development, 569

missionaries, 114, 126, 128–29

missions: Alamo, 151; along Rio Grande, 114, 121, 127; architecture of, 129, *p129*; Concepción, 110; Corpus Christi de la Isleta, 114; La Bahía, 126, 131, 137, 139; layout of, *p113*; Nuestra Señora del Espíritu Santo de Zúñiga, 126, *p127*; Nuestra Señora del Refugio, 151; Nuestro Padre San Francisco de los Tejas, 122; Rubí's report on, 137; in San Antonio, 110, 123–24, 126, 129; San Antonio de Béxar, 137; San Antonio de Valero, 151; San Francisco de los Tejas, 110; San José y San Miguel de Aguayo, 126, 128; San Miguel de Linares de los Adaes, 125; Santa Cruz de San Sabá, 127; San Xavier, 127; system of, 112–13, 119, 151. *See also* churches, forts, specific missions

Mississippi, 374–75, 377

Mississippians, 71

Mississippi River, 22, 61, 71, 102, 110, 115–16, 126, 136, 140–41, 523

Mississippi River valley, 121

Missouri, 160, 162, 164, 174, 372

Missouri River, 115

mitotes, 74

Mobile Army Surgical Hospital (MASH), 616

mock government sessions, *p672*

Moctezuma II, 92, 93

mohair, 36, 56

Molina, Miguel de, 126

Monahans, 2

monarchs, 110

Monks Mound, 71

monopoly, 503

Monterrey (Mexico), 33

Montgomery (Alabama), 375

Moody, Dan, 538, R6

Moore, Edwin W., 298

Moore, John H., 269

Morelos y Pavón, José María, 148

Morfi, Juan Agustín, 134, 141

Morfit, Henry, 295

Morgan, James, 304

Morse, Samuel, 292

Moscoso Alvarado, Luis de, 102–03, 109

mosques, 31

Mothers Against Drunk Driving (MADD), 673

Motorola, 621

mountains, 21, 44, 557–58. *See also* specific mountain ranges

Mount Everest, 3

movies, 526

mud volcanoes, 119

Muldoon, Michael, 176, *p189*

multigenerational families, *p33*

Munich (Germany), 526

municipalities, 664

Murad, Dr. Ferid, 621

Murchison, Clint, 541

Murphy, Audie, 562, *p562*, 565–66

Murrah, Pendleton, 387, R3

museums, 526

music: blues, 31, 542–43, 627–28; classical, 627; country, 628; folk, 627; jazz, 31, 534, 542, 621; polka, 31; popular, 621; ragtime, 31, 525; rap, 627; Tejano, 627–28

Mussolini, Benito, 564

mustangs, 105, *p105*, 143. *See also* horses

NAACP. *See* National Association for the Advancement of Colored People

Nacogdoches, 134, 138–39, 145, 147, 149, *p203*, 210, 212

NAFTA. *See* North American Free Trade Agreement

Nagasaki, 567

Narrative of Álvar Núñez Cabeza de Vaca, The, 96–97

Narváez, Pánfilo de, 95, 97, 102

NASA. *See* National Aeronautics and Space Administration

Natchez (Mississippi), 147

Natchitoches (Caddo), 76

Natchitoches (Louisiana), 125, 142, 164

Nation, Carry, 511

National Aeronautics and Space Administration (NASA), 596–97

National Association for the Advancement of Colored People (NAACP), 538, 577

National Colonization Law of 1824, 172

National Guard, 536, 546

National Parks, 59, *m61*, 495

National Wildflower Research Center, 28–29

Native Americans. *See* American Indians, Paleo–Indians

native plants, 28–29, 59, 74. *See also* plants, vegetation

natural gas. *See* gas (natural)

natural regions, 44

natural resources: and agriculture, 35; caverns, 20; coal, 18; demands on, 8; energy, 36–37; of Grand Prairie, 52; oil, 18, *p38*; and timber, 35

Nava, Pedro de, 255

naval bases, 566

Navarro, José Antonio, 148, 174, 206, 281, *p281*, 297–98, 319

Navarro County, 518

Neches River, 22, 46, 119

Neff, Pat, 537, 652, R5

Neighbors, Robert S., 342

Neiman, Abraham Lincoln, 520

Neiman, Carrie Marcus, 520, *p520*

Neiman Marcus department store, 517, 520

Nelson, Willie, 585, *p585*, 628

Netherlands, 161, 292, 296, 337

Neutral Ground, 142

neutrality, 530

New Braunfels, 32, 283, 625

New Deal, Texas and the, 550–53

New England, 456

New Mexico, 20–23, 57–58, 66, 70, 79, 81, 84, 98, 100, 103–06, 114–15, 297–98, 323, 333

New Orleans, 110, 136, 146, 164, 165, 294, 314, 402, 466

New Spain, 93, 98, 103–04, 115, 120–23, 131, 137, 143, 162

New York City, 315, 460, 507, 538, 627

New York Stock Exchange. *See* stock market

New Zealand, 497

newspapers, 358, 519, 666

Ney, Elizabet, 526, *f526*

Nile River, 2

Nimitz, Chester W., 565

Niña (ship), 90

Nineteenth Amendment, 512

Nixon, Lawrence A., 539

Nixon, Richard, 603

Nobel Prize, 622

Nocona, Peta, 422

Nolan, Philip, 135, 143–44

nomads, 72, 79, 105

nonrenewable resources, 36

nonviolent resistance, 578

North Africa, 567

North America, 91, 93, 99, *m133*, 136–37, *m137*

North American Free Trade Agreement (NAFTA), 205, 608, 622, 632

North Carolina, 376

North Korea, 568

North Pole, 10, 12, 20, 24

North Texas, 7, 21–22, 42–43

northers, 25

Nueces County, 449, 540

Nueces River, 22, 175, 260, 330–31

Nuestra Señora del Espíritu Santo de Zúñiga, 126, *p127*

Nuestra Señora del Pilar de Adaes (presidio), 126

Nuestra Señora del Refugio, 151

Nuestro Padre San Francisco de los Tejas, 122

Obnoxious Acts, 405

O'Connor, Sandra Day, 639

occupations, *c623*. *See also* employment

ocean, 78

O'Daniel, W. Lee, 553, R6

Odessa, 55, 487, 568

Office of Budget and Planning, 655

Ogallala Aquifer, 18, 23, 36, 55, 450, 541

O. Henry. *See* Henry, O.

Ohio, 115, 441

Ohio River valley, 136

oil: boom and bust, 480–81, 486, 488–89, 496, 619; in Central Texas, 482, 484; companies, 491, 619–20; drilling, 485, 488; in East Texas, 482, 540–41; and economy, 46, 485–86, 605; fields, 540, 613, *m482*; in the Gulf Coast, 478–83; and horizontal integration, *c484*, 485; in North Texas, 482–84; in the Panhandle, 482, 484; prices, *c605*; production, *c491*; refinery, 479; in South Texas, 482, 484; and Spindletop, 479–83, 486, 491;

R48 Index

supplies of, 18, 36, 46–49, 53, 55, 58, 102, 516, 520–21, 531, 569, 645; and vertical integration, c484, 485; and West Texas, 482, 484; and wildcatters, 483, 485

Oklahoma, 20, 71, 76–77, 323, 342, 541

"Old Chisholm Trail," 453

Old San Antonio Road, 170–71. *See also* El Camino Real

Old Three Hundred, 169–70

Old Yeller (Gipson), f407

Olivares, Antonio de San Buenaventura y, 123

Oñate, Juan de, 89, 103–04, 106, 108

OPEC. *See* Organization of Petroleum Exporting Countries

open range. *See* ranges

Operation Desert Storm, 614

Orbison, Roy, 575

ordinances, 658

Oregon Trail, 292

Organization of Petroleum Exporting Countries (OPEC), 603–04

O'Sullivan, John, 315

outlaws, 182

override, 642

Owen Falls Reservoir (Uganda), 19

PAC. *See* political action committee

Pacific Ocean, 94, 328

Padre Island, 6, 48, 88

Paleo–Indians, 69

Palm, Swante, 359

Palmetto State Park, 119

Palmito Ranch, 390

Palo Alto, 328, 331

Palo Duro Canyon, 54, 101, 108, p426, 427, 450

Panama Canal, 517

Pancho Villa. *See* Villa, Francisco "Pancho"

Panhandle: Coronado in, 88; explorers in, 101, 104, 106; farming in, 36; and High Plains, 54; name of, 42; de Oñate in, 89; as perceptual region, 6; plains of, 21; population of, 520; ranches on, 450; vegetation of, 28; weather of, 24–28

Panic of 1819, 160, 182

Panic of 1837, 262

panthers, 184

Papadakis, James, 20

Paraguay, 97

pardon, 644

Parker, Cynthia Ann, 422, p422

Parker, Quanah, p415, 422, 425, 427

parks, 19

Parrilla, Colonel Diego Ortiz, 136

party platform, 665

Pastry War, 298

Pearl Harbor (Hawaii), 562, 564–65

Pease, Elisha M., 323, f323, p323, 324, 357, 374, R3

Pecos River, 22, 44, 58

Peñalosa, Diego de, 115

Pennybacker, Anna, 153

Pensacola Bay, 125

Pentagon, 616

People's Party. *See* Populist Party

perceptual region, 6

peregrine falcon, 59

Permanent School Fund, 323

Permanent University Fund, 489

Permian Basin, 484

Perry, Henry, 146

Perry, Rick, 612, 629, p641, R7

Pershing, John "Black Jack," 528–29

Persian Gulf War. *See* Gulf War

petition, 242

petit jury, 654

Petri, Friedrich Richard, f341, 359

petrochemical industry, 47, 488, 569

petroleum. *See* oil

Petticoat Lobby, 512–13

philanthropy, 489

Phillip II, King of Spain, 104

Phillippines, 94, 528, 566

physical maps, 12

physical systems, 8

pie chart, 14–15

Piedras, José de las, 210

Pig War, 296

Pike, Zebulon, 142

Pilgrim, Thomas J., 181

Pineda, Alonso Álvarez de, 88, 94–95

Piney Woods, 28, 40, 45–47, 49, 138, 176, 471

Pinta (ship), 90

Piper, Edward, 441

pirates, 146

Piro, 114

Pizarro, Francisco, 88

places and regions, 8

plains, 21, 106

Plains cultural region, 71, 81–83, p86

Plains Indians, 82–85, 414–31. *See also* American Indians

Plan de San Diego, 529

Plano, 50

plantation, 170, 286, 361

planters, 349

plants (native), 28–29, 59, 79, 107

plants (non–native), 105, 107, c107, m107

plateaus, 21, 44, 57, m58

platform, 502

plaza, 80

plumbing, 518

Point Bolivar, 147

poison gas, 530

Poison Springs (Arkansas), 385

Poland, Polish, 284, 337, 521, 562, 564

police protection, 657–58, 669

political action committee (PAC), 673–74

political campaigns, 673

political maps, 12

political parties, 316, 322, f406, 669, 671–72, 674

politics: African Americans and, 394, 402, 404, 408–09, 590–92; Asian Americans and, 639; during Civil War, 387; during early statehood, 321–24, 374–75; during

Great Depression, 550–53; Mexican Americans and, 499, 510, 513, 593, 661; in the 1920s, 538; after Reconstruction, 455, 499–511; during Reconstruction, 398–409; in the Republic, 259–60, 265, 271, 303–04; after World War II, 570–71, 603–04, 613–15

Polk, James K., 316–17, 330–31, 333–34

Polk County, 342

polka music, 31

poll tax, 513

pollution, 37

Pony Express, 311

pooling, 500

Poor Richard's Almanac (Franklin), 111

popular sovereignty, 641

population: of African Americans, 31, c34, 338, 625; and age distribution, 33, c34; of American Indians, 30–31, c34, 76; of Asian Americans, 31; of Austin, 524, 650, c17; and birthrate, 32–33; of Dallas, c17, 32, 524, 624; and death rate, 33; and diversity, 31–32, c34; and environment, 31–32, c34; and gender distribution, 33, c34; growth of, 8, c14, c34, 32–33, 149, 182–83, m183, 278, 292, 337, 601, 624; of major cities, g17, 32; of Mexican Americans, 31; and migration, 7, 33; of Panhandle, 520; ranking of, 4, c179; of San Antonio, c17, 32, 122, 149, 624; and urbanization, c533; water demands of, 26

Populist Party, 501–02

populists, 501

Port Arthur, 47, 566

Porter, Katherine Anne, 574, f574, p574

Porter, William Sydney. *See* Henry, O.

Port Isabel Lighthouse, 312, p313

Port Lavaca, 28

Portugal, 98

Post Oak Belt, 49, 176

Potter, Robert, 240, 242

Power, James, 175

prairies, 29, 44

precincts, 656

precious metals, 91, 93, 103

precipitation, m26. *See also* rainfall

precontact period, 70

prehistory, prehistoric, 68–69

presidios, 113, 121, 123, 126–27, 129–30, 137, 145

presumption of innocence, 666

primary elections, 539, 669

prime meridian, 10

Princip, Gavrilo, 530

profit, 192, 443, 447

progressives, 507

prohibition, 511–12

projections (maps), 12

property rights, 320

property taxes, 669

proration, 546

Protestantism, 31, 104

protests, p666

Providence, 315

provisional government, 232

public health, 524

public school, 180, 395, 657. *See also* education

public service, 668–69

Public Works Administration, 551
Pueblo cultural region, 71, 79, 81, *p86*, 103
Pueblo (Indians), 79–81, *p86*, 104, 106, 114
Pueblo Revolt, 114
Pueblo villages, 84, 100, 104
Puerto Rico, 528
Pulitzer Prize, 608, 626
pyramids, 70

Quakers, 419
Quarter Circle T Ranch, 450
quilting bees, 187
Quintanilla, Selena. *See* Selena
Quivira, 89, 100–01, 104

Rabb, Mary, 191
race, 659
Radical Republicans, 400–401, 403
radio, 542–43
ragtime, 31, 525, *f525*
Railroad Commission. *See* Texas Railroad Commission
railroads, 50–51, 323, 325, 356, 460–65, *m463*, 471–72, 520, 650–51; after the Civil War, 460–66; before the Civil war, 356, *p460*, *p462*, *m463*, 469, 472–73; and the cattle industry, *p438*, 444–45, *m445*, 447; and growth of, 356, 462–66, *m463*, *c464*, *f465*; impact on development of West Texas, *c464*, 465–66; impact on farming, 356, 465–66, *c464*, *p468*, 468–70; impact on trade, *c464*, 466, 471–72; impact on urbanization, 464–66, *c464*; land grants and, 356, 463, *c464*; political reforms and, 499–500, 502, 503–05
rainfall, 26–27, *m26*, 35, 45, 56, 58. *See also* precipitation
Ramón, Diego, 121
Ramón, Domingo, 122
Ramsdell, Charles William, 399
ranchers, 150, 350, 437, 441, 451–52, 456
ranching, 26, 36, 48, 53–58, 131, 150, *m176*, 450, *m457*. *See also* cattle industry, individual
ranchos, 113; *See also* ranching
Randolph Air Force Base, 566
range wars, 455
ranges, 21, 456
Rankin, Melinda, 363
Rauschenberg, Robert, 574, *f575*
Raven, the, *f263*
Rayburn, Sam, *f551 p551*, 669
Rayner, John, 502
Reagan, John H., 375, 505
Reagan, Nancy, *p608*
Reagan, Ronald, 608, *p608*
real estate, 619; and boom–and–bust cycles, 603, 619–20

Reconstruction, 397–98, *m401*, 603, 642, 665; African Americans during, 396–97, *f398*, 399, 402, 409–11; Black codes and segregation, 399, 409–10; Congressional Plan, 400–03; and Edmund J. Davis, 402–03, 404–06; Freedmen's Bureau, 397, *f398*; Ku Klux Klan, 404; and military districts, 401–02, *m401*; opposition to, 405–06; Presidential Plan, 398; Radical Republicans, 400–03; results of, 405–06, 408–11; and sharecropping, *c410*, 411
Reconstruction Acts, 401
recreation, 59
recycling, 37
red backs, 267
Red River, 22, 49, 54, 77, 134, 142, 385
Red River Campaign, 385
Red River War, 427
Redeemers, 409
Redlands, 42
reference maps, 12
referendum, 670
refineries, 479
reform movements: during the 1800s, 498–505; during the 1900s, 505–13; in education, 505–06, 509–10. *See also* individual movements
Reformation, *f104*
refugees, 529
Refugio, 247, 299
regions: Blackland Prairie, *m43*, 44, *m46*, 50; Central Plains, *m43*, 44, 51–52, *m52*, 53; Central Texas, 6–7, 21, 23, 36, 521, *p22*; climates of, 44–50; Coastal Bend, 42; crossroad of natural, 44; Cross Timbers, *m43*, 51–53, *m52*; definition of, 5, 43; East Texas, 22, 26, 28, 35, 40, 42, 68, 119, 122–24, 126, 137–38; Edwards Plateau, *m43*, *m55*, 55–56; features of, 6, *m43*; formal, 5; functional, 5–6; Grand Prairie, *m43*, 50–52, *m52*; Great Plains, *m43*, 55, *m55*; Gulf Coast Plain, 21, 25, 35–36, *m46*, 47, 72–73, 94, 141, 164, 168, 484; Gulf Coastal Plain, *m43*, 44–45, *m46*, 47, 55; High Plains, *m43*, 54–55, *m55*; Hill Country, 4, 21, 27, 31, 54, 84, 337, 521; Intermountain Basins and Plateaus, *m43*, 57–59, *m58*; mapping of, 43; of Native Americans, 71; natural, *m43*, 44; North Texas, 7, 21–22, 42–43; Panhandle, 6, 21, 24–28, 36, 42, 520; Piney Woods, *m43*, 45–46, *m46*; perceptual region, 6; population of, 58; Post Oak Belt, *m43*, *m46*, 49, 174, 176; Rio Grande valley, 24, 48; Rolling Plains, *m43*, 51, *m52*, 53; South Texas Plain, 18, 21, 35–36, 42, *m43*, *m46*, 48–49; and subregions, 45; West Texas, *p3*, 7, 20–21, 23, 28, 42–43, 56–57, *p104*, 466–67, 520
Regulator–Moderator War, 273
Reid, Thomas Mayne, 359
relative location, 9
religion, *f31*, 188–89, 289, 357–58, 665–66; *See also* specific denominations
"Remember Goliad!", 251
"Remember the Alamo!", 251
Remington, Frederic, 300
remuda. *See* wrangler
renewable resources, 36
republic, 140
Republic of Texas, 256, *m257*, 318–20, 322, 325, 634; and African Americans, 280; and annexation, 305, 314–17; and Archives War, 299, *p299*; boundaries of, 257, *m257*; capitals of, 260, 266–67,

p267; conflicts of the, 268–69, *m268*, *p269*, 273, *m302*; conflicts with Mexico, 299–300, *m302*; economic problems and debt, 262, 267, 270–71, 304, *f325*; and the election of 1836, 258; Europeans, 282–84; foreign relations of, 294–305; Houston's first administration, 259–64; Houston's second administration, 271–73; and immigration, 278–80, *p279*, 282–84, *f285*, *m285*; and Indian Policy, 263–64, 268–70, 272; Jones's administration, 303–05; Lamar's administration, 265–70; land policy of, 262, 267; and Mier Expedition, 300–01, *p300*, *m302*; and New Mexico, 297–98, *m302*; and Tejanos, 281; and Texas Rangers, 261, *f261*, *p261*
Republican Army of the North, 145
Republican Party, 323, 373, 402, 404, 603, 608–12, 632, 660–61, 670–72
Resaca de las Palmas, 331
reservations, 340–42, *m343*, 429–30
reservoirs, 23, 46, 525
residential neighborhoods. *See* suburbs
revenue, 620, 656
revolt, 114, 373
revolver, 159
Reynolds, George Thomas, 311
Reynolds, Joseph J., 644
rice, 35, 47
Rice Hotel, 523
Richards, Ann, 609–11, 649, *f649*, *p649*, 656, R7
Richards, Chelsea, 631
Richardson, 50
Richardson, Sid, 541
Richmond (slave), 161–62
Ricklis, Robert A., 73
right to bear arms, 667
Río de las Palmas, 94
Rio Grande: basins of, 57; big bend in, 59; borders of, 142, 334–35, *m335*; discovery of, 94; and La Salle, 115–17; length of, 2, 22; life along, 69, 79–80, 100, 104, 150, 330, 339, 521; missions along, 114–15, 121, 123, 127; mountains near, 58; pollution of, 662; sediment from, 48; and Texas's boundaries, 297, 300, 331; tributaries of, 22
Rio Grande valley, 31–32, 48, 84, 470, 529
rivers, 21–22, *m39*; Brazos, 22–23, 27, 164–66, 170, 210, 340, 355; Canadian, 22; Colorado, 22, 56, 164–66, 171; Comal, 22; Cumberland, 71; and floods, 27; Guadalupe, 158, 174; and Gulf of Mexico, 21–22; Hudson, 89; mapping of, 12, *m39*; Mississippi, 22, 61, 71, 102, 125, 136, 140–41, 523; Missouri, 115; Neches, 22, 46, 119; Nueces, 22, 175, 260, 330–31; number of, 22; Pecos, 22, 44, 58; Red, 22, 49, 54, 77, 134, 142, 385; Río de las Palmas, 94; Rio Grande, 2, *p2*, 22, 57–59, 69, 79, 94, 104, 114–17, 150, 297, 330–31, 334–35, 339, 521, 662; Sabine, 19, 22, 46–47, 78, 142, 163; San Antonio, 8, 123, 150; San Gabriel, 127; San Marcos, 119; Soto la Marina, 94; system of, 21–22, *p161*; Tennessee, 71; Trinity, 22, 46, 51, 137, 207, 338–39
roads. *See* transportation
Roberts, Dora Nunn, 470, *f470*, *p470*
Roberts, John, 470
Roberts, Oran M. 39, 400, R4
Robertson, Felix H., 377

Robertson, Sterling C., 179

Robinson, Andrew, 166

Robinson, James W., 675

rock art, 69, *f69, p69*

rock 'n' roll, 572, *f573,* 575

Rodriguez, Benito, 495

Rolling Plains, 51, 53

Roman Catholic Church. *See* Catholicism

romances corridos, f131

Roosevelt, Franklin, 535, 639

Roosevelt, Theodore, *p516,* 527–28

"Rosie the Riveter", 566

Rosier, Lance, 45, *p45*

Ross, Lawrence Sullivan, R4

Ross's Texas Brigade, 377

Rough Riders, *p516,* 528

Rove, Karl, 673

Rubí, Marqués de, 134, 136–37

Ruby, George T., 394, 402

Ruiz, José Francisco, 241

Runaway Scrape, 247–48, 278, 295, 342

runaway slaves, 373

Runnels, Hardin, 324, R3

runoff election, 670

Rusk, Thomas J., 242, 312, *p312,* 318, 320–21, 640–41

Russell, Charles M., 339

Russia, 530

Russians, 521

rustlers, 441

Rutersville College, 266, 289

S & Ls. *See* savings and loans

Sabeata, Juan, 81

Sabine National Forest, 46

Sabine Pass, 371

Sabine River, 19, 22, 46–47, 78, 142, 163

Saint Patrick, 175

Salado Creek, 299–300

salaries, *c304*

sales tax, 656

Saligny, Alphonse Dubois de, 295–96

Salt Creek Raid, 420–21, *m421*

salt domes, 480, 483

Saltillo, 196,

Sam Houston National Forest, 46

Sam Houston Normal Institute, 526

Sam Rayburn Reservoir, 46

Sampler, Samuel M., 530

San Angelo, 56, 568

San Antonio, *f122;* capture of, 230–31; and Civil War, 370; early days of, *p123,* 170, 299, 338; economy of, 122; and fault line, 55; founding of, 48–49; history of, 122; immigration to, 521; libraries in, 526; longitude and latitude of, 10; march on, 228–30; Mexican capture of, 145, 293, 300; and Mexican Revolution, 528; military bases in, 520, 530, 566; missions in, 110, 123–24, 126–27, 129; Moses Austin in, 161; movies in, 526; O. Henry on, 519; population of, *c17,* 32, 122, 149, 624, *c17;* and railroads, 463–65; refugees in, 529; as settlement, 8, 123; Stephen F. Austin in,

164; and Tejanos, 184, 192, 281; and the Texas revolution, 229–30; and trade, 49, 192, 354; traffic in, 524; water sources for, 23

San Antonio de Béxar, 137, 148

San Antonio de Valero, 151

San Antonio Register, 539

San Antonio River, 8, 123, 150

San Antonio Settlements, 123

Sánchez, Tomás, 111, 150, 440

San Diego (California), 111

San Elizario, 104

San Felipe, 170, 231, 235

San Felipe de Austin. *See* San Felipe

San Fernando de Béxar, 130

San Francisco de los Tejas, 65, 118–20, *p118*

San Gabriel River, 127

Sängerfest, 32

San Jacinto Monument, *f554*

San José y San Miguel de Aguayo, 126, 129

San Juan Bautista, 121

San Juan Hill, 527

San Luis, 95

San Marcos River, 119

San Miguel de Linares de los Adaes, 125

San Patricio de Hibernia, 175

San Salvador, 91

Santa Anna, Antonio López de, 209–11, *f210, p210,* 211, 214, 225–26, 233–42, 247–48, 298, 300, 332–33; and Constitution of 1824, 209–12, 215–17, *c216;* and Goliad massacre, 248; Mexican war, 332–33; and Mier Expedition, 300–01; and Siege of the Alamo, 234–39; Texas Revolution, 226, 228, 234–39, 241–42, 246–51, 256–57, 275, *p275*

Santa Cruz de San Sabá, 127

Santa Fe (New Mexico), 104

Santa Fe County (Texas), 335

Santa Fe Expedition, 297–98, *m302*

Santa Fe Trail, 297

Santa María (ship), 90

Santiago de Cuba, 527

San Xavier, 127

Satanta, *f419, p419*

Saucedo, José Antonio, 171

savings and loans, 620. *See also* banking industry

sawmills, 193

Sayers, Joseph D., R5

scalawags, 405

Scarborough, Dorothy, 56

school boards, 657

school districts, 657, 664

schools. *See* education

science. *See* technology

Scott, Dred, 372–73

Scott, Winfield, 332–33

Scott, Harriet, 372

Screwmen's Benevolent Association, 473

scrip, 547

Scull, Sarah, 350

sculpture, 526, 627

sea life, 29

secession, 370, 374–75, *m393*

Seco Creek, 339

secretary of state, 304–05, 331, 611, 649, 669

secularize, 151

Sedalia Trail, 444

Seguin, 336

Seguín, Erasmo, 148, 163, 171, 206, 213, 332

Seguín, Juan, 229, *f229, p229,* 238, 281

Selena, 628

Seminole, 2

Seminole Canyon, 69

Seneca Falls Convention, 312, 660

separation of powers, *c320,* 642

settlements: attacks on, 148; in Austin, 157, 165, 167, 169; in California, 111; on the frontier, 112, *m431;* German, *m291;* in Mexico, 103; and Moses Austin, 161–62; in New Mexico, 104; patterns of, 5, 32, 105, 141, 325; population in, 130–31; in San Antonio, 123

settlers, 141, 150, 180, *p181,* 182, *m183,* 341, 346; African Americans, 184, 192, 278, 280, 337; Asian, 31, 69, 465, 521; Czech, 31–32, 284, 337, 521; daily life of, *f169,* 186–90, *f187;* European, 31–32, 184, 282–84, 337, 521; French, 284, 337; German, 31–32, 282–83, 337, *f337,* 521; Irish, 31–32, 284, 521; Spanish, 111, *p132;* teenagers, *f157;* Tejano, 138–39, 174–75, 184, 190, 192, 278, 281, 336, 521; from United States, 88, 160–67, 168–71, 182–84, 279–80, 337

Seven Cities of Gold, 98–99, *m99,* 102

Seven Years' War, 134, 136

Seventeenth Amendment, 507

Seymour, 2

sharecroppers, 410–11, *c410,* 519

Sharpstown stock–fraud scandal, 604

sheep ranching, 36, 56, *m107,* 455–56, *p455, f457, m457*

Shepard, Alan Jr., 597

Sheridan, Philip, 402

sheriffs, 663

Sherman, 50

Sherman, William Tecumseh, 371, 390, *f421*

Shivers, Allan, 563, 580, 603, R6

shrimping, 21, 47

Sibley, Henry H., 381–82

siege, 145

Siege of the Alamo, 234–39, *m236, p238*

Sierra, Joe, 625

Sierra Blanca, 464

Sikh, *f31*

silver, 92–93, 102, 104

Siringo, Charles A., 453, 526

sit–ins, 590

skyscrapers, 523

slander, 666

slave culture, 360–61

slave labor, 360–61

slavery, 31, 130, 164, 169, 181, 295, 312–14, 323, 335, 338, *m365,* 370, 372–74, 394

Slidell, John, 330–31

smallpox, 105, 127

Smith, Edward, 50

Smith, Henry, 232–33

Smith, Jedediah, 158

Smith, Preston, R7

INDEX

Smith v. Allwright, 577–78
Smithwick, Noah, 17, 170, 174, 179, 318, 340
Social Security, f552
society, 7–8
Society of Friends. *See* Quakers
Socorro de Cielo, 103
soil, 28–29, 32, 35, 37, 42–47, 49–56, 75, 161, 176
Somervell, Alexander, 300
Soto la Marina, 94
soup kitchens, 546
South America, 88, 93, 95
South Carolina, 370
South Dakota, 23
South Korea, 568
South Pole, 10, 12
South Texas, 18, 28, 35–36, 42
South Texas Plains, 21, 48–49
Southeastern cultural region, 71
Southern Farmers' Alliance, 500–02
Southern Pacific Railroad, 460, 464
sovereignty, 375
Soviet Union, 563, 565, 597, 633
Spain, 31, 89, 91–93, c93, 97, 101, 104–05, 115, 121, 135–36, 140, 147, 151, 527. *See also* New Spain
Spanish: and American Indian relations, 105, 136, 139; and cattle industry, 113, 131, 440–42, 452; colonization, f93, 112–14, 123–24, 128–31, 138–39; conquistadores and explorers, 88, p89, 91, 93, m96, 99, f102; culture, 131; descent, 138; flag, 148; and France, 125–26; on frontier, 126; and gold, f93; law, 131, 141, 320; on Louisiana Purchase, 142; missions, 110–14, 118–19, f129; and New Spain, 143; rule of Texas, 120, m121; and early settlements in Texas, 123–24, 130–31, 138–39; soldiers, 145; Spaniards, 12, 54–55, 73–74, 77, 80–84, 88, 94–95, 98–106, 110–11, 160; and United States, 140–42
Spanish American War, 516, 527–28
Spanish place–names, f55, f114, f144
Spanish West Indies, 89
spatial terms, 8
speaker of the house, 646
special district, 664
special elections, 670
spending, 656
Spindletop, 479–80, f479, 483, 486, 491; and boom–and–bust cycles, 480–81
sports, 288, 525; and baseball, 516, p516, 525; and football, 516, 525; and horse racing, 276, 288, 525
Sputnik, 563, 596
St. Anthony's Day, 625
St. Augustine (Florida), 88
St. Denis, Louis Juchereau de, 121–22, 126, 139
St. Louis (Missouri), 160
stagecoach, 353–54
stalactites, 20
Stalin, Joseph, 568
Star Film Ranch, 526
State Baseball League, 516
State Colonization Law 1825, 173
state government. *See* Texas government
State of the State address, 650

states' rights, 372, 375
Statue of Liberty, 638, p638
steam power, 522
steamboats, 355
Stephens, John Henry, 447
Sterling, Ross, 545, R6
Stevenson, Coke, 566
Stinson, Katherine, 530
Stinson, Marjorie, 530
Stinson School of Flying, 530
stock market, 534, 544–45
stockyards, 439, 443
Strait, George, 628
streetcars, 523, p523
streetlights, 522–23
strikes, 473, f473
subregions, 45
suburbs, 523
suffrage movement, 512. *See also* voting
Suma, 114
Sunbelt, 42, 600–01, m607
supply and demand, 349, f352, 469–70, 481
Supreme Court, Texas. *See* Texas Supreme Court
Swartwout, Samuel, 304
Sweatt, Heman, 580
Swinford, Jerome, 472
synagogues, 31

T. & B. Gardner, 468
tables, 14–15
tallow, 350
Tampa Bay, 95
tanneries, 351
Tanoes, 114
Taovaya, 66
tariff, 372
Tatum, Lawrie, 419, 421
taxes, 205, 602, 656–57, 662–64, 669
Taylor, Richard, 332–33, 385
Taylor, Zachary, 331–33, f331
TEA. *See* Texas Education Agency
technology, 41, 56, 522–23, 596–99, 608, 620–23, c623, 629, 631, 660; and air conditioning, f601; and barbed wire, 454–56, f456; and cattle industry, 450, 454–56, f456; and electronics 598–99, 620–21; and employment, f623, c623; and the future, 623–24, f625; and geographical information systems, f5; and government, f641; and La Belle, f116; and oil industry, 478–80, 485–86, 487–88, f488, 540; and windmills, 450, f456, 468
Tejanos, 138, 140, 145, 149–51, 158, 171–75, 205–06, 231, p276, 281, 298, 319, 336, 529; and the cattle industry, 174, 286–87, 452, m459; and culture, f175; and education, 190; and the Mexican War, 332, 336; and music, 628 f622; and the Republic, 281, 298; and the Texas Revolution, 206, 228–30, 236, 239, 241, 250–51. *See also* Hispanics, Mexican Americans

Tejas, 77, 119, 121–22, 138–39
telecommunications, 620–21
telegraph, 292, p292, 358
Telegraph and Texas Register, 170, 358
telemedicine system, 621
telephones, 522
temperance movement, 511–12
temperature. *See* weather
Ten Bears, Chief, 418
tenant farmers, 410–11, c410, 470, 519
Tennessee, 212, 235, 319, 376, 377
Tennessee River, 71
Tenochtitlán, 92–93
Tenorio, Antonio, 215
tepees, 82–83
terrain, 2
Terrell Election Law, 507
terrorism, 616; and anthrax, 618
Terry, B. F., 377
Terry's Texas Rangers, 377
Texans for Lawsuit Reform, 673
Texarkana, 46, 465, 516, 525
Texas A & M University, 49, 116, 496, 516, 525, 670
Texas Admission Act, 317, 330
Texas and Pacific Railway (T&P), 460, 464–65
Texas Bill of Rights, 642, 654, 665–67, 669, 674; and freedom of the press, 642, 665–66; and freedom of speech, 642, 665–66
Texas Board of Education, 657
Texas Capitol, 647, f651
Texas Congress, 317
Texas Constitution, 240–42, 319–21, 395, 638–45, 647–52, 654, 656, 658, p658; and the influence of the U.S. Constitution, 240–42, 641, 643
Texas Corporate Recycling Council, 37
Texas Cowboy, A (Siringo), 526
Texas Declaration of Independence, 241, 243–45, f243, 640
Texas Department of Health, 524
Texas Education Agency, 638, 657
Texas Equal Rights Amendment, 581
Texas fever, 442
Texas Folklife Festival, 625
Texas Gazette, 159
Texas government: function of 644–57; size of, f272; structure of, 640–59
Texas governor's mansion, 9, 313, p324, f324, p638, 665
Texas Highway Department, 524
Texas Historical and Landmarks Association, 523
Texas Independence, 292
Texas Institute of Texan Culture, 619
Texas Instruments, 50, 598
Texas Land Company, 175
Texas League of Professional Baseball Clubs, 525
Texas Mortgage Bankers Association, 672
Texas Natural Resource Conservation Commission (TNRCC), 630
Texas Navy, 293–94, 298–99
Texas: Observations, Historical, Geographical, and Descriptive (Holley), f194

Texas Parks and Wildlife, 1

Texas Railroad Commission, 461, 488, 650–51

Texas Rangers, 53, 261, *f261*, 269, 299, 329, 332, 338–39, 473, 529; in Battle of Plum Creek, 269; in Civil War, 377; and the frontier, 338–39; and Mexican War, 332–33; and the Republic of Texas, 261, *f261, p261*, 269

Texas Republican Party, 402, 603–04, 610–11, 665–66

Texas Revolution, *m227, m249*, 324; and the Battle of San Jacinto, 250–51, *p250, m253*; and the capture of San Antonio, 228–30; causes of, 200–1; and daily life during, *f230*; and declaring independence, 231–32, 240–41; early battles of the, 226–30, *m227*; first battle of, 227; and Goliad 227; and Gonzales, 226–27; and massacre at Goliad, 247–248, *p248*; and the Runaway Scrape, 246–47; and the siege of the Alamo, 234–239, *p238*; Stephen F. Austin, 228–29, 232; and teenagers, *f223*; treaties following, 256–57, *p275; See also* specific individuals and battles

Texas Secession Convention of 1861, 400

Texas Senate, 644–647, 658–59

Texas Siftings (Flemmons), 183

Texas Southern University, 627

Texas State Budget, 655–56

Texas State Legislature, 319–20, 610–11, 644–47, 651

Texas Supreme Court, 312, 319, *c320*, 652–53, *c653*, 661

Texas Technological College. *See* Texas Tech University

Texas Tech University, 538

Texas Trial Lawyers Association, 673

Texas Water Commission, 525

Texas Women's Political Caucus, 595

textiles, 456, 520

thematic maps, 12

thirteen colonies, 140

Thirteenth Amendment, 397

Thomas, David, 242

threshers, 468

Throckmorton, James W., 374, 377, 398, 402, 417, R4

tidelands dispute, 571, *p571*

Tiguas, 100–101, 114, 625

Tiguex, 100

timber, 35, 40, 45–46, 471–72, 531

TNRCC. *See* Texas Natural Resource Conservation Commission

Toledo Bend Reservoir, 19, 46

Toltec, 70

Tonkawas, 83, 168–69, 171, 340

Tonkin Gulf Resolution, 589

"Tornado Alley", 27

tornadoes, 24, *p24*, 27, *f27*

tourism, 49, 56, 58–59

Tower, John, 603, 670

T&P. *See* Texas and Pacific Railway

trade, 49–50, 56–58, 90, 96, 139, 295, 297, 378, 520, 622, 631; foreign trade, *f205*, 622, 631; and interstate highways, *f576. See also* economy, global trade

traffic, 524

Trans–Pecos area, *f58*

transcontinental railroad, 460, 463

transportation center, 51

Trask, Frances, 189

transportation, 50–52, 325, 353, *m355*, 522–24, 573, 609, 629, *m355;* air, 530, 566, 569, 586–98; automobile, 487–88; camel experiment, 353; roads, 193, 287, 353–54, *m355*; stage and freight lines, 353–54, *m355*; railroads, 356, 462–66; water, 193, 287, 355–56, *m355*

Travis, William B., 208, 235–38, *f235, p235, f239*

Travis County, *c14*

Travis's Letter, *f237*

treason, 373

Treaties of Velasco, 256–57

Treaty of Guadalupe Hidalgo, 328, 334, 336, 373

Treaty of Little Arkansas, 417

Treaty of Medicine Lodge, 418

Treaty of Paris, 134, 136

Treaty of Techuacana Creek, 272

trench warfare, 530

trial courts, 653

tributaries, 22, 47

Trinity River, 22, 46, 51, 138, 207, 337, 339

Trist, Nicholas, 334

trolleys, 181

Truman, Harry S, 562

trusts, 503

Tulia, 2

Turk, The, 100–01

Turkey, 530

Turtle Bayou Resolutions, 209, *f209*, 211

Twiggs, David E., 378

Twin Sisters, 249

two–party system, 603–04, 610–12

Tyler, 49, 378

Tyler, John, 314–16

Uganda, 19

Umlauf Sculpture Garden, 621

Umlauf, Charles, 621

Uncle Tom's Cabin (Stowe), 373

Union army, 369, 370, 375, 385, 404, 442, 566

Unionists, 374, 376

Union League, 402

Union states, *m374*

unions, *f473*

United Nations, 568

United States, 370, *p374*; and annexation of Texas, 295, 296, 301, 304–05, 312, 314–17, 323, 325, 330, 334; first settlement in, 88; and Great Britain, 295, 328; immigration to, 372; and Louisiana Purchase, 20, 160; and Mexican Revolution, 529; and Mexico border, 22, 330–31; and Mexico relations, 295, 328; oil production in, 18; political parties in, 671–72; Texas entry to, 317; Texas secedes from, 370; and war with Mexico, 323, 328–42; and World War I, 517, 530–31

United States Army, 329, 378

United States attorney general, 531

United States Congress, 141, 292, 295, 316, 331, 335, 397–98, 638, 644

United States Constitution, 242, 375, 397–98, 403, 641–43, 665; and influence on the Texas constitution 240–42, 641–43

United States Declaration of Independence, 240–41, 243

United States Department of Energy, 37

United States Environmental Protection Agency, 37

United States House of Representatives, 395, 611, 661, 670

United States Marines, 529

United States Navy, 146, 564, 566, 613

United States Patent Office, 159

United States postmaster general, 531

United States Senate, 315, 321, 670

United States Senate Banking Committee, 611

United States Supreme Court, 372–73, 505, 562, 639

universities, 325. *See also* specific universities and colleges

University of Texas, 28, 53, 56, 496, 506, 510, 516, 525

urbanization, 7, 522–25, *c533*, 572–73, 602, *f602*; economic factors of, 465–66, 480–81, 486–87, 519–520, 600–03, *f602*

Urrea, José de, 234, 247

uses of geography, 8

USS *West Virginia*, 564

utilities, 664

Uvalde, 336

valleys, 21

Van Cliburn International Piano Competition, 628

vaqueros (cowboys), 131, 174, 286–87, 452, *m459. See also* cowboys

Vara, Sara Castro, 565

Vásquez, Ráfael, 299, 301

vaudeville shows, 525–26

Vaughan, Stevie Ray, 608, 628

vegetation, 28–29, 52, 59, *m107. See also* native plants

Velasco, *m208*, 210

Venezuela, 135, 146

Veracruz, Mexico, 211, *p332*, 333, 529

vertical axis, 13–14

vertical integration, 485

veto, 642

viceroy, 98

Vicksburg (Mississippi), 371

Victoria, 172, 174, 299

Victorio, 428

victory gardens, 566

Vietnam War, 588–89, *p589*

Vietnamese, 31, 33, 588–89

Vigness, David M., 126, 141

Villa, Francisco "Pancho," 528–529

Villa de Béxar, 123

Virginia, 160, 162, 164, 375, 377

volcanoes, 21

volunteers, 668
voter registration, 669
voting, *f305,* 320, 394, 398, *f403,* 538–39, *c594,* 661, 663, 668–69, *c675*
Voting Rights Act of 1965, 592
Voting Rights Act of 1975, 594

WAAC. *See* Women's Auxiliary Army Corps
Waco, 50, 143, 465, 523, 530, 649
Waco (Indians), 77, 340
Waerenskjold, Elise, 363
Wagner, Mathilda Doebbler, 348
Walker, Jerry Jeff, 628
Walker, Samuel H., 328, *p328*
Walker, Walton Harris, 568
Wallace, Daniel W., 452
Wallace, Ernest, 238, 332
Wallace, Miriam Amanda. *See* Ferguson, Miriam "Ma"
Waller, Edwin, 266
Waller County, 170, 369
Walsh, W. C., 278
War Between the States. *See* Civil War
war bonds, 566
war chief, 85
War of 1812, 146
Washington, 296
Washington, Maggie, 518
Washington-on-the-Brazos, 238, 240, 242, 246, 640
WASP. *See* Women's Airforce Service Pilots
water: as basic need, 8; conservation of, 37; shortages of, 7, 26, 79, 81, 523; sources of, 5, 40
Waterloo. *See* Austin
water resources, 23; scientific and technological innovations effects on, 23, 450, 456, *f456,* 467–68
Wavell, Arthur G., 175
WAVES. *See* Women Accepted for Volunteer Emergency Service
weather: and economy, 7, 27; and El Niño, *f25;* and environment, 6, *p38;* and location affect, 24–25; and northers, 25; and precipitation, *m26;* severe, 27–28, *f27; f508,* and temperatures, 24–25; and wind patterns, 24–25. *See also* climate
Weatherford, 53
Webb, Walter Prescott, 53, *f53, p53,* 61
West, the. *See* frontier
West Texas, *p3,* 7, 20–23, 28, 42–43, 56–57, *p104,* 338–40, 466–67, 520;

development of, 282–84, 337, 464–68, 484, *f487,* 520–21
Western Cross Timbers, 52
Western gulf cultural regions, 71
western swing, *f553*
Western Trail, 445–46
Westward Ho! (Kingsley), 329
Wharton, John, 377
Wharton, William H., 212, *p212,* 232, 292, *p292,* 294, 296
Whig Party, 316, 323, 373
White, Mark, 610, 675
White, Thomas, 183
white primary, 577–78
whooping crane, *p19,* 29
Wichita Falls, 53, 484–85
Wichita (Indians), 77–78, 136
Wichita (Kansas), 101
Wightman, Mary, 189
wigwams, 73
Wild West shows, 443, 453
wildcats, *p29*
wildcatters, 483, 485, *f485*
wildflowers, 29
wildlife, 29, 40, 74, *c109*
Wilkinson, James, 142–43
Williams, Samuel May, 169, 216
Williamson, Robert M.,170, *p171,* 216
Wills, Bob, *f553,* 554
Wilson, Hiram, 363
Wilson, Woodrow, 529, 531, 672
Wind, The (Scarborough), *f56*
windmills, 450, 456, *f456,* 468; impact on farming and ranching, 450, 456, *f456,* 468
Wink, 3
Wittenberg Church, 104
Woll, Adrián, 293, 299–300
wolves, 83, *p83,* 101
Woman's Christian Temperance Union, 511
women: age distribution of, 33; in Congress, 661; equal rights for, 563, 595; on the frontier, 170, *f170,* 187, 189, 194, 348–49, 447, 449–50; as judges, 652; and jury duty, 639; in military service, 565; in politics, 509–13, 538, *f538,* 578, 581, 590, 592, 595, 611–12, 649, *f649,* 652; property rights of, 320; and right to vote, 312, 320, 512, 654; and war effort, 566; working during war, 531
Women Accepted for Volunteer Emergency Service (WAVES), 565
Women's Airforce Service Pilots (WASP), 565
Women's Auxiliary Army Corps (WAAC), 565
Women's Joint Legislative Council, 512

women's movement, 512, 581, 595
Wood, George T., 312, 323–24, 339, R2
Woodman, David Jr., 286
Works Progress Administration (WPA), 551
world competition. *See* global trade
World Trade Center, 615–18
World War I, 517, 530–31, 534, 536, 541, 564; origins of, *f530*
World War II: Allies in, 565–66; D–Day, 562; and Harm de Blij, 9; and Europe, 562, 567; and France, 564–65; and George H. W. Bush, 613; and Germany, 562, 564; and Great Britain, 564–65; and Japan, 562, 564–65, 567; and medicine, 621; and military bases, 569; rationing during, 566; soldiers in, *f565;* and Texas economy, 566; veterans of, 568
Worth, William Jenkins, 51, *p51*
Wrangell–St. Elias Park, 41
wrangler, 447
Wueste, Louise Heuser, 359
Wurstfest, 625
Wyoming, 323, 439

XIT Ranch, 451, *f451*

Yale University, 613
Yarborough, Charles R., 39
Ybarbo, Antonio Gil, 134, 138, 139, *f139, p139*
Yellow Stone (boat), 277, *p277*
Yeltsin, Boris, 621
Ysleta, 114
Yucatán, 175, 298–99
yucca, 28

Zambrano, Juan, 190
Zapata, Emiliano, 529
Zavala, Adina Emilia De, 523, *f523, p523*
Zavala, Lorenzo de, 175, 216, 240, 242, *f242, p242*
Zuni, 100

Acknowledgments

For permission to reprint copyrighted material, grateful acknowledgment is made to the following sources:

Bantam Books, a division of Random House, Inc.: Quote by James Farmer from *Voices of Freedom, A History of the Civil Rights Movement from the 1950's through the 1980's* by Henry Hampton and Steve Fayer, with Sarah Flynn. Copyright © 1990 by Blackside, Inc.

Susan Bergholz Literary Services, New York: From "Interview with Sandra Cisneros" by Reed Dasenbrock, accessed August 3, 2001, at http://acunix.wheatonma.edu/rpearce/MultiC Web/Authors/Sandra Cisneros/body sandra cisneros.html.

Barbara J. Bullard, Attorney for Annie Mae Hunt: From *I Am Annie Mae* by Annie Mae Hunt and Ruthe Winegarten. Copyright © 1983 by Annie Mae Hunt.

The Center for American History, The University of Texas at Austin: From interview with E. M. Friend by Mody C. Boatright and Louise Kelly from *Oral History of the Texas Oil Industry.* Copyright 1953 by The Center for American History, The University of Texas at Austin.

The Chandler Historical Society: Quote by Charles R. Yarborough from *The Chandler Area: Its History and People, 1880-1980.* Copyright © 1980 by The Chandler Historical Society.

Joy Chou: From poem "Go Wild in Texas!" by Joy Chou, Sugar Land Middle School from *Texas Parks and Wildlife,* accessed July 26, 2000 at http:www.tpwd.state.tx.us.expo/expo2000/ contest/htm. Copyright © 2000 by Joy Chou.

The Encino Press: From *The Slave Narratives of Texas,* edited by Ronnie C. Tyler and Lawrence R. Murphy. Copyright © 1974 by The Encino Press.

Mark Furr: From "Reservist Called Up" by Mark Furr from *Virtual Texan: Texas War Veterans,* accessed April 30, 2001, at www.virtualtexan.com.com/veterans/memories/furr.htm.

HarperCollins Publishers, Inc.: From "The Buffalo Go" by Old Lady Horse from *American Indian Mythology* by Alice Marriott and Carol K. Rachlin. Copyright © 1968 by Alice Marriott and Carol K. Rachlin.

Houghton Mifflin Company: From "Why I Write About Mexico" from *The Collected Essays and Occasional Writings of Katherine Anne Porter.* Copyright © 1970 by Katherine Anne Porter. All rights reserved.

Keep Texas Beautiful: From "El Paso to Honor Dia del Rio: Cleanup events need volunteers" by Keith Floyd from *Keep Texas Beautiful,* accessed October 18, 2000, at http://www.ktb.org/Dia%20Rio%20Press%20Rel.htm. Copyright © 2000 by Keep Texas Beautiful.

Little, Brown and Company: From "Mustang Gray" from *I'll Tell you a Tale* by J. Frank Dobie. Copyright 1928, 1930, 1931, 1935, 1936, 1938, 1939, 1941, 1947, 1949, 1950, 1951, 1952, © 1955, 1960 by J. Frank Dobie.

Robert Richards for Chelsea Richards: Quote from interview with Chelsea Richards, July 21,2000, about being a member of the Young Democrats Club.

Simon and Schuster, Inc.: From *The Mexican War, 1846-1848* by K. Jack Bauer. Copyright © 1974 by Simon & Schuster, Inc.

Thad Sitton: From interview by Thad Sitton with elderly woman from Bell County. Copyright © 1979 by Thad Sitton.

Time, Inc.: Quote by Holland McCombs from *Fortune Magazine*, 1949. Copyright 1949 by Time, Inc.

Alexandra Villarreal: From poem "Coast...ing" by Alexandra Villarreal from Goodnight Junior High from *Texas Parks and Wildlife,* accessed July 26, 2001, at http.www.tpwd.state.tx.us.expo/expo2000/contest/htm. Copyright © 2000 by Alexandra Villarreal.

Abbreviations used: (t) top, (c) center, (b) bottom, (l) left, (r) right, (bkgd) background

ILLUSTRATIONS

All work, unless otherwise noted, contributed by Holt, Rinehart & Winston.

All icons created by Argosy.

Table of Contents: Page xxiv (tr), MapQuest.com, Inc., xxviii (cl), Argosy; xxxiii (b), Argosy.

Atlas: Page A1 MapQuest.com, Inc.; A2 MapQuest.com, Inc.; A4 MapQuest.com, Inc.; A6 MapQuest.com, Inc.; A7 MapQuest.com, Inc.; A8 (b), (t), MapQuest.com, Inc.

Chapter One: Page 6 (b), Mark Heine; 10 (bl), MapQuest.com, Inc.; 11 (t), MapQuest.com, Inc.; 12 (tl), MapQuest.com, Inc.; 14 (t), Argosy; 15 (tr), Argosy; 16 (t), Argosy; 17 (tl), Argosy.

Chapter Two: Page 21 (b), Ortelius Design; 26 (t), MapQuest.com, Inc.; 34 (tr), Argosy; 34 (cr), Argosy; 38 (bl), Argosy; 39 (tl), MapQuest.com, Inc.

Chapter Three: Page 43 (b), MapQuest.com, Inc.; 46 (b), MapQuest.com, Inc.; 52 (t), MapQuest.com, Inc.; 55 (t), MapQuest.com, Inc.; 58 (t), MapQuest.com, Inc.; 60 (t), Argosy; 61 (tl), MapQuest.com, Inc.

Chapter Four: Page 70 (t), MapQuest.com, Inc.; 84 (bl), MapQuest.com, Inc.; 86 (t), Argosy; 87 (tl), MapQuest.com, Inc.

Chapter Five: Page 96 (t), MapQuest.com, Inc.; 107 (tr), MapQuest.com, Inc.; 108 (t), Argosy; 109 (tl), Argosy.

Chapter Six: Page 113 (b), Argosy; 117 (br), MapQuest.com, Inc.; 121 (b), MapQuest.com, Inc.; 132 (l), Argosy; 133 (tl), MapQuest.com, Inc.

Chapter Seven: Page 137 (br), MapQuest.com, Inc.; 141 (b), MapQuest.com, Inc.; 149 (b), Argosy; 152 (t), Argosy; 153 (tl), MapQuest.com, Inc.

Chapter 8: Page 165 (b), MapQuest.com, Inc.; 173 (b), MapQuest.com, Inc.; 177 (r), MapQuest.com, Inc.; 178 (t), Argosy; 179 (tl), Argosy.

Chapter 9: Page 183 (b), MapQuest.com, Inc.; 196 (t), MapQuest.com, Inc.; 198 (t), Argosy; 199 (tl), MapQuest.com, Inc.

Chapter 10: Page 208 (t), MapQuest.com, Inc.; 216 (t), Argosy; 218 (l), Simon Shaw; 219 (tl), Argosy.

Chapter 11: Page 227 (b), MapQuest.com, Inc.; 236 (t), Argosy; 249 (t), MapQuest.com, Inc.; 252 (l), Dartmouth Publishing, Inc.; 253 (tl), MapQuest.com, Inc.

Chapter 12: Page 257 (b), MapQuest.com, Inc.; 268 (t), MapQuest.com, Inc.; 274 (t), Kenneth Batelman.

Chapter 13: Page 285 (b), MapQuest.com, Inc.; 290 (l), Argosy; 291 (tl), MapQuest.com, Inc.

Chapter 14: Page 302 (r), MapQuest.com, Inc.; 304 (b), Argosy; 306 (t), Argosy; 307 (tl), Argosy.

Chapter 15: Page 320 (t), Argosy; 326 (t), Argosy.

Chapter 16: Page 331 (b), MapQuest.com, Inc.; 335 (b), MapQuest.com, Inc.; 343 MapQuest.com, Inc.; 344 (l), Argosy.

Chapter 17: Page 349 (b), Argosy; 352 (b), Argosy; 355 (t), MapQuest.com, Inc.; 362 (t), Argosy; 364 (l), Argosy; 365 (tl), MapQuest.com, Inc.

Chapter 18: Page 374 (t), MapQuest.com, Inc.; 379 (b), MapQuest.com, Inc.; 382 (t), MapQuest.com, Inc.; 387 (b), MapQuest.com, Inc.; 392 (t), Argosy; 393 (tl), MapQuest.com, Inc.

Chapter 20: Page 401 (b), MapQuest.com, Inc.; 410 (t), Argosy; 412 (l), Kenneth Batelman; 421 (b), MapQuest.com, Inc.; 431 (b), MapQuest.com, Inc.; 432 (t), Argosy; 433 (tl), Argosy.

Chapter 21: Page 445 (b), MapQuest.com, Inc.; 457 (tr), MapQuest.com, Inc.; 458 (l), Argosy; 459 (tl), MapQuest.com, Inc.

Chapter 22: Page 463 (b), MapQuest.com, Inc.; 464 (b), Argosy; 469 (r), Argosy; 474 (t), Argosy.

Chapter 23: Page 482 (tr), MapQuest.com, Inc.; 482 (br), MapQuest.com, Inc.; 484 (t), Argosy; 490 (l), Dartmouth Publishing, Inc.; 491 (tl), Argosy.

Chapter 24: Page 501 (t), MapQuest.com, Inc.; 505 (br), MapQuest.com, Inc.; 514 (l), Argosy; 515 (tl), MapQuest.com, Inc.

Chapter 25: Page 532 (t), Argosy; 533 (tl), Argosy.

Chapter 26: Page 547 (t), Argosy; 549 (tr), MapQuest.com, Inc.; 549 (br), Argosy; 556 (t), Argosy.

Chapter 27: Page 576 (t), MapQuest.com, Inc.; 576 (br), Argosy; 582 (l), Argosy; 583 (tl), Argosy.

Chapter 28: Page 594 (bl), Argosy; 602 (t), Argosy; 605 (tr), Argosy; 605 (br), Argosy; 606 (l), Argosy; 607 (tl), MapQuest.com, Inc.

Chapter 29: Page 611 (b), Argosy; 623 (bl), Argosy; 623 (tr), Argosy; 630 (tl), Argosy; 632 (t), Argosy.

Chapter 30: Page 646 (t), Argosy; 653 (br), Argosy; 656 (tl), Argosy; 658 (t), Argosy.

Chapter 31: Page 663 (b), Argosy; 674 (l), Argosy; 675 (tl), Argosy.

PHOTOGRAPHY

Front Cover, HRW Photo by Peter Van Steen. **Front Matter**: Page iii, Courtesy Larry Willoughby; Courtesy Janice C. May; Courtesy Randolph Campbell, University of North Texas Office of Public Affairs Information Services Courtesy Dr. Frank De La Teja; Courtesy Terry Jordan and Third Eye Photography; Courtesy Barbara Mayo; v (t), © Steve Kaufman/CORBIS; v (c), David Muench Photography; v (b), HRW Photo by Victoria Smith; vi (l), Courtesy Institute of Texan Cultures, University of Texas, San Antonio/HRW Photo by Joseph Armendariz; vi (tr), Wallace Collection, London, UK/Bridgeman Art Library, New York/London; vi (br), SuperStock; vii (t), Texas Western Press/University of Texas at El Paso; vii (b), Laurence Parent; viii (l), The Center for American History, The University of Texas at Austin; viii (r), Isaac Geib/Grant Heilman Photography; ix (l), *Reading of the Texas Declaration of Independence* by Charles and Fanny Normann, Collection of the Joe Fultz estate, Navasota, Texas/Courtesy of the Star of the Republic Museum; ix (r), Private Collection/The Bridgeman Art Library, New York/London; x (t), Dallas Historical Society; x (b), Archives Division-Texas State Library, courtesy Texian Press; xi (t), History Division, Los Angeles County Museum. Photo by Henry Groskinsky; xi (b), Bob Daemmrich Photo, Inc.; xii (t), Don Couch Photography; xii (b), The Granger Collection, New York; xiii, Sophia Smith Collection, Smith College; xiv (t), PRC Archive; xiv (b), © Museum of Flight/CORBIS; xv, Courtesy Texas Department of Transportation; xvi, The Granger Collection, New York xvii (l), AP/Wide World Photos; xvii (tr), David Muench Photography; xvii (br), *Cartooning Texas* by Maury Forman and Robert Calvert, Texas A&M University Press, College Station, © 1993; xix (t), HRW Photo by Sam Dudgeon; xx (t), From the collection of the Yoakum Heritage Museum; xx (b), David Spindel/Superstock; xxi, Dembinsky Photo Associates; xxii (t) Victoria Smith/HRW Photo; xxii (b), Dennis Fagan; xxvii, HRW Photo by Sam Dudgeon; xxviii, Dallas Historical Society; xxxi (t) Rebecca McEntee/Austin American Statesman; (b) HRW Photo by Sam Dudgeon; xxxii (t), Eggenhoffer, Nick, *The Stagecoach*, 1972, mixed media, 14x17, 82.09c.2, National Cowboy and Western Heritage Museum, Oklahoma City; xxxii (bl) Stockbyte; xxxii (br) CPIO Partners; xxxiii (t), Bob Daemmrich Photo, Inc.; xxxiii (b), Sam Dudgeon/HRW; xxxiv (tl) NASA; xxxiv (tr) AP/Wide World Photos; xxxiv (b), *Reading of the Texas Declaration of Independence* by Charles and Fanny Normann, Collection of the Joe Fultz estate, Navasota, Texas/Courtesy of the Star of the Republic Museum; xxxv, S0, HRW Photo by Sam Dudgeon; S1 (t), Laurie Platt Winfrey/Woodfin Camp & Associates; S1 (b), Courtesy of *Texas Highways* Magazine; S2 (l), Texas Memorial Museum; S2 (tr), PRC Archive; S2 (br), HRW Photo by Sam Dudgeon; S3 (l), Texas State Library and Archives Commission; S3 (r), HRW Photo by Sam Dudgeon S4, S5, S6, S8, (t), HRW Photo by Sam Dudgeon; (b) University of Houston Libraries, George Fuermann City of Houston Collection; S9, S12, S14, HRW Photo by Sam Dudgeon.

Section Opener Masters: ; 4, 9, 13, 20, 24, 30, 35, 42, 45, 51, 54, 57, 90, 372, 376, 381, 386, 389, 396, 416, 420, 425, 428, © Laurence Parent; 51, 98, 160, 163, 168, 172, 182, 186, 191, 195, 202, 207, 211, 215, Texas Department of Transportation; 45, 68, 72, 75, 79, 82, 90, 94, 98, 103, 112, 115, 120, 125, 128, 136, 140, 143, 148, Texas Department of Transportation; 54, 103, 226, 231, 234, 240, 246, 256, 259, 265,271, 278, 282, 286, 294, 297, 303, Wyman Meinzer Photography; 330, 334, 338, 348, 353, 357, 360, © Corbis Images; 498, 503, 507,511,518, 522, 527, Bob Daemmrich/Picture Quest; 640, 644, 648, 646, 649, 662, 665, 668, 671, Courtesy of Tx DOT/HRW Photo; 440, 443, 449, 454, 462, 467, 471, 478, 483, 486, Laurence Parent; 562, 566, 570, 575, 586, 590, 596, 600, 610, 613, 624, 629, NASA.

Unit 1: Page lxviii, Laurence Parent Photography; 1, © Bod Daemmrich/Stock, Boston/PictureQuest. **Chapter 1:** ; 2 (t), David Muench Photography; 2 (t), AP/Wide World Photos; 2 (bl), Fritz Polking/Peter Arnold, Inc.; 3 (t), Laurence Parent; 3 (t), Wyman Meinzer Photography; 3 (br), Victoria Smith/HRW Photo; 4 (cl), Wyman Meinzer Photography; 5 (b), David Muench Photography; 7 (t), Peter Van Steen/HRW Photo. Courtesy of Rodney Desmond; 9 (cr), Courtesy of Harm De Blij; 11 (br), HRW Photo by Sam Dudgeon; 12 (cl), MapQuest.com, Inc.; 13 (cr), United States Census Bureau; 17 (bl), HRW Photo by Sam Dudgeon. **Chapter 2**: Page 18 (t), Bruce Hands/Stock Boston/Picture Quest; 18 (tl #1), © Bill Brooks/Masterfile; 18 (tl #2), Digital Image ® copyright 2003 PhotoDisc, Inc.; 18 (tl #3) Digital Image ® copyright 2003 PhotoDisc, Inc.; 18 (bl), SuperStock; 19 (tc), David Muench Photography; 19 (t), © Steve Kaufman/CORBIS; 19 (cl), Stockbyte; 19 (br), HRW Photo by Sam Dudgeon; 20 (cl), Laurence Parent; 22 (t), David Muench Photography; 23 (tr), John Graves, *Goodbye to a River,* © 1960 by Random House, Inc., New York. 24 (cl), Paul & Linda Marie Ambrose/FPG International; 25 (bl), Wyman Meinzer Photography; 27 (b), © Annie Griffiths Belt/CORBIS; 28 (t), Dennis Fagan; 29 (cr), Corbis Images; 30 (cl), © Morton Beebe, S.F./CORBIS; 31 (br), Michael A. Murphy/TxDOT; 32 (t), Kevin Stillman/TxDOT; 33 (t), Courtesy Rosie and Henry Montalvo/HRW Photo by Terry Janecek; 35 (cl), ; 36 (t), Victoria Smith/HRW Photo; 37 (cl), Mark Lewis/Tony Stone Images; 39 (bl), HRW Photo by Sam Dudgeon. **Chapter 3:** Page 40 (t), Rebecca Shepherd/Stock Connection/Picture Quest; 40 (t), HRW Photo Research Library; 40 (bl), Image © Copyright PhotoDisc, Inc.; 41 (t), Laurence Parent; 41 (t), Digital Imagery copyright 2001 PhotoDisc, Inc.; 41 (br), HRW Photo by Sam Dudgeon; 42 (cl), Jeff Foott/Bruce Coleman, Inc./Picture Quest; 44 (t), James Newberry; 45 (cr), Photo by Peter Koch; 47 (t), Stone; 48 (b), © Laurence Parent; 50 (t), SuperStock; 51 (cr), North Wind Picture Archives; 53 (t), The Center For American History, The University of Texas at Austin; 54 (cl), Grant Heilman Photography; 56 (tc), HRW Photo/Victoria Smith; 57 (cr), Zon International Publishing, courtesy the Mackin Collection. Photo © William Manns; 59 (t), SuperStock; 61 (bl), HRW Photo by Sam Dudgeon; 63, HRW Photo by Victoria Smith.

Unit 2: Page 64, SuperStock; 65, Bob Daemmrich Photo, Inc. **Chapter 4:** Page 66 (t), CORBIS/Jonathon Blair; 66 (bl), Rich Buzzelli/Tom Stack & Associates; 66 (cr), Courtesy of Texas Highways Magazine; 67 (tc), Courtesy Institute of Texan Cultures, University of Texas, San Antonio/HRW Photo by Joseph Armendariz; 67 (c), National Park Service/Chaco Culture National Historic Park; 67 (t), Courtesy of Ray Olachia and the Brazoria County Historical Museum; 67 (br), HRW Photo by Sam Dudgeon; 68 (cl), Jonathan Blair/CORBIS; 69 (t), Wyman Meinzer Photography; 70 (bl), Institute of Texan Cultures, University of Texas, San Antonio/Victoria Smith; 71 (cr), Courtesy of Texas Highways Magazine; 72 (cl), Marc Segers/HRW/courtesy of the Baytown Historical Museum; 73 (br), Lino Sanchez y Tapia, Carancabueses, 4016.336, From the Collection of Gilcrease Museum, Tulsa; 74, Biblioteca Nazionale Firenze/Art Resource, NY; 74, Biblioteca Nazionale Firenze/Art Resource, NY; 74 (t), ; 75 (cr), Ken Wagner/Phototake/Picture Quest; 76 (cl), The Texas Archeology Research Library/The University of Texas at Austin; 77 (t), George Catlin, *Catching the Wild Horse*, Oil, 0126.2174, Thomas Gilcrease Institute of American History and Art, Tulsa, Oklahoma; 78 (tc), Superstock; 79 (cr), Bruce Coleman, Inc.; 80 (t), Victoria Smith/HRW Photo/Courtesy Institute of Texan Cultures; 82 (cl), Panhandle-Plains Historical Museum, Research Center, Canyon, Texas; 83 (bl), George Catlin/Smithsonian Art Museum, Washington, D.C. USA/Art Resource, NY; 83 (cr), Bruce Coleman, Inc.; 84 (t), Victoria Smith/HRW Photo/Courtesy of The Institute of Texan Cultures; 85 (t), The Granger Collection, New York; 87 (bl), HRW Photo by Sam Dudgeon**.** **Chapter 5**: Page 88 (t), Scala/Art Resource, NY; 88 (b), Ulrich Zillman/AKG Photo, London; 88 (t), The Granger Collection, New York; 89 (t), Wallace Collection, London, UK/Bridgeman Art Library, New York/London; 89 (c), 1998/FoodPix; 89 (b), HRW Photo by Sam Dudgeon; 90 (b), Victoria Smith/HRW Photo; 91 (b), The Granger Collection, New York; 91 (t), Image © PhotoDisc, Inc.; 92 (t), The Granger Collection, New York; 92 (b), Berlin, SMPK, Museum fuer Voelkerkunde/AKG Photo, London; 94 (cl), The Granger Collection, New York; 95 (t), Cartographic History Library/The University of Texas at Arlington; 95 (b), NASA; 97, Hulton Getty/Archive Photos; 98 (b), CORBIS/Jeffrey L. Rotman; 99 (t), The Granger Collection, New York; 99 (b), The Trustees of the British Library, courtesy American Heritage Library 100, Bridgeman Art Library, London/New York; 101, Hulton Getty/Archive Photos; 102, © David Muench/CORBIS; 103 (b), ©John Houser/XII Travelers Memorial of the Soutwest/photo by Jody Polk Schwartz; 104 (t), CORBIS/David Muench; 104 (b), © John Houser/XII Travelers Memorial of the Southwest/photo by Jody Polk Schwartz; 106 , Jerry Jacka Photography; 109 (l), HRW Photo by Sam Dudgeon. **Chapter 6**: Page 110 (tl), The Granger Collection, New York; 110 (tr), Laurence Parent; 110 (b), The Granger Collection, New York; 111 (tr), Mark Nohl/New Mexico Magazine; 111 (tl), Daughters of the Republic of Texas Library; 111 (c), The Art Archive/Museo del Prado Madrid/Dagli Orti (A); 111 (b), HRW Photo by Sam Dudgeon; 112 (cl), Church of San Francesco, Pescia, Italy/Canali PhotoBank, Milan/SuperStock; 115 (cr), Giraudon/Art Resource, NY; 116 (t), Wyman Meinzer Photography; 118 (t), Laurence Parent; 120 (cl), Victoria Smith/HRW Photo/Courtesy Rosie and Henry Montalvo; 122 (t), CORBIS/Phil Schermeister ; 123 (t), Josef Armendariz/HRW Photo/J.R. Rubio, San Antonio/courtesy of the Institute of Texan Cultures, University of Texas; 124 (t), Institute of Texas Cultures, University of Texas; 125 (cr), SuperStock; 126 (t), Institute of Texas Cultures, University of Texas; 127 , 128, 129 (t), Laurence Parent; 130 (t), Daughters of The Republic of Texas Library at the Alamo; 131, The Metropolitan Museum of Art, Purchase Clara Mertens Bequest, in memory of Antre Mertens, 1992 (1992.1.2). Photograph © 1997 The Metropolitan Museum of Art; 133, HRW Photo by Sam Dudgeon. **Chapter 7**: Page 134 (tl), HRW Photo by Victoria Smith; (tr), Benson Latin American Collection, University of Texas at Austin; (b), The Granger Collection, New York; 135 (tl), Institute of Texas Cultures, University of Texas; (tr), The Granger Collection, New York; (bl), From *The National Museum of American History* by Shirley Abbott, Published by Harry N. Abrams, Inc., New York; (br), HRW Photo by Sam Dudgeon; 136 (b), Peter Van Steen/Texas Memorial Museum; 138, Institute of Texan Cultures; 139 (t), East Texas Folklife Center; 140, US Postal Service; 142, National Archives (NARA); 143, Dominique Braud/Dembinsky Photo Associates; 144, Institute of Texan Cultures, University of Texas; 145, Park Street Photography; 146 (t), Courtesy of the Rosenberg Library, Galveston, Texas; (b), Radeka/SuperStock; 147, The Center for American History, The University of Texas at Austin; 148, The Granger Collection, New York; 150, Peter Newark's Western Americana; 151 (t), Courtesy The Texian Press, Waco, TX; 153, 155, Sam Dudgeon/HRW Photo.

Unit 3: Page 156 (t), *George Allen's Residence* by F. J. Rothhass, 1845, Texas Memorial Museum, University of Texas at Austin; 157, © 2003 Scott Teven/All Rights Reserved; **Chapter 8**: Page 158, (tl #1), HRW Photo by Victoria Smith 158, (tl #2) Dallas Historical Society; 158 (tr), The Center for American History, The University of Texas at Austin; 158 (b), Bettmann/CORBIS; 159 (tl), The Center for American History, The University of Texas at Austin; 159 (tc), Institute of Texan Cultures at San Antonio.; 159 (cl), The Hermitage/Woodfin Camp & Associates; 159 (br), HRW Photo by Sam Dudgeon; 160 (cl), Digital Image Copyright ©2003 PhotoDisc, Inc.; 161 (bl), Laurence Parent; 161 (cr), Digital Imagery Copyright © 2003 PhotoDisc, Inc./HRW; 162 (t), Institute of Texan Cultures, University of Texas/Texas State Archives; 163 (cr), Courtesy Albert Seguin Gonzales; 164 (t), Texas State Library and Archives Commission; 165 (cr), Texas Memorial Museum/The University of Texas at Austin; 166 (t), Courtesy of the Witte Museum, San Antonio, Texas; 167 (t), Texas State Library and Archives Commission; 168 (cl), © L. F. Van Landingham; 169 (b), Illustration by Norman Price, Texas State Library and Archives Commission; 170 (t), The Institute of Texas Cultures at San Antonio, University of Texas, Courtesy of James P. Prowell; 171 (t), Texas State Library and Archives Commission; 172 (cl), Christie's Images; 173 (t), Courtesy Texas General Land Office, HRW Photo by Peter Van Steen; 174 (cl), Institute of Texan Cultures, University of Texas at San Antonio; 175 (b), Daughters of the Republic of Texas Library; 176 (t), David Muench Photography; 179 (bl), HRW Photo by Sam Dudgeon, **Chapter 9:** Page 180 (tl), Texas State Library and Archives Commission; 180 (tr), Institute of Texas Cultures, University of Texas at San Antonio; 180 (bl), Courtesy Boston Latin School; 181 (tl), The Granger Collection, New York; 181 (tr), Picture Research Consultants, Inc.; 181 (cl), National Museum of American History 1999/Smithsonian Institution; 181 (b), Sam Dudgeon/HRW Photo; 182 (cl), 354, Terry Janecek/HRW Photo/Courtesy More Primitives Furniture & Accessories, Austin, TX; 184, © Indiana University Art Museum, Photograph by Michael Cavanagh, Kevin Montague; 185 (cr), © Tom Lazar/Animals Animals/Earth Scenes; 186 (cl), Bob Daemmrich Photo, Inc.; 187 (t), From the collection of the Yoakum Heritage Museum.; 188, Sam Dudgeon/HRW; 189 (t), © Judy Courtwright/Brazoria County History Museum; 190 (t), The Texas Collection, Baylor Unversity; 191 (cr), Isaac Geib/Grant Heilman Photography; 192 (t), Texas Memorial Museum; 193 (t), Art by Charles Shaw, Courtesy Nacogdoches Folklife Center; 194 (t), The Center for American History, The University of Texas at Austin; 195 (cr), Texas State Library and Archives Commission; 196 (bl), Gallery of the Republic; 197 (t), Kim Neilsen/Smithsonian Institution, Washington, DC; 199, Sam Dudgeon/HRW Photo. **Chapter 10**: Page 200 (tl), Institute of Texas Cultures, University of Texas; 200 (tr), Sanchez y Tapia, Lino, Soldado Mexicano Presidial, (?-1838), watercolor on paper, 4016.336 , From the Collection of Gilcrease Museum, Tulsa; 200 (b), D. Donne Bryant Stock Photography; 201 (tl), Doug Kubicek; 201 (tr), The Newberry Library, Chicago/SuperStock; 201 (c), *Democracy in America* by Alexis de Tocqueville. Courtesy the Perry-Castenda Library, The University of Texas at Austin. HRW Photo/Victoria Smith; 201 (b), HRW Photo by Sam Dudgeon; 202, SuperStock; 203, The Center for American History, The University of Texas at Austin; 204 (cl), Bob Daemmrich Photo, Inc.; 205, Frederic Remington, *Drum Corps, Mexican Army, 1889*; The Amon Carter Museum, Fort Worth, Texas; 206, Chicago Historical Society, #X.1354; 207, Institute of Texas Cultures, University of Texas; 208, Benninghoff Foundation; 209, Texas State Library and Archives Commission; 210, The Granger Collection, New York; 211 (cr), Courtesy Camp Mabry Military Museum, HRW Photo by Peter Van Steen; 212, Institute of Texas Cultures, University of Texas, San Antonio/Courtesy of the Texas State Archives; 213, Newberry Library, Chicago/SuperStock; 214, Austin Papers, CN07586, The Center for American History, The University of Texas at Austin; 215, Courtesy James Townsend & Son, Inc.; 217, Laurie Platt Winfrey/Woodfin Camp &

Associates; 219, HRW Photo by Sam Dudgeon; 221, HRW Photo by Sam Dudgeon. **Unit 4**: Page 222, Sam Dudgeon/HRW, courtesy of Texas State Library and Archives Division; 223, Chuck Pefley/Stock, Boston. **Chapter 11**: 224 (tl), Courtesy of Texas Highways Magazine; 224 (tr), San Jacinto Museum of History, Houston; 224 (b), National Portrait Gallery, Smithsonian Institution, Washington, DC. Gift of the Swedish Colonial Society/Art Resource, NY; 225 (t), Texas State Library and Archives Commission; 225 (cl), Reunion des Musees Nationaux/Art Resource, NY; 225 (cr), Gallery of the Republic; 225 (b), HRW Photo by Sam Dudgeon; 226, Doug Kubicek; 227, HRW Photo/Sam Dudgeon; 228, Daughters of the Republic of Texas Library; 229, Institute of Texan Cultures, University of Texas, San Antonio; 230, Christie's Images; 231, TEXAS HIGHWAYS Magazine; 233, Texas Southern University Archives; 234, Texas State Library and Archives Commission; 235 (t), Texas State Library and Archives Commission; 235 (br), The Center for American History, The University of Texas at Austin; 236, Institute of Texas Cultures, University of Texas; 238, *Fall of the Alamo* by Robert Onderdonk, Courtesy of Friends of the Governor's Mansion, Austin, Texas; 239, Benninghoff Foundation; 240, Will Van Overbeek; 241, Courtesy of the Joe Fultz Estate, Navasota, Texas/The Star of the Republic Museum; 242, San Jacinto Museum of History, Houston; 245, The Center for American History, The University of Texas at Austin; 246, R.W. Parvin; 247, Daughters of the Republic of Texas Library; 248 (t), Texas State Library and Archives Commission; 248 (b), Texas Parks and Wildlife; 249, San Jacinto Museum of History, Houston; 250, Texas State Library and Archives Commission; 251, San Jacinto Museum of History, Houston; 253, HRW Photo by Sam Dudgeon. **Chapter 12**: Page 254 (tl), © Bettmann/CORBIS; 254 (tr), San Jacinto Museum of History, Houston; 254 (b), WOOLAROC MUSEUM, BARTLESVILLE, OKLAHOMA; 255 (t), The Granger Collection, New York; 255 (c), Punch Limited; 255 (b), HRW Photo by Sam Dudgeon; 256, HRW Photo Research Library; 257, The State Preservation Board, Austin, Texas; 259, San Jacinto Museum of History, Houston; 260 (bc), Pearce-Moses; 261, Texas State Library and Archives Commission (colorized); 262, The Granger Collection, New York; 263 (t), Private Collection/The Bridgeman Art Library, New York/London; 263 (b), San Jacinto Museum of History, Houston;264 (t), Texas State Library and Archives Commission (colorized); 265 (cr), Department of Anthropology, National Museum of American History, Smithsonian Institution, Washington, DC. Smithsonian Photo no. 79-5058; 266, San Jacinto Museum of History, Houston; 267 (br), The Center for American History, The University of Texas at Austin ; 269 (bc), William Adams, Dallas; 270 (t), (detail), *George Allen's Residence* by F. J. Rothhass, 1845, Texas Memorial Museum, University of Texas at Austin; 271 (cr), HRW Photo by Peter Van Steen, courtesy General Land Office; 272 (t), Courtesy of Pierce and Susan Butler, Nashville, Temmessee. Photo: Sam Ratcliffe, SMU Hamon Arts Library.; 273 (cr), San Jacinto Museum of History, Houston; 275 (t), Library of Congress; 275 (b), HRW Photo by Sam Dudgeon. **Chapter 13**: Page 276 (tl), Zon International Publishing, courtesy the Esterly Collection. Photo © William Manns; (tr), Courtesy of the Witte Museum, San Antonio, Texas 276 (bl), HRW Photo/Josef Armendariz/Courtesy of The Institute of Texas Cultures, University of Texas at San Antonio 277 (tl), Harley Murray; 277 (tr), Courtesy of The Sophienburg-New Braunfels Archives and Museum of History; 277 (c), Mary Evans Photo Library, England; 277 (b), Sam Dudgeon/HRW; 278 (b), The Granger Collection, New York; 279 (cl), From the Collections of Henry Ford Museum and Greenfield Village; 280 (bl), The Granger Collection, New York; 280 (t), Texas Southern University Archives; 281 (t), Daughters of the Republic of Texas Library; 282 (cl), Daughters of the Republic of Texas Museum, Austin TX, HRW Photo by Peter Van Steen; 283 (bl), Janet Fish, courtesy Texas Memorial Museum; 283 (cr), Courtesy Nacogdoches Visitors Center/HRW Photo by Rick Benavides; 284 (t), Courtesy of the Witte Museum, San Antonio, Texas; 286 (cl), San Jacinto Museum of History, Houston; 287 (cr), SuperStock; 288 (t), Daughters of the Republic of Texas Library; 289, Daughters of the Republic of Texas Museum, HRW Photo by Peter Van Steen; 291 (bl), Sam Dudgeon/HRW. **Chapter 14**: Page 292 (bl), National Museum of American History, Smithsonian Institution, neg. no. 91-6501; 292 (tl), Texas State Library and Archives Commission (colorized); 292, (tr) © 1998 Stockbyte; 293 (tl), Texas State Library and Archives Commission, courtesy of Peter Flagg Maxson, Austin, Texas; 293 (tr), HRW Photo by Peter Van Steen; 293 (c), Henry Groskinsky; 293 (b), Sam Dudgeon/HRW; 294, San Jacinto Museum of History, Houston; 295, Allison Wade/Bob Daemmrich Photo, Inc.; 296, Ralph A. Reinhold/Animals Animals/Earth Scenes; 297, Texas Memorial Museum; 298 (b), Image © 2003 PhotoDisc, Inc.; 298 (t), North Wind Picture Archives; 299, Texas State Library and Archives Commission (colorized); 300, Museum of Fine Arts, Houston, TX, USA/Bridgeman Art Library, New York/London; 301, Dallas Historical Society, HRW Photo by Kristen Darby; 302 (bc), Institute of Texan Cultures, University of Texas at San Antonio; 303, Sam Houston Memorial Museum, Huntsville, Texas; 304 (t), Bob Daemmrich Photo, Inc.; 305 (t), Courtesy Rick Benavides; 305 (c), Courtesy Rick Benavides; 305 (b), Courtesy Rick Benavides; 307 (bl), Sam Dudgeon/HRW Photo; 309, HRW Photo by Victoria Smith.

Unit 5: Page 310, Eggenhoffer, Nick, *The Stagecoach*, 1972, mixed media, 14x17, 82.09c.2, National Cowboy and Western Heritage Museum, Oklahoma City. ; 311, St. Joseph Museum, St. Joseph Missouri; 311, © Philip Gould/CORBIS. **Chapter 15**: Page 312 (tl), Archives Division - Texas State Library, courtesy Texian Press; 312 (tr), Institute of Texas Cultures, University of Texas at San Antonio; 312 (bl), Private Collection/Bridgeman Art Library, New York/London; 313 (tl), © Laurence Parent; 313 (tr), Janice L. and David J. Frent Collection of Political Americana; 313 (c), Department of Anthropology, Smithsonian Institution, Washington, DC; 313 (b), HRW Photo by Sam Dudgeon; 314 (cl), Janice L. and David J. Frent Collection of Political Americana ; 315 (t), Archive Photos; 315 (b), The Granger Collection, New York; 316 (b), The Janice. L. and David J. Frent Collection of Political Americana; 316 (t), Library of Congress; 317, Texas State Library and Archives Commission; 318 , Lone Star Flag, Republic Period. Collection of the Star of the Republic Museum. Gift of L. Cletus Brown, Jr.; 319 (t), Casa Navarro State Historical Site; 319 (b), North Wind Picture Archives; 321, Bonhams, London, UK/Bridgeman Art Library, New York/London; 322, Sam Houston Memorial Museum, Huntsville, Texas; 323, Texas State Library and Archives Commission; 324, Bob Daemmrich Photo, Inc.; 327 (t), The Center for American History, Broadsides Collection,The University of Texas at Austin, photo no. CN00694; 327 (b), HRW Photo by Sam Dudgeon. **Chapter 16**: Page 328 (t), Library of Congress; 328 (b), Society of California Pioneers; 329 (tl), Courtesy Frank Kent Cadillac/Provided by Special Collections and Archives, UT at Arlington Libraries; 329 (tr), Panhandle-Plains Historical Museum, Canyon, Texas; 329 (c), Reprinted with the permission of Atheneum Books for Young Readers, an imprint of Simon & Schuster's Children's Publishing Division from WESTWARD HO! by Charles Kingsley, illustrated by N.C. Wyeth. Cover illustration by N.C. Wyeth. © 1920 Charles Scribner's Sons; renewed 1948 Charles Scribner's Sons and Carolyn B. Wyeth; 329 (b), Sam Dudgeon/HRW; 330 (cl), © D. Donne Bryant/DDB Stock Photo; 331 (t), Special Collections Division, UT at Arlington Libraries; 332 (t), Sipa Press/Woodfin Camp & Associates, Inc.; 333 (t), Institute of Texas Cultures, University of Texas/Library of Congress, Prints and Photographs Division; 334 (cl), National Archives (NARA); 335 (t), Stock Montage, Inc.; 336 (t), Library of Congress; 337 (cr), CORBIS/Darrell Gulin; 338, Zon International Publishing, courtesy the Spangenberger Collection. Photo © William Manns; 339 (bl), Courtesy of The Snook Trading Post, Billings, Montana/Institute of Texan Cultures, University of Texas at San Antonio; 340 (cl), CORBIS/Tim Thompson; 341, Texas Memorial Museum; 342 (cl), US Army Photo Provided by Fort Bliss; 345 (t), The Granger Collection, New York; 345 (b), Sam Dudgeon/HRW. **Chapter 17**: 346 (t), Texas State Library and Archives; Page 346 (b), © 1997 North Wind Picture Archives; 347 (t), Everett Collection/CSU Archives; 347 (cr), CORBIS/Shai Ginott; 347 (cl), Nancy Gewitz/Antique Textile Resources; 347 (b), Sam Dudgeon/HRW; 348 (cl), Josef Armendariz/HRW Photo/Mr. & Mrs. Frank Aelvoet, San Antonio, TX/Courtesy of the Institute of Texas Cultures/The University of Texas; 349 (b), Daughters of the Republic of Texas Library; 350 (cl), Josef Armendariz/HRW Photo/Courtesy of the Institute of Texas Cultures/The University of Texas; 351 (cr), Courtesy of Texas Highways Magazine; 352, HRW Photo by Terry Janecek; 353 (cr), SuperStock; 354 (br), North Wind Picture Archives; 354, Terry Janecek/HRW Photo/Courtesy More Primitives Furniture & Accessories, Austin, TX; 356 (t), Josef Armendariz/HRW Photo/Courtesy of the Institute of Texas Cultures/The University of Texas; 357 (cr), Courtesy The Heritage Museum, Seguin, Tx.; 358 (t), Courtesy of Texas Highways Magazine; 358 (b), Culver Pictures, Inc.; 359 (t), Courtesy of the Witte Museum, San Antonio, Texas; 360 (cl), Louisiana State Museum; 361 (b), Christie's Images; 362, Bulgarini Publishing, 1991/English language edition © 1998 by Barnes & Noble, Inc./HRW Photo by Victoria Smith; 363 (t), Courtesy of the Witte Museum, San Antonio, Texas. HRW Photo by Joseph Armendariz; 365, HRW Photo by Sam Dudgeon; 367, HRW Photo by Victoria Smith.

Unit 6: Page 368, Painting by Donald Yena, courtesy the Texian Press, Waco, TX; 369, Texas State Library & Archives Commission. **Chapter 18**: Page 370 (t), © R.J. Marrion, Fellow of The Company of Military Historians of America. Published by Victoria Gallery, London; 370 (tr), Texas State Library and Archives Commission; 370 (bl), Anne S. K. Brown Military Collection, Brown University. Courtesy Picture Research Consultants, Inc.; 371 (tl), Photography by Larry Sherer, ©2001 High Impact Photography; 371 (tr),HRW Photo Research Library; 371 (c), The Museum of the Confederacy Richmond, Virginia. Photo by Katherine Wetzel; 371 (br), Sam Dudgeon/HRW; 372, The Granger Collection, New York; 374 (t), The Museum of the Confederacy, Richmond, Virginia; 375, Corbis-Bettmann; 376 (cl), Confederate Museum, United Daughters of the Confederacy; 377 (bl), Courtesy of the Witte Museum, San Antonio, Texas; 378 (l), Picture Research Consultants, Inc.; 378 (r), The Museum of the Confederacy Richmond, Virginia. Photography by Katherine Wetzel; 380 (cl), The Museum of the Confederacy Richmond, Virginia. Photography by Katherine Wetzel; 381 (cr), The Museum of the Confederacy Richmond, Virginia. Photography by Katherine Wetzel; 383 (t), The State Preservation Board, Austin, Texas; 383 (b), Institute of Texas Cultures, University of Texas; 384, Don Couch Photography; 385, Picture Research Consultants, Inc.; 386, John Deere Museum/Picture Research Consultants, Inc.; 387, The Museum of the Confederacy Richmond, Virginia. Photography by Katherine Wetzel; 388, Comfort Historical Museum, Comfort, Texas/Courtesy Picture Research Consultants; 389, From *The Civil War: Forward to Richmond*. Photograph by Al Freni, © 1983 Time-Life Books, Inc. Courtesy, Troiani Collection; 390, Tom Lovell/National Geographic Image Collection; 391 (t), Library of Congress; 393 (bl), Sam Dudgeon/HRW; 393, HRW Photo by Sam Dudgeon. **Chapter 19**: Page 394 (tl), The Lincoln Museum, Fort Wayne, IN; 394 (tr), Texas State Library and Archives Commission; 394 (b), Library of Congress; 395 (t), PRC Archive; 395 (cl), Janice L. and David J. Frent Collection of Political Americana ; 396 (cl), Chicago Historical Society; 397 (cr), Bob Daemmrich Photo, Inc.; 398 (bl), Library of Congress ; 399 (t), The Granger Collection, New York; 401 (cr), © 2000 N. Carter/North Wind Picture Archives; 402, Texas State Library and Archives Commission; 403, North Wind Picture Archives; 404, Texas State Library and Archives Commission; 405 (b), The Granger Collection, New York; 405 (t), Paul Quinn College, Dallas, TX; 406, Courtesy Jack Wilson Collection, HRW Photo by Sam Dudgeon; 407, Victoria Smith/HRW Photo; 408, Austin History Center/Austin Public Library; 409 (t), The State Preservation Board, Austin, Texas; 409 (br), The Granger Collection, New York; 411, John Deere and Co. **Chapter 20**: Page 412 (tl), © 2000 N. Carter/North Wind Picture Archives; 412 (tr), Smithsonian American Art Museum, Washington, DC/Art Resource, NY; 412 (b), Library of Congress/PRC Archive; 413 (cl), Courtesy Lawrence T. Jones III Collection, Austin,TX; 413 (t), Nawrocki Stock Photo; 415 (t), The Granger Collection, New York; 415 (c), The Bradfor Collection, Plains Indian Museum, Buffalo Bill Historical Center, Cody, Wyoming. Photo © Werner Forman/Art Resource, NY; 415 (br), Sam Dudgeon/HRW Photo; 416 (cl), Christie's Images; 417 (bl), Witte Museum, San Antonio, Texas; 418 (t), The Granger Collection, New York; 419 (t), The Granger Collection, New York; 420 (cl), Courtesy of the Museum of the Big Bend, Alpine, Texas; 422 (t), Brown Brothers; 423 (bl), Russell, Charles M. *Shooting The Buffalo*; 424 (t), First National Bank, Amarillo; 425 (t), Panhandle-Plains Historical Museum, Research Center, Canyon, Texas; 425 (cr), Christie's Images; 426 (bl), Archive Photos; 428 (cl), SuperStock; 429 (bl), Courtesy of Texas Highways Magazine; 429 (t), National Archives (NARA); 430 (cl), © Lindsay Hebberd/CORBIS; 433 (bl), Sam Dudgeon/HRW; 435, HRW Photo by Sam Dudgeon.

Unit 7: Page 436, SuperStock; 437, HRW Photo by Sam Dudgeon; **Chapter 21**: Page 438 (tl), Dallas Museum of Art, gift of LIFE Magazine; 438 (tr), History Division, Los Angeles County Museum. Photo by Henry Groskinsky; 438 (b), The Granger Collection, New York; 439 (tc), The Granger Collection, New York; 439 (cr), Brooks Walker; 439 (bc), HRW Photo by Sam Dudgeon; 440 (cl), Laurence Parent; 441 (bl), Courtesy of the Witte Museum, San Antonio, Texas; 443 (cr), The Granger Collection, New York; 444 (t), Christie's Images; 445 (t), Boltin Picture Library; 446 (t), Christie's Images; 447 (t), Western History Collection, University of Oklahoma Library; 448 (t), Laurence Parent; 449 (cr), Panhandle-Plains Historical Museum, Research Center, Canyon, Texas; 450 (tl #1) © John Elk III; 450 (tl #2) Danny Lehman/CORBIS; 451 (bl), E.E. Smith Photo Collection, Library of Congress; 452 (t), Christie's Images; 453, Bygone Designs; 454 (cl), The Granger Collection, New York; 455 (bl), I. N. Hall; 456 (cl), Charles Phillips. **Chapter 22**: Page 460 (tl), Age of Steam Railroad Museum; 460 (tr), Don Couch Photography; 460 (b), Marion County Historical Society, Marion, OH; 461 (tl) Courtesy Austin Steam Train Association, Photo by Ross Cravens; 461 (tr), Valley House Gallery; 461 (b), HRW Photo by Sam Dudgeon. Page 462, Texas State Library and Archives Commission; 464 , The Center for American History, The University of Texas at Austin; 465, Collection of Daniel K. E. Ching/PRC Archive; 467, Texas State Library and Archives Commission; 468 (t), Replica courtesy Deere & Company; 468 (b), University of Houston Libraries, George Fuermann City of Houston Collection; 470 (t), (detail), Courtesy, Fort Worth Star-Telegram Photography Collection, The University of Texas at Arlington Libraries, Arlington, Texas; 471, Smithsonian Institution, Division of Electricity, photo no. 75-2343; 472, Courtesy of the Witte Museum, San Antonio, Texas; 475 (t), *Cartooning Texas* by Maury Forman and Robert Calvert, Texas A&M University Press, College Station, © 1993; 475 (b) HRW Photo by Sam Dudgeon. **Chapter 23**: Page 476 (tl), Courtesy North Texas University; 476 (tr), Charles C. Stephenson/Courtesy Art Museum of Southeast Texas; (bl) Cindy Lewis Photography (br) Culver Pictures, Inc.; 477 (t), Photo by Larry Murphy/The University of Texas at Austin, News and Information Services; 477 (b), HRW Photo by Sam Dudgeon; 478, Woodfin Camp & Associates; 479 (t), Photo by Kevin Gilliam; 479, The Granger Collection, New York; 480 (t), HRW Photo Research Library; 480, *Cartooning Texas* by Maury Forman and Robert Calvert, Texas A&M University Press, College Station, © 1993; 480, Bob Daemmrich Photo, Inc.; 481, Brown Brothers; 483, Brown Brothers; 485, CORBIS/Kit Kittle; 486, Hughes Tool Company, Houston; 487 (l), Courtesy of *Texas Highways* Magazine; 487 (r), Mark Swindler; 488 (t), Courtesy of Basil Clemons Photograph Collection/Special Collections Division, UT at Arlington Libraries; 488 (b), Nawrocki Stock Photo; 489, Peter Van Steen; 491, HRW Photo by Sam Dudgeon; 493, HRW Photo by Victoria Smith.

Unit 8: Page 494, *Boomtown* (detail) 1927-28, by Thomas Hart Benton. Memorial Art Gallery of the University of Rochester, Marion Stratton Gould Fund; 495, National Association of Civilian Conservation Corps Alumni. **Chapter 24**: Page 496 (tl), Culver Pictures, Inc.; 496 (tr), HRW Photo by Terry Janecek/Courtesy the Texas A&M Corp of Cadets Center; 496 (bl, Brown Brothers; 497 (tl), Photograph by Robert Mihovil; 497 (tr), HRW Photo by Sam Dudgeon; 497 (c), Collection of Janice L. and David J. Frent/PRC Archive; 497 (b), Sam Dudgeon/HRW; 498, Courtesy of The National Grange; 499, Wayne McSpadden Photography; 500, The Granger Collection, New York; 501, CORBIS/© David J. & Janice L. Frent Collection; 502 (t), The Granger Collection, New York; 503 (cr), Courtesy, Age of Steam Railroad Museum; 504 (t), The State Preservation Board, Austin, Texas 504 (br), *Cartooning Texas* by Maury Forman and Robert Calvert, Texas A&M University Press, College Station, © 1993; 506 (t), The State Preservation Board, Austin, Texas. Photo by Eric Beggs; 507 (cr), HRW Photo by Victoria Smith; 508, Brown Brothers; 509, Laurence Parent; 510, Courtesy The Heritage Museum, Seguin, TX. HRW Photo/Victoria Smith; 511 (cr), HRW Photo by Victoria Smith; 512, (cl) Sophia Smith Collection; 513 (t), Courtesy Jovita Lopez; 515 (bl), Sam Dudgeon/HRW. **Chapter 25**: Page 516 (tl), Texas State Library and Archives Commission, colorized by HRW; 516 (tr), National Archives, (NARA), photo 111-SC-93574; 516 (bl), PRC Archive; 517 (tl), Dallas Public Library; 517 (tr), University of Houston, George Fuermann City of Houston Collection; 517 (bl), PRC Archive; 517 (bl), HRW Photo by Sam Dudgeon; 518, Panhandle-Plains Historical Museum, Research Center, Canyon, Texas; 519 (b), Detail from #PICB 12866, Austin History Center, Austin Public Library; 519 (t), Ohio Historical Society; 520 (l), Dallas Public Library, photo by Gittings; 520 (r), Rosenberg Library; 521, Institute of Texas Cultures, University of Texas; 522, Cindy Lewis Photography; 523 (t), Texas State Library and Archives Commission (colorized); 523 (b), University of Houston Libraries, George Fuermann City of Houston Collection; 524, Ron Kimball Photography; 525 (b), Collection of Sandy Marrone/PRC Archive; 525 (t), National Baseball Hall of Fame; 526, Bob Daemmrich Photo, Inc.; 527, Janice L. and David J. Frent Collection of Political Americana; 528 (t), Library of Congress; 528 (b), Bettmann/CORBIS; 529, E.E. Mireles and Jovita G. deMireles Papers, Special Collections & Archives, Texas A&M University-Corpus Christi Bell Library; 530 (b), Collection of Col. Stuart S. Corning. Photo © Rob Humtley/Lightstream/PRC Archive; 530 (t), Texas State Library and Archives Commission (colorized); 531, Ohio Historical Society; 533 (b), HRW Photo by Sam Dudgeon. **Chapter 26**: Page 534 (tl, San Antonio Light Collection at The Institute of Texas Cultures, University of Texas; 534 (tr), Janice L. and David J. Frent Collection of Political Americana; 534 (b), The Granger Collection, New York; 535 (tl), Library of Congress; 535 (tc), Carolyn Brown Photography; 535 (tr), Dallas Historical Society; 535 (c), HRW Photo by Lance Schriner; 535 (b), HRW Photo by Sam Dudgeon; 536, Digital Imagery® copyright 2003 PhotoDisc, Inc.; 537, Center for American History, The University of Texas at Austin; 538 (t), Texas State Library and Archives Commission; 538 (b), Courtesy Jack Wilson Collection. HRW Photo/Sam Dudgeon; 539, Courtesy of The Crisis Publishing Co., Inc., the publisher of the magazine of the National Association for the Advancement of Colored People. General Research and Reference Division; Schomburg Center for Research in Black Culture; The New York Public Library; Astor, Lenox and Tilden Foundations; 540, Texas Energy Museum, Beaumont, Texas; 541, The Center for American History, The University of Texas at Austin; 542, © John Elk III; 543, EyeWire, Inc. Image Club Graphics ©1998 Adobe Systems, Inc.; 544, CPIO Partners; 545 (t), Dembinsky Photo Associates; 545 (b), Otis Dozier, *The Annual Move*, 1985.125, Dallas Museum of Art; 546, Library of Congress; 548, Franklin D. Roosevelt Library; 550, Janice L. and David J. Frent Collection of Political Americana; 551 (t), The State Preservation Board, Austin, Texas; 551 (b), Library of Congress; 552 (t), PRC Archive; 552 (b), Mural by Maxwell B. Starr, Rockdale Post Office; 553, Don Couch Photography, courtesy the Bob Wills Museum, Turkey, TX; 554, Bob Daemmrich Photo, Inc.; 555 (t), Harry Ransom Humanities Research Center, University of Texas at Austin; 555 (b), *I'll Tell You A Tale* by J. Frank Dobie, © 1960 by the author, published by University of Texas Press, Austin TX/HRW Photo by Sam Dudgeon; 557 (t), Cartooning Texas, by Maury Forman and Robert Calvert, courtesy Texas A&M University Press, © 1993; 557 (b), HRW Photo by Sam Dudgeon; 558, HRW Photo by Victoria Smith; 559, HRW Photo by Victoria Smith.

Unit 9: Page 560, NASA; 561, HRW Photo by John Langford. **Chapter 27**: Page 562 (tl), HRW Photo by Victoria Smith; 562 (tr), AP Wide World Photos; 562 (bl), Archive Photos; 562 (br), Michael Barson Collection/Past Perfect; 563 (tl), Ewing Galloway; 563 (tr), Bill Griggs Rockin' 50s Collection, Lubbock, TX; 563 (c), Sovfoto/Eastfoto; 563 (b), HRW Photo by Sam Dudgeon; 564, PRC Archive; 565, Denver Public Library Western History Department, Photo No. TMD-780; 566, Library of Congress; 567, PRC Archive; 567, © Museum of Flight/CORBIS; 568, © The Curtis Publishing Company; 569 (t), Michael Barson/Archive Photos; 570 (t), Dwight D. Eisenhower Presidential Library; 570 (b), United States Postal Service; 571, Cartoon by Bob Taylor, Dallas Times Herald; 572, Michael Ochs Archives; 573 (b), David Spindel/SuperStock; 574, Hershenson-Allen Archives; 574, Photo # 2582, Katherine Anne Porter Collection, Hornbake Library, University of Maryland Special Collections. Photo by Paul Porter; 55, Robert Rauschenberg/License by VAGA, New York, NY/SuperStock; 577, AP/Wide World Photos; 578, AP/Wide World Photos; 579 (b), Dr. Hector P. Garcia Papers, Special Collections and Archives, Texas A&M University-Corpus Christi Bell Library; 579 (t), Dr. Hector P. Garcia Papers, Special Collections & Archives, Texas A&M University-Corpus Christi Bell Library; 580, Timepix; 581, Bettmann/CORBIS. **Chapter 28**: Page 584 (tl), Courtesy the Gary Job Corps; (tr), NASA; (bl), ©Underwood & Underwood/CORBIS; 585 (t), Scott Newton/Austin City Limits; 585 (cl), Bruce Kliewe/Jerobam 1972; 585 (t), Courtesy Jack Wilson Collection. HRW Photo/Sam Dudgeon; 585 (b), HRW Photo by Sam Dudgeon; 586 (cl), AP/Wide World Photos, Inc.; 587 (bl), © CORBIS; 588 (cl), Arnold Newman/Lyndon Baines Johnson Library Collection; 588 (t), H. Armstrong Roberts/American Stock Photo; 589 (cr#2) ©Bettmann/CORBIS; 589 (cr#1), HRW Photo by Sam Dudgeon; 590 (cl), COURTESY HOUSTON METROPOLITAN RESEARCH CENTER, HOUSTON PUBLIC LIBRARY; 591 (t), AP/Wide World Photos; 591 (bl), Austin History Center, Austin Public Library, #AS-60-27281-14; 592 (t), AP/Wide World Photos; 593 (t), HRW Photo Research Library; 594 (t), Courtesy Elisabeth Martinez; 595 (t), Wally McNamee/CORBIS; 596 (cl), AP/Wide World Photos; 597 (b), Sheldon Cohen/Bell Helicopter Textron; 597 (t), NASA; 598 (bl), NASA/TimePix; 599 (t), Ralph Morse/TimePix; 600 (cl), ©James Lemass/Index Stock Imagery/Picture Quest; 601 (b), ©Bettmann/CORBIS; 603 (br), Ryan Brown; 604 (t), Herc Ficklen, The Dallas Morning News, March 11, 1973; 605, © Corbis Images; 607, Sam Dudgeon/HRW Photo. **Chapter 29**: Page 608 (tl), *Lonesome Dove* © 1985 by Larry McMurtry, published by Scribner Paperback Fiction, a trademark of Macmillan Library Reference, Inc. published by Simon & Schuster, Inc., New York/HRW Photo by Sam Dudgeon; 608 (tc), Kimberleh Jones/Shooting Star International; 608 (tr), HRW Photo by Lyndol Descant; 608 (b), Ronald Reagan Presidential Library; 609 (tl), Courtesy Jack Wilson Collection. HRW Photo/Sam Dudgeon; 609 (tc), HRW Photo by Sam Dudgeon; 609 (tr), Bob Daemmrich Photo, Inc.; 609 (bl), HRW Photo by Sam Dudgeon; (br), Thomas E. Franklin/The Record (Bergen County, NJ)/CORBIS/SABA; 610 , Courtesy Jack Wilson Collection, HRW Photo/Sam Dudgeon 611, White House Photo by Eric Draper 612 (t), Susan Biddle/CORBIS; 613, HRW Photo/Lance Shriner; 614, Susan Biddle/CORBIS; 615 (t), Hyungwon Kang/Reuters/TimePix; (b), Monica Graff/The Image Works; 616, AP/Wide World Photos; 617, Bob Daemmrich/Corbis Sygma; 619, Kelly-Mooney Photography/CORBIS; 620, Bob Daemmrich/Stock Boston; 621, AP/Wide World Photos; 622, Bob Daemmrich/Stock, Boston; 623 (cl), Courtesy of the Office of Secretary of State Henry Cuellar; 624, HRW Photo by Victoria Smith; 625, Bob Daemmrich/Stock Boston; 627, *The Four Sisters*, by Dr. John Biggers/HRW Photo by Victoria Smith; 628, EyeWire, Inc. Image Club Graphics ©1998 Adobe Systems, Inc.; 629, Bob Daemmrich Photo, Inc.; 630, Bob Daemmrich, Stock, Boston; 631 (cl), David Sams/Stock Boston; 633 (t), Cartoon by Bill Saylor, The Houston Post. From *Cartooning Texas* by Maury Forman and Robert A. Calvert, Texas A&M University Press; (b) Sam Dudgeon/HRW Photo; 635, Jeffrey Titcomb/Newsmakers.

Unit 10: Page 636, Courtesy of *Texas Highways* Magazine; 637, Sam Dudgeon/HRW. **Chapter 30**: Page 638 (t), Bob Daemmrich Photo, Inc.; 638 (t), Courtesy of Texas Education Agency; 638 (bl), AP/Wide World Photos/Larry Lettera; 639 (tc), ©Rebecca McEntee/Courtesy Austin American Statesman; 639 (br), HRW Photo by Sam Dudgeon; 640 (cl), The UT Institute of Texan Cultures at San Antonio, Courtesy of the Center for American History, The University of Texas, Austin; 641 (bl), Bob Daemmrich/Stock, Boston; 642 (bl), ©Adam Woolfitt/CORBIS; 643 (t), Texas House of Representatives Photo Archive; 644 (cl), Gay Shackelford Photography; 645 (t), The UT Institute of Texan Cultures at San Antonio No. 76-229. The San Antonio Express-News Collection; 645 (b), AP/Wide World Photos/Harry Cabluck; 647 (cr), Bob Daemmrich Photo, Inc.; 648 (cl), The Texas Collection, Baylor University; 649 (t), AP/Wide World Photos/Joe Marquette; 649 (b), AP/Wide World Photos/Harry Cabluck; 650 (t), Gay Shackelford Photography; 651 (cr), Texas State Library and Archives Commission, colorized; 652 (cl), HRW Photo/Peter Van Steen; 653 (t), Bob Daemmrich/Stock Boston; 654 (t), Bob Daemmrich/Stock Boston; 654 (cr), © CORBIS; 656 (bl), HRW Photo/Charlie Fonville; 657 (cr), HRW Photo by Victoria Smith; 659 (t), Bill McClanaghan, Dallas Morning News; 659 (b), Sam Dudgeon/HRW. **Chapter 31**: Page 660 (tl), Brian K. Diggs/Austin American-Statesman; 660 (tr), Courtesy Jack Wilson. HRW Photo/Sam Dudgeon; 660 (bl), PRC Archive; 660 (br), AP/Wide World Photos; 661 (tl), ©Christopher Brown/Stock Boston; 661 (tr), Project Vote, www.sos.state.tx.us; 661 (c), Texas State Library and Archives Commission; 661 (b), HRW Photo by Sam Dudgeon; 656, HRW Photo by Larry Kolvoord; 657, © Craig Aurness/CORBIS; 664, © Bob Daemmrich/Stock, Boston, Inc./PictureQuest; 665, HRW Photo Research Library; 666, Bob Daemmrich Photo, Inc.; 667, Laurence Parent; 668, Bob Daemmrich Photo, Inc.; 669, © Bob Daemmrich/Stock, Boston, Inc./PictureQuest; 669 (b), HRW Photo by Sam Dudgeon; 671, AP/Wide World Photos; 672, Texas Democratic Party; 673, Bob Daemmrich Photo, Inc.; 674, Courtesy Mothers Against Drunk Driving, Austin, TX; 677, HRW Photo by Victoria Smith.

Back Matter: Page; 678 (tr), History Division, Los Angeles County Museum. Photo by Henry Groskinsky; 678 (r), Laurence Parent; 678 (bl), Laurence Parent; 678 (br), Don Couch Photography; 678 (bkgd), Texas State Library and Archives Commission; 680 (t, c) Texas State Library and Archives Commission; 680 (tl, c),Texas State Library and Archives Commission; 680 (cl, cr, b), The State Preservation Board, Austin, Texas; 681 (t, cl, cr), The State Preservation Board, Austin, Texas; 681 (c, b), Texas State Library and Archives Commission; 682 (tl, tc, c, cl, bc), The State Preservation Board, Austin, Texas; 682 (tr, cr, bl, br), Texas State Library and Archives Commission; 683 (t, c), The State Preservation Board, Austin, Texas; 683 (b), Texas State Library and Archives Commission; 684 (t, cl, cr), Texas State Library and Archives Commission; 684 (c), The State Preservation Board, Austin, Texas; 684 (b), Texas State Library and Archives Commission; 685 (tl, tr, cl, cr), Texas State Library and Archives Commission; 685 (tc, c, bl), The State Preservation Board, Austin, Texas; 685 (bc), Darren Carroll/Liaison Agency; 685 (br), Office of the Governor; 686, 687, Texas Department of Transportation; 688 (t), One Mile Up, Inc.; 688 (b), Texas Department of Transportation; 689 (t), *Texas, Our Texas*, words by Gladys Yoakum Wright and William J. Marsh, Music by William J. Marsh. © 1925, 1953 by W.J. Marsh. Distributed by Southern Music Company; 689 (b), HRW Photo by Eric Beggs.